ACCADEMIA ITALIANA
DELLA CUCINA

THE ITALIAN ACADEMY OF CUISINE

La Cucina

THE REGIONAL COOKING OF ITALY

TRANSLATED BY JAY HYAMS

RIZZOLI
NEW YORK

Accademia Italiana della Cucina
The Italian Academy of Cuisine
Via Napo Torriani 31, 20124 Milano

President: **GIOVANNI BALLARINI**
Coordination and supervision: **PAOLO PETRONI**

The Accademia Italiana della Cucina would like to offer acknowledgment
to all its delegates and members for the research and editing of the recipes.

FOR THE ENGLISH-LANGUAGE EDITION:

Translator: **JAY HYAMS**
Typesetter: **TINA HENDERSON**
Designer: **ERICA HEITMAN-FORD** *for* **MUCCA DESIGN**
Copy editor: **SARA NEWBERRY**
Editor: **CHRISTOPHER STEIGHNER**
Assistant Editor: **JONO JARRETT**
Translation and typesetting coordinated by **LIBRISOURCE INC.**
The publisher wishes to gratefully acknowledge **FRED PLOTKIN**
for his invaluable services as a consultant on the text.

Originally published in the Italian language as *La Cucina del Bel Paese*,
© Copyright by Bolis Edizioni - Azzano San Paolo (BG).

First published in the United States of America in 2009
by **RIZZOLI INTERNATIONAL PUBLICATIONS, INC.**
300 PARK AVENUE SOUTH, NEW YORK, NY 10010

www.rizzoliusa.com

© 2009 RIZZOLI PUBLICATIONS, INC.

2021 2022 2023 2024 / 15 14 13 12

Printed in China

ISBN: 978-0-8478-3147-0

Library of Congress Control Number: 2009931239

TABLE *of* CONTENTS

Preface ✦ vi

Introduction ✦ vii

Editor's Notes ✦ viii

. . . .

Antipasti, Pizza, & Sauces ✦ 1

Soups ✦ 91

Pasta, Polenta, & Rice ✦ 211

Fish ✦ 425

Meat & Poultry ✦ 507

Vegetables ✦ 671

Cheese Dishes ✦ 737

Desserts ✦ 747

. . . .

Conversion Chart ✦ 893

Index by Region ✦ 894

Index by Principal Ingredient ✦ 908

PREFACE

The Accademia Italiana della Cucina, founded by Orio Vergani in 1953, has as its primary purpose the safeguarding of Italy's culinary traditions. From its very beginning, the academy has worked to record, study, and spread knowledge of Italy's most genuine regional dishes. Today, thanks to the dedicated work of more than 7,600 academy members organized in 300 delegations, we have succeeded in collecting the fruits of this long labor, assembling a collection of recipes that is unprecedented in its scope.

One of the strengths of the Accademia is its reach across the entire territory of Italy. Our members have been able to canvas the country, investigating even the most remote and isolated localities—areas that would escape the attention of any single author working alone.

Only by living in Italy, by knowing its traditions, by being in constant contact with its day-to-day reality, is it possible to understand, evaluate, and select the dishes that constitute true home cooking—not only the dishes being prepared today but also the ones that were prepared in years past and those that persist only in the memories of our elders.

Thus was born the idea of taking a kind of census, so far as doing so was possible, of Italy's enormous patrimony of local cooking traditions. But such a huge task necessarily presented certain challenges. The overall editing had to be both wide-sweeping and delicate. On the one hand we hesitated to change the idiosyncratic regional language of the individual contributors; on the other hand, we had to put together a clear and readable collection that would be easy to consult.

The resulting work presents more than 2,000 recipes, from the well-known classics to some obscure gems, with the inclusion of traditions that have been nearly forgotten even by the inhabitants of many Italian cities.

Any Italian knows that a cherished heirloom dish is sure to vary in its preparation, depending on who is in the kitchen. It will be made in a certain way at home, in another way at a relative's, and in yet another way by a friend. Sometimes the differences are minimal (or at least they appear so on the surface); sometimes they are substantial. Interpretation, improvisation—these are essential characteristics of traditional Italian cooking. Thus while we have strived to present the most iconic version of key regional dishes, it is up to you, the home cook, to make them your own.

This is not intended to be a history book but a living cookbook. The ultimate goal is to keep these recipes alive so that future generations might continue to enjoy them. We are especially delighted that now this body of culinary knowledge is available in the English language—a true world to discover.

Paolo Petroni
Editorial Coordinator and Supervisor
Accademia Italiana della Cucina

INTRODUCTION

Such a genial idea: an Italian culinary academy called on its many members, located in every part of the country, to collect favorite recipes for traditional local dishes from relatives, friends, and neighbors. Genial because it goes to the heart of Italian culture: the home, family, food. In Italy a restaurant earns praise if its creations can be described as "homemade"—recognition that the home cook is the best cook. It is also true that traditions are carried on most enthusiastically, and most accurately, at the local level, at the source.

The result was a cookbook the size of a phonebook—an accurate comparison since each recipe leads back to a province, a city, a street, ultimately a kitchen table. That intimacy has contributed to the book's enduring popularity in Italy. Also appealing is what the book reveals about Italy, still very much a patchwork quilt of constant, often striking, variations (backed by stubborn opinions). From region to region—even from the seacoast to the interior of the same region—everything changes in little ways, and many things change in very large ways. Whether or not the sauce contains tomatoes or eggplant or pecorino can often tell you, as accurately as a compass, exactly where you are.

The most striking aspect of the book remains the enormous quantity of recipes and their close relationship to the places where they are eaten. Plenty of them—page after page—have been prepared on the same site using the same ingredients since the Middle Ages or before. Which doesn't mean there aren't local variations, which are also duly noted.

All of which makes the English-language edition a surprise and a treasure, presenting as it does the original, historical version of famous dishes known until now only from their toned-down modern versions. These genuine versions reveal their roots, and their close relationships with local ingredients, customs, and history. In addition to famous recipes there are recipes for dishes previously unknown to American cooks, dishes known only to travelers in Italy. And not all travelers: only those knowledgeable enough to seek them out or lucky enough to be invited into an Italian home.

How much was lost in translation? Certain jokes and witticisms in local dialect resisted translation into standard Italian and thus could not be brought into English. Otherwise every effort has been made to maintain the varying local flavors of the original. The royal history of Naples is unmistakable in many Neapolitan recipes; the rustic past of the Veneto, along with that region's wry humor, is also made abundantly clear. From every region there are recipes that give a sense of the hardships of the past. There can be no better example of Italy's famous *cucina povera* than the "fish" soup that calls for no fish and gets its seaside flavor from beach rocks, boiled in the cooking water. Being such a clear mirror of Italian culture, Italian food reflects that nation's history and geography. *La Cucina* documents not just the cooking of Italy, but the country's character as well.

EDITOR'S NOTES

Family recipes present certain caveats. These recipes were not tested in a professional kitchen, thus not simplified or standardized. They are instead originals, handed down over many generations. The original book endeavored to maintain the individual voices of each recipe's contributor, and we have done the same. Thus you will notice that the language varies from recipe to recipe. Some delve into greater detail than others regarding technique. In terms of ingredients, almost all are less precise than the recipes that fill today's cookbooks. Embrace this flexibility and vary the ingredients based on your own taste, seasonality, and availability. Some of the ingredients may be hard to find outside of Italy, but there are valid substitutions for any regional herb or mushroom or cheese.

We have attempted to remain true to the spirit of this book as it was originally published in Italy. However, we have made some changes to open the book to a broader audience. Approximately one hundred recipes were cut, mainly because they depended upon ingredients rarely found outside of Italy. In other cases, we transformed recipes into "Local Tradition" sidebars, so that the reader may learn a dish's history and principal components. In general, for every chapter except Desserts, the recipes yield four servings, unless otherwise stated. Here are some general guidelines concerning ingredients.

BAY LEAVES Used to infuse sauces and stews with flavor, bay leaves themselves should not be eaten, and can be removed before serving, if desired.

BEANS The two most common types of beans used are *borlotti* (cranberry beans) and *cannellini* (white beans), though lentils, chickpeas, and favas also feature prominently. If the type of bean is not specified, choose whichever you prefer, but be prepared to adjust cooking times. When dried beans are called for, they should always be soaked first.

BREAD In the Italian country kitchen, when bread goes stale it is not discarded. Slices are topped with soup or stew to soak up their savory liquids. Or the bread is ground into crumbs for coating other ingredients or tossing with pasta. Good stale bread results from bread that is left at room temperature in a perforated plastic or paper bag or box, not refrigerated. If none is on hand, you can approximate stale bread by drying fresh bread slices in a 350° oven for a few minutes.

BROTH In general, use a broth that corresponds to the principal component of a dish. For instance, use beef broth for a beef recipe. Chicken broth is the default for recipes that do not specify.

CAPERS The larger capers from the islands near Sicily and Sardinia have the most flavor. Capers preserved in salt are preferable to those brined in vinegar, but both should be rinsed well and drained before using.

CHEESE Here are some of the cheeses most commonly used in this book:

✦ **Asiago**, named for the plateau at the foot of the Dolomites to the north of Vicenza in the Veneto region, is a pale cow's-milk cheese with a slightly sweet taste; aged and hardened it can be grated. It is made in several versions, from a hard, half-fat cheese to a soft, full-fat version.

✦ **Bitto**, from the Sondrio province of Lombardia (the Valtellina), is made of cow's milk and ten percent goat's milk.

✦ **CACIOCAVALLO** comes from Southern Italy, where it is stretched and shaped by hand, like *mozzarella* and *provolone*. Made with cow's milk, *caciocavallo* when it is young has a firm, smooth texture and a mildly salty flavor that grows more pungent as it is aged. It is often made into a gourd shape, and smoked versions are available.

✦ **Fior di latte** is a soft, fresh cheese from cow's milk—literally, "flower of milk."

✦ **Fontina** is an unpasteurized cow's-milk cheese, the most authentic and delicious examples of which come from the slopes of the Valle d'Aosta. With its delicate, buttery, nutty flavor, fontina is a favorite for cooking, as it melts beautifully.

✦ **Gorgonzola** is Italy's most famous blue cheese. It was born in Lombardia, but almost all of it today is produced in Piemonte. Made of cow's milk, most *gorgonzolas* are aged from three to six months. The mildest, sweetest versions (aged for the minimum) are called *gorgonzola dolce*; the most pungent, *gorgonzola piccante*.

✦ **Grana** is a general term for a hard, grainy-textured cheese often used for grating. The original recipes here often called simply for *grana,* the expectation being that one would use the *grana* of that recipe's region. Since these local *grana* cheeses are not widely available outside Italy, we have usually substituted the quintessential Parmigiano-Reggiano.

✦ **Montasio** is a firm cow's-milk cheese similar to Asiago, available aged or fresh. It comes from Friuli-Venezia Giulia.

✦ **Mozzarella** is one of the most famous and widely available cheeses in Italy, though southern versions are considered the best. *Mozzarella di bufala* is made from buffalo milk rather than cow's milk, as is most common today. Buffalo milk is creamier than cow's and imparts a more velvety texture and tangier fragrance.

✦ **Parmigiano-Reggiano** is a hard cheese made from partly skimmed cow's milk by a centuries-old method in the provinces of Parma, Reggio Emilia, Modena, and Bologna in Emilia-Romagna and Mantova in Lombardia.

✦ **Pecorino** refers to any Italian sheep's-milk cheese (*pecora* is Italian for "sheep"); of the dozens of varieties of *pecorino* cheeses, the most famous version is *pecorino Romano*, which has a sharp and pungent flavor that makes it mainly appropriate for cooking or for grating like *Parmigiano-Reggiano*. *Pecorino dolce* is a young and fresh *pecorino* with a notable sweetness and softer texture.

✦ **Provolone** is a sharp and tangy, firm-textured cow's-milk cheese that originated in the Basilicata region of southern Italy; like *gorgonzola*, it has lighter-flavored versions referred to as *dolce*, and stronger-flavored, aged versions referred to as *piccante*. Both versions can also be smoked and are good for cooking.

✦ **Ricotta** in Italian means "re-cooked," and refers to a soft, mild creamy-white cheese traditionally made from the whey remaining after making *pecorino*. Today, most *ricotta* is made from cow's milk. It has a very mild, lightly tart flavor and slightly grainy texture. It is also often used in desserts and baking. *Ricotta salata* refers to *ricotta* to which salt has been added as a preservative, making it less moist and more pungent in flavor than fresh *ricotta*. *Robiola* is a goat's milk cheese that often contains cow's and sheep's milk. It has a creamy texture and is not aged beyond three weeks.

✦ **Scamorza**, from Abruzzo and Molise, is a *pasta filate* ("pulled or spun dough") cheese that is shaped by hand, like *provolone* or *mozzarella*. A cow's-milk cheese with a mild, creamy flavor similar to *mozzarella*, it is sometimes smoked.

✦ **Taleggio** is made in the Taleggio Valley north of Bergamo as well as in other centers in Lombardia and in Treviso in the Veneto. Made in square forms, it is a semisoft cow's-milk cheese with a delicate creamy taste but a pungent aroma.

✦ **Toma** (also known as *tuma*) can mean different kinds of cheeses. The first is a smooth, firm, cow's-milk cheese from Lombardia and Piemonte, traditionally aged between three and eighteen months. In Sicilia, *toma* refers to fresh ewe's-milk curds molded in a basket. In the north, *tuma* refers to an unsalted goat's-milk cheese.

CHILE PEPPER Note that sometimes, in order to impart a more subtle flavor to a dish, whole dried hot peppers are used and left in the dish at serving time (but in this case they are not meant to be eaten).

CITRUS When a recipe calls for citrus zest, it is important to use organically grown fruit, in order to avoid the ingestion of pesticides and other harmful chemicals found in the peel of conventionally grown fruit. Always zest the fruit before you juice it.

FLOUR Italy's famous hard durum wheat provides the semolina flour used to make dried pasta and some breads. However, for homemade pasta, a softer flour should be used. In all recipes here, unless otherwise specified, use unbleached all-purpose flour.

GARLIC European garlic cloves tend to be smaller than much garlic found in American markets, so it's best to err on the side of using less rather than more to avoid overwhelming the other flavors in a dish. All garlic should be peeled unless otherwise stated. In many recipes in this book, whole garlic cloves are left in the dish at the time of serving but are not intended to be eaten—a custom that is in accord with the recipes' rustic origins.

GREENS Spring and summer in the Italian countryside means fields of tender wild greens, which enterprising foragers turn into flavorful salads, soups, sauces, or side dishes. While the wild varieties may be hard to find, many of these greens are widely available at grocers and especially farmers' markets today.

✦ **Arugula** is used in salads and soups, cooked as a vegetable, or added to sauces.

✦ **Chicory**, radicchio, endive, and escarole are all members of the chicory family and share a pleasantly bitter taste. Chicory's curly leaves somewhat resemble those of dandelion's. "Curly endive" is quite similar, but with slightly darker green leaves. Curly endive and chicory are roughly interchangeable in recipes.

+ **Escarole** is most often cooked, baked, or stirred into soups. Its leaves are broader and wavier, resembling lettuce. It has a milder flavor than the rest of the chicory family.

+ **Radicchio** comes in several varieties, the most familiar of which may be the tight, round, bright crimson heads of *radicchio rosso di Verona* (or *rosa di Chioggia*), which is often served raw or lightly wilted in salads. *Radicchio di Castelfranco* has a looser shape and more of a marbleized pink coloration. Shaped similarly to a head of romaine lettuce and markedly less bitter than its cousins, *radicchio di Treviso* can be served fresh but is also often used in sauces and risottos, baked, or grilled.

+ **Swiss chard** is actually a native Italian plant with no real botanical or historic connection to Switzerland; in Italian cuisine it's used in much the same manner as spinach.

MARINADES While many of the recipes did not originally call for refrigerating a dish while it is marinating, it is best to do so for safety reasons in the modern kitchen.

MEAT AND POULTRY In this book are recipes from the countryside, where cooks have access to all kinds of animals, and where almost every part of the animal is used. Thus sometimes a recipe will specify the age and/or gender of an animal. This detail is key to the ideal qualities and taste of the dish. Try your farmers' markets and other local sources to see if you can obtain these meats. Substitute as needed, but note that quantities and cooking times will need to be adjusted.

OIL Each region imparts different characteristics to its native olive oils. Northern oils, especially from Liguria, are often considered the most elegant; those from central Italy are known for their peppery character; olive oils from the south often carry hints of Mediterranean herbs. Try to use an olive oil from the region of the recipe or, failing that, from a nearby region. Use extra-virgin olive oil for all of these recipes. For deep-frying, you may substitute vegetable oil.

PARSLEY Italian parsley has flat, sharply pointed leaves, and a clean, bright flavor fundamental to Italian cooking. Curly parsley is a poor substitute.

PINE NUTS The best pine nuts come from Pisa. If these are unavailable, you may still be able to find pine nuts from Italy.

PORK Every region of Italy has its own distinctive pork products, many of which have become essential to general Italian cuisine. *Ciccioli* are the flavorful bits left over after the fat has been rendered, similar to cracklings. The jowls (guanciale) and belly (pancetta) are often seasoned and cured and used in a similar manner as American bacon, though not smoked. The ham of a pig that is salted and air-cured has the great honor of becoming prosciutto, the finest type of which is prosciutto di Parma. The rind, or skin, of the pig is used to give flavor and body to many stews. *Lardo* is a delicacy of the white fat from the pig's rump that has been cured and seasoned with spices. *Lardo,* as well as other types of fatty meat, are used in the larding of meat before cooking. To lard a piece of meat, first cut small slits every inch or so across the surface of the meat. Then insert small pieces of the larding fat into the slits, using either a larding needle, a skewer, or even the tip of a knife. This helps the meat to stay moist and augments its flavor. *Lardo* should not be confused with lard (*strutto*), which is simply rendered pork fat. Lard is a staple in the Italian country kitchen, used often for sautéing. Avoid supermarket lard that has been hydrogenated. You can substitute olive oil for lard in most cases.

RICE Arborio, Vialone Nano, and Carnaroli are the three most common and popular varieties of Italian rice used in risotto. In individual recipes, a particular kind of rice is often specified based upon the region. If none is specified, try to use an Italian variety.

SALAME There are many types of local salame throughout Italy, with various ingredients, flavorings, sizes, shapes, and curing processes. Most Italian salame, however, is uncooked, air-dried and cured, and made with pork along with other meats, lard, or pancetta, and boldly flavored with garlic, wine, herbs, and spices. Unless otherwise directed, it is recommended that you use a salame from the same region as the recipe. The English "salami" is a catch-all term for Italian-style dried sausage, and this will serve as a decent substitute in some recipes using dried sausage. Fresh sausage (*salsiccie*) is called for in some recipes; here you can use the generally available "Italian sausage" that is sold from the butcher's case in many supermarkets; use the spicy or sweet variety depending upon the recipe and your taste. Cotecchino is a fresh pork sausage that contains bits of pork skin in its mixture. Finocchiona is a sausage made with fennel seed. Note that the word *salumi* refers to the entire family of cured or preserved meats, including but not limited to bresaola (air-dried salted beef), collo or coppa (cured pork neck), culatello (salt-cured aged ham), guanciale, mortadella (sausage made of pork and often beef or veal), pancetta, prosciutto, soppressata (pressed salame usually made with pork), or speck (smoked ham shoulder).

SALT Sea salt is generally preferable. Rarely are measurements given; add salt to taste.

WINE Specific recommendations are given when a recipe calls for wine as an ingredient. It is always wise to use (and drink) a wine from the same region as the recipe.

VANILLA In Italy, vanilla-sugar packets are more often used than vanilla extract, which we have substituted throughout. If you would like to make your own vanilla sugar, split a vanilla bean, place it in a jar, and cover it with granulated sugar. Shake it occasionally, and after a few days, the sugar will have taken on the vanilla flavor. Use this in place of extract, reducing the amount of sugar otherwise in the recipe.

VINEGAR Always use wine vinegar in Italian cooking—red or white depending upon the flavors of the dish. The exception would be that apple cider vinegar is fine in certain dishes from the northern regions. True balsamic vinegar comes from the provinces of Modena and Reggio Emilia, just north of Bologna in Emilia-Romagna, and it always bears the appellation *Aceto Balsamico Tradizionale di Modena*. It should be used sparingly, added at the very end of cooking, at the time of serving, or in dressings and light sauces.

YEAST For leavening, the original recipes called for *lievito di birra* and other kinds of yeast. In all cases we have approximated equivalents using active dry yeast, which is more universally available.

THE REGIONS of ITALY

CHAPTER ONE

ANTIPASTI, PIZZA, & SAUCES

ANCHOVIES IN TOMATO SAUCE

ACCIUGHE IN SALSA ROSSA

PIEMONTE

1 lb. salt-cured anchovies
1 garlic clove, minced
1 piece chili pepper, minced
1 tbsp. capers
¼ cup chopped flat-leaf parsley
6 tbsp. tomato purée
1 tsp. sugar

Rinse the anchovies, fillet them, and place in a container. Combine the remaining ingredients to make a sauce. Cover the anchovies with this sauce and let stand at room temperature for several hours before use.

SAGE-AND-ANCHOVY FRITTERS

ACCIUGHINI

YIELDS
12 FRITTERS

TOSCANA

24 large sage leaves, rinsed and patted dry
1½ cups all-purpose flour, plus more for dredging the sage leaves
6 salt-cured anchovies, rinsed and filleted
½ cup white wine
1 large egg white, beaten until foamy
Olive oil

This dish is popular in Piombino, a town on the southern coast of Toscana.

Dredge the sage leaves in flour. Cut the anchovies in half lengthwise and sandwich each half between two sage leaves, squeezing to make them stick together. ✦ Whisk together the flour, wine, egg white, and 1 tablespoon olive oil to make a batter. Heat 3 inches of olive oil in a saucepan. Dip the sage-and-anchovy sandwiches in the batter, then fry them until golden brown and crunchy. Serve hot.

ONION PIZZAS

AGNOLOTTI CON CIPOLLA

SARDEGNA

2 lbs. medium onions, chopped
1¾ lbs. plum tomatoes, peeled and chopped
7 oz. *casu de fitta* (aged pecorino sheep cheese; can use ricotta salata), grated
7 oz. *lardo* (see note), minced
¼ cup diced zucchini
2 cups all-purpose flour, plus more as needed
Outer leaves from 1 head of cabbage
Salt

Lardo is pork fatback, from the strip of fat that runs along the pig's back. The *lardo* used for cooking is most often fresh, not to be confused with the *lardo* that is cured and seasoned (see page 42). If fatback is unavailable, you could trim just the white fat portion from unsmoked bacon and use that as a substitute.

Preheat the oven to 400°F. Combine the onions, tomatoes, cheese, *lardo*, and zucchini. Blend this with the flour and about ½ cup warm salted water to obtain a somewhat firm dough. Divide the dough into 6-inch pizzas that are 1½ inches thick. ✦ Arrange the cabbage leaves on the bottom of a baking pan, place the pizzas on top of them, and bake until golden. Serve warm.

ORANGES WITH ANCHOVIES

ANTIPASTO D'ARANCE

MOLISE

4 large, juicy oranges
(preferably organic)

6 oz. salt-cured anchovies,
packed in oil

⅓ cup extra-virgin olive oil

Salt

Rinse and dry the oranges. Do not peel them. Cut them crosswise in thin slices. ✦ Arrange the slices on a *sperlunga* (large serving plate). Garnish with anchovy fillets and dress with olive oil and salt.

✦ **LOCAL TRADITION** ✦

ALBORELLE OR SARDINE SALATE

Fish prepared by this traditional method, typical of the Lake Iseo area of Lombardy, go very well with spaghetti or fresh polenta. Fresh alborelle, or sardines, are slightly dried on a rack and then layered in an earthenware pot with a mixture of chopped garlic, sage, and rosemary and coarse sea salt. The pot is then covered and weighted and left undisturbed for a period of up to 2 months, after which time the fish are soaked in water and then milk to remove the salt before eating.

SEAFOOD RICE BALLS

ARANCINI AL SAPORE
DI MARE

SICILIA

2 ½ cups Arborio rice

A few threads saffron,
steeped in 1 tbsp. warm water

3 large eggs, lightly beaten

½ cup grated Parmigiano-Reggiano

Extra-virgin olive oil

1 garlic clove, chopped

½ medium onion, chopped

CONTINUED

This dish is typical of Caltanissetta. The fritters can also be made smaller, about the size of a large nut, and served with an aperitif. In that case, the fish stuffing should be mixed together with the rice, but otherwise the fritters would be prepared the same way.

Boil the rice in 4 cups lightly salted water until it is al dente; drain it well. Add the saffron and its water, half the eggs, and Parmigiano-Reggiano, mixing well. Set aside to cool. ✦ Prepare the filling: Heat 2 tablespoons olive oil in a large pan and sauté the garlic and onion; add the tomatoes, then the seafood, beginning with the pieces that require the most cooking. The baby shrimp

½ cup plum tomatoes, peeled and chopped

½ lb. sliced swordfish, pieces of cuttlefish (all carefully boned); baby shrimp

½ cup dry white wine

All-purpose flour

Breadcrumbs

should come last. Pour in the white wine and let it evaporate, then complete the cooking, adding warm water if necessary, bearing in mind that the result should be soft but not soupy. Let cool enough to handle, then chop the fish into small pieces. ✦ Take a tangerine-size ball of rice mixture and press your thumb in the center to make a hollow. Add a little filling, then close the rice around it, and form into a ball. Roll the balls in the flour, then the remaining eggs, then breadcrumbs. Heat 3 inches of olive oil in a saucepan, enough to deep-fry the balls. The oil must be hot, but not smoking, before adding the balls. Working in batches (being careful not to crowd the pan), fry until golden. Drain well and serve hot.

ARANCINI DI RISO

RICE BALLS
WITH MEAT AND PEAS

SICILIA

2 ½ cups Arborio rice

2 large eggs, beaten

4 tbsp. (½ stick) unsalted butter

1 cup grated caciocavallo cheese (if possible from Ragusa)

1 tbsp. chopped flat-leaf parsley

For the filling:

7 oz. browned ground veal or pork, minced, with a little of its gravy

Pinch powdered saffron

½ cup fresh peas, cooked with onion

4 oz. fresh tuma (unsalted goat's-milk cheese), cut in bits

6 oz. breadcrumbs

Olive oil for frying

Salt and pepper

Boil the rice in 4 cups lightly salted water, cooking it over moderate heat for about 15 minutes and stirring continuously until all the water is absorbed. Remove from the heat and quickly add half the eggs, butter, and half the caciocavallo. When blended, stir in the parsley and season with salt and pepper. ✦ While the rice cools, prepare the filling. Mix the meat, saffron, peas, tuma, and the remaining caciocavallo until blended. ✦ With damp hands take a small quantity of rice (about ¼ cup), spread it out on your palm, and place a teaspoonful of the filling in the center, then close the rice over, forming a ball roughly the size of a small orange. Heat 3 inches of oil in a saucepan until hot. Dip the balls in the remaining eggs and then breadcrumbs. Working in batches (being careful not to crowd the pan), fry until golden, drain well, and serve warm.

ASPARAGUS
WITH GORGONZOLA

**ASPARAGI
AL GORGONZOLA**

PIEMONTE

1 ¾ lbs. asparagus,
woody ends trimmed

7 oz. Gorgonzola dolce, sliced

4 tbsp. (½ stick) unsalted butter,
melted

Salt

There are two types of Gorgonzola, a luscious blue-veined cheese. Gorgonzola dolce, which is creamy and yellow, is more suitable for this recipe than Gorgonzola piccante, which is crumbly and white.

Preheat the oven to 400°F. Cut the asparagus stalks to equal length, and boil briefly in lightly salted water until very bright green. ✦ Dry the asparagus stalks, place them in a baking dish, and cover with Gorgonzola and butter. Bake until the cheese is melted and lightly browned, about 10 minutes.

✦ **LOCAL TRADITION** ✦

ASPIC

From the area of Lombardy, this preparation for aspic incorporates veal sweetbreads, *filoni* (spinal cord with marrow), cock's comb, beef tongue, and pistachios. The sweetbreads, *filoni*, and cock's comb are cleaned, rinsed, and boiled separately in water and lemon juice. The tongue and pistachios are layered in a traditional mold or loaf pan, topped with gelatin, and chilled until set. The boiled meats are then arranged in overlapping layers with more gelatin used to keep the layers intact. Once the whole dish has set and chilled, slice it at the table.

GREEN SAUCE
FOR BOILED MEAT

BAGNETTO VERDE

PIEMONTE

1 large bunch flat-leaf parsley

2 garlic cloves, chopped

3 salt-cured anchovies, chopped

½ cup breadcrumbs

1 tbsp. red wine vinegar

Pinch chili pepper flakes (optional)

⅔ cup olive oil

In Piedmont this sauce is indispensable as an accompaniment to mixed boiled meats.

Carefully wash and dry the parsley, finely chop it, and combine well with the other ingredients except the oil. Then whisk in the oil.

BAGNA CAÔDA

Literally "hot bath," *bagna caôda* is a pungent dip and sauce first devised by ancient Piedmontese winemakers. This is the traditional process: In a large earthenware pot, over a low flame and stirring constantly for at least 30 minutes, slowly dissolve thinly sliced garlic cloves in extra-virgin olive oil and butter. Once they have become a creamy, homogenous sauce, add the Spanish red anchovies and more oil and cook slowly until the anchovies dissolve, blending with the garlic and oil to create a light brown sauce. The secret of the preparation, critical if one wants a good, healthy, and easy-to-digest *bagna caôda,* is to heat it over a low flame and to never overcook it. Firm traditionalists insist on a full head of garlic per person, up to 15 cloves, though 2 to 3 cloves, soaked in cold water for a couple hours or placed under running water, per person will suffice. Use 2 to 3 anchovies per person, cleaned in water and wine, well dried, and boned. The oil must be extra-virgin olive oil, with at least 2 tablespoons per person. When serving at the table, add oil if needed, gradually augmenting the sauce.

The vegetables to dip into the sauce should be those typical of Piedmontese kitchen gardens: cardoons (the Gobbi "hunchback" of Nice or Spadoni di Chieri variety); red peppers, both raw and roasted; pickled red peppers; Jerusalem artichokes; green, white, and red cabbage; white hearts of escarole and chicory; fresh leeks; white turnips; roasted beets; boiled cauliflower; roasted onions; white potatoes boiled in their skins; apples; slices of roasted or fried pumpkin; as well as slices of hot roasted or fried polenta. Long spring onions were also sometimes served for dipping, first sliced crosswise at the base and presented at the table in bunches of 3 or 4, half-immersed in a glass of Barbera. Fresh eggs could be scrambled in the last spoonfuls of the *bagna caôda* remaining in the earthenware pot.

FRIED SQUASH RAVIOLI

BARBAGIOAN

LIGURIA

2 lbs. yellow squash
2 garlic cloves, minced
2 tbsp. chopped flat-leaf parsley
4 large eggs, beaten
⅔ cup grated Parmigiano-Reggiano
⅔ cup grated pecorino
CONTINUED

Preheat the oven to 350°F. Peel the squash and pass it through a food mill. Put the purée in a baking pan and bake 10 minutes; when cool enough to handle, remove it from the pan, wrap in a dishcloth, and squeeze dry. ✦ Put the squash purée in a bowl. Let cool for 10 minutes. Add the garlic, parsley, eggs, cheeses, oregano, rice, butter, and olive oil; salt and pepper to taste and mix carefully to blend. ✦ Use the flour to prepare a pasta dough as on page 10, using 1 teaspoon olive oil and ½ cup

Fresh oregano

½ cup rice, cooked al dente

4 tbsp. (½ stick) unsalted butter, melted

⅓ cup extra-virgin olive oil, plus more for the dough and for frying

1⅔ cups all-purpose flour, plus more as needed

Salt and pepper

water in place of the eggs, and roll out the dough to form a sheet (see note, page 212). Drop the filling in evenly spaced nut-size dollops 1½ inches apart along the sheet. Roll out a second sheet, cover the bottom sheet. Press down using your fingertips to separate the dollops of filling and flatten the dough between the dollops. Cut the dough to form square ravioli. Heat about 2 inches of olive oil in a pan and fry the ravioli until golden brown. Serve very hot.

◆ **LOCAL TRADITION** ◆

BARBAZZA SCOTTATA

This is a preparation one finds in Umbria. Take two thin slices of *barbazza* (*guanciale*, or pork cheek) and fry them in a pan with a little olive oil and several sage leaves. When the *barbazza* is browned, add a little red wine vinegar. Nothing is more fragrant and appetizing. Serve piping hot.

BRIOCHE RUSTICA

STUFFED BRIOCHE

CAMPANIA

3 cups all-purpose flour, plus more as needed

2¼ tsp. active dry yeast

¾ cup (1½ sticks) unsalted butter

½ cup sugar

½ cup grated Parmigiano-Reggiano

3 large eggs

⅔ cup milk

6 oz. mixed salame, cubed

6 oz. fresh provolone, cubed

CONTINUED

Combine ½ cup of the flour, yeast, and enough water to form a dough. Knead into a small loaf; cover and let rise until doubled in size. ◆ Butter and flour a tube or Bundt pan. Combine the remaining flour, sugar, Parmigiano-Reggiano, and salt with the eggs and butter. Work this mixture a long time, slowly adding milk until it is soft but compact and, finally, add the small yeasted loaf, which by then will have doubled in size. Knead this energetically until the mixture comes away from the bowl as a single piece. Form the dough into a ball, inscribe it with a cross, cover, and let rise. ◆ After about an hour, rework the dough and roll it out into a large strip about 6 inches wide. ◆ Distribute the pieces of salame and cheese along the length of the strip of dough then roll the dough over on itself to enclose the filling, forming a narrow roll. ◆

2 cups peas sautéed in unsalted butter and prosciutto (or 2 cups stewed eggplant or 2 cups sautéed mushrooms)

Salt

Fit the roll in the prepared pan, cover with a cloth, and let it rise until the brioche has expanded to reach the edges of the pan. ✦ Preheat the oven to 350°F. Bake the brioche 25 to 30 minutes, or until it becomes a dark blond color. ✦ Remove from the oven, transfer to a serving dish, and fill the central cavity with the cooked peas and prosciutto, or with eggplant or mushrooms.

✦ **LOCAL TRADITION** ✦

BÈLECÒT

This fresh salame is connected to the *Fira di sette dulur* ("Fair of the seven sorrows") held annually around the third Sunday of September at Russi, an important center on the Romagna plain leading from Ravenna to Faenza. Known in dialect as *bèlecòt* ("already cooked"), this salame falls halfway between cotechino and the traditional (and nearly extinct) *zuzzezza màta* sausage (the name of which does not express its dominant reddish color).

BRUSCHETTA

BRUSCHETTA

LAZIO

4 slices peasant-style bread
1 garlic clove, peeled and cut in half
Olive oil
Salt

The word *bruschetta* is derived from the dialect word *bruscare*, meaning "to scorch." According to the late Secondino Freda of the Accademia Italiana della Cucina, bruschetta was once known to the common people as *cappone* ("capon"). This popular term reflects the fact that the less well to do, not having the financial means to enjoy a true capon (perhaps cooked with the spicy "diavolo" sauce), made do with "*bruscato,*" bread seasoned with garlic and olive oil, leading to the name *cappone*. Without doubt, this savory antipasto came into being in the vicinity of olive presses where, since ancient times, the quality of the freshly pressed oil was assessed by drizzling some of it over slices of grilled bread. If desired, freshly ground pepper can be added, increasing the flavor of the bruschetta.

Grill the slices of bread and rub them with the garlic. Arrange them on a serving plate, season with salt, and sprinkle with olive oil.

BREAD RINGS WITH BAKED EGGS

BUCCELLATI OR CIAMBELLE CON LE UOVA

CALABRIA

Olive oil

1 lb. bread dough (see page 13)

1 heaping tbsp. lard

Pinch chili pepper flakes

Eggs

Salt

Grease a baking sheet with olive oil. Knead the bread dough with the lard, salt, and chili pepper flakes until it is soft and elastic. Divide it in pieces and shape them into rings. Arrange the rings on the greased pan; let them rise in a warm spot before putting in the oven. ✦ Preheat the oven to 350°F. Crack a raw egg into the center of each ring. Bake until the rings are golden and the eggs are set, about 25 minutes.

FRIED FLATBREAD

BURTLEINA

EMILIA-ROMAGNA

3 cups all-purpose flour, plus more as needed

1 cup lard or olive oil

Salt

This dish is typical of Piacenza and the Faenza area.

Put the flour in a bowl and slowly whisk in enough warm water to obtain a somewhat liquid batter (about 2 cups); add salt to taste. ✦ In a frying pan heat lard or ½ inch of olive oil and when it is hot pour in a thin layer of the batter. Cook at a high heat on both sides until the mixture is crisp and browned. ✦ Dry on paper towels and serve hot with a dusting of salt.

FRIED CHEESE

CÁCIÙ ALL'ARGINTÉRA

SICILIA

¼ cup olive oil

2 garlic cloves

1 lb. fresh cheese (pecorino or caciocavallo), sliced into ½-inch slices

2 tbsp. vinegar

1 tbsp. chopped fresh oregano

Pepper

This dish's Sicilian name means "silversmith's cheese," almost certainly a reference to the color of the cooked cheese.

In a pan heat the olive oil over medium heat. Lightly sauté the garlic until blond, then discard it. ✦ Cook the cheese pieces in the oil, turning them as soon as they take on color, then quickly sprinkle in the vinegar, and add oregano and pepper. Cover for a few minutes, then serve the cheese very hot.

BAKED DUMPLINGS
WITH SAUSAGE AND CHEESE

LAZIO

For the dough:

1½ cups all-purpose flour, plus
more as needed

2 large eggs

1 tsp. lard

2 tbsp. olive oil

Salt

For the filling:

¾ cup grated Parmigiano-Reggiano

½ cup grated pecorino

4 oz. sausage, cut in pieces

2 tbsp. chopped flat-leaf parsley

3 large eggs, beaten

For the glaze:

1 large egg yolk, beaten

These appetizers may well have a Neapolitan origin since they can be found in several towns that were once part of the Kingdom of Naples.

Here is an essential, all-purpose method for making pasta dough: Pour the flour onto a work surface or into a mixing bowl and shape it into a mound. Use your hand or the bottom of a measuring cup to hollow out the center of the mound to form a crater. ✦ Break the eggs into the crater, add a pinch of salt, the lard, and olive oil (note that in some pasta recipes, no fat is used). Beat the egg mixture lightly with a fork, as if making scrambled eggs. When the eggs begin to look homogeneous, use the fork to pull a little of the flour into the eggs, gradually adding more flour just until the eggs are no longer runny. Push aside about 3 tablespoons of flour, then use your hands to work the rest of the flour into the eggs until the dough is smooth. ✦ When you think you have achieved the right texture, wash and dry your hands. Press your finger into the center of the ball dough. If the dough does not stick to your finger as you pull it out, you do not need to add more flour. If the dough is still sticky, knead in flour in small increments (heaping tablespoons) until the dough passes the test. ✦ Use a towel or pastry scraper to remove any loose flour or crumbs from your work surface—it should be clean when you knead the dough. Press the ball of dough forward with the palm of your hand, then fold the dough over on itself, then give the dough a half turn. Repeat, pressing forward with your palm, folding in half, and turning, always in the same direction. When the dough is smooth and slightly "leathery" (anywhere from 5 to 10 minutes), it is ready to be rolled out. ✦ Preheat the oven to 400°F. In a bowl mix together the cheeses and sausage. Add the parsley and the eggs and knead to blend. ✦ Roll the pasta out into a thin sheet (see note, page 212). Cut out circles about 2½ inches in diameter and spoon walnut-size portions of the prepared filling in the center of each. Close each by placing another pasta circle on top, pressing down along the edges with a thumb to seal. ✦ Brush the *calascioni* with egg yolk and bake for 5 minutes, or until golden.

FRIED DUMPLINGS WITH PROSCIUTTO AND CHEESE

MOLISE

For the filling:

1 lb. sheep's-milk ricotta

2 large egg yolks, beaten

4 oz. prosciutto crudo, cut in thick slices, then cut in slightly large cubes

4 oz. provolone piccante cheese, cut in slightly large cubes

Chopped flat-leaf parsley

Salt and white pepper

For the dough:

2 ⅓ cups all-purpose flour, plus more as needed

2 large eggs, beaten

4 oz. lard

Juice of 1 lemon

Extra-virgin olive oil

Mix the ricotta and egg yolks in a bowl until blended. Add the prosciutto, provolone, and parsley, salt to taste, and a little freshly ground pepper. Knead well to obtain a homogenous ball, firm to the touch. Let this rest in the same bowl. ✦ Use the flour and eggs to prepare a pasta dough as on page 10, adding the lard and lemon juice with the eggs. Roll the dough out into a somewhat thin sheet (see note, page 212). On one-half of the sheet arrange little lumps of the filling; these should be about the size of a large walnut, spaced about 2 inches apart. Cover the half of the sheet with the other half. Use your fingertips to separate the *calcioni*. Using a pastry wheel, cut out the *calcioni* one by one, pressing down slightly with the fingers along the edges to seal. ✦ Pour 2 inches of olive oil in an iron pan and, when it is hot, lower in the *calcioni*, a few at a time, letting them cook until well browned. Remove them with a slotted spoon, drain on paper towels, and serve hot.

OLIVE AND RICOTTA CALZONES

PUGLIA

For the dough:

2 cups all-purpose flour, plus more as needed

2 ½ tsp. active dry yeast, dissolved in 2 tbsp. warm water

Extra-virgin olive oil

For the filling:

1 medium onion, sliced

¾ lb. ripe plum tomatoes, peeled and chopped

⅓ cup pitted and chopped black olives

4 oz. ricotta salata, passed through a sieve

Salt and pepper

CONTINUED

During the period of Lent in Puglia, it was once customary to enrich the filling of these *calzoni* with the addition of salted anchovies, boned and cut up, added together with the olives.

Pour the flour onto a flat surface and work it together with the yeast mixture, a dash of salt, and ¼ cup of the olive oil. Knead the dough, turning and folding it onto itself, until it becomes soft and elastic, adding water by the tablespoon as necessary—you may need to add as much as ¾ cup. Then cover it with a clean kitchen towel and let it rise for about an hour. ✦ Preheat the oven to 450°F. Grease a baking dish. In a saucepan, heat 3 tablespoons olive oil and sauté the onion until pale, then add the tomatoes. Cook the sauce down for a few minutes, then add salt, pepper, and olives. Remove the pan from the heat and add the ricotta salata and mix well. ✦ Roll out the dough on a floured board into two sheets, one larger than the other. With the larger one line the greased pan. Pour in the sauce, spread it out, and cover with the other sheet, folding the edges over each other. Bake for approximately 20 minutes or until the top is golden.

CALZONE DI CARNEVALE

CARNIVAL CALZONE

PUGLIA

Olive oil

For the dough:
6½ cups all-purpose flour, plus more as needed
1¼ cups sugar
1 tbsp. active dry yeast
5 large eggs, beaten
¾ cup (1½ sticks) plus 2 tbsp. unsalted butter, softened

For the filling:
Olive oil
2 lbs. mixed ground pork and veal
5 large eggs, beaten
⅔ cup grated Parmigiano-Reggiano
Sugar
1¾ lb. ricotta
2 fresh scamorza cheese, thinly sliced
1 large egg yolk, beaten

Like the preceding one, this dish is served in Bari at Carnival time.

Preheat the oven to 350°F. Grease a round baking pan with olive oil and dust it with flour. ✦ Make a well with the flour on the work surface or in a bowl. Add the sugar and yeast in the center and mix well. Make a well again and add the eggs and butter; knead well. The dough should be soft; add another egg if necessary. ✦ Divide the dough in two parts, one larger than the other. Roll out the larger portion to form a ⅛-inch-thick sheet and use it to line the pan. ✦ Heat 1 tablespoon olive oil in a pan and add the meats. Sauté until brown and put the meat in a mixing bowl. Add the eggs and Parmigiano-Reggiano; mix well to obtain a homogeneous mixture. ✦ Sprinkle sugar on the dough in the baking pan and top with an even layer of meat mixture; cover with ricotta. Arrange the slices of scamorza over the ricotta and sprinkle on more sugar. ✦ Roll out the remaining dough to form a 1/16-inch-thick sheet and use this to cover the pan, sealing the edges. Pierce the top with a fork, brush with egg yolk, and sprinkle with sugar. Bake until the top is well browned.

CALZONE RIPIENO AL FORNO

BAKED CALZONE

CAMPANIA

Ciccioli are made during the process of rendering lard: Pork fat is cut in cubes and "melted" in copper pots over low heat. The result still contains small bits of pork meat; these are removed, flavored with salt and pepper, pressed, and aged to create *ciccioli*, also called *sfrizzoli*. There are also *spergoli (spapagliati)*, which are of a darker color. The use of tomatoes in *calzoni* is relatively recent, dating to the 1940s, and there are still Neapolitan pizzerias where *calzone* is made without them.

Olive oil

2 lbs. bread dough (see recipe below)

1 lb. ricotta

4 oz. *ciccioli* (see note)

6 oz. salame (Neapolitan if possible), cut in pieces

10 oz. fresh provolone or *fior di latte* cheese, cubed

½ cup grated Parmigiano-Reggiano

4 tbsp. lard

¼ cup fresh tomato purée (optional)

Salt and pepper

Preheat the oven to 450°F. Grease a baking sheet with olive oil. Divide the dough in four pieces, roll out to form disks, and place them on the sheet. Each will become a calzone. ✦ Combine the ricotta with the *ciccioli,* salame, provolone (or *fior di latte*), and Parmigiano-Reggiano; mix well. Put a quarter of this filling at the center of each disk. ✦ Close each calzone by folding the dough over and pressing down along the edges with the tines of a fork. Put a pat of lard on each calzone and, if desired, a tablespoon of tomato purée. ✦ Bake for about 10 minutes.

CALZUNCIELLI DI SCAMMARO

FASTING DAY (MEATLESS) CALZONE

FOR 6 PERSONS

CAMPANIA

For the dough:

3 cups all-purpose flour, plus more as needed

⅔ cup extra-virgin olive oil

2¼ tsp. active dry yeast, dissolved in 2 tbsp. warm water

For the filling:

2 anchovy fillets packed in oil

1 garlic clove

2 heads of escarole, boiled, drained, and chopped

¾ cup capers, crushed

½ cup pitted and chopped black olives (Gaeta if possible)

½ cup each pine nuts and raisins (optional)

Olive oil

Salt

Mix together the flour, a dash of salt, ⅓ cup of the olive oil, yeast with its water, and enough additional water (¾ to 1 cup should be sufficient) to obtain a somewhat soft dough. Knead well, until the dough is smooth and elastic. Cover the dough with a kitchen towel and let rise for 2 hours. This is a standard dough (of about 1½ pounds) that can be used for many bread and pizza recipes. ✦ Flour a sheet pan and set aside. Heat the anchovy fillets in a pan with their olive oil over very low heat until they are melted. Raise the heat slightly and sauté the garlic, removing it and discarding it when it is golden. Add the escarole and stir to blend. Continue cooking, adding the capers and olives and, if desired, pine nuts and raisins. ✦ Divide the dough into egg-size lumps, then with floured hands pat them out to form disks about 4 inches in diameter. Arrange these disks on the pan and put a little of the escarole mixture at the center of each. Fold over the disks to close and press down along the edges with the tines of a fork to seal. ✦ Heat 1½ inches of olive oil in a wide high-sided pan. Fry the *calzoni* until golden, drain on paper towels, and serve.

CAPONATA 1

4 salt-cured anchovies

1 lb. cauliflower, cleaned, boiled, and chopped

6 oz. mixed pickled vegetables, chopped

2 *papaccelle* (pickled peppers), chopped

1 head escarole, chopped

1 head lettuce, chopped

½ cup capers

½ cup black olives (preferably Gaeta), pitted and chopped

⅔ cup olive oil

¾ cup white wine vinegar

4 *freselle* (bread biscuits)

1 cup white wine

½ lb. mackerel, poached and seasoned with olive oil and lemon

Salt and pepper

This dish is typical of Maddaloni.

In a large salad bowl combine the anchovies, cauliflower, pickled vegetables, *papaccelle,* escarole, lettuce, capers, and olives. Season with a little salt, pepper, olive oil, and ¼ cup of the vinegar and mix energetically. ✦ Place the *freselle* in a bowl and add the wine and remaining vinegar and let stand; when they are softened crumble them into the salad mixture, mixing well to make the mixture smooth. Top with the mackerel.

CAPONATA 2

4 *taralli* (savory biscuits similar to pretzels)

Splash white wine vinegar

4 firm plum tomatoes, chopped

2 celery stalks, chopped

1 large and fleshy sweet pepper, chopped

1 cucumber, cleaned and chopped

2 garlic cloves, chopped

Green and black olives as desired

2 large hard-boiled eggs, sliced

4 oz. anchovies in oil

Pinch dried oregano

¼ cup extra-virgin olive oil

Salt

Briefly soak the *taralli* in lightly salted water, sprinkle them with the vinegar, and let them dry for 5 minutes on a kitchen cloth. ✦ Place the *taralli* on a serving plate and cover them with the tomatoes, celery, pepper, cucumber, garlic, and olives; garnish this with slices of hard-boiled eggs and anchovies. ✦ Season the caponata with oregano, salt, and olive oil, and let it sit for about half an hour in the refrigerator before serving.

CAPONATA 3

LIGURIA

2 hardtack crackers

1 small can tuna in oil, drained and broken up

3 anchovies, boned and chopped

2 oz. *mosciame* (salt-cured tuna loin), sliced

½ cup green olives

1 tbsp. capers, rinsed

Extra-virgin olive oil

White wine vinegar

Salt

This dish is typical of Imperia.

Soak the crackers in water until soft, drain thoroughly, and put them in a salad bowl with the tuna, anchovies, *mosciame*, olives, and capers. Season with olive oil, vinegar, and salt to taste. Mix carefully and let stand at least 1 hour before serving.

✦ **LOCAL TRADITION** ✦

CARNE 'NCARTARATA

Following the method for *carne 'ncartaratai*, or "aged meat," from Calabria entails thickly slicing both fat and lean portions of pork and arranging the slices in layers within an enameled earthenware crock—preferably a *salaturi*, a traditional wide-mouthed container about 8 inches in diameter. Each layer is spread with salt and pieces of Calabrian red chili pepper and pressed. A wooden plank is placed on top of the vessel and weighted, and the *carne* is left to age for several months in a cool place.

BOILED CHESTNUTS WITH BUTTER

CASTAGNE BOLLITE CON BURRO

VALLE D'AOSTA

This dish is typical of the German-speaking Walser community in Aosta. The chestnuts can be used as a side dish to accompany other specialties of the area, such as *lard d'Arnad* (see page 42), *jambon de Bosses*, Valdostan sausages, and cooked blood pudding. Dried chestnuts can be used in place of fresh, but they must be soaked in lukewarm water overnight before being cooked. Instead of boiling the chestnuts in water, you can use whey or buttermilk.

½ lb. fresh chestnuts
4 tbsp. (½ stick) unsalted butter
¼ cup superfine sugar or to taste
Salt

Shell the chestnuts, cover them with several inches of lightly salted water, and boil them. When cooked (between 30 minutes and an hour, depending on how fresh the chestnuts are), drain well. Heat the butter in a pan and add the chestnuts, tossing to coat. If desired, add sugar and cook until the sugar has melted.

CHIOCCIOLE A PICCHI PACCHI

SNAILS WITH PICCHI PACCHI SAUCE

SICILIA

2 lbs. *vaccareddi* (large snails)
2 tbsp. olive oil
1 medium onion, cut in thin slices
4 ripe plum tomatoes, peeled and seeded
Pinch chili pepper flakes (optional)
2 tbsp. chopped flat-leaf parsley (or basil)
Salt and black pepper

Before being cooked the snails must be purified: Put them in a large basket, firmly sealed so they cannot escape, and leave them for 24 hours. Wash them carefully, then put them in a pan, cover with cold water, and place over low heat, letting them cook for about 2 hours. Drain well and set aside. ✦ Heat the olive oil in a pan and sauté the onion. Add the snails and stir them around a little, then add the tomatoes, salt, black pepper, chili pepper (if desired), and parsley (or basil). Carefully stir and cook, covered, another 15 minutes. The dish can be served hot or cold.

CIAMBELLE COL FORMAGGIO | RING CAKES WITH CHEESE

UMBRIA

3 tbsp. olive oil

5 oz. pecorino dolce cheese

3 tbsp. extra-virgin olive oil

1¾ lbs. bread dough already leavened (see page 13)

These are typical of the area around Todi, where they are made using that area's excellent pecorino.

Preheat the oven to 400°F. Grease a baking sheet with olive oil. Grate half the pecorino and break the other half into small pieces. Work the cheese and olive oil into the bread dough, eventually forming it into a loaf; let this rise again. ✦ Divide the dough into 10 equal pieces. Roll each piece into a rope and form into a ring, pinching the ends together to close the ring. Arrange them on the baking sheet, leaving space between them, and bake for about 20 minutes, until golden. Let cool before serving.

✦ **LOCAL TRADITION** ✦

CIALDE

This traditional dish of Genoa for fried wafers stuffed with veal calls for *cialde*, large wafers only found in certain bakeries. The preparation begins with onion and parsley sautéed in butter and olive oil, to which is added veal, including ground veal, chopped cow's udder, chopped sweetbreads, and *granelli* (testicles). This mixture is cooked slowly and thinned with broth, and after an hour sliced artichokes and *schienale* (spinal marrow) are added to the pan. The mixture can be either finely chopped by hand or in a blender. Fresh peas and egg yolks are added once the mixture has cooled. One tablespoon of the mixture is spooned into the center of a *cialde* that has been dampened with broth only enough to become pliable. The wafer is then closed like a package and the edges sealed, then dipped in whipped egg whites and breadcrumbs, and fried in olive oil.

CIARLA

This basic recipe for pizza dough from Lazio is the same as that used to make bread: A simple mixture of flour, water, and yeast is prepared in the same method as on page 13. The dough is baked in a pizza oven heated to its highest temperature; when the pizza is well cooked, it should be removed from the oven, halved crosswise, and seasoned with a layer of ricotta, thin slices of fresh pecorino, or prosciutto crudo. It was also once common to spread a thin layer of honey over freshly baked pizza dough and eat it folded while still hot.

CIPOLLE RIPIENE DI CARNE

ONIONS STUFFED WITH MEAT

PIEMONTE

2 lbs. onions (preferably the flat onions called *cipolline*)

1 tbsp. aromatic herbs (flat-leaf parsley, sage, rosemary, thyme), finely chopped

½ cup (1 stick) unsalted butter, plus more for topping

8 oz. ground veal

1 stale roll, grated, then soaked in milk until soft

½ cup raisins, softened in warm water

4 large eggs, beaten

¾ cup grated Parmigiano-Reggiano

Salt

Preheat the oven to 350°F. Boil the onions in lightly salted water to cover until soft. Cut off the tops of the onions and scoop out the insides to form bowls. ✦ Mix the herbs with the onion pulp. Add the veal. Heat the butter and sauté the veal mixture; salt to taste. ✦ Drain the bread (reserve the milk) and raisins, then work them into the meat mixture, adding half the eggs and 2 table-spoons cheese. ✦ Stuff this mixture into the onion bowls and place them on a baking sheet. Beat the remaining eggs with the remaining cheese and add 1 tablespoon of the milk. Pour this over the onions almost to cover them. Dot each onion with butter. ✦ Bake until the surface is browned, about 20 minutes.

CIPOLLE RIPIENE DI MAGRO

MEATLESS STUFFED ONIONS

PIEMONTE

This is the main dish in the traditional cooking of Caravino, the town that was the source of this recipe. In the past it was prepared only for the feast day of the local patron saint, James, and for that of the Assumption.

4 tbsp. (½ stick) unsalted butter

2 lbs. medium yellow onions, with the tops cut off

½ lb. stale bread, soaked overnight in milk

3 large eggs, beaten

½ cup grated Parmigiano-Reggiano

½ cup golden raisins, softened

Pinch grated nutmeg

Various spices (marjoram and thyme)

Salt

Preheat the oven to 350°F. Grease a baking sheet with butter. Peel the onions and cook them in lightly salted water to cover. When they begin to open, remove them from the water, drain upside down in a colander, and let cool. ✦ Remove the center from each onion, being careful not to break the resulting "cup." Arrange these cups on the baking sheet. ✦ For the filling, squeeze the bread dry and pass it through a food mill. Finely chop the interiors of the onions and mix them into the bread. ✦ In a large pan melt 2 tablespoons butter and sauté the bread and onion for about 10 minutes, stirring continuously to keep it from sticking to the bottom of the pan. Put the mixture in a bowl and add the eggs, Parmigiano-Reggiano, raisins, nutmeg, spices, and salt. ✦ Fill the onion cups with this mixture and dot each with butter. Bake until a golden crust has formed on each onion. These can be served hot or cold, as an appetizer or entrée. As a light meal, they can replace the main dish.

✦ **LOCAL TRADITION** ✦

ONIONS IN THE PIEDMONTESE TRADITION

Onions have been cultivated in Piedmont since ancient times, as indicated by numerous medieval documents. According to Sandro Doglio, author of a dictionary of Piedmontese gastronomy, stuffed onions originated in the area around Turin, in particular at Settimo Torinese, where they have long represented the typical dish served on the last Sunday in August. Even so, the cultivation of onions has always been traditionally tied to the area around Canavese, where even today onions—filled with a variety of mixtures that vary from town to town—are a constant in meals prepared for important occasions. The versions change from place to place, and aside from those given here, there are those based on yellow squash, amaretti cookies, *mostarda*, and eggs. A curious version popular in old Piedmont called for baked onions stuffed with a mixture of powdered cacao, amaretti, egg yolks, and chopped onion (thus very much like the classical stuffing used for peaches). Such chocolate-filled onions were served as a side dish to meats.

Another filling for onions is cooked rice, with the addition of roast meat or salame or herbs. It seems likely that in the past onions were filled with whatever happened to be left over from the previous day's meals.

POTATO SALAD WITH ANCHOVIES, OLIVES, AND TOMATO

CONDIÔN

LIGURIA

1 lb. plum tomatoes, not overly ripe, sliced

1 cucumber, sliced

2 potatoes, boiled and sliced

1 chili pepper, cut in strips

½ cup pickled green olives, pitted and diced

5 salt-cured anchovies, rinsed of the salt

Several basil leaves, chopped

3 tbsp. extra-virgin olive oil

2 tbsp. white wine vinegar

2 large hard-boiled eggs, cut in sections

Salt

This dish is typical of the Riviera di Ponente.

Combine the tomatoes, cucumber, potatoes, chili pepper, olives, and anchovies; add the chopped basil. Season with a little salt, olive oil, and vinegar and mix carefully. Top with the eggs and serve.

✦ **LOCAL TRADITION** ✦

COPPA

The Umbrian pork sausage known as *coppa* is emblematic of the custom of making use of every part of a slaughtered pig. In a sense, everything that is not used in some other way goes into it, from tendons and gristle to fat, cartilage, and rind. The cleaning of the animal, the so-called *toletta*, is thus of primary importance. The better the variety of parts is, the better the *coppa* will be. The procedure goes as follows: Collect bones from which the meat has already been roughly removed and combine them with a few pork rinds, trotters, head, and ears (carefully cleaned and washed several times), and set all this to boil in water perfumed with fennel seeds, orange zest, and a few cloves. When it has cooked, detach the meat from the still-hot bones and chop it all up in a rough way, flavoring with salt, pepper, garlic cloves, and grated orange zest. Add salt as needed, working all this together by hand and then stuffing the mixture into a canvas sack. Tie it tightly closed and place it under a weight for a few days. The *coppa*, cut in thin slices, is excellent as part of an antipasto plate, but is also great on its own with a slice of peasant-style bread or a piece of hot foccacia.

COPPIETTA | # SMOKED SPICED VEAL | FOR 6 PERSONS

TOSCANA

2 lbs. veal tenderloin or top round
Wild fennel
Chili pepper flakes
3 garlic cloves, finely chopped
⅓ cup salt
Pepper

This dish is typical of the *butteri* ("cowboys") of the Maremma area. When a horse or donkey being raised in the wild e died, its hind quarters were used to make *coppietta*. Today, given the scarcity of animals raised wild, steers are used instead.

Cut the meat into strips about 8 inches long and 1 inch wide. Combine all the other ingredients with the meat in a large container. Mix well and let rest a few hours. ✦ Smoke the strips of meat by attaching them to the top of a fireplace for 2 or 3 days (or use a barbecue smoker). ✦ The strips can be eaten cut in pieces with stale bread and red wine.

COPPIETTE | # MEAT JERKY

LAZIO

2 lbs. tender donkey, horse, or steer meat
½ tsp. chili pepper flakes
Salt

This dish is typical of Rome and the Viterbo and Pontino areas.

Cut the meat into 4-inch strips. Season with salt and chili pepper. Attach near the heat of a fireplace so that it can dry and smoke well. ✦ When the strips have been smoked, preheat the oven to 275°F and bake for a few minutes to dry further. ✦ Eat at room temperature, accompanied by a good dry white wine. If you prefer them softer, thread onto skewers and heat over charcoal.

COZZE GRATINATE | # MUSSELS AU GRATIN

ABRUZZO

4 tbsp. breadcrumbs
3 tbsp. extra-virgin olive oil
1 large garlic clove, chopped
2 tbsp. chopped flat-leaf parsley
1 tsp. lemon juice
1 tbsp. tomato purée
4 lbs. mussels, washed and opened

This dish can be prepared without the tomato purée, and the mussels can be served with just a dusting of pecorino.

Preheat the oven to 400°F. In a bowl combine the breadcrumbs, olive oil, garlic, and parsley with a little lemon juice and tomato purée just to bind. ✦ Stuff this mixture into the mussels and bake them until the stuffing is golden, about 15 minutes.

STUFFED MUSSELS

COZZE RIPIENE

MOLISE

1 cup extra-virgin olive oil, or as needed

2 lbs. mussels (use somewhat large seaside mussels)

½ cup stale bread without crust

2 tbsp. grated pecorino

2 tbsp. chopped flat-leaf parsley

2 garlic cloves, minced

1 *diavolillo* (see note), minced

Diavolillo means "little devil" and is a very hot chili pepper. Thai bird chilies or several red serrano peppers can be used in place of the *diavolillo*.

Preheat the oven to 400°F. Grease a baking pan with olive oil. Scrape off any barnacles or beards from the mussels, brush, and rinse under running water. ✦ Arrange the mussels in a pot, cover, and cook them over high heat in nothing more than the seawater they give up until they open. As soon as they are all open, remove the pan from the heat. ✦ Crumble the bread into a bowl, adding the pecorino, parsley, garlic, and *diavolillo*. Work in just enough olive oil to bind; use this mixture to fill the mussels. ✦ Arrange the stuffed mussels on the pan, sprinkle with more olive oil, and bake in the oven 10 minutes, or until they are lightly browned.

EASTER CHEESE BREAD

CRESCIA DI PASQUA COL FORMAGGIO

FOR 10 PERSONS

UMBRIA

2 lbs. all-purpose flour, plus more as needed

1 lb. bread starter (see note), dissolved in 1 ½ cups slightly warmed milk and 1 ½ cups lukewarm water

½ cup (1 stick) plus 3 tbsp. unsalted butter

½ cup slightly warmed milk

1 oz. active dry yeast

10 large eggs, beaten

1⅔ cups grated Parmigiano-Reggiano

4 oz. Gruyère, cubed

4 tbsp. lard

⅓ cup salt

There is also an Easter pizza, typical of the area of Foligno, that is made without butter, Parmigiano-Reggiano, milk, or Gruyère, but instead with sharp aged pecorino. When, after about 10 days, it begins to harden, it is cut into cubes and added to broth (meat or vegetable). To make a bread starter, mix together ½ teaspoon active dry yeast, 2 cups of warm water, and 4 ½ cups all-purpose flour. Let rise at room temperature overnight. Then refrigerate until needed.

On the night before the preparation, form a well with the flour on a work surface, add the starter and enough water to bind, and form a loaf. Cut a cross into the surface to facilitate its rising and cover with a cloth to hold in the heat. ✦ The next morning preheat the oven to 400°F. Grease several deep pans with butter or lard. Rework the loaf with the milk and active dry yeast. In a large bowl mix the eggs, Parmigiano-Reggiano, Gruyère, butter, lard, and salt; mix well and work into the dough. Knead this mixture until it is soft. ✦ Divide the dough among the prepared pans, using an amount for each that does not extend more than halfway up the pan. Bake until golden and the loaves sound hollow when tapped, about 45 minutes.

FLATBREAD WITH GREENS AND SAUSAGE

CRESCIONE

EMILIA-ROMAGNA

For the dough:

4 oz. lard

2 cups all-purpose flour, plus more as needed

1 cup milk

For the filling:

2 tbsp. olive oil or unsalted butter

3 oz. *lardo* (see page 2)

3 oz. pancetta

2 garlic cloves

6 cups mixed greens (spinach, collard greens, beet greens, radicchio, chicory)

¼ lb. meat from a prosciutto bone, diced

¼ lb. fresh *ciccioli* (see note, page 12), chopped

¼ lb. fresh sausage meat, crumbled

Aromatic herbs (flat-leaf parsley, sage, rosemary, thyme), chopped

Salt

Preheat the oven to 350°F. Grease a baking pan with lard. Combine the ingredients as on page 13 to form an elastic, soft dough. Divide into loaves (balls) and let rest for 30 minutes covered by a cloth. Roll out the balls to form disks about 6 inches in diameter and a quarter of an inch thick. ✦ Heat the olive oil or butter in a pan and add the *lardo* and pancetta. Cook until lightly golden, then add the garlic and cook until golden. Remove and discard the garlic. Add the greens and toss briefly until wilted; remove from the pan and set aside. Add the prosciutto, *ciccioli*, and sausage and cook until browned, then add to the greens and work together; add the herbs. ✦ Top each disk of dough with the filling. Fold the dough over to form a half-moon shape, then seal closed with the tines of a fork, much like making a large raviolo. Bake until golden, about 20 minutes.

RING-SHAPED FRITTERS

CRESPELLE

LAZIO

1⅔ cups all-purpose flour, plus more as needed

1 large egg

¾ oz. active dry yeast

Extra-virgin olive oil

Salt

In the Ciociaria area, these are made for the midday "fast" on Christmas Eve. They are quite different from the crepe-like *crespelle* from other regions.

Knead the flour with 6 tablespoons lukewarm water, egg, yeast, and salt; the resulting dough should be soft. Put it in a bowl and let rise for about 1 hour. ✦ Heat several inches of oil in a saucepan. Using a spoon or wet fingers form hunks of dough into rings and put them immediately into the hot oil. Fry until light golden, drain on paper towels, and serve.

| # MYRTLE CREAM CROSTINI

TOSCANA

¾ cup fresh myrtle berries
½ garlic clove
½ cup (1 stick) unsalted butter
2 tbsp. olive oil
Slices of wholegrain bread, toasted
Salt and pepper

This dish is typical of Empoli. The distinctive flavor of myrtle, a Mediterranean evergreen shrub that grows commonly on the coasts and islands, is somewhat like that of juniper and rosemary, and was once as common as pepper in Italian cuisine. On the island of Sardinia, it's used to make a famous liqueur called mirto.

Chop together the berries and garlic. Work together with the other ingredients to obtain a mixture with the prevalent perfume and flavor of myrtle. ✦ Spread on slices of toasted wholegrain bread.

CROSTINI
ALLA PROVATURA | # CROSTINI WITH ANCHOVIES AND PROVATURA

CAMPANIA

½ cup (1 stick) unsalted butter
1 lb. stale bread
1 lb. *fior di latte* cheese (or provola)
3 tbsp. milk
6 anchovies in oil

Crostini have a long history in Italy: There are recipes for this dish that date back to the 1500s. The *provatura* in the title of this dish from Campania is a kind of buffalo-milk cheese, similar to mozzarella.

Preheat the oven to 450°F. Butter a tall, rectangular baking dish. Cut the crust from the bread to create slices the size of a playing card. Cut the *fior di latte* (or provola) in slices of the same size. ✦ Arrange alternating layers of bread and cheese in the baking dish; this can be done more easily by threading them on a long wooden skewer to keep them together. Brush the crostini with cold milk. ✦ Bake until the cheese has softened and the bread is toasted. Meanwhile, heat the butter and add the anchovies. Cook over low heat, stirring until the anchovies are melted. Pour the mixture over the bread and cheese, then let bake another minute and serve hot.

CROSTINI CON LE COZZE | # CROSTINI WITH MUSSELS

MOLISE

For the crostini:
Olive oil
CONTINUED

Heat an inch of olive oil in a high-sided pan. Dampen the slices of bread in the vinegar; let dry for several minutes on a clean cloth. Fry the bread until golden brown and crunchy. Remove them with a slotted spoon, drain, and set aside to dry on paper towels. ✦ Clean the mussels,

8 slices stale peasant-style bread

½ cup white wine vinegar

For the mussels:

2 lbs. mussels

2 tbsp. extra-virgin olive oil

2 garlic cloves, chopped

1 *diavolillo* (hot chili pepper; see note, page 22)

2 bay leaves

¾ cup dry white wine

2 tbsp. chopped flat-leaf parsley

removing the beards, scraping them, and rinsing under running water. Put them in a covered pot and cook them over high heat until they open. Drain the mussels, preserving the liquid and discarding the shells. ✦ Prepare the seasoning: Heat 2 tablespoons olive oil in a pan and sauté the garlic and *diavolillo*. Add the mussels, a cup of their liquid (add water as need to make a cup of liquid), and bay leaves; cook 5 minutes, then add the wine. As soon as the liquid has evaporated add the parsley. ✦ Arrange the bread on individual plates, and pour over each a ladleful of mussels with their cooking sauce and serve.

CROSTINI
DI FEGATINI E MILZA

CROSTINI WITH LIVER AND SPLEEN

TOSCANA

6 oz. calf's spleen

3 chicken livers

2 tbsp. extra-virgin olive oil

½ medium onion, finely chopped

1 celery stalk, finely chopped

⅓ cup white wine

1 cup broth

1 tbsp. capers, rinsed

Unsalted butter

8 slices stale peasant-style bread, toasted

Salt and pepper

This typical dish of Siena can also be made without the spleen.

Remove the skin from the spleen and clean the livers; cut both into somewhat large pieces. ✦ Heat the olive oil in a pan and sauté the onion and celery. Add the spleen and livers to the pan. Add the white wine and continue cooking, stirring often. When the wine has evaporated add the broth and capers. Cook until the sauce has thickened. ✦ Remove the meats and slice thinly. Return them to the mixture and add a little butter, salt, and pepper to taste. Sprinkle the bread with lukewarm broth to soften slightly, then spread the slices with the meat mixture.

CROSTINI
DI PÂTÉ DI FEGATINI

CHICKEN-LIVER PATÉ CANAPES

TOSCANA

2 chicken livers

1 cup beef broth

4 tbsp. (½ stick) unsalted butter, cut into small pieces

1 tsp. chopped capers

Slices of peasant-style bread, toasted

Flat-leaf parsley leaves

Salt

Rinse and clean the chicken livers. Simmer in the broth until the liver is just pink in the center. Crush with a fork and mix in the butter, salt, and capers until a paste is formed. ✦ Spread this mixture on small pieces of lightly toasted peasant-style bread and decorate each with a parsley leaf.

CRUDO DI CALAMARETTI | MARINATED SQUID

ABRUZZO

10 oz. small tender squid
1 medium onion, thinly sliced
½ cup extra-virgin olive oil
½ cup red wine vinegar
Pinch chili pepper flakes
Salt

This dish is typical of the fishermen of Pescara.

Put the squid and the onion in a bowl. Salt and season with olive oil, vinegar, and chili pepper flakes. Let stand briefly before serving.

ERBAZZONE | SPINACH PIE

FOR
6 PERSONS

EMILIA-ROMAGNA

3 lbs. spinach or Swiss chard, washed
4 tbsp. (1 stick) unsalted butter
2 oz. *lardo* (see page 2)
1 medium onion, finely diced
1 garlic clove, minced
⅔ cup grated Parmigiano-Reggiano
2 tbsp. olive oil
1⅔ cups all-purpose flour, plus more as needed
2 oz. pancetta, minced
Salt and pepper

This dish is typical of Reggio Emilia, where a rustic vegetable pie was long a traditional standby for picnics in the countryside, washed down with Lambrusco wine. Today, it also appears as an appetizer and is eaten in bars and cafes as a quick morning snack.

Preheat the oven to 350°F. Steam the spinach or Swiss chard in about ½ cup water until wilted, drain, pat dry, and chop. Heat the butter and *lardo* in a pan and sauté the onion until soft; add the spinach and garlic and cook 5 minutes. Cool and work in the Parmigiano-Reggiano, olive oil, salt, and pepper. ✦ Use the flour to prepare a pasta dough as on page 10, using ½ cup water in place of the eggs. Roll out half the dough to form a sheet (see note, page 212) to line a large pan; put the filling over this in a single thick layer. Roll out the other half of the dough to form a sheet to cover and place it over the filling, pleating the dough slightly to create ripples. Decorate with the pancetta. ✦ Bake until the surface is completely browned. Serve hot.

FARINATA | CHICKPEA CREPE

LIGURIA

1⅔ cups chickpea flour, plus more as needed
Olive oil

CONTINUED

This dish is typical of San Remo.

Whisk together the chickpea flour with ¾ cup water and a pinch of salt to form a thick batter; set aside to rest 12 hours. ✦ Spoon off the foam that will have formed and remix the batter; pass through a sieve. ✦ Preheat the oven to 425°F. Generously grease a baking sheet with olive oil.

1 medium onion, minced
Salt and pepper

Add the batter, spreading it across the oil with a wooden spoon. Sprinkle the onion over the surface along with a few grindings of black pepper. ✦ Bake for about 20 minutes, or until the crust has become golden. Serve warm.

FARINATA DEL TIGULLIO | # CHICKPEA FLATBREAD

LIGURIA

6 cups chickpea flour, plus more as needed
1 tsp. salt
½ cup olive oil

The final product should possess the following sensory traits: pleasing odor and tasty *sui generis* flavor. It should be no more than one-quarter of an inch thick with a soft interior and crunchy surface.

Blend the chickpea flour, salt, and enough water (about 2 cups) to make a soft dough. Set aside for 4 hours. ✦ Preheat a wood-burning oven or grill. Skim off the mixture and carefully mix with a wooden spoon before transferring it to a copper baking pan. Cover evenly with the olive oil. ✦ Bake for 10 minutes, or until the surface forms a golden crust. Serve warm on heated plates.

FIORI DI ZUCCHINI ACCOCCOLATI | # STUFFED ZUCCHINI BLOSSOMS

PIEMONTE

For the blossoms:
4 tbsp. (½ stick) unsalted butter
7 oz. ground veal
4 oz. sausage meat, crumbled
½ cup chopped Swiss chard
2 baby zucchini
1 tbsp. chopped aromatic herbs (flat-leaf parsley, sage, rosemary, bay leaf, thyme basil)
Crustless bread, softened in milk and squeezed dry
2 tbsp. grated Parmigiano-Reggiano
1 large egg, beaten
8 zucchini blossoms, trimmed

For the sauce:
2 large eggs, beaten
1 tbsp. milk
2 tbsp. unsalted butter
Salt

Heat half of the butter in a pan and cook the veal and sausage meat until brown. In another pan heat the remaining butter and sauté the Swiss chard. Simmer the zucchini in a little water until softened, then slice thin. ✦ Combine the meats, chard, zucchini, herbs, bread, Parmigiano-Reggiano, and egg. Salt to taste. Stuff the blossoms with this mixture and arrange them upside down in a pan. ✦ Separately mix the eggs and milk and pour over the stuffed blossoms (they will not be completely covered). Dot with butter. ✦ Cook over high heat until the sauce has thickened and the flowers are golden. Serve hot.

| # FOCACCIA

LIGURIA

3 cups all-purpose flour,
plus more as needed

2¼ tsp. active dry yeast

1 cup extra-virgin olive oil

Fennel seeds

Salt

Combine the flour with the yeast, salt, and 1 cup water as instructed on page 13 to make a smooth dough. Cover with a cloth and let rise for at least 3 hours. ✦ Preheat the oven to 400°F. Grease a baking sheet with olive oil. Roll the dough to form a sheet with a thickness of about ⅛ inch and place on the baking sheet. ✦ Using the fingers push down on the dough to form slight indentations in it. Sprinkle with salt, olive oil, and fennel seeds. Bake for about 20 minutes or until golden.

GUASTELLA | **FILLED FOCACCIA**

CALABRIA

3 cups all-purpose flour,
plus more as needed

2¼ tsp. active dry yeast,
dissolved in a little lukewarm water

1 oz. *lardo* (see page 2)

2 oz. dry spicy sausage, chopped

2 large hard-boiled eggs,
cut into wedges

4 oz. provolone, cubed

4 oz. pork rind, boiled and sliced

2 tbsp. unsalted butter

Pepper

This dialect name, *guastella,* recalls the derivation of the word *gastel* from Old French. An excellent rustic focaccia, this version is prepared in Calabria on Easter Monday.

Sift the flour and form it into a well. Work in enough water and the dissolved yeast to form an elastic dough. Knead for 5 to 6 minutes, cover, and let rise in a warm place for about 1 hour; when it has risen divide the dough in two parts. ✦ Preheat the oven to 350°F. Grease a baking pan with the *lardo* and use half of the dough to line it; fill evenly with the sausage, eggs, provolone, and pork rind. Sprinkle with pepper. Cover with the other half of the dough, using damp hands to press down to make level. Dot with butter and bake for about 30 minutes until golden.

FOCACCIA CON LA POLPA DI OLIVA | **FOCACCIA WITH OLIVES**

LIGURIA

3 cups all-purpose flour,
plus more as needed

2¼ tsp. active dry yeast,
dissolved in warm water

½ cup extra-virgin olive oil

CONTINUED

Sift the flour and form about half of it into a well on a work surface or in a bowl. Pour in the yeast mixture and add 1 cup of water. Knead to form a dough for 5 to 6 minutes, cover, and let rise in a warm place for about 2½ hours. ✦ When the dough has risen, form a well with the remaining flour and put the risen dough in the middle of it. Add 2 tablespoons olive oil, olives, salt, and 1 tablespoon water. Knead for about 6 minutes and let rest

1 cup pitted small black olives (preferably Taggiasca olives from Liguria), roughly chopped

Salt

covered for another 2½ hours. ✦ Preheat the oven to 350°F. Grease a baking pan with olive oil. Roll out the dough or flatten it with your hands to a uniform thickness. Sprinkle with the remaining olive oil and bake for about 20 minutes until golden.

FOCACCIA WITH OIL, TUNA, AND TOMATO

PITTEDDA CHICCHIULIATA

CALABRIA

3 cups all-purpose flour, plus more as needed

2¼ tsp. active dry yeast

1¼ lbs. plum tomatoes, peeled and seeded

¼ cup olive oil

6 oz. tuna in oil, drained and cut in small pieces

2 oz. anchovies, boned

⅔ cup pitted black olives, halved

2 tbsp. salted capers, rinsed

Salt

Using the flour, yeast, and water, prepare a dough as on page 13. Place it in a baking pan and let rise for 1 hour. ✦ Preheat the oven to 400°F. Combine the tomatoes and olive oil and cook over high heat; season with salt. Mix in the tuna, anchovies, olives, and capers. ✦ Spread this mixture over the risen dough, and bake for about 30 minutes until golden. This focaccia can be served hot or cold.

FOCACCIA WITH RICOTTA

PITTA CIU CASARICA

CALABRIA

FOR 6 PERSONS

1 tbsp. extra-virgin olive oil

1 lb. bread dough (see page 13)

2 tbsp. lard

1 cup ricotta

4 oz. caciocavallo cheese, finely sliced

4 oz. soppressata, sliced

1 tbsp. chopped flat-leaf parsley

2 large hard-boiled eggs, thinly sliced

Salt and pepper

Work the olive oil into the dough and knead to blend well. Divide the dough into two parts, one slightly larger than the other. ✦ Preheat the oven to 425°F. Grease a baking pan with 1 tablespoon lard. Roll out the dough to obtain 2 disks. Use the larger one to line the pan, allowing the dough to extend half an inch over the sides. ✦ Break up half the ricotta with the tines of a fork and spread it over the dough in the pan. Add the caciocavallo, soppressata, parsley, and eggs. Cover with the remaining ricotta and sprinkle with salt and pepper. ✦ Place the remaining dough over this, folding the edges inward and brushing them with a little water to better seal this large "pitta." Pierce the surface with the tines of a fork and dot with the remaining lard. Bake for about 40 minutes or until golden.

FRIED SAGE LEAVES

SALVIADE

FRIULI-VENEZIA GIULIA

⅔ cup all-purpose flour,
plus more as needed

1 large egg, beaten

40 large sage leaves

Olive oil

Salt

Combine the flour, egg, and salt to form a batter and let rest at least 1 hour. ✦ Heat about 1 inch of olive oil in a pan. Wash and dry the sage leaves, dip in the batter, and fry until golden. Serve immediately with a dash of salt.

MARINATED TOMA CHEESE

FORMAGGINO
DI PERANCHE

VALLE D'AOSTA

½ cup white wine vinegar

1 cup extra-virgin olive oil

2 tbsp. chopped flat-leaf parsley

1 garlic clove, crushed

Pinch chili pepper flakes

1 sage leaf

2 celery stalks, chopped

Pinch grated nutmeg

1 sprig thyme
(mountain thyme if possible)

12 small rounds of fresh *toma*
(can substitute unsalted
goat's-milk cheese)

Slices of toasted bread

Salt and pepper

This dish is typical of Courmayeur at the foot of Mont Blanc.

Whisk together the vinegar and salt. Slowly drizzle in the oil, whisking to emulsify. Add the other ingredients (except the *toma* and bread) and stir until they are well mixed; season with salt and pepper. ✦ Arrange the *toma* in a serving bowl, top with the mixture, and let marinate for several hours, covered. Serve with bread.

SAUSAGE FRITTATA

FRITTATA COL SALAME

LOMBARDIA

In Milan this frittata is made using raw salame, cut in small pieces and added to the beaten eggs with a little grated Parmigiano-Reggiano. The frittata must be kept pale and soft, for otherwise the salame will change flavor. In Monza and in the area of Lomello this is made using *luganega*. This frittata is excellent with a salad composed of finely chopped chicory and new onions.

2 tbsp. unsalted butter

7 oz. sausage (preferably *luganega*), removed from the casings and crumbled

1 tbsp. dry white wine

6 large eggs, beaten

2 tbsp. grated Parmigiano-Reggiano

Salt and pepper

Heat the butter in a cast-iron pan over medium heat and sauté the sausage meat. After about 3 minutes pour in the white wine and let it evaporate. Spread the sausage in an even layer in the pan. ✦ Meanwhile combine the eggs, Parmigiano-Reggiano, and salt and pepper. Reduce the heat to low and pour the egg mixture over the sausage. Cook, carefully turning the frittata before its underside becomes too browned. Serve warm.

FRITTATA CON IL GHIOZZO

FRITTATA WITH WHITEBAIT

FRIULI-VENEZIA GIULIA

Olive oil

10 oz. freshwater whitebait *(Gobius fluviatilis)*, cleaned

All-purpose flour

6 large eggs, beaten

⅓ cup chopped flat-leaf parsley

Salt

This dish is typical of the area north of Trieste.

Heat ½ inch of olive oil in a pan until hot. Dredge the fish in flour and fry quickly until golden. Season the eggs with salt and add the fish and parsley. Heat ¼ cup olive oil in a cast-iron pan over medium heat, and add the egg mixture. Cook until the bottom is set, then carefully turn the frittata before its underside becomes too browned and cook the other side quickly, just until set. Serve warm.

✦ **LOCAL TRADITION** ✦

FRITTATA CON LE ERBE

This traditional herb frittata from Friuli-Venezia Giulia uses the buds of various plants commonly eaten as cooked greens, primarily bladder campion *(Silene vulgaris)*, long pricklyhead poppy *(Papaver argemone)*, oregluzze *(Lychuis abba)*, and hops. It is popular in spring and summer and is always prepared on June 24, the feast day of St. John.

HOPS FRITTATA

LOMBARDIA

2 cups *luvértis* (hops)
4 tbsp. (1 stick) unsalted butter
6 large eggs, beaten
2 tbsp. grated Parmigiano-Reggiano
Salt and pepper

Chop the freshly gathered *luvértis* (hops). Heat half the butter over low heat and add the hops. Sauté very briefly to give them flavor without frying, thus not making them lose their very mild natural flavor by boiling. ✦ Season the eggs with salt and pepper and Parmigiano-Reggiano. Heat the remaining butter in a cast-iron pan, add the egg mixture, and cook as on page 31, topping with the sauteed hops toward the end of cooking.

TRUFFLE FRITTATA

FRITTATA DI TARTUFI
ALLA SPOLETINA

UMBRIA

7 oz. black truffles
5 large eggs, beaten
2 tbsp. olive oil
Salt

Thoroughly clean the truffles under running water. Dry them with a cloth and finely chop, grinding the larger pieces in a mortar. ✦ Season the eggs with salt. Heat the olive oil in a pan and add the eggs, tilting the pan to create an even layer. Add the truffles and cook the frittata, stirring with a wooden spoon. Carefully turn the frittata onto a plate and turn off the heat. Let stand for about 30 seconds, then serve.

✦ LOCAL TRADITION ✦

FRITTATA DI VITALBA

This classic springtime frittata, typical of Garfagnana, has the flavor of asparagus and uses the tips of young clematis, which grows wild in the woods of Tuscany. The clematis tips are washed, chopped, parboiled, and lightly floured before being cooked in a hot pan with a little olive oil and garlic. To ensure a good, somewhat soft frittata, the egg whites are beaten separately, then combined with the yolks and salt and pepper to taste; up to 2 tablespoons of flour can be added, as well, if desired.

EASTER FRITTATA

FRITTATA PASQUALE

UMBRIA

1 artichoke, outer leaves and
fuzzy choke removed

Juice of 1 lemon

½ cup aromatic herbs
(Roman mint, costmary,
basil, marjoram, sage,
rosemary, mint, thyme)

½ cup olive oil

2 oz. sausage, crumbled

1 oz. pancetta, diced

½ blood sausage

4 oz. spinach

3 cups arugula

½ medium onion, minced

½ garlic clove

A few stalks asparagus,
woody ends trimmed,
stalks chopped

1 bunch flat-leaf parsley

1 oz. salame, diced

4 large eggs, beaten

Salt and pepper

The sight, smell, and taste of this dish will make it abundantly clear that spring has finally arrived. Serve cold at Easter lunch. The serving dish can be garnished with leaves of the hearts of chicory around the edges, making a sort of big daisy, with room for the frittata in the center.

Slice the artichoke and place in water acidulated with lemon juice. Grind the aromatic herbs in a mortar, blending with 2 tablespoons olive oil to form a mush. Heat 2 tablespoons olive oil in a pan and cook the sausage, pancetta, and blood sausage; add the spinach and arugula. In a separate pan, heat 2 tablespoons olive oil and sauté the onion and garlic. Remove the garlic when blond and add the artichoke and asparagus. Reduce the heat to low. ✦ Add the sausage and herb mixtures to the onion mixture and cook at low heat, adjusting for salt and pepper. Remove from heat and add the salame. Add to the eggs and mix well. ✦ Heat 2 tablespoons olive oil in a cast-iron pan and cook the frittata as on page 31, making it thick and soft.

SALAME FRITTATA 1

FRITTATA ROGNOSA 1

PIEMONTE

5 large eggs, beaten

2 tbsp. grated
Parmigiano-Reggiano

2 tbsp. olive oil

4 oz. *salame d'la duja*
(pork sausages covered in lard),
crumbled

Salt and pepper

Season the eggs with salt, pepper, and Parmigiano-Reggiano. Heat the oil in a cast-iron pan and sauté the salame. Add the eggs. Cook well, turning to cook both sides, as on page 31.

SALAME FRITTATA 2

4 large eggs, beaten

4 oz. salame, minced

2 tbsp. chopped flat-leaf parsley

2 tbsp. olive oil

1 medium onion, chopped

Salt

Season the eggs with salt; add the salame and parsley. In a pan heat the olive oil and cook the onion; when just golden add the egg mixture and cook at low heat as on page 31. Serve hot.

FRITTATA WITH GROUND MEAT

FRITTATA ROGNOSA DEL GARDA

VENETO

1 celery stalk

3 tbsp. extra-virgin olive oil

1 tbsp. unsalted butter

1 large onion, finely chopped

2 oz. smoked pancetta, diced

¼ lb. ground meat (pork or mixed beef, veal, and salame)

5 large fresh eggs, beaten

¼ cup grated Parmigiano-Reggiano

Salt

Boil the celery in water to cover for at least 30 minutes, drain, then finely chop. Heat 1 tablespoon of the olive oil and the butter in a pan and sauté the celery and onion. Add the pancetta and salt to taste. Add the ground meat and cook for 40 minutes. ✦ In a large bowl, beat the eggs together with the Parmigiano-Reggiano. Add the cooked ingredients to the egg mixture. Heat the remaining olive oil in a pan and add the egg mixture. When it has cooked on one side turn it over onto a lightly greased hot plate. Let stand for 30 seconds and serve on warmed plates.

ANCHOVY FRITTERS

FRITELLE DI ACCIUGHE

CALABRIA

6½ cups all-purpose flour, plus more as needed

½ oz. active dry yeast, diluted in 2 tbsp. lukewarm water

10 oz. salt-cured anchovies

Olive oil for frying

Salt

Put the flour in a terra-cotta pan, preferably a fully enameled pan with flaring sides (a *bavanu*). Add the yeast mixture, a dash of salt, and blend. Work the dough, adding lukewarm water, until it is very soft; continue for another 30 minutes, beating the dough to make it stringy. Cover the dough with a cloth and let it rise 4 or 5 hours. ✦ Remove the bones from the anchovies, clean them, and chop them. ✦ When the dough has risen, heat a couple of inches of oil in a pan, grease your hands with oil, take a little of the dough (about 1 tablespoon), elongate it, insert a piece of anchovy, enclose it, and fry until golden. Repeat this procedure until the dough is used up. Serve very hot.

FRITTELLE DI ANEMONI DI MARE

Blue sea anemones appear so commonly along the coast running from Cirella to Diamante in the spring and autumn that the reefs seem to turn blue in the early morning hours. The anemones themselves have gelatinous bodies that nearly dissolve in the strong heat of a sunny day. This recipe for sea anemone fritters, typical of Calabria, is based on an older one used by the local fishermen at Diamante, where the anemones are known as *jújime*. Flour, eggs, parsley, salt, and pepper are combined to make a simple batter for the fresh anemones, which should still be fragrant from the reef. A couple of tablespoons of the battered anemones are added to hot olive oil to make fritters. The fritters are fried until golden, drained, and served simply sprinkled with salt and pepper.

FRITTELLE DI BIANCHETTI

BIANCHETTI FRITTERS

FOR
6 PERSONS

CALABRIA

1 ¼ cups flour, plus more as needed

2 tbsp. chopped flat-leaf parsley

1 lb. *bianchetti* (whitebait)

Olive oil for frying

Salt and pepper

Bianchetti are tiny white fish in an almost larval state (neonates, hence they are called *nunnate* in the area around Reggio, *rosamarina* in the province of Cosenza).

In a bowl, mix the flour, salt, parsley, and pepper, adding ½ cup water to create a smooth batter. Carefully and delicately wash the *bianchetti* and fold them into the batter. ✦ Heat 1 inch of olive oil in a pan and fry tablespoons of the fish batter until golden, then drain on paper towels. Sprinkle with salt and serve hot.

FRITTELLE
DI FARINA DI CECI

CHICKPEA-FLOUR FRITTERS

LIGURIA

1 ⅔ cups chickpea flour,
plus more as needed

1 tsp. active dry yeast

Pinch fresh marjoram, finely chopped

Extra-virgin olive oil for frying

Salt

Mix ¾ cup water into the chickpea flour to obtain a thick dough; add the yeast and set aside to rest overnight. ✦ Knead the dough well, salt to taste, and add the marjoram. ✦ Heat three inches of olive oil in a heavy pan until hot but not smoking. One by one form the dough into roughly 3-inch balls and fry in olive oil. Serve hot.

FRITTELLE DI MARESINA

This dish is typical of the valley of the Agno and Chiampo in Veneto. *Maresina* is an Italian name for feverfew *(Chrysanthemum parthenium)*, a sort of wild chrysanthemum. According to the quantity of *maresina* used, and whether it is bitter or sweet, this dish is used as an appetizer or side dish to meat or even as a dessert at the end of the meal. It involves rice cooked until it is mushy, then combined with eggs, milk, and chopped *maresina* to make a dough. Flat-shaped fritters are formed and deep-fried in olive oil.

FRITTO MISTO ALLA PIAZZESE

MIXED FRIED VEGETABLES

SICILIA

4 ½ cups all-purpose flour, plus more as needed

4 large eggs, beaten

2 ¼ tsp. active dry yeast

4 artichokes

1 lb. fresh anchovies

2 apples, peeled and cored

1 lb. cardoons, boiled

1 small cauliflower, cut in florets and blanched (veal brains were once used)

Olive oil

1 tbsp. salt

This dish is typical of Piazza Armerina.

Combine the flour, eggs, and yeast to make a batter with a fluid consistency. ✦ Clean and chop the artichokes, clean the anchovies, slice the apples, and slice the cardoons. ✦ Heat several inches of olive oil in a high-sided pan until hot. One by one immerse the vegetables in the batter, then fry in olive oil until golden. Drain on paper towels and serve hot.

FUNGHI AL GUAZZETTO

MUSHROOMS IN BROTH

EMILIA-ROMAGNA

1 ½ lbs. porcini mushrooms

1 garlic clove

CONTINUED

If possible use only the caps of porcini mushrooms from Borgotaro (in Parma); or use as few stems as possible. Scrape clean the ends of the stems and clean the mushroom caps with a damp cloth. Never use water, least of all running water: The mushrooms would lose the patina

36

1 cup chopped flat-leaf parsley

¼ cup olive oil

1 cup meat broth, skimmed of fat if necessary

2 tbsp. unsalted butter

Salt and pepper

that covers them, and with it they would lose their flavor and aroma. Slice the cleaned mushrooms. ✦ Chop together the garlic and parsley, adding a little salt and pepper; do not mince too finely. ✦ Using, if possible, a terra-cotta pot on a cast-iron stove, heat the olive oil over low heat and sauté the garlic mixture. Add the mushrooms, and when they have given up their water, add the broth and butter. Cook until the mushrooms are soft.

MUSHROOMS WITH TOMATOES

FUNGHI CON I POMODORI

CALABRIA

¾ lb. *vavusi (Suillus luteus)* mushrooms (can substitute porcini)

2 tbsp. extra-virgin olive oil

1 medium onion, finely chopped

¾ lb. plum tomatoes, peeled

1 *diavolillo*, cut in pieces (see note, page 22)

Several basil leaves, torn up

Peasant-style bread, sliced and toasted

Salt

Delicately clean the mushrooms, eliminating the outer film. Cut in pieces. Heat the oil in an earthenware pot and cook the mushrooms and the onion. ✦ After about 10 minutes add the tomatoes with their seeds and sauce, *diavolillo*, and salt. When cooked, add the basil. Serve with bread.

✦ **LOCAL TRADITION** ✦

GELATINA

This recipe for gelatin from Calabria was typically served as an appetizer for Easter dinner in the area around Trieste. A veal hoof (with hide), a beef hoof (without hide), 2 pig's ears, a smoked pork shank, 1 veal tongue (with holes), and 1 pound of lean beef are simmered gently for 6 hours, while salting lightly and constantly skimming fat, to create a broth; after about 3½ hours some white wine vinegar should be added. As much garlic as is desired per person, sliced hard-boiled eggs, and a bay leaf (for decoration) are then portioned into individual bowls, and topped with the hot liquid. The gelatin should be chilled until it has set completely.

FRIED BREAD

EMILIA-ROMAGNA

3 cups all-purpose flour,
plus more as needed

2¼ tsp. active dry yeast

1 tsp. baking powder

2 tbsp. lard, plus more for frying

1 cup lukewarm milk,
plus more as needed

Salt

In Parma this is called a "fried cake." Serve it with thinly sliced prosciutto di Parma or salumi.

Combine the flour, yeast, baking powder, 2 tablespoons lard, and salt with enough milk as on page 13 to make a soft dough and let it rise for about 1 hour, covered, at room temperature. ✦ Roll out the dough to a thickness of about ¼ inch, cut in squares. Heat 1 inch of lard in a pan and fry the dough, turning, until golden. Drain on paper towels and serve hot.

SPIDER CRAB CANAPES

GRANSEOLA
ALLA TRIESTINA

FRIULI-VENEZIA GIULIA

1 spider crab

1 tbsp. unsalted butter

½ medium onion, finely chopped

1 tbsp. breadcrumbs

Chopped flat-leaf parsley as desired

Juice and grated zest of 1 lemon

1 tbsp. olive oil

Slices of bread, warmed

This appetizer is based on the traditional Istrian cuisine in terms of its special method and for the characteristic flavor of the mixture, based on the sweet taste of the crustacean.

Boil and carefully clean the spider crab; when cool enough to handle, remove the meat over a bowl so the liquid is reserved also. Mix the meat and liquid. Heat the butter in a pan and add the onion. When the onion is translucent, add the breadcrumbs and sauté briefly until golden. Remove from the heat, and add the crab meat and liquid. Mix in the parsley, lemon juice and zest, and olive oil. ✦ Spread the mixture on slices of warm bread.

BREADSTICKS

GRISSINI

PIEMONTE

2 cups all-purpose flour,
plus more as needed

1 tbsp. extra-virgin olive oil

1 tsp. active dry yeast,
dissolved in ¾ cup warm water

Semolina flour

Salt

This dish is typical of Turin.

Combine the all-purpose flour with the olive oil, a little salt, and the yeast mixture as on page 13. Knead at least 30 minutes. ✦ Divide the dough into 12 pieces and let rest for a few minutes. Form the pieces into oblong rolls. Set them out on a damp surface, flatten them by hand, and let them rise for 1 hour. ✦ Preheat the oven to 400°F. Sprinkle a baking sheet with semolina. Cut the dough into strips and set them out on the semolina. By hand, draw each out to at least 12 inches in length. Bake until crisp and golden, about 10 minutes.

INSALATA DI FUNGHI E TARTUFI | MUSHROOM AND TRUFFLE SALAD

PIEMONTE

⅔ cup extra-virgin olive oil

Juice of 1 lemon

Yolks of 2 large hard-boiled eggs

2 tbsp. chopped flat-leaf parsley

2 anchovies, cleaned,
boned, and finely chopped

¾ lb. *ovolo* mushrooms
(Caesar's, or royal, or any good,
firm mushroom)

1 white truffle

Salt and pepper

Mix the olive oil, lemon juice, and egg yolks, then push through a sieve and blend well. Add the parsley and anchovies and stir together to obtain a homogenous sauce. ✦ Remove the film from the stems of the mushrooms and chop them finely; clean the truffle and shave with a truffle slicer. ✦ Add the mushrooms and truffle to the sauce in the bowl, taste for salt, add a few grindings of fresh pepper, and stir delicately so that the mushrooms and truffle pick up the flavors without breaking. Let stand for a few minutes before serving.

INSALATA DI MAIALE | PORK SALAD

MOLISE

2 pig's ears

2 pig's trotters

¼ cup white wine vinegar

2 garlic cloves, chopped

2 stalks white celery, chopped

Juice of 1 lemon

1 cup olive oil

Salt and black pepper (optional)

Clean the ears and trotters, scraping well with the blade of a knife and burning off remaining bristles with a flame. Wash carefully and place in a pot; add water to cover, season with salt and vinegar, and simmer for about 2 hours. ✦ When fully cooked, chop the ears and trotters in small pieces, and while still warm arrange them on a serving plate and season them with the garlic, celery, lemon juice, olive oil, and, if desired, a grinding of pepper.

INSALATA DI MARE 1 | SEAFOOD SALAD 1

FOR
6 PERSONS

CAMPANIA

2 lbs. mussels

1 lb. clams (or *lupini* or *telline*)

1 medium onion, chopped

2 celery stalks, chopped

2 carrots, chopped

1 sprig fresh rosemary

1 sprig fresh marjoram

CONTINUED

This dish is typical of Salerno.

Clean the mussels and rinse them well. Put them in water to cover in a large covered pot without seasoning and cook over high heat to make them open, setting aside the cooking liquid. Repeat with the clams. ✦ Remove the mussels and clams from their shells. Put the empty shells in a pan with a quart of water and add the onion, celery, carrots, rosemary, marjoram, and thyme; bring to a boil, then simmer for 20 minutes. Remove the shells from the broth and discard. ✦ Add the shrimp to

1 sprig thyme
1 lb. baby shrimp
1 lb. baby octopus
1 lb. squid, cleaned and cut in rings
⅔ cup extra-virgin olive oil
2 tsp. strong French mustard
Juice of 1 lemon, or to taste
2 garlic cloves, chopped
2 tbsp. chopped flat-leaf parsley
Salt and pepper

the broth and simmer for 3 minutes, then remove them from their shells. Filter the broth through cheesecloth. ✦ In the strained broth simmer the cleaned octopus and squid. Drain them and cut the octopus in pieces. ✦ On a large serving plate combine the mussels, clams, shrimp, squid, and octopus. ✦ Whisk together the olive oil, mustard, lemon juice, garlic, parsley, salt, and pepper. ✦ Mix the seafood with the dressing, cover, and chill for at least 30 minutes before serving.

✦ **LOCAL TRADITION** ✦

INSALATA DI GALLINA COTTA NEL FIENO

Typical of Val Pellice in Piedmont, this recipe for an old hen cooked with May hay called for simmering onion, carrots, celery, sage, bay leaves, and rosemary with the hay to create a flavorful broth. To this is added a cup of dry white wine and a hen and then all are cooked together over low heat for about 3 hours. The meat is removed from the hen and shredded, then dressed with salt, pepper, walnut oil, and a little vinegar, and is traditionally served with a salad of potatoes and chervil.

INSALATA DI MARE 2

SEAFOOD SALAD 2

FOR
6 PERSONS

SICILIA

¾ lb. octopus
¾ lb. squid
1 lb. shrimp
¾ lb. mussels
¾ lb. clams
Olive oil
White wine vinegar
2 celery stalks, chopped
9 cups mixed salad greens
Salt and pepper

Simmer the octopus and squid separately in lightly salted water to cover. Separately boil the shrimp in lightly salted water to cover. Put the mussels and clams in a pan over high heat, cover, and cook until they open. Remove from heat, preserving the liquid, and remove and discard the shells. Drain the octopus and shrimp; cut the octopus in small pieces and the squid in rings. ✦ Arrange all the seafood on a serving plate and drizzle with oil, vinegar, pepper, and salt; filter a little of the cooking liquid from the mussels and clams and sprinkle it over the seafood. Add the celery and salad greens. Chill and serve.

INSALATA DI NERVETTI

Nervetti are tendons from a veal or beef hoof that have been cooked down until they fall away from the bone. The meat is then put into a container under pressure so that, when cooled, it forms a single mass that can then be sliced. In this salad from Lombardy, the *nervetti* are usually sliced thinly and seasoned with some thinly sliced onion (soaked in cold water to lose their sharpness), lemon juice or vinegar, olive oil, and chopped flat-leaf parsley.

INSALATA DI RISO NOVARESE

RICE SALAD WITH ANCHOVIES

PIEMONTE

2 cups Arborio rice
¼ cup extra-virgin olive oil
1 garlic clove
4 fresh anchovies, cleaned and boned
2 tbsp. chopped flat-leaf parsley
Juice of 2 lemons
Salt and black pepper

This dish is typical of Novara, near Lago Maggiore.

Boil the rice in lightly salted water to cover until al dente, drain, and set aside in a bowl to cool. ✦ Pour the olive oil in a saucepan and add the garlic and anchovies; turn on the heat to low and, without frying them, cook the anchovies until they become mushy. Remove from heat and cool. ✦ Pour the anchovy mixture over the rice and add the parsley and lemon juice. Let this cool, add a few grindings of fresh black pepper, salt to taste, and serve.

INTINGOLO CON FAGIOLI

PORK ROLL-UPS

LOMBARDIA

2 pork loins
4 oz. sausage meat
2 oz. ground beef, cooked
1 garlic clove, chopped
1 tbsp. chopped flat-leaf parsley
1 large egg
2 tbsp. grated Parmigiano-Reggiano
½ cup (1 stick) unsalted butter
CONTINUED

Polenta is the ideal accompaniment for this dish. To flatten the pork loins, it may be easiest to first sprinkle the surface of the meat with water. Then cover with plastic wrap, and use a heavy mallet, or the underside of a heavy iron skillet, to pound to a ¼ inch thickness.

Slice the pork loins into medallions and pound them flat. Lay them out on a surface. ✦ Mix the sausage meat, ground beef, garlic, parsley, egg, and Parmigiano-Reggiano. ✦ Place a dollop of this filling at the end of each pork loin and roll it up, tying each one closed with kitchen twine. Heat the butter and olive oil in a pot and brown the pork loins. Add broth to cover them. ✦

2 tbsp. olive oil	Reduce the heat to low and cook for at least 30 minutes, then add the beans and tomato paste. Let cook another 30 minutes and serve warm.
Beef broth, warmed	
2 cups cooked borlotti beans	
1 tbsp. tomato paste	

INVOLTINI
DI CARNE TONNATI

BEEF ROLL-UPS
WITH TUNA SAUCE

PIEMONTE

1 slice white bread, crust removed
10 salt-cured anchovy fillets
1 tbsp. capers
Juice of 2 lemons
1 tbsp. olive oil
¾ lb. thinly sliced roast beef
3 oz. canned tuna, drained
3 tbsp. broth
½ cup mayonnaise
Chopped flat-leaf parsley

Chop the bread in a blender with 6 anchovies, half of the capers, lemon juice, and olive oil. Divide this mixture among the beef slices, spread into an even layer, then roll them up. In a blender combine the tuna, the remaining capers, anchovies, broth and mayonnaise, Blend just until a chunky sauce forms. Cover the beef slices with this mixture and sprinkle with parsley. ✦ Cover and refrigerate until just before serving.

✦ **LOCAL TRADITION** ✦

LARDO DI ARNAD

The lard (actually *lardo*, but written in French) made in the town of Arnad in the Val d'Aosta is especially famous. It is treated and flavored by being soaked in a special brine with aromatic herbs. Given its high price this *lardo* is not used in cooking, but only as an appetizer typical of the Valdostan area. With a highly delicate flavor, it is especially soft, literally melting in the mouth. It is eaten raw, cut into thin slices.

LATTE BRUSCO

FRIED MILK

LIGURIA

⅔ cup all-purpose flour, plus more as needed

CONTINUED

Whisk the flour into the milk; add a good dash of salt, then the eggs. Pass this mixture through a sieve and add the lemon zest and parsley. ✦ Cook this mixture, which will be decidedly liquid, for about 1 hour over low heat

4 cups milk

4 large eggs, beaten

Grated zest of 1 lemon

2 tbsp. chopped flat-leaf parsley

Olive oil

1 large egg white

Breadcrumbs

Salt

(or in a water bath). Grease a high-sided bowl with olive oil, add the mixture, and refrigerate until firm. ✦ Cut it into 1-inch cubes. Heat 1 inch of olive oil in a pan until hot. Beat the egg white until frothy. Dip the cubes in the egg white, roll in the breadcrumbs, and fry until golden. Serve hot.

LISOGNI

FRIED POTATO DUMPLINGS

LIGURIA

2 lbs. top-quality potatoes

1 cup all-purpose flour, plus more as needed

2 tbsp. milk

1 garlic clove, minced

1 cup olive oil

Salt

This dish is typical of the Val Bormida. As a variation, you can add chopped parsley; you can also add, if desired, the crumbled yolk of an egg.

Preheat the oven to 400°F. Peel and boil the potatoes, put them through a food mill, and shape into a well on the work surface. ✦ Knead the potatoes together with the flour, milk, and salt to create a firm dough. Shape it into a long loaf. ✦ Cut the loaf into many small pieces and flatten them by hand. Bake until golden on one side, then turn and bake on the other. As soon as they are ready, and piping hot, arrange them on a serving plate in layers. ✦ Heat the olive oil and add the garlic, cooking just until blond. Pour the oil over the dumplings and serve.

✦ **LOCAL TRADITION** ✦

MAMMELLA DI MUCCA

In ancient Rome, the udders of various animals were considered delicacies. This dish for brined udders, typical of Val d'Aosta and most often served as an appetizer, can be tasted during the Feast of the Tetin (udder), held every year at Gignod, and found in some specialty food shops. To prepare it, several cows' udders are cleaned, divided into several pieces, and layered in a wooden container with coarse sea salt, garlic, fresh sage, and bay leaves. The mixture should be covered and weighted so that for at least two weeks the udders remain immersed within the briny liquid that is produced. After such time, the meat is removed and left hanging to dry. The dried udders are then cooked again for a couple of hours and sliced.

LUMACHE ALLA VIGNAIOLA

WINEMAKER-STYLE SNAILS

PIEMONTE

2 dozen snails

2 tbsp. olive oil

2 tbsp. unsalted butter

1 oz. *lardo* (see page 2), chopped

1 medium onion, chopped

1 garlic clove, chopped

1 celery stalk, chopped

2 sage leaves

2 tbsp. chopped flat-leaf parsley

1 anchovy

2 tbsp. red wine (preferably Barbera)

1 tbsp. tomato purée

1 tbsp. all-purpose flour

Salt and pepper

Clean the snails and boil them in water to cover for about 1½ hours. When they are cool, remove them from their shells, cut off the intestinal sack, and dry them. Heat the olive oil and butter in a pan and add the *lardo*, onion, garlic, celery, sage leaves, and parsley. Add the snails and sauté. ✦ Add the anchovy and let it dissolve, then add the red wine and tomato purée, then add the flour. Simmer the sauce at high heat for 10 minutes to thicken; season with salt and pepper to taste.

MACCHERONCINI NEL "MACCU" FRITTO

PASTA AND FAVA-BEAN CUBES

SICILIA

1½ cups dried fava beans

1 sprig wild fennel

Roughly ½ lb. small macaroni, preferably homemade

Extra-virgin olive oil

4 tbsp. all-purpose flour

Salt and pepper

Made of dried fava beans, *maccu* is typical of the peasant cooking of the Syracuse area. Its preparation involves two stages: In the evening of one day the favas and macaroni are cooked; the slicing and frying of the cubes takes place the next day.

The night before, begin cooking the fava beans and the fennel in lightly salted water just to cover. Cook until the beans become a dense purée. This requires patience, with constant stirring to keep the mixture from sticking. ✦ Remove the sprig of fennel and pour in macaroni, basing the quantity on what, "to an expert eye," the quantity of remaining liquid will cook. Season with pepper generously. Grease a rectangular baking pan with olive oil. As soon as the macaroni are cooked al dente transfer them along with the fava purée to the pan; the layer should be no more than half an inch thick. Refrigerate overnight. ✦ You'll find that the next day the fava-bean *maccu* will have solidified around its macaroni "prisoners." Slice the *maccu* into small squares. Heat 1 inch of olive oil in a pan. Dip them in the flour, then fry them until golden. They can be eaten hot or cold; you'll find that both their fragrance and flavor are surprisingly good.

| MOCCETTA SU CROSTINI DI PANE | # CURED CHAMOIS ON CROSTINI |

VALLE D'AOSTA

½ cup (1 stick) unsalted butter

¼ cup honey
(preferably unrefined
Valdostan honey)

8 slices of black rye bread,
slightly stale

½ lb. chamois *moccetta* (cured
meat, similar to prosciutto),
finely sliced

Work the butter and honey together to form a homogenous paste. Spread this over slices of black bread. Place a slice of *moccetta* over each and serve.

| MOUSSE DI PROSCIUTTO | # PROSCIUTTO MOUSSE |

EMILIA-ROMAGNA

2 lbs. prosciutto cotto

½ cup brandy

4½ cups cream, whipped

4 large hard-boiled eggs,
sliced into rounds

Pepper

Grind the prosciutto several times in gradually smaller plates of a meat grinder to make it almost creamy. Mix in the pepper and brandy, then gently fold in the whipped cream. Line a baking dish with aluminum foil or waxed paper, pour in the mixture, and refrigerate overnight. ✦ Before serving, overturn onto a plate and garnish with hard-boiled eggs.

✦ **LOCAL TRADITION** ✦

MIGLIACCIO

The name of this baked blood pudding, which is typical of Arezzo in Tuscany, comes from the word *miglio*, meaning "millet." Cakes like this date to ancient times, when millet was combined with the blood of a freshly slaughtered pig and baked. The millet has dropped out of most such recipes, replaced by other grains but leaving the name. The pig's blood has also disappeared (see page 76 for another example of this evolution). In this Tuscan version, a few cups of blood were mixed with an egg, Parmigiano-Reggiano, breadcrumbs, fennel seeds, a little pork fat, and salt and pepper. This mixture was spread out to form a layer no more than 1 inch thick and then baked until the *migliaccio* became softly set like custard and detached easily from the bottom of the pan.

MISSOLTINI ALLA GRATELLA

In the central area of Lake Como in Lombardy, at Lecco, and in all the small lakes of the Pian d'Erba, *agoni,* a variety of shad, are fished during their spawning season and hung out to dry in the sun on triangular trestles. *Missoltini* are *agoni* that have been gutted and then arranged in regular rows with bay leaves and pressed under wooden boards on which weights are placed. This way of preserving fish in Como dialect is called "*far la missolta,*" which is the derivation of the final product: *missoltini.* The traditional preparation is to cook the *missoltini* on a grate over a fire, if possible wood-burning, being careful to keep them from burning. After grilling, the *missoltini* would be served with a sprinkling of extra-virgin olive oil and vinegar. Sliced polenta makes the ideal side dish, or they also go well with finely sliced fresh chicory seasoned with oil and vinegar.

MOZZARELLA IN CARROZZA

FRIED MOZZARELLA SANDWICH

LAZIO

8 slices stale peasant-style bread about 6 inches long

2 cups milk

8 slices mozzarella

8 salt-cured anchovy fillets

Extra-virgin olive oil

2 large eggs, beaten

1 ¼ cups all-purpose flour, plus more as needed

This dish is typical of Rome and Lazio.

Cut the crust off the slices of bread, then dip them in the milk, but only briefly to soften them. ✦ Create sandwiches, putting two slices of mozzarella and two anchovy fillets in each. Press down to make the slices adhere well. ✦ Heat ½ inch of olive oil in a pan. Mix the eggs with 2 tablespoons milk, dip the sandwiches in the egg mixture, then dredge in the flour. Fry the sandwiches, turning so they brown on both sides. Serve hot.

OLIVE ALL'ASCOLANA

STUFFED OLIVES

MARCHE

If possible, use large and tender Ascolan olives. Remove the pits with a sharp knife, making a spiral cut from top to bottom without breaking them; the resulting hollow can be filled with a wide variety of mixtures, such as the one here.

Extra-virgin olive oil
1 carrot, cut into 3 pieces
1 celery stalk, cut into 3 pieces
1 medium onion, cut into 4 wedges
studded with 2 cloves each
½ lb. beef chuck
½ lb. pork loin
½ lb. boneless chicken
1 chicken liver, cleaned
1 tbsp. tomato purée
½ cup grated Parmigiano-Reggiano
⅓ cup grated pecorino
2 large eggs, beaten
Grated zest of 1 lemon
Pinch grated nutmeg
1 cup crustless bread, soaked
in broth and squeezed dry
1 lb. olives (or ¾ lb. pitted olives)
Breadcrumbs
Salt and pepper

Heat 2 tablespoons olive oil in a saucepan and add the carrot, celery, and onion and sauté; add the meats and salt and pepper to taste. Add the chicken liver and tomato purée. When the meats are cooked, remove the carrot, celery, and onion and finely chop the meats. Add the cheeses, half the eggs, lemon zest, a hint of nutmeg, and make a filling by adding the soaked bread. ✦ Stuff this mixture into the olives, which should become large and fat. Heat 1 inch olive oil in a pan. Dip the olives in the remaining egg, then breadcrumbs, then fry until golden. Serve immediately.

CAESAR'S MUSHROOMS WITH TRUFFLES

OVOLI E TARTUFI

PIEMONTE

1 lb. *ovolo* mushrooms
(*Amanita caesarea*)
1 garlic clove
⅓ cup extra-virgin olive oil
Juice of 1 lemon
1 tbsp. chopped flat-leaf parsley,
plus whole parsley leaves
for garnish
1 anchovy, minced
2 hard-boiled egg yolks
7 oz. white Alba truffle
Salt and pepper

Carefully clean the mushrooms and cut them in thin slices, reserving 1 whole mushroom for garnish. ✦ Stick the garlic clove onto the end of a fork. Combine the olive oil, lemon juice, salt and pepper, chopped parsley, anchovy, and egg yolks in a bowl; use the fork with the garlic to beat the mixture. ✦ Pour this dressing over the sliced mushrooms on a serving plate and cover with shavings of the white truffle. Garnish with the whole mushroom and parsley.

PADELLATA DI FUNGHI SILANI | PAN-COOKED MUSHROOMS

CALABRIA

2 lbs. mushrooms, preferably "coppulini" (Lepiota procera, known in English as "parasol" mushrooms), vavusi (Suillus luteus), porcini, rositi (Lactarius deliciosus), and ditole (Ramaria aurea)

⅔ cup extra-virgin olive oil

3 garlic cloves, slivered

¾ lb. plum tomatoes, chopped

Pinch chili pepper flakes

Pinch oregano

A few basil leaves

1 tbsp. chopped flat-leaf parsley

Salt

Mushrooms prepared this way can be served hot or cold.

Clean the mushrooms, dry in a cloth, and cut in pieces. ✦ Heat the olive oil in a pan and cook the garlic and mushrooms; after about 15 minutes add the tomatoes, chili pepper, oregano, basil, and parsley. Salt only at the end.

✦ **LOCAL TRADITION** ✦

MOSTARDA DI CARPI

Typical of Emilia-Romagna, this thick, slow-cooked fruit sauce is excellent with *zampone* and *cotechino*, as well as all boiled meats and roasts. Must from fermented grapes is simmered over low heat in a terra-cotta pot until reduced to a dense syrup. Chopped fruit—typically apples, pears, and quince—and orange zest that has been soaked in water is added and the sauce is again reduced by half. The very thick syrup is poured into terra-cotta containers or glass jars and kept in a cool, dry, dark place.

PALLE DI RISO | RICE BALLS

FOR 6 PERSONS

CAMPANIA

For the filling:

¼ oz. dried mushrooms

CONTINUED

Soak the dried mushrooms in warm water for half an hour, then boil them in the same liquid. When cooked, drain them from the liquid, reserving the liquid, and chop them. ✦ Heat the *lardo* and pancetta in a pan over low heat. Add the onion and cook until lightly golden. ✦

48

¼ oz. *lardo* (see page 2)

2 oz. pancetta, chopped

1 small onion, sliced

1½ cups shelled peas

3 oz. prosciutto cotto, minced

1 tbsp. tomato paste

¼ cup white wine

2 tbsp. unsalted butter
for the livers

3 chicken livers

7 oz. mozzarella or
fior di latte cheese,
cut into small cubes

For the rice:

2½ cups rice

1 oz. *lardo* (or 2 tbsp.
unsalted butter)

⅔ cup grated Parmigiano-Reggiano

2 tbsp. chopped flat-leaf parsley

2 tbsp. chopped basil

3 large eggs, beaten

Salt and pepper

For frying:

Olive oil

Breadcrumbs

Add the peas, prosciutto, tomato paste, wine, and a little of the mushroom water. Simmer until there is no trace of liquid, by which time the peas should have become soft. ✦ Heat a little butter in a separate pan and quickly brown the chicken livers at high heat, cut them in small pieces, and add to the pea mixture along with the mushrooms and their broth; cook another 10 minutes. ✦ Let it cool and add the mozzarella. Check for salt. ✦ Cook the rice in boiling lightly salted water until al dente (15 to 25 minutes, depending on the kind of rice), drain, and rinse under cold running water. ✦ Mix in the *lardo* (or melted unsalted butter), Parmigiano-Reggiano, parsley, and basil. Stir in the eggs; season with salt and pepper. ✦ Take a little bit of rice (about the size of a large walnut) at a time and flatten it against the palm of your dampened hand. Put a little of the stuffing on it and close over the rice, forming balls. Heat several inches of oil in a saucepan. Roll the rice balls in the breadcrumbs and fry until they are golden brown.

✦ **LOCAL TRADITION** ✦

MORTADELLA DI FEGATO

The Lombardian tradition of *mortadella di fegato*, typical of the areas of Brianza and central and upper Lake Como, derived from the inspiration of the area's butchers. To make this characteristic mortadella, a mixture of pig's liver, ground pork, and pork fat would be stuffed into a large intestine, folded in on itself, and boiled. The preferred serving method was to present warm, thick slices with polenta. While versions of *mortadella di fegato* are still sold in specialty food shops today, the occasional addition of isinglass can cause the slices to crumble.

OLIO SANTO

This method of flavoring extra-virgin olive oil with chili pepper and garlic is typical of Puglia and results in a very tasty seasoning for those with strong palates. Olive oil is barely warmed and then poured into a bottle with crumbled dried chili pepper and a couple garlic cloves. The oil is then steeped for several days before using. Note: In today's kitchen, it is important for safety to keep oil like this, with garlic, not hermetically sealed and in the refrigerator both during and after steeping.

PALLINE D'ALPEGGIO

POLENTA BALLS

VALLE D'AOSTA

2 cups cornmeal
1 lb. *toma* (cheese from Gressoney, can substitute strained ricotta), cut into 1-inch chunks
Unsalted butter

This recipe is from the German-speaking Walser community and is typical of Issime and Gressoney. In other valleys a similar recipe is called *"lo poutcho."*

Preheat the oven to 350°F. Grease a baking pan. Make a very dense polenta (see page 289), turn it out on a cutting board, and using your hands shape balls about the size of eggs. ✦ Poke a finger into each ball to form a hole and fill the cavity with a chunk of *toma* and 1 teaspoon butter. Close the ball with polenta and arrange the balls on the pan. ✦ Cover the pan and bake slowly until the balls are browned and a crust has formed on them. Serve hot.

PALLOTTE CACE E OVA

CHEESE AND EGG FRITTERS

ABRUZZO

½ lb. stale bread without crust, crumbled
2 cups grated pecorino
5 large eggs, beaten
3 tbsp. garlic, minced
3 tbsp. chopped flat-leaf parsley
Extra-virgin olive oil
Tomato sauce (optional)

Combine the bread, pecorino, and eggs in a bowl and work together to form a dough. Complete the dough by adding the garlic and parsley, then shape into balls. Heat several inches of oil in a saucepan and fry the bread balls until golden. ✦ The balls can be served as they are or seasoned with tomato sauce, in which case they should be heated in the sauce at low heat for about 15 minutes.

PAN NOCIATO | BREAD WITH WALNUTS

FOR
6 PERSONS

UMBRIA

2 tbsp. extra-virgin olive oil
6 oz. pecorino
20 walnut halves
1 lb. bread dough (see page 13)
Salt and pepper

This dish is typical of Todi.

Preheat the oven to 350°F. Grease a baking sheet with olive oil. Cut the pecorino in half; dice one half and grate the other. ✦ Roughly chop the walnut halves. ✦ Work the remaining olive oil into the bread dough, then add the walnuts, pecorino, and a little salt and pepper. Shape into a loaf and place on the pan, cover with a cloth, and let rest for about 30 minutes. ✦ Bake for at least 45 minutes, raising the heat to 450°F near the end of the cooking time to brown the outside of the loaf. Let cool before serving.

PANE A CAPONATA | BREAD AND TOMATO SALAD

SICILIA

1 lb. peasant-style bread,
cubed or sliced, toasted
⅔ cup extra-virgin olive oil
2 garlic cloves, minced
2 ripe plum tomatoes, sliced
Salt and pepper
(or chili pepper flakes)

This dish is typical of the Lipari Islands.

Briefly dip the pieces of bread in warm water, to soften, then arrange in a salad bowl; season with olive oil, garlic, salt, and pepper (or chili pepper flakes), and slices of tomato with their liquid. ✦ Toss and let rest 15 to 20 minutes; mix again before serving.

PANE CON OLIVE | BREAD WITH OLIVES

PUGLIA

3 cups all-purpose flour,
plus more as needed
2¼ tsp. active dry yeast,
dissolved in 2 tbsp. warm water
⅔ cup pitted small black olives
Salt

Work together the flour with the yeast mixture, 1 cup lukewarm water, and 1 level tablespoon of salt to form a smooth dough. ✦ Dredge the olives in flour and shake off the excess. Add them to the bread dough. Form the dough into loaves and let rise for 1½ hours. ✦ Preheat the oven to 400°F and bake for 45 minutes until golden and the loaves sound hollow when tapped.

MUSIC-PAPER-BREAD SALAD

PANE FRATTAU

SARDEGNA

1 lb. plum tomatoes, peeled
1 garlic clove
2 tbsp. extra-virgin olive oil
Basil
1 lb. *pane carasau*
(music-paper bread)
⅔ cup grated pecorino
4 large eggs
Salt

Combine the peeled tomatoes, garlic, olive oil, and basil in a pan; cook over low heat for 10 to 15 minutes. ✦ In a large pot bring 4 or 5 cups of lightly salted water to a boil. ✦ Break up the bread and immerse it piece by piece for a few moments in the water, then set out on plates. ✦ Alternate a layer of bread and one of sauce with a dusting of pecorino. ✦ Soft-boil the eggs in the same water, peel them, and add them to the plates on top of the bread and tomato layers.

FAVA-BEAN FRITTERS

PANELLE DI FAVE

SICILIA

2 lbs. dried fava beans
½ medium onion, sliced
Tops of wild fennel
Olive oil for frying
Pinch chili pepper flakes (optional)
Salt

Soak the fava beans in water overnight, then drain. The next morning boil them in lightly salted water with the onion and fennel. ✦ Cook over low heat for 2 to 3 hours until the beans dissolve to form a purée; pass them through a sieve. Grease a work surface, preferably marble, with olive oil and pour the mixture onto it. ✦ Roll the mixture out to a thickness of about 1 inch and let cool. Cut into 2-inch strips. Heat a few inches of olive oil in a saucepan and fry the strips until golden. Drain and, if desired, dust with chili pepper flakes. Serve warm.

PASTRY LEAVES

PANIGACCI O PANIGAZI

TOSCANA

6½ cups all-purpose flour,
plus more as needed
1 tbsp. extra-virgin olive oil
plus oil for greasing
Half a potato
Salt

This dish, typical of Aulla, is served with salumi or fresh pecorino. In Podenzana they are cooked on earthenware disks.

Mix the flour, olive oil, a pinch of salt, and enough water (about 3 cups) to form a smooth dough. ✦ Dip the cut side of the potato in oil and use it to grease an iron griddle (4½ to 6 inches in diameter), then heat it. When the disk is smoking hot, pour over a scant ladleful of the batter and cook on one side, moving the disk in a spiral motion so that the batter covers the entire surface. Use a table knife to detach batter, turn, and cook on the other side. As you proceed (greasing the griddle with the potato each time), put the cooked leaves in a basket covered with a cloth in a warm spot.

CHICKPEA POLENTA

PANISSA

LIGURIA

1⅔ cups chickpea flour,
plus more as needed

Salt

This can be eaten hot, poured into soup bowls and seasoned with olive oil, a few drops of lemon juice, and a dash of pepper. It can also be allowed to cool, after which it can be sliced and then fried or baked.

Warm 3 cups of water with a pinch of salt and, removing the pan from the heat, very slowly pour in the chickpea flour, stirring constantly. Continue to stir until it is perfectly blended. Put the pan back over low heat and cook 45 minutes, stirring constantly.

MARINATED BREAD SALAD

PANZANELLA

TOSCANA

1 lb. stale peasant-style bread,
cut into slices

2 plum tomatoes not overly ripe,
chopped

2 medium red onions, chopped

1 cucumber (optional), chopped

½ bunch basil, chopped

3 tbsp. extra-virgin olive oil

1 tbsp. red wine vinegar

Salt and pepper

This dish is typical of Florence.

Soak the bread for a few minutes in cold water. When sodden, take pieces of bread a little at a time and squeeze them between your hands to remove the liquid. Rub the pieces between your hands to form small cubes of bread. ✦ Put these in a salad bowl, add all the vegetables and basil; season only with olive oil, salt, and pepper and put in a cool place. Just before serving add the vinegar.

STUFFED PEPPERS

PAPACCELLE AL VINCOTTO

CAMPANIA

½ lb. stale bread without crust

1 bunch flat-leaf parsley, chopped

2 garlic cloves, chopped

3 oz. pitted Gaeta olives

½ cup golden raisins

2 tbsp. capers

1 ½ cups extra-virgin olive oil

8 *papaccelle* (pickled peppers),
stems and seeds removed

2 tbsp. *vin cotto* (see note)

Salt

This dish is typical of Avellino. *Vin cotto* ("cooked wine") is a kind of dark, sweet vinegar.

Mix the bread, parsley, garlic, olives, raisins, capers, ½ cup olive oil, and salt. Use this mixture to stuff the peppers. ✦ Put them in a skillet large enough to accommodate all 8 *papaccelle* easily, pour the remaining olive oil over them, and cook at medium heat for about 15 minutes. ✦ When the lower half of the *papaccelle* has browned, delicately turn them over to permit the part where the stuffing was inserted to brown equally. ✦ After about 20 minutes, by which time the *papaccelle* should be nearly cooked, add the *vin cotto* and cook for another 10 minutes.

VEGETABLE PIE

PIEMONTE

3 lbs. *ravisse* (turnip leaves)
4 oz. fresh *lardo* (see page 2), minced
3 or 4 garlic cloves, crushed
2 ½ cups Arborio rice
1 ¼ cups cornmeal
3 oz. pork rind, cut in pieces
Salt

Pasticcio verde is a dish typical of the fall since it requires *ravisse,* the green and healthful leaves of turnips, which are planted in local fields on July 29, feast day of St. Martha. This vegetable can also be chopped and fried together with sausage or, even better, with *salame d'la duja*: an excellent variation. Pieces of red chili pepper fried together with the *ravisse* heighten its flavor.

Carefully clean and wash the *ravisse;* boil in unsalted water to cover by several inches just until wilted (do not overcook). Drain and immerse in cold water for at least 1 hour to make them lose their typical bitter flavor. Drain the *ravisse* and squeeze them into little balls using both hands. Finely chop them. Heat the *lardo* over low heat and fry the garlic until golden. ✦ Combine the chopped *ravisse* with the rice, cornmeal, and pork rind in an oven-proof pot; stir in as much water as necessary to obtain a somewhat thick paste; season with salt. ✦ Put the pot over medium heat and bring to a boil, carefully stirring. When it boils, lower the heat and, still stirring, let it cook slowly for 15 minutes. Meanwhile, preheat the oven to 400°F. All this stirring serves to blend the ingredients and, at the same time, will prevent the cornmeal from sinking to the bottom of the container when the mixture is baked. ✦ Bake until it forms a beautiful dark crust.

POLENTA PIE WITH SAUSAGE AND RAISINS

PASTUCCIA

ABRUZZO

2 cups cornmeal, plus more for serving
1 cup raisins
¾ lb. sausage meat, minced
2 large egg yolks
¼ lb. pork pancetta (or *guanciale*), minced
2 tbsp. lard
Salt

Put the cornmeal and a little salt in a bowl and work in enough lukewarm water to obtain a solid dough (about ½ cup), kneading and turning until it pulls away from the bowl dry. ✦ Add the raisins and sausage to the dough, then work in the egg yolks. ✦ In a pan (preferably copper) over low heat, fry the pancetta (or *guanciale*) until golden; add the dough, pressing it down and flattening it with a wooden spoon. Brush the surface of the dough with lard, adding the remaining pancetta (or *guanciale*). Brown well on both sides and serve hot.

PÂTÉ DI CONIGLIO | RABBIT AND PORK PÂTÉ

PIEMONTE

2 cups prepared gelatin
1 lb. rabbit meat, cubed
½ lb. pork loin, cubed
Sage leaves
1 tbsp. lard
4 oz. prosciutto cotto, diced
Salt and pepper

Pour a little gelatin into a plum-cake mold or loaf pan and put in the refrigerator to harden. Put the meats and sage in a saucepan with the lard. Cook, covered, 40 minutes, stirring occasionally. Let cool. ✦ Add salt and pepper and purée the meat with its cooking juices in a blender until smooth. Add the prosciutto and let cool. ✦ Fill the mold with the meat mixture, cover with the remaining gelatin, and refrigerate 4 or 5 hours or until firm.

PÂTÉ DI FEGATO | LIVER PÂTÉ

VENETO

¾ lb. chicken livers
2 cups white wine
1 garlic clove
A few sage leaves
1 sprig rosemary
1½ cups (3 sticks) unsalted butter
1 tsp. brandy
Salt and pepper

Anise seeds, mushrooms whipped in a blender, asparagus tips, or cooked Treviso radicchio can be added. Spread on toasted bread.

Simmer the livers in the wine with the garlic, sage, rosemary, salt, and pepper. Remove the livers with a slotted spoon, pass through a sieve, and work together with the butter, adding the brandy. Put the mixture in molds and refrigerate; this pâté will remain good for many days.

PÂTÉ NAPOLETANO | NEAPOLITAN PÂTÉ

FOR
6 PERSONS

CAMPANIA

1 lb. boneless veal
1 lb. very lean boneless pork
1 lb. chicken breast
4 large egg yolks, beaten
6 tbsp. grated Parmigiano-Reggiano
1 slice white bread, softened in milk and squeezed dry
A few tbsp. milk
Bay leaves
1 large black truffle, shaved

CONTINUED

Preheat the oven to 450°F. Pass the veal, pork, and chicken through a meat grinder twice and blend well in a large bowl with the egg yolks, Parmigiano-Reggiano, salt, pepper, and bread. ✦ Work the mixture well for a long time to blend it thoroughly, adding a little milk from time to time. ✦ Pass the mixture through the meat grinder again. ✦ Put a few bay leaves in the bottom of a pâté terrine or rectangular mold and spread a layer of the meat mixture over them, smoothing it to form a flat surface and pressing down with the hands. ✦ Sprinkle with black truffle, prosciutto, and lard; repeat the layers until the ingredients are used up. Cover the last layer with bay leaves. ✦ Close the mold and place it in a large

6 oz. prosciutto crudo, minced

6 oz. lard

Salt and pepper

pan. Add cold water to reach halfway up the sides of the mold. Heat over low heat, until the water boils; transfer the whole thing to the oven and bake about 2 hours, or until the surface has browned. ✦ Remove from the oven; eliminate any liquid that has formed in the terrine or mold. Remove the lid from the mold, cover the pâté with a wooden cover, and on that place a weight of more than 10 pounds. ✦ When the pâté has cooled, refrigerate for 12 hours, still being pressed. Serve cold, accompanied by slices of bread toasted in the oven.

PEARÀ | # MARROW SAUCE

VENETO

4 oz. beef marrow

½ cup olive oil, preferably from Liguria

3 lbs. fine breadcrumbs

4 cups broth, warmed

3 tbsp. grated Parmigiano-Reggiano

Salt and pepper

Pearà calls for a great deal of pepper; the aroma and spicy flavor should remain on the palate. Some of the pepper can be added near the end of the cooking. Serve this sauce with all kinds of boiled meats, from chicken to beef. It is the classic accompaniment for *bollito misto* (see page 522).

In a terra-cotta pot over low heat, melt the marrow with the olive oil and add the breadcrumbs slowly, working the mixture together well. ✦ Add the broth and salt and pepper. Boil slowly over low heat for 2 hours; never stir until the last moment, when you add the Parmigiano-Reggiano, about 10 minutes before serving.

PEPERONI ALLA PIEMONTESE | # PAN-COOKED PEPPERS

PIEMONTE

¼ cup olive oil

4 yellow or red peppers, cut into somewhat large pieces

8 salt-cured anchovies, rinsed of salt

2 tbsp. mixed chopped flat-leaf parsley and basil

1 garlic clove, chopped

1 tbsp. capers

4 tbsp. red wine vinegar

Heat the olive oil in a pan and cook the peppers quickly, keeping them somewhat crisp. Chop the remaining ingredients and add to the pan, sprinkling on vinegar and raising the heat to make it evaporate. Let cool, stirring from time to time.

UNLEAVENED FLATBREAD

PIADA OR PIADINA

EMILIA-ROMAGNA

2 cups all-purpose flour,
plus more as needed

¼ lb. *lardo* (see page 2)
(or ⅓ cup extra-virgin olive oil)

1 cup milk

Salt

The *piada* has ancient origins. Over time the idea developed of a kind of flatbread or salted *piada* or *"schiacciata"* or *piada* made with salt and *lardo*, but usually without sweet ingredients, which can be found—speaking specifically of honey—in the area of Cervia. Over the centuries the *piada* has been considered a kind of bread, in general made without yeast and eaten hot. It was during the postwar period that the *piada* assumed its current consolidated shape and taste, along with a richness that has helped it become a typical specialty of the Romagna, correctly referred to as *piada* and in dialect *pié*. The good *piadina* represents the nurturing and domestic arts that are the basis of Romagnan conviviality. Historically speaking, what did our ancestors eat with their *piada*? Herbs from the garden and field, such as cabbage, nettles, corn poppies, and radicchio. They also ate greens fried with garlic, onion, shallots, pancetta, and *lardo*. They ate cheeses, like *raviggiolo* or *squacquarone* or pecorino, *caprino*, mixed chesses, and aged cow's-milk cheeses. They also ate cured meats in general, including *lardo*, pancetta, and *ciccioli*, or topped it with *sapa* (see page 69).

Combine the ingredients to form an elastic, soft dough (add water if necessary) and divide into loaves (balls) and let rest for 30 minutes covered by a cloth. Roll out the balls to form disks about 6 inches in diameter and ¼ inch thick. ✦ Put each disk on a heated griddle or cast-iron skillet and cook until just colored, then turn with a fork so it will cook evenly without bubbles.

PISSALADIÈRE

PISCIALANDREA

LIGURIA

3 cups all-purpose flour,
plus more as needed

2¼ tsp. active dry yeast

⅓ cup milk

2 tbsp. extra-virgin olive oil

2 medium onions, sliced

4 salt-cured anchovies,
rinsed of salt and chopped

CONTINUED

This dish is typical of the Riviera di Ponente. Popular legends attribute the name of this pizza to the Genoese naval hero Andrea Doria, claiming he variously invented it or was offered it in homage; a very different view traces the name to *pissaladière*, a flatbread from the nearby Côte d'Azur.

Mix the flour, yeast, milk, 1 tablespoon of the olive oil, and a dash of salt. Turn out onto a clean work surface and knead, turning and folding, until the dough is smooth and elastic. You may need to add a few tablespoons of water if the dough feels too dry. Cover with a cloth and let it rise for at least 2 hours. ✦ Meanwhile

1 lb. plum tomatoes, peeled and drained, seeded and chopped

Several small basil leaves

½ cup pitted black olives, halved

5 garlic cloves

2 tbsp. chopped oregano

Salt

preheat the oven to 350°F. Grease a baking pan with olive oil. Heat the remaining olive oil in a pan and add the onions and sauté; add the anchovies, tomatoes, basil, and salt to taste. Cook for about 15 minutes. ✦ Roll out a 1-inch-thick layer of dough and place it in the prepared pan. Sprinkle with the olives and garlic. Spread over the tomato sauce, then sprinkle with oregano. Bake for about 30 minutes. Serve hot.

PIZZA ALLA CAMPOFRANCO

LAYERED PIZZA

FOR 6 PERSONS

CAMPANIA

3 cups all-purpose flour, plus more as needed

⅔ cup milk

2¼ tsp. active dry yeast

3 large eggs

½ cup (1 stick) unsalted butter

7 oz. *fior di latte* cheese, sliced

½ cup tomato purée

¼ cup grated Parmigiano-Reggiano

Combine the flour, milk, yeast, eggs, and butter to prepare a dough as though making brioche (see page 7). Set it to rise in a loaf pan with somewhat high sides. ✦ Preheat the oven to 350°F. Bake until browned and golden, then let it cool. Increase the oven temperature to 450°F. Remove the loaf from the pan and slice it in half horizontally. Put the lower part back in the pan and cover it with slices of *fior di latte*, half the tomato purée, and half the Parmigiano-Reggiano. Cover with the top half and add the remaining *fior di latte*, tomato purée, and Parmigiano-Reggiano. Bake 15 minutes. Serve hot.

PIZZA ALLA NAPOLETANA

NEAPOLITAN PIZZA

CAMPANIA

1 lb. risen pizza dough (see page 13)

5 or 6 San Marzano plum tomatoes, peeled, seeded, and chopped

1 tsp. dried oregano, crumbled

2 tbsp. small basil leaves

2 garlic cloves, chopped

Extra-virgin olive oil

Salt

There are many variations, such as the Margherita, which is similar with the addition of diced mozzarella. Many other versions use various ingredients: anchovies, mushrooms, olives, hard-boiled eggs, prosciutto, and so on.

Preheat the oven to 450°F. Put the dough on a flat surface, divide in half, and make a somewhat thick disk out of each half, making them a little thicker at the edges. ✦ Distribute the pieces of tomato across the disks and spread with oregano, basil, and garlic. Sprinkle with oil and salt and bake for about 15 minutes.

PIZZA ALLA SICILIANA | SICILIAN PIZZA 1

SICILIA

For the dough:

3 cups all-purpose flour, plus more as needed

2¼ tsp. active dry yeast, dissolved in 2 tbsp. water

For the seasoning (the *conza*):

3 medium onions, sliced

2 tbsp. olive oil, plus more for the pan

6 plum tomatoes, peeled

2 garlic cloves

6 anchovies, boned and chopped, or as desired

½ lb. cheese (caciocavallo or, in its absence, pecorino), thinly sliced

1 tbsp. chopped oregano

Salt

According to tradition, you can determine when the ball of dough is done by knocking on it: If the ball responds with a certain hollow sound not unlike that of a muffled drum, it's done. If the sauce is not thick enough, it is common to add breadcrumbs to the cheese; these breadcrumbs should be toasted in a greased pan.

Form a well with the flour; add the yeast with its water, a dash of salt, and enough additional water to make a soft dough (¾ to 1 cup). Knead until the dough becomes solid and homogenous, then form into a ball, cover, and let rise for several hours. ✦ Prepare the *conza*: Heat 2 tablespoons of the olive oil over low heat and add the onions. Cover the pan to create steam and keep the onions from darkening. Add the tomatoes and the whole garlic cloves. Continue cooking until the sauce is fragrant and dense. Remove and discard the garlic cloves. ✦ Preheat the oven to 425°F. Grease a baking sheet with olive oil. Make a layer of dough about 2 inches high on the pan. Push into the dough as many pieces of anchovy as desired; also push in some thin slices of cheese. ✦ Cover with the *conza* and sprinkle with cheese and oregano. Generously drizzle with more olive oil and bake for approximately 15 minutes, until the cheese has melted and the dough is crisp on the bottom.

PIZZA ARROTOLATA | ROLLED PIZZA

SICILIA

⅔ cup all-purpose flour, plus more as needed

4 tbsp. lard

2 tbsp. *ciccioli* or *frittuli* (see note, page 12)

1 lb. fresh sausage, crumbled

2 medium onions, chopped

½ cup grated pecorino

Salt and pepper

This dish is typical of Campofranco. The dialect name for this pizza, *'Mpriolata,* is probably derived from *'impriola,* a sailor's word for a sail attached to a mast with a wooden ring.

Preheat the oven to 425°F. Mix together the flour and ¼ cup water and a little salt to form a smooth dough. Knead until soft and elastic. Cover with a kitchen cloth and let rest for 1 hour. ✦ Roll the dough out into a thin sheet and cut out 4 disks 10 to 12 inches in diameter. Spread each disk with 1 tablespoon lard; sprinkle each with some of the *ciccioli,* sausage meat, onions, pecorino, and top with pepper. Roll each disk of dough up, then coil the roll to create a ring shape. Bake 15 to 30 minutes or until golden.

PIZZA WITH TURNIP GREENS

LAZIO

1 ¾ lbs. turnip greens,
washed and dried

1 garlic clove, chopped

Extra-virgin olive oil

Pinch chili pepper flakes

1 ½ cups all-purpose flour,
plus more as needed

1 ½ tsp. active dry yeast,
dissolved in 2 tbsp. lukewarm water

1 large egg yolk

Salt and white pepper

The leafy tops of turnips are used like broccoli rabe; the type called for in this recipe, locally called *tanni*, is grown in the southern part of Lazio and has a particularly bitter flavor.

Slowly cook the turnip greens in a pan over low heat with salt, garlic, olive oil, and chili pepper flakes. ✦ Combine the flour with the yeast mixture and 3 tablespoons water. Turn out onto a work surface and knead until smooth. Let rise until doubled in volume, about an hour. When the dough has risen, add a dash of salt and enough water to make an elastic dough that is not too firm. ✦ Preheat the oven to 400°F. Roll the dough out on a floured board to 2 ⅛-inch-thick sheets and use one sheet to line a baking pan. Spoon a layer of greens no more than 1 inch thick; cover this with the other sheet of dough. Puncture the top with a fork, brush with the egg, and dust with white pepper. ✦ Bake about 25 minutes, until the top is browned.

PIZZA WITH ANCHOVIES AND CAPERS

CALABRIA

Extra-virgin olive oil

¾ lb. bread dough (see page 13)

¼ cup capers in vinegar

6 to 8 fillets of salt-cured anchovies,
chopped

Salt

Preheat the oven to 400°F. Grease a baking pan with olive oil. Roll out the dough and lay it into the pan. Spread with capers and anchovies. Season with a drizzle of olive oil, salt if needed, and bake about 25 minutes, until golden brown.

PIZZA WITH ARTICHOKES AND RICOTTA

CALABRIA

Extra-virgin olive oil

Leaves of 1 artichoke, boiled until soft

6 oz. sheep's-milk ricotta

2 tbsp. chopped flat-leaf parsley

CONTINUED

A good idea is to use artichoke leaves left over from other preparations.

Preheat the oven to 350°F. Grease a baking pan with olive oil. Pass the boiled artichoke leaves through a food mill. Combine the resultant purée with the ricotta, parsley, salt, and pepper. ✦ Divide the dough in half and spread the first half across the pan. Cover this with the

¾ lb. bread dough (see page 13)

Salt and pepper

artichoke mixture then cover with the remaining dough, pressing down on the edges with a fork to seal them. ✦ Bake about 25 minutes, until golden brown.

PIZZA WITH CRACKLINGS AND RAISINS

PIZZA CON CICCIOLI
E UVA PASSA

FOR
6 PERSONS

CALABRIA

3 cups all-purpose flour, plus more as needed

1 tbsp. active dry yeast, dissolved in 2 tbsp. warm water

2 tbsp. lard

6 oz. *ciccioli* (see note, page 12)

⅓ cup raisins, soaked in warm water and drained

Salt

Preheat the oven to 400°F. Grease a baking pan. Combine the flour, yeast mixture, and salt with enough water (¾ to 1 cup) to make a smooth dough. Knead until smooth and elastic. Let rest covered with a kitchen towel for 1 hour. ✦ Roll the dough out to obtain a square or rectangle about ½ inch thick. Let rest while making the filling. ✦ Heat the lard in a pan and sauté the *ciccioli* and raisins until the pork begins to take on a little color. Spread the filling over the dough and roll it up. Join the ends to form a ring. Place on the pan and bake until golden brown, about 30 minutes.

PIZZA WITH CRACKLINGS

PIZZA CON GLI SFRIZZOLI

UMBRIA

3 tsp. active dry yeast

⅔ cup milk, warmed

4 ¼ cups all-purpose flour, plus more as needed

4 large eggs

7 oz. *sfrizzoli* (*ciccioli;* see note, page 12)

Parmigiano-Reggiano, to taste

Olive oil

Salt

Dissolve the yeast in the milk, then work together all the ingredients (except the olive oil). Turn out onto a work surface and knead together until the dough is smooth and elastic. Cover with a kitchen cloth and let the dough rest and rise for 1 hour. ✦ Preheat the oven to 400°F. Grease a pan with olive oil. Pat the dough to a thickness of 2 inches and bake until golden.

PIZZA WITH ESCAROLE

PIZZA DI SCAROLA

CAMPANIA

3 large heads escarole

CONTINUED

Preheat the oven to 350°F. Grease a pie pan. Wash the escarole, boil it in lightly salted water, and drain well. Coarsely chop. Heat the olive oil in a pan over low heat and add the anchovies, cooking them to break them up;

2 tbsp. extra-virgin olive oil
2 anchovies in oil
1 garlic clove
2 tbsp. capers, crushed
½ cup pitted Gaeta olives
1 lb. risen pizza dough (see page 13)
Salt

add the garlic and fry until golden, then remove it. Add the escarole, capers, and olives. Cook at high heat until the escarole is completely dry; taste for salt. ✦ Take two-thirds of the dough and roll it out on a floured board to a sheet large enough to line the pie pan. Cover with the greens mixture and then roll out the remaining dough to create a cover; pinch the edges to seal. ✦ Bake 30 to 40 minutes until golden. This can be served either hot or at room temperature.

CORNMEAL PIZZA

Several sage leaves
1 celery stalk, chopped
1 sprig rosemary
2 or 3 whole cloves
2⅓ cups cornmeal
2 tbsp. olive oil
½ cup golden raisins
2 tbsp. pine nuts (optional)
2 tbsp. chopped herbs (optional)
Salt

This "pizza" is typical of Orvieto and goes well with the town's golden white wine.

Preheat the oven to 350°F. Boil the sage, celery, rosemary, and cloves in 4 cups of salted water; add the cornmeal and stir energetically until the mixture thickens; then add the olive oil, raisins, pine nuts, and herbs, if using. Immediately turn the dough out into a pan and bake until firm and a golden crust forms.

✦ **LOCAL TRADITION** ✦

PIZZA DI VERDURE

This dish, typical of Ferrazzano, in Molise, is even better the next day, reheated in a pan with a little olive oil. Traditionally, the cornmeal "pizza" was baked on the hearth, on top of a layer of chestnut leaves. Then this "pizza" was broken up and mashed together with cooked greens and pork.

EASTER PIZZA WITH CHEESE

PIZZA PASQUALE DI FORMAGGIO

UMBRIA

6 ½ cups all-purpose flour, plus more as needed

1 tbsp. active dry yeast, dissolved in ½ cup warm water

1 cup milk

10 large eggs, beaten

1 ¼ cups grated pecorino

¾ cup grated Parmigiano-Reggiano

½ cup lard

2 tbsp. extra-virgin olive oil

Juice of 1 lemon

Splash of white wine

Salt

This dish is typical of Terni and goes well with salame, most especially capocollo. It is an element in the traditional Easter meal, eaten "after the ringing of the bells" along with Lamb offal with artichokes (see page 562) and the Easter frittata (see page 33).

Make a well with the flour, add half the yeast mixture, and knead well until the dough is smooth. (You may need to add a little water if the dough is too dry.) Form into a loaf shape. Let this rest, covered with a kitchen towel, overnight in a warm spot. ✦ The next morning work the milk and the remaining yeast mixture into the dough. Let it rise for at least 2 hours in a warm spot. ✦ Preheat the oven to 425°F. Add the remaining ingredients and prepare a soft and elastic dough. ✦ Divide into loaves and put in somewhat high but not wide molds. Bake until golden, about 30 minutes.

STUFFED PIZZA

PIZZA PIENA

CAMPANIA

For the dough:

3 cups all-purpose flour, plus more as needed

1 large egg, beaten

2 tbsp. lard (or unsalted butter), plus more for topping

For the filling:

8 large eggs, beaten

1 lb. fresh mozzarella, sliced

7 oz. salame or prosciutto, minced

½ cup grated pecorino

½ cup ricotta (optional), whipped with a fork

Salt and pepper

Combine the flour with the egg, salt, and enough water to form a soft dough (about 1 cup). Roll out to make a thin round sheet as large as possible. Grease the sheet of dough with the lard (or butter) then roll it up tightly and put it in the refrigerator for 30 minutes. ✦ Preheat the oven to 350°F. Lay out the roll on a cutting board and cut it in half lengthwise. Place one of these halves on the board, seam side down, and roll it up from one end, allowing it to stick together but without adding any pressure so that it eventually forms a cylinder with a distinct spiral. Seal the end by moistening the last end. ✦ Using a floured rolling pin, delicately flatten the cylinder from the center outward toward the edges in such a way that the edges of the spiral fold under to form a disk. ✦ Use the disk to line a round pan, making certain the spiral adheres to the pan. ✦ Mix the eggs, mozzarella, pepper, salame, pecorino, and, if desired, ricotta. Pour this mixture in the lined pan and cover with the remaining sheet of dough, prepared like the first. Dot the surface with lard (or butter), and bake for 40 minutes, until golden. Let rest and serve.

PIZZA CON FIORI DI SAMBUCO

This pizza recipe from Calabria, typical of the area of Serra San Bruno, makes use of elderberry flowers, which grow wild along roadsides and in the verdant woods of both Italy and America. A basic bread dough would be used to create a pizza crust, which would then be completely covered with the elderberry flowers and sprinkled with a small amount of olive oil. This simple pizza would then be rolled up and baked in a greased pan until golden brown.

PIZZA RUSTICA 1

MEAT PIZZA

CAMPANIA

1 lb. ricotta

7 oz. provola or *fior di latte* cheese

3 large eggs, separated

⅓ cup grated Parmigiano-Reggiano

4 oz. prosciutto cotto, diced

2 oz. salame (preferably Neapolitan), diced

2 oz. mortadella, diced

1 lb. puff pastry or short-crust pastry, according to taste

Salt and pepper

Preheat the oven to 350°F. Mix the ricotta, provola, egg yolks, salt, pepper, and Parmigiano-Reggiano until blended. Add the prosciutto, salame, and mortadella. Whip the egg whites to soft peaks and fold them into the mixture. ✦ Use two-thirds of the pastry dough to line a pie pan and fill with the mixture. Roll the remaining pastry dough out to form a disk and cover the filling. Use the tines of a fork to seal the edges all around. Bake for 30 to 40 minutes, or until the top is golden. Serve hot or at room temperature.

PIZZA RUSTICA 2

PIZZA WITH POTATOES AND OLIVES

PUGLIA

2 medium potatoes

3 cups all-purpose flour, plus more as needed

2 tsp. active dry yeast, dissolved in 2 tbsp. lukewarm water

Pinch sugar

CONTINUED

This dish is typical of Brindisi.

Boil the potatoes, peel them when still warm, then pass them through a food mill. Knead in the flour, adding the yeast and enough water to obtain a solid dough, about 1½ cups. Add salt, sugar, and 2 tablespoons olive oil; let rest and rise for at least 2 hours in a warm spot. ✦ Meanwhile boil the onions in a little water for 5 to 10 minutes. At the end of that time, drain the water and remove

½ cup extra-virgin olive oil

4 medium onions, thinly sliced

1 heaping tbsp. capers

4 ripe San Marzano plum tomatoes, cut in pieces

30 pitted black olives

Salt

onions. Add 3 tablespoons olive oil to the pan. Sauté the onions without letting them take on color. Add the capers and tomatoes and work the mixture well to combine thoroughly. Remove from the heat and add the olives. ✦ Preheat the oven to 350°F. Grease a baking pan with olive oil. Arrange the risen dough in the prepared pan and distribute the onion mixture over it; cover with another layer of dough and brush the top with olive oil. Bake for nearly 1 hour or until golden.

PIZZA SICILIANA 2

SICILIAN PIZZA 2

SICILIA

For the dough:

3⅔ cups all-purpose flour, plus more as needed

1 tsp. baking powder

1⅛ tsp. cream of tartar or active dry yeast

2 tbsp. extra-virgin olive oil

Salt

For the topping:

½ cup tomato purée

1 medium onion, cut in thin slices

4 oz. tuma (unsalted goat's-milk cheese), cubed

6 anchovies, in pieces

½ cup black olives, pitted and chopped

1 tsp. dried oregano, crumbled

1 tbsp. extra-virgin olive oil

Pepper

Slowly combine the flour and salt with 1½ cups lukewarm water, baking powder, and cream of tartar (or yeast) and work to obtain a homogenous dough. When the dough has risen, knead it again, adding 1 tablespoon oil. ✦ Preheat the oven to 350°F. Grease a baking pan with olive oil and spread out the dough to create a layer about ½ inch high. Season the top of the dough with the tomato purée, onion, tuma, anchovies, olives, oregano, pepper, and olive oil. ✦ Bake for 20 minutes until golden. Cut it in slices when warm; it is easier to cut this using kitchen shears than a knife.

POLENTA IN TORTIERA

BAKED POLENTA WITH TURNIPS AND SAUSAGES

CAMPANIA

¼ cup olive oil

1¼ cups cornmeal

⅔ cup milk

CONTINUED

This polenta's pleasingly bitter flavor makes it suitable as an appetizer, preferably served warm.

Preheat the oven to 475°F. Grease a baking pan with olive oil. Prepare polenta, combining the cornmeal, milk, and salt in a pot with 5 cups water, stirring until cooked and smooth. ✦ Heat half the olive oil in a pan and cook

2 garlic cloves

1 *diavolillo* (see note, page 22) (optional)

2 bunches *friarielli* (can substitute broccoli rabe), chopped

2 pork sausages, crumbled

Salt

the garlic and (if desired) the *diavalillo*. Add the *friarielli* and sausage meat and, when these are cooked, mix them into the polenta. ✦ Pour the mixture into the pan, spreading it with the back of a fork. Bake for about 30 minutes, or until a crust forms.

MUSHROOM MEATBALLS

POLPETTE DI FUNGHI ROSITI

FOR 6 PERSONS

CALABRIA

1 ½ lbs. mushrooms (preferably *rositi* [*Lactarius deliciosus*])

¾ lb. ground beef

4 oz. peasant-style bread without crust, soaked in milk and squeezed dry

⅓ cup grated pecorino

2 garlic cloves, minced

1 tbsp. chopped flat-leaf parsley

2 large eggs

Extra-virgin olive oil

2 cups tomato sauce, for serving

Salt and pepper

Clean and carefully wash the *rositi* (so called for their pinkish hue), dry them with a cloth, and cut in very small pieces. ✦ In a bowl mix the beef, *rositi,* bread, pecorino, garlic, parsley, eggs, salt, and pepper. ✦ Prepare a sauce with ½ cup olive oil and the tomato purée. Shape the mushroom-meat mixture into meatballs. Heat ½ inch of olive oil in a pan and brown the meatballs. Drain on paper towels and serve with tomato sauce.

FRIED BACCALÀ BALLS

POLPETTINE DI BACCALÀ

MARCHE

Olive oil

1 medium onion

1 garlic clove, crushed

1 ½ lbs. baccalà, soaked overnight and cut in pieces without bones and skin

2 tbsp. dry white wine

2 tbsp. milk

½ cup bread without crust

1 tbsp. chopped flat-leaf parsley

Pinch grated nutmeg

1 ½ cups all-purpose flour

2 large eggs, beaten

2 cups breadcrumbs

White pepper

Heat 2 tablespoons olive oil in a pan. Chop together the onion and garlic and sauté. Add the pieces of baccalà and toss. Pour in the wine, and cook until it evaporates. Add water to cover the fish and continue cooking for 2 minutes more. Let cool. ✦ When the baccalà has cooled, pass it through a meat grinder or blender. Add the milk to the baccalà liquid and soak the bread in it to soften. Add the baccalà, white pepper, parsley, and nutmeg. ✦ Work together to form balls about the size of large olives. Heat ½ inch of olive oil in a pan, until hot but not smoking. Flour the balls, then dip in beaten egg and breadcrumbs. Fry, in batches if necessary to prevent crowding, until golden, serve hot.

PROSCIUTTO DI BOSSES
JAMBON DE BOSSES

This rare Valdostan prosciutto crudo is made with the haunch of small local gray pigs raised in the Alps together with cows. The pigs feed on fresh grass along with residues from the manufacture of milk; they live at 1,800 meters altitude near the opening of the Great St. Bernard Tunnel. The tradition of making this prosciutto is very ancient, being pre-Roman, perhaps dating back to the Salassians; today, its production is very limited. The meat is brined in a mixture enriched with aromatic mountain herbs, and it is aged on the site (at 1,800 meters) in *rascards*, typical Valdostan wooden haylofts built off the ground. The period of aging lasts from a minimum of two years to a maximum of three. The prosciutto is dark red with white veins and has a very flavorful taste with an aromatic fragrance. The prolonged aging period is related to the special climatic conditions. In general, the jambon de Bosses is still prepared, as in the past, by private producers.

PUCCE | **OLIVE BREAD**

PUGLIA

5 tbsp. extra-virgin olive oil

3 *cipolotti* (salad onions)

3 ripe plum tomatoes, peeled and chopped

1 cup pitted olives in water

3 cups all-purpose flour, plus more as needed

2¼ tsp. active dry yeast, dissolved in 2 tbsp. warm water

Salt

Heat 2 tablespoons olive oil in a pan. Clean the onions, cut them in strips, then sauté. Add the tomatoes and cook, stirring constantly, until they have broken down some. Add the olives and a dash of salt. Keep on heat a few minutes, then let cool. ✦ Work together the flour, yeast mixture, 1 cup water, and salt to form a smooth dough. Knead until the dough is elastic. Add the cooled mixture to the dough, form into loaves, and let rise at least 1 hour. ✦ Preheat the oven to 400°F. Bake until golden, about 40 minutes.

PROSCIUTTO DI SAURIS

This type of prosciutto, typical of Friuli-Venezia Giulia, is made from young pigs raised on natural foods: cornmeal, barley, potatoes, whey. The prosciutto is slowly smoked with juniper and silver fir wood, giving it a special flavor and aroma.

RAMACCHÉ

PROSCIUTTO AND CHEESE FRITTERS

SICILIA

2 tbsp. unsalted butter

1 ¼ cups all-purpose flour, plus more as needed

5 large eggs

2 oz. prosciutto crudo, diced

½ cup grated caciocavallo cheese

2 tbsp. chopped flat-leaf parsley

Lard

Salt

This dish is typical of Acireale.

Heat water (about 1 cup), salt, and butter in a saucepan, preferably of copper, and when it boils remove the pan from heat and stir in the flour with a wooden spoon. Return the pan to the heat and work the mixture continuously with the spoon; after a great deal of stirring the mixture will have formed a solid and homogeneous ball of dough. Let it cool, then incorporate the eggs one at a time, constantly kneading (using a mixer can save some of this effort). ✦ When the dough forms bubbles, work in the prosciutto, caciocavallo, and parsley. When this is done, set the dough aside in a cool place. ✦ Heat several inches of lard in a high-sided pan until hot (but not smoking), then drop in 1-inch balls of dough. (You can make the balls with a spoon or spread out the dough and cut it into cylinders to roll directly in the pan.) Let these fry slowly, reducing the heat if they start to brown too quickly. ✦ Remove the *ramacché* with a slotted spoon, put them on a serving plate covered with paper towels, and serve hot.

BUCKWHEAT FLATBREAD

RUNDITT

PIEMONTE

4¼ cups all-purpose flour, plus more as needed

1¼ cups buckwheat flour, plus more as needed

2 tbsp. unsalted butter

1 garlic clove (optional)

Salt

The trick in this dish, typical of the Valle Vigezzo, is in making the thinnest possible sheet of dough.

Sift together the two flours, then mix with 1¾ cups water and salt to form a smooth dough as explained on page 13. Let rest for a few hours, then roll out into a thin sheet of dough. ✦ Cut into squares that will fit on an iron griddle. Place on the griddle and put the griddle over a burning flame, and when the dough is cooked remove it and grease it with a little butter and salt; if desired it can be rubbed with a cut clove of garlic.

GRAPE SYRUP

SAPA

MAKES ABOUT 3 LBS.

EMILIA-ROMAGNA

15 lbs. ripe sweet grapes

2-inch cinnamon stick

16 cloves

Zest of 2 lemons, with the pith removed

A simple way to see if the *sapa* (or *saba*) has cooked enough is to pour a few drops onto a sheet of paper and hold the sheet at an angle; if the drops resist gravity and stay in place, your *sapa* is ready. There are those who add 5 to 6 walnuts in their shell to the pot while it is cooking. The idea is that the walnuts, by hitting the bottom and walls of the pot, keep the syrup from sticking. Traditionally, *sapa* was put in the pantry in bottles that were sealed with wax.

Carefully clean the grapes, checking them one by one. Dry them and put them in a large terra-cotta pot. ✦ With a pestle (or even better, by hand) crush the grapes as completely as possible, creating a must. Put the must through a sieve to remove the skins and seeds, then return it to the pot. Cover with a cloth and let rest in a cool spot. ✦ After 24 hours add the cinnamon, cloves, and lemon zest and turn on the heat. Simmer, stirring occasionally to avoid sticking, for at least 12 hours, or until the must has reduced by about two-thirds. ✦ Skim off any impurities and let cool; remove the cinnamon. ✦ The result will be a sweet and very viscous liquid; pour it into sterilized bottles. The *sapa* will keep well, refrigerated, for a month or more.

SALAME D'OCA

This dish is typical of the Friulian plain. Chop together equal amounts of goose and pork, then season with lard, salt, pepper, garlic, and white wine. Stuff into casings to create salame. If desired, these can be smoked under the hood of the fireplace or preserved in goose fat.

SALSA AGRODOLCE

SWEET-AND-SOUR SAUCE

TOSCANA

1 tbsp. sugar
Juice of 1 lemon
½ cup white wine
4 oz. bittersweet chocolate
4 tbsp. (½ stick) unsalted butter
1 apple, peeled and grated
½ cup grappa
1 tbsp. raisins (optional)
1 tbsp. pine nuts (optional)
1 tbsp. chopped almonds (optional)

Put the sugar in a small copper pot, add the lemon juice, and caramelize the sugar at high heat. ◆ As soon as the sugar has developed a golden color remove from the heat and add the wine to dissolve it. Put it back on the heat and add the chocolate and butter. Let this dissolve. ◆ Mix in the apple. Add the grappa, and if desired, raisins, pine nuts, and almonds. Cook at low heat for a few minutes more.

**SALSA AGRODOLCE
ALLA PARMIGIANA**

SWEET-AND-SOUR SAUCE PARMA STYLE

EMILIA-ROMAGNA

3 tbsp. unsalted butter
3 tbsp. olive oil
1 garlic clove, chopped
2 tbsp. chopped flat-leaf parsley
1 heaping tbsp. tomato paste, dissolved in 2 tbsp. warm water
2 tbsp. white wine vinegar
1 tsp. sugar
Salt

In a saucepan heat the butter and olive oil and sauté the garlic and parsley. When the garlic is golden, add the tomato paste mixture, vinegar, sugar, and salt and simmer for a few minutes until thickened. Serve cool.

HORSERADISH SAUCE

SALSA DI CREN

EMILIA-ROMAGNA

9 oz. fresh horseradish root
½ cup breadcrumbs
2 tbsp. white wine vinegar
Salt

Wash the horseradish root under running water, dry well, then scrape off the peel with a knife and grate. (Do this in a well-ventilated place; the fumes are rather strong.) ✦ Mix the horseradish, breadcrumbs, vinegar, and a little salt, until combined. (The breadcrumbs temper the strong flavor of the horseradish.) ✦ This sauce can be preserved if stored in sealed sterilized glass jars covered with a film of olive oil. Preserved this way the sauce keeps for several weeks, bearing in mind that the sauce will gradually lose its characteristic sharp flavor. Store in the refrigerator.

TARRAGON SAUCE

SALSA AL DRAGONCELLO

TOSCANA

1 bunch fresh tarragon
A few basil leaves
3 garlic cloves
2 oz. crustless bread,
soaked in white wine vinegar
½ cup olive oil
Salt and pepper

This sauce is best served with boiled chicken or capon. It is prepared with tarragon, the herb of Siena. Following the wisdom of the farmer's wife, let it rest as long as possible: The more it rests, the better it tastes as the garlic dissolves.

Mix chopped tarragon, basil, and garlic with a little salt and pepper. ✦ Add the bread to the mixture; work these together for a long time to create the creamiest sauce possible. Let it rest for a few hours, then add the oil.

TRUFFLE SAUCE

SALSA AL TARTUFO

UMBRIA

¾ cup olive oil
2 garlic cloves
2 anchovies (needed only if the truffles are not highly fragrant)
2 oz. black truffles, grated
Salt and pepper

Heat the olive oil in a pan and cook the garlic and anchovies (if needed). Remove from heat, discard the garlic, and let cool slightly. Add the truffles, salt, and if necessary pepper (but only a little).

SALSA DELLA BORMIDA | BORMIDA SAUCE

LIGURIA

1 celery stalk, finely chopped

1 carrot, finely chopped

Extra-virgin olive oil

2 salt-cured anchovies

½ small garlic clove

1 handful flat-leaf parsley

Heart of 1 onion
(peel away the outer layers to
obtain a piece the size of a walnut)

Bread without crust from
a baguette (about 1 cup)

¾ cup vinegar

2 yolks of large hard-boiled eggs

Juice of 1 lemon, or as needed

Salt and pepper

This sauce should be eaten with boiled meats.

Heat 2 tablespoons oil and cook the vegetables for 10 minutes. ✦ Chop the anchovies, garlic, parsley, and onion. ✦ Soak the bread in the vinegar, squeeze dry, and work together with the egg yolks. ✦ Mix anchovy and bread mixtures into the celery and carrot, and add the lemon juice, salt, pepper, and additional oil as desired.

SALSA BARBERINA | BARBERINA SAUCE

TOSCANA

½ cup dry white wine

½ cup broth

Juice of 1 lemon

1 cup breadcrumbs

2 tbsp. extra-virgin olive oil

3 tbsp. chopped onion

2 tbsp. chopped flat-leaf parsley

1 bay leaf

Pinch grated nutmeg

Salt and pepper

This sauce, typical of Bolgheri, is especially good on roast game.

In a saucepan, combine all the ingredients, adding salt and pepper to taste. Mix and bring to a boil. Cook for several minutes.

SALSA DI FIORI DI ZUCCA | SQUASH-BLOSSOM SAUCE

ABRUZZO

2 tbsp. extra-virgin olive oil

1 garlic clove, chopped

CONTINUED

This is a pasta sauce typical of Sulmona. Put part of the sauce over the pasta in the pan; add the rest of the sauce when the pasta is served, using it primarily as decoration.

Heat the olive oil and lightly cook the garlic; add the squash blossoms and sauté briefly. Add a little water

Squash blossoms, chopped

A few threads saffron

1 large egg yolk

Grated pecorino

Lemon juice

and saffron, and boil for 10 to 15 minutes. Pass through a sieve; add the egg yolk, pecorino, and a few drops of lemon juice.

SALSA DI NOCI

WALNUT SAUCE

LIGURIA

2 cups walnut halves

Bread from a roll, soaked in milk and squeezed dry

½ cup pine nuts

½ garlic clove

¼ cup grated Parmigiano-Reggiano

½ cup extra-virgin olive oil

A few marjoram leaves

This is the classic sauce to use with *pansotti* (see page 292) and is typical of the Tigullio area.

Grind the walnuts in a mortar and pestle, adding the bread, pine nuts, garlic, and a little salt; grind until you have a thick paste (you can choose instead to perform this operation with a blender on low, beginning with the nuts and adding the other ingredients). ✦ Put the mixture in a bowl and work with a wooden spoon, incorporating the Parmigiano-Reggiano and olive oil. Add the marjoram last.

SALSA DI SALSICCE

SAUSAGE SAUCE

TOSCANA

2 tbsp. extra-virgin olive oil

1 large onion, chopped

9 oz. sausage meat, removed from its casing and crumbled

7 oz. fresh porcini mushrooms (or 1 oz. dried porcini soaked in lukewarm water 30 minutes and drained), roughly chopped

1 lb. ripe plum tomatoes, peeled, seeded, and crushed

¼ cup red wine (if needed)

This dish is typical of the area near Monte Amiata and is most often served on the thick Tuscan pasta called *pici* (see page 316) or another similar pasta.

Heat the oil in a pan and add the onion; when the onion begins to become transparent, add the sausage meat and mushrooms. Cook about 10 minutes, stirring occasionally. ✦ Add the tomatoes, salt and pepper to taste, and, if needed to thin the sauce, the red wine. ✦ Continue cooking at very low heat for another 30 minutes.

SALSA FERRARESE

GREEN-PEPPER SAUCE

EMILIA-ROMAGNA

¼ cup olive oil

CONTINUED

Heat the olive oil in a pan over low heat and sauté the onions until translucent; add the green peppers. Cook until the peppers have wilted completely, then add the tomatoes. ✦ Cook at low heat, stirring often, for about

6 oz. red onions, sliced very thin

1 ¾ lbs. green peppers, sliced very thin

2 lbs. ripe plum tomatoes, chopped

1½ hours. This sauce should be preserved in sterilized well-sealed glass jars and stored in a cool spot.

GREEN SAUCE

2 tbsp. pine nuts

1 tbsp. capers, well drained

1 salt-cured anchovy, without bones or head and cleaned

Yolk of 1 large hard-boiled egg

3 pitted green olives

1 garlic clove

1 bunch flat-leaf parsley, chopped

1 small amount of bread, soaked in vinegar, salt, and pepper

½ cup extra-virgin olive oil, plus more as needed

1 tbsp. vinegar, or to taste

Salt

This sauce is ideal for use on boiled fish.

Combine all the ingredients. Grind them in a mortar, then pass through a sieve; adjust the sauce for salt and vinegar, adding more olive oil for a creamier sauce.

OLIVE OIL, LEMON, AND GARLIC SAUCE 1

Juice of 1 lemon

½ cup extra-virgin olive oil

1 tsp. fresh oregano

1 bunch flat-leaf parsley, chopped

2 garlic cloves, roughly chopped

Salt and pepper

Use this sauce on fish about to be cooked or pour on cooked fish before serving.

Whisk the lemon juice and olive oil until blended; add the oregano, parsley, a little pepper, salt, and garlic.

OLIVE OIL, LEMON, AND GARLIC SAUCE 2

The many variations of this sauce include one made without parsley and another in which the lemon is replaced by an equal amount of red wine (the version used on the Lipari Islands).

½ cup olive oil

Juice of 2 or 3 lemons

2 tbsp. chopped flat-leaf parsley

1 or 2 garlic cloves, minced

1 tbsp. oregano

Salt and pepper

Whisk together the olive oil and ¼ cup of warm water. Gradually whisk in the lemon juice, parsley, garlic, oregano, salt, and pepper. ✦ When the sauce is thoroughly blended cook it in the top of a double boiler for 3 minutes, whisking until thickened slightly.

ALMOND-AND-ANCHOVY SAUCE

SALSETTA DI MANDORLE E ACCIUGHE

SICILIA

6 tbsp. almonds, toasted

½ cup breadcrumbs, toasted

6 fillets of salt-cured anchovies, minced

Several mint leaves, chopped

Pinch ground cinnamon

1 tbsp. vinegar

1 tbsp. lemon juice

¾ cup olive oil, or as needed

Use this sauce on meats and boiled fish.

Pound the almonds into small pieces and mix with the breadcrumbs and anchovies. Blend in the mint leaves, cinnamon, vinegar, lemon juice, and enough olive oil to make a creamy sauce. Blend well.

CORNMEAL FRITTERS

SCAGLIUOZZOLI

CAMPANIA

1⅔ cups cornmeal

Olive oil

Salt

Setting aside ⅔ cup of the cornmeal, use the rest to prepare a somewhat dense polenta, cooking it in 5 cups of lightly salted boiling water. ✦ When it is fully cooked, turn it out on a slightly damp work surface (preferably marble). Using damp hands, spread it out to a thickness of ½ inch and let it cool completely. ✦ When the polenta has cooled, cut it in rectangles 1 to 1½ inches wide and 2 to 3 inches long. Dip these one at a time in the reserved cormeal. ✦ Heat 1 inch of olive oil in a large pan and fry the polenta sticks a few at a time, removing them when they form a golden crust. Drain on paper towels, sprinkle with a little salt, and serve hot.

| # STUFFED PIZZA

PUGLIA

For the dough:

3 cups all-purpose flour,
plus more as needed

1 tbsp. active dry yeast

Salt

For the filling:

4 fresh anchovies,
boned and lightly fried

½ cup pitted black olives, chopped

4 tbsp. capers

4 tbsp. golden raisins,
soaked in warm water to plump

1 lb. leeks, sliced lengthwise

2 tbsp. olive oil

This rustic stuffed pizza is traditional on Good Friday, consumed to end the fast that many of the faithful practice on that day.

Mix the flour, yeast, a pinch of salt, and 1 cup water to prepare a dough. Knead together until soft and elastic. Cover with a kitchen towel and let rest for 1 hour. ✦ Divide the dough into two equal parts. Roll out each part to form a disk. Preheat the oven to 400°F and grease a baking pan. Place the first disk in the pan and spread over it (as in a Sicilian baked pie) anchovies, black olives, capers, raisins, leeks, and olive oil. Close with the second disk, seal the edges, puncture the top with the tines of a fork, and bake for about 20 minutes, until golden.

✦ **LOCAL TRADITION** ✦

SANGUINACCIO VALDOSTANO

In the Valle d'Aosta, blood pudding (blood sausage) is known as *bouden (bodin)*, a name that comes from a French-Provençal dialect that dates back to the 13th century and is derived from the old medieval French *boudine*, which meant a large belly. The sausage was already known to the Celts, Greeks, and Romans who made a mixture of blood, milk or cream, *lardo*, and aromatic herbs thickened with the addition of fruit and legumes. Pliny called blood sausages *sanguiculi*, but it seems they were invented by Phoenician butchers or royal Assyrian cooks. When pig's blood was in ready supply, this typical sausage was made by mixing a portion of blood with lard, potatoes, milk or cream, beets, and spices (pepper, cinnamon, nutmeg, cloves, coriander). Of course there were variations: using both potatoes and beets or only one of them; using milk or cream instead of potatoes. The sausages were consumed fresh or were preserved and dried. They were eaten cold with dark rye bread or warm with boiled potatoes (the ideal was *tartifles perboulies*, to use the old Savoiard term for a kind of potatoes). In the first instance they were served as an appetizer; in the second as a meat course.

SCAPECE ALLA VASTESE | PICKLED FISH 1

ABRUZZO

3 lbs. good-size fish (skate or shark)

All-purpose flour for dredging

Extra-virgin olive oil

4 cups good white wine vinegar

A few saffron threads

Salt

Scapece is found in Abruzzo, Molise (see below), and Campania; there is also the *scapace* of Naples and the *scabeccio* of Liguria. All come from a word for pickling that may well be derived from the Portuguese *escabeche* ("marinated"). Traditionally, the copious amount of vinegar served to preserve the fish for about a month.

Clean the fish, cut in equal-size pieces, and dredge in flour. Heat ¼ inch of olive oil until very hot in a large pan, and, working in batches, cook the fish until golden. As the fish is cooked, drain on paper towels and sprinkle with salt. ✦ Heat the vinegar in a nonreactive pan. As soon as the vinegar boils, remove the pan from the heat and add the saffron. Arrange the pieces of fish in layers in a bowl or earthenware pan and pour over the vinegar mixture to cover completely. Refrigerate 12 hours or overnight. ✦ The fish is excellent after a day in this marinade; serve it drained as an appetizer.

SCAPECE DE LICETTE | PICKLED FISH 2

MOLISE

1 lb. fresh anchovies

1 handful hard durum wheat flour

Olive oil for frying

For the marinade:

A few sage leaves

1 garlic clove, chopped

1 cup white wine vinegar

Salt

Ideally, this dish calls for *alicette*—small anchovies which can be eaten whole—but these fish are available only in the spring. Anchovies or sardines can be used as a substitute, making it possible to make *scapece* year-round. Fish prepared this way are excellent after a few days.

Gently rinse the anchovies in a colander. Drain them, pat dry, then dredge in flour. Heat ½ inch of olive oil over high heat and as soon as the oil shimmers, fry the fish; when they are golden, remove them with a slotted spoon and drain on paper towels. Sprinkle with salt and layer them in a glass or earthenware bowl. ✦ Spread sage leaves and garlic over each layer. ✦ Bring the vinegar and ½ cup water to a boil in a pan and pour this liquid over the fish while it is still hot. Refrigerate at least one day.

SCARPACCIA | VEGETABLE TART

TOSCANA

Extra-virgin olive oil

¾ lb. small zucchini
(best if with blossoms)

2 large eggs, beaten

4 tbsp. all-purpose flour

5 tbsp. plus 1 tsp. milk mixed with
an equal amount of water

3 baby onions, in thin slices

4 tbsp. grated Parmigiano-Reggiano,
plus more for topping

½ garlic clove, crushed

Salt and pepper

A sweet version of this dish typical of Camaiore is made without the garlic and onions, on the Tuscan coast.

Preheat the oven to 425°F. Grease a baking pan. Cut the zucchini in thin slices, salt to taste, and let rest 20 minutes. Rinse the zucchini to remove the salt and pat them dry. Heat 2 tablespoons olive oil in a pan and cook the zucchini until lightly golden. ✦ Whisk the eggs, flour, and milk mixture to make a batter. Combine the zucchini, onions, Parmigiano-Reggiano, and garlic with the egg mixture and pour it all into the prepared pan (the mixture should not be much more than half an inch thick). Drizzle with 3 tablespoons olive oil and bake for about 30 minutes, or until the result is a firm, golden tart. ✦ Serve sprinkled with additional Parmigiano-Reggiano.

SCIACAROTTI O FAZZEGNI | SMALL FOCACCIAS WITH TOMATO SAUCE

LIGURIA

For the dough:

3 cups all-purpose flour,
plus more as needed

2 ¼ tsp. active dry yeast

Salt

For the sauce:

2 tbsp. extra-virgin olive oil

2 lbs. ripe plum tomatoes

1 garlic clove

10 basil leaves, chopped

Salt and pepper

Make bread dough with the flour, yeast mixture, salt, and 1 cup water. Knead together until the dough is soft and elastic. Let rest, covered with a kitchen towel, for 1 hour. ✦ Divide the dough into 8 small pieces. Flatten each piece by hand to form small focaccias about 4 by 8 inches and let rest. ✦ In a pan mix the olive oil, tomatoes, garlic, basil, salt, and pepper and cook for about 30 to 35 minutes to form a thick sauce. ✦ Preheat the oven (if possible a wood-burning oven) to 400°F. Cover the little focaccias with the sauce and bake them until the dough is golden.

SCIATT | BUCKWHEAT FRITTERS

LOMBARDIA

1 ⅔ cups buckwheat flour,
plus more as needed

CONTINUED

Mix the two flours with salt, adding ¾ cup water to obtain a dough that is not overly soft. Add the cheese and knead until the dough becomes stringy, then let it rest for about 2 hours. ✦ Just before frying blend in the baking powder (or yeast). Heat the oil (or lard) in the pan

1 ¼ cups all-purpose flour,
plus more as needed

10 oz. *bitto* (or other cow's-milk
cheese), cut in small dice

½ tbsp. baking powder
(or ½ tsp. active dry yeast)

Olive oil (or lard)

Salt

until it shimmers, then use a spoon to scoop out a little of the dough, being careful to include a few bits of cheese, and drop in the oil. Fry until golden, then drain on paper towels. Serve hot, usually with a salad, preferably of chicory.

SEDANO AL GORGONZOLA

GORGONZOLA-STUFFED CELERY

PIEMONTE

6 celery hearts
4 oz. Gorgonzola piccante
4 oz. mascarpone

Cut the celery into lengths about 3 inches long; blend the two kinds of cheese and stuff into the celery.

✦ **LOCAL TRADITION** ✦

SPALLA COTTA DI SAN SECONDO

This boiled pork salame is typical of the area of San Secondo in the lowlands of Parma, in Emilia-Romagna. The shoulder is the most ancient pork specialty of the Parma area; it has been known since 1170 and was a favorite of Giuseppe Verdi's. The boiled version is particularly good served warm. It is made of pork shoulder with the addition of only kitchen salt and crushed pepper in established quantities. The average *spalla* weighs more than 10 pounds. The salt is removed from the meat by soaking it in lukewarm water for 8 to 12 hours. Then it is put in a pot with a great deal of water and boiled at low heat for about 8 hours.

SPICY TOMATO SAUCE

SFRICONE

PUGLIA

¼ cup extra-virgin olive oil

2 or 3 garlic cloves

1 *diavolillo* (spicy chili pepper; see note, page 22)

1 lb. ripe plum tomatoes, peeled, seeded, and chopped

Salt

Hunks of stale bread make the best dip for this sauce typical of Bisceglie.

Heat the olive oil until hot and cook the garlic and *diavolillo* until the garlic is golden; add the tomatoes and salt and cook until a thick sauce forms. You can increase the volume by thinning with a little water.

SPICY CHEESE SPREAD

SPUMA PICCANTE DI FORMAGGIO

FRIULI-VENEZIA GIULIA

1 tbsp. capers

1 tbsp. mustard

1 tbsp. flat-leaf parsley, chopped

9 oz. ricotta or stracchino

¼ medium onion, sliced

½ tsp. caraway seeds

4 tbsp. unsalted butter

2 tbsp. chopped chives

1 anchovy, boned and head removed

1 tbsp. paprika

Blend all of the ingredients, except the paprika, to form a creamy mixture. Stir in the paprika.

RICE CROQUETTES

SUPPLÌ AL TELEFONO

LAZIO

4 tbsp. extra-virgin olive oil

1 medium onion, minced

1 celery stalk, minced

12 oz. ground beef

½ cup white wine

½ cup broth

2 cups tomato purée

CONTINUED

They're called *supplì al telefono* ("telephone style") because the strands of melted mozzarella resemble telephone wires. *Supplì* can be made without meat and using many ingredients, such as chicken giblets or mushrooms or peas. Some food writers see this variation in the filling as the derivation of the word *supplì*, which they claim is from *surprise*. The diner simply doesn't know what to expect in the filling.

Heat the olive oil in a pan and sauté the onion and celery; add the ground beef and brown. ✦ Pour in the wine and let it evaporate. Add the broth and tomato purée and cook until a thick sauce forms. ✦ Cook the rice in

2½ cups rice

5 tbsp. unsalted butter

¾ cup grated Parmigiano-Reggiano

Pinch grated nutmeg

4 large eggs, beaten

5 oz. mozzarella, diced

4 cups extra-virgin olive oil for frying

1¼ cups all-purpose flour, plus more as needed

1¼ cups breadcrumbs

Salt

4 cups of lightly salted boiling water, drain, and combine with the meat mixture, butter, Parmigiano-Reggiano, and nutmeg. Adjust for salt. ✦ Spread the rice on a work surface (preferably of marble), using a wooden spoon to level it out. Let it cool. ✦ Season the eggs and add half of them to the rice. ✦ With the palms of your hands shape the rice mixture into flattened ovals the size of a small orange. Poke a hole in the middle of each and insert 2 pieces of mozzarella, then close the rice around the cheese to form a ball. Continue this until you have used up all the rice. ✦ Heat several inches of oil in a saucepan. One by one dip the *suppli* in the flour, then eggs, then breadcrumbs. Fry a few at a time in the olive oil until crisp and golden and drain on paper towels. Serve hot.

TARTUFI BIANCHI
ALLA PARMIGIANA

WHITE TRUFFLES WITH PARMIGIANO-REGGIANO

EMILIA-ROMAGNA

3 tbsp. unsalted butter

2½ oz. white truffles

¾ lb. Parmigiano-Reggiano, cut in slivers

Toasted bread slices

Salt

Preheat the oven to 350°F and butter a baking pan. Clean the truffles with a brush, eliminating any dirt, then finely shave using a truffle slicer. ✦ Form a layer of truffle slices on the bottom of the pan, salt, and cover with half the Parmigiano-Reggiano. Make a second layer of truffles, add salt again, and cover with the remaining Parmigiano-Reggiano. ✦ Add a few pats of butter and bake for about 15 minutes, or until it forms a golden crust. Serve with toasted bread.

TARTUFI IN TEGAMINO

BAKED TRUFFLES

CAMPANIA

2 oz. black truffles (the ideal would be the *scorzoni del Laceno* from Bagnoli Irpino)

⅔ cup crumbled pecorino

2 tbsp. unsalted butter, cut into 4 pieces

This dish is typical of Bagnoli Irpino.

Preheat the oven to 350°F. Clean the truffles and cut them in slices about 1 to 1½ inches in width and place them, together with the pieces of pecorino and the butter, in 4 ovenproof bowls or ramekins. Bake until the cheese begins to melt, about 12 minutes.

DUCK TERRINE

TERRINA DI ANATRA

PIEMONTE

2 large eggs, beaten
2 tbsp. chopped flat-leaf parsley
1 lb. duck breast, sliced
¾ cup *lardo* (see page 2), sliced
1 oz. pancetta, minced
7 oz. mushroom caps
1 bay leaf
Salt and pepper

Mix the eggs, parsley, salt, and pepper. ✦ Preheat the oven to 400°F. Line a loaf pan with the slices of *lardo*, extending them above the rim. Cover the bottom with a layer of duck, a layer of pancetta, then one of mushrooms, then pour over the egg mixture. Close by folding over the lard. ✦ Place a bay leaf on top, cover with aluminum foil, and bake for about 1 hour. Let cool before removing it from the pan.

RICOTTA AND SAUSAGE DUMPLINGS

TESTI DI TURCO

SICILIA

1⅔ cups all-purpose flour, plus more as needed
3 large eggs, separated
Lard
1¼ cups fresh ricotta, passed through a sieve
12 oz. fresh pork sausage
Pinch ground cinnamon
1 oz. bitter chocolate, melted
Salt and pepper

This dish is typical of San Cataldo.

Use the flour, 3 egg yolks, and 1 white (set aside the remaining whites) as on page 10 to form a smooth dough; let it rest 30 minutes. ✦ Preheat the oven to 325°F and generously grease a pan with lard. Roll the dough out to a sheet, then use a large glass to cut an even number of disks. ✦ Beat the reserved egg whites until frothy. Mix the ricotta, sausage, cinnamon, and salt and pepper. Place a spoonful of the ricotta mixture at the center of half the disks, then cover with the other disks. Firmly close, then press down to seal. Brush the edges with the reserved egg whites. Mix the remaining egg whites with the chocolate and a few tablespoons water to make a glaze. ✦ Bake for 20 minutes, then "polish" the dumplings with the egg mixture and bake 5 minutes more.

SAUSAGE TIMBALE

TIMBALLO CON SALSICCIA

SICILIA

Olive oil
4 oz. fresh sausage
CONTINUED

This dish is typical of Gela.

Preheat the oven to 325°F. Grease a baking pan with olive oil. Heat 2 tablespoons olive oil in a pan and brown the sausage. Drain and cut in pieces. Add the potatoes to the pan, and season with salt; sauté and set aside when tender. Boil the cauliflower until half cooked. Drain then

1 large potato, peeled and
cut in large chunks
½ lb. cauliflower
1 medium onion, sliced
4 pitted black olives
Yeasted bread dough
(see page 13)
1 tbsp. lard
Salt and pepper

chop in small pieces. ✦ Cook the onion in the same pan the sausage and potatoes were cooked in. Add the cauliflower; salt to taste. Add the sausage and potatoes to the pan; add the olives and sprinkle with pepper. ✦ Blend the lard into the dough and roll out on a floured board to about ¼ inch thick. Divide this in two uneven parts. Use the larger part cover the bottom and sides of the pan. Fill with the mixture, then cover with the smaller sheet of dough, carefully sealing the edges. Brush the surface with olive oil. ✦ Bake for 30 to 40 minutes, or until the top is golden.

MEAT PIE
WITH ELDERBERRY

TORTA COL SAMBUCO

SICILIA

For the dough:
3 cups all-purpose flour,
plus more as needed
2¼ tsp. active dry yeast
3¼ oz. lard
2 large eggs
2 large eggs, separated
2⅓ cups milk
1 tbsp. olive oil
Salt

For the filling:
¼ cup olive oil
7 oz. *guanciale*, chopped
7 oz. salame, preferably rustic,
sliced
7 oz. tuma (unsalted
goat's-milk cheese)
6 oz. elderberry flowers, chopped

This dish is typical of Triona. In Sicily this dish is made in May and June, the season of the elderberry flowering.

Use the flour, yeast, lard, 2 eggs, 2 whites (reserve 2 yolks), milk, and a dash of salt to prepare a dough. Knead together until soft and elastic. Let the dough rise in a warm spot for at least 2 hours. ✦ Preheat the oven to 350°F. Meanwhile, make the filling. Heat 2 tablespoons olive oil and brown the *guanciale*, then drain on paper towels. ✦ Work 1 tablespoon olive oil into the dough. Divide the dough in half and roll out half of it to a sheet large enough to line the bottom of a high-sided baking pan. Layer the dough with the salame, *guanciale*, tuma, a few elderberry flowers, and drizzle with 1 tablespoon oil. Cover with the other half of the dough. Mix the reserved egg yolks with 1 tablespoon olive oil and brush on the dough. Sprinkle with more elderberry flowers. ✦ Bake for about 40 minutes until golden. Serve hot.

CHEESE TART

BASILICATA

For the dough:

1 ¼ cups all-purpose flour,
plus more as needed

¼ cup sugar

1 large egg yolk

½ cup (1 stick) unsalted butter,
cut in small pieces

1 large egg, beaten

For the filling:

Olive oil

5 oz. ricotta, pressed
through a sieve

3 oz. fresh caciotta cheese, cubed

1 small mozzarella, cubed

3 oz. prosciutto crudo, diced

¼ cup sugar

1 large egg

1 large egg yolk

2 tbsp. grated pecorino

Salt

Mix together the flour, sugar, egg yolk, a pinch of salt, and butter. Knead together until the dough is soft and elastic. Shape the dough into a ball and let it rest, covered, in a cool spot for 1 hour. ✦ Preheat the oven to 350°F and grease a baking pan with olive oil. Mix the ricotta, caciotta, mozzarella, and prosciutto until blended. Add the sugar, egg, egg yolk, and pecorino, kneading the mixture well. ✦ Divide the dough into two parts, one larger than the other. Roll these out to make two thin disks. Use the larger disk to line the pan, extending it over the sides. Add the filling, spreading it out to make it even. Cover with the other disk of dough, folding the borders to seal. Brush the dough with the beaten egg. Bake for 1 hour or until golden.

POTATO PIE OR "TARTLETS"

TRENTINO

Lardo (see page 2) (or olive oil)

8 medium-size mature potatoes

3 tbsp. all-purpose flour

Grated Parmigiano-Reggiano

Salt

Instead of this potato pie, one can make excellent and fast "tartlets" using the same mixture to make small flatbreads and frying them in olive oil.

Preheat the oven to about 400°F. Generously grease a baking pan with *lardo* or olive oil. Peel the potatoes and grate them with a cheese grater. Add the flour and a dash of salt and work to blend evenly. Turn this mixture into the pan, sprinkle with Parmigiano-Reggiano, and bake until the surface forms a golden crust.

TORTA PASQUALINA | **EASTER TART**

LIGURIA

6 cups plus 2 tbsp. all-purpose flour, plus more as needed

4 tbsp. extra-virgin olive oil

2 lbs. vegetables (leeks, spinach, artichokes, chard)

1 cup grated Parmigiano-Reggiano

1 tbsp. marjoram leaves

1 ½ cups ricotta

4 large eggs

Salt

Use 6 cups flour, 1 tablespoon of the olive oil, a pinch of salt, and 2 cups water to form a dough. Knead together until the dough is soft and elastic. Divide the dough in six equal balls and let them rest for 1 hour, covered with a kitchen cloth. ✦ Clean the vegetables, removing any ribs; rinse well. Blanch in lightly salted boiling water until wilted. Drain well, roughly chop, and mix with ½ cup Parmigiano-Reggiano and marjoram leaves. ✦ Preheat the oven to 350°F. Grease a baking pan with olive oil. Roll out three of the six balls of dough to form very thin sheets. Brush with olive oil and layer to line the pan. Put the vegetable mixture in the pan and spread to an even layer. Mix the ricotta with 2 tablespoons flour, then spoon over the vegetables. Salt to taste. ✦ Using a spoon make four wells in the surface of the vegetable mixture and break an egg into each one. Cover with the remaining Parmigiano-Reggiano. ✦ Roll out the remaining three balls of dough to form sheets, brush them with olive oil and layer them to cover the pan. Seal the edges. Brush the surface with a little olive oil and bake for about 45 minutes. Serve warm.

TORTA SALATA DI ZUCCA | **SQUASH CAKE**

LOMBARDIA

3 lbs. winter squash, seeded and cut in pieces

3 tbsp. *mostarda di Cremona* (see note), chopped, with 2 tbsp. of its liquid

2 cups finely chopped almonds

Juice and grated zest of ½ lemon

¾ cup breadcrumbs

¾ cup grated Parmigiano-Reggiano

2 large eggs, beaten

Pinch grated nutmeg

4 tbsp. (½ stick) unsalted butter

2 garlic cloves

Salt

It is best to make the mixture a day ahead. *Mostarda di Cremona* is a kind of savory preserves made from fruit.

Preheat the oven to 350°F and bake the squash for about 40 minutes, or until soft. Let cool, then squeeze out any liquid. Scoop out the flesh and discard the peel. ✦ Mix the *mostarda*, its liquid, almonds, lemon juice and zest, ½ cup breadcrumbs, cheese, eggs, nutmeg, and salt; last, add the squash. Heat the butter and cook the garlic until golden. Discard the garlic, then use half of the butter to grease a baking pan. Pour in the squash mixture. Dust with the remaining breadcrumbs and drizzle with the remaining butter. Bake for about 1 hour until set.

TORTANO CON CIGOLI | BREAD WITH PORK BITS

CAMPANIA

4 ¼ cups all-purpose flour, plus more as needed

4 tbsp. lard (or ½ stick unsalted butter)

4 ½ tsp. active dry yeast

½ lb. *cigoli (ciccioli;* see note, page 12)

Salt and pepper

This dish is typical of Salerno.

Use the flour, lard (or butter), salt and pepper, and yeast to form a very soft dough as done on page 13, then knead it a long time to make it elastic and velvety. Add the *cigoli* and let rise in a warm spot covered by a cloth. Form the dough into a ring and let it rest, 1 hour. ✦ Preheat the oven to 300°F. Place the ring into a pie pan and bake until golden, about 45 minutes.

FRITÀ AN BAGNA | STEWED FRITTATA STRIPS

PIEMONTE

½ cup (¼ lb.) chopped flat-leaf parsley

1 medium onion, chopped

2 tbsp. olive oil

2 tbsp. tomato purée

1 tbsp. all-purpose flour, dissolved in 1 cup warm broth, plus more as needed

Unsalted butter

6 large eggs, beaten

¼ cup milk

2 tbsp. grated Parmigiano-Reggiano

Salt and pepper

This dish is typical of Vercelli.

Chop together the parsley and onion. Heat the olive oil over low heat and cook until the onion is translucent. Add the tomato purée and broth mixture, then add salt and pepper. Simmer, adding more broth if needed. ✦ Mix the eggs, milk, and Parmigiano-Reggiano. In a large cast-iron pan over low heat, cook the eggs to form a wide, thin frittata. Roll the frittata and slice it; put the slices in the pan with the parsley and onion mixture, stir, and let it cook at low heat for another 10 minutes. This can also be served at room temperature.

✦ **LOCAL TRADITION** ✦

ZEAIA

Another economical recipe for a rustic meat gelatin (see page 37), *zeaia*, typical of Ceriana de Imperia in Liguria, is made of meat broth and bits of pork, pork rind, trotters, and boiled rabbit. Like many dishes made with game, it is best with a dusting of black pepper.

TROTELLE DI SESIA IN CARPIONE | MARINATED TROUT

PIEMONTE

Olive oil

3 medium onions, finely chopped

1 carrot, finely chopped

2 bay leaves

1¼ cups dry white wine

1¼ cups white wine vinegar

All-purpose flour

2 trout, about 1 lb. each, cleaned and filleted

Salt and pepper

To create the *carpione* (marinade), heat 2 tablespoons olive oil in a pan, sauté the onions and carrot, then add bay leaves. When the mixture has browned, add the wine and vinegar and remove from the heat. ✦ Flour the trout fillets. Heat 1 inch of olive oil in a large pan and fry the trouts until golden. Dry them and place them in a deep pan. ✦ Cover with the marinade and let stand until at room temperature. Cover with plastic wrap and refrigerate for at least 48 hours. Serve cold.

UOVA AL CIRIGHET | FRIED EGGS IN SAUCE

PIEMONTE

4 salt-cured anchovies, boned and chopped

4 garlic cloves, chopped

2 tbsp. chopped flat-leaf parsley

2 sage leaves, chopped

2 tbsp. chopped capers

½ *spagnolino* (chili pepper), chopped

⅓ cup extra-virgin olive oil

⅓ cup red wine vinegar

Juice of 1 lemon

8 large eggs

In a wide pan, combine the anchovies, garlic, parsley, sage, capers, and *spagnolino*. Add the olive oil and sauté over low heat for 2 minutes (being careful not to darken it!). ✦ Add the vinegar and lemon juice and cook another 2 minutes, then remove from the heat. ✦ In another pan, fry the eggs to over-easy, then pour the cooked mixture over them, blending well to combine the flavors.

UOVA ALLA MONACHINA | STUFFED EGGS | FOR 6 PERSONS

CAMPANIA

6 large hard-boiled eggs

Thick béchamel sauce made with 1½ cups milk (see page 339) (or 1⅔ cups ricotta)

2 tbsp. grated Parmigiano-Reggiano

CONTINUED

Shell the hard-boiled eggs and cut in half lengthwise; separate the yolks from the whites. ✦ Using a fork, mix the yolks with the béchamel sauce (or ricotta), Parmigiano-Reggiano, salt, pepper, and nutmeg. Arrange this mixture in half the egg whites, shaping it to give it the rounded form of a whole yolk, then top with the other halves of the whites. Flour the "eggs," then dip them in the beaten egg, then delicately dip them in breadcrumbs, being careful

Pinch grated nutmeg
All-purpose flour
1 large egg, beaten
Breadcrumbs
Olive oil
Salt and pepper

that they maintain their shape. ✦ Heat several inches of olive oil in a large pan and fry the eggs a few at a time until golden. Drain on paper towels and serve hot.

EGGS IN GARLIC SAUCE

UOVA CON L'AGLIO

TOSCANA

10 garlic cloves
2 salt-cured anchovies, cleaned and boned
1 handful capers
⅔ cup extra-virgin olive oil
3 tbsp. white wine vinegar
Salt and pepper
10 large hard-boiled eggs, cut in half lengthwise
Bread, fried in butter, for serving

This dish is typical of Cecina.

Boil the garlic cloves in water to cover for 10 minutes. Drain and grind in a mortar with the anchovies and capers. ✦ Mix into this the olive oil, vinegar, salt, and pepper to create a sauce. Put half of this sauce in a bowl to serve at the table. Spread the other half over the eggs. Serve with bread.

EGGS AND MUSHROOMS

UOVA IN FUNGHETTO

FRIULI-VENEZIA GIULIA

6 large hard-boiled eggs
¾ lb. mushrooms (or leeks), thinly sliced
¼ cup finely chopped flat-leaf parsley
2 tbsp. unsalted butter
Salt and pepper

This dish is served most often in homes, not restaurants, for it is looked upon as "humble"; yet it is very tasty, simple, and open to many variations.

Preheat the oven to 350°F. Shell the eggs and cut in half lengthwise. Spread an even layer of mushrooms or leeks in a baking pan, then set the eggs on it with the yolks upward. Salt and pepper and sprinkle with parsley and pats of butter. Bake for several minutes, until the butter has melted and the eggs are heated through.

VOL-AU-VENT WITH RADICCHIO AND CHEESE

VOL AU VENT CON RADICCHIO E FONDUTA

VENETO

2 large egg yolks
1⅔ cups milk
CONTINUED

In a blender, combine the egg yolks with 2 tablespoons of the milk; set aside. ✦ Mix the flour into the remaining milk and add the cheese. Heat over very low heat and whisk energetically. When the mixture begins to thicken, add in the yolk mixture and, still stirring, cook for

1 level tbsp. all-purpose flour

7 oz. fresh Monte Baldo cheese (or Fontina), without rind and finely chopped

1 tbsp. unsalted butter (if needed)

¾ lb. red radicchio, cut in pieces

1 large vol-au-vent pastry shell, baked

1 black truffle

Salt

another 10 minutes. Salt, add a pat of butter if necessary, and remove from the heat. ✦ Add the radicchio. Return to the heat briefly, just to heat the mixture. Fill the pastry shell, grating some black truffle over the top.

ZEPPULELLE 'E PASTA CRISCIUTA | FRIED BREAD PUFFS

CAMPANIA

½ oz. active dry yeast, dissolved in ¼ cup warm water

3 cups all-purpose flour, plus more as needed

Sunflower oil

Salt

Zeppulelle are best if a piece of anchovy or boiled cod is inserted in them.

Mix the yeast mixture with the flour, ¾ cup water, and a dash of salt and knead as instructed on page 13 to form a smooth and elastic dough. Cover with a clean dishtowel and set it aside to rise. ✦ After about 2 hours, by which time the dough will have expanded, use a spoon to make large gnocchi, about the size of an egg. Heat several inches of oil in a pan and fry the gnocchi until golden. Drain on paper towels and serve hot.

ZUCCA GIALLA "CA GGHIATA" | FRIED SQUASH

CALABRIA

2 lbs. yellow winter squash

¾ cup olive oil, plus more for frying

¼ cup white wine vinegar

3 tbsp. capers

1 garlic clove, sliced

Several mint leaves

1 cup breadcrumbs, toasted

Salt

Peel the squash, remove the seeds, and cut in thin slices. Mix a gallon of water with ½ cup salt and add the squash. Keep the slices in the brine about 1 hour, then rinse and dry well. Heat an inch of olive oil in a pan and fry the squash until golden; drain and set aside. ✦ Mix ¾ cup olive oil, vinegar, capers, garlic, mint leaves, and breadcrumbs and stir until thoroughly blended. ✦ Put a layer of squash slices on a serving plate and spread over this a little of the sauce; form another layer of squash and cover with more of the sauce, continuing until all the ingredients have been used. Sprinkle with breadcrumbs, press down with the palms of the hand, and let rest for about 1 hour before serving.

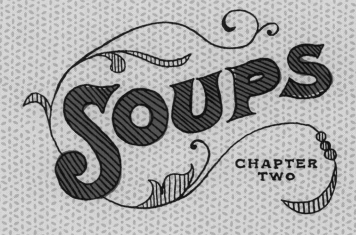

SOUPS

CHAPTER
TWO

ACQUA PAZZA | "CRAZY WATER" SOUP

TOSCANA

6 garlic cloves

¼ cup *nepetella* (see note)

Pinch chili pepper flakes

1 cup olive oil

2 lbs. *zerri,* cleaned but with the heads still on (see note)

Slices of peasant-style bread

Salt

Recipes throughout central Italy (most of all Toscana, Umbria, and Lazio), like this one typical of the Maremma area, call for local types of small-leafed mint that go by a variety of names. Some cookbook authors suggest substituting calamint, should it be available. There are also those who claim the only way to duplicate the flavor is to buy *nepetella* seeds (available from seed catalogs and on the Internet) and grow it. Of course, you can choose to experiment with your own locally available types of mint. *Zerri* are small reef fish; whitebait can be substituted.

In a mortar, grind together the garlic, *nepetella*, and chili pepper flakes. ✦ Put enough water for soup in a pot (at least 1 cup per person) over high heat and when it boils, add the garlic mixture, which will become homogeneous. ✦ Add the olive oil and salt as needed. Boil at a high heat for 10 minutes, then add the fish. ✦ Lower the heat and continue cooking the fish; very little time is needed. Pay attention to keep them from breaking up. ✦ Place a slice of bread (best if toasted) in a serving bowl and pour over the *acqua pazza*, then the fish.

ACQUACOTTA CASENTINESE | "COOKED WATER" CASENTINO-STYLE SOUP

TOSCANA

2 tbsp. olive oil

1 lb. porcini mushrooms, cleaned and roughly chopped

1 garlic clove

¼ cup *nepetella* (see note above)

¼ cup tomato purée

4 large eggs, beaten

¼ cup grated Parmigiano-Reggiano

Warm slices of toasted bread

Salt and pepper

Acquacotta is a traditional soup that started among peasant farmers of the hilly, coastal area of Toscana. Legend says that each diner would bring something to add to the boiling water that would become the soup. *Acquacotta* is unique in that it is one of the few soups not made from stock.

Heat the olive oil in an earthenware pot. Add the mushrooms, garlic, and *nepetella,* adding salt and pepper as needed. Sauté until the mushrooms have taken on a little color. ✦ Add the tomato purée and cook until the sauce thickens. When that happens, add 4 cups of warm water (plus 1 or 2 more cups for the pot, if you want to stretch the soup among many diners). ✦ Cover and cook over low heat for 20 minutes. ✦ Meanwhile, mix the eggs and cheese and pour into a large bowl. Whisk in the mushroom-tomato broth. The result should be a smooth liquid, not a suspension like *stracciatella*. ✦ Cover the bowl and let it sit for 4 or 5 minutes. ✦ Serve warm in bowls over warm toasted bread.

ACQUACOTTA CON LE "ERBARELLE"

"COOKED WATER" SOUP WITH WILD HERBS

LAZIO

2 lbs. *erbarelle* (see note)

3 garlic cloves, unpeeled

¼ tsp. chili pepper flakes

2 cups grape tomatoes, chopped

1 medium onion, chopped

1 slice of stale peasant-style bread per person (preferably homemade)

1 bunch fresh wild fennel, chopped

1 large egg per person (optional)

Olive oil

Salt

In Viterbo, the term *erbarelle* is applied to a large group of wild greens that can be gathered in local fields in both the fall and spring. Among these are *"caccialepre"* (*Picridium volgare*), chicory (*Cichorium intybus*), prickly lettuce (*Lactuca seriola*), yellow rattle (*Rhinanthus crista-galli*), sow thistle (*Sonchus oleraceus*), narrowleaf plantain (*Plantago lanceolata*), parsnips (*Pastinaca sativa*), salad burnet (*Poterium sanguisorba*), dandelions (*Taraxacum officinalis*), rampion (*Campanula rapunculus*), bladder campion (*Silene inflata*), lamb's lettuce (*Valerianella olitoria*), and wild beet. Several soups can be made using even just one of these greens, or you can work with a mix in this recipe. The dialect names vary throughout the area, much as the names for these plants vary from area to area in the English-speaking world, for which reason we have also given the scientific names.

Carefully wash the *erbarelle* and combine with the garlic, chili pepper, tomatoes, and onion in a saucepan. Add water to cover and season with salt. Cook over low heat until the *erbarelle* are tender. ✦ Pour into individual bowls over slices of stale bread and top with fennel. ✦ If desired, and if you want to turn the soup into a one-dish meal, toward the end of the cooking add 1 egg per person, poached or beaten directly into the broth. ✦ Let it rest a few minutes in covered bowls, then remove any broth that has not been absorbed by the bread and sprinkle the *acquacotta* with olive oil, preferably from Toscana.

ACQUACOTTA MARCHIGIANA

MARCHE-STYLE "COOKED WATER" SOUP

MARCHE

1 lb. potatoes, peeled and sliced

1 medium onion, in thick slices

A few slices of stale bread

1 garlic clove, cut in half

A few leaves of *nepetella* (see note, page 92), preferably gathered in the wild

Cook the potatoes and onion in lightly salted boiling water to cover until tender. ✦ Meanwhile, toast the bread, then rub with the garlic. Line a serving bowl with the bread. Add the *nepetella,* and pour the entire contents of the pot into the prepared serving bowl (the bread will soak up the cooking water).

ACQUACOTTA LAZIALE

Acquacotta is the most typical and traditional dish of central Italy, still prepared today throughout the province of Viterbo using ingredients that vary from place to place. The term *acquacotta* means "cooked water" and for centuries this dish has been the daily meal of the people of the countryside of the Tuscia region and, in particular, of the cattle herdsmen, the famous *butteri,* the "cowboys" of the Maremma region of Toscana-Lazio. *Acquacotta* differs from true soups because, while soups always involve a fried fatty cut of meat—bacon, prosciutto, guanciale, salt pork, or lard—the ingredients in *acquacotta* are cooked directly in water, without the presence of any fat except olive oil. *Acquacotta* is thus a poor person's food, prepared with the products of the land available at that moment.

Its fundamental base is the bread, often stale and hard, which peasants and *butteri,* shepherds as well as fishermen, put in their knapsacks on their way to work. Peasant families tended to bake bread once a week, either in large ovens near the farmhouse or in communal, village ovens. Inevitably, the bread would get hard after a few days, and since it was out of the question to throw away even a stale crust, this hard bread became the basis for various simple dishes, including *acquacotta* and other bread soups. The other fundamental element, olive oil, was always available in the homes of peasants since there were always a few olive trees on the land they cultivated, no matter how small that land might be. Versions of *acquacotta* made in Lazio differ from those made in nearby Toscana in that raw, unfiltered olive oil is added to each individual plate.

The third necessary element is the aromatic herbs, first among them the highly fragrant *nepetella* (see note, page 92), easily found in the sunny fields of the Maremma, followed by garlic still in its skin and by onion, which often enough, instead of being cooked together with the other herbs, was eaten raw like an apple as an accompaniment to the *acquacotta*. Vegetables are the final necessary component, and aside from the constant presence of potatoes and tomatoes, these vary according to the season and local availability. Most often these include wild herbs, such as cardoons, campion, hops, mushrooms, asparagus, beets, parsnips, and nettles. But the most common and typical is wild chicory. Homemade versions of this dish also make use of legumes, since they add to the dish's caloric value. Also used were the vegetables available to peasants in their gardens, such as broccoli, cabbage, spinach, turnips, squash blossoms, and artichokes; the shepherd could add such sheep's-milk cheeses as pecorino; and fishermen enriched it with lake fish. Home-style versions of *acquacotta* might also be enriched with the addition of dried cod or eggs, usually one per person.

ACQUACOTTA MAREMMANA 1

MAREMMA-STYLE "COOKED WATER" SOUP 1

LAZIO

4 large potatoes

4 garlic cloves

2 medium onions, sliced

1 lb. plum tomatoes (preferably small ones), chopped

2 or 3 sprigs fresh *nepetella* (see note, page 92)

1 dried chili pepper

Meat or vegetable broth, as needed

2 lbs. wild chicory

1 lb. salt-dried cod or 1 large egg per person (if desired)

Stale peasant-style bread (preferably homemade)

Olive oil (preferably from Tuscia)

Salt

Peel the potatoes, cut them in half, and put them in a pot with lightly salted water to cover by several inches. Add the garlic, onions, tomatoes, *nepetella*, and chili pepper and bring to a boil. In order to have sufficient liquid to pour over the bread, warm water or broth should be added during the cooking to maintain the quantity of liquid. ✦ Cook the chicory separately in lightly salted water to cover for a few minutes to eliminate its bitter flavor, which not everyone likes. Drain and stir into the soup just before serving. ✦ To turn this into a one-dish meal, and also to make it more flavorful, you can add salt-dried cod: Cut the cod into medium-size pieces and soak it in water or milk to cover in the fridge overnight. When the soup has cooked 15 minutes, add the cod. Or, instead of cod, some prefer at the end to add 1 egg per person, poached directly in the broth. ✦ When the cooking has finished, arrange the slices of stale bread in individual soup bowls and pour over them the cooking broth together with the chicory, potatoes, and a piece of cod or poached egg. ✦ Let this rest a few minutes with the plates covered, so that the bread will soak up liquid, then dispose of any residual liquid not absorbed by the bread. ✦ Sprinkle on top the olive oil, preferably one with a robust and typical local flavor.

ACQUACOTTA MAREMMANA 2

MAREMMA-STYLE "COOKED WATER" SOUP 2

TOSCANA

¼ cup olive oil

1 medium onion, sliced

2 tbsp. aromatic herbs (basil, celery leaves)

4 chard leaves, chopped

1 tbsp. grated pecorino, plus more for serving

¼ cup red wine

CONTINUED

The original *acquacotta* was prepared only with onions and was flavored only with pecorino; the addition of an egg was rare, not to mention mushrooms, asparagus, and so on. Furthermore, it was made using water, not broth.

Heat the olive oil in a pot over low heat, add the onion, and sauté until golden. ✦ Add the herbs, chard leaves, and pecorino. Cook 2 minutes, then add the wine. ✦ Add the tomato purée, and broth. You may need to add water if the mixture is too dense. Simmer for 15 minutes. ✦ Prepare the bowls (preferably earthenware) by lining them with slices of toasted bread. ✦ Break the eggs gently and

¾ lb. tomato purée

4 cups broth

Slices of bread, toasted

4 large eggs

poach them in the broth for 3 minutes. Ladle out 1 egg per person and place in each bowl along with a portion of soup. ✦ Wait several minutes for the bread to soak up the liquid, sprinkle each serving with more pecorino, and serve.

ACQUASALA | # "SALTED WATER" SOUP 1

PUGLIA

4 slices of stale black bread, preferably toasted, about ½ inch thick

2 garlic cloves

2 fresh plum tomatoes, preferably very juicy

Olive oil

2 sprigs oregano, chopped

1 medium onion, minced

This soup, typical of the Tavoliere plains, is quite simple, but the most important—and most difficult—part is finding the right kind of bread, which should be whole wheat and which should ideally be baked in a wood-burning oven. The slices of bread can be toasted, but must be stale. Variations can be made by eliminating the onions or the garlic or adding a little sweet red pepper, a little basil, celery leaves, or even a few pieces of anchovy, whether fresh or salt-cured.

Dampen the bread slightly with water to make it soft (but without making it too soggy). ✦ Chop the garlic and sprinkle pieces over each slice; cut open the tomatoes and rub a half across each slice to add tomato seeds and liquid; sprinkle with olive oil, oregano, and onion. ✦ Set aside the bread slices and let them rest at least 2 hours before being served so they can completely soak up the flavors.

ACQUASALE | # "SALTED WATER" SOUP 2

BASILICATA

4 slices of stale bread

1 tbsp. extra-virgin olive oil

1 medium onion, finely chopped

Garlic to taste

Flat-leaf parsley to taste

3 plum tomatoes, peeled and cut in half

Pinch chili pepper flakes (optional)

Salt

Place a slice of stale bread in each bowl. ✦ Heat a little olive oil in a saucepan and sauté the onion until translucent. ✦ Chop together the garlic and parsley and add to the onion with a little salt. When the onion has changed color, add the tomatoes and a little boiling water to keep the mixture liquid. ✦ When it begins to boil, pour the *acquasale* directly on the bread in the bowls and serve hot. If desired, add a little chili pepper.

RICOTTA AND EGG SOUP

BASILICATA

This soup is typical of Avigliano.

1 lb. ricotta salata

1 bunch aromatic herbs
(such as basil, mint, rosemary,
sage, and celery leaves)

4 large eggs

Slices of bread, toasted

Extra-virgin olive oil

Simmer the ricotta and herbs in water to cover for 15 minutes. ✦ Add the eggs and cook a few minutes. ✦ Pour this liquid over slices of bread arranged in bowls; season with olive oil.

ANOLINI PARMIGIANI

ANOLINI WITH BEEF FILLING

FOR
6 PERSONS

EMILIA-ROMAGNA

This recipe is typical of Parma.

For the filling:

¼ lb. (1 stick) plus 3 tbsp. butter

1 celery stalk, finely chopped

1 carrot, finely chopped

1 tbsp. finely chopped chives

3 oz. lean beef roast
(bottom round or chuck)

A few tbsp. red wine

1 tbsp. tomato purée

2 cloves

1⅔ cups breadcrumbs

2 tbsp. grated Parmigiano-Reggiano

5 large eggs

Pinch grated nutmeg, optional

Beef or capon broth

For the pasta:

6½ cups all-purpose flour,
plus more as needed

5 large eggs

Heat the butter in an earthenware pot. Sauté the celery, carrot, and chives; add the beef and cover with warm water. ✦ Cover the pot with several sheets of wax paper and on the sheets put a soup plate in which red wine should be poured, in accordance with tradition. ✦ Return the pot to the heat and cook very slowly for about 12 hours. ✦ Halfway through this period add the tomato purée and cloves. ✦ When it has finished cooking, the meat will have become a thick sauce. Remove any remaining vegetables and chop them. Put the breadcrumbs and Parmigiano-Reggiano in a bowl; pour in the meat sauce and the vegetables, eggs, and nutmeg. ✦ Work well to combine and set aside in the refrigerator to rest for 1 night. ✦ The next day, use the flour and eggs to prepare a pasta dough as in the recipe on page 10. Let the dough rest, covered with a cloth, for 30 minutes. Knead well and roll out to the thinnest possible sheet (see note, page 212). ✦ Cut the dough into small circles and place about ½ tablespoon of filling on each circle; fold in two and press down along the edges to make them adhere well so as to keep the anolini from opening during cooking. ✦ Cook the anolini in beef or capon broth until they float. Serve in the broth.

PIACENZA-STYLE ANOLINI

ANOLINI PIACENTINI

EMILIA-ROMAGNA

For the filling:

4 tbsp. butter

1 medium onion, finely chopped

1 carrot, finely chopped

1 celery stalk, finely chopped

9 oz. beef chuck roast

2 garlic cloves

½ cup red wine

2 cups broth

¾ cup breadcrumbs

2 large eggs

1⅔ cups grated Parmigiano-Reggiano, preferably from Piacenza

Pinch grated nutmeg

For the pasta:

3 cups all-purpose flour, plus more as needed

6 large eggs

Salt and pepper

Cook these anolini in broth made with beef, hen or capon, and pork, being careful to cook the three meats separately and combine their broths only later, measuring the quantities to obtain a flavorful but not fatty broth, clear and tasty, with a delicate flavor. This is the classic "broth in three," a preparation typical of Piacenza.

Heat the butter in a sauté pan and in it cook the onion, carrot, and celery until fragrant. Make a slit in either side of the beef, inserting a clove of garlic into each one, and add it to the pan, seasoning with salt and pepper. ◆ When the beef has browned, pour in the red wine and let it evaporate. Add broth to cover and let this simmer, partially covered, over low heat for at least 2 hours. ◆ Remove from the heat, cool to room temperature, and refrigerate overnight; the next day return it to low heat for 3 hours; repeat this for a third day. ◆ Chop up the stew thus obtained; sauté the breadcrumbs in the sauce remaining in the pot. Remove it from the heat, then return the chopped stew to the pot along with the eggs, cheese, and nutmeg. Work this well to form a homogeneous mixture. ◆ Use the flour and eggs to prepare a pasta dough as in recipe on page 10. Let the dough rest, covered with a cloth for 30 minutes. Roll the dough out to form a thin sheet (see note, page 212). ◆ Align small balls of the stuffing down one side of this sheet, making each ball about ½ inch in diameter and spacing them by about 2 to 2½ inches. Fold the pasta over onto itself to cover the balls of stuffing. Press the edges to seal and cut them out to form squares or half-moons. ◆ Cook the anolini in broth until al dente. Serve in the cooking liquid.

BATHED BREAD

BAGNONE

LAZIO

6 sun-dried tomatoes

2 garlic cloves

1½ lbs. dried cod, soaked the night before and cut into pieces

CONTINUED

This dish is typical of Vallerano.

In a pot, preferably earthenware, combine the sun-dried tomatoes with the garlic, cod, and fennel. Add water to cover. ◆ Cook for 1 hour over low heat so the flavors blend, adding water if necessary to maintain the quantity of broth (needed to pour over the bread). ◆ Place

2 bunches dried wild fennel

4 slices stale bread, ½ inch thick, or more as needed

Extra-virgin olive oil, for serving

Black pepper

one slice of bread in each individual serving bowl. When the soup has cooked, pour some over each slice of bread. Give the bread 10 minutes to soak up the liquid, and before serving drizzle with olive oil and add a few gridings of black pepper.

BAGNUN D'ANCIÖ

ANCHOVY SOUP

LIGURIA

2 lbs. fresh anchovies

¼ cup olive oil

2 garlic cloves

1 medium onion, finely chopped

1 bunch flat-leaf parsley, chopped

1 lb. fresh plum tomatoes, peeled, seeded, and chopped

½ cup dry white wine

12 hardtack crackers (or toasted bread)

Salt and pepper

Clean the anchovies, cutting off the heads and tails, and rinse them (if possible in seawater). ✦ Heat the olive oil in a sauté pan and add 1 of the garlic cloves, the onion, and parsley; add the tomatoes and cook for 15 minutes. ✦ Add salt and pepper to taste. Add the wine, 2 tablespoons water, and the anchovies. Cook for another 15 minutes. ✦ Rub the crackers (or slices of toasted bread) with the other garlic clove and put them in soup bowls. Pour over the soup and serve after a few minutes.

BIETA IN BRODO

CHARD IN BROTH

CALABRIA

¾ lb. Swiss chard

Chicken broth (about 12 oz. per person)

4 large eggs

Ricotta salata, crumbled

Remove the outer leaves from the Swiss chard, rinse it, chop it, and cook it in broth to cover until tender, about 10 minutes. ✦ When it has cooked, reduce the heat to a gentle simmer. Add the eggs, which should coagulate without breaking and without becoming poached. ✦ Pour the chard with the broth and eggs into bowls and top with a little ricotta salata.

BORDATINO

POLENTA WITH BLACK KALE

TOSCANA

½ cup olive oil

1 medium carrot, chopped

CONTINUED

This dish, typical of both Pisa and Livorno, uses *cavolo nero*, which is also called lacinato kale, Tuscan kale, and black kale.

Heat the olive oil in a sauté pan and add the carrot, celery, onion, garlic cloves, and parsley. Cook until soft. Add

1 celery stalk, chopped

1 medium onion, chopped

2 garlic cloves, chopped

3 tbsp. chopped flat-leaf parsley

1 tbsp. tomato purée

6 cups broth from cooking beans, mixed with a few beans run through a vegetable mill and some (only a few) whole beans

2 cups roughly chopped black kale leaves

1⅔ cups cornmeal

Salt

the tomato purée diluted with a little warm water and then pass the entire mixture through a vegetable mill. ✦ Bring the broth to a boil and add to it the blended vegetables. Add the black kale leaves and cook for about 15 minutes. Add salt to taste. ✦ At this point, add the cornmeal, pouring it in a steady drizzle while constantly stirring with a wooden spoon; cook for about 30 minutes. ✦ Serve in individual bowls, pouring a little olive oil over each.

WINTER VEGETABLE SOUP

BRIZA

FRIULI-VENEZIA GIULIA

½ winter squash (about 2 lbs.)

1 lb. potatoes, peeled and chopped

⅔ cup fresh shelled beans

1 carrot, chopped

1 bay leaf

½ medium onion, chopped

1 celery stalk, chopped

4 cups buttermilk

Salt

This soup, typical of Friuli-Venezia Giulia, is light and flavorful, with a slightly sour taste.

Peel the squash, removing its skin, seeds, and inner filaments. Cut it in slices and soak them in lightly salted water for about 2 hours, then drain very well. ✦ Meanwhile, cook the potatoes in lightly salted boiling water to cover; when cooked pass them through a vegetable mill and set aside in a warm spot. ✦ In a saucepan simmer the beans, carrot, bay leaf, onion, and celery in water to cover by 1 inch until almost tender, about 1½ hours. ✦ Heat the buttermilk in a large pan. Add the squash, potatoes, and beans with their cooking water, being careful to remove the bay leaf. ✦ At this point raise the heat and wait for the mixture to boil, stirring often. Immediately reduce the heat to low and cook for about 15 minutes. ✦ Adjust for salt and let cool to almost room temperature before serving.

FISH SOUP
ANCONA-STYLE

BRODETTO ALL'ANCONETANA

MARCHE

How many fish should go into a *brodetto*? What is the magic number, arrived at through long experimentation and experience? In Ancona, they say thirteen, the same number as the diners at the Last Supper. And each fish should perform a precise role in contributing to the final harmony of a soup

¼ cup olive oil

1 garlic clove, chopped

1 medium onion, finely chopped

2 tbsp. white wine vinegar

2 tbsp. chopped flat-leaf parsley

1 ½ lbs. tomato purée

5 lbs. mixed seafood: cuttlefish, octopus, prawns, shrimp, mussels, clams, cod, red snapper, skate, scorpion fish, mullet, mackerel, John Dory, goby, turbot, monkfish, squid

Peasant-style bread, toasted and rubbed with garlic if you like

that has become the favorite dish for all important occasions. Which fish? Best of all are those the fisherman brings home after his long labors at sea; then there are those that have just arrived in the market today and are absolutely fresh.

Heat the olive oil over low heat in a large enameled earthenware pot. Add the garlic and onion and cook slowly until golden. Add the vinegar and cook until it evaporates, at which point add the parsley and tomato purée. ✦ Add the fish in this order: cuttlefish, squid, octopus, prawns, shrimp, mussels, and clams, larger fish, and so on to the most delicate. ✦ Cook for about 30 minutes, then let sit. Place one slice of bread in each individual serving bowl. Bring the pot of soup to the table. Spoon the soup over the bread.

BRODETTO DI MARANO | FISH SOUP MARANO-STYLE

FRIULI-VENEZIA GIULIA

¼ cup extra-virgin olive oil

1 medium onion, finely minced

1 garlic clove, finely minced

About 4 lbs. fish, cleaned and cut in pieces but not filleted

2 tbsp. white wine vinegar

¼ cup white wine

1 carrot, chopped

1 celery stalk, chopped

2 ripe plum tomatoes, peeled, seeded, and chopped

1 bay leaf

Crusts of stale bread, toasted and fried in a little olive oil

Salt and pepper

It is difficult to give precise numbers or varieties for the fish in this recipe. Some prepare this dish with a single type, such as *gò* (goby; *Gobius venetisrum*), a plentiful fish and very flavorful. Others add eel, *passerine* (little flounder), gray mullet, cuttlefish, or prawns.

Heat the olive oil in a pot (preferably earthenware) over low heat; add the onion and garlic and cook slowly. After a few minutes add the fish, then add the vinegar and let it evaporate. ✦ Add the wine and enough water to cover. ✦ Add the carrot, celery, tomatoes, bay leaf, salt, and pepper. ✦ Simmer at low heat for about 2 hours, then pass the soup through a food mill. ✦ Serve hot, accompanied by crusts of stale bread.

FISH SOUP
FANO-STYLE

MARCHE

4 lbs. mixed fish (cuttlefish or squid,
shrimp or prawns, tub gurnard,
scorpion fish, mackerel or dog fish,
sole or turbot, red snapper or
John Dory, monkfish, sea bream,
skate or ray, etc.)

¼ cup olive oil

1 medium onion, finely chopped

1 tsp. tomato purée

¾ cup white wine vinegar
(or white wine)

Salt and pepper

The characteristics of a genuine *brodetto* consumed in Fano, north of Ancona, like this one have long been the subject of debate. In truth, the basic elements used (olive oil, garlic, onion, vinegar, wine, pepper or chili pepper, tomatoes or tomato purée) come from the area and are themselves distinctive. There is then the great variety of fish used, for which reason one can readily affirm that no two *brodetti* could ever be identical. Those who have had the opportunity to accompany fishermen from Fano and to taste the *brodetto* they prepare on their boats will note that even among the same group of fishermen one encounters different methods of preparation. The *brodetti* made on boats are sometimes based on one type of fish, such as shrimp, prawns, spider crabs, or cuttlefish, and these are slightly sweet; or the *brodetto* is made from a mixture, depending on what is being fished that day. Because of the freshness of the fish, the results are always notable.

Wash and carefully clean the fish. ✦ Heat the olive oil in a sauté pan and cook the onion until golden. Add the tomato purée, salt and pepper, vinegar, and 1 cup of water (or use equal measures of wine and water). ✦ Boil for several minutes to blend the ingredients. Add the fish, beginning with the largest or those that require the longest cooking (cuttlefish, tub gurnard). ✦ When you have finished adding fish, simmer until the cooking is complete. It is essential to pay close attention to the cooking times of the fish, for since they are of different sizes and composition, cooking them for the right amount of time requires putting them in at different times, otherwise some fish will not cook long enough and others will be overcooked.

FISH SOUP FROM
PORTO RECANATI

MARCHE

2 tbsp. olive oil

1 medium onion, finely minced

8 oz. cuttlefish

4 cups fish broth (or water)

⅛ oz. saffron (if possible wild)

CONTINUED

Heat the olive oil in a sauté pan; cook the onion until golden; add the cuttlefish cut in little pieces. ✦ Add salt and pepper to taste, cover with broth or water and the saffron, and continue cooking. ✦ When the cuttlefish is cooked, adjust for salt and pepper. ✦ Dredge the assorted fish in flour and place them in a large pot, beginning with the cooked cuttlefish (reserving their cooking liquid) and the larger or firmer fish and moving on to

4 ½ lbs. assorted fish (mullet, sole, cod, monkfish, angler, scorpion fish, John Dory, prawns, etc.)
All-purpose flour for dredging the fish
½ cup dry white wine
Slices of toasted bread
Salt and pepper

those more delicate, thus ending with the sole and mullet. ✦ Cover with the cuttlefish liquid, and add the white wine and as much water as needed. ✦ Cook over high heat for no more than 15 minutes, occasionally shaking the pan to move the fish (thus avoiding the use of spoons, which will break up the fish). ✦ Serve hot over slices of toasted bread.

**BRODETTO DI ROMBO
ALLA GRADESE**

TURBOT GRADO-STYLE

FRIULI-VENEZIA GIULIA

2 lbs. turbot
1 tbsp. olive oil
½ cup sunflower oil
4 whole garlic cloves
¼ cup white wine vinegar
Coarse salt and pepper

This is often served with soft white polenta.

Clean the turbot, removing the gills, and cut in slices, setting aside the heads; rinse and dry the fish. ✦ In a heavy pan heat the olive and sunflower oils, then sauté the garlic until it becomes dark brown. ✦ Remove the garlic and put the fish slices and heads in the pan and cook for 5 to 8 minutes, then add a pinch of salt and pepper and sprinkle with the vinegar. ✦ When the vinegar has evaporated, cover with warm water, turn up the heat to high, and boil for about 20 minutes. ✦ Taste for salt and serve.

**BRODETTO DI SARDONCINI
E CAVOLFIORE**

ANCHOVY AND
CAULIFLOWER STEW

MARCHE

1 lb. sardoncini (anchovies)
1 head cauliflower
¼ cup olive oil
1 medium onion, cut in thin slices
1 shallot, cut in thin slices
½ cup dry white wine
2 plum tomatoes
1 tbsp. chopped flat-leaf parsley
½ tsp. thyme leaves
Salt and pepper or chili pepper flakes

This is an ancient recipe from the coast of Pesaro.

Carefully clean the *sardoncini*, split them open, bone them, and set them aside to dry. ✦ Cut the cauliflower in florets, wash them, and cook until al dente in lightly salted boiling water to cover. ✦ Heat the olive oil in a sauté pan and cook the onion and shallot. When the onion begins to become transparent, add the wine and let it evaporate; add the tomato, parsley, and thyme leaves, and cook for about 10 minutes. ✦ Cover the bottom of a large pot with the cauliflower, add the anchovies, and pour in the sauce; cook over low heat for about 30 minutes. Serve hot.

FISH STEW TERMOLI-STYLE

BRODETTO TERMOLESE

MOLISE

1½ lbs. fresh fish (not anchovies or sardines): stargazer, *frascine*, cod, mullet, prawns, small cuttlefish

1 tbsp. olive oil

1 garlic clove, chopped

½ hot dried chili pepper

¼ fresh green pepper, chopped

2 tbsp. chopped flat-leaf parsley

¾ lb. plum tomatoes, peeled, seeded, and chopped

2 lbs. mussels, scrubbed and beards removed

4 lbs. clams, cleaned

Salt

Clean the fish carefully and cut any large ones in pieces. ✦ Heat the olive oil in a pot (preferably earthenware) and add the garlic, chili pepper, green pepper, parsley, and tomatoes. Cook until the sauce has reduced. ✦ Add all the fish, water to cover, and salt and cook for 15 minutes. Add the mussels and clams and let cook another 5 minutes. ✦ Serve in the same pot.

TOASTED BROTH

BRODO ABBRUSTOLITO

FOR 6 PERSONS

FRIULI-VENEZIA GIULIA

2 tbsp. butter

2 tbsp. all-purpose flour

½ tsp. ground cumin

2 large eggs, beaten

1 sprig sweet marjoram

Slices of bread, toasted

Grated aged Montasio cheese

Salt and pepper

Cook the butter in a pot over medium-low heat until it is nut brown in color, then whisk in the flour and cumin. ✦ Gradually whisk in 4 cups water, carefully avoiding the formation of lumps, and simmer slowly for 30 minutes. ✦ Meanwhile, mix the eggs with the salt, pepper, and marjoram and pour into the broth, stirring constantly. ✦ Place slices of bread in the bottoms of bowls, sprinkle with cheese, and pour in the broth.

"BURNED BROTH"

BRODO BRUCIATO

FRIULI-VENEZIA GIULIA

2 tbsp. butter

2 tbsp. all-purpose flour

1½ cups milk

This dish is typical of Carnia, where it is sometimes made with the addition of boiled potatoes.

Slowly melt the butter in a pot over low heat, mixing in the flour. ✦ Gradually whisk in the milk until smooth, and cook until the raw taste of the flour is gone.

BRODO BRUCIATO COI FUNGHI | MUSHROOM SOUP

FOR
6 PERSONS

TRENTINO

4 tbsp. butter
1¼ cups all-purpose flour
2 tbsp. olive oil
½ medium onion, finely chopped
¾ lb. fresh porcini mushrooms, sliced
2 tbsp. white wine
1 tbsp. chopped flat-leaf parsley
Broth, if necessary
Salt and pepper

Melt the butter in a pot over medium heat and stir in the flour, mixing well with a wooden spoon. Cook until the mixture takes on a golden color. ✦ Whisk in 4 cups cold water to obtain a somewhat thick broth. ✦ Meanwhile, heat the olive oil in a pan and add the onion, cooking until translucent. Add the mushrooms; let them cook for about 10 minutes. Sprinkle with the wine and add salt, pepper, and the parsley. ✦ Pass half of the mushrooms through a food mill and blend them and the other mushrooms into the broth, mixing well. ✦ Cook slowly for 30 minutes, adding broth if necessary.

BRODO DI CARDI | CARDOON AND MEATBALL SOUP

FOR
6 PERSONS

MOLISE

1 turkey wing
1 cardoon
Juice of 1 lemon
¾ pound ground veal
8 large eggs
1 cup grated pecorino
Extra-virgin olive oil
Giblets from 1 turkey
1 tbsp. butter
¼ cup white wine
6 slices stale bread
Salt

Place the turkey wing in a large pot and cover with 8 cups of water. Bring to a boil over high heat, skim the surface, reduce the heat, and simmer for at least 1 hour. ✦ Meanwhile, remove the hard outer ribs from the cardoon and strip away the stringy fibers from the more tender areas. Cut it into small pieces and boil in salted water acidulated with the lemon juice (to keep the cardoon pieces from browning) until tender. Drain, let cool, and pat dry. ✦ In a bowl combine the veal, 1 of the eggs, 1 tablespoon of the pecorino, and salt. Work together well, then gently form this mixture into tiny meatballs (the size of fat chickpeas). Heat 2 tablespoons of the olive oil in a pan and brown the meatballs on all sides until they are fully cooked. ✦ Dice the turkey giblets. Heat 1 tablespoon of the olive oil and the butter in another pan and cook the giblets until browned. Add the white wine and let it evaporate. ✦ Remove the turkey wing from its broth and discard the wing. Add the cardoon and the giblet mixture to the broth. Simmer together for about 15 minutes. ✦ Heat ¼ inch of olive oil in a high-sided pan until hot. Beat one of the eggs in a deep plate. Dip the bread into the beaten egg, then fry the bread, turning, until golden on all sides. ✦ In another bowl beat the remaining 6 eggs with the remaining pecorino. Fold the meatballs, the fried bread, and the egg mixture into the soup and let it cook 3 or 4 minutes before serving.

BRODO DI FAGIOLI	# BEAN SOUP

EMILIA-ROMAGNA

1½ cups dried beans,
if possible of the *saluggia* variety
(called "old lady's teeth"
in the Modenese dialect)

Pistadein (see page 169)

This recipe is typical of Modena.

Boil the beans in lightly salted water to cover, cooking them until tender, about 2 hours. ✦ Add the *pistadein* and cook until the pasta is al dente. ✦ Serve hot in soup bowls. This dish can be also eaten cold, which concentrates its body and its flavor.

BRODO DI PESCE CON VERDURE	# FISH AND VEGETABLE SOUP	FOR 6 PERSONS

MOLISE

2 prawns
4 medium shrimp
1 head of a monkfish
1 scorpion fish
1 lb. plum tomatoes, peeled and crushed
1 garlic clove
1 bunch flat-leaf parsley
1 small piece sweet green pepper
½ cup extra-virgin olive oil
1 hot dried chili pepper (optional)
2 lbs. Swiss chard (or chicory)
Salt

Put all the ingredients except the Swiss chard (or chicory) in a pot with 8 cups of water and cook until the liquid is reduced by half. ✦ Remove the fish and filter the broth. ✦ Meanwhile, boil the chard in water to cover until tender, about 10 minutes. When cooked, blend with the fish broth, cooking them together for 5 minutes.

BROT AD FASEUI E CASTAGNI	# BEAN AND CHESTNUT SOUP

PIEMONTE

1½ cups dried beans
1½ cups dried chestnuts
¼ cup olive oil
Salt

This simple soup was brought to the Vercelli area by Valesian shepherds moving their flocks.

In separate containers, soak the beans and chestnuts in lightly salted water overnight. ✦ The next day, in a pot combine the two with their water and the olive oil and cook until tender, about 2 hours. Add a little salt. ✦ Serve hot in bowls.

BEAN AND RICE SOUP

BRUVÒIRA

PIEMONTE

2 ½ cups beans
1 ½ cups rice
4 cups milk
Salt

This bean soup is typical of Biella.

If the beans are dried, they must be soaked overnight to soften; if they are of the *faseu dël papa* type, they must be shelled. ✦ Cook the beans in lightly salted water without bringing them to a boil until nearly cooked, about 1 ½ hours. ✦ Add the rice, salt as needed, and the milk and cook for 30 minutes. ✦ Serve hot.

TRIPE SOUP

BUSECCA

FOR
6 PERSONS

PIEMONTE

2 lbs. fresh white tripe
2 medium onions, peeled
½ cup loosely packed
flat-leaf parsley leaves
1 garlic clove
⅓ cup lard
1 celery stalk
8 cups flavorful broth
¼ cup mixed herbs
(such as sage and thyme)
Slices of toasted bread
Grated Parmigiano-Reggiano

This is a dish typical of Biella.

Wash the tripe, place it in a pot, and add water to cover. Boil several minutes, stirring, then remove and cool in cold water. ✦ Clean the tripe again, then cut in slices about 3 inches long. ✦ Finely chop together the onions, parsley, garlic, lard, and celery and put in a pot with the tripe. ✦ Cook over high heat for a few minutes, then add the broth. ✦ Cover and slowly cook for 2 hours, adding the herbs toward the end. ✦ Skim off any fat and serve with bread. Sprinkle with Parmigiano-Reggiano at the table.

✦ **LOCAL TRADITION** ✦

CALLARIEDDE

This is a soup made of chicory or fennel broth with slices of salame, mozzarella, beaten eggs, and lamb. It would typically be served on Easter Monday in Gravina, in the area of Puglia.

RAZOR CLAMS IN BROTH

VENETO

1¾ cups olive oil
2 garlic cloves
2 tbsp. flat-leaf parsley
3 lbs. razor clams, cleaned
4 cups beef broth
Hunks of bread, sautéed in a little oil

Make a *guazzetto* (oil infused with garlic and parsley) by slowly simmering the garlic and parsley in the olive oil in a large pan over very low heat. ✦ When the garlic takes on color, raise the heat to medium and add the clams. ✦ When the clams open, remove the shells and add the broth. Bring to a simmer. ✦ Arrange the bread in bowls and pour the soup over.

CAPPELLETTI IN BROTH

CAPPELLETTI IN BRODO

EMILIA-ROMAGNA

For the filling:
4 tbsp. butter
½ lb. pork loin
4 oz. boneless chicken breast
7 oz. prosciutto crudo, minced
1⅔ cups grated
Parmigiano-Reggiano
1 large egg
Pinch grated nutmeg
Salt

For the dough:
3 cups all-purpose flour,
plus more as needed
4 large eggs
1 tbsp. olive oil
1 cup capon broth (see page 226)
per person, brought to a simmer
Grated Parmigiano-Reggiano

This is a dish typical of Forlì and Reggio Emilia. At Imola it is customary to add one oversized *cappelletto* (known as a *caplitaz*) to the bowl at the New Year's meal; it is destined to bring good luck to the diner who is served it. The version given here is the classic stuffing, but there are many variations. There are those who use mortadella in place of prosciutto or roast veal instead of pork; some use turkey breast in addition to the pork, and some use chicken fat (even better, capon fat) in place of butter; and those, finally, who add ¼ pound calf's brains. At Novellara (Reggio Emilia) the filling is prepared using only braised beef with cloves and chopped onion.

Heat the butter in a pan over low heat until melted. Finely chop the pork and chicken and add them to the pan. Cook for about 15 minutes, then add the prosciutto crudo. ✦ Leave the pan on the heat for a few minutes, then transfer it to a bowl and let it cool. ✦ Work the Parmigiano-Reggiano and egg into the mixture and knead to obtain a soft consistency, adding salt and the nutmeg. ✦ Use the flour, eggs, and olive oil to prepare a pasta dough as on page 10, adding the oil with the eggs. Let it rest under a kitchen towel for about 30 minutes. ✦ Roll out a sheet of pasta about 1/16 inch thick (see page 212) and cut it in horizontal and then vertical strips to obtain squares 1 to 1½ inches on a side. ✦ Put a small amount of the filling at the center of each square and fold over to form a triangle, making sure the edges adhere well. ✦ Pick up each triangle, holding it by the ends between the thumb and forefinger of each hand, then twist the triangle around the tip of your left index finger until the two ends overlap. Press the ends together to join them well, forming a "little cap" (*cappelletto*). ✦ Set the *cappelletti* aside to rest and harden for several hours, then cook in boiling capon broth for 10 minutes. ✦ Serve with broth and sprinkle with Parmigiano-Reggiano at the table.

CAPRIATA	**BEAN AND GRAIN MUSH**

BASILICATA

About 1 lb. in total of a mixture of grain, dried beans, lentils, flat peas, dried peas

Extra-virgin olive oil

Salt

The evening before, soak the grain and legumes in lightly salted water. ✦ Drain and rinse them and put them in an earthenware pot. Add enough water to cover them by a few inches, season with salt, and cook, covered, for about 2 hours over medium heat, or until the beans are very soft, almost a purée. ✦ Serve warm in the winter and cold in the summer after drizzling with olive oil.

✦ **LOCAL TRADITION** ✦

CANNELICCHJE E FAFE

According to various period chroniclers, the nourishing soup common to Puglia and known as *cannelicchje e fafe*—made from dried fava beans reduced to a mush and combined with raw or boiled razor clams—was served to the thirteen Italian soldiers led by Ettore Fieramosca in the 1503 battle known as the "Challenge of Barletta."

CARABACCIA	**SWEET ONION SOUP**	FOR 6 PERSONS

TOSCANA

4 tbsp. olive oil

1 carrot, chopped

1 celery stalk, chopped

CONTINUED

Heat the olive oil in a large earthenware pot. Add the carrot, celery, and basil and cook for 5 minutes. ✦ Add the onions and one third of the broth and cook over low heat for at least 1 hour, by which time all the liquid will have evaporated. ✦ Raise the heat and add the wine. ✦ When the wine has evaporated, add the legumes. ✦ After about 1 minute, add the rest of the broth and lower the heat;

1 large sprig of basil, roughly chopped

2 lbs. medium onions, finely chopped

4 cups broth

3 tbsp. white wine

⅔ cup mixed fresh legumes (peas, beans, etc.)

3 tbsp. grated Parmigiano-Reggiano or pecorino

6 slices toasted bread

Salt and pepper

simmer until the legumes are tender. Add salt and pepper to taste. ✦ Before serving sprinkle the soup with cheese and mix in well. Place a slice of bread in each bowl and pour over the soup. Let it rest a few minutes, then serve hot.

CARDOONS IN BROTH 1

FOR 6 PERSONS

CAMPANIA

2 large cardoons

Juice of 1 lemon

7 cups beef or chicken broth

2 whole large eggs and 2 yolks

4 tbsp. grated Parmigiano-Reggiano, plus more for serving

Salt and pepper

This preparation is typical of Avellino.

Remove the outer ribs and fibers from the cardoons, then cut the inner ribs into 4-inch-long strips. To keep them from discoloring, immerse them immediately in water acidulated with lemon juice. ✦ Cook the strips of cardoons in lightly salted boiling water for 10 minutes, remove, and thoroughly drain. ✦ Heat the broth to boiling, add the cardoons, reduce the heat to low, and cook for another 10 minutes. Beat together the eggs and yolks, Parmigiano-Reggiano, salt, and pepper; at the moment of serving the dish add the egg mixture to the cardoons in their broth, stirring rapidly to make the eggs congeal slightly. Serve more Parmigiano-Reggiano at the table.

CARDONI IN BRODO 2

CARDOONS IN BROTH 2

ABRUZZO

1½ lbs. cardoons

Juice of 1 lemon

6 cups broth (best if made from free-range chicken or beef)

3 large eggs, beaten

Grated pecorino

1 recipe cheese and egg fritters (see page 50)

Clean the cardoons, cut them in cubes, and put them in cold water acidulated with the lemon juice. ✦ Boil the cardoon cubes in lightly salted water to cover for about 1½ hours. ✦ Remove the cubes and drain them. Bring the broth to a boil and add the cardoons. Cook for 5 minutes. Beat the eggs with 3 tablespoons pecorino and pour it into the broth, stirring briskly; simmer for a few minutes, then serve hot with the addition of pecorino and cheese and egg fritters.

CAVATELLI, RUGHETTA E PATATE | CAVATELLI WITH ARUGULA AND POTATOES

PUGLIA

2 tbsp. extra-virgin olive oil
1 garlic clove, sliced
½ cup basil leaves
1 lb. plum tomatoes, peeled
1 lb. potatoes, peeled and cubed
2 lbs. arugula, washed and drained
1 lb. cavatelli
Salt and pepper

This dish is typical of Foggia.

Heat the olive oil in a pot over low heat, add the garlic, and cook until fragrant; add the basil, tomatoes, and salt and cook over low heat. ✦ Meanwhile, boil the potatoes in a pot with lightly salted water to cover. When they are almost done add the arugula. Remove the potatoes and arugula from the pot. Heat the water and as soon as the water returns to a boil, add the cavatelli. ✦ When the cavatelli is cooked, drain it and put everything back in the pot, including the tomato mixture. Serve hot.

CIALDA | PEASANT SOUP

PUGLIA

2 medium onions
2 plum tomatoes, not overly ripe
2 tbsp. chopped flat-leaf parsley
2 tbsp. olive oil
4 slices stale bread
4 tbsp. chopped oregano
Salt

This humble repast of peasants is good enough to please connoisseurs as well.

Roughly chop the onions and tomatoes and put them in a pot with the parsley, salt, and olive oil; add water to cover and boil for 10 minutes to create a broth. ✦ Slice the bread and place in bowls, sprinkling with the oregano. ✦ Pour the broth over and serve.

✦ **LOCAL TRADITION** ✦

CROSTINI ALLA MILZA PER MINESTRA

In this recipe for spleen crostini, typical of Alto Adige, a veal spleen is pounded with a meat mallet, halved, and the membrane removed before being seasoned with salt and pepper. Three slices of stale, crustless bread are then spread with butter and stacked with the spleen. The stacked bread and veal spleen is then sliced and cubed into "striped croutons," which are sautéed until just browned in butter and served in beef broth with chives.

CIANFOTTA FAICCHIANA | VEGETABLE STEW

CAMPANIA

¼ cup extra-virgin olive oil

3 zucchini, cubed

2 medium potatoes, peeled and cubed

2 large sweet peppers, seeded and cubed

3½ cups cubed eggplant, tossed with salt and allowed to drain of its juices

1 garlic clove, thinly sliced

1 medium onion, thinly sliced

3 medium plum tomatoes, peeled and seeded

1 tbsp. chopped basil

1 tbsp. chopped oregano

1 tbsp. chopped flat-leaf parsley

Salt and pepper

Heat 2 tablespoons olive oil in a pan. Add the zucchini, potatoes, peppers, and eggplant and cook until golden. ✦ In a saucepan, heat the remaining olive oil and cook the garlic and onion. ✦ When this mixture takes on a golden color, add the tomatoes and let cook for 5 minutes. ✦ At this point transfer the zucchini mixture to the pan with the garlic and onion; add the basil, oregano, parsley, salt, and pepper and cook, covered, for about 30 minutes. ✦ When the cooking is almost completed take off the cover, turn up the heat, and cook until the liquid evaporates. Serve at room temperature.

CISRÀ | CHICKPEA SOUP

PIEMONTE

¾ cup dried chickpeas

1 tsp. baking soda

1 tbsp. all-purpose flour

¼ cup extra-virgin olive oil

1 tbsp. chopped sage leaves

1 cup dried mushrooms, softened in hot water

½ lb. string beans

Slices of toasted bread

This preparation is typical of Vercelli. One variation adds *ossette di suino* (pork ribs with meat attached), pork rind, and also raw salame to the bean pot at the beginning of cooking. When the soup has been cooked to perfection, add chopped onion, carrots, celery, Swiss chard, or spinach. Continue to cook at least half an hour with the addition of string beans and serve with hunks of toasted bread.

Soak the chickpeas in water to cover and baking soda overnight, then drain them and combine with the flour and olive oil. ✦ Mix until the flour adheres to the chickpeas but without forming lumps. Add the sage, mushrooms, salt to taste, and lukewarm water to cover. ✦ Cook for several hours over low heat without stirring, maintaining a constant simmer. ✦ Separately, blanch the string beans in salted boiling water until bright green. Stir them into the soup just before serving. Serve with the toasted bread.

FISH SOUP WITH HERBS

CIUPPIN

LIGURIA

½ cup extra-virgin olive oil
1 medium onion, finely chopped
1 celery stalk, finely chopped
1 carrot, finely chopped
1 bunch flat-leaf parsley,
finely chopped
1 garlic clove, finely chopped
Pinch oregano, finely chopped
¼ cup aromatic herbs, finely chopped
½ cup white wine
3 ripe plum tomatoes,
peeled, seeded, and chopped
2 lbs. mixed fish (sea bream, white
bream, gurnard, or scorpion fish),
cleaned and cut into pieces
4 slices bread, toasted
Salt and pepper

This is a soup typical of the Riviera di Levante.

Heat the olive oil in a large pan. Add all the vegetables and herbs and sauté them. ✦ As soon as the mixture begins to take on color add the wine and cook until it evaporates. Add the tomatoes and season with salt and pepper. Cook slowly for 20 minutes, stirring frequently. ✦ Add the fish to the pot; it can cook slowly until it begins to fall apart. If necessary add a little hot water. ✦ Remove any bones and pass the mixture through a mill, collecting the resulting broth in a pot. ✦ Adjust for salt and pepper and bring to a boil. The result should be dense. ✦ Serve hot with toasted bread.

CREAM OF ZUCCHINI SOUP

CREMA DI ZUCCHINE

PIEMONTE

5 zucchini, cubed
2 leeks, cut in half lengthwise
and sliced
4 cups chicken or vegetable broth
1 large egg yolk
¾ cup milk
2 tbsp. grated Parmigiano-Reggiano
Chopped flat-leaf parsley
Salt and pepper

Put the zucchini and leeks in a saucepan with ½ cup water and salt. ✦ Cover and cook over low heat for 25 minutes, then pass through a food mill. ✦ Add the broth. Beat the egg yolk with the milk and add to the soup, then add the Parmigiano-Reggiano. ✦ Add salt and pepper and sprinkle with parsley before serving.

TURNIP GREENS SOUP

ERBE DA "BRUO"

VENETO

2 lbs. turnip greens
CONTINUED

Traditionally, the turnip leaves used in this recipe must have experienced frost.

Boil the greens for a few minutes and drain them. Put them in a pan with cold water to cover, salt, pork bones,

3 pork bones	and *lardo* and cook over low heat for about 1½ hours. ✦ Add the milk and let it cook another 10 minutes. ✦ Place a slice of polenta in each bowl and pour the steaming soup over. Serve hot.
1 piece of *lardo* (see page 2)	
2 cups milk	
Slices of cooked firm polenta	
Salt and pepper	

FAGIOLI "GRASSI" | PORK AND BEANS

PIEMONTE

4 *preive* (rectangles of pork rind flavored with pepper, nutmeg, garlic, and finely chopped rosemary tightly tied with string)

1 *zampino* (a pig's trotter, optional)

5 pork loins

½ lb. dried beans, soaked for several hours in cold water

1 bunch herbs (rosemary, sage, bay leaf)

In the area of Ivrea this dish is prepared using the small dark beans called "*del granoturco,*" or "*d'la melia,*" whereas white or borlotto beans are used in other towns of the Cavanese area. In the past it was the custom to bake the beans in a bread oven, putting them in just after the bread. Older residents of the area are in the habit of accompanying this dish with Barbera wine.

The ideal pot for making this dish is one of the typical earthenware containers of Castellamonte; the best is known as the *tofeja,* which is also the dialect name for this dish. ✦ Preheat the oven to 300°F. Put all the ingredients in the pot, cover with water, and bake for several hours to obtain a somewhat dense soup.

FAGIOLI E PASTELLA | BEANS WITH DUMPLINGS

FRIULI-VENEZIA GIULIA

1⅔ cup dried beans, soaked overnight and drained

1 potato, peeled and cut into pieces

¼ cup mixed herbs (to your taste)

1 oz. pancetta, minced

¾ cup all-purpose flour

Salt

This recipe is typical of the upper Friuli.

Combine the beans, potato, herbs, and pancetta in a pot. Add water to cover and simmer until the beans are tender, then raise the heat slightly to bring the mixture to a boil. ✦ Prepare *lis mignàculis* with the flour, a pinch of salt, and just enough water to make a somewhat fluid batter (about ½ cup). ✦ When the soup boils, slowly drizzle in the batter, stirring, and cook for several minutes more.

FARRO ALLA LEONESSANA | FARRO PORRIDGE

LAZIO

1½ cups farro (spelt)

1½ cups meat broth

CONTINUED

Even today one can still have the good fortune to taste this dish at Leonessa, the town for which it is named.

Cook the farro, or *farricello,* like polenta (see page 289), using a good meat broth. Cook over low heat, paying special attention that it does not stick during the cook-

Sauce of mixed meats (see page 635)
Grated pecorino

ing. ✦ Serve in soup bowls with a sauce, prepared separately, of mixed meats or only pork or only sausage. ✦ Serve with pecorino at the table.

FARRO CON FIORI E ZUCCHINE

FARRO WITH ZUCCHINI FLOWERS

MARCHE

⅔ cup extra-virgin olive oil
2 garlic cloves, finely chopped
½ medium onion, finely chopped
8 zucchini flowers, quartered
2 zucchini, cut in thin rounds
½ cup white wine
2 cups beef broth
2 cups farro (spelt)
½ cup grated pecorino
Mint leaves
Pepper

Heat the olive oil in a pot. Add the garlic and onion and sauté until they take on a little color; add the zucchini flowers and zucchini. ✦ Sprinkle with the wine, let it evaporate slightly, then add the broth and farro. Cook over high heat, stirring until the broth has been absorbed by the farro. ✦ Sprinkle with pecorino and add a few twists from a pepper mill. Put in warm plates and garnish with mint leaves.

FOGLIOLO

TRIPE AND BEAN STEW

LOMBARDIA

1 ¼ cups dried cannellini beans
1 lb. curly tripe
3 lbs. *fogliolo (centopelli)* tripe
¼ lb. (1 stick) butter
1 medium onion, sliced
1 slice pancetta, finely chopped
1 tbsp. fat from roasted meat, or as needed
2 ladlefuls broth
1 can (28 oz.) crushed plum tomatoes
2 stalks celery, chopped
2 large carrots, chopped
Grated Parmigiano-Reggiano
Salt and pepper

Purchase curly tripe that has already been cleaned and slightly precooked.

The night before, soak the beans in water to cover. ✦ Wash the curly tripe in cold water (otherwise you risk dissolving its rich load of fat) and cut in large rectangular pieces. ✦ Soak the *fogliolo* tripe in boiling water for a few minutes and cut it in very thin strips. ✦ Melt the butter in a pot, add the onion and sauté, then add the pancetta, *fogliolo*, fat, broth, tomatoes, and salt and pepper. ✦ After 1 hour add the curly tripe and after another hour the celery and carrots. Continue cooking for another 2 hours, adding broth if the tripe gets dry. ✦ Meanwhile, cook the beans separately and add them. (Don't stir too often to keep them from falling apart as they cook.) ✦ If the mixture does not seem flavorful enough, add more of the fat from the roast meat, salt, and Parmigiano-Reggiano to taste. The result should be somewhat dry and should be served with more cheese at the table.

POLENTA SOUP WITH CAVOLO NERO

FRASCADEI

TOSCANA

1 lb. *cavolo nero* (black kale)
(see note, page 199)
2 medium potatoes,
peeled and cut in large chunks
1¼ cups cornmeal
⅔ cup lard
2 oz. mortadella
½ bunch flat-leaf parsley
1 garlic clove
½ cup extra-virgin olive oil
Coarse salt

This is a recipe typical of Pontremoli.

Roughly chop the inner leaves of the *cavolo nero* and cook them in lightly salted boiling water to cover. ✦ Add the potatoes and cook for 40 minutes. ✦ Pass the cornmeal through a sieve and slowly rain it into the pot, stirring to avoid the formation of lumps. Stir often and cook for 1 hour. ✦ The mixture should be relatively liquid; add a little warm water if it becomes too thick. ✦ Meanwhile, finely chop together the lard, mortadella, parsley, and garlic. Add this and the olive oil to the pot after 30 minutes. Mix well and serve in individual soup bowls.

TINY DUMPLINGS IN HERB BROTH

FRASCARELLI

LAZIO

1⅔ cups all-purpose flour,
plus more as needed
2 tbsp. extra-virgin olive oil
4 oz. pancetta (or lard)
1 garlic clove
1 medium onion
1 celery stalk
Herbs (a few sage leaves,
a thyme sprig)
½ lb. plum tomatoes, peeled
1 cup chicken broth, warmed
Salt and pepper

This dish, typical of Viterbo and the area surrounding it, was once made almost exclusively for the nourishment of pregnant women and new mothers, for it was believed to help in the creation of milk for nursing. The dish gets its name from the fact that, in times gone by, a leafy branch (*frasca*) was used to sprinkle the boiling water over the flour, so as to avoid burning the hands. In the area of Lake Bolsena (Bolsena, San Lorenzo Nuovo, and so on), *frascarelli* are also called *'nsaccheragatti,* a colorful dialect expression. At Corchiano they are instead called *'nsaccagnotti.*

Spread the flour evenly on a flat surface, and sprinkle ½ cup boiling water over it. Gather up the flour gently, then rub your hands together. (The success of the *frascarelli* depends on the sureness and delicate quickness with which this operation is performed.) ✦ Place the resulting balls in a sieve and shake to eliminate any flour that has not been mixed with water. What remains are the *frascarelli*, small, irregularly shaped balls of pasta not unlike grated pasta. ✦ Heat the olive oil in a large pot. Chop together the pancetta (or lard), garlic, onion, celery, and herbs and sauté until the pancetta takes on a little color; add the tomatoes, broth, salt, and pepper and let cook over low heat for 30 minutes. ✦ Bring this broth to a boil and add the *frascarelli*. Cook just until al dente, which will take just a few minutes.

FREGULA | FREGULA SOUP

1½ cups *fregula*

½ cup olive oil

Large pinch saffron,
steeped in ¼ cup warm water

6 cups beef broth

7 oz. *casu de fitta*
(fresh sheep's cheese in brine;
can use feta), drained

½ cup grated pecorino piccante

Salt

Fregula is a tiny round pasta that resembles large-grain couscous. It is made with hard durum wheat.

Put the *fregula* on a pastry board together with the olive oil and a pinch of salt and knead it with the saffron water. ✦ Slowly rub the damp grains between the palms of the hands until they are swollen. ✦ Spread the grains on a cloth to dry, then place in a pot with the broth and cook until al dente. ✦ Place the *casù de fitta* in a bowl and pour the *fregula* over it; sprinkle with pecorino and mix thoroughly. Serve hot.

GANEFFE 1 | RICE BALLS IN SOUP 1

2 cups rice

3 large eggs

¼ cup grated pecorino (or
caciocavallo), plus more for serving

Large pinch saffron, steeped in
2 tbsp. warm water

All-purpose flour, for dredging

Extra-virgin olive oil for frying

Beef broth, for serving
(about 1 cup per person)

Salt

This recipe is typical of Enna.

Boil the rice in lightly salted water to cover. Drain when al dente and pour it into a shallow bowl to cool. ✦ When the rice has cooled, add 2 eggs, cheese, and the saffron water. ✦ Work well and form into balls the size of hazelnuts. ✦ Heat 1 inch of olive oil in a skillet until hot. Beat the remaining egg. Dredge the rice balls in flour, dip in the egg, then fry until golden. ✦ Serve in bowls with the beef broth and pecorino.

GANEFFE 2 | RICE BALLS IN SOUP 2

2½ cups Arborio rice

4 cups milk

⅔ cup grated Parmigiano-Reggiano

4 tbsp. butter

CONTINUED

In a pot cook the rice in milk (add enough water so the liquid covers the rice by 2 inches) until it has absorbed all the cooking liquid. ✦ When the rice is cooked stir in the Parmigiano-Reggiano and butter and transfer to a shallow bowl to cool. ✦ When the rice has cooled add the egg yolks. Beat the whites until frothy. ✦ Mold the rice into small balls. ✦ Heat 2 inches of olive oil in a skillet until hot. Dip the rice balls in the egg whites, then in

2 large eggs, separated

Olive oil for frying

All-purpose flour, for dredging

Broth made from veal and chicken meat (about 1 cup per person)

Salt

flour, and fry until golden. ✦ Heat the broth, add the rice balls, and serve.

LUCCA SPRING VEAL AND VEGETABLE STEW

GARMUGIA LUCCHESE

FOR 6 PERSONS

TOSCANA

¼ cup extra-virgin olive oil

2 oz. pancetta, finely chopped

4 new onions, sliced

4 oz. veal, diced

¼ cup fresh, shelled fava beans

¼ cup fresh peas

4 artichokes, cleaned and cut in pieces

¼ cup asparagus tips, cooked just until very bright green

4 cups beef broth

Peasant-style bread, cut into cubes and toasted

Salt

Heat the olive oil in a pot over medium-low heat. Add the pancetta and cook slowly so it will release its fat without burning. Add the onions. ✦ When the onions turn golden, add the veal, fava beans, peas, artichokes, and asparagus tips. ✦ Let cook until the vegetables are brightly colored, then add the broth and slowly bring to a boil and cook until the vegetables are softened. Season with salt. ✦ Serve with cubes of toasted bread.

FAVA BEAN SOUP

GRANERISE E FAFE

PUGLIA

1 ¼ cups fresh, shelled fava beans

¼ cup extra-virgin olive oil

½ medium onion, sliced

½ cup tomato purée

A few basil leaves

1 ¼ cups rice

4 cups broth

Salt and pepper

Peel the fava beans and parboil in lightly salted water to cover for a few minutes. Drain well. ✦ Reserve 1 tablespoon olive oil, and heat the remaining olive oil in a pan. Add the onion and sauté until golden; add the drained fava beans and after a few minutes, the tomato purée and cook for 10 minutes. ✦ Add pepper and the basil. Stir in the rice, then slowly add the broth, stirring to absorb. ✦ Toward the end stir in the reserved olive oil. Serve hot.

KNÖDEL CON LO SPECK IN BRODO | DUMPLINGS WITH SPECK IN BROTH

ALTO ADIGE

2 tbsp. butter

4 to 5 oz. speck, cubed

3 oz. prosciutto crudo, cubed

1 bunch flat-leaf parsley, chopped

1⅔ cups stale bread cubes

2 or 3 large eggs

1¼ cups milk

2 tbsp. all-purpose flour

Beef broth, for serving

Snipped chives, for serving

Salt and pepper

Heat the butter in a pan over low heat until melted. Sauté the speck and prosciutto. ✦ Remove from the heat and add salt and pepper, the parsley, and bread cubes. ✦ Beat the eggs with the milk and pour over the bread mixture. Add the flour and mix well. ✦ Let this mixture rest for 15 minutes then shape into *knödel* (dumplings) about 2 to 2½ inches diameter. ✦ Cook the *knödel* in lightly salted boiling water, reduce the heat, and simmer for 15 minutes. ✦ Drain. Serve in beef broth sprinkled with chives.

LAGNE CON FAGIOLI | PASTA WITH BEANS

LAZIO

1 cup all-purpose flour

1 lb. dried beans (white or colored), soaked overnight and drained

2 medium onions, chopped

2 garlic cloves, minced

1 tbsp. minced rosemary

1 tsp. minced thyme

1 tsp. *serpillo* minced (wild thyme)

4 oz. pork rind

2 oz. lard or prosciutto fat

Olive oil

1 tbsp. tomato purée, mixed with 1 tbsp. water

Salt

This is a dish typical of Sermoneta.

Use the flour to prepare a pasta dough as in the recipe on page 10, using 3 tablespoons water in place of the egg. Roll the dough out into a thin sheet (see note, page 212). ✦ Cut into irregular shapes (*maltagliati*) or wide tagliatelle. ✦ Combine the beans with 1 onion, 1 garlic clove, the rosemary, thyme, wild thyme, and a little pork rind in a pot, earthenware if possible. Add water to cover and bring to a simmer. Gently simmer until the beans are cooked. ✦ When this has cooked, pass half of it through a food mill and return all of it to the pot and cook to make the mixture thicker. ✦ Finely chop together the lard (or prosciutto fat) with the remaining onion and garlic clove. Heat 2 tablespoons olive oil and the lard mixture in a skillet. Sauté until the mixture begins to take on a little color. ✦ Add the tomato purée mixture. ✦ Cook until it forms a thick sauce and add to the bean broth. Let this simmer to blend the flavors. ✦ Cook the pasta in lightly salted boiling water. When half cooked drain almost all the water, then add the pasta and the remaining water to the bean mixture. ✦ Continue cooking for a few minutes until the pasta is cooked. Let it rest before serving. If desired, olive oil can be drizzled on before serving.

BAKED LASAGNE WITH BROTH

LASAGNE AL FORNO IN BRODO

PUGLIA

1 lb. egg pasta (see page 10), rolled into sheets (see note, page 212)

Meat from preparing broth below, chopped

¾ lb. tiny meatballs (see page 105)

1 cup grated pecorino

6 oz. prosciutto cotto, cubed

1 lb. fresh mozzarella, cubed

2 cups grated provolone

Several pinches grated nutmeg

Homemade broth (made with turkey, chicken, beef, or capon, see page 226)

This lasagne is typical of Francavilla Fontana.

Preheat the oven to 400°F. Cook the egg pasta in lightly salted boiling water until very al dente, then drain. In a baking pan, make a layer of pasta, then top it with some of the meat, meatballs, pecorino, prosciutto, mozzarella, provolone, and nutmeg. Repeat until the ingredients have been used up. ✦ Cover with a final layer of pasta and add a few tablespoons of the broth. ✦ Bake for 30 minutes, until the liquid is bubbling. Serve with the remaining warm broth on the side.

LETTUCE ROLLS

LATTUGHE RIPIENE

LIGURIA

¼ oz. dried mushrooms

8 small heads lettuce

2 tbsp. extra-virgin olive oil

7 oz. ground veal

4 oz. sweetbreads, membrane removed

4 oz. veal brains (optional), membrane removed

½ cup grated Parmigiano-Reggiano, plus more for serving

2 large eggs

Soft breadcrumbs, made from 1 roll soaked in broth and crumbled

1 tbsp. marjoram leaves

Beef broth (about 1 cup per person)

Toasted bread, for serving

Salt

Soak the dried mushrooms in warm water until soft, then drain. ✦ Wash the lettuce, blanch in boiling water until wilted (about 2 minutes), and drain. Cut out the hearts and set aside. ✦ Heat the olive oil in a pan, then sauté the veal until it takes on a little color. Simmer the sweetbreads and brains in water to cover. ✦ Mince together the lettuce hearts, veal, sweetbreads, brains (if using), and mushrooms. ✦ Add the Parmigiano-Reggiano. Reserve 1 egg white. Add the yolk and the other whole egg, the breadcrumbs, and marjoram to the lettuce mixture. Knead together until blended. ✦ Spread open the parboiled lettuce leaves. ✦ Beat the reserved egg white until frothy. Place 1 tablespoon of the stuffing in each leaf, fold the end of the leaf over the filling, then roll up to enclose the filling. Tie closed with kitchen twine and brush with the egg white. ✦ Bring the broth to a simmer, then add the lettuce rolls and cook for about 15 minutes. ✦ Remove the string and serve the lettuce with the broth and toasted bread. Sprinkle with Parmigiano-Reggiano at the table.

MACCARONI DI NATALE

CHRISTMAS MACARONI

LIGURIA

Capon broth (see page 226)
1 cardoon
1 tbsp. olive oil
1 tbsp. butter
1 carrot, chopped
1 medium onion, chopped
2 tbsp. chopped flat-leaf parsley
½ lb. tripe, cooked and cut into 1-inch pieces
½ cup white wine
10 oz. macaroni (see note)
4 oz. sausage (*Luganega*, if possible), crumbled
Grated Parmigiano-Reggiano

Any tubular pasta, large or small, is suitable for this Genoese dish. The traditional shape is a kind of very long, smooth penne—which absolutely must not be broken before being put in the cooking water. These macaroni are not easy to find in Genoa, except on Christmas Eve. They can be seen as the close heirs to the pasta shapes of the Middle Ages and Renaissance, which were often stuffed with meat, cheese, or vegetables, much like today's cannelloni. Traditionally, the type of tripe used here is *centopelle*, which is sometimes called "paunch" tripe.

While the broth is heating, boil the heart of the cardoon in lightly salted boiling water. Heat the olive oil and butter in a skillet until hot, add the carrot, onion, and parsley, and cook until the vegetables are soft. Add the tripe and cook for a few minutes; end the cooking by pouring in the wine. ✦ Skim any fat from the broth and add in the macaroni, cardoon, and tripe mixture. ✦ Just before removing the pan from the heat add the sausage. Serve with Parmigiano-Reggiano.

MACCO DI FAVE 1

FAVA BEAN PURÉE 1

FOR
6 PERSONS

CALABRIA

1 lb. dried fava beans
6 basil leaves
1 dried hot chili pepper (optional)
1 tbsp. tomato paste
Extra-virgin olive oil
Grated pecorino

This dish gets its name from the Latin *maccus*, meaning "crushed." In the rural areas of Calabria this exquisite dish is served as a soup over slices of toasted peasant-style bread.

Soak the fava beans overnight in lukewarm water to soften. ✦ Grind the basil to a paste in a mortar. Drain the beans and put them in a terra-cotta pot with cold water to cover by 2 inches; add salt, the basil, chili pepper, if desired, and tomato paste. ✦ Cook over medium heat, stirring often, until the beans soften and are reduced to a purée. Drizzle with olive oil and sprinkle with pecorino.

| # FAVA BEAN PURÉE 2

SICILIA

2 lbs. dried fava beans
1 frond wild fennel, chopped
¼ tsp. chili pepper flakes

This preparation is typical of Paternò and can be eaten as a sauce for pasta (preferably homemade) by diluting it with enough boiling water to create a thick soup. Season with olive oil on the plate. In the area of Sicilia's Madonie Mountains, ripe tomatoes are added to this dish; closer to Palermo there are those who use, in place of the fennel, 6 ounces peeled yellow winter squash and peeled tomatoes chopped into small pieces.

Soak the fava beans overnight to soften them. ✦ Remove any skins or threads. Put them in an earthenware pot, and cover with water by 2 inches. ✦ Bring to a boil, then reduce the heat to low and cook for at least 3 hours, until all the beans are reduced to a pulp in a brothy purée (you can speed up the process by mashing the beans with a wooden spoon against the side of the pot). ✦ Add the fennel and chili pepper flakes. ✦ When the fennel is soft the dish is ready.

MACH 1 | # CHESTNUT MASH 1

LOMBARDIA

1⅔ cups dried chestnuts
6 cups milk
1⅔ cups cooked rice (optional)
Salt

This dish is typical of the entire area above Milan. It gets its name from the Milanese dialect phrase "*a mach,*" meaning "without expense": in fact, this dish, cooked without the milk, was used as fodder for pigs.

Soak the chestnuts in water to cover by an inch for at least 12 hours. ✦ Drain them, then remove the skins. Boil them in a pot with water to cover by an inch with a pinch of salt. ✦ As soon as the chestnuts are cooked and have absorbed almost all the water, crush them roughly with a fork, pour in the milk, and return to a boil. ✦ Add the rice (if desired) and adjust for salt. Serve when the rice is tender and fully cooked.

MACH 2 | # CHESTNUT MASH 2

PIEMONTE

1 lb. dried chestnuts
CONTINUED

This *mach*, typical of Biella, is excellent the next day eaten cold or fried in a little butter.

Shell the chestnuts and break them up in a mortar. ✦ Boil them in a pot with lightly salted water to cover for

3 tbsp. all-purpose flour

2 cups milk

Salt

about 1 hour, by which time it should have formed a dense mush; mix the flour with the milk and add to the mush. Add salt to taste. ✦ Let the mixture simmer for about 20 minutes, stirring occasionally. ✦ This soup, typical of the winter season, is served either hot or warm.

MALAFANTI

WHITE BEAN PURÉE

VENETO

1¼ cups dried beans

5 or 6 pork ribs (with meat attached)

½ cup *lardo* (see page 2), cubed

¼ medium onion, chopped

1⅔ cups cornmeal

Salt

This dish can be varied by adding rice, potatoes, Savoy cabbage, or celery.

Soak the beans overnight to soften them. Drain. ✦ Add the beans, together with the pork ribs and a pinch of salt, to a pot. Add 6 cups water. Simmer over low heat for about 2 hours. ✦ Meanwhile, heat the *lardo* in a pan until it starts to give off its fat, then add the onion; when the onion turns a golden color, add it to the pot with the pork. ✦ Stir energetically, adding the cornmeal in a steady stream; let simmer slowly for 45 minutes, stirring occasionally. ✦ The result should be a creamy mixture. Serve hot.

MANFRIGÙL

MANFRIGÙL PASTA BALLS

EMILIA-ROMAGNA

1½ cups all-purpose flour, plus more as needed

2 large eggs

½ cup grated Parmigiano-Reggiano

1 tsp. grated lemon zest

Pinch grated nutmeg

2 tbsp. olive oil

1 medium onion, chopped

1 celery stalk, chopped

1 carrot, chopped

¼ cup tomato purée

2 lbs. spinach, finely chopped

4 cups beef broth

Salt

In the past, the place of the beef broth was taken by a broth made using pork bones or prosciutto, and the dish, typical of Forlì, was sometimes further enriched with leftovers of the *piadina* (see page 57) from the day before.

Use the flour and eggs to prepare pasta dough as directed on page 10, adding the Parmigiano-Reggiano, lemon zest, nutmeg, and salt with the eggs. ✦ Cut this dough into small pieces and roll them to obtain tiny pasta balls. ✦ Heat the olive oil in a pan and add the onion, celery, and carrot. Cook until slightly soft, then add the tomato purée and cook for 15 to 20 minutes. ✦ Add the spinach and cook gently for 30 minutes. ✦ Combine the broth and pasta balls in a large pot. As soon as they come to the surface with the first boil, add the spinach mixture. Serve immediately.

SOUP WITH BREAD DUMPLINGS 1

MARICONDA 1

EMILIA-ROMAGNA

4 heaping tbsp. all-purpose flour
4 large eggs
4 tbsp. grated Parmigiano-Reggiano
¼ lb. (1 stick) butter
Pinch grated nutmeg
Beef broth

Mix all the ingredients except the broth to form a dough, then knead well for 15 minutes, adding flour as needed, until the dough is no longer sticky. ✦ Form the dough into a ball, then let it rest for 30 minutes. ✦ Wrap the dough in a clean dish towel, tie it closed, and simmer in broth to cover for 2½ hours. ✦ Remove from the broth, cool, and cut into ½-inch cubes. ✦ Heat and serve in additional warm broth.

SOUP WITH BREAD DUMPLINGS 2

MARICONDA 2

LOMBARDIA

1 lb. stale bread
1 quart milk, or as needed
6 tbsp. butter
Grated Parmigiano-Reggiano
4 large eggs, beaten
Pinch grated nutmeg
6 cups beef broth
Salt and white pepper

This soup is typical of the Veneto-Lombardia area around Brescia and part of the area of Mantua.

Put the bread in a bowl, add milk to cover, and let stand for 30 minutes. ✦ Remove the bread and squeeze out the excess milk. ✦ Melt the butter in a pan and add the bread. Cook over low heat, stirring constantly, until all the milk has evaporated, while at the same time making sure the mixture remains soft. ✦ Remove from the heat and let cool. When the bread has cooled, put it in a bowl with 3 tablespoons cheese, the eggs, salt, pepper, and the nutmeg. ✦ Mix the ingredients to blend well. ✦ Cover with a dish towel and let stand for 30 to 40 minutes. ✦ Heat the broth to a boil in a pot. Meanwhile, use a spoon to form the bread mixture into nutmeg-size dumplings. Drop them into the broth; when they float to the surface, they are cooked. ✦ Pour the warm soup into a tureen and serve with more Parmigiano-Reggiano. ✦ Finely chopped leftover boiled chicken can be added to the mixture.

CHICKPEA AND BEAN SOUP

MESCIÜA

LIGURIA

2 cups each dried cannellini beans, dried chickpeas, and farro (spelt)

CONTINUED

Fresh pecorino can be used, but it can add an acidic taste to this vegetable soup typical of La Spezia.

In three different pots, soak the cannellini beans, chickpeas, and farro, adding a pinch of baking soda to the

Pinch baking soda
Olive oil
Freshly ground black pepper
Grated pecorino (optional)

beans to make them more tender. ✦ After at least 12 hours of soaking, cook the cannellini beans, chickpeas, and farro separately since their cooking times differ. ✦ When cooked, drain them and mix in a single bowl with a little of their cooking water. ✦ Drizzle with olive oil and sprinkle with pepper and pecorino, if using. Serve warm.

MINESTR' E COCCIULA

CLAM SOUP

SARDEGNA

2 lbs. clams (preferably those from the Cabras pond at Marceddì, above Oristano)
⅓ cup extra-virgin olive oil
1 garlic clove, minced
½ cup flat-leaf parsley leaves
Fregula (see note and page 117)

Fregula is obtained from hard wheat flour worked by hand into a dough and then treated to create small balls of pasta to which 2 tablespoons of white Nuragus wine is added. This soup is typical of Campidano di Cagliari.

Put the clams in clean seawater so they can purge themselves well. ✦ Heat the olive oil in a pot and sauté the minced garlic, taking care not to burn it. ✦ Pour in the cleaned clams and parsley, along with about 1 quart of water. ✦ Add the *fregula* and cook together. Serve warm in a serving bowl.

**MINESTRA
"DEL BATE 'L GRAN"**

TAGLIATELLE WITH CHICKEN LIVERS

FOR
6 PERSONS

PIEMONTE

¼ cup extra-virgin olive oil
1 medium onion, finely chopped
10 oz. chicken livers, cut in small pieces
2 tbsp. tomato purée
6 cups meat and chicken broth
10 oz. tagliatelline (narrow tagliatelle)
Grated Parmigiano-Reggiano
Salt

This dish is typical of Alba.

Heat the olive oil in a sauté pan and sauté the onion. Add the chicken livers and cook until browned, then add the tomato purée and salt. ✦ Add the broth, heat until boiling, then pour in the pasta and cook. ✦ Sprinkle with Parmigiano-Reggiano and serve hot.

| # MINESTRONE WITH BASIL

FRIULI-VENEZIA GIULIA

10 oz. young Swiss chard

4 potatoes, cut into chunks

1 small carrot, chopped

6 celery leaves

2 zucchini, chopped

1 small onion, chopped

1 garlic clove, minced

1 cup string beans,
cleaned and cut into pieces

½ cup fresh shelled beans

½ cup barley

½ cup peas

2 tbsp. olive oil

2 tbsp. butter

30 basil leaves, finely chopped
or pounded in a mortar

Salt and pepper

Cook the Swiss chard, potatoes, carrot, celery, zucchini, onion, and garlic in a pot of lightly salted boiling water until the potatoes are tender. Season generously with pepper. ✦ When the vegetables are cooked, put them in a blender and purée. Return to the pot and keep warm. ✦ Meanwhile, in four different pots cook the string beans, beans, barley, and peas. ✦ When these have finished cooking, add them to the blended vegetables. Stir in the olive oil, butter, and basil and serve.

| # WHITE CELERY SOUP

BASILICATA

1 lb. white celery
(*accio*; or celery hearts)

1 tbsp. extra-virgin olive oil

1 tbsp. lard

1 medium onion, chopped

4 oz. *soppressa* or sausage, sliced

6 cups beef broth

Slices of bread, toasted

4 large hard-boiled eggs,
sliced or quartered

Grated pecorino

Salt and pepper

Clean the celery and cut it in long (2-inch) pieces; boil in a pot of lightly salted water and drain. ✦ Heat the olive oil and lard in a sauté pan and cook the celery and onion; before removing it from the heat add the *soppressa* or sausage. ✦ Bring the broth to a boil in a pot and arrange toasted bread slices in bowls. ✦ Add to each bowl hard-boiled eggs, celery, and *soppressa* or sausage. ✦ Cover with broth and generously sprinkle with pecorino and a little black pepper.

RICE AND EGG SOUP

MINESTRA ALL'UOVO

LOMBARDIA

10 oz. chard leaves
1 oz. *lardo* (see page 2)
1 tsp. olive oil
1 tbsp. butter
1 leek, finely chopped
2½ cups rice
1 large egg, beaten
1 tbsp. Parmigiano-Reggiano
Salt and pepper

Remove the white ribs from the chard leaves. Finely chop them and wash them several times in cold water. ✦ In a pan with high sides, fry the *lardo* with the olive oil and butter. As soon as the butter turns golden, add 4 cups of water, chard, and leek. ✦ Cook for 15 minutes, then add the rice. ✦ Mix the egg with a little salt and pepper and the cheese. ✦ When the rice has finished cooking (about 20 minutes), add the egg mixture, beating again, and let it cook for no more than 1 minute. Serve hot.

BEAN SOUP WITH CHICORY AND FENNEL

MINESTRA ALLA MURESE

BASILICATA

1 lb. chicory (about 8 cups)
7 oz. wild fennel
1 handful fresh shelled beans
2 or 3 potatoes, sliced
2 oz. pecorino, cubed
1 tbsp. lard
1 tbsp. olive oil
1 tbsp. diced pork fat
1 garlic clove, minced
Toasted white bread
Salt

This dish is typical of Muro Lucano. Chard can be used in place of the chicory.

Boil the chicory and the tender parts of the fennel in a pot of salted water; cook the beans separately. ✦ In another pot place the potatoes and add water to cover. Stir in the cheese and a little salt. ✦ Boil, and when the potatoes are nearly cooked, add the chicory, fennel, and beans and complete the cooking. ✦ In a frying pan, heat the lard, olive oil, and pork fat, add the garlic, and cook until golden. Pour this mixture over the soup in serving plates. ✦ Top with the toasted bread.

SKATE SOUP WITH PASTA

MINESTRA WITH L'ARZILLA

LAZIO

1 skate wing, weighing 3 lbs.
(or a piece of skinless skate)
1 medium onion, cut into wedges
1 carrot, chopped
1 celery stalk, chopped
CONTINUED

This flavorful soup is a typical Christmas Eve dish.

Gently simmer the skate, onion, carrot, and celery in a pot of lightly salted water for about 2 hours; remove the cooked fish with a slotted spoon, and when it is cool enough to handle, remove and discard the cartilage and bones. Strain the broth and discard the vegetables. Chop the remaining flesh and return it to the broth. ✦ In a separate large pot, heat the olive oil and cook the garlic,

¼ cup extra-virgin olive oil

1 garlic clove

5 anchovy fillets

¼ cup flat-leaf parsley leaves

3 plum tomatoes, peeled and chopped

6 oz. spaghetti, broken into short pieces

Salt and pepper

anchovies, and parsley until the anchovies begin to break down. Add the broth and skate, tomatoes, and a little pepper. ✦ Let stand 10 minutes. Add the spaghetti, bring the broth to a boil, and cook until the pasta is al dente.

MINESTRA DEI MORTI | ## SOUP OF THE DEAD

LOMBARDIA

2 cups dried chickpeas

2 lbs. bone-in pork loin

2 tbsp. sage leaves

1 sprig rosemary

6 medium onions, sliced

2 large carrots, chopped

3 celery stalks, chopped

Grated Parmigiano-Reggiano

Pickled gherkins, peppers, and onions, for serving

Salt

This dish, practically confined to the city of Milan and its immediate environs, is eaten on November 2, All Souls' Day. It is probably derived from an ancient Roman dish. Typical of the area of Lomellina is the Minestra de Scisger, a chickpea soup made using beef bones, pork rind, leeks, and tomato sauce.

Soak the chickpeas in water for 48 hours, then boil them in a pot of water without salt for 3 hours. ✦ Cook the pork in a separate pot with water to cover (in the past a pig's head) with the sage, rosemary, onions, carrots, celery, and salt. ✦ When the meat is cooked, add the chickpeas, adjust for salt (the chickpeas were cooked without any), and let simmer for another 30 minutes. ✦ Eat the chickpeas with the soup as a first course, adding Parmigiano-Reggiano at the table; eat the meat as a second course, along with pickled gherkins, peppers, and onions.

MINESTRA DI CARDI | ## CARDOON SOUP

LAZIO

2 chicken livers

½ cup (8 tbsp.) butter

2 oz. ground veal

1 large egg

1 tbsp. grated Parmigiano-Reggiano, plus more for serving

Pinch grated nutmeg

2 lbs. cardoons (use only the very tender stalks), chopped

CONTINUED

This is a dish often eaten during Christmas in several areas of the Ciociaria zone south of Rome.

Rinse and dry the chicken livers and chop them. Melt 4 tablespoons of the butter in a pan and add the livers. Sauté them over medium heat just until lightly browned. ✦ Make small meatballs by mixing together the ground veal, egg, Parmigiano-Reggiano, salt, and the nutmeg. Melt 2 tablespoons butter in the same pan and cook the meatballs until browned. ✦ Simmer the vegetables separately in a pot with lightly salted water to cover until tender, then remove from the heat and let cool. Cut them

3 or 4 celery stalks, strings removed and chopped into sticks

1 small endive, chopped

Capon or chicken broth (see page 226)

Salt

into smaller pieces. ✦ Heat the remaining butter in another pan and cook the vegetables briefly, just so they will take on flavor and lose moisture. ✦ Skim any fat off the broth, heat it, and add the vegetables, meatballs, and chicken livers; cook and stir to blend. Serve very hot, sprinkled with Parmigiano-Reggiano.

CARDOON AND JERUSALEM ARTICHOKE SOUP

MINESTRA DI CARDI E TOPINAMBUR

FOR 6 PERSONS

PIEMONTE

1 large cardoon

6 Jerusalem artichokes

Juice of 1 lemon mixed with 2 tbsp. all-purpose flour

3 tbsp. olive oil

6 tbsp. butter

2 garlic cloves

6 cups chicken or capon broth (see page 226)

2 large eggs

2 large egg yolks

¼ cup grated Parmigiano-Reggiano, plus more for serving

3 tbsp. heavy cream

Sliced peasant-style bread, toasted and rubbed with a cut clove of garlic (optional)

Salt and pepper

Jerusalem artichokes are tubers; they are also found under the name sunchokes. They are not interchangeable with globe artichokes.

Carefully clean the cardoon, removing the harder outer ribs and any filaments. ✦ Peel the Jerusalem artichokes and cut into ¼-inch slices. ✦ Cut the core and ribs of the cardoon into relatively small pieces and put them in water acidulated with the lemon mixture. Put the artichoke slices in the same water. ✦ Bring water to boil in a pot and add the cardoons. After about 30 minutes, add the Jerusalem artichokes and boil them until al dente, about 2 minutes; drain. ✦ Heat the olive oil and butter in a separate pot and add the garlic, removing it from the pot and discarding when it takes on color. ✦ Add the cardoon and artichokes to the pan, stir well, then pour in the broth. ✦ Cook until the vegetables are cooked but not too mushy, about 15 minutes. Adjust for salt and pepper. ✦ Beat the eggs and yolks in a bowl with the Parmigiano-Reggiano and cream and pour over the soup, mixing carefully. ✦ Place a slice of bread in each bowl, then spoon the soup over. Serve immediately with more Parmigiano-Reggiano.

CHESTNUT AND RICE SOUP

MINESTRA DI CASTAGNE

VALLE D'AOSTA

3 cups milk

1¼ cups dried chestnuts

CONTINUED

This soup is typical of the Bassa Valle and Walser. It was typically eaten on the day of grain threshing. A variation involves the addition of two cloves to flavor the milk.

Combine the milk with 1 cup lightly salted water in a pot and bring to a boil. ✦ Add the chestnuts and cook for at

½ cup converted rice
(can use long-grain rice)
2 tbsp. butter
1 tbsp. lard
Salt

least 3 hours to reduce the liquid somewhat. ✦ Pour in the rice, stirring, and add the butter and lard. Continue to cook another 15 minutes, until the rice is cooked. Serve hot.

MINESTRA DI CASTAGNE
E PORRI

CHESTNUT AND LEEK SOUP

CAMPANIA

2 tbsp. butter
2 tbsp. extra-virgin olive oil
4 leeks, finely chopped
2 celery stalks, finely chopped
1 tbsp. finely chopped
flat-leaf parsley
1 garlic clove
1 lb. chestnuts
Broth or milk (as needed)
Bread, cut into hunks
Salt and pepper

This soup is typical of Benevento.

Heat 1 tablespoon each of the butter and oil in a pot; sauté the leeks, celery, parsley, and garlic clove until golden; remove and discard the garlic. ✦ Peel the chestnuts and cook them in a pot of boiling water for 10 minutes, then drain and skin them and add them to the cooked vegetables. Add 4 cups water and salt and pepper to taste. ✦ Boil until the chestnuts are completely cooked, then pass the entire mixture through a food mill or sieve. ✦ If the resulting mixture seems too thick, add water, broth, or, even better, milk, and return it to the heat until it boils. ✦ Meanwhile, heat the remaining oil and butter in a skillet and fry the bread until golden. Serve with the soup.

MINESTRA DI CECI

CHICKPEA SOUP

MARCHE

1 lb. dried chickpeas
1 tbsp. baking soda
2 tbsp. olive oil
4 tbsp. butter
1 medium onion, chopped
2 tbsp. chopped flat-leaf parsley
1 garlic clove, chopped
2 oz. prosciutto crudo, chopped
1 lb. plum tomatoes,
peeled and chopped
1 celery stalk, chopped
3 endive leaves, cut in pieces
10 oz. pork rib meat, cut in pieces
Slices of stale bread, toasted
½ cup grated pecorino
Salt and pepper

Place the chickpeas in a pot and add water to cover. Stir in the baking soda. Let soak for 1 day and 1 night. ✦ In a pot, heat the oil and butter and sauté the onion, parsley, garlic, and prosciutto. ✦ Drain the chickpeas and add them to the pot; add the tomatoes. Stir, then add 12 cups of cold water. ✦ Raise the heat and add the celery, endive, pork, salt, and pepper. ✦ Continue cooking over low heat for 3 hours, or until the water is reduced by half. Serve in bowls over slices of toasted bread. Sprinkle a spoonful of pecorino over each bowl.

MINESTRA DI CICERCHIE | CICERCHIA SOUP

UMBRIA

7 oz. *cicerchie* (see note)
3 tbsp. olive oil
1 garlic clove, chopped
2 tbsp. chopped flat-leaf parsley
A few mint leaves, torn by hand
6 oz. tomato purée
Salt and pepper

The *cicerchia* is a type of dried bean not unlike a chickpea. Today *cicerchie* show up quite often in restaurants, but they were once among the foods most commonly found on the tables of poor Umbrian peasants. This version of *cicerchia* soup, given an aromatic through the addition of mint, is typical of southern Umbria. Chickpeas can be used if necessary.

Soak the *cicerchie* in a pot of water for 24 hours. Drain and refill with water to cover. Simmer until soft (which will take roughly 2 hours). ✦ Heat the olive oil in a pot, add the garlic, parsley, and mint, and cook a few minutes, then add the tomato purée. Let this cook into a sauce. ✦ Add salt and pepper to taste and add the *cicerchie*; after 10 minutes, pour in enough warm water to make a soup and continue cooking for 10 minutes. Adjust for salt and serve.

MINESTRA DI ERBE DI PRATO | WILD HERB SOUP

VALLE D'AOSTA

10 oz. wild herbs (alpine yarrow, bladder campion, hops, sorrel)
2 baking potatoes, peeled and sliced
1 ¼ cups long-grain rice
2 tbsp. butter
Grated Parmigiano-Reggiano
Salt

This dish is typical of the lower valley and the Walser communities. Other wild herbs can be used, including nettles, silene, primrose, wild spinach, mallow, bistort, yellow goatsbeard, wild chervil, borage leaves, lemon balm, and pellitory.

Cook the herbs and sliced potatoes in a pot of lightly salted water to cover for 20 minutes. ✦ As they cook, crush the potatoes with a fork. ✦ Add the rice, butter, and salt. Stir and continue cooking for another 10 minutes. ✦ Serve hot with Parmigiano-Reggiano.

MINESTRA DI FAGIOLI 1 | BEAN SOUP 1

FRIULI-VENEZIA GIULIA

1 ⅔ cups dried cranberry beans
1 tbsp. olive oil
1 medium onion, chopped
Salt

Soak the beans in water for 12 hours; drain. ✦ Heat the olive oil in a pot and sauté the onion until it is well colored. Add the beans and pour in enough water to cover by 2 inches. Bring to a boil, then reduce the heat and simmer for about 3 hours. ✦ When this has cooked, salt to taste, then pass a small quantity of the beans through a food mill and return the resulting purée to the soup to thicken. ✦ Heat again before serving.

MINESTRA DI FAGIOLI 2 | BEAN SOUP 2

PIEMONTE

1 ¼ cups dried cranberry beans
1 carrot, chopped
1 potato, chopped
1 celery stalk, chopped
1 bay leaf
1 oz. *lardo* (see page 2)
1 garlic clove
1 medium onion
A few sage leaves
2 tbsp. chopped flat-leaf parsley
Salt and pepper

Soak the beans in cold water to cover by a few inches the night before. ✦ Drain, pour them into a pot with water to cover, and bring to a boil. Simmer until softened; drain the cooked beans and discard the cooking water. ✦ Cook the carrot, potato, and celery with the bay leaf in a pot with 8 cups of water until soft. ✦ Crush the cooked vegetables and put them back in the pot. ✦ Remove the bay leaf, add the beans, and adjust for salt and pepper. ✦ Melt the *lardo* over low heat and lightly sauté the garlic, onion, sage, and parsley. Add this mixture to the soup and continue cooking for about 20 minutes. Serve hot.

MINESTRA DI FAGIOLI 3 | BEAN SOUP 3

TOSCANA

2 cups dried cannellini beans, soaked overnight and drained
1 tsp. tomato paste
⅓ cup olive oil
3 garlic cloves
1 sprig rosemary
6 oz. short curled pasta (such as *gramigna*)
Salt and pepper

This dish, typical of Volterra, is good hot, at room temperature, or even cold. Traditional cooks say that the beans are best when cooked in rainwater.

Cook the beans in water to cover until tender and let them stand for 2 hours so they can soak well. ✦ Pass the beans through a food mill, diluting them with a cup or so of their cooking water. Add the tomato paste, salt, and pepper to the purée. Place the purée in a large pot and cook over low heat. ✦ Meanwhile, in a separate pot, heat the olive oil and cook the garlic and rosemary until they both turn light brown in color. ✦ Add the bean mixture to the pot and add the pasta, cooking it until al dente, about 15 minutes.

MINESTRA DI FAGIOLI 4 | BEAN SOUP 4

UMBRIA

1 lb. fresh beans, shelled
4 cups broth, plus more as needed
CONTINUED

Boil the beans in a pot with broth to cover until tender, about 25 minutes, then set aside. ✦ Finely chop together the celery, carrot, onion, and *lardo* (or prosciutto fat). Heat 2 tablespoons of the olive oil in a large pot. Add the celery mixture and lightly sauté; add salt and pepper to

132

1 celery stalk

1 carrot

1 small onion

1 oz. *lardo* (see page 2)
or prosciutto fat

3 tbsp. extra-virgin olive oil

1 tsp. tomato paste

Salt and pepper

taste and add the tomato paste. ✦ Cook for several minutes, then add the beans and their broth. ✦ Continue to simmer for a few minutes. Serve in bowls, adding a little olive oil and pepper at the table.

**MINESTRA DI FAGIOLI
ALLA LAMONESE**

LAMON BEAN SOUP

VENETO

1 lb. dried Lamon beans

7 oz. pork rind

⅔ cup lard or 4 oz. pancetta, minced

2 potatoes, cut into chunks

2 celery stalks, chopped

3 bay leaves

7 oz. homemade broad tagliatelle
(made without egg, see page 119)

Salt and pepper

Fagioli di Lamon are among the most prized beans in Italy. If unavailable, use cranberry beans.

Soak the beans in water to cover for at least 12 to 14 hours, changing the water at least once. ✦ Scald the pork rind in boiling water, scrape, cut into strips, and rinse. ✦ Put all the ingredients except the pork rind and tagliatelle in a pot, preferably earthenware. ✦ Cover with cold water by several inches and season with salt and pepper. Cook over very low heat for several hours (at least 3), until the beans are soft. ✦ Pass half of the beans through a food mill and return to the pot, return to a boil, and add the tagliatelle. ✦ When the tagliatelle is al dente, turn off the heat, add the pork rind, and let the soup rest for several minutes. ✦ The soup should be served hot or lukewarm (it is excellent reheated) with several grindings of black pepper, but without the addition of olive oil.

**MINESTRA DI FAGIOLI
COL MUSETTO**

BEAN SOUP
WITH MUSETTO

FRIULI-VENEZIA GIULIA

10 oz. dried beans

1 pork *musetto* (see note)

2 oz. *lardo* (see page 2)

1 medium onion

1 garlic clove

1 tbsp. chopped flat-leaf parsley

A few sage leaves

Musetto is sausage made in part using the pig's snout (muso). You may use cotechino.

Soak the beans in water for 24 hours, then drain them and cook in a pot with water to cover with a cleaned and washed *musetto*. ✦ In a pan heat the *lardo* and sauté the onion, garlic, parsley, and sage until fragrant; when the beans are half cooked, pour this mixture into the pot, mixing it in thoroughly. Cook until the beans are tender and serve hot.

BEAN SOUP WITH FERMENTED TURNIPS

FRIULI-VENEZIA GIULIA

10 oz. dried beans

2 oz. *lardo* (see page 2)

1 medium onion, chopped

1 lb. potatoes,
peeled and cut into chunks

¼ cup all-purpose flour

2 tbsp. butter

1½ cups cooked *brovada*
(see note, page 721)

Salt and pepper

Brovada is a vegetable soup common in Friuli-Venezia Giulia. Its primary ingredient is turnips, although sausages are sometimes added.

Soak the beans in water to cover by 1 inch for 24 hours, then drain. ✦ Heat the *lardo* in a pot and sauté the onion until golden; add the beans and potatoes. ✦ Stir in enough water for soup and cook until the beans are tender. Slowly stir in the flour. ✦ Add the butter, salt, and pepper and just before serving, the *brovada*.

BEAN SOUP WITH MUSHROOMS

BASILICATA

2 cups dried beans

1 lb. pork rind, cleaned and
parboiled a few minutes

2 tbsp. extra-virgin olive oil

2 medium onions, sliced

1 garlic clove

12 oz. cleaned mushrooms,
preferably the oyster mushrooms
known as *cardoncelli*

Slices of stale bread

Pinch chili pepper flakes

Salt

Soak the beans overnight. Drain them and cook with the pork rind in lightly salted water to cover until tender. ✦ Heat the olive oil in a sauté pan over low heat and sauté the onions and garlic. When the garlic becomes transparent, stir in the mushrooms. ✦ After a few minutes, add this to the beans and cook for 10 minutes. ✦ Put the slices of stale bread in bowls and pour the soup over. Add the chili pepper flakes and drizzle with olive oil.

FARRO SOUP 1

ABRUZZO

2½ cups farro (spelt)

2 tbsp. extra-virgin olive oil

7 oz. pancetta, diced

CONTINUED

This dish is typical of Pescara.

Grind the farro in a mortar to a coarse meal; clean and wash it. ✦ Half fill an earthenware pot with lightly salted water and put over high heat; when the water boils, reduce the heat to low and pour in the farro in a steady stream, stirring constantly, as when making polenta (see

1 medium onion, finely chopped
Grated pecorino (optional)
Salt and pepper

page 289). Cook for about 3 hours, resulting in a soup that is not too liquid. ◆ Heat the olive oil in a sauté pan and sauté the pancetta until it starts to take on a little color; add the onion and a pinch of pepper and cook until the onion and pancetta are golden. ◆ Pour the farro into warmed bowls; season with the pancetta mixture and, if desired, sprinkle with pecorino.

MINESTRA DI FARRO 2

FARRO SOUP 2

MARCHE

1⅔ cups farro (spelt)
2 oz. pork rind
2 tbsp. extra-virgin olive oil
3 oz. guanciale (cured pork jowl), diced
1 garlic clove, minced
1 sprig fresh marjoram
1 medium onion, chopped
10 oz. plum tomatoes, chopped
1 tbsp. chopped flat-leaf parsley
Several basil leaves
Grated pecorino, for serving
Salt and pepper

Soak the farro in warm water for about 8 hours; cook the pork rind in a pot with water to cover, reserving the cooking liquid. ◆ Heat the olive oil in a pot and cook the guanciale, garlic, and marjoram. ◆ Add the onion and let it cook; add the tomatoes, parsley, basil, salt, and pepper, and cook until the flavors have blended, about 30 minutes. ◆ Add the pork rind with its cooking water; cook for 20 minutes longer. ◆ Drain the farro and add it to the soup; cook for about 20 minutes. Serve with pecorino.

MINESTRA DI FARRO 3

FARRO SOUP 3

MOLISE

1¼ cups farro (spelt)
1 lb. fresh shelled beans
1 tbsp. extra-virgin olive oil, plus more for serving
2 garlic cloves, minced
Pinch chili pepper flakes
½ lb. plum tomatoes, peeled and chopped
Basil leaves, for serving (1 for each bowl)
Salt

Soak the farro for about 8 hours in a pot with water to cover and cook it in the same water for 40 minutes. ◆ Boil the beans in a separate pot with lightly salted water to cover until tender. ◆ Heat the olive oil in a pot and sauté the garlic and chili pepper flakes. ◆ When the garlic is golden, add the tomatoes and cook for about 15 minutes, then add a pinch of salt and the beans and farro with their cooking liquids. Let stand for 5 minutes. ◆ Add a drizzle of olive oil and a basil leaf to each bowl before serving.

FARRO SOUP 4

TOSCANA

1 ½ cups dried red beans, soaked overnight and drained

4 oz. prosciutto from near the bone, diced

¼ cup extra-virgin olive oil

1 medium onion, chopped

9 oz. plum tomatoes, peeled, seeded, and drained

1 carrot, chopped

1 potato, chopped

½ Savoy cabbage, outer leaves removed and chopped

1 celery stalk, chopped

2 cups farro (spelt)

Salt and pepper

Cook the beans with the prosciutto in a pot with water to cover by 1 inch; when the beans are cooked, pass half of them through a food mill and return to the broth. ✦ In another pan, heat the olive oil and sauté the onion. ✦ When it begins to color, add it to the bean broth, along with the tomatoes, carrot, potato, cabbage, and celery and cook for 20 minutes. ✦ Season with salt and pepper as needed and add the farro, continuing to cook for 40 minutes over low heat.

FARRO SOUP 5

UMBRIA

1 prosciutto bone

1 medium onion, chopped

1 celery stalk, chopped

1 carrot, chopped

2 ripe plum tomatoes, chopped

1 ¼ cups farro (spelt)

Grated pecorino, for serving

Salt

Soak the prosciutto bone overnight in lukewarm water. ✦ The next morning, rinse it, break it up, put the pieces in a pot with cold water, and boil for 15 minutes; discard the water and cover with new water. ✦ Add the onion, celery, carrot, and tomatoes and cook for about 3 hours. ✦ At this point, strain the broth into another pot (reserve the prosciutto pieces). Heat the broth, and when it boils, add the farro, pouring it in a steady stream and stirring constantly with a wooden spoon for the entire cooking period (about 20 minutes). ✦ Put in bowls and serve with prosciutto and pecorino.

WHITEBAIT SOUP

LIGURIA

¾ lb. zucchini, cut in small cubes

CONTINUED

In a pot, boil the zucchini in the fish broth. ✦ Remove any remaining algae or stones from the whitebait, but clean it with care so it will not lose its typical flavor. ✦ Mix the egg with the Parmigiano-Reggiano and marjo-

4 cups fish broth

7 oz. *gianchetti* (*bianchetti;* whitebait)

1 large egg, beaten

1 tbsp. grated Parmigiano-Reggiano

1 tsp. minced fresh marjoram

¼ lb. capellini

ram. ✦ When the zucchini is nearly cooked, add the capellini and whitebait. Stir in the egg and cook just until it coats the pasta. Serve hot.

MINESTRA DI GRANO

WHEAT BERRY SOUP

FOR 6 PERSONS

CALABRIA

2 cups wheat berries

1 prosciutto bone with meat

12 oz. cooked goat and pork meat, chopped

8 oz. Calabrian provolone, sliced

Salt

Preheat the oven to 400°F. Put the wheat berries in a bowl with enough water to cover to soften them. ✦ In an ovenproof earthenware pot, boil the prosciutto bone in water to cover for about 30 minutes. ✦ In a separate pot, cook the wheat berries in lightly salted boiling water to cover by 1 inch until soft, about 45 minutes. Drain the wheat berries and add to the pot with the prosciutto. ✦ Add the goat and pork meat, top with slices of provolone, add salt to taste, and bake until the cheese has melted and the flavors have blended, about 20 minutes.

MINESTRA DI GRANOTURCO, FAGIOLI, E PATATE

CORN, BEAN, AND POTATO SOUP

FOR 6 PERSONS

FRIULI-VENEZIA GIULIA

1⅔ cups fresh shelled beans

3 potatoes

1 plum tomato

1 fresh pig's trotter

3 tbsp. olive oil

2 ears corn

1 tbsp. lard

1 garlic clove

Salt and pepper

In a pot, boil the beans, potatoes, tomato, trotter, and 2 tablespoons olive oil. ✦ Cut the kernels off the ears of corn and boil them in a separate pot until the outer skin becomes soft. ✦ Pass half of the beans and corn through a food mill, return to the pot, and crush the potatoes with a fork. ✦ In another pot, heat the remaining olive oil and the lard, add the garlic, and sauté until golden. Add to the soup, season with salt and pepper, and serve.

GOULASH SOUP

ALTO ADIGE

6 oz. potatoes, peeled and cubed
2 tbsp. olive oil or butter
1 large onion, finely chopped
10 oz. beef, cubed
1 tbsp. sweet paprika
Pinch caraway seeds
2 tbsp. tomato paste
¼ cup dry white wine
1 sprig fresh thyme
1 sprig fresh marjoram
1 bay leaf
1 garlic clove, slivered
2 tbsp. all-purpose flour
8 cups broth
Salt and pepper

This soup can be varied according to taste by adding some hot paprika.

Boil the potatoes in a pot with lightly salted water to cover until tender. Drain and set aside. ✦ Heat the olive oil or butter in a pot and sauté the onion until translucent. Add the beef, paprika, caraway seeds, and tomato paste; season with salt and pepper and cook well. ✦ Pour in the wine and a little water, and add the thyme, marjoram, bay leaf, and garlic and continue cooking. ✦ Add the flour, broth, and potatoes, stir to cook the raw taste out of the flour, and serve.

LENTIL SOUP

PIEMONTE

1 ¼ cups dried lentils
⅔ cup lard
1 carrot, chopped
1 medium onion, chopped
1 celery stalk, chopped
1 garlic clove
1 ¼ cups rice
Grated Parmigiano-Reggiano
Salt and pepper

Soak the lentils in water to cover overnight, then drain. ✦ Heat the lard in a soup pot until melted, then add the carrot, onion, celery, and garlic and cook until softened; add 8 cups water, a little salt, and lentils. ✦ Cook for about 2 hours. ✦ Add the rice and continue cooking until it is tender. Add Parmigiano-Reggiano and pepper to taste before serving.

MONTASIO CHEESE SOUP

FRIULI-VENEZIA GIULIA

4 tbsp. butter
1 small onion, minced
CONTINUED

Fresh Montasio cheese is aged 9 months or fewer; aged Montasio is aged more than a year.

Heat 2 tablespoons of the butter in a pot over low heat until melted. Add the onion and sauté until translucent, then slowly add the flour and cook it for 5 minutes.

½ cup all-purpose flour
1½ cups milk
½ cup broth
⅓ cup grated fresh Montasio
⅓ cup grated aged Montasio
½ cup dry white wine
Pinch grated nutmeg
1 tsp. grated lemon zest
1 garlic clove, finely chopped
4 oz. black bread
Salt and pepper

Whisk in the milk and broth and bring to a boil. ✦ Reduce the heat to a simmer, add the cheeses, wine, salt, pepper, the nutmeg, lemon zest, and garlic. ✦ Cook for another 10 minutes. ✦ Pass through a food mill. Melt the remaining butter in another pan, add the bread, and sauté until crisp. Serve with the soup.

MINESTRA DI NOCI | WALNUT SOUP

PIEMONTE

2 cups walnut halves
½ cup milk
4 cups beef broth
½ cup heavy cream
Sliced bread
Butter
Salt and pepper

Blanch the walnut halves in lightly salted water; dry them on a cloth and carefully rub off the skins. ✦ Grind the walnuts, then stir in the milk to obtain a dense, creamy mixture. ✦ Heat the beef broth in a large pot, and add the nut mixture and cream; adjust for salt and pepper and boil for several minutes. ✦ Serve hot with buttered bread.

MINESTRA DI ORZO 1 | BARLEY SOUP 1

VALLE D'AOSTA

¼ cup (4 tbsp.) butter
1 leek, cut in thin strips
1 medium onion, cut in thin strips
3 potatoes, peeled and cubed
1 carrot, grated
½ cup pearl barley
1 bay leaf in winter or 1 sprig *parrietta* (thyme) in summer

This soup's name in dialect is *Seupa de Pelon—pelon* meaning "pestle"—probably in reference to the fact that in the past, barley was ground with a mortar and pestle to facilitate its cooking. It is typical of the valley of the Colle del Gran San Bernardo.

Heat the butter in a saucepan over low heat until melted. Add the leek and onion and cook until the leek begins to soften. ✦ Add the potatoes and carrot and cook for about 10 minutes, then cover with boiling water. ✦ When the mixture returns to a boil, add the barley and bay leaf or thyme. Let cook, uncovered, over medium heat for 1 hour, until the barley is tender.

BARLEY SOUP 2

ALTO ADIGE

1 ¼ cups pearl barley
10 cups broth
1 carrot, chopped
1 celery stalk, chopped
2 potatoes, peeled and cubed
1 tbsp. chopped flat-leaf parsley
1 sage leaf
1 small sprig rosemary
1 sprig fresh marjoram
1 tbsp. all-purpose flour
1 smoked pork shank or loin
(about ½ lb.), cubed
Salt and pepper

In former times, when animal fats were not plentiful, pork was often boiled together with barley. The soup can be made even more flavorful by cooking the onion and vegetables in olive oil before adding them to the soup.

Rinse the barley and put it in a pot. Add the broth, lightly salt it, and bring to a boil. Reduce the heat and cook for 2 hours; after the first hour of cooking, add the vegetables, herbs, flour, and pork. ✦ Before serving, add salt and pepper to taste.

BARLEY SOUP 3

TRENTINO

1 ¼ cups pearl barley
2 tbsp. olive oil
1 leek, chopped
1 tbsp. all-purpose flour
2 cups broth
1 tbsp. chopped flat-leaf parsley
1 celery stalk, chopped
1 carrot, chopped
1 potato, peeled and cubed
½ cup milk
Grated Parmigiano-Reggiano

Rinse the barley in cold water and drain. ✦ Heat the olive oil in a pot, add the leek, and sauté until it softens. Add the flour, mixing for a few seconds, then add 6 cups cold water, the barley, broth, parsley, celery, carrot, and potato. ✦ Cook over low heat for about 2 hours; after the first 30 minutes, add the milk. ✦ Add a little cheese just before serving.

BARLEY SOUP 4

LOMBARDIA

Variously called *urgiàda*, *duméga*, or *orzàda*, barley soups like this were made in the past by farmers well off enough to raise and butcher pigs. Those parts of the animal that were not used in the preparation of salame (ears, snout, tail,

2½ cups pearl barley

1 lb. pork rind or other pork parts leftover after carving

3 garlic cloves

¼ cup (4 tbsp.) butter

1¼ cups grated Parmigiano-Reggiano

Salt

bones, and some of the rinds) were thrown into a large pot and boiled for an entire day with the addition of smooth barley. Given the notable quantity of such scraps, this made for quite a large amount of soup, which was then consumed over a period of many days. Friends and neighbors were invited over for the first such meal, which took place on the day of the slaughter itself. The soup was then consumed on a daily basis for twenty or more days. After each day, the remaining soup was put in vats; the amount needed the next day was then drawn from these vats, remixed (each time the soup cooled the fat rose to the surface), and boiled. Despite the monotony of this process, the soup undoubtedly became more flavorful each time it was reheated.

Soak the barley in water to cover for 12 hours, then drain. ✦ Partially cook the pork rind or other pork parts in a pot with water to cover. Drain. ✦ Rub the bottom of a pot with 1 of the garlic cloves, cut in half, and add enough water for soup, at least 4 cups. Add the butter and pork cut in small pieces. Add salt and bring to a boil. ✦ Mince the remaining garlic, add to the soup, and let simmer for a few minutes. ✦ Add the barley in a thin stream, stirring, and cook for 45 minutes. Serve with the cheese sprinkled on top.

MINESTRA DI ORZO 5 | ## BARLEY SOUP 5

FOR 6 PERSONS

VENETO

1 carrot, chopped

1 celery stalk, chopped

1 medium onion, finely chopped

1 cup pearl barley

1 garlic clove

2 bay leaves

1 piece smoked pork (about ¼ lb.)

4 large potatoes

1 cup milk

Instead of smoked pork for this soup typical of the Veneto, one can use pork rind, lard, a piece of bacon, a pig's trotter, or a piece of mutton. This soup tends to stick and thus requires frequent stirring while it cooks.

Combine all the ingredients except the potatoes and milk in a pot and cook for 2½ hours. ✦ Add the potatoes; after 1 hour of cooking crush them with a fork and add the milk; return to a boil and serve.

BARLEY AND VEGETABLE SOUP

MINESTRA DI ORZO E VERDURE

FRIULI-VENEZIA GIULIA

6 to 7 tbsp. barley
2 carrots, chopped
1 celery stalk, chopped
A few sage leaves
1 garlic clove
1 bay leaf
6 oz. smoked pancetta, minced
4 potatoes, peeled and sliced
¼ cup (4 tbsp.) butter
1 tbsp. minced flat-leaf parsley
Salt and pepper

Rinse the barley and put it in a pot with the carrots, celery, sage, garlic, bay leaf, and pancetta. Add water to cover all; cook slowly for 30 minutes, then add the potatoes. ✦ When the potatoes are tender, add the butter and parsley. Season with salt and pepper and serve.

BREAD SOUP

MINESTRA DI PANE

LOMBARDIA

1 tbsp. butter, melted
2 large egg yolks
Pinch grated nutmeg
½ cup breadcrumbs, or as needed
6 cups broth
Grated Parmigiano-Reggiano
Salt

This dish from the Lake Como area shows the clear influence of Austro-Hungarian cooking, most of all the celebrated *knödel*.

Mix the butter, egg yolks, a pinch of salt, the nutmeg, and enough breadcrumbs to obtain a smooth, compact paste. ✦ Bring the broth to a boil in a pot. Form the breadcrumb mixture into walnut-size balls and simmer in the broth for 10 minutes. Serve the soup sprinkled with Parmigiano-Reggiano.

SOUP WITH SHAVED PASTA 1

MINESTRA DI PASTA RASA

LOMBARDIA

3 large eggs, beaten
3 tbsp. breadcrumbs
6 tbsp. grated Parmigiano-Reggiano, plus more for serving
Pinch grated nutmeg
2 quarts broth
1 cup bean purée (see page 131)
Salt

Combine the eggs, breadcrumbs, cheese, and nutmeg and knead to form a firm dough; season with salt. ✦ Let stand for 30 minutes, then grate the mixture, letting the "shaved pasta" fall onto a cloth to dry. ✦ Add the broth to the bean purée to create a broth. Bring this to a boil and cook the grated pasta in it quickly, stirring carefully. Pour into bowls and serve with cheese.

SOUP WITH SHAVED PASTA 2

MINESTRA DI PASTA TRIDA

LOMBARDIA

1⅔ cups all-purpose flour, plus more as needed

3 large eggs

1 tbsp. grated Parmigiano-Reggiano, plus more for serving

Pinch grated nutmeg

1 medium onion, chopped

1 carrot, chopped

1 celery stalk, chopped

Salt and white pepper

At Ferrara, this soup is called *gratin*.

This is very similar to *pasta rasa* (see page 142) and is prepared following the same procedure. Use the flour and eggs to prepare a pasta dough as directed on page 10, adding the cheese and nutmeg with the eggs (the dough will be very firm). Grate the mixture and let dry on a clean kitchen towel. ✦ Boil the onion, carrot, and celery in a pot with lightly salted water to cover until the vegetables are nearly dissolving. Strain the broth, return it to the pot, and bring it to a boil. Then cook the grated pasta for a few minutes in the broth. ✦ Serve in a tureen after letting it rest for a few minutes so the soup can thicken slightly. Add more cheese at the table.

POTATO AND PASTA SOUP

MINESTRA DI PATATE ALLO ZAFFERANO

ABRUZZO

FOR 6 PERSONS

½ cup olive oil

½ medium onion, chopped

1 carrot, chopped

1 celery stalk, chopped

A few threads of saffron (if possible from L'Aquila)

1 lb. potatoes

10 oz. *cannarozzetti* or broken spaghetti

Salt

This soup, a typical Christmas dish of L'Aquila, is good even without the pasta, in which case you should use less water.

Heat the olive oil in a pot and lightly sauté the onion, carrot, and celery. ✦ Remove from the heat; as soon as it cools, stir in the saffron. Let stand. ✦ Peel and boil the potatoes in a pot of salted water until tender, then drain and cut into small pieces. ✦ Add the potatoes to the vegetables, along with 8 cups of lightly salted water. Bring to a boil and add the pasta. ✦ When the pasta is cooked, let stand for a few minutes off the heat and serve.

PEA SOUP

MINESTRA DI PISELLI

FRIULI-VENEZIA GIULIA

FOR 6 PERSONS

1½ cups dried peas

1 potato, cut into chunks

CONTINUED

Cragno sausages, typical of Trieste, have a higher fat content than most sausages, and are delicious.

Soak the peas in a pot with water to cover for 2 hours, then cook them in the same water with the potato and sausages until the peas are very bright green. ✦ Heat the olive oil in a sauté pan and add the flour. Cook until the

143

8 oz. sausages (ideally the local "skull" sausages called "*luganighe di cragno*"), crumbled

3 tbsp. olive oil

5 tbsp. all-purpose flour

1 tbsp. minced flat-leaf parsley

Bread slices

Butter

Salt and pepper

paste is golden, then add it to the soup, adding salt and pepper. ✦ Cook until the peas form a purée. If the peas do not cook down to become a mush, pass the entire mixture through a food mill. Add the parsley. ✦ Serve with bread toasted with butter.

MINESTRA DI PORRI E CASTAGNE

LEEK AND CHESTNUT SOUP

PIEMONTE

½ lb. fresh chestnuts

3 tbsp. butter

1 lb. leeks, sliced

1 lb. potatoes, peeled and sliced

1 cup beer

Beef broth

1 ¼ cups heavy cream

2 large egg yolks

Bread slices

Clean and peel the chestnuts. Melt the butter in a pot and sauté the chestnuts, leeks, and potatoes. ✦ Pour in the beer, let it evaporate, add broth to cover by 1 inch, and continue cooking. ✦ Pass the mixture through a food mill, reheat, and whisk in the cream and egg yolks. Heat, stirring until thickened, but do not let the mixture boil. Serve with bread.

✦ **LOCAL TRADITION** ✦

MINESTRA DI RISO

Typical of the area of Monferrato in the Asti wine zone of Piedmont, this rustic soup calls for two plants that grow wild on the local hillsides: *rônséle,* delicate plants of the poppy family, and *luvertìn,* which are related to the wild hops that grow along riverbanks in spring. To prepare the soup, a one-pound veal lung would be boiled in water along with bay leaf, sage, thyme, and rosemary for about half an hour before being diced (the bronchia and bronchioles being carefully removed) and cooked in meat broth for two more hours, or until tender. The *rônséle* and *luvertìn* are then sautéed in olive oil and butter, minced, and added to the broth along with rice and parsley. The final dish would be seasoned with salt and pepper and served hot with raw olive oil and grated Parmigiano-Reggiano.

MINESTRA DI RISO | RICE SOUP

VALLE D'AOSTA

6 cups vegetable broth
3 turnips
4 tbsp. butter
1½ cups rice
Salt

Bring the broth to a boil in a pot. Meanwhile, rinse and peel the turnips; cut into thin slices. ✦ In a saucepan, melt the butter and add the turnips; stir for 5 minutes, then add the rice. ✦ Stir for 2 minutes, slowly adding the boiling vegetable broth and continue cooking for at least another 15 to 20 minutes. Add salt and serve hot.

MINESTRA DI RISO CON LA ZUCCA | RICE SOUP WITH SQUASH

PIEMONTE

1 medium potato, peeld and cut into chunks
3 medium winter squash, peeled and cut into chunks
3 cups milk
1¼ cups rice
Grated Parmigiano-Reggiano
Salt

Boil the potato and squash in a pot with lightly salted water to cover until soft. Drain, reserving the cooking liquid. Purée the potato and squash in a blender, adding cooking liquid as needed. ✦ Transfer to a saucepan, add the milk, and bring to a boil. ✦ Pour in the rice and cook at a simmer for another 20 minutes. Add salt and sprinkle with Parmigiano-Reggiano before serving.

MINESTRA DI RISO E PATATE 1 | RICE AND POTATO SOUP 1

VENETO

3 medium white-skinned potatoes
3 tbsp. butter
1 tbsp. olive oil
1 large onion, chopped
1 celery stalk, chopped
6 cups beef or chicken broth
1½ cups *Vialone Nano* rice, cooked
1 tbsp. chopped flat-leaf parsley
Grated Parmigiano-Reggiano (optional)
Salt and pepper

Peel the potatoes and boil them in a pot with water to cover until they are half cooked. ✦ Drain and cut into thin slices. ✦ Heat the butter and oil in a sauté pan and add the onion and celery; add the potatoes and cook for 30 minutes. ✦ In a pot, bring the broth to a boil. Pour in the mixture and cook for another 15 minutes. ✦ Pour in the rice and parsley and salt and pepper. Serve hot. If desired, sprinkle with Parmigiano-Reggiano.

MINESTRA DI RISO ALLA VALDOSTANA

This rustic rice soup is typical of Walser cooking in the Valle d'Aosta and combines turnips, which have medieval origins in the region, with rice brought to the Lys River valley from the Biella area of Piedmont, in a preparation reminiscent of risotto. In a saucepan, turnips and butter would be lightly cooked, then mixed with rice, and hot vegetable broth would then slowly be mixed in.

MINESTRA DI RISO E PATATE 2	RICE AND POTATO SOUP 2

FRIULI-VENEZIA GIULIA

¼ cup olive oil

1 medium onion, chopped

4 potatoes, peeled and cut into large pieces

2 cups broth

⅔ cup rice, cooked

Chopped flat-leaf parsley

Grated aged Montasio

Pepper

Heat the olive oil in a sauté pan over low heat and cook the onion. Add the potatoes and cook until golden. ✦ When the potatoes are almost completely cooked, add the broth, and when it comes to a boil, add the rice. ✦ Sprinkle with parsley, pepper, and Montasio, and serve.

MINESTRA DI SONDALO

To make this soup from Lombardia, ripe bunches of elderberries were crushed and passed through a strainer. The juice would then be boiled down, while in another pan a little milk would be whisked with flour to make a paste; more milk would then be added to the paste and warmed through but not boiled. The reduced elderberry juice would then be mixed into the milk mixture and seasoned with salt, and finally a quantity of butter and sugar were added to reach the desired level of sweetness and thickness.

RICE AND FRANKFURTER SOUP

MINESTRA
DI RISO E WÜRSTEL

TRENTINO

1 tbsp. butter
1 medium onion, chopped
1 yellow carrot, chopped
1 celery stalk, white part only, sliced
1 leek, chopped
1 potato, chopped
2 tbsp. chopped flat-leaf parsley
1 ¼ cups rice
Beef broth
2 frankfurters,
cut in quarter-inch rounds

Heat the butter in a saucepan until melted, and add the vegetables, parsley, and rice; stir to coat the rice. Add broth to cover and cook for about 20 minutes. ✦ At this point, when the rice is almost completely cooked, add the frankfurters. Cook until the rice is tender.

ESCAROLE SOUP

MINESTRA DI SCAROLA

LAZIO

2 lbs. escarole
2 tbsp. olive oil (or butter)
1 garlic clove
Broth (or water)
1 large egg, beaten
2 tbsp. grated Parmigiano-Reggiano
Slices of bread toasted in butter
or olive oil

This dish is typical of the Ciociara area and is eaten at room temperature in the summer.

Rinse the escarole in cold water. ✦ Drain it and cut it in pieces. Heat the olive oil or butter in a saucepan and add the garlic. When it is golden, add the endive, then add broth or water to cover and cook until soft. ✦ When it has cooked, add the egg and Parmigiano-Reggiano. Stir it well and remove from the heat. ✦ Place a slice of bread in each bowl and spoon the soup over.

TAGLIATELLE AND CHESTNUT SOUP

MINESTRA DI TAGLIATELLE
E CASTAGNE

PIEMONTE

7 oz. sweet, dried chestnuts
¼ cup olive oil
3 tbsp. butter
1 medium onion, chopped
10 oz. fresh tagliatelle (see page 397)
Grated Parmigiano-Reggiano
Salt

Soak the dried chestnuts overnight in lightly salted water to cover. ✦ Rinse them in cold water and carefully shell them. ✦ Heat the oil and butter in a sauté pan and sauté the onion until golden. ✦ Boil the chestnuts in a pot with lightly salted water to cover by 2 inches. When they are soft, add the tagliatelle and onion; stir with a wooden spoon. ✦ Simmer until the tagliatelle is cooked to al dente. ✦ Serve the soup in bowls, preferably brown earthenware. Sprinkle with cheese at the table.

TENCH AND TAGLIOLINI SOUP 1

LAZIO

1 tench, weighing about 1 lb. (or several small tench) (can use carp if tench is unavailable), cleaned

1 carrot, chopped

1 celery stalk, chopped

1 medium onion, chopped

1 bay leaf

2 tbsp. extra-virgin olive oil

1 garlic clove

3 salt-cured anchovies, desalted

2 tbsp. chopped flat-leaf parsley

1 dried hot chili pepper, crumbled

2 or 3 tbsp. tomato purée

1 tbsp. tomato paste

½ cup white wine (*Est! Est!! Est!!!*, see note, or Orvieto)

½ lb. egg tagliolini (best if homemade)

Est! Est!! Est!!! is a semisweet white wine created in Montefiascone, near the Lago di Bolsena, from trebbiano and malvasia grapes. Legend says that it was named in the 1100s when a German bishop named Fugger who needed to go to Rome for his ordination sent a servant ahead to mark the inns serving the best wines with "Est!" (standing for *vinum est bonum*—the wine is good) on their doors in chalk. When the servant reached Montefiascone, he liked the wine there so much that he wrote "Est! Est!! Est!!!" on the doors. The bishop stayed in Montefiascone, preferring to enjoy the wine. Once a year he is celebrated in a ceremony during which wine is poured on his grave.

Add the fish to a pot with the vegetables and bay leaf, and water to cover. Simmer until the fish is opaque. Strain and reserve the broth, discarding the vegetables and saving the fish to eat separately. ✦ In a separate pot heat the olive oil and cook the garlic until golden. Add the anchovies, parsley, chili pepper, then add the reserved broth, tomato purée, tomato paste, and wine. ✦ Let this soup cook over low heat for 30 minutes, then bring it to a boil and add the tagliolini. The soup is finished when the pasta is al dente.

TENCH AND TAGLIOLINI SOUP 2

UMBRIA

2 tbsp. extra-virgin olive oil

1 medium onion, finely chopped

1 celery stalk, finely chopped

1 sprig rosemary, finely chopped

1 garlic clove, finely chopped

1 tench, weighing about 1½ lbs., cleaned

2 small plum tomatoes, peeled and chopped

Salt and pepper

For the pasta:

1 cup all-purpose flour, plus more as needed

2 large eggs

Heat the olive oil in a soup pot until hot and sauté the onion, celery, rosemary, and garlic. ✦ Add the whole tench and cook for 15 minutes, then add the tomatoes. ✦ Add warm water to cover and season with salt and pepper. ✦ Remove the tench and cut it in large pieces, discarding the head. ✦ Boil the broth for 10 minutes more, then pass it through a sieve. Return it to the pot and bring to a boil. ✦ Use the flour and eggs to prepare a pasta dough as in the recipe on page 10. Roll out a sheet of dough (see note, page 212) and cut it to form tagliolini. ✦ Add them to the broth, cook for 2 minutes, and serve.

MINESTRA DI TRIPPE ALLA TRENTINA | TRIPE SOUP

TRENTINO

1 lb. tripe
⅓ cup olive oil
3 tbsp. butter
2 medium onions, chopped
2 carrots, chopped
2 celery stalks, chopped
2 garlic cloves
Broth
3 tbsp. breadcrumbs
1 potato, diced
Grated Parmigiano-Reggiano
Salt and pepper

Boil the tripe in a pot of water, for 2 hours if veal and 4 hours if beef, then drain and cut in strips. ✦ Heat the oil and butter in a soup pot and sauté the onions, carrots, celery, and garlic until soft. ✦ Add the tripe, carefully stirring for about 10 minutes. ✦ Add broth to cover and season with salt and pepper. Sprinkle with breadcrumbs. Add the potato and simmer over low heat until all the ingredients are cooked. ✦ Just before serving, add the cheese.

MINESTRA DI VERZE E COTENNE | CABBAGE AND PORK-RIND SOUP

PIEMONTE

1½ lbs. pork rind
1 Savoy cabbage
2 cups meat broth
Toasted bread
Salt and pepper

Sear the pork rind in a skillet, scrape off any remaining soft fat, and cut into strips about 1 inch thick. ✦ Cut away the outer leaves of the cabbage and slice in long strips. ✦ Bring about 6 cups of water to a boil in a soup pot, then add salt and the broth, then add the pork rind and cabbage. ✦ Cook, covered, for about 3 hours. Serve hot with pepper and toasted bread.

MINESTRA DI VIRZI E RISI | CABBAGE AND RICE SOUP

CAMPANIA

2 tbsp. extra-virgin olive oil
1 small onion, finely chopped
4 oz. pancetta, minced
1 cabbage, outer leaves removed
1⅔ cups rice
Broth, if needed
⅔ cup grated Parmigiano-Reggiano
Salt

To make this soup more flavorful, it is a popular custom to add (before the cooked rice goes in) hunks of cheese rinds, which melt while it cooks and give the vegetables a creaminess that bonds wonderfully with the rice.

Heat the olive oil in a pot over low heat. Add the onion and pancetta and sauté slowly so the fat renders without burning. ✦ Rinse the cabbage, cut it in long strips, and add to the onion and pancetta. Add salt and cover the pot; cook, stirring occasionally, until the cabbage has wilted and is a golden color. ✦ Meanwhile, boil the rice in a separate pot to al dente, drain, and add it to the cabbage. Stir well and complete the cooking, adding a cup or so of broth if necessary. ✦ Pour into a tureen, sprinkle with Parmigiano-Reggiano, and serve.

SQUASH SOUP

MINESTRA DI ZUCCA

FRIULI-VENEZIA GIULIA

1 butternut squash, peeled and cut in large slices

1 tbsp. olive oil

1 tbsp. butter

2 tbsp. all-purpose flour

1 garlic clove, minced

1 cup ricotta

1 tbsp. grated Parmigiano-Reggiano

Pinch ground cinnamon

Pepper

This soup is typical of the Pedemontana Maniaghese.

Boil the pieces of squash in a pot with water to cover until tender, then drain and squeeze dry, reserving the cooking water. ✦ Heat the oil and butter in a pot; whisk in the flour and garlic and stir to make a paste. ✦ Add the squash, ricotta, Parmigiano-Reggiano, pepper, and cinnamon. Stir in enough of the squash cooking water to make a thick, soupy consistency. Bring to a boil. Serve hot.

SOUP WITH SALT CHEESE

MINESTRA E MERCA

SARDEGNA

10 oz. potatoes, peeled and diced

10 oz. cabbage, outer leaves removed and chopped

2 ripe plum tomatoes

A few basil leaves

7 oz. salted sheep's-milk cheese (ricotta salata, *merca, quagliato,* salted *caxagedu,* salted *frue*), rinsed 1 hour before use

½ cup olive oil

1 tbsp. finely chopped *lardo* (see page 2)

Fregula (see page 117)

Put the potatoes and cabbage in a pot, add water to cover, and bring to a boil. As soon as the water boils, add the tomatoes, then remove them almost immediately. Peel them, crush them, and put them back in the pot. Add the basil. ✦ Crush the cheese well with a fork. ✦ Heat the olive oil in a pan. Add the *lardo* and cook slowly until golden. ✦ Check the potatoes and cabbage; when they are almost cooked, add the *fregula* and *lardo* and complete the cooking. ✦ Turn off the heat and add the cheese and stir until it melts completely. Let stand for 20 minutes before serving.

WEDDING SOUP 1

CALABRIA

1⅔ cups dried fava beans

½ medium onion, chopped

2 tbsp. olive oil

4 oz. guanciale (cured pork jowl), chopped

3 cups beef broth

2 lbs. chicory

2 bunches wild fennel

Pinch chili pepper flakes

Peasant-style bread, cubed and fried in olive oil

Salt

The popular English name for this soup is a mistranslation. The only things "married" here are the vegetables and meat, which get along perfectly.

Soak the fava beans overnight in a pot with water to cover. ✦ Drain, add fresh water to cover, and cook until tender. Drain and put them through a food mill. ✦ In a pan, sauté the onion in the olive oil with the guanciale. Add a few tablespoons of the broth. ✦ Meanwhile, clean the chicory and fennel and boil them in a pot with lightly salted water to cover; drain and add to the fava mixture; stir in the rest of the broth. ✦ Cook for 10 minutes; serve the soup with the chili pepper and the bread.

✦ **LOCAL TRADITION** ✦

MINESTRA MARITATA 2

This version of Wedding Soup, typical of Campania, can be prepared according to an older method or in a more modern preparation. The more traditional version calls for a prosciutto bone, pork rind, salame (any will do, including cotechino), *tracchiolelle* (spare ribs), and fresh pork loin cooked with aromatic herbs in water to create a flavorful broth. In the modern preparation, fresh sausages take the place of the *tracchiolelle*. The meat is then removed from the various bones, chopped, and set aside in a small portion of the broth. Various vegetables, which in the modern version can include broccoli rabe, broccoli florets, chicory, escarole, or cabbage, are blanched in boiling water and drained, then cooked together with crumbled *caciocavallo secco* or rinds of other cheeses and crumbled chili peppers in the boiling meat broth. The meat is added back to the broth with the vegetables at the end but traditionally is served separately so that each diner can choose whether to add the meat to his or her plate together with grated cheese.

WEDDING SOUP 3

PIEMONTE

2 tbsp. olive oil

2 tbsp. butter

1 garlic clove, minced

1 bunch flat-leaf parsley, chopped

A few sage leaves, chopped

1 celery stalk, chopped

6 ¼ cups spinach, roughly chopped

6 cups beef broth

3 ½ cups rice

½ cup milk

3 large egg yolks and
1 large egg white, beaten

½ cup grated Parmigiano-Reggiano

This soup is typical of the Tanaro Valley.

Heat the olive oil and butter in a pot over low heat. Add the garlic, most of the parsley, the sage, and celery and sauté for 3 minutes. ✦ Add the spinach and cook, stirring, for another 10 minutes. ✦Add the broth and boil for about 10 minutes. ✦ Add the rice and cook until al dente. ✦ When it has half cooked, about 15 minutes, add the milk. ✦ Meanwhile, mix the egg yolks and white with the Parmigiano-Reggiano and the remaining parsley. ✦ Remove the soup from the heat and pour in this mixture, stirring rapidly to combine the ingredients. Serve hot.

WEDDING SOUP 4

PUGLIA

1 prosciutto bone

1 head curly endive

2 bulbs fennel

1 bunch garden chicory

1 bunch Swiss chard

Grated pecorino

Salt

This soup is typical of Lucera.

Put the prosciutto bone in a pot with cold water to cover and boil for about 2 hours. ✦ Trim all bits of meat from the bone and return them to the broth. ✦ Meanwhile, remove the tough outer layers of the vegetables and chop them into medium-size pieces; boil in a pot with lightly salted water to cover until they are barely al dente, about 3 minutes, drain well, and add them to the broth. ✦ Stir and bring to a boil to blend the flavors. ✦ Pour the soup in bowls and sprinkle each portion with pecorino.

WEDDING SOUP 5

VENETO

Giblets from 1 chicken

8 cups chicken broth

CONTINUED

This soup is typical of Padua.

Chop the giblets into small pieces, taking care to first boil the *durello* (stomach) in a pot of water briefly; simmer all of the chopped giblets in 7 cups of the broth for about 6 minutes. ✦ Bring to a boil and add the rice; after about 8 minutes, add the tagliolini. ✦ When the pasta is

1 ¼ cups *Vialone Nano* rice

6 oz. egg tagliolini, cut very narrow and short

1 heaping tbsp. all-purpose flour

Grated Parmigiano-Reggiano

Salt

nearly cooked, dissolve the flour in 1 cup of broth and stir in gently; simmer for another 2 minutes. Serve in bowls and sprinkle with Parmigiano-Reggiano.

MINESTRA SPERSA

WILD HERBS AND MEAT SOUP

BASILICATA

1 head escarole, chopped

2 medium onions, chopped

2 potatoes, chopped

½ cup chopped fresh herbs

1 lb. stew beef or pork meat

6 oz. guanciale

1 small piece pork rind

2 tbsp. extra-virgin olive oil

2 garlic cloves

Salt

For the herbs, use a combination of whatever is available, such as parsley, rosemary, marjoram, and/or thyme.

Simmer the escarole, onions, potatoes, and herbs in a pot with lightly salted water, either together or separately according to type. ✦ Cook the meat, guanciale, and pork rind in another pan in a little water. ✦ Combine with the vegetables and cook until the meat is tender. ✦ Heat the olive oil in a skillet over low heat and sauté the garlic. Add to the soup just before serving.

✦ **LOCAL TRADITION** ✦

MINESTRA PRIMAVERILE DI ERBE DI PRATO

This fresh spring herb soup, typical of the Bassa Valle and Walser regions of the Valle d'Aosta, is traditionally made with yarrow, bladder campion, hop sprouts, and sorrel leaves, but can be prepared with a variety of different wild herbs, including nettles, catchfly, primrose, wild spinach, mallow, bistort, salsify, wild chervil, borage leaves, lemon balm, and pellitory. Potatoes, preferably from the mountains, are cooked with the field herbs in water. Once tender, the potatoes should be crushed with a fork and cooked rice added to the pot with butter. The mixture should be cooked together briefly, stirring, and served hot with Parmigianno-Reggiano.

CHICKEN AND PASTA SOUP

LOMBARDIA

3 tbsp. unsalted butter

½ chicken, cut in small pieces

3 chicken livers

2 chicken gizzards, cleaned and chopped

Chicken giblets, cleaned and chopped

2 cups beef broth

1¼ cups pastina for soup

2 tbsp. chopped flat-leaf parsley

Grated Parmigiano-Reggiano

This dish is typical of the area around Brescia.

Heat 2 tablespoons butter in a pot over low heat and sauté the pieces of chicken until golden. Add the livers, gizzards, and giblets, pour in the broth, raise the heat, and bring to a boil. Reduce the heat to low and cook. ✦ When the chicken is cooked through, pour in the pastina (if you have a choice, use the largest type available). ✦ When the pastina is done, mix in the remaining butter, parsley, and cheese to taste.

MINESTRONE

FOR 6 PERSONS

TOSCANA

5 tbsp. olive oil

2 oz. pancetta, diced

½ medium onion, finely sliced

½ cup chopped basil

½ lb. potatoes, peeled and diced

1 carrot, diced

½ lb. Swiss chard, chopped

1 celery stalk, cut in small pieces

1 head lettuce, chopped

2 or 3 small zucchini, diced

4 oz. string beans

2 or 3 ripe plum tomatoes, peeled and roughly chopped

⅔ cup fresh borlotti beans

Broth

½ lb. short pasta

In a deep pot, heat 4 tablespoons olive oil and sauté the pancetta, onion, and basil, then add all the vegetables except the tomatoes. ✦ Add salt to taste, cover, and cook over low heat for about 10 minutes. ✦ Add the tomatoes and beans, then add enough broth to cover. ✦ Cook slowly for about 2 hours, stirring to prevent the mixture from sticking and adding water or broth as needed. ✦ Add the short pasta and cook for 10 minutes; when the pasta is done the soup is finished. ✦ Finish with the remaining olive oil and serve hot.

MINESTRONE WITH PESTO

MINESTRONE COL PESTO

LIGURIA

3 lbs. vegetables: onions, garlic, flat-leaf parsley, celery, potatoes, peas, squash, cabbage, fava beans, zucchini, green beans, fresh beans (cannellini and borlotti), plum tomatoes (1 or 2 at the most), eggplant, carrots

¾ cup extra-virgin olive oil

Several rinds of Parmigiano-Reggiano

½ lb. pasta, as desired: tagliatelle, broken spaghetti, or macaroni

¼ cup pesto sauce (see page 418)

Coarse salt

Ideally this soup is served in terra-cotta bowls called *xatte* from the Ligurian town of Albissola.

Peel or clean the vegetables and chop into small pieces. Heat a little olive in a sauté pan and sauté the onion, garlic, parsley, and celery; set aside. ✦ Put the remaining vegetables into a pot, add water to cover, and bring to a boil. Boil vigorously over high heat for a few minutes, then lower the heat to a simmer. Cover and cook, stirring often to keep the mixture from sticking to the bottom of the pot. ✦ Halfway through, add the remaining olive oil, the onion mixture, cheese rinds, and salt. ✦ Using a wooden spoon, crush the potatoes and beans to gradually thicken the mixture. ✦ When the vegetables begin coming apart and the soup is dense and creamy, add the pasta. When the pasta is cooked, remove the pot from the heat and stir in the pesto. Pour the minestrone into bowls. ✦ Let the soup rest in the bowls for 15 minutes and serve at room temperature.

BARLEY AND POTATO SOUP

MINESTRONE D'ORZO E PATATE

FRIULI-VENEZIA GIULIA

1 garlic clove, finely chopped

1 bunch flat-leaf parsley, finely chopped

1 medium onion, finely chopped

1 cup chopped *erba porcina* (burdock root)

2 tbsp. olive oil

3 potatoes, peeled and cut in chunks

1¼ cups barley, soaked in water to soften and drained

1 or 2 fresh plum tomatoes, cut in small pieces

2 tbsp. Parmigiano-Reggiano

Salt and pepper

Finely chop the garlic, parsley, onion, and *erba porcina*. Heat a little olive oil in a pot and sauté the vegetables; add the potatoes and barley. ✦ Stir in the tomatoes. ✦ Cover with water, season with salt and pepper to taste, and simmer for 1 hour; if the soup is too liquid, crush some of the potatoes. Let rest for 15 minutes and serve lukewarm, sprinkled with Parmigiano-Reggiano.

TOMATO SOUP

PUGLIA

1 ½ lbs. plum tomatoes
2 tbsp. olive oil
Pinch sugar
1 medium onion, cut in thin slices
2 potatoes, peeled and sliced
3 eggplants, sliced
3 large peppers (1 green, 1 yellow, and 1 red), roughly chopped
¼ cup chopped basil
¼ cup chopped flat-leaf parsley

This dish is typical of Foggia.

Wash the tomatoes, slice them, and put them in a pan over low heat with the olive oil, sugar, and onion; after 10 minutes add the potatoes, cook for a few minutes, then add the eggplants and peppers. ✦ Add the basil and parsley. ✦ Cook the mixture over low heat for another 10 to 15 minutes, or until all the ingredients are cooked through. Serve hot in a tureen.

CHICKPEA AND PORK SOUP

MINESTRONE DI CECI E COSTINE

PIEMONTE

1 cup dried chickpeas
1 tsp. baking soda
2 tbsp. extra-virgin olive oil
1 medium onion, sliced
¼ cup chopped flat-leaf parsley
¼ cup dried mushrooms, soaked in warm water for 20 minutes, drained, and chopped
1 tbsp. tomato purée
1 lb. pork rind
4 potatoes, peeled, boiled, and crushed
Chunks of bread, toasted
Grated Parmigiano-Reggiano
Salt and pepper

Soak the chickpeas in water to cover for 12 hours. ✦ Drain, then place the chickpeas in a pot with water to cover. Add the baking soda and cook until starting to soften. Strain and return to the pot; add water to cover and season with salt. ✦ In a sauté pan, heat the olive oil and sauté the onion. Add the parsley, mushrooms, and tomato purée. ✦ Add this mixture to the chickpeas. Add the pork rind and potatoes and cook for 2 hours. ✦ Serve hot with chunks of toasted bread and a sprinkling of Parmigiano-Reggiano.

BEAN, CABBAGE, AND POTATO SOUP

MINESTRONE DI FAGIOLI, CAVOLO, E PATATE

FOR 6 PERSONS

CALABRIA

1 ¼ cups dried beans

CONTINUED

Soak the beans in water to cover overnight. ✦ The next day, drain, then cook the beans in a pan (preferably earthenware) in water to cover until tender. ✦ Slice the cabbage, then peel the potatoes, rinse, and cut into dice.

½ medium head of cabbage, outer leaves removed

1 lb. potatoes

1 tbsp. lard

10 oz. pancetta, diced

Hot red pepper

Salt

✦ Cook each of these ingredients separately in pots of lightly salted boiling water, then combine them, reserving a little of the cooking liquid. ✦ Heat the lard in a skillet and sauté the pancetta until golden, then add it to the pot; add hot red pepper, but only an instant before removing the pot from the heat.

MINESTRONE DI VERDURA

VEGETABLE SOUP

PIEMONTE

1 lb. potatoes, cut in chunks

¼ lb. green beans

2 small eggplants (optional), chopped

3 medium zucchini, chopped

2 carrots, chopped

1 medium onion, chopped

4 celery stalks, chopped

1½ cups fresh beans, shelled

½ cup fresh peas, shelled

½ cup fresh fava beans, shelled and peeled

¼ cup chopped basil

½ cup chopped flat-leaf parsley

¼ lb. Swiss chard or other leafy greens according to taste and season, washed and chopped

¼ cup extra-virgin olive oil

2 cups short pasta or rice

Grated Parmigiano-Reggiano

Salt

This minestrone is pleasantly thick; instead of short pasta or rice, some families use tagliatelle or *maltagliati*.

Put all the vegetables and herbs, setting aside a little of the chopped basil, in a pot with the olive oil. ✦ Add water to cover, and add salt, bearing in mind that the soup will cook down and should not end up overly salty. ✦ Cook over low heat, using the tines of a fork or a wooden spoon to crush the potatoes as they cook to thicken the soup. ✦ After a few hours of slow cooking, add the short pasta or rice. Just before the end of cooking, add the remaining chopped basil, which should cook only a short time. ✦ Serve sprinkled with cheese. This minestrone can be served cold in the summer.

PALLOTTE IN BRODO

CHEESE BALLS IN BROTH

MOLISE

1⅔ cups sheep's-milk ricotta

4 large eggs, beaten

CONTINUED

Heat the oven to 400°F. Work together the ricotta, eggs, and pecorino in a bowl. Add the parsley and salt and mix well. ✦ Use this mixture to create balls about the size of hazelnuts. ✦ Roll the balls in flour. Heat 1 inch of olive oil in a high-sided pan and fry the *pallotte* until

½ cup grated pecorino

¼ cup chopped flat-leaf parsley

All-purpose flour

Olive oil

Slices of stale peasant-style bread

8 cups broth (preferably made with a free-range chicken), heated to boiling

Grated pecorino

Salt and pepper

golden. Remove with a slotted spoon and let drain on paper towels. ✦ Meanwhile, toast the slices of bread in the oven, cut them in pieces, and arrange in a bowl; add the *pallotte*, pour over the boiling broth, and sprinkle with pecorino. Serve immediately.

BREAD SOUP 1

4 cups beef broth

¾ lb. stale bread, cut in pieces

4 tbsp. unsalted butter

2 tbsp. olive oil

⅓ cup grated Parmigiano-Reggiano

Salt and pepper

Pour the broth into a pan, add the stale bread, and cook over low heat for about 20 minutes. ✦ Add the butter, olive oil, salt, pepper, and cheese and cook for another 20 minutes. ✦ If the *panada* is prepared properly, the bread should congeal in the center with a circle of clear broth all around. Serve immediately.

BREAD SOUP 2

6 cups broth

¼ cup fine breadcrumbs

2 tbsp. unsalted butter

2 large eggs, beaten

¼ cup grated Parmigiano-Reggiano, plus more for serving

Salt and pepper

This is a typical Easter dish in Milan.

Bring the broth to a boil in a pot, then add the breadcrumbs. ✦ After 15 minutes, add the butter and cook over medium heat for 5 minutes. ✦ Divide the eggs evenly among 4 bowls and add a tablespoon of grated Parmigiano-Reggiano to each. Pour the broth over the egg mixture, stirring with a wooden spoon to prevent the formation of lumps. ✦ Add salt and pepper to taste and add more cheese at the table.

BREAD SOUP 3

PIEMONTE

¼ cup (4 tbsp.) unsalted butter
3 medium onions, cut in thin slices
¾ lb. dried bread, cubed
2 cups milk, warmed
6 cups broth
Salt

Heat the butter in a pot over low heat and sauté the onion. ✦ Add the bread and milk. ✦ Add the broth, cover, and cook for 30 minutes. Add salt to taste and serve boiling hot.

BREAD SOUP 4

TOSCANA

6 cups broth
1 lb. stale bread, grated
1 garlic clove
1 large egg yolk per person
Grated Parmigiano-Reggiano

Store-bought breadcrumbs are too small for this recipe, which is why the bread is grated at home.

Bring the broth to a boil. Pour the bread into the broth and add the garlic. Cook, stirring often to avoid lumps, on low heat for 10 minutes. ✦ Remove from the heat and add the egg yolks, mixing well. Add Parmigiano-Reggiano and serve hot.

BREAD SOUP 5

FOR
6 PERSONS

BASILICATA

6 or 7 potatoes
4 lbs. small turnips, cleaned and trimmed
1 lb. stale white bread, crumbled in rough pieces
2 tbsp. olive oil
1 garlic clove
Salt

This dish is typical of the Melfi area.

Cut the potatoes in slices about ⅛ inch thick and put in a pot. Add the turnips and water to cover and cook. ✦ When the turnips have almost finished cooking, mix in the bread, then drain. ✦ Meanwhile, heat the olive oil and sauté the garlic. Add to the potato mixture. Serve hot.

BREAD SOUP WITH BAY LEAF

PANCOTTO CON L'ALLORO

MOLISE

½ cup olive oil

1 bay leaf

8 slices stale bread, crumbled or in slices

Grated pecorino, for serving

Salt

Add the olive oil and bay leaf to a pot with 4 cups lightly salted water and bring to a boil. ✦ After a few minutes, add the bread. ✦ Boil for 5 to 6 minutes, add salt to taste, then serve sprinkled with pecorino.

BREAD SOUP WITH ARUGULA AND POTATOES

PANCOTTO, RUGHETTA, E PATATE

PUGLIA

1 lb. potatoes, peeled and sliced

1½ lbs. arugula, trimmed and cleaned

8 slices stale peasant-style bread

2 tbsp. extra-virgin olive oil

1 garlic clove, minced

1 hot chili pepper

Salt and pepper

This dish is typical of the Daunia Mountains area.

Boil the potatoes in a pot of lightly salted water; when they are about half cooked, about 10 minutes, add the arugula. ✦ When the potatoes and arugula are cooked, add the slices of bread and immediately turn off the heat (be careful not to let the bread become too soft—it is best to use only the crust with about ½ inch of bread). ✦ Heat the olive oil in a skillet and sauté the garlic and chili pepper until fragrant. Season the soup with the garlic mixture and serve.

CHEESE AND ONION BREAD IN BROTH

PANE CONCIO

LOMBARDIA

1 cup beef broth

¾ lb. rye bread

1¼ cups grated aged *bitto* (or another aged cow's-milk cheese)

¼ cup (4 tbsp.) unsalted butter

1 medium onion, thinly sliced

A few sage leaves (optional)

This dish is typical of the Valtellina.

Heat the broth in a pot. Cut the rye bread in small pieces. Toss the bread with just enough broth to dampen the bread, being careful not to soften it too much, and add the grated *bitto*. ✦ Heat the butter in a large pan over low heat and sauté the onion until caramelized. Spoon onto the bread and garnish with sage leaves, if desired.

| # SHEPHERD'S BREAD SOUP

BASILICATA

½ lb. stale bread, sliced

1 bay leaf

A few sprigs of oregano

2 tbsp. olive oil

1¼ cups plum tomatoes, peeled, seeded, and diced

4 large eggs

Broth, heated

Salt

Simmer the stale bread in a pot with 5 cups of lightly salted water with the bay leaf, oregano, olive oil, and tomatoes for 5 minutes. ✦ Add the eggs; they should remain whole, as though poached. Serve with a little broth in fairly deep bowls.

| # SPINACH-CORNMEAL SOUP

FRIULI-VENEZIA GIULIA

2 lbs. spinach, well washed and any large stems removed

4 tbsp. unsalted butter

1 or 2 garlic cloves

¾ cup flour

8 cups broth

⅔ cup cornmeal

Salt and pepper

This soup should be somewhat thick and is served hot.

Boil the spinach in a pot with a little lightly salted water; drain, strain, and chop. ✦ Heat the butter in a separate pot over low heat and sauté the garlic until golden. Remove the garlic and discard; add the spinach and cook for a few minutes. ✦ Whisk in the flour, then add half the broth, stirring to prevent the formation of lumps. ✦ Pour in the remainder of the broth, then add the cornmeal and cook over medium heat for 30 to 40 minutes, stirring constantly. Add salt and pepper to taste.

| # TOMATO SOUP

TOSCANA

½ cup extra-virgin olive oil

3 garlic cloves, chopped together with several basil leaves

1 lb. plum tomato pulp, crushed with the tines of a fork

4 thick slices of bread

Salt and pepper

Heat the olive oil in a pot and sauté the garlic mixture. ✦ Stir and add the tomato pulp. Season with salt and pepper to taste and cook over medium heat for 20 minutes. ✦ Add the bread, cover with warm water, and continue cooking until the bread has turned to mush. ✦ Let it rest, uncovered, about 1 hour. ✦ Before serving, stir again to break up the bread. If necessary, warm it up for a few minutes.

PAPPONE DI TORNOLA

This meal, known as the Fisherman's Dinner and typical of Molise, should be eaten among friends along the shore at dusk by the light of a driftwood fire. After selling the day's catch, the fishermen of Termoli would make this Fisherman's Dinner by combining whatever remained in their nets, the "small catch," in a single communal pot. Traditional ingredients besides the fish included fresh tomatoes, basil, parsley, garlic, spicy green peppers, and olive oil. Each fisherman would shake out the remains of his fishing net and clean and rinse the fish in seawater. In a large cauldron they would cook the other ingredients for a few minutes, then add the fish depending on how long each took to cook. Stale bread collected from the fishing boats' galleys would be layered across the bottom of individual dishes, and each fisherman would then pour over some of the broth and serve himself from the pot.

CHICKPEA PURÉE WITH SHRIMP AND CLAMS

PASSATA DI CECI
CON SCAMPI E VONGOLE

PUGLIA

1¼ cups dried chickpeas
1 lb. fresh shrimp
½ cup extra-virgin olive oil
1 garlic clove
½ lb. clams
2 tbsp. chopped flat-leaf parsley
Toasted peasant-style bread
Salt and white pepper

Soak the chickpeas in lukewarm salted water overnight. ◆ Drain, then cook the chickpeas in a pot with water to cover. Drain and put them through a food mill to form a purée; set aside. ◆ Remove the shrimp from their shells. Heat a little olive oil in a pan over medium heat and cook the garlic just until golden; remove the garlic from the pan. Add the shrimp and cook just until opaque, then remove from the pan. Put the clams in the pan and cover the pan. When the clams have opened, season with some of the parsley and pepper. ◆ Divide the chickpea purée among bowls and top with the shrimp and clams in their shells; sprinkle with parsley, white pepper, and the remaining olive oil. ◆ Serve with slices of toasted peasant-style bread.

PASSATELLI IN BROTH

EMILIA-ROMAGNA

1 oz. beef marrow
⅔ cup breadcrumbs
1¼ cups grated
Parmigiano-Reggiano
3 large eggs
Pinch nutmeg or
grated zest of ½ lemon
8 cups meat or chicken broth
Salt

In the past, *passatelli* was a special dish made only for Easter or confirmation celebrations.

Melt the beef marrow in a pan over low heat. ✦ Combine the breadcrumbs, 1 cup Parmigiano-Reggiano, the eggs, marrow, and nutmeg (or lemon zest) in a bowl; knead to create a firm dough. ✦ Ideally, the dough should be pressed through a special *passatelli* utensil; if you don't have one, force the dough through the holes in a potato ricer or colander to create *passatelli,* which are somewhat thick spaghetti, 1½ to 2 inches long. ✦ Let the *passatelli* rest for 10 minutes, then cook them in a pot with boiling broth. As soon as they float to the surface, they are done. ✦ Serve the *passatelli* in their broth in bowls with the remaining Parmigiano-Reggiano.

PASSATELLI IN FISH BROTH

PASSATELLI
IN BRODO DI PESCE

MARCHE

For the broth:
1 medium onion, chopped
1 celery stalk, chopped
1 carrot, chopped
1 ripe plum tomato,
seeded and chopped
1 lb. fish (see note)

For the *passatelli*:
½ cup breadcrumbs
½ cup grated Parmigiano-Reggiano
1 tbsp. all-purpose flour
Pinch nutmeg
1 tsp. grated lemon zest
1 large egg
Salt

Passatelli were made for important celebrations and were cooked in broth. The availability of fish in fishing areas resulted in particularly flavorful broths. Whatever fish was available was used. Many different types can be used, each of which will give the broth a different flavor, and different types can be used together. In Italy, small white fish are believed to create a broth of particular delicacy. Among these are hake, cod, and whiting; there are also broths made with sea toad or John Dory; a more flavorful broth is made with *mazzole* or *ghiozzi.* Local variations are based on the quantity and type of grated cheese used, the quantity of flour in the dough (increasing it results in firmer *passatelli*), whether nutmeg or lemon zest is used, and the amount of broth used to give the dough the right consistency.

Prepare the broth by mixing the onion, celery, carrot, tomato, and fish in a pot; add water to cover and simmer for about 1 hour. Strain, pressing on the solids to extract all the liquid. Return the broth to the pot and bring to a boil just before adding the *passatelli.* ✦ Prepare the *passatelli*: Mix the breadcrumbs, cheese, flour, salt, the nutmeg, lemon zest, and egg. Knead together to form a smooth dough. ✦ Press the mixture through the holes in a *passatelli* utensil or use the holes in a potato ricer or colander.

The resulting spaghetti should be about 2 inches long and ¼ inch thick. ✦ Cook them in the boiling broth until they float, 2 to 5 minutes. Serve with the broth.

SOUPY PASTA WITH CAULIFLOWER AND BLACK OLIVES

PASTA E CAVOLFIORE DI S. AGATA DEI GOTI

CAMPANIA

1 lb. cauliflower
¼ cup olive oil
1 garlic clove
½ cup black olives
1 lb. mixed pasta
Salt and pepper

Rinse the cauliflower, break it up, rinse again, and cook in a pan over low heat with a little of the olive oil and the garlic, stirring occasionally. ✦After 10 minutes, add the olives. ✦ Boil the pasta in a pot of lightly salted water until al dente, drain, and put aside a cup of the cooking water. ✦ Add the cooked pasta to the cauliflower in the pan, add salt and pepper, and finish cooking, adding a little of the pasta cooking water if necessary. ✦ Sprinkle with ground pepper before serving.

PASTA AND CHICKPEA SOUP 1

PASTA E CECI 1

LAZIO

¾ lb. dried chickpeas
½ cup olive oil
2 garlic cloves
1 sprig rosemary
2 salt-cured anchovies, rinsed and chopped
1 tbsp. tomato purée
6 oz. short pasta (cannolicchi, conchiglie, broken spaghetti)
Salt and pepper

This dish is typical of Rome. In the past, soups like this were made using finely chopped *lardo*, prosciutto fat, or guanciale, which gave them greater depth of flavor. Pasta and chickpeas was once a typical Lenten dish in Rome. In the area of Viterbo, this soup, together with the soup of chestnuts and chickpeas (see page 194), is one of the typical dishes served on Christmas Eve, and the pasta used is *anellini* ("small rings"). Before *anellini* was used, a pasta similar to small gnocchi was made. These were called *cecetti* in the area of Viterbo, *ceciarelli* toward the Maremma area, and *gnocchetti* in the area of Monti Cimini. In Rieti, the pasta most commonly used in this soup was broken spaghetti or cannolicchi.

Soak the chickpeas in water to cover overnight, then drain. ✦ Heat 2 tablespoons olive oil in a pot and sauté 1 garlic clove; add the chickpeas, stir, and add enough water to cover; season with salt and pepper and add the rosemary. Cook for 3 hours over low heat. ✦ Heat 4 tablespoons olive oil in a pot (preferably earthenware) over low heat. Chop the second garlic clove and sauté it with the anchovies; add the tomato purée diluted in a little of the chickpea cooking water. Cook for 10 minutes, then add the chickpeas with their cooking water;

remove the rosemary. ✦ When the liquid returns to a boil, add the pasta and cook until al dente. The soup should be somewhat dense. Serve seasoned with the remaining olive oil and a pinch of freshly ground pepper.

PASTA AND CHICKPEA SOUP 2

PASTA E CECI 2

PUGLIA

1 lb. dried chickpeas
1 celery stalk, chopped
1 garlic clove
6 tbsp. olive oil
Salt and pepper

For the pasta:
1½ cups all-purpose flour, plus more as needed

Soak the chickpeas overnight in salted lukewarm water to cover. ✦ The next morning, drain them, rinse, and cook in a pot, preferably earthenware, with the celery, garlic, salt, and lukewarm water to cover. ✦ The chickpeas will need at least 3 hours' cooking. ✦ Meanwhile, use the flour to prepare a smooth but firm pasta dough as in recipe on page 10, using ½ cup water in place of the eggs. Roll the dough into cylinders about ½ inch thick. Cut these in short lengths and give each length a hollow shape by pressing it against the tines of a fork or a grater to make cavatelli. ✦ When the chickpeas are cooked (make sure there is enough water in the pan), add the cavatelli and bring to a boil. ✦ Serve in a tureen or in the same earthenware pot, adding the olive oil and pepper at the end. The soup should be fairly thin.

PASTA AND CHICKPEA SOUP 3

PASTA E CECI 3

UMBRIA

¾ lb. dried chickpeas, soaked overnight in water to cover
1 cup drained and chopped peeled plum tomatoes
2 tbsp. lard
¼ cup olive oil
1 garlic clove
1 sprig rosemary
7 oz. *maltagliati* (irregularly shaped pasta)
Salt and pepper

Drain the chickpeas, then boil them in fresh water to cover until tender. Put the tomatoes through a food mill. ✦ Meanwhile, heat the lard and half the olive oil in a pot and sauté the garlic and rosemary until the garlic is golden. ✦ Add the chickpeas and tomatoes and salt and pepper to taste. ✦ Cover with water and cook, adding more water if necessary so there is enough to cook the pasta. ✦ Add the pasta; when it has cooked, the soup is done. ✦ Add the remaining olive oil before serving, along with a few grindings of black pepper.

PASTA AND BEAN SOUP 1

CAMPANIA

1½ cups fresh shelled beans
1 tbsp. extra-virgin olive oil
1 celery stalk, minced
2 garlic cloves
¾ cup peeled plum tomatoes
1 tbsp. tomato paste
1 small piece hot chili pepper
(or pepper)
¾ lb. mixed pasta
1 tbsp. chopped oregano
1 tbsp. chopped flat-leaf parsley
Salt

Cook the beans in water to cover in a covered pot over low heat. ✦ When the beans are almost done, heat the olive oil in a pot and sauté the celery and garlic. ✦ When the garlic is browned, remove and discard it. Take the pan off the heat and add the tomatoes, tomato paste, chili pepper, ¼ cup water, and salt; stir, and cook for 10 minutes over low heat, then immediately add to the beans (which by then should be coming apart) and continue cooking over low heat for 15 minutes. ✦ Purée a small quantity of the beans in a food mill and return them to the pot. ✦ Add the pasta, oregano, and parsley; raise the heat to high to return the pot to a boil as soon as possible. Cook, adding a little boiling water if necessary, until the pasta is al dente. ✦ Let the soup rest for 10 minutes before serving. It should be dense with a creamy texture.

PASTA AND BEAN SOUP 2

FRIULI-VENEZIA GIULIA

1⅔ cups dried beans
3 cloves
1 medium onion
1 celery stalk, chopped
½ lb. potatoes, chopped
½ bay leaf
1 pig's trotter, trimmed of fat
½ lb. short pasta
1 garlic clove
1 rosemary sprig
2 sage leaves,
fried in a few drops of olive oil
1 tbsp. chopped flat-leaf parsley
1 tablespoon olive oil
Salt and pepper

This dish is typical of Pordenone, in western Friuli.

Soak the beans overnight in a pot with water to cover; drain and add cold water to cover. ✦ Use the cloves to stud the onion and add to the beans. Add the celery, potatoes, bay leaf, pig's trotter, and salt. Bring to a boil, then reduce the heat and simmer until the beans are cooked. ✦ Remove the trotter and cut in half lengthwise. ✦ Remove 1 cup of the beans and pass the rest through a food mill. ✦ Return the purée, trotter, and whole beans to the pot, bring to a boil, and add the pasta. ✦ When the pasta is still very al dente, add the garlic, rosemary, sage, and parsley. Continue cooking until the pasta is done. ✦ Put the soup in a serving bowl and add the olive oil and a little pepper.

PASTA E LENTICCHIE | PASTA AND LENTIL SOUP

PUGLIA

1⅔ cups dried lentils
1 celery stalk, chopped
1 small onion, sliced
2 garlic cloves
Olive oil
5 plum tomatoes, peeled
¾ lb. broken spaghetti
or ditalini
Salt and pepper

This dish is typical of Foggia.

Clean and rinse the lentils and combine in a pot (preferably earthenware) with the celery, onion, and 1 garlic clove. Add water to cover, bring to a boil, and lower the heat. ✦ Meanwhile, in a saucepan, heat 6 tablespoons olive oil and sauté the other garlic clove until golden, then add the tomatoes. ✦ When the sauce has cooked down, add the lentil mixture. ✦ Meanwhile, cook the broken spaghetti (or ditalini) in lightly salted boiling water; drain when still very al dente. Add to the pan with the lentils and finish cooking. ✦ Serve sprinkled with pepper.

GRATED PASTA IN BROTH

PASTA GRATTUGIATA

FOR 6 PERSONS

FRIULI-VENEZIA GIULIA

6 cups broth
1 cup all-purpose flour,
plus more as needed
1 large egg
⅔ cup grated cheese

The cheese should be aged Montasio; if unavailable, use Parmigiano-Reggiano.

In a pot, heat the broth to boiling. Use all of the remaining ingredients to prepare a pasta dough as in the recipe on page 10, adding 5 tablespoons water with the egg. ✦ Using a vegetable grater, grate the dough into small pieces on the board, then cook them in the boiling broth until they float. Serve in the broth.

CHICKEN BROTH WITH GRATED PASTA

PASTARÉSA

EMILIA-ROMAGNA

2 large eggs, beaten
¼ cup grated Parmigiano-Reggiano
2 oz. breadcrumbs
Pinch nutmeg
8 cups chicken broth, heated
Salt

This dish is typical of Reggio Emilia.

Use all of the ingredients except the broth to prepare a firm pasta dough as in the recipe on page 10, using the Parmigiano-Reggiano and breadcrumbs in place of the flour. (It should be firm enough to be easily grated with a grater.) ✦ Grate the dough, let the pasta dry, then cook it in the broth until it floats. ✦ Serve immediately in terra-cotta bowls.

167

PASTINA IN
FISH SAUCE

PUGLIA

¼ medium onion, thinly sliced

1¼ cups extra-virgin olive oil

6 plum tomatoes, peeled and
seeded (can use canned),
thinly sliced

1 lb. mixed fresh soup fish
(see page 447)

¾ lb. small-size pasta

2 tbsp. chopped flat-leaf parsley

Salt and pepper

Cook the onion in the olive oil in a covered pot over low heat. When the onion has browned, add the tomatoes. ✦ Clean the fish, taking care to remove all the scales, and put them in the sauce when it boils. Add salt to taste and cook the sauce for 15 to 20 minutes, adding water if needed. ✦ When the fish is cooked, remove it from the broth, reserving the broth. ✦ Meanwhile, in a separate pot boil the pasta in lightly salted water and drain when still very al dente; add to the fish broth and complete the cooking. ✦ Serve the pasta hot with the chopped parsley and pepper. The cooked fish is the second course.

POTATO AND
CELERY SOUP

BASILICATA

2 tbsp. extra-virgin olive oil

2 tbsp. chopped flat-leaf parsley

A few garlic cloves

1 lb. peeled plum tomatoes

Pinch chili pepper flakes

1½ lbs. celery,
chopped in pieces

1½ lbs. potatoes,
peeled and cut in pieces

Slices of toasted bread

Salt

This dish is typical of Melfi.

In a high-sided pan, heat the oil and sauté the parsley and garlic. Add the tomatoes, pour in 4 cups water, then add salt to taste and sprinkle in some chili pepper flakes. ✦ When the liquid begins to boil, add the celery and cook for 15 minutes. ✦ At this point, add the potatoes and continue cooking until the potatoes begin to fall apart. Serve in bowls with slices of toasted bread.

MARJORAM BROTH
WITH POACHED EGGS

TOSCANA

1 handful marjoram

4 garlic cloves, crushed

½ cup olive oil

4 large eggs

Toasted slices of bread

This dish is typical of Elba.

Bring a pot of lightly salted water to a boil and add the marjoram, 3 garlic cloves, and olive oil. ✦ Cook for about 30 minutes, by which time the garlic and marjoram should have flavored the water. ✦ At this point, add the eggs one at a time and let them cook for a few minutes, removing them from the broth with a slotted spoon and setting them aside. ✦ Meanwhile, rub the crusts of bread with the remaining garlic and arrange in bowls.

Pour the broth over the slices of bread and add the poached eggs.

PASTA AND BEAN SOUP 3

PISAREI E FASÒ

FOR 6 PERSONS

EMILIA-ROMAGNA

For the pasta:

1 ¼ cups all-purpose flour, plus more as needed

4 oz. breadcrumbs

Pinch salt

For the broth:

7 oz. *lardo* (see page 2) (or pancetta)

1 garlic clove

1 bunch flat-leaf parsley

1 small onion

1 small celery stalk

1 carrot

2 basil leaves

1 tbsp. unsalted butter

2 tbsp. olive oil

7 oz. dried borlotti beans, soaked in water 8 to 10 hours and drained

6 oz. pork rind

⅔ cup grated Parmigiano-Reggiano

Salt and pepper

This dish is typical of Piacenza.

Use the flour to prepare a pasta dough as in the recipe on page 10, using the breadcrumbs and ½ cup hot water in place of the eggs. ✦ Let the dough rest for about 30 minutes, then shape it into long strips about ¼ inch wide. Cut the strips into lengths about 1 inch long. ✦ Using your thumb, create a hollow in each piece of pasta. ✦ For the broth, finely chop together the *lardo* (or pancetta), garlic, parsley, onion, celery, carrot, and basil. Heat the butter and olive oil in a pan over very low heat; add the *lardo* mixture and cook for about 15 minutes. ✦ When the mixture has softened completely, stir in the beans, then add 12 cups of water and slowly bring to a boil. ✦ Burn off any remaining bristles from the pork rind and rinse in cold running water to remove the burnt odor. ✦ Put the pork rind in a pot, cover with water, and boil for several minutes; remove the rind from the pot when still hot and scrape it carefully to remove any remaining fat and bristles. Cut the pork rind in ½-inch cubes. ✦ When the beans are about half cooked (after about 1 hour), add the pork rind to the pan and finish cooking. ✦ When the beans have finished cooking, add the pasta; it should cook in about 10 minutes. ✦ Turn off the heat, add half the cheese, and blend well; the mixture should be compact. Sprinkle the remaining cheese over the plated soup. Add salt and pepper to taste.

TINY PASTA IN BEAN BROTH

PISTADEIN MODENESI

EMILIA-ROMAGNA

1 ⅔ cups all-purpose flour, plus more as needed

1 large egg

Bean broth

Pistadein—tiny pasta—calls for a very dense dough, so dense it is difficult to knead.

Use the flour and egg to prepare a pasta dough as in the recipe on page 10. It should be very firm. Work the dough into the shape of a square loaf. ✦ On a cutting board, cut the loaf into strips about ¼ inch thick. Leave the strips to dry long enough so that they no longer stick

169

together. ✦ Cut them with a sharp knife to create bits of pasta about the size of grains of rice (if possible even smaller!). This pasta does not need to rest before using and will keep for a few days. Cook the *pistadein* in bean broth.

POLENTA AND BEANS

POLENTINA CON I FAGIOLI

LAZIO

1 ½ cups dried cannellini beans

5 oz. pork rind, cut in strips

2 tbsp. olive oil

4 oz. *lardo* (see page 2) (or pancetta)

1 medium onion

2 tbsp. chopped basil

1 sprig rosemary

6 oz. tomato purée

2 ⅓ cups cornmeal

½ cup grated pecorino piccante

Salt and pepper

In the area of Viterbo, any leftover polenta, a rare thing, was left to harden and the next day or evening was reheated directly over the fire of the fireplace and lightly toasted.

Wash the beans and soak them in water to cover overnight. ✦ Cook the beans and the pork rind in a pot, earthenware if possible, with water to cover. ✦ Heat the olive oil in a pan. Finely chop together the *lardo* (or pancetta), onion, basil, and rosemary and sauté. ✦ When the fat dissolves, add a few tablespoons of the tomato purée and salt and pepper. Cook for 20 minutes, then add this mixture to the beans. ✦ Bring to a boil, then add the cornmeal in a steady stream while stirring constantly. Continue cooking until the polenta reaches the desired thickness. ✦ Add the pecorino and serve on a board or in soup plates.

✦ **LOCAL TRADITION** ✦

PESCE FUIUTE

"Fake fish" soup is the name given to this dish, which is truly a reflection of the stark poverty that afflicted the peasantry in Molise and the resourcefulness with which they fed themselves. The fish of the title is present only in the saltiness conferred on the cooking water by placing 3 or 4 sea rocks in a pan with olive oil and slowly heating them, allowing the flavor of the sea to permeate the oil. Half an onion and some fresh, ripe tomatoes would then be sautéed in the oil to form the base of the soup. After flavoring the tomato and onion, the rocks were removed, and small pasta, such as tubetti—cooked until still very al dente—were added to the tomato mixture. When the pasta was fully cooked, the soup would be ready to eat.

RYE-FLOUR PORRIDGE

POLENTINA DI FARINA DI SEGALE

VALLE D'AOSTA

2 ⅓ cups rye flour, plus more as needed

¼ lb. (1 stick) unsalted butter

2 medium onions, sliced

4 oz. fontina, grated

½ lb. whole wheat rye bread

Salt

This dish is typical of the Bassa Valle.

In a copper pot, bring 4 cups (or more if you want a more liquid polenta) of lightly salted water to a boil and pour in the rye flour in a steady stream, stirring continuously with a wooden spoon; cook the polenta over low heat for 45 minutes. ✦ Meanwhile, heat the butter in a pan and sauté the onions. ✦ When the polenta is cooked, stir the onions and cheese into it and serve in individual bowls with slices of whole wheat rye bread.

RICOTTA DUMPLINGS IN BROTH

POLPETTE DI RICOTTA IN BRODO

CALABRIA

Vegetable or beef broth

2 ⅓ cups fresh sheep's-milk ricotta

6 oz. bread, crust removed

2 large eggs, beaten

1 bunch flat-leaf parsley, chopped

Salt and pepper

In a pot, bring the broth to a boil. ✦ Mix the other ingredients to form a dough. Form this mixture into 1-inch balls and cook in the boiling broth. Serve the dumplings in the broth.

TINY SQUARE PASTA AND FAVA BEANS

QUADRUCCI CON LE FAVE

LAZIO

¾ cup all-purpose flour

1 large egg

2 tbsp. extra-virgin olive oil

2 oz. prosciutto cotto, diced, with the fat reserved

Mint leaves

½ medium onion

Olive oil

½ cup beef broth (more if necessary)

6 oz. plum tomatoes, peeled and drained

1 ¾ lbs. fresh fava beans (the smaller ones are more tender), shelled and peeled

Salt and pepper

This dish is typical of upper Lazio.

Use the flour and egg to prepare a pasta dough as in the recipe on page 10. Roll out a sheet (see note, page 212) and cut it into *quadrucci*, tiny squares used in soup. ✦ Heat the olive oil in a pot. Finely chop the prosciutto fat, mint leaves, and onion and sauté, adding salt and pepper. ✦ After a few minutes, add the prosciutto, broth, tomatoes, and fava beans. ✦ Cook over low heat for 1 hour, adding more broth if necessary. ✦ When the beans are cooked, add the *quadrucci*, and when they are cooked the dish is finished. Serve hot.

TINY SQUARE PASTA AND PEAS

QUADRUCCI E PISELLI

ABRUZZO

1⅔ cups all-purpose flour,
plus more as needed

3 large eggs

1 medium onion, finely chopped

2 oz. pancetta

¼ cup white wine

1 cup fresh peas

Salt

Use the flour and eggs to prepare a pasta dough as in the recipe on page 10. Roll out the dough to create a thin sheet (see note, page 212) and cut into strips about ¼ inch thick, then into squares. Dry the *quadrucci* in a well-floured bowl. ✦ Cook the onion and pancetta with the wine in a pan over low heat until soft; add the peas and a little water. ✦ Simmer for about 20 minutes, then pour in the *quadrucci*. Adjust for salt and continue cooking over medium heat until the pasta is cooked. The dish should be somewhat soupy.

"ROOTS" AND BEAN SOUP

RADICI E FASÌOI

VENETO

2 cups dried borlotti beans

2 tbsp. extra-virgin olive oil

4 oz. *ciccioli* (see note, page 12)

1 tbsp. vinegar

2 cups arugula

½ medium onion, minced

2 sage leaves

1 tbsp. tomato paste

Salt

Traditionally, this is made with wild radicchio; arugula is a fine substitute.

Soak the borlotti beans in water to cover overnight; drain. ✦ Heat the olive oil in a pan and cook the *ciccioli* until crisp. Remove from the heat and sprinkle with the vinegar. Put the arugula in a bowl; add the *ciccioli* and set aside. ✦ Cook the beans, onion, and sage leaves in a pot with water to cover by 1 inch to obtain a compact mass, crushing the beans with a wooden spoon. ✦ Stir in the tomato paste and salt. Cook until thick (a spoon should stand up in it!), then mix into the arugula mixture by the spoonful.

VEGETABLE RAGÙ

RAGÙ DI VERDURE

FOR 6 PERSONS

CAMPANIA

2 lbs. bell peppers

1½ cups extra-virgin olive oil

1 garlic clove

1 lb. onions, sliced

CONTINUED

This dish is typical of Sessa Aurunca.

Cut the peppers in strips. Heat the olive oil in a pot and cook the peppers and garlic; remove from the pan and set aside. ✦ In the same olive oil, sauté the onions, eggplant, potatoes, and tomatoes. Add salt and cook over low heat, covered, for 30 minutes; check the density and if too liquid let it thicken by cooking with the pot

1 ½ lbs. eggplant (3 medium), chopped
1 lb. potatoes, peeled and chopped
2 plum tomatoes, chopped
Salt

open. ✦ Add the peppers and salt to taste. Serve at room temperature.

RIBOLLITA

VEGETABLE AND BEAN STEW

FOR
6 PERSONS

TOSCANA

1 lb. dried cannellini beans
2 tbsp. olive oil
1 medium onion, sliced
1 celery stalk, sliced
1 carrot, sliced
1 cup peeled plum tomatoes, chopped
1 cabbage, cored and chopped
½ Savoy cabbage, outer leaves removed, cored and chopped
Slices of stale peasant-style bread, for serving
Salt and pepper

This soup's name—*ribollita* means "reboiled"—reflects the fact that it is meant to be prepared a day in advance and then "reboiled" (at least reheated) for about 10 minutes before being served. It is best served with a drizzle of olive oil.

Soak the cannellini beans in water to cover for at least 12 hours; drain. ✦ In an earthenware pot, heat the olive oil and sauté the onion. Add the celery and carrot and cook, stirring, then add the tomatoes, cabbage, and salt and pepper to taste. ✦ Meanwhile, cook the beans in a pot with water to cover, then drain them, reserving their cooking liquid. ✦ Set aside about half the beans and pass the other half through a food mill, then directly back into the cooking liquid. Pour the milled beans with their liquid into the pot with the vegetables and cook, very slowly, for about 1 hour, adding water if needed. ✦ Just before serving, turn off the heat and add the whole beans. ✦ Put slices of bread in a tureen and pour half the soup over them; then put in more slices of bread and cover with the remaining half of the soup.

RIS CUN TARDÚRA

RICE WITH EGGS AND CHEESE

EMILIA-ROMAGNA

3 large eggs, beaten
½ cup grated Parmigiano-Reggiano
1 ⅔ cups rice
2 cups broth
Salt and pepper

This dish is typical of Reggio Emilia.

Beat the eggs, cheese, salt, and pepper: This is the *tardúra*. Set aside. ✦ Cook the rice in the broth, then remove it from the heat and let stand for a few minutes. ✦ Using a wooden spoon, slowly work the *tardúra* into the rice, mix well, and serve.

RIS E LAIT E CASTAGNI BIANCHI

RICE WITH MILK AND CHESTNUTS

PIEMONTE

7 oz. dried chestnuts

4 cups milk, heated to lukewarm, plus more as needed

1 tbsp. unsalted butter

2 cups rice

Pinch grated nutmeg (optional)

This dish is typical of Vercelli.

Soak the chestnuts in a pot with water to cover overnight. ✦ The next day, boil the chestnuts in the soaking water for 30 minutes, then add the milk, butter, and rice. ✦ Complete the cooking until the rice is tender, adding more milk if necessary and the nutmeg, if desired.

RIS E MALASTRE

RICE AND PANSIES

PIEMONTE

1 lb. potatoes, peeled

1 handful *malastre* (mountain pansies: *Viola tricolor hortensis*)

1 cup rice

2 tbsp. unsalted butter

½ cup milk, heated to a boil

This pale yellow soup, with its floating flowers, is typical of Biella. Any edible pansies may be substituted for the *malastre*.

Combine the potatoes and pansies in a pot and add water to cover. Cook over medium heat. ✦ When cooked halfway, about 10 minutes, add the rice. ✦ When the potatoes are cooked, remove them from the pan (let the rice continue to cook) and put them in a bowl; add the butter. Crush them with a fork to incorporate the butter. ✦ Add the potatoes and milk to the soup and add salt to taste. Stir well and serve hot.

RISO CÖ PREBOGGION

RICE AND WILD HERBS

LIGURIA

2 bunches *preboggion* (see page 292 for an explanation of these herbs)

1½ cups rice

½ cup pesto made without pine nuts (see page 418)

¼ cup grated Parmigiano-Reggiano

A note of caution: This dish is not easy to make because the goal is to make something halfway between a soup and a risotto. There is always the risk of ending up with a mixture that is either too dry or too soupy.

Wash and finely chop the *preboggion*, then simmer for 30 minutes in a pot with 6 cups salted water. ✦ Add the rice to the pot and let it boil over high heat for 5 minutes. ✦ Use a little of the cooking water to dilute the pesto. Pour half of the pesto sauce into the pot and let it cook for another 10 minutes, or until the rice is cooked. ✦ Pour the soup in a tureen and add the remaining pesto and the Parmigiano-Reggiano and serve hot.

RICE WITH CHICKEN LIVERS

RISO CON I FEGATINI

VENETO

4 tbsp. unsalted butter
1 medium onion, finely chopped
1 celery stalk, finely chopped
2 chicken livers
2 gizzards
½ cup dry white wine
4 cups broth, boiling
1⅔ cups rice
Grated Parmigiano-Reggiano

This dish is typical of Padua.

Heat the butter in a pan over low heat. Sauté the onion and celery; add the chicken livers, gizzards, and white wine and continue cooking over low heat. ✦ Add the broth and rice, and cook, stirring, until the rice is cooked through. Sprinkle with Parmigiano-Reggiano and serve.

BAKED RICE AND BEANS WITH CHEESE

RISO E FAGIOLI

VALLE D'AOSTA

Unsalted butter, melted, as needed
1 lb. dried beans
2½ cups rice
7 oz. *toma grassa di Gressoney*, sliced (can substitute fontina)
Salt

This dish is typical of Issime.

Preheat the oven to 350°F. Coat a baking dish with high sides with melted butter. Put the beans in a pot with cold water to cover, add salt, and cook. ✦ When the beans are almost tender, add the rice and cook until done. ✦ Put a layer of rice and beans in the baking dish, cover with slices of toma, and repeat the layers, ending with a covering of toma. ✦ Drizzle with melted butter and bake for 10 minutes.

RICE, BEANS, MILK, AND SALAME

RISO, FAGIOLI, LATTE, E SALAME

FOR 6 PERSONS

PIEMONTE

2 cups dried beans (soaked as needed in water) or 3 cups fresh shelled beans
1 *salam ëd l'ola* (salame in fat) that is very lean and of pure pork
4 cups milk
3 cups rice
Salt and pepper

This dish is typical of Fraschea di Sandigliano.

Put the beans and *salam ëd l'ola* (with fat removed) in a pot with cold water, cover, and cook for about 2 hours; add the milk and bring to a boil. ✦ Pour in the rice, add salt and pepper to taste, and cook for another 20 minutes, or until the rice is done. ✦ When serving, put the soup in bowls with the salame along the edges. Eat the salame first while the soup cools.

RICE WITH CELERY AND TOMATO

RISO, SEDANO, POMODORO

VENETO

3 tbsp. unsalted butter
1 tbsp. olive oil
1 small onion, finely chopped
2 celery stalks, finely chopped
¾ lb. fresh plum tomatoes, chopped
4 cups chicken or beef broth
1⅔ cups rice
Grated Parmigiano-Reggiano
Salt and pepper

This dish is typical of Padua.

In a pot, heat the butter and oil and cook the onion, celery, and tomatoes for several minutes over low heat. ✦ Add the broth and rice, and cook, adding salt to taste and a little pepper and Parmigiano-Reggiano. Serve at room temperature.

RISOTTO WITH EELS

RISOTTO CON ANGUILLE ALLA COMACCHIESE

EMILIA-ROMAGNA

2 lbs. small eels
4 tbsp. unsalted butter
1 tbsp. olive oil
½ medium onion, finely chopped
2 small celery stalks, finely chopped
2½ cups rice
1 tbsp. tomato paste
1¼ cups grated Parmigiano-Reggiano

Clean and skin the eels, cut them in small pieces, and simmer in a pot with water to cover for about 30 minutes, setting aside the cooking liquid. ✦ Heat half the butter and the olive oil in a pan and lightly sauté the onion and celery. ✦ Add the rice, toast it well, then add the eels. ✦ Proceed with the cooking of the rice, slowly adding the water from the cooking of the eels. ✦ When the rice is about half cooked, add the tomato paste. Once the rice is cooked, remove the pan from the heat and work in the remaining butter and Parmigiano-Reggiano. Serve immediately.

BAKED PASTA WITH HEN AND BROTH

SAGNA IN BRODO

MOLISE

1 hen
Several whole cloves
Pinch grated nutmeg
1 cinnamon stick
1 cup all-purpose flour
2 large eggs
CONTINUED

This dish, typical of the Lower Molise, was eaten in noble homes on special occasions, such as baptisms, communions, and weddings.

Simmer the hen in a pot with water to cover with the cloves, nutmeg, and cinnamon. ✦ Use the flour and eggs to prepare a pasta dough as in the recipe on page 10. Roll out to a very thin sheet (see note, page 212) and cut in squares as for lasagne. ✦ When the hen is cooked through, cut the breasts in pieces and the neck meat in

2 cups grated pecorino dolce
8 oz. scamorza cheese, cut up
Broth

small pieces. ✦ Boil the pasta squares in a pot of lightly salted water until al dente. ✦ Preheat the oven to 300°F. In an earthenware pan with high sides, make a layer of pasta and top with ½ cup pecorino dolce, then a layer of scamorza, a layer of hen meat, then a cup of the broth. Continue making these layers until the ingredients are used up. Bake until a fork inserted in the mass comes out with threads of scamorza; this is when the dish is cooked to perfection. Cut in quarters and serve hot with the addition of more broth.

SBĬRA

TRIPE SOUP

LIGURIA

¾ lb. tripe (*foiolo*)
2 cups wine
4 cups beef broth
Toasted slices of bread
Sauce from roast meat
(see page 584)
Grated Parmigiano-Reggiano

Cut the tripe into strips and cook Ligurian style, meaning stewed in a pot with wine mixed with enough water to cover by a couple of inches until it has softened. ✦ Transfer the tripe to the broth and cook for a few minutes. ✦ Put a slice of toasted bread at the bottom of each individual bowl and pour the broth and tripe over it, adding a spoonful of the sauce from the roast meat and a sprinkling of cheese. Serve hot.

SCATTONE

PASTA-WATER PICK-ME-UP

MOLISE

Water from cooking pasta
Red wine
Pepper

Born as a simple and popular relief against winter chills, *scattone* owed most of its invigorating effect to a pinch of pepper or even the addition of a chopped *diavolillo* chili pepper. Because of these healthful benefits or simply for the pleasure of remaining true to tradition, it can sometimes still be found served as a kind of rustic "consommé." For the woman of the house, making this is like showing off a small jewel that belonged to her grandmother.

Draw off 1 cup of water from the pan in which you are cooking *sagne* (or *taccozze*), preferably when the pasta is about half cooked; pour this liquid into a cup, and add ¼ cup red wine and a pinch of pepper. Serve piping hot.

VEAL MEATBALLS WITH RICOTTA IN BROTH

SCIUSCEDDU

SICILIA

½ lb. ground veal

3 large eggs, beaten

½ cup breadcrumbs

⅔ cup grated caciocavallo
or Parmigiano-Reggiano

2 tbsp. chopped flat-leaf parsley

⅔ cup ricotta,
passed through a sieve

4 cups beef broth

Salt and pepper

This dish is typical of Messina.

Combine the veal, 1 of the eggs, the breadcrumbs, half of the caciocavallo (or Parmigiano-Reggiano), the parsley, and a little water and make meatballs (roughly the size of a pigeon's egg). ✦ In a bowl, beat the remaining eggs, the ricotta, and the remaining caciocavallo with a little salt and pepper. ✦ Heat the broth in a pot, and when it is boiling, add the meatballs. ✦ Simmer for 20 minutes, add the egg mixture, and quickly stir for a few seconds. Remove from the heat, and serve the *sciusceddu* boiling hot.

CREPES IN BROTH

SCRIPPELLE "MBUSSE"

ABRUZZO

½ cup all-purpose flour

4 large eggs, beaten

Lard

6 cups chicken broth

4 cups grated pecorino
or Parmigiano-Reggiano,
plus more for serving

2 tbsp. ground cinnamon

In a bowl, slowly add the flour to the eggs to obtain a homogeneous mixture; whisk in 3 cups water to make a thin batter. ✦ Grease a pan (about 10 inches wide) with the lard and put over low heat. When the pan is hot, pour in about ½ cup of the batter, tilting the pan to get the mixture to cover the bottom. The result will be a very thin, almost transparent *scrippella* (if not, reduce the quantity for each *scrippella*). ✦ Cook each one about 30 seconds; when half cooked gently turn over the *scrippella*. ✦ Repeat until all of the batter has been used up. Place the *scrippelle* on a surface and let them dry. ✦ Meanwhile, heat the broth. ✦ One at a time sprinkle the *scrippelle* with the 4 cups of cheese and a pinch of cinnamon, roll them tightly, and arrange them in soup bowls, putting 7 or 8 in each bowl. Pour over the hot broth, dust with more cheese, and serve.

SOUP FROM COGNE

SEUPPETTA DE COGNE

FOR
10 PERSONS

VALLE D'AOSTA

¾ cup (1½ sticks)
plus 2 tbsp. unsalted butter

Preheat the oven to 350°F. Melt a third of the butter in a high-sided pan and toast the bread until golden. ✦ Add a second third of the butter to the pan and toast the rice. Make a risotto as directed on page 349 omitting fennel

CONTINUED

2 lbs. bread, sliced

3 cups Arborio rice

Beef broth, warmed

¾ lb. fontina, in small pieces

Salt

and sausage. Just before the rice is completely cooked, remove it from the heat. ✦ Arrange a layer of bread in a bowl, cover it with a layer of rice, then one of fontina, continuing these alternating layers, ending with a layer of fontina. ✦ Add a little broth. Melt the remaining butter, pour over the mixture, and bake about 10 minutes.

SGUAZZABARBUZ

PASTA WITH BEANS

EMILIA-ROMAGNA

1⅔ cups dried borlotti beans

1 tsp. baking soda

4 oz. *lardo* (see page 2)

Olive oil

1 medium onion, chopped

1 garlic clove

2 tbsp. tomato paste

1 small piece pork rind

¾ lb. *maltagliati*
(irregularly shaped pasta)

Parmigiano-Reggiano

Salt and pepper

Soak the beans in cold water to cover for 12 hours with the baking soda to soften their skins. ✦ Heat the *lardo* and a little olive oil in a pot and sauté the onion and garlic. ✦ Add the tomato paste, beans, pork rind, and 10 cups of lukewarm water. ✦ Bring to boil, then simmer until the beans are nearly cooked (about 1½ hours), remove about half, put them through a food mill, and return the purée to the pan. ✦ Cook for 20 minutes more, then bring to a boil and add the *maltagliati*. Cook until the pasta is al dente, then serve hot with Parmigiano-Reggiano or a drizzle of olive oil.

SOPA COÀDA

"BROODING" PIGEONS (SQUAB) STEW

FOR
5 PERSONS

VENETO

4 young pigeons (squab)

3 tbsp. olive oil

½ cup (1 stick) plus
3 tbsp. unsalted butter

1 celery stalk, finely chopped

2 large onions, finely chopped

3 carrots, finely chopped

½ cup dry white wine

6 cups beef broth

1 bunch flat-leaf parsley, chopped

1 lb. stale white bread

⅔ cup grated Parmigiano-Reggiano

Salt and pepper

Clean the pigeons and cut them in half. ✦ Heat the olive oil and butter in a pot and sauté the celery, onions, and carrots. ✦ When the onions are translucent, add the pigeons and wine. Let simmer a few minutes. ✦ Add the broth and salt and pepper. Add the parsley and cover; cook until the pigeons are well done. ✦ Cut the bread in ½-inch-thick slices. ✦ Remove the bones from the pigeons without breaking them up too much. ✦ Preheat the oven to 200°F. In a large baking dish or earthenware pan, create a layer of bread slices. On each slice place a half pigeon in pieces, sprinkle with Parmigiano-Reggiano, and cover with another slice of bread. ✦ Cover this with broth and place in the oven to very slowly "brood" for at least 5 hours, or until the broth has almost completely evaporated. ✦ If necessary, moisten with the addition of a little broth and a few pats of butter. Serve hot.

PASTA AND BEAN SOUP

SOUPA D'PASTA E FASEN

PIEMONTE

7 oz. *lardo* (see page 2), minced

1 large onion, chopped

1 garlic clove

2 lbs. fresh cranberry beans, shelled

¼ cup white wine

Beef broth

1 lb. potatoes, peeled and chopped

½ lb. pasta

1 sprig rosemary, finely chopped

1 bunch flat-leaf parsley, finely chopped

1 tbsp. unsalted butter

Slices of toasted bread, rubbed with the cut side of a garlic clove

Salt

This dish is typical of Orta San Giulio.

Heat the *lardo* in a pot over low heat and sauté the onion, garlic, and beans; when the onions are translucent, sprinkle with the wine. ✦ Add beef broth and salt to taste. Add the potatoes and let cook for about 1 hour over medium heat. ✦ Pass the potatoes and one third of the beans through a food mill. Return the purée to the soup; when the broth boils again, add the pasta and cook until al dente, about 15 minutes. ✦ Add the rosemary, parsley, and butter. Serve in bowls with slices of toasted bread flavored with garlic.

CABBAGE AND CHEESE SOUP

SOUPA DIJ BARBÉT

FOR 6 PERSONS

PIEMONTE

1 head Savoy cabbage, outer leaves removed

1½ lbs. stale bread, sliced

¾ lb. hard toma (unsalted goat's-milk cheese), grated

¼ cup seasonings to taste (salt, black pepper, chopped basil, chopped flat-leaf parsley)

Beef or chicken broth

¼ lb. (1 stick) unsalted butter

This dish is typical of the Valli Valdesi (Torre Pelice).

Cover the bottom of a large pan with cabbage leaves; cover the leaves with slices of stale bread; sprinkle toma over the bread and add half of the seasonings. Continue in this way layer by layer until the pan is filled, then cover with broth. ✦ Cook at low heat without stirring. ✦ Toast the remaining seasonings in the butter in a skillet. When the cabbage mixture is half cooked, pour it into another pan of the same size and add the seasoned butter. This can be served at room temperature in the summer.

ITALIAN EGG-DROP SOUP

STRACCIATELLA

LAZIO

4 cups meat broth

3 large eggs, beaten

CONTINUED

This dish, typical of Rome and Lazio, gets its name from the resemblance of the eggs to shredded rags, from *stracetti* ("little rags").

Bring the broth to a boil in a pot. ✦ Season the eggs with Parmigiano-Reggiano, semolina, and a pinch each of salt,

4 tbsp. grated Parmigiano-Reggiano
2 tbsp. semolina
Pinch grated nutmeg
Pinch grated lemon zest
Salt

nutmeg, and lemon zest; mix well. ✦ Pour the egg mixture into the broth and beat with a whisk long enough for the eggs to set. Simmer 10 minutes and serve hot.

BEEF BROTH WITH BARLEY FLOUR, MINT, AND PECORINO

SU FARRE

SARDEGNA

2 cups beef broth
1⅔ cups barley flour
10 leaves dried mint, chopped
¼ lb. fresh pecorino, in small chunks
Salt

This dish is typical of Gallura.

Bring the broth to a boil in a pot, then turn down the heat to low and pour in the barley flour in a thin stream, stirring continuously as though making polenta. Cook for 30 minutes at low heat, resulting in a dense soup. ✦ Add the mint and pecorino, which should melt immediately. Salt to taste and serve hot.

✦ **LOCAL TRADITION** ✦

SOUPE PAYSANNE

Typical of the Valle d'Aosta, this "Peasant Soup" is another rustic dish made with stale bread. Alternating layers of stale sliced bread and fontina, toma, and grated grana cheeses are spread in the bottom of a large baking dish. Beef broth is poured over the whole, and the dish goes into a hot oven to bake until the cheese is melted.

TAGLIATELLE WITH CHICKPEAS

TAGLIATELLE CON I CECI

CALABRIA

1⅔ cups dried chickpeas
1 tsp. baking soda
1 celery stalk
⅔ cup olive oil
2 garlic cloves, crushed
CONTINUED

Soak the chickpeas overnight in water to cover with the baking soda. ✦ Cook them with the celery in a pot with double their volume of water. When the water boils, lower the heat and continue to cook at very low heat; when the chickpeas are cooked remove with a slotted spoon and set aside. ✦ Heat half of the olive oil in a pan and sauté the garlic and guanciale. ✦ Remove the garlic, and add the *pipi russu*, tomatoes, and parsley. ✦ Cook a

2 oz. guanciale, diced

Pinch *pipi russu* (dried and ground sweet chili pepper, can use paprika)

2 fresh plum tomatoes, seeded and chopped

1 tbsp. chopped flat-leaf parsley

¾ lb. *lagane* (fresh tagliatelle, up to 1 inch wide, see page 397)

Freshly ground pepper

Salt

few minutes then add the boiled chickpeas. Let stand. ✦ Meanwhile cook the *lagane* (adding a drizzle of oil to the cooking water to keep them from sticking to one another), adding some of the cooking water, if needed, to loosen the chickpea mixture. ✦ When the *lagane* are al dente, add them to the chickpea mixture and cook for another few minutes. ✦ Before serving sprinkle the soup with the remaining oil, and season delicately with salt and pepper. This can also be eaten at room temperature.

✦ **LOCAL TRADITION** ✦

TRIPPA DEL "VECCHIO SALERA"

Typical of Piedmont, tripe cooked in the style of Vecchio Salera is a dish in which all types of tripe can be used, from *millefogli* to *rotondino* to *nido d'api*. The tripe should be boiled along with celery leaves, bay leaf, parsley stalks, rosemary, and an onion. After cooking, the broth should be discarded and the tripe cut into strips and sautéed in a hot pan with *lardo*, prosciutto crudo, olive oil, carrot, celery, and herbs, along with veal breast and a parboiled trotter, cut in half, and potatoes. Once this has cooked, a splash of strong white wine or Marsala, a few tablespoons of tomato paste, and at least one cup of good beef broth are added and left to cook for 2 or more hours, with cooked borlotti beans added near the end. Off the heat, once the fat has been skimmed, the dish can be enlivened with the addition of some finely chopped parsley, basil, and garlic. The tripe should be served in its dense sauce—the sauce must never be watery, always thick and concentrated—with fresh black pepper and grated cheese.

TAGLIOLINI CON I GARGANELLI DI MAIALE

TAGLIOLINI WITH PORK GULLETS

LAZIO

2 lbs. *garganelli* (pork gullets)

1 carrot, chopped

1 celery stalk, chopped

1 medium onion, chopped

CONTINUED

This dish is typical of the Viterbo area. These *garganelli* should not be confused with the garganelli pasta of Emilia-Romagna.

Carefully wash the pork gullets (also called *gargarozzo*) and immerse briefly in boiling water. ✦ Cut them in small pieces and cook in a pot with lightly salted water with the carrot, celery, onion, basil, and tomato to obtain

2 tbsp. chopped basil

1 plum tomato, chopped

½ lb. tagliolini, preferably homemade (see page 399)

Grated Parmigiano-Reggiano or pecorino (optional)

Salt and pepper

a thick broth; cook the tagliolini in this liquid. ✦ Before serving, if desired, sprinkle with pecorino or Parmigiano-Reggiano. ✦ The gullets can be left in pieces in the sauce, but most often they are served separately as a dish of boiled meat.

TAGLIOLINI IN BRODO CON FEGATINI

TAGLIOLINI IN BROTH WITH GIBLETS

FOR 6 PERSONS

TOSCANA

2 lbs. beef (tail, middle brisket, lean roast)

1 free-range chicken (breast and wing)

½ large onion, chopped

1 large carrot, chopped

1 celery stalk, chopped

1 plum tomato, seeded and chopped (optional)

Several basil leaves

Giblets of 2 chickens, cleaned and cut in small pieces

½ lb. egg tagliolini (see page 399)

Grated Parmigiano-Reggiano

Salt and pepper

Put the beef and chicken in a pot with about 12 cups of water. ✦ Add the vegetables, basil, and salt. Simmer at low heat until the meat is tender, removing the chicken from the pot first. ✦ When the beef is well cooked, remove it and let the broth stand, skimming off the fat. Cover and keep the chicken and beef warm. ✦ Put the giblets in a small pan and simmer them in a little of the broth; set aside when cooked. ✦ Move 4 cups of the broth from the pot to another pan, bring it to a boil, and add the tagliolini. Cook until al dente; drain. ✦ Put the cooked pasta and giblets in the pot with the remaining broth, heat, and serve in bowls. Sprinkle with cheese and pepper. The beef and chicken make the second course.

TORTELLINI BOLOGNESI

TORTELLINI BOLOGNESE IN BROTH

FOR 6–8 PERSONS

EMILIA-ROMAGNA

4 tbsp. unsalted butter

4 oz. pork loin, diced

4 oz. prosciutto crudo

4 oz. mortadella

1 large egg, beaten

1¼ cups grated Parmigiano-Reggiano

1 nutmeg, grated

4 sheets egg pasta (see page 377)

8 cups broth made from beef and capon

Prepare the filling ahead of time. Heat the butter and a little water in a pan and sauté the loin for a few minutes. ✦ When the loin is cooked, finely chop it together with the prosciutto and mortadella. ✦ Combine this mixture with the egg, cheese, and half the nutmeg, and knead together. ✦ Roll out a thin sheet of pasta (see note, page 212) and cut out disks 1½ inches in diameter. At the center of each disk place a teaspoon of the filling, fold the disk in half to form a semicircle, and press down along the edges. (You can also arrange small teaspoons of filling in rows along one sheet of pasta, cover with

another, then use a pasta cutter to cut out the tortellini.)
✦ Fold each tortellino around the tip of your index finger
to connect the two tips and press down to unite them. ✦
In a pot, bring the broth to a boil and cook the tortellini.
The pasta should be cooked thoroughly, including where
the connections were made. Even if served without a
sauce, the tortellini should always be cooked in broth.

BEEF SOUP WITH MEATBALLS AND EGGS

TRUSCELLO

SICILIA

12 oz. beef stew meat
(chuck or bottom round)

1 celery stalk, chopped

1 plum tomato, peeled,
seeded, and chopped

1 medium onion, chopped

8 oz. ground beef

6 large eggs

1 bunch flat-leaf parsley, chopped

6 oz. bread without crust

Salt and pepper

This dish is typical of Milazzo.

Simmer the stew meat in water to cover along with the
celery, tomato, onion, salt, and pepper. ✦ Meanwhile,
begin making the meatballs by working together the
ground beef, 2 of the eggs, and parsley with salt and
pepper. Use the resulting mixture to make small meatballs; set aside. ✦ When the boiling meat is cooked, remove it from the water and set aside; filter the broth and
return it to the heat; bring to a boil. ✦ Put in the meatballs and simmer, covered, for 10 minutes. ✦ Meanwhile,
beat the 4 remaining eggs. Add the bread and knead the
mixture until the eggs are completely absorbed by the
bread. ✦ Pour this mixture in the broth and stir carefully,
letting the soup simmer for another 10 minutes, then
remove from heat and serve.

PASTA AND PRAWNS IN BROTH

TUBETTI IN BRODO DI PANNOCHIE

ABRUZZO

2 lbs. mantis prawns
(the *pannocchie*)

1 medium onion, chopped

1 celery stalk, chopped

1 carrot, chopped

1 plum tomato, chopped

1 each sweet and spicy pepper

½ lb. short pasta, penne, or rigatoni

This dish is typical of Pescara.

Put the prawns in a large pot with 1 cup of water. ✦
Bring to a boil and boil over high heat until the prawns
are pink and opaque. When the prawns are cool enough
to handle, remove them from their shells and return the
meat to the cooking water. ✦ Combine the onion, celery,
carrot, tomato, and peppers in a pot with enough water
to make broth and boil for 40 minutes. ✦ Add the prawn
meat and the prawn cooking water. ✦ Cook the pasta in
this broth; when it is done, the dish is cooked.

VIGNAROLA | SPRING VEGETABLE STEW

LAZIO

½ cup olive oil
1 medium onion, thinly sliced
6 oz. pancetta, diced
1 lb. fresh fava beans, shelled and peeled
1 lb. fresh peas
5 artichoke bottoms, sliced
Salt

Vignarola is associated with the spring in Rome because it is made using the tender early produce from local gardens. It can be prepared in a more liquid version simply by adding water or broth.

Heat 4 tablespoons of the olive oil in a pan over low heat and slowly sauté the onion and the pancetta; add the fava beans and after 15 minutes add the peas; after another 10 minutes add the artichoke bottoms; let cook at low heat for 15 minutes and salt to taste.

✦ **LOCAL TRADITION** ✦

LE VIRTÙ

The Festival of the Virtù is held on May 1 in many areas of the Abruzzo but most of all in the region of Teramo. This soup, traditionally prepared at this time and known simply as Virtues Soup, was made using legumes left over from the winter combined with fresh vegetables from the new season. According to the ancient pagan rites from which this soup originated, seven virgins are to bring each seven ingredients so that the dish has 49 different elements. A few handfuls of dried legumes, such as beans, chickpeas, lentils, peas, and fava beans, would be soaked in cold water for at least a day, then drained and cooked until still very al dente. A few handfuls of fresh greens, including spinach, carrots, celery, beets, fennel, and endive, were then cleaned and also cooked in salted water, drained, and set aside. In a second pot, ground pork meat—and, if possible a prosciutto bone or the bone from a pig's snout—would be simmered in the water, then chopped, boned, and returned to the broth along with the legumes and leaves of marjoram and mint. In a third pan, parsley, tomato purée, onion, and garlic would be sautéed in *lardo*, to which was then added the broth with the meat and legumes and the fresh vegetables. Once the fresh vegetables were almost cooked, dried pasta would be added to the pot. This dense and delicious soup was eaten either hot or cold.

| # CHICKPEA STEW

LIGURIA

1 ½ cups dried chickpeas, soaked in water at least 24 hours

2 tbsp. extra-virgin olive oil

1 medium onion, finely chopped

1 celery stalk, chopped

1 garlic clove, chopped

1 oz. dried mushrooms, soaked in water, dried, and chopped

3 or 4 ripe plum tomatoes, peeled, seeded, and chopped

¾ lb. Swiss chard, cut in strips

Toasted bread (optional)

Salt

Boil the chickpeas in a pot with lightly salted water about 3 hours. Drain and set aside, reserving the liquid. ✦ Heat the olive oil in a pan and sauté the onion, celery, garlic, and mushrooms; add the tomatoes, then the chard. ✦ Add the drained chickpeas and cook 10 minutes. Add a few cups of the chickpea liquid, adjust for salt, bring to a boil, and serve hot over toasted bread, if desired.

✦ LOCAL TRADITION ✦

ZUPPA AL RAPERONZOLO

Haller's rampion (*raperonzolo*) is an ancient wild green now slightly out of favor; its roots were often boiled and served like parsnips, and the leaves, like those in this rampion soup typical of Valle d'Aosta, could be substituted for spinach out of season or eaten as a winter salad. Rampion was already commonly used in rustic cooking by the early seventeenth century, and its use had even been discussed by Horace—one of the greatest Roman poets—in his third satire. In this recipe, the rampion would be simmered with potatoes, carrots, onions, and zucchini, while in a separate pot barley would be cooked with pork rind or pancetta. The vegetables were then combined with the barley and rendered fat of some prosciutto crudo in a large baking pan and the top covered with slices of toasted black rye bread (preferably Valdostan), olive oil, fontina, and chopped fresh parsley, basil, and garlic. The dish would be baked for about 10 minutes, until the cheese melted, and was served hot.

PIQUANT TRIPE SOUP

ZUPPA ACIDA DI TRIPPA

ALTO ADIGE

1 lb. veal or pork tripe
4 tbsp. olive oil
2 medium onions, chopped
2 tbsp. all-purpose flour
6 cups broth
2-inch strip lemon zest, diced
1 bay leaf
1 pimiento (Jamaican pepper)
2 garlic cloves, finely diced
½ cup red wine vinegar
Grated Parmigiano-Reggiano
Salt and pepper

In place of the vinegar, some cooks use the juice of a lemon and a half cup of white wine. The true (and best) recipe calls for vinegar; in the past, it was customary to serve it at the table, allowing the diners to decide for themselves how much they wanted.

Cut the tripe into thin strips. Heat the oil in a pot and sauté the onions and tripe. ✦ Sprinkle with flour, cook until the flour forms a paste, then cover with broth. ✦ Add salt and pepper, lemon zest, bay leaf, pimiento, and garlic. Simmer for at least 30 minutes. ✦ Season with vinegar and serve with Parmigiano-Reggiano.

CHEESE SOUP

ZUPPA AL PIATTO

VALLE D'AOSTA

6 oz. peasant-style bread, sliced and toasted
6 oz. fontina
Beef broth, heated
4 tbsp. unsalted butter, melted

This dish is typical of Cogne. A version of this dish is served for wedding lunches in the Alta Valle (Valdigne), but in place of the beef broth it is made with a thick vegetable soup prepared a day in advance.

Preheat the oven to 350°F. In a baking dish alternate layers of bread slices with slices of fontina. ✦ Pour over hot broth until the bread is soaked, resulting in a soft soup. ✦ Pour the butter over this and bake for about 10 minutes, until the cheese is melted. Serve hot in the winter, room temperature in the summer.

SCALIGER SOUP

ZUPPA ALLA SCALIGERA

VENETO

½ young female turkey
½ free-range chicken
2 young squabs
All-purpose flour, for dredging
CONTINUED

The Scaligers are one of the grand old families of Verona and might be thought of as either the Capulets or the Montagues in *Romeo and Juliet*.

Cut the turkey, chicken, and squabs in pieces, and dredge the pieces in flour. In a large pot, heat half of the olive oil over high heat, add the bird pieces, and sauté until lightly browned, turning as necessary. Reduce the heat to

187

¼ cup extra-virgin olive oil
1 celeriac, cut in thin slices
3 large onions, cut in thin slices
3 carrots, cut in thin slices
3 potatoes, peeled and sliced
1 lb. plum tomatoes, peeled, seeded, and chopped
1 bay leaf
6 cups dry white wine
6 cups beef broth
¾ lb. bread, sliced and toasted
Grated Parmigiano-Reggiano, for topping
Salt and pepper

medium, cover, and complete the cooking (until the juices run clear when the birds are pierced with a long fork). (You may have to use two pots for this). ✦ In another pot, heat the remaining olive oil over low heat and sauté the celeriac, onions, carrots, and potatoes for 15 minutes. ✦ Bone the birds and put the meat in the pot with the cooked vegetables; add the tomatoes, salt, pepper, bay leaf, wine, and half the broth. ✦ Simmer at low heat for at least 2 hours. Preheat the oven to 350°F. ✦ In a high-sided baking dish create a layer of toasted bread and over that a layer of the meat-and-vegetable mixture; pour over this the remaining broth and sprinkle with cheese. ✦ Bake for 1 hour. ✦ Sprinkle more cheese over the top, raise the heat to 400°F, and bake 20 minutes more. Serve warm, not piping hot.

BAKED VEGETABLE SOUP WITH BLACK BREAD AND BARLEY

ZUPPA ALLA UECA

VALLE D'AOSTA

2 potatoes
2 carrots
1 small onion
2 zucchini
1¼ cups barley
10 oz. pork rind or pancetta
Sliced black bread, toasted
2 tbsp. extra-virgin olive oil
7 oz. fontina, sliced
2 tbsp. chopped flat-leaf parsley
2 tbsp. chopped basil
1 garlic clove, chopped

This dish is typical of Aosta.

Preheat the oven to 350°F. Chop the vegetables and combine them in a pot with water to cover; simmer about 30 minutes to make a soup. ✦ Separately cook the barley with the pork rind until the grains are tender; add them to the vegetable soup. ✦ Put this mixture in a large baking dish, cover it with toasted black bread, olive oil, and fontina. Mince together the parsley, basil, and garlic and sprinkle this mixture over the fontina. ✦ Bake for about 10 minutes until the cheese melts, then heat the broiler and broil for about 3 minutes, or until the cheese is golden.

MOUNTAIN SOUP FROM VALPELLINE

ZUPPA ALLA VALPELLINESE

VALLE D'AOSTA

To braise the cabbage, remove the outer leaves of the cabbage, then shred the inner leaves very fine. Heat a little olive oil in a pan and add the cabbage. Sauté until it starts to wilt, then add salt, pepper, and 1 tablespoon red wine vinegar. Cover, reduce the heat to low, and cook 1½ hours or until very tender. The liquid given off by the cabbage should be sufficient, but if needed, add 2 tablespoons water.

¼ cup (4 tbsp.) unsalted butter

8 slices black bread

7 oz. fontina, sliced

½ Savoy cabbage, braised (see note)

Grated Parmigiano-Reggiano

2 cups beef broth

Preheat the oven to 350°F. Melt the butter in a pan and toast the slices of bread. Place them in a baking dish. ✦ Alternate layers of bread with fontina and leaves of the braised cabbage, covering with Parmigiano-Reggiano; then pour over beef broth and bake for 10 minutes, until the cheese is melted.

ZUPPA CON I BULBI DEI MUSCARI

WILD ONION SOUP

FOR
6 PERSONS

CALABRIA

1 ¼ cups olive oil

1 garlic clove, crushed

¾ lb. *cipuddizzee* (wild onions that resemble the Puglian *lampascioni*, hyacinth bulbs), cleaned and quartered

4 cups broth, either beef or vegetable

1 *diavolillo* (hot chili pepper, see note, page 22), cut in small pieces

1 lb. stale peasant-style bread slices, toasted

½ cup grated pecorino

Salt

If you can find them from a trusted source, wild lily bulbs are an appropriate substitute for the *cipuddizzee*. Or, you could substitute half and half of peeled pearl onions and shallots.

In an earthenware pot heat the olive oil, then sauté the garlic until light golden. Add the wild onions, cover with broth, add salt, and cook until the onions are tender. ✦ At the end of cooking add the *diavolillo*. ✦ Place the slices of toasted peasant-style bread in the bottom of bowls, pour over the broth with the onions, and sprinkle with pecorino.

ZUPPA CON L'AGNELLO

LAMB SOUP

LAZIO

2 tbsp. extra-virgin olive oil

4 oz. prosciutto or guanciale fat

1 carrot, chopped

1 garlic clove, chopped

1 medium onion, chopped

2 lbs. lamb shoulder, cut in pieces

½ cup dry white wine

1 lb. plum tomatoes, peeled and passed through a food mill

Stale peasant-style bread

CONTINUED

This dish is typical of the shepherds around Viterbo—its popular name, *giubba e calzoni* ("vest and trousers"), apparently refers to the satisfying completeness of its ingredients. Indeed, it represents a kind of prototype of the nutritious and substantial one-dish meal. In the variation most common in the area of the Maremma Laziale, one artichoke is added per person, cooked in the broth in which the lamb was cooked. In this case chili pepper takes the place of pepper, and not much use is made of the pecorino. There are still those who add pecorino at the table.

In an earthenware pot heat the olive oil and sauté the prosciutto or guanciale fat, adding the carrot, garlic, and onion. ✦ Season the lamb with salt and pepper and add to the pan; sauté until lightly browned, then pour in the

Grated aged pecorino Romano (optional)

Salt and pepper

white wine. ✦ When the wine evaporates add the tomatoes and a few tablespoons of warm water; let cook slowly, adding water occasionally to maintain the quantity of liquid that will be needed to soak the bread. Add salt and pepper to taste. ✦ When it has cooked, arrange slices of bread in a serving bowl and pour the entire mixture over them. Let rest for a few minutes to allow the bread to soak up liquid, then serve, sprinkled with pecorino, if using.

ZUPPA CON LE FAVE

FAVA BEAN SOUP

FOR
6 PERSONS

LAZIO

2 tbsp. extra-virgin olive oil

8 oz. pancetta, diced

4 oz. prosciutto fat

1 garlic clove, chopped

Several sprigs fresh spearmint (or marjoram)

12 lbs. fresh fava beans, shelled and peeled

½ cup vegetable broth (optional)

2 medium white onions, sliced

1 head butter lettuce, outer leaves removed, inner leaves washed and removed from the core

1 lb. plum tomatoes, peeled and passed through a food mill

7 oz. pork rind, cleaned and parboiled

Pinch chili pepper flakes

Stale peasant-style bread, sliced

This dish is typical of Viterbo. The dialect name for this soup is *scafata*, itself based on the dialect word for favas (*scafi*). At Montefiascone this soup is called *baggianata*, an Italian word most often applied to a foolish act or statement or an object of little value. The word comes from *baggiana*, the name for a variety of fava beans; according to some sources it is from a Latin word meaning "fava from Baia," referring to a town near Naples. To achieve success with this soup it is best to use fresh fava beans, only recently harvested, and small in size. The pork rind should be carefully scraped to remove any remaining bristles and then washed in warm water; scrape away any superfluous fat and parboil before adding it to the soup. In some areas of the Maremma Laziale, artichokes cut in sections are added to the soup.

Heat the olive oil in a pan and sauté the pancetta, prosciutto fat, garlic, and spearmint (or marjoram). ✦ Add the fava beans and a half cup of water or hot broth, letting it cook for 10 minutes. ✦ At this point add the onions, lettuce leaves, tomatoes, pork rind, and chili pepper; continue cooking at low heat for about 1½ hours, until the fava beans are completely cooked, adding more salt and water if necessary. ✦ When the soup is cooked place the bread in bowls, spoon the soup over, and let it rest for a few minutes before serving.

ZUPPA CON RAPE
E FAGIOLI

TURNIP AND BEAN SOUP

LAZIO

1 lb. dried beans

CONTINUED

Soak the beans overnight in water to cover. ✦ The next day, drain them, then boil in a pot of lightly salted water. ✦ Combine the most tender turnip greens and turnips, rinse, and add to the beans along with the tomatoes. ✦ In

2 lbs. turnips, cut in pieces,
with greens

3 plum tomatoes, cut in pieces

2 tbsp. extra-virgin olive oil

1 garlic clove

1 medium onion, chopped

2 oz. *lardo* (see page 2)

Salt and pepper

Stale peasant-style bread slices

a pan with a little olive oil sauté the garlic, onion, and *lardo*; add salt and pepper. ✦ When the fat melts add to the soup pot. Continue cooking, adding hot water if necessary, and at the end pour the soup into a tureen with slices of stale bread.

ZUPPA DEI "TRAPPETARI"

FAVA, BROCCOLI, AND CHICORY SOUP

PUGLIA

1 lb. dried unshelled fava beans

2 small plum tomatoes, chopped

1 bunch flat-leaf parsley, chopped

4 lbs. mixed broccoli and chicory

4 slices dark stale bread

Olive oil

Salt and freshly ground pepper

This dish is typical of Macchia (Gargano). You can also season the soup with olive oil in which some garlic and a little chili pepper have been browned; if doing so, eliminate the fresh pepper and the unheated olive oil. The favas should be shelled by hand: only the interior is eaten, the shell discarded.

Soak the fava beans in their shells overnight in water to cover. ✦ The next morning peel them, then boil them in a pot with water to cover at very low heat for 1 hour, then set aside some of the water. Add the tomatoes and salt and continue cooking until tender, about 1 hour more. ✦ When the beans are thoroughly cooked, almost to a purée, add the parsley. ✦ In a separate pot simmer the broccoli and chicory in water to cover until tender, then drain. ✦ Put ½-inch-thick slices of dark stale bread in soup bowls, pour the reserved water from boiling the fava beans over the bread, add the broccoli and chicory, and top with the fava beans. ✦ Season with olive oil and pepper.

ZUPPA DEL MONACO

CHICORY SOUP

BASILICATA

8 cups chicory, cleaned

4 cups chicken broth

¼ cup olive oil

½ cup *lardo* (see page 2), diced

1 medium onion, sliced

Grated pecorino

In a pot, boil the chicory in the broth; strain, reserving the liquid. ✦ Chop the chicory and set aside. ✦ Heat the olive oil in a pan and sauté the *lardo* and onion. Add the cooked chicory. ✦ Put the chicory and its cooking liquid in a tureen, sprinkle with pecorino, and serve hot.

ZUPPA DI ASPARAGI | ASPARAGUS SOUP

CALABRIA

1 lb. wild asparagus

2 tbsp. extra-virgin olive oil

2 garlic cloves, chopped

6 cups beef broth

4 large eggs, beaten

2 tbsp. grated pecorino

2 tbsp. chopped flat-leaf parsley

Slices of toasted bread

Salt and pepper

Clean and peel the asparagus, keeping only the tips and the more tender areas of the stalks; rinse and set aside. ✦ Heat the olive oil in a pot and sauté the garlic; when it has browned add the asparagus and cook for a few minutes. ✦ Add the broth and cook until the asparagus is bright green and tender. ✦ Add the eggs, pecorino, parsley, salt, and pepper. ✦ Mix with a wooden spoon. Place slices of bread in bowls and pour the soup over.

ZUPPA DI AVOLE E COREGONI | LAKE GARDA FISH SOUP

VENETO

2 lbs. whitefish

1 lb. butterfish

1 lb. carp

1 lb. perch fillets

2 garlic cloves, crushed

4 bay leaves

⅔ cup olive oil

2 medium onions, thinly sliced

Juice of ½ lemon

¼ cup chopped flat-leaf parsley

1 lb. freshwater shrimp

Slices of bread, toasted or sautéed in oil

Salt and pepper

This fish soup, known locally as *brodetto*, has origins that lead back to the famous *brodetto* of Venice, which is made with fish and crustaceans from the sea. Renowned since ancient times, this soup has been a constant presence in the cooking of the area around Lake Garda and Verona.

Rinse and carefully clean all the fish. ✦ Cut all the fish except the perch in pieces and put them in a pot with the garlic and bay leaves; cover with water and simmer at least 1 hour. ✦ Turn off the heat and let the liquid cool; strain and reserve the broth. Bone the fish and pass the fillets through a food mill, returning the mixture to the broth. ✦ In a separate pan heat the olive oil and cook the onions and lemon juice; add salt to taste, then parsley. ✦ Add the perch and shrimp and cook for 10 minutes. ✦ Add this mixture to the broth, bring to a boil, then reduce the heat and simmer another 10 minutes. ✦ Place a slice of bread in each soup bowl. Pour over the broth and distribute the seafood. Season with a pinch of pepper. Serve hot.

ZUPPA DI BORRAGINE | BORAGE SOUP

CALABRIA

2 potatoes, peeled and
cut in small pieces

3 shallots, peeled and
roughly chopped

¼ cup extra-virgin olive oil

6 oz. borage leaves

1 *diavolillo* (hot chili pepper,
see note, page 22)

Slices of peasant-style bread, toasted

Cook the potatoes and shallots in a pot of lightly salted water; when they are still very al dente season with the olive oil. ✦ Add the borage leaves and chili pepper and continue cooking until the potatoes are tender. Place a slice of bread in each bowl and spoon the soup over.

ZUPPA DI BRODO CON SALSICCE | SAUSAGE SOUP

ABRUZZO

8 slices peasant-style bread

4 large eggs, beaten

½ cup grated pecorino

1 lb. sausages, sliced

2 large hard-boiled eggs, sliced

6 cups beef broth

Toast the bread and dip each slice in the beaten eggs. ✦ Align the slices in a pan and sprinkle with cheese. ✦ Arrange the slices of sausage and boiled eggs over the bread slices. ✦ Pour in the broth and when it boils, serve the soup.

ZUPPA DI CARDONE | CARDOON SOUP

CAMPANIA

1 cardoon stalk, hard parts
and ribs removed

Juice of 1 lemon

¾ lb. ground veal

1 cup crumbs of stale bread

3 large eggs

¼ cup extra-virgin olive oil

4 cups chicken broth

2 tbsp. grated Parmigiano-Reggiano

½ tbsp. pine nuts

½ tbsp. raisins

Salt and pepper

Crostini

Soak the cardoon for a few hours in water with lemon juice so it loses some of its bitter flavor. ✦ Boil the cardoon, drain it, and cut in small pieces. ✦ Mix the ground veal, breadcrumbs, 1 egg, and salt. Form tiny meatballs. ✦ Heat the olive oil in a pan and quickly brown the meatballs. Set aside. ✦ Skim any fat off the broth, heat it, strain it, and put it back over heat. ✦ As soon as it boils add the cardoon. Cook 15 minutes. ✦ Beat the remaining eggs with cheese, salt, and pepper and add this mixture to the broth. ✦ Let it thicken without stirring, then pour the soup into bowls, and add the meatballs, pine nuts, and raisins. Serve with crostini.

CHESTNUT AND CHICKPEA SOUP 1

LAZIO

1⅔ cups dried chickpeas

1⅔ cups dried chestnuts

1 sprig rosemary

½ cup olive oil

1 garlic clove

1 chili pepper

1 celery stalk, chopped

1⅔ cups peeled plum tomatoes

Stale peasant-style bread, sliced

Salt

This soup comes from the countryside around Viterbo, an area with abundant chestnut trees. In the past it was a traditional dish made on the day of Christmas Eve (hence the presence of the relatively expensive chickpeas). In fact, during the fall chestnut harvest, a portion of chestnuts, with the husks removed, was kept soaking for several days, put in the cellar to dry, and preserved to be eaten during the winter. According to the older farmers in the area, the presence of chestnuts in this soup was not the result of some elaborate and skilled combination of flavors but was simply because chestnuts, which could be collected freely along the roads and in many chestnut groves on the Ciminian Hills, were available at no cost and were thus used to supplement the chickpeas which had to be bought. All this demonstrates the great poverty and frugality that reigned in times not really so distant.

Soak the chickpeas overnight in water and salt. ✦ Parboil the chestnuts to make them easier to shell, shell them, and break the larger ones in half. ✦ In a pot, earthenware if possible, partially cook the chickpeas with the rosemary (later discarded). ✦ In a separate pot heat the olive oil in a pan and sauté the garlic, adding the chili pepper, a few rosemary leaves, and celery. ✦ Pass the tomatoes through a food mill and add them to the garlic mixture; let this cook for several minutes. ✦ Add the dried chestnuts and, a little later, add the mixture to the chickpeas, removing a few tablespoons of chestnuts and chickpeas, crushing them or passing them through a food mill before returning them to the soup to make it denser and more flavorful. ✦ Place a slice of bread in each bowl and when the soup is cooked, pour it over the bread. Cover the bowls for a few minutes to allow the bread to soak up the liquid, then serve.

ZUPPA DI CASTAGNE E CECI 2
CHESTNUT AND CHICKPEA SOUP 2

UMBRIA

1 ¼ cups dried chickpeas
1 cup fresh chestnuts
1 garlic clove
½ cup flat-leaf parsley leaves
2 tbsp. olive oil
6 tbsp. tomato purée
4 slices of peasant-style bread
Salt and pepper

This dish is typical of Todi, where it is traditionally served on Christmas Eve.

Soak the chickpeas in water to cover for 24 hours. ✦ At the end of that time, drain the chickpeas, put them in a pot, cover with water, and boil at low heat for at least 2 hours. Drain. ✦ Roast the chestnuts, peel them, and chop them in small pieces. ✦ Finely chop the garlic and parsley and put them in a pan together with the chestnuts and olive oil. ✦ Cook, add the tomato purée, and after a few minutes the chickpeas. ✦ After 10 minutes add enough water to make a soup and cook for 1 hour. ✦ Taste for salt, add pepper, and serve over slices of toasted bread arranged in soup bowls.

ZUPPA DI CIPOLLE
ONION SOUP

FOR 6 PERSONS

PIEMONTE

¼ cup (4 tbsp.) unsalted butter, plus more for buttering the bread
1 lb. onions, sliced
½ cup dry white wine
2 tbsp. all-purpose flour
6 cups beef broth
Slices of stale bread
Grated Parmigiano-Reggiano
Grated Gruyère

Preheat the oven to 350°F. Melt the butter in a large pot over low heat. Add the onions and slowly sauté them until golden. ✦ Add the wine and let it evaporate. ✦ Sprinkle the flour over the onions, stir, then slowly add the broth, creating a creamy but not too thick soup. ✦ Butter slices of bread and toast them in the oven. Put the slices of bread in individual bowls, pour the soup over, and sprinkle with Parmigiano-Reggiano and Gruyère.

ZUPPA DI CIPOLLE E FAVE
ONION AND FAVA BEAN SOUP

CAMPANIA

4 tbsp. olive oil
1 lb. new onions, finely chopped
2 lbs. fresh fava beans, shelled
Salt

Heat the oil in a large pot over low heat, then add the onions and sauté for a few minutes. ✦ Add the fava beans. ✦ Add a little water and salt, cover, and cook for about 30 minutes. Stir often to break up the beans.

ONION SOUP WITH BREAD

ZUPPA DI CIPOLLE E PANE

CALABRIA

2 tbsp. lard

2 or 3 medium onions
(best are the red onions of
Parghelia-Tropea), finely sliced

2 spicy dried red chili peppers,
crumbled

Slices of toasted
peasant-style bread

Grated pecorino

Salt

Heat the lard in a large pot. Add the onions and sauté slowly until golden, gradually adding water to make soup. ✦ When the onions are nearly cooked, add the chili peppers and salt. ✦ Place the bread in bowls, then pour the soup over and sprinkle with pecorino.

BEAN SOUP 5

ZUPPA DI FAGIOLI

PUGLIA

1 lb. dried beans

1 celery stalk, chopped

2 garlic cloves

A few threads of saffron

4 large slices peasant-style bread,
toasted

¾ cup olive oil

Chili pepper flakes (optional)

This dish is typical of Foggia.

Soak the beans overnight in lukewarm salted water. ✦ The next morning rinse them, drain, and put in an earthenware pot with the celery, garlic, saffron, and water to cover by several inches. ✦ Bring to a boil, then simmer for about 2 hours. ✦ Serve in bowls over toasted bread. Season with olive oil and, if desired, chili pepper flakes.

BEAN AND WILD FENNEL SOUP

ZUPPA DI FAGIOLI
COL FINOCCHIETTO

LAZIO

1 bunch fresh wild fennel

1½ cups dried beans

¼ cup extra-virgin olive oil

1 garlic clove

1 lb. tomato purée

Salt and pepper (or chili pepper)

Peasant-style bread, sliced

This dish is typical of Viterbo. Wild fennel is an aromatic plant widely used in the area. It shows up in porchetta, dried chestnuts, stewed snails, various soups, and other dishes.

Select the more tender parts of the wild fennel leaves, slice them in finger-length pieces, and parboil them in a pot with water to cover 2 minutes. ✦ Cook the beans in a pot with lightly salted water and, in a pan, heat half the olive oil and sauté the garlic until lightly golden. Add the tomato purée, parboiled fennel, salt, and pepper (or chili pepper) and cook for 10 minutes at low heat, then add to the beans. ✦ Add hot water (or broth) and continue cooking, adding more water if necessary so that there is enough liquid in the end to pour over the slices of bread arranged in a tureen or individual bowls. ✦ Pour the soup over the bread, cover, and let it rest for a few minutes. Just before serving drizzle with olive oil.

BEAN AND PORK SOUP

ZUPPA DI FAGIOLI
CON COTENNE

ABRUZZO

6 oz. pork rind
1 lb. fresh cranberry beans, shelled
1 celery stalk
1 medium onion
1 carrot
1 garlic clove
2 tbsp. olive oil
Salt and pepper

Scrape and carefully clean and defat the pork rind. ✦ Boil it in a pot of water, then cut it in thin strips. ✦ Cover the beans with water by several inches, bring to a boil, then simmer until half cooked, about 30 minutes. ✦ Finely chop together the celery, onion, carrot, and garlic. Heat the olive oil in a pot and sauté the vegetables, adding salt and pepper. ✦ When this is about half cooked, add the pork rind, beans, cooking liquid and let cook for another 30 minutes, or until the beans are tender.

BEAN AND PASTA SOUP

ZUPPA DI FAGIOLI
WITH TAGLIOLINI

ABRUZZO

1 lb. fresh white beans
(*sgrano* beans if possible)
2 tbsp. extra-virgin olive oil
1 celery stalk, chopped
1 garlic clove, chopped
1 medium onion, chopped
1 carrot, chopped
1 cup purée of fresh
plum tomatoes
1 cup all-purpose flour
Grated fresh pecorino
Salt

Shell the beans. Heat the olive oil in a pot and sauté the celery, garlic, onion, and carrot. Add the beans and stir to coat them with the oil. ✦ Add water to cover and the tomato purée, salt to taste, and cook until the beans are tender, about 1 hour. ✦ Use the flour to prepare a pasta dough as in the recipe on page 10, using 6 tablespoons water in place of the eggs. Roll the dough into a sheet (see note, page 212) and cut it into thick strips no more than 2 inches long. ✦ Add the tagliolini to the beans and cook until al dente, about 10 minutes. Serve hot with a sprinkling of fresh pecorino.

BEAN, ESCAROLE, AND PORK SOUP

6 oz. pork rind

6 oz. dried sausage

1 small piece prosciutto bone

1 ½ lbs. dried beans

1 lb. escarole

½ cup lard

1 garlic clove

1 celery stalk

6 peeled plum tomatoes

¼ cup chopped flat-leaf parsley, plus more for serving

1 small piece red chili pepper

4 oz. salame, diced

Salt

Slices of peasant-style bread, toasted

This dish is typical of Naples.

Clean the pork rind, sausage, and prosciutto bone and combine them in a pot with the beans. Add cold water to cover and bring to a boil. Reduce the heat and simmer until the beans are completely cooked. ✦ Put the escarole in a pot with lightly salted boiling water, cover the pot, and when the water returns to a boil, remove the pot from the heat, drain, and mash the escarole. ✦ Heat the lard in a pot and add the garlic, celery, and tomatoes. Cook until it thickens into a sauce. Just before it is finished, add the parsley. ✦ Remove the prosciutto bone and pork rind from the beans. Stir in the escarole, tomato sauce, and red chili pepper. Cook at low heat for another 20 minutes, adding the salame and a little more parsley at the end of cooking. Serve over slices of toasted bread.

FRESH FAVA BEAN SOUP

6 artichokes

Lemon juice

2 lbs. fresh shelled fava beans

1 ½ lbs. fresh shelled peas

4 small onions

4 oz. pancetta, diced

⅔ cup olive oil

1 lb. potatoes, peeled and chopped

1 lb. asparagus, woody ends trimmed

½ cup chopped flat-leaf parsley

Salt and pepper

This dish is typical of Aversa.

Cut each artichoke into eight sections, removing all the hard outer leaves and the fuzzy choke; put them in water with lemon juice. ✦ Clean and dry the fava beans and peas. ✦ Set aside 2 of the onions and cut the others in half to add to the pancetta. ✦ Heat the olive oil in a pot over medium heat and add the halved onions and pancetta. When the onions begin to turn golden, add the potatoes, fava beans, pepper, salt, and the 2 whole onions. ✦ Reduce the heat to low, cover, and stew slowly for 10 minutes, then add the peas and the artichokes, stirring and mixing so that the artichokes are completely covered by the other ingredients so they do not turn black. ✦ Add the asparagus and continue cooking with the pan covered, adding a little water if needed. ✦ Add the parsley about 2 minutes before removing the soup from the heat. The vegetables should very soft, almost mushy.

ZUPPA DI FUNGHI | MUSHROOM SOUP

EMILIA-ROMAGNA

1½ lbs. small, fresh porcini mushrooms

2 tbsp. unsalted butter

2 tbsp. olive oil

1 medium onion, finely minced

1 carrot, minced

1 celery stalk, minced

1 oz. dried mushrooms, minced

4 cups beef broth

1 potato, peeled, boiled, and crushed

1¼ cups heavy cream

Salt

This dish is typical of Borgotaro. Serve with boiled rice or toasted croutons.

Clean the mushrooms, and finely slice the tops and some of the stalks; grate the remaining stalks. ✦ Heat a little butter and olive oil in a pot over medium heat and cook the onion, carrot, celery, and dried mushrooms; when these have browned add the fresh mushrooms. ✦ Add salt and let the mushrooms take on a light color. ✦ Add the broth and potato. ✦ Simmer for a few minutes, then add the cream.

ZUPPA DI LEGUMI CON ZUCCA E ORZETTO | VEGETABLE SOUP WITH SQUASH AND BARLEY

PUGLIA

¼ cup olive oil

4 oz. yellow winter squash, peeled and cut into cubes

2 cups broth

1 celery stalk

1 carrot

1 garlic clove

1 medium onion

½ lb. legumes (chickpeas, cannelli, and/or cranberry beans), cooked, liquid reserved

6 oz. barley, cooked in water

1 tsp. chili-pepper flakes or 1 tbsp. chopped flat-leaf parsley

Peasant-style bread, sliced and toasted

Salt

Heat half the olive oil in pot; add the squash and sauté until it begins to take on a little color. ✦ Add the broth, and simmer until the squash is done; set aside and keep warm. ✦ Chop together the celery, carrot, garlic, and onion. Heat the remaining olive oil in a pot and sauté the vegetables; add the legumes and their water, then add the squash and barley. ✦ Adjust for salt and add chili pepper flakes or parsley. Serve with slices of toasted peasant-style bread.

LENTIL AND CROSTINI SOUP

ABRUZZO

2 ½ cups dried lentils
2 bay leaves
1 potato, peeled and sliced
¼ cup olive oil
1 garlic clove
1 sprig marjoram
1 sprig basil
1 cup tomato purée
Slices of peasant-style bread, cut into cubes

The soup can be made without tomatoes, in which case it should be served with a drizzle of olive oil.

Boil the lentils in 8 cups water in an earthenware pot together with the bay leaves and potato until cooked, about 1 hour. ✦ Heat 2 tablespoons olive oil in a pan and add the garlic, marjoram, basil, and tomato purée. Cook until the sauce thickens and set aside. In a separate pan, heat the remaining olive oil and toast the bread cubes until golden. ✦ Add the tomato sauce to the lentils and serve the soup with the toasted bread.

ZUPPA DI MAGRO
CON CAVOLO NERO

BLACK KALE AND RICE SOUP

LIGURIA

1 medium onion
1 celery stalk
1 bunch flat-leaf parsley
1 bunch black kale (see page 99; can substitute kale)
5 tbsp. olive oil
8 cups fish broth
1 ¼ cups rice
Salt

Chop together the onion, celery, and parsley; slice the black kale. Heat ¼ cup olive oil in a pan and sauté the onion mixture, then add the kale. ✦ Add the fish broth, salt to taste, and let simmer about 30 minutes. ✦ Add the rice and cook until tender. Drizzle with the remaining olive oil. This dish can be served hot or at room temperature.

✦ **LOCAL TRADITION** ✦

ZUPPA DI PANE

This bread soup, typical of Friuli-Venezia Giulia, made use of the excellent native Istrian olive oil, which would impart a particular flavor to the soup, along with fennel or cumin seeds. Stale bread would be boiled with water, the oil, and seeds to make a dense, rustic soup, traditionally enriched with egg yolks.

ZUPPA DI MUSCOLI | MUSSEL SOUP

LIGURIA

2 lbs. mussels, scrubbed and beards removed

½ cup olive oil

1 garlic clove, chopped

¼ cup chopped flat-leaf parsley

2 tbsp. tomato paste

½ cup dry white wine

Toasted bread slices

Place the mussels in a pot and add a little water. Cover and heat over high heat until they open. Drain them and reserve the cooking liquid. ✦ Heat the olive oil in another pan and sauté the garlic and parsley. Add the tomato paste, then the white wine; cook for 10 minutes then add the mussels and 2 or 3 spoonfuls of their lukewarm cooking liquid. ✦ Cook another 5 minutes. Serve hot over slices of toasted bread in bowls.

ZUPPA DI ORTAGGI | VEGETABLE SOUP

FOR 6 PERSONS

CALABRIA

1 celery stalk

1 medium onion, quartered

1 carrot

2 potatoes, peeled and quartered

Pinch dried oregano

4 large eggs

1 bunch flat-leaf parsley

1 sprig fresh marjoram

Slices of bread, toasted

Grated pecorino

Salt

The name for this dish, *sciscillu,* is a diminutive of *sciscia,* meaning "a happy thing; a toy." In fact, such is the simplicity of this dish that a child could almost make it.

Put the celery, onion, carrot, potatoes, and oregano in a pot with about 8 cups of salted water and simmer 40 minutes. ✦ Strain the broth, discard the vegetables (or eat them separately), and pour the broth into a small pan; crack the eggs into the liquid delicately to keep the yolks from breaking. Simmer until the eggs are poached. ✦ Chop together the parsley and marjoram. Stir the herbs into the soup. Serve with bread. Dust with pecorino.

BARLEY SOUP

ZUPPA DI ORZO

PIEMONTE

2 cups pearl barley

1 ¼ cups fresh shelled beans

2 tbsp. extra-virgin olive oil

2 carrots, chopped

1 medium onion, chopped

3 celery stalks, chopped

1 garlic clove, chopped

2 oz. speck, diced

2 tbsp. chopped flat-leaf parsley

Salt and pepper

Soak the pearl barley in cold water for 1 hour; drain. ✦ Boil the beans in a pot with lightly salted water to cover until done, drain, and set aside. ✦ Heat the olive oil in a pot and sauté the carrots, onion, celery, garlic, and speck. ✦ Add the barley, beans, 4 cups of water, and the parsley. Salt and cook, covered, for 15 minutes. ✦ Turn off the heat, uncover, and let rest for 30 minutes. Reheat and add pepper before serving.

✦ **LOCAL TRADITION** ✦

ZUPPA DI PESCE

On the beaches of Crotone, beneath the promontory of Capo di Colonne, the sure sign of a bountiful catch would be the sight of the local fishermen gathered around enormous copper pots called *quadaro* over open fires of olive branches, cooking this traditional fish soup famous throughout Calabria. Onion, garlic, and hot red chili would be sautéed in olive oil, and the fish, shellfish (typically scorpion fish, *lumera*, *cocio* or red bandfish, grouper, octopus, cuttlefish, crayfish, limpets, mussels, and clams), and fresh seaweed would be added to the *quadaro* and cooked for a few minutes before the addition of chopped fresh tomato and seawater. Stale peasant-style bread completed their rustic meal.

STUFFED-BREAD SOUP

ZUPPA DI PANE FARCITO

CALABRIA

8 slices stale peasant-style bread

6 large egg yolks, beaten

CONTINUED

Cut the crusts off the bread and lay 4 of the slices out on a cutting board. ✦ Brush the slices with egg yolk and cover them evenly with the meat, parsley, black pepper, and cheese. ✦ Brush the remaining bread with egg yolk, then place them on top of the meat mixture. With a ser-

¾ lb. chicken and veal, finely ground

¼ cup chopped flat-leaf parsley

Grated pecorino

Sprigs of oregano (optional),
as needed

1 cup lard

6 cups chicken broth,
heated to boiling

Salt and pepper

rated knife cut each sandwich into cubes. ✦ Hold them closed with a sprig of oregano or a wooden toothpick. Heat the lard in a pan and cook the cubes so that the egg yolks fasten them together as they cook. Place in bowls and pour over the broiling broth.

ZUPPA DI PATATE
AI FUNGHI E CRESCIONE

POTATO AND
MUSHROOM SOUP

TRENTINO

¾ lb. mushrooms, preferably
marzaioli (*Pleurotus*), cubed

1½ cups olive oil

4 shallots, sliced

1 garlic clove, minced

¼ cup white wine

1 lb. potatoes, peeled,
cut in cubes, and steamed

4 cups beef broth

1½ cups heavy cream

2 large egg yolks, beaten

1 bunch chervil, chopped

Trentino is famous for its great variety of mushrooms. *Marzaioli* arrive in March. Fresh porcini may be substituted.

Carefully clean the mushrooms. Heat the olive oil in a pot and cook the shallots, garlic, and mushrooms. ✦ Add the wine, potatoes, and broth. ✦ Cook for 15 minutes, then remove from the heat and whisk in the cream and egg yolks. Garnish with chervil.

ZUPPA DI PATATE
E PORRI GRATINATI

POTATO AND LEEK SOUP

PIEMONTE

4 leeks, sliced and rinsed

4 potatoes, peeled and cubed

4 cups beef broth

Bay leaf

Bread

4 tbsp. unsalted butter,
in small pieces

¼ cup grated Parmigiano-Reggiano

Salt and pepper

In a bowl, combine the leeks, potatoes, and broth with the bay leaf and bring to a boil over medium heat. Lower the heat and simmer for about 1 hour. Season to taste with salt and pepper. ✦ Preheat the oven to 400°F. Pass the mixture through a food mill and divide among four ovenproof bowls. Cover each serving with a slice of bread, add pats of butter to each, then sprinkle with Parmigiano-Reggiano. Bake until the cheese is lightly browned.

ZUPPA DI PESCE | FISH SOUP

VENETO

2 lbs. mixed fish (scorpion fish, bass, mullet, shrimp, clams, etc.)

2 cups white wine

½ lemon

1 celery stalk

2 carrots

2 plum tomatoes, cut into quarters

1 medium onion, quartered, plus ½ cup chopped onion

4 tbsp. unsalted butter

½ cup olive oil

1 garlic clove, chopped

¼ cup tomato purée

⅓ cup chopped flat-leaf parsley

Salt and pepper

Clean the fish and place in a pot. Add 12 cups of water and the wine, lemon, celery, carrots, tomatoes, and quartered onion. ✦ As soon as the fish have cooked remove them from the liquid and bone them. ✦ Heat the butter and olive oil in a pot and sauté the chopped onion and garlic. Add the fish, tomato purée, and salt and pepper. ✦ Strain the broth and add it to the pot. Serve the soup sprinkled with parsley.

✦ **LOCAL TRADITION** ✦

ZUPPA DI PESCE DI LAGO

This fish soup constituted the usual meal of the fishermen of Lake Bolsena in Lazio. When they were forced to spend several days away from home, they would prepare it outside their small reed huts on the banks of the lake. According to the fishermen, the fish had to be added in a particular sequence, beginning with the so-called black fish—the fattest, including tench, rudd, and eel—and ending with those most delicate, such as whitefish, perch, and pike. In a large pot filled with lake water—preferably from the lake where the fish were caught—fresh tomatoes, onion, potatoes (traditionally 2 per person), a few leaves of pennyroyal, celery, and chili pepper would be cooked for a few minutes before the various fish were added. When the fish were cooked the soup was done and most often served on hunks of stale bread in bowls, topped with raw olive oil.

ZUPPA DI PESCE GALLIPOLINA

It is widely believed—especially in Italy—that the ancient Greeks ate very poorly. A story goes that Dionysius of Syracuse (in what is now Sicily) heard tales of a cook in Sparta who could work wonders. Dionysius had the man brought to Syracuse, but sent him packing after only a few days, because according to legend his "delicacies" were no good at all. This idea combined with the soup's overall excellence makes the supposed Greek origins of this ancient and distinctive Gallipoli-style fish soup, typical of the area of Puglia, somewhat suspect. In its very simple preparation, onions are sautéed in a generous amount of olive oil and when browned, the fish—any and all varieties available to the cook—are added. A dash of vinegar and enough water to make it a soup complete the recipe, which is traditionally served with toasted bread.

ZUPPA DI PESCE ALLA BRINDISINA

FISH SOUP BRINDISI-STYLE

PUGLIA

1 ½ lbs. scorpion fish

¾ lb. squid

½ lb. cuttlefish

¾ lb. mussels

½ lb. clams

¼ cup olive oil

1 medium onion, finely chopped

1 celery stalk, finely chopped

¾ lb. plum tomatoes, peeled and chopped

1 diavolillo (hot red chili pepper, see note, page 22), chopped

4 slices stale peasant-style bread, toasted

1 bunch flat-leaf parsley

1 garlic clove

Salt

This dish is typical of Brindisi.

Remove the larger external scales from the scorpion fish and clean them, then cut into pieces. ✦ Clean out the squid and cuttlefish, removing their eyes and mouths and roughly chop; scrub the mussels and clams and wash carefully. ✦ In a large pot (preferably earthenware), heat the olive oil and sauté the onion and celery until they begin to take on a little color. ✦ Add the tomatoes and sauté 5 to 6 minutes. ✦ Add the cuttlefish and squid; after about 8 to 10 minutes add the rest of the seafood. ✦ Put in the red chili pepper and cook for half an hour at low heat. Add salt only if necessary. ✦ Heat 4 oven-proof bowls and put a slice of toasted bread in each; spoon the soup over them. Finely chop the parsely and garlic together. At the moment of serving top each bowl with a tablespoon of the garlic mixture.

RICE AND CHESTNUT SOUP

ZUPPA DI RISO E CASTAGNE

PIEMONTE

40 fresh chestnuts, boiled and shelled
½ cup (1 stick) unsalted butter
4 cups milk
2 cups beef broth
1 ¼ cups rice

Peel the chestnuts. Heat the butter in a pot and cook the chestnuts for a couple of minutes. ✦ Add the milk and broth and simmer 30 minutes. ✦ Add the rice and boil 15 more minutes. ✦ Remove the soup from the heat and let rest 5 minutes before serving.

ST. LUCY'S SOUP

ZUPPA DI SANTA LUCIA

CAMPANIA

¾ cup all-purpose flour
¾ cup cornmeal
1 ¼ cups dried chickpeas
1 ¼ cups dried beans
⅔ cup olive oil
2 garlic cloves
1 sprig rosemary
6 *papaccelle* (round pickled peppers), seeded and chopped into small pieces
Chopped flat-leaf parsley, for serving
Salt

This dish from the area of Avellino is eaten on the eve of St. Lucy's Day. It is related to the miracle of St. Lucy della Quaglia, which occurred in Syracuse in 1646. In that city, however, tradition calls for a different dish called *Cuccia* (see page 787), which is eaten on the first Sunday in May.

In four different pots boil the flour, cornmeal, chickpeas, and beans in 3 cups lightly salted water each. ✦ Drain off almost all the cooking liquid from the chickpeas and beans. ✦ Adjust for salt, and combine the chickpeas and beans with the flour and cornmeal with their liquid all in one large pot. Heat the olive oil in a large pot and sauté the garlic, rosemary, and 3 of the *papaccelle* until the garlic is lightly golden. Discard the garlic and rosemary. Add the grain-legume mixture and sauté until slightly thickened. ✦ Serve in bowls, garnishing each portion with the remaining *papaccelle* and parsley.

✦ LOCAL TRADITION ✦

ZUPPA DI SOFFRITTO

This soup from Campania is based on using the lung, heart, and kidney from veal or lamb. The offal is simmered until soft and then chopped. Sautéed tripe is mixed with tomato purée, salt, and herbs, then stewed together for several hours. Just before serving, the offal is added, and the soup is served over toasted bread.

ZUPPA DI SPINACI | SPINACH SOUP

EMILIA-ROMAGNA

1 lb. spinach

4 cups beef broth

¼ cup (½ stick) unsalted butter

Pinch grated nutmeg

Grated Parmigiano-Reggiano

Salt and pepper

Slices of peasant-style bread, fried or toasted

Wash the spinach thoroughly and simmer in a pot with a little lightly salted water. ✦ Remove from the pot, pat dry on paper towels, and finely chop. ✦ Heat the broth to a boil. Melt the butter in a pot; add the spinach, salt, pepper, a pinch of nutmeg, and cheese. ✦ While stirring carefully, slowly add the boiling broth, 1 spoonful at a time. Salt to taste and serve over bread.

ZUPPA DI TRIPPE 1 | TRIPE SOUP 1

VENETO

2 lbs. tripe (beef or veal)

4 tbsp. olive oil

4 tbsp. unsalted butter

1 celery stalk, chopped

2 carrots, chopped

2 medium onions, chopped

8 cups beef broth

2 tbsp. tomato purée

2 tbsp. all-purpose flour

1 sprig rosemary

1 bay leaf

Grated Parmigiano-Reggiano

Slices of peasant-style bread

Salt and pepper

This dish is typical of Padua.

In a pot, boil the tripe, then cut in long strips. ✦ Heat the oil and butter in a pot and sauté the vegetables until they start to soften. ✦ Stir in the tripe, then pour in the broth and tomato purée. ✦ Whisk together the flour and a couple tablespoons broth to form a paste, then stir the paste into the pot. ✦ Add the rosemary and bay leaf. Cook 4 hours. ✦ Salt to taste. Sprinkle with cheese and pepper and serve with bread.

ZUPPA DI TRIPPE 2 | TRIPE SOUP 2

FRIULI-VENEZIA GIULIA

1 lb. fresh beef or pork (*doppione*) tripe

1 carrot, chopped

1 medium onion, chopped

CONTINUED

Clean the tripe and boil it in a pot of water for 10 minutes; drain, discarding the cooking water, and cut the tripe in thin strips. ✦ Finely chop the carrot, onion, and lard. Heat the olive oil in a pot and sauté the chopped mixture along with the bay leaf and cloves. ✦ Add the tripe and continue cooking. ✦ Add the wine, let it

1/3 cup lard

2 tbsp. extra-virgin olive oil

1 bay leaf

5 cloves

1/2 cup white wine

8 cups beef broth, warmed

Slices of Montasio cheese

evaporate, and cover with warm broth. Simmer until the tripe is cooked. Place a slice of cheese in each bowl and spoon the soup over.

| ZUPPA DI TRIPPE ALLA TREVIGIANA | ## TRIPE SOUP 3 |

VENETO

1 lb. *doppione* tripe

1 lb. veal *millefoglie* tripe

1 celery stalk, chopped

3 medium onions, chopped

1 bunch flat-leaf parsley

A few sprigs rosemary

A few leaves sage

Juice of 1 lemon

A few cloves

2 tbsp. lard

2 tbsp. unsalted butter

Beef broth

Salt and white pepper

This may well be the most popular dish in the area of Treviso.

Cook and clean the tripe and soak it overnight along with the celery, one of the onions, parsley, 1 sprig of the rosemary, sage, lemon juice, and white pepper. ✦ The next morning boil the tripe in fresh water to cover for 1½ hours with another onion and cloves. ✦ Remove the tripe from the liquid and chop it into sections. Heat the lard and butter and sauté the remaining onion and rosemary. Add the tripe and toss to coat with the oil. ✦ Add enough beef broth to cover, taste for salt and pepper, and continue cooking for another hour, until tender.

| ZUPPA DI VINO TERLANO | ## WINE SOUP |

ALTO ADIGE

2 cups beef broth, chilled so the fat has separated completely

3 large egg yolks, beaten

1½ cups white wine, preferably one from the Alto Adige, such as Gewurztraminer, Terlano (Terlaner), Riesling, or Pinot Grigio

4 tbsp. heavy cream

¼ tsp. ground cinnamon

¼ cup (½ stick) unsalted butter

Stale bread, cut into cubes

Salt

Skim the fat from the broth and pour it in a pot; add the egg yolks, wine, cream, half the cinnamon, and salt. ✦ Place the pot over very low heat and heat the broth, which must not boil. Then beat the broth vigorously until it thickens. ✦ Meanwhile, heat the butter in another pan and add the remaining cinnamon. Add the bread and toast until golden. Serve the broth over the bread.

PEASANT SOUP

VALLE D'AOSTA

1 lb. stale peasant-style bread, sliced

7 oz. fontina, finely sliced

7 oz. Valdostan toma (unsalted goat's-milk cheese), finely sliced

4 cups beef broth, heated to boiling

This dish is popular in the Aosta as a peasant *seupa*. Like our word *soup*, this is a very ancient term derived from the French *sup*, meaning to eat a liquid, whether broth, milk, or wine. When made with the highly regarded toma of Gressoney, this is quite an elegant dish, reflecting traditional Walser cooking.

Preheat the oven to 350°F. Arrange several slices of bread across the bottom of a baking dish then cover each with slices of cheese. Make another layer of bread and cheese. ✦ Cover with boiling broth and bake for about 10 minutes. Serve hot.

CHAPTER THREE

PASTA, POLENTA, & RICE

HALF-MOON PASTA WITH MEAT-AND-SPINACH FILLING

PIEMONTE

For the filling:

6 tbsp. unsalted butter

¾ lb. beef chuck,
cut in regular pieces

1 medium onion, chopped

1 garlic clove, minced

1 tbsp. all-purpose flour

1 cup broth

1 tbsp. fresh purée of tomatoes

3¾ cups spinach,
boiled and drained

1 egg yolk

Freshly grated Parmigiano-Reggiano

Pinch grated nutmeg

Salt and pepper

For the pasta:

2 cups all-purpose flour,
plus more as needed

3 large eggs

Because rolling pasta by hand is a craft that takes years of practice, we have included directions for rolling out pasta with a machine. Before you begin, cover a large work surface with kitchen towels upon which to lay out the pasta. ✦ Cut the ball of dough into twice as many pieces as eggs used to make the dough: Dough made with 2 eggs should be cut into 4 pieces; 3 eggs, 6 pieces, and so on. If the dough was made with just water, cut one piece for every 2 tablespoons of water. ✦ Set the pasta machine to its widest setting (usually "1"). Flatten the ball of pasta slightly, then pass it through the rollers once. Fold the dough lengthwise in half, then roll it again. Do this 3 times for each sheet of pasta. ✦ Set the rollers to the next setting ("2") and roll each piece of dough out once. (Do not fold and re-roll; after the first pass, send each piece of dough through each setting just once.) Repeat, turning the rollers to the next thinner setting each time. Most pasta shapes are rolled to the "4" or "5" setting; check your machine's specific instructions. ✦ Roll the entire batch of dough through each setting as you go, rather than rolling each sheet out completely before moving on to the next one. (Except when the pasta is to be stuffed: In this case, roll each sheet of pasta to the right thickness, then stuff it immediately, so the sheets do not dry out and crack.) For long pasta shapes, rest rolled-out sheets 10 minutes before cutting.

Heat half the butter in a saucepan over medium heat until hot. Add the meat, onion, and garlic; sauté slowly, until the meat is browned and the onions are translucent. Season with a little salt. ✦ Dust the browned meat with the flour, place in a pot, and cover with the broth and fresh tomato purée. Cook until the meat is done and the sauce has thickened. ✦ Use a slotted spoon to remove the meat, then chop it together with the boiled spinach. In a bowl, add to this mixture the egg yolk and several tablespoons Parmigiano-Reggiano, a pinch of pepper, and nutmeg. ✦ Use the flour and eggs to prepare a pasta dough as in the recipe on page 10. Let it rest 20 minutes before rolling it out. ✦ Divide the pasta in half, then roll it out into two thin sheets; on the first sheet, place scant tablespoons of the filling evenly spaced one from the next; cover with the second sheet, pressing down well between the lumps to close the agnolotti. Then cut into squares with a knife. ✦ Cook the agnolotti in lightly salted boiling water, remove with a slotted spoon, and toss with the sauce, remaining butter, and Parmigiano-Reggiano. Serve hot.

HALF-MOON PASTA WITH RICOTTA AND PRUNE FILLING

AGNOLOTTI (CJALSONS) DI PONTEBBA

FRIULI-VENEZIA GIULIA

For the pasta:

1½ cups all-purpose flour, plus more as needed

1 large egg

Salt

For the filling:

¼ lb. pitted prunes

¼ lb. dried figs

1 ½ cups ricotta

1 heaping tbsp. sugar

¼ cup unsalted butter, melted, for serving

1 tsp. cinnamon

Salt

This dish is typical of the Canal del Ferro near the border of Austria and Slovenia.

Use the flour and egg to prepare a pasta dough as in the recipe on page 10 and let it rest for 20 minutes before rolling it out. ✦ Make the filling: Cook the prunes in a pot of simmering water until they have softened; drain very well and repeat with the figs. Chop the fruit together, then mix with the ricotta and half the sugar until blended. ✦ Roll the dough out into a very thin sheet (see page 212). ✦ Cut disks 1½ to 2 inches in diameter and in the middle of each put a heaping teaspoon of the filling. Dampen the edges of the disks with water, then fold the disks to form half moons, pressing down on the edges to seal completely, and cook them in boiling salted water for 10 minutes. ✦ Drain and toss with the melted butter, remaining sugar, and cinnamon. Serve hot.

✦ **LOCAL TRADITION** ✦

AGNOLOTTI GOBBI ASTIGIANI– ALBESI AI TRE ARROSTI

This stuffed pasta recipe from Piedmont took its complex flavors from the drippings of three roasted meats—veal or beef, rabbit, and pork—as well as cabbage or escarole, sausage, cheese, eggs, nutmeg, and herbs. The people of Asti would sometimes substitute horse meat for the veal, with quite tasty results. After roasting and chopping up the meats and sautéing the greens, the meat and vegetables would be passed through a food mill to make a filling. The agnolotti would be stuffed with the fragrant filling and cooked either in broth perfumed with celery, onion, and olive oil, or more simply in boiling salted water. Traditionally, the cooked agnolotti were to be dressed only in the remaining pan juices from the roasts and cheese, or an even thriftier sauce of butter and herbs. Later variations calling for a heavier sauce of ground or chopped meat are vulgarizations of this ancient dish, and adding tomato to the sauce was considered almost a crime.

HALF-MOON PASTA
WITH POTATO FILLING

For the pasta:

1½ cups all-purpose flour,
plus more as needed

1 large egg

Salt

For the filling:

¾ lb. potatoes, peeled

4 tbsp. unsalted butter

1 medium onion

3 tbsp. ground cinnamon

⅔ cup golden raisins

2 tsp. sugar

1 pinch dried mint

1 tbsp. grated lemon zest

1 large egg, beaten

Salt and pepper

For the sauce:

6 tbsp. unsalted butter

⅔ cup freshly grated smoked ricotta

1 pinch cinnamon

Sugar

This dish is typical of the Carnia.

Use the flour and eggs to prepare a pasta dough as in the recipe on page 10 and let the pasta rest for 20 minutes before rolling it out. ✦ Make the filling: boil the potatoes until soft enough to be easily pierced with a fork, then drain and pass them through a food mill. Heat the butter in a pan over medium heat until melted, then add the onion and cook until golden. Add the onion to the potatoes along with the cinnamon, raisins, sugar, mint, and lemon zest; season with salt and pepper. ✦ Roll out the pasta to form a thin sheet (see page 212). Cut disks about 3 inches in diameter, and place a tablespoon of the filling on each one. ✦ Brush the edges of the disks with a little egg, then fold over the disks and press along the edges to seal them. ✦ Cook the pasta in lightly salted boiling water. As soon as they float remove them with a slotted spoon. ✦ Make the sauce: Melt the butter, then mix it with the ricotta. Stir in a pinch of cinnamon and a little sugar. Add the pasta, toss gently, and serve hot.

HALF-MOON PASTA WITH
SPINACH AND RICOTTA FILLING

For the filling:

1½ cups ricotta,
passed through a food mill

½ lb. spinach, boiled, dried, cooled,
and finely chopped (to make ½ cup)

½ cup grated Parmigiano-Reggiano,
plus more for serving

4 large egg yolks

1 large slice prosciutto cotto,
cut into 4 squares (about 4 oz.)

CONTINUED

It is important to prepare this dish at the last moment since the pasta must be fresh and not dry, so the cooking time must be short since the egg must remain soft.

Combine the ricotta, spinach, and half the Parmigiano-Reggiano in a bowl and mix well to obtain a homogeneous mixture; set aside in a cool place. ✦ Use the flour and eggs to prepare a pasta dough as in the recipe on page 10 and let rest 20 minutes before rolling out. ✦ Roll the dough out to obtain thin sheets (see page 212), then use a pastry wheel to cut out 8 squares about 6 inches on a side. ✦ At the center of four of the squares place a lump of one-fourth of the ricotta and spinach mixture,

For the pasta:

1 ¼ cups all-purpose flour,
plus more as needed

2 large eggs

For the sauce:

4 tbsp. unsalted butter

1 shallot, finely chopped

Salt

forming this into a kind of nest with a well in the middle. Put an egg yolk into each of these openings, covering it with a square of prosciutto; cover the prosciutto with a second square of pasta dough and press down around the edges to seal. (If necessary, dampen the dough with a little water to make a better seal.) ✦ Melt the butter in a small pan over low heat, add the shallot, and gently cook until it is translucent. Remove from the heat and set aside. ✦ Fill a pot two-thirds full with lightly salted water. Heat over high heat, and when the water boils, lower the heat and delicately lower the agnolotti into the water one at a time, cooking for a few minutes and then removing them with a slotted spoon and setting them out to dry on a plate. ✦ When all the agnolotti are cooked sprinkle them with Parmigiano-Reggiano. Rewarm the shallot butter and pour over the agnolotti.

ANATRA AL RISO

DUCK WITH RICE

MARCHE

One 2-lb. duck

4 oz. prosciutto crudo, diced

1 medium onion, finely chopped

1 garlic clove, minced

2 cups converted rice

¼ cup red wine vinegar

6 tbsp. unsalted butter

Salt and pepper

Clean the duck and prepare it for cooking, then boil it in a pot with water to cover with the prosciutto, onion, garlic, salt, and pepper. ✦ When the duck is cooked transfer its cooking liquid to a medium saucepan and bring it to a boil. Add the rice. ✦ When it is nearly cooked, stir in the vinegar and butter. ✦ Preheat the oven to 400°F. Cut the duck into serving pieces. Grease a baking dish and pour in half the cooked rice; top with the duck pieces and prosciutto. ✦ Cover with the remaining rice and bake 15 minutes, until the rice is cooked and the duck is heated through.

ANGIULOTTOS

STUFFED PASTA

SARDEGNA

For the pasta:

3 cups all-purpose flour,
plus more as needed

2 tbsp. olive oil

CONTINUED

There are those who add a bit of boiled and chopped chard to the cheese fillings for these ravioli, but this is looked down upon as a continental—meaning mainland Italian—influence.

Use the flour to prepare a pasta dough as in the recipe on page 10, using the olive oil and 1 cup water in place of the eggs. Let rest 30 minutes before rolling out. ✦ Meanwhile make the filling, which can be of three different types:

Salt

For the filling (meat or cheese):

1 tbsp. olive oil

¾ lb. ground meat or
¾ lb. pecorino, finely chopped,
or ¾ lb. sheep's-milk ricotta

4 large eggs, beaten

Pinch saffron, if making
cheese filling

¼ cup unsalted butter,
melted, for serving

1 to 1¼ cups freshly grated pecorino

Pepper, if making meat filling

Salt

with meat (*Angiulottos de pezza*), with cheese (*Angiulottos de casu*), or with ricotta (*Angiulottos de arrescottu*). ✦ For a meat filling, heat the olive oil in a pan and cook the ground meat until cooked through. Let the meat cool slightly then work it together with ¼ cup of the grated pecorino, 3 eggs, pepper, and a pinch of salt until blended. ✦ For a cheese filling, mix the chopped pecorino or ricotta with 3 eggs and saffron. ✦ Roll out the dough to form two thin sheets (see note, page 212). ✦ Beat the remaining egg with a little water and salt. Brush one side of the sheet with egg mixture. Arrange lumps of the filling along the sheet of dough, making sure they are evenly spaced. Brush over the other sheet of dough with the egg mixture, then place it brushed side down over the filling. Press down on the edges and cut out with a pastry wheel. ✦ Cook in lightly salted boiling water, drain, and toss with butter and remaining grated pecorino.

BACIALLI

POTATO DUMPLINGS
WITH MUSHROOM SAUCE

LIGURIA

For the pasta:

3 lbs. russet potatoes

3 cups all-purpose flour,
plus more as needed

For the sauce:

2 tbsp. extra-virgin olive oil

1 medium onion, minced

2 oz. dried mushrooms,
soaked in warm water,
drained, and chopped

1 tbsp. tomato paste,
diluted in 2 tbsp. water

¼ cup red wine (optional)

¼ cup broth, plus more as needed

Grated Parmigiano-Reggiano
(optional)

Salt

This dish is typical of Calizzano and the Alta Valle Bormida.

Bake the potatoes until completely soft. Cut in half and scoop out the flesh. Stir in just enough flour to form a smooth dough that is not sticky. (You may not use all of the flour, depending on how starchy the potatoes are.) ✦ Form the dough into thin cylinders, then cut them with a knife into pieces about 1 inch long. ✦ Using your thumb, press each length of dough against a floured fork, then let it fall onto the work surface. When all the *bacialli* have been made, cover them with a cloth and let them rest. ✦ Heat the olive oil in a medium saucepan over medium heat. Add the onion and mushrooms and sauté until the onions are golden. Add the tomato paste mixture. Stir in the red wine, if using. Add the broth, reduce the heat to low, and cook very slowly, stirring every once in a while, adding a little more broth if the mixture dries out. ✦ Cook the *bacialli* in boiling salted water; as soon as they float to the surface they are done. ✦ Drain them with a slotted spoon and arrange them in a deep serving dish, alternating layers of them with sauce. If desired, the plate can be completed with a sprinkle of Parmigiano-Reggiano.

BAZOTT | BAKED TAGLIOLINI

EMILIA-ROMAGNA

¼ cup unsalted butter, melted and cooled slightly

1 lb. tagliolini (see page 399), cooked

½ cup freshly grated Parmigiano-Reggiano

⅔ cup breadcrumbs

Meat broth (preferably pork)

Bazott are long, thin tagliolini, less than ⅛ inch wide, made of fresh egg pasta worked by hand with a rolling pin. They should be cooked in the broth left after cooking pork bones until al dente. This dish is typical of Faenza.

Preheat the oven to 400°F. Grease a baking pan with butter. Make an even layer of the tagliolini in the bottom of the pan, sprinkle with Parmigiano-Reggiano and butter, and dust with breadcrumbs. Bake until the topping is browned; remove the pan from the oven and pour in just enough broth to cover the pasta, then return the pan to the oven and bake again until all the liquid has evaporated. ✦ Remove from the oven, cut the crunchy *bazott* into squares, and serve.

BIGOLI CON AOLE DE LAGO SALADE | BIGOLI WITH SALTED FRESHWATER SARDINES

VENETO

4 cups all-purpose flour, plus more as needed

4 large eggs

¼ cup milk

4 oz. salted *aole* (preserved freshwater sardines)

¼ cup white wine

¼ cup olive oil

Freshly grated Parmigiano-Reggiano

Salt

Making genuine *bigoli* requires a special kind of press (*torchio*), a tool that was once common in all homes but has now nearly disappeared. You can use a pasta extruding machine today. *Bigoli* are thicker and longer than spaghetti. *Pici* or thick spaghetti would also work in this recipe. This recipe can be made using regular sardines, which are easier to find, but the result will be a less delicate flavor.

Use the flour, eggs, and milk to prepare a pasta dough as in the recipe on page 10, adding the milk with the eggs. Let rest 30 minutes. Knead the dough again until smooth and firm, then let rest 20 minutes more. Divide the pasta into small balls and using a *torchio*, extrude the pasta and lay in a single layer on a floured baking sheet. ✦ Remove the *aole* from the salt, rinse in the wine, and bone them. ✦ Heat the olive oil in the top of a double boiler until warm. Add the *aole* and stir them until they break up and the mixture becomes homogeneous. ✦ Cook the *bigoli* in lightly salted boiling water for about 15 minutes. Drain well and toss with the *aole* sauce. Sprinkle with Parmigiano-Reggiano.

BIGOLI WITH DUCK 1

PIEMONTE

1 duckling of about 3½ lbs.
with its giblets

1 medium onion, chopped

1 carrot, chopped

1 celery stalk, chopped

1 garlic clove, minced

⅓ cup lard

1 tbsp. olive oil

3 tbsp. unsalted butter

3 bay leaves

Sage leaves

1 lb. bigoli (see page 217)

Chopped flat-leaf parsley,
for garnish (optional)

Freshly grated Parmigiano-Reggiano

Salt and pepper

Serve the duck as a second course, with a side dish of boiled potatoes or cooked chard.

Clean the duckling and add it to a large pot. Add the giblets, onion, carrot, celery, and garlic, then add water to cover. Simmer for about 70 minutes, or until the duck is tender. ✦ Remove the duck from the broth; use a slotted spoon or strainer to remove the giblets and vegetables. Reserve the broth. Chop the giblets into small pieces. ✦ Heat the lard, olive oil, and butter in a pan, add the giblets and vegetables, bay leaves, sage leaves, salt, and pepper, and cook until the mixture reaches the density of a thick sauce. ✦ Bring the duck broth to a boil and add the bigoli. Cook until al dente, drain, and toss with the sauce. Sprinkle with parsley, and if desired, cheese.

BIGOLI WITH DUCK 2

VENETO

1 duckling weighing more than
2 lbs. with its liver and giblets

1 medium onion, chopped

1 carrot, chopped

1 celery stalk, chopped

1 garlic clove, minced

4 bay leaves

⅓ cup lard

⅓ cup olive oil

¼ cup (4 tbsp.) unsalted butter

A few sage leaves

1 lb. bigoli (see page 217)

Chopped flat-leaf parsley
or Parmigiano-Reggiano,
for garnish

Salt and pepper

Serve the duck as a second course, perhaps with boiled potatoes or cabbage.

Clean the duckling and add it to a large pot. Add the liver and giblets and the onion, carrot, celery, garlic, and bay leaves. Add water to cover. Cook for about 70 minutes, or until the duck is tender. ✦ Remove the duck from the broth; use a slotted spoon or strainer to remove the giblets and vegetables. Reserve the broth. Chop the giblets into small pieces. ✦ Heat the lard, olive oil, and butter in a pan, add the giblets and vegetables, sage leaves, salt, and pepper, and cook until the mixture reaches the density of a thick sauce. ✦ Bring the duck broth to a boil and add the bigoli. Cook until al dente, drain, and toss with the sauce. Sprinkle with parsley or Parmigiano-Reggiano.

THICK BIGOLI WITH GOOSE AND MUSHROOM SAUCE

BIGOLI GROSSI CON L'OCA E PORCINI

VENETO

1 lb. fresh porcini mushrooms

2 tbsp. olive oil

1 medium onion, finely minced

1 garlic clove, finely minced

2 tbsp. unsalted butter

1 goose breast, skin removed and boned, meat diced

1 lb. bigoli (see page 217)

Chopped flat-leaf parsley, for garnish

Freshly grated Parmigiano-Reggiano

Salt

Clean the mushrooms, chop them in somewhat large strips, and place in a small pan. Add water to cover and heat over medium-high heat. When the water begins to boil, remove the mushrooms and drain them. ✦ Heat the olive oil in a sauté pan and sauté the onion and garlic until fragrant, then add the mushrooms. Cook at moderate heat, adding water as necessary to keep the mixture moist. ✦ Heat the butter in a large sauté pan and add the goose. Cook until all the liquid has been absorbed and the meat is golden brown. ✦ Bring a pot of lightly salted water to boil, add the bigoli, and cook until al dente. Drain and toss with the goose and mushrooms. Sprinkle with parsley and Parmigiano-Reggiano and serve.

BIGOLI WITH ANCHOVIES

BIGOLI IN SALSA

VENETO

3 oz. salt-cured or canned anchovies

2 medium onions, chopped

½ cup extra-virgin olive oil

1¾ lbs. bigoli (see page 217)

Salt and pepper

No other flavors are added to this simple composition, both traditional and popular, with its extremely limited ingredients and easy preparation. If desired, two or three crushed cloves of garlic can be used in place of the onion. The result will be more flavorful, but it will also have a heavier taste.

Rinse the salt from the anchovies and chop them into small pieces together with the onions. ✦ Heat the olive oil in a sauté pan and add the anchovy mixture. Add 2 tablespoons water and cook over medium-low heat. ✦ When the mixture has softened and the onion is golden, season with salt and pepper, and stir for a few minutes to blend, creating a thick sauce. ✦ Cook the bigoli in a pot of lightly salted boiling water until al dente. Drain and toss with the sauce, adding a drizzle of olive oil.

BUCKWHEAT PASTA WITH TOASTED CORNMEAL

BLÉCS

FRIULI-VENEZIA GIULIA

⅔ cup buckwheat flour

CONTINUED

This dish is typical of the Carnia, Prato Carnico, Treppo, and Ovaro.

Sift together the flours and use them and the eggs to prepare a pasta dough as in the recipe on page 10. Let

⅔ cup all-purpose flour, plus more as needed

2 large eggs

¼ lb. (1 stick) plus 3 tbsp. unsalted butter, cut into pieces

½ cup cornmeal

2 oz. grated aged cheese, such as Parmigiano-Reggiano

Salt

the dough rest 20 minutes. ✦ Roll the dough out to form as thin a sheet as possible (see note, page 210), then cut into triangles 2 inches on a side. Cook in lightly salted boiling water for 3 minutes. Remove with a slotted spoon, reserving the liquid. ✦ Heat the butter in a pan until melted. Add the cornmeal and sauté 10 minutes or until golden. Add the pasta triangles and quickly toast them (if they become too dry, add a little of their cooking water). Serve dusted with cheese.

BOMBA DI RISO
CON PICCIONI

RICE BOMBE WITH SQUAB

EMILIA-ROMAGNA

½ cup (8 tbsp.) unsalted butter

2 tbsp. breadcrumbs

3 tbsp. extra-virgin olive oil

3 medium onions, finely chopped

1 carrot, finely chopped

1 celery stalk, finely chopped

1 bunch flat-leaf parsley, chopped

1 tbsp. dried porcini mushrooms, softened in warm water, drained, and chopped

2 squabs, cut into small pieces

½ cup dry red wine (preferably Gutturnio)

Several cups broth

2 cups Vialone nano rice

¼ cup dry white wine (preferably Trebbiano)

Grated Parmigiano-Reggiano

Salt

Don't increase the quantity of mushrooms: just a few are better. This preparation is typical of Piacenza; if desired, you can add sweetbreads to the squab sauce, chopping them first and cooking in butter.

Preheat the oven to 350°F. Butter a baking dish and dust with breadcrumbs. Heat the olive oil in a large high-sided pot. Add 2 of the onions, carrot, celery, and parsley and cook until the onions are golden. ✦ Add the mushrooms. Season the squabs with salt, then cook until browned. ✦ Add the red wine, cover the pot, and continue cooking. If necessary, add a little broth to maintain the liquid. ✦ In another pan, heat 2 tablespoons butter until melted, then sauté the remaining onion until golden; remove and discard the onion and add the rice. Mix well, slightly toasting the rice. ✦ Pour in the white wine and let it evaporate. ✦ Cook the rice until al dente, stirring in ladlefuls of broth as needed. ✦ Blend in the cheese and 2 tablespoons butter. ✦ Use a little more than half the rice to line the bottom and sides of the baking dish. ✦ Place the birds and sauce in the opening. Cover with the remaining rice, then top with a few pats of butter and dust with more breadcrumbs. ✦ Bake for 15 minutes, or until the rice forms a light golden crust. ✦ Remove from the oven and let it stand a few minutes. Turn out into a serving dish and serve immediately.

BUCATINI IN MACKEREL SAUCE

BUCATINI AL SUGO DI SURI

ABRUZZO

¼ cup olive oil

2 medium-size mackerel, cleaned and boned

1 cup chopped, peeled, and seeded ripe plum tomatoes

2 tbsp. shredded basil

1 lb. bucatini

Salt

The mackerel used in this dish, typical of Giulianova, is easier to scale if you first remove the backbone and head. Or of course you can buy the fish already cleaned.

Heat the olive oil in a sauté pan until very hot. Add the mackerel and cook them until they take on a golden color. ✦ Use a wooden spoon to break up the fish, then add the tomatoes and basil, and continue cooking to reduce and concentrate the sauce. ✦ Cook the bucatini in lightly salted boiling water until al dente. Drain and toss with the sauce.

BUCATINI WITH GUANCIALE, HOT PEPPER, AND TOMATO

BUCATINI ALL'AMATRICIANA

LAZIO

6 oz. guanciale or pancetta, diced

3 ripe plum tomatoes, peeled, seeded, and chopped

1 dried hot chili pepper (or ¼ tsp. chili pepper flakes)

1 lb. bucatini

⅓ cup grated pecorino Romano

Salt and pepper

This dish is typical of Rome.

Heat the guanciale and 2 tablespoons water in a saucepan over medium-low heat to render the fat. ✦ Remove the guanciale with a slotted spoon and set aside. Add the tomatoes to the fat in the pan. Crumble in the chili pepper and add a little salt and pepper. ✦ Cook for 10 minutes or until thickened. Add the guanciale to the sauce, and heat to warm it. ✦ Cook the bucatini in a pot of lightly salted boiling water until al dente. Drain, and toss with the pecorino and sauce. Mix well and serve hot.

BUCATINI WITH MULLET SAUCE

BUCATINI ALLE TRIGLIE

MARCHE

3 sardines, boned, heads removed

5 tbsp. olive oil

1 garlic clove, crushed

2 tbsp. tomato paste

1 pinch thyme

1 pinch chili pepper flakes

8 mullet, cleaned and boned

1 tbsp. chopped flat-leaf parsley

1 lb. bucatini

Salt

Chop the sardines. ✦ Heat the olive oil in a large pan and add the garlic and sardines; cook until fragant. Add the tomato paste, thyme, salt, and red pepper flakes. ✦ Cook for several minutes then add the mullet. ✦ When the mullet are cooked remove them from the pan. ✦ Add the parsley and salt to the pan. ✦ Cook the bucatini in a pot of lightly salted boiling water until al dente. Drain them and add them to the pan with the sauce. Toss until mixed, then serve topped with the mullet.

BRUSAROL

This very simple recipe for grilled polenta balls from the mountain folk of the Val d'Ossola entailed little more than cooking a basic polenta until firm and cooling it. Once cooled, the polenta was shaped—damp hands worked best—into spheres, filled with the local soft mountain cheese, and placed on a warm grill.

BUSIATI COL PESTO TRAPANESE

BUSIATI WITH PESTO

SICILIA

For the pasta:

1⅔ cups all-purpose flour, plus more as needed

2 large eggs

1 tbsp. olive oil

Salt

For the sauce:

⅓ cup blanched almonds

10 ripe plum tomatoes, peeled, seeded, and roughly chopped

¼ cup shredded basil

6 garlic cloves, minced

3 tbsp. olive oil

⅓ cup breadcrumbs

Salt and pepper

In the area of Trapani, this pasta is known as *busiato* because with a fast movement of the hands it is rolled around a *busu* (knitting needle) resulting in a shape similar to fusilli.

Use the flour, eggs, and olive oil to prepare a pasta dough as in recipe on page 10, adding the olive oil with the eggs. Let the dough rest 20 minutes. To form the *busiati*, roll the dough very thin (see page 212). Cut into ¼-inch strands. Wrap a strand very tightly around a large skewer or knitting needle. Roll on a board to flatten the pasta (and to make it adhere to itself a little), then push the coiled strand of pasta off the skewer, then lay on a floured baking sheet in a single layer to dry. ✦ Preheat the oven to 350°F. ✦ Toast the almonds and chop very fine. ✦ Grind the tomatoes in a mortar with salt, basil, pepper, and garlic. ✦ When this sauce is thoroughly mixed, add 1 tablespoon olive oil and the almonds. ✦ Meanwhile, heat the remaining olive oil in a medium pan. Add the breadcrumbs and toast until golden. ✦ Cook the *busiati* for 5 minutes in lightly salted boiling water, drain, and toss with the tomato and almond sauce. Put the pasta in serving plates, dust with breadcrumbs, and serve hot.

RICOTTA CALZONI

For the pasta:

1 ¼ cups semolina flour, plus more as needed

4 large eggs

For the filling:

1 cup ricotta

1 tsp. sugar

1 large egg, beaten

1 tsp. ground cinnamon

Salt

Meat sauce, preferably lamb or pork (see page 330)

This dish is typical of the Carnival period.

Use the semolina and eggs to prepare a pasta dough as in the recipe on page 10. Let dough rest 20 minutes. ✦ Meanwhile mix the ricotta, sugar, egg, and cinnamon until blended. ✦ Roll the dough out to form as thin a sheet as possible (see note, page 212). Cut the sheet into circular shapes with a somewhat narrow-mouthed glass. Put small dollops of ricotta filling on the disks, then fold them over to close them like ravioli. Press on the edges to seal completely. Cook in a pot of lightly salted boiling water and toss with the meat sauce.

PASTA, POLENTA & RICE

CHEESE DUMPLINGS

4 tbsp. (¼ cup) unsalted butter

1 lb. stale bread, sliced

1 medium onion, finely chopped

¾ lb. hard or semi-hard cheese (such as fresh Asiago or Montasio), cubed

½ cup grated Parmigiano-Reggiano

1 tbsp. minced chives

2 tbsp. heavy cream

3 or 4 large eggs, beaten

A few tbsp. milk

Broth or melted butter, for serving

Salt

This recipe is often a means of using up any leftover cheese.

Heat the butter in a large pan until hot, then toast the bread until golden. Put it in a bowl. ✦ Sauté the onion in the same butter just until translucent and lightly golden, then add it to the bread. ✦ Add the cubed cheese, Parmigiano-Reggiano, chives, and cream to the bread. ✦ Mix carefully and add the eggs, mix again and pour in just enough milk to make a soft but workable dough. ✦ Shape the dough into small balls. ✦ Cook the balls in lightly salted boiling water for 20 minutes. Serve in broth or with a sauce of melted butter.

CANNAROZZETTI WITH RICOTTA AND SAFFRON

Pinch saffron threads (best if from L'Aquila)

CONTINUED

This dish is typical of L'Aquila.

Heat the saffron and 3 tablespoons of water in a small saucepan to boiling. Remove from the heat and set aside to steep. Heat the olive oil in a large pan. Add the guanciale and cook until browned. ✦ Meanwhile cook the

1 tbsp. olive oil

4 oz. guanciale, cut in pieces

1 lb. *cannarozzetti* (or other short-ribbed pasta, such as penne)

1⅔ cups sheep's-milk ricotta

Freshly grated pecorino (optional)

Salt and pepper

cannarozzetti in a pot of lightly salted boiling water until al dente, drain, and add them to the pan with the guanciale. ✦ Add the ricotta, a pinch of pepper, and saffron water. ✦ Blend the ingredients, warming the ricotta, and serve immediately. If desired, top with pecorino.

CANNELLONI ALLA SORRENTINA

CAMPANIA

½ cup olive oil

¾ lb. cubed lean beef or pork

1 medium onion, finely chopped

¼ cup dry white wine

1⅔ cups tomato paste

¼ cup shredded basil

2 cups ricotta

6 oz. *fior di latte* cheese, in small cubes

½ cup freshly grated Parmigiano-Reggiano

12 squares of fresh pasta, 5 to 6 inches on a side (see page 377)

Salt

CANNELLONI WITH MEAT SAUCE

Preheat the oven to 400°F. ✦ Heat the oil in a large pan and add the meat and onion. Cook until the meat is browned and the onion is golden. ✦ Pour in the wine and let it evaporate, then add the tomato paste, a pinch of salt, and basil. ✦ Add 1 cup water and cook until the meat has broken down nearly to a paste. Remove from the heat and add the ricotta, *fior di latte,* and a little Parmigiano-Reggiano. ✦ Cook the pasta squares a few at a time in lightly salted boiling water, removing them from the water with a strainer when they rise to the surface and aligning them on a countertop (preferably marble) dampened with cold water. ✦ Put a tablespoon of the meat and ricotta filling across the center of each square and roll them up to form cannelloni. ✦ Spoon some of the meat sauce in the bottom of a rectangular baking dish, then align the cannelloni in the dish in a single layer. ✦ Cover the cannelloni with more sauce, sprinkle with Parmigiano-Reggiano, and bake 15 to 20 minutes, until the sauce is bubbling.

CAPPELLACCI DI ZUCCA

EMILIA-ROMAGNA

For the filling:

3 lbs. yellow winter squash

1 large egg, beaten

¾ cup grated Parmigiano-Reggiano, plus more for serving

Pinch freshly grated nutmeg

CONTINUED

PASTA STUFFED WITH SQUASH

This pasta, typical of Ferrara, can also be served with meat sauce.

Preheat the oven to 400°F. Cut the squash into quarters, remove the seeds, and bake until completely soft, about 30 minutes. ✦ Let cool slightly, then scoop out the flesh and set aside. Discard any liquid that may drain from the squash. ✦ Use the flour and eggs to prepare a pasta dough as in the recipe on page 10. Let dough rest 20 minutes. ✦ Roll the dough out to form as thin a sheet as possible (see

¼ cup (4 tbsp.) unsalted butter, melted

2 tbsp. chopped sage

For the pasta:

2 cups all-purpose flour, plus more as needed

4 large eggs

Salt

note, page 212). Cut in small squares about 2½ inches on a side. ✦ Mix the squash flesh, egg, cheese, and nutmeg until blended. Arrange this filling atop the pasta squares. Fold the squares diagonally to create triangles, pressing the edges to seal. Wrap each triangle around the thumb and press the ends together to make *cappelletti* (little hats). (These will be larger than usual.) ✦ Cook in a pot of lightly salted boiling water until they float. Drain and toss with butter, sage, and Parmigiano-Reggiano.

CAPPELLI DEI PRETI | **"PRIEST CAPS"**

CALABRIA

For the pasta:

2 cups all-purpose flour, plus more as needed

4 large eggs

For the sauce:

Lamb sauce, pork sauce, or tomato-basil sauce (see pages 330, 539, and 327)

½ cup grated pecorino

Salt

Use the flour and eggs to prepare a pasta dough as in the recipe on page 10. Let the dough rest 30 minutes. ✦ Roll the dough out to form as thin a sheet as possible (see note, page 212). Cut into small squares. ✦ Fold the squares in half to make triangles. Fold the top point of the triangle down and press, to create a shape similar to the three-ridged *biretta* worn by priests. ✦ Let the pasta dry slightly on a floured baking sheet. Cook in lightly salted boiling water until al dente, drain, and toss with a pork or lamb sauce or a sauce of tomato and basil. Top with pecorino.

CAPPELLO DA GENDARME | **"GENDARME HAT" PASTA PIE**

PUGLIA

Extra-virgin olive oil

1 medium eggplant

¾ cup all-purpose flour, plus more for the vegetables

½ lb. lean pork, cubed

2 zucchini, cleaned and cut in thin rounds

½ lb. short pasta or macaroni

2 large hard-boiled eggs, cut into quarters

CONTINUED

Preheat the oven to 400°F. Grease a baking pan with a little olive oil. Clean the eggplant and cut it in thin slices. Salt the slices and set aside for 1 hour. ✦ Use the flour to prepare a dough as in the recipe on page 10, using 2 tablespoons olive oil and 1 teaspoon lukewarm water in place of the eggs. Cover with a kitchen towel and set aside for 30 minutes. ✦ Heat 2 tablespoons olive oil in a sauté pan, add the pork, and season with a pinch of salt. Cook until golden. ✦ Heat ½ inch of olive oil in a second sauté pan until hot. Dip the zucchini rounds in flour, then fry them in olive oil until golden. ✦ Repeat with the eggplant, adding more oil to the pan if necessary. ✦ Meanwhile, cook the macaroni until al dente in lightly salted boiling

6 oz. mozzarella, sliced

⅓ cup tomato sauce

2 tbsp. chopped flat-leaf parsley

1 pinch oregano

⅓ cup grated pecorino

Salt and pepper

water. ✦ Roll out the dough on a floured board to make two thin sheets, one slightly larger than the other. Use the larger one to line the baking pan; top with a layer of macaroni, a layer of zucchini and eggplant, then the eggs, mozzarella, meat, tomato sauce, parsley, and oregano. ✦ Dust with pecorino. ✦ Cover with the other sheet of dough, sealing the edges. Puncture the top with a fork and bake about 30 minutes, or until the top is lightly browned.

CAPON WITH ANOLINI AND PROSCIUTTO SAUCE

5 tbsp. unsalted butter, plus more for finishing the dish

1 capon (or chicken), weighing about 4 lbs.

1 carrot, chopped

1 medium onion, cut into wedges

1 celery stalk, chopped

¼ cup all-purpose flour

4 oz. prosciutto crudo

1 cup grated Parmigiano-Reggiano

1¼ lbs. *anolini* (see pages 97 and 98)

Salt and pepper

This recipe is from Carlo Nascia and was cooked at the court of the Farnese family in Parma in 1500. It is adapted for today's kitchen.

Make the capon broth: Simmer the capon (or chicken) in water to cover with the carrot, onion, celery, a pinch of salt, and pepper. Cook on very low heat for 3 hours. ✦ Drain the capon and remove all the meat from the bones, cutting it into medium-size pieces. ✦ Skim the fat off the broth. ✦ Melt the remaining butter in a saucepan. Add the flour, stir to blend, then whisk in some broth from the capon to make a sauce the consistency of cream. Set aside. ✦ Pass this sauce through a sieve. Add the prosciutto and a third of the Parmigiano-Reggiano. ✦ Preheat the oven to 400°F. Grease a baking pan with a little butter. Cook the anolini in the remaining broth until al dente and drain. Spread the capon meat into an even layer across the bottom of the baking pan. Sprinkle with half the remaining Parmigiano-Reggiano. Cover this with the cooked anolini, adding pats of butter and the remaining Parmigiano-Reggiano. ✦ Pour the sauce over and bake for about 15 minutes, or until the top is lightly browned.

CAPUNTI WITH LAMB SAUCE

⅔ cup extra-virgin olive oil

1 medium onion, thinly sliced

CONTINUED

Heat the oil in a saucepan until hot. Add the onion, then the lamb. ✦ Sauté until browned, add the wine, and when that has evaporated add the tomato purée. ✦ Cook over low heat about 50 minutes, adding water as needed, then break up the lamb. ✦ Cook the *capunti* in lightly salted

½ lb. boneless leg of lamb or
lamb shoulder, chopped

½ cup dry white wine

⅔ cup tomato purée

¾ lb. *capunti* (canoe-shaped
fresh pasta)

⅔ cup grated pecorino

Salt

boiling water until al dente, drain, and toss with the
sauce. Sprinkle with pecorino and serve.

CASONCELLI DI SALSICCIA
AL BURRO

SAUSAGE-FILLED PASTA
WITH BUTTER

LOMBARDIA

For the pasta:

1¼ cups all-purpose flour,
plus more as needed

2 large eggs

1 tbsp. olive oil

Salt

For the filling:

2 tbsp. unsalted butter

7 oz. fresh sausage

½ medium onion, chopped

½ cup grated Parmigiano-Reggiano,
plus more for serving

½ cup breadcrumbs

¼ cup (4 tbsp.) unsalted butter,
melted

Use the flour, eggs, olive oil, and salt to prepare a pasta
dough as in the recipe on page 10, adding the olive oil
and salt with the eggs. Cover the dough and let it rest 30
minutes. ✦ Meanwhile, heat the butter in a pan over high
heat until melted. Add the sausage and onion and cook
until the sausage is browned and the onion is golden. ✦
Pass this through a meat grinder, then return to the pan
and add the Parmigiano-Reggiano and breadcrumbs;
blend well. ✦ Roll out the dough to form a thin sheet (see
note, page 212), then use a pastry wheel to cut out
squares about 2 inches on a side. Fill each with a lump
of the filling, fold over, and seal the edges. ✦ Cook the
casoncelli in a pot of lightly salted boiling water until they
float. Toss with Parmigiano-Reggiano and melted butter
and serve.

CASONSEI DI BERGAMO

BERGAMO-STYLE
STUFFED PASTA

LOMBARDIA

For the pasta:

3 cups all-purpose flour,
plus more as needed

4 large eggs

For the filling:

5 oz. stewed beef, chopped

6 oz. salame (preferably
from Bergamo), chopped

CONTINUED

The pasta dough in this recipe is made without eggs so it will
be quite firm.

Use the flour and eggs to prepare a pasta dough as in the
recipe on page 10. Let the dough rest 20 minutes. ✦
Combine the filling ingredients until blended, adding a
little milk to bind the mixture as needed. ✦ Roll the
dough out to form as thin a sheet as possible (see note,
page 212). Cut in small disks about 2½ inches on a side.
✦ Place a dollop of filling at the center of each disk, then
fold over the disk, dampening the edges to seal them

1 tbsp. breadcrumbs

1 large egg, beaten

Pinch freshly grated nutmeg

Pinch ground cinnamon

3 tbsp. grated Parmigiano-Reggiano

1 pear, seeded, chopped,
and puréed in a food mill

A few tbsp. milk

For serving:

1 tbsp. chopped sage

¼ cup (4 tbsp.) unsalted butter

Grated Parmigiano-Reggiano

Salt

well. Cook the pasta in a pot of lightly salted boiling water. Meanwhile, sauté the sage in the butter in a skillet until fragrant. Add the pasta and toss gently. Sprinkle with Parmigiano-Reggiano and serve hot.

CASONSEI DI BRESCIA

BRESCIA-STYLE STUFFED PASTA

LOMBARDIA

For the pasta:

3 cups all-purpose flour,
plus more as needed

5 large eggs

For the filling:

2 tbsp. unsalted butter

½ lb. ground beef

A few tbsp. beef broth

¾ cup breadcrumbs

¾ cup grated Parmigiano-Reggiano

1 large egg, beaten

1 heaping tbsp. chopped
flat-leaf parsley

1 garlic clove, chopped

Salt

For the sauce:

¼ cup (4 tbsp.) unsalted butter

A few sage leaves

Grated Parmigiano-Reggiano

This recipe is typical of the area around Brescia, but the dish is hotly contested between that city and Bergamo, with versions often characterized by the use of herbs, mortadella, and sausage. This Brescian version and the preceding one from Bergamo (see page 227) resemble the original recipe, which dates to the late Middle Ages, although the ancient versions used a filling made with pears, whether in syrup or candied, almonds, and fruit cake bound with eggs and butter. Although the many modern versions vary from place to place, they all have fillings similar to those of normal ravioli.

Use the flour and eggs to prepare a pasta dough as in the recipe on page 10, then let the dough rest 20 minutes. ✦ For the filling: Heat the butter until melted. Add the meat, breaking it up with a wooden spoon and cooking until brown. ✦ Add a few tablespoons of beef broth, breadcrumbs, cheese, and salt. ✦ Cook at low heat for about 15 minutes, stirring constantly. ✦ Remove the pan from the heat, then add the egg, parsley, and garlic. ✦ Roll the dough out to form as thin a sheet as possible (see note, page 212). Cut into small squares about 2½ inches on a side. ✦ Arrange the filling atop the pasta squares. Fold the squares, pressing the edges to seal. ✦ Cook in a pot of lightly salted boiling water until al dente, then drain. Meanwhile, sauté the sage in the butter until fragrant. Add the pasta and toss gently. Sprinkle with Parmigiano-Reggiano and serve on warmed plates.

BEET STUFFED PASTA WITH POPPY SEEDS

VENETO

For the pasta:

2 cups all-purpose flour, plus more as needed

4 large eggs

1 ½ tbsp. olive oil

Salt

For the filling:

1 lb. beets

1 turnip, weighing about 6 oz.

Pinch grated nutmeg

Pinch ground cloves

¼ cup olive oil

2 garlic cloves

Salt and pepper

For the sauce:

¼ cup (4 tbsp.) unsalted butter

1 tbsp. poppy seeds

Freshly grated Parmigiano-Reggiano

Use the flour, eggs, and olive oil to prepare a pasta dough as in the recipe on page 10, adding the oil with the eggs. Let the dough rest 20 minutes. ✦ For the filling, boil the beets and turnip, peel them, and pass them through a food mill. Discard any liquid. ✦ Season with salt, nutmeg, black pepper, and cloves. ✦ Heat the olive oil in a large pan, add the filling mixture and garlic, and cook until the liquid has evaporated. ✦ To make the *casunziei*, roll out thin sheets of dough (see note, page 212) and use a pastry wheel to cut out rounds. ✦ Put a little of the filling at the center of each round, then fold it over to form a half moon, making sure the edges are sealed. ✦ Cook them in a pot of lightly salted boiling water until they float, then drain. ✦ Meanwhile, to make the sauce, heat the butter until melted, then add the poppy seeds. Arrange the *casunziei* on a serving plate, drizzle with the butter mixture, then sprinkle with Parmigiano-Reggiano.

✦ **LOCAL TRADITION** ✦

CAVATELLI CON CIME DI COCOZZE

A simple preparation of pasta and vegetables in a light olive oil–based sauce, this cavatelli recipe comes from Basilicata and is made with the green tops of a squash. The vegetables would first be very simply cooked and chopped and then added to the pasta pot halfway through cooking the cavatelli. A simple sauce would be made from olive oil, garlic, a dried chili, and tomato, if desired and available. The dish would be tossed together as soon as the pasta was finished cooking and the sauce done, and then left to rest for a few minutes.

CAVATELLI WITH WALNUTS

CAMPANIA

For the cavatelli:
1 ⅓ cups durum wheat flour
2 large eggs, beaten

For the sauce:
2 garlic cloves
1 spicy red chili pepper
4 tbsp. olive oil
⅔ cup walnuts, pounded to a paste, preferably in a mortar
2 tbsp. chopped flat-leaf parsley
Salt

The dialect name in Vallesaccarda for the cavatelli in this recipe is *triilli*, a word of Arabic origin. During the period when they ruled Sicilia, the Arabs made a certain kind of long pasta like spaghetti that was dried so it could be preserved and sold even outside Sicilia. The *triilli* of this recipe are made using fresh pasta and resemble cavatelli or even *strozzapreti*.

Use the flour and eggs to prepare a pasta dough as in the recipe on page 10 (the dough will be soft). Roll the dough into cylinders similar to breadsticks about half an inch thick. ✦ Using a knife, cut them into inch-long lengths. Press a finger into each one to make them hollow. ✦ Cook these in a pot of lightly salted boiling water until al dente, then drain. ✦ Meanwhile heat the olive oil until hot, then add the garlic and chili pepper and cook until the garlic is golden. Add the walnuts and cook for 5 minutes; add the parsley and cook 30 seconds more. ✦ Add the cavatelli, toss gently and serve hot.

CAVATELLI AND BEANS

BASILICATA

1 ⅔ cups fresh beans, shelled
1 ⅔ cups durum wheat flour
2 tbsp. lard
1 garlic clove
1 dried chili pepper
Salt

Boil the beans in lightly salted water. ✦ Use the flour to prepare a soft pasta dough as in the recipe on page 10, using ⅔ cup water in place of the eggs. ✦ Roll out a thin sheet of dough (see note, page 212), let it dry, then cut in wide strips (like wide tagliatelle). ✦ Cook these in lightly salted boiling water until al dente, then drain. ✦ Meanwhile, heat the lard until hot. Add the garlic and chili pepper and cook until fragrant. Add the beans and cook until warmed through. Put the pasta in a serving bowl and add the bean mixture. Toss to mix and serve hot.

CAVATELLI WITH EGGS AND PANCETTA

MOLISE

Use the flour to prepare a soft pasta dough as in the recipe on page 10, using 1 ⅛ cups water in place of the eggs. Let it rest 20 minutes, then roll it with the palms of your hands to create long cylinders about the thickness

For the pasta:

3 cups durum wheat flour, plus more as needed

For the sauce:

¼ cup olive oil

⅔ cup diced pancetta

5 large eggs, beaten

Salt and pepper

of a pencil. Cut these in lengths of about 1 inch, pressing a finger against them to give each a slight hollow. ✦ Cook in lightly salted boiling water until al dente; drain. ✦ Meanwhile, heat the olive oil in a large pan until hot. Add the pancetta and cook until it starts to get a little brown. Add the cooked cavatelli to the pan, mix, then add the eggs along with a pinch of salt and a dusting of pepper. ✦ Stir until the eggs have cooked and coat the cavatelli. Serve immediately.

CECI E LAGANELLE

PASTA WITH CHICKPEAS

CAMPANIA

1¼ cups dried chickpeas

1 tsp. baking soda

2 cups all-purpose flour, plus more as needed

½ cup extra-virgin olive oil

2 garlic cloves

1 tbsp. chopped fresh oregano

1 tbsp. chopped flat-leaf parsley

Salt and pepper

This dish is typical of Caserta. *Laganelle* **are thin noodles similar to fettuccine, nicknamed "lightning and thunder."**

Put the chickpeas in a soup pot and add water to cover. Stir in the baking soda and soak overnight. ✦ Use the flour to prepare a soft pasta dough as in the recipe on page 10, using ¾ cup water in place of the eggs. ✦ Roll out the dough to a thin sheet (see note, page 212), let it dry slightly, then cut into *laganelle*. Let dry on a floured baking sheet in a single layer for a few hours before cooking. ✦ Drain and rinse the chickpeas thoroughly and cook them in unsalted water to cover in a pot that is large enough to also accommodate the *laganelle*. Cook at low but constant heat (it should never boil) for about 4 hours. ✦ When the chickpeas are well cooked, in fact almost dissolving, add the olive oil, garlic, salt, and pepper and then the *laganelle*. Keep some boiling water handy to add if extra liquid is needed to cook the *laganelle*. ✦ A few minutes before removing from the heat add some oregano and parsley. ✦ Let rest for about 10 minutes before being served. The dish should be thoroughly blended, not brothy.

PASTA WITH CHICKPEAS AND ONION

CICERI E TRIA

PUGLIA

1 lb. dried chickpeas

1 sprig rosemary

CONTINUED

This dish is typical of Salento.

Soak the chickpeas overnight in lukewarm salted water, then drain and boil with a sprig of rosemary in a large pot with water to cover. Drain and discard the rosemary. ✦ Prepare a soft pasta dough as in the recipe on page 10

1⅔ cups all-purpose flour, plus more as needed

3 tbsp. olive oil

1 medium onion, sliced

Salt and pepper

using ⅔ cup water in place of the eggs. ✦ Roll out the dough to a thin sheet (see note, page 212) and cut it into strips about ½ inch wide; set these on a floured cloth and let them dry a few hours before cooking. Cook in lightly salted boiling water until al dente; drain. ✦ Heat 1 tablespoon of the olive oil in a pot, then add the onion and cook until translucent. Add half of the chickpeas; purée the remaining chickpeas in a food mill, then add them to the pot. ✦ Add half of the cooked pasta to the chickpeas and cook them together; heat the remaining olive oil in a large sauté pan. Add the other half of the pasta and toast until lightly browned. Add it to the chickpea mixture just before serving. ✦ Season with freshly ground black pepper and serve.

TERNI-STYLE PASTA WITH GARLIC AND OIL

CIRIOLE ALLA TERNANA

UMBRIA

For the pasta:
1⅔ cups all-purpose flour, plus more as needed

For the sauce:
¾ cup olive oil

1 garlic clove

1 tbsp. chopped flat-leaf parsley (optional)

Salt

Ciriole have always been made using only water, flour, and a pinch of salt. You should cook the pasta immediately after it is made because it will begin to contract almost as soon as it is made, much like the mortar of bricklayers. Otherwise it would be necessary to bind it with eggs and it would no longer be *ciriole*.

Use the flour to prepare a soft pasta dough as in the recipe on page 10, using ⅔ cup water in place of the eggs; set it aside to rest for about 30 minutes. ✦ Work the dough in small portions, giving each the shape of rough spaghetti. These should be firm. ✦ Cook the *ciriole* in lightly salted boiling water to cover until al dente and drain. ✦ Heat the olive oil in a large pan and add the garlic. Cook over low heat just to color the garlic slightly; it should not be brown. ✦ Before serving drizzle the hot olive oil over the *ciriole*. If desired, sprinkle with parsley.

PASTA WITH MUSHROOMS AND GARLIC

CIRIOLE CON I FUNGHI DI PIOPPO

UMBRIA

1 recipe *ciriole* (see note above)

CONTINUED

This dish is typical of Terni.

Cook the *ciriole* in lightly salted boiling water until al dente. Meanwhile, heat the mushrooms in a dry pan over medium heat just until their liquid has evaporated.

For the sauce:

1 lb. pioppino mushrooms
(*Pholiota aegerita*), cleaned

2 tbsp. olive oil

1 garlic clove

1 plum tomato, peeled,
seeded, and chopped

1 dried chili pepper

Finely chopped flat-leaf parsley
(optional)

✦ Heat the olive oil in a saucepan and add the garlic. Sauté until fragrant, then add the mushrooms. ✦ Stir the mushrooms to keep them from sticking and add the tomato. Add the chili pepper. ✦ Pour this over the drained *ciriole,* adding parsley if desired.

CORONA DI RISO
CON CALAMARI

CROWN OF RICE WITH SQUID

SICILIA

4 cups fish broth

4 tbsp. unsalted butter

2 medium onions, finely chopped

2 cups Vialone nano rice

¼ cup extra-virgin olive oil

1 garlic clove, minced

1 tbsp. chopped flat-leaf parsley

3 lbs. squid, cut in rings

¼ cup dry white wine

7 oz. tomato purée

7 oz. tomato paste

Salt and pepper

Preheat the oven to 350°F. Heat the fish broth until it is boiling. Heat half the butter in an ovenproof pot over low heat until melted, then add 1 onion and cook until it becomes soft. ✦ Add the rice, stirring constantly for 3 or 4 minutes, until the grains become shiny and translucent. ✦ Slowly add the boiling broth, and when the liquid returns to a boil cover the pot and bake for 45 minutes, or until the rice has cooked. ✦ When the rice has cooked remove the cover from the pot, add the remaining butter (cut into pats), and delicately mix it in using two forks. ✦ Meanwhile prepare the sauce. Heat the olive oil in a sauté pan over medium heat. Mix the remaining onion, garlic, and parsley, sauté until fragrant, and add the squid. ✦ Sauté at high heat until the squid become opaque, then add the wine. When the wine has cooked down a little add the tomato purée and paste. ✦ Add salt and pepper to taste and cook, adding a little water if necessary, until the sauce has reduced and become dense and the squid are cooked through and tender. ✦ To serve, form a crown with the rice in a bowl and put the squid in the center.

CORZETTI

PASTA "CROSSES"

LIGURIA

This recipe is typical of the Val Polcevera. There is a variation in the Riviera di Levante in which the dough is cut in round shapes 1 or 1½ inches in diameter and them stamped with wooden stamps bearing traditional patterns or arabesques or friezes like coins. These are then served with a sauce of

1⅔ cups all-purpose flour, plus more as needed

1 large egg

Salt

olive oil, marjoram, and pine nuts or with a meat or mushroom sauce (see pages 330 and 412).

Use the flour and egg to prepare a pasta dough as in the recipe on page 10. Let the dough rest 20 minutes, then divide it into pieces the size of a large nut. Roll the pieces into cylinders and twist these to give them the form of a figure eight. ✦ Cook the *corzetti* in lightly salted boiling water until al dente.

✦ **LOCAL TRADITION** ✦

CONGLUFI

This very involved recipe for brioche filled with chicken and mushrooms from the area of Campania called for homemade brioche called *conglufi*, two separate béchamel sauces, and making quenelles of ground chicken, mushrooms, peas, and prosciutto cotto. The *conglufi* were baked in small molds about two inches across and four inches high. After baking, a cylinder was cut out of the center to hold the filling and what was cut out became the "cap." A very thick béchamel would be mixed with ground chicken, egg, and cheese and then formed into balls. The mushrooms were cooked in butter and sherry, and the peas just lightly cooked in boiling water and flavored with butter. The second béchamel became the sauce for the filling and mixed with the quenelles, cooked mushrooms, peas, and prosciutto cotto. The *conglufi* were stuffed with the hot filling and served immediately.

CRESPELLE AL RADICCHIO

RADICCHIO CREPES

VENETO

This recipe is typical of Treviso.

For the crespelle:

4 large eggs, beaten

2 cups all-purpose flour, plus more as needed

2¼ cups milk

4 tbsp. (¼ cup) unsalted butter

CONTINUED

Preheat the oven to 350°F. Prepare the crespelle (crepe) batter: Mix the eggs, flour, and milk to make a batter with the consistency of heavy cream. Refrigerate for 30 minutes. ✦ Meanwhile, make the filling: Heat the olive oil in a large pan over high heat. Add the radicchio and garlic, sauté until the radicchio is just starting to wilt, then sprinkle with wine. Remove from the heat. ✦ Use the butter, flour, milk, and broth to make a béchamel

For the filling:

2 tbsp. extra-virgin olive oil

1 lb. radicchio (preferably from Treviso), cored and chopped into small pieces

1 garlic clove, minced

¼ cup white wine

For the béchamel:

5 tbsp. unsalted butter

1 cup all-purpose flour

1¼ cups milk

1¼ cups broth

3 large egg yolks

4 tbsp. grated Parmigiano-Reggiano

Salt and pepper

sauce as in the recipe on page 339. Whisk in the egg yolks and cheese, then add the radicchio. ✦ Cook the crespelle: Heat a nonstick sauté pan over medium heat and add 1 tablespoon butter. Pour in ¼ cup batter and swirl the pan to coat the bottom with a thin layer of batter. When the bottom becomes firm, flip the crespelle. Cook on the other side, then remove to a warm plate. Repeat with the remaining batter, adding butter to the pan as needed. ✦ In a baking pan arrange alternating layers of crespelle and radicchio sauce and bake until golden, about 20 minutes.

CULINGIONIS DE CASU OR DE ARRESCOTTU

SARDEGNA

For the pasta:

3 cups all-purpose flour

6 large eggs

For the stuffing:

1 lb. grated fresh pecorino or 1 lb. grated pecorino ricotta dolce

½ lb. steamed spinach, drained and chopped

2 large eggs, beaten

Pinch Sardegnan saffron

Grated aged pecorino, for serving

Salt

SARDINIAN-STYLE STUFFED PASTA WITH SPINACH

Pecorino ricotta dolce is fresh sheep's-milk ricotta.

Use the flour and eggs to prepare a pasta dough as in the recipe on page 10. Make a ball, wrap it in a cloth, and let it rest 30 minutes. ✦ Prepare the stuffing by combining all the ingredients and seasoning with salt to taste. ✦ Roll out the dough into thin sheets (see note, page 212) about 4 inches wide; align teaspoons of the stuffing along the sheets, spacing them evenly; fold over the sheets and press down around the piles of stuffing. ✦ Cut out 1-inch *culingionis* using a pastry wheel. ✦ Cook in lightly salted boiling water for a few minutes, until they float. Drain and dress as desired with a sauce of tomatoes or meat, adding pecorino to the serving bowl. Serve hot.

CULINGIONIS DE PATATA

SARDEGNA

1½ lbs. potatoes

CONTINUED

SARDINIAN-STYLE STUFFED PASTA WITH POTATO AND MINT

Boil the potatoes, then peel and crush them. Season with ¼ cup olive oil, garlic, and mint. ✦ Add a pinch of salt and the fresh cheese (or ½ cup grated pecorino). Knead and set aside. ✦ Use the flour to prepare a pasta dough

1 ½ cups olive oil

2 garlic cloves, minced

4 mint leaves, finely chopped

6 oz. pecorino without crust in brine or ½ cup grated pecorino

3 cups all-purpose flour, plus more as needed

9 oz. fresh pecorino, for serving

Salt

as in the recipe on page 10, using the remaining olive oil in place of the eggs. Let the dough rest 20 minutes. ✦ Roll the dough out to form as thin a sheet as possible (see note, page 212). Cut into small disks about 2½ inches in diameter. ✦ Put a dollop of the filling in the middle of each disk, fold it over, and press down along the edges to seal. ✦ Cook in lightly salted boiling water for a few minutes (they will float when they are cooked), drain, arrange on a serving plate, and top with pecorino.

✦ **LOCAL TRADITION** ✦

CUSCUS

In Sicily, where this recipe for couscous with fish soup originated, homemade couscous was made *incucciata*, meaning the semolina was worked between the palms of the cook's hands. On a large flat surface, dry semolina would be sprinkled with cold salted water and then worked in wide circles—in a single direction—to create tiny lumps. Once the lumps were achieved, more semolina and salted water were added and the mixture worked further, until the flour and water were absorbed together and the tiny couscous "beads" formed, and olive oil was added. The couscous would then be cooked on a bed of onions for ninety minutes in a terra-cotta steamer, the water perfumed with salt, garlic, olive oil, and parsley, while the fish soup was prepared. Onion, garlic, lemon juice, parsley, and chopped fresh tomatoes formed the soup's broth, and the fish—a mixture of readily available meaty "soup fish," shrimp, squid, cuttlefish, octopus, and if desired mussels and clams—was added in the order of how long each took to cook. Once the couscous and soup were done cooking, the couscous would be placed in a large bowl and the fish added; the complete dish would then be covered and left to rest for an hour. Any leftover broth was flavored with more garlic and parsley and used to season individual servings at the table.

DITALI CON ZUCCHINI E RICOTTA

DITALI WITH ZUCCHINI AND RICOTTA

CAMPANIA

2 tbsp. extra-virgin olive oil

1 small onion, thinly sliced

CONTINUED

In a saucepan heat the olive oil over medium-low heat. Add the onion and sauté until transparent. ✦ Add the zucchini, season with salt, and cover the pan. ✦ After about 15 minutes open the pan and turn up the heat to high to sauté the zucchini while letting the liquid evapo-

1 lb. zucchini, finely diced
1 lb. ditali
1 ¼ cups ricotta
½ cup grated Parmigiano-Reggiano
Salt

rate. ✦ Cook the ditali in lightly salted boiling water until al dente; drain. ✦ Pour them into a bowl and toss with the zucchini and ricotta, breaking the cheese up with the tines of a fork and stirring to coat the pasta. ✦ Add Parmigiano-Reggiano and serve hot.

DITALINI RIGATI
CON ACCIUGHE E
POMODORI SECCHI

DITALINI WITH ANCHOVIES AND SUN-DRIED TOMATOES

SICILIA

¾ lb. ditalini rigati
¼ cup extra-virgin olive oil
6 anchovies in oil, cut in small pieces
4 sun-dried tomatoes in oil, drained and chopped
½ cup white wine
1 garlic clove, crushed
1 pinch chili pepper flakes
A few sprigs of flat-leaf parsley, chopped
½ cup breadcrumbs, toasted very dark
Coarse sea salt

Ditalini rigati are small, hollow tubular pasta with ridges.

Cook the ditalini in lightly salted boiling water until very al dente; drain. ✦ Heat the olive oil in a large pan over low heat, and add the anchovies, stirring them with a wooden spoon to break them up. Do not let them burn: they should cook only about 1 minute in the hot oil. ✦ Add the tomatoes and stir to blend with the anchovies. ✦ Add the wine and garlic, increase the heat to medium, and stir until the wine has nearly evaporated. ✦ Remove the garlic and add the chili flakes and parsley. ✦ Add the ditalini and cook until al dente. Complete the dish with the addition of toasted breadcrumbs and a sprinkling of sea salt.

✦ **LOCAL TRADITION** ✦

CUSCUS CON ZUPPA DI PESCE

In this variation of Sicilian couscous with fish soup, the couscous was cooked along with sliced onion and a small cleaned, skinned, and chopped eel, and the steaming water fragranced with bay leaves, cinnamon, peppercorns, and onion. After sautéing onion and garlic in olive oil, tomato purée and an assortment of "soup fish" (grouper, scorpion fish, angler, squid, octopus, etc.) were cooked together to make the soup, flavored with parsley or basil, saffron, and chopped toasted almonds. The smallest fish from the soup would be passed through a food mill to make a thickening purée. The cooked couscous was placed in a serving bowl and a little of the fish sauce was poured over, but in this version the couscous and hot soup were served separately.

CUSCUS SICILIANO

This third variation on Sicilian couscous with fish soup required a special pan called the *mafaradda*. The couscous would be formed into larger beads, about the size of peppercorns—which required much skill on the part of the cook to keep consistent—and then dried for at least three hours. The dried couscous would then be cooked in a special, tightly-sealed earthenware steamer called a *cuscusèra* (known as a *couscoussière* in French). Halfway through the thirty-minute cooking time, the couscous was removed from the *cuscusèra* and returned to the *mafaradda*. A little cold water was sprinkled over and the couscous allowed to swell slightly before being returned to the steamer to finish cooking. Once cooked, the couscous would be placed in a serving bowl and the piping hot fish soup—either of the above versions, as desired—poured over.

FAVE BIANCHE E LOANE	# FETTUCCINE WITH WHITE FAVA BEANS

PUGLIA

2 cups fresh, shelled white fava beans, peeled

¾ lb. *loane* (tagliatelle made without egg; see page 119) or fettuccine

½ cup olive oil

1 garlic clove

1 dried chili pepper

Salt

Loane are tagliatelle made using only water and flour. This is a typical peasant dish since the fava beans cost little but are rich in protein. Following the rotating crop system of farming, fava beans were cultivated in alternation with wheat, the beans serving to refresh the fallow ground. This dish can be enriched with the addition of bits of bread sautéed in a pan and brought to the table in a bowl so that every diner can take some. To prepare the bread, tear up stale bread and put it in a pan with heated olive oil. Cook it while stirring constantly to keep it from sticking or burning. The bread is ready when it becomes golden.

Cook the fava beans in a saucepan in water to cover for 1 hour. ✦ When they are cooked (and already disintegrating) purée them in a food mill to obtain a liquid purée. ✦ Meanwhile cook the *loane* or fettuccine in lightly salted boiling water until al dente, then drain them and add them to the bean purée. ✦ Heat the olive oil in a small saucepan, add the garlic and chili pepper, season with salt, and when the garlic becomes translucent (this happens very quickly) pour the contents of the pan into the pasta mixture. ✦ Let rest for a few minutes and serve.

FERRETTI IN MEAT SAUCE

BASILICATA

For the pasta:

3 cups white durum wheat flour, plus more as needed

For the sauce:

2 tbsp. extra-virgin olive oil

½ cup chopped flat-leaf parsley

1 medium onion, chopped

1 garlic clove

4 oz. ground pork

4 oz. ground veal

4 oz. ground lamb

2 thick sausages, casing removed, meat crumbled

1 lb. plum tomatoes, peeled

1 tbsp. tomato paste

Grated pecorino

Grated horseradish

Chili pepper flakes

Salt

Tube pasta such as ziti can be used in place of the *ferretti*.

Prepare the pasta as in the recipe on page 10, using ¾ cup water in place of the eggs. Roll as for *strascinati* (see page 388), but instead of being rolled by hand, *ferretti* are made using a square iron 20 to 25 inches long and 1 to 1½ inches thick that creates a kind of hollow strand almost half as long as the iron itself. ✦ For the sauce, heat the oil in a sauté pan, then add the parsley, onion, and garlic and cook until fragrant, then add the meats and sausages. ✦ When the meats have begun to cook add the tomatoes and reduce the heat to low to cook slowly. ✦ Near the end of the cooking add the tomato paste and salt to taste. ✦ Cook the pasta in lightly salted boiling water until al dente, drain, and toss with the sauce. Serve topped with pecorino, horseradish, and chili pepper, to taste.

PASTA, POLENTA & RICE

FERRETTI WITH ANCHOVIES AND BREAD

BASILICATA

½ cup extra-virgin olive oil

8 anchovies, well cleaned and chopped

2 garlic cloves

1 dried chili pepper, crumbled

1 lb. *ferretti* (see above)

1 cup dried and crumbled crustless bread

1 tbsp. chopped flat-leaf parsley

Salt

In place of the anchovies, *ferretti* can be tossed with raisins plumped in a little water and chopped almonds.

Preheat the oven to 400°F. Heat the olive oil in a sauté pan and add the anchovies, garlic (which should be discarded later), and chili pepper. ✦ Cook the *ferretti* in lightly salted boiling water until al dente. ✦ Just before draining the pasta, mix the bread and parsley in a baking pan. Bake for a few minutes, until the bread is lightly toasted. ✦ Drain the pasta, pour into a serving plate; add the anchovy sauce (removing the garlic cloves) and the bread mixture and mix well. Serve hot.

FETTUCCINE "ALFREDO"

FETTUCCINE
AL TRIPLO BURRO

LAZIO

3 cups durum wheat flour
mixed with 1 tbsp. semolina flour,
plus more as needed

5 large eggs

1¼ cups grated
Parmigiano-Reggiano

1½ sticks plus 2 tbsp. unsalted
butter, cut into small pieces

Salt and pepper

This dish was the renowned specialty of the Roman restaura-teur Alfredo, known as the "king of fettuccine," who invented it during the 1930s in his restaurant in Via della Scrofa. He made the final blending of the butter into the pasta into a true spectacle, using gold utensils given to him, it was said, by Mary Pickford and Douglas Fairbanks. He opened another restaurant later on Piazza Augusto Imperatore, but Alfredo, sadly, is no more.

Sift together the flours and use them and the eggs to prepare a pasta dough as in the recipe on page 10. Let rest 20 minutes. ✦ Roll the dough out to form a sheet (see page 212), then cut into strips about ⅜ inch wide. ✦ Cook these fettuccine in a pot of lightly salted boiling water until al dente, then drain and put in a warmed serving dish, adding 2 tablespoons of the cooking water (to help blend the ingredients). ✦ Add the Parmigiano-Reggiano and butter; toss to melt the butter. Serve in warmed bowls. A pinch of pepper makes an excellent final touch.

FETTUCCINE WITH RICOTTA

FETTUCCINE
CON LA RICOTTA

LAZIO

For the pasta:

3 cups all-purpose flour,
plus more as needed

4 large eggs

For the sauce:

2⅓ cups fresh ricotta Romana

3 to 4 tbsp. extra-virgin olive oil

Salt and freshly ground pepper

This dish is typical of Rieti.

Use the flour and eggs to prepare a pasta dough as in the recipe on page 10. Let the dough rest, covered with a cloth, for 30 minutes. ✦ Roll out a sheet that is not too thin (see page 212), fold it over on itself several times, and cut into fettuccine not wider than ¼ inch. ✦ Arrange the fettuccine, spaced widely apart, on a floured cloth placed over a bowl and let them dry. ✦ Cook the fettuc-cine in lightly salted boiling water until al dente, drain, and arrange on a serving dish. ✦ Meanwhile, make the sauce. Press the ricotta through a sieve, then mix into it 3 to 4 tbsp. olive oil, a little of the pasta cooking water, and a good grinding of pepper. Mix and serve hot.

CHESTNUT FETTUCCINE
WITH CABBAGE AND PORK

VALLE D'AOSTA

For the sauce:
1 lb. pork spareribs
1 medium onion, minced
1 carrot, minced
1 celery stalk, minced
¾ cup dry white wine
Vegetable broth
1 Savoy cabbage,
cored and chopped

For the pasta:
¾ cup chestnut flour
⅔ cup all-purpose flour
2 large eggs, beaten, plus 1 yolk
Salt and pepper

This dish is typical of Saint Vincent.

Preheat the oven to 300°F. Place the pork ribs in a baking pan and add the onion, carrot, and celery. Add the wine and vegetable broth to cover. Cover and bake until the meat is falling off the bones, about 1½ hours. Meanwhile, blanch the cabbage. ✦ Bone the ribs, cut the meat in small pieces, and mix with the cabbage. ✦ Sift together the flours and use them and the eggs to prepare a pasta dough as in the recipe on page 10, adding the egg yolk with the eggs. Let the dough rest 20 minutes. ✦ Roll out a very thin sheet of dough (see page 212), cut fettuccine, and cook them in lightly salted boiling water until al dente. Drain and toss them with the meat and cabbage sauce. A grinding of pepper is recommended.

PASTA, POLENTA & RICE

FIADONE

BAKED CHEESE PIE

ABRUZZO

For the pasta:
½ cup milk
1½ tsp. active dry yeast
3 cups all-purpose flour,
plus more as needed
½ cup extra-virgin olive oil
3 large eggs
Salt

For the filling:
6 large eggs, beaten
3½ cups grated pecorino
Pinch grated nutmeg
2¼ tsp. active dry yeast
Salt and pepper

Preheat the oven to 325°F. Warm the milk slightly and add the yeast, stirring to dissolve. Set aside. ✦ Use the flour, yeast mixture, olive oil, and eggs to prepare a pasta dough as in recipe on page 10, adding the yeast mixture and olive oil with the eggs. Let the dough rest, covered with a kitchen towel, 20 minutes. ✦ Roll out to form a sheet (see page 212). ✦ Set aside one-fourth of the dough and use the rest to line a pan, letting the edges of the dough extend above the lip of the pan. ✦ Make the filling: Combine 5 of the eggs, pecorino, and nutmeg. Add the yeast and salt and pepper, and stir with a wooden spoon to obtain a creamy mixture. ✦ Put this in the pan and cover it with the edges of dough left extending over the pan. ✦ Roll out the remaining portion of dough and cut it into strips like fettuccine and arrange these across the top of the *fiadone*. ✦ Whisk the remaining egg and brush it over the surface. ✦ Bake for about 45 minutes or until the dough is dark golden. Let it cool before serving.

PASTA IN ANCHOVY SAUCE

FILETTI DI ACCIUGHE SOTTO SALE

CALABRIA

For the pasta:

3 cups all-purpose flour, plus more as needed

For the sauce:

¼ cup extra-virgin olive oil

4 or 5 salt-cured anchovy fillets, broken up into pieces

2 garlic cloves, minced

1 cup crustless peasant-style bread, crumbled and toasted

Chili pepper flakes

Chopped flat-leaf parsley

Salt and pepper

Use the flour to prepare a pasta dough as in the recipe on page 10, using ¾ cup water in place of the eggs. Let rest, covered with a cloth, 20 minutes. ✦ Roll it out (see page 212), and by hand work it into long threads. ✦ Heat a little olive oil in a sauté pan until hot, and add the anchovy fillets, garlic, and bread; cook until fragrant. ✦ Cook the pasta in lightly salted boiling water, drain, and toss with the sauce. Before serving sprinkle with chili flakes, black pepper, and parsley.

FIORONI FILLED WITH SALAME AND CHEESE

FIORONI DI MORCONE

CAMPANIA

Olive oil

For the pasta:

3 cups all-purpose flour, plus more as needed

½ cup lard

2 large eggs

Salt

For the filling:

2 large eggs, beaten

7 oz. salame (best if Neapolitan), cubed

½ cup grated pecorino

4 oz. fresh pecorino, in pieces

Salt

The ingredients of this recipe can be used to make smaller disks, which can then be fried in a pan and served as an appetizer.

Preheat the oven to 350°F. Grease a baking sheet with olive oil. Use the flour, lard, and eggs to prepare a pasta dough as on page 10, adding the lard with the eggs. Let the dough rest, covered with a cloth, for 20 minutes. ✦ Roll out the dough to a thin sheet (see page 212), and cut into two disks about 8 inches in diameter. ✦ Mix the eggs, salame, and cheeses until blended. ✦ Spread this mixture across one of the two pasta disks and cover it with the other, pressing down to seal the edges tightly. Place on the prepared baking sheet and bake until nicely golden, about 20 minutes. Make as many of these disks— the *fioroni*—as you like.

BAKED SEAFOOD RISOTTO

CAMPANIA

For the filling and rice:

1¼ cups unsalted butter

1 lobster

1 bouquet garni

¾ lb. small head-on shrimp, shelled, shells and heads reserved

2 lbs. mussels, scrubbed and beards removed

2 lbs. clams, cleaned

1 cup all-purpose flour

1 tbsp. curry powder

1⅔ cups Patna rice (can substitute any long-grain white rice)

⅔ cup grated Parmigiano-Reggiano

For the dough:

1 oz. active dry yeast

4½ cups all-purpose flour, plus more as needed

5 large eggs, beaten

¼ lb. (1 stick) plus 3 tbsp. unsalted butter

2 tbsp. sugar

Salt

Butter an 8-inch-round deep baking dish. Bring 12 cups of water to a boil. Add the lobster and cook for 20 minutes. ✦ Remove from the water. When cool enough to handle break it apart, setting aside its meat. ✦ Roughly chop the carcass and claws and put them back in its cooking water with the bouquet garni. ✦ Roughly chop the shells and heads of the shrimp and add them to the lobster pot. ✦ Heat 4 tablespoons butter in a pan and sauté the shelled shrimp for a few minutes. Set aside. ✦ Simmer the lobster cooking water for 2 hours, adding water if necessary to maintain the same level. ✦ Strain the liquid through cheesecloth and set it aside. ✦ Cook the mussels in a covered pot without water. Remove them when they are fully open, remove their shells, and set aside. ✦ In a pot, heat 10 cups of water to a simmer, add the clams, and cook until they open. Strain their liquid through cheesecloth and mix with the lobster liquid. ✦ Make the dough. Dissolve the yeast in 2 tablespoons lukewarm water and mix it in a bowl with a small amount of the flour to form a very soft small loaf. ✦ Set this small loaf aside to rise, covered by a kitchen towel, until it has tripled in volume. ✦ Use the flour, eggs, risen loaf, butter, and sugar to prepare a pasta dough as in recipe on page 10, adding the risen loaf, butter, and sugar with the eggs. ✦ Knead the dough a long time, pushing against it with the palms of your hands to stretch it upward (the dough should be stringy), and then bang it on the work surface to enclose as much air in the dough as possible. The resulting dough should be very soft and elastic, so it may be necessary to add water. Normally this kneading lasts around 20 to 30 minutes, by which time the dough should come away from the surface in a single lump. Set it aside to rest under a cloth. ✦ Continue with the filling: melt the remaining 1 cup butter in a saucepan, then add the flour and curry powder, stirring well. ✦ A little at a time add enough broth from cooking the shellfish to obtain a velvety sauce. ✦ Mix in the mussels, clams, shrimp, and lobster meat cut in pieces. Let this cool. ✦ Use the rice, remaining broth, and remaining butter to prepare a risotto (see page 349) ✦ Cover the bottom of the baking dish with a 2-inch-thick layer of dough; cover this with a 1-inch-thick layer of risotto, leaving an open space all around of about ¾ inch. ✦ Now pour in a layer of filling about 2 inches thick, leaving the same space around the edge. ✦ Fill this open space with the remaining dough, also using it to make a ½-inch cover for the pan. ✦ Let the dough rise for a few hours, until doubled. ✦ Preheat the oven to 350°F. Bake until the surface is crisp and golden, about 40 minutes. ✦ Take out of the oven, invert onto a serving plate, and serve warm.

PASTA STUFFED WITH BEEF AND SAUSAGE

FREGNACCE

ABRUZZO

For the sauce and filling:
¼ cup olive oil
½ lb. ground beef
2 sausages, casings removed
1 medium onion, sliced
1½ lbs. ripe plum tomatoes, chopped
¼ tsp. chili pepper flakes
2 large eggs, beaten
Grated pecorino

For the pasta:
3 cups all-purpose flour, plus more as needed
5 large eggs
Salt

Preheat the oven to 400°F. Heat the olive oil in a large pot, then add the beef, sausage meat, and onion and cook until the meat is browned, breaking it up with a wooden spoon. Stir in the tomatoes and chili pepper and cook until the sauce has thickened. Divide this sauce in two parts. Set aside one portion and to the other add the eggs and enough pecorino to form a filling of a thick consistency. ✦ Use the flour and eggs to prepare a pasta dough as in the recipe on page 10, then finish as for *Maccheroni all chitarra* (see page 278). ✦ Roll out a sheet (see page 212), and cut it into squares about 8 inches on a side. ✦ Cook these in lightly salted boiling water for 3 minutes. ✦ Put the pasta squares on a table and put a little of the filling at the center of each. Fold the pasta over to close, pressing to seal the edges. ✦ Arrange these *fregnacce* in a pan, sprinkle with pecorino and the remaining meat sauce, and bake for a few minutes until the sauce is bubbling. Serve hot.

LEFTOVER PASTA OMELET

FRITTATA DI MACCHERONI AUSATI

CAMPANIA

¼ cup extra-virgin olive oil
¾ lb. leftover cooked pasta (preferably short macaroni)
2 large eggs, beaten
Grated Parmigiano-Reggiano

The great Eduardo De Filippo, with his sharp Neapolitan sensibility, baptized this dish macaroni *ausati*, as in "used." This recipe calls for leftover pasta. Any kind will do, and it does not matter what kind of sauce or seasoning the pasta was made with.

Preheat the broiler. Heat the olive oil in a broilerproof pan and add the pasta, spreading it into an even layer.

Pour over the eggs, shaking the pan to make sure they are evenly distributed. Cook for a few minutes without stirring, then lift up one edge to check that there is a golden crust on the bottom. Place the pan under the broiler until the top is browned, about 1 minute. Cut into wedges and serve, topped with some cheese to taste.

✦ **LOCAL TRADITION** ✦

LA FRIGOLADA

In Lombardia, there is a special way of preparing polenta, called *la frigolada*. Polenta is made with cornmeal, milk, water, and chopped costmary (erba di San Pietro). It is then poured into a pan, left to cool, and sliced into chunks. The chunks are set in hot oil in a pan and crushed with a fork until they turn golden.

FUSILLI ALLA PAESANA

FUSILLI WITH MUSHROOMS AND OLIVES

CALABRIA

⅔ cup extra-virgin olive oil

½ medium onion, finely chopped

1 garlic clove

1 lb. plum tomatoes, peeled and seeded

7 oz. porcini mushrooms in oil (or 1 oz. dried, softened in lukewarm water and drained), chopped

½ cup pitted black olives, halved

½ fresh hot chili pepper, chopped

1 bunch flat-leaf parsley, chopped

1 pinch fennel seeds

3 oz. capocollo, cut into strips

1 lb. fusilli

½ cup grated aged or smoked sheep's-milk ricotta (or pecorino)

Salt

To season the fusilli more thoroughly, spread a layer of cheese (in this case grated ricotta) on the bottom of the serving plate, then pour in the drained pasta and mix with the sauce.

Heat the olive oil in an earthenware pan and add the onion and garlic and cook; remove and discard the garlic when golden brown. ✦ Add the tomatoes, mushrooms, olives, chili pepper, parsley, fennel seeds, and capocollo. ✦ Salt to taste and cook at low heat. ✦ Cook the fusilli in lightly salted boiling water until al dente and drain well. Put them in a large serving bowl and toss with the sauce, adding ricotta. Blend well with a wooden fork and serve.

FUSILLI ALLA MOLISANA

In the area of Molise, homemade fusilli was made by wrapping fresh pasta noodles around knitting needles to obtain the perfect, consistent spiral. To make this traditional meat sauce to dress the fusilli, a single piece of lamb and a single piece of veal would be seasoned on one side with parsley, garlic, and *lardo*, then rolled up and pinned with toothpicks. The meat rolls would be sautéed in a hot pan with olive oil, garlic, onion, and parsley. Crumbled sausage meat and red wine would then be added and cooked down, then peeled whole tomatoes would be added to cook for two hours to finish the hearty sauce. Chili flakes were added last to retain their bite. The sauce would then be tossed with the fusilli—cooked just al dente—and served with pecorino at the table.

FUSILLI ED ORECCHIETTE IN TEGAMINO

BAKED FUSILLI AND ORECCHIETTE

CAMPANIA

½ lb. ground beef

1 medium onion, minced

1 large egg, beaten

½ cup crustless bread, soaked in milk until soft, then squeezed dry

½ cup grated pecorino

⅓ cup extra-virgin olive oil

4 cups tomato sauce

6 oz. fusilli

6 oz. orecchiette

6 oz. scamorza cheese, sliced

⅔ cup grated Parmigiano-Reggiano

Salt

This dish is typical of Avellino.

Preheat the oven to 400°F. Form the ground beef, onion, egg, bread, pecorino, and a pinch of salt into meatballs. Heat the olive oil in a pan and cook the meatballs until browned. ✦ Add the tomato sauce and let it cook over medium-low heat until it thickens. ✦ Cook the fusilli and orecchiette in separate pots of lightly salted boiling water until very al dente; drain. ✦ Mix the two types of pasta and divide among four ovenproof bowls, adding the meatballs, sauce, and scamorza. ✦ Bake about 30 minutes or until the liquid is bubbling and the cheese is melted and browned. Serve in the bowls, sprinkled with Parmigiano-Reggiano.

GARGANELLI WITH PEAS AND PROSCIUTTO

EMILIA-ROMAGNA

1 lb. pasta in sheets (see page 10 and note, page 212)

2 tbsp. unsalted butter

3 oz. prosciutto di Parma (ideally prosciutto dolce from Langhirano), diced

1 ½ cups heavy cream

3 oz. boiled peas, cooled in cold water

3 sweet red peppers, peeled and cubed

⅔ cup grated Parmigiano-Reggiano

Salt

Garganelli came into being as pasta eaten in soup but are now used most often in sauces, as in this recipe typical of Imola. *Penne rigate* can be used in place of the *garganelli*.

Cut the sheets of pasta into squares about 2½ inches on each side. Holding one end, wrap each around a cylindrical stick about the thickness of a pencil, then roll it along a regular comb, a weaver's comb, or, if possible, along the special ribbed metal tool made for the purpose. The resulting *garganelli* will be shaped like small *penne rigate;* set them out on a cloth and let them dry several hours. ✦ Heat the butter in a pan over medium-low heat until melted; add the prosciutto and cook for a few seconds. ✦ Add the cream, peas, and peppers and cook over low heat until the mixture begins to boil; remove from the heat and keep warm. ✦ Cook the *garganelli* in lightly salted boiling water until al dente, drain, pour into a serving bowl, and toss with the sauce and cheese. Serve immediately.

SMALL GNOCCHI MADE WITH BREADCRUMBS IN BEAN SAUCE

GNOCCHETTI ALLA COLLESCIPOLANA

UMBRIA

For the pasta:

1 ¼ cups all-purpose flour, plus more as needed

⅔ cup breadcrumbs

Salt

For the sauce:

½ cup extra-virgin olive oil

¼ medium onion, minced

1 garlic clove, minced

1 celery stalk, finely chopped

1 carrot, finely chopped

⅔ cup diced pancetta

2 sausages, crumbled

1 ¼ cups tomato purée

1 ¼ cups boiled beans

Grated pecorino

Salt

This dish is typical of Terni.

Sift together the flour and breadcrumbs, then use them to prepare a pasta dough as in the recipe on page 10, using ½ cup water in place of the eggs. Let rest 30 minutes. ✦ Shape the dough into long, thin ropes, then cut these crosswise to create pieces about ¼ inch thick and ½ inch long. ✦ Heat the olive oil in a pot over low heat, then add the onion, garlic, celery, and carrot and cook until softened; add the pancetta and sausage meat. ✦ After 15 minutes add the tomato purée and continue cooking; after about 10 minutes, add the beans and cook 10 minutes more. ✦ Boil the gnocchetti in lightly salted water to cover, and as they rise to the surface toss them into the sauce. Add pecorino as desired.

SMALL BUTTER GNOCCHI IN BROTH

GNOCCHETTI DI BURRO

TRENTINO

4 tbsp. unsalted butter

2 tbsp. all-purpose flour

¼ cup meat broth,
plus more for serving

¼ cup grated Parmigiano-Reggiano,
plus more for serving

2 large eggs, beaten

Melt the butter in a saucepan over medium heat and stir in the flour. Add just enough meat broth to obtain a dense paste, then let it cool. ✦ Add the cheese and eggs to the mixture, working them in well with a spoon. ✦ Shape this mixture into small gnocchi. Heat the remaining broth to boiling and cook the gnocchi until they float. Serve in the broth with additional cheese.

SPÄTZLE

GNOCCHETTI DI FARINA

ALTO ADIGE

1⅔ cups all-purpose flour,
plus more as needed

4 tbsp. (¼ cup) unsalted butter

Salt

These *gnocchetti*, unsalted, can accompany *Castrato alla cacciatora* (see page 544) or game. When using a sieve—and a special version exists for making spätzle—the dough should be made a little damper (by adding more water).

In a mixing bowl, combine the flour with ¾ cup water and stir the resulting dough until it forms air bubbles. ✦ Using the round tip of a knife spread out very small portions of the dough on a floured board; cut these into tiny strips and drop them into lightly salted boiling water (a better method is to push the dough through the holes of a sieve or colander placed directly over the water). ✦ When the *gnocchetti* float, remove them with a strainer, run them under cold water, and set out to dry. ✦ Before serving, sauté them in butter until golden.

SMALL GNOCCHI WITH RICOTTA AND PORCINI

GNOCCHETTI DI RICOTTA
AI FUNGHI TRIFOLATI

PIEMONTE

For the gnocchi:

1 lb. ricotta (preferably
from Piemonte)

¾ cup grated Parmigiano-Reggiano

⅔ cup all-purpose flour

2 large eggs plus 2 yolks

Salt

CONTINUED

Combine the ricotta, Parmigiano-Reggiano, flour, eggs and yolks, and a pinch of salt, then knead to create a soft dough; divide the dough into balls and form these into long sticks. ✦ Cut these sticks into short cylinders and press each against the curved back of a fork to obtain the traditional gnocchi shape, but smaller than those made of potato. ✦ Heat 2 tablespoons of the olive oil in a pan until hot, add the garlic then the mushrooms, and cook until lightly browned. Stir in the parsley and butter. ✦ Cook the *gnocchetti* in lightly salted boiling water with

For the sauce:

¼ cup extra-virgin olive oil

1 garlic clove, minced

2 lbs. fresh porcini mushrooms, cleaned and sliced

2 tbsp. chopped flat-leaf parsley

2 tbsp. unsalted butter

Salt

the addition of the remaining olive oil. ✦ As soon as they float, remove them from the water and toss with the mushroom sauce. Stir gently and serve hot.

GNOCCHETTI
DI SPINACI CON SALSA
DI PROSCIUTTO

SMALL SPINACH GNOCCHI IN PROSCIUTTO SAUCE

ALTO ADIGE

For the sauce:

2 tbsp. unsalted butter

4 oz. prosciutto, cut in thin strips

¼ cup white wine

1 cup heavy cream

1 large egg yolk

Pinch grated nutmeg

2 tbsp. grated
Parmigiano-Reggiano

For the gnocchi:

6 cups spinach, drained and chopped fine to make 1 cup

¾ cup all-purpose flour

1 tbsp. milk

Salt and pepper

Prepare the sauce: heat the butter and prosciutto in a pan over medium heat until the prosciutto is slightly golden, then add the white wine and let it evaporate. Add the cream and let it reduce by half. ✦ Make the gnocchi: combine the spinach, flour, and milk to form a paste, mixing well. ✦ Transfer to a pastry bag. Squeeze the bag to drop pieces of the mixture into lightly salted boiling water. Cook 2 to 3 minutes, drain the *gnocchetti*, and put them in the pan with the sauce. ✦ At this point add the egg yolk, nutmeg, salt, and pepper and cook for about 5 minutes. Serve hot with a dusting of Parmigiano-Reggiano.

GNOCCHETTI FRITTI

FRIED SMALL GNOCCHI

PIEMONTE

For the gnocchi:

⅓ cup all-purpose flour

½ cup semolina flour

2 large egg yolks

2 cups milk

1 tbsp. sugar

4 tbsp. unsalted butter

CONTINUED

These *gnocchetti* are often included in the large Piemontese fritto misto or are served as a sweet fried dish.

Put the flour, semolina, and egg yolks in a saucepan and stir to mix. Add the milk, sugar, and salt and pepper. Cook, stirring, until thickened. ✦ Remove from the heat and, stirring constantly, add the butter, Parmigiano-Reggiano, Gruyère, and truffle. ✦ Heat this mixture for a few minutes then turn it out on a lightly greased work surface. Spread it out, smoothing it and leveling it with the blade of a knife to form a uniform thickness of about

⅓ cup grated
Parmigiano-Reggiano

½ cup grated Gruyère

Slices of white truffle

Salt and pepper

For frying:

Extra-virgin olive oil

2 cups all-purpose flour,
plus more as needed

1 large egg, beaten

2 cups breadcrumbs

½ inch. Let it cool completely. ✦ Heat 2 inches of olive oil in a high-sided pan until hot. Using the dampened blade of a knife cut out small rectangles of gnocchi, roll them in flour, then egg, then breadcrumbs. Fry until golden and serve hot.

GNOCCHI AL FORMAGGIO

CHEESE GNOCCHI

ALTO ADIGE

3 dinner rolls,
cut into small cubes
(or stale bread)

6 oz. Emmenthal Appenzell,
Gruyère, or other Alpine cheese

2 large eggs, beaten

1 ¼ cups milk

1 tbsp. all-purpose flour

Salt and pepper

Melted butter, for serving

Grated Parmigiano-Reggiano or
local *graukäse* (soft cow's-milk
cheese), for serving

Combine all the ingredients except the melted butter and Parmigiano-Reggiano to form a dough; mix well and make into gnocchi, pressing lumps of dough into the bowl of a spoon to form them. ✦ Cook the gnocchi in lightly salted boiling water for about 5 minutes. Serve hot with butter and Parmigiano-Reggiano or *graukäse*.

GNOCCHI
AL MODO ANTICO

STUFFED POTATO GNOCCHI

FRIULI-VENEZIA GIULIA

For the gnocchi:

1 lb. potatoes, peeled

1 large egg

⅔ cup all-purpose flour

½ cup grated Montasio cheese

CONTINUED

This dish is typical of the area of Carnia.

Steam the potatoes until cooked then drain well. ✦ Crush them on a pastry board, then add the egg and work in the flour, cheese, nutmeg, and salt and pepper. ✦ Knead well to obtain an elastic dough then make into sticks. Cut these sticks into pieces about 1 inch long and flatten them slightly. ✦ Make the filling by combining the sausage meat with the rye bread, egg, and cheeses. ✦ Place some of this mixture at the center of each flattened gnocchi

Pinch grated nutmeg

Salt and pepper

For the filling:

Meat of 1 sausage

2 slices of rye bread, softened in
water and squeezed dry

1 large egg, beaten

⅓ cup grated Montasio cheese

⅓ cup grated smoked ricotta

For the sauce:

¼ cup unsalted butter,
melted, for serving

2 tbsp. shredded sage leaves,
for serving

Salt and pepper

and fold over, pressing the edges to seal. Cook them in lightly salted boiling water and toss with butter and sage leaves. Season with salt and pepper.

GNOCCHI
AL SUGO D'OCA

GNOCCHI WITH
GOOSE SAUCE

UMBRIA

For the gnocchi:

2 lbs. potatoes

All-purpose flour

For the sauce:

¼ cup extra-virgin olive oil

2 carrots, chopped

1 celery stalk, chopped

1 medium onion, minced

1½ lbs. goose meat, cut in pieces

½ cup dry white wine

Broth (if needed)

1 lb. peeled plum tomatoes

Grated pecorino

Salt

Boil the potatoes in lightly salted water, peel them while still warm, crush them, and combine them with just enough flour to obtain a smooth dough. ✦ Shape the dough into long sticks similar to breadsticks and cut crosswise with a knife to form gnocchi. Set aside. ✦ Prepare the sauce: Heat the olive oil in a pan and add the carrots, celery, and onion. Cook until the onion is golden, then add the goose. ✦ Add the wine and a pinch of salt, and cook for about 1 hour, taking care to add more wine (or broth) if needed. ✦ Add the tomatoes and continue cooking at low heat for 30 minutes. ✦ When cooked, remove the goose with a slotted spoon, remove any bones, cut the meat in small pieces, and return to the sauce. Adjust for salt. ✦ Put the gnocchi in lightly salted boiling water, remove with a slotted spoon when they rise to the surface, and toss with sauce and pecorino.

GNOCCHI WITH RABBIT SAUCE

ABRUZZO

For the gnocchi:

2 lbs. starchy potatoes

2 cups all-purpose flour, plus more as needed

1 large egg, beaten (optional)

For the sauce:

1 rabbit, weighing 2 lbs., cut in pieces

2 tbsp. extra-virgin olive oil

1 medium onion, studded with 3 cloves

1 carrot, chopped

1 cup tomato sauce

Chili pepper flakes (as much as desired)

¾ cup grated pecorino

Salt

This preparation is typical of Pescara. In place of the rabbit one can make the sauce with mutton.

Heat the oven to 300°F. Boil the potatoes, peel, and put through a food mill or potato ricer. ✦ On a floured pastry board or in a mixing bowl, knead the potatoes, slowly adding flour to obtain a soft and elastic dough, adding salt and, if desired, an egg. ✦ Divide the mixture in small pieces and roll these to form finger-size lengths. Cut these crosswise to create the gnocchi. ✦ Press each of these gnocchi against the back of a fork or a grater. Arrange the gnocchi on floured parchment paper and set aside. ✦ Brush the rabbit pieces with olive oil, then place them in a roasting pan with the onion studded with cloves, carrot, and tomato sauce; season with salt and chili pepper flakes and bake for about 2 hours. ✦ Remove the rabbit from the pan and pass the sauce through a strainer. Shred the rabbit meat and mix with the sauce. ✦ Cook the gnocchi in a pot in lightly salted boiling water; as they come to the surface remove them with a strainer and put them on a warmed serving platter; top with rabbit sauce, mixing well. Dust with pecorino.

GNOCCHI IN MEAT SAUCE

PIEMONTE

For the gnocchi:

1 ¼ cups all-purpose flour, plus more as needed

⅔ cup breadcrumbs

½ cup grated Parmigiano-Reggiano

1 large egg plus 1 yolk

Pinch cinnamon

Pinch grated nutmeg

½ cup finely chopped prosciutto cotto

½ cup milk

Salt

CONTINUED

Sift together the flour and breadcrumbs, then prepare a dough as in the recipe on page 10, adding the Parmigiano-Reggiano, egg yolk, cinnamon, nutmeg, prosciutto cotto, and milk with the egg. ✦ Put the dough in a warm place, covered with a cloth, and let it rest for 1 hour. Although it contains no yeast, it will tend to rise a little. ✦ When the hour has passed, return the dough to the work surface, knead it again, divide it in pieces, then form the pieces into lengths about the size of an index finger. ✦ Cut each of these crosswise with a knife in lengths of about ½ inch. Press a finger against each lump to make it slightly hollow. ✦ Put a pot of water over high heat and when it boils, salt it and drop in the gnocchi, letting them boil slowly for a few minutes. ✦ When they float to the surface, drain and put them in a

For the sauce:

Sauce from roast meat
(see page 584)

Parmigiano-Reggiano

2 tbsp. unsalted butter

warmed serving bowl and toss with the meat sauce and Parmigiano-Reggiano. ✦ Put the butter in a pan and heat until melted and golden. Pour it over the gnocchi and serve.

GNOCCHI ALLA ROMANA

ROMAN-STYLE GNOCCHI

LAZIO

3 cups all-purpose flour,
plus more as needed

4 large eggs, beaten

⅔ cup diced Gruyère
or Swiss cheese

2 ¼ cups milk

¼ lb. (1 stick) unsalted butter,
melted

Grated Parmigiano-Reggiano

Salt

Semolina flour can be used in place of the all-purpose flour, resulting in "semolina gnocchi," a dish that originated in Piemonte.

Combine the flour and eggs in a saucepan, then add the diced cheese. ✦ Slowly add the milk, stirring well with a wooden spoon and breaking up lumps to obtain a very liquid mixture. ✦ Put the pan over low heat and continue stirring to obtain a mixture with the thickness of polenta; at that point remove from the heat. ✦ Add a pinch of salt and half the butter; stir. ✦ Pour the mixture onto a work surface and using a knife spread it into a sheet with the thickness of a finger. ✦ When this cools use a knife to cut it into small squares or use an upside-down glass to create disks. ✦ Preheat the oven to 450°F. Grease a baking pan with a little butter and arrange the gnocchi in layers. Drizzle each layer with butter and sprinkle with Parmigiano-Reggiano. ✦ Bake for 20 minutes or until the gnocchi are golden.

GNOCCHI ALLA SORRENTINA

BAKED GNOCCHI WITH FIOR DI LATTE CHEESE AND TOMATO SAUCE

CAMPANIA

1 lb. gnocchi (see page 252)

Tomato sauce seasoned with basil
(see page 327)

⅔ cup grated Parmigiano-Reggiano

7 oz. *fior di latte* cheese, sliced

½ cup basil leaves

Salt

Preheat the oven to 450°F. Cook the gnocchi in lightly salted boiling water and drain as soon as they rise to the surface. ✦ Put them in a baking dish and toss them with a dense sauce of tomato and Parmigiano-Reggiano. ✦ Cover with a layer of *fior di latte*, adding more sauce, more Parmigiano-Reggiano, and some basil. Bake until the cheese melts, about 12 minutes. Serve immediately.

PUMPKIN-POTATO GNOCCHI

PIEMONTE

1 lb. peeled and seeded pumpkin
1 lb. potatoes
½ cup chestnuts
¾ cup all-purpose flour
¾ cup breadcrumbs
2 large egg yolks
Pinch grated nutmeg
1 tbsp. olive oil
Salt and pepper

Serve these gnocchi with brown butter with sage.

Boil the pumpkin, potatoes, and chestnuts separately until tender. Drain and pass through a food mill. ✦ Mix, then combine with all the other ingredients to form a dough. Shape into balls the shape of gnocchi. ✦ Cook in lightly salted boiling water until they float. Serve hot.

GNOCCHI WITH DUCK SAUCE

MARCHE

For the gnocchi:
2 lbs. potatoes
¾ cup all-purpose flour
1 large egg, beaten
2 tbsp. grated Parmigiano-Reggiano
Salt

For the sauce:
¼ cup olive oil
1 medium onion, finely chopped
1 celery stalk, finely chopped
1 carrot, finely chopped
1 duck, weighing 2 lbs., cleaned and cut into serving pieces
½ cup white wine
1 pint tomato sauce
⅓ cup tomato paste
⅔ cup grated Parmigiano-Reggiano
Salt and pepper

Boil the potatoes in lightly salted water to cover until soft. Drain, peel, and let cool. ✦ Pass them through a food mill and combine with the flour, egg, cheese, and a pinch of salt. Knead to form a soft, elastic dough. ✦ Form the dough into long cylinders, then cut the cylinders crosswise to form pieces about ¾ inch long and press these against the tines of a fork. Set aside. ✦ Heat the oil in a large pan and add the onion, celery, and carrot. Add the duck pieces and sauté until golden. ✦ Adjust for salt and pepper and pour in the wine. ✦ When it evaporates, add the tomato sauce and tomato paste dissolved in hot water. Simmer until the duck is cooked through and the sauce has thickened. ✦ Cook the gnocchi in lightly salted boiling water, drain, and toss with the sauce and Parmigiano-Reggiano.

GNOCCHI CON LE SARDELLE DEL TRENTINO | GNOCCHI WITH SARDINES

TRENTINO

For the dough:

2 lbs. potatoes

1⅔ cups all-purpose flour, plus more as needed

2 large egg yolks

Pinch grated nutmeg

For the sauce:

6 tbsp. unsalted butter

¾ lb. fresh sardines, rinsed, boned, and finely chopped

Grated Parmigiano-Reggiano (optional)

Peel and rinse the potatoes and cook them in lightly salted boiling water. ✦ When cooked, drain them and pass them through a food mill or potato ricer. Spread them on a work surface and sprinkle with the flour. ✦ Add the egg yolks and nutmeg; knead well to form a smooth dough. ✦ Shape the dough into cylinders and cut into the desired size. ✦ Cook them in lightly salted boiling water and drain as soon as they rise to the surface. ✦ Heat the butter in a pan, and as soon as it melts, add the sardines and cook for 1 minute. Pour this over the cooked gnocchi, adding cheese as desired.

GNOCCHI DI CASTAGNE | CHESTNUT-FLOUR GNOCCHI

TOSCANA

1⅔ cups chestnut flour

¾ cup all-purpose flour, plus more as needed

Extra-virgin olive oil

Grated pecorino

Salt

These gnocchi are typical of Pontremoli, Zeri, and Bagnone.

Sift the flours together then use them to prepare a pasta dough as in the recipe on page 10, using ¾ cup water in place of the eggs. ✦ Roll out the dough to form a sheet about ⅛ inch thick (see page 212). ✦ Let this dry for 20 minutes then cut in squares 1½ inches on a side and dust with flour. ✦ Put the gnocchi in a pot with lightly salted boiling water; cook for 10 minutes. ✦ Drain and layer in a serving bowl, sprinkling olive oil and pecorino over each layer.

GNOCCHI DI GRANO SARACENO ALLO SPECK | BUCKWHEAT GNOCCHI WITH SPECK

VALLE D'AOSTA

1 lb. potatoes

½ cup all-purpose flour

⅔ cup buckwheat flour

4 tbsp. unsalted butter

CONTINUED

This dish is typical of Gressoney St. Jean (Walser cuisine).

Boil the potatoes in lightly salted water until soft. Peel them when still warm, and put through a food mill or potato ricer. ✦ Mix the potato purée with the flours to form a soft dough, then shape the dough into gnocchi. ✦ Cook the gnocchi in lightly salted boiling water and drain with a strainer as soon as they float. ✦ In a large pan heat

¾ cup diced speck

1 tbsp. chopped flat-leaf parsley

1 tbsp. chopped thyme

2 tbsp. seasonal aromatic herbs, chopped fine

Salt

the butter over low heat, add the speck, and cook it without letting it brown. ✦ Add the gnocchi to the pan and cook them at high heat for a few moments. ✦ Spoon onto serving plates and dust with herbs.

GNOCCHI DI PATATE 1

POTATO GNOCCHI 1

EMILIA-ROMAGNA

For the pasta:

2 lbs. potatoes

3 cups all-purpose flour, plus more as needed

2 tbsp. unsalted butter

1 large egg

Salt

For the sauce:

¼ cup unsalted butter, melted

2 tbsp. grated Parmigiano-Reggiano, for serving

This preparation is typical of Parma. If desired, add tomato sauce or, even better, fresh tomatoes browned in butter.

Boil the potatoes, peel them, and put them through a food mill or potato ricer. Mix them with the flour, butter, and egg to make a soft dough. ✦ Make cylinders about the thickness of a finger. ✦ Cut these crosswise in lengths of about 1 to 1½ inches. Press each of these little cylinders against the work surface with a finger, dragging them lengthwise to shape them into little curls. ✦ Cook the gnocchi in lightly salted boiling water, drain well, and toss with butter and Parmigiano-Reggiano.

GNOCCHI DI PATATE 2

POTATO GNOCCHI 2

EMILIA-ROMAGNA

2 lbs. potatoes

1⅔ cups all-purpose flour, plus more as needed

2 large eggs, beaten

1 recipe Romagna-style sauce (see page 330)

⅔ cup grated Parmigiano-Reggiano

Salt

This dish is typical of Romagna.

Boil the potatoes in lightly salted water, peel them, and put them through a potato ricer. ✦ Mix with the flour and eggs to obtain a smooth dough. ✦ Shape the dough into strips and cut them into pieces about 1 inch long. Press these against the tines of a fork to create gnocchi. Cook the gnocchi in lightly salted boiling water. ✦ Drain as soon as they float and toss in a serving bowl with sauce and Parmigiano-Reggiano.

GNOCCHI DI PATATE ALLA ROMAGNOLA

ROMAGNA-STYLE POTATO GNOCCHI

EMILIA-ROMAGNA

For the dough:

3 ¼ lbs. starchy potatoes

1 ⅔ cups all-purpose flour, plus more as needed

Salt

For the sauce:

4 tbsp. unsalted butter

½ small onion, finely chopped

½ celery stalk, finely chopped

1 small carrot, finely chopped

2 oz. *lardo* (see page 2), chopped

½ lb. beef (rump or topside), coarsely ground

Pinch grated nutmeg

1 bay leaf

½ cup dry red wine

1 ¼ cups finely chopped plum tomatoes (or 4 oz. tomato paste diluted in water to make 1 ¼ cups)

¼ lb. (1 stick) butter, melted

1 cup grated Parmigiano-Reggiano

Beef broth (if necessary)

Salt and pepper

Boil the potatoes in lightly salted water until al dente, drain and peel, and pass through a food mill to obtain a purée. ✦ Combine the flour with the still lukewarm potato purée to obtain a thick but soft mixture. ✦ Divide this in portions and with floured hands roll out cylinders about 1 inch in diameter. ✦ Cut these crosswise in lengths of about 1½ inches and carefully press against them to make them slightly hollow. Arrange the gnocchi on a floured cloth. ✦ Prepare the sauce: heat the butter in a pot and add the onion, celery, carrot, and *lardo* and cook until golden. ✦ Add the ground meat and season with a little salt and pepper, nutmeg, and bay leaf (remember to remove it before serving the sauce). ✦ Add the wine and raise the heat so it evaporates, stirring; add the chopped tomatoes (or paste). ✦ Bring to a boil, lower the heat, and continue cooking at low heat for 1 hour or until thickened. ✦ Cook the gnocchi in a large pot of lightly salted boiling water and remove with a slotted spoon when they float. ✦ Drain well and put on a serving plate, drizzle with butter, dust with Parmigiano-Reggiano, and top with about 1¼ cups of the sauce. ✦ Add the rest of the Parmigiano-Reggiano, also adding a little broth if the mixture gets too thick. Serve immediately.

GNOCCHI DI PATATE ALLA ROMANA

ROMAN-STYLE POTATO GNOCCHI

LAZIO

2 lbs. yellow potatoes

1 ½ cups all-purpose flour, plus more as needed

1 lb. meat sauce made with beef, mutton, pork, or boar (see pages 413, 634, or 635)

Grated Parmigiano-Reggiano

Salt

In Rome and other areas of Lazio, pecorino Romano cheese is used instead of Parmigiano-Reggiano.

Boil the potatoes. As soon as they are cooked, peel them, pass them through a food mill or potato ricer, and let them cool slightly. ✦ Mix them with the flour and a pinch of salt and knead. It is difficult to determine the precise amount of flour to add since different kinds of potatoes absorb more or less; either way, the result should be a soft dough. ✦ Cut the dough in pieces and roll out the pieces on a floured board to form tubes the size of a finger; cut these tubes into inch-long lengths. ✦ Press a finger against each gnocco to give it a small cavity. As you finish them arrange the gnocchi on a floured cloth. ✦ Heat a large pot of lightly salted water, and when the water boils, drop in the gnocchi a few at a time, removing them with a skimmer as soon as they float. ✦ Drain well and form into layers in a serving bowl with a sauce made with meat. Top with Parmigiano-Reggiano and serve.

POTATO GNOCCHI VERONA-STYLE

GNOCCHI DI PATATE ALLA VERONESE

VENETO

2 lbs. white potatoes

1 ¼ cups all-purpose flour, plus more as needed

1 large egg, beaten

¼ lb. (1 stick) plus 1 tbsp. unsalted butter, melted

⅔ cup grated Parmigiano-Reggiano

Salt

Rinse the potatoes and boil in lightly salted water to cover. ✦ When cooked, peel and crush with a masher. ✦ Place the potato mixture on a floured board and add the flour and egg. Knead well to obtain a smooth dough. ✦ Roll into cylinders ¾ inch in diameter and cut crosswise to make pieces about 1 inch long. ✦ Press the gnocchi one at a time against a fork or grater. ✦ Cook in lightly salted boiling water; they are cooked when they float. ✦ Collect them with a strainer and transfer them to a serving plate and top with butter. Sprinkle with cheese and serve hot.

STUFFED GNOCCHI IN CHEESE SAUCE

GNOCCHI DI RESIA

FRIULI-VENEZIA GIULIA

For the dough:

1 ¼ cups all-purpose flour, plus more as needed

Salt

For the filling:

1 lb. Swiss chard (wild if possible)

4 large eggs, beaten

⅔ cup raisins

1 ½ cups grated smoked ricotta

⅓ cup sugar

Salt and pepper

For the sauce:

¼ cup unsalted butter, melted

2 tbsp. grated Parmigiano-Reggiano

Use the flour to prepare a pasta dough as in the recipe on page 10, using ¼ cup water in place of the eggs. Let rest, covered with a cloth, for 30 minutes. Make the filling: Cook, drain, and mince the chard. Mix the chard with all of the other filling ingredients until blended. Roll the dough out to a thin sheet (see page 212), and cut it into disks. ✦ Top each disk with a spoonful of filling, then fold over and press the edges to seal them. Cook in lightly salted boiling water until they float; drain and toss with melted butter and cheese.

BUTTERNUT-SQUASH GNOCCHI 1

VALLE D'AOSTA

3 lbs. butternut squash

1⅔ cups all-purpose flour, plus more as needed

2 large eggs, beaten

Pinch grated nutmeg

Milk, if necessary

¼ lb. (1 stick) unsalted butter, melted

4 sage leaves, chopped

Grated Parmigiano-Reggiano

8 oz. sliced fontina

Salt and pepper

This dish is typical of Gressoney St. Jean.

Preheat the oven to 350°F. Cut the squash in large slices, remove the seeds, and bake until tender, about 45 minutes. Let cool.✦ When cooled peel the slices and pass through the large holes of a food mill into a bowl. Add the flour, eggs, nutmeg, and salt and pepper. Mix well; if the dough is too stiff add a little milk; if too soft add more flour. Scoop out small balls of dough with a teaspoon and drop them into lightly salted boiling water, dipping the spoon in the cooking water to make the dough slip off more easily. ✦ When the gnocchi float remove with a slotted spoon. ✦ Place in a baking dish and drizzle with butter and sprinkle with sage. Dust with Parmigiano-Reggiano and cover with slices of fontina. ✦ Bake for about 10 minutes, or until the fontina melts.

PASTA, POLENTA & RICE

BUTTERNUT-SQUASH GNOCCHI 2

FRIULI-VENEZIA GIULIA

For the dough:

2 lbs. butternut squash

1⅔ cups all-purpose flour, plus more as needed

2 large egg yolks

⅓ cup grated smoked ricotta

Salt and pepper

For the sauce:

¾ cup breadcrumbs

⅓ cup grated smoked ricotta

¼ cup chopped sage leaves

¼ cup unsalted butter, melted

Preheat the oven to 350°F. Grease a baking pan. Peel and seed the squash, cut it in large hunks, and arrange on the baking pan. Cover with a sheet of aluminum foil. Poke a few holes in the foil and bake until tender, about 30 minutes. ✦ When the squash is cooked, pass it through the larger holes of a food mill into a bowl and let it cool. ✦ Knead in the flour and egg yolks, cheese, and salt and pepper to form a soft and slightly sticky dough. ✦ Make gnocchi by dropping spoonfuls of the mixture into lightly salted boiling water, greasing the spoon with olive oil to keep the dough from sticking. ✦ When the gnocchi float, remove from the water and put them in a baking dish. Sprinkle with breadcrumbs, cheese, and sage leaves. Drizzle with butter. Bake until the breadcrumbs are golden, about 10 minutes.

BUTTERNUT-SQUASH GNOCCHI BELLUNO-STYLE

GNOCCHI DI ZUCCA ALLA BELLUNESE

VENETO

For the dough:

1 lb. firm butternut squash

1 large egg yolk

⅔ cup all-purpose flour, plus more as needed

Salt

For the sauce:

4 tbsp. unsalted butter

½ cup grated smoked ricotta

Preheat the oven to 350°F. Cut the squash into large pieces, remove the seeds, and bake until tender. Let cool. ✦ Scoop the flesh from the squash and pass through a food mill into a bowl. Add the egg yolk and salt, and work in the flour, kneading until soft and homogeneous. Form gnocchi the size of small nuts. ✦ Hollow the gnocchi with the tip of a spoon and cook in boiling salted water for a few minutes until they float (the cooking time will depend on the kind of squash used); drain. ✦ Meanwhile, make the brown butter sauce: cut the butter into pieces, then heat in a heavy saucepan over medium heat without stirring until the butter is a light brown color and gives off a nutty aroma. Be careful not to burn the butter or it will be bitter. Toss the gnocchi with brown butter and ricotta.

GNOCCHI STUFFED WITH MUSHROOMS

GNOCCHI RIPIENI DI BARBONI

VENETO

For the filling and sauce:

¼ lb. (1 stick) unsalted butter

1 lb. *barboni* (*Polyporus pescaprae*) mushrooms (may substitute porcini), sliced

1 tsp. chopped flat-leaf parsley

4 tbsp. heavy cream

½ cup grated Parmigiano-Reggiano, plus more for serving

2 tbsp. chopped sage leaves

2 tbsp. poppy seeds

Salt and pepper

For the dough:

1¾ lbs. potatoes

1 large egg

1½ cups all-purpose flour, plus more as needed

Salt

In a pan, heat 2 tablespoons butter until melted, then add the *barboni* and sauté for about 10 minutes. Add pepper and parsley. Finely chop and mix with the cream and Parmigiano-Reggiano. ✦ Put this filling in the refrigerator for 2 hours. ✦ Prepare the dough for the gnocchi: boil, peel, and crush the potatoes; add the egg, a pinch of salt, and enough flour to make a somewhat firm dough. ✦ Shape the dough into cylinders about 1½ inches in diameter. Cut these in pieces, and make a hollow in each big enough to hold ½ tablespoon of filling. ✦ Close the dough over the filling, sealing the edges and giving them the shape of a ball. ✦ Cook the gnocchi in boiling salted water about 1 minute, or until they float. ✦ Drain and sauté them in the remaining butter with the sage. Serve sprinkled with Parmigiano-Reggiano and poppy seeds.

GNOCCO MEDIEVALE | MEDIEVAL GNOCCHI

FRIULI-VENEZIA GIULIA

1 lb. stale bread, coarsely grated

8 cups beef broth

¼ lb. (1 stick) unsalted butter

½ medium onion, cut into 3 wedges

1¼ cups raisins

⅔ cup pine nuts

½ cup sugar

1 large egg plus 3 yolks

1 handful wild garlic, chopped

1 tsp. ground cinnamon

½ nutmeg nut, grated

Grated Montasio cheese

Salt

Dampen the bread with some of the broth to make a stiff mush. Heat the butter until melted and add the onion. Cook until translucent, then remove and discard the onion. Add the butter to the bread. ✦ Add the other ingredients one at a time along with as much broth as needed to make a dough suitable for making gnocchi the size of a finger, 2½ to 3 inches long. ✦ Cook the gnocchi in the broth until al dente, drain, and serve without sauce.

GNOCCOLI CON RAGÙ DI TONNO | GNOCCOLI WITH TUNA SAUCE

SICILIA

1¾ lbs. fresh tuna (preferably the tail)

Juice of 1 lemon

4 garlic cloves

½ cup mint leaves

3 tbsp. olive oil

1 medium onion, chopped

1 tsp. anchovy paste

1 cup tomato paste

2 cups tomato sauce

¼ cup red wine

½ tbsp. sugar

1 lb. *gnoccoli*

Salt and pepper

Gnoccoli are similar to *busiati* (see page 222), except after the pasta has been rolled on the skewer or knitting needle, the ends are pinched together to form a long thin shape with narrow ends. Other similarly long, thin types of homemade pasta can be used in place of the *gnoccoli*.

Soak the tuna in salted water acidulated with the juice of a lemon, keeping it completely covered until it turns lighter pink. ✦ Dry the tuna, make slits in the flesh, and stuff it with garlic and mint leaves. ✦ Heat the olive oil in a pan and sear the tuna on all sides. Remove the tuna and set aside. ✦ Add the onion to the pan, then add the anchovy paste, tomato paste, and tomato sauce. When this mixture simmers, add the tuna, a few more mint leaves, pepper, red wine, and sugar and stir to break up the tuna. ✦ Cook the *gnoccoli* in lightly salted boiling water until al dente; drain. Mix the pasta with the sauce.

MEAT (OR VEGETABLE OR FISH) PASTRIES

SARDEGNA

For the meat filling:

½ lb. cooked ground pork or beef

2 pork sausages,
cooked and crumbled

¼ lb. mild or aged pecorino, grated

For the vegetable filling:

½ cup cooked artichokes

¼ cup cooked peas

¼ cup chopped pitted olives

½ cup cooked green vegetables

For the fish filling:

¾ lb. cooked fish and crustaceans

Seasoning for all fillings:

1 garlic clove, minced

1 tbsp. minced flat-leaf parsley

1 tbsp. minced sage leaves

2 plum tomatoes,
peeled and crushed

1 tbsp. olive oil

Pinch saffron

For the dough:

1⅔ cups all-purpose flour,
plus more as needed

6 oz. lard

Salt

For frying:

Lard for the meat impanadas

Olive oil for the meatless impanadas

Follow the same procedure for meatless impanadas, filling them with the vegetables indicated. Of course, the filling can also be fish or shellfish, making use of vegetables, cheese, and olives.

Cut the meats (or vegetables or fish) in rough pieces and mix with the cheese and seasonings. ✦ Put this mixture in a covered bowl and refrigerate it for 1 day. ✦ Pour the flour into a bowl. Add the lard and a pinch of salt and knead together until a smooth dough forms. Let it rest for about 1 hour, then roll it out to a sheet about ⅛ inch thick (see page 212). ✦ Using a pastry wheel, cut the sheet into 4-by-3-inch rectangles. Put ¼ cup filling on each and close to form small impanadas, folding the shorter edge over to seal. Heat about 2 inches of lard or olive oil until it is hot, then fry the impanadas until golden. Drain on paper towels and serve hot.

| # MEAT PASTRIES

SARDEGNA

For the dough:

1 ¼ cups all-purpose flour, plus more as needed

½ cup lard (or 4 tbsp. unsalted butter)

Salt

For the filling:

¼ cup extra-virgin olive oil

3 oz. chicken giblets

1 medium onion, finely chopped

2 sun-dried tomatoes

½ lb. beef, diced

½ lb. pork, diced

½ lb. peas, shelled and cooked in a little olive oil until bright green

4 oz. prosciutto crudo, minced

Pinch grated nutmeg

1 sprig flat-leaf parsley, chopped

Pinch saffron (if possible Sardegnan)

Salt

Pour the flour into a bowl. Add the lard and a pinch of salt and knead together until a smooth dough forms. Let the dough rest for 30 minutes, covered, in a warm spot. ✦ Meanwhile, heat the olive oil in a large saucepan and sauté the giblets. Remove them when brown and set aside. Add the onion and tomatoes to the same pan. ✦ Add the beef and pork to the saucepan and cook for several minutes. ✦ Chop the giblets, add them, stirring thoroughly, and continue cooking several minutes. ✦ Then take the pan off the heat and add the peas, prosciutto, nutmeg, parsley, salt, and saffron. ✦ Preheat the oven to 350°F. Grease and flour a baking pan. Roll out a thin sheet of dough (see page 212), and make disks about 4 inches in diameter. Put a dollop of filling on half of them. ✦ Cover each disk with another, sealing the edges, then place on the prepared pan and bake for about 15 minutes or until golden. Serve hot.

POLENTA WITH BEANS AND CABBAGE

INTRUGLIA

TOSCANA

1 ¼ cups dried red or white beans, soaked overnight (2 cups if fresh)

4 cups beef broth

2 tbsp. extra-virgin olive oil

1 celery stalk, chopped

2 carrots, chopped

1 medium onion, chopped

1 potato, diced

1 bunch *cavolo nero* (or ½ Savoy cabbage), cut in strips

1 tsp. tomato paste

1 ⅔ cups cornmeal

Salt

This dish is typical of Versilia. If the polenta is made a little more dense, it can be sliced when cool and fried.

Cook the beans in broth (or water) and pass half through a food mill. Reserve the broth. ✦ Heat the olive oil in a pot and add the celery, carrots, and onion and sauté; when browned add to the broth. Stir in the beans. ✦ Add the potato, cabbage, and tomato paste. ✦ Bring to a boil, and add salt to taste. After about 15 minutes add the cornmeal, pouring it in a steady drizzle while stirring constantly. Cook for another 40 minutes. ✦ The result will be a somewhat soft polenta; if necessary, add boiling water to make it thinner.

CHEESE-STUFFED DUMPLINGS

ALTO ADIGE

10 oz. stale rolls, cut in cubes

3 tbsp. unsalted butter

½ medium onion, chopped

½ leek, chopped

4 oz. cheese, cut in tiny cubes
(*tilsiter* and *graukäse*; see note)

1 tbsp. chopped chives

1 tbsp. chopped flat-leaf parsley

3 large eggs, beaten

2 cups milk

3 to 4 tbsp. all-purpose flour

1 ½ oz. Gorgonzola,
cut in 8 equal cubes

1 tbsp. sunflower oil

Grated Parmigiano-Reggiano

Salt

For the *tilsiter* and *graukäse* cheese, you may substitute any or a combination of the following: young Asiago, young Montasio, Appenzeller, or Munster.

Put the cubed bread in a bowl. Heat 1 tablespoon of the butter in a pan and sauté the onion and leek. Add to the bread, followed by the cubes of *tilsiter* and *graukäse*, chives, and parsley. ✦ Mix the eggs and milk, pour over the bread mixture, and let rest 3 hours. ✦ Bind with just enough flour to form a dough. ✦ Using wet hands shape the *knödel*, inserting a piece of Gorgonzola into each. ✦ Melt the remaining butter. Cook the *knödel* slowly for 15 minutes in lightly salted boiling water to which sunflower oil has been added. Drain, and sprinkle with Parmigiano-Reggiano and the melted butter.

BLACK-BREAD GNOCCHI WITH HOPS

ALTO ADIGE

¼ cup extra-virgin olive oil

2 oz. shallots, chopped

2 oz. scallions (or leeks), chopped

4 oz. *bruscandoli*: hop shoots (see note), lightly blanched and chopped

¾ lb. black bread, cubed and salted

¼ cup milk

2 large eggs plus 1 yolk,
lightly beaten

Grated Parmigiano-Reggiano

3 tbsp. unsalted butter

4 oz. pancetta

Salt and pepper

Bruscandoli are the shoots of the hop flowers that give beer its bitter flavor; the tender tops of the shoots of the same plant are eaten in the northeast of Italy. They can be cooked like asparagus and are used in risottos and frittatas. As in this recipe, they are usually boiled or blanched to reduce their bitterness.

Heat half the olive oil in a pan and sauté the shallots, scallions, and hops. ✦ Moisten the bread with the milk and mix in the eggs and yolk. ✦ Add the bread to the mixture in the pan, season with 2 tablespoons Parmigiano-Reggiano and pepper, and let sit 30 minutes. ✦ Use a wet spoon to form oblong gnocchi and cook them in lightly salted boiling water for a few minutes. ✦ Meanwhile heat the remaining olive oil and the butter in a pan and sauté the pancetta. ✦ Remove the gnocchi from the water when they float and add to the pancetta sauce. ✦ Sprinkle with Parmigiano-Reggiano and serve.

SPINACH DUMPLINGS 1

ALTO ADIGE

2 tbsp. extra-virgin olive oil

1 medium onion, finely chopped

6 rolls, diced

⅔ cup boiled and chopped spinach

3 large eggs

3 tbsp. all-purpose flour

2 tbsp. grated Parmigiano-Reggiano

4 tbsp. (¼ cup) unsalted butter, melted

Salt and pepper

Heat the olive oil in a pan and sauté the onion and bread until golden. ✦ In a bowl combine the spinach, eggs, flour, grated cheese, and salt and pepper to taste. ✦ Add the sautéed bread and onions to the bowl. Knead well and shape into balls (large gnocchi). ✦ Cook in boiling lightly salted water about 7 to 8 minutes. ✦ Drain, sprinkle with cheese, drizzle with melted butter, and serve.

SPINACH DUMPLINGS 2

VENETO

4 tbsp. (¼ cup) unsalted butter

10 cups spinach, finely chopped

1 bunch chives, chopped

1 lb. stale bread, cut into small cubes

½ cup diced *tilsiter* cheese (may substitute young Asiago or Gruyère)

All-purpose flour

4 large eggs, beaten

3 tbsp. milk, or as needed

Grated Parmigiano-Reggiano

Salt

Heat 1 tablespoon butter in a pan and quickly cook the spinach and chives; season with salt and let cool. ✦ Mix the bread, cheese, flour, and eggs with the spinach mixture and enough milk to form a soft dough. ✦ Using wet hands shape the dough into balls (about the size of tennis balls) and cook them in lightly salted boiling water for 20 minutes. ✦ Meanwhile, heat the remaining butter in a pan over low heat until lightly brown. Place the *knödel* on a serving plate. Cover with Parmigiano-Reggiano and pour the butter over.

PASTA FOR HARD TIMES (WITH BROCCOLI AND ANCHOVIES)

LA PASTA DEL CATTIVO TEMPO

SICILIA

1 garlic clove, crushed

2 tbsp. extra-virgin olive oil

CONTINUED

This dish requires slow cooking.

Rub the garlic across the bottom of a saucepan then add the extra-virgin olive oil and heat it over low heat. When the oil is warm, return the garlic to the pan and sauté it. ✦ As soon as the garlic begins to darken, add the parsley

¼ cup chopped flat-leaf parsley

12 salt-cured anchovy fillets, cut in small pieces

1 tbsp. dry white wine

1 head boiled broccoli (tender leaves and stems with flowers attached), cut in pieces

¾ lb. ditalini rigati

4 tbsp. breadcrumbs, well toasted

12 black olives, pitted and chopped

Salt and pepper or chili pepper flakes

and anchovies; dissolve the anchovies in the oil, crushing them with a wooden spoon; do not let them burn. ✦ Add the wine and stir until it has nearly evaporated. ✦ Add the broccoli and mix very delicately to avoid breaking it up; remove the garlic and discard it. ✦ Add salt and ground pepper or chili pepper flakes. Meanwhile, cook the pasta until very al dente, then pour the hot sauce over and delicately toss for a few minutes until the pasta goes from being very al dente to merely al dente and at the same time takes on flavor. ✦ Serve in warmed plates and finish with breadcrumbs and black olives.

LAGANE DI SAN GIUSEPPE | ST. JOSEPH'S PASTA

PUGLIA

½ cup breadcrumbs

1 tbsp. extra-virgin olive oil

⅔ cup finely chopped chestnuts

2 anchovies, finely chopped

1 lb. *lagane* (or flat lasagne, pappardelle, or other broad, flat pasta)

1 lb. tomato purée

This dish is typical of Mola and is eaten on March 19, the feast day of St. Joseph.

In a cast-iron skillet toast the breadcrumbs, sprinkling with olive oil. ✦ As soon as they are ready add the chestnuts and anchovies. Stir well and cook for a few minutes. ✦ Meanwhile cook the *lagane* in lightly salted boiling water, drain, and toss with the tomato purée. ✦ Add the bread mixture and serve.

LAGANE E CECI | PASTA AND CHICKPEAS

BASILICATA

For the sauce:

1 ¼ cups dried chickpeas

¼ cup extra-virgin olive oil

1 garlic clove

3 ripe plum tomatoes, peeled and chopped

1 tbsp. chopped rosemary

Salt

For the dough:

1 ⅔ cups all-purpose flour, plus more as needed

Salt

Soak the chickpeas overnight in water to cover. Use the flour to prepare a pasta dough as in the recipe on page 10, using ½ cup water in place of the eggs. ✦ Roll out to make a thin sheet (see page 212) and cut into fettuccine about ½ inch wide. ✦ Meanwhile cook the chickpeas in unsalted water over low heat, if possible in an earthenware pot. ✦ Heat the olive oil in a pan and sauté the garlic until golden. Remove it, then add the tomatoes, rosemary, and salt and let cook down for 10 minutes. ✦ When the chickpeas are almost cooked, cook the *lagane* in lightly salted boiling water until al dente; drain. ✦ Pour the chickpeas in a bowl, add the pasta, and toss with the sauce. Let rest a few minutes before serving.

LANGAROLI OR AGNOLOTTI

PIEMONTE

For the broth:

2 lbs. veal bones

2 medium onions, chopped

4 oz. pork rind, cut in strips

3 celery stalks, chopped

3 carrots, chopped

¼ cup chopped flat-leaf parsley

3 bay leaves

1½ cups white wine

Unsalted butter

Sliced Alba truffle

Salt and pepper

For the fondue:

4 oz. fontina

½ cup milk

1 large egg yolk

½ tbsp. unsalted butter

For the dough:

6½ cups all-purpose flour

5 large eggs, beaten

2 tbsp. extra-virgin olive oil

Salt

FONDUE-STUFFED PASTA WITH VEAL BROTH

This dish is typical of the Langhe.

Preheat the oven to 400°F. Put the veal scraps, bones, and cartilage in a baking pan with the onions and pork rind and roast until brown. ✦ Transfer all this to a large pot and add the celery, carrots, parsley, bay leaves, salt, and pepper. ✦ Add 12 cups water and 1 cup wine. (If necessary, add additional water to cover, adding ½ cup wine for every 4 cups water.) Simmer over low heat for at least 3 hours, periodically skimming off the fat. ✦ When it has cooked down (and is clear), strain it and keep in the refrigerator until cold and thickened. ✦ For the fondue, soften the fontina in a pan with lukewarm milk over low heat; let it stand 1 hour or more, then heat over very low heat with the egg yolk and butter, whisking until slightly thickened. Refrigerate until cold. ✦ Use the flour, eggs, ⅔ cup lukewarm water, and olive oil to prepare a pasta dough as in the recipe on page 10, adding the water and oil with the eggs. Roll out a thin sheet (see page 212). Fill the pasta as in the recipe on page 212, using about 1 teaspoon fondue for each *langarolo* or *agnolotto*. ✦ Meanwhile, heat the stock in a pot with butter and add the remaining wine when it melts. ✦ Cook the pasta in lightly salted boiling water and toss them with the stock on a serving plate. Top with slices of truffle and serve hot.

LASAGNE BENEVENTANA

CAMPANIA

For the dough:

3 cups all-purpose flour, plus more as needed

5 large eggs plus 1 yolk (optional)

For the sauce:

1 lb. veal in a single piece

CONTINUED

BENEVENTO-STYLE LASAGNE WITH VEAL MEATBALLS AND EGGS

Use the flour and eggs to prepare a pasta dough as in the recipe on page 10. ✦ Roll out a sheet (see page 212) and using a pastry wheel cut it into tagliatelle a little wider than normal. (These can be prepared a day ahead to divide the amount of work.) ✦ Season the veal with parsley, garlic, a little pepper, and Parmigiano-Reggiano, then roll it up and tie it. ✦ Heat the olive oil in a pot and brown the veal. Pour in the wine, and when it has evaporated add the tomato purée. Reduce the heat to very low,

2 tbsp. chopped flat-leaf parsley

1 garlic clove, minced

Grated Parmigiano-Reggiano

3 tbsp. extra-virgin olive oil

¼ cup dry white wine

4 cups tomato purée

Pepper

For the filling:

¾ lb. ground veal

2 large eggs, beaten

Crustless bread of 1 roll, finely crumbled

3 tbsp. chopped flat-leaf parsley

½ cup extra-virgin olive oil

7 oz. mozzarella, hardened by spending a few days in the refrigerator, sliced into strips

5 large hard-boiled eggs, cut into wedges

⅔ cup grated pecorino dolce

Salt and pepper

cover the pot, leaving the lid slightly ajar, and simmer 2 hours. Remove the string from the veal. The meat should be tender and fall apart into the sauce. ✦ Preheat the oven to 350°F. ✦ For the filling, combine the ground veal, beaten eggs, bread, salt, pepper, and parsley and use the mixture to make tiny meatballs. Heat the olive oil in a pan and brown the meatballs. ✦ Boil the tagliatelle until very al dente and drain well. ✦ In a baking pan, make a layer of pasta with one-third of it. Over this form a circle of half the mozzarella strips, then half the meatballs, then half the hard-boiled-eggs, then half the tomato-veal sauce. Repeat with another layer of pasta and then the remaining half of all the filling components. Finish with a layer of the remaining third of the pasta. ✦ Sprinkle with pecorino dolce and add a final tablespoon of the tomato sauce. Bake until bubbling, about 20 minutes. Let stand for 10 minutes before serving.

NEAPOLITAN LASAGNE

CAMPANIA

1⅔ cups extra-virgin olive oil (or pork fat)

1 lb. stew beef or pork

1 medium onion, minced

1¼ cups dry white wine

½ cup tomato paste

Several basil leaves

1 lb. ground beef or pork

½ lb. *cervellatine* (thin sausages)

1 lb. ricotta

1 lb. fresh lasagne

10 oz. *fior di latte* cheese, diced

⅔ cup grated Parmigiano-Reggiano

Salt

Heat ⅔ cup olive oil (or pork fat) in a pan and sauté the meat and onion; when the onion darkens add the wine. ✦ When the wine evaporates add the tomato paste and ¾ cup water, then add salt to taste and basil and cook at low heat. This is the tomato sauce. ✦ Shape the ground meat into small meatballs, then heat ⅔ cup olive oil in a pan and brown the meatballs. ✦ In another pan, heat the remaining olive oil and brown the *cervellatine*, then cut them in rounds. ✦ Mix the ricotta with half of the tomato sauce. ✦ Preheat the oven to 350°F. Cook the lasagne in lightly salted boiling water, drain, and lay out on a work surface to cool. ✦ Pour a little of the tomato sauce into a rectangular baking pan and spread it across the bottom; arrange one layer of the lasagne over this, one noodle beside the next without overlapping. ✦ Spread over this a few tablespoons of the ricotta-tomato sauce, then add some of the meatballs, some of the *cervellatine,* and some of the *fior di latte* and Parmigiano-Reggiano. ✦ Add a few tablespoons of the tomato-ricotta sauce and make another layer of lasagne, this time aligning them in the opposite direction, repeating the layers and ending with a layer of lasagne. Cover with tomato sauce and Parmigiano-Reggiano. ✦ Bake for 30 to 40 minutes, then turn off the oven and and let stand for a few minutes before serving.

✦ **LOCAL TRADITION** ✦

LASAGNE WITH RICOTTA E MELANZANE

In the area of Siracusa, most of all at Noto, certain homemade lasagne—such as the pasta used in this traditional recipe for lasagne with ricotta and eggplant—made with durum wheat flour, salt, and water were known as *taccuna di mulinu*, which might loosely be translated as "the miller's heel." What distinguished this from other lasagne was the specific shape and consistency of the pasta dough, described as *'ncutugnári.* To achieve this distinction, the sheets of pasta would be rolled up and cut by a single blow of a sharp knife into a long strip of *taccuna.* After being laid out to dry in the shade, the *taccuna* would then be tossed with a simple tomato sauce and slices of fried eggplant and covered with ricotta salata.

LASAGNE IMBOTTITE

STUFFED LASAGNE

CALABRIA

For the lasagne:

3 cups all-purpose flour, plus more as needed

Extra-virgin olive oil

For the filling:

½ lb. ground beef

1 large egg yolk

All-purpose flour for dredging

4 oz. *lardo* (see page 2)

2 bay leaves

1 medium onion, finely sliced

1 lb. fresh peas, boiled and drained

5 artichokes, boiled and drained

CONTINUED

Use the flour to prepare a pasta dough as in the recipe on page 10, using 1 cup lukewarm water in place of the eggs; set the dough aside to rest for 30 minutes. ✦ Roll out sheets (see page 212) and cut them in squares about 3 inches on a side. ✦ Preheat the oven to 400°F. ✦ Cook the pasta squares a few at a time in lightly salted boiling water to which a few tablespoons of olive oil have been added to keep them from sticking together. When al dente, drain and set them out on a cloth to cool. ✦ In a bowl, mix the beef, egg yolk, a pinch of salt, and some pepper and shape into meatballs about the size of walnuts. ✦ Roll them in flour and shake off the excess. Heat half the *lardo* in a pan with the bay leaves and brown the meatballs; drain well and set aside. ✦ Heat the remaining *lardo* in the same pan and sauté the onion, peas, artichokes, and mushrooms; drain and set aside. ✦ Cover

269

¾ lb. mushrooms,
boiled and drained

2 hard-boiled eggs, cut into wedges

¼ lb. mozzarella, sliced

⅔ cup grated pecorino

Salt and pepper

the bottom of a large baking pan with a layer of lasagne. ✦ Over this spread the hard-boiled egg, the mozzarella, meatballs, vegetables, and pecorino. ✦ Bake for about 40 minutes; as soon as the surface is golden brown remove from the oven and serve.

LASAGNE RICCE
CON RICOTTA E
CAVOLFIORE FRITTO

CURLY LASAGNE WITH RICOTTA AND CAULIFLOWER

SICILIA

¾ lb. cauliflower
(with the core removed)

¼ cup extra-virgin olive oil

¾ lb. lasagne *ricce* (curly edged ribbons about ⅜ inch wide) or fettuccine

1 cup ricotta

Salt

This dish is typical of Caltanissetta.

Cook the cauliflower in lightly salted boiling water to cover; drain when still firm. ✦ When it has cooled detach the florets and their stems; chop the remainder. Heat the olive oil in a pan and sauté the cauliflower until the edges are golden. ✦ Cook the pasta until al dente, drain, reserving a few tablespoons of cooking water, and transfer to a serving bowl. ✦ Add the cauliflower to the pasta. ✦ Mix the ricotta with enough of the cooking water to make a sauce, then add to the pasta. Stir and serve.

LASAGNE VERDI
ALLA BOLOGNESE

GREEN LASAGNE WITH MEAT SAUCE

FOR
6 PERSONS

EMILIA-ROMAGNA

¾ lb. spinach

3 tbsp. unsalted butter

½ medium onion, sliced

1 carrot. chopped

1 celery stalk, chopped

6 oz. ground beef

6 oz. ground pork

4 oz. chicken livers

½ cup tomato purée

3 cups all-purpose flour, plus more as needed

2 large eggs

1 recipe béchamel sauce (see page 339)

Grated Parmigiano-Reggiano, as needed

Salt and pepper

Wash the spinach and cook it in very little water just until wilted. Drain well, put through a food mill, and set aside. ✦ Heat 2 tablespoons butter and sauté the onion, carrot, and celery until softened, then add the meat and chicken livers and cook a few minutes longer. ✦ Add the tomato purée and salt and pepper to taste and set aside. ✦ Use the flour, eggs, and spinach to prepare a dough as in the recipe on page 10; add the spinach with the eggs. ✦ Roll the dough into a fairly thin sheet (see page 212) and cut into strips no longer than the pan in which the lasagne will be baked. ✦ Cook the lasagne in lightly salted boiling water, drain, and set aside on a cloth. Preheat the oven to 325°F. Butter a rectangular baking pan. ✦ In the baking pan arrange alternating layers of lasagne, cheese, meat sauce, and béchamel, repeating the layers until the ingredients are used up. End with a final layer of béchamel and dot with the remaining butter. ✦ Bake for about 30 minutes, or until the surface is golden brown.

CORNMEAL PASTA WITH TOMATOES

LI PAPPICCI

FOR
6 PERSONS

ABRUZZO

1 ¼ cups cornmeal

1 ½ cups all-purpose flour,
plus more as needed

2 tbsp. extra-virgin olive oil

7 oz. pancetta, diced

1 medium onion, finely sliced

¾ lb. plum tomatoes,
peeled and chopped

Grated pecorino

Salt

This dish is typical of the area of Vomano.

Sift the cornmeal and flour together and use them and 1 ¼ cups water to make a dough as in the recipe on page 10; the dough will be stiff. Roll out a ⅛-inch-thick sheet (see page 212) and cut in irregular triangles to make *pappicci*. ✦ Heat the olive oil in a pot and cook the pancetta and onion. When these brown add the tomatoes and cook 15 minutes. ✦ Boil the *pappicci* in lightly salted boiling water until al dente, drain, leaving a little of the cooking water, and toss with the sauce and pecorino.

LINGUINE WITH MUSHROOMS

LINGUE DI PASSERO AI FUNGHI

CAMPANIA

¼ cup extra-virgin olive oil

1 medium onion, finely sliced

1 lb. shelled peas

1 garlic clove

2 artichokes, cut in small pieces

7 oz. *chiuovetielli* mushrooms,
thinly sliced

⅔ cup pitted black olives

⅓ cup capers

2 tbsp. chopped flat-leaf parsley

1 lb. *lingue di passero* (linguine)

Salt

This dish is typical of Caserta.

Heat half the olive oil in a large pan and sauté the onion; when it is translucent add the peas. ✦ In another pan heat the remaining olive oil and sauté the garlic until golden, then add the artichokes; discard the garlic. ✦ Add the artichokes to the peas, then add the mushrooms, olives, capers, and parsley. ✦ Cook at low heat for about 15 minutes. ✦ Meawhile cook the pasta in lightly salted boiling water until al dente, drain well, and add it to the sauce. Serve hot in a serving bowl without cheese.

LINGUINE WITH WALNUTS

LINGUE DI PASSERO CON LE NOCI

CAMPANIA

⅔ cup extra-virgin olive oil

1 garlic clove, chopped

2 to 3 tbsp. breadcrumbs

⅔ cup roughly chopped walnuts

1 lb. *lingue di passero* (linguine)

Salt and pepper

In a large pan heat the olive oil and sauté the garlic until golden. Add the breadcrumbs and toast well. ✦ Add the walnuts, salt, and pepper and stir. ✦ Cook the pasta in lightly salted boiling water until very al dente, drain, and add to the sauce. Toss and serve hot.

271

LINGUINE WITH RAZOR CLAMS

LINGUINE AI DATTERI

PUGLIA

¼ cup extra-virgin olive oil
1 garlic clove
1 lb. razor clams, cleaned
1 cup dry white wine
1 tbsp. chopped oregano
2 tbsp. chopped flat-leaf parsley
¾ lb. linguine
Salt

The only salt used in this recipe, typical of Brindisi, goes into the cooking water for the pasta.

Heat the oil in a pot and sauté the garlic. When it takes on color add the clams, cover, and cook them at high heat for 5 minutes. ✦ Add the wine, oregano, and 1 tablespoon parsley. ✦At the same time cook the pasta in salted boiling water until al dente. ✦ Drain and toss with the clams; sprinkle with the remaining parsley. Serve hot.

BAKED SEAFOOD LINGUINE

LINGUINE AL CARTOCCIO

PUGLIA

⅓ cup extra-virgin olive oil
1 garlic clove
6 oz. squid, chopped
3 oz. shrimp
3 oz. cleaned mussels
½ cup chopped flat-leaf parsley
1 cup tomato purée
1 lb. linguine

Preheat the oven to 400°F. Heat the olive oil in a pot and sauté the garlic until golden. Add the squid, shrimp, and mussels then add the parsley and tomato purée. ✦ Cook the linguine in lightly salted boiling water until al dente; blend well with the seafood sauce and transfer to a baking pan; cover with foil and fold over the edges to seal. ✦ Bake for about 5 minutes. Serve immediately.

LINGUINE WITH CUTTLEFISH RAGÙ

LINGUINE AL RAGÙ
DI SEPPIA

FOR
6 PERSONS

PUGLIA

4 cuttlefish, weighing about 4 oz. each
⅔ cup extra-virgin olive oil
1 medium onion, sliced
1 ½ lbs. fresh peeled plum tomatoes
1 lb. linguine
⅔ cup grated pecorino (preferably from Puglia)
½ cup chopped flat-leaf parsley
Salt and pepper

Clean the cuttlefish, being careful to avoid detaching the heads. ✦ Heat the olive oil in a pan and sauté the onion; add the cuttlefish and sauté for a few minutes. ✦ Purée the tomatoes in a food mill and add them to the pan; cook over low heat for about 45 minutes, adjusting for salt and pepper. ✦ Remove the cuttlefish and keep warm. ✦ Cook the pasta in lightly salted boiling water until al dente, and toss with the sauce and pecorino, and arrange on a serving plate. ✦ Serve the pasta with the cuttlefish on top and sprinkle with parsley.

LINGUINE WITH LOBSTER

LINGUINE ALL'ARAGOSTA

CAMPANIA

¼ cup (4 tbsp.) unsalted butter
½ medium onion, finely chopped
½ lb. pieces of boiled lobster
⅔ cup brandy
1 tbsp. tomato paste
1⅔ cups heavy cream
1 lb. linguine
½ cup grated
Parmigiano-Reggiano
Salt and pepper

Heat 3 tablespoons of the butter in a large pan and sauté the onion. Add the pieces of lobster and cook a few minutes, then add the brandy and cook until it evaporates. ✦ Add salt, pepper, tomato paste, and cream and boil a few minutes to thicken slightly. ✦ Cook the linguine in lightly salted boiling water until al dente, drain, and add to the pan with the sauce, mixing them well in the sauce over a low heat. ✦ Finish with Parmigiano-Reggiano and the remaining butter. Serve hot.

LINGUINE WITH ANCHOVIES, OLIVES, AND CAPERS

LINGUINE ALLA PUTTANESCA

CAMPANIA

½ cup extra-virgin olive oil
1 garlic clove
1 *diavolillo* (hot chili pepper, see note, page 22)
2 salt-cured anchovy fillets, boned and rinsed
1 lb. peeled plum tomatoes
⅔ cup pitted Gaeta olives
⅓ cup capers, crushed
1 lb. linguine
2 or 3 tbsp. chopped flat-leaf parsley
Salt

In a large pan, heat the olive oil and sauté the garlic and chili pepper. Add the anchovies and stir until they break down completely. ✦ Remove and discard the garlic; add the tomatoes, olives, and capers. ✦ Add salt to taste and cook at high heat, crushing the tomatoes with a fork until they are completely broken up. ✦ Cook the pasta in lightly salted boiling water until very al dente, drain, and add to the sauce in the pan. Cook, stirring often. ✦ Transfer to a serving plate, sprinkle with parsley, and serve.

LINGUINE WITH SEAFOOD

LINGUINE CON FRUTTI DI MARE

ABRUZZO

¼ cup extra-virgin olive oil
1 garlic clove
CONTINUED

Heat the olive oil in a pan and sauté the garlic, chili pepper, parsley, and tomatoes. ✦ When the garlic has colored remove it and add the squid and cuttlefish. ✦ Cook at high heat for a few minutes then add the shrimp, mussels, and clams. ✦ Season with a little salt and cook at

1 *diavolillo* (hot chili pepper,
see note, page 22)

3 tbsp. chopped flat-leaf parsley

¾ lb. plum tomatoes, chopped

6 oz. young squid

6 oz. cuttlefish

6 oz. shelled shrimp

¾ lb. cleaned mussels,
opened in a pan at high heat

¾ lb. cleaned clams,
opened in a pan at high heat

1 lb. linguine

Salt

low heat for about 20 minutes. ✦ Cook the linguine until al dente, drain, and combine with the sauce.

THICK PASTA WITH TOMATO RAGÙ

LOMBRICHELLI

LAZIO

3 cups all-purpose flour,
plus more as needed

¼ cup extra-virgin olive oil

4 oz. pork fat, finely chopped

1 garlic clove, minced

1 carrot, finely chopped

1 celery stalk, finely chopped

½ medium onion, finely chopped

1 lb. peeled plum tomatoes

½ *diavolillo* (hot chili pepper,
see note, page 22)

Chopped flat-leaf parsley

Grated pecorino piccante

Salt

This dish is typical of Viterbo. This type of pasta represents the most ancient and most common type of pasta in Tuscia made at home using just water and flour; a reflection of this fact is that this shape of pasta is known by a different name in nearly every town of the province. Without doubt *lombrichelli* is the most common of these names, with its obvious derivation from the Italian word for earthworm, *lombrico*. Another name used references walking sticks, which in the local dialect are called *tortoro*. Among many other names are *l'ombreicheelli, pici, pisciarelli, visciarelli, tortorelli, torcolacci, filarelli, chicarelli, lilleri, scifulati, cechi, cultitonni, ghighi, bighi, bichi, brigoli, ceriole, ciuci, spunafusi, stratte, stringoli*, and still others. The usual sauce for this pasta was known in the past as "fake" sauce because it was made without meat.

Use the flour to prepare a pasta dough as in the recipe on page 10, using 1 cup water in place of the eggs. ✦ Pinch off hunks of dough and shape them into slightly tapering noodles ¹⁄₁₂ to ⅛ inch thick and 6 to 8 inches long (these are the *lombrichelli*). Let them dry a few hours before cooking them in lightly salted boiling water. ✦ Meanwhile heat the olive oil in a pot and sauté the pork fat, garlic, carrot, celery, and onion; after a few minutes add the tomatoes and chili pepper. ✦ Cook this for about 1 hour at low heat with the pot covered, adding warm water if necessary to maintain the liquid. ✦ Spoon the sauce over the *lombrichelli*, sprinkle with parsley and pecorino, and serve.

PASTA "SNAILS" WITH SAUSAGE

LUMACHE ALLA PERUGINA

UMBRIA

1 lb. *lumache* (snail-shaped pasta; *conchiglie* can be used instead)

2 tbsp. unsalted butter

2 tbsp. extra-virgin olive oil

1 medium onion, sliced

4 oz. sausage, chopped

½ cup white wine

¼ cup grated pecorino

Salt and pepper

This dish is typical of Castel Rigone (Perugia).

Cook the pasta in lightly salted boiling water until half-cooked. ✦ In a pan heat the butter and olive oil; add the onion and sausage and a pinch of salt and pepper. ✦ Sauté at low heat for about 5 minutes, then add the wine. ✦ Drain the pasta and add to the sauce in the pan, tossing well to mix. When the pasta is thoroughly cooked add the pecorino.

PASTA SCHEGGINO-STYLE

LUMACHINE ALLA SCHEGGINESE

UMBRIA

6 tbsp. extra-virgin olive oil

1 small onion, finely chopped

1¾ lbs. trout fillets

1 lb. tomato purée

3 oz. black truffle, thinly sliced

1 lb. *lumachine* pasta ("little snails"; small *conchiglie* can be used instead)

Salt and pepper

Scheggino, the town for which the dish is named, is to the east of Spoleto. This dish is typically served at Christmas.

Heat the olive oil in a pan and sauté the onion. ✦ Add the trout fillets and cook 5 minutes. ✦ Add the tomato purée and salt and pepper to taste, and cook 10 minutes more. ✦ Remove the pan from the heat and remove the trout from the pan. Add the truffle. ✦ Cook the pasta in lightly salted boiling water, drain when al dente, and toss with the sauce. Serve immediately with the trout as a second course.

BUCATINI IN TOMATO SAUCE

MACCARONI ALLA MARATEOTA

BASILICATA

1¾ lbs. ripe plum tomatoes

2 garlic cloves, roughly chopped

¼ cup extra-virgin olive oil

1 lb. bucatini

Salt

This dish is typical of Maratea.

Parboil the tomatoes to loosen the skins. Peel them, then remove the seeds. Cut into small pieces and combine with the garlic in a heatproof serving bowl. ✦ Drizzle with olive oil. ✦ Cook the bucatini until still very al dente. Drain, saving the cooking water. Add the bucatini to the tomato and garlic and mix well. Set the serving plate on the pot with the cooking water and heat. After 15 minutes, add a little more oil; mix once and serve immediately.

| # MACARONI
WITH ARUGULA

PUGLIA

For the pasta:

1⅔ cups whole-wheat flour,
plus more as needed

⅔ cup semolina flour,
plus more for the cloth

For the sauce:

¼ cup extra-virgin olive oil

2 garlic cloves

1 tbsp. chopped flat-leaf parsley

1 lb. ripe plum tomatoes, peeled,
seeded, and puréed in a food mill

1 *diavolillo* (hot chili pepper,
see note, page 22), chopped

1 lb. arugula (best if wild)

⅓ cup grated pecorino

Salt

Sift together the two flours and use them and ¾ cup water to make a dough as in the recipe on page 10. ✦ Shape the pasta into strands about ½ inch in diameter; cut in lengths of about 1½ inches and twist these around a knitting needle to form macaroni. Sprinkle a cloth with semolina and add the pasta in a single layer; let rest until the moment of cooking. ✦ Heat 3 tablespoons olive oil in a pan and add the garlic. Sauté until golden, then remove the garlic and add the parsley. ✦ Add the tomatoes, salt, and chili pepper, and cook to reduce for 15 to 20 minutes. ✦ Wash the arugula to remove any grit, then cook it in lightly salted boiling water just until bright green. After 2 minutes add the pasta and cook until al dente. ✦ Drain and put on a serving plate; sprinkle with pecorino, then add the tomato sauce. Serve immediately.

✦ **LOCAL TRADITION** ✦

MACCARONARA DI MONTEMARANO

The secret to the *maccaronara* for this dish from Campania was to work the pasta dough without egg, and its distinctive shape came from the fluted rolling pin, also known as a *maccaronara*, which both flattened and cut the dough. The thin strips of pasta had to be cooked immediately after rolling and then rinsed with hot water to remove the starch. The hearty sauce for this dish was made with onion, garlic, guanciale, pine nuts, raisins, tomato, and the stomach (called "pancetta") of a lamb stuffed with an egg mixture and sewn closed with white thread. Fresh parsley and basil were added to the sauce after two hours, and the lamb stomach removed, sliced, and served (with some of the remaining sauce) after the *maccaronara* as a second course.

MACCHERONCINI DI CAMPOFILONE

For the pasta:

2½ cups all-purpose flour, plus more as needed

5 large eggs

For the sauce:

¼ cup extra-virgin olive oil

1 celery stalk, finely chopped

1 carrot, finely chopped

1 medium onion, finely chopped

4 oz. ground pork

4 oz. ground veal

4 oz. giblets and bone marrow

½ cup white wine

2 lbs. plum tomatoes, peeled and chopped

Pinch ground cloves

Pinch grated nutmeg

Grated pecorino

PASTA WITH CAMPOFILONE-STYLE MEAT SAUCE

The sauce for this pasta is intentionally abundant.

Use the flour and eggs to prepare a pasta dough as in the recipe on page 10; do not add additional water. The *maccheroncini* require a hard, thin sheet of dough made using only flour and eggs. ✦ Roll out to a sheet (see page 212). Cut this sheet into long strips as fine as angel hair pasta. ✦ Heat the olive oil in a pot and sauté the celery, carrot, and onion until softened. Add the meats, giblets, and marrow. ✦ When the meat has browned, pour in the wine and add the tomatoes, cloves, and nutmeg. ✦ Add the *maccheroncini* to a pot of lightly salted boiling water. When the water returns to a boil and the *maccheroncini* float to the surface, drain immediately. ✦ Ladle some sauce onto a serving plate, add the pasta, then more sauce, reserving any additional sauce for the individual serving plates. Serve with pecorino.

MACCHERONI AGLIO E OLIO

1 lb. spaghetti

4 garlic cloves, thinly sliced, any green core removed

1 cup extra-virgin olive oil

1 *diavolillo* (hot chili pepper, see note, page 22)

Chopped flat-leaf parsley

SPAGHETTI WITH GARLIC AND OIL

The dish can be made even more flavorful by adding ground pepper to the garlic. For those who are not fond of garlic, the dish can be made using whole cloves that can then be removed before adding the spaghetti.

Add the spaghetti to a pot of lightly salted boiling water. While the spaghetti cooks, sauté the garlic in a pan with the olive oil at low heat with the chili pepper; let the garlic take on color without burning. ✦ When the garlic is golden, add a ladleful of water from the pasta cooking water to stop its cooking and take the pan off the heat. ✦ Drain the pasta when very al dente and toss with the garlic and oil on a serving plate, adding chopped parsley.

PASTA AU GRATIN

¼ cup (4 tbsp.) unsalted butter, cut into cubes, plus more for the dish

⅔ cup all-purpose flour, plus more as needed

6 cups milk

Pinch grated nutmeg

1 lb. *mezzani* (can use ziti or long macaroni if necessary)

⅔ cup grated Parmigiano-Reggiano

6 oz. *fior di latte* cheese, thinly sliced

Salt and pepper

This dish is typical of Naples.

Preheat the oven to 350°F. Butter a baking dish. Use the flour, 2 tablespoons butter, and 5½ cups milk to make a thin béchamel sauce (see page 339). Add nutmeg and salt. ✦ Break up the *mezzani* and cook in lightly salted boiling water until very al dente. ✦ Drain and toss with 1 tablespoon butter. Stir in 3 tablespoons of Parmigiano-Reggiano and 1 tablespoon of béchamel. ✦ Make an even layer with half the pasta in the baking dish, sprinkle with Parmigiano-Reggiano, cover with *fior di latte*, and spoon over more béchamel sauce. ✦ Cover with the rest of the pasta, add the rest of the sauce, spread over the rest of the Parmigiano-Reggiano, and pour in ½ cup cold milk. ✦ Dust with more Parmigiano-Reggiano and dot with the remaining butter. ✦ Bake about 15 minutes, or until the top is golden; let cool 15 minutes before serving.

HOMEMADE PASTA WITH MEAT AND TOMATO

For the pasta:

3 cups semolina flour, plus more as needed

3 large eggs

Salt

For the sauce:

¼ cup extra-virgin olive oil

1 medium onion

4 oz. veal

4 oz. pork

4 oz. lamb

1 lb. tomato purée

Grated pecorino

1 pinch chili pepper flakes, crumbled

Salt

To make true macaroni *alla chitarra* requires a *chitarra* (guitar), the wooden frame with steel strings set about ⅛ inch apart over which sheets of pasta are laid and then pressed through using a rolling pin. The *chitarra* requires sheets of pasta cut to its length and width; these are laid over it so that moving a rolling pin over them presses them down and cuts them into square-sided spaghetti. A pasta roller's spaghetti attachment is an acceptable substitute.

Use the flour and eggs to prepare a pasta dough as in the recipe on page 10. ✦ When finished pour a few drops of oil on your hands and give the dough a final kneading; set it aside to rest a few hours. ✦ Meanwhile make the sauce: heat the olive oil in a pot and add the onion. When it is soft add the veal, pork, and lamb. When the meats are browned add the tomato purée. Stir in the pecorino and chili pepper. ✦ Roll out the pasta (see above and page 212). Cook the pasta in lightly salted boiling water until al dente, then toss with the sauce.

PASTA WITH MEAT SAUCE AND ONIONS

FOR
8 PERSONS

CAMPANIA

2 lbs. beef chuck roast
1 ⅓ cups extra-virgin olive oil
¼ lb. (1 stick) unsalted butter
4 medium onions, thinly sliced
6 oz. salame, preferably Neapolitan, minced
1 celery stalk, chopped
1 carrot, chopped
4 small plum tomatoes
1 ⅓ cups dry white wine
1 ¼ lbs. macaroni (*mezzani* or ziti)
⅔ cup grated Parmigiano-Reggiano
⅔ cup grated Romano
Salt

This preparation is also known, perhaps disparagingly, as "meat alla Genovese" since the meat is used only to flavor the macaroni. (It is common in Italy to think of the Genoese as a frugal people.) The dish is absolutely unknown in the city of Genoa, and the name most probably dates back to a group of Genoese who lived in the Spanish Quarter of Naples during the late 1800s and prepared this onion glaze. Others claim the dish was prepared by a cook from Geneva (*Ginevrino*) in the service of an aristocratic family in Naples. As so often happens with recipes, there are variations, some of which use a piece of prosciutto or even a piece of the muscle of the pig's trotter known as the *gallinella* in addition to the beef.

Tie the meat with butcher's twine. Heat the olive oil and butter in a pot and add the onions, salame, celery, carrot, and tomatoes. Add the meat and brown. ✦ Add 1 cup of water, cover, and cook over very low heat, turning the meat occasionally, for about 2 hours, or until the water has nearly cooked away. Do not let the sauce boil. ✦ Remove the meat and raise the heat to reduce the sauce, stirring with a wooden spoon to prevent it from sticking to the bottom. Add a little wine from time to time, letting it evaporate before adding more. ✦ When the sauce has become shiny and dark, return the meat to the pot, add ½ cup of water, taste for salt, and cook at low heat for about 10 minutes. Remove the meat. ✦ Meanwhile, cook the macaroni in lightly salted boiling water until al dente, then drain and toss with the sauce, reserving some of the sauce to serve with the meat as a second course. Mix the cheeses and serve with both courses.

LONG-COOKED PASTA WITH STEW AND BROTH

PUGLIA

2 lbs. macaroni
¾ lb. grated Parmigiano-Reggiano
Sauce from a stew (see page 329)
Broth
½ lb. (1 cup) butter, melted

The preference for pasta cooked "al dente" dates to the last century. During the nineteenth century pasta was cooked a bit longer, as indicated by this period recipe from Bari, which gives the ingredients for a macaroni dish named for Napoleon's Marshal Murat.

Cook the macaroni in lightly salted boiling water for 30 minutes. Drain, and dress the macaroni with the cheese, spreading over some stew and broth. ✦ Add the butter. While still warm bring the macaroni to the table.

MACCHERONI ALLA MULINARA

The method for this special pasta from Abruzzo was to form the pasta dough into a loaf shape and create a hole in the center; then, working the dough as though winding wool, a single long cylinder would be formed and cut into the desired lengths. The pasta was cooked in salted boiling water until al dente and dressed with a simple meat sauce of pancetta or pork guanciale, onion, parsley, sage, tomato sauce, chopped duck, goose, beef, and chili pepper.

MACCHERONI ALLA TORANESE

CALABRIAN-STYLE PASTA WITH LARDO AND ONION

CALABRIA

1 lb. macaroni

4 oz. fresh *lardo* (see page 2), cubed

1 medium onion, sliced

Grated pecorino

Salt

This dish is typical of Torano Castello.

Heat a pot with lightly salted water. When it boils stir in the macaroni. Heat the *lardo* in a pan over low heat, add the onion, and sauté. ✦ When the macaroni are cooked, drain them and toss with the sauce, adding pecorino. Serve hot.

MACCHERONI CON AGLIO, OLIO, E DIAVOLILLO

SPAGHETTI WITH GARLIC AND CHILI PEPPER

ABRUZZO

½ cup extra-virgin olive oil

3 garlic cloves, crushed

1 *diavolillo* (hot chili pepper, see note, page 22)

1 lb. spaghetti, cut in pieces about 4 inches long

1 tbsp. chopped flat-leaf parsley

Salt

This dish is typical of Chieti.

Heat the olive oil in a pan and sauté the garlic. ✦ As soon as the garlic colors, mix in the *diavolillo*. ✦ Cook the spaghetti in lightly salted boiling water; drain when al dente and put in a large heated serving bowl. ✦ Pour the sauce over the spaghetti, adding parsley. Toss and serve immediately.

HOMEMADE PASTA IN PORK SAUCE

MACCHERONI CON LE CEPPE

ABRUZZO

3 cups all-purpose flour, plus more as needed
4 large eggs
¼ cup olive oil
1 medium onion, sliced
1 lb. ground pork
1 lb. tomato purée
Grated pecorino

This dish is typical of Civitella del Tronto.

Use the flour and eggs to prepare a pasta dough as in the recipe on page 10. ✦ Let the dough rest several hours, then roll out to form a sheet (see page 212) and cut into small 1-inch pieces. Wrap the pieces around a knitting needle to form macaroni. ✦ Heat the olive oil in a pan and add the onion. When it is soft add the pork. When the pork is brown, add the tomato purée and cook until slightly thickened. ✦ Cook the macaroni in lightly salted boiling water until al dente and toss with the sauce, adding pecorino.

HOMEMADE PASTA WITH CHICKEN GIBLETS

MACCHERONI CON LE RIGAGLIE

UMBRIA

For the pasta:
1⅔ cups all-purpose flour, plus more as needed
3 large eggs
3 tbsp. extra-virgin olive oil
1 tbsp. white wine

For the sauce:
½ lb. chicken giblets
2 tbsp. extra-virgin olive oil
1 medium onion, finely chopped
1 carrot, finely chopped
1 celery stalk, finely chopped
¾ lb. peeled plum tomatoes
Grated pecorino
Salt

Use the flour, eggs, oil, and wine to prepare a pasta dough as in the recipe on page 10, adding the oil and wine with the eggs. Roll out to a thin sheet (see page 212) and cut it into narrow strips. ✦ Parboil the giblets until cooked. Drain and chop into small pieces. ✦ Heat the olive oil in a pan and sauté the onion, carrot, and celery until soft. Add the giblets, tomatoes, and salt and cook at low heat. ✦ Cook the pasta in lightly salted boiling water until al dente, drain, and toss with the sauce, adding pecorino.

PASTA WITH WHITE MULLET

MACCHERONI CON LE TRIGLIE

MARCHE

¼ cup extra-virgin olive oil
CONTINUED

Heat the olive oil in a pan and sauté the garlic until golden. Add the pieces of mullet, and after a minute, add the tomatoes and wine. ✦ Adjust for salt, and let the sauce cook for 10 to 15 minutes, or until it reaches the

2 cloves garlic, minced

1 lb. mullet filets,
cut in pieces

2 cups peeled plum tomatoes

¼ cup white wine

2 tbsp. chopped flat-leaf parsley

1 lb. macaroni

Salt and pepper

desired thickness. ✦ Add a little pepper and parsley. ✦ Cook the macaroni in lightly salted boiling water until al dente, drain, and toss with the sauce. Serve immediately.

MACCHERONI DI CASA COL SUGO DI NEONATA

HOMEMADE PASTA WITH BABY ANCHOVIES

SICILIA

3 tbsp. all-purpose flour,
plus more as needed

2 large eggs

4 oz. *neonata* (baby anchovies
or sardines)

¼ cup chopped flat-leaf parsley

Extra-virgin olive oil

1 medium onion, finely chopped

3 garlic cloves

2 anchovy fillets

1 tbsp. tomato paste

1 tbsp. red wine

1 ¼ lbs. macaroni

½ cup breadcrumbs

Salt

This can be a one-dish meal.

Use the flour and eggs to prepare a batter, adding the *neonata* and parsley with the eggs. ✦ Heat 2 inches of olive oil in a skillet. Fry walnut-size spoonfuls of dough until golden, then drain on paper towels. ✦ Heat 2 table-spoons olive oil in a pan and sauté the onion, 1 garlic clove, and anchovies. Add the tomato paste, salt, and red wine. ✦ Add the fried dough to the sauce and cook a few more minutes. ✦ Meanwhile cook the macaroni in lightly salted boiling water until al dente, then drain and toss with the sauce. ✦ Grind the remaining garlic in a mortar with 2 tablespoons olive oil until a paste forms. Mix in the breadcrumbs and add them to the macaroni mixture. Stir to mix and serve.

MACCHERONI E PEPPERONI SECCHI

PASTA WITH DRIED PEPPERS

BASILICATA

6 tbsp. extra-virgin olive oil

4 garlic cloves

6 dried peppers

1 lb. macaroni

Salt

Heat ¼ cup olive oil in a pan and sauté 3 of the garlic cloves; let this cook a moment then add the peppers and toss, then remove the pan from the heat. Transfer the mixture to a mortar and grind to make a sauce. ✦ Cook the macaroni in lightly salted boiling water. When it is almost cooked add the remaining oil to the pan and sauté the remaining garlic clove; as soon as the garlic has colored add the chili sauce to the pan. ✦ Quickly drain the pasta and toss it in the pan with the sauce.

PASTA WITH BEANS AND MUSHROOMS

MACCHERONI CON FAGIOLI E FUNGHI

CALABRIA

⅔ cup dried borlotti or cranberry beans

¼ cup extra-virgin olive oil, plus more for serving

1 garlic clove

6 oz. fresh porcini or other mushrooms, cleaned and chopped

¾ lb. rigatoni

2 tbsp. chopped flat-leaf parsley

Salt

Soak the beans in water overnight then cook them in lightly salted water to cover by several inches, stirring often with a wooden spoon until tender. Drain and set aside. ✦ Heat the olive oil in a pan and sauté the garlic until golden. Add the mushrooms and cook until the water they give off has evaporated; add the beans. ✦ Cook the pasta in lightly salted boiling water until al dente; drain and combine with the mushrooms and beans. ✦ Sprinkle with oil and parsley before serving.

PAN-COOKED PASTA WITH PORK, TOMATO, AND RED WINE

MACCHERONI IN PADELLA

CALABRIA

¼ cup extra-virgin olive oil

2 garlic cloves

¾ lb. pork, cubed

¼ cup red wine

1 lb. peeled plum tomatoes, seeded and drained

Bay leaf

1 *diavolillo* (hot chili pepper, see note, page 22)

1 lb. macaroni

2 tbsp. grated pecorino

Salt

Heat the olive oil in a saucepan and sauté the garlic until golden; add the pork and wine. ✦ Add the tomatoes, bay leaf, and chili pepper. ✦ Thicken the sauce at low heat, stirring often. ✦ Cook the macaroni in lightly salted boiling water until al dente, drain, and add to the saucepan with the sauce, adding pecorino before serving.

ZITI WITH LARDO

MACCHERONI ZITI CON IL LARDO

CAMPANIA

2 ½ oz. *lardo* (see page 2), cubed

2 cups extra-virgin olive oil

⅔ cup chopped, peeled plum tomatoes

1 lb. ziti

Grated Parmigiano-Reggiano

Salt and pepper

This dish is typical of Naples.

In a pot heat the *lardo* and olive oil over low heat until the *lardo* has started to take on color. Add the tomatoes and cook for about 30 minutes. ✦ Cook the ziti in lightly salted boiling water until al dente, drain, and toss with the sauce. Add Parmigiano-Reggiano and a little pepper, and serve.

PASTA WITH BEANS

This dish is typical of the Upper Molise. In the Lower Molise, tomato, fresh peppers, and parsley are added to this dish.

For the sauce:

1⅔ cups dried cannellini beans

4 oz. pork rind

1 celery stalk, chopped

1 garlic clove, chopped (not crushed)

1 *diavolillo* (hot chili pepper, see note, page 22)

2 tbsp. extra-virgin olive oil

Salt

For the pasta:

3 cups semolina flour, plus more as needed

1 tbsp. extra-virgin olive oil

Salt

Soak the beans in water overnight. Drain and cook in an earthenware pot in lightly salted water to cover by several inches until tender. Drain and set aside. ✦ Scrape the pork rind with a serrated knife and pass it over a flame to burn away any remaining bristles. After this cleaning simmer it in lightly salted water. ✦ When the pork rind is cooked, cut it in strips or cubes and mix with the beans in a large pot over low heat; add the celery, garlic, chili pepper, and olive oil. Sauté all this for about 10 minutes. ✦ Meanwhile use the flour and olive oil to prepare a pasta dough as in the recipe on page 10, using 1 cup water in place of the eggs. ✦ Roll the dough out to form a very thin sheet (see page 212). Cut this into ribbons about 5 inches long and ¾ to 1 inch wide: the *malefante*. Cook in lightly salted boiling water until al dente. Drain well and add to the beans, mixing well. Serve hot.

SMALL SARDINIAN GNOCCHI WITH MEAT SAUCE

3 cups semolina flour, plus more as needed

2 tbsp. extra-virgin olive oil

All-purpose flour

1 medium onion, finely sliced

4 oz. *lardo* (see page 2), diced

4 oz. ground veal

4 oz. ground pork

1 sprig flat-leaf parsley

1 sprig rosemary

3 cups tomato purée

½ cup grated pecorino piccante

Salt

This dish is typical of the Campidano.

Use the semolina to make a dough as in the recipe on page 10, using 1 cup water and 1 tablespoon olive oil in place of the eggs. ✦ Divide the dough into small pieces and roll into ropes about the thickness of a pencil. ✦ Cut the ropes of dough into ½-inch-long pieces. Press each piece over the tines of a fork or other rough surface to form hollowed gnocchi: these are the *malloreddus*. ✦ Dust the *malloreddus* with flour and arrange on a work surface. ✦ Meanwhile prepare the sauce. Heat the remaining olive oil in a pan and sauté the onion and *lardo*. ✦ Add the meats, parsley, and rosemary and continue cooking. ✦ Add the tomato purée and 1 cup of water and cook slowly for about 1 hour, adding more water if necessary. ✦ Cook the *malloreddus* in lightly salted boiling water until they float, drain, and toss with the sauce. Add pecorino and serve hot.

ROUGH-CUT PASTA WITH BEANS

MALTAGLIATI COI FAGIOLI

LOMBARDIA

1⅔ cups dried borlotti or cranberry beans

2 tbsp. unsalted butter

½ medium onion, chopped

1 garlic clove, chopped

2 tbsp. tomato paste

¾ lb. *maltagliati* (see note and below)

Grated Parmigiano-Reggiano

Salt and pepper

This can also be seasoned with a drizzle of olive oil and a grinding of pepper. The dish can be served at room temperature in the summer. Maltagliata are roughly or randomly cut pieces of pasta from sheets.

Soak the beans in cold water overnight; drain, then boil until tender, about 2 hours. ✦ In a large pot over low heat, melt the butter and sauté the onion and garlic. Add the beans and their cooking liquid and tomato paste. ✦ Add enough warm water (if necessary) to cook the pasta with the bean mixture. Taste for salt and pepper, and continue cooking at low heat. ✦ Bring the liquid to a boil and cook the maltagliati until al dente. Serve hot with Parmigiano-Reggiano.

HOMEMADE ROUGH-CUT PASTA WITH LEEKS

MALTAGLIATI DI PORRO

PIEMONTE

For the pasta:

3 cups all-purpose flour, plus more as needed

4 large eggs

For the sauce:

2 tbsp. unsalted butter

4 leeks, cleaned and sliced in rounds

½ cup heavy cream

Grated Parmigiano-Reggiano

Salt

This dish is typical of Alba.

Use the flour and eggs to prepare a pasta dough as in the recipe on page 10. ✦ Roll out in a thin sheet (see page 212) and cut in medium-size squares. Cook the pasta in lightly salted boiling water. ✦ Meanwhile, heat the butter in a pan over low heat. Sauté the leeks until softened. ✦ Drain the pasta and add to the pan with the leeks. ✦ Stir in the cream, add cheese, and serve hot.

PASTA STUFFED WITH SWEETBREADS AND BORAGE

MANDILI 'NVERSOI

PIEMONTE

For the pasta:

2 cups semolina flour, plus more as needed

CONTINUED

This dish is typical of Alessandria and is a traditional recipe for *Mandili 'nversoi*. This shape of pasta holds sauce very well.

Use the flour to prepare a pasta dough as in the recipe on page 10, using ¾ cup water in place of the eggs. It should be as firm as possible. ✦ Let this rest for several hours, then knead again, adding more flour if possible. ✦ Make

PASTA, POLENTA & RICE

285

Salt

For the filling:

4 oz. sausage meat, finely sliced

8 oz. sweetbreads (cooked in butter), finely ground

6 cups borage, boiled, finely chopped, and sautéed in unsalted butter

¼ cup extra-virgin olive oil, or as needed

2 tbsp. grated Parmigiano-Reggiano, or as needed

2 large eggs, or as needed

Pasta sauce, as desired

the filling. Combine the sausage, sweetbreads, and borage. Add just enough olive oil, cheese, and eggs to bind the mixture. ✦ Roll out a thin sheet of dough (see page 212) and let this rest for several hours to dry well. ✦ Make the *mandili 'nversoi* by cutting the sheet into squares. Put a dollop of the filling in the middle of each, then fold the sheet closed diagonally, joining the two far ends and folding back the other two ends. ✦ Cook these in boiling lightly salted water, drain, and combine with the sauce.

✦ **LOCAL TRADITION** ✦

MANATELLE

Perhaps originally from the area of Vaglio in Basilicata, *manatelle* are a cultural as well as a culinary phenomenon. This particular type of pasta (exclusively homemade) is unknown even to many Lucanians (people from Basilicata). Its preparation is something of a rite—a rite composed of faith, patience, skill, and many hours of labor. This also explains why the number of women still making *manatelle* in Basilicata can probably be counted on the fingers of two hands. It starts with durum wheat flour that is kneaded with a little lard (or olive oil) and lukewarm water. (A certain elderly Lucanian peasant also added some eggs to this, as well as a dash of salt.) The dough rests, covered by a cloth, for at least 30 minutes, then is kneaded to form small loaves weighing about 10 ounces each. A hole is made in the center of each loaf and it is gradually widened with the hands, to create a sort of large ring. The pasta-maker keeps working this ring, stretching it out more and more, then folds it over itself in the middle to form a figure eight without breaking the dough or letting it stick together. Next these two rings are similarly expanded and folded over onto each other to make four separate rings. This process is continued again and again, going from 4 rings to 8 to 16, then 32 and, if possible, even up to 64! At this point the dough rests and then is gently cut all the way through at two opposite ends. The result is lengths of pasta about 1 foot or more. Having been worked so intensely and for such a long time, these lengths of pasta will be of an unequalled softness and lightness. After cooking, they are served with the typical Lucano sauce.

BAKED CREPES WITH BREAD AND CHEESE FILLING

MANFRIGULI

FOR 8 PERSONS

LOMBARDIA

For the crepes:
½ cup buckwheat flour, plus more as needed
½ cup all-purpose flour, plus more as needed
½ cup milk
1 large egg, beaten
1 tbsp. extra-virgin olive oil
Unsalted butter, as needed

For the filling:
1 lb. stale bread
⅔ cup milk
1¼ cups heavy cream
1⅔ cups *fior di latte* cheese, cubed
Pinch grated nutmeg
1 large egg, beaten
Salt and pepper

This dish is typical of the Valtellina.

Combine the flours, milk, half of the egg, and olive oil to make a batter the consistency of heavy cream. Heat a 12-inch nonstick pan over medium heat and melt 1 tablespoon butter. Add ½ cup batter and swirl the pan to make a very thin layer of batter. When firm, flip to cook the other side. Make as many crepes in this manner as possible, using up all of the batter and adding more butter to the pan as needed. ✦ Soak the bread in the milk and cream for about 3 hours, then add the cheese and a pinch of nutmeg. Pass the mixture through a food mill twice to obtain a homogeneous dough. ✦ Preheat the oven to 350°F. Brush the upper edge of the crepes with the remaining egg then arrange a cylinder of the filling down the center of each; roll up the crepes around the filling. ✦ Cut each crepe in 1-inch-long lengths and arrange the cylinders with an open (filling) end facing upward. Bake for about 10 minutes, or until the filling is lightly browned.

LAYERED POLENTA WITH SAUSAGE AND MUSHROOMS

MATUFFI

TOSCANA

½ cup extra-virgin olive oil
1 carrot, chopped
1 celery stalk, chopped
1 medium onion, chopped
4 large lean sausages
1½ cups red wine
¼ oz. dried mushrooms, soaked in lukewarm water, drained, and chopped
1¼ lbs. plum tomatoes, peeled and chopped
1 bay leaf
1½ cups cornmeal

CONTINUED

This is a fine old peasant dish typical of Versilia and around Lucca. It is robust, with the cheese and sausage. It can be eaten with a spoon and, naturally, should be washed down with plenty of full-bodied red wine.

Heat the olive oil in a saucepan and sauté the carrot, celery, and onion. ✦ Remove the sausage from the casing and crush with the tines of a fork and add it to the pan. Skim off any fat if necessary and add the wine. ✦ When the wine has almost evaporated add the mushrooms. ✦ Cook this mixture until the mushrooms are lightly browned, then add the tomatoes and bay leaf. Simmer for 20 minutes. ✦ Meanwhile make polenta by bringing 3 cups of lightly salted water to a boil in a pot. Slowly pour the cornmeal into this, stirring continuously with a wooden spoon to keep it from forming lumps. ✦ Continue cooking, stirring, for 45 minutes, until the polenta

Grated Parmigiano-Reggiano
or aged pecorino

Salt and pepper

is cooked. ✦ When the polenta is done, put a tablespoon of it in every bowl, add a dollop of the sauce, then some cheese. Then add another tablespoon of polenta, another dollop of sauce, and so on, layer by layer, until the ingredients have been used up.

MEZZANELLI
AL CACIOCAVALLO

BUCATINI WITH CACIOCAVALLO CHEESE

CAMPANIA

This dish is typical of Caserta.

¼ cup extra-virgin olive oil

1 garlic clove

1 lb. plum tomatoes, peeled and chopped

Several basil leaves, chopped, and several whole basil leaves, for garnish

1 lb. *mezzanelli* (can use bucatini or long macaroni if necessary)

1 cup roughly grated caciocavallo

Salt

In a large pan heat the olive oil and sauté the garlic. Add the tomatoes and basil; salt lightly and cook at low heat. ✦ Cook the *mezzanelli* in lightly salted boiling water and drain when al dente. ✦ Pour the *mezzanelli* into the pan with the sauce, adding half the caciocavallo and stirring constantly. Serve in a bowl decorated with basil leaves and the remaining cheese.

✦ **LOCAL TRADITION** ✦

MIGNUIC OR CAVATIELLI

Mignuic are homemade wheat-flour gnocchi, made by the same method as more traditional gnocchi. Because of their ability to absorb seasonings and to take on aromas, *mignuic* are an excellent pasta to use with hare or with a sauce made with olive oil, wine, and bay leaves. In typical recipes from Puglia, the boiled *mignuic* would be tossed with a substantial sauce made from beef or hare, tomato, olive oil, and spices.

BAKED POLENTA WITH SAUSAGE AND CICCIOLI

MIGLIACCIO RUSTICO

CAMPANIA

½ lb. fresh sausage

2 cups cornmeal

½ lb. *ciccioli* (see note, page 12)

2 oz. *lardo* (see page 2)

⅓ cup grated Parmigiano-Reggiano

⅓ cup grated pecorino

Salt and pepper

This dish is typical of Avellino. The various recipes called *migliaccio* refer to dishes that were once prepared using millet (*miglio*).

Preheat the oven to 400°F. Simmer the sausages in a saucepan with ½ inch of water. ✦ When they are cooked let them cool, reserving their pan juices, then cut them into thin rounds and set aside.✦ Heat 6 cups of lightly salted water in a large pot (copper is best) over medium heat to boiling and add the pan juices from the sausages. ✦ Whisking constantly, pour a steady stream of cornmeal very slowly into the boiling water. ✦ Cook for about 40 minutes, stirring constantly to prevent the formation of lumps. It's not a bad idea to have extra boiling water on hand in case the polenta gets too thick before it is cooked. ✦ The polenta is cooked enough when the grains are no longer crunchy and it pulls away from the walls of the pot as you stir it. ✦ Grease a 12-inch ovenproof pan with *lardo*. ✦ Heat the *ciccioli* in a pan and add to the polenta. Add the sausage, Parmigiano-Reggiano and pecorino, and a generous grinding of pepper. ✦ Pour the mixture into the ovenproof pan and bake until it forms a golden crust. Serve hot.

TAGLIOLINI CROQUETTES

ORDURA (OR PALLE) DI TAGLIOLINI

FOR 12 OR 15 CROQUETTES

CAMPANIA

1 lb. tagliolini

¼ lb. (1 stick) unsalted butter

⅔ cup grated Parmigiano-Reggiano

7 large eggs

All-purpose flour

4 oz. prosciutto cotto, finely diced

5 oz. *fior di latte* cheese, finely diced

Breadcrumbs

Olive oil, for frying

Salt

This dish is typical of Naples. It is best to dress the tagliolini with the butter, Parmigiano-Reggiano, and eggs several hours prior to making the croquettes so the pasta will have time to cool. This will make it easier to form into the right shape and will help prevent it from coming open while boiling.

Cook the tagliolini in lightly salted boiling water until very al dente, drain, and toss in a bowl with butter, Parmigiano-Reggiano, and 4 of the eggs beaten with a little salt. ✦ Spread a layer of flour across the work surface and assemble across it small heaps of the cooked tagliolini. ✦ Fill each of these heaps with small portions of prosciutto and *fior di latte*, trying (with damp hands) to give them the shape of large eggs. ✦ Heat a couple of inches of oil in a large pot until hot. Beat the remaining eggs. Roll the croquettes in flour, then dip in the eggs, then roll in breadcrumbs. ✦ Fry in olive oil a few at a time until golden.

<table>
<tr><td>ORECCHIETTE CON CIME DI RAPE</td><td># ORECCHIETTE WITH TURNIP TOPS</td></tr>
</table>

ORECCHIETTE WITH TURNIP TOPS

ORECCHIETTE CON CIME DI RAPE

PUGLIA

3 ¼ lbs. turnip greens

1 lb. orecchiette (homemade if possible; see below)

¼ cup extra-virgin olive oil

2 garlic cloves

1 *diavolillo* (hot chili pepper, see note, page 22)

4 salt-cured anchovy fillets, boned and crushed to a paste

Salt

If the turnip tops are tender, it is better to cook the orecchiette first or there is the risk that they will become mushy before the orecchiette are cooked.

Clean the turnip tops, using only the tender parts, and rinse in cold water. ✦ Bring a large pot of lightly salted water to a boil; add the turnip tops, and after a few minutes the orecchiette. ✦ Drain when the pasta is still very al dente. ✦ Heat the oil in a pan and sauté the garlic; add the chili pepper, then the anchovies. Then add the orecchiette mixture. ✦ Toss to blend well (if needed, add more extra-virgin olive oil). Serve.

ORECCHIETTE WITH ARTICHOKES

ORECCHIETTE CON I CARCIOFI

PUGLIA

For the pasta:

1 ⅔ cups whole-wheat flour, plus more as needed

⅔ cup semolina flour, plus more for the pan

Salt

For the sauce:

4 large artichokes (if possible from Puglia)

Juice of 1 lemon

¼ cup extra-virgin olive oil

1 garlic clove

½ medium white onion, finely chopped

5 oz. pork loin, in small pieces

¼ cup dry white Malvasia wine

9 oz. plum tomatoes

¼ cup finely chopped flat-leaf parsley

⅓ cup ricotta

½ cup grated pecorino

This dish is typical of Brindisi.

Combine the flours and use them to make a pasta dough as in the recipe on page 10, using ¾ cup water in place of the eggs. ✦ Shape the dough into cylinders about ½ inch in diameter, cut in lengths of 1 inch, and flatten them with the blade of a knife. Squeeze them between your fingers to form orecchiette. ✦ Sprinkle a clean dishcloth with semolina and spread the orecchiette out; leave to dry until cooking. ✦ Clean the artichokes, blanch them in water acidulated with lemon juice, cut them in slices, and set aside. ✦ Heat the olive oil in an earthenware pan, add the garlic, and cook until browned; remove and discard. ✦ Add the onion and cook it until it becomes pale, then add the pork and brown it; add the wine. ✦ Add the tomatoes, parsley, and ricotta. ✦ At this point, add the artichokes to the sauce and slowly cook 40 to 45 minutes, adding water if the sauce reduces too much. ✦ Cook the orecchiette in boiling lightly salted water, drain, put in a bowl, and toss with the pecorino and then with the artichoke sauce. Mix and serve.

ORECCHIETTE WITH RICOTTA

ORECCHIETTE
CON LA RICOTTA

PUGLIA

1 lb. orecchiette (if possible homemade; see page 290)

9 oz. ricotta

Salt

Cook the orecchiette in lightly salted boiling water until al dente. Meanwhile mix the ricotta in a bowl with a pinch of salt and a few tablespoons of the pasta cooking water. ✦ Drain the orecchiette and toss with the ricotta, mixing well. Serve immediately.

MUSIC-PAPER BREAD WITH POACHED EGGS

PANI FRATTAU

SARDEGNA

1 garlic clove

¼ cup extra-virgin olive oil

Several basil leaves

2 cups tomato purée

1¼ lb. *pane carasau* (music-paper bread)

4 poached large eggs

⅔ cup grated pecorino

Salt

This is a typical rustic preparation from Nuoro that uses *pane carasau*, known as "music paper" bread. There are many variations of this recipe; for example, using meat sauce in place of tomato, fried eggs instead of poached, and so on.

Combine the garlic, olive oil, basil, and tomato purée in a saucepan and cook at high heat for a few minutes. ✦ Break the bread and dip the pieces in the sauce, draining them immediately. ✦ Form layers of the bread in individual serving plates, one piece after another. ✦ Put a poached egg on top of each and break it so it covers the surface well. Sprinkle with pecorino and serve.

RICE WITH BEANS, CABBAGE, AND SALAME

PANISCIA

PIEMONTE

1 celery stalk, roughly chopped

1 carrot, roughly chopped

½ lb. cabbage, roughly chopped

2 ripe plum tomatoes, peeled and chopped

1 cup fresh shelled beans

2 oz. pork rind, cut in strips

2 tbsp. unsalted butter

2 tbsp. lard

1 medium onion, chopped

1 *salam d'la duja* (pork sausage covered in lard), skinned and diced

1⅔ cups Arborio rice

½ cup red wine

Grated Parmigiano-Reggiano

Salt and pepper

This dish is typical of Novara. For the wine use Barbera or Dolcetto.

Put the celery, carrot, cabbage, and tomatoes in a pan; add the beans. ✦ Add the pork rind, water to cover, then salt and pepper to taste. Cook uncovered for about 2 hours. ✦ Meanwhile heat the butter and lard in a large pan and sauté the onion and *salam d'la duja*. ✦ Add the rice and toast it. Add the wine, then slowly add the broth and the vegetables. ✦ Cook for about 20 minutes, let rest 5 minutes, then serve hot with Parmigiano-Reggiano.

RICE WITH BEANS, CABBAGE, AND PORK

PANISCIA NOVARESE

PIEMONTE

1 ¼ cups fresh shelled borlotti
or cranberry beans
½ lb. cabbage
1 carrot, chopped
1 celery stalk, chopped
2 or 3 plum tomatoes, chopped
4 tbsp. unsalted butter
1 medium onion, chopped
2 oz. pork rind, in thin strips
2 oz. *lardo* (see page 2), diced
1 ⅔ cups Arborio rice
½ cup red wine
Salt and pepper

Put the beans, cabbage, carrot, celery, and tomatoes in a pot with 6 cups of water. ✦ Add salt and pepper and cook for about 2 hours, uncovered. ✦ Meanwhile heat the butter in a pan and sauté the onion; add the pork rind and *lardo* and sauté briefly. Add the rice, toasting it well. ✦ Add the wine and then slowly add the broth from the cooking vegetables, then the vegetables themselves. ✦ Simmer for about 20 minutes, let rest covered 5 minutes, then serve seasoned with plenty of pepper.

RICE WITH BEANS

PANISSA

PIEMONTE

1 ¼ cups dried borlotti
or cranberry beans,
soaked overnight
3 tbsp. extra-virgin olive oil
2 oz. *lardo* (see page 2), chopped
½ medium onion, finely sliced
1 garlic clove, minced
2 ½ cups Arborio rice
1 tbsp. unsalted butter
Salt

This dish is typical of Vercelli.

Boil the beans in lightly salted water to cover by a couple of inches with 1 tablespoon olive oil until tender, about 2 hours; drain the beans, reserving the liquid. ✦ Heat the olive oil and *lardo* in a pan and sauté the onion and garlic. ✦ When the garlic is well colored, add the rice, stir, then slowly add cups of the bean cooking liquid. ✦ Give it a good stir every so often to keep the rice from sticking, and after 10 to 12 minutes of cooking add the beans and the butter. ✦ Continue cooking a few minutes to reach the desired thickness, stirring only when necessary to keep it from sticking. Serve hot.

HERB-STUFFED PASTA

PANSOTTI

LIGURIA

"Pansotti" is Ligurian dialect meaning "pot-bellied," evoking the shape of these filled pasta. *Preboggion* is a Genoese dialect word meaning "cooking herbs" and refers to a combination of Ligurian herbs (including wild herbs) and plants sold in bunches. A legend as outlandish as it is philologically

For the filling:

¾ lb. borage

1 lb. chard

1 lb. *preboggion* (see note)

¼ cup extra-virgin olive oil

1 garlic clove, chopped

1 pinch ground marjoram

2 large eggs, beaten

6 oz. fresh ricotta

Grated Parmigiano-Reggiano

For the pasta:

3 cups all-purpose flour, plus more as needed

2 tbsp. white wine

Salt

For the sauce:

Walnut sauce (see page 73)

unfounded attributes the word to Godfrey of Bouillon, a leader of the First Crusade; its ingredients were "for Bouillon," the phrase becoming in Genoese *pro Buggiun* and eventually *preboggion*. As for the ingredients, the *Cuciniere* (Ratti and Rossi) gives chard, cabbage, and parsley as fixed components. Whereas for the *pansotti*, the tradition of Tigullio (the area east of Genoa) calls for "seven wild herbs" that must be collected in the morning along the edges of paths, on river banks, and along the cracks of dry walls. We can be "almost sure" of several of these herbs: sow thistle, talegua, burnet, dog tooth, and borage. Adding chard and parsley (forget the cabbage) we reach seven. Some of these are difficult to find today, so one must make do with what is available.

Boil the borage, chard, and herbs in lightly salted water; drain. ✦ Chop them finely and put in a pan over medium heat with the olive oil, garlic, and marjoram. ✦ When this is warm, add the eggs and cheeses, stirring with a wooden spoon to obtain a compact mixture. ✦ Use the flour to make a pasta dough as in the recipe on page 10, using ¾ cup water and the wine in place of the eggs. ✦ Roll out a thin sheet of dough (see page 212). The *pansotti* can be made as triangles or as large *tortelli*. ✦ Stuff them high with the filling, cook in lightly salted boiling water, drain, and toss with the walnut sauce.

PANZAROTTI SANNITI

STUFFED DUMPLINGS

CAMPANIA

3 cups all-purpose flour, plus more as needed

½ cup plus 2 tbsp. lard

2 large eggs, beaten

6 oz. salame, chopped

6 oz. caciotta cheese (can substitute provolone), in pieces

⅔ cup grated Parmigiano-Reggiano

2 tbsp. chopped flat-leaf parsley

Extra-virgin olive oil, for frying

Salt and pepper

Use the flour to make a pasta dough as in the recipe on page 10, using the lard and ¼ cup water in place of the eggs. Let the dough rest 30 minutes, covered with a cloth. ✦ Prepare the filling: combine the eggs, salame, caciotta, Parmigiano-Reggiano, parsley, and pepper. Work the mixture to thoroughly blend the ingredients. ✦ Roll out a thin sheet of pasta (see page 212), and using a glass cut out disks. ✦ Fill the disks with the filling and cover with another disk, sealing the edges to close. Heat ½ inch of olive oil in a large pan and fry until golden. Drain on paper towels and serve hot.

LITTLE STUFFED
DUMPLINGS

CAMPANIA

For the pasta:

1 ¼ cups all-purpose flour

1 ½ sticks plus 2 tbsp. butter,
softened

For the 1st filling:

1 ⅔ cups diced mozzarella

8 anchovy fillets, chopped

2 tbsp. grated Parmigiano-Reggiano

1 tbsp. chopped flat-leaf parsley

Pinch pepper

For the 2nd filling:

1 lb. button mushrooms, chopped

1 cup thick béchamel sauce
(see page 339)

1 tbsp. grated Parmigiano-Reggiano

For the 3rd filling:

4 tbsp. unsalted butter

1 tbsp. all-purpose flour,
plus more as needed

1 cup chicken broth

1 large egg yolk

6 oz. white mushrooms, chopped

2 oz. prosciutto cotto, diced

2 oz. cooked chicken, chopped

Pinch pepper

For cooking:

1 large egg, beaten

Extra-virgin olive oil for frying

Use the flour to prepare a pasta dough as in the recipe on page 10, using the butter in place of the eggs. Roll out the dough to a thickness of ⅛ to ¼ inch and with a pastry wheel with a jagged edge cut out disks about 4 inches in diameter; brush these with beaten egg on one side. ✦ To prepare the 1st and 2nd fillings simply combine the ingredients and blend well. ✦ The 3rd filling requires the preparation of a velvety sauce following the procedure for a normal béchamel (see page 339), using chicken broth in place of milk. Let the sauce simmer, stirring until it is very thick. Mix it with the egg yolk, mushrooms, prosciutto cotto, and chicken. ✦ Fill the center of each disk with one of the three fillings and fold it over on itself, sealing the edges to obtain half-moon shapes. ✦ Brush with the beaten egg. Heat 1 inch of olive oil in a pan and fry the *panzarottini* until golden. Drain on paper towels and serve hot.

PAPPARDELLE
IN HARE SAUCE

TOSCANA

¼ cup extra-virgin olive oil

1 carrot, chopped

CONTINUED

This dish is typical of Florence. For the wine use Chianti.

Heat the olive oil in a large earthenware pan and sauté the carrot, onion, and celery. ✦ Add the shoulder, breast, lungs, and heart. Cook a few minutes then add the wine, letting it evaporate. ✦ Add the tomato purée, milk, and

½ medium onion, chopped

1 celery stalk, chopped

Shoulders, breast, lungs, heart, and liver of a young hare

¼ cup red wine

1 tbsp. tomato purée

¼ cup milk

1 lb. fresh pappardelle (see below)

Grated Parmigiano-Reggiano

Salt and pepper

salt and pepper to taste. ✦ Cook to the desired consistency, adding a little warm water if necessary. ✦ Remove the meat from the pan, chop with the liver, return to the pan, and cook another 5 minutes. ✦ Cook the pappardelle in lightly salted boiling water, drain when al dente, and toss with the sauce. Add cheese at the table.

✦ **LOCAL TRADITION** ✦

PANZEROTTI

More of a preparation or type of dish than a specific recipe, *panzerotti* from Puglia are half-moon-shaped ravioli. They were filled with beaten eggs and cheese, a mixture of tomato, onion, and anchovies, or even simply mozzarella or ricotta—often the skill and imagination of the cook would suggest different combinations and variations. Certain occasions required *panzerotti* filled with spaghetti dressed with olive oil, anchovies, and olives. There are also delicious sweet *panzerotti*, filled with marmalade and dusted with confectioners' sugar. All types of filled *panzerotti* would be fried in olive oil and eaten hot.

PAPPARDELLE AL SUGO
DI PAPERA MUTA

PAPPARDELLE IN DUCK SAUCE

FOR
12 PERSONS

ABRUZZO

This dish is typical of Pescara.

For the pasta:

10 cups sifted all-purpose flour, plus more as needed

5 large eggs

For the sauce:

7 oz. stew beef

1 duck, weighing 4½ lbs., feathered and seared, cleaned

CONTINUED

Use the flour and eggs to prepare a pasta dough as in the recipe on page 10. Let rest for 30 minutes. ✦ Roll out a sheet of dough (see page 212) and slice in strips about ¾ inch wide and 2½ inches long. ✦ Combine the beef with half of the vegetables and chile and add water just to cover. Bring to a simmer and cook until the beef is tender. ✦ Cut off the legs from the duck at the joint and tie up the bird with butcher's twine. ✦ Arrange the duck in a medium-size pan with the other half of the vegetables and a little water. Cook over low heat for about 3

2 carrots, chopped

3 medium potatoes, chopped

1 medium onion, sliced

1 celery stalk, chopped

1 pinch chili pepper flakes

1⅔ cups grated Parmigiano-Reggiano

Salt

hours. ✦ Purée the beef and its vegetables in a food mill; untie the duck; mix the duck's cooking sauce with that of the beef, adding salt only if necessary ✦ In a large pot cook the pappardelle in lightly salted boiling water; drain when al dente and place in a serving bowl. Pour over the sauce, which will be somewhat dense, and mix; put back on the heat for 2 to 3 minutes. ✦ Sprinkle with cheese and serve immediately. The duck can be served as a second course, with a side dish of fresh seasonal vegetables.

PAPPARDELLE ALLE
QUAGLIE IN PORCHETTA

PAPPARDELLE WITH QUAIL AND FENNEL

MARCHE

4 quail (one for each diner), with their livers

¼ cup extra-virgin olive oil

1 medium onion, sliced

4 chicken livers

½ cup dry white wine

2 or 3 tbsp. finely chopped wild fennel

1 tbsp. potato starch (or a mixture of 1 tbsp. all-purpose flour and 1 tbsp. butter)

¾ lb. fresh pappardelle (see page 295)

Grated pecorino dolce

Salt and pepper

Clean the quail and pass a flame over them to remove any feathers. ✦ Heat the olive oil in a pan and sauté the onion until pale, add the quail, and sauté them; add the chicken and quail livers with a little water and white wine. ✦ Add the fennel and salt and pepper to taste, and cook over low heat. ✦ Remove the quail from the pan and set aside, then whisk in the potato starch (or flour and butter) to thicken the sauce. ✦ Cook the pappardelle in lightly salted boiling water until al dente, toss with the quail sauce, and sprinkle with pecorino. Add a whole quail to each plate.

PAPPARDELLE
SUL CINGHIALE

PAPPARDELLE WITH BOAR

TOSCANA

1½ lbs. boar

1½ cups red wine

2 cups red wine vinegar

3 garlic cloves, crushed

4 sprigs rosemary

½ cup chopped flat-leaf parsley

CONTINUED

This dish is typical of the Maremma. Remember that the pappardelle should be at least 1 inch wide. In order to give the boar meat a good red color the Etruscans added a large portion of the animal's blood.

Put the boar in a container and pour over 1 cup wine, the vinegar, a good pinch of salt, garlic, and rosemary. Refrigerate and let it marinate 12 hours. ✦ Remove the meat from the marinade and cut it in pieces. Put the meat in a pan over high heat. ✦ After 2 minutes take the pan off the

1 large onion, finely sliced

7 oz. pancetta, in small dice

½ cup extra-virgin olive oil

1 very spicy red chili pepper

2 lbs. peeled plum tomatoes

⅔ cup tomato paste

Beef broth (if necessary)

1 lb. fresh pappardelle
(see page 295)

Grated pecorino

Salt

heat, pressing against the meat with the lid, and drain off and discard the liquid. Repeat this to make certain the meat gives up all its liquid. ✦ Combine the parsley, onion, and pancetta in a pan, making sure they are all finely chopped (or pass these ingredients through a food mill). ✦ Add the olive oil, turn on the heat to low, and sauté for 4 minutes. Add the boar meat, along with salt and the chili pepper. ✦ Add the remaining wine, tomatoes, and tomato paste so that the sauce turns a vibrant red color. ✦ Let cook for about 2 hours at low heat, adding a little warm broth if necessary. Taste and adjust for salt. ✦ Cook the pappardelle in boiling lightly salted water and remove when al dente. ✦ Add them to the sauce and stir over high heat so they soak up the flavor and stay hot. Sprinkle with pecorino and serve hot.

PASTA 'NCASCIATA

BAKED PASTA WITH EGGPLANT

CALABRIA

1½ medium eggplants

Olive oil, for frying

¾ lb. *paccheri* (or rigatoni)

1 recipe meat sauce (beef or pork)
(see page 635)

3 oz. fresh provolone,
in narrow slices

½ cup grated Parmigiano-Reggiano

Salt

Slice the eggplants lengthwise, cover with a good amount of salt, and put a weight over them (a plate) for about 20 minutes to remove the bitter flavor. Rinse and pat dry. ✦ Heat ½ inch of olive oil in a large pan and fry the eggplant until golden. ✦ Preheat the oven to 350°F. Cook the *paccheri* in lightly salted boiling water and drain when very al dente. Put them in a baking pan and dress with some of the meat sauce, mixing well. ✦ Cover with a layer of the provolone. ✦ Cover this with a layer of eggplant, add more meat sauce, and sprinkle with Parmigiano-Reggiano. Bake for 10 to 15 minutes.

PASTA AL FORNO
INVERNALE

BAKED WINTER PASTA

SICILIA

¼ lb. (1 stick) unsalted butter

Breadcrumbs

¼ cup extra-virgin olive oil

2 medium onions, chopped

2 lbs. ground lean beef

CONTINUED

Preheat the oven to 375°F. Grease a baking pan with butter and dust with breadcrumbs. Heat 2 tablespoons butter and the olive oil in a pan and sauté the onions. ✦ Add the meat, sausage, and wine; when the wine evaporates add the tomato paste. ✦ Add the broth and continue cooking until the meat is done and the sauce is reduced. ✦ Use the butter, flour, and milk to prepare a béchamel sauce as in the recipe on page 339. ✦ Add

7 oz. chopped sausage
½ cup white wine
2 tbsp. tomato paste
1 cup beef broth
Grated Parmigiano-Reggiano
2 lbs. *mezze penne rigate*
Salt and pepper

For the béchamel:
4 tbsp. unsalted butter
½ cup all-purpose flour
2 cups milk

Parmigiano-Reggiano to the béchamel. ✦ Cook the pasta in lightly salted boiling water and drain it when al dente; toss with the meat sauce and béchamel, adding more cheese. ✦ Pour the pasta into the pan and dot with the remaining butter. Bake for 20 minutes.

PASTA WITH MASCARPONE

PASTA AL MASCARPONE

LOMBARDIA

½ lb. *maltagliati* (see page 285) made with semolina flour
⅔ cup mascarpone
1 large egg yolk
Pinch grated nutmeg
Grated Parmigiano-Reggiano
Salt

This dish is typical of Lodi.

Cook the maltagliati in lightly salted boiling water for about 20 minutes at low heat. ✦ Mix the mascarpone, egg yolk, salt, and nutmeg. ✦ Whisk well to obtain a homogeneous mixture, adding a few tablespoons of the pasta cooking water if needed. ✦ When the pasta is cooked (and still hot) add it to the mascarpone mixture, adding Parmigiano-Reggiano to taste. Serve the pasta in heated plates.

SPAGHETTI WITH CUTTLEFISH INK

PASTA AL NERO DI SEPPIE

SICILIA

1 lb. cuttlefish
½ cup extra-virgin olive oil
2 garlic cloves
1⅔ cups chopped plum tomatoes
1 lb. spaghetti
Salt and black pepper

Remove the ink sac from the cuttlefish without breaking it and dice the fish. ✦ Heat the olive oil in a pan and sauté the garlic until golden. Add the tomatoes and cuttlefish; season with salt and pepper and at the last moment add the ink sac. ✦ Cook for another 30 minutes. ✦ Cook the spaghetti in lightly salted boiling water. Drain and toss with the sauce. Serve hot.

SPAGHETTI WITH PEPPERS, TOMATOES, AND GUANCIALE

PASTA ALLA JONICA

CALABRIA

¾ lb. fresh plum tomatoes, chopped
2 peppers, sweet or hot, chopped
¼ cup extra-virgin olive oil
2 garlic cloves
5 oz. guanciale, diced
Several basil leaves, chopped
1 lb. spaghetti
Grated pecorino
Salt

Cook the tomatoes and peppers in boiling water for a few minutes, drain, then pass them through a food mill. ✦ Heat the olive oil in a pan and sauté the garlic and guanciale. Add the tomato-pepper sauce and basil. ✦ Cook the spaghetti in lightly salted boiling water, drain when al dente, and toss with the sauce. Sprinkle with pecorino and serve immediately.

SPAGHETTI WITH EGGPLANT AND RICOTTA SALATA

PASTA ALLA NORMA

SICILIA

1¼ lbs. eggplant
2 lbs. tomato purée
Extra-virgin olive oil
1 medium onion, sliced
1 lb. spaghetti
4 oz. ricotta salata
1 bunch basil leaves
Salt and pepper

This dish was named in honor of the opera *Norma*, written by Vincenzo Bellini, born in Catania. Garlic can be used in place of the onion.

Peel the eggplant, slice, sprinkle with salt, and leave in a colander or under a weight for one hour to let the bitter taste drain out. ✦ Combine the tomato purée, ¼ cup olive oil, salt, pepper, and onion in a pan and cook until the mixture has reduced in volume by one-third. ✦ Heat 1 inch of olive oil in a pan and fry the eggplant until golden. ✦ Cook the spaghetti, drain well, and put in a bowl. ✦ Toss with half the ricotta salata, add the tomato sauce, basil, and more pepper and blend well. ✦ Transfer the pasta to individual bowls, and add slices of eggplant and the remaining ricotta salata. Decorate with basil leaves.

LINGUINE WITH SWORDFISH

PASTA ALL'USO DI BAGNARA

CALABRIA

½ lb. swordfish fillets
¼ cup extra-virgin olive oil
CONTINUED

This dish is typical of Bagnara.

Chop the fish into large chunks. Heat the olive oil in a pan and add the garlic and fish. ✦ After a few minutes add the tomatoes. When the fish has cooked and the sauce reduced, add the parsley and chili pepper. ✦ Cook

2 garlic cloves

¾ lb. peeled plum tomatoes

¼ cup chopped flat-leaf parsley

1 *diavolillo* (hot chili pepper,
see note, page 22), chopped

1 lb. linguine

the pasta in lightly salted boiling water; drain and add to
the pan. Serve immediately.

PASTA ASCIUTTA CON
LE MELANZANE FRITTE

PASTA WITH
FRIED EGGPLANTS

SICILIA

1 ½ fresh, large, ripe eggplants

Extra-virgin olive oil, for frying

1 lb. semolina pasta
(in the shape of your choosing)

Sprigs of basil for garnish

1 cup crumbled ricotta salata,
for dusting, optional

Coarse salt

Cut the eggplants in ½-inch-thick slices and arrange in
layers on a plate; spread each layer with coarse salt. Set
another plate over the eggplant and on top of this put
something heavy (at least 4 pounds). ✦ After 2 hours the
eggplants will have lost their bitter juice; rinse and set
them out to dry on paper towels, then cut them in ½-inch
dice. ✦ Heat ½ inch olive oil in a cast-iron skillet and fry
the eggplant until golden, stirring constantly to cook on
all sides. Using a slotted spoon remove the diced eggplant from the pan and drain on paper towels. ✦ Meanwhile cook the pasta in lightly salted boiling water; drain
when very al dente and leave in the colander. ✦ Transfer
the pasta to the pan and heat for a few minutes until it goes
from very al dente to al dente and picks up the flavor from
the cooking oil. ✦ Add the eggplant and stir over medium
heat for a few minutes. ✦ Serve the pasta and eggplant in
warmed plates decorated with sprigs of basil. The dish
can be completed with a dusting of ricotta salata.

PASTA CON BROCCOLO
IN TEGAME

PASTA WITH BROCCOLI
AND ANCHOVIES

SICILIA

Unsalted butter

1 head broccoli

½ cup extra-virgin olive oil

1 medium onion, finely chopped

2 salt-cured anchovy fillets,
dissolved in oil (or anchovy paste)

½ cup tomato paste

1 lb. peeled plum tomatoes

CONTINUED

Preheat the oven to 350°F. Grease a baking dish with butter. Parboil the broccoli in lightly salted water just until
very bright green; drain, reserving the cooking liquid.
Break off the florets, and set aside. ✦ Heat the olive oil
and sauté the onion, anchovies, tomato paste, and tomatoes. Add the florets. ✦ Cook, stirring often, and add the
cooked tomato sauce. ✦ Cover the pan and simmer until
the broccoli florets begin to come apart. ✦ Cook the bucatini in the broccoli cooking water; drain when al dente and
add to the pan with the broccoli sauce, mixing well. ✦

2 tablespoons cooked tomato sauce
(see page 327)
1 lb. bucatini
2 tbsp. pine nuts
2 tbsp. raisins
Grated Parmigiano-Reggiano

Add the pine nuts and raisins. ✦ Place in the prepared pan, dust with Parmigiano-Reggiano, and bake for about 1 hour, stirring often, until the sauce has thickened.

PASTA CON I BROCCOLI 1 | # PASTA WITH BROCCOLI 1

SICILIA

1 lb. broccoli
¼ cup extra-virgin olive oil
2 garlic cloves, chopped
1 lb. short pasta (ditalini)
¼ cup grated pecorino piccante
4 oz. fresh caciocavallo
4 oz. aged caciocavallo
Salt

This dish is typical of Siracusa.

Clean the broccoli and steam it in a colander over a pan of water until very bright green. ✦ When the broccoli is cooked break it into pieces. Heat the olive oil in a pan and sauté the garlic. Add the broccoli and salt. ✦ Cook the pasta in lightly salted boiling water until al dente. Drain and pour it into the pan with the broccoli and toss for a few minutes. ✦ Transfer to a serving bowl. Add the pecorino and two kinds of caciocavallo and serve.

✦ **LOCAL TRADITION** ✦

PASTA ASCIUTTA ALLA PUGLIESE

The breadth and variety of pasta dishes from Puglia reflect the place of honor these dishes—ranging from the simplest to the most elaborate preparations—held in the traditional Pugliese kitchen. Basic macaroni dishes dressed with artichokes, ricotta, cuttlefish sauce, or a fragrant sauce made with rue and tomatoes—especially common around Andria—represent some of the simpler pasta dishes common in Puglia. More complex dishes include baked pastas, layered with tomato sauce, mozzarella, and possibly mortadella, salame, or meatballs, and covered with breadcrumbs mixed with tomatoes. Special occasions would see a timbale at the table, another baked pasta dish characterized by a taller, narrower pan and sheets of a somewhat sweeter pasta forming the bottom and sides and topped with alternating layers of boiled macaroni, meatballs, sliced hard-boiled eggs, and soppressata, all blended with tomato sauce and olive oil. Timbales were traditionally served in thick slices on warm plates at ceremonial lunches. Stuffed rigatoni was another alternative for festive meals: The pasta would be half cooked, then filled with a mixture of cooked ground beef, mozzarella, provolone, and mortadella, layered with grated pecorino and tomato sauce, and baked.

PASTA WITH BROCCOLI 2

1 lb. broccoli

¼ cup extra-virgin olive oil

1 medium onion, finely sliced

1 pinch saffron

1 tbsp. raisins

1 tbsp. pine nuts

2 anchovies, dissolved in
extra-virgin olive oil

1 lb. short pasta

¼ cup grated pecorino

Several basil leaves, chopped

Salt

This dish is typical of Palermo. There is a wealth of variations of this recipe with the addition or omission of ingredients; the most interesting call for putting the mixture in an oven after arranging the pasta and broccoli in a pan, covering with cheese to give the dish a crust, and adding a little tomato sauce (in which case the saffron is omitted).

Boil the broccoli just until al dente (saving the water), and cut in pieces. Heat the olive oil in a pan and sauté the onion. Add the broccoli and toss. ✦ Add the saffron, raisins, pine nuts, and anchovies. ✦ Boil the pasta in the broccoli cooking water, drain, and add to the pan, tossing with the broccoli for a few minutes. Add the cheese and basil and serve.

PASTA WITH BROCCOLI 3

2 lbs. vegetables (preferably
broccoli rabe, otherwise broccoli
or cauliflower)

1 lb. pasta (preferably homemade)

½ cup extra-virgin olive oil

2 garlic cloves, unpeeled

8 salt-cured anchovies, boned,
cleaned, and finely chopped

1 *diavolillo* (hot chili pepper,
see note, page 22), minced

½ cup toasted breadcrumbs

Salt

Clean the vegetables and cut into pieces that are not too small. Put them in a pot with lightly salted water to cover and bring to a boil. ✦ When the vegetables are only just tender drain them, reserving the cooking water, and add the pasta to the water. ✦ When the pasta is nearly cooked return the vegetables to the pot to finish cooking with the pasta. ✦ Meanwhile heat the olive oil in a pan and sauté the garlic until it darkens; remove the pan from the heat and add the anchovies and chili pepper. ✦ Peel the garlic, return it to the pan, and mash these ingredients to form a paste. ✦ Drain the pasta and vegetables thoroughly and pour the sauce over them, mixing well and adding more olive oil if needed and the breadcrumbs. Serve hot.

PASTA WITH
FRIED BROCCOLI

1 lb. broccoli

¼ cup extra-virgin olive oil

This dish is typical of Enna.

Cook the broccoli in boiling lightly salted water until tender but firm, drain (reserving the water for the pasta), and cut in pieces. Heat the olive oil in a pan and sauté the

CONTINUED

2 garlic cloves, chopped

2 cups cooked tomato sauce
(see page 327)

1 lb. spaghetti

Grated pecorino

broccoli and garlic. ✦ Heat the tomato sauce. ✦ Cook the spaghetti in the broccoli cooking water, drain, and combine with the tomato sauce and broccoli. Add pecorino and serve.

**PASTA CON
LA BOTTARGA 1**

PASTA WITH BOTTARGA 1

CALABRIA

4 oz. *bottarga* of tuna (see note)

½ cup capers

½ cup extra-virgin olive oil

1 lb. spaghetti or linguine

Salt and black pepper

Bottarga is the Italian term for cured roe from gray mullet or from tuna. It is sometimes referred to as Mediterranean caviar. Most *bottarga* comes from the west coast of Sardegna.

Thinly slice the *bottarga,* crumble it, and mix with the capers, oil, salt, and pepper. ✦ Cook the pasta until al dente in boiling water (do not add salt); drain and toss with the *bottarga* sauce.

**PASTA CON
LA BOTTARGA 2**

PASTA WITH BOTTARGA 2

SICILIA

4 oz. *bottarga* (see note above)

2 garlic cloves

¼ cup finely chopped
flat-leaf parsley

¼ cup extra-virgin olive oil

1 lb. spaghetti or bucatini

Salt

Grate the *bottarga* into a bowl and add the garlic and parsley. ✦ Add the olive oil and, using a fork, work the mixture to form a paste. If this operation proves difficult, add a few tablespoons of lukewarm water, but doing so should not be necessary if the *bottarga* is of good quality, pink, and compact. ✦ Cook the pasta in unsalted boiling water (*bottarga* is very salty) and drain when al dente; mix with the sauce and serve hot.

PASTA CON LA MOLLICA 1

PASTA WITH BREADCRUMBS AND ANCHOVIES 1

SICILIA

1 cup breadcrumbs

1 lb. spaghetti

¼ cup extra-virgin olive oil

10 salt-cured anchovies,
cleaned and boned

Salt

Known as *Pasta con la mollica* around Siracusa, this dish changes name in other locales, becoming *Pasta c'anciovi* and *Pasta a muddica.* Some people add chopped garlic to the anchovy sauce. The most popular local type of pasta for this dish is called "tagghiarini," meaning tagliolini, but spaghetti works just as well.

Toast the breadcrumbs in a pan over medium heat until they darken (turning the shade of a monk's tunic, according to a local saying); set aside. ✦ Cook the pasta in lightly salted boiling water. Heat the olive oil in a pan and cook the anchovies until they break down to form a sauce. ✦ Drain the pasta and toss with the anchovy sauce, adding the breadcrumbs.

PASTA WITH BREADCRUMBS AND ANCHOVIES 2

PASTA CON LA MOLLICA DI PANE

CALABRIA

4 salt-cured anchovies
½ cup extra-virgin olive oil
4 tbsp. breadcrumbs
Good pinch chili pepper flakes
1 lb. long pasta (bucatini, spaghetti)
Salt

This is a traditional meatless dish for Christmas Eve.

Clean and fillet the anchovies. Heat the olive oil in a pan and sauté the anchovies until they dissolve and become a paste. ✦ In another pan toast the breadcrumbs. Add the chili pepper flakes. ✦ Cook the pasta in lightly salted boiling water to cover. Drain and toss with the anchovy paste then the breadcrumbs. Serve hot.

PASTA WITH SARDINES, ANCHOVIES, AND BREADCRUMBS

PASTA CON LA MOLLICA 2

SICILIA

1 fennel bulb
½ cup extra-virgin olive oil
1 medium onion, finely chopped
1 lb. fresh sardines, boned
1 tbsp. tomato paste, diluted in 2 tbsp. water
4 oz. salt-cured anchovies, boned
¼ cup breadcrumbs
1 lb. short pasta

This dish is typical of Catania.

Boil the fennel until softened, drain (reserving the liquid), and cut in pieces. ✦ Heat half the olive oil in a pan and sauté the onion. Add the sardines and toss. Add the tomato paste mixture. ✦ Simmer 20 minutes, adding a little water from time to time so the pan doesn't go completely dry, then add the fennel. ✦ In a separate pan heat the remaining olive oil and cook the anchovies until they break down; add the breadcrumbs, stirring constantly to achieve a brown color. ✦ Boil the pasta in the fennel cooking water; toss it with the sardine mixture. Spoon onto plates and add some of the breadcrumb mixture to each.

PASTA WITH TURNIP TOPS

PASTA CON LE CIME DI RAPA

BASILICATA

For the pasta:
2 cups semolina flour, plus more as needed
CONTINUED

To give the dish even more flavor, toast the breadcrumbs in butter and sprinkle over the cooked pasta like cheese.

Use the flour to prepare a pasta dough as in the recipe on page 10, using 6 tablespoons water in place of the eggs. ✦ Roll out a sheet of dough ⅛ inch thick (see page 212) and cut out pieces shaped like almonds. ✦ Cook the pieces of pasta in boiling lightly salted water together

For the sauce:

8 cups chopped turnip tops

½ cup extra-virgin olive oil

3 garlic cloves

Salt

with the turnip tops; drain when the pasta is cooked to al dente. ✦ Heat the olive oil in a pan and sauté the garlic. ✦ Toss this with the cooked pasta and turnip tops.

PASTA CON LE FAVE

PASTA AND FAVA BEANS

ABRUZZO

¼ cup extra-virgin olive oil

2 oz. pancetta, diced

1 large onion, thinly sliced

1¼ lbs. fresh peeled fava beans

2 tbsp. chopped fresh marjoram

Pinch chili pepper flakes

¼ cup tomato purée

¾ lb. maltagliati (see page 285)

Salt

This dish is typical of the Vomano valley. It is best not to use cheese, but if desired grated pecorino would be best. Instead of the maltagliati, the local peasants used to prepare tagliolini using durum wheat flour (fettuccine), water, and salt without eggs.

Heat the olive oil in a pan and sauté the pancetta and onion. Add the fava beans and marjoram, salt, and a pinch of chili pepper. ✦ After about 15 minutes add the tomato purée. ✦ Cook the maltagliati until al dente, but do not drain off all the cooking water. ✦ Mix the maltagliati and a little cooking water in the pan with the fava bean sauce, cover, and let sit 5 minutes before serving.

PASTA CON LE SARDE 1

PASTA WITH SARDINES 1

SICILIA

½ cup extra-virgin olive oil

1 large head wild fennel

1 medium onion, chopped

3 salt-cured anchovies, boned and rinsed

¾ lb. fresh sardine fillets

¼ cup raisins

¼ cup pine nuts

2 tbsp. ground, toasted chestnuts

1 pinch saffron threads

8 whole fresh sardines, butterflied

6 tbsp. breadcrumbs

1½ lbs. pasta (*perciatelli, cannolicchi,* bucatini)

Salt and pepper

This is the standard Palermo recipe, but of course there are several variations. One version does without the breadcrumbs; another skips the time in the oven and has the pasta served immediately after being seasoned; yet a third puts the dish in the oven but with the pasta and seasonings arranged in layers rather than being mixed together.

Preheat the oven to 425°F. Grease a baking pan with olive oil. Wash the fennel and put it in a pot of boiling lightly salted water; cook it for 15 minutes after the water returns to a boil. ✦ Drain the fennel, reserving the water, and press it against a hard surface to remove all the water, then cut it in thin slices ½ to 1 inch in length. ✦ Heat half the olive oil in a pan and sauté the onion; add the anchovies, stirring them until they dissolve, then add the sardine fillets, raisins, pine nuts, chestnuts, and saffron. ✦ Taste for salt and pepper, stir delicately, and cook for 10 minutes. ✦ In another pan heat the remaining olive oil and cook the whole sardines. ✦ In another pan toast the breadcrumbs until they darken slightly. ✦ Boil the pasta in the fennel cooking water and drain when al dente. ✦ Toss the pasta with the sardine sauce, and transfer to the baking pan. Dust the surface with breadcrumbs, and cover with the whole sardines. ✦ Bake for 8 to 10 minutes.

PASTA WITH SARDINES 2

PASTA CON LE SARDE 2

SICILIA

Several bunches wild fennel
¼ cup extra-virgin olive oil
2 medium onions, finely sliced
2 salt-cured anchovies
2 lbs. fresh sardines, boned and butterflied
3 tbsp. white wine
¼ cup pine nuts
¼ cup raisins
1 pinch saffron
1 tsp. anchovy paste
½ cup breadcrumbs
1 lb. bucatini
Salt

Boil the fennel in water to cover, drain well, chop in pieces, and set aside. ✦ Heat half the olive oil in a pan and sauté the onions with the anchovies; add about half of the sardines. ✦ Add the fennel, 2 tablespoons water, wine, and salt. ✦ When this is well mixed and the sardines are crumbling, add the remaining sardines, which will remain more intact than the first, along with the pine nuts, raisins, and saffron. ✦ Heat the olive oil in a pan and add the anchovy paste. Add the breadcrumbs and toast until lightly browned. ✦ Cook the bucatini in lightly salted boiling water until al dente, drain, and toss with the sardine mixture. Sprinkle with the breadcrumb mixture and serve.

PASTA WITH BREADED TOMATOES

PASTA CON POMODORI GRATINATI

PUGLIA

1 cup extra-virgin olive oil
10 ripe plum tomatoes
1 cup breadcrumbs
2 garlic cloves, chopped
1 lb. pasta, preferably *mezza zita* or bucatini
1 tbsp. chopped oregano
Salt

This dish is typical of Foggia.

Preheat the oven to 350°F. Grease a baking pan with olive oil. Cut the tomatoes in half and remove the seeds. Arrange them cut side up across the bottom of the pan; sprinkle the breadcrumbs over the tomatoes and drizzle with olive oil, then sprinkle with salt and garlic. ✦ Put the pan in the oven and at the same time begin heating the water to cook the pasta. ✦ By the time the pasta is cooked to al dente the tomatoes should be gratinéed. ✦ Drain the pasta and mix with the tomatoes. Add oregano and, if needed, more olive oil. Serve hot.

PASTA WITH CAULIFLOWER

PASTA E CAVOLFIORE DI S. AGATA

CAMPANIA

1 medium cauliflower
½ cup extra-virgin olive oil
2 garlic cloves
½ cup pitted Gaeta olives
1 lb. mixed pasta
Salt and pepper

Clean the cauliflower and chop it in pieces, cutting away the hard parts; cook it in a covered pan over low heat with olive oil and garlic until tender but still firm. ✦ When it is almost cooked add the olives. ✦ Meanwhile cook the pasta until al dente. Drain, setting aside a cup of the cooking water. ✦ Add the pasta to the cauliflower and cook together, adding a little of the pasta water from time to time. Before serving add a few grinds of fresh pepper and salt to taste.

PASTA, POLENTA & RICE

PASTA AND WHITE BEANS

PASTA E FAGIOLI BIANCHI

BASILICATA

1 lb. dried white beans
1 celery stalk, chopped
2 garlic cloves
1 lb. smooth tubular pasta (ziti or penne)
¼ tsp. *peperone crusco* (may substitute paprika, sweet or hot according to taste)
¼ lb. pancetta, finely diced

Peperone crusco is sweet or hot pepper, which comes from Matera and Potenza and is considered a specialty of Basilicata.

Soak the white beans overnight to soften them. ✦ The next day drain, then add fresh water to cover by several inches. Add the celery and 1 clove garlic; boil until the beans are tender, about 2 hours. Drain. ✦ Cook the pasta in lightly salted boiling water until very al dente and drain. ✦ Add the pasta to the beans. Heat the olive oil in a pan and sauté the remaining garlic. Add the red pepper and pancetta and stir until lightly browned. ✦ Cook these together until the pasta goes from being very al dente to al dente, then combine everything and serve.

BAKED PASTA AND POTATOES

FOR
6 PERSONS

PASTA E PATATE AL FORNO

CALABRIA

½ lb. fresh plum tomatoes, peeled, seeded, and chopped
½ medium onion, sliced
¼ cup extra-virgin olive oil
1 green pepper, sweet or spicy, seeded
Several basil leaves, chopped

CONTINUED

Preheat the oven to 400°F. Combine the tomatoes with the onion in a pan and cook in olive oil over low heat for a few minutes. ✦ Add the pepper, basil, and salt and continue cooking. ✦ Cook the pasta in lightly salted boiling water together with the potatoes, draining them and separating them. ✦ In a large ovenproof pan arrange a layer of potatoes; add some of the sauce and add some of the sausage (or salame) and cheese. Follow this with a layer of pasta; add more sauce then more sausage and

½ lb. ziti or penne

½ lb. potatoes, peeled and sliced

6 oz. sausage (or *soppressata*), chopped

3 oz. caciocavallo, sliced

Salt

cheese. ✦ Having used up the ingredients, bake until the cheese is melted and golden, about 20 minutes.

PASTA E PATATI
CA TRIMMA

PASTA WITH POTATOES AND EGGS

CALABRIA

¼ cup extra-virgin olive oil

4 new potatoes, rinsed and diced

4 large eggs, beaten

½ cup grated pecorino

¼ cup chopped flat-leaf parsley

¾ lb. pasta (ditali or other short tubes)

Salt and black pepper

Heat the olive oil in a large pan and sauté the potatoes until golden. Add salt, remove with a slotted spoon, and drain on paper towels. ✦ Mix the eggs, pecorino, and parsley and set aside. ✦ Cook the pasta in lightly salted boiling water and drain when very al dente. ✦ Put the pasta in the pan with the remaining oil from frying the potatoes; add the potatoes, egg mixture, and a pinch of black pepper. Stir until the eggs begin to set and in that instant serve.

PASTA FATTA IN CASA
CON RAGÙ DI MAIALE

HOMEMADE PASTA WITH PORK SAUCE

CALABRIA

For the pasta:

1 ⅔ cups semolina flour, plus more as needed

For the sauce:

2 tbsp. extra-virgin olive oil

1 garlic clove, chopped

1 small onion, chopped

2 or 3 tbsp. chopped flat-leaf parsley

¾ lb. lean pork, diced

¼ cup red wine

1 ¼ lbs. plum tomatoes, peeled and seeded

1 *diavolillo* (hot chili pepper, see note, page 22)

½ cup grated pecorino

Salt

Use the flour and ½ cup water to make a pasta dough as in the recipe on page 10. Roll out into a sheet ½ inch thick; cut this into 1-inch pieces. By hand flatten each piece and stretch it out to obtain strips 2 ½ inches long and 1 inch wide. ✦ Arrange on a clean dishcloth, cover with a second cloth, and let dry. Meanwhile, heat the olive oil and sauté the garlic, onion, and 1 tablespoon parsley. Add the pork and brown it, then pour in the wine. ✦ When the wine has evaporated add the tomatoes, the remaining parsley, salt, and chili pepper. ✦ Cook the sauce at low heat for 1 hour. ✦ Cook the pasta in lightly salted boiling water and drain when somewhat al dente. Toss the pasta with the sauce and pecorino. Serve hot.

PASTA WITH POTATOES AND PANCETTA

PASTA RUSTIDA

PIEMONTE

2 lbs. ditalini
6 potatoes, peeled and diced
3 tbsp. unsalted butter
½ lb. toma cheese, diced
1 medium onion, sliced
1 lb. pancetta, diced
Salt

This dish is typical of the Valle Vigezzo.

Combine the pasta and potatoes in a pot with water to cover by several inches. Heat, adding salt the moment the water boils. ✦ Drain when very al dente and toss with 1 tablespoon butter and 1 tablespoon cheese to keep the pasta from sticking together. ✦ Heat the remaining butter over low heat and sauté the onion, making sure it doesn't burn. ✦ Add the pancetta and when it is golden put it in the pan with the pasta and potatoes and toss. ✦ Add the remaining cheese, toss again briefly, and serve piping hot.

ZITI AND MEATBALLS

PASTA SEDUTA

PUGLIA

¾ lb. ziti
Light meat sauce (see page 329)
Fried meatballs (see page 105)
¼ cup grated Parmigiano-Reggiano

Cook the pasta in lightly salted boiling water and drain it when al dente. ✦ Meanwhile, heat the sauce and add the meatballs. Bring to a simmer and cook until the pasta is cooked. ✦ Toss the pasta with the cheese, meat sauce, and meatballs in the top of a double boiler. ✦ Cover and heat for 5 to 7 minutes before serving.

UNCLE VINCENZO'S RIGATONI (RIGATONI WITH ANCHOVIES, BROCCOLI, AND BREADCRUMBS)

FOR 6 PERSONS

PASTASCIUTTA DI ZIO VINCENZO

SICILIA

⅔ cup tomato purée
2 garlic cloves
2 salt-cured anchovy fillets
1 *diavolillo* (hot chili pepper, see note, page 22)
1 lb. rigatoni
1⅔ cups small pieces steamed and chopped broccoli, still warm
½ cup toasted breadcrumbs
1 tbsp. chopped flat-leaf parsley
½ cup pitted and finely chopped black olives

Put the tomato purée, garlic, anchovies, and chili pepper in a blender and pulse until combined. ✦ Cook the rigatoni in boiling salted water and drain when al dente. ✦ Toss the rigatoni in a bowl with the tomato mixture, adding the broccoli. ✦ Before serving sprinkle with breadcrumbs, parsley, and olives.

BAKED MUSHROOM CRESPELLE

TRENTINO

For the crespelle:

3 large eggs, beaten

3 tbsp. all-purpose flour, plus more as needed

2½ cups milk

Salt

For the filling:

¼ cup extra-virgin olive oil

3 tbsp. unsalted butter

1 garlic clove, minced

1¾ lbs. porcini mushrooms, thinly sliced

2 tbsp. flat-leaf parsley

1¼ lbs. spinach

1 recipe (3 cups) béchamel sauce, made with half broth and half milk (see page 339)

Grated Parmigiano-Reggiano

Salt and pepper

Mix the eggs, flour, milk, and a pinch of salt to prepare a batter. Prepare 20 very thin crespelle (crepe) as in the recipe on page 234. ✦ Preheat the oven to 400°F. Heat the olive oil and 1 tablespoon butter in a pan. Add the garlic and mushrooms and sauté. Add the parsley, salt, and pepper and set aside. ✦ Steam the spinach in about 1 inch of water until bright green; drain very well and chop, then mix in the remaining butter, salt, and pepper. ✦ Combine half the béchamel with the spinach mixture and 2 tablespoons Parmigiano-Reggiano until blended. ✦ Reserve ½ cup mushrooms. Place one crespelle in a round baking pan, spread with 1 tablespoon of the green béchamel, cover with another crespelle, spread with 1 tablespoon mushrooms, and dot with butter. Cover with another crespelle, spread with 1 tablespoon white béchamel, and so on until the ingredients are used up. ✦ Bake for a few minutes, garnish with the reserved mushrooms, and serve.

MACARONI PIE 1

FOR 6 PERSONS

EMILIA-ROMAGNA

For the sauce:

½ cup (¼ lb.) unsalted butter

¼ cup dry white wine

1 tbsp. Marsala

½ cup extra-virgin olive oil

6 oz. ground veal

6 oz. ground beef

6 oz. ground chicken breast or squab

6 oz. chicken giblets

1 celery stalk, chopped

1 medium onion, chopped

1 carrot, chopped

CONTINUED

This dish is typical of Ferrara. The version of this *pasticcio*, which is made in Piacenza, has very little veal and pork and instead a rich stuffing made of sweetbreads combined with the meat of boned stewed squab.

Butter a baking pan. ✦ Mix the wine and Marsala. Heat 1 tablespoon each of the olive oil and butter in a pan and sauté the ground veal, adding and cooking off 1 tablespoon of the wine mixture. Repeat with the remaining meats, cooking them separately, then combine all of them. Heat the remaining olive oil and sauté the celery, onion, and carrot until soft, then mix with the meat mixture. ✦ Use the butter, flour, milk, and nutmeg to prepare a béchamel sauce as in the recipe on page 339; set aside. ✦ Preheat the oven to 400°F. Cook the macaroni in lightly salted boiling water until al dente. Drain and toss with the béchamel, meat sauce, and Parmigiano-

For the béchamel sauce:

1 tbsp. unsalted butter

2 tsp. all-purpose flour

2 cups milk

Pinch grated nutmeg

For the stuffing:

¾ lb. macaroni rigati

½ cup grated Parmigiano-Reggiano

Salt

Truffle (optional)

For the pasta:

3 cups all-purpose flour,
plus more as needed

⅔ cup sugar

5 large egg yolks

1½ sticks plus 2 tbsp. unsalted butter

1 tbsp. lemon zest

Salt

Reggiano. Mix delicately and season with salt. ✦ Sift together the flour and sugar, then use them and 4 egg yolks to prepare a pasta dough as in recipe on page 10, adding the butter and lemon zest with the egg yolks. Roll out the pasta to form two sheets (see page 212). Use one to line the baking pan. ✦ Fill this with the pasta mixture, adding some shavings of truffle if desired, and cover with the second sheet, sealing the edges. ✦ Brush the surface with the remaining egg yolk then bake until the surface has browned, about 25 minutes.

PASTICCIO
DI MACCHERONI 2

MACARONI PIE 2

FOR
12 PERSONS

VENETO

For the stuffing:

6 oz. dried mushrooms
(preferably porcini)

¼ cup extra-virgin olive oil

1 garlic clove, minced

2 tbsp. chopped flat-leaf parsley

1 tbsp. all-purpose flour,
plus more as needed

1 tbsp. butter, softened

1¼ lb. ziti (or penne), not too large

1¼ cups grated Parmigiano-
Reggiano

Salt

For the pastry dough:

4½ cups all-purpose flour,
plus more as needed

2½ sticks (10 oz.) butter, softened

⅔ cup sugar

2 large eggs plus 2 yolks

¼ cup Marsala

Salt

Soak the dried mushrooms for a few hours, then rinse them carefully and drain. Heat the olive oil in a pan and sauté the garlic, parsley, and flour. Add 1 cup of water and simmer for about 30 minutes. ✦ Use all the dough ingredients except for 1 yolk to prepare a dough as in the recipe on page 10. Let it rest for 15 minutes in a cool place. ✦ Preheat the oven to 350°F. Grease a high-sided baking dish with butter. Cook the ziti (or penne) in lightly salted boiling water, drain, and toss with the mushrooms, one third of the cheese, and 1 tablespoon butter. ✦ Roll out the dough to form two sheets, one larger than the other, and use the larger to line the baking dish. Fill this with the pasta mixture. Cover the pie with the second sheet of pastry dough, seal the edges, and brush with the remaining egg yolk. ✦ Bake for 45 minutes until golden.

PASTA AND PROSCIUTTO PIE

FOR 6 TO 8
PERSONS

FRIULI-VENEZIA GIULIA

4 tbsp. unsalted butter, softened

1⅔ cups all-purpose flour,
plus more as needed

4 large eggs (separate 2 of them)

1 tbsp. extra-virgin olive oil

6 oz. prosciutto crudo,
cut in small cubes

⅔ cup heavy cream

Salt

Preheat the oven to 350°F. Grease a baking pan with butter. Use the flour and 2 eggs to prepare a pasta dough as in the recipe on page 10. ✦ Roll out the dough to a thin sheet (see page 212), then use a pastry wheel to cut the dough into 6-inch squares. ✦ Add 1 tablespoon olive oil to a pot of water and bring to boil. Add the pasta and cook until al dente, then drain and set out to dry on a cloth. ✦ Whip the remaining egg whites until stiff. Mix the butter with the remaining egg yolks and add the prosciutto and cream. Fold in the egg whites. ✦ In the prepared pan alternate layers of pasta with the mixture until the ingredients are used up, ending with a layer of pasta. ✦ Bake for about 45 minutes until the pasta is golden.

BAKED PROSCIUTTO AND HERB PIE

PASTICCIO DI
PROSCIUTTO ED ERBE

FOR
6 PERSONS

VENETO

For the dough:

1½ cups all-purpose flour,
plus more as needed

6 tbsp. unsalted butter

2 tbsp. extra-virgin olive oil

1 large egg yolk

Salt

For the stuffing:

10 oz. prosciutto crudo

2 large eggs, beaten

4 oz. fresh Asiago, sliced

1⅔ cups mixed herbs,
sautéed in olive oil until fragrant

This recipe from the area of the Euganean Hills near Padua dates to the nineteenth century.

Use the flour, butter, olive oil, and egg yolk to make a dough as in the recipe on page 10; let the dough rest 2 hours. ✦ Preheat the oven to 350°F. Roll out the dough to form two sheets, one larger than the other, and use the larger one to line a high-sided narrow oven pan. ✦ Cut the prosciutto into small cubes. Mix the eggs and prosciutto, and pour this into the pan to form a layer. ✦ Cover this with the Asiago, then the herbs. Close with the second sheet of dough, seal the edges, and pierce with a fork. ✦ Bake for 45 minutes until golden.

BAKED TORTELLINI

3 cups all-purpose flour,
plus more as needed

⅓ cup sugar

½ cup (¼ lb.) unsalted butter,
chilled and cut into pieces

2 large eggs, beaten

1 lb. tortellini

6 cups meat broth

1 ½ cups Bolognese meat sauce
(see page 330)

⅔ cup grated Parmigiano-Reggiano

1 large egg yolk

Salt

This dish is typical of Bologna.

Sift the flour, sugar, and a pinch of salt together. Using your fingers, work in 6 tablespooons butter to create a mixture the consistency of wet sand, then mix in the eggs, kneading to create a smooth dough. Add more flour if the dough is at all sticky. ✦ Let the dough rest under a clean cloth for about 30 minutes. ✦ Preheat the oven to 350°F. Butter and flour a baking dish. On a floured surface, roll out slightly more than half of the dough, then use it to cover the bottom and sides of the prepared dish. Refrigerate this (and the other half of the dough) while preparing the filling. ✦ Cook the tortellini in the broth, draining when still slightly al dente. ✦ Put them in a bowl and toss with half of the meat sauce. ✦ Form a layer of tortellini in the dish, dot with half of the remaining butter, some of the remaining meat sauce, and some of the cheese. ✦ Continue making these layers, using up all the ingredients. ✦ Roll out the remaining dough and cover the filling, using the tines of a fork to seal the two edges together. ✦ Brush the surface with egg yolk and prick it a few times with a fork. ✦ Bake for about 40 minutes until golden. Let cool in the pan for 10 minutes before serving.

HOMEMADE PASTA WITH TOMATOES AND GARLIC

For the pasta:

3 cups all-purpose flour,
plus more as needed

For the sauce:

¼ cup extra-virgin olive oil

1 garlic clove

1 lb. peeled plum tomatoes,
chopped

Pinch chili pepper flakes

Salt

Use the flour to prepare a pasta dough as in the recipe on page 10, using 1 cup water in place of the eggs. Taking small pieces at a time, work the dough by hand to obtain thick spaghetti about 8 inches long. ✦ Cook these in boiling lightly salted water and drain when al dente. ✦ Meanwhile heat the olive oil in a pan and sauté the garlic until golden. Add the tomatoes and cook 15 minutes until thickened. Season with salt and chili pepper. Toss with the cooked pasta and serve hot.

HOMEMADE PASTA WITH GUANCIALE AND SAUSAGE

PENCHI

UMBRIA

For the pasta:

3 cups all-purpose flour, plus more as needed

2 large eggs

For the sauce:

2 oz. guanciale, diced

3 sausages, crumbled

2 large eggs, beaten

3 tbsp. lemon juice

3 tbsp. butter, melted and cooled slightly

1 pinch grated nutmeg

Grated Parmigiano-Reggiano

Salt and pepper

Use the flour and eggs to prepare a pasta dough as in the recipe on page 10. Roll out to a sheet ⅛ inch thick (see page 212), then cut into 1-inch strips; these are the *penchi*. ✦ Heat the guanciale in a saucepan until it starts to give off its fat, then add the sausage. ✦ When the guanciale and sausage are cooked, drain off some of the fat. ✦ Mix the eggs, lemon juice, butter, nutmeg, salt, and pepper. ✦ Cook the *penchi* and drain when al dente, then add them to the pan with the guanciale mixture. ✦ Add the egg mixture and stir together over low heat. Season with Parmigiano-Reggiano and serve right away.

PENNE WITH HOT CHILES, PROSCIUTTO, AND TOMATO

PENNE ALL'ARRABBIATA

LAZIO

4 tbsp. extra-virgin olive oil

6 oz. prosciutto crudo, cut in small cubes

½ *diavolillo* (hot chili pepper, see note, page 22)

2 garlic cloves, crushed

1 lb. plum tomatoes, peeled and seeded

2 basil leaves, chopped

1 lb. penne

½ cup grated Parmigiano-Reggiano, mixed with ½ cup grated pecorino

Salt

This dish was created in the 1930s by Giovanni Cotellesi, owner of the restaurant Alfredo alla Chiesa Nuova, frequented by the poet Carlo Alberto Salustri (a.k.a. Trilussa) and other well-known Roman gourmets. It was originally made with spaghetti, but penne are now preferred.

Heat the oil in a pan and sauté the prosciutto, chili pepper, and garlic. ✦ Remove the garlic and chili pepper and add the tomatoes. ✦ Season with salt, add the basil, and cook 15 minutes. ✦ In lightly salted boiling water cook the penne and drain when al dente. ✦ Transfer to a heated serving bowl, dress with the blended cheeses, and cover with the sauce. Mix and serve hot.

PENNE WITH TOMATOES AND BASIL

PENNETTE E POMODORINI
D'O PIENNULO

CAMPANIA

1 garlic clove
Pinch chili pepper flakes
⅔ cup extra-virgin olive oil
½ lb. plum tomatoes (if possible
Ischian), peeled and chopped
1 lb. pennette
Several basil leaves, chopped
Salt

This dish is typical of Ischia.

Crush the garlic and combine it with the chili pepper and olive oil in a large pan over low heat. ✦ Remove the garlic when golden and add the tomatoes. Add salt to taste and cook for 15 minutes at high heat. ✦ Cook the pennette in boiling lightly salted water and drain when al dente. ✦ Put the pennette in the pan with the sauce, adding a few basil leaves. Serve hot.

PEPPERS STUFFED WITH PASTA

PEPERONI DI PULCINELLA

CAMPANIA

4 sweet peppers,
halved lengthwise and seeded
⅓ cup extra-virgin olive oil
1 *diavolillo* (hot chili pepper,
see note, page 22)
1 garlic clove
2 salt-cured anchovies,
boned and cleaned
¾ lb. peeled plum tomatoes
¼ cup capers, crushed
½ cup pitted Gaeta olives
2 tbsp. chopped flat-leaf parsley
½ lb. bucatini
Salt and pepper

This dish is typical of Naples. The dish has increased visual appeal if different colored peppers are used.

Preheat the oven to 450°F. Roast the peppers in the oven until their skins are wrinkled. Cover the pan with foil and let them stand until they are cool enough to handle, then peel them, taking care to crush them as little as possible. Reduce the oven temperature to 350°F. ✦ Meanwhile, in a pan heat the olive oil over medium heat. Sauté the chili pepper and garlic (remove and discard the garlic when golden). Add the anchovies and cook them until they dissolve. ✦ Add the tomatoes, crushing them with a fork. Salt to taste and add the capers, olives, and parsley and simmer. ✦ As the sauce thickens, cook the bucatini in lightly salted boiling water until very al dente, then drain and add to the sauce, tossing to mix. ✦ Stuff the peppers with the bucatini mixture, then arrange the stuffed peppers in a baking pan, season with salt and pepper, and bake for 15 to 20 minutes, or until the bucatini is al dente.

PASTA WITH SNAILS

PERCIATELLI
CON LE LUMACHE

CALABRIA

40 snails (give or take)
¼ cup extra-virgin olive oil
CONTINUED

Purge and clean the snails as in the recipe on page 16. Boil them for about an hour, then pull them out of their shells and cut off the bitter black tails. ✦ In a large pan heat the olive oil and sauté the onion, garlic, and chili pepper. ✦ Add the parsley, tomatoes, salt, and pepper. ✦

315

1 medium onion, chopped
1 garlic clove
1 *diavolillo* (hot chili pepper, see page 22), chopped
3 tbsp. chopped flat-leaf parsley
3 ripe plum tomatoes, chopped
1 lb. pasta (perciatelli)
Grated pecorino
Salt and black pepper

After about 10 minutes add the snails, pour in about 1 cup of water, and cook at medium heat about 45 minutes. ✦ Meanwhile cook the pasta in lightly salted boiling water until al dente, drain it, and put it in the pan with the snails for a few minutes, stirring well. Serve with pecorino.

HOMEMADE TWISTED PASTA

PICI

TOSCANA

2½ cups all-purpose flour, plus more as needed
Pasta sauce as on page 331
Salt

This dish is typical of the Amiata. *Pici* date back to antiquity.

Use the flour to prepare a pasta dough as in the recipe on page 10, using ¾ cup water in place of the eggs. ✦ Let the dough rest, covered, for about 20 minutes. ✦ Roll the dough out to the thickness of ¼ inch (see page 212) and cut it in strips ½ inch wide. Twist each ribbon by hand to create *pici,* a kind of very long, twisted shape. As you make them, keep the *pici* covered by a cloth. ✦ Cook the *pici* in boiling lightly salted water, drain, and toss with tomato sauce, a meat sauce, or with the sauces for the recipes *Salsa briciolata* (see below) or *Salsa di salsicce* (see page 73).

TWISTED PASTA IN BREAD SAUCE

PICI CON SALSA BRICIOLATA

TOSCANA

4 stale rolls, without crusts
½ cup extra-virgin olive oil
1 garlic clove
1 recipe *pici* (see above), cooked until al dente and drained, but still hot
Salt

This dish is typical of Cortona. Be careful that the end result is seasoned but not oily pasta. A touch of chili pepper added to the pan is by no means out of place.

Grate the bread so that it will not be as finely ground as what is sold in stores. Heat the olive oil in a cast-iron skillet and add the garlic. Add the grated bread and toast until golden; season for salt. ✦ Toss with the cooked *pici.*

CORN PONE
WITH TURNIPS

MOLISE

For the pizza:
3 ½ cups cornmeal
3 tbsp. extra-virgin olive oil
Salt

For the sauce:
As many pork rinds as desired
2 lbs. white turnips
1 *diavolillo* (hot chili pepper,
see note, page 22)
Salt

This dish is typical of Ripalimosani.

Preheat the oven to 375°F. Use the cornmeal, ¾ cup water, the olive oil, and a pinch of salt to create a dough as in the recipe on page 10. Pat the dough out to ¼ inch thick on a baking sheet, then bake until golden and lightly browned. ✦ Clean the pork rinds, flame them, scrape with the blade of a knife to remove any remaining bristles, then rinse and cook them in a pan with enough water to cover. ✦ Salt and cook at moderate heat, skimming the broth from time to time; when cooked remove them and cut in pieces. ✦ Meanwhile peel the turnips and cut them into wedges. Boil them in lightly salted water until they are tender but not falling apart. ✦ Drain and mix with the pork rind pieces; when the crust is cooked, cut it up and add it to the turnips, crushing it with a fork. Work until well mixed. ✦ Add the chili pepper and return to the oven for 15 minutes, or until the crust is browned and the turnips are golden. Serve hot.

✦ **LOCAL TRADITION** ✦

PIZZICONI

While this dish of dumplings in tomato sauce from Lazio, especially the area of Cittaducale, is very simple, true *pizziconi* require the unique flavor that comes from *cruschello*, or whole-wheat flour. Using the thumb and index finger, the cook would simply tear small chunks off of the ball of pasta dough and toss them immediately into boiling salted water. While the *pizziconi* were technically finished cooking as soon as they floated, tradition dictated that they were cooked a few moments longer before being tossed with a simple sauce of olive oil, garlic, tomato purée, and chili pepper.

BUCKWHEAT PASTA WITH CABBAGE

LOMBARDIA

2 ⅓ cups buckwheat flour,
plus more as needed

⅔ cup all-purpose flour,
plus more as needed

1 lb. Savoy cabbage, outer leaves
removed and head cored and
cut into 2-inch strips (or
torn into strips by hand)

1 ⅔ cups grated Parmigiano-
Reggiano

1 lb. young *casera* cheese
(may substitute Taleggio)

3 ½ sticks (14 oz.) unsalted butter

4 garlic cloves, sliced,
any green core removed

Salt

This dish is widespread in the Valtellina area of northern Lombardia and also in the bordering upper Val Camonica. The amount of butter—nearly 8 tablespoons per person—may seem excessive, but this is the original dish, from Teglio, where the portions of *pizzoccheri* are served in plates drowned in butter.

Blend the two flours, then use them and 1 cup water to make a dough as in the recipe on page 10. ✦ Roll out a sheet to a thickness just under ¼ inch (see page 212) and cut into strips ½ inch wide and 3 inches long; stack them, and cut lengthwise into strips about ¼ inch wide to form the *pizzoccheri*. ✦ Put the pieces of cabbage in lightly salted boiling water. ✦ After 5 minutes salt the water and add the *pizzoccheri*, which should cook in rapidly boiling water 7 to 10 minutes. ✦ Before draining taste them to be sure they are soft but not overly cooked; do this also with the cabbage, which should maintain a certain resistance. ✦ Using a slotted spoon or strainer, remove some *pizzoccheri* and cabbage from the pot and place in a bowl. ✦ Sprinkle with Parmigiano-Reggiano and cover with *casera*, continuing the layers until using up the ingredients. ✦ Meanwhile heat the butter in a pan and cook the garlic just until golden, then pour the mixture over the *pizzoccheri*. Serve in warmed plates.

ROMAGNA-STYLE POLENTA

EMILIA-ROMAGNA

3 cups cornmeal

Salt

This dish is typical of Romagna. In the past, polenta was cooked in large copper pots positioned over the wood fire in the kitchen fireplace. Dress with Romagnola meat sauce (see page 330) or a sauce made with sausages (page 73) or pancetta.

Use the cornmeal and 9 cups lightly salted boiling water to prepare a polenta as in the recipe on page 289. To serve, pour it out onto a kitchen table or cutting board.

POLENTA WITH SALTED PORK

POLENTA CON CARNE SOTTO SALE

CALABRIA

¾ lb. salted pork
1⅔ cups tomato purée
¼ cup extra-virgin olive oil
2 cups cornmeal
Salt

Soak the pork in cold water for 12 hours to remove the salt, then simmer it in the tomato purée and olive oil. ✦ Meanwhile, use the cornmeal and 6 cups lightly salted water to prepare a polenta as in the recipe on page 289. ✦ When the polenta is ready pour it on a board and top with the meat sauce.

POLENTA WITH WHITE BEANS AND CABBAGE

POLENTA CON CAVOLI

PIEMONTE

1 pork rind
1¼ cups white beans, soaked overnight and drained
2 potatoes, peeled and cut in pieces
4 cups chopped cabbage leaves
2 cups cornmeal
1 tbsp. unsalted butter

Cut the pork rind into strips and combine it with the white beans. Add water to cover and boil until the beans are tender. ✦ In another pan combine the potatoes and the cabbage with water to cover and cook, salting to taste. ✦ Use the cornmeal and 6 cups lightly salted water to prepare the polenta. Combine the polenta with the bean mixture, using just enough polenta to obtain an even mixture. Stir in the butter and serve.

POLENTA WITH LEEKS

POLENTA CON I PORRI

PIEMONTE

¼ cup (4 tbsp.) unsalted butter
6 tbsp. extra-virgin olive oil
4½ lbs. leeks, cut in thin rounds
6 oz. salt-cured anchovies, boned, cleaned, and chopped
7 oz. fontina, cut in strips
1 small *Robiola di Roccaverano* (see note)
2 tbsp. grated Parmigiano-Reggiano
3 cups cornmeal
2 large egg yolks

Robiola is a soft, creamy cheese made in Italy's alpine valleys, most of all in Lombardia and Piemonte. It is known for its pungent or aromatic flavor. *Robiola di Roccaverano* comes from a town in Piemonte. While this is the cheese that is truly authentic, any *Robiola* will do. This dish is typical of Novara.

Preheat the oven to 425°F and butter a baking pan. Heat half the olive oil in a pan over low heat and cook the leeks; when the leeks have begun to fall apart add the anchovies. ✦ Put the fontina in a separate bowl, add the *Robiola*, and mix in the Parmigiano-Reggiano. ✦ Use the cornmeal and 8 cups water to make a thick polenta as in the recipe on page 289; stir in the remaining olive oil. ✦ Pour a layer of polenta into the baking pan no more than ¾ inch thick; top with half of the cheese mixture and half the butter; then add a few spoonfuls of the leeks and anchovies. ✦ Make another layer and end with a thin cover of polenta. Mix the egg yolks with 2 tablespoons water and brush on the polenta. ✦ Dot with the remaining butter and bake for about 10 minutes. Serve hot.

POLENTA WITH PORK LOIN

POLENTA CON LE SPUNTATURE DI MAIALE

LAZIO

2 oz. *lardo* (see page 2)
3 tbsp. extra-virgin olive oil
½ medium onion, finely chopped
½ carrot, finely chopped
1 sprig marjoram
½ celery stalk, finely chopped
2 lbs. pork loin
¼ cup white wine
1½ lbs. peeled plum tomatoes, seeded and chopped
½ cup broth
1⅔ cups cornmeal
½ cup grated pecorino
Salt and pepper

In Rome and Lazio, in the past and also today, polenta is served on a wooden cutting board spread with sauce and pecorino; the entire family sits around this flavorful dish, each member eating his or her portion.

In a pan heat the *lardo* and oil. Sauté the onion, carrot, marjoram, and celery until softened, then add the pork loin. ✦ Sprinkle in the wine and continue cooking over moderate heat for 30 minutes, then add the tomatoes and broth. ✦ Season with salt and pepper to taste. ✦ Complete cooking at low heat for 2 hours. ✦ Use the cornmeal and 5 cups lightly salted water to prepare a polenta as in the recipe on page 289. ✦ Turn off the heat and pour the polenta into wooden bowls (*schifetti*) or into serving plates and add the pork loin with its sauce. Sprinkle with pecorino.

POLENTA WITH SALTED GREEN TOMATOES

POLENTA CON POMODORI VERDI SALATI

CALABRIA

2 cups cornmeal
2 tbsp. extra-virgin olive oil
1 tbsp. fennel seeds
¾ lb. green tomatoes preserved in salt, rinsed in cold water
Salt

Use the cornmeal and 6 cups water to make a polenta as in the recipe on page 289. ✦ When the polenta is done pour it onto a wooden board. Heat the olive oil in a pan and toast the fennels seeds until fragrant. Cook the tomatoes until golden. Spoon the tomatoes on top of the polenta and serve.

POLENTA WITH PORK SAUCE

POLENTA CON SUGO DI MAIALE

LAZIO

2 cups cornmeal
1½ tbsp. extra-virgin olive oil
CONTINUED

This dish is typical of the Roman plain. Let the pork be the second course, accompanied by seasonal vegetables cooked in a pan with olive oil and garlic.

Use the cornmeal and 6 cups lightly salted water to make a polenta as in the recipe on page 289. ✦ Heat the olive

1 ¼ lbs. pork thigh, cut into cubes and dredged in all-purpose flour (can use pork loin if necessary)

2 oz. prosciutto fat, minced

1 celery stalk, minced

¼ medium onion, minced

1 carrot, minced

2 sprigs marjoram, minced

3 peppercorns

4 tbsp. cloves and cumin, chopped together

Broth, if needed

1 ¼ lbs. peeled plum tomatoes, drained of sauce

½ cup grated pecorino

Salt and pepper

oil in a pan until it slightly smokes, then add the pork. ✦ Brown the meat on all sides, add the prosciutto fat, celery, onion, carrot, and marjoram, and give it a good stir, then add the peppercorns and cloves and cumin. ✦ Continue cooking, bathing the pork every so often with pan juices, adding a few tablespoons of broth if necessary, until the meat is nearly cooked but still mostly pink inside. ✦ At that point add the tomatoes, season with salt if necessary and a little pepper, stirring occasionally, and cook until the sauce has thickened. ✦ Pour the polenta into warmed bowls and cover with sauce and pecorino.

POLENTA CONCIA OR PASTICCIATA

VALLE D'AOSTA

1 ½ cups cornmeal *fioretto* (finely ground)

1 ½ cups cornmeal *bramata* (coarsely ground)

¾ lb. fontina, diced

1 ½ sticks plus 2 tbsp. butter

POLENTA WITH FONTINA

This is a soft polenta that is not put in the oven, as is the classical Valdostan polenta, which is firmer, with a golden crust. This dish is prepared throughout Aosta but most of all in Gressoney and other Walser zones, where it is seasoned with toma of Gressoney instead of fontina.

Use the cornmeal and 9 cups lightly salted water to make a polenta as in the recipe on page 289. ✦ When the polenta is cooked, stir in the fontina and half the butter. ✦ Pour the polenta into a bowl. Melt the remaining butter and pour over the polenta. Serve hot.

POLENTA DI GRANO E VERDURA

SICILIA

1 lb. broccoli florets

3 oz. pancetta, diced

2 garlic cloves

1 ½ cups semolina flour

2 tbsp. extra-virgin olive oil

Pinch chili pepper flakes

Salt

POLENTA WITH BROCCOLI AND PANCETTA

This typical winter dish is also found in a variation that uses mountain fennel in place of the broccoli.

Cook the broccoli florets in 6 cups boiling water, just until bright green. Drain and reserve the cooking water. ✦ In a pan sauté the pancetta and garlic until golden. Add the broccoli, crushing them with the tines of a fork to combine all the ingredients. ✦ Use the semolina and broccoli cooking water to make a "polenta" as in the recipe on page 289. ✦ When the polenta is finshed, add the broccoli, season with olive oil and chili pepper flakes as desired, and serve immediately.

POLENTA WITH PORK AND TURNIPS

LAZIO

¼ cup extra-virgin olive oil

1 garlic clove

2 lbs. turnip tops

1⅔ cups cornmeal

Pasta sauce made with pork
(see page 539)

Grated Parmigiano-Reggiano

Salt

Heat the olive oil in a pan and sauté the garlic until golden, then add the turnip tops. Season with salt; add 1 cup of water. ✦ Cover and cook at low heat. ✦ Use the cornmeal and 5 cups lightly salted water to make a polenta as in the recipe on page 289. ✦ When the polenta is done stir in the turnip tops. ✦ Pour the polenta on a flat surface or in plates. Cover with the meat sauce and sprinkle with Parmigiano-Reggiano.

POLENTA E FAGIOLI

POLENTA AND BEANS

ABRUZZO

2 cups dried borlotti
or cranberry beans

¼ cup extra-virgin olive oil

9 oz. pancetta, cut in small pieces

1 medium onion, sliced

Pinch chili pepper flakes (optional)

4 cups large-grain cornmeal

4 sausages

½ cup dry white wine

Salt and pepper

This dish is typical of Pescara. For the wine use Trebbiano.

Soak the beans in cold water to cover by several inches for 12 hours. ✦ At the end of that time, rinse the beans in cool water then put them in cool salted water in an earthenware pan and cook over moderate heat. ✦ Meanwhile heat the olive oil in a pan and add the pancetta. Cook until golden; add the onion and sauté. Add salt to taste and, if desired, some chili pepper. ✦ Drain the beans and combine them with half of the mixture in the pan; continue slowly cooking the remaining portion. ✦ Using the cornmeal and 6 cups of lightly salted water make a polenta as in the recipe on page 289. ✦ When the polenta is cooked add the rest of the onion mixture to the pot, stirring it in quickly; combine the polenta and beans and cook a few more minutes. Meanwhile, pierce the sausages and cook them in a pan with the wine and ¼ cup water until browned and cooked through. ✦ Pour the polenta into warmed bowls; add a sausage to each bowl.

POLENTA E LUMACHE
ALLA TRENTINA

POLENTA AND SNAILS

TRENTINO

With a few small exceptions, this recipe follows the old methods, those typical of Trentino, of preparing snails served with steaming polenta, a festive dish that was traditional for the feast of All Saints' Day. With respect to tradition, snails

2 lbs. snails
1 medium onion
1 garlic clove
1 carrot
1 bunch flat-leaf parsley
1 celery stalk
2 tbsp. extra-virgin olive oil
2 tbsp. unsalted butter
½ cup dry white wine
(preferably from Trentino)
1 tbsp. breadcrumbs
1 heaping tbsp. grated
Parmigiano-Reggiano
3 cups cornmeal
Salt and pepper

thus prepared along with their sauce should be served with warm, somewhat soft polenta. The side dishes should include crisp lettuce, all of this enlivened by a wine worthy of such a flavorful plate, a wine with an aroma and body as substantial as Trentino polenta and snails. The choice thus falls on a bottle from a good year of the famous Teroldego Rotaliano with its unmistakable fragrance of violets and spring.

Having cleaned the snails and separated them from their shells as in the recipe on page 16, boil them for at least 2 hours, then drain them, setting aside their cooking water, which will be used later for the sauce. ✦ Finely chop together the onion, garlic, carrot, parsley, and celery. Heat the olive oil and butter and sauté the vegetables. ✦ Finely chop some of the snails then add the chopped and whole snails to the pan with the onion mixture. ✦ Pour in the wine and 2 cups of the snail cooking water; add the breadcrumbs and simmer for at least 1½ hours, being careful at the end that the sauce is neither too dense nor too liquid. Toward the end of the cooking add salt and pepper to taste and the cheese. ✦ Meanwhile use the cornmeal and 9 cups water to make a polenta as in the recipe on page 289. Pour it onto a board and top with the snails and their sauce.

POLENTA GRASSA
VALDOSTANA

VALDOSTAN BAKED POLENTA

VALLE D'AOSTA

1½ cups cornmeal *fioretto*
(finely ground)
1½ cups cornmeal *bramata*
(coarsely ground)
1 lb. fontina, sliced
¾ cup plus 2 tbsp. unsalted butter,
melted
Salt

This dish is typical of Aosta.

Blend the two types of cornmeal and cook them in 8 cups of lightly salted boiling water as in the recipe on page 289. Transfer the polenta to a wooden board and let it cool completely before cutting it into slices (best done with a string). ✦ Preheat the oven to 350°F. In a copper pan or baking sheet, alternate layers of polenta with layers of fontina. ✦ Cover with melted butter and end with a layer of polenta slices. ✦ Bake until it forms a golden, shiny crust. Serve immediately, while still very hot.

| # BLACK POLENTA

4 cups heavy cream

4 cups black buckwheat flour

1 lb. young and lean Valtellina cheese (may substitute Taleggio), cut in large chunks

Salt

This dish is typical of the Valtellina and of the Val Poschiavo, in Engadine.

Heat the cream in a copper pot. ✦ When it boils add the flour and cook as in the recipe on page 289. ✦ A few minutes before the polenta has cooked (about 40 minutes), add the cheese. ✦ Give the mixture a few final stirs then turn out onto a board before the cheese has completely melted.

POLENTA WITH BEANS AND CAVOLO NERO

1 cup fresh borlotti beans

¾ lb. *cavolo nero* (see page 99), outer leaves removed, finely chopped

¼ cup extra-virgin olive oil

1 cup cornmeal

Grated Parmigiano-Reggiano

Salt

This dish is typical of Fivizzano and the Lunigiana.

Put the beans in a pan with lightly salted water to cover by several inches. ✦ Cook for 10 minutes, add the *cavolo nero* then the olive oil and cook another 30 minutes. ✦ Put the cornmeal through a sieve then cook as in the recipe on page 289, using 3 cups water. Cook for 1 hour. ✦ The polenta should be soft; add a little warm water if necessary. ✦ Serve the polenta with the sauce in individual bowls, topping each serving with Parmigiano-Reggiano.

BAKED POLENTA WITH MEAT SAUCE 1

3 cups cornmeal

2 cups milk

¼ lb. (1 stick) plus 3 tbsp. unsalted butter

1 small onion, finely chopped

3 tbsp. all-purpose flour

1¼ cups grated Parmigiano-Reggiano

1 pinch grated nutmeg

¾ lb. sausage meat, removed from its casing and broken up

CONTINUED

This dish is typical of the Brianza and the central and upper Lario River valley.

Preheat the oven to 350°F. Prepare the polenta as in the recipe on page 289, using the cornmeal and 8 cups salted water. ✦ Turn it out onto a baking sheet or wooden board and let it cool. ✦ Bring the milk to a boil in a saucepan over low heat. Heat 4 tablespoons butter in a pan and sauté the onion. ✦ Add the flour a little at a time at low heat, stirring well, and let it cook 3 minutes. ✦ Slowly pour in the boiling milk, stirring constantly. ✦ Add the Parmigiano-Reggiano, a pinch of salt, pepper, and nutmeg. ✦ Keeping the heat low, stir to obtain a somewhat thick sauce. ✦ At this point add the sausage meat and mushrooms. Simmer for 15 minutes. ✦ Cut

1 oz. dried porcini mushrooms, softened in warm water and drained

1 to 2 oz. white truffle, sliced in thin shavings

6 oz. Gruyère, sliced

Salt and pepper

the polenta in slices about half an inch thick. ✦ Pour a little of the sausage sauce in the bottom of a baking pan and dot with butter. ✦ Create layers of polenta, covering each layer with more sauce, truffle, and slices of Gruyère, until all the polenta is used. ✦ Cover the last layer with the remaining sauce and bake for 45 minutes or until set. Serve in slices.

POLENTA PASTICCIATA 2

BAKED POLENTA WITH MEAT SAUCE 2

EMILIA-ROMAGNA

2 oz. *lardo* (see page 2)

1 medium onion, finely chopped

1 celery stalk, finely chopped

1 carrot, finely chopped

2 oz. dried mushrooms, soaked in water and softened, drained, and chopped

¾ lb. ripe plum tomatoes, peeled, seeded, and diced

½ lb. sausage, removed from its casing and broken up

¼ cup white wine

3 cups cornmeal

¼ cup (4 tbsp.) unsalted butter

½ cup grated Parmigiano-Reggiano

Salt

Preheat the oven to 350°F. Butter a baking pan. Heat the *lardo* in a pan and sauté the onion, celery, and carrot. Add the mushrooms, tomatoes, then the sausage. ✦ Cook for about 10 minutes, adding a little water and white wine. ✦ Use the cornmeal and 8 cups lightly salted water to make a polenta as in the recipe on page 289. ✦ Cover the bottom of the prepared pan with a little of the mushroom sauce, follow with a layer of polenta and one of Parmigiano-Reggiano, continuing layers until the ingredients are used up. ✦ End with a layer of sauce, pats of butter, and cheese. ✦ Bake until the surface forms a golden crust.

POLENTA TARAGNA

BUCKWHEAT AND CORNMEAL POLENTA WITH CHEESE

LOMBARDIA

1 lb. (2 cups) butter

1½ cups cornmeal

2 cups buckwheat flour

Bread of 1 roll, grated to make ½ cup

1½ lbs. semifat Valtellina cheese, roughly chopped (see note, may substitute Taleggio)

Salt

This polenta is known for its speckled color and coarse texture; the name probably comes from *tarel*, the long stick formerly used to stir the polenta. The recipe works best if some of the cheese is aged and some fresh, as for example from Talamona or Gerola. The dish is usually eaten with sausages and pickled vegetables.

Heat 7 cups lightly salted water in a copper pot and add ½ cup plus 2 tablespoons butter. ✦ When the water boils, add the cornmeal then the buckwheat flour and make a polenta as in the recipe on page 289. ✦ During the cooking (about 1 hour) gradually add the remaining butter, then add the bread. ✦ A few minutes before removing the pot from the heat add the Valtellina cheese. ✦ Give a final stir and turn out the polenta before all the cheese melts.

POLENTA UNCIA | "DROWNED" POLENTA

LOMBARDIA

½ lb. (2 sticks) unsalted butter
1 ¼ cups all-purpose flour
1 ¼ cups cornmeal
10 garlic cloves, slivered
7 oz. Taleggio or fontina,
cut in small cubes
7 oz. young, soft Asiago,
cut in small cubes
Coarse salt

Polenta uncia should drown in butter, following an ancient custom. This version is typical of the western shore of Lake Como and Rogaro, an area of Tremezzo.

In a copper pot boil 6 cups of lightly salted water and add 2 tablespoons of the butter. ✦ Pour in both the flour and the cornmeal in a slow but steady stream, stirring constantly. ✦ When the mixture begins to thicken, add ¼ cup more butter. ✦ Meanwhile melt the remaining butter and sauté the garlic until softened. When the polenta is almost finished (after about 1 hour) add the butter with the garlic along with the cheeses. ✦ Stir well so the cheeses melt, and serve.

POLENTINA D'ORZO | BARLEY POLENTA

VALLE D'AOSTA

1 lb. potatoes
⅔ cup all-purpose flour
⅔ cup barley flour
3 oz. aged fontina, without rind,
in thin slices
3 oz. Valdostan toma cheese,
without rind, in slices
6 tbsp. clarified butter, melted
Salt

This dish is typical of Cogne. *Toma* is a soft cow's-milk cheese.

Peel and boil the potatoes in water to cover until soft. Drain, reserving the liquid. ✦ Put them through a ricer into the same pot with the cooking water. ✦ Combine the flours and pour them into the water in a steady stream, adding salt and stirring as in the recipe on page 289 for about 30 minutes. ✦ Transfer to a bowl and add the cheeses, mixing them in until they melt. ✦ Level off the surface; pour the butter over the top.

POLENTINA GRIGIA | POLENTA WITH SPRING GREENS

PIEMONTE

1 lb. *ajucche* (rampion),
or other fresh spring greens
1 ¼ cups cornmeal
10 oz. toma cheese, diced
CONTINUED

Boil the greens in 4 cups lightly salted water. ✦ When it is cooked (10 minutes should suffice for rampion, less for other greens), add the cornmeal and cook as in the recipe on page 289, then stir in the toma. ✦ Heat the butter in a pan and sauté the pancetta until golden. Add a few tablespoons of the pancetta pan juices to the polenta. ✦ Drain off any remaining liquid from the

2 tbsp. unsalted butter

2 oz. pancetta, diced

pancetta and cook a few moments more so the pancetta will be dry. Add the pancetta to the polenta at the moment of serving.

BAKED POLENTA AND SAUSAGE

POLENTONE

MARCHE

2 tbsp. extra-virgin olive oil

5 oz. pancetta, diced

3 sausages, removed from casings and crumbled

4 cups cornmeal

Grated pecorino

Heat the olive oil in a pan and sauté the pancetta and sausage meat until lightly browned; set aside. ✦ Prepare a somewhat thick polenta with the cornmeal and 6 cups water as in the recipe on page 289. Pour the polenta on a damp cloth and let it cool. ✦ Preheat the oven to 350°F. With a length of string, cut the polenta in slices and arrange the slices in layers in a baking pan. ✦ Season each layer with some of the meat sauce and sprinkle generously with pecorino. ✦ Bake for about 10 minutes. Serve immediately.

BREAD BALLS IN TOMATO SAUCE

POLPETTE DI PANE

PUGLIA

1½ large onions, thinly sliced

3¼ lbs. San Marzano plum tomatoes, seeded and crushed

1 tbsp. chopped basil (or flat-leaf parsley)

1¼ cups extra-virgin olive oil

5 large eggs, beaten

1 tbsp. grated pecorino

About 6 oz. stale bread (not too soft, not too hard: about 2 days old), grated

Salt

This dish is typical of the Capitanata, an area of Puglia corresponding to today's province of Foggia.

Prepare a sauce by cooking the onions and tomatoes in a pan over low heat without seasoning; when they have released their liquid but are not colored pass them through a food mill. Return them to the pan and cook again for about 10 minutes with 1 teaspoon basil (or parsley), ¼ cup olive oil, and salt. ✦ Mix the eggs in an earthenware bowl with salt, cheese, and the rest of the basil. ✦ Add the bread and work together to form a soft dough. ✦ Make the dough into balls, then flatten them. Heat the remaining olive oil in a pan and sauté the bread balls until golden. Drain on paper towels then add them to the tomato sauce. Cook for 10 minutes at low heat.

RICE-STUFFED TOMATOES 1

POMODORI COL RISO 1

LAZIO

½ cup extra-virgin olive oil

CONTINUED

This dish is typical of Rome and Lazio.

Preheat the oven to 350°F. Grease a baking pan with olive oil. Clean the tomatoes and cut around the stems to form tops; set aside. ✦ Remove the seeds and some of

327

4 large ripe tomatoes
¾ cup parboiled rice (it will still be a little crunchy)
1 garlic clove, chopped
5 basil leaves, shredded
2 tbsp. chopped flat-leaf parsley
1 tsp. oregano
½ cup tomato purée
Salt and pepper

the interior pulp from the tomatoes. ✦ In a bowl combine the parboiled rice, garlic, basil, parsley, and oregano; pass the tomato pulp through a food mill and add to the bowl. ✦ Add 2 tablespoons of the tomato purée, a good pinch of salt, and a pinch of freshly ground black pepper; mix well and let sit to marinate for 1 hour. ✦ Arrange the tomatoes and their tops on a work surface. Sprinkle the insides with olive oil and lightly salt. ✦ Arrange the tomatoes in the prepared pan. Fill each about ⅔ full of the rice mixture and cover each with its top. ✦ Pour the remaining tomato sauce around the tomatoes, then sprinkle with olive oil and salt. ✦ Bake for 1 hour, until the rice is tender and the tomatoes are soft.

✦ **LOCAL TRADITION** ✦

ST. JOSEPH'S LUNCH

The origins of this tradition are lost in time. In the beginning of summer, when the people of Molise were short of food, the well-to-do had to respond to the needs of the poor. So for this symbolic meal, these thirteen courses were devised: 1) appetizer: pickled peppers and pears; 2) spaghetti with marinara sauce (olives, anchovies, and tomato sauce); 3) codfish, first dipped in egg yolk and fried, then cooked with tomato sauce; 4) cod baked with cauliflower, in which the cod was seasoned with breadcrumbs, pepper, parsley, garlic, and extra-virgin olive oil then covered with a layer of boiled cauliflower and more breadcrumbs, parsley, garlic, olive oil, and a few tomato fillets; 5) dried cod fried with a side dish of beans; 6) lentils; 7) codfish balls with a side dish of broccoli; 8) golden-fried cod fillets with golden-fried cauliflower; 9) orange salad; 10) rice cooked in milk; 11) sweet-and-sour dessert made with almonds 12) *calzoni*, a pastry typical of this festival; 13) mixed fruit.

POMODORI COL RISO 2 | # RICE-STUFFED TOMATOES 2

LAZIO

If desired, you can bake potatoes together with the stuffed tomatoes, placing large hunks of peeled potatoes around the tomatoes and seasoning them with olive oil, salt, and a little pepper.

8 medium-size plum tomatoes, not overly ripe

8 heaping tbsp. rice

2 garlic cloves, crushed

Basil, chopped

Flat-leaf parsley, chopped

2 tbsp. tomato sauce diluted in a few tbsp. water

½ cup extra-virgin olive oil

Potatoes (optional)

Salt and pepper

Preheat the oven to 350°F. Wash the tomatoes then cut off their tops, making the horizontal cut near the stems. ✦ Scoop out the pulp from the bodies of the tomatoes and set aside; also clean out the seeds and liquid. ✦ In a bowl combine the tomato pulp with the rice, garlic, basil, parsley, the diluted tomato sauce, a good pinch of salt, and a little pepper and mix well. ✦ Line up the tomatoes with their tops on a work surface, sprinkle them with olive oil, and lightly salt them. ✦ Pour half the olive oil into a baking pan and line up the tomatoes on it, filling each two-thirds full of the rice mixture, and closing each with its top. ✦ Pour the rest of the tomato sauce around the tomatoes, sprinkle again with olive oil and salt, and bake for about 40 minutes until the tomatoes are softened and the rice is cooked.

MALTAGLIATI WITH ARTICHOKE SAUCE

PREAGGE AL SUGO DI CARCIOFI

LIGURIA

1⅔ cups all-purpose flour, plus more as needed

2 large eggs

2 artichokes

2 tbsp. extra-virgin olive oil

1 garlic clove

1 sprig flat-leaf parsley, chopped

2 cups chicken or vegetable broth

Grated Parmigiano-Reggiano

Salt and pepper

This recipe is typical of the Riviera di Levante.

Use the flour and eggs to prepare a pasta dough as in the recipe on page 10. ✦ Let the pasta rest for 20 minutes before rolling it out. ✦ Roll out a sheet (see page 212) and cut it to make *maltagliati* (see page 285). ✦ Clean the artichokes and cut them in slices that are not too thin. ✦ Heat the olive oil in a pan and cook the garlic until golden; add the artichokes, parsley, salt, and pepper and cook until lightly browned. Add the broth and simmer uncovered until the mixture reduces to a sauce. ✦ Meanwhile cook the *maltagliati* in lightly salted boiling water, drain, and toss with artichoke mixture. Sprinkle with Parmigiano-Reggiano and serve hot.

PUGLIAN MEAT SAUCE

RAGÙ ALLA PUGLIESE

FOR 12 PERSONS

PUGLIA

1 medium onion, finely sliced

2 garlic cloves

Extra-virgin olive oil

CONTINUED

Use this sauce on pasta (it is especially well suited to orecchiette), adding the pieces of meat that did not come apart during the long cooking and some good grated pecorino.

Put the onion and garlic in a covered pot with ½ cup water and ¼ cup olive oil. Cook at very low heat, stirring frequently to keep the onion from sticking to the pot. ✦

9 oz. pancetta, minced

½ cup white wine

9 oz. beef, in 1- to 1½-inch cubes

9 oz. lamb, in 1- to 1½-inch cubes

4 cups tomato purée

6 tbsp. tomato paste

Pinch chili pepper flakes

Meat of ½ chicken,
in 1- to 1½-inch cubes

4 pieces of sausage,
in 1- to 1½-inch cubes

Grated pecorino

Salt

When the onion is caramelized add the pancetta and raise the heat to medium. ✦ When the pancetta has begun to brown add ¼ cup wine and reduce the heat to very low. Cover and simmer 30 minutes. ✦ Add the beef, lamb, the remaining wine, tomato purée, tomato paste, chili pepper, and salt. Continue cooking very slowly, always with the pot covered, for about 3 hours, or until the meats are well cooked and the pork fat has dissolved in the tomato sauce. ✦ During the last 45 minutes of cooking add the chicken and sausage. Serve over pasta sprinkled with pecorino.

RAGÙ ALLA ROMAGNOLA

ROMAGNA-STYLE MEAT SAUCE

EMILIA-ROMAGNA

1 medium onion

1 carrot

1 celery stalk

1 oz. pancetta, minced

¼ cup olive oil (or 4 tbsp.
unsalted butter)

6 oz. lean beef (bottom round)

3 oz. chicken livers, diced

¼ cup wine, red or white

¾ lb. ripe peeled plum tomatoes

Pinch of grated nutmeg

2 tbsp. meat broth

Salt and pepper

Finely chop together the onion, carrot, and celery. Heat the olive oil (or butter) in a pan over medium heat and add the vegetables; cook until softened. ✦ Add the pancetta, then the beef and chicken livers. ✦ Pour in the wine, and when it has evaporated add the tomatoes, salt, pepper, nutmeg, and broth. Cover and cook at low heat 50 to 60 minutes.

RAGÙ D'AGNELLO

LAMB RAGÙ

UMBRIA

1 sprig rosemary

2 garlic cloves, minced

5 tbsp. extra-virgin olive oil

1 lb. lamb, cut in pieces
but not minced

½ cup dry white wine

1½ lbs. tomato purée

Salt and pepper

This sauce, typical of Foligno, is traditionally served with homemade tagliatelle.

Chop together the rosemary leaves and garlic. Heat the olive oil in a pan over medium heat and sauté the garlic and rosemary until fragrant. ✦ Add the lamb pieces and let them brown. ✦ Pour in the wine, and when it has evaporated, add salt and pepper. ✦ Add the tomato purée and cook over low heat until the sauce has thickened, about 40 minutes.

RAGÙ TOSCANO | TUSCAN RAGÙ

TOSCANA

1 medium onion

1 carrot

1 celery stalk

¼ cup extra-virgin olive oil

¾ lb. choice lean beef chuck, diced

¼ cup red wine

1 tbsp. tomato paste, diluted in 3 tbsp. water

Salt and pepper

This sauce is typical of Pistoia.

Finely chop together the onion, carrot, and celery. Heat the olive oil at very low heat, add the vegetables, and cook for 30 minutes. ✦ Add the beef and cook a few minutes, then pour in the red wine; add the tomato paste and salt and pepper to taste. ✦ Cover and cook slowly for at least another 30 minutes, or until the sauce has thickened considerably.

RAMICCIA | FETTUCCINE WITH MEAT SAUCE

LAZIO

For the pasta:

3 cups all-purpose flour, plus more as needed

4 large eggs, beaten

Salt

For the sauce:

½ cup extra-virgin olive oil

1 medium onion, finely sliced

1 garlic clove, minced

1 to 1¼ lbs. beef, cubed not ground

½ cup dry white wine

Tomato purée or peeled plum tomatoes

Chili pepper

Grated pecorino

Salt

This dish is typical of Norma.

Use the flour and eggs to prepare a pasta dough as in the recipe on page 10. Roll out a thin sheet (see page 212) and cover with a clean kitchen towel so that the dough will dry uniformly. ✦ Meanwhile make the sauce: heat the olive oil in a pan and sauté the onion and garlic. Add the meat. ✦ When the meat has browned, pour in the wine and let it evaporate rapidly. ✦ Add the tomatoes, chili pepper, and salt. Let cook until the sauce has thickened, about 40 minutes. Cut the pasta sheet into fettuccine no wider than a quarter inch. ✦ Cook in lightly salted boiling water and dress with the meat sauce. Sprinkle with pecorino.

RAVIÊU | MIXED MEAT RAVIOLI

LIGURIA

For the filling:

4 heads escarole

CONTINUED

There is also the alternative of cooking the pasta and serving it in beef or capon broth.

Boil the escarole and borage in a little water until bright green; drain and set aside. ✦ Heat a little butter in a pan and sauté the pine nuts until lightly golden. Add the veal,

2 bunches borage

2 tbsp. unsalted butter

⅓ cup pine nuts

7 oz. veal, cubed

10 oz. sweetbreads

8 oz. sausage, crumbled

2 large eggs plus 2 large yolks, beaten

Bread from a roll, without crust,
soaked in broth or meat sauce

¼ cup grated Parmigiano-Reggiano,
plus more for serving

1 tbsp. chopped marjoram leaves

1 garlic clove, chopped

Salt

For the pasta:

4 ¼ cups all-purpose flour,
plus more as needed

2 large eggs

sweetbreads, and sausage meat and sauté until browned. ✦ Chop all this together with the greens and put the mixture in a bowl, adding the eggs and yolks, bread, Parmigiano-Reggiano, marjoram, and garlic. Work together to obtain a homogeneous mixture. Add salt to taste. ✦ Use the flour and eggs to prepare a pasta dough as in the recipe on page 10. Roll out a sheet (see page 212) and divide it in two parts. Deposit spoonfuls of the filling along one of the sheets. Cover with the other sheet and press down, then cut out square ravioli with a pastry wheel. ✦ Lightly flour the ravioli and let them dry on a kitchen towel for several hours. ✦ Cook the ravioli in lightly salted boiling water; drain, and toss with the meat sauce, adding cheese at the table.

BAKED RAVIOLI

CALABRIA

For the sauce:

1 carrot

1 medium onion

1 celery stalk

2 oz. lard

1 ½ cups tomato purée

⅓ cup grated pecorino

For the pasta:

3 cups all-purpose flour,
plus more as needed

5 large eggs

1 tbsp. extra-virgin olive oil

Salt

For the filling:

¾ lb. ground pork or veal

4 oz. sausage, roughly chopped

4 oz. salame, minced

4 large hard-boiled eggs

⅓ cup grated pecorino

Finely chop together the carrot, onion, and celery. Heat the lard in a saucepan and add the vegetables. Cook until golden, then add the tomato purée and simmer for about 30 minutes. ✦ Meanwhile, make the pasta: Use the flour and eggs to prepare a pasta dough as in the recipe on page 10, adding the olive oil with the eggs. ✦ Roll out a sheet (see page 212) and cut it in squares about 4 inches on a side. ✦ Slice the boiled eggs. Make the filling by combining the meat, sausage, salame, and hard-boiled eggs, then add the pecorino. ✦ Preheat the oven to 425°F. Fill each pasta square with a little filling and fold it closed, pressing down along the edges. ✦ Cook the ravioli for 7 to 8 minutes in lightly salted boiling water, drain, and arrange some of them across the bottom of a baking dish. ✦ Cover these with a layer of sauce and cheese, then make another layer of ravioli, sauce, and cheese, and so on, ending with sauce and cheese. ✦ Bake for 15 minutes and serve hot.

BAKED MEAT RAVIOLI

LAZIO

For the filling:

1 ¼ cups grated Parmigiano-Reggiano, plus more as needed

1 lb. ricotta

4 oz. salame, minced

4 oz. spicy sausage meat, diced

1 pinch nutmeg

For the pasta:

3 cups all-purpose flour, plus more as needed

4 large eggs

For the sauce:

½ cup extra-virgin olive oil

1 medium onion, minced

7 oz. sausage, finely chopped

3 cups tomato purée

¼ cup white wine

Basil leaves

¼ cup (4 tbsp.) unsalted butter

Salt and pepper

Begin by combining the ingredients for the filling. Using the tines of a fork work the Parmigiano-Reggiano into the ricotta, adding the salame, sausage meat, and nutmeg, then tasting for salt and pepper. ✦ Use the flour and eggs to prepare a pasta dough as in the recipe on page 10. Roll it out into a very thin sheet (see page 212). ✦ Using an upside-down glass cut disks from the sheet. Arrange a small dollop of the filling at the center of each disk; fold the disks over on themselves, pressing around the edges to seal them. ✦ Make the sauce. Heat the olive oil in a saucepan. Add the onion and sauté until soft. ✦ Add the sausage meat and tomato purée. ✦ Cook over medium heat, sprinkling with wine from time to time and adding salt, pepper, and basil leaves. ✦ Preheat the oven to 325°F. Cook the ravioli in lightly salted boiling water for 5 to 6 minutes. ✦ Drain and toss with the sauce. ✦ In a baking pan arrange layers of ravioli and sauce, dusting each layer with Parmigiano-Reggiano and adding a few pats of butter. ✦ Bake about 15 minutes, until the sauce has thickened, and serve warm.

RICOTTA RAVIOLI

BASILICATA

For the filling:

1 ½ cups ricotta

2 large eggs, beaten

2 tbsp. chopped flat-leaf parsley

3 tbsp. grated pecorino

For the dough:

3 cups all-purpose flour, plus more as needed

4 large eggs, beaten

Salt

These cheese-filled ravioli go well with a meat sauce.

Begin with the filling, putting the ricotta in a bowl and working in the eggs, parsley, and pecorino to obtain a smooth mixture. ✦ Use the flour and eggs to prepare a pasta dough as in the recipe on page 10. Divide it in two and roll out each portion to form a thin sheet (see page 212). ✦ Arrange the filling in small piles in rows along one sheet, then cover with the other, making certain the edges line up all around and that the ricotta-mixture piles are not moved. ✦ Using an upside-down glass cut out ravioli, sealing the edges. Set them aside to dry. ✦ Cook the ravioli in lightly salted boiling water, drain, and dress with a meat sauce, if desired, and additional pecorino.

FRIED SAUERKRAUT RAVIOLI

RAVIOLI DELLA VAL PUSTERIA

ALTO ADIGE

For the filling:

3 tbsp. unsalted butter

1 small onion, finely chopped

1 tbsp. all-purpose flour, plus more as needed

½ cup dry white wine

1 lb. sauerkraut (or white cabbage), chopped

3 juniper berries, crushed

6 black peppercorns, crushed

1 pinch cumin seeds

For the dough:

1½ cups rye flour, plus more as needed

1½ cups all-purpose flour, plus more as needed

2 large eggs

1 tbsp. extra-virgin olive oil

2 tbsp. unsalted butter, melted

Lard

Salt and pepper

Sauerkraut used in Italy is less acidic than that found in North America. If your sauerkraut is very tart, rinse it before use here. A variation of this recipe calls for a filling of ricotta and potatoes: combine 1¼ cups (about 7 ounces) ricotta with 4 ounces of grated boiled potatoes, add some chopped chives, a minced onion, and salt. Again, let the filling cool before using it to make ravioli.

Heat the butter in a pan and add the onion; cook until golden. Dust with the flour and add the wine to thicken. ✦ Add the sauerkraut, juniper berries, peppercorns, and cumin and cook at low heat for about 30 minutes (even better a full hour). Let the filling cool before using it. ✦ Sift together the flours and use them and the eggs to make a pasta dough as in the recipe on page 10, adding the oil and butter with the eggs. Let the dough rest 1 hour. Roll the dough out to form a cylinder about 2 inches in diameter; cut this into slices that when rolled out with a rolling pin form circles about the width of the palm of your hand. Fill each circle of dough with the sauerkraut filling and cover with another circle of dough, sealing the edges carefully by hand and using a pastry wheel to trim the edges. ✦ Heat lard to about ½ inch in a large pan and fry the ravioli until golden and crisp.

MEATLESS RAVIOLI 1

RAVIOLI DI MAGRO 1

LIGURIA

For the filling:

2 tbsp. extra-virgin olive oil

1 medium onion, finely chopped

1 garlic clove, crushed

2 tbsp. chopped flat-leaf parsley

2 bunches borage, finely chopped

7 or 8 bunches escarole (or spinach), finely chopped

1 large egg, beaten

Grated Parmigiano-Reggiano

Lard

Salt

For these ravioli the classic sauce is the *tocco di funzi* (mushroom sauce; see page 412). The same sauce also goes very well with green tagliatelle.

Heat the olive oil in a pan and sauté the onion, garlic, and parsley; add the borage and escarole (or spinach). ✦ Remove from the heat and add the egg and cheese. ✦ Use the flour and eggs to prepare a pasta dough as in the recipe on page 10. Let the dough rest 1 hour. Roll the dough out to form a cylinder about 2 inches in diameter; cut this into slices that when rolled out with a rolling pin form circles about the width of the palm of your hand. Fill each circle of dough with the filling and cover with another circle of dough, sealing the edges carefully by hand and using a pastry wheel to trim the edges. ✦ Let

For the dough:

4½ cups all-purpose flour, plus more as needed

2 large eggs

the ravioli rest for at least an hour. Cook in boiling water and remove when tender, about 5 minutes. Drain and dress with sauce.

RAVIOLI DI MAGRO 2 | **MEATLESS RAVIOLI 2**

TOSCANA

For the filling:

6 oz. Swiss chard, finely chopped

1 potato, boiled and passed through a sieve

½ cup grated Parmigiano-Reggiano, plus more for serving

1 pinch grated nutmeg

2 tbsp. extra-virgin olive oil

2 large eggs, beaten

Breadcrumbs

For the dough:

1⅔ cups all-purpose flour, plus more as needed

2 large eggs, beaten

Salt

Grind up the chard, if possible in a mortar, to obtain a purée and combine it in a bowl with the potato purée. ✦ Add the Parmigiano-Reggiano, nutmeg, olive oil, eggs, breadcrumbs, and a little salt. ✦ Mix and carefully knead. ✦ Use the flour and eggs to prepare a pasta dough as in the recipe on page 10. Roll out to form two sheets (see page 212). ✦ On one sheet distribute rows of the filling, formed into balls; cover with the second sheet and seal the edges. ✦ Cut out ravioli using a pastry wheel. ✦ Cook the ravioli in lightly salted boiling water, drain, and dress with your favorite sauce, adding more Parmigiano-Reggiano at the table.

RAVIOLI DI MARE | **FISH RAVIOLI**

LIGURIA

For the filling:

1 gurnard or grouper (the weight will depend on how many ravioli you intend to make)

Extra-virgin olive oil

2 garlic cloves, chopped

1 tbsp. finely chopped rosemary

1 tbsp. finely chopped flat-leaf parsley

2 tbsp. grated Parmigiano-Reggiano

1 or 2 large eggs (depending on the quantity of fish), beaten

CONTINUED

Preheat the oven to 400°F. Carefully scale the fish, cutting away the gills and removing any intestines. ✦ Clean the fish, rinse it, put it in a roasting pan with ¼ cup olive oil, half of the garlic, and rosemary, and bake until cooked through, about 15 minutes, depending on the size of the fish. ✦ When the fish is cooked cut away the meat and put it in a bowl, adding the remaining garlic, parsley, Parmigiano-Reggiano, and the egg (or eggs). ✦ Work well to create a firm filling. ✦ Use the flour and eggs to prepare a pasta dough as in the recipe on page 10. Knead until a smooth dough forms, adding water as necessary. Roll it out and fill as for making meat ravioli (see page 212). ✦ Cut out the ravioli with a knife or pasta wheel and let rest 1 hour before cooking. ✦ Cook

2 sprigs marjoram, minced

For the dough:

4 ½ cups all-purpose flour, plus more as needed

2 large eggs

Salt

the ravioli in lightly salted boiling water; as the ravioli float to the surface remove them with a strainer or slotted spoon. ✦ Place the cooked ravioli in a serving bowl and serve hot, sprinkled with marjoram.

SPINACH RAVIOLI

ALTO ADIGE

For the filling:

1½ lbs. spinach

½ cup (¼ lb.) unsalted butter

Salt

For the dough:

2 cups rye flour, plus more as needed

½ cup milk

1 large egg

Grated Parmigiano-Reggiano

Salt

This highly "primitive" recipe is typical of the *cucina povera* of the past. It can be modernized and made more flavorful by frying the spinach with a little minced onion, prosciutto crudo, and brains.

Clean and wash the spinach, then boil in water just until very bright green. ✦ Drain very well and chop. Heat 2 tablespoons butter in a pan and cook the spinach until its liquid evaporates, then salt to taste and set aside. ✦ Use the flour and eggs to prepare a pasta dough as in the recipe on page 10, adding the milk with the egg. ✦ Roll out a sheet (see page 212) and cut it in half. ✦ Arrange the filling in small balls along one sheet of pasta, placing the balls about 2 inches apart in rows; cover with the second sheet and using a pastry wheel cut out square ravioli. Press down along the edges to seal. ✦ Cook in lightly salted boiling water; as they float to the surface remove them with a slotted spoon. Melt the remaining butter and toss with the ravioli. Sprinkle with Parmigiano-Reggiano and serve.

SWEET RICOTTA RAVIOLI

FOR
6 PERSONS

ABRUZZO

For the filling:

1½ cups sheep's-milk ricotta

6 large egg yolks

1 tbsp. chopped marjoram

1 tbsp. grated lemon zest

Sugar to taste

Ground cinnamon to taste

CONTINUED

Ravioli are to be found all over Italy, with fillings of meat, vegetables, or ricotta, but sweet ravioli like these, typical of Teramo, can be found only in the Abruzzo. Even today, connoisseurs dress these ravioli only with sugar and cinnamon. Those who are not fond of such "antique" flavors can replace the sugar, cinnamon, and marjoram with salt and parsley.

Mix the ricotta, egg yolks, marjoram, lemon zest, sugar, cinnamon, and salt to make the filling; set aside. ✦ Use the flour and eggs to prepare a pasta dough as in the recipe on page 10. Roll out a thin sheet of dough (see

For the pasta:

2 ⅓ cup all-purpose flour, plus more as needed

4 large eggs

Salt

page 212) to use to make square ravioli (1 inch on a side). ✦ Fill these with the ricotta filling, seal, and cook in lightly salted boiling water, being careful to keep them from breaking. ✦ Drain and toss with a light tomato sauce, adding a little Parmigiano-Reggiano if desired.

RAVIUOLI ALLA
MONTICCHIANA

SPINACH-RICOTTA RAVIOLI

FOR
6 PERSONS

BASILICATA

For the sauce:

2 medium onions, chopped

1 carrot, chopped

1 celery stalk, chopped

¼ cup extra-virgin olive oil

9 oz. veal

9 oz. lamb

2 lbs. plum tomatoes, peeled

1 tbsp. chopped flat-leaf parsley

Pinch chili pepper flakes

For the dough:

3 cups all-purpose flour, plus more as needed

3 large eggs

For the filling:

2 cups ricotta

2 cups spinach

2 large eggs, beaten

1 tbsp. chopped flat-leaf parsley

1 tbsp. cognac

Grated pecorino (or aged ricotta)

Salt

These ravioli are typical of Monticchio Bagni. Ravioli are made in more or less the same way throughout Basilicata.

Make the meat sauce: In a pan, sauté the onions, carrot, and celery in the oil over medium heat until soft. Add the meats, cook until browned, then add the tomatoes. Simmer until the meat is tender, about an hour. Stir in the parsley and chili. ✦ Use the flour and eggs to prepare a pasta dough as in the recipe on page 10. ✦ After letting the dough rest 30 minutes roll it out with a rolling pin. Cut it in disks about 3 inches in diameter using a pastry wheel or, as was the custom in the past, with a glass. ✦ Make the filling: Stir the ricotta in a bowl. Blanch the spinach in lightly salted boiling water for a minute. Drain, squeeze dry, and chop roughly. Add to the ricotta and mix in the eggs, parsley, and cognac. Place a dollop of 1½ tablespoons of the filling in the center of each pasta disk. Fold over the disks to form half-moon ravioli and seal the edges by pressing along them with dampened fingers. ✦ Cook in lightly salted boiling water, drain, and toss with the meat sauce. Add pecorino (or ricotta) before serving.

RIGATONI AI
CAVOLFIORI VERDI

CAULIFLOWER RIGATONI

CAMPANIA

1 large green cauliflower

CONTINUED

This dish is typical of Naples.

Boil the cauliflower whole in lightly salted water to cover; drain when still very al dente and set aside. ✦ When cool enough to handle, chop into small pieces. ✦ Heat the

4 tbsp. extra-virgin olive oil

2 garlic cloves

Hot chili pepper

½ cup pitted and chopped Gaeta (black) olives

¼ cup crushed capers (best if from Pantelleria)

4 salt-cured anchovies

1 lb. rigatoni

olive oil in a pan over low heat; very slowly sauté the garlic and chili pepper until golden. Discard the garlic cloves and add the olives, capers, and anchovies. ✦ Cook at low heat, stirring, until the anchovies disintegrate. ✦ Add the cauliflower and blend with the sauce, mixing well for 5 minutes. ✦ Cook the rigatoni in lightly salted boiling water until al dente, drain, and quickly toss with the cauliflower sauce. Serve piping hot.

✦ LOCAL TRADITION ✦

RIGATONI CON LA PAGLIATA

In the past, this rigatoni dish typical of Rome was prepared—by preference—using the intestines of oxen, but *pagliata* means literally the intestines of a milk-fed calf, usually including some of their milky contents. The skin would be removed from the underlying meat of the intestine, and the whole cut into long pieces; the cut ends of each piece would then be tied together to form "rounds," to keep the contents from dispersing during cooking. The *pagliata* would then be cooked in a large, heavy pot in olive oil and *lardo* flavored with onion, celery, and carrot, just until it browned. White wine would be added and evaporated before the addition of tomato purée. The whole dish would then cook for a further two hours until the sauce became dense and flavorful. Tradition dictated that each person was served two "rounds" over boiled rigatoni mixed with the sauce and pecorino.

RIGATONI ALLA SILANA

RIGATONI WITH SAUSAGE AND MUSHROOMS

CALABRIA

1 lb. plum tomatoes, peeled, seeded, and chopped

1 medium onion, chopped

2 garlic cloves

2 tsp. chopped flat-leaf parsley

½ cup torn basil leaves

CONTINUED

This dish is typical of the Sila Massif, the little-known mountain forest inland from the Calabrian shoreline.

In a saucepan (terra-cotta if possible), combine the tomatoes, onion, garlic, parsley, basil, prosciutto, sausage, guanciale, mushrooms, olive oil, and chili pepper. ✦ Let this cook slowly for a few hours, adding salt to taste and also a little water if too much liquid seems to cook away. ✦ Cook the rigatoni in lightly salted boiling water, drain when still very al dente, and add to the sauce in the pan

6 oz. prosciutto crudo, diced

6 oz. dry sausage, sliced

4 oz. guanciale, cut in strips

1 oz. porcini mushrooms,
soaked, dried, and chopped
in small pieces

⅔ cup olive oil

1 dried chili pepper, crumbled

1 lb. rigatoni

½ cup grated pecorino

4 tbsp. unsalted butter

4 oz. fresh caciocavallo

Black peppercorns to taste,
ground in a mortar

at very low heat. ✦ Toss well to season and sprinkle with pecorino, pepper, butter, and caciocavallo. When well blended transfer to a serving bowl and serve hot.

BAKED PASTA WITH EGGPLANT

RIGGIDANELLA

CALABRIA

4 tbsp. unsalted butter

4 tbsp. all-purpose flour,
plus more as needed

2 cups milk, heated

½ cup extra-virgin olive oil

1¾ lbs. ripe plum tomatoes
(or 1 28-oz. can peeled tomatoes)

4 or 5 basil leaves

2 garlic cloves

1 small piece chili pepper

1 lb. eggplant (about 2 medium)

1 lb. short pasta (short rigatoni
or a similar kind)

Salt

Make a béchamel sauce: Heat 4 tablespoons of the butter in a saucepan. Stir in the flour and cook for a minute; do not allow it to brown. Add the hot milk very slowly, whisking constantly. Continue to cook on medium-low heat, until the sauce has thickened. Salt to taste. ✦ Preheat the oven to 400°F. Butter a baking pan. Heat half of the olive oil in saucepan and add the tomatoes, basil, garlic, and chili pepper. ✦ Cook over low heat until very thick, then pass it through a food mill and set it aside. ✦ Clean the eggplants, cut off the ends, then slice them lengthwise. ✦ Salt them, then drain them a little. Heat the remaining olive oil in a pan, add the eggplant, and cook until golden. Drain on paper towels. ✦ Boil the pasta in salted water until al dente, pass it under cold water to stop the cooking, and drain well. ✦ Cover the bottom and sides of the prepared pan with slices of eggplant; on top of the eggplant spread a layer of béchamel. Next, place a layer of the cooked pasta, then add some of the tomato sauce, then another layer of eggplant over this, and so on, layer after layer, ending with a layer of eggplant and béchamel sauce. ✦ Bake for about 15 minutes, or until the liquids evaporate. If it has become compact, you can turn it out onto a serving plate; otherwise, serve it directly from the baking pan.

| # FILLINGS FOR TIELLAS

PUGLIA

With octopus (or squid or cuttlefish):

2 lbs. octopus (those with two rows of suckers on their tentacles) or squid or cuttlefish

2 tbsp. chopped flat-leaf parsley

3 garlic cloves

¾ lb. plum tomatoes, peeled, drained, and cut in pieces

Chili pepper (as much as desired)

¼ cup extra-virgin olive oil

¼ cup dry white wine

1 pinch salt

With onions:

¼ cup extra-virgin olive oil

2 lbs. onions, thinly sliced

4 large eggs, beaten

2 tbsp. chopped flat-leaf parsley

Grated Parmigiano-Reggiano

7 oz. scamorza cheese or cheese from Itri, cut in small pieces

Salt and pepper

With escarole and cod:

4½ lbs. escarole

1½ lbs. salt-dried cod, soaked and chopped in pieces (or anchovies, boned and soaked in olive oil overnight)

3 garlic cloves, chopped

Pinch chili pepper flakes

2 tbsp. chopped flat-leaf parsley

1⅔ cups pitted Gaeta (black) olives

2 tbsp. extra-virgin olive oil

2 or 3 tbsp. coarse salt

With anchovies or sardines:

1½ lbs. fresh anchovies or sardines

1½ cups dry white wine

CONTINUED

The *tiella* (or *teglia*) is the layered dish so typical of Puglia. Prepare the dough as in recipe on page 411.

Put the octopus (or squid or cuttlefish) whole in a pan, adding neither olive oil nor water; cover, and cook them in their own liquid. Let them cool, then slice in pieces. ✦ Combine the sliced octopus with all the other ingredients, let them sit to absorb the flavors, then use the mixture to fill the *tiella*. Bake as in the recipe on page 411.

Heat half the olive oil in a pan over low heat and add the onions. ✦ When the onions begin to take on color, pour in the eggs, parsley, 2 tablespoons olive oil, and Parmigiano-Reggiano. Season with salt and pepper and stir to mix well. Fill the *tiella* with this. ✦ Lay the slices of scamorza on top of the filling. ✦ Then cover with another disk of dough. Pinch the edges to seal them well. Pierce the top of the *tiella* and brush with the remaining olive oil before placing in the oven. Bake as in the recipe on page 411.

Wash the escarole, drain, toss with salt, and cover it with a weight over it to make it wilt. Stir it every so often and after a few hours squeeze dry. ✦ Meanwhile combine the cod, garlic, chili pepper, parsley, olives, and olive oil. ✦ Mix all of these ingredients with the escarole. ✦ Place this filling in the dough lining the *tiella*. Bake as in the recipe on page 411.

Wash and bone the fish, removing the heads and tails. ✦ Let them sit for about 30 minutes in white wine mixed with vinegar. Drain well and pat dry. ✦ Crush the fish and mix them with the olive oil, garlic, chili pepper,

¼ cup white wine vinegar
¼ cup olive oil
1 garlic clove, minced
Pinch chili pepper flakes
Black olives, pitted
Salt

olives, and salt. ✦ Use mixture to fill the lined *tiella* and bake as in the recipe on page 411.

With spinach and ricotta:
3 cups fresh ricotta
2 tbsp. pine nuts
1 tbsp. raisins, soaked in warm water and drained
2 tbsp. unsalted butter, softened
12 cups spinach, washed, dried, and chopped
Pepper

Work together the ricotta, pine nuts, raisins, butter, and pepper. ✦ Add the spinach and blend well. ✦ Use this mixture to fill the lined *tiella* and bake as in the recipe on page 411.

RISO A ROSTO

BAKED RICE AND MEAT

LIGURIA

4 tbsp. unsalted butter
½ cup coarsely chopped flat-leaf parsley
1 small onion, chopped
6 oz. lean veal (loin)
4 oz. veal breast
2⅓ cups Arborio rice
3 cups meat sauce (*sugo di carne*, see page 634)
Meat broth (if necessary)
3 tbsp. grated Parmigiano-Reggiano

Preheat the oven to 350°F. Butter a baking dish. Heat the butter in a pan over low heat; add the parsley and onion and cook until fragrant. Remove them from the pan. Chop together the two kinds of veal and cook. ✦ Cook the rice for 10 minutes in the meat sauce, thinning it with a little broth if necessary. ✦ Add the onion mixture, veal, and Parmigiano-Reggiano. ✦ When cooked (the rice, al dente, should be somewhat dry) pour the rice mixture into the dish, pat it down with a fork, and bake until it has a nice crust, about 25 minutes.

RISO ALLA GENOVESE

GENOESE RICE

LIGURIA

¼ cup extra-virgin olive oil
1 tbsp. unsalted butter
1 medium onion, minced
6 oz. sausage meat, crumbled
CONTINUED

Preheat oven to 350°F, heat the oil and butter in an ovenproof pan; add the onion. ✦ When the onion is golden add the sausage meat, peas, artichoke, and mushrooms. ✦ Cook slowly with the addition of a little broth. ✦ Meanwhile, cook the rice in lightly salted boiling water but for only 5 minutes; drain and add to the sauce. ✦ Add more broth and Parmigiano-Reggiano and bake

¼ cup fresh shelled peas

1 artichoke, cut in thin slices

½ cup dried mushrooms, soaked in warm water, drained, and chopped

1 cup meat broth

3 cups rice

Grated Parmigiano-Reggiano

until the rice is cooked and the top has formed a crust, about 30 minutes.

✦ **LOCAL TRADITION** ✦

RISO CO-I FIDÊ

This dish, typical of Sestri Levante in Liguria, took its fresh flavors from sea anemones and sea urchin roe. The anemones would be sautéed in butter before adding rice to the pan to toast. Broth of reef fish or limpets would be gradually added and cooked into the rice. When the rice was nearly cooked, it was removed from the heat and immediately poured over the roe, stirred, and covered for two to three minutes. Salt was never added to either the anemones or the broth.

RISO CON GRANSEOLA E DATTERI

RICE WITH CRABS AND RAZOR CLAMS

FRIULI-VENEZIA GIULIA

2 lbs. razor clams

1 tbsp. olive oil

1 small onion, minced

2 cups Vialone nano rice

Cooked meat of 2 large crabs

½ cup flat-leaf parsley

Salt and pepper

Wash the clams and put them in a pan without water. Cover and cook at high heat until the shells open and the clams give up all their liquid. ✦ Drain, reserving the liquid, and discard the shells. ✦ In the same pan heat the olive oil and cook the onion until soft. ✦ Add the rice, let it toast, then add the clams and their liquid. Add salt and pepper. Cover and cook, stirring occasionally, over low heat. ✦ Chop together the crab meat and parsley. When the rice is nearly cooked, about 25 minutes, add the crab mixture and any liquid contained in the crabs.

RISO CON LA ZUCCA | # RICE WITH SQUASH

EMILIA-ROMAGNA

6 tbsp. unsalted butter

1 small onion, minced

2 ¼ lbs. winter squash, peeled, seeded, and coarsely chopped

1 tbsp. sugar

6 cups milk

1 ⅓ cups Carnaroli rice

Grated Parmigiano-Reggiano

Salt

This dish is typical of Ferrara. *All'onda* means "wavy," which means when you tilt the pan the surface of the rice should ripple like waves in the ocean, that is, move fluidly.

Heat half the butter in a large pan and sauté the onion. Add the squash, salt, and sugar and cook until the squash cooks to a purée. ✦ Pour in the milk and as soon as it boils add the rice. Lower the heat and simmer the rice until it is *all'onda*. ✦ If the rice is still not fully cooked when the milk has been absorbed, add warm water. ✦ Season with the remaining butter and Parmigiano-Reggiano. Serve immediately.

PASTA, POLENTA & RICE

✦ **LOCAL TRADITION** ✦

RISO CON I FEGATINI

This dish of rice and livers from the Veneto was an abundant feature at festive country weddings, since the traditional slaughter of poultry at such events meant the ingredients would all be in ready supply. The giblets of hens, geese, and other poultry were roasted with onion, celery, cinnamon sticks, black pepper, and white wine until cooked through, before the rice was added and cooked with ladles of fine broth from boiled meats to be served later. The finished soup would be served boiling hot and "fixed," meaning with a high relationship between rice and liquid, with abundant grated cheese.

RISO E ASPARAGI | # RICE AND ASPARAGUS

LOMBARDIA

1 ½ lbs. asparagus

2 cups Carnaroli or Arborio rice

4 oz. Taleggio or similar cow's-milk cheese, cubed

3 tbsp. unsalted butter

Grated Parmigiano-Reggiano may also be added at the end of the cooking of this dish.

Cut away any rough areas on the asparagus stalks and remove the outer layer with a vegetable peeler. ✦ Tie the stalks in bunches with the tips all at the same height and trim the bottoms of the stalks so that they are all the same length. ✦ Stand them in lightly salted boiling water, cover, and let them simmer about 15 minutes. ✦ Drain, reserving the liquid, and cut off the tips. Discard the stalks. ✦ Add water to the cooking liquid to bring it to around 8 cups, return it to a boil, and add the rice. ✦ Cook the rice, stirring it occasionally so that it absorbs the liquid. ✦ Before serving fold in the cheese, asparagus tips, and butter. Mix well and serve.

RICE AND BEANS

RISO E FAGIOLI

VENETO

2 oz. salted *lardo* (see page 2), finely minced

A few sage leaves

1 medium onion, thinly sliced

1 garlic clove, thinly sliced

4 oz. pork rind, chopped

¾ lb. dried beans, soaked in water overnight and drained

2 tbsp. tomato purée

A few basil leaves

4 cups rice

Heat the *lardo* with the sage in a pan (preferably earthenware) until fragrant, then sauté the onion, garlic, and pork rind; add the beans. ✦ Add the tomato purée, basil, and as much water as needed to cook the beans. Cook until the beans are tender but not mushy. ✦ Add the rice along with more water if needed, although the result should be dense. Cook until the rice is tender.

FELTRE-STYLE RICE AND BEANS

RISO E FAGIOLI ALLA FELTRINA

VENETO

2 cups dried cranberry beans (Lamon), soaked overnight and drained

1 bay leaf

1 sage leaf

3 cups Vialone nano rice (can use Arborio)

4 tbsp. unsalted butter

2 oz. cheese, preferably *Piave stravecchio*

Salt

Boil the beans in lightly salted water to cover with a bay leaf and sage leaf; when cooked put through a food mill and set aside. ✦ Cook the rice until al dente in 7 cups lightly salted water. Drain, mix in the butter and cheese, and pack it into a round mold with a hole in the center; turn it out on a serving plate. ✦ Fill the hole in the center of the mold with bean purée and serve.

RICE AND PEAS 1

VENETO

2 lbs. fresh peas

¼ cup (4 tbsp.) unsalted butter

2 tbsp. extra-virgin olive oil

1 garlic clove, minced

2 medium onions,
1 minced, 1 chopped

½ cup chopped flat-leaf parsley

1 carrot, chopped

1 celery stalk, chopped

1⅔ cups rice (Vialone nano
or Carnaroli)

Grated Parmigiano-Reggiano

Salt

Popularly known as *risi e bisi*, this dish, typical of the Lumignano (a mountainous area in the province of Vicenza), is prepared like this: finely chop pancetta, parsley, and onion and sauté in butter and oil. When cooked add Lumignano peas of the correct ripeness, cook until just tender, then add the rice and the right amount of broth. When the soup is about medium thickness add grated Parmigiano-Reggiano. Some of the broth can be replaced by water in which the fresh pods were boiled, for this will add aroma and delicacy to the soup.

Shell the peas, setting aside the pods. ✦ Heat half the butter and the olive oil in a pan and sauté the garlic and the minced onion. ✦ Add the peas with a little water, sprinkle in the parsley, and cook at medium heat. ✦ Meanwhile clean the pea pods, cutting away the stems, wash them, and put them in a pot of lightly salted boiling water, with the remaining onion, carrot, celery, and salt; simmer for 1 hour, making sure the level of the water does not diminish too much. ✦ Strain the resulting broth and adjust for salt. ✦ When the peas are almost cooked, add the rice, let it toast a few minutes, then slowly add the broth from cooking the pods. ✦ When the rice is done, add the cheese and the remaining butter. Serve the rice *all'onda* (see page 343).

RICE AND PEAS 2

VENETO

2 lbs. fresh peas

2 tbsp. extra-virgin olive oil

3 tbsp. unsalted butter

1 garlic clove, chopped

2 medium onions,
1 minced, 1 chopped

2 tbsp. chopped flat-leaf parsley

1 carrot, chopped

1 celery stalk, chopped

1⅔ cups Vialone nano rice

½ cup grated Parmigiano-Reggiano

This recipe was much in use in Venice during the doge's (chief magistrate's) festivities, but Padua claims to have invented it. The dispute is the subject of ongoing controversy.

Shell the peas, setting aside the pods. ✦ Heat the olive oil and half of the butter in a pan and sauté the garlic and the minced onion. ✦ Add the peas, a little water, and parsley and cook at medium heat. ✦ Clean the pods then cook in lightly salted boiling water with the chopped onion, carrot, and celery. Add salt. ✦ After about 1 hour of cooking (the water should not diminish too much) strain the broth. ✦ Add the rice to the peas, toast for a few minutes, then begin adding the broth, a little at a time, to cook the rice, stirring constantly. ✦ When the rice is cooked add the remaining butter and the Parmigiano-Reggiano, and mix well.

RICE AND TURNIPS

LOMBARDIA

¾ lb. tender turnips

½ cup flat-leaf parsley leaves

2 oz. *lardo* (see page 2)
(or 4 oz. prosciutto fat)

1 garlic clove, crushed (if desired)

5 cups meat broth

1 ¼ cups Vialone nano rice

1 cup grated Parmigiano-Reggiano

This dish is typical not only of the Milan area but also all of Lombardia. A widespread variation begins with a minced half onion and 4 ounces of prosciutto fat cooked in butter; 10 cups of water are poured over this, then salt and pepper and the rice. Before the rice is cooked slices of boiled turnip are added, then butter and parsley. Grated cheese is added at the table.

Clean the turnips, trim and peel them, and cut in very thin slices. ✦ Immerse the slices in cold water for 30 minutes, then drain. ✦ Wash the parsley and mince it together with the *lardo*, adding garlic, if desired. ✦ Bring the broth to a boil, add the turnips, and when the water returns to a boil, add the rice and parsley mixture. ✦ Cook at high heat 15 to 20 minutes and when the rice is cooked add ½ cup Parmigiano-Reggiano, mix well, and put in a tureen. Serve with more cheese.

RICE AND CELERY

VENETO

1 celery stalk, diced

1 medium onion, thinly sliced

1 carrot, minced

½ cup olive oil

4 tbsp. unsalted butter

¼ cup white wine

6 cups broth, plus more as needed

3 cups Vialone gigante rice
(can use Arborio)

Salt

This dish can be served almost dry, brothy like a soup, or with a medium risotto consistency, *all'onda*.

Combine the celery, onion, carrot, olive oil, and butter in a saucepan. ✦ Add salt, then cook over very low heat for about 30 minutes, or until completely softened (almost to a mush), adding the wine halfway through the cooking. ✦ Transfer this mixture to a pot and add the broth. ✦ When the broth comes to a boil pour in the rice and stir to keep it from sticking. ✦ When the rice has absorbed all the liquid add tablespoons of boiling broth until reaching the desired thickness.

VERONESE RICE AND TRIPE

VENETO

2 lbs. tripe

¼ cup olive oil

CONTINUED

Wash and cook the tripe in water to cover for at least 1½ hours. ✦ Cut it in strips. ✦ Heat the olive oil and butter in a pan and sauté the onion, carrot, celery, parsley, and rosemary. Salt and pepper to taste. ✦ Dredge the tripe in the cornmeal and add it to the pan, then add half

4 tbsp. unsalted butter

1 medium onion, chopped

1 carrot, chopped

2 celery stalks, chopped

2 tbsp. chopped flat-leaf parsley

1 sprig rosemary

½ cup cornmeal

6 cups meat broth

1⅔ cups Vialone nano rice (can use Arborio)

2 tbsp. grated Veronese monte cheese (can use Parmigiano-Reggiano), plus more for serving

Salt and pepper

the broth. ✦ Cook at low heat for at least 2 to 3 hours, according to the thickness of the tripe. ✦ When the tripe is tender add the remaining broth and when it returns to a boil pour in the rice. ✦ In about 20 minutes the mixture will have reached the right thickness for a good soup. Sprinkle with cheese and add more to each plate.

RICE WITH MEAT SAUCE

RISO IN CAGNON

LIGURIA

2⅓ cups rice (Arborio or Carnaroli)

4 cups meat sauce with sausage (see page 413)

2 tbsp. unsalted butter

Grated Parmigiano-Reggiano

Salt

According to Waverley Root, this dish gets its name from the resemblance of the grains of rice to a kind of black-headed worm called, in the local dialect, *cagnon*.

Boil the rice until half cooked in water to cover with only a little salt; drain and put it in a saucepan with a meat sauce made with a good deal of crumbled sausage meat. ✦ When the rice is cooked *all'onda* (see page 343), turn off the heat and mix in the butter and Parmigiano-Reggiano. Serve hot.

RICE WITH CHEESE SAUCE

RISO IN CAGNON

PIEMONTE

2 cups Baldo or Carnaroli rice (can use Arborio)

7 oz. *toma* from Maccagno or *bettelmatt* (can substitute fontina), cubed

4 tbsp. unsalted butter

½ cup grated Parmigiano-Reggiano

Salt

Bring lightly salted water to a boil in a pot and add the rice. ✦ Cook it and drain it, leaving it very soft, and pour it into a warmed bowl. ✦ Add the cubed cheese, stirring well until it melts and blends thoroughly. ✦ In pan over medium heat, heat the butter and when it browns pour it over the rice. Add the cheese.

347

GREEN RICE

MARCHE

¼ cup extra-virgin olive oil

2 celery stalks, finely chopped

2 carrots, finely chopped

2 leeks, finely chopped

1 small onion, minced

1 large head of spinach, cleaned, drained, and finely chopped

1⅔ cups Vialone nano or Carnaroli rice

1 tbsp. unsalted butter

2 tbsp. chopped flat-leaf parsley

Salt and pepper

Heat the olive oil in a saucepan and when it is hot add the vegetables. ✦ As soon as they are soft add the rice, stirring well and slowly adding warm water. ✦ Add the butter, then salt and pepper, and when the rice is tender stir in the parsley.

RICE WITH FENNEL AND RICOTTA

RISO, FINOCCHIO E RICOTTA

CALABRIA

2 bunches fennel (wild if possible)

1⅔ cups rice (Vialone nano or Carnaroli)

6 oz. ricotta

Clean, rinse, and chop the fennel. Boil it in lightly salted water to cover until it is cooked through, about 10 minutes. ✦ Drain and set aside, reserving the cooking liquid. ✦ Use the liquid to cook the rice, and when the rice is tender drain it and carefully blend in the ricotta and fennel. Serve hot.

RICE AND MUSHROOMS

RISOT E FONSC

PIEMONTE

4 tbsp. unsalted butter

1 medium onion, minced

1⅔ cups rice

3 tbsp. very dry cognac

4½ cups broth (if possible half beef and half chicken), heated to boiling

Fresh mushrooms (in season), finely chopped (or dried mushrooms, soaked, drained, and chopped)

Grated Parmigiano-Reggiano

This dish is typical of Novara.

Melt half of the butter in a saucepan and add the onion. When the onion has taken on some color pour in the rice and turn the heat up. Toast the rice lightly, and when it has taken on color add the cognac and turn the heat up to high to evaporate the alcohol. ✦ Cover the rice with boiling broth and let it cook, at low heat, without stirring. ✦ Meanwhile melt the remaining butter in a pan. Add the mushrooms and cook for a few minutes. When the rice is nearly cooked, add the mushrooms, stir well, and serve hot. Serve the Parmigiano-Reggiano at the table.

RISOTTO AI FINOCCHI | # RISOTTO WITH FENNEL

PIEMONTE

This dish is typical of Asti.

2 tbsp. extra-virgin olive oil
4 tbsp. unsalted butter
1 medium onion, finely chopped
1 leek, finely chopped
¼ stalk celery, finely chopped
½ carrot, finely chopped
4 oz. sausage meat
2 ⅓ cups fennel hearts, chopped
Pinch fennel seeds
1 ⅔ cups Carnaroli rice
(can use Arborio)
½ cup dry white wine
5 cups chicken or vegetable broth
½ cup grated Parmigiano-Reggiano
1 tbsp. finely chopped
flat-leaf parsley
1 tbsp. finely chopped fennel fronds

Heat the olive oil and half the butter in a pan and sauté the onion, leek, celery, and carrot. ✦ Add the sausage meat, breaking it up with a wooden spoon. ✦ Stir in the fennel and fennel seeds and cook 2 minutes. Add the rice, and toss to coat with the oil. When the rice is translucent, add the wine and stir until the wine evaporates. ✦ Add ½ cup broth, stirring with a wooden spoon, until all of the liquid has been absorbed. Continue adding liquid ½ cup at a time, stirring constantly. After about 20 minutes, taste the rice for texture and seasoning. It should be al dente: tender, but not mushy. ✦ When the rice is al dente, turn off the heat and stir in the remaining butter and cheese. ✦ Before serving sprinkle on the parsley and fennel fronds.

RISOTTO AI FUNGHI | # RISOTTO WITH MUSHROOMS

PIEMONTE

6 tbsp. unsalted butter
1 medium onion, minced
1 lb. porcini mushrooms, sliced
2 cups Arborio rice
5 cups broth
Grated Parmigiano-Reggiano
Salt

Heat 4 tablespoons butter in a pan and sauté the onion, then add the mushrooms. ✦ When they are browned add the rice and cook as in the recipe above. ✦ Remove from the heat and work in the remaining butter with a little Parmigiano-Reggiano and cover it for a few minutes before serving.

RISOTTO AL BARBERA | # RISOTTO WITH BARBERA

PIEMONTE

3 tbsp. extra-virgin olive oil

CONTINUED

This risotto is typical of Monferrato.

Heat the olive oil and half the butter in a saucepan. Add the marrow, bay leaves, and onions. ✦ When the onions are pale, add half the wine and the potato flour and cook

349

6 tbsp. unsalted butter
2 oz. beef marrow, minced
2 bay leaves
2 medium onions, minced
2 ½ cups Barbera wine
Pinch potato flour
2 ⅓ cups rice (Roma or Baldo, if possible, or Arborio)
Meat broth
3 tbsp. tomato purée
1 bunch sage
⅔ cup grated Parmigiano-Reggiano
Pinch grated nutmeg
Black pepper

down the liquid. ✦ Then add the rice, raise the heat, and while stirring with a wooden spoon, let the rice absorb the liquid. ✦ Mix half the remaining wine with ½ cup of broth, and add it when the rice is well toasted. Add the tomato purée and sage (which should be removed when the rice is cooked). Warm the remaining wine. ✦ When this second helping of wine has been absorbed cook the risotto as in the recipe on page 349. ✦ When the rice is tender work in the remaining butter and Parmigiano-Reggiano, give it a generous grinding of black pepper, and finish with nutmeg plus another 3 to 4 tablespoons of warmed Barbera.

RISOTTO WITH BAROLO

PIEMONTE

4 tbsp. unsalted butter
1 bay leaf
1 medium onion, finely chopped
2 ½ cups Arborio rice
1 cup Barolo red wine, slightly warmed
2 cups beef broth
Grated Parmigiano-Reggiano

This dish is typical of Cuneo.

Heat half the butter with the bay leaf in a saucepan. Add the onion and sauté until soft, then pour in the rice. ✦ Stir a few minutes then add the Barolo and cook until it evaporates. ✦ Gradually add the broth, stirring until the rice is al dente, as in the recipe on page 349. ✦ Add the remaining butter and cheese. Serve hot.

RISOTTO WITH GORGONZOLA

PIEMONTE

5 tbsp. unsalted butter
1 medium onion, minced
2 cups Arborio rice
½ cup dry white wine
4 cups meat broth
3 oz. Gorgonzola dolce, chopped
3 oz. Gorgonzola piccante, chopped
1 cup heavy cream
Salt and pepper (if necessary)

Heat half the butter in a pan and sauté the onion until it is soft. Add the rice and toast it for a few minutes. ✦ Pour in the white wine, let it evaporate, then continue cooking the rice by adding the stock a little at a time as in the recipe on page 349. ✦ About 20 minutes through the cooking add the two types of Gorgonzola and cream, stirring well to make them blend into the rice. If necessary, add salt and pepper. ✦ When the rice is cooked to al dente, add the remaining butter, cover for about 3 minutes, then serve.

RISOTTO AL NERO DI SEPIA

BLACK RISOTTO WITH CUTTLEFISH INK

VENETO

3 tbsp. extra-virgin olive oil

1 small onion, minced

1 garlic clove, minced

1 lb. cuttlefish, cleaned and cut into strips (with ink sacs)

3 tbsp. finely chopped flat-leaf parsley

¼ cup red wine

1⅔ cups Vialone nano rice

4 cups vegetable broth (or fish stock from cooking crustaceans or small fish)

Salt and pepper

Heat the olive oil in a saucepan and sauté the onion and garlic, adding salt and pepper. ✦ Add the cuttlefish and parsley. ✦ Pour in the red wine and crush 2 of the ink sacs. Cook at low heat for about 40 minutes, stirring from time to time. ✦ Add the rice and continue cooking, stirring constantly and adding ladlefuls of the broth as needed, as in the recipe on page 349. ✦ Complete the cooking in about 20 minutes. Remove the pan from the heat, give it one final energetic stir, and serve.

PASTA, POLENTA & RICE

RISOTTO AL SOUFFLÉ E PISTILLI DI ZAFFERANO

SAFFRON RISOTTO SOUFFLÉ

PIEMONTE

For the rice:

¼ lb. (1 stick) unsalted butter

⅓ cup chopped onion

1⅔ cups Arborio rice

2 tsp. saffron threads

2 cups chicken or vegetable broth

1 cup heavy cream

⅔ cup grated Parmigiano-Reggiano

For the soufflé:

¼ lb. (1 stick) plus 3 tbsp. unsalted butter

2 tbsp. all-purpose flour

1 cup milk

10 large eggs, beaten

⅔ cup grated Parmigiano-Reggiano

2 large egg whites, beaten stiff

Preheat the oven to 400°F. Melt half the butter in a saucepan, then add the onion and sauté until translucent. Add the rice and saffron and toast, then add the broth gradually as in the recipe on page 349. Stir in the cream, remaining butter, and cheese at the end of cooking. ✦ Meanwhile, use the butter, flour, and milk to prepare a béchamel sauce as in the recipe on page 349. Whisk a little of the béchamel into the eggs to warm them, then whisk the eggs back into the béchamel in the pan. Remove from the heat and stir in the cheese. Gently fold in the egg whites. ✦ Put the cooked risotto into a deep baking dish and cover evenly with the egg mixture. ✦ Bake 20 minutes until the top is golden and serve immediately.

RISOTTO WITH RED WINE

4 tbsp. unsalted butter

1 small onion, minced

2½ cups Vialone nano rice (can use Arborio)

½ cup red wine

4 cups meat broth, heated to boiling

Grated Parmigiano-Reggiano

For the wine use Dolcetto, Freisa, or Grignolino.

Melt the butter in a pan, add the onion, and cook without letting the onion brown. ✦ Add the rice, stirring well. ✦ Pour in the wine and when it has evaporated begin adding, as needed, ladlefuls of boiling broth to cook the rice as in the recipe on page 349. ✦ Cook, stirring constantly, for about 20 minutes, then remove from the heat, stir in Parmigiano-Reggiano, cover, and let rest about 5 minutes before serving hot.

RISOTTO ALL'ANATRA DI VALLE

WILD DUCK RISOTTO

EMILIA-ROMAGNA

Half a wild duck, about 2 lbs.

½ cup extra-virgin olive oil

1 medium onion, minced

4 oz. pancetta, diced

¼ cup Trebbiano wine (or other dry white wine)

1 tbsp. tomato paste, diluted in a little water

1⅔ cups Vialone nano rice

6 cups broth (duck, capon, or rich chicken), heated to boiling, as needed

2 tbsp. unsalted butter

Grated Parmigiano-Reggiano

Salt and pepper

This dish is typical of Cesena.

Pluck and clean the duck inside and out. Heat the olive oil in a large pan and add the onion and pancetta. Add the duck. Add salt and pepper and the wine, simmering until the wine has evaporated. ✦ When the duck has browned, stir in the tomato paste mixture. ✦ Cook over low heat about 90 minutes. ✦ Remove the duck and cut in pieces; use the less attractive pieces to make a sauce: pull the meat off the bone and return to the pan. ✦ Heat the butter and add the rice. Cook until the grains are translucent, then pour in ladles of boiling broth as needed. ✦ When the rice is half cooked add the duck sauce. ✦ When the rice is done add the butter and a good amount of Parmigiano-Reggiano. ✦ Serve the duck meat (breast, thigh) atop the risotto on a serving plate and provide cheese at the table.

RISOTTO ALLA CERTOSINA

FROG LEG RISOTTO

LOMBARDIA

3½ lbs. freshwater prawns

2 lbs. frogs, skinned and without heads

CONTINUED

Frogs were once abundant in the rice paddies of northern Italy. This dish is a specialty of the province of Pavia. For the wine use a white from the area of Oltrepò Pavese if possible.

Remove the tails from the prawns and the legs from the frogs, grind what remains in a mortar, and boil it in a little lightly salted water with the bay leaves. ✦ Pass the

2 bay leaves

6 cups fish broth from fish that has been cooked without lemon or vinegar

½ cup extra-virgin olive oil

1½ cups finely chopped celery, carrot, garlic, and onion

3¾ cups Carnaroli or Arborio rice

1 lb. fresh peas, shelled

1 lb. perch fillets

All-purpose flour

2 tbsp. unsalted butter

1 medium onion, sliced

½ cup dry white wine

Flat-leaf parsley, chopped

Salt

resulting liquid through cheesecloth and keep warm, adding fish broth. ✦ Heat the olive oil in a pan and sauté the vegetables. ✦ Add the rice and cook as in the recipe on page 349, adding the peas with the first addition of broth. Add the frogs legs after 10 minutes, then add the prawns 5 minutes later. ✦ Meanwhile, cook the fish. Dip the fish fillets in flour. Heat the butter and sauté the onion until golden. Add the fish and cook until browned. Sprinkle with wine. Sprinkle the rice with parsley and serve with the fish on top.

RISOTTO ALLA CREMA DI PORRI

RISOTTO WITH CREAM OF LEEK

PIEMONTE

½ cup (¼ lb.) unsalted butter

½ cup finely chopped onion

1 small garlic clove, finely chopped

½ cup chopped carrot

2 oz. mushrooms, chopped

½ lb. leeks, white parts sliced in rings and rinsed, greens chopped fine and rinsed well

6 cups chicken or vegetable broth

1⅔ cups rice (S. Andrea, if possible or Arborio)

⅓ cup heavy cream

⅓ cup Parmigiano-Reggiano

Heat half the butter in a pan over low heat and slowly sauté the onion, garlic, carrot, mushrooms, and leeks. ✦ When they begin to brown, add the broth and slowly cook for 1 hour, adding more warm water as the broth evaporates. ✦ Blend, then strain to create a smooth mixture. ✦ Heat 2 tablespoons of the butter in a saucepan. Add the rice and cook as in the recipe on page 349, adding the leek purée in place of the broth. ✦ When the rice is al dente add the cream and take the rice off the heat. ✦ Stir in the remaining butter and cheese. Serve in individual bowls, decorating the bowls with the remaining leek greens.

RISOTTO ALLA MARINARA

SEAFOOD RISOTTO

SICILIA

1 lb. clams

1 lb. mussels

CONTINUED

Rinse the clams and scrub and clean the mussels. Steam the clams and mussels in a covered pan with no additional water until the shells open; shell them (discarding the shells) and reserve the liquid they have given off, straining it and setting it aside. ✦ Cook the shrimp in

1 lb. small shrimp

Zest of 1 lemon, in strips

¼ cup extra-virgin olive oil

1 medium onion, minced

1 celery stalk, minced

1 carrot, minced

2 small squid, cleaned and cut in strips

½ cup white wine

1 tbsp. tomato paste

2½ cups Vialone nano rice

1 spicy chili pepper, minced

½ cup grated aged caciocavallo

2 tbsp. finely chopped flat-leaf parsley (or basil)

Salt and pepper

lightly salted water with the lemon zest until pink; shell them and reserve their broth, straining it and combining it with the mussel and clam broth. ✦ Heat the olive oil in a saucepan and sauté the onion, celery, and carrot. ✦ Add the squid, shrimp, mussels, and clams. Stir for a few minutes, pour in the wine, and let it evaporate. ✦ Add the tomato paste, stir, dilute with a cup of the fish broth (from cooking the clams, mussels, and shrimp), add pepper, and cook, covered, for 10 minutes. ✦ Meanwhile, cook the rice in a little less than 4 cups of lightly salted water; when half cooked add the seafood and, if necessary, a few tablespoons of the fish liquid. ✦ Incorporate the chili pepper, caciocavallo, parsley (or basil), and let rest a few minutes before serving.

RISOTTO ALLA MILANESE

SAFFRON RISOTTO WITH MUSHROOMS

LOMBARDIA

½ cup pan juices from cooking meat

1 oz. bone marrow (double this amount if you have no pan juices), chopped

5 tbsp. unsalted butter

1 small onion, finely sliced

2 cups rice (Carnaroli, Arborio, or Vialone nano)

4 cups veal or chicken broth

2 tsp. saffron threads, soaked in warm broth and drained

1 cup dried porcini mushrooms, soaked in warm water, drained, and chopped

1 cup grated Parmigiano-Reggiano

Until 1909, in the years when Milan was still populated chiefly by L'Aquila Milanese, risotto was always made without wine or (horror of horrors) beer, as indicated in recipes from 1809, 1821, and 1843. The *cervellato* (brains) were no longer used, having been replaced by marrow or pan juices. The saffron threads (not powder), guarantee of authentic saffron, could be found at herbalists or in the area of production, such as at San Gavino in Sardegna or L'Aquila in the Abruzzo. The true Milanese eat risotto with a spoon. Serve with red wine. If desired add 1 ounce of dried mushrooms or slices of white truffle over the risotto at the moment of serving it.

Put the pan juices, bone marrow, 4 tablespoons butter, and onion in a saucepan over low heat; cook slowly until the onion takes on a golden hue. ✦ Add the rice and stir well to let it absorb the flavors. ✦ Turn up the heat and cook as in the recipe on page 349. ✦ Add the saffron threads to the rice about two-thirds of the way through the cooking time (about 12 minutes). ✦ Add the mushrooms. ✦ Last add the remaining butter and cheese. The rice should be *all'onda* (see page 343), not dry, with the grains visibly separate but joined by a creamy mixture.

COUNTRY-STYLE RISOTTO

RISOTTO ALLA PAESANA

LOMBARDIA

4 tbsp. unsalted butter
1 medium onion, finely sliced
2 cups rice
2 oz. *lardo* (see page 2)
(or pancetta), minced
4 cups meat broth
Grated Parmigiano-Reggiano

This risotto is typical of the Alta Brianza and Milano.

Heat the butter in a saucepan at low heat and sauté the onion. ✦ Stir in the rice with the *lardo* (or pancetta) and add broth, cooking as in the recipe on page 349. Serve with cheese.

RISOTTO WITH PARMIGIANO-REGGIANO

RISOTTO ALLA
PARMIGIANA

EMILIA-ROMAGNA

4 tbsp. extra-virgin olive oil
¼ lb. (1 stick) plus 3 tbsp.
unsalted butter
1 medium onion, finely chopped
2 ½ cups Carnaroli rice
(can use Arborio)
½ cup white wine
4 cups capon broth (skimmed of fat)
½ cup grated Parmigiano-Reggiano
Salt

Heat the olive oil and 4 tablespoons butter in a high-sided pan over low heat. Sauté the onion until golden, then add the rice and stir it to coat with the mixture. Cook as in the recipe on page 349, adding wine first, then broth. ✦ Adjust for salt. ✦ When the rice is al dente, add the remaining butter and Parmigiano-Reggiano. Mix well and serve immediately.

RISOTTO WITH SALAME

RISOTTO ALLA PILOTA

LOMBARDIA

1 ⅔ cups Vialone nano rice
6 oz. salame (preferably
Castiglione delle Stiviere)
or lean pork, cubed
4 tbsp. unsalted butter
½ cup grated Parmigiano-Reggiano,
plus more for serving
Salt and pepper

The name has nothing to do with airplanes and refers instead to rice huskers, known as *pilarini* or *piloti*. Very similar is the *Riso col puntel*, traditionally eaten during the celebrations accompanying the slaughter of a pig. A grilled pork chop is added to each plate, standing up with the meat end pointing up like a handle (*puntel*). Mantuan salame is made with a mixture of lean shoulder meat. At Castiglione delle Stiviere, a typical area for this rice dish, until a few years ago it was cooked over the embers of a fireplace, using a pot covered by rags with bricks placed on top to guarantee the hermetic closure.

In a heavy pot that holds heat well, boil 1 ⅔ cups water. ✦ Carefully pour in the rice a little at a time so that it forms a cone, the tip of which extends just above the water. ✦

Shake the pot from right to left in sudden jerks to mix around the rice without touching it with a spoon. ✦ Cook the rice at high heat for 10 to 12 minutes, then turn off the heat, stir the rice, and seal it shut by covering it with a cloth, putting on the lid, and placing a weight on it. ✦ Let it sit like that for 15 minutes. ✦ Meanwhile remove the salame from its casing. Heat the butter in a pan over low heat and brown the salame. ✦ When the rice has had its 15 minutes, uncover it, add the cooked salame, stir again, add some of the Parmigiano-Reggiano, and stir, then serve with more cheese on the side.

RISOTTO WITH SAUSAGE AND RUM

RISOTTO ALLA SALSICCIA
CON IL RHUM

PIEMONTE

¼ cup extra-virgin olive oil

2 medium onions, finely chopped

2 celery stalks with leaves,
finely chopped

1 carrot, finely chopped

2 garlic cloves

7 oz. lean sausage meat,
casings removed

½ cup rum

2⅓ cups Arborio rice

4 or 5 tbsp. tomato paste,
diluted in 1 cup warm broth

Bouquet garni wrapped in
cheesecloth (1 sprig rosemary,
sage, 2 bay leaves)

6 cups pork or chicken broth

4 tbsp. unsalted butter

¼ cup grated Parmigiano-Reggiano

Black pepper

Heat the olive oil in a saucepan and sauté the onions, celery, carrot, and garlic (remove when it is golden). ✦ Crumble in the sausage meat and brown. ✦ Setting aside a few tablespoons of meat, pour in half the rum and cook, stirring, until it is absorbed. ✦ Add the rice and toast it, stirring with a wooden spoon. ✦ Add the tomato paste mixture. ✦ Then cook the rice as in the recipe on page 349. ✦ Add the bouquet garni along with the first addition of broth (and remove it at the end of cooking). ✦ When the rice is *all'onda* (see page 343) and al dente, stir in the butter, the remaining rum, remaining meat, and cheese. Let it rest 3 minutes and serve hot.

RISOTTO WITH TROUT AND SAFFRON

RISOTTO ALLA TROTA
CON ZAFFERANO

ABRUZZO

6 medium-size trout

½ cup extra-virgin olive oil

CONTINUED

Simmer the medium trout in lightly salted water to cover, drain, and strain the cooking water, setting it aside. ✦ Clean the trout, bone them thoroughly, cut them in small pieces, and set aside. ✦ Heat half the olive oil in a saucepan and sauté the onion until soft. Mince the small trout

1 medium onion, finely chopped

2 small trout

Pinch saffron threads
(if possible from L'Aquila)

2½ cups Vialone nano rice

¼ cup dry white wine

2 tbsp. chopped flat-leaf parsley

Salt

and add to the pan. ✦ Dissolve the saffron threads in a little of the trout cooking liquid and set aside. ✦ Add the rice to the onion mixture and cook the risotto as in the recipe on page 349, adding the saffron liquid first. ✦ When the rice is almost cooked add the trout and wine. Transfer the rice to a serving bowl and dust with parsley. Drizzle with the remaining olive oil and serve.

RISOTTO WITH PORK AND VEAL

RISOTTO ALL'ISOLANA

VENETO

4 oz. lean veal, diced

4 oz. pork loin, diced

¼ lb. (1 stick) unsalted butter

1 sprig rosemary

6 cups veal broth

1⅔ cups Vialone nano rice
(can use Arborio)

½ cup grated Parmigiano-Reggiano

1 tsp. ground cinnamon

Salt and pepper

This meaty rice dish takes its name from the town of Isola della Scala in the Veneto, the region where the special Vialone nano rice is grown.

Season the meat with salt and pepper; let rest for 1 hour. Melt the butter in a pan over low heat. Add the rosemary, then the meat. Brown the meat and cook it slowly, removing and discarding the rosemary. Bring the broth to a boil in a pot, pour in the rice, and lower the heat. Simmer, covered, until the rice has completely absorbed the liquid, about 25 minutes. At this point add the meat mixture, cheese, and cinnamon. Stir well and serve immediately.

RISOTTO WITH SPUMANTE, FONTINA, AND MUSHROOMS

RISOTTO ALLO SPUMANTE, FONTINA, E FUNGHI

PIEMONTE

4 tbsp. unsalted butter

1 medium onion, minced

2 porcini mushrooms, sliced

2 cups rice

4 cups broth

5 oz. fontina, cubed

½ cup dry Asti Spumante

½ cup grated Parmigiano-Reggiano

Heat half the butter in a large saucepan over low heat. Add the onion and sauté until soft, then add the porcini. ✦ When the onion is brown add the rice, toast it, and cook as in the recipe on page 349. ✦ After about 15 minutes of cooking add the fontina, stirring until it is melted. ✦ When the rice is al dente, stir in the remaining butter and the spumante, stirring until it is absorbed. ✦ Remove from the heat and stir in the Parmigiano-Reggiano. Cover and let stand 5 minutes before serving.

RISOTTO WITH SAFFRON AND ZUCCHINI FLOWERS

PIEMONTE

¼ lb. (1 stick) plus 1 tbsp. unsalted butter

1 shallot, chopped

2 small zucchini, diced

1⅔ cups Baldo (or other superfine) rice

½ cup white wine

6 cups vegetable broth

Pinch saffron threads

8 zucchini flowers, cleaned and chopped

4 tbsp. grated Parmigiano-Reggiano

Salt and pepper

Heat 3 tablespoons butter in a pan over low heat and sauté the shallot. Add the zucchini and then the rice, stirring to toast it. ✦ Add the wine, and when it has evaporated cook the risotto as in the recipe on page 349. ✦ After about 15 minutes add the saffron and the zucchini flowers and continue cooking until the rice reaches the desired doneness. ✦ At that point adjust for salt, put in a good grinding of pepper, and stir in the remaining butter and cheese. Let stand for a few minutes before serving.

RISOTTO WITH PERCH AND ZUCCHINI FLOWERS

PIEMONTE

½ lb. (2 sticks) plus 2 tbsp. unsalted butter

1 medium onion, finely chopped

2⅓ cups Carnaroli or Baldo rice (can use Arborio)

½ cup dry white wine

6 cups fish broth (preferably made with lake fish)

20 zucchini flowers, cut in strips

20 perch fillets

Breadcrumbs

2 tbsp. chopped flat-leaf parsley

Melt 3 tablespoons butter in a saucepan and sauté the onion. ✦ Add the rice and toast, then pour in the white wine. ✦ When the wine has evaporated begin cooking the rice by adding the fish broth as in the recipe on page 349. ✦ Meanwhile heat 5 tablespoons butter in a second pan and sauté the zucchini flowers. ✦ Add them to the rice when it is nearly cooked. ✦ Lightly dip the perch fillets in the breadcrumbs. Heat the remaining butter in the pan in which the flowers were cooked and fry the perch until browned. When the rice is cooked set the fish on top and sprinkle with parsley.

RISOTTO WITH FRESHWATER PRAWNS

PIEMONTE

1¼ lbs. freshwater prawns

CONTINUED

Clean the prawns and shell them, putting the shells in a pot. ✦ Add the onion, celery, garlic, parsley, a few peppercorns, and about 6 cups of cold lightly salted water. ✦ Bring to a boil and simmer for about 30 minutes, then

1 medium onion, chopped

1 celery stalk, chopped

1 garlic clove, slivered

2 tbsp. chopped flat-leaf parsley

A few peppercorns

2 tbsp. extra-virgin olive oil

2 shallots, finely chopped

2 cups Vialone nano rice
(can use Arborio)

¼ cup dry white wine

1 tbsp. tomato purée

1 tbsp. unsalted butter

Salt and pepper

strain the broth and set aside. ✦ Heat the olive oil in a pan and sauté the shallots, then add the rice, stirring it around to toast it for a few minutes. ✦ Add the wine and when it has evaporated begin adding the fish broth and cook as in the recipe on page 349. ✦ After about 20 minutes add the prawns and tomato purée. ✦ Adjust for salt and pepper, and when the rice is done add the butter and serve.

RISOTTO CON
GLI STRIGOLI

RISOTTO WITH BLADDER CAMPION AND ONION

LOMBARDIA

¼ lb. (1 stick) plus 1 tbsp.
unsalted butter

1 medium onion, chopped

9 oz. *strigoli* (bladder campion;
see note, page 729), chopped

2 cups Carnaroli rice
(can use Arborio)

Chicken or vegetable broth

½ cup grated Parmigiano-Reggiano

Salt

Bladder campion can also be used to make a soup: having sautéed the onion and campion, cook the rice, thinning it with the broth, then bind it with egg yolks and cheese. This recipe is typical of the area of Brescia.

Heat half the butter in a saucepan over low heat and sauté the onion. Add a little salt and the bladder campion. After a minute or two add the rice, and when the rice is well coated with butter begin adding the broth and cook as in the recipe on page 349. When the rice is al dente, remove it from the heat and mix in the remaining butter and cheese. Serve very soft.

RISOTTO CON
GLI STRIGOLI

RISOTTO WITH WILD GREENS

UMBRIA

5 tbsp. extra-virgin olive oil

1 garlic clove, crushed

10½ oz. *strigoli* (bladder campion;
see note, page 729), chopped

2⅓ cups Carnaroli rice

6 cups chicken or vegetable broth

Salt

This risotto from the recent past is widespread in the area between Foligno and Spoleto. It uses the local extra-virgin olive oil and a wild herb dear to the gastronomic tradition of the areas around Foligno and Spoleto.

Heat the olive oil in a saucepan and add the garlic and bladder campion. ✦ Cover the pan and cook 5 to 6 minutes, then add the rice and toast it for 1 to 2 minutes. ✦ Cook the rice as in the recipe on page 349. Season with salt. Serve without cheese.

RISOTTO WITH HONEY MUSHROOMS

RISOTTO CON I CHIODINI

VENETO

¼ cup extra-virgin olive oil

1 garlic clove

2 tbsp. chopped flat-leaf parsley

1 cup honey mushrooms (*chiodini*, "nails," in Italian; can use pioppini)

¼ cup (4 tbsp.) unsalted butter

1 medium onion, minced

1½ cups Vialone nano rice

5 cups chicken or vegetable broth

2 tbsp. grated Parmigiano-Reggiano

This recipe is typical of the Montello area.

Heat the olive oil in a low, wide pan at high heat and add the garlic, parsley, and honey mushrooms; cook until all the liquid is absorbed. ✦ To make a risotto, in a separate pan heat half the butter and sauté the onion. Add the rice and toast to coat the grains, then gradually add the broth, cooking as in the recipe on page 349. ✦ After about 20 minutes begin adding the cooked mushrooms. ✦ When the rice is al dente, remove it from the heat and stir in the remaining butter and the cheese.

RISOTTO WITH BEANS

RISOTTO CON I FAGIOLI DELL'OCCHIO

LOMBARDIA

1¼ cups small dried beans, shelled

6 cups chicken broth

2 tbsp. extra-virgin olive oil

2 tbsp. unsalted butter

1 small onion, chopped

1 leek, chopped

1 small salame, chopped with fat removed

½ cup red wine

2½ cups Carnaroli or Arborio rice

This dish is very popular in the area of Lomellina. For the wine use Bonarda.

Soak the beans in water to cover by several inches at least 12 hours before use. ✦ Drain them, then put the beans in the broth and simmer them for about 1 hour. ✦ Heat the olive oil and butter in a saucepan and cook the onion and leek until soft. ✦ Add the salame and let it brown for a few minutes. ✦ Pour in the wine and let it evaporate. ✦ Add the rice and, after a brief toasting, slowly add the broth with the beans as in the recipe on page 349 until the rice is cooked al dente.

RISOTTO WITH CAMPION

RISOTTO CON IL GRISO

FRIULI-VENEZIA GIULIA

1 lb. bladder campion (*Silene agustifolia;* see note, page 93)

2 tbsp. unsalted butter

1 garlic clove

3 cups Vialone nano rice

CONTINUED

Boil the campion until wilted, drain, and finely chop. ✦ Heat half the butter in a saucepan and cook the garlic, removing it when light brown. ✦ Add the campion and sauté, then add the rice; stir quickly then begin slowly adding the broth as with a normal risotto (see page 349). ✦ When the rice is almost cooked add the Parmigiano-Reggiano, adjust salt and pepper, and add the remaining

4 to 6 cups chicken or vegetable broth

⅓ cup grated Parmigiano-Reggiano

Salt and pepper

butter. In the end the rice should be somewhat fluid (*all'onda*; see note, page 343).

RISOTTO CON IL TASTASAL

SPICED RISOTTO WITH SALAME

VENETO

4 tbsp. unsalted butter

1 small onion, chopped

1 garlic clove, crushed

¼ cup dry white wine

10 oz. fresh, soft salame (preferably *tastasal*), minced

1⅔ cups Vialone nano rice

6 cups pork broth, skimmed of fat

½ cup grated cheese (such as Parmigiano-Reggiano)

Pinch ground cloves

Pinch ground cinnamon

Ground pepper

This dish is typical of the Veronese countryside and was originally made following the slaughter of a pig and the butchering of its meat.

Heat the butter in a pan and sauté the onion and garlic. ✦ Pour in the wine and let it evaporate. ✦ Add the salame and slowly cook it thoroughly. ✦ Mix the rice into this mixture and let it soak up the flavors. ✦ Add the broth as in the recipe on page 349, stirring until the rice is al dente. ✦ Complete the risotto by working in the cheese, cloves, cinnamon, and pepper.

RISOTTO CON LA SALSICCIA

RISOTTO WITH SAUSAGE 1

EMILIA-ROMAGNA

4 tbsp. unsalted butter

1 small onion, finely chopped

1⅔ cups Carnaroli rice

¼ cup dry red wine

6 cups pork broth

6 oz. pork sausage meat, diced

4 tbsp. tomato purée

½ cup grated Parmigiano-Reggiano

Salt

This risotto is typical of Ferrara.

In a large saucepan heat half the butter; add the onion. ✦ When the onion has begun to brown add the rice and mix well to make it pick up the flavors. ✦ Pour in the wine and raise the heat to cook it off. ✦ Add the broth to the rice a little at a time, as in the recipe on page 349. ✦ When the rice has cooked about 15 minutes add the sausage and tomato purée. ✦ When the rice is al dente remove the pan from the heat, adjust for salt, and stir in the remaining butter and Parmigiano-Reggiano; serve immediately.

PASTA, POLENTA & RICE

RISOTTO WITH SAUSAGE AND CABBAGE

RISOTTO CON LA SALSICCIA E IL CAVOLO

VENETO

5 tbsp. unsalted butter

1 medium onion, minced

1 celery stalk, minced

3 *luganeghe* sausages (can use fresh, mild pork sausage), crumbled

1 head Savoy cabbage, outer leaves removed, head cored and chopped

2 cups rice

½ cup dry white wine

6 cups pork broth, skimmed of fat and boiling

½ cup milk

¼ cup grated Parmigiano-Reggiano

Heat 4 tablespoons butter in a saucepan. Add the onion, celery, sausage meat, and cabbage and sauté. ✦ Add the rice and stir constantly with a wooden spoon until it shines with oil. ✦ Pour in the white wine, stirring until the wine is absorbed. ✦ Add the broth to the rice a little at a time as in the recipe on page 349. ✦ Finish cooking the rice, constantly stirring, and making sure the mixture remains very soft, meaning *all'onda* (see note, page 343). ✦ A moment before the rice is cooked add the remaining butter, milk, and a generous amount of Parmigiano-Reggiano. Stir vigorously and serve hot.

RISOTTO WITH TENCH

RISOTTO CON LA TINCA

PIEMONTE

2 lake tench

1 tbsp. white wine vinegar

1 medium onion, quartered

1 carrot, roughly chopped

1 celery stalk, chopped

¼ lb. (1 stick) unsalted butter

2 tbsp. finely chopped flat-leaf parsley

1 garlic clove, minced

2 cups rice

Clean the tench, removing the heads and scales (setting them aside), and gutting them. ✦ Simmer the fish in water with the vinegar and set aside when cooked. ✦ When they have cooled, fillet them. ✦ Meanwhile bring 6 cups of water to a boil, add the fish heads and scales, onion, carrot, and celery, and cook for about 30 minutes; strain this liquid into another pot. ✦ Heat half the butter in a pan and cook the fish fillets, turning them to cook both sides while trying not to break them. ✦ Heat the remaining butter in a pot and sauté the parsley and garlic. ✦ Add the rice, toast it, then slowly add the fish broth. ✦ When the rice is al dente, break the tench fillets into small pieces and stir them in.

RISOTTO CON LA TINCA DEL GARDA

RISOTTO WITH LAKE GARDA TENCH

VENETO

2 tench, 1¾ lbs. each

4½ tsp. all-purpose flour

½ cup extra-virgin olive oil
(if possible from Lake Garda)

¼ lb. (1 stick) unsalted butter,
plus more for serving

5 sage leaves

1 medium onion, thinly sliced

1 lb. plum tomatoes, peeled,
seeded, and chopped

Pinch grated nutmeg

1 tbsp. chopped tarragon

1 tbsp. chopped flat-leaf parsley

½ cup dry white wine

2 cups Vialone nano rice

Salt and pepper

Carefully clean the tench, removing the guts and cutting off and reserving the heads. ✦ Cut the fish in pieces, dredge the pieces in the flour, and salt them. Heat the olive oil and butter in a pan and sauté the sage and onion. Add the fish and fry them until golden. Remove them and set them aside; pass the pan remains through a sieve and set aside. ✦ Put the fish heads in 3 cups of water and simmer for about 30 minutes; strain, discarding the heads, and set aside. ✦ Put the tomatoes, nutmeg, tarragon, parsley, and wine in a large pan and simmer for at least 30 minutes. ✦ Meanwhile carefully take apart the pieces of tench, removing every scale, bone, or piece of hard skin. Add the resulting pulp and the pan remains to the tomato mixture and continue cooking for at least 20 minutes. ✦ Use this mixture, which should be abundant, to proceed with the preparation of a risotto as in the recipe on page 349, using as the liquid the broth obtained from boiling the fish heads. ✦ Serve the risotto hot, adding a tablespoon of butter to each plate and using very little pepper.

RISOTTO CON LA ZUCCA E I FAGIOLI FRESCHI

RISOTTO WITH SQUASH AND BEANS

LOMBARDIA

7 oz. fresh shelled beans

1 lb. winter squash, peeled
and roughly chopped

3 cups rice

¼ lb. (1 stick) unsalted butter
(fresh if possible)

3 tbsp. grated
Parmigiano-Reggiano

A generous pinch of
grated nutmeg

Grated Parmigiano-Reggiano

This risotto is very good hot, but some people prefer it just warm.

Cook the beans and the squash in 10 cups of water until tender. ✦ When the two vegetables are cooked, use a ladle to scoop up the squash pieces; crush them with a spoon and return to the pot. ✦ Add the rice and immediately after it 6 tablespoons butter and simmer for about 15 minutes. ✦ At this point add the Parmigiano-Reggiano, nutmeg, and the remaining butter; let it cook for another 5 minutes. ✦ If the cooking times and the ingredients have been followed, the result will be dense, almost like a risotto *all'onda* (see note, page 343). It should be served with a sprinkling of cheese.

RISOTTO CON LE LUMACHE | RISOTTO WITH SNAILS

PIEMONTE

24 snails

2 tbsp. unsalted butter

1 medium onion, minced

1 garlic clove, minced

1 oz. unsweetened chocolate

1 tbsp. white wine vinegar

All-purpose flour for dredging

½ cup dry white wine

¼ cup flat-leaf parsley, chopped

2 cups rice

4 cups chicken broth

½ cup heavy cream

Purge the snails (see page 16), clean them, and take them out of their shells. ✦ Heat the butter in a pan over low heat and sauté the onion and garlic. ✦ Add the chocolate and vinegar. ✦ Dredge the snails lightly in flour, then add them to the pan. ✦ When the snails have taken on color, add the wine. ✦ Add the parsley followed by the rice and proceed with cooking the risotto as in the recipe on page 349, using the broth. When the rice is al dente, stir in the cream and serve.

RISOTTO CON LE POVERACCE | RISOTTO WITH CLAMS

EMILIA-ROMAGNA

2 oz. prosciutto fat, minced, or ¼ cup (4 tbsp.) unsalted butter

½ cup olive oil

3 garlic cloves, crushed

1 tbsp. each chopped flat-leaf parsley and fresh marjoram

1 medium onion, minced

1 carrot, minced

1 celery stalk, minced

¼ oz. dried mushrooms, soaked, drained, and chopped

1 clove

4 oz. dry white wine

2 lbs. plum tomatoes, peeled, seeded, and chopped

10 oz. clams (if possible *poveracce* from Emilia-Romagna)

6 tbsp. unsalted butter

1 tbsp. chopped flat-leaf parsley

4 oz. dry white wine

6 cups clam or fish broth

CONTINUED

This recipe is typical of Porto Garibaldi.

Begin by making the sauce. Heat the prosciutto fat (or butter) and 1 tablespoon olive oil in a pot over low heat, then add 1 garlic clove, parsley, marjoram, onion, carrot, celery, mushrooms, clove, and a pinch of pepper. Sauté until softened, then pour in the wine and cook it down almost completely; add the tomatoes and season with salt. Cover the pot and cook over medium-low heat for about 1 hour, adding a little water if necessary. When cooked pass the sauce through a food mill. ✦ Wash the clams in cold water then put them in a pan with a little water over medium heat. Cover and, shaking the pan by the handle, heat them until they open. ✦ Remove the clams from their shells and drain off the broth, straining it to eliminate any sand. ✦ Put the remaining olive oil and half the butter in an earthenware pan and add the remaining garlic; as soon as the garlic browns remove it and add the parsley then the clams and wine. ✦ Raise the heat to cook off about half of the wine then add the sauce diluted with a little of the clam broth. ✦ Cook for 10 minutes then add the broth. ✦ Bring to a boil and add the rice, season with salt, stir, and cook the rice as in the

1⅔ cups Carnaroli rice
(can use Arborio)

Salt and pepper

recipe on page 349, stirring with a wooden spoon. Finish the risotto with the remaining butter and a good pinch of pepper. Serve hot.

FROG RISOTTO

RISOTTO CON LE RANE

PIEMONTE

24 frogs
3 tbsp. extra-virgin olive oil
¼ cup chopped flat-leaf parsley
1 garlic clove, minced
2 carrots, minced
2 small onions, finely sliced
1 celery stalk, diced
2 cups Arborio rice
¼ cup white wine
6 cups vegetable broth
Salt and pepper
2 tbsp. unsalted butter
Grated Parmigiano-Reggiano
Salt and pepper

This recipe is typical of Novara.

Clean the frogs, wash them, and use only the legs, removing the bone. ✦ Heat half the olive oil in a saucepan and sauté the parsley, garlic, carrots, 1 of the onions, and celery. ✦ Add the frog legs, cover, and let slowly cook. ✦ Heat a little olive oil in a pot, add the other onion, and sauté it. Add the rice and toast it. ✦ Add the wine and let it evaporate. Cook the rice as in the recipe on page 349. ✦ A minute before taking it off the heat, taste for salt and pepper then add the frog legs and their sauce and work in the butter and Parmigiano-Reggiano. Serve piping hot.

RISOTTO WITH GIBLETS

RISOTTO CON LE RIGAGLIE

PIEMONTE

3 gizzards
4 chicken livers
4 tbsp. unsalted butter
Sage
5 cups chicken broth
2 tbsp. olive oil
1 small carrot, chopped
1 small celery stalk, chopped
1 medium onion, chopped
2 cups fine or superfine rice
(Arborio, Carnaroli, Vialone nano)
1 tbsp. tomato purée
Grated Parmigiano-Reggiano
Salt

Clean the gizzards and boil them. ✦ When they are cooked cut them in slices together with the livers. Heat half the butter in a pan and add the sage, then the liver mixture. Brown them, then add salt. ✦ Heat the broth. Heat the olive oil and 1 tablespoon butter in a saucepan and sauté the vegetables. Add the rice and stir it around to toast it. ✦ Add the broth a little at a time to cook the rice as in the recipe on page 349, then add the tomato purée. ✦ After about 20 minutes add the gizzards and their cooking liquid, setting aside a little to add at the end along with the remaining butter and Parmigiano-Reggiano.

RISOTTO WITH SALAME AND ONION

RISOTTO CON LE SALAMELLE

LOMBARDIA

¼ lb. (1 stick) unsalted butter

1 medium onion, finely sliced

7 oz. soft salame (preferably from Cremona), peeled and chopped

3 cups Vialone nano rice

6 cups chicken broth

⅔ cup grated Parmigiano-Reggiano

Heat the butter in a pan and sauté the onion and salame. ✦ Add the rice, stirring with a wooden spoon to toast it. ✦ Slowly add broth as in the recipe on page 349, constantly stirring until the risotto is al dente. Sprinkle with cheese and serve.

RISOTTO WITH SÈCOLE

RISOTTO CON LE SÈCOLE

VENETO

⅓ cup olive oil

2 tbsp. unsalted butter

1 small onion, minced

1 celery stalk, minced

1 carrot, minced

10 oz. beef *sècole* (see note)

2 cups Vialone nano rice (can use Arborio)

4 cups beef broth

½ cup grated Parmigiano-Reggiano

Salt and pepper

Sècole are strips of meat from along the vertebrae of cows. They are highly prized today by connoisseurs for their particular flavor.

Heat the olive oil and butter in a saucepan over low heat and sauté the onion, celery, and carrot. Add the *sècole*, salt, and pepper and cook slowly for about 2 hours. ✦ When cooked pour in the rice, stir to blend, then cook the risotto as in the recipe on page 349. ✦ When the rice is cooked add the cheese. The rice should be very *all'onda* (see note, page 343).

RISOTTO WITH SAUSAGE 2

RISOTTO CON SALSICCIA

LOMBARDIA

1½ sticks plus 2 tbsp. unsalted butter

3 tbsp. olive oil

1 small onion, finely chopped

1⅔ cups Carnaroli or Arborio rice

1 cup dry white wine, such as Gari

6 cups chicken broth (to which 2 tsp. of tomato paste have been added)

CONTINUED

Heat half the butter in a pan at low heat and add the olive oil and onion. ✦ Cook until the onion is golden then add the rice and stir well for a few minutes. ✦ Add ½ cup of the wine and cook at high heat another 5 minutes. ✦ Then add the broth mixture and continue cooking the rice as in the recipe on page 349. ✦ A minute before the end of cooking work in a tablespoon of butter and a good helping of Parmigiano-Reggiano. ✦ Heat the remaining butter in a pan and cut the sausage into 2-inch lengths. When the butter is golden add the sau-

Grated Parmigiano-Reggiano
1 sausage

sage. ✦ After a few minutes, pour in the remaining white wine. ✦ Pour the sausage mixture over the risotto and serve hot.

RISOTTO WITH SAUSAGE AND CAULIFLOWER

VENETO

4 tbsp. (½ stick) unsalted butter
1 celery stalk, finely sliced
1 small onion, finely sliced
3 *luganeghe* sausages, crumbled
Florets of 1 cauliflower, chopped
2⅓ cups Vialone nano rice
½ cup dry white wine
6 cups broth, boiling
¼ cup grated Parmigiano-Reggiano

For the wine use Soave or bianco di Custoza.

Heat 3 tablespoons butter in a pan and sauté the celery, onion, sausage meat, and cauliflower. ✦ Add the rice and toast well then pour in the wine, stirring constantly until the wine has evaporated. ✦ Cook the rice by slowly adding the boiling broth as in the recipe on page 349. ✦ Just before taking the rice off the heat add the remaining butter and the cheese.

RISOTTO AL BRANZINO

RISOTTO WITH SEA BASS

FOR
6 PERSONS

VENETO

1 sea bass, about 1 lb. 5 oz.
1 bay leaf
Several thyme leaves
6 tbsp. unsalted butter
2 tbsp. extra-virgin olive oil
1 small shallot, minced
1⅔ cup Vialone nano rice
½ cup white wine
1 tbsp. chopped flat-leaf parsley
Salt and peppercorns

Clean and scale the sea bass and simmer it in lightly salted water flavored with a few peppercorns. ✦ When it is almost cooked remove it from the liquid, reserving the liquid, and separate the fish from the bones, cutting the meat in small pieces. ✦ Return the head, skin, and bones to the cooking liquid along with a bay leaf and a few thyme leaves; heat to make a broth. ✦ Heat 4 tablespoons butter and the olive oil in a pan and sauté the shallot. Add the rice, stirring to toast. ✦ Pour in the wine and turn up the heat to make it evaporate. Cook the risotto by adding ladlefuls of the fish liquid as in the recipe on page 349 (finishing with hot water if needed). ✦ When the rice is cooked turn off the heat and add the remaining butter and parsley. Serve hot.

RISOTTO WITH HOP SHOOTS

RISOTTO DI BRUSCANDOLI

VENETO

¼ cup olive oil

1 bunch flat-leaf parsley, chopped

1 garlic clove, minced

10 oz. tips of *bruscandoli* (hop shoots; see note, page 264), cleaned and chopped in pieces

5 cups Vialone nano rice

6 cups broth (beef or chicken)

Grated Parmigiano-Reggiano

¼ lb. (1 stick) unsalted butter, cut into pieces

Salt and pepper

Heat the olive oil in a pan over medium heat and add the parsley, garlic, and hop shoots. Let cook for at least 15 minutes. ✦ Add the rice and stir, raising the heat to cook it a few minutes, then add the broth a little at a time as in the recipe on page 349, and wait for the rice to absorb the liquid before adding more. ✦ Continue calmly stirring; a little before the rice is finished (it should be al dente) taste for salt and add cheese, pepper, and butter. ✦ At this point turn off the heat, cover the pan, and let the risotto rest for 2 minutes before serving.

"FREE-RANGE" RISOTTO WITH GIZZARDS

RISOTTO DI RUSPANTE

VENETO

1 celery stalk, chopped

2 tbsp. chopped flat-leaf parsley

1 carrot, chopped

2 cups dry white wine, such as Soave

10 oz. intestines, gizzards, liver, and heart of a free-range chicken

1 bay leaf

1 sprig rosemary

2 cups Vialone nano rice

Chicken broth blended with beef broth

Simmer the celery, parsley, and carrot in white wine to cover. ✦ Cover and cook at moderate heat for about 1 hour. ✦ Clean the intestines as you would tripe. ✦ Cook the gizzards, liver, heart, and intestines separately in water to cover, then add to the vegetables with the bay leaf and rosemary. ✦ Add the rice and cook the risotto as in the recipe on page 349.

RISOTTO WITH SHRIMP AND ASPARAGUS

RISOTTO DI SCAMPI AGLI ASPARAGI

VENETO

½ lb. white asparagus

¾ lb. shrimp (with shells)

1 carrot

1 medium onion, chopped

CONTINUED

Trim the asparagus and peel the stalks with a vegetable peeler. Cut off the tips along with about 1 inch of the stalks and set aside. ✦ Boil the remaining stalks in a little lightly salted water. ✦ Strain the cooking liquid and set it aside. ✦ Put the stalks through a food mill and put the purée in the reserved cooking liquid. ✦ Shell the shrimp, reserving the shells. Combine the heads and shells of the

1 celery stalk
Bay leaf
6 tbsp. unsalted butter
¼ cup extra-virgin olive oil
1 garlic clove, minced
¼ cup white wine
2 tbsp. chopped flat-leaf parsley
3 tbsp. cognac
1⅔ cups Vialone nano rice
½ cup Grated Parmigiano-Reggiano
Salt and pepper

shrimp with the carrot, half of the onion, celery, and bay leaf and add water to cover. Boil 30 minutes. ✦ Strain this liquid and add to the asparagus liquid. ✦ Heat 3 tablespoons butter in a pan and cook the asparagus tips for a few minutes. ✦ Heat the olive oil in a pot, add the remaining onion and garlic, and brown. ✦ Add the shrimp, and when it has taken on color pour in the wine; add the parsley and cognac. Cook to evaporate. ✦ Add the asparagus tips and rice. ✦ Cook the risotto as in the recipe on page 349 using the reserved broth. Taste for salt and pepper. ✦ When the rice is nearly cooked work in the remaining butter and Parmigiano-Reggiano.

PASTA, POLENTA & RICE

SHRIMP RISOTTO WITH ZUCCHINI FLOWERS

RISOTTO DI SCAMPI
E FIORI DI ZUCCA

MARCHE

2 tbsp. extra-virgin olive oil
1 small onion, minced
1⅔ cups Vialone nano rice
½ cup white wine
16 zucchini flowers
6 cups fish broth
1 lb. shrimp
1 tbsp. unsalted butter
Salt

Heat the olive oil in a pan and cook the onion until soft, then add the rice and toast it for 2 minutes. ✦ Add the wine and let it evaporate. ✦ Remove the pistils and stamens from the zucchni flowers. Cook the risotto as in the recipe on page 349, adding the zucchini flowers and shrimp after about 10 minutes. ✦ Taste for salt, add the butter, and complete cooking the risotto until the rice is tender.

SEAS AND MOUNTAINS RISOTTO

RISOTTO MARI E MONTI

FRIULI-VENEZIA GIULIA

Olive oil
1 tsp. chopped garlic
10 oz. peeled and deveined shrimp
2 oz. porcini mushrooms
1⅓ cups Canaroli rice
½ cup white wine, such as Pinot Grigio
6 cups fish broth
CONTINUED

This is a variant of the shrimp risotto that is typical of the Venezia Giulia coast. With its flavor reinforced by porcini mushrooms from Cadore, the rice, cooked in fish broth with the addition, near the end of the cooking, of arugula, has a flavor that by now has been forgotten by the modern era.

Heat the olive oil in a saucepan and add the garlic, stirring with a wooden spoon for 2 to 3 minutes. ✦ Add the shrimp and mushrooms and brown. ✦ Add the rice and toast it for a few minutes, sprinkling in the white wine. Adjust for salt and pepper. ✦ When the wine has cooked off cook the risotto as in the recipe on page 349. After

2 tbsp. chopped arugula
(if possible wild)
2 tbsp. unsalted butter
1 dash cognac
Salt and pepper

about 20 minutes add the arugula. ✦ Turn off the rice when it is still somewhat brothy and stir in the butter and cognac.

RISOTTO WITH BAKED SOLE, SHRIMP, AND HOLLANDAISE

RISOTTO MONTELERA

PIEMONTE

4 tbsp. unsalted butter
2 small onions, minced
1½ oz. porcini mushrooms, chopped
1⅔ cups Carnaroli rice
6 cups chicken broth,
skimmed of any fat, boiling
⅓ cup grated Parmigiano-Reggiano
2 sole fillets
¼ cup dry spumante
7 oz. shelled shrimp
¼ cup dry white wine, such as Gari
4 oz. cognac

For the hollandaise sauce:
2 large egg yolks
¼ cup white wine
1 tbsp. lemon juice
¼ lb. (1 stick) unsalted butter,
melted
Salt and pepper

Preheat the oven to 350°F. Grease a baking dish with butter. Heat 1 tablespoon of the butter in a large saucepan and sauté one of the onions, the mushrooms, and the rice. Continue cooking the rice with the broth as in the recipe on page 349. ✦ When the rice is cooked stir in 2 tablespoons of the remaining butter and the Parmigiano-Reggiano. ✦ Arrange the sole in the prepared dish. Sprinkle with salt and pepper, pour in the spumante, and cover the pan with a sheet of aluminum foil. ✦ Bake for about 12 minutes. ✦ Heat the remaining 1 tablespoon butter in a pan and cook the remaining onion and shrimp; pour in the white wine, sprinkle in the cognac, and ignite carefully with a match, to burn off the alcohol. ✦ Meanwhile, make the sauce: Place a copper pot with high sides on top of another pan filled with simmering water. In this whisk the egg yolks, white wine, salt, pepper, and the lemon juice. ✦ Whisk until thickened, then gradually whisk in the melted butter. ✦ Spoon the risotto in a serving dish, garnish with the shrimp mixture and the sole fillets; cover with the hollandaise sauce.

BLACK RISOTTO WITH CUTTLEFISH INK AND CHARD

RISOTTO NERO

TOSCANA

1 lb. cuttlefish
Extra-virgin olive oil
1 medium onion, chopped
1 garlic clove, chopped
¾ lb. Swiss chard
CONTINUED

Clean the cuttlefish, skinning them and removing the bones, eyes, mouth, and intestines but setting aside at least one of the ink sacs. ✦ Clean well and cut in pieces. ✦ Heat the olive oil in a pot and cook the onion and garlic. When these begin to change color add the cuttlefish and cook at low heat for about 10 minutes. ✦ Clean and trim the chard, rinse, and chop into slices; add to the pan. ✦ Cook for a few minutes and add the rice. ✦ After

2 cups Vialone nano rice
Freshly ground black pepper

the rice has had time to pick up the flavors, cook it like a risotto, as in the recipe on page 349, using 6 cups of lightly salted water in place of the broth. ✦ A few minutes before the rice is done add 1 or 2 of the ink sacs, stir well, and serve, but not before sprinkling with freshly ground black pepper.

RISOTTO PRIMAVERA

SPRING RISOTTO

VENETO

1 carrot
1 slice eggplant
1 section of yellow pepper
1 section of red pepper
1 zucchini
1 artichoke bottom
4 asparagus stalks
2 tbsp. unsalted butter
2 tbsp. shelled fresh peas
1 tbsp. extra-virgin olive oil
6 cups chicken broth
(skimmed of any fat)
1 medium onion
¼ cup dry white wine
(Soave, if possible)
1⅔ cups Vialone nano rice
3 tbsp. Parmigiano-Reggiano
Salt and pepper

Trim and clean the carrot, eggplant, peppers, zucchini, artichoke, and asparagus as needed, then cut into small cubes, keeping the different vegetables separate. ✦ Heat half the butter in a pan and sauté the vegetables one at a time, still keeping them separate. ✦ Also cook the peas and set them aside. ✦ In a pan heat the olive oil and 3 tablespoons of broth and cook the onion. ✦ Add the wine and let it slowly evaporate. ✦ Add the rice and toast it, then cook as in the recipe on page 349. ✦ When the rice is done add the cooked vegetables with the remaining butter and the cheese. Serve immediately.

RISOTTO RICCO
ALLA PADOVANA

RICH RISOTTO
PADUA-STYLE

VENETO

¼ cup olive oil
1 celery stalk, minced
1 medium onion, minced
1 carrot, minced
2 oz. chicken
2 oz. duck liver
CONTINUED

Heat the olive oil in a pot and sauté the celery, onion, and carrot. ✦ Without oil or butter brown the meats and giblets in a saucepan; add half the wine and cook until the meats are almost completely done. ✦ Add the contents of the meat pan to the vegetables, then add the peas (or mushrooms), tomato sauce, marrow, and cloves, and taste for salt and pepper. ✦ Cook this at low heat for a few minutes. ✦ In another pot heat 2 tablespoons butter and toast the rice. Add the meat sauce, pour in the

371

2 oz. chicken gizzards

2 oz. turkey

2 oz. pork

2 oz. chicken hearts

2 oz. sausage

1 cup wine

3 oz. peas (or porcini mushrooms)

4 oz. tomato sauce

2 oz. marrow

A few cloves

1⅔ cups Vialone nano rice

4 tbsp. unsalted butter

6 cups hen or guinea hen broth

½ cup grated Parmigiano-Reggiano

Salt and pepper

remaining wine, and cook as in the recipe on page 349.
✦ Just before taking it off the heat stir in the remaining
butter and Parmigiano-Reggiano.

HAND-CUT PASTA WITH CHEESE AND SAGE SAUCE

RITAGLI DI PASTA (BLECS)

FRIULI-VENEZIA GIULIA

1½ cups all-purpose flour,
plus more as needed

½ cup cornmeal

3 large eggs, beaten

7 oz. smoked ricotta, grated

4 oz. grated aged cheese

½ cup unsalted butter, melted

2 tbsp. chopped sage

This dish is typical of the Carnia area near Austria.

Use the flour, cornmeal, and eggs to prepare a pasta
dough as in the recipe on page 10. ✦ Roll it out to sheet
about ⅛ inch thick (see page 212). ✦ Cut this in irregular pieces and cook them in lightly salted boiling water
until al dente. ✦ Drain and mix with the ricotta, aged
cheese, butter, and sage.

PASTA ROLL WITH SPINACH

ROTOLO DI PASTA VARIA CON SPINACI

FOR 8 PERSONS

FRIULI-VENEZIA GIULIA

1 lb. potatoes

1 large egg yolk
plus 1 large egg, beaten

3 tbsp. unsalted butter, softened

¾ cup all-purpose flour,
plus more as needed

1 lb. spinach

6 oz. ricotta

CONTINUED

Boil the potatoes, put them through a food mill, then
combine the purée with the egg yolk, 2 tablespoons butter, salt, and flour. ✦ Knead as in the recipe on page 10 to
obtain a smooth dough. ✦ Roll out the dough on top of a
floured cloth to a thickness of ¼ inch. ✦ Meanwhile boil,
drain, and chop the spinach. Heat the remaining butter in
a pan and sauté the spinach. Remove the pan from the
heat and add the egg, ricotta, and Parmigiano-Reggiano.
✦ When this is well mixed spread it across the sheet of
pasta evenly and then, somewhat like rolling a strudel, roll
up the cloth. ✦ Tie up the ends with string, adding an-

½ cup grated Parmigiano-Reggiano
Salt and pepper

other length around the middle. ✦ Cook this in lightly salted boiling water to cover, leaving it alone to cook for 20 minutes. Remove from the water and let cool.

SAGNE ALLA FURESE

LASAGNE IN MEAT SAUCE

PUGLIA

For the wine use Trebbiano.

2 tbsp. extra-virgin olive oil
2 garlic cloves, minced
1 small onion, minced
7 oz. sausage meat
7 oz. mushrooms
7 oz. fresh green beans
½ cup white wine
1 lb. tomato sauce
1¼ cups grated pecorino
1 lb. fresh lasagne
Salt

Heat the olive oil in a pan and sauté the garlic and onion. Add the sausage, mushrooms, and green beans. ✦ Pour in the wine and let it evaporate. ✦ Add the tomato sauce, salt to taste, and simmer for about 45 minutes. ✦ Mix in the pecorino. ✦ Cook the *sagne* (lasagne) in boiling lightly salted water, drain, and dress with the sauce. Serve hot.

PASTA, POLENTA & RICE

SAGNE E FAGIOLI

PASTA WITH BEANS

ABRUZZO

1⅔ cups all-purpose flour, plus more as needed
3 tbsp. extra-virgin olive oil
1 medium onion, minced
1 carrot, minced
1 celery stalk, minced
2 tbsp. chopped basil
1 *diavolillo* (spicy chili pepper, see note, page 22)
1¼ cups fresh borlotti beans
4 oz. pork rind
1 prosciutto bone
1½ cups peeled plum tomatoes
Salt

Use the flour to prepare a pasta dough as in the recipe on page 10, using ½ cup water in place of the eggs. Roll this out to a thin sheet (see page 212). ✦ Cut the sheet into 1-inch-wide strips then cut the strips unevenly to obtain many small diamond shapes. Set the pasta on a floured dish cloth to dry. ✦ In an earthenware pan heat the olive oil and sauté the onion, carrot, celery, and basil. Add the chili pepper; when these are cooked add some water with the beans, pork rind, and prosciutto bone. ✦ After about 30 minutes skim off any fat and remove the rind and prosciutto bone. ✦ Cut the pork rind and the meat from the prosciutto bone in small pieces and return them to the pot; add the tomatoes. ✦ Meanwhile cook the pasta. When they are nearly cooked drain them and add them to the beans and pork in the pan. ✦ Cook the mixture all together for another 4 to 5 minutes, stirring. Season with salt, then serve.

| # RICE TIMBALE 1

For the sauce:

1 oz. pancetta

1 ¼ cups fresh shelled peas

1 small onion, sliced

¼ cup dry red wine,
such as Aglianico

1 tbsp. lard

4 artichokes, trimmed and
each sliced into 8 sections

1 garlic clove, chopped

2 tbsp. chopped flat-leaf parsley

For the rice:

1 ⅔ cups Arborio or Carnaroli rice

2 large eggs, beaten

⅔ cup grated Parmigiano-Reggiano

2 tbsp. chopped flat-leaf parsley

Salt and pepper

For the filling:

½ cup lard

½ cup breadcrumbs

7 oz. mozzarella or provola

2 large hard-boiled eggs, sliced

7 oz. prosciutto crudo, diced

7 oz. cooked meatballs
(see page 105)

7 oz. fresh sausage, sliced

4 oz. salame, sliced

½ cup grated Parmigiano-Reggiano

One must remember that in the robust gastronomy of Naples, rice was looked upon as a food for invalids (it was "reviving") and could be rendered acceptable only if heavily doused with meat sauce and combined with rich fillings, such that the abundance of seasonings outweighed the quantity of rice (such fillings varied from place to place). In other words, to the cook at court or employed in a noble home (and such cooks were almost always of French origin, following the style of the 1800s), rice was an accessory to set atop everything else, *sur tout*, which in the Neapolitan dialect became *sartù*.

Cook the pancetta, peas, onion, and red wine in a pan over low heat. ✦ In another pan heat the lard and cook the artichokes, garlic, and parsley. ✦ Set aside portions of this artichoke sauce as follows: 1) 4 or 5 tablespoons in a serving dish to pass at the table; 2) 6 or 7 tablespoons to add to the pancetta mixture, which should then be simmered over low heat for 10 minutes; 3) 2 or 3 tablespoons to finish off the timbale. ✦ Dilute what remains of the sauce with as much water as needed to obtain 3 cups of sauce and pour it into a saucepan, together with the rice. ✦ Cook this at a moderate heat in a covered pot without stirring it even once for exactly 10 minutes. ✦ Let the rice cool, then stir in the eggs, Parmigiano-Reggiano, a little pepper, parsley, and salt to taste. ✦ Preheat the oven to 350°F. Grease a large, deep baking dish that is 9 inches in diameter and about 6 inches high with some of the lard, then sprinkle it with some of the breadcrumbs. Put three-quarters of the cooked rice into the dish, pressing to make it adhere well to the sides and the bottom. ✦ At the center of this put, first, half of the slices of mozzarella, half of the hard-boiled eggs, and half of the prosciutto. ✦ Cover this with the meatballs, sausage, salame, and Parmigiano-Reggiano. Spread in all of the pancetta sauce. Then add the remaining mozzarella, eggs, and prosciutto. Cover with the remaining rice and reserved artichoke sauce. ✦ Sprinkle with the remaining breadcrumbs and 5 or 6 teaspoons of the remaining lard. Bake for about 1 hour until the breadcrumbs are a beautiful golden color. Let this cool for 10 minutes then turn it out on a round plate and serve.

RICE TIMBALE 2

¼ lb. (1 stick) unsalted butter
Breadcrumbs
2 cups rice
Grated Parmigiano-Reggiano
Olive oil, for frying
1 lb. zucchini, cut in disks
1 lb. mozzarella, sliced
Salt

Preheat the oven to 350°F. Grease a baking pan with butter and sprinkle with breadcrumbs. Cook the rice in lightly salted boiling water until al dente, drain, and stir in the butter and 2 tablespoons Parmigiano-Reggiano. ✦ Heat ½ inch of olive oil in a pan and fry the zucchini until golden. ✦ Pour a layer of rice into the prepared pan, then a layer of zucchini, then mozzarella and Parmigiano-Reggiano. Repeat the layers, using all of the ingredients, and end with a layer of rice. ✦ Bake for 15 minutes. Turn out onto a serving plate and serve.

SBOMBATA

BAKED PASTA PIE

FOR
8 PERSONS

Unsalted butter

For the pasta:
5¾ cups all-purpose flour,
plus more as needed
8 large eggs, beaten
Pinch of salt

For the pie dough:
5¾ cups all-purpose flour,
plus more as needed
8 large eggs, beaten
Pinch of salt

For the sauce:
1 large cup of goose sauce
(see page 635)
1 large cup of giblet sauce
(see page 281)
⅔ cup grated pecorino

Preheat the oven to 350°F. Grease a baking pan with butter. Use the flour and eggs to prepare a pasta dough as in the recipe on page 10. ✦ Roll out to a sheet (see page 212) and cut into somewhat large squares. ✦ Boil them, drain them, and set them out to dry on a cloth. ✦ Use the flour and eggs to prepare a pasta dough as in the recipe on page 10 to make the pie dough; set one small portion of this dough aside. Roll out the larger piece of dough to make a sheet and use it to line the sides and bottom of the baking pan. ✦ Pour into this a little of the two sauces and a little pecorino then cover with some of the cooked pasta squares. ✦ Continue making such layers until the ingredients are used up. ✦ Roll out the remaining portion of dough and use it to cover the pan. ✦ Bake until golden brown, about 25 minutes.

PASTA, POLENTA & RICE

PASTA WITH GUANCIALE

BASILICATA

1 lb. pasta (*schiaffoni* or
mezze maniche)

2 tbsp. extra-virgin olive oil

5½ oz. guanciale (or *lardo*, see
page 2, or bacon), finely minced

1 garlic clove, chopped

½ cup white wine

2 tbsp. chopped flat-leaf parsley

1 tsp. paprika (optional)

½ cup grated pecorino

Pepper

For the wine use Trebbiano or Falanghina.

Cook the pasta until al dente. Meanwhile, in a saucepan heat the olive oil and sauté a good part of the guanciale (or *lardo* or bacon) and the garlic. ✦ When the garlic begins to brown add the wine and let it evaporate. ✦ Cut the remaining guanciale in strips and add it to the pan, adding the parsley and paprika (if desired) at the last minute. ✦ Drain the pasta well and dress it in a bowl with cheese and pepper, then pour the hot sauce over it.

BUCKWHEAT PORRIDGE

FOR
6 PERSONS

PIEMONTE

4 cups buckwheat flour,
plus more as needed

Milk (or Alpine cheese
or minced *lardo*, see page 2)

Salt

This preparation from the Valle Vigezzo near the Swiss border is truly ancient. It was only after the discovery of the New World that buckwheat flour was gradually supplanted by other cereals, most especially corn, which eventually replaced it entirely.

Bring 8 cups lightly salted water to a boil in a large pot, if possible made of copper, and pour in the buckwheat flour, stirring to avoid the formation of lumps. ✦ Add salt and cook for about 40 minutes, stirring constantly with a wooden spoon. ✦ Serve, as is the popular tradition in the Valle Vigezzo, with milk or Alpine cheeses or minced *lardo*.

PASTA WITH BLACK OLIVES AND MUSHROOMS

MARCHE

Extra-virgin olive oil

1 lb. mixed fresh mushrooms,
finely sliced

1 garlic clove, minced

1¼ cups pitted and chopped
black olives

1 lb. tubular pasta (such as *sedanini*)

¼ cup grated pecorino

Heat a little olive oil in a pan and sauté the mushrooms and garlic. ✦ As soon as they are cooked add the olives. ✦ Cook the pasta in lightly salted boiling water, drain, and toss with the sauce. ✦ Add pecorino and serve.

SFOGLIA

This is a cardinal technique in Italian cuisine, the foundation for almost all fresh pasta. These sheets of homemade pasta common to Emilia-Romagna, known as *sfoglia*, are made in the traditional method of forming a well with the flour on a pastry board, and adding eggs, salt, and a little water (according to lore, two half eggshells' worth) before working the ingredients together with a fork and then by hand to form a smooth ball of dough. The eventual quality of the pasta is determined by how much the dough is kneaded. Flour is added in very small quantities to keep the dough from getting too soft. The final step is to use a rolling pin to create a sheet of dough—the thickness of which depends on what sort of dish the pasta is to be used for.

SFORMATO DI ORTAGGI
IN TEGLIA

VEGETABLE TIMBALE

CALABRIA

¼ cup extra-virgin olive oil

1 cup roughly cubed homemade breadcrumbs

½ cup grated pecorino

1 tbsp. oregano

1 tsp. chili pepper flakes

2 lbs. fresh plum tomatoes, peeled, seeded, and finely chopped

4 or 5 large potatoes, peeled and sliced in thick rounds

1 medium onion, sliced

½ cup basil leaves

Salt

Aside from this version, there are other ways of preparing the *tiedda* (as it is known in Calabria). For example, it can be made with mushrooms or with wild artichokes. Another variation of this recipe calls for the addition to the potatoes and tomatoes of a little broken-up bucatini pasta. The addition of this ingredient makes the *tiedda* more flavorful.

Preheat the oven to 425°F. Grease a baking pan (if possible earthenware) with olive oil. ✦ In a bowl combine the breadcrumbs, cheese, the oregano, and chili flakes. ✦ Cover the bottom of the pan with a layer of tomatoes. Sprinkle with salt, and continue with a layer of potatoes; place onion slices here and there; add some of the breadcrumb mixture. ✦ Over this put a few basil leaves, then drizzle with olive oil. ✦ Repeat with another layer of tomatoes, ending with the breadcrumb mixture and a little more olive oil. ✦ Add ¼ cup water, pouring it in slowly from the side, and bake for about 1 hour, or until a golden crust forms on the surface. This dish can be served hot or cold.

RICE WITH SMOKED CHEESE

PIEMONTE

2 tbsp. extra-virgin olive oil
1 small onion, chopped
1 ⅔ cups Arborio rice
½ cup dry white wine
6 cups boiling chicken broth
1 tbsp. grated Parmigiano-Reggiano
2 tbsp. unsalted butter
6 oz. smoked provola, sliced

Heat a little olive oil in a pan and sauté the onion. ✦ Add the rice, toast it, then pour in the white wine. ✦ When the wine has evaporated cook the rice with the broth as in the recipe on page 349. ✦ When it is al dente stir in the Parmigiano-Reggiano. ✦ Preheat the oven to 425°F. Butter a high-sided baking dish and add one third of the cooked rice. Cover the layer of rice with half of the smoked provola. Cover this with another third of the rice, then add the remaining provola. Cover this with the remaining rice. ✦ Flatten and smooth the top. Cover the mold with a sheet of aluminum foil. ✦ Place the dish in a larger pan and place in the oven. Fill the larger pan with two inches of warm water and bake 15 to 20 minutes. ✦ Remove from the oven, turn out onto a serving plate, and serve hot, with the desired garnish.

SFORMATO FERDINANDEO

PASTA TIMBALE

FOR
6 PERSONS

CAMPANIA

For the meat sauce:
2 tbsp. extra-virgin olive oil
1 tbsp. lard
10 oz. veal *locena* (see note)
1 lb. *gallinella* of pork
(pork tenderloin)
1 lb. *trachiole* of pork (neck)
1 medium onion
1 whole clove
4 oz. *lardo* (see page 2),
finely minced
2 oz. prosciutto crudo,
finely minced
1 basil leaf
1 bay leaf
1 sprig fresh marjoram
½ cup red wine
1 lb. tomato sauce
Salt

CONTINUED

This dish is typical of Naples. *Locena* is a Neapolitan term for a cut of veal that runs from the tip of the breast to the shoulder.

Prepare a meat sauce: heat the olive oil and lard in a pot. Add the meats, onion, clove, *lardo*, prosciutto crudo, basil, bay leaf, and marjoram. ✦ Brown the meats at low heat, stirring often. ✦ When the ingredients have colored well, pour in the wine a little at a time then slowly add the tomato sauce with 2 cups hot water. ✦ Test for salt and cook at very low heat for several hours. ✦ Preheat the oven to 375°F. ✦ Grease the inside of a baking pan with lard, and sprinkle in breadcrumbs. Use the ground meat to prepare meatballs the size of a small nut. Heat half the olive oil in a pan and brown the meatballs well on all sides. ✦ Heat the olive oil in a pan and cook the mushrooms. ✦ Heat the butter in another pan and cook the peas and add them, with the mushrooms, to a little of the meat sauce. ✦ Cook the mezzanelli in lightly salted boiling water until al dente, drain, and toss with the meat sauce and some Parmigiano-Reggiano. Arrange a layer of the pasta in the prepared pan with some of the

For the filling:
Lard
Breadcrumbs
½ lb. ground meat
¼ cup olive oil
1 oz. dried mushrooms, soaked and drained
2 tbsp. unsalted butter
½ lb. peas, shelled
1 lb. mezzanelli (or other short pasta)
1 cup grated Parmigiano-Reggiano
2 large hard-boiled eggs, sliced
9 oz. *fior di latte* cheese, diced
Salt

mushroom-pea filling, slices of egg, pieces of *fior di latte*, meatballs, and more Parmigiano-Reggiano; cover with more pasta and repeat the layering operation, ending with a layer of pasta. ✦ Sprinkle breadcrumbs over the top and bake for about 40 minutes.

SMACAFAM

"APPETITE-BUSTER" SAUSAGE CASSEROLE

TRENTINO

4 tbsp. unsalted butter
1 oz. *lardo* (see page 2), diced
2 oz. *lucanica* (fresh pork sausages), thinly sliced
2 cups buckwheat flour, plus more as needed
1 cup cold pork broth
2 tbsp. lard (or olive oil)
Grated Parmigiano-Reggiano

Preheat the oven to 350°F. Place a baking pan in the oven and heat it. Heat 3 tablespoons butter in a pan and add the *lardo* and about half the *lucanica*. Transfer to a mixing bowl. ✦ Add the flour and broth and mix well. ✦ Put a good piece of lard (or a fair amount of olive oil) in the baking pan, and heat in the oven. When it has melted pour in the *lucanica* mixture, spreading it out and topping it with the remaining *lucanica,* grated cheese, and remaining butter. ✦ The *smacafam* should be about ½ inch deep. ✦ Bake for about 1 hour, by which time it should have formed a nice brown crust on the top and bottom.

SPAGHETTI AGLIO, OLIO, E PEPPERONCINO

SPAGHETTI WITH GARLIC, OLIVE OIL, AND HOT PEPPER

LAZIO

1 lb. spaghetti
½ cup extra-virgin olive oil
2 garlic cloves, sliced
2 fresh or dried red chili peppers, seeded and shredded
1 tbsp. finely chopped flat-leaf parsley
Salt

Cook the pasta in lightly salted boiling water. ✦ At the same time heat the olive oil in a pan and sauté the garlic and chili peppers in the olive oil without letting them burn; when the garlic is browned remove it and the chilies and discard. ✦ When the pasta is cooked drain it well and put in the pan with the oil over medium heat, tossing and adding the parsley. ✦ Cook about 1 minute and serve.

SPAGHETTI BAKED IN FOIL

ABRUZZO

1 garlic clove
¼ cup extra-virgin olive oil
4 oz. shrimp, cleaned
10 oz. clams, shelled
7 oz. squid, cleaned
1 large prawn for every diner
¼ cup white wine
1 lb. plum tomatoes, chopped in pieces
1 tbsp. chopped flat-leaf parsley
Chili pepper flakes, to taste
1 lb. spaghetti
Salt

This dish is typical of Chieti. For the wine use Trebbiano d'Abruzzo.

Preheat the oven to 375°F. In a saucepan over low heat sauté the garlic in the olive oil; as soon as the garlic browns add the seafood. ✦ After about 10 minutes, or when the liquid from the seafood has cooked away, add the wine and let it reduce for a few more minutes. ✦ Add the tomatoes, parsley, and chili pepper. ✦ Boil the spaghetti in lightly salted water; when just half done, drain and toss with the sauce. ✦ Spread a large sheet of foil over a shallow baking dish and pour in the spaghetti mixture. Fold together the ends of the foil to seal and bake for several minutes, until the heat puffs up the foil and the pasta is al dente.

SPAGHETTI WITH GUANCIALE

ABRUZZO

1 lb. spaghetti
2 tbsp. lard
¼ lb. guanciale, diced
1 tbsp. vinegar or white wine
Grated pecorino
Salt

This simple dish is quickly prepared.

Cook the spaghetti in lightly salted boiling water. Heat the lard in a pan and cook the guanciale. ✦ Keep it from drying out too much by sprinkling with vinegar or white wine. ✦ When the spaghetti is done, drain it and toss it with this sauce, adding pecorino to taste.

SPAGHETTI WITH CUTTLEFISH INK

CALABRIA

2 squid, weighing about 4 oz. each
¼ cup extra-virgin olive oil
2 garlic cloves
2 tbsp. chopped fresh flat-leaf parsley
Dried chili pepper
½ lb. plum tomatoes
¾ lb. spaghetti
Salt

This dish is typical of Diamante and Cirella.

Clean the squid, removing and setting aside the black ink sac in the center of the tentacles. (Alternatively, squid ink can be purchased in many fish stores.) ✦ Cut the squid into strips and, after cleaning them, set them out to drain in a strainer. ✦ Heat the olive oil in a pan and cook the garlic, most of the parsley, and chili pepper. ✦ As soon as the garlic browns remove it and add the squid and the ink sacs, breaking them with a spoon and stirring to blend. ✦ Add the tomatoes and salt, and cook over low heat. ✦ Cook the spaghetti in lightly salted boiling water and drain when al dente. ✦ Pour some of the sauce into the bottom of a bowl; add the spaghetti and mix well, then add the remaining sauce and dust with the remaining parsley.

SPAGHETTI WITH BLACK TRUFFLE

SPAGHETTI AL TARTUFO NERO

MARCHE

1 garlic clove
¼ cup extra-virgin olive oil
2 anchovy fillets
½ cup tomato purée
1 lb. spaghetti
3 oz. black truffle, shaved
Flat-leaf parsley, chopped
Salt and pepper

Crush the garlic clove to extract the maximum amount of its flavoring. Heat the olive oil in a pan and cook the garlic until golden. ✦ Add the anchovy fillets and break them up with a fork; add the tomato purée. ✦ Cook the sauce for a few minutes, adding salt and pepper. ✦ Cook the spaghetti until al dente and while still very hot toss with black truffle; add the sauce and parsley.

SPAGHETTI WITH TUNA

SPAGHETTI AL TONNO

SICILIA

2 tbsp. extra-virgin olive oil
1 lb. fresh tuna fillet
4 cups tomato sauce
2 tbsp. chopped flat-leaf parsley
1 lb. cooked spaghetti
Salt

This sauce, typical of Messina, can also be prepared with canned tuna. To make this variation, prepare a tomato sauce (4 cups) and as soon as it is at the right point add 10½ ounces of canned tuna that has been completely drained and cut into small pieces. Stir well, add chopped parsley and a chopped clove of garlic, and cook at low heat for 10 minutes.

Heat the olive oil in a pan and cook the tuna until it takes on a golden color, then drain it, season it with salt, and cut it in small pieces. ✦ Prepare a tomato sauce (see page 327) and when it is nearly finished add the tuna and parsley. ✦ Cook together for 10 minutes at low heat and use this sauce on the spaghetti, making certain that each serving gets a quantity of tuna.

SPAGHETTI WITH GUANCIALE SAUCE

LAZIO

2 tbsp. extra-virgin olive oil
1 medium onion, sliced
Chili pepper flakes
4 oz. guanciale
1 ½ cups tomato purée
1 lb. spaghetti
Grated pecorino Romano
Salt

From time immemorial the origin of this recipe, typical of Rome, has been the subject of heated debate. Secondino Freda provides an enlightening explanation. This flavorful dish, which many believe originated in Amatrice, a pleasant town in Lazio in the Alta Valle del Tronto, is, on the contrary, a creation of Rome. It came into being about a century ago from the imagination of a cook from Amatrice living in Rome who designed a sauce composed of guanciale and certain local tomatoes grown only in the suburbs of Rome that give the sauce the special sweet-sour flavor that is its essential characteristic. Its inventor called it "alla Amatriciana," but this name was later reworked into "alla matriciana." Thus, the dish has nothing to do with spaghetti "in the style of Amatrice," but rather spaghetti "in the style of a cook from Amatrice." The recipe is the source of other disputes, such as whether or not to use the onion and if it is acceptable to flavor the sauce with a dash of wine.

Heat the olive oil in a pan and cook the onion and chili pepper. Cut the guanciale in slices then crosswise to make small rectangles and add to the pan. ✦ When the guanciale is well browned remove it and the chili pepper and onion and set them aside. ✦ Add the tomato purée to the pan juices and add salt. ✦ Cook this sauce for 10 minutes then return the guanciale mixture, stir well, and turn off the heat. ✦ Cook the pasta in lightly salted boiling water until al dente, drain, and pour it into the sauce, quickly placing the pan back over the heat and flavoring with pecorino. Serve hot.

SPAGHETTI WITH CARBONARA SAUCE

LAZIO

1 lb. spaghetti
2 tbsp. extra-virgin olive oil
3 oz. guanciale (or pancetta), cut in strips
2 large eggs, beaten

CONTINUED

Is *spaghetti alla carbonara* an authentic Italian dish? One school of thought traces it back to a Neapolitan recipe that supposedly (no details survive) called for cheese and beaten eggs. Another school attributes the recipe to the presence of American GIs in Italy at the end of World War II. These soldiers were in the habit of taking their daily rations to local restaurants, where the cooks combined them with Italian foods to create hearty "American-style" meals.

Cook the spaghetti in lightly salted boiling water. ✦ Meanwhile in a large pan heat the olive oil and cook the

²⁄₃ cup grated pecorino or Parmigiano-Reggiano (or a combination of both)

Salt and freshly ground pepper

guanciale; when it is well browned remove the pan from the heat. ✦ Season the eggs with salt, 2 tablespoons cheese, and a generous amount of pepper to taste. ✦ When the pasta is cooked, drain and put it in the pan with the guanciale, heat on a low flame, and add the eggs. ✦ Mix for a few seconds then remove from the heat, combine with the remaining cheese, mix again, and serve hot.

SPAGHETTI WITH GUANCIALE AND CHILI PEPPER

SPAGHETTI ALLA GRICIA

LAZIO

1 small chili pepper (optional)

4 oz. guanciale, in small dice

2 tbsp. extra-virgin olive oil

1 lb. spaghetti

Grated pecorino

Salt

This dish is typical of Rieti.

If using, remove the seeds from the chili and chop it finely. Heat a little olive oil in a pan and sauté the guanciale and chili. ✦ Cook the spaghetti in lightly salted boiling water, drain when al dente, and toss with the guanciale sauce along with pecorino. Serve hot.

SPAGHETTI WITH FRIED EGGS

SPAGHETTI ALLA POVER'UOMO

CAMPANIA

1 lb. spaghetti

¼ cup extra-virgin olive oil

Small amount of lard

4 large eggs

Salt

Pepper (optional)

This dish, "poor man's spaghetti," is typical of Naples.

Cook the spaghetti in lightly salted boiling water. ✦ Meanwhile, heat half of the olive oil and lard in a pan and fry the eggs just until sunny-side up. ✦ Drain the spaghetti when al dente, pour it in a serving bowl, and place the eggs—not overdone—on top of it together with all their seasonings. ✦ If desired add a little pepper. Serve immediately, while hot, making sure the eggs remain whole and each serving gets its share.

SPAGHETTI WITH ANCHOVIES, OLIVES, AND CAPERS

LAZIO

2 tbsp. unsalted butter

2 tbsp. extra-virgin olive oil

2 garlic cloves, thinly sliced

4 tsp. anchovy paste

6 oz. black olives, pitted and sliced

1 tbsp. capers, rinsed and roughly chopped

A few plum tomatoes, peeled and cut in slices

1 lb. spaghetti

1 tbsp. chopped flat-leaf parsley

This dish, typical of Rome, is a somewhat recent invention, related to the vogue for strong flavors. Literally its title translates as spaghetti in the style of the prostitute.

Combine in a saucepan the butter, olive oil, garlic, and anchovy paste and sauté. ✦ As soon as the garlic browns add the olives, capers, and tomatoes. ✦ Turn up the heat and stir the sauce for a few minutes to blend the flavors. ✦ Meanwhile cook the spaghetti in lightly salted boiling water, drain when al dente, and put in a serving bowl. ✦ Add the sauce and sprinkle with parsley. Mix and serve hot.

SPAGHETTI WITH PECORINO AND PEPPER

SPAGHETTI CACIO E PEPE

LAZIO

1 lb. spaghetti

½ cup grated pecorino (pecorino Romano is best)

1 tbsp. black pepper (ground in a mortar if possible)

Salt

This dish is typical of Rome.

Cook the spaghetti in lightly salted boiling water, drain when al dente, reserving some of the cooking water, and pour into a heated serving bowl. ✦ Toss the spaghetti with the cheese and pepper, pour over a few tablespoons of the cooking water, and mix well to thoroughly blend the ingredients. Serve hot.

✦ **LOCAL TRADITION** ✦

SPAGHETTI ALLA COLATURA

Colatura is a preparation famously made by the fishermen of Cetara, a town on the Amalfi coast, in Campania. It is a by-product of preserving anchovies by packing them in layers of sea salt in wooden barrels; from time to time a hole is made in the barrel out of which a liquid drips. This liquid, when distilled, becomes translucent—and a potent fish sauce. Spaghetti, dressed with olive oil, sautéed garlic and chili pepper, and some *colatura*, makes for a delicious yet simple dish.

SPAGHETTI WITH BABY ANCHOVIES

SPAGHETTI CON I BIANCHETTI

CALABRIA

½ cup extra-virgin olive oil
4 tbsp. *nudilla* (see note)
1 chili pepper, chopped and ground
1 lb. spaghetti

Nudilla (or *rosamarina* or *nonnata* or *neonati*) are baby anchovies and sardines—also known as *bianchetti*—which in Calabria are preserved in salt with a great deal of chili pepper.

Heat the olive oil in a pan, remove the pan from the heat, and pour in the *nudilla,* breaking it up with the tines of a fork to separate the tiny fish. Add the chili pepper. ✦ Cook the spaghetti until al dente in lightly salted boiling water, drain well, and toss with the *nudilla.* Serve hot.

SPAGHETTI WITH TRUFFLES

SPAGHETTI CON I TARFUTI ALLA SPOLETINA

UMBRIA

6 oz. black truffles
1 garlic clove
1 oz. anchovy paste
4 tbsp. olive oil
1 lb. spaghetti
Salt

Clean the truffles, wash under running water, rub with a medium-hard brush, and make certain there are no pebbles hidden in the folds. ✦ Grind the smaller pieces in a mortar together with a small piece of garlic and mix this with the anchovy paste. ✦ Add in the olive oil and warm in the top of a double boiler while the spaghetti cooks. ✦ Cook the spaghetti in lightly salted boiling water, drain well, and toss with the truffle sauce.

SPAGHETTI WITH GUANCIALE AND TOMATO SAUCE

SPAGHETTI CON IL RANCETTO

UMBRIA

¼ cup extra-virgin olive oil
1 medium onion, sliced
4½ oz. guanciale, diced
2⅓ cup tomato purée
½ tbsp. chopped fresh marjoram
1 lb. spaghetti
¼ cup grated pecorino
Salt

This dish, typical of Spoleto and Foligno, is best if made with guanciale that is old enough to be somewhat rancid, which is what the *rancetto* of the title means.

Heat the olive oil in a saucepan and sauté the onion and guanciale; add the tomato purée, taste for salt, and cook 30 minutes at low heat. ✦ Add the marjoram and cook a little longer. ✦ Cook the spaghetti in lightly salted boiling water, drain when al dente, and dress with this sauce, adding pecorino before serving.

SPAGHETTI CON LE VONGOLE | SPAGHETTI WITH CLAMS

CAMPANIA

2 lbs. clams
¼ cup extra-virgin olive oil
1 garlic clove, crushed
1 lb. plum tomatoes, peeled, seeded, and chopped
1 lb. spaghetti
1 tbsp. chopped flat-leaf parsley
Salt and black pepper

There is also a white version of this typical Neapolitan dish. In that version, open the clams, and strain and reserve the cooking liquid. Heat ¼ cup olive oil in a pan and cook 2 cloves of garlic; remove the garlic and add the clams and their liquid. Let the sauce reach a boil then mix with the spaghetti, adding parsley and pepper. It can be made more flavorful by adding 1 pound of shelled *telline*.

Carefully wash the clams, put them in a large pan with 1 tablespoon of the olive oil, cover the pan, and cook at high heat. ✦ In a few minutes the clams will open. Reserve their cooking liquid after straining it through a fine cheesecloth. ✦ In another pan heat the remaining olive oil and add the garlic; when the garlic begins to brown remove it and pour in the tomatoes. Add salt and the clam liquid. ✦ At the last moment add the clams to the sauce and let it just return to a boil. ✦ Meanwhile cook the spaghetti in lightly salted boiling water. Drain when very al dente and add to the pan with the sauce, mixing well. ✦ Complete the dish with parsley and a grinding of black pepper.

SPAGHETTI DEL MARINAIO | MARINER'S SPAGHETTI

MARCHE

4½ oz. fresh anchovies
7 oz. mussels
½ cup extra-virgin olive oil
1 small onion, sliced
1 garlic clove, slivered
2 tbsp. chopped flat-leaf parsley
2 salt-cured anchovies
1 tsp. capers, rinsed
1 *diavolillo* (spicy chili pepper, see note, page 22), chopped
¼ cup white wine
2⅓ cups peeled plum tomatoes
1 lb. spaghetti
Salt

Clean and fillet the anchovies, then cut them in small pieces. ✦ Scrub the mussels and remove their beards. Open the mussels, reserving and straining their liquid. ✦ Heat the olive oil in a pan and sauté the onion. Add the garlic, parsley, salted anchovies, capers, and chili pepper; slowly cook together, adding the pieces of fresh anchovies then a little later the mussels and their strained liquid. ✦ Brown this mixture, then add the wine and salt. ✦ When the wine has evaporated add the tomatoes and simmer for about 30 minutes. ✦ Cook the pasta in lightly salted boiling water until very al dente. ✦ Drain and add to the pan with the sauce, tossing well and completing the cooking.

WHOLE-WHEAT SPAGHETTI WITH ANCHOVIES AND BREADCRUMBS

SPAGHETTI NERI
CON LA MOLLICA

MOLISE

½ cup extra-virgin olive oil

1 medium onion, in very thin slices

4 oz. salt-cured anchovies, boned and rinsed

A hunk of stale bread, crumbled into pieces (about ½ cup)

1 lb. whole-wheat spaghetti

2 tbsp. chopped flat-leaf parsley

The type of pasta traditionally used to make this dish, known as *zengarielle*, is brownish vermicelli, a result of the use of dark grains, which have more fiber and thus are healthier. *Zengarielle* flavored with olive oil and anchovies were a traditional dish for Christmas Eve.

Heat half the olive oil in a pan and sauté the onion. ✦ Add the anchovies and a little water and cook for 10 minutes. ✦ Meanwhile heat the remaining olive oil in another pan and fry the bread until it is golden and crunchy. ✦ Boil the spaghetti until al dente, drain, and toss with the anchovy sauce and parsley and sprinkle with breadcrumbs as you would for grated cheese.

PASTA, POLENTA & RICE

SPAGHETTI AND LOBSTER

SPAGHETTI TAGLIUZZATI
CON ZUPPA DI ARAGOSTA

SICILIA

¼ cup olive oil

5 medium onions, diced

1¾ lbs. plum tomatoes, peeled or in chunks

1 medium fresh lobster, cut in half

Pinch chili pepper flakes

2 tbsp. chopped flat-leaf parsley

1 lb. spaghetti, broken in pieces

Salt

Heat the olive oil in a pan over low heat and cook the onions until golden; add the tomatoes. ✦ Cook, stirring, 15 minutes, then stir in 1 cup warm water to form a creamy mixture. ✦ Add the lobster with all its shell. ✦ Add the chili pepper and enough warm water to cover and cook the lobster until opaque. ✦ When the lobster is cooked remove it from the pot and cut it open to remove the meat. ✦ Chop the meat and return it to the sauce; add the parsley. ✦ Cook the spaghetti in lightly salted boiling water until al dente and toss with the sauce. Let it rest 5 minutes before serving to blend the flavors.

"PRIEST STRANGLERS" GREEN GNOCCHI IN BUTTER AND SAGE SAUCE

STRANGOLAPRETI 1

LOMBARDIA

For the pasta:

1½ lbs. stale bread

2 cups milk

CONTINUED

While typical of the area of Bergamo, this dish is widespread throughout the former territory of the Venetian republic.

Soak the bread in the milk for at least an hour. ✦ Parboil the spinach or chard in lightly salted water, drain, and chop. ✦ Combine the bread with the spinach or chard, add the egg yolks, and pass the mixture through a food

10 oz. spinach or chard

2 large egg yolks

½ cup all-purpose flour

Pinch grated nutmeg

Grated bread, if needed

Salt and pepper

For the sauce:

2 tsp. unsalted butter, melted

⅓ cup grated Parmigiano-Reggiano

2 tbsp. chopped sage leaves

mill. ✦ Place it on a board and knead in the flour. ✦ Add nutmeg, salt, and pepper, and grated bread, if necessary, to form a smooth dough. ✦ Shape into gnocchetti and cook in lightly salted boiling water; as soon as they float remove with a slotted spoon and put in a dish, sprinkling with butter, cheese, and sage leaves. Serve hot.

STRANGOLAPRETI 2

"PRIEST STRANGLERS" GREEN GNOCCHI IN BUTTER SAUCE

TRENTINO

4 stale rolls, cut in pieces

½ cup whole milk, heated to lukewarm

1 lb. spinach or chard

2 large eggs, beaten

All-purpose flour, plus more as needed

½ cup (1 stick) unsalted butter, melted

4 tbsp. grated Parmigiano-Reggiano

Salt

Soak the bread in the milk for 30 minutes; squeeze to drain. ✦ Cook the spinach or chard, squeeze dry, and chop. ✦ Combine the bread, spinach, eggs, and enough flour to make a soft but firm dough. ✦ Bring lightly salted water to a boil and use a spoon to drop in lumps of the dough. ✦ When the gnocchetti float, drain and dress with butter and Parmigiano-Reggiano.

STRASCINATI CON LA MENTA

PASTA WITH MINT

BASILICATA

For the pasta:

4 cups all-purpose flour, plus more as needed

Salt

For the sauce:

2 tbsp. extra-virgin olive oil

CONTINUED

This dish, typical of Tito, is the white version; you can make it red by adding 2 or 3 dried sweet peppers.

Use the flour to prepare a pasta dough as in the recipe on page 10, using ½ cup water in place of the eggs. ✦ Cut the dough into sections and roll them out to form strips; cut the strips into 1-inch pieces. Place a piece of dough on the work surface and stretch the center (*strascinati,* as in the name of the recipe) to form long ovals, sort of like stretched-out orecchiette. ✦ Let the pasta dry on the floured work surface then cook it in lightly salted

1 tbsp. each unsalted butter and *lardo* (see page 2), minced

1 garlic clove, minced

2 tsp. chili pepper flakes (optional)

Fresh mint leaves

boiling water; the *strascinati* are cooked when they float. ✦ While the pasta is cooking, sauté all the ingredients for the sauce except the mint until the garlic takes color, then, add some chili pepper flakes. A moment before putting the sauce on the pasta add the mint leaves.

STRASCINATI
DI GRANO SARACENO

BUCKWHEAT PASTA WITH ZUCCHINI

PUGLIA

1⅔ cups buckwheat flour, plus more as needed

1 cup all-purpose flour, plus more as needed

2 tbsp. milk

1 large egg

6 oz. zucchini, cleaned and cut in rounds

¼ cup olive oil

1 garlic clove, crushed

1 lb. plum tomatoes, peeled and cubed

5½ oz. ricotta

Basil leaves

Salt

Use the flours and egg to prepare a pasta dough as in the recipe on page 10, adding the milk and ½ cup water with the egg. Roll out and form into *strascinati* as in the recipe on page 212. Bring a pot of lightly salted water to a boil and add the zucchini; after a few minutes add the *strascinati*. ✦ Separately heat the olive oil in a pan and add the garlic. Cook until light golden and add the tomatoes and cook briefly. ✦ Drain the zucchini and pasta when the pasta is al dente, combine with the sauce, and season with the ricotta and basil. Serve immediately.

STRENGOZZI
ALLA SPOLETINA

STRENGOZZI PASTA WITH GARLIC, CHILI, AND TOMATOES

UMBRIA

For the pasta:

2 cups all-purpose flour, plus more as needed

Salt

For the sauce:

2 tbsp. extra-virgin olive oil

2 garlic cloves

1 chili pepper

12 oz. plum tomatoes, peeled

2 tbsp. chopped flat-leaf parsley

Use the flour to prepare a pasta dough as in the recipe on page 10, using ¾ cup water in place of the eggs. Roll out a ¹⁄₁₆-inch-thick sheet (see page 212). ✦ Cut the sheet in narrow strips. ✦ Heat the olive oil in a pan and cook the garlic and chili pepper. Add the tomatoes and, when these are cooked, the parsley. ✦ Cook the *strengozzi* until al dente in boiling lightly salted water, drain, and combine with the sauce.

"PRIEST-CHOKERS" WITH MEAT SAUCE

STROZZAPRETI 1

CAMPANIA

2 ¼ cups all-purpose flour, plus more as needed

2 ¼ cups semolina flour

2 ½ oz. lard

Neapolitan meat sauce (see page 539)

Parmigiano-Reggiano, for serving

Salt

Mix the flour and semolina together on a clean work surface. Form a well in the center and add the lard and salt to taste in the center. Work together with the flours, slowly adding enough warm water to obtain a soft dough. ✦ Break off bits of the dough and shape them into finger-size cylinders. Cut these into inch-long pieces, and press them against a fork. ✦ Cook the pasta in a large pot of boiling salted water until al dente. ✦ Drain and toss with the sauce and sprinkle with Parmigiano-Reggiano to taste.

"PRIEST-CHOKERS" WITH SALSIFY SAUCE

STROZZAPRETI 2

EMILIA-ROMAGNA

For the pasta:

2 ⅓ cups all-purpose flour, plus more as needed

1 large egg

Salt

For the sauce:

4 tbsp. unsalted butter

7 oz. pancetta, diced

4 oz. boiled *lischi* (see note), chopped (may substitute Swiss chard leaves)

1 cup dry red wine, preferably Sangiovese di Romagna

⅔ cup grated Parmigiano-Reggiano

These "priest chokers," typical of Forlì, get their name for their white color, like that of priests' collars. Like so many *cucina povera* dishes there was originally no trace of an egg in the dough: it was just flour, water, and salt and served with a homemade sauce. This is a classic recipe from nineteenth-century Romagna only slightly revised and altered, most of all to ease its digestion (the original *strozzapreti* were indeed heavy enough to stick in the throat and cause a bit of "choking"). Wine, *lischi*, and meat were the ingredients used in the country. *Lischi*, also known as *barba di frate*, are the young leaves of the salsify plant. The shape of the *strozzapreti* varies, as does the sauce. Among the most commonly encountered are sauces based on sausage, meat sauce, or herbs.

Use the flour and egg to prepare a pasta dough as in the recipe on page 10, adding 3 tablespoons water with the egg. ✦ Roll out a large sheet (see page 212) and cut it into strips, then roll these with the palms of your hands into vermicelli about 4 to 6 inches long. Make a knot in the middle of each one. Cook in lightly salted boiling water until al dente, drain, and rinse. ✦ Heat 1 tablespoon of butter in a pan over low heat and sauté the pancetta. Add the *lischi* (or the chard) and the wine. ✦ When the wine has evaporated add the *strozzapreti* and the rest of the butter, and toss to heat. Sprinkle with Parmigiano-Reggiano and serve.

BAKED BREAD AND CHEESE WITH BROTH

SUPPA QUATTA

SARDEGNA

12 oz. peasant-style bread

12 oz. young pecorino or smooth-texture cheese

2 cups broth of mixed meats (lamb is indispensable)

Preheat the oven to 350°F. Cut the bread in thick slices and the cheese in thin ones. ✦ In a large baking pan arrange alternating layers of bread and cheese, ending with a layer of cheese. ✦ Cover with the broth. ✦ Bake for 20 minutes. Serve hot in the pan it was cooked in.

PASTA SQUARES WITH MEAT SAUCE

TACCONCELLE

MOLISE

3 cups all-purpose flour, plus more as needed

4 large eggs

Grated pecorino

1 recipe mixed meat sauce, made without tomato (see page 635)

Salt

Use the flour and eggs to prepare a pasta dough as in the recipe on page 10. ✦ Roll out a sheet to ⅛-inch (see page 212) and cut it into medium-size squares. ✦ Cook these *tacconcelle* in lightly salted boiling water, drain, and toss with pecorino and a good sauce made of mixed meats (veal, lamb, pork) without tomato.

PASTA SQUARES WITH JOHN DORY

TACCONCELLE CON SANPIETRO

MOLISE

1 potato, chopped

1 ripe plum tomato, seeded and chopped

1 medium onion, chopped

1 celery stalk, chopped

1 John Dory (orata), about 3½ lbs., cleaned

2 tbsp. extra-virgin olive oil

1 lb. *tacconcelle* (see above)

Grated pecorino

Salt

Mix the vegetables in a soup pot, then add water to cover. Bring to a boil, then simmer for 30 minutes to make a broth, then add the fish. ✦ Simmer gently for about 20 minutes, being careful to keep it whole. ✦ Remove the fish from the broth and set aside; add the olive oil to the broth and then use it to cook the *tacconcelle* (small squares of homemade pasta; see preceding recipe). ✦ Cook them until they float to the surface, a sign that they are cooked. Serve the pasta sprinkled with pecorino; serve the fish separately.

TAGLIATELLE
WITH HERB SAUCE

EMILIA-ROMAGNA

2 tbsp. extra-virgin olive oil

1 carrot, finely chopped

1 medium onion, finely chopped

1 celery stalk, chopped

½ cup diced pancetta

½ cup *striduli* (see note)

2 or 3 tbsp. tomato paste, diluted in ¼ cup water

10½ oz. tagliatelle

Grated Parmigiano-Reggiano

Salt

This same sauce can be used on *manfrigoli* or *quadrucci* (see page 171), diluting the sauce with broth and water. *Striduli* are small herbs gathered in the wild. You can substitute a mix of your favorite herbs, chopped.

Heat the olive oil in a pan over low heat and sauté the carrot, onion, celery, and pancetta. ✦ When this mixture has browned add the *striduli* and the tomato paste mixture. Cook at low heat until the sauce reduces. ✦ Meanwhile prepare the pasta, which should be handmade tagliatelle (see page 397). Boil in lightly salted water just until al dente and drain. ✦ Toss the tagliatelle with the *striduli* sauce, adding cheese to serve.

TAGLIATELLE
WITH MEAT SAUCE

EMILIA-ROMAGNA

2 tbsp. unsalted butter

1 tbsp. lard

1 celery stalk, finely chopped

1 carrot, finely chopped

1 medium onion, finely chopped

6 oz. pork, ground

4 oz. veal, ground

4 oz. chicken breast, finely chopped

½ cup dry red wine

10 oz. plum tomatoes, peeled

1 tbsp. tomato paste

12 oz. homemade egg tagliatelle (see page 397)

Grated Parmigiano-Reggiano

Salt and pepper

When peas are in season, they can be added to this typical Bolognese meat sauce at the end of its cooking. For the wine use Sangiovese di Romagna.

Heat the butter and lard in a saucepan (if possible earthenware) over low heat. Slowly sauté the celery, carrot, and onion for about 30 minutes. ✦ Add the meats, salt, and pepper, and cook for a few minutes. Add the wine and let it evaporate, then add the tomatoes and tomato paste. Continue cooking at very low heat with the pan covered for about 1 ¼ hours, stirring often with a wooden spoon and using the tines of a fork to break up the meats. ✦ When the sauce is almost ready cook the tagliatelle in boiling lightly salted water. Cook the pasta just until al dente, drain carefully, and pour it in the pan to mix with the meat sauce. ✦ Add a little Parmigiano-Reggiano, which will help adhere the sauce to the pasta.

TAGLIATELLE IN SQUAB SAUCE

TAGLIATELLE AL RAGÙ DI PICCIONE

VENETO

For the sauce:

¾ cup extra-virgin olive oil

1 medium onion, minced

1 celery stalk, minced

1 boned squab, 9 oz.

3 oz. lean ground pork

2½ oz. white wine

1 small sprig rosemary

2 plum tomatoes, peeled

For the pasta:

2 cups all-purpose flour, plus more as needed

3 large eggs, beaten

¾ cup grated Parmigiano-Reggiano

Salt

Heat the olive oil in a pan and cook the onion and celery. ✦ Add the squab and pork. ✦ Add the white wine, rosemary, and tomatoes, and cook for 30 minutes. ✦ Remove the rosemary and let the sauce rest 30 minutes before preparing the pasta. ✦ Use the flour and eggs to prepare a pasta dough as in the recipe on page 10. Roll out the dough (see page 212) and cut out tagliatelle (see page 397). ✦ Cook them in lightly salted boiling water; drain well and toss with the sauce, adding Parmigiano-Reggiano.

TAGLIATELLE WITH ZUCCHINI, ROASTED PEPPERS, AND TOMATOES

TAGLIATELLE ALLA REGGINA

CALABRIA

2 tbsp. extra-virgin olive oil

1 small onion, sliced

2 garlic cloves

6 oz. zucchini, cleaned and diced

6 oz. roasted peppers, peeled and cut in strips

6 oz. plum tomatoes, peeled, seeded, and chopped

12 oz. homemade tagliatelle (see page 397)

2 tbsp. grated pecorino

1 tbsp. chopped oregano

Salt and pepper

Heat the olive oil in a pan and sauté the onion. Add the garlic cloves. ✦ Add the zucchini, peppers, and tomatoes to the pan. ✦ Salt and pepper and continue cooking until the sauce is done. ✦ Cook the pasta until al dente, drain it, and toss with the sauce, pecorino, and oregano.

TAGLIATELLE WITH ROMAGNA-STYLE MEAT SAUCE

TAGLIATELLE ALLA ROMAGNOLA

EMILIA-ROMAGNA

For the pasta:

2 ⅓ cups all-purpose flour, plus more as needed

4 large eggs, beaten

Salt

For the sauce:

3 tbsp. olive oil

1 carrot, minced

1 celery stalk, minced

1 small onion, minced

4 oz. pancetta, diced

4 oz. ground beef

4 oz. ground pork

½ cup dry white wine

4 oz. tomato purée

1 ¼ cups grated Parmigiano-Reggiano

Salt and pepper

This dish is typical of Romagna.

Use the flour and eggs to prepare a pasta dough as in the recipe on page 10. Roll out a thin sheet (see page 212) and cut it in strips (see page 397). ✦ Prepare the meat sauce: heat the olive oil in a saucepan and sauté the carrot, celery, and onion. Add the pancetta and brown it, then add the other meats. Salt and pepper to taste. ✦ After about 10 minutes add wine, and as soon as it evaporates add the tomato purée and cook at low heat for 1 hour. ✦ Cook the tagliatelle in lightly salted boiling water, drain, and put in a serving bowl; toss with the meat sauce and add Parmigiano-Reggiano.

TAGLIATELLE WITH WILD FENNEL

TAGLIATELLE COL FINOCCHIO SELVATICO

CALABRIA

4 shallots, minced

2 garlic cloves, crushed

2 bunches of wild fennel, cleaned and chopped

6 oz. pancetta, diced

1 tbsp. chopped flat-leaf parsley

Extra-virgin olive oil

1 lb. homemade tagliatelle (see page 397)

Grated pecorino

Salt and black pepper

Put the shallots, garlic, and fennel in an earthenware pan; add the pancetta, parsley, and olive oil. Add salt and pepper. ✦ Cover with water and cook at low heat until the sauce has reduced by half. ✦ Use the sauce on tagliatelle cooked until al dente in lightly salted boiling water; add cheese and serve hot.

TAGLIATELLE WITH BABY SQUID

TAGLIATELLE
CON CALAMARETTI

MARCHE

2 tbsp. extra-virgin olive oil
1 garlic clove, minced
1 chili pepper, diced
10½ oz. small squid
½ cup dry white wine
(preferably Verdicchio)
2 tbsp. chopped flat-leaf parsley
12 oz. tagliatelle (see page 397)
Salt

Heat the olive oil in a pan and sauté the garlic and chili pepper until fragrant. ✦ Add the squid and, a little at a time, the wine. Cook until the wine has completely evaporated. ✦ Add a little salt and parsley. ✦ Cook the tagliatelle in boiling lightly salted water. Drain and toss with the sauce at high heat.

TAGLIATELLE WITH BEANS

TAGLIATELLE
CON FAGIOLI

MARCHE

2 tbsp. extra-virgin olive oil
½ cup diced prosciutto crudo
½ cup diced pancetta
1 medium onion, thinly sliced
1 carrot, thinly sliced
1 celery stalk, thinly sliced
1 ripe plum tomato,
seeded and chopped
1 cup leftover cooked beans
1 lb. tagliatelle (see page 397)
Salt and pepper

This dish is quite common among local peasants since it uses leftover beans cooked with pork, or stewed beans, to sauce homemade tagliatelle. The tagliatelle should be of medium thickness. The beans can be fresh or dried and may require being soaked for a period of time; the beans will thus require differing cooking times and also different quantities of water.

Heat the olive oil in a pan over low heat and add the prosciutto and pancetta. Sauté until golden, then add the onion, carrot, and celery. ✦ Add the tomato, then the beans and salt and pepper. ✦ Let the sauce cook over low heat until the beans begin to break down and the sauce assumes a creamy consistency. ✦ Cook the tagliatelle in boiling lightly salted water until al dente, drain, and toss with the sauce in a bowl. It is best to wait a few minutes before serving.

TAGLIATELLE WITH SQUASH BLOSSOMS

TAGLIATELLE
DI PAPARDURA

SICILIA

½ cup chicken broth
1 pinch saffron
CONTINUED

Heat the broth to boiling and add the saffron. Remove from the heat, cover, and let steep for 5 minutes. ✦ Clean and chop the squash blossoms. Heat the olive oil in a large pan and sauté the squash blossoms and onion until golden. Add the saffron broth, salt, pepper, and red

15 squash blossoms

2 tbsp. extra-virgin olive oil

1 medium onion, minced

Pinch chili pepper flakes

2 large egg yolks

½ cup grated pecorino

1 lb. tagliatelle (see page 397)

Salt and pepper

pepper flakes. ✦ When the sauce has cooked down pass it through a sieve and whisk in the egg yolks and pecorino. ✦ Cook the pasta until al dente, drain well, and dress with the sauce.

TAGLIATELLE WITH BROCCOLI

TAGLIATELLE E BROCCOLI
NERI COI CICCIOLI

CALABRIA

10 oz. broccoli,
trimmed and chopped

1 lb. tagliatelle (see page 397),
broken up

Pork *ciccioli* (see note, page 12)

Hot chili pepper flakes

Salt

Cook the broccoli in boiling lightly salted water just until crisp-tender. ✦ Meanwhile, cook the pasta in lightly salted boiling water until al dente. ✦ Drain the broccoli and pasta and mix in a serving bowl with *ciccioli* and chili pepper.

TAGLIATELLE AND CHICKPEAS WITH DRIED PEPPERS

TAGLIATELLE E CECI
CON PEPERONI SECCHI

CALABRIA

7 to 10 oz. dried chickpeas

Bay leaves

7 to 10 oz. homemade tagliatelle
(see page 397)

2 tbsp. extra-virgin olive oil

4 or 5 dried peppers,
seeded and thinly sliced

Salt

This dish is typical of Mottafallone.

Soak the chickpeas overnight then cook them in a terra-cotta pan in water, salt, and bay leaves until tender. ✦ Cook the tagliatelle in boiling lightly salted water, drain, and add to the chickpeas. ✦ Heat the olive oil in a large saucepan and add the peppers. Immediately add the tagliatelle mixture, stir well with a wooden spoon, and serve warm.

TAGLIATELLE PIE

TAGLIATELLE
IN PASTICCIO

EMILIA-ROMAGNA

½ lb. (2 sticks) unsalted butter,
softened to room temperature

CONTINUED

Butter a glass deep-dish pie plate. Use the flour, 1 stick plus 1 tablespoon of the butter, the wine, and eggs to prepare a pasta dough as in the recipe on page 10. Set this aside to rest for 1 full hour, covered, in a cool spot.

3 cups all-purpose flour,
plus more as needed

¼ cup dry white wine

2 large eggs plus 1 large egg yolk,
beaten

1 lb. egg tagliatelle

1 ¼ cups heavy cream

6 tbsp. grated Parmigiano-Reggiano

Salt

+ Preheat the oven to 350°F. Meanwhile cook the tagliatelle in lightly salted boiling water and drain when very al dente. + At the same time melt 2 tablespoons of the butter in a pan and add to this the drained tagliatelle. Stir in 3 tablespoons of the pasta cooking water, the cream, the remaining butter, and cheese. Cook this, stirring, for a few seconds at medium heat. + Divide the dough into two parts, one larger than the other, and roll these out to form disks. Use the larger disk to line the pie plate. Add the tagliatelle and cover with the remaining disk of dough, crimping the edges to form a braid. + Bake for about 30 minutes, until golden.

+ **LOCAL TRADITION** +

TAGLIATELLE

Tagliatelle are about 6 inches in length and about ½ inch in width. According to one story that made the rounds during the 1930s, tagliatelle had been invented by a certain Mastro Zafirano, cook to Giovanni Bentivoglio in 1487—a story that is completely false. Artusi said, "Short accounts and long tagliatelle," because short noodles only attest to the ineptness of the person who prepared them and, when served that way, they seem more like kitchen leftovers.

TAGLIATELLE
IN SALSA D'UOVO

TAGLIATELLE IN EGG SAUCE

PIEMONTE

2 ⅓ cups all-purpose flour,
plus more as needed

5 large eggs

3 anchovies, boned, rinsed,
and chopped in pieces

⅔ cup cubed mozzarella

¼ lb. (1 stick) unsalted butter

Salt

Use the flour and 3 eggs to prepare a pasta dough as in the recipe on page 10 (using more water as needed). + Knead it well, roll it out not too thin, then cut into wide tagliatelle. Boil them in lightly salted water. + While the tagliatelle cook put the yolks of the 2 remaining eggs in a bowl with the anchovies and mozzarella; mix thoroughly. + Melt the butter in a large pan. + When the tagliatelle are al dente, drain them and put them in the pan with the butter over low heat. + Stir in the egg mixture along with a few tablespoons of the pasta cooking water, and when the mozzarella begins to melt and the eggs form a cream, transfer the tagliatelle to a serving bowl and serve hot.

BLACK TAGLIATELLE WITH CUTTLEFISH

TAGLIATELLE NERE ALLE SEPPIE GROSSE

VENETO

1¾ cups all-purpose flour, plus more as needed

2 large eggs, beaten

1 cuttlefish ink sac

¼ lb. (1 stick) unsalted butter

⅓ cup chopped shallots

2 garlic cloves, peeled

1 lb. large cuttlefish, cut in pieces

¼ cup white wine

3 oz. tomato purée

⅓ cup grated Parmigiano-Reggiano

Salt and pepper

Use the flour and eggs to prepare a pasta dough as in the recipe on page 10, adding the ink sac and 1 tablespoon water with the eggs. ✦ Roll the dough out and cut to the measure desired. Hang up the tagliatelle to dry. ✦ Prepare the sauce: Heat 3 tablespoons of the butter in a pan and sauté the shallot and garlic, removing the garlic when it turns golden. ✦ Add the cuttlefish, wine, tomatoes, and salt and pepper. Cook slowly over low heat until done. ✦ Cook the tagliatelle in lightly salted boiling water, drain them but not completely, and add them to the sauce. Add the remaining butter and Parmigiano-Reggiano and cook for a few minutes.

THIN TAGLIATELLE WITH SQUID AND SHRIMP

TAGLIATELLINE CON CALAMARI E SCAMPETTI

MARCHE

2 tbsp. extra-virgin olive oil

¼ medium onion, finely chopped

2 garlic cloves, chopped

10 oz. squid, cut in small pieces

¼ cup dry white wine, preferably Verdicchio

1¼ cups tomato sauce diluted with a little warm water

10 oz. small shrimp

1 lb. thin tagliatelle (see page 397), cooked until al dente

1 tbsp. chopped flat-leaf parsley

Heat the olive oil in a pan over low heat and sauté the onion, adding the garlic but not letting it brown. ✦ Add the squid and cook until it has given up all its liquid. ✦ Pour in the wine and let it evaporate, then add the diluted tomato sauce (in the end the sauce should be a nice rosy color). ✦ Near the end add the shrimp, which will cook in 3 minutes. ✦ Use this sauce on thin tagliatelle; sprinkle with the parsley.

TAGLIOLINI WITH BLACK TRUFFLE

TAGLIOLINI AL TARTUFO NERO

MARCHE

1 lb. tagliolini, homemade (see below) or purchased

Salt

For the sauce:

3 tbsp. unsalted butter

1 tsp. demiglace

3 oz. black truffle, shaved using a truffle shaver

or

3 tbsp. olive oil

1 clove garlic

3 oz. black truffle, grated

Make tagliolini using only egg yolks (4 yolks to each cup of flour) or use the classic tagliolini of Campofilone.

Cook the tagliolini until al dente in lightly salted boiling water. ✦ There are two variations for the sauce. 1) Mix the butter and demiglace. Use this sauce on the tagliolini, adding the remaining truffle to the plate. ✦ 2) Heat the olive oil in a large pan and cook the garlic (removing it as soon as it turns brown!), and pour in the tagliolini and the truffle. Serve immediately in serving bowls.

TAGLIOLINI WITH BLACK TRUFFLE FROM NORCIA

TAGLIOLINI AL TARTUFO NERO DI NORCIA

UMBRIA

For the pasta:

1⅔ cups all-purpose flour, plus more as needed

3 large eggs

For the sauce:

3 tbsp. extra-virgin olive oil

1 garlic clove

2 oz. black truffle, sliced

Salt

Norcia is a town in eastern Umbria and is famous for its black truffles.

Use the flour and eggs to prepare a pasta dough as in the recipe on page 10. Roll it out to form thin sheets (see page 212). Cut these into tagliolini (much thinner than tagliatelle), roll them in flour, and set them aside to rest under a cloth for 30 minutes. ✦ Cook the tagliolini till al dente in lightly salted boiling water; drain. Pour the olive oil in a pan large enough to hold the pasta and heat the garlic over low heat, but do not let it take on any color. Add the cooked tagliolini and truffle, toss, and serve.

TAGLIOLINI WITH SQUID AND SHRIMP

TAGLIOLINI DI CAMPOFILONE

MARCHE

7 oz. squid, cut in thin slices

4 oz. small shrimp, sliced in half

CONTINUED

For the wine use Verdicchio.

Combine the squid, shrimp, olive oil, and garlic in a pan. ✦ Cook over low heat for about 15 minutes, then add the chili pepper. ✦ Pour in the wine and stir well. ✦ Separately, cook the tagliolini in lightly salted boiling water;

2 tbsp. extra-virgin olive oil

1 garlic clove

Pinch red chili pepper flakes

½ cup dry white wine

1 lb. homemade tagliolini
(see page 399)

2 tbsp. chopped flat-leaf parsley

Salt

drain when al dente. Add the tagliolini to the squid and shrimp and toss. Add the parsley. Serve hot.

TAJARIN DELLE LANGHE

TAGLIERINI
IN MEAT SAUCE

PIEMONTE

For the dough:

3 cups all-purpose flour,
plus more as needed

6 large eggs

Salt

For the sauce:

2 tbsp. extra-virgin olive oil

4 tbsp. unsalted butter

1 oz. scraped *lardo* (see page 2)

1 celery stalk, finely minced

1 carrot, finely minced

1 medium onion, finely minced

1 garlic clove, finely minced

1 bunch flat-leaf parsley, chopped

1 tbsp. chopped sage

1 tbsp. chopped rosemary

½ cup red wine

2 chicken livers

Kidneys, hearts, and gizzards
from several chickens

Fresh mushrooms, chopped, or
dried mushrooms, soaked in water
and Marsala, drained, and chopped

4 oz. fresh sausage meat, crumbled

2 tbsp. tomato purée

2 tbsp. grated Parmigiano-Reggiano

It is traditional to add to the sauce along with the chicken gizzards, cockscombs, rabbit livers, and unlaid eggs found in hens that have been slaughtered.

Use the flour and eggs to prepare a pasta dough as in the recipe on page 10. Roll the dough out into a thin sheet (see page 212). ✦ Cut the taglierini as fine as hair and set them aside to dry covered by a cloth. ✦ Heat the olive oil, 2 tablespoons butter, and *lardo* in a pan; add the celery, carrot, onion, garlic, parsley, sage, and rosemary; when this mixture begins to take on color begin adding small amounts of wine. ✦ Cut all the giblets into pieces and brown. ✦ Then add the mushrooms and sausage meat, the remaining wine, and the tomato purée. ✦ Cook at very low heat, remembering that the more it cooks the better it tastes. ✦ Cook the taglierini until al dente, drain, and toss them with the sauce. Stir in the remaining butter and cheese and serve.

TAGLIATELLE WITH TRUFFLE

TAJARIN TRIFOLÀ

PIEMONTE

For the pasta:

2⅓ cups all-purpose flour, plus more as needed

2 large eggs

1 tbsp. grated Parmigiano-Reggiano

For the sauce:

¼ lb. (1 stick) unsalted butter

1 garlic clove

Several sage leaves

½ cup grated Parmigiano-Reggiano

¼ cup chicken broth

Shaved white truffle, as much as needed

Salt and pepper

This dish is typical of Alba.

Use the flour and eggs to prepare a pasta dough as in the recipe on page 10, adding the Parmigiano-Reggiano and 4 tablespoons water with the eggs (the dough will be very dense). ◆ Roll out a very thin sheet (see page 212). Roll up the sheet and cut it into wide tagliatelle. ◆ Heat the butter in a pan and add the garlic, sage, cheese, salt, and pepper. ◆ Add the broth and reduce the heat to low. ◆ Cook the pasta in lightly salted boiling water until al dente, drain, and pour the sauce over the tagliatelle. Add slices of white truffle to the serving plate.

BAKED RICE MOLD

TAMBURO DI RISO

SICILIA

Lard

Breadcrumbs

1 large hen

2 cups chopped vegetables (celery, onion, carrot)

Broth

1½ lbs. ground veal (enough to make at least 30 tiny meatballs)

2¾ cups Arborio rice

¼ cup grated pecorino

6 oz. tuma or caciocavallo, sliced

Sausage or salame, chopped

4 large eggs, beaten

Parmigiano-Reggiano

This dish, typical of Catania, is prepared for the midday meal on Christmas. Some families enrich the preparation by adding layers of meat sauce to the layers of hen meat.

Preheat the oven to 400°F. Grease a baking dish with lard and sprinkle it with breadcrumbs. Simmer the hen and vegetables in broth to cover. ◆ Use the veal to make meatballs about as large as almonds (about thirty should be enough) and add them to the broth; remove them when cooked and set aside. ◆ When the hen is cooked through remove it from the broth, drain it, and when it is cool enough to handle, remove the skin and bones and chop the meat into strips. ◆ Add the rice to the broth and cook it until al dente (add water if necessary). Add the pecorino (the result should be quite dry). ◆ Make a layer of rice in the baking dish; over this place the tuma and/or caciocavallo; next add a good layer of hen meat, meatballs, and sausage or salame; cover this with rice. ◆ Make as many layers as desired, ending with one of rice. ◆ Pour the eggs over the rice, then sprinkle with Parmigiano-Reggiano. ✦ Bake for 25 to 30 minutes, or until the eggs are set.

TRUFFLE RAVIOLI

TARTUFIOLI AQUILANI

ABRUZZO

1⅔ cups all-purpose flour, plus more as needed

4 large eggs

12 oz. ricotta, drained of most of its liquid

2 oz. grated black truffle, plus some sliced truffle for serving

Unsalted butter, melted

Grated pecorino

1 bunch flat-leaf parsley, chopped

Salt

This dish, typical of L'Aquila, is called a *tartufioli*, a word that combines *tartufo* (truffle) with *ravioli*. Instead of butter, it can be seasoned with tomato sauce.

Use the flour and 3 of the eggs to prepare a pasta dough as in the recipe on page 10. Let the pasta rest for 20 minutes before rolling it out. ✦ Beat the remaining egg and mix it with the ricotta. Add a pinch of salt, then stir in the truffle. ✦ Divide the dough in half and roll out half to form a sheet (see page 212). ✦ Arrange little balls of the ricotta filling at regular intervals in rows along the sheet; roll out the other half and cover the first. ✦ Using a round cutter cut out the ravioli, pinching the edges to make sure they are well sealed. ✦ Boil these *tartufioli* in boiling lightly salted water until they float. Drain and dress with butter, pecorino, and a little parsley. ✦ Before serving add a few slices of truffle to the plate.

BAKED RIGATONI WITH BRAISED PORK AND EGGS

FOR 16 PERSONS

TEGAME (IL)

SICILIA

Lard or unsalted butter

1⅓ lb. rigatoni

1¼ lb. pork loin

40 large eggs

2½ cups grated pecorino

1 bunch flat-leaf parsley, finely chopped

2¾ lbs. tuma cheese, cut in thin, wide slices (can substitute caciocavallo)

Salt

This recipe, originally from an ancient noble family of Aragonese origin, is rich with eggs and seasonings. It has many variations, all of which merely decrease the quantity of the ingredients but do not alter the technique. At Aragona Caldaro and in various other locales around Agrigento, this is a devotional dish for Easter that is eaten on Holy Saturday. The "tanánu," a kind of earthenware pot typical of old Sicilia, performs an important role in this preparation. In fact, the ritual called for it to be broken so that the contents could retain the form they had assumed while cooking. The dish can be made in another pan, provided it is deep and round and does not have straight sides. The sides should instead have the shape of a panettone.

Grease an earthenware baking dish with lard or butter. Cook the rigatoni in boiling lightly salted water until al dente; drain. Divide in three parts and arrange them in a single layer on a cloth so that their openings remain open to later absorb sauce. ✦ Braise the pork: heat 2 tablespoons lard in a heavy pot and brown the pork. Add 1 inch of water, cover, and cook over low heat, turning the loin occasionally until cooked through, about 1½ hours. ✦ Preheat the oven to 300°F. When the meat is cooked remove it from the liquid (which will not be used) and chop it. ✦ Now come the 40 eggs. Take 36 of them and beat them together with 2¼ cups of the pecorino. Add the parsley and pork. This mixture must then be divided into three portions. ✦ Beat the 4 remaining eggs with the remaining 4 tablespoons pecorino (to make the topping). ✦ Divide the slices of tuma into 4 portions: the first 3 should amount to about 12 oz. each, leaving about 6 oz. for the last. ✦ Now begins the *tegame:* use one of the three larger portions of tuma to line the bottom and also the sides of the baking dish; over this goes a first portion of the pasta, which should be put in without pressing. ✦ Over this goes one of the portions of egg-meat mixture. ✦ Proceed now with the second layer, arranging another of the large portions of tuma over the last layer and not forgetting the sides, then a portion of pasta, and the second portion of the egg-meat mixture. ✦ The third layer should be identical to the second. ✦ The remaining tuma (the smallest portion) goes over the last layer of pasta, followed by the egg and cheese mixture. ✦ Now the *tegame* is finally ready. ✦ Bake for 30 minutes. ✦ Remove from the oven and when it has cooled break the pan (or turn it over) and you'll have a perfect timbale. ✦ It should be served at room temperature, neither hot nor cold, immediately after it is plated. It serves as both a first and second course.

TESTAROLI

GRIDDLED PASTA

TOSCANA-LIGURIA

3¾ cups all-purpose flour, plus more as needed

Salt

This ancient recipe is typical of the Lunigiana and the upper Val di Magra. It is a home version; the true *testo* was a stone disk kept in the embers of the fireplace.

Preheat the oven to 350°F. Grease a *testo* (or a griddle or baking pan). Mix the flour, water, and salt to make a batter that is not overly thick, being careful to avoid the formation of lumps. ✦ Pour this onto the *testo* (or griddle or baking pan) and bake until firm, about 25 minutes. ✦ After letting it cool, cut it in strips that can then be boiled in lightly salted water. ✦ *Testaroli* can be flavored with a dressing of garlic and oil or, as has been customary for quite a while now, with pesto (see page 418).

BAKED RICE WITH MUSSELS AND POTATOES

TIELLA ALLA BARESE

PUGLIA

Extra-virgin olive oil
1 cup rice
1 lb. mussels in their shells
1 garlic clove, minced
4 or 5 yellow potatoes, peeled and sliced
8 plum tomatoes, peeled and sliced
1 medium onion, thinly sliced
¼ cup grated pecorino
¼ cup finely chopped flat-leaf parsley
Breadcrumbs (optional)
Pepper

This preparation is typical of Bari. One variation is to make a bed of chopped onions cooked in olive oil followed by a layer of raw zucchini sliced in thin rounds instead of making the first layer of potatoes.

Preheat the oven to 350°F. ✦ Grease a large baking dish with olive oil. ✦ Boil the rice until al dente, setting it aside. ✦ Scrape the mussels to clean the shells and wash under running water. Put them in a pan with the garlic and heat until they open. ✦ Drain, strain the liquid (and reserve), and remove the mussels from their shells. Arrange a layer of potatoes along the bottom of the baking dish and top with a layer of mussels. On top of this place a layer of the rice, tomatoes, and onion; sprinkle with pecorino and dust with parsley and pepper. ✦ Arrange another layer of potatoes, rice, tomatoes, onion, and pecorino, and continue alternating layers until the ingredients are used up, ending with a layer of potatoes. ✦ When you have finished this final layer, drizzle with olive oil, the liquid from cooking the mussels, then the liquid from boiling the rice. If desired, add some breadcrumbs. ✦ Bake for about 45 minutes. There is no need to add salt since the liquid from the mussels has salt.

BAKED RICE FOGGIA-STYLE

TIELLA ALLA FOGGIANA

PUGLIA

This is a typically Pugliese preparation, particularly of Foggia. *Tiella* (the dish is named for the kind of pan it is traditionally cooked in) is always made on a base of onions, potatoes, and tomatoes, but there are many local variations. In Bari it is made with rice, mussels, and potatoes; in Foggia cod, mushrooms, or zucchini and black olives or mushrooms and *lampasciuni* (hyacinth bulbs, a kind of wild onion typical of the

Extra-virgin olive oil

4 medium onions, peeled and sliced (or as many as needed)

1¾ lbs. potatoes, peeled, chopped, and seasoned in olive oil and salt

¾ lb. salt-dried cod, soaked to soften and chopped

¾ lb. fresh oyster mushrooms (or other firm mushrooms), chopped

4 plum tomatoes, peeled and sliced

2 tbsp. chopped flat-leaf parsley

1 garlic clove, chopped

½ cup breadcrumbs

2 tbsp. grated pecorino

1 tbsp. chopped oregano

Salt

Mediterranean area, also known as *cipollaccio col fiocco*). A dish with ancient peasant origins, fruit of the creativity of local women, it is a one-dish meal that can be eaten cold, maintaining all its pleasant flavor and the blending of its aromas.

Preheat the oven to 400°F. Grease the bottom of a 12-inch ovenproof pan with olive oil and put in a layer of the onions, making it less than half an inch high. ✦ Follow this with a layer of the seasoned potatoes; between the pieces of potato insert pieces of cod and mushrooms. ✦ Season this layer with a few pieces of tomato, parsley, garlic, breadcrumbs, pecorino, salt, and oregano. ✦ Drizzle with a little olive oil and add a little water, bearing in mind that the potatoes, mushrooms, and tomatoes will give off their own liquid and that more water can be added during cooking, if necessary. ✦ Put the pan in the oven and bake for 45 minutes, or until the surface has browned and is crusty. Let it rest a few minutes before serving.

POTATO-MUSHROOM GRATIN

TIELLA DI FUNGHI

PUGLIA

½ lb. potatoes, peeled and sliced

½ lb. onions, thinly sliced

1 lb. mushrooms, chopped

Extra-virgin olive oil

2 tbsp. chopped flat-leaf parsley

2 tbsp. grated pecorino

½ cup breadcrumbs

Salt and pepper

Preheat the oven to 350°F. ✦ Form alternating layers in an ovenproof pan: potatoes, onions, mushrooms. ✦ Drizzle with olive oil and sprinkle with parsley, salt, pepper, and pecorino; dust the last layer with breadcrumbs, drizzle with more olive oil, and add a little water. ✦ Bake for about 30 minutes. Let cool before serving.

POTATO AND VEGETABLE GRATIN

TIELLA DI VERDURE

PUGLIA

Extra-virgin olive oil

¾ lb. fresh plum tomatoes, peeled and thinly sliced

CONTINUED

Preheat the oven to 400°F. Drizzle some olive oil into an ovenproof baking pan and follow it with a layer of tomatoes (reserve a few for the top layer); follow this with layers of potatoes, eggplant, peppers, mozzarella, and a few basil leaves. Season every third layer with salt and pepper. ✦ Repeat the layers in the same sequence until

1 lb. potatoes, peeled and sliced

2 eggplants, sliced

2 yellow peppers, cleaned, seeded, and sliced

9 oz. mozzarella, cubed

1 bunch basil leaves

½ cup grated pecorino

½ cup breadcrumbs

1 tbsp. oregano

Salt and pepper

using up the ingredients, ending with a layer of mozzarella. ✦ Mix the breadcrumbs, pecorino, oregano, salt, and pepper and sprinkle over the final layer. Add the reserved tomato slices and drizzle them with oil. ✦ Bake for about 1 hour.

TIELLA TARANTINA

BAKED RICE WITH SEAFOOD

PUGLIA

1½ lbs. mussels (see note)

2 medium onions, thinly sliced

2 zucchini, sliced in disks

2 medium potatoes, peeled and sliced

1¼ cups Vialone nano rice

2 ripe plum tomatoes, peeled and sliced

Grated pecorino

½ cup basil leaves

Extra-virgin olive oil

This recipe, typical of Taranto, uses Pugliese mussels, which can be opened like oysters. If these are not available, use and cook regular mussels, reserving some of their cooking liquid.

Preheat the oven to 350°F. Scrape the mussels under running water. ✦ Open them, reserving their liquid, and discard the top shell from each. ✦ Arrange the onion slices on the bottom of an ovenproof pan, and add the zucchini. ✦ Make a layer of potato slices and on these place the mussels. ✦ Spread the rice over the mussels and pour on the reserved mussel liquid. ✦ Make a layer of tomatoes over the rice. ✦ Dust with the pecorino, add basil leaves, and drizzle with olive oil. Bake for 45 minutes.

✦ LOCAL TRADITION ✦

TIELLE DE GAETA

In this simple pie recipe from Lazio, homemade pastry dough would be made with flour, olive oil, yeast, and water, and after rising filled with a savory mixture of chopped fresh anchovy fillets, tomatoes, garlic, parsley, chili flakes, and meaty Gaeta olives. The top of the pie would be brushed with olive oil before baking.

CHICORY TIMBALE

4 ½ lbs. wild chicory
(can use dandelion)

2 tbsp. extra-virgin olive oil

½ medium onion, chopped

2 lbs. tomato purée

½ cup grated pecorino

6 oz. mozzarella, cubed

4 oz. mortadella, minced

2 large hard-boiled eggs, sliced

Salt

An old variation uses sautéed meatballs instead of the mortadella.

Preheat the oven to 400°F. Boil the chicory in lightly salted water until tender, drain, and chop. ✦ Heat the olive oil in a pan and add the onion. Cook until translucent, add the tomato purée, and cook until the sauce has darkened and thickened slightly. Season with salt and 2 tablespoons of the pecorino. ✦ In a bowl combine the chicory with a little salt. ✦ Put a cup of the sauce in a baking dish, top with half the chicory, then add the other ingredients, sprinkle with pecorino, and top with sauce. ✦ Make another layer of chicory and season it as the first, ending with a layer of tomato sauce. ✦ Bake for 30 minutes. Serve immediately.

TIMBALLO DI MACCHERONI 1 **BAKED MACARONI WITH EGGPLANT**

3 eggplants, cut in thin
lengthwise strips

Extra-virgin olive oil

1 tbsp. *lardo* (see page 2), minced

1 medium onion, thinly sliced

1 garlic clove, crushed

¾ lb. fresh plum tomatoes,
chopped and seeded

¾ lb. macaroni rigati

2 oz. caciocavallo, sliced

2 tbsp. unsalted butter

Salt

This dish is typical of Messina.

Preheat the oven to 350°F. Grease a baking dish. Put the eggplant slices in a colander, sprinkle with salt, and leave for 30 minutes to make them lose their bitter juice. ✦ Heat ¼ inch of olive oil in a pan. Dry the eggplant slices and fry them; set aside. ✦ In a saucepan heat the *lardo* and 2 tablespoons olive oil and sauté the onion and garlic; add the tomatoes and season with salt; cover and cook at low heat. ✦ Cook the macaroni in salted boiling water; drain when al dente. ✦ In the baking dish arrange alternating layers of macaroni, tomato sauce, eggplant, and caciocavallo, continuing the layers until no ingredients are left. Place pats of butter across the surface and bake for about 10 minutes. ✦ Unmold onto a serving dish and cut in wedges to serve.

BAKED MACARONI
AND RICE WITH PORK

SICILIA

2 tbsp. extra-virgin olive oil

¼ cup grated Parmigiano-Reggiano

1 medium onion, minced

¼ cup chopped flat-leaf parsley

1 lb. ground pork

½ lb. tomato purée

2 lbs. cauliflower

1 lb. short pasta

2½ cups Arborio rice

½ lb. tuma cheese
(can substitute caciocavallo),
cut in pieces

Salt and pepper

Grease a baking pan (preferably a drum-shaped mold) with olive oil and dust with a little Parmigiano-Reggiano. Heat the remaining olive oil in a large saucepan and sauté the onion and parsley. Add the pork and cook until browned. ✦ Add the tomato purée, season with salt and pepper, and simmer slowly for at least 2 hours; when cooked set aside some of the meat. ✦ Boil the cauliflower until al dente, drain well, and chop. Heat some olive oil in a sauté pan and cook the cauliflower until lightly browned. ✦ Preheat the oven to 350°F. In separate pots cook the pasta and rice in lightly salted boiling water. ✦ Flavor the cooked rice with some of the sauce. Reserve a quarter of the rice and use the rest to line the bottom and sides of the baking pan (it will be thick). ✦ Toss the cooked pasta with the remaining sauce and spread it over the rice. ✦ Over this place the cooked cauliflower, the meat set aside from the sauce, and tuma. ✦ Cover with the reserved rice, dust with more Parmigiano-Reggiano, and bake until it forms a fine golden crust.

RICE AND PASTA
BAKED WITH
MEATBALLS

SICILIA

For the rice:

¼ lb. (1 stick) unsalted butter

About 2 tbsp. breadcrumbs

5 cups rice

⅔ cup grated caviocavallo

3 large eggs

Salt

For the filling:

1 lb. spaghettini or macaroni

1 recipe béchamel sauce
(see page 339)

1 recipe pasta sauce
made with pork (see page 539)

CONTINUED

This dish is made exceptional by its mixture of rice and pasta, making it somewhat elaborate but always enormously successful. A historic dish, it is still prepared for important occasions.

Preheat the oven to 350°F. Grease a baking dish with butter and dust with breadcrumbs. Boil the rice in lightly salted water and drain when still al dente; combine with the caciocavallo and eggs and set aside. ✦ Cook the pasta in lightly salted boiling water and drain when still very al dente. ✦ Toss the pasta with most of the béchamel and meat sauce. ✦ Line the pan with half the cooked rice mixture. ✦ Cut the eggs in half lengthwise. Pour in the pasta and top with the hard-boiled eggs, tuma, and meatballs. ✦ Cover with more of the sauce and the remaining rice. ✦ Dust with breadcrumbs and dot with butter. ✦ Bake for about 1 hour, by which time it should

5 large hard-boiled eggs

7 oz. fresh tuma cheese (can substitute caciocavallo), in pieces

1 recipe veal meatballs (the size of a peanut), sautéed in oil (see page 105)

2 tbsp. unsalted butter, cut into cubes

have a fine golden color. Remove from the oven and unmold onto a serving plate. Serve immediately.

TIMBALLO DI SCRIPPELLE

BAKED LAYERED CREPES WITH ARTICHOKE

FOR
6 PERSONS

ABRUZZO

Extra-virgin olive oil

Breadcrumbs

For the *scrippelle*:

6 large eggs, beaten

¾ cup all-purpose flour

Lard or olive oil

For the sauce:

1 (28-oz.) can tomato purée

1 celery stalk, minced

1 small carrot, minced

1 small onion

6 oz. ground beef

6 oz. ground lamb

6 oz. ground pork

½ cup extra-virgin olive oil

For the filling:

6 artichokes, trimmed, chokes removed, and sliced

All-purpose flour

2 tbsp. extra-virgin olive oil

3 scamorza cheeses (6 oz. each), diced

3 large hard-boiled eggs, cut in pieces

⅔ cup grated pecorino

1 large egg, beaten

2 tbsp. unsalted butter

1 tbsp. milk

Salt

You can use 2 pounds spinach or 1 pound peas or porcini mushrooms, chopped, floured, and sautéed in place of the artichokes.

Lightly grease a baking dish with oil and coat with breadcrumbs. Combine the eggs and flour and dilute with 3 cups of water; you will have a very thin batter. Grease a sauté pan with a little lard (or olive oil), let it heat a few moments, then pour in a cup or so of the batter and cook the *scrippelle* (crepes) one at a time at low heat, setting them aside as they finish. ✦ Preheat the oven to 350°F. Combine the tomato purée, celery, carrot, and whole onion (to discard at the end of the cooking), the three kinds of meat, and olive oil in a large saucepan. Cook until the sauce has thickened, adding salt as needed. ✦ Dredge the artichoke slices in flour and sauté in a pan in olive oil, turning, until golden. ✦ Set aside two of the *scrippelle* and arrange the others around the inside of the baking dish so that they extend past the rim. ✦ Begin with a layer of sauce, follow with one of artichokes, then scarmoza, then hard-boiled eggs, and a dusting of pecorino as desired; beat together the egg, a little of the pecorino, milk, and salt; brush on the hard-boiled eggs and continue the series of layers. ✦ Fold over the extending edges of the *scrippelle*, cover with the two remaining *scrippelle*, and add pats of butter. Bake for about 90 minutes.

TIMBALLO ALLA BONIFACIO VIII

This hearty timbale recipe from the area of Ciociaria in Lazio was reportedly created for Pope Bonifacio VIII. To assemble the timbale, a baking pan would be lined with slices of prosciutto crudo to form the shell. Homemade fettuccine would be tossed with Parmigiano-Reggiano and a small amount of savory sauce made from tomatoes, sautéed chicken gizzards and giblets, mushrooms, and veal meatballs. More sauce would then be poured over the pasta and the dish covered with a final layer of prosciutto slices before baking. At the table, the baked timbale would be unmolded onto a serving plate and sliced.

TIMBALLO DI SFOGLIE

BEEF AND VEGETABLE PIE

FOR 6 PERSONS

ABRUZZO

Unsalted butter

For the dough:
About 2 ⅓ cups all-purpose flour
4 large eggs
Salt

For the sauce:
2 tbsp. extra-virgin olive oil
¾ lb. ground beef
2 lbs. canned tomatoes
1 medium onion, chopped
Salt

For the filling:
¼ cup extra-virgin olive oil, for frying
7 oz. zucchini, cut in rounds
3 artichokes, cut in pieces
1 ¼ lbs. scamorza cheese, cubed
1 large egg, beaten
1 ½ cups milk
Grated Parmigiano-Reggiano

A variation of this recipe (typical of Pescara) includes the addition of boiled peas to the sauce.

Preheat the oven to 325°F. Grease a 10-inch-round baking dish with butter. Use the flour and eggs to prepare a pasta dough as described on page 10. ✦ Roll out a very thin sheet (see page 212); cut the sheet in strips about 8 inches long and 6 inches wide. ✦ Cook these in boiling lightly salted water for 3 minutes until very al dente, drain, and dry on a cloth. ✦ In another pan prepare the sauce: heat the olive oil in a pan and brown the ground beef. Add the tomatoes, onion, and salt to taste. ✦ In another pan heat the olive oil and fry the zucchini and artichokes until golden, then combine them with the scamorza. ✦ Mix the egg into the milk. ✦ In the prepared pan, arrange alternating layers of pasta, scamorza, sauce, pats of butter, Parmigiano-Reggiano, and half of the egg mixture; repeat, then end with a final layer of pasta and bake 50 minutes.

PASTA AND MEAT PIE

CAMPANIA

For the sauce:

2 tbsp. extra-virgin olive oil

1 medium onion, minced

A few pieces of leftover meat
and their fat (about ¼ lb.)

½ cup red wine

2 tbsp. tomato paste

12 oz. tomato purée

⅔ cup grated Parmigiano-Reggiano

For the filling:

6 oz. ground beef

2 oz. stale bread, soaked in milk

½ cup grated pecorino

1 tbsp. chopped flat-leaf parsley

Olive oil

½ lb. sausage

1 tbsp. lard

2 oz. pork belly

1 medium onion, sliced

1 (15 oz.) can peas, drained

1¾ lbs. short macaroni

4 large hard-boiled eggs,
cut in quarters

7 oz. *fior di latte* cheese, cubed

For the pastry dough:

4 cups all-purpose flour

3 large egg yolks

1 large egg white

½ lb. (2 sticks) unsalted butter

1¼ cups sugar

1 tsp. grated lemon zest

Salt

This recipe is typical of Naples.

Preheat the oven to 350°F. Grease a high-sided baking dish. Prepare a "fake" meat sauce, meaning a tomato sauce almost without meat: Heat the olive oil and cook the onion with the leftover meat and fat, browning slowly and adding a little wine from time to time. ✦ When the onion and meat have taken on a nice brown color, add the tomato paste and cook until it too darkens and becomes velvety. ✦ At this point dilute the sauce with the tomato purée and water and cook at very low heat until the sauce thickens. ✦ Combine the ground beef, bread, pecorino, and parsley to make meatballs. Heat ½ inch of olive oil in a large pan until hot and brown the meatballs in it. ✦ Heat 2 tablespoons olive oil in another pan, cook the sausage, then cut it in disks. ✦ Mix the meatballs and sausage with a few tablespoons of the tomato sauce. ✦ In another pan, heat the lard until sizzling. Cook the pork belly and onion until golden, then add the peas. ✦ Use the flour and eggs to prepare a pasta dough as on page 10, adding the butter, sugar, lemon zest, and salt with the eggs. Cover the dough with a kitchen towel and set aside to rest at least 30 minutes. Roll out about two thirds of it to a sheet large enough to line the baking dish (see page 212). ✦ Cook the macaroni in lightly salted boiling water, just until half cooked, then drain and toss with the sauce, Parmigiano-Reggiano, and pea mixture. ✦ Arrange a layer of the macaroni mixture along the bottom of the baking dish and over that pour part of the filling: hard-boiled eggs, *fior di latte*, and sausage mixture. Repeat this operation so as to end with a layer of macaroni. ✦ Roll out the remaining portion of pastry to make a disk with which to cover the top. ✦ Bake until the top is nicely browned. Invert onto a serving plate and serve hot.

PASTA AND CHEESE PIE

CAMPANIA

¼ lb. (½ cup) unsalted butter,
softened

1½ cups all-purpose flour

2 large egg yolks

4 tbsp. Marsala

1 lb. perciatelli (can use bucatini
or thick spaghetti)

⅔ cup grated Parmigiano-Reggiano

3 oz. grated Gruyère

2 oz. prosciutto cotto, diced

Pinch grated nutmeg

Salt and pepper

Preheat the oven to 350°F. Butter a deep baking dish. Use the flour and egg yolks to prepare a dough as on page 10, adding the butter and Marsala with the egg yolks. Let the dough rest, covered with a cloth, 30 minutes. ✦ Meanwhile, cook the perciatelli until al dente, drain, and toss with 3 tablespoons butter, Parmigiano-Reggiano, Gruyère, prosciutto, nutmeg, and pepper. ✦ Divide the dough into two parts, one larger than the other. Roll out the larger part on a floured board to ¹⁄₁₆ inch thick and use it to line the baking dish. ✦ Pour in the perciatelli mixture, and dot with the remaining butter. Roll out the remaining dough to form a sheet ¹⁄₁₆ inch thick and cover the timbale, sealing the borders all around with a fork and flattening the top. ✦ Bake about 30 minutes, or until the top has turned golden. ✦ Remove from the oven, let it rest 10 minutes, invert onto a serving plate, and serve hot.

MUSHROOM SAUCE

LIGURIA

¼ cup extra-virgin olive oil

1 medium onion, minced

1 carrot, minced

1 celery stalk, minced

2 garlic cloves, minced

1 lb. fresh mushrooms (or 2 to 3 oz.
dried porcini mushrooms,
soaked and drained), sliced

4 ripe plum tomatoes,
peeled, seeded, and chopped

1 tbsp. tomato paste

1 pinch oregano

6 small basil leaves, chopped

¼ cup minced flat-leaf parsley

Salt and pepper

This is a classic sauce for tagliolini or corzetti.

Heat 2 tablespoons of the olive oil in a pan and add the onion, carrot, celery, and garlic; cook over medium heat until the onion is golden. If needed, dilute with a few tablespoons of warm water. ✦ Add the mushrooms, then the tomatoes, tomato paste, oregano, and salt and pepper to taste. ✦ Lower the heat and cook, stirring with a wooden spoon while the sauce thickens. ✦ In a separate bowl combine the remaining olive oil with the basil and parsley. Add the mushroom mixture and toss to mix.

GENOESE MEAT SAUCE

TOCCO DE ROSTO

LIGURIA

2 tbsp. extra-virgin olive oil
1 lb. veal leg (or beef)
1 carrot, minced
1 celery stalk, minced
1 medium onion, minced
2 tbsp. chopped flat-leaf parsley
2 tbsp. unsalted butter
2 oz. beef marrow
½ cup dry wine
(white for veal, red for beef)
1 sprig rosemary
3 tbsp. tomato paste
A few dried mushrooms (softened in warm water), chopped
Beef broth
1 tbsp. all-purpose flour

And the meat that was used to make the sauce? In Genoa (and not only there) there can be but one response: it is used to make meatballs for the next day. Many Genoese add a basil leaf to the ingredients.

Heat the olive oil in a large saucepan with high sides over high heat. Add the veal, carrot, celery, onion, parsley, butter, and marrow and brown. ✦ Delicately turn the meat during this first phase to make certain it browns on all sides. ✦ Add the wine, rosemary, tomato paste, and mushrooms. Lower the heat and cook 15 to 20 minutes. ✦ At this point add enough meat broth to cover the meat. With the heat very low, add the flour and continue cooking the sauce, to make it reduce, for about 1 hour. ✦ At that point remove the meat and pass the sauce through a sieve. ✦ It is now ready to use on ravioli.

MACARONI WITH CHARD SAUCE

TORTELLATA

TOSCANA

1 cup boiled chard, finely chopped
¾ lb. ricotta
2 tbsp. unsalted butter
Pinch grated nutmeg
2 tbsp. grated Parmigiano-Reggiano
3 or 4 tbsp. Tuscan meat sauce (see page 331)
1 lb. macaroni
1 tbsp. olive oil
Salt and pepper

This dish is typical of Pistoia and Lucca.

Combine the chard with the ricotta, butter, nutmeg, half the Parmigiano-Reggiano, and meat sauce in a large saucepan. ✦ Heat this for a few minutes, stirring constantly and never letting it boil, until it becomes a smooth and homogeneous sauce. ✦ Cook the pasta in lightly salted boiling water to which the olive oil has been added until al dente; drain. (Draining the pasta properly is important: it should be neither too dry nor too watery.) ✦ Put a little of the meat sauce in the bottom of a serving bowl, cover with pasta, sprinkle with more Parmigiano-Reggiano, then top with the chard sauce. Serve hot.

TUSCAN TORTELLI

For the dough:

3 cups all-purpose flour, sifted,
plus more as needed

4 large eggs

3 tbsp. milk

For the filling:

10 oz. sheep's-milk ricotta

10 oz. chard, parboiled
and finely chopped

⅔ cup grated Parmigiano-Reggiano

2 large eggs, beaten

1 pinch nutmeg

1 recipe meat sauce (see page 331)

Grated pecorino Romano

Salt and pepper

Tortelli from the Maremma should be made so there is a thick layer of dough around the filling.

Use the flour, eggs, and milk to prepare a pasta dough as on page 10, adding the milk with the eggs. Roll out a sheet (see page 212) to achieve a medium thickness. (You can also use the kind of dough sold commercially.) ✦ In a salad bowl thoroughly combine the ricotta, chard, Parmigiano-Reggiano, eggs, nutmeg, salt, and pepper. ✦ Using a spoon arrange dollops of the mixture in rows along the sheet of dough, folding over the edge to cover. ✦ Cut out with a knife and press down with a finger to make certain they won't open during cooking. ✦ Cook the tortelli in lightly salted boiling water for about 15 minutes, or until they float. Drain, using a skimmer to avoid breaking them, and arrange some of them in a single layer in a bowl. ✦ Top with an excellent meat sauce and sprinkle with pecorino. Repeat with more tortelli and sauce, making layers.

PIACENZA TORTELLI

For the dough:

About 3 cups all-purpose flour,
sifted, plus more as needed

2 large eggs

Salt

For the filling:

7½ cups spinach

7 oz. ricotta

1 large egg, beaten

⅓ cup grated Parmigiano-Reggiano,
plus more for serving

Pinch grated nutmeg

½ cup unsalted butter,
melted, for serving

Use the flour and eggs to prepare a pasta dough as on page 10. ✦ Roll out a thin sheet (see page 212) and cut it into strips about 3 inches wide. Cut the strips lengthwise to form squares about 1½ inches long on the side. ✦ Prepare the filling: steam the spinach with a couple tablespoons of water until bright green (this happens very quickly), drain it, squeeze it dry, and chop it together with the ricotta. Work in the egg, Parmigiano-Reggiano, and nutmeg. ✦ Put a dollop of this filling on each pasta square, folding it over to form a triangle. Twist two corners to close, or, even better, press two ends together between the thumb and forefinger. ✦ Cook the tortelli in lightly salted boiling water. Drain, toss with melted butter, and sprinkle with Parmigiano-Reggiano.

TORCINELLI

This recipe for stuffed lamb's intestines comes from Molise. The entrails of suckling lambs would first be cleaned with a mixture of water and salt, and left to soak through several changes of water for at least a day. The lambs' sweetbreads and stomachs would also be cleaned and made into a chopped filling with onion, carrot, and parsley and stuffed into the cleaned *torcinello*, or intestine. The tradition in upper Molise was to then cook and chop up the *torcinello* to make a hearty tomato sauce with onion, parsley, and basil to serve over homemade pasta, especially fusilli; the *torcinello* could also be cooked whole over hot coals.

TORTELLI DI ERBETTE

TORTELLI FILLED WITH SWISS CHARD

EMILIA-ROMAGNA

For the filling:
1 bunch Swiss chard
1½ lbs. ricotta
½ cup grated Parmigiano-Reggiano
2 tbsp. unsalted butter
1 large egg
Pinch grated nutmeg
Salt

For the dough:
3 cups all-purpose flour, plus more as needed
2 large eggs
Salt

For the sauce:
1 cup unsalted butter, melted
½ cup grated Parmigiano-Reggiano

This dish is typical of Parma.

Clean the greens, cutting away the stalks, and boil them just until bright green. ✦ Remove them from the water, squeeze them dry, and leave to drain. ✦ Combine the ricotta with the Parmigiano-Reggiano and butter. ✦ Chop the boiled greens and work together with the cheese mixture along with the egg, a pinch of salt, and nutmeg. ✦ Use the flour and eggs to prepare a dough as on page 10, then roll out the dough to make the thinnest sheet possible (see page 212). ✦ Arrange small amounts of the filling in rows along the sheet. ✦ Fold over the sheet and cut in rectangles, closing the edges and pressing them with the tines of a fork. ✦ Cook the tortelli in lightly salted boiling water for about 15 minutes until they float, then drain thoroughly. ✦ Combine the melted butter and Parmigiano-Reggiano. Arrange some of the tortelli in a single layer in a deep bowl. Spoon over some of the sauce and repeat the layers, using all of the tortelli.

RICOTTA TORTELLI WITH SAGE SAUCE

EMILIA-ROMAGNA

For the filling:

¼ cup finely chopped flat-leaf parsley

½ cup grated Parmigiano-Reggiano

7 oz. ricotta

1 large egg, beaten

Pinch grated nutmeg

Salt

For the pasta:

About 2⅓ cups all-purpose flour

3 large eggs

¼ cup dry white wine

Salt

For the sauce:

2 tbsp. unsalted butter

8 sage leaves

⅔ cup heavy cream

½ cup grated Parmigiano-Reggiano

This recipe is typical of Imola.

Thoroughly combine the filling ingredients, season with salt, then set aside. ✦ Use the flour and eggs to prepare a pasta dough as in the recipe on page 10, adding the wine with the eggs. Let the dough rest, wrapped in a damp kitchen towel (about 10 minutes). ✦ Meanwhile, heat the butter in a large pan and sauté the sage, adding the cream and simmering for about 3 minutes. ✦ Roll out the dough to make the thinnest sheet possible (see page 212). ✦ Arrange small amounts of the filling in rows along the sheet. ✦ Fold over the sheet and cut in rectangles, closing the edges and pressing them with the tines of a fork. Cook the tortelli in lightly salted boiling water until very al dente, drain, and add them to the sauce. ✦ Cook them in a pan over medium heat and stir in the Parmigiano-Reggiano until the tortelli are coated with the sauce. ✦ Divide them among warmed individual serving plates and serve immediately.

PUMPKIN RAVIOLI 1

EMILIA-ROMAGNA

For the filling:

1¼ lbs. pumpkin

4 oz. amaretti cookies (about 6)

1¼ cups grated Parmigiano-Reggiano

1 tbsp. grated lemon zest

Salt

For the pasta:

About 2⅓ cups all-purpose flour

2 large eggs

For the sauce:

½ cup unsalted butter, melted

2 tbsp. chopped sage

¼ cup grated Parmigiano-Reggiano

Preheat the oven to 400°F. Cut the pumpkin into large slices, remove the seeds, and bake until soft, about 30 minutes. ✦ When baked scrape the flesh off the rind and wrap it in a kitchen towel. Place in a colander to drain for 10 minutes. ✦ Crumble the amaretti and combine with the Parmigiano-Reggiano and lemon zest. Add the drained pumpkin and a pinch of salt and work together to obtain a homogeneous filling; set aside. ✦ Use the flour and eggs to prepare a pasta dough as in the recipe on page 10; the dough will be soft. ✦ Roll out to form a sheet (see page 212) and on this arrange small amounts of the filling (about the size of an egg yolk). Fold the sheet over and cut rectangles. Make certain to seal the edges of the pasta. ✦ Cook in lightly salted boiling water for about 15 minutes. ✦ Drain well and arrange in layers in a deep dish, topping each layer with melted butter, sage, and Parmigiano-Reggiano.

PUMPKIN RAVIOLI 2

2 lbs. pumpkin
(preferably from Mantua)

6 oz. amaretti cookies, crushed

7 oz. *mostarda di Cremona*
(in a jar or homemade), minced

1 cup grated Parmigiano-Reggiano,
plus more for serving

Pinch grated nutmeg

1 large egg, beaten

2 tbsp. breadcrumbs

Pinch sugar, if necessary

1 sheet of pasta dough
(see page 10)

½ cup unsalted butter, melted

Salt

This recipe is typical of the area of Mantua.

Clean the pumpkin and cut into large slices, removing the rind and seeds. ✦ Steam the pumpkin or, if you prefer, boil it or bake it in an oven; when cooked drain it. ✦ Pass the flesh through a sieve and work it with a fork to create a uniform purée. ✦ Add the amaretti, *mostarda di Cremona*, Parmigiano-Reggiano, a pinch of salt, a pinch of nutmeg, egg, and breadcrumbs. (Add a pinch of sugar if the pumpkin is not sweet enough. The filling should not be overly sweet, but this is a question of delicate balances.) ✦ Let the filling rest in a warm place. ✦ The sheet of dough should be cut in rectangles about 3 inches by 1½ inches. At the center of each goes a spoonful of the filling. Fold over the dough to obtain little envelopes about 1½ inches on a side; close the edges with a fork. ✦ Cook in lightly salted boiling water. ✦ When they float lift them out and toss with melted butter and Parmigiano-Reggiano.

TORTELLI CREMASCO-STYLE

For the filling:

9 oz. amaretti cookies, crushed

1 large egg, beaten

½ cup raisins

2 oz. candied citron peel, minced

⅔ cup grated Parmigiano-Reggiano

1 dry cracker, crumbled,
or 1 tsp. breadcrumbs

For the dough:

3 cups all-purpose flour,
plus more as needed

1 large egg

Salt

For the sauce:

½ cup unsalted butter, melted

This dish is typical of Cremasco.

For the filling: grind the amaretti and combine with the egg, then chop and add all the other filling ingredients, stirring to blend. ✦ Refrigerate at least 1 day. ✦ Prepare a pasta dough as in the recipe on page 10, adding 2 tablespoons water to the egg. ✦ Roll out a thin sheet (see page 212) and cut disks with a glass. ✦ Fill the disks of dough, fold them over, then seal the edges by pinching them closed with the thumb and forefinger. ✦ Cook in lightly salted boiling water until they float; drain. Dress while hot with butter.

SARDINE AND ARTICHOKE CASSEROLE

TORTIERA DI SARDE E CARCIOFI

PUGLIA

10 oz. fresh sardines

8 artichokes
(preferably from Brindisi)

Juice of 1 lemon

½ cup breadcrumbs

3 garlic cloves, chopped

1 bunch flat-leaf parsley, minced

½ cup grated pecorino

Olive oil

Salt and pepper

Preheat the oven to 350°F. Grease a baking dish. ✦ Clean the sardines, removing the heads, then cut open and remove the bones. ✦ Clean the artichokes, snapping off the tough outer leaves and trimming green areas from the stem, then cut in lengthwise slices as thin as possible and immerse in water mixed with lemon juice. ✦ Arrange a layer of artichokes along the bottom of the baking dish, add salt and pepper, then spread with breadcrumbs, garlic, parsley, and pecorino, and drizzle with olive oil. ✦ Form a second layer using the sardines, and continue, making more layers. ✦ Drizzle the final layer with olive oil and 2 tablespoons water. ✦ Bake until the artichokes are tender, about 30 minutes, checking every so often to see how the artichokes are cooking.

✦ **LOCAL TRADITION** ✦

TROCCOLI AL RAGÙ DI POLPO

In Puglia, thick-cut spaghetti is sometimes served with a sauce made with octopus. This sauce, or ragù, can be made in the same way as a meat ragù (such as that on page 329). Simply replace the beef and lamb with an equal quantity of octopus and omit the sausage and chicken at the end. When used to flavor *troccoli*, its wonderful fragrance is integrated with the unmistakable perfume of the grated pecorino.

TRENETTE WITH PESTO SAUCE

TRENETTE CON IL PESTO

LIGURIA

2 bunches of small basil leaves, cleaned and dried

1 garlic clove, crushed

½ cup pine nuts

CONTINUED

Grind a little coarse salt in a mortar with the basil leaves, garlic, and pine nuts to form a dry paste. Still mixing, drizzle in the olive oil. ✦ When this forms a creamy paste mix in the cheeses, which will bind it. ✦ Cook the pasta until al dente in lightly salted boiling water, drain well (reserve ½ cup of cooking water), and transfer to a

6 tbsp. extra-virgin olive oil

2 tbsp. grated Parmigiano-Reggiano

1 tbsp. grated pecorino,
plus more for serving

1 lb. trenette or linguine

Coarse salt

bowl. ✦ Toss with the pesto and, if it seems too dry, dilute with some of the pasta cooking water. Add cheese and serve immediately.

TRILLI CON LE NOCI

TRILLI PASTA IN WALNUT SAUCE

CAMPANIA

For the dough:

About 1⅔ cups all-purpose flour

2 large eggs

Salt

For the sauce:

4 tbsp. olive oil

3 garlic cloves

1 dried spicy chili pepper

¼ lb. (about 1 cup) walnuts,
finely chopped

2 tbsp. chopped flat-leaf parsley

This dish is typical of Avellino.

Use the flour and eggs to prepare a pasta dough as in the recipe on page 10; the dough will be soft, but should not be sticky. Let the dough rest, covered with a cloth, 30 minutes. ✦ Form the dough into cylinders with the width of a breadstick. ✦ With a knife cut each cylinder into 1-inch cubes, then, using one finger, roll each one to form 3-inch ropes; these are the *trilli*. ✦ Cook these in lightly salted boiling water, then drain. Meanwhile, make the sauce. Heat the olive oil in a pan and add the garlic and chili pepper. When the garlic is browned, add the walnuts and cook for a minute, then add a little water and the parsley and simmer for another 5 minutes. Add the pasta to the pan and toss.

TURTUNETT

FONTINA GNOCCHI WITH SAGE CREAM

PIEMONTE

For the gnocchi:

1 lb. potatoes

⅔ cup all-purpose flour

1 tbsp. chopped flat-leaf parsley

4 oz. fontina, cubed

Salt

For the sauce:

¼ lb. (1 stick) unsalted butter

A few sage leaves, chopped

⅔ cup heavy cream

Grated Parmigiana-Reggiano,
for serving

Cook the potatoes in lightly salted boiling water, peel them, put them through a potato ricer, then set aside to cool. ✦ Add the flour, parsley, and fontina, then knead to form a soft dough and shape the dough into small gnocchi (see recipe, page 247). ✦ Melt the butter in a pan, then add the sage and cream. ✦ Cook the gnocchi in lightly salted boiling water until they float, drain, then add them to the sauce and cook for 1 minute. Serve hot with more cheese at the table.

VERMICELLI IN GARLIC AND OIL

CAMPANIA

1 lb. vermicelli
½ cup extra-virgin olive oil
3 garlic cloves, thinly sliced
1 dried chili pepper
Chopped flat-leaf parsley
Salt

An extremely simple dish, yet to Neapolitans it ranks among the most difficult to prepare since there will always be a critic on hand: there is too much oil, or not enough garlic, the pasta is overcooked. One flavorful variant consists of the addition of ground pepper to the garlic and oil.

Cook the pasta in lightly salted boiling water until very al dente. While the pasta cooks, heat the olive oil in a sauté pan over low heat. Add the garlic and chili and cook slowly so they will color without burning. ✦ When the garlic has colored add a ladleful of water from the pasta cooking water to stop it from cooking and take the pan off the heat. ✦ Drain the pasta, toss it in a serving bowl with the sauce, and sprinkle with parsley. Serve hot.

✦ **LOCAL TRADITION** ✦

LE TROFIE RECCHESI

In the area along the Ligurian coastline running from Bogliasco to Camogli, there was a custom of preparing small gnocchi made by hand with white "sack" flour (meaning flour without the bran), salt, and water. These gnocchi are called *trofie Recchesi*, after Recco, which is just above Camogli. They are about 1½ inches long, thin, and rounded like a kind of corkscrew. Sometimes a little chestnut flour was added in. They were tossed with pesto alla Genovese, sometimes supplemented with green beans and boiled potatoes or with a few boiled fresh white beans.

VERMICELLI AND SEAFOOD BAKED IN FOIL

CAMPANIA

1 lb. vermicelli
¼ cup extra-virgin olive oil
1 garlic clove, chopped

CONTINUED

This dish is typical of the Amalfi coast.

Preheat the oven to 350°F. Cook the vermicelli in lightly salted boiling water until very al dente; drain. Heat the olive oil over low heat in a large ovenproof pan. Add the garlic and chili pepper and cook until the garlic takes on

½ dried chili pepper
¾ lb. mussels, cleaned
¾ lb. clams, cleaned
¾ lb. octopus, cleaned
¾ lb. fresh shelled shrimp
¾ lb. fresh plum tomatoes, crushed
½ cup chopped flat-leaf parsley

a little color. Add the seafood and stir 2 minutes, then add the tomatoes and parsley. ✦ After about 10 to 15 minutes of cooking combine this sauce with the vermicelli and cover the pan with aluminum foil, sealing the edges. ✦ Bake for 5 minutes.

VERMICELLI AL SUGHETTO DI ANGUILLA

VERMICELLI WITH EEL SAUCE

MOLISE

½ cup extra-virgin olive oil
1 garlic clove
8 pieces of eel (about 2 lbs.), cleaned
¼ cup dry white wine
1 lb. vermicelli
¼ cup chopped flat-leaf parsley
Coarse sea salt

Heat the olive oil in a terra-cotta pan, add the garlic and eel, and cook until they take on a little color. Pour in the wine; add salt. ✦ When the eel is thoroughly cooked remove it from the pan, skin and bone it, and return only the flesh to the sauce. ✦ Cook the vermicelli in lightly salted boiling water until al dente, drain, and then add them to the pan. Cook at high heat a few minutes, adding the parsley at the end. Serve immediately.

VERMICELLI ALLA SICILIANA

SICILIAN-STYLE VERMICELLI

SICILIA

½ cup extra-virgin olive oil
1 garlic clove
10 oz. plum tomatoes, chopped
1 eggplant, cleaned and diced
1 sweet pepper
½ cup pitted and chopped green olives (if possible Sicilian)
1 tbsp. capers, rinsed and chopped
2 salt-cured anchovies, cleaned, boned, and chopped
A few basil leaves
1 lb. vermicelli
Grated caciocavallo or pecorino
Salt

This dish is typical of Messina.

Heat the oil in a saucepan, add the garlic, and cook until golden. Remove it and add the tomatoes and eggplant. ✦ Spear the sweet pepper on a fork and pass it over a flame to burn the skin, then scrape off the skin with a knife. Cut the pepper in half and remove the seeds. Rinse the halves, then cut in strips and add to the pan. ✦ Stir in the olives, capers, and anchovies, then add the basil leaves. ✦ Cook at low heat. ✦ Cook the vermicelli in lightly salted boiling water, drain when slightly al dente, then toss with the sauce and sprinkle with caciocavallo or pecorino.

MARCHE-STYLE LASAGNE

For the sauce:

4 tbsp. unsalted butter

2 oz. pancetta, minced

2 oz. prosciutto crudo, finely chopped

1 medium onion, finely chopped

1 garlic clove, finely chopped

1 celery stalk, finely chopped

1 carrot, finely chopped

A few tbsp. dry white wine

4 oz. chicken giblets, chopped

12 oz. tomato purée

½ cup grated Parmigiano-Reggiano

1 recipe béchamel sauce (see page 339)

Salt and pepper

For the pasta:

About 2 cups all-purpose flour

3 large eggs

This dish is supposedly named for Austrian Prince Alfred zu Windisgrätz, who in 1799 commanded the troops occupying Ancona. It would be impossible to present a definitive recipe since every local kitchen makes a highly personal version. It is a good idea to prepare this well in advance of the meal in question, because the assembled dish has to be set aside for several hours of "meditation." This period of "reflection" will permit the flavors to blend, only to then be exalted by baking in a slow oven, which will result in a beautiful outward appearance. There are also those who add ground meat and sweetbreads, brains, and chicken livers to the sauce with the giblets.

Begin by preparing the sauce: Heat the butter in an earthenware pot over low heat, add the pancetta and prosciutto, and sauté until they have taken on a little color. Add the onion, garlic, celery, and carrot and cook slowly, adding small sprinkles of white wine and letting them evaporate. ✦ Add the giblets and tomato purée and season with salt and pepper; let this sauce then simmer over low heat for at least 2 hours. ✦ Use the flour and eggs to prepare a pasta dough as in the recipe on page 10. Let the dough rest, covered with a kitchen towel, 30 minutes. ✦ Preheat the oven to 300°F. Roll the dough out to form thin sheets (see page 212). Cut it into sheets of lasagne about 4 inches wide and 6 inches long. ✦ Boil these, a few at a time, in lightly salted boiling water and when still very al dente drain and put them in cold water. ✦ Lay them out to dry on a cloth. ✦ Pour some of the tomato sauce in a baking pan, then put in a first layer of the pasta. ✦ Add more tomato sauce and a dusting of Parmigiano-Reggiano, then more pasta, tomato sauce, and Parmigiano-Reggiano, and so on until you've used up the pasta. ✦ End with a final layer of sauce and cover with the béchamel. ✦ Bake for 45 minutes or until the top is golden.

PASTA "SNAKES" WITH SAUSAGE

VIPERE CIECHE

LAZIO

For the pasta:
3 cups all-purpose flour,
plus more as needed

For the sauce:
2 tbsp. extra-virgin olive oil
1 chili pepper
4 oz. sausage meat, crumbled
2 oz. pancetta, minced
Grated pecorino

Use the flour to prepare a pasta dough as in the recipe on page 10, using about 1⅛ cups of water in place of the eggs. Let the dough rest, covered with a cloth, 30 minutes. ✦ Form this dough into thin rods about as long as the palm of a hand (these are the *vipere*). ✦ Cook the pasta in lightly salted boiling water and remove them from the pot as soon as they float. ✦ Heat the olive oil in a large pan and sauté the chili pepper until it takes on a little color. Add the sausage and pancetta and cook until browned, then add the pasta and cook over high heat to dry the cooking water of the "vipers." ✦ Pour into a serving bowl and dress with pecorino to taste. Serve hot.

ZITI WITH TUNA SAUCE

ZITI AL SUGO CON TONNO

CALABRIA

4 salt-cured anchovies
1 lb. plum tomatoes, peeled
4 oz. canned tuna
2 tbsp. extra-virgin olive oil
1 small onion, chopped
2 garlic cloves, chopped
1 pinch oregano
1 lb. ziti
½ cup grated caciocavallo
Salt and pepper

Chop the anchovies and tomatoes, discarding the tomato seeds and juice. Drain the tuna and mince it. Heat the olive oil in a terra-cotta pan. Add the onion and garlic and cook until golden. ✦ Add the anchovies, tomatoes, salt and pepper, and oregano. ✦ When this has thickened, add the tuna. ✦ Cook the ziti in lightly salted boiling water until al dente, then drain and and toss them with this sauce and caciocavallo. Serve hot.

PASTA WITH ANCHOVIES AND TUNA

ZITONCINI ALLA CAMPOLATTARO

CAMPANIA

2 salt-cured anchovies, boned
6 oz. canned white meat tuna
1¼ cups chicken broth
Pinch chili pepper flakes
1 lb. penne or other small pasta
¼ cup extra-virgin olive oil
2 tbsp. chopped flat-leaf parsley
Salt and white pepper

Chop the anchovies and tuna together to blend. ✦ Put the mixture in a bowl with half the chicken broth, put it through a food mill, and transfer the result to a pan. ✦ Add the second half of the broth, chili pepper flakes, and white pepper. ✦ Cook this sauce at very low heat until it has thickened. ✦ Cook the pasta in lightly salted boiling water until al dente. Drain, toss it with the olive oil, and add the parsley. Stir the pasta into the sauce andcook over low heat for 3 minutes and serve hot.

FISH

CHAPTER
FOUR

ACCIUGHE AL BAGNETTO ROSSO

ANCHOVIES IN RED SAUCE

PIEMONTE

For the sauce:

2 whole anchovies preserved in oil, bones removed and cut lengthwise

1 tbsp. capers

3 oz. canned tuna (preferably Italian)

1 garlic clove

1 small piece of red chili pepper

10 basil leaves

2 bay leaves

Pinch thyme or oregano

6 tbsp. tomato purée, blended with 1 tbsp. yellow mustard

1 tbsp. sugar

1 tbsp. red wine vinegar

¾ lb. salt-cured anchovies (if possible Spanish anchovies)

½ cup extra-virgin olive oil

For serving:

Olives

Hard-boiled eggs, sliced

Lemon wedges

Basil leaves

Mushrooms in oil, drained

This dish is typical of Asti.

Combine all the ingredients for the sauce except the salt-cured anchovies and olive oil in a blender. Blend until a coarse paste forms. ✦ Stir in extra-virgin olive oil to taste. Arrange the anchovies side by side on a serving plate and spoon the sauce over them. Garnish with olives, hard-boiled eggs, lemon wedges, basil, and mushrooms. ✦ Refrigerate at least 24 hours before serving.

ACCIUGHE AL BAGNETTO VERDE

ANCHOVIES IN GREEN SAUCE

PIEMONTE

½ lb. salt-cured anchovies

½ cup plus 1 tbsp. red wine vinegar

1 garlic clove, chopped

⅓ cup chopped flat-leaf parsley

1 chili pepper (preferably *spagnolino*; can substitute cherry pepper)

Extra-virgin olive oil

This dish is typical of Biella.

Cover the anchovies with a solution of ½ cup water and ½ cup vinegar. Soak overnight to desalt them. ✦ Rub the anchovies with your hands under a *pisciola* (thin stream of running water), splitting them in half lengthwise and removing the bones. Place in a colander and rinse again under running water, then set them aside to dry. ✦ Prepare *êl bagnet verd* ("the green sauce") with the garlic, parsley, and chili pepper by blending them together in a mortar. Add extra-virgin olive oil as needed to loosen the sauce. Add the remaining 1 tablespoon vinegar. ✦ Put the anchovies in layers in a glass container and cover each layer with the green sauce. Refrigerate and serve after a few days.

MARINATED ANCHOVIES

¾ lb. fresh anchovies
Juice of 2 lemons
½ cup red wine vinegar
1 tbsp. chopped fresh oregano
Extra-virgin olive oil
Salt

This dish is typical of Oneglia.

Butterfly, clean, and bone the anchovies. Wash them in cold running water. Dry with a cloth. ✦ Arrange them in a dish in layers with the lemon juice, salt as desired, a little vinegar, and oregano. ✦ Refrigerate in that mixture for 24 hours, then drain them. Put them in another container and barely cover with olive oil. They are now ready to be served.

FRIED STUFFED ANCHOVIES

1¼ lbs. fresh anchovies
⅓ cup pine nuts
1 bunch flat-leaf parsley
1 garlic clove
1 small sprig fresh marjoram
The bread of a roll, soaked in milk
⅓ cup grated Parmigiano-Reggiano
2 large eggs, separated
Olive oil for frying
1½ cups breadcrumbs
Salt and pepper

The same technique can be applied to sardines.

Clean the anchovies and remove the heads and bones. ✦ Finely chop the pine nuts with the parsley, garlic, and marjoram. Add the bread, cheese, egg yolks, salt, and pepper. ✦ Fill half of each anchovy with the mixture and fold over the other half. ✦ Heat 1 inch of olive oil in a pan until hot. Beat the egg whites until frothy. Dip the anchovies in the egg whites, then in the breadcrumbs. ✦ Fry until golden, then drain on paper towels and serve.

FRIED SHAD

Olive oil for frying
2 large eggs, beaten
1 lb. shad, cleaned
All-purpose flour, for dredging
Lemon slices, for garnish
Salt

Heat 1 inch of olive oil in a pan until hot. Season the eggs with salt. Dredge the cleaned fish in the flour, then in eggs, and fry them until golden. ✦ Drain on paper towels and serve hot with slices of lemon.

FISH

SOUSED SHAD

1 lb. *agoni* (shad), cleaned

Olive oil for frying

All-purpose flour, for dredging

1 cup red wine vinegar

1 tbsp. chopped flat-leaf parsley

1 medium onion, chopped

1 garlic clove, chopped

1 sprig *segrigiola* (wild thyme)

Salt

Agoni are a kind of shad; this recipe is popular in the Lario area, meaning around Lake Como, as well as in all the other Lombard lakes.

Rinse and dry the shad. ✦ Heat 1 inch of olive oil in a pan until hot. Dredge the fish in flour, removing any excess, and fry them. ✦ When golden, drain them on paper towels. ✦ Put them in a bowl. Combine the vinegar, parsley, onion, garlic, salt, and *segrigiola* in a saucepan and heat just until boiling. Pour over the fish. ✦ Leave the fish in this infusion for about 6 hours before serving.

SHAD IN GREEN SAUCE

For the fish:

1 lb. shad or freshwater sardines, cleaned

All-purpose flour, for dredging

Extra-virgin olive oil

For the sauce:

1 bunch flat-leaf parsley

½ cup pickled salad onions

¼ cup pickles

1 tbsp. capers

2 salt-cured anchovies

2 garlic cloves, chopped

Yolks of 2 hard-boiled eggs, crumbled

1 cup extra-virgin olive oil

This dish is typical of the Lario, which is what Lake Como is called based on its Latin name, *Larius*.

Choose somewhat small fish because they're tastier. ✦ Heat a cast-iron griddle or skillet until hot. Meanwhile, chop together the parsley, onions, pickles, capers, anchovies, garlic, and egg yolks. Whisk in the olive oil to form a sauce. Dip the fish in flour and sprinkle them with a little olive oil. Cook them for 2 minutes on each side. ✦ Put the cooked fish in a bowl and pour the sauce over them.

BAKED ANCHOVIES

1 cup roughly chopped stale bread without crust

CONTINUED

This simple recipe from the cuisine of Reggio Calabria was invented by fishermen. The number of ingredients may be very small, but the result is truly flavorful.

Preheat the oven to 325°F. Grease a baking pan. Combine the bread, parsley, salt as desired, capers, chili pepper

2 tbsp. chopped flat-leaf parsley

1 tbsp. capers

Pinch chili pepper flakes

1 garlic clove, chopped

1¾ lbs. fresh anchovies, cleaned and filleted

A few tbsp. extra-virgin olive oil

Salt

flakes, and garlic. ✦ Arrange ⅓ of the anchovies in a layer in the prepared pan. ✦ Cover with a thin layer of the bread mixture. Repeat the layers, ending with a thicker layer of the bread mixture. Sprinkle the surface with olive oil and bake until the top has formed a golden crust.

✦ LOCAL TRADITION ✦

AGONI ALLA NAVETT

The name *agoni alla navett*, shad "boat-style," is no fantasy. The *navett* is the boat used by Larian fishermen in Lombardy, with three oarsmen. The fishermen set out from their homes on Monday and return Saturday, eating and sleeping all that time on the boat. On the boat there is always a small charcoal grill. During the work week, some of the fish caught are grilled for nourishment. The *agoni* (a kind of shad) are prepared by being laid across the grill, sprinkled with coarse salt, and cooked, first on one side, then on the other. The side dish is cold polenta.

ALICIOTTI CON INDIVIA

ANCHOVIES WITH ENDIVE

LAZIO

2 lbs. fresh anchovies

2 lbs. white endive

½ cup extra-virgin olive oil

Salt

Preheat the oven to 400°F. Grease a baking dish. Clean and fillet the anchovies and remove the heads; salt them and let them drain well. ✦ Clean the white area of the endive, wash and salt it, and drain well. ✦ Arrange alternating layers of endive and anchovies in the prepared baking dish, repeating the layers three or four times, but the first and last layer must be endive. ✦ Drizzle generously with olive oil and bake for about 45 minutes, or until the water in the endive has evaporated and it is well cooked and the olive oil has taken on a dark gold color.

BOLSENA EELS IN THE STYLE OF BISENTINA

LAZIO

2 lbs. eels, cleaned, heads and skin removed

5 sprigs rosemary

3 sage leaves

1 dried bay leaf, crumbled almost to a powder

¼ cup extra-virgin olive oil

2 cups white wine vinegar

2 or 3 garlic cloves

½ lb. plum tomatoes, peeled

Dried chili pepper, broken in pieces

Salt and pepper

Bisentina is the name of a small island in the middle of Lake Bolsena.

Slice the eels into 4-inch-long lengths. Mix the herbs together. ✦ Heat a little olive oil in a pan (preferably earthenware) and sauté the eels with 1 tablespoon vinegar. Add the garlic and herbs. ✦ Let this cook for several minutes, then add 2 or 3 tablespoons olive oil, the tomatoes, salt, pepper, chili pepper, and the remaining vinegar. Cook a while longer, adding warm water if necessary to maintain a dense and flavorful sauce. Remove the cloves of garlic before serving.

HUNTER-STYLE EELS

ANGUILLA ALLA CACCIATORA

LAZIO

3 garlic cloves

1 bunch flat-leaf parsley

1 sprig fresh marjoram

1 sprig fresh rosemary

1 leaf fresh sage

½ cup extra-virgin olive oil

2 lbs. eels, cleaned, heads and skin removed

All-purpose flour, for dredging

¼ cup white wine vinegar

¼ cup dry white wine

Finely chop together the garlic, parsley, marjoram, rosemary, and sage; mix with olive oil to make a paste. Heat this mixture in a pan over low heat. ✦ Cut the eels into 2-inch-long sections. Dust them with the flour, then slowly sauté in the oil mixture. ✦ When the eels are well browned, add the vinegar, then the wine; let this evaporate, then serve hot.

EELS GIOVI-STYLE

ANGUILLA ALLA GIOVESE

TOSCANA

¼ cup extra-virgin olive oil

1 medium onion, chopped

1 celery stalk, chopped

CONTINUED

Heat 3 tablespoons of the olive oil in a pan over medium heat. Sauté the onion, celery, carrot, and parsley until soft. Add the tomatoes and salt and pepper to taste. Cook until it begins to thicken. ✦ Chop together the garlic and sage. Heat the remaining tablespoon of oil in another pan and cook the garlic and sage over low heat until the garlic

1 carrot, chopped

1 bunch flat-leaf parsley, chopped

2 lbs. plum tomatoes, peeled and chopped

1 garlic clove

4 sage leaves

2 lbs. eels, cleaned, heads and skin removed

2 tbsp. all-purpose flour

Salt and pepper

begins to take on color. Dust the eels with the flour, cut in lengths of a couple inches each, and add salt. Add the eels to the pan with the garlic and cook, turning, until browned on all sides and cooked through. ✦ Transfer the cooked eels to the tomato sauce, let them soak up the flavor for a few minutes, then serve.

EELS LABRESE-STYLE

LAZIO

2 lbs. eels, cleaned, heads and skin removed

Grated zest of 1 orange

Grated zest and juice of 1 lemon

Bay leaves as needed

Salt and pepper

Cut the eels into short lengths. Put the eels in a dish and season with salt, pepper, orange and lemon zests, a little lemon juice, and bay leaves. ✦ Let the eels marinate for more than 2 hours. ✦ Meanwhile, prepare a grill, letting the fire burn down to low. ✦ Thread the pieces of eel on a spit or several skewers crosswise, alternating each piece of eel with a bay leaf. ✦ Cook over charcoal very slowly. Serve hot.

GLASSMAKER'S EEL

VENETO

1 large eel (about 2 lbs.), cleaned, skin and head removed

Vinegar

Bay leaves as needed

Salt

This ancient recipe comes to us from the glassmakers of Murano, who used the heat of their glass furnaces to cook it.

Cut the eel in pieces about 2½ inches long, but don't make the cuts all the way through, thus leaving the pieces not completely separated one from the next. ✦ Thoroughly rinse the eel in equal parts water and vinegar. ✦ Arrange the lengths of eel curled in a ring over a bed of bay leaves on the bed of a glass furnace, salt, and cover with another abundant layer of bay leaves. Leave in the furnace about 1 hour. ✦ Naturally, this special way of cooking eel can be adapted to home cooking, making use of the oven while following the same procedure. Preheat the oven to 450°F. Place the eel in the oven and cook for 2 hours. Lower the temperature by 50 degrees about every 20 minutes until turning it off.

FISH

EEL WITH PLUMS

VENETO

1 large eel (about 2 lbs.), cleaned,
skin and head removed

1 cup cornmeal

¼ cup extra-virgin olive oil

1 medium onion, minced

1 garlic clove, minced

1 lb. plums (wild, if possible),
halved and pitted

½ cup white wine

This dish is typical of Venice, Padua, and Treviso. Tart, wild plums can be preserved year-round in the freezer. Use Soave or bianco di Custoza for the wine.

Remove the fat from the eel by dipping it in the cornmeal and then rubbing it with a paper towel. ✦ Wash in cold water, pat dry, and cut it in pieces. ✦ Heat the eel in a pan over very low heat with the olive oil, onion, and garlic; add the plums and raise the heat. Brown the eel, then add the white wine. Let simmer 20 minutes.

SPIT-ROASTED EEL

ANGUILLA
ALLO SPIEDO

UMBRIA

1½ lbs. eels, cleaned,
skin and heads removed

3 tbsp. white wine vinegar

Juice of 1 lemon

¼ cup olive oil

Bay leaves as needed

1 cup breadcrumbs

Lemon slices

Salt and pepper

Heat a rotisserie to medium heat. Cut the eels in sections, wash piece by piece, dry, and place in a bowl. ✦ Pour the vinegar over the eels, then the lemon juice and olive oil; sprinkle on salt and pepper. Stir these ingredients to blend and let the eels marinate for about 2 hours. ✦ Thread the sections of eel on the rotisserie skewer, inserting a bay leaf between the sections, and roast, turning the skewer over the heat and basting the eel with olive oil, adding salt, and dusting with breadcrumbs. ✦ When the pieces of eel have taken on a good golden tint, serve with slices of lemon.

EEL WITH SAVOY CABBAGE

ANGUILLA
CON LE VERZE

EMILIA-ROMAGNA

5 lbs. Savoy cabbage

2 lbs. medium-size eels, cleaned,
skin and heads removed

1 tbsp. tomato paste

Salt and pepper

Set aside several of the outer leaves of the cabbage, cut what remains into four parts, and simmer half of them in 2 cups of water until soft. ✦ Remove half of the cabbage from the pan and add half the raw leaves. Cut each of the eels into 3 or 4 lengths. To the cabbage in the pan, add the eels, salt, and a generous amount of pepper. ✦ Cover with the remaining cabbage and add the tomato paste. ✦ Cook for about 1 hour, shaking the pan occasionally.

FRIED EEL

ANGUILLA FRITTA

VENETO

Several small eels (about 2 lbs. total), cleaned, skin and heads removed

Sunflower oil for frying

All-purpose flour, for dredging

Salt

This dish is typical of the province of Treviso.

It is best to use smaller-size eels. Cut the eels into pieces about 2 inches long. ✦ Heat a couple of inches of sunflower oil in a pan until hot. Dust the eels with the flour and fry them. ✦ When they are a good golden color, remove them from the oil and drain on pieces of paper towels. Salt and serve.

STEWED EEL

ANGUILLA IN UMIDO
ALLA LARIANA

LOMBARDIA

1 large eel, weighing about 2 lbs., cleaned, skin and head removed

½ cup all-purpose flour

1 medium onion

1 carrot

1 celery stalk

2 tbsp. extra-virgin olive oil

2 tbsp. unsalted butter

½ cup dried mushrooms, soaked in warm water and chopped

2 plum tomatoes, peeled

1 bunch aromatic herbs (sage, flat-leaf parsley, thyme, bay leaves), tied with string

2 cups red wine

Salt and pepper

For the wine use Bonarda or rosso della Valtellina.

Cut the eel in short lengths (2 inches), salt and pepper them, then dust them with the flour. ✦ Chop together the onion, carrot, and celery. Heat the oil and butter and sauté the vegetables until soft. Add the pieces of eel, mushrooms, tomatoes, and herbs. ✦ Let it all cook over high heat for 5 minutes, then pour in the wine. Lower the heat and cover the pan. ✦ When it has finished cooking, remove the bunch of herbs before serving.

STEWED EEL WITH PEAS

ANGUILLA IN UMIDO
COI PISELLI

VENETO

½ cup extra-virgin olive oil

½ medium onion

½ cup white wine

CONTINUED

Serve this with a side dish of polenta.

Heat half the olive oil in a pan and cook the onion until it turns golden, then remove and add the wine. ✦ Add the tomatoes, peas, broth, and vinegar and continue cooking. ✦ Meanwhile, heat the remaining olive oil in another pan, add the bay leaves, and cook the eels until they

½ lb. plum tomatoes, peeled

1 lb. peas

2 cups broth

2 cups white wine vinegar

2 bay leaves

2 lbs. eels, cleaned,
skin and heads removed,
cut into 2- to 2½-inch pieces

All-purpose flour

Salt and pepper

render out all their fat. ✦ Remove the eels from the pan, dust them with flour, and add to the tomato mixture. Cook for a few minutes. Season to taste with salt and pepper.

ANGUILLA IN UMIDO
CON PISELLI

STEWED EEL WITH PEAS

EMILIA-ROMAGNA

2 lbs. eels, cleaned,
skin and heads removed

2 tbsp. all-purpose flour

2 tbsp. extra-virgin olive oil

2 tbsp. unsalted butter

1 celery stalk

1 carrot

½ cup chopped flat-leaf parsley

½ medium onion

1 garlic clove

1 sprig rosemary,
tied with 4 sage leaves

1 lb. peas

½ cup broth

2 cups chopped fresh plum
tomatoes or tomato purée

Salt and pepper

This dish is typical of Piacenza.

Cut the eels in lengths of about 1½ to 2 inches. ✦ Dust the pieces of eel with the flour. Heat the olive oil and butter in a saucepan and brown the eels on all sides, turning, over medium-high heat; set aside. ✦ Finely chop the celery, carrot, parsley, onion, and garlic; sauté these in the same pan with the sprig of rosemary for a few minutes. Remove the herb and discard. ✦ Add the peas and broth and stir to mix. ✦ When the peas are about half-cooked and still firm, add the tomatoes or tomato purée. ✦ When the peas are fully cooked, add the eels and continue simmering until the eels are cooked through, stirring the mixture and adding salt and pepper to taste.

ANGUILLA MARINATA

MARINATED EEL

EMILIA-ROMAGNA

2 lbs. medium-size eels, cleaned,
skin and heads removed

Olive oil for frying

All-purpose flour, for dredging

CONTINUED

This dish is typical of Ferrara.

Using a sharp knife, open the eels lengthwise and remove the bones, carefully rinsing away all blood. ✦ Heat 2 inches of olive oil in a large pan until hot. Cut the eels into 3-inch lengths, dredge them well in the flour, sprinkle with salt, and fry, turning several times until completely browned. Transfer to a large flameproof pan. ✦

3 cups white wine vinegar
10 sage leaves
2 garlic cloves
Salt

Meanwhile, mix the vinegar, sage leaves, and garlic in a saucepan. Bring this to a boil and pour over the eels, making sure they are completely covered by the liquid (add water if necessary). ✦ Put the pan over heat and bring to a boil for a few minutes. ✦ When the eels have cooled, put them in glass jars rinsed with the vinegar used in the marinade and hermetically seal.

ANGUILLE CON
LA CICORIA DI CAMPO

EEL WITH WILD CHICORY

CAMPANIA

This dish is typical of the Mazzoni di Capua.

1 lb. wild chicory (can substitute store-bought chicory)
⅔ cup extra-virgin olive oil
2 garlic cloves, chopped
¾ lb. plum tomatoes, peeled, seeded, and chopped
1½ oz. lard
1 medium onion, sliced
1½ lbs. eels, cleaned, skin and heads removed, cut in 4-inch lengths
Pinch chili pepper flakes
Salt

Parboil the chicory, drain, and leave in the colander with a weight over to drain it well. ✦ Heat half the olive oil in a pan over low heat and sauté the garlic. Add the tomatoes, raise the heat, add salt, and cook for 20 minutes. ✦ In a saucepan heat the lard and remaining olive oil over medium heat. Add the onion and when the onion is brown, put in the chicory, letting it cook for 10 minutes, then add the eels, chili pepper, and salt and cook for about 5 minutes. ✦ At this point, add the sauce and, according to the size of the eels, cook for about 20 minutes.

ANGUILLE E TROTE
IN SALSA PICCANTE

EELS AND TROUT
IN A SPICY SAUCE

SARDEGNA

3 trout (about 1½ lbs.), cleaned
4 medium-size eels (about 1½ lbs.), cleaned, skin and heads removed
Extra-virgin olive oil
½ cup semolina
½ cup all-purpose flour
4 garlic cloves, chopped
1 cup tomato paste
¼ cup white wine vinegar
1 dried chili pepper
Salt

Cut each of the trout in three pieces and each of the eels in four pieces. ✦ Heat 1 inch of olive oil in a pan until hot. Mix the semolina and flour with a little salt and dust the eel with this mixture. Fry, turning, until golden. ✦ In another pan, heat 2 tablespoons of olive oil and sauté the garlic until golden; add the tomato paste and ½ cup of water. ✦ After 5 minutes add salt, the vinegar, and chili pepper. ✦ The eventual sauce should be somewhat dense; put the pieces of trout and eel in the sauce, which should cover them completely. ✦ Let cool completely and if possible put off serving until the next day. Reheat before serving.

ANGUILLA INFILZATA

In Friuli-Venezia Giulia they identify three different kinds of eels used in their cuisine: the *bisato fiumàn* (river eel), *bisato marìn* or *grongo* (sea eel), and the *bisato de palùo*, an eel that swims upriver from the sea in springtime and is prized—especially in the area's renowned fish soup recipes—for its thin skin and fine flavor. For this dish, eels would be cut into segments, with the skin left on, and threaded onto wooden skewers for grilling over a wood fire. Tradition dictated that the skewers be obtained from a plank that had been eroded by seawater, so that the sea itself would flavor the eel.

ANGUILLE IN GINOCCHIONI

EEL IN SAUCE

TOSCANA

1 lb. eel, cleaned, skin and head removed

2 tbsp. extra-virgin olive oil

1 lb. tomatoes, chopped and peeled

Handful of aromatic herbs (sage, parsley, thyme, bay leaves)

1 garlic clove, sliced

1 medium onion, sliced

Salt and pepper

This dish, typical of the Fuecchio marshes at Ponte Buggianese and Massarella, should be served with polenta.

Cut the eel into lengths 1½ to 2 inches long. ✦ Heat the olive oil in a pan (earthenware, if possible) over low heat and add the eel, tomatoes, herbs, garlic, onion, and salt and pepper to taste. Simmer until the eel is cooked through.

ARAGOSTA BOLLITA

BOILED LOBSTER

SARDEGNA

1 medium-size lobster

3 tbsp. extra-virgin olive oil

Juice of 1 lemon

2 tbsp. white wine vinegar

This dish is typical of Cala Gonone.

Fold the lobster claws inward and tie it with kitchen twine. ✦ Immerse it in a pot of boiling salted water. ✦ As soon as it is cooked, take it off the heat and let it cool in the water. ✦ When it is cool enough to handle, lay it out and cut it along its entire length. Carefully remove the meat and divide it in medallions a little more than ½ inch in length and arrange on a serving plate. ✦ Collect its yellowish liquid (tomalley) and mix with olive oil, lemon juice, and vinegar to form a thin sauce. ✦ Pour this sauce over the medallions of lobster and use the roe (coral, if there is any) and the larger claws to garnish. Serve cold.

BACCALÀ 'MBRIACHE

COD IN WINE

MOLISE

1 lb. or more salt-dried cod (see note)

½ cup extra-virgin olive oil

1 bay leaf

1 medium onion, finely sliced

2 cups dry white wine

Generally, throughout Italy, *baccalà* is the name used for salt-dried cod (and this is not to be confused with the unsalted *stoccafisso*). Salt-dried cod requires much soaking to get rid of its intense salinity before cooking. Put it in a large container and cover with cold water, cover, and refrigerate for two days, changing the water often—every eight hours if possible. Drain, and if you are not working with fillets, remove the skin and bones at this point.

Cut the cod in pieces and soak in water to cover 2 to 4 hours. ✦ Preheat the oven to 450°F. Drain the cod and put it in a baking pan. Drizzle with the olive oil, then add the bay leaf and onion, and wine to cover. ✦ Bake until completely cooked, about 20 minutes.

BACCALÀ AGGHIOTTA

COD IN SAUCE

SICILIA

½ cup extra-virgin olive oil

1 medium onion, finely chopped

1 celery stalk, chopped

¾ lb. plum tomatoes, peeled, seeded, and chopped

1½ lbs. salt-dried cod, soaked, drained, and cut in pieces (see note above)

1 tbsp. pine nuts

1 tbsp. raisins, softened in warm water and drained

1 tbsp. pitted green olives, chopped

1 tbsp. capers

2 medium potatoes, peeled and cubed

Salt and pepper

This dish is typical of Messina.

Preheat the oven to 325°F. Pour the olive oil into a pan (preferably terra-cotta) and add the onion and celery; when they have browned, add the tomatoes. ✦ Continue cooking a few minutes, then add the cod and cook awhile to soak up the flavors. Add the pine nuts, raisins, olives, capers, and potatoes; add salt and pepper to taste. ✦ When the liquid in the pan begins to boil, turn off the heat and cover the pan. ✦ Transfer to the oven and bake for about 1 hour, until the potatoes are tender.

BACCALÀ ALLA BRACE

GRILLED COD

PUGLIA

2 lbs. salt-dried cod, softened in water for 2 days (see note, page 437)

5 tbsp. extra-virgin olive oil

2 tbsp. white wine vinegar

2 tbsp. chopped flat-leaf parsley

Salt and pepper

Divide the cod into 8 pieces and remove the skin. ✦ In a bowl prepare a sauce by combining the olive oil, vinegar, pepper, a pinch of salt, and parsley. ✦ Add the cod and marinate for a few hours. ✦ Heat the grill to high heat. Grill the cod, turning them from time to time and brushing them with the sauce in which they were marinated. Serve hot.

BACCALÀ ALLA CAPPUCCINA

COD IN SAUCE

FRIULI-VENEZIA GIULIA

1½ lbs. *unsalted* dried cod, soaked and drained (see note, page 491)

All-purpose flour, for dredging

Olive oil

1 medium white onion, finely chopped

1 bay leaf

2 sardines, cleaned and chopped

⅓ cup pine nuts

⅓ cup golden raisins

Zest of 1 lemon

1 tsp. sugar

Pinch cinnamon

½ piece of candied citron, chopped

Pinch grated dark chocolate

2 cups fish broth, plus more as needed

½ cup white wine

½ cup breadcrumbs

Salt and pepper

For the wine use Ribolla gialla, malvasia istriana, or Vitorska. Serve piping hot with very soft yellow polenta.

Remove the skin and bones from the cod, cut it into somewhat large pieces, and dust them with the flour. Heat ½ inch of olive oil in a high-sided saucepan and add the cod, arranging the pieces close to one another without spaces in between. ✦ Spread the onion over them. Add the bay leaf, sardines, pine nuts, raisins, lemon zest, sugar, cinnamon, citron, chocolate, salt, and pepper. ✦ Cover with 2 cups broth, bring to a boil, then reduce the heat to low and cook very slowly for about 3 hours without stirring, only gently shaking the pan from time to time to keep the cod from sticking to the bottom. Add more broth if needed. ✦ Preheat the oven to 400°F. When the broth is finally absorbed, add the white wine and let it evaporate. ✦ Sprinkle with breadcrumbs and bake until it forms a crusty surface.

BACCALÀ ALLA FIORENTINA

COD FLORENCE-STYLE

TOSCANA

For the sauce:

2 tbsp. extra-virgin olive oil

CONTINUED

Begin by preparing the sauce. Heat 2 tbsp. olive oil in a pan (preferably earthenware) and slowly sauté the leek and half of the garlic clove. ✦ When these take color, add the tomatoes. Add salt and pepper to taste and cook at low heat while preparing the cod. ✦ In another pan, heat

1 leek, finely chopped

1 garlic clove, cut in half

¾ lb. ripe plum tomatoes, peeled and cut in pieces

For the cod:

Extra-virgin olive oil for frying

1½ lbs. salt-dried cod, already soaked and dried, boned and cleaned (see note, page 437)

All-purpose flour, for dredging

1 sprig rosemary

1 tbsp. chopped flat-leaf parsley

Salt and pepper

½ inch of olive oil until hot. Meanwhile, cut the cod into somewhat large pieces (1½ by 3 inches) and dust them with the flour. Add the remaining garlic and rosemary to the pan and fry the cod until golden. ✦ Drain them on paper towels. ✦ When the tomato sauce is ready, add the pieces of cod in a single layer and let them soak up the flavor for 5 minutes, still at low heat. Before serving sprinkle with parsley.

COD TRENTINO-STYLE

TRENTINO

1 cup olive oil

3 potatoes, peeled and thinly sliced

1¾ lbs. salt-dried cod, soaked and drained (see note, page 437)

1 celeriac (celery root), peeled and sliced

2 tbsp. finely chopped onion

2 tbsp. chopped flat-leaf parsley

2 garlic cloves, minced

Several sage leaves, chopped

1 tbsp. minced rosemary needles

2 cups milk, or as needed

¼ cup grated Parmigiano-Reggiano

Salt and pepper

Preheat the oven to 350°F. Grease a copper pot or baking pan with 2 tablespoons of the olive oil. Line the bottom with the slices of potato. ✦ Carefully clean the pieces of cod, removing all skin and bones while trying to keep the individual slices intact. ✦ Arrange the slices of cod over the layer of potatoes in rows, each slice near the next; fill in the spaces between the slices with more potato and celeriac, using more of the celeriac than the potato. ✦ Mix the onion, parsley, garlic, sage, and rosemary. Add enough of the remaining olive oil to make a thin paste; spread over the cod in the pan, pressing to get it into the spaces between the slices. ✦ Bake 30 minutes, then add salt and pepper and enough milk to nearly cover the cod. ✦ Return it to the oven and bake for about 2½ hours, checking during that time to make certain the uppermost part of the fish does not dry out (press down on the fish to keep it covered by the liquid). Sprinkle with cheese, bake 5 minutes more, and serve hot.

COD VICENZA-STYLE

VENETO

½ cup olive oil

CONTINUED

This dish should be served without any side dishes, with only yellow polenta just made or slightly grilled—but never fried.

Heat the olive oil in a pan and sauté the onions and garlic. Add the anchovies and parsley and stir well to keep

2 medium onions, minced

2 garlic cloves, minced

8 salt-cured anchovy fillets

2 tbsp. chopped flat-leaf parsley

2 lbs. *unsalted* dried cod (stockfish), soaked, drained, cleaned, and cut in half (see note, page 491)

½ cup grated Parmigiano-Reggiano

1 cup all-purpose flour

3 cups (or more) whole milk

Salt and pepper

the mixture from burning. ✦ Distribute a good part of this mixture on the cod. Mix the Parmigiano-Reggiano with the flour; season with salt and pepper. Sprinkle the cod with the mixture, then unite the two halves. ✦ Cut the fish in slices 2 to 2½ inches wide, dust them again with the flour mixture, and arrange the pieces in a pan (preferably earthenware). Pour over the remaining onion mixture, then add enough milk to completely cover the fish. ✦ Cook for about 4 hours over low and continuous heat. Do not stir the pot, but shake it from time to time to keep the fish from burning. ✦ The dish will be more fully appreciated if served 24 hours after being cooked; remember to reheat it slowly.

ROAST COD

1 *baccala ragno* (Norwegian cod from the Spider Islands; can substitute any *unsalted* dried cod) (see note, page 491)

1 lb. *lardo*, finely chopped

3 garlic cloves, minced

1 bunch flat-leaf parsley, chopped

7 salt-cured anchovies, rinsed and chopped

1 cup olive oil

¼ cup white wine

Pepper

For the wine use Soave or Lugana.

Beat the dried cod on a work surface using a wooden mallet until it becomes soft, then soak it in cold water for at least 3 days. ✦ Cut it open lengthwise, bone it, and stuff it with the *lardo*, pepper, garlic, parsley, and anchovies. ✦ At this point, roll it up well, tie with twine, and put it in a wide terra-cotta pan with ½ cup water and the olive oil. ✦ Cook over low heat for 2 hours and add the wine just before removing it from the heat.

BRAISED COD AND POTATOES

1 lb. salt-dried cod, soaked and dried (see note, page 437)

1 ¼ cups all-purpose flour

3 cups extra-virgin olive oil

CONTINUED

Cut the cod in pieces roughly 1½ to 2½ inches long and dust them with the flour. Heat 2⅓ cups olive oil in a pan until hot and fry the cod until golden; remove the cod from the pan and set aside on paper towels. ✦ Heat the remaining olive oil in a pan and sauté the onion and garlic; as soon as they have darkened, add the potatoes. ✦ After about 45 minutes of cooking, adjust

1 medium onion, thinly sliced

2 garlic cloves, thinly sliced

1 lb. potatoes, peeled and thinly sliced

1 lb. plum tomatoes,
peeled and chopped

A few bay leaves

2 tbsp. chopped flat-leaf parsley

Salt

for salt, then add the tomatoes, bay leaves, and cod. Cook for about 10 minutes to blend the flavors, then sprinkle with parsley.

BACCALÀ CON
UVETTA E PRUGNE

COD WITH RAISINS AND PRUNES

UMBRIA

¼ cup extra-virgin olive oil

1 medium onion, chopped

1 celery stalk, chopped

2 cups tomato purée

1 lb. salt-dried cod, soaked,
drained, skinned, and boned, and
cut in pieces (see note, page 437)

1 oz. pitted prunes

½ cup raisins

Salt

In the past, this was the central dish of the Christmas Eve dinner in Perugia.

Heat the olive oil in a pan and sauté the onion and celery until they begin to color, then add the tomato purée. ✦ Cook until it begins to thicken, then add the cod and cook about 20 minutes; add the prunes and raisins and complete the cooking. ✦ Add salt if necessary and serve hot.

BACCALÀ CROGIATO

COD AREZZO-STYLE

TOSCANA

1 lb. salt-dried cod, soaked
and drained (see note, page 437)

Extra-virgin olive oil

¼ cup chopped flat-leaf parsley

2 tbsp. capers, chopped

2 or 3 anchovies
(or sardines), chopped

1 cup breadcrumbs

Pepper

The ideal accompaniment is hot boiled chickpeas dressed with olive oil, salt, and pepper.

Preheat the oven to 350°F. Parboil the cod (5 minutes) in water to cover, dry it well, and put it in a baking dish. Drizzle with a little olive oil. ✦ Add the parsley, capers, and anchovies (or sardines), pepper, and breadcrumbs. ✦ Drizzle with olive oil and cover. Bake for about 30 minutes and serve hot.

COD IN PARSLEY

VENETO

1 lb. *unsalted* dried cod
(see note, page 491)
2 tbsp. chopped flat-leaf parsley
3 garlic cloves, minced
¼ cup olive oil
Salt and pepper

Soak the cod in a pan of water for 1 full day and 1 night. ✦ The next morning drain it and boil it for 30 minutes in fresh water. ✦ Drain again, dry with a cloth, squeezing it dry. ✦ At this point, cut the cod in pieces and put them in a bowl. Cover with the parsley, garlic, olive oil, salt, and pepper. ✦ Cover the bowl with a plate slightly smaller than the diameter of the bowl and let the mixture rest for at least 30 minutes. ✦ Do not eat immediately; this is truly good after 5 to 6 hours or the next day.

COD WITH TOMATOES, RAISINS, AND PINE NUTS

LAZIO

1 lb. salt-dried cod, softened,
cleaned, boned, and cut in pieces
(see note, page 437)
All-purpose flour, for dredging
⅔ cup extra-virgin olive oil
2 garlic cloves, crushed
(or 1 medium onion, finely chopped)
6 cups tomato purée
1 tbsp. chopped flat-leaf parsley
1 tbsp. golden raisins
1 tbsp. pine nuts
Salt and pepper

Preheat the oven to 325°F. Rinse the pieces of fish in cold running water, dry with a cloth, and lightly coat them with the flour. ✦ Heat ½ cup of the olive oil in a pan and add the cod; lower the heat and cook, removing the pieces when browned on all sides and setting aside in a warm place. ✦ Heat the remaining oil and sauté the garlic (or onion), add the tomato purée, season with pepper, a little salt, and mix in the parsley, raisins, and pine nuts. ✦ Return the fish to the pan and heat 15 to 20 minutes. Bake for a few minutes and serve hot.

POACHED COD

CAMPANIA

1 ¾ lbs. salt-dried cod,
soaked (see note, page 437)
½ cup extra-virgin olive oil
1 cup chopped onion
½ cup white wine
3 tbsp. chopped flat-leaf parsley
Pepper

Serve accompanied by potatoes or fried chicory or even better with polenta, for although polenta is not precisely Neapolitan, it is indicated by Cavalcanti, duke of Buonvicino.

Rinse the cod, leaving it whole. ✦ Heat the olive oil in a pan at low heat and add the onion, letting it slowly sauté. Add 3 tablespoons of water. ✦ When the water evaporates, add the cod in a single layer and after a few minutes pour in half the wine; let it evaporate, then pour in the other half and add pepper and 1 tablespoon parsley.

✦ Continue cooking for 15 minutes, adding water, pepper, and parsley as needed so the cod will cook covered by liquid and will end up in a little sauce.

CREAMED COD VENETO-STYLE

BACCALÀ MANTECATO

VENETO

2 lbs. *unsalted* dried cod
(stockfish, see note, page 491)

2 garlic cloves

Delicate extra-virgin olive oil
as needed

Salt and white pepper

For those who are not fond of garlic, marinate several crushed cloves in the olive oil for several hours, then remove the garlic before using the oil with the fish. This way only the perfume will remain and the dish will be easier to digest.

The dried cod, well beaten to soften, should simply be cooked in water. ✦ When the water boils, skim off the surface. If the fish is not yet tender enough, continue cooking for a while. ✦ Take the pan off the heat and let the fish cool in the broth for about 30 minutes. ✦ Remove the fish from the liquid and remove the skin and bones. Put the fish in a pan over very low heat with the garlic and pour in a thin trickle of olive oil, using a wooden spoon to beat the fish into the oil until the result is a creamy mixture; add salt and pepper to taste.

CREAMED COD VICENZA-STYLE

BACCALÀ MANTECATO ALLA VICENTINA

VENETO

1½ lbs. *unsalted* dried cod
(stockfish, see note, page 491)

4 cups milk

½ cup extra-virgin olive oil

1 cinnamon stick

Salt and white pepper

The inhabitants of the Veneto call *baccalà* what all other Italians call *stoccafisso* (stockfish), meaning cod dried in the air, without salt. Serve with grilled polenta.

Begin with beating the fish, then soak it in water for two days, clean it, and go back to beating it until it is reduced to chunks that are not too small. ✦ After this first preparation, put the fish in a pot with the milk over medium heat. When the milk begins to take on a little color from the fish, add the olive oil. ✦ When the mixture begins to dry out, add salt and pepper and (if you wish to continue an old custom, as some do) a piece of cinnamon. ✦ Continue cooking to obtain a dense and flavorful mixture.

FISH

443

BAKED WHITEBAIT

PUGLIA

Extra-virgin olive oil

1 lb. whitebait

1 cup breadcrumbs

4 tbsp. grated pecorino
(from Puglia if possible)

1 garlic clove, chopped

2 tbsp. chopped flat-leaf parsley

Salt and pepper

Preheat the oven to 350°F. Grease a baking pan with olive oil. ✦ Place the whitebait in a colander and rinse them in cold running water. ✦ Arrange the fish in an even layer in the prepared pan. ✦ Mix the breadcrumbs and pecorino; season with salt, pepper, garlic, and parsley. Drizzle with olive oil and bake for about 15 minutes.

BATTER-DIPPED WHITEBAIT

LAZIO

2 large eggs, beaten

1 cup all-purpose flour

1 tbsp. chopped flat-leaf parsley

1 garlic clove, finely minced

1 tsp. lemon juice

Extra-virgin olive oil for frying

¾ lb. whitebait

Salt

Mix the eggs, flour, parsley, garlic, lemon juice, and salt to form a batter. ✦ Heat several inches of olive oil in a saucepan until hot. Immerse the whitebait in the batter, and drop into the oil. ✦ Fry until golden brown on all sides, remove with a slotted spoon, and drain on paper towels. ✦ Give them a light dusting of salt before serving them hot.

PAN-FRIED WHITEBAIT

CALABRIA

¼ cup extra-virgin olive oil

2 garlic cloves

2 bay leaves

1 lb. whitebait

Salt

This dish is typical of Amantea.

Heat the olive oil until hot and sauté the garlic until golden. Remove it and add the bay leaves and fish and cook quickly. ✦ Add salt, stir, and serve immediately.

SOUSED BREAM

BOGHE IN CARPIONE

LIGURIA

1 lb. bream, fresh anchovies, or (more rarely) fresh sardines
All-purpose flour, for dredging
Extra-virgin olive oil for frying
2 cups white wine vinegar
2 garlic cloves, chopped
A few sage leaves
1 tbsp. coarse salt

Ligurian *carpione*, the marinade used here, is very different from that of the Veneto because of its far stronger flavors.

Clean and bone the fish and dredge in flour. Heat ½ inch olive oil until hot and fry the fish until golden. ✦ Drain on paper towels and let cool. Meanwhile, stir together the vinegar and coarse salt. Add the fish, garlic, and sage leaves and let marinate at least 6 hours.

ANCHOVY ROLL-UPS

BRACIOLETTE DI ALICI

CALABRIA

½ cup breadcrumbs
⅓ cup grated pecorino
Pinch dried oregano
2 tbsp. chopped flat-leaf parsley
½ cup dry white wine
2 or 3 garlic cloves, finely chopped
1 dozen large, fresh anchovies
Olive oil for frying
All-purpose flour, for dredging
Salt

These fish can also be served with a tomato sauce. For the wine use Cirò or Coda di Volpe.

Mix the breadcrumbs, cheese, oregano, parsley, a pinch of salt, 2 tablespoons wine, and garlic. ✦ Work together well. ✦ Clean the anchovies, rinse, and open them halfway; dip them in the remaining wine, drain, then top them with the breadcrumb mixture. ✦ Roll them up like veal rolls, holding them closed with a toothpick. Heat ½ inch of olive oil in a pan until hot. Dredge the anchovies in the flour and fry until golden. Drain on paper towels and serve hot.

SWORDFISH STEAKS

BRACIOLETTE DI PESCE SPADA

SICILIA

1½ lbs. swordfish steaks, cut in thin slices
1¼ cups breadcrumbs
¼ cup chopped flat-leaf parsley
1 tbsp. capers
⅓ cup grated caciocavallo

CONTINUED

This dish is typical of Messina.

Heat a grill to high heat or preheat the oven to 450°F. Delicately flatten the slices of swordfish with a meat pounder, then cut them in half. ✦ Season the breadcrumbs with salt, pepper, and parsley. ✦ Take about three-quarters of the breadcrumb mixture and blend with the capers, caciocavallo, and 2 tablespoons olive oil and spread over the swordfish pieces. ✦ Roll up the slices and thread them on skewers, alternating them with

½ cup extra-virgin olive oil

1 or 2 medium onions, quartered

Salt and pepper

onion quarters. ✦ Dip the skewers in olive oil, then in the remaining breadcrumb mixture. ✦ Grill over charcoal, turning them only once; or put in a very hot oven for a few minutes. Serve hot.

BRANZINO GUARNITO
IN SFOGLIA DORATA

SEA BASS AND SHELLFISH IN DOUGH

FOR 8–10 PERSONS

FRIULI-VENEZIA GIULIA

1 sea bass, weighing about 10 lbs., cleaned and filleted

3 tbsp. unsalted butter

2 lbs. clams

2 lbs. mussels

½ lb. razor clams

4 oz. small shrimp, shelled and deveined

1 sheet of pasta dough (see page 10)

Preheat the oven to 350°F. Rinse and dry the fillets of sea bass. Heat the butter in a large pan over medium-high heat and sear the fish, flesh-side down, until the first side is golden. ✦ Turn the fish over and add the clams, mussels, and razor clams and cover the pan. Cook until they open, then remove them from their shells. ✦ Add the shrimp and cook until opaque, about 2 minutes. ✦ Leaving the sea bass in the pan, put the rest of the seafood in a blender and chop just until a coarse mixture forms. ✦ Place the sea bass on the pasta, then top with the shellfish mixture. Fold the ends and sides of the pasta over the fish to seal. Bake for about 15 minutes, or until golden. Serve very hot.

BRANZINO IN
CROSTA DI SALE

SEA BASS IN SALT

FRIULI-VENEZIA GIULIA

About 4 lbs. sea salt

2 large, fresh sea bass, weighing about 1 lb. each, cleaned

4 tbsp. delicate extra-virgin olive oil (Ligurian or from Lake Garda)

Preheat the oven to 450°F. Pour ½ inch of sea salt into a 3-inch-deep baking pan large enough to hold the fish with 1 inch of space around each of them. Give the fish a good, long rinse under running water to remove any residue of blood or other impurities; dry them thoroughly with paper towels and put them in the pan with at least 1 inch of space between them. ✦ Cover the fish with the remaining sea salt, leaving no part of the fish uncovered, and bake for at least 25 minutes. ✦ Test for doneness by inserting a skewer at the thickest part of the fish (near where the head is attached to the body): the skewer should come away hot but not wet. ✦ Now the fish is ready and, after having cracked through the crust that will have formed during cooking, cut the fish into fillets, sprinkle 1 tablespoon of olive oil over each fillet, adjust for salt, and serve very hot.

FISH SOUP PESCARA-STYLE

BRODETTO ALLA PESCARESE

ABRUZZO

3 tbsp. extra-virgin olive oil

1 medium onion, thinly sliced

A few dried peppers (*bastardoni* or *fuffoloni* are best)

4 lbs. mixed, cleaned fish: monkfish, scorpion fish, octopus, dogfish, skate, and if possible John Dory, rock lobster, mussels, clams (no "pesce azzurro," meaning anchovies, sardines, mackerel)

Tomato paste can be used instead of the peppers (which give flavor and color), but the flavor will be different, less authentic.

Heat the olive oil in a pan over low heat and sauté the onion and dried peppers; let cool and then pulverize in a mortar. ✦ Pour this into a pot with 4 cups of water, then slowly add the fish according to their size and cooking requirements. When the most delicate fish is cooked through, the soup is ready to serve.

FISH SOUP RAVENNA-STYLE

BRODETTO ALLA RAVENNATE

EMILIA-ROMAGNA

½ cup extra-virgin olive oil

2 garlic cloves

9 oz. tomato purée

½ cup white wine

½ cup white wine vinegar

4 lbs. mixed, cleaned fish, according to the time of year and what the market offers: scorpion fish, mazzola, shark, turbot, squill fish, calamari, cuttlefish, eels, clams

Fishermen from the port of Ravenna are credited as being the first to make *brodetto*, doing so aboard their boats using the least valuable fish, since the best fish could be sold to support their families. It is said that Dante, when in exile at Ravenna, was fond of the *brodetto* made in Porto Corsini.

Heat the olive oil in a pot over low heat and sauté the garlic until golden. Add the tomato purée, wine, and vinegar. ✦ When the wine and vinegar have evaporated, add 4 cups water, then add the fish according to their size and cooking time, beginning with the cuttlefish and ending with the clams, if there are any. The heat should always be low. When the fish is cooked, the soup is ready.

TENCH SOUP

BRODO DI TINCA

UMBRIA

¼ cup extra-virgin olive oil

1 garlic clove, sliced

1 small fresh plum tomato, peeled, seeded, and chopped

A few sage leaves

1 medium-size tench, cleaned (can substitute pike)

Sliced bread, toasted

Salt and peppercorns

Using a pan large enough to hold the entire fish, heat the olive oil and cook the garlic. Add a few peppercorns, salt, tomato, and sage. ✦ Add the fish and enough water to cover. ✦ Cook a long time, occasionally skimming off any fat. ✦ Filter the soup through a sieve and serve it in bowls, very hot, with slices of toasted bread. Serve the tench as a second course with a sauce of parsley and garlic.

BURIDDA | FISH STEW

LIGURIA

¼ cup extra-virgin olive oil

1 carrot, chopped

1 medium onion, minced

1 celery stalk, chopped

1 garlic clove, minced

1 bunch flat-leaf parsley, chopped (with the stalks and leaves kept separate)

2 oz. salt-cured anchovies, rinsed and chopped

3 or 4 lbs. mixed fish, cleaned, boned, and cut in pieces, preferably including anglerfish, monkfish, smooth hound, hake, scorpion fish, skate

1 oz. dried mushrooms, soaked, drained, and chopped, or as needed

2 plum tomatoes, peeled, seeded, and diced

Heat the oil in a pot and sauté the carrot, onion, celery, garlic, and parsley stalks. ✦ While this takes color, add 1 or 2 anchovies and let them melt into the sauce. ✦ At this point add the fish. ✦ After the fish have cooked a few minutes, add the mushrooms along with the tomatoes. ✦ When all the fish have cooked, add the parsley leaves. Serve hot.

BURRIDA A SA CASTEDDAIA | FISH IN WALNUT SAUCE

SARDEGNA

1 dogfish, weighing about 1 lb., cleaned

20 walnut halves (preferably Sardinian)

½ cup extra-virgin olive oil

3 garlic cloves

2 cups white wine vinegar

Salt

This dish is typical of Cagliari and in particular of Carloforte.

After rinsing the dogfish, remove its liver and parboil it in water to cover. Boil the fish in lightly salted water to cover for about 15 minutes; then remove it, skin it, and cut it in small pieces. ✦ Chop the walnuts, adding ¼ cup olive oil to a form a paste. ✦ Heat the remaining olive oil in a pan and add the garlic and the parboiled liver. Add the walnut paste, letting this cook slowly and stirring it until completely blended. ✦ Pour in the vinegar and simmer until the sauce becomes smooth and creamy. ✦ In a bowl arrange the pieces of dogfish in layers, covering each layer with some of the sauce just taken off the heat. Cover and let it rest at least 1 day before serving.

FISH STEW LIVORNO-STYLE

TOSCANA

1 lb. reef octopus, cleaned
½ cup extra-virgin olive oil
4 garlic cloves
A few sage leaves
Pinch chili pepper flakes
1 lb. calamari and/or cuttlefish,
cleaned, rinsed, and chopped
½ cup red wine, such as Chianti
1 tbsp. tomato paste
1 medium onion, roughly chopped
1 celery stalk, roughly chopped
½ lb. soup fish (see page 447)
1 lb. ripe plum tomatoes,
peeled, seeded, and chopped
1 lb. mollusks (clams, cockles,
mussels, periwinkles),
scrubbed and rinsed
¾ lb. dogfish fillets
Slices of bread

On a work surface, pound the octopus with a mallet to tenderize it. Cut it into pieces. ✦ Heat half of the olive oil in a large pan over low heat with 2 of the garlic cloves, the sage, and chili pepper. ✦ As soon as the garlic browns a little, add the octopus and slowly sauté. ✦ After about 20 minutes, add the calamari and/or cuttlefish and continue cooking, adding the wine and tomato paste. ✦ Meanwhile, in another smaller pan, heat the remaining olive oil and sauté the onion, celery, and 1 of the garlic cloves until golden. Add the soup fish, tomatoes, and ½ cup water. ✦ Simmer for about 20 minutes, then put the tomato mixture through a food mill; add this purée to the large pan of the octopus mixture. ✦ Add the mollusks, and when half have opened, add the fish fillets. Cook for a few more minutes until the fillets are opaque through and through. Remove from the heat. ✦ Toast the bread. Smash the remaining garlic clove and rub on the bread. Arrange the slices on the bottoms of individual serving bowls, then spoon the stew over.

FISH

FISH STEW VIAREGGIO-STYLE

FOR
6 PERSONS

TOSCANA

½ cup extra-virgin olive oil
5 garlic cloves, 4 finely chopped
and 1 cut in half
¼ lb. cuttlefish,
cleaned and cut into strips
1 small octopus, cleaned
4 squill fish, cleaned
¼ lb. medium shrimp, peeled
½ cup white wine
1 shark fillet
1 monkfish tail, filleted
2 or 3 fish heads
2 celery stalks, chopped
2 carrots, chopped
CONTINUED

For the wine use Vernaccia di San Gimignano or Vermentino.
Heat half the olive oil in a pan and add the 4 chopped garlic cloves, keeping the heat low so the garlic does not change color. ✦ Add the cuttlefish, octopus, squill fish, and shrimp. ✦ Add the white wine and cook a few more minutes, then add the shark and monkfish fillets. Remove from the heat. ✦ Boil the fish heads separately in water to cover with the celery, carrots, onion, bay leaves, and salt. ✦ When they are boiled, pass the liquid through a sieve and add to the fish fillet mixture. ✦ In another pan, heat the remaining olive oil and sauté the parsley until bright green. Add the mussels and clams and 1 cup water. Cover and let cook just until the shells open. ✦ Shell half of them and add all of them to the pan with the fish fillets. ✦ Add the tomato and the cooking liquid from the mussels and clams (passed through a sieve) and

1 medium onion, chopped

3 bay leaves

½ cup finely chopped flat-leaf parsley

1 lb. mussels, scrubbed and rinsed

1 lb. clams, scrubbed and rinsed

1 plum tomato, chopped

Slices of bread

Salt

simmer everything together for a few minutes, until the fillets are opaque through and through. ✦ Toast the bread, rub it with the remaining cut clove of garlic, and put it in separate soup bowls or layered in a large soup tureen. Pour the stew over the bread and serve.

CALAMARETTI RIPIENI

STUFFED SQUID 1

MOLISE

4 squid

¼ cup chopped flat-leaf parsley

2 garlic cloves (1 chopped, 1 whole)

2 salt-cured anchovies, rinsed, boned, and chopped

1 tbsp. capers

1 or 2 tbsp. breadcrumbs

1 cup extra-virgin olive oil, or as needed

¼ cup dry white wine

Salt and pepper

Clean the squid, removing the small bones, eyes, and mouth. ✦ Empty the ink sacs, clean, and dry them. ✦ Put the parsley, chopped garlic clove, anchovies, and capers in a bowl, add the breadcrumbs, dampen with water, then stir in enough olive oil to obtain a thick mixture. ✦ Put this mixture into the squid sacs, not quite filling them, and close with toothpicks or sew closed with kitchen twine. ✦ Heat 3 tablespoons of olive oil in a pan (preferably earthenware) and sauté the garlic until golden; remove and discard the garlic, then add the squid. ✦ Turn up the heat to cook away their liquid, sprinkling them with wine, and as soon as the wine has evaporated add salt and pepper and 1 cup of warm water, and continue cooking. ✦ The dish is done when the squid are soft and their sauce is thickened. Serve warm.

CALAMARI RIPIENI

STUFFED SQUID 2

PUGLIA

4 medium-size squid

1 garlic clove, chopped

¾ cup breadcrumbs

¼ cup chopped flat-leaf parsley

¼ cup extra-virgin olive oil

Salt and pepper

Preheat the oven to 425°F. Clean the squid and remove the tips of the tentacles. ✦ Chop the tips and combine with the garlic, ½ cup breadcrumbs, salt, pepper, and parsley. Mix in just enough olive oil to make a soft, homogeneous mixture. ✦ Stuff this mixture into the squid and put them in an ovenproof saucepan. Add the olive oil and a little water, and bake until cooked, about 10 minutes. ✦ When the squid are cooked, remove from the oven and heat the broiler. Sprinkle the squid with the remaining breadcrumbs, and lightly gratinée under the broiler. Serve hot.

TUSCAN SEAFOOD STEW

TOSCANA

1 medium onion, chopped

1 bunch flat-leaf parsley, chopped

1 cup extra-virgin olive oil

¾ lb. reef octopus, cleaned and cut into pieces

¾ lb. cuttlefish, cleaned and cut into pieces

½ cup white wine

Pinch chili pepper flakes

1 tbsp. tomato paste

1 conger eel, cleaned, head and tail removed, cut into pieces

1 moray eel, cleaned, head and tail removed, cut into pieces

2 scorpion fish, cleaned

1 John Dory, cleaned, cut into pieces

1 sea bream, cleaned, cut into pieces

1 lb. mantis prawns

1 loaf of stale peasant-style bread, sliced

2 garlic cloves, cut in half

Salt and pepper

This dish is typical of the Maremma. For the wine use Vernaccia di San Gimignano or Vermentino. John Dory fish is also known as gilthead bream or orata.

Put the onion and parsley in a large earthenware pot with about half the olive oil and heat over low heat. ✦ When the onion begins to change color, add the pieces of octopus and cuttlefish. ✦ After about 10 minutes add the white wine, chili pepper flakes, and tomato paste. Add 2 cups warm water and cook 10 minutes more. ✦ Now add the eels and 1 cup water, then the other fish and let cook. ✦ Toast the bread, rub with garlic, and drizzle with the remaining olive oil. Taste the soup for salt, and when the broth tastes somewhat concentrated but is still fairly liquid, pour it along with the fish into individual serving bowls on top of the slices of toasted bread.

SQUILL FISH WITH GARLIC

FRIULI-VENEZIA GIULIA

6 garlic cloves, slivered

2 tbsp. chopped flat-leaf parsley

1 cup breadcrumbs

1½ lbs. squill fish, cleaned and cut lengthwise

½ cup white wine

Salt and pepper

For the wine use pinot grigio or malvasia istriana.

Combine the garlic, parsley, and breadcrumbs and spread them over the slices of fish, arranging them in layers in a saucepan. ✦ Pour in the white wine and add salt and pepper. ✦ Cover the pan and cook over medium heat for 10 minutes. The sauce is delicious!

GRILLED EEL
IN GRAPE LEAVES

EMILIA-ROMAGNA

1½ lbs. eel, cleaned,
with head and tail removed

1 medium onion, roughly chopped

1 carrot, roughly chopped

1 celery stalk, roughly chopped

1 cup extra-virgin olive oil

Grape leaves
(1 for each piece of eel)

1½ cups tomato purée

¼ cup coarsely chopped
flat-leaf parsley

Salt and pepper

This dish is typical of Ferrara.

Heat a grill to high heat. Skin the eel by making an incision around the head with a knife and pulling off its skin like a glove. ✦ Carefully rinse in cold running water and cut in sections about 2½ inches long. ✦ Combine the chopped vegetables with half the olive oil. ✦ Dip the eel sections in this marinade, then wrap the individual sections in grape leaves and tie each closed with kitchen twine. Soak the packages in the marinade for 10 minutes. Grill the packages, turning, about 4 minutes a side. ✦ Meanwhile, heat the tomato purée in a saucepan. As soon as it begins to boil, add the remaining olive oil and the parsley and taste for salt and pepper. ✦ Untie the packages, discarding the twine and grape leaves; put a little of the tomato sauce in the bottom of individual serving bowls and add the eels. Serve immediately.

MARINATED EEL

LAZIO

1½ lbs. eels, cleaned,
with heads and tails removed

1¼ cups extra-virgin olive oil

2 bay leaves, broken in pieces

2 garlic cloves, crushed

1¼ cups very strong
white wine vinegar

Salt and freshly ground pepper

This dish is typical of Rome.

Rinse the eels in cold running water, dry them, then roll each one up on itself, holding them closed with a toothpick. ✦ Mix the olive oil, bay leaves, garlic, and vinegar. Put the eels in a pan and pour over half the marinade; adjust for salt and pepper. The eels must be covered completely by the liquid. ✦ At this point, put the pan over heat and bring to a boil as slowly as possible; reduce the heat and simmer until the eels are cooked. ✦ Remove the eels from the pan and put them in a bowl to cool, pouring over the remaining marinade. ✦ Refrigerate for 48 hours in order for the flesh to macerate and pick up its inimitable flavor.

SEAFOOD AND VEGETABLE PLATTER

Bread of 1 roll, without crust

¼ cup white wine vinegar

2 garlic cloves, 1 chopped, 1 cut in half

1 small red chili pepper, chopped

2 salt-cured anchovies, rinsed and chopped

2 tbsp. chopped flat-leaf parsley

A few capers, chopped

Juice of 2 lemons

1 cup olive oil

1 small cauliflower, cored and chopped

2 carrots, each cut in several pieces

½ lb. slender string beans

1 celery stalk, cut in several pieces

2 potatoes, peeled and chopped

2 bunches black salsify (*scorzonera*, also called goat's beard), cut in pieces

1 red beet, quartered

2 artichokes, trimmed, chokes removed, and cut in half

1 fish, weighing about 2 lbs. (sea bass, scorpion fish, hake), cleaned

1 small lobster

10 shrimp

4 large hardtack crackers

4 oz. mushrooms, preserved in olive oil

6 oysters, removed from their shells

Salt

This dish is typical of the Riviera di Ponente.

Soften the roll by soaking it in a mixture of ¼ cup water and the vinegar. ✦ Combine the chopped garlic clove, chili pepper, anchovies, parsley, and capers with half the lemon juice; drain the bread and work it into this mixture, then pass it all through a sieve. ✦ Whisking the mixture as if you were making mayonnaise, slowly add half the olive oil in a thin stream, then set aside. ✦ Boil the cauliflower, carrots, string beans, and celery in lightly salted water to cover; separately boil the potatoes, salsify, beet, and artichokes in lightly salted water to cover. Drain the vegetables and set aside. ✦ Poach the fish and separately boil the lobster and shrimp. Season the fish and shellfish with 2 tablespoons of the remaining olive oil and lemon juice to taste; add salt if needed. ✦ Rub the crackers with the cut clove of garlic, then arrange them on a serving plate. Mix ¼ cup water with 1 teaspoon of the remaining lemon juice. Dampen the crackers with this acidulated water and then pour over the remaining olive oil. ✦ Arrange alternating layers of vegetables, fish, pieces of lobster, and shrimp, cover with crackers, then pour on a little of the prepared anchovy sauce. ✦ Finish with more lobster, a few more shrimp, and the mushrooms. ✦ Pour on the remaining sauce and decorate the edges of the plate with the oysters. Serve at room temperature.

FISH

CARP ROASTED WITH WILD FENNEL

4 oz. prosciutto fat, minced

4 bulbs wild fennel, chopped

CONTINUED

Combine the prosciutto fat, fennel, and sage leaves and blend with ½ cup of the olive oil, adding salt and pepper to taste. ✦ Make a series of transverse cuts along the carp's body and insert some of the fennel mixture into them, also adding some inside the fish and finally spreading it

Several chopped sage leaves

½ cup plus 3 tbsp. extra-virgin olive oil

1 carp, weighing about 4½ lbs., cleaned

1 tbsp. white wine vinegar

1 sprig rosemary

Salt and pepper

over the exterior. ✦ Let the fish sit for at least 2 hours. ✦ Preheat the oven to 400°F. Mix the remaining olive oil and vinegar. Bake the carp for 2 hours, basting it every so often by dipping the rosemary sprig in the olive oil mixture and spreading over the fish.

✦ **LOCAL TRADITION** ✦

CARBONARETTI DEL LAGO DI PIEDILUCO

In this recipe typical of the lake fishermen in Umbria, the fish are cooked at the end of a long day's work right on the water. The fishermen scorch the local perch over small fires in their boats, giving the dish its name, *carbonaretti*. This process served a dual purpose since the flames scorch off most of the scales while cooking the inner flesh. After scorching, the fishermen would then remove any burned parts on the outside as well as the intestines and other internal organs, and separate the two fillets from the skeleton. A simple sauce made of olive oil, salt, pepper, garlic, and parsley would be used to dress the fresh fillets.

CARPIONE | **SOUSED FISH**

VENETO

1 lb. mixed fish: sardines, mullet, lemon sole, sole, cleaned and boned

All-purpose flour, for dredging

Extra-virgin olive oil

3 medium onions, sliced

1 cup white wine vinegar

1 cup white wine

This dish, typical of the Venetian coast, can be consumed immediately, but improves if allowed to marinate a few days. Following an ancient tradition, raisins, pine nuts, and various spices (cloves, cinnamon, anise, pepper, and so on) can be added. For the wine use Soave or Lugana.

Dust the fish with the flour. Heat 1 inch of olive oil in a pan until hot and fry until golden. ✦ Heat 2 tablespoons oil over low heat and add the onions. Cook very slowly, adding the vinegar and white wine. ✦ Let this simmer about 10 minutes. ✦ Arrange alternating layers of fish and onions in a bowl, then pour over the wine-vinegar mixture to cover completely.

CUTTLEFISH BAKED IN FOIL

CARTOCCIO DI SEPPIOLINE

PUGLIA

1 cup breadcrumbs

3 tbsp. olive oil

2 tbsp. flat-leaf parsley

1 garlic clove, chopped

2 small cuttlefish, cleaned and cut in pieces

2 whole shrimp, shelled

Pepper

Preheat the oven to 350°F. Mix the breadcrumbs, 2 tablespoons olive oil, parsley, garlic, and pepper. ✦ Arrange the cuttlefish and shrimp on a sheet of aluminum foil and spread the breadcrumb mixture over them, adding the remaining olive oil and parsley. ✦ Fold shut the aluminum foil, crimping around the edges to seal. Bake until the fish is cooked through, about 10 minutes.

FISH SOUP

CASSOLA

SARDEGNA

3½ lbs. mixed, cleaned fish (mullet, cuttlefish, bream, octopus, eel, scorpion fish, conger eel, a small lobster)

½ cup olive oil

1 large onion, finely chopped

2 garlic cloves, 1 finely chopped, 1 whole

2 tbsp. chopped flat-leaf parsley

1 lb. plum tomatoes, peeled and strained of seeds

2 dried chili peppers

Bread

Salt

Heat the oven to 400°F. Rinse all the fish, cut in pieces, and drain well; the lobster must be left whole. ✦ Heat the olive oil in a pan and sauté the onion, chopped garlic, and parsley. ✦ When the onion becomes translucent, add the tomatoes, a pinch of salt, and 1 chili pepper. ✦ Let this cook a few minutes, then add the fish, beginning with those that take longest to cook and, after a few minutes, the rest. ✦ After the fish have cooked in the sauce for a few minutes, add 2 cups of warm water and cover the pot; cook for about 1 hour at very low heat. ✦ Slice the bread, rub the slices with the whole garlic and remaining chili pepper, then toast in the oven for a few minutes. Put the slices of bread in bowls, pour over the soup, and serve piping hot.

ROAST STRIPED MULLET

CEFALO ARROSTO

SARDEGNA

1 striped (gray) mullet, cleaned

Bay leaves, as needed

¼ cup lard, melted and kept hot

This dish is typical of Campidano.

Heat a grill to medium-high heat. ✦ Rinse the fish under cold running water, then cut into six equal-size pieces. Pat dry with paper towels. ✦ Slide the pieces of fish on skewers, alternating them with bay leaves, and grill, turning the skewer often. ✦ When the fish is almost done, drizzle hot lard onto it, letting it drain off. ✦ Remove the

FISH

fish from the skewers as soon as it is cooked and serve immediately.

GROUPER IN SAUCE

SICILIA

Extra-virgin olive oil
1 large onion, chopped
8 garlic cloves, whole
Several celery stalks, chopped
1 carrot, chopped
1 cup dry white wine
(preferably Sicilian)
3½ lbs. grouper, cleaned
1 or more pieces dried chili pepper,
or as desired
1 tbsp. capers, rinsed
⅔ cup pitted green olives
1 lb. ripe plum tomatoes,
peeled, seeded, and chopped
2 tbsp. chopped flat-leaf parsley
Salt

This is a very ancient preparation, which is part of the seaside tradition. The same recipe can also be used for salt-dried cod and unsalted dried cod, the latter with the addition of potatoes. Grouper is one of the few fish that, like game, must be allowed to ripen two or three days in the refrigerator before being cooked. The recipe results in an abundance of sauce that can be used to dress spaghetti, or even better *trenette* or *bucatini*, always remembering to set aside enough to pour over the fish, served as a second course. In terms of the cooking time for the fish, a grouper that weighs about 4 pounds will need 40 to 45 minutes; those weighing 10 or more pounds are going to have cooking times as long as 2 hours.

In a cooking pan large enough to hold the grouper, heat the olive oil and sauté the onion, garlic, celery, and carrot. ✦ When they are lightly colored, pour in the white wine. ✦ Add the fish and chili pepper, but only a little salt (because of the capers), capers, and olives. ✦ Cook the fish in this sauce for about 10 minutes, then add the tomatoes and, if desired, more chili pepper. ✦ Spoon the sauce over the fish, then seal the pot closed using a sheet of aluminum foil or waxed paper under the lid. ✦ Cook the fish like this until opaque. ✦ A few minutes before turning off the heat, open the pan and add the parsley. Taste for salt. Cook another 5 minutes.

DIAMANTE-STYLE GROUPER

CALABRIA

2 lbs. grouper, cleaned
½ cup pitted black olives
⅓ cup capers, rinsed
6 oz. tomato purée
2 bay leaves
2 garlic cloves, chopped
CONTINUED

This dish is typical of Diamante. The remaining sauce, flavored with the addition of the pulpy and fragrant part of the fish's head, is excellent for dressing pasta.

Preheat the oven to 350°F. Rinse the fish and pat it dry with a cloth. Season it with salt and pepper and put it in a high-sided cooking pan. ✦ Add the olives, capers, tomato purée, bay leaves, and garlic, then pour in the wine and olive oil. ✦ Cover the pan with aluminum foil and bake for about 30 minutes. ✦ At the end of that time, be

1 ¼ cups dry white wine
½ cup extra-virgin olive oil
1 tbsp. chopped flat-leaf parsley
Salt and pepper

careful when lifting the grouper from the pan not to break it. Place the fish on a serving platter, pour over a tablespoon of the cooking juices, and sprinkle with parsley before bringing to the table.

HALIBUT AND SEAFOOD STEW

CIAMBOTTA DI ROMBO

PUGLIA

¼ cup extra-virgin olive oil
1 garlic clove, minced
2 tbsp. chopped flat-leaf parsley
2 halibut fillets
2 medium shrimp, opened lengthwise
4 or 5 mussels
½ cup dry white wine
15 grape tomatoes
Pinch chili pepper flakes
Sliced peasant-style bread, toasted

Heat the oil in a large pan and sauté the garlic and half the parsley; after a few minutes add the halibut, shrimp, and mussels. Add the white wine and cook 5 minutes. Add the tomatoes and chili pepper. ✦ Cook for 10 to 15 minutes, then serve in a bowl with slices of toasted bread, and sprinkle with the remaining parsley before serving.

SWEET-AND-SOUR MUSSELS

COGNOTTI

PUGLIA

2 lbs. mussels,
or oysters if you prefer
All-purpose flour, for dredging
Extra-virgin olive oil for frying
1 ½ lbs. honey
5 cups white wine vinegar
⅔ cup almond meats,
toasted and chopped
½ cup chopped chestnuts
2 oz. chopped candied oranges

This specialty, with its sweet-and-sour flavor, has very ancient origins.

Whether using mussels or oysters, open them by hand and remove them from their shells, making certain they remain whole. ✦ Drain them, then dredge them in flour. ✦ Heat 1 inch of olive oil in a pan until hot and fry the mussels or oysters until golden. Drain on paper towels. ✦ Heat the honey and vinegar in a saucepan to 200°F on a candy thermometer. Stir in the mussels or oysters and all the other ingredients, cook for a few minutes, then let cool. Pour into glass jars and keep in refrigerator or seal according to manufacturer's instructions.

FISH

FRIED TUNA WITH LEMON AND PARSLEY

CONNETTO FRITTO

SICILIA

1½ lbs. *sangusu* (common tombarello; can substitute fresh tuna), cleaned and sliced

All-purpose flour, for dredging

Olive oil for frying

2 lemons, sliced

½ cup chopped flat-leaf parsley

Salt

This dish is typical of Milazzo.

Rinse the slices of fish under running water to remove the dark blood that is its distinguishing trait as much as possible. ✦ Drain them, dust them with flour, and shake them in a large sieve to eliminate any extra flour. ✦ Heat a couple inches of olive oil in a pan until hot and fry the fish until golden. Drain on paper towels. ✦ Salt the fish, then arrange them on a serving plate decorated with lemon slices and chopped parsley.

STUFFED GAR FISH OR PIKE

COSTARDELLE RIPIENE

CALABRIA

6 medium gar fish

1½ garlic cloves, chopped

1 tbsp. chopped flat-leaf parsley

Pinch dried oregano

½ cup breadcrumbs

½ cup extra-virgin olive oil

6 plum tomatoes, peeled, seeded, and chopped

Salt and pepper

Remove the head, tail, and spine of the gar fish, then rinse clean and dry. ✦ In a bowl combine the garlic, parsley, oregano, breadcrumbs, salt, pepper, and olive oil to make a mixture that sticks together when pressed between your fingers. ✦ Stuff the gar fish with this mixture. ✦ Arrange the stuffed fish in a pan, keeping the stuffing side upward. ✦ Spoon a little tomato onto each fish, drizzle with olive oil, and add salt. Cover the pan and cook at low heat for about 20 minutes.

PUGLIA-STYLE MUSSELS

COZZE ALLA PUGLIESE

PUGLIA

4½ lbs. mussels

1 garlic clove, sliced

2 tbsp. extra-virgin olive oil

½ cup white wine

2 tbsp. tomato paste

1 cup fish broth (or water)

⅔ cup béchamel sauce (see page 339) or ½ cup grated pecorino

⅔ cup breadcrumbs

Preheat the oven to 425°F. Scrub the mussels and remove the beards. Shell them, then combine with the garlic in a saucepan; add the olive oil and heat over very low heat. ✦ When the garlic changes color, add the wine. Let the wine evaporate. Dilute the tomato paste in the broth (or water), then add to the pan. ✦ Reduce the sauce, then transfer the mixture to a large earthenware pan. ✦ Thicken the sauce with some béchamel or pecorino. ✦ Sprinkle with the breadcrumbs, then bake until the top is browned.

MUSSELS AU GRATIN WITH LEMON

COZZE GRATINATE

CAMPANIA

4 ½ lbs. mussels, scrubbed, with beards removed

2 tbsp. chopped flat-leaf parsley

4 garlic cloves, finely chopped

⅔ cup breadcrumbs

¼ cup extra-virgin olive oil

Juice of 2 lemons

Salt

Preheat the oven to 425°F. Put the mussels in a pan over high heat. Cover and cook for about 5 minutes, discarding any that do not open; also discard the top shells. ✦ Arrange the mussels in a baking pan and sprinkle with parsley and garlic, then sprinkle with breadcrumbs, salt, and drizzle with olive oil. ✦ Bake for a few minutes, until the breadcrumbs color. Sprinkle with lemon juice and serve.

MUSSELS AU GRATIN

COZZE GRATINATE

PUGLIA

4 ½ lbs. mussels, scrubbed, with beards removed

1 garlic clove, finely chopped

½ cup flat-leaf parsley

¼ cup breadcrumbs

Extra-virgin olive oil

Preheat the oven to 400°F. Clean the mussels (scraping the shells if necessary). Place them in a pan, cover, and heat over high heat for a few minutes until they open; discard any that do not open and discard the top shell from the rest of them. ✦ Arrange them in a baking dish. Mix the garlic, parsley, and breadcrumbs, and sprinkle over the mussels; spoon a little olive oil over each one and lightly brown in the oven.

STUFFED MUSSELS

COZZE RIPIENE

PUGLIA

½ cup extra-virgin olive oil

1 garlic clove, chopped

1 ½ cups tomato purée

1 ½ lbs. mussels, scrubbed, with beards removed

2 large eggs, beaten

⅔ cup breadcrumbs

½ cup grated pecorino

¼ cup chopped flat-leaf parsley

Salt and pepper

Preheat the oven to 400°F. Grease a baking pan with olive oil. Heat the olive oil in a pan and sauté the garlic. ✦ As soon as the garlic colors, add the tomato purée and cook at low heat for 10 minutes. ✦ Heat the mussels in a pan over high heat until they open; discard any that do not open. ✦ Mix the eggs, breadcrumbs, cheese, parsley, salt, and pepper. Work the mixture well to combine thoroughly (it should not be overly dense), then stuff it into the mussels, closing the shells over it. ✦ Place the mussels in the pan and bake about 15 minutes.

FISH

PIKE CROQUETTES

CALABRIA

1 lb. pike, cleaned

1 tbsp. chopped flat-leaf parsley

⅓ cup grated pecorino

2 large eggs

3 oz. stale bread, softened in water
and squeezed dry

Extra-virgin olive oil

All-purpose flour, for dredging

Breadcrumbs

Salt and pepper

Boil the fish in water to cover by 1 inch until cooked through. Let cool and drain, then remove its bones and skin with great care. Pass the fish through a food mill and mix with the parsley, cheese, 1 egg, and bread. ✦ Season with salt and pepper, then knead together and make croquettes. ✦ Heat 2 inches of olive oil in a high-sided pan until hot. Dredge the fish in the flour. Beat the remaining egg, dip the fish into it, then in breadcrumbs. Fry until golden and drain on paper towels.

BAKED FRESH TUNA

FETTE DI TONNO FRESCO
AL FORNO

SICILIA

Extra-virgin olive oil

Slices of fresh tuna fillet,
½ inch thick, as many as
are the portions to prepare

1 or more medium onions,
finely minced

1 or more ripe plum tomatoes,
peeled and chopped

Pinch dried oregano, crushed

Salt

This dish is typical of the Ortigia neighborhood of Siracusa.

Preheat the oven to 350°F. Lay out a sheet of aluminum foil and drizzle a little olive oil down the center. ✦ Add the tuna, top with onion and tomatoes, and sprinkle with salt and oregano. ✦ Fold the foil closed, put it on a baking sheet, and bake for 20 minutes. ✦ Around the end of this time open the foil package and bake to dry up the sauce that the tuna will have given up. ✦ When well cooked the tuna will change color from red to a pale gray and will become firm. Serve them hot; it is permissible to complete the seasoning with a few grindings of black pepper should anyone so desire. Lemon juice is not recommended.

FRIED COD FILLETS

FILETTI DI BACCALÀ

LAZIO

8 salt-dried cod fillets
(see note, page 437)

2 cups all-purpose flour,
plus more as needed

CONTINUED

Clean away any bits of skin and scales from the fillets, and if they are not already softened, soak them in cold water for 24 hours, changing the water several times. ✦ Mix the flour, salt, 1 tablespoon olive oil, and a dash of vinegar with just enough water (about 1 cup) to create a thick batter. ✦ Heat a couple of inches of olive oil in a

Extra-virgin olive oil
Dash white wine vinegar
Salt

large pan until hot. Dry the fillets with a cloth, dip them lightly in flour, then in the batter, and fry them. ✦ Use a skimmer or slotted spoon to keep the fillets submerged until they are golden. Remove them and drain on paper towels. Serve hot.

FRITTATA CON ACCIUGHE

ANCHOVY FRITTATA

ABRUZZO

6 salt-cured anchovy fillets,
rinsed of salt and boned
½ cup roughly chopped
flat-leaf parsley
3 tbsp. extra-virgin olive oil
1 garlic clove, crushed
1⅔ cups tomato purée
Pinch chili pepper flakes
10 large fresh eggs, beaten
Salt

Finely chop the anchovy fillets and parsley, then crush them together in a mortar to form a paste and set aside. ✦ Heat 1 tablespoon of the olive oil in a pan and add the garlic. ✦ As soon as the garlic colors, remove and discard it and add the anchovy mixture; immediately add the tomato purée. ✦ Season with a little salt and chili pepper flakes and continue cooking for 8 minutes. ✦ Pour this mixture into a bowl and let it cool, then mix in the eggs and season with another pinch of salt and chili flakes. ✦ Heat another tablespoon of olive oil in the skillet and put in the mixture. Stir it around for a few seconds, then let it brown on one side. When it has browned, turn it out onto a large plate. ✦ Heat the remaining tablespoon of olive oil in the skillet and return the frittata to the skillet to cook the other side. When the second side has also cooked, slide the frittata out onto a serving plate and serve.

FRITTATA DI BIANCHETTI

WHITEBAIT FRITTATA

LIGURIA

3 large eggs, beaten
¾ lb. whitebait, rinsed and drained
1 garlic clove, minced
2 tbsp. chopped flat-leaf parsley
2 tbsp. extra-virgin olive oil
Salt and pepper

Mix the eggs, whitebait, garlic, parsley, salt, and pepper, and stir well. ✦ Heat the olive oil in a cast-iron skillet and pour in the mixture, stirring it with a wooden spoon. ✦ Cook at moderate heat to cook the first side, then turn the frittata and cook the other side.

FISH

FRITTELLE DI BACCALÀ | COD FRITTERS

UMBRIA

¾ lb. salt-dried cod
(see note, page 437)

1 large egg

1 ¼ cups (more or less)
all-purpose flour

Olive oil for frying

Salt

Begin soaking the cod the morning before the day you plan to use it or buy it already softened. ✦ Drain (if necessary), bone, and skin it, then cut it into fillets. ✦ Mix 1 egg, ½ cup water, a pinch of salt, and as much flour as needed to make a thick batter. ✦ Heat 1 inch of olive oil in a pan until hot. Dip the fillets in the batter, then fry them until they are golden. Drain on paper towels and serve hot.

GAMBERI IN SALSA VERDE | SHRIMP IN GREEN SAUCE

UMBRIA

2 lbs. freshwater (rock) shrimp

For the sauce:

½ cup minced flat-leaf parsley

½ cup minced mint

2 garlic cloves, crushed

2 tbsp. white wine vinegar

½ cup extra-virgin olive oil,
or as needed

Salt and pepper

This dish is typical of the Valnerina.

Cook the shrimp in lightly salted boiling water until opaque, drain, and shell them. ✦ Make the sauce by grinding together all the other ingredients in a wooden mortar, adding enough olive oil to make a thin paste. ✦ Arrange the shrimp on a serving plate. Cover them with the sauce and drizzle generously with additional olive oil.

GAMBERI DI S. POLO | TREVISO SHRIMP

VENETO

2 tbsp. extra-virgin olive oil

2 or 3 garlic cloves, crushed

1 lb. freshwater (rock) shrimp

1 medium onion, minced

1 celery stalk, minced

1 carrot, minced

Pinch fresh oregano

½ cup dry white wine

Pinch paprika

Salt

Serve this dish, typical of S. Polo di Piave (Treviso), hot with polenta. For the wine use pinot grigio, Soave, or Lugana.

Heat the olive oil in a pan; sauté the garlic until golden, then remove and discard it. ✦ Add the shrimp, onion, celery, carrot, and oregano, then pour in the wine. ✦ Add some paprika and salt and cook for 3 minutes with the lid on the pan and 3 minutes with the lid off.

CRESPELLE DI "MUCCO ROSSO"

In Sicily, *mucco rosso* (*muccu russu*, in dialect) is the name given to tiny red newborn fish, which are not only rare but also highly prized for their delicate flavor and perfume. They are used to make this special dish of *crespelle* or fritters, which highlights their fresh lightness and delicacy and must be prepared with great care. The *mucco rosso* would first be separated from any other tiny fish or bits of shell and then lightly seasoned with garlic, parsley, salt, pepper, a little sharp pecorino, and just a splash of white wine. A fork was the traditional utensil used to gently stir the mixture so as not to reduce it to a mush. By hand, a small pinch of the mixture was coated very gently in a little flour and then placed into hot oil to fry to a burnt red color. Each fritter was to be served immediately and without any further seasoning to preserve its freshest flavors.

FISH

LAVARELLI AL VINO BIANCO

WHITEFISH IN WHITE WINE

LOMBARDIA

2 lbs. medium-size whitefish
½ garlic clove, crushed
½ cup chopped flat-leaf parsley
¼ lb. (½ cup) unsalted butter
1 medium onion, minced
Juice of ½ lemon
½ cup dry white wine
Salt

For the wine use Lugana or bianco di Custoza.

Clean the whitefish, setting aside the heads and scales, then fillet them. ✦ Put the heads and scales in a pot with 1 cup water, garlic, and half the parsley and boil to make a broth. ✦ Heat 4 tablespoons butter in a saucepan and add the onion; when the onion pales, add the fish. ✦ Filter the broth and pour it over the fish. ✦ Add the lemon juice and wine. ✦ Taste for salt and cook at low heat. Whitefish cook quickly and 5 minutes should be enough time. ✦ Remove the fillets carefully, so as not to break them, and set them aside where they will stay warm. ✦ Turn up the heat and reduce the remaining liquid to form a sauce. ✦ Mix in the remaining butter and parsley. Pour this over the fish and serve immediately.

| **PIKE IN TOMATO SAUCE**

EMILIA-ROMAGNA

6 small pike, cleaned
½ cup all-purpose flour
Extra-virgin olive oil for frying
1 bunch flat-leaf parsley, chopped
1 cup extra-virgin olive oil
¼ cup tomato purée or
½ cup tomato paste diluted in
1 cup warm water
Salt and pepper

This dish is typical of Imola.

Rinse and dry the pike, then dust with the flour. Heat 1 inch of olive oil in a large, heavy pan until hot, and fry the pike until golden, turning. Drain them on paper towels. ✦ Sprinkle with a little salt and pepper—and they're good just like that. ✦ If you are able to resist eating all the fish at this point, then go ahead and finish the preparation: Heat the parsley and olive oil in a terra-cotta pan, add salt and pepper and tomato purée or paste mixture. ✦ As soon as this sauce thickens, add the fried pike and turn them to coat with the sauce. Serve hot.

| **PIKE—FRIED, GRILLED, OR BAKED**

VENETO

2 lbs. pike, cleaned
4 oz. *lardo*
1 sprig rosemary
2 garlic cloves
½ cup extra-virgin olive oil
Salt and pepper

Cut the pike lengthwise along the belly; rinse and dry it. ✦ Grind together the *lardo*, salt, and pepper in a mortar; add the rosemary and garlic. ✦ Use this to fill the pike, then sew it closed and brush it with olive oil and sprinkle with salt. ✦ The fish can be fried in olive oil over low heat, cooking it for a long time; or it can be grilled, placing it a good distance from the charcoal and, again, cooking for a long time. ✦ Yet another quite popular way is to roast pike in a 400°F oven until it is completely browned.

| **FRIED PIKE CROQUETTES**

VENETO

1½ lbs. pike, cleaned
½ cup white wine
Grated zest of 1 lemon
The bread of 3 stale rolls,
soaked in milk
3 large eggs, beaten
⅔ cup all-purpose flour
2 garlic cloves, crushed
CONTINUED

Cut the pike in pieces and boil for at least 15 minutes in lightly salted water to cover, with the addition of the wine and lemon zest. ✦ Remove the fish, let them cool, then bone them carefully. ✦ Put the resulting pieces in a bowl and work them into a pulp by hand. ✦ Mix in the rolls, eggs, some of the flour, garlic, anchovies, pepper, parsley, butter, and breadcrumbs if needed to bind the mixture better. ✦ Heat 1 inch of olive oil in a deep pan until it is so hot that it shimmers on the surface, but not so hot that it smokes. Form the mixture into medium-size balls and fry them until golden and crusty, turning

3 salt-cured anchovies, boned, rinsed, and minced

¼ cup chopped flat-leaf parsley

4 tbsp. unsalted butter

Breadcrumbs (if needed)

Extra-virgin olive oil for frying (preferably from Lake Garda)

Salt and pepper

occasionally. You may need to work in batches; avoid crowding the pan. Remove the croquettes with a slotted spatula and set them on paper towels. Serve hot with a sprinkling of salt if you like.

LUCCIO ALLA PESCATORA CON POLENTA

PIKE IN ANCHOVY SAUCE

LOMBARDIA

2 lbs. pike, cleaned

2 carrots

1 celery stalk

3 medium onions, 2 whole, 1 finely chopped

2 cups extra-virgin olive oil

2 garlic cloves, finely chopped

6 anchovies, filleted

3 tbsp. capers, rinsed

2 tbsp. flat-leaf parsley, finely chopped

Salt

Pike prepared this way should be served hot with fresh polenta.

Preheat the oven to 350°F. Simmer the pike, carrots, celery, and 2 whole onions in lightly salted water to cover. ✦ When the pike is cooked, drain and discard the vegetables. Fillet the pike carefully and place the fillets in a baking dish. ✦ Heat the olive oil in a pan and add the chopped onion, then the garlic, anchovies, and capers. ✦ When the onion has browned, remove the pan from the heat, add the parsley, and mix. ✦ Pour this mixture over the pike. Bake 10 minutes, or until the sauce is bubbling.

LUCCIO IN SAOR

PIKE IN SAUCE

VENETO

1 pike, weighing about 2 lbs., cleaned

2 bay leaves

½ medium onion

2 celery stalks

For the sauce:

½ lb. salt-cured sardines, rinsed

Extra-virgin olive oil (preferably from Lake Garda)

Combine the pike, bay leaves, onion, and celery in a pot. Add water to cover and heat to boiling. Reduce the heat and simmer for 20 minutes. ✦ When the fish is cooked, let it cool, then fillet it and put the fillets on a serving plate. ✦ Prepare the sauce: Put the sardines in a pan and pour in enough olive oil to cover them. Put this over very low heat and cook, stirring, until the sardines have dissolved to form a paste. ✦ Let this cool, then pour it over the pike.

BOILED PIKE

1 pike, weighing about 1¾ lbs., cleaned

½ cup extra-virgin olive oil

1 garlic clove, minced

1 tbsp. white wine vinegar

Bread for serving

Salt and pepper

Place the pike in a pot large enough to contain it lengthwise and add water to cover. ✦ Bring to a boil, then simmer for 20 minutes. When cooked, delicately remove it from the pot without breaking it, and set it on a serving plate. ✦ Season with olive oil, salt, pepper, garlic, and a little vinegar. Do not overdo it with the pepper since the dish should have a delicate flavor. As for the olive oil, any extra can be soaked up with bread.

BAKED ANCHOVIES

2 cups breadcrumbs

1 tbsp. chopped flat-leaf parsley

1 garlic clove, chopped

1 tsp. capers, rinsed and chopped

½ cup pitted black olives, chopped

Pinch chili pepper flakes

1 tbsp. chopped basil

1½ lbs. fresh anchovies, cleaned

2 tbsp. extra-virgin olive oil

Salt

Preheat the oven to 300°F. Grease a baking pan. ✦ In a bowl, combine the breadcrumbs, parsley, garlic, capers, olives, chili pepper, and basil with a little salt. ✦ Butterfly the anchovies and arrange half of them in rows along the bottom of the pan; cover this with a layer of the breadcrumb mixture, alternating layers until using up the ingredients, ending with a layer of breadcrumbs. Drizzle with olive oil over the top and bake for 15 minutes.

COD WITH GREEN OLIVES

2 lbs. cod

⅔ cup extra-virgin olive oil

2 garlic cloves, minced

⅔ cup pitted green olives, chopped

1 tbsp. chopped flat-leaf parsley

Salt

This dish is typical of Fuscaldo.

Clean and gut the cod and cut it in somewhat thick slices. ✦ In a pan, heat the olive oil and cook the garlic, then add the olives and cook for 10 minutes. ✦ Add the fish, and when they are nearly cooked through, taste for salt and sprinkle with parsley. Serve immediately.

TUNA-AND-ANCHOVY CREPES

TOSCANA

1 can (6½ oz.) tuna in olive oil

2 oz. anchovies

1 tbsp. chopped flat-leaf parsley

½ cup all-purpose flour

3 large eggs, beaten

1 medium onion, finely chopped

Extra-virgin olive oil

Salt and pepper

This dish is typical of Pitigliano, a historically Jewish town in southern Toscana.

Preheat the oven to 375°F. Make the filling by chopping together the tuna, anchovies, parsley, salt, and pepper. ✦ Make the batter by combining the flour with ½ cup water. Stir until the mixture no longer sticks to the sides of the bowl; at that point add another ½ cup of water. ✦ Add the eggs, onion, a pinch of pepper and mix well. ✦ Grease a skillet with olive oil, turn on the heat, pour in 2 tablespoons of the batter, and make thin *migliaccini* (crepes). Cook for 3 minutes, until the bottom is cooked and the top part is still soft; put 1 tablespoon of the tuna filling at the center, close the *migliaccio*, and remove from the pan. Repeat with the remaining batter and filling. Arrange the *migliaccini* in a baking pan and bake for 5 minutes. Serve cold.

FISH

MOLECHE FRITTE

FRIED SOFT-SHELL CRABS

VENETO

2 large eggs, beaten

4 soft-shell crabs (the smaller the better; about 1 lb.), rinsed

Olive oil for frying

All-purpose flour, for dredging

Salt

These are a wonder of the lagoon. In the fall and in the spring, the crabs change their shells, with the old shell discarded and replaced by the soft new one. Serve them with large slices of polenta, preferably white.

Put the eggs into a shallow baking dish. Add the crabs in a single layer (there should be enough egg to cover them; if necessary beat an additional egg and add). ✦ Let the crabs sit in the eggs a little while. ✦ Heat 1 inch of olive oil in a pan until hot. Dredge the crabs in flour, then fry them until golden. ✦ Drain the crabs on paper towels and sprinkle them with salt. Serve them warm.

| # SWORDFISH PIE

SICILIA

For the filling:

Extra-virgin olive oil

1 medium onion, finely chopped

1 celery stalk, finely chopped

1 can (28 oz.) peeled plum tomatoes

2 lbs. swordfish steaks,
cut in large pieces

½ cup capers,
rinsed and finely chopped

⅔ cup pitted green Sicilian olives,
thinly sliced

2 zucchini, cut in short sticks

For the crust:

1¼ cups all-purpose flour

⅔ cup superfine sugar

¼ lb. (1 stick) cold unsalted butter,
cut into pieces

2 large egg yolks

Salt

This is a kind of turnover, made using pie crust that is not very sweet, containing swordfish and sautéed zucchini (you can use sautéed eggplant instead of the zucchini).

Heat the olive oil and sauté the onion and celery. When they have colored, add the tomatoes and cook for about 20 minutes. ✦ Add the swordfish, capers, and olives and cook for another 15 minutes. ✦ In a separate pan, heat a little more oil and cook the zucchini until golden; drain on paper towels. ✦ Meanwhile, make the crust, first sifting together the flour and sugar, then kneading in the butter until the mixture looks like wet sand. Add the egg yolks and a pinch of salt. ✦ Knead this mixture briefly, then set aside and let it rest for 30 minutes. ✦ Preheat the oven to 350°F. Roll out the dough to make a sheet and use it to line a baking pan, leaving enough extra at the sides to fold closed. ✦ Make a first layer of sauce, then put in a layer of zucchini, then more sauce, then swordfish. Follow with more zucchini, sauce, and fish; close over the dough to seal it. ✦ Bake for 1 hour, or until the surface of the dough is well browned. This is best served cold.

✦ **LOCAL TRADITION** ✦

MUSTICA DI CRUCOLI

Reminiscent of an ancient Roman recipe called *garum*, this spread made from salted newborn sardines was typical of Calabria. The newborn fish would be put under salt in a terra-cotta container to age for about two months. After said time, the mixture would be flavored with spicy red chili peppers that had been crushed with a mortar and pestle along with fennel seeds. Sealed terra-cotta jars were used to preserve the spread, which was often served on toasted peasant-style bread and sprinkled with olive oil.

FISH COOKED IN SALT

OMBRINA AL SALE

PUGLIA

2 *ombrine* or sea bass, 1 lb. each
(or any other fish that
can be roasted)

2 lbs. coarse salt

Pepper

Preheat the oven to 400°F. Make a thick layer of coarse salt in a baking pan. Gut the fish and rinse very carefully; do not scale them. ✦ Place the fish on the salt, then cover with another layer of salt. ✦ Bake for about 30 minutes. ✦ Bring the fish to the table still covered by its crust of salt, then break open the crust, remove the fish, and serve it seasoned, at the most, with a little pepper.

HERB-STUFFED GILTHEAD BREAM

ORATE ALLA SAN NICOLA

PUGLIA

1 ½ lbs. gilthead bream (orata)

¾ cup fragrant herbs
(bay leaves, rosemary, sage, thyme)

1 cup olive oil

In the old San Nicola section of Bari, bream and other kinds of fish are prepared in the most ancient and most delicious way.

Heat a grill to high heat. Clean the fish without scaling them and bathe them in seawater. ✦ Fill them with fragrant herbs and soak them in a bath of olive oil for a few minutes, then grill them over charcoal or wood.

MARINATED TOPE (SHARK)

PALOMBO A SCAPECE

SICILIA

1 ¼ lbs. tope fillets (shark)

All-purpose flour, for dredging

Olive oil

2 cups white wine vinegar,
or as needed

1 medium onion, finely sliced

⅔ cup tomato purée

⅓ cup pine nuts

⅓ cup golden raisins

4 garlic cloves, coarsely chopped

2 tbsp. chopped flat-leaf parsley

Salt and pepper

The word *scapece* is from the Spanish *eschabeche* and refers to a dish of marinated fish.

Dip the tope fillets in flour. Heat ½ inch of olive oil in a pan until hot and fry until golden, then put them in a bowl and pour in enough vinegar to cover them. ✦ Drain off nearly all of the oil from the pan, then add the onion. As soon as the onion changes color, add the tomato purée and cook for 10 minutes, then add the pine nuts, raisins, garlic, parsley, salt, and pepper. Stir this around to blend. ✦ Remove the fish from the vinegar, drain well, and add them to the pan. ✦ Cover the pan, lower the heat, and cook for another 15 minutes. This dish is best if served 1 hour after its preparation.

FISH

TOPE AND MUSHROOMS

2 oz. dried chanterelle mushrooms

4 tbsp. extra-virgin olive oil

4 tbsp. unsalted butter

3 garlic cloves, crushed

1 sprig rosemary

2 ½ lbs. tope fillets (shark)

¼ cup dry white wine, such as
Vernaccia di San Gimignano

Juice of 2 lemons

2 tbsp. chopped flat-leaf parsley
or chives

Salt and freshly ground pepper

Finferle (one of the many local names for chanterelle mushrooms) are small highly perfumed mushrooms that grow in the woods of the Maremma area around the end of November, especially if the season has been rainy. They are a darkish yellow color with an uneven cap, and they grow in large groups. They must be threaded on a needle and set to dry near a fireplace. Before being used they must be revived in warm water. They are excellent for the preparation of sauces for pasta and polenta.

Soak the mushrooms in warm water, drain, and squeeze dry. ✦ Put them in a pan with olive oil and butter and cook them for 10 minutes at low heat. ✦ Remove the mushrooms from the pan with a slotted spoon and set aside. ✦ Put the garlic in the pan with the rosemary. Add the tope fillets and cook at low heat. Taste for salt. ✦ When the fillets are opaque, add the mushrooms, then pour in the wine and lemon juice. ✦ Cook the sauce down for about 5 minutes, then add the parsley or chives and freshly ground pepper to taste.

FRIED TOPE

1 lb. tope (shark)

Extra-virgin olive oil

1 bunch flat-leaf parsley, chopped

Juice of 1 lemon

All-purpose flour, for dredging

2 large eggs, beaten

Salt and pepper

Scale the tope and cut them in small pieces. ✦ Marinate the pieces for a few hours in a bowl with olive oil, salt, pepper, parsley, and lemon juice; add olive oil to cover. ✦ Heat 1 inch of olive oil in a large pan until hot. Drain the fish. Dredge them in flour, dip in the eggs, and fry until golden. Serve very hot.

FRIED CATFISH

2 lbs. small catfish

1 ½ cups milk

CONTINUED

Clean the fish, removing the fins on the back, rinse, and dry well. ✦ Soak the fish in milk for 30 minutes. ✦ Mix the rosemary, garlic, salt, and pepper and add the fish, turning to coat. Cover and let stand 1 hour. ✦ Heat 1 inch of olive oil in a pan until hot. Remove them from the herbs,

1 sprig rosemary
1 garlic clove, chopped
Extra-virgin olive oil for frying
1 ½ cups all-purpose flour
Salt and pepper

dust them with the flour, and fry until brown on both sides, then drain on paper towels. ✦ Salt and pepper and serve while still very hot.

PESCE GATTO IN UMIDO 1

BRAISED CATFISH 1

EMILIA-ROMAGNA

4 medium-size catfish
3 tbsp. lard
1 medium onion, minced
1 bunch flat-leaf parsley, minced
1 garlic clove, minced
All-purpose flour, for dredging
½ cup dry white wine
4 tbsp. tomato purée
Salt and pepper

Serve with hot polenta. For the wine use Trebbiano or Albana di Romagna.

Clean and gut the catfish, leaving the heads but removing the backbones. ✦ Heat the lard and sauté the onion, parsley, and garlic; dredge the catfish in the flour and add them to the pan. ✦ Pour in the wine, let it evaporate, and add the tomato purée. ✦ Taste for salt and pepper. ✦ Cook for about 1 hour at low heat and serve.

PESCE GATTO IN UMIDO 2

BRAISED CATFISH 2

VENETO

1 large catfish, cleaned
All-purpose flour, for dredging
Sunflower oil
5 garlic cloves, finely chopped
1 bunch flat-leaf parsley, chopped
¼ cup tomato paste diluted in a little warm water
Salt and pepper

Dust the catfish in the flour. Heat 1 inch of oil in a pan until hot and fry until browned. ✦ Meanwhile, heat a little more oil in another pan and sauté the garlic and parsley; when the garlic begins to change color, add the catfish. ✦ Add salt and pepper to taste, then pour in the tomato paste mixture. ✦ Bring to a boil, cover, and simmer until the liquid has completely evaporated, leaving in the pan only about a half inch of sauce. Serve with slices of polenta.

PESCE PERSICO

PIKE-PERCH IN CREAM

PIEMONTE

4 perch, cleaned
½ cup extra-virgin olive oil
CONTINUED

This dish is typical of Verbania. For the wine use Arneis or Gavi.

Fillet the fish and place the fillets in the refrigerator as you continue. Use the fish bones and heads to make a broth, simmering in water to cover for 3 hours. The broth should be done before you begin the rest of the

1 scallion (or a small bunch
of chives), chopped

All-purpose flour, for dredging

¼ cup dry white wine

2 tbsp. cream

Salt and pepper

recipe. ✦ Heat the olive oil in a pan and sauté the scallion (or chives). Dredge the fish in the flour and add them to the pan. ✦ Add the wine and 1 cup of the fish broth. ✦ When the liquid has cooked away, add the cream; season with salt and pepper to taste. (Reserve the remaining fish broth for use in another recipe.)

FISH IN VEGETABLE SAUCE

PESCE SALSITO

SICILIA

1 celery heart, minced

⅓ cup chopped flat-leaf parsley

3 medium onions, finely chopped

Extra-virgin olive oil

10 green Sicilian olives, pitted

⅓ cup capers, rinsed and chopped

¼ cup tomato purée

2 tbsp. white wine vinegar

2 tbsp. sugar

2 lbs. sea bass, boiled and filleted

Cook the celery in a little water to cover. Remove with a slotted spoon and set aside. ✦ Repeat with the parsley and onions. ✦ Heat the olive oil in a pan and sauté the cooked vegetables until they begin to color. Add the olives and capers. ✦ After a few minutes add the tomato purée, vinegar, and sugar. ✦ Put the fish fillets on a serving plate and pour the sauce over them.

SWORDFISH ROLL-UPS

PESCE SPADA A GHIOTTA

CALABRIA

½ lb. crustless bread

½ cup pitted black olives, chopped

⅓ cup capers, rinsed

½ cup chopped flat-leaf parsley

Pinch chili pepper flakes

1¾ lbs. swordfish steaks,
1 inch thick

2 tbsp. olive oil

2 cups tomato sauce with basil
(see page 327)

Salt

This dish is typical of Reggio Calabria. Any remaining sauce can be used to dress spaghetti.

In a bowl, combine the bread, olives, capers, parsley, salt, chili pepper, and a little water; work these ingredients together well to blend them. ✦ Slice the steaks into ½-inch strips. Place a dollop of the bread mixture on each strip, roll up, and fix them with a toothpick. ✦ Heat the olive oil in a pan and cook the roll-ups, browning them on both sides. ✦ Meanwhile, heat the tomato sauce in a wide pan, and when the roll-ups are well cooked, transfer them to the sauce and cook them in it for a few minutes. ✦ Serve the roll-ups hot.

PESCE SPADA AL FORNO

BAKED SWORDFISH

CALABRIA

1 ¾ lbs. swordfish steaks
⅔ cup extra-virgin olive oil
Pinch chili pepper flakes
2 garlic cloves, minced
Salt

Preheat the oven to 400°F. Rinse the swordfish steaks. ✦ Put them in a baking pan, pour the olive oil over them, and season with salt, chili, and garlic, then bake until they are golden, about 20 minutes.

PESCE SPADA AL VAPORE 1

STEAMED SWORDFISH 1

CALABRIA

1 ¾ lbs. swordfish steaks
½ cup extra-virgin olive oil
¼ cup chopped flat-leaf parsley
Salt

Set up a steamer: Heat a large pot of water to boiling and place a perforated pan or heatproof colander on top so it does not touch the water. Add the fish in a single layer, cover, and steam until it is opaque, about 10 minutes. ✦ Season with olive oil, parsley, and salt and serve.

FISH

PESCE SPADA AL VAPORE 2

STEAMED SWORDFISH 2

SICILIA

1 ½ lbs. swordfish steak, in one piece
Pinch dried oregano
1 strip of lemon zest
Extra-virgin olive oil
Juice of 4 lemons
½ cup chopped flat-leaf parsley
1 garlic clove, minced
Salt and pepper

Put the swordfish steak in an earthenware pan. ✦ Season with oregano, lemon zest, and salt and pepper to taste, and cover with olive oil. ✦ Cover, place the pan in a larger pan, and pour in 1 inch water into the larger pan. Cook over low heat for about 2 hours. ✦ At the end of that time add the lemon juice, parsley, and garlic. Serve hot on a serving plate without removing the whitish coating that will have formed on the surface, which will make the fish tastier.

PESCE SPADA ALL'USO REGGINO

SWORDFISH WITH CAPERS

CALABRIA

Extra-virgin olive oil
CONTINUED

This dish is typical of Reggio Calabria. For the wine use Cirò or Code di Volpe.

Choose a pan big enough to hold the fish in a single layer. Heat the olive oil and sauté the onion until soft. ✦

1 medium onion, finely minced

1 ¾ lbs. swordfish steaks, skin removed

Pinch chili pepper flakes

¼ cup white wine

¼ cup chopped flat-leaf parsley

½ cup capers

1 tbsp. tomato purée

Salt

Add the swordfish and brown them a little on each side. ✦ Salt to taste, sprinkle with chili pepper, and add the wine. ✦ When the wine has evaporated, add the parsley, capers, and tomato purée and continue cooking at low heat for 3 to 4 minutes. Serve piping hot.

PESCE SPADA MENTA | SWORDFISH WITH MINT

CALABRIA

1 ¾ lbs. swordfish steaks

2 garlic cloves, cut in half

Homemade stale bread, grated (for breading)

Extra-virgin olive oil

2 tbsp. white wine vinegar

¼ cup mint leaves, chopped (or as many as desired)

Salt

Rub the fish steaks with garlic, salt them, then bread them. ✦ Heat ¼ inch olive oil and cook the fish until golden on both sides, then drain on paper towels and let cool. ✦ Arrange them on a serving plate, sprinkle with vinegar, and dust with mint leaves. ✦ Let rest for at least 30 minutes before serving.

PESCE SPADA CON PEPERONI | SWORDFISH WITH PEPPERS

SICILIA

¼ cup olive oil

1 medium onion, finely sliced

2 sweet yellow peppers, seeded and cut in strips

3 carrots, peeled

1 cup tomato purée

¼ cup chopped flat-leaf parsley

1 ½ lbs. swordfish steaks

Salt and pepper

This dish is typical of Catania. In some families there is the custom of frying the swordfish slices in olive oil before adding them to the other ingredients; in that case, the cooking time is reduced by half.

Heat half the olive oil and sauté the onion, adding salt and pepper. ✦ Heat the remaining olive oil in another pan and cook the peppers for a few minutes; in another pan boil the carrots in water to cover until just tender, then dice them. ✦ Combine the onion, peppers, carrots, and tomato purée in a pan. ✦ Add pepper to taste, parsley, and finally the swordfish. ✦ Stir, taste for salt, and bring to a simmer over low heat. Cook at low heat for 30 minutes. Serve hot.

SWORDFISH WITH CAPERS AND LEMON

PESCE SPADA CON CAPPERI E LEMON

CALABRIA

¼ cup extra-virgin olive oil
2 or 3 garlic cloves
1¾ lbs. swordfish steaks
½ cup capers
2 tbsp. chopped flat-leaf parsley
Pinch dried oregano
Juice of 1 lemon
Salt

Heat the olive oil in a pan and sauté the garlic; remove (and discard) the garlic, then add the swordfish and capers. ✦ Salt to taste and add the parsley and oregano; add the lemon juice and cook until the fish is cooked through.

SWORDFISH WITH OLIVES AND CAPERS

PESCE SPADA CON OLIVE E CAPPERI

CALABRIA

¼ cup extra-virgin olive oil
2 medium onions, finely sliced
1¾ lbs. swordfish steaks
1 cup tomato purée
½ cup pitted black olives, chopped
1 tbsp. capers
Salt

The dialect name of this dish, *Pisci-spatu a ra matalotta*, is from the French phrase *à la matelote*, meaning "marinated."

Heat the olive oil in a pan, sauté the onions, then add the swordfish, stirring so that the pieces cook on both sides. ✦ Add the tomato purée, olives, and capers, and salt to taste. ✦ Serve at room temperature, arranging the steaks on a serving plate and covering them with the sauce.

SWORDFISH WITH CAPERS

PESCE SPADA DI BAGNARA

CALABRIA

1¼ lbs. swordfish steaks, skin removed
1 cup extra-virgin olive oil, or as needed
½ cup capers
2 garlic cloves, minced
1 bunch flat-leaf parsley, chopped
1½ lemons, sliced
Salt and freshly ground black pepper

This dish is typical of Bagnara.

Arrange the steaks in layers in a terra-cotta pan with a wide bottom and high sides, seasoning each layer with olive oil, capers, garlic, parsley, a few lemon slices, and salt and pepper to taste. Sprinkle the last layer with more olive oil. ✦ Place the pan in a water bath and cook, preferably using a copper pot, about 1½ hours, during which time the pan with the fish should remain uncovered. Do not stir.

SWORDFISH IN SALMORIGLIO SAUCE

PESCE SPADA IN SALMORIGLIO

CALABRIA

Extra-virgin olive oil
1¾ lbs. swordfish steaks
Lemon juice
2 tbsp. chopped fresh oregano
2 tbsp. chopped flat-leaf parsley
1 garlic clove, minced
A few capers, chopped
1 tsp. grated lemon zest
Salt and pepper

Grease a grill grate with olive oil, put it over hot coals, and as soon as it is hot, cook the swordfish, turning, until the flesh is opaque when prodded. ✦ Make the *salmoriglio* sauce: Mix 3 parts olive oil with 1 part lemon juice with the oregano, parsley, garlic, and salt and pepper to taste. ✦ Add the capers and lemon zest. Serve on top of the fish.

BAKED SWORDFISH

PESCE SPADA IN TEGAME

CALABRIA

1¾ lbs. swordfish steaks
All-purpose flour, for dredging
½ cup extra-virgin olive oil
¼ cup dry white wine
Juice of ½ lemon
2 garlic cloves, minced
½ medium onion, finely chopped
1 tbsp. minced flat-leaf parsley
Bread dough (see page 13) or foil
Salt and pepper

For the wine use Cirò or Coda di Volpe.

Preheat the oven to 400°F. Dust the fish with the flour, place in a pan, and season with olive oil, salt, and pepper. Add the wine and lemon juice, then the garlic, onion, and parsley. ✦ Cover the pan, sealing the edges with bread dough or wrapping the entire pan in aluminum foil. ✦ Bake for about 30 minutes, until the dough is golden or the liquid is bubbling and the fish is opaque.

SOUSED FISH

PESCHERIA IN CARPIONE

LOMBARDIA

1 lb. small fish,
such as baby sardines
All-purpose flour, for dredging
2 tbsp. extra-virgin olive oil
2 tbsp. unsalted butter

CONTINUED

Without cleaning them, dust the fish in the flour. Heat half the olive oil in a pan until hot and fry them until golden; set aside. ✦ In another pan, heat the remaining olive oil and butter and cook the carrot, celery, scallions, and sage leaves. ✦ Add the garlic and peppercorns. ✦ When the vegetables begin to pale, add the vinegar, bring the contents to a boil, and add the fish. ✦ Cover the pan, take it off the heat, and let it cool. This dish is

1 carrot, sliced

1 celery stalk, sliced

3 scallions, chopped

2 sage leaves, chopped

1 garlic clove

½ cup white wine vinegar

Salt and 4 peppercorns, cracked

excellent alone the next day, but is even tastier when served with polenta.

PIKE-PERCH IN SHRIMP AND MUSHROOM SAUCE

PESCI PERSICI
CON IL RAGOTTINO

LOMBARDIA

¼ lb. (1 stick) unsalted butter

4 tbsp. all-purpose flour

2 lbs. pike-perch fillets

2 cups fish broth

¾ lb. shrimp, shelled and cut in half lengthwise

1 oz. dried mushrooms, soaked in lukewarm water, drained, and chopped (may substitute ½ lb. fresh porcini, chopped)

2 small truffles (about 2 oz.), thinly sliced

Salt

The *"ragottino"* in the Italian name means "little ragù," meaning a prepared sauce made with various elements. This is a long-forgotten nineteenth-century recipe from Lake Como.

Put 4 tablespoons of the butter in a pan and as soon as it melts add 2 tablespoons of the flour and brown it. ✦ Add the fish fillets, salt, and enough broth to cover the fish with an inch of liquid. ✦ Continue cooking. ✦ In another pan heat the remaining butter and stir in the remaining flour. Add the shrimp, mushrooms, and ½ cup of the remaining broth. Let this simmer until thickened. ✦ Remove the pan from the heat and add the truffles. Put the fish on a serving plate and cover with the sauce.

FRIED FISH

PESCI PETTINE FRITTI

CALABRIA

Extra-virgin olive oil for frying

4 *sùrici* (grenadier fish; can use turbot), cleaned

All-purpose flour, for dredging

2 lemons, cut in half

Salt

Sùrici, a flat fish with delicate flesh and of the species *Xyrichthys novacula*, are common in the sea off Calabria. At Tropea and Sant'Eufemia there is the custom of giving the fish a sharp blow with the back of a knife just above the tail to break the spine so that the fish, while cooking, will swell up.

Heat 1 inch of olive oil in a pan until hot. Rinse and dry the fish, dust them with the flour, add salt, and fry until golden and crunchy. Drain on paper towels. Serve with lemon halves.

POLIPETTI AFFOGATI ALLA CIVITAVECCHIESE

LAZIO

¼ cup extra-virgin olive oil
4 garlic cloves, finely minced
¼ cup chopped flat-leaf parsley
2 lbs. baby octopuses, cleaned and rinsed
¼ cup dry white wine
Pinch chili pepper flakes
Salt

OCTOPUS IN WINE

For the wine use Frascati or Orvieto.

Heat half the olive oil in a pan and cook the garlic and parsley. Add the remaining olive oil and the octopuses and let them color a little. ✦ Add the wine and chili pepper, and when most of the wine has evaporated, add 1 cup of boiling water. Salt to taste and slowly cook with the pan covered. Serve lukewarm.

POLPETTE DI ALICI

CALABRIA

¾ lb. fresh anchovies
Extra-virgin olive oil for frying
2 large eggs, beaten
2 tbsp. grated pecorino
1 tbsp. chopped flat-leaf parsley
All-purpose flour, for dredging
Salt

ANCHOVY BALLS

Bone the anchovies and cut off their heads. Heat 2 tablespoons olive oil in a pan and lightly sauté them. ✦ Break them up into small pieces, then add the eggs, pecorino, parsley, and salt. ✦ When all of these ingredients are thoroughly blended, take the pan off the heat. When the mixture is cool enough to handle, form it into balls, then roll the balls in flour. Heat 1 inch of oil in a pan until hot and fry them until golden. Drain on paper towels.

POLPI AFFOGATI

CALABRIA

2 lbs. octopuses
1 lb. fresh plum tomatoes, peeled, seeded, and cut in pieces
3 garlic cloves, chopped
Salt and pepper

OCTOPUS IN WINE

A recommended variation includes ¼ cup each capers, olives, and parsley or oregano.

O purpe se coce int'all'acqua soia ("Octopus should cook in its own water") says a Neapolitan proverb so, after having cleaned the octopuses, not forgetting to remove their eyes but without touching the skin, put them in a somewhat tall earthenware pan together with the tomatoes, salt, pepper, and garlic. ✦ Cover the pan and cook at medium heat for about 30 minutes. Serve lukewarm.

STEWED OCTOPUS "IN PURGATORY"

POLPI IN PURGATORIO

MOLISE

1 lb. octopus
2 medium onions, finely chopped
¼ cup extra-virgin olive oil
2 tbsp. chopped flat-leaf parsley
Pinch chili pepper flakes
Salt and pinch pepper

Clean the octopus in salted water, then rinse it well.
✦ Put the octopus in a pan with the onions, olive oil, parsley, chili pepper flakes, salt, and pepper and cook at low heat for about 2 hours, stirring from time to time with a wooden spoon. ✦ Add a little water and cook it away. Serve tepid.

STEWED OCTOPUS

POLPO ALLA LUCIANA

CAMPANIA

1 octopus, weighing about 1¾ lbs., cleaned
¼ cup extra-virgin olive oil
2 tbsp. chopped flat-leaf parsley
1 garlic clove, minced
Salt and pepper

This dish is typical of Naples.

Put the octopus in a terra-cotta pan big enough to hold it. ✦ Add salt and pepper to taste and the olive oil. ✦ Cover the pan with two sheets of wax paper, tying them around the rim, put on the lid, and cook at very low heat for about 2 hours, shaking the pan from time to time to keep the octopus from sticking. ✦ Remove the paper and let the octopus cook for a few minutes more. Add the parsley and garlic and serve hot.

ANGLER IN TOMATO SAUCE

RANA PESCATRICE ALL'OTRANTINA

PUGLIA

½ cup extra-virgin olive oil
1 medium onion, thinly sliced
1 garlic clove, minced
1½ lbs. angler, cleaned and cut in small hunks
All-purpose flour, for dredging
½ cup dry white wine
1¼ cups chopped plum tomatoes
Pinch dried oregano
2 tbsp. chopped flat-leaf parsley
1 cup vegetable broth, warmed
Sliced peasant-style bread
Salt and pepper

This dish is typical of Lecce.

Heat a little olive oil in a pan and add the onion, then the garlic. ✦ When these have browned, dredge the pieces of fish in the flour and add them to the pan. ✦ Fry the pieces on both sides, adding salt and pepper and then the wine. ✦ When the wine evaporates, add the tomatoes, oregano, and parsley. ✦ Add a cup of vegetable broth, cover, and cook at moderate heat for 15 to 20 minutes. Serve hot on slices of peasant-style bread.

FISH

| # MARINATED SKATE

1 skate wing, cleaned and filleted
Extra-virgin olive oil for frying
All-purpose flour, for dredging
2 cups white wine vinegar
Pinch saffron threads
Pickled vegetables (peppers, olives, etc.), for serving

Rinse and pat dry the skate, then cut it into slices about 2 inches wide and 4 inches long. ✦ Heat ¼ inch of olive oil in a pan until hot. Dredge the fish in the flour and fry until golden. Drain and let cool. ✦ Meanwhile, bring the vinegar and saffron to a boil, remove from the heat, cover, and let steep. When the skate is cool enough to handle, cover them with the vinegar infusion and refrigerate for about 1 week. ✦ Drain and serve at room temperature.

ROTOLO DI TONNO | # TUNA ROLL

PIEMONTE

10 oz. (or so) canned tuna
2 large eggs, beaten
3 large egg yolks
2 tbsp. grated Parmigiano-Reggiano
1 tsp. sugar
1 tsp. strong yellow mustard
Juice of 1 lemon
1 cup extra-virgin olive oil
Salt

This dish is typical of Turin.

Crumble the tuna and mix it with the eggs, 1 egg yolk, cheese, and sugar and pass this mixture through a fine strainer. ✦ Shape the resulting purée into a log, cover with a cloth, and sew the cloth closed. ✦ Place in a pot of boiling lightly salted water and simmer for about 15 minutes. ✦ Remove the roll from the water and set it aside to cool. ✦ Meanwhile, make the mayonnaise. In a blender, combine the remaining egg yolks, mustard, and lemon juice. Turn the blender on and add the olive oil in a thin stream to make a pale creamy mixture. ✦ When the tuna roll has cooled, remove it from the cloth and slice it in lengths about ½ to 1 inch thick. ✦ Serve these on a plate with the mayonnaise. This can be served cold in the summer.

SARDE A BECCAFICO | # STUFFED SARDINES

SICILIA

In eastern and central Sicilia stuffed sardines like these are joined in pairs, tied with kitchen twine, and dipped in egg and breadcrumbs and fried in olive oil. The *beccafico* is a kind of warbler fond of figs; in the summer it becomes plump and tasty. The sardine dish is thus named for the bird by way of analogy: Stuffed sardines resemble the birds. There is a great deal of diversity in terms of the filling used (varying from town to town and from one side of the island to the other) and in terms of the preparation: In some places the

Olive oil for the pan

1½ lbs. fresh sardines, cleaned

8 bay leaves

½ cup fresh breadcrumbs

For the filling:

⅔ cup toasted breadcrumbs

1 tbsp. extra-virgin olive oil

1 tbsp. lemon juice

Grated zest of 1 lemon

½ tsp. sugar

4 anchovies in olive oil,
minced with their oil

2 tbsp. chopped flat-leaf parsley

½ cup capers

½ cup pitted black olives,
finely chopped

⅓ cup golden raisins, chopped

⅓ cup pine nuts, chopped

½ cup toasted and
chopped almonds

Salt and pepper

stuffing is put in the fish singly (eastern Sicilia), in others (eastern and central) two sardines are put together. This recipe is typical of Palermo.

Preheat the oven to 425°F. Grease a baking pan with olive oil. Rinse the sardines and open them lengthwise like a book. ✦ Mix together all the filling ingredients. When the filling mixture is thoroughly blended, spread a little on each sardine, then fold it closed, pressing lightly with your fingers. ✦ Twist the sardines, being careful not to squeeze out any of the filling, and shape them into rings with the tail sticking upward. ✦ Arrange these rings in the baking pan with the tails sticking up, placing bay leaves between them. ✦ Sprinkle with a little olive oil and the breadcrumbs and bake for 10 to 15 minutes.

SARDINES IN VINEGAR

SARDE IN SAÒR

VENETO

1¾ lbs. fresh sardines, cleaned

All-purpose flour, for dredging

Extra-virgin olive oil

1 lb. onions, sliced in rings

2 cups white wine vinegar

Several whole cloves

2 bay leaves, crumbled

Salt

This is a dish of the sea, reminiscent of the Venetian fleet and its constant problems providing victuals in days long before the refrigerator. This dish lasts a long time thanks to the *saòr*, meaning its marinade, which combines the humble queen of Venetian gardens, the white onion, with the modest but equally flavorful sardine.

Dust the sardines with the flour. Heat 1 inch oil in a pan until hot and fry the sardines. Drain on paper towels. ✦ In another pan, heat 2 tablespoons oil over low heat and slowly sauté the onions. Add the vinegar and when it boils, immediately turn off the heat. ✦ Arrange the sardines in a terra-cotta bowl and cover them with some of the onion mixture. ✦ Add salt, cloves, and bay leaves, then cover with the remaining marinade. Cover the container and refrigerate overnight. ✦ The sardines can be eaten beginning the next day, used either as a main dish or an appetizer.

SARDE SALATE

Salting sardines in this traditional Sicilian manner is still done in summer by many families near the seaside. The fresh fish, after cleaning in salt water—never in fresh water—would be layered in a tin barrel with heavy amounts of coarse salt and covered with a heavy weight. While the fish would be ready after about two weeks, tradition dictated waiting closer to a month. The salted fish would then be rinsed in vinegar and enjoyed with slices of bread and onion doused in olive oil, or used in myriad traditional Sicilian recipes calling for sardines.

SARDINE RIPIENE ALLA PUGLIESE

STUFFED SARDINES

FOR 10 PERSONS

PUGLIA

1 cup extra-virgin olive oil, or as needed

30 fresh sardines, cleaned and filleted

3 large eggs, beaten

½ cup grated pecorino

⅔ cup breadcrumbs

1 tbsp. chopped flat-leaf parsley

Preheat the oven to 400°F. Grease a baking pan with olive oil. ✦ Set the sardines out on a cloth to dry. ✦ Mix the eggs, cheese, breadcrumbs, parsley, and enough olive oil to form a mixture (it should not be too compact). ✦ Put some of the filling inside each sardine and fold it closed; arrange the stuffed sardines in the baking pan. ✦ Sprinkle with the remaining olive oil and bake for about 15 minutes.

SARDONCINI AL COCCIO

SAUTÉED BABY SARDINES

EMILIA-ROMAGNA

About 1 lb. *sardoncini* (see note)

Extra-virgin olive oil

1 small onion, chopped

Juice of ½ lemon

Pepper

This dish is typical of the spring in Cesenatico. *Sardoncini* (also known as *bagigi*) are tiny baby sardines.

Pull the heads off the young sardines by hand, then rinse them well under running water. ✦ In an earthenware pan, heat a little olive oil over low heat and sauté the onion, then delicately (so they will not break) add the sardines. ✦ Cover the pan and cook the fish very quickly at high heat. ✦ After no more than 1 minute open the pan and add a generous amount of pepper and the lemon juice, then cover the pan and continue cooking, still at high heat, for another 30 seconds. Serve at once.

SAUTÉED CLAMS
SAUTÉ DI VONGOLE

CAMPANIA

4 ½ lbs. clams
2 tbsp. extra-virgin olive oil
1 garlic clove, minced
2 tbsp. chopped flat-leaf parsley
Salt and pepper

Variation: This sauté can also be performed with tomatoes. In that case, crush 3 or 4 plum tomatoes in the saucepan after frying the garlic. Let them cook a few minutes before adding the clams.

Purge the clams in water and salt or in seawater, then rinse them well. ✦ Heat the olive oil in a large pot and sauté the garlic. Add the clams and some pepper; cover the pan and raise the heat to high. ✦ After about 10 minutes, stir the clams around; when they open, add the parsley and serve hot.

BOILED COD
SBURRITA DI BACCALÀ

TOSCANA

¾ lb. salt-dried cod, soaked and drained (see note, page 437)
4 garlic cloves, crushed
½ cup *nepitella*, chopped (see note, page 92)
2-inch piece of ginger, chopped
½ cup extra-virgin olive oil
Sliced bread

This dish is typical of Elba.

Cut the soaked cod in 1-inch pieces. ✦ Put the garlic in a pot half-filled with cold water, adding a handful of *nepitella* and ginger. ✦ Put the pot over heat, and when the water begins to boil, add the olive oil. Let it boil for about 30 minutes, then add the cod. ✦ Let it boil again for about 10 minutes at very low heat. ✦ When the cod is cooked, arrange slices of bread in a tureen, pour over the broth, and top with the cod. Serve hot.

FRIED EEL MARINATED IN VINEGAR SAUCE
SCAVECCIO

TOSCANA

3 cups white vinegar (made from good white wine)
½-inch piece fresh chili pepper
2 garlic cloves, crushed
½ tsp. whole peppercorns

CONTINUED

This dish is typical of Orbetello and this same procedure can be used with small fried fish. Marinated eel, eel in *carpione*, etc., are dishes that resemble *scaveccio*, which differs, however, in several small ways. For example, marinated eel is made using roast eel, whereas in *scaveccio* the eel is fried.

Dilute 2 cups of the vinegar with 1 cup water (or, even better, with white wine). ✦ Add the chili pepper, garlic, peppercorns, and rosemary and bring to a boil; now the

Several sprigs rosemary

2 lbs. eels, cleaned, heads and tails removed

Extra-virgin olive oil for frying

sauce is ready. ✦ Cut the eels into sections about 4 inches long, rinsing these in the remaining 1 cup of vinegar. ✦ Heat ½ inch olive oil in a pan until hot and add the eels. Fry, turning, until browned on all sides and cooked through. Remove with a slotted spatula and drain on paper towels. ✦ Put the eels in an earthenware pot or a glass jar. Pour over the vinegar sauce, cover, and refrigerate. ✦ After three or four days the eel will be ready to eat.

SEPPIE A ZEMINO

STEWED CUTTLEFISH 1

LIGURIA

2 lbs. cuttlefish

½ cup olive oil

¼ cup chopped flat-leaf parsley

2 celery stalks, finely chopped

1 medium onion, finely chopped

1 garlic clove, minced

1 lb. chard, cored, tough rib removed

1 oz. dried mushrooms, soaked in warm water, drained, and chopped

¼ cup pine nuts, ground in a mortar

1 tbsp. all-purpose flour

Clean and rinse the cuttlefish and cut in strips or small pieces. Rinse and drain them, then put them in a saucepan with the olive oil and the parsley, celery, onion, and garlic. Heat over low heat. ✦ Meanwhile, parboil the chard, squeeze dry, chop, and add to the cuttlefish. ✦ After 10 or 15 minutes, add the mushrooms, pine nuts, flour, and 1 tablespoon water. ✦ Cook for about 45 minutes, or until the cuttlefish is tender.

SEPPIE IN ZIMINO

STEWED CUTTLEFISH 2

TOSCANA

1½ lbs. cuttlefish, cleaned

3 tbsp. extra-virgin olive oil

1 medium onion, minced

1 celery stalk, minced

2 tbsp. chopped flat-leaf parsley

1½ lbs. chard, cored and coarsely chopped

1 tbsp. tomato purée

Salt and pepper

This dish is typical of Antignano (Livorno).

Clean the cuttlefish and cut them in pieces. ✦ Heat the olive oil in a pan and cook the onion, celery, and parsley until the vegetables are soft. Add the chard. ✦ Cover and cook 15 minutes; add the cuttlefish and salt and pepper to taste; after another 10 minutes, add the tomato purée and continue cooking. Serve lukewarm.

SCHILLE OR CRAGNONI
CON AGLIO E OLIO

Schille, known in Venice as *schie*, are gray saltwater crustaceans that superficially resemble crayfish; even after cooking they retain their gray color. In this recipe typical of the Veneto, the *schille* would be cooked in salted water in a terra-cotta container only until a thick foam formed on the surface of the water. The *schille* would then be cooled, removed from their shells, seasoned with olive oil, garlic, and parsley, and served over soft white polenta.

SEPPIE RIPIENE 1 | # STUFFED CUTTLEFISH 1

LIGURIA

1 cup breadcrumbs
⅓ cup grated Parmigiano-Reggiano
1 garlic clove, minced
1 bunch flat-leaf parsley, chopped
½ cup extra-virgin olive oil, or as needed
4 medium cuttlefish, cleaned
White wine
Pitted olives

For the wine use Pigato or Vermentino.

Preheat the oven to 350°F. Combine the breadcrumbs, cheese, garlic, and parsley to make a filling, adding olive oil as needed. ✦ Stuff into the cuttlefish and arrange them in a pan. Add white wine to cover and olives to taste. Cover and bake for 20 minutes. Serve lukewarm.

SEPPIE RIPIENE 2 | # STUFFED CUTTLEFISH 2

PUGLIA

2 lbs. cuttlefish
1 cup breadcrumbs
½ cup grated pecorino
CONTINUED

Preheat the oven to 400°F. Clean the cuttlefish without cutting them in half; rinse them well, then drain. ✦ Combine the breadcrumbs, cheese, garlic, parsley, capers, salt and pepper, and black olives; mix well, then add the eggs, combining thoroughly to make the filling. ✦ Stuff the cuttlefish and arrange them in a baking pan; drizzle

1 garlic clove, minced
2 tbsp. chopped flat-leaf parsley
¼ cup capers
¼ cup pitted black olives, chopped
2 large eggs, beaten
Extra-virgin olive oil
½ cup white wine
Salt and pepper

generously with olive oil, add the wine, and bake about 1 hour. Let rest a few minutes before serving.

STUFFED SMALL CUTTLEFISH 1

SEPPIOLINE RIPIENE 1

EMILIA-ROMAGNA

Extra-virgin olive oil
6 black cuttlefish, each weighing 4 oz.
1 cup breadcrumbs
1 garlic clove, minced
3 tbsp. chopped flat-leaf parsley
Salt

Preheat the oven to 350°F. Grease a baking pan with olive oil. Clean the small cuttlefish, using scissors to cut away the belly but leaving the bone attached; chop the tentacles and set them aside. ✦ Prepare a filling by combining the breadcrumbs, garlic, parsley, salt, and enough olive oil to bind. ✦ Stuff the cuttlefish with the filling, adding the chopped tentacles. ✦ Tie closed with kitchen twine. ✦ Place in the prepared pan and bake for about 30 minutes.

STUFFED SMALL CUTTLEFISH 2

FOR 6 PERSONS

SEPPIOLINE RIPIENE 2

SICILIA

2 lbs. small cuttlefish, cleaned
1 lb. crustless bread, crumbled
1 garlic clove, minced
2 tbsp. chopped flat-leaf parsley
1 tbsp. capers, chopped
2 tbsp. grated Parmigiano-Reggiano
1 tbsp. grated caciocavallo
3 tbsp. extra-virgin olive oil
Salt and pepper

Preheat the oven to 350°F. Drain the cuttlefish well. ✦ Mix the bread, garlic, parsley, capers, Parmigiano-Reggiano, caciocavallo, salt, pepper, and olive oil. ✦ Stuff this into the cuttlefish and arrange them in a baking pan. Bake for 30 minutes.

BAKED PASTA WITH ANCHOVIES

¾ lb. fresh anchovies, cleaned

Pinch chili pepper flakes

2 tbsp. white wine vinegar

¼ cup dry white wine

Juice of ½ lemon

1 cup breadcrumbs

2 tbsp. unsalted butter, melted

1 ½ cups tomato purée

½ medium onion, finely chopped

1 garlic clove, minced

⅓ cup extra-virgin olive oil

2 cups fish stock

½ lb. fresh egg pasta
(see page 337), cooked

Salt and pepper

For the béchamel:

3 tbsp. unsalted butter

3 tbsp. all-purpose flour

2 cups milk

Pinch grated nutmeg

Salt and pepper

Fish stock is used here to make the béchamel lighter and more suitable to the strong taste of the anchovies. For the wine use Soave, Lugana, or bianco di Custiza.

Preheat the oven to 400°F. Arrange the anchovies in a single layer in a baking pan. ✦ Season the anchovies with salt, pepper, chili pepper, vinegar, wine, lemon juice, breadcrumbs, and melted butter. ✦ Bake for 10 minutes. ✦ Remove from the oven and when cool enough, remove the bones from the anchovies and put them with their cooking liquid in a saucepan. ✦ Separately combine the tomato purée, onion, garlic, and olive oil and pour this in the saucepan with the anchovies, diluting with fish stock. Bring to a boil and add salt and pepper. ✦ Use the butter, flour, and milk to make the béchamel as on page 339. Add the nutmeg. ✦ In the baking pan, alternate layers of pasta, béchamel sauce, and the anchovies, making at least 2 layers of each in total. Bake for 10 minutes until hot and bubbling.

SHRIMP AND PORCINI GRATIN

¼ lb. (½ cup) unsalted butter

½ cup all-purpose flour

4 cups milk, warmed

1 ⅓ cups grated
Parmigiano-Reggiano

2 garlic cloves

¾ lb. shelled shrimp

¼ cup white wine

Pinch nutmeg

½ cup cognac

2 tbsp. olive oil

CONTINUED

Preheat the oven to 400°F. Use 3 tablespoons of the butter, the flour, and milk to make a béchamel sauce (see page 339). Season with salt and pepper. ✦ Simmer over very low heat for 10 minutes; pass this mixture through a sieve to eliminate any lumps. ✦ Remove the pan from the heat and whisk in half the Parmigiano-Reggiano. ✦ Heat the remaining butter in a pan and add 1 garlic clove, discarding the clove as soon as it darkens. ✦ Add the shrimp and wine and continue cooking. Add the nutmeg, salt, pepper, and cognac. ✦ In another pan, heat the olive oil and cook the mushrooms with the remaining garlic, salt, and pepper; add the parsley. ✦ Add the mushrooms to the shrimp, then add the egg yolk, cream,

1⅔ cups chopped
porcini mushrooms
¼ cup chopped flat-leaf parsley
1 large egg yolk
⅓ cup cream
Salt and pepper

and the remaining Parmigiano-Reggiano. ✦ Mix with the béchamel and transfer to a baking dish. Gratinée in the oven for 10 minutes, or until lightly browned.

SGOMBRI ALL'ACETO

MACKEREL IN VINEGAR

PUGLIA

2 lbs. mackerel or mackerel fillets
White wine vinegar
½ cup olive oil
8 mint leaves
2 garlic cloves, finely chopped
Salt

Typical of Bari, this preparation has been used as a way to preserve fish. After the fish are marinated, you can pack them in sterilized glass jars and cover with olive oil; place a lid on the jars but do not seal. This way they will keep, in the refrigerator, for at least a week. As for how long to cook the fish, in Puglia it is said the fish should be boiled for the time it takes to recite the "Our Father."

Cut off the heads of the fish, remove the bones, and wrap each pair of fillets in cheesecloth. ✦ Cook the wrapped fillets a few minutes in lightly salted boiling water. ✦ Remove them from the water, drain them, put them in a bowl, and cover them with vinegar, leaving them to marinate for about 1 hour. ✦ After that time, drain off the vinegar, remove the cheesecloth, and line up the fillets on a serving plate. ✦ Sprinkle with olive oil, mint, and garlic. Chill the fish and eat them cold.

SOGLIOLA AI FERRI

GRILLED SOLE

EMILIA-ROMAGNA

1 cup olive oil
Juice from ½ lemon
3 tbsp. breadcrumbs
1¾ lbs. sole, cleaned
Salt and pepper

This is a classic preparation in the Romagna area. It requires a fish grill so that the fish can remain in position during the cooking and can be turned without being damaged.

Mix the olive oil, lemon juice, a little salt, very little pepper, and breadcrumbs. Turn the fish in the mixture and let marinate for about 1 hour refrigerated. ✦ Prepare a grill so that it is very hot. Remove the fish from the marinade, place in a fish basket, and cook over the very hot grill, turning as necessary, until the flesh of the fish is opaque when prodded.

SOLE IN WINE

SOGLIOLA AL VINO

EMILIA-ROMAGNA

1¾ lbs. sole, cleaned
All-purpose flour, for dredging
½ cup unsalted butter
½ cup dry white wine
Juice of 1 lemon
1 cup fish broth
2 tbsp. chopped flat-leaf parsley
Salt and pepper

For the wine use Trebbiano or Albana di Romagna.

For this dish the sole should be lightly dusted with the flour. Heat ¼ cup butter in a pan over low heat, add the fish, and brown lightly. ✦ Add the wine and let it evaporate, then add the lemon juice and fish broth. Add salt and pepper to taste. ✦ Brown the remaining butter in a pan until it gives off a nutty fragrance. Serve the sole in their cooking liquid, garnished with parsley and browned butter.

GRILLED SOLE

SOGLIOLA IN GRATICOLA

EMILIA-ROMAGNA

3 lbs. sole, each weighing about ¾ lb., cleaned
1⅔ cups olive oil
½ cup breadcrumbs
Salt and pepper

This dish is typical of Romagna.

Heat a grill to high heat. Rinse the fish, then dry with a cloth. ✦ Mix the olive oil, salt, pepper, and breadcrumbs and add the fish. Let stand about 20 minutes, then put them on a hot grill, turning them several times as they cook. Serve immediately.

SOLE WITH PEPPERS

SOGLIOLE CON I PEPERONI

CALABRIA

⅓ cup extra-virgin olive oil
1 medium onion, thinly sliced
2 garlic cloves, minced
¾ lb. sweet peppers, cored, seeded, and minced
1⅔ cups chopped fresh plum tomatoes
2 lbs. *sunici* (sole), cleaned, rinsed, and dried
Salt

Heat the olive oil in a pan and cook the onion and garlic until they take on color, then add the peppers and tomatoes. ✦ Cook at low heat for 15 minutes, then add the sole. ✦ Add salt to taste, cover the pan, and cook at low heat, shaking the pan from time to time.

FISH

SEA BASS WITH TOMATO

SPIGOLA ALLA PITARILLARA

MOLISE

¼ cup extra-virgin olive oil

1 garlic clove

6 plum tomatoes, peeled and chopped

1 basil leaf

½ sweet pepper, minced

2 tbsp. minced flat-leaf parsley

1 fresh sea bass, cleaned and cut into slices

Salt

Heat the olive oil in a pan and cook the garlic. Add the tomatoes, basil, sweet pepper, parsley, and salt to taste. ✦ When the tomatoes have cooked down, add the sea bass. ✦ Stir, add 1 tablespoon water, then cover the pan and cook for 15 minutes. Serve hot.

SEA BASS STUFFED WITH SEAFOOD

SPIGOLA IMBOTTITA DI FRUTTI DI MARE

CAMPANIA

1 small cuttlefish, cleaned

1 squid, cleaned

Extra-virgin olive oil

2 garlic cloves

½ lb. mixed shellfish, shelled

¼ lb. shelled shrimp

1 fresh anchovy

2 tbsp. chopped flat-leaf parsley

2 lbs. sea bass fillet

Dash white wine vinegar

Pepper

Preheat the oven to 350°F. Cut the cuttlefish and squid into small pieces. Heat half of the olive oil in a large pan and sauté 1 garlic clove. ✦ When the garlic has colored, remove it and add the cuttlefish and squid; turn off the heat and add the shellfish, shrimp, anchovy, half of the parsley, and pepper. ✦ Arrange these ingredients along the inside of the sea bass, then sew it closed with kitchen string. ✦ Mince the remaining garlic clove and add it to a baking pan with the fish, the remaining olive oil, vinegar, the remaining parsley, and salt. ✦ Bake until the fish is cooked through, about 30 minutes. Slice and serve.

SEA BASS IN WINE SAUCE

SPIGOLE ALL' ORISTANESE

SARDEGNA

3 tbsp. extra-virgin olive oil

1 medium onion, finely sliced

1 bunch flat-leaf parsley, chopped

4 medium sea bass (about 2 lbs.), cleaned and rinsed

1 cup pitted olives

½ cup Vernaccia di Oristano wine

This dish is typical of Oristano.

Heat the olive oil and cook the onion and parsley. ✦ As soon as the onion colors, add the fish and cook it at low heat for about 10 minutes. ✦ Add the olives and wine, cover the pan, and cook until opaque.

SQUADRO ALLA MATALOTTA

MONKFISH WITH OLIVES

SICILIA

2 tbsp. extra-virgin olive oil

½ medium onion, finely sliced

2 garlic cloves, minced

12 green olives, pitted and chopped

1 tbsp. capers

2 tbsp. chopped flat-leaf parsley

A few basil leaves

½ cup tomato purée

2 lbs. monkfish or halibut fillets, sliced

Like the recipe on page 475, this is another fish preparation named for the French *matelote*. This method can be applied to any saltwater fish, but is best if the fish has firm, compact flesh. Fresh plum tomatoes can be used instead of the prepared sauce. In that case, cook the tomatoes for 10 minutes before adding the fish.

Heat the olive oil in a pan and sauté the onion and garlic. ✦ Add the olives, capers, parsley, basil, and tomato purée. ✦ Stir, then add the fish and cook for 15 to 20 minutes, depending on the thickness of the slices.

STOCCAFISSO ACCOMODATO

STOCKFISH AND POTATO STEW

LIGURIA

¼ cup extra-virgin olive oil

3 salt-cured anchovies, boned and rinsed

1 large onion, finely chopped

1 carrot, finely chopped

1 celery stalk, finely chopped

¼ cup dried mushrooms, soaked in warm water, drained, and chopped

1 garlic clove, minced

2 lbs. *unsalted* dried cod, cleaned, skinned, and chopped (see note)

½ cup pitted green olives (or as many as desired)

½ cup pine nuts (or as many as desired)

1 cup vegetable broth (or warm water)

2 medium potatoes, peeled and cubed

Salt and pepper

Throughout Italy, *stoccafisso* is generally the name used for unsalted dried cod. Not to be confused with *baccalà* (salt-dried cod), *stoccafisso* is made with little or no salt. *Stoccafisso* requires much less soaking than *baccalà* before cooking. *Stoccafisso* should be soaked in water to cover for an hour, drained, and then beaten with a mallet on a clean work surface. This beating tenderizes the fish. Then it should be boiled in fresh water to cover for about 10 minutes, and drained. If the *stoccafisso* is not a fillet, then remove the skin and bones at this point.

Heat the olive oil in a pan (preferably earthenware). Add the anchovies and cook, breaking them up with the tines of a wooden fork, keeping the heat low. ✦ When the anchovies have dissolved, add the onion, carrot, celery, and mushrooms. ✦ Raise the heat to medium, stirring often to keep the vegetables from burning, and when they have become a good brown color, add the garlic, then add the cod. ✦ Lower the heat to the minimum, taste for salt and pepper, cover, and cook for about 30 minutes. ✦ Add the olives and pine nuts to taste and dilute the sauce with 1 cup of warm water or, better, vegetable broth. ✦ Cover the pan and cook for about 2½ hours, keeping the heat at the minimum. Add the potatoes and cook 30 minutes more. Serve hot.

STOCCAFISSO ALL'ACQUESE 1

COD AND POTATO STEW 1

PIEMONTE

3 salt-cured anchovy fillets, boned and rinsed

1 garlic clove, minced

3 tbsp. extra-virgin olive oil

2 lbs. *unsalted* dried cod (see note, page 491)

½ cup white wine

2 lbs. potatoes, boiled, peeled, and cubed

1 bunch flat-leaf parsley, chopped

6 olives (preferably Ligurian), pitted and chopped

Pine nuts (as desired)

Pinch chili pepper

For the wine use Gavi or Pigato.

Heat the anchovies and garlic in olive oil over low heat, then add the cod. ✦ After 10 minutes, add the white wine. ✦ When the wine has evaporated, add the potatoes, parsley, olives, pine nuts, and chili pepper. ✦ Cook a few minutes longer to blend the flavors, then serve hot.

STOCCAFISSO ALLA CALABRESE 2

COD AND POTATO STEW 2

CALABRIA

¾ cup extra-virgin olive oil

2 medium onions, sliced

1⅔ cups peeled and chopped plum tomatoes

3 tbsp. chopped flat-leaf parsley

1 chili pepper (preferably Calabrian), chopped

1¾ lbs. *unsalted* dried cod, cut in pieces (see note, page 491)

½ cup red wine

2 medium potatoes, peeled and coarsely chopped

½ cup capers

½ cup black olives, pitted

Salt

For the wine use Cirò or Aglianico. For the olives use Gaeta or Cerignola.

Heat the olive oil in a pan (preferably terra-cotta) and sauté the onions. ✦ After a few minutes, add the tomatoes and parsley. ✦ Add salt and chili pepper and cook for about 15 minutes. ✦ Add the cod and wine. ✦ When the wine has evaporated, add the potatoes and capers and dilute with a few cups of warm water. ✦ Add the olives and continue cooking for another 10 minutes. Serve hot.

MARINER'S STOCKFISH

1¾ lbs. *unsalted* dried cod
(see note, page 491)

2 bay leaves

1 lemon, sliced in rounds

2 tbsp. olive oil

2 salt-cured anchovy fillets, rinsed
and boned

2 tbsp. chopped flat-leaf parsley

1 garlic clove

2 tbsp. capers

¾ lb. plum tomatoes,
seeded and chopped

½ cup mixed green and black olives,
pitted and chopped

Pine nuts (as desired)

Dry white wine (if necessary)

For the wine use Vermentino or Gavi. For the olives, you can use Gaeta.

Parboil the cod with the bay leaves and lemon slices in water to cover; when done, chop in bite-size pieces. ✦ Separately, heat the olive oil and anchovies, stirring until the anchovies break down. Add the parsley and garlic. ✦ As soon as these take color, add the capers and tomatoes and raise the heat to high. ✦ After 15 minutes, add the cod, olives, and pine nuts. ✦ Reduce the heat to low, cover, and cook for about 15 minutes. Stir occasionally to keep the mixture from sticking to the bottom and add white wine if necessary. Serve hot.

FISH

BOILED STOCKFISH
WITH POTATOES

1 bouquet garni

1 bunch flat-leaf parsley

1 carrot, chopped

1 small onion, quartered

1 celery stalk, chopped

1¾ lbs. *unsalted* dried cod,
soaked, cleaned, and cut in pieces
(see note, page 491)

2 potatoes

Juice of 1 lemon

A variation involves adding plum tomatoes (not peeled) to the pot when it is half cooked. When the dish is served, crush the tomatoes over the potatoes and cod, removing the peel. Then season with olive oil, salt, pepper, and lemon and serve hot.

Put the bouquet garni in a large pot of cold water and add the parsley, carrot, onion, and celery. ✦ Bring to a boil, and when it boils, add the cod and simmer at high heat for no more than 10 minutes. ✦ Separately boil the potatoes in lightly salted water to cover, drain, peel, and cut in pieces. ✦ Drain the cod and put it in a bowl with the potatoes. Adjust for salt and pepper and add olive oil and lemon juice to taste.

STOCCAFISSO CON IL POMODORO ALLA TRIESTINA

STOCKFISH WITH TOMATO SAUCE

FRIULI-VENEZIA GIULIA

¼ cup extra-virgin olive oil

½ lb. *unsalted* dried cod, cut in pieces (see note, page 491)

2 plum tomatoes, blanched, peeled, and chopped

2 garlic cloves, crushed and peeled

1 bay leaf

Salt and pepper

Preheat the oven to 350°F. Cover the bottom of a baking pan with a little of the olive oil. Arrange the pieces of cod in the pan. ✦ Add salt and a little water to keep the fish from sticking, cover, then bake. ✦ After about 1 hour, add the tomatoes, garlic, bay leaf, pepper, and the rest of the olive oil. ✦ Add water to cover, put the lid on the pan, and bake for another hour. Serve with a pinch of salt and yellow polenta.

STOCCAFISSO CON PATATE

STOCKFISH AND POTATOES 1

CAMPANIA

¾ cup extra-virgin olive oil

1½ lbs. potatoes, peeled and sliced

2 medium onions, sliced

1 lb. plum tomatoes, peeled and chopped

1 tsp. dried oregano

1½ lbs. *unsalted* dried cod, soaked, beaten, and cut in pieces (see note, page 491)

Salt and pepper

Pour ½ cup olive oil into a pan and form a layer of half the potatoes and onions in the bottom of the pan. ✦ Add half the tomatoes and sprinkle with half of the oregano and salt and pepper. ✦ On this layer put the cod. ✦ Cover the cod with a second layer of potatoes and onions, then add the remaining tomatoes, the remaining oregano, salt, and pepper. ✦ Sprinkle with the remaining olive oil, cover, and cook over low heat, stirring as little as possible. Serve hot.

STOCCAFISSO CON PATATE ALLA BOLZANINA

STOCKFISH AND POTATOES 2

ALTO ADIGE

¾ lb. *unsalted* dried cod (see note, page 491)

1½ lbs. potatoes

5 tbsp. unsalted butter

1 medium onion, sliced

1 garlic clove, minced

1 bay leaf

½ cup cream

2 tbsp. chopped flat-leaf parsley

Salt and pepper

Soak the cod in water to cover for 1 day. ✦ The next day drain it, then boil it in fresh water to cover until the meat easily comes away from the bones. ✦ Boil the potatoes with their skins, peel while still hot, then let cool and slice. ✦ Drain the cod, cut away the skin and bones, and break it up by hand. ✦ Heat the butter in a pan and cook the onion and garlic, then add the cod and the potatoes. ✦ Salt and pepper to taste. ✦ Brown well, adding the bay leaf. Add the cream, stirring delicately, and serve hot, sprinkled with parsley.

STOCKFISH WITH TOMATOES AND POTATOES

STOCCAFISSO CON PATATE ALLA PISANA

TOSCANA

½ cup extra-virgin olive oil

1 medium white onion, thinly sliced

½ lb. ripe plum tomatoes, peeled, seeded, and chopped

1 bouquet garni
(basil and flat-leaf parsley)

1 lb. *unsalted* dried cod,
soaked and beaten, boned and
cut in small chunks with its skin
(see note, page 491)

2 or 3 potatoes,
peeled and cut in hunks

Salt and pepper

Heat the olive oil in a saucepan and sauté the onion; add the tomatoes and bouquet garni. ✦ At this point, add the cod and its skin cut in strips. ✦ Salt and pepper to taste, add a little water, and cook at low heat. ✦ After 2 hours, add the potatoes and cook 30 minutes more. Serve hot.

STOCKFISH WITH POTATOES AND ONIONS

STOCCAFISSO CON PATATE E CIPOLLE

LIGURIA

1¼ lbs. *unsalted* dried cod, soaked and drained (see page 491)

3 potatoes, peeled

1 medium onion

1 garlic clove, finely chopped

2 tbsp. chopped flat-leaf parsley

2 tbsp. extra-virgin olive oil

Juice of 1 lemon

This dish is typical of Imperia.

Boil the cod, potatoes, and onion for 10 minutes. ✦ Separately combine the garlic, parsley, olive oil, and lemon juice; stir to blend and set aside. ✦ Chop the cod into smaller pieces, also chopping the onion and potatoes. ✦ Put these in a pan and season with the olive oil mixture. ✦ Mix well, then cover the pan. ✦ Cook this, stirring it repeatedly and energetically to whip it. Serve hot or at room temperature.

STOCKFISH WITH CAPERS

STOCCU AMMUDICATU

CALABRIA

1¾ lbs. *unsalted* dried cod
(see note, page 491)

½ cup extra-virgin olive oil

1 tbsp. breadcrumbs

1 tbsp. capers

Pinch dried oregano

Beat the cod with a mallet to soften it. Boil the cod in lightly salted water to cover and when it is cooked, drain it, dry it on a cloth, and cut into large pieces. ✦ Heat the olive oil in a pan, add the cod, and brown it; add the breadcrumbs, capers, and oregano. ✦ Stir to blend and serve hot.

BAKED STURGEON

VENETO

1 sturgeon, weighing about 7 lbs., cleaned

4 oz. *lardo*

½ cup extra-virgin olive oil

Juice of 1 lemon

Grated zest of 1 lemon

¼ lb. (1 stick) unsalted butter

½ cup white wine

3 tbsp. Marsala

1 scant tbsp. all-purpose flour

Salt and pepper

For the wine use Lugana, bianco di Custoza, or Soave.

Preheat the oven to 300°F. Skin the sturgeon, then wrap it with the *lardo*. ✦ Brush it with olive oil and lemon juice, then salt and pepper and add the lemon zest. ✦ Put the sturgeon in a flameproof baking pan and add the remaining olive oil and 2 tablespoons butter. ✦ Bake for 40 minutes, brushing with wine and cooking liquid. ✦ When cooked, remove the fish, then dilute the sauce with the Marsala, then thicken it with the remaining butter and the flour. Pour this sauce over the fish and serve hot.

STURGEON WITH CAPERS AND OLIVES

FOR 12 PERSONS

STORIONE IN ACQUA FERVENTE CON CAPPERI E UVETTE

VENETO

½ cup fresh thyme

1⅔ cups chopped flat-leaf parsley

½ cup aromatic herbs (sage, rosemary, thyme, bay leaves)

1⅔ cups capers

1¼ cups golden raisins

2 garlic cloves

Juice and zest from 5 lemons

1 cup cider vinegar

2 tbsp. extra-virgin olive oil

1 sturgeon, weighing about 10 lbs., cleaned

Lettuce leaves (or grape leaves)

This dish was served in honor of Michele Savonarola, a respected Paduan doctor and philosopher, in the fifteenth century. It can be made using slices of sturgeon, but the result will not be the same.

Prepare an aromatic liquid by boiling thyme, some of the parsley, and other herbs as desired in 4 cups of water for about 10 minutes. ✦ Chop together half of the capers, half the raisins, and the remaining parsley, garlic, and lemon juice and zest. (Put the remaining capers and raisins in cider vinegar and set aside until serving.) ✦ Add olive oil to this and use it to season the sturgeon, making incisions into the flesh of the fish to facilitate the penetration of the flavor. ✦ Wrap the fish in lettuce or grape leaves and tie up with kitchen twine. ✦ Simmer in the aromatic liquid over very low heat for about 3 hours. Serve in slices accompanied by the vinegar mixture.

STEWED EELS AND PERCH

TEGAMACCIO

UMBRIA

½ cup extra-virgin olive oil

CONTINUED

Tegamaccio is best served on slices of toasted bread.

Heat the olive oil in a large earthenware pan and cook the garlic and parsley; as soon as the garlic changes color, add the tomatoes, salt, and chili pepper. ✦ Cook for 15 min-

1 garlic clove

2 tbsp. chopped flat-leaf parsley

1 lb. ripe plum tomatoes,
peeled, seeded, and chopped

Pinch chili pepper

2 lbs. medium-size eels,
cleaned, with heads and tails
removed, cut in 2-inch lengths

1 lb. perch fillets

Salt

utes. ✦ Add the eels and cook at low heat for 20 minutes, then add the perch and cook for another 10 minutes.

TUNA CALABRIA-STYLE

TONNO ALLA CALABRESE

CALABRIA

1½ lbs. fresh tuna fillet, cut in 4 slices

All-purpose flour, for dredging

⅓ cup extra-virgin olive oil

½ cup dry white wine

2 oz. pancetta, finely chopped

1 garlic clove, finely chopped

1 medium onion, finely chopped

¼ cup chopped flat-leaf parsley

4 salt-cured anchovy fillets,
boned and rinsed

1⅔ cups plum tomatoes,
peeled, seeded, and
passed through a sieve

Pinch chili pepper
(preferably Calabrian)

Salt and pepper

Rinse the tuna slices, drain them, and pat dry with paper towels. ✦ Salt and pepper the fish, then lightly dredge them in flour. ✦ Heat the olive oil in a large skillet and as soon as the oil is hot, add the tuna. Brown on one side, then the other, then sprinkle with a little white wine. ✦ Turn up the heat to evaporate the wine. Remove the tuna with a slotted spoon and set aside on a plate. ✦ In the same skillet cook the pancetta, garlic, and onion; after a few minutes add half of the parsley and the anchovies, crushing them with a fork. ✦ Stir, and after 1 minute add the tomato purée, salt, and chili pepper. ✦ Boil the sauce at moderate heat for 15 minutes, stirring from time to time. ✦ Add the tuna to the pan and cook for a few minutes. Turn them and add the remaining parsley. Turn off the heat and serve.

FISH

TUNA COSENZA-STYLE

TONNO ALLA COSENTINA

CALABRIA

1 cup extra-virgin olive oil

1¾ lbs. fresh tuna fillet, cut in
4 slices about ¾ inch thick

1 medium onion, finely sliced

1 tbsp. all-purpose flour

¼ cup dry white wine,
mixed with ¼ cup water

CONTINUED

For the wine use Cirò or Coda di Volpe.

In an earthenware pan, heat the olive oil until it is so hot that it shimmers on the surface. Fry the tuna slices in the oil, turning, until both sides are browned. ✦ Remove them from the pan, drain, salt, and set aside. ✦ In the same pan, cook the onion until golden, then stir in the flour. ✦ Pour in the wine mixture, then the vinegar. Season with salt, chili pepper, thyme, bay leaf, and tomatoes. ✦ As soon as the sauce begins to boil, return the tuna to the pan and cook at very low heat for about

3 tbsp. white wine vinegar

Pinch chili pepper flakes

Pinch thyme

1 bay leaf

⅔ cup peeled and seeded plum tomatoes

1 tbsp. chopped gherkins

1 tbsp. capers

1 tbsp. chopped flat-leaf parsley

Salt

1 hour. ✦ Just before serving add the gherkins, capers, and parsley.

TUNA REGGIO-STYLE

TONNO ALLA REGGITANA

CALABRIA

1 ½ lbs. fresh tuna fillet, cut in 4 thick slices

All-purpose flour, for dredging

Extra-virgin olive oil

1 medium onion, finely sliced

1 garlic clove, crushed

2 tbsp. chopped flat-leaf parsley

4 salt-cured anchovy fillets, boned, rinsed, and ground in a mortar

1 lb. ripe plum tomatoes, peeled, seeded, and passed through a sieve

Salt and pepper

This dish is typical of Reggio Calabria.

Season the slices of tuna with salt and pepper. ✦ Dip them in the flour. Heat a few tablespoons olive oil and cook the tuna just until golden. ✦ Remove them from the pan with a slotted spoon and set them aside in a warm place. ✦ Add a few tablespoons of olive oil to the pan if necessary, then sauté the onion and garlic until soft. Add the parsley and anchovies, then add the tomatoes. ✦ Cook at low heat for 15 minutes. Return the tuna to the pan, cook for a few minutes, and serve covered with the sauce.

BOILED TUNA

TONNO BOLLITO

CALABRIA

1 carrot

1 medium onion

1 celery stalk

1 bay leaf

½ cup flat-leaf parsley leaves

2 garlic cloves

1 ¾ lbs. fresh tuna, cleaned

Olive oil

Freshly ground pepper

Heat about 8 cups of lightly salted water to a boil, then add the carrot, onion, celery, bay leaf, half the parsley, and 1 garlic clove. ✦ Boil for 45 minutes, then filter the broth and let it cool. ✦ Remove the skin from the tuna, then tie it with kitchen twine so it will maintain its shape. Place in the broth; bring to a boil and cook. ✦ When the tuna is cooked, drain it, untie it, and cut it in equal-size slices. ✦ Arrange these on a serving plate. ✦ Chop the remaining parsley and garlic and sprinkle on the tuna. Dust with pepper, season with olive oil, and serve.

TUNA AND ONIONS

1 ¾ lbs. fresh tuna fillet, sliced

All-purpose flour, for dredging

¼ cup extra-virgin olive oil

4 medium onions, sliced

¼ cup white wine vinegar

½ cup mint leaves

Salt and pepper

Rinse the tuna in cool running water, then drain and pat dry. ✦ Dust the slices with the flour, shaking off any excess. Heat the oil in a pan and brown the tuna; set aside on a plate. ✦ Add the onions to the pan and cook over low heat until soft. ✦ Add the vinegar, salt, pepper, and mint and cook for a few minutes. ✦ Pour this sauce over the tuna, then cover with another plate and let it soak up the flavor for at least 30 minutes before serving.

STUFFED SQUID

4 squid

½ cup extra-virgin olive oil

2 garlic cloves

1 lb. dry caciocotta cheese, grated (may substitute Parmigiano-Reggiano)

2 large eggs, beaten

½ cup grated Parmigiano-Reggiano

1 sprig fresh marjoram

½ cup dry white wine

Salt and chili pepper

This preparation is typical of Capri. The recipe can be varied with the addition of chopped plum tomatoes and a few basil leaves. Choose a wine from Capri or Ischia.

Clean the squid, removing the head and tentacles. ✦ Mince the tentacles and set aside. Heat half the olive oil in a pan; add 1 garlic clove and the squid bodies and brown lightly. ✦ Mix the tentacles, caciocotta, eggs, Parmigiano-Reggiano, marjoram, and a pinch of salt. ✦ Stuff this mixture into the body cavities and close them with a toothpick or, even better, sew them shut with kitchen string. ✦ Heat the remaining olive oil, garlic, salt, and chili pepper. Add the squid and cook at low heat for about 1 hour until the stuffing is cooked and the squid is tender, basting with wine and being careful to turn them every so often. ✦ The cooking time will vary, longer or shorter, according to the size and type of squid.

MULLET BAKED IN PARCHMENT 1

8 large mullet, each weighing about 6 oz., cleaned

2 tsp. garlic

½ cup extra-virgin olive oil

Salt

Preheat the oven to 350°F. Rinse the mullet and dry them. ✦ Lay the fish on sheets of parchment paper and add a pinch of salt, ¼ teaspoon garlic, and 1 tablespoon olive oil to each. ✦ Fold the paper over the fish, crimp the edges to seal them, and bake for about 25 minutes. ✦ When the mullet are done, they will be fragrant and the packets will have puffed up. Serve immediately, still closed in the packets.

FISH

MULLET BAKED IN PARCHMENT 2

CAMPANIA

1 bunch flat-leaf parsley, chopped

4 salt-cured anchovies, chopped

⅓ cup pitted green olives, chopped

⅓ cup capers

1 garlic clove, minced

8 large mullet, each weighing 4 oz., cleaned

Extra-virgin olive oil

Pepper

This dish is typical of the Amalfi coast.

Preheat the oven to 350°F or heat a grill to medium heat. Mix the parsley, anchovies, olives, capers, and garlic and stuff the fish with this mixture. ✦ Spread olive oil over the fish, sprinkle them with pepper, then wrap up the fish in parchment paper, crimping the edges to close them well. ✦ Bake or roast on the grill until cooked, about 25 minutes.

BAKED MULLET

CALABRIA

⅔ cup extra-virgin olive oil

8 mullet, each weighing about 4 oz.

Juice of 1 lemon

1 sprig oregano

Salt

This dish is typical of Crotone.

Preheat the oven to 400°F and grease a baking pan with olive oil. Clean, rinse, and dry the mullet. ✦ Place the mullet in the pan, salt them, and add the lemon juice and oregano. ✦ Drizzle with olive oil and bake for about 20 minutes. Serve immediately.

MULLET WITH PLUM TOMATO

TOSCANA

8 mullet, each weighing 4 to 5 oz.

½ cup extra-virgin olive oil

2 garlic cloves, minced

2 tbsp. chopped flat-leaf parsley

1 lb. ripe plum tomatoes, peeled, seeded, drained, and chopped

Salt and pepper

Scale the mullet, removing the fins (but not the tail); rinse and dry them well. ✦ Heat the olive oil in a pan and sauté the garlic and parsley. ✦ Before the garlic takes color, add the tomatoes and salt and pepper to taste. ✦ Cook 5 minutes, then add the mullet and cook for about 10 minutes without moving the pan. Let cool in the pan and serve at room temperature.

MULLET WITH VERNACCIA

TRIGLIE ALLA VERNACCIA

SARDEGNA

8 gray mullet, about 4 oz. each, cleaned

½ cup extra-virgin olive oil

½ cup breadcrumbs

Grated zest of 1 lemon

½ cup Vernaccia wine

Salt

Put the mullet in a pan with the olive oil and sprinkle with the breadcrumbs and lemon zest. ✦ Season with salt and add the wine. ✦ Simmer over low heat until the fish is cooked through, about 20 minutes. Let cool and serve at room temperature.

STUFFED MULLET

TRIGLIE SETTEMBRINE ALLA 'NGORDA

MOLISE

Stale bread, crusts removed, crumbled to make 2 cups

½ cup extra-virgin olive oil

1 garlic clove, finely minced

1 bunch flat-leaf parsley, minced

Dried chili pepper (hot or sweet as desired)

8 fresh mullet, cleaned

In order for the flavors to blend, it is best to prepare the filling at least 2 hours before using it.

Mix all the ingredients except the fish. ✦ Rinse the mullet in cold water. ✦ Preheat the oven to 350°F. Stuff the fish (stomach cavity and gills), arrange on a pan, and bake about 20 minutes. Serve at room temperature.

FISH

TROUT IN RED WINE

TROTA AL VINO ROSSO DI SAINT PIERRE

VALLE D'AOSTA

4 brook trout, each weighing about 12 oz., cleaned

4 tbsp. unsalted butter

1 medium onion, minced

1 carrot, finely chopped

A few sage leaves, chopped

1 sprig rosemary, chopped

1 bottle red wine, slightly warmed

Salt and pepper

This dish is typical of *Courmayeur*. Preferably the wine should be from Saint-Pierre; dolcetto is an acceptable substitution.

Preheat the oven to 350°F. Rinse the trout and dry them well. ✦ Melt the butter in a cast-iron pan over low heat and add the vegetables and herbs. ✦ Cook until the onion is pale, then add the trout with salt and pepper as desired. ✦ When the trout begin to brown, pour the wine over them. ✦ Raise the heat to high, cook 5 minutes, then put in the oven to finish the cooking, about 15 minutes or until the flesh flakes easily. Serve with boiled potatoes.

TROUT WITH
TRUFFLE SAUCE

**TROTA DEL NERA
AL TARTUFO**

UMBRIA

2 trout, each about 12 oz., cleaned
Extra-virgin olive oil
Black truffle sauce
Salt and pepper

Heat a grill to high heat. Rinse the trout and pat them dry. Season them with salt and pepper and grill them 4 minutes per side, basting them on both sides with olive oil about every 2 minutes. ✦ When they are cooked, remove their bones and season the fillets with black truffle sauce.

TROUT WITH
PARSLEY SAUCE

TROTA IN BIANCO

UMBRIA

1 trout, weighing about 1 lb., cleaned
½ cup chopped flat-leaf parsley
1 garlic clove, minced
Juice of 1 lemon
Extra-virgin olive oil
Salt and pepper

Place the trout in a pan with lightly salted water just to cover. Simmer until cooked, about 10 minutes. Meanwhile, prepare the sauce, mixing the parsley and garlic to form a paste. Butterfly the trout and place it on a serving plate. Spoon the sauce over and season with lemon juice, pepper, and olive oil.

✦ LOCAL TRADITION ✦

VENTRICIEDDI DI STOCCO
AL POMODORO

To prepare this traditional Calabrian dish of the tripe from unsalted dried cod, the dark film would first be removed and the tripe sliced. It would then be added to a hot pan of olive oil and garlic just as the garlic began to color. After a brief sauté, tomato purée, oregano, and a hot chili pepper would be added and the dish simmered for about an hour.

GRILLED TROUT

ABRUZZO

4 trout, each weighing about 12 oz.
1 garlic clove, minced
1 bunch flat-leaf parsley, minced
Extra-virgin olive oil
Juice of 1 lemon
Salt and pepper

Heat a grill to medium-high. Clean and rinse the trout. Mix the garlic and parsley and stuff the trout with the mixture. ✦ Salt and pepper and grill until the skin is browned and blistered and the flesh flakes easily. ✦ Before serving sprinkle them with olive oil and lemon juice.

TROUT BAKED IN TOMATO SAUCE WITH POLENTA

TROTE IN UMIDO
CON POLENTA

FRIULI-VENEZIA GIULIA

¼ cup extra-virgin olive oil
1 garlic clove, minced
1 lb. plum tomatoes,
peeled, seeded, and chopped
4 trout, each weighing about
6 to 8 oz., cleaned
1 tbsp. all-purpose flour
1 tbsp. chopped flat-leaf parsley
Salt and pepper

This dish is typical of the valleys of the Torre River.

Heat the olive oil in a pan and add the garlic and tomatoes; cook for a few minutes. ✦ Dust the trout with the flour and add them to the pan. Cook for about 15 minutes; add salt and pepper and parsley. Serve with warm polenta.

FISH

CLAMS IN PARSLEY AND WINE

VONGOLE ALLA
PESCATORA

MARCHE

¼ cup extra-virgin olive oil
1 medium onion, sliced
(or 1 garlic clove)
1 small bunch flat-leaf parsley,
chopped
1 lb. clams, scrubbed and rinsed
⅔ cup white wine
Pepper

Tasty, simple, and quick to prepare, this dish was originally part of the *cucina povera* tradition of fishermen families and is now popular in many restaurants and trattorias along the coast. For the wine use Verdicchio.

Heat a little olive oil in a pan and cook the onion (some prefer garlic) and parsley until the onion is soft. ✦ Add a pinch of pepper and the clams. Toss, then add the white wine. Cook for 10 to 15 minutes until the clams have all opened.

SALT COD FRITTERS

1 ¼ cups all-purpose flour

1 tsp. active dry yeast, dissolved in 2 tbsp. warm water

½ cup minced flat-leaf parsley

1 lb. salt-dried cod, soaked, drained, and broken up with a fork (see note, page 437)

Olive oil for frying

Salt

This dish is typical of Caserta.

In a large bowl, combine the flour with the yeast mixture; add a pinch of salt and enough water to make a thick batter (about ¾ cup). ✦ Mix with an electric mixer on medium speed for 3 minutes. ✦ Let this rest, covered by a cloth, until it rises, about 1 hour. ✦ Add the parsley and cod. ✦ Heat 3 inches of olive oil in a saucepan until hot. Drop spoonfuls of the batter into the oil and fry until golden. Drain on paper towels and serve hot.

SWEET-AND-SOUR COD STEW

¼ cup extra-virgin olive oil

1 garlic clove, minced

2 chili peppers, cut in strips

16 walnut halves, chopped

4 dried figs

4 pitted prunes

1 tsp. golden raisins

1 tbsp. pine nuts

1 head cauliflower, cooked al dente and chopped

4 cups peeled plum tomatoes

1 ½ lbs. salt-dried cod, soaked and rinsed of salt (see note, page 437)

Slices of peasant-style bread, toasted

The quantity of dried fruit (along with the kinds) can be varied according to taste.

In a large pan, heat the olive oil and sauté the garlic. Add the chili peppers, walnuts, figs, prunes, raisins, pine nuts, and cauliflower. ✦ Add the tomatoes, bring to a boil, and cook about 20 minutes. ✦ When this mixture seems well blended, add the pieces of cod, adding salt and water if necessary. ✦ Since the cod cooks quickly, the stew will be done in about 10 minutes. It should be moderately thin and should be served over toasted slices of peasant-style bread.

CRAYFISH SOUP

2 tbsp. extra-virgin olive oil

1 garlic clove, minced

CONTINUED

This dish is typical of Ciociaria.

Heat the olive oil in an earthenware pan over medium heat and add the garlic, chili pepper, and anchovy. Sauté until the anchovy starts to fall apart, then add the parsley and crayfish. ✦ Add 4 cups water and stir the mix-

1 chili pepper

1 salt-cured anchovy,
rinsed and chopped

2 tablespoons chopped
flat-leaf parsley

1 pound crayfish, cleaned

4 slices of toasted stale bread,
optional

ture counter-clockwise constantly, until the crayfish are cooked, about 12 minutes. ✦ If desired, cut the toasted bread in triangles, put the triangles in earthenware serving bowls, and pour the hot soup on top.

SARDINE AND LETTUCE STEW

**ZUPPA DI SARDE
E LATTUGA**

SICILIA

1 head lettuce

1½ lbs. fresh sardines,
cleaned and boned

Extra-virgin olive oil

Salt and pepper

This dish is typical of Vittoria. For the lettuce try Boston limestone, or bibb; you may need 2 heads depending upon the size.

Core the head of lettuce and cut it in ½-inch strips. ✦ Arrange alternating layers of lettuce and sardines in a pan, seasoning each layer with olive oil, salt, and pepper and continuing the layers until the ingredients are used up. ✦ Cover and cook for 30 minutes at low heat.

FISH

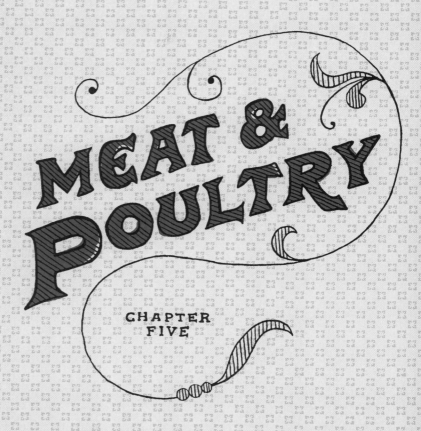

MEAT &
POULTRY

CHAPTER
FIVE

ROAST SUCKLING LAMB WITH POTATOES

ABBACCHIO AL FORNO CON LE PATATE

LAZIO

4½ lbs. suckling lamb, nourished only with mother's milk (leg and rib, if possible with kidneys)

2 garlic cloves, chopped

4 sprigs rosemary

½ cup extra-virgin olive oil

½ cup dry white wine

1½ lbs. potatoes, peeled and cut in large chunks

Salt and ground pepper

Sheep have been raised on the Roman plains since time immemorial.

Using a knife with a narrow, sharp blade, cut ½-inch-deep slits in the meat and insert some garlic and a few rosemary leaves into each slit. ✦ Place the meat in a baking pan and spread the olive oil over it. Pour on the wine; season with salt and pepper, add 2 sprigs of rosemary, and let the lamb rest for 12 hours. ✦ Preheat the oven to 350°F and bake for 1 hour. After the meat has cooked 1 hour, add the potatoes to the pan. Cook 1 more hour, basting the lamb and potatoes from time to time with the cooking juices. ✦ Place the cooked meat on a serving dish with the potatoes and serve hot.

HUNTER-STYLE SUCKLING LAMB

ABBACCHIO ALLA CACCIATORA

LAZIO

2 garlic cloves

1 tsp. rosemary leaves

2 anchovies, boned

¼ cup red wine vinegar

2¼ lbs. leg of spring lamb, cut in pieces weighing about 1 oz. each

½ cup extra-virgin olive oil

¼ cup dry white wine, such as Orvieto

Salt and pepper

This dish is typical of Rome and Lazio.

In a wooden mortar grind the garlic, rosemary, and anchovies to obtain a paste. ✦ Add the vinegar, a little at a time, and mix to obtain a dense sauce. ✦ Rinse and pat dry the pieces of lamb. Heat the olive oil in a pan. Season the lamb with salt and pepper and brown it over moderate heat. Stir from time to time with a wooden spoon to cook them evenly. ✦ Pour in the wine and turn up the heat; when the wine has evaporated, add the vinegar sauce. ✦ Cover and cook for 2 hours at low heat, stirring often. ✦ Let the lamb rest for at least half an hour before serving; the longer the lamb rests in its pan, the greater will be its flavor. Serve hot.

STEWED SUCKLING LAMB ROMAN-STYLE

ABBACCHIO BRODETTATO ALLA ROMANA

LAZIO

½ cup extra-virgin olive oil

1 medium onion, finely chopped

2 oz. prosciutto fat, finely chopped

CONTINUED

This dish is typical of Rome and Lazio. For the wine use Frascati or Orvieto.

Heat the olive oil in a pan (preferably terra-cotta) over medium heat and cook the onion and prosciutto fat. ✦ As soon as the onion takes on color, add the lamb, season with salt and pepper, and brown. Pour in the white

508

2 ¼ lbs. suckling lamb, cut in small
pieces, cleaned and dried

½ cup dry white wine

1 tbsp. all-purpose flour

1 garlic clove, finely chopped

1 tbsp. chopped flat-leaf parsley

4 large egg yolks, beaten

Juice of 1 lemon

1 tbsp. grated Parmigiano-Reggiano

Salt and pepper

wine. ✦ When the liquid has nearly evaporated, sprinkle with flour, then add 2 cups hot water. Bring to a simmer. ✦ Cover and continue cooking, adding more water when necessary to maintain the liquid while also being careful not to let the sauce become too watery. ✦ When the lamb is cooked, add the garlic and parsley. ✦ Mix the egg yolks and lemon juice. Remove the pot from the heat and pour in the egg mixture and Parmigiano-Reggiano. Blend well and let the sauce thicken, stirring constantly. Serve hot.

AGGLASSATO

ONION-GLAZED BEEF

FOR
6 PERSONS

SICILIA

2 lbs. beef round or 1 large chicken (or both)

½ cup extra-virgin olive oil

2 lbs. or more medium onions, roughly chopped (the quantity of onions determines the amount of glaze)

¼ cup (4 tbsp.) unsalted butter

¼ cup or more Marsala (the amount of Marsala depends on the quantity of meat)

Salt and pepper

This dish from the family of braised meats and stews is the prince of the meat dishes of Palermo. It was a traditional Sunday family dinner since the sauce—the glaze—could be used for other preparations during the coming week. The recipe is ancient and of French derivation.

Put the beef round or chicken in a large saucepan and cover with water, olive oil, salt, pepper, and all the onions. ✦ Bring the liquid to a boil, then lower the heat and braise the meat until the almost total reduction of the liquid (being careful to remove the chicken when it has cooked to keep it from coming apart). In another saucepan, melt the butter. ✦ Remove the beef or chicken from the onion sauce and drain it. Add it to the pan with the butter and brown it on all sides. ✦ When it reaches a good brown color, add the Marsala. ✦ When the Marsala has evaporated, begin the process of transferring the cooked onions from the first pan to the pan with the meat. Do this by collecting a cupful of onion with a slotted spoon, then holding the onion over the meat and breaking it up with a wooden spoon so that the onion purée will fall onto the meat as it continues to brown. Repeat this operation until all the onions have been transferred. ✦ Pour the remains of the broth over the meat and continue to cook down the sauce, which should be becoming a creamy glaze, while also paying close attention since at this point the glaze may tend to stick to the bottom. ✦ At this point the glazed meat is done. ✦ According to age-old tradition, the meat should be served very hot covered by the glaze and accompanied by cooked peas and fried potato cubes flavored with some of the glaze.

MEAT & POULTRY

LEG OF LAMB
BAKED IN EMBERS

TOSCANA

1 sprig rosemary

2 garlic cloves

A few sage leaves

2 oz. *lardo*

3 ¼ lbs. leg of lamb

5 tbsp. extra-virgin olive oil

2 ¼ lbs. potatoes,
peeled and cut in pieces

Salt and pepper

This dish is typical of Pontremoli.

Heat a grill to medium. Finely chop together the rosemary, garlic, sage, and *lardo*. ✦ Using the tip of a knife, make a series of incisions in the lamb and insert the mixture. Salt and pepper. ✦ Put the olive oil in a flameproof pan and add the lamb and potatoes. Cover the pan with a lid and put the pan directly over a bed of coals. Place embers and cinders on the lid. ✦ Cook for 40 minutes until the lamb is cooked and tender.

HUNTER-STYLE LAMB

MARCHE

1 garlic clove, finely minced

1 tbsp. finely chopped
flat-leaf parsley

2 sprigs rosemary, finely chopped

1 tbsp. anchovy paste

Pinch chili pepper flakes

¼ cup red wine vinegar

¼ cup white wine

½ cup extra-virgin olive oil

2 ¼ lbs. leg of lamb,
cut in 2-inch pieces

Prepare the sauce by combining the garlic, parsley, and rosemary with the anchovy paste and chili pepper; stir in the vinegar and wine and set aside. ✦ Heat the olive oil in a pan over high heat and brown the lamb; reduce the heat to low and cook slowly partially covered, for about 1 hour, until tender. Add the sauce and cook 5 minutes more. Serve hot.

BAKED LEG OF LAMB

ABRUZZO

1 leg of lamb

¼ cup extra-virgin olive oil

1 medium onion, finely minced

Pinch chili pepper flakes

Juice of 1 lemon

Freshly grated pecorino

Salt and pepper

Preheat the oven to 400°F. Rub the lamb with olive oil, season with salt and pepper, and place it in a pan. Add the onion and chili pepper. ✦ Bake until cooked through, turning it from time to time, about 30 minutes. ✦ When the meat is brown, remove the pan from the oven, sprinkle with lemon juice, dust with pecorino, and serve.

ABUOTTO

Typical of the area of the Ciociaria in Lazio, this recipe involved cooking slices of a lamb's liver on a warm grill. The liver would be sliced into pieces about the length of a finger, seasoned with some pepper, parsley, and garlic, and then wrapped in sheets of caul from the same animal. The caul-wrapped sections of liver would in turn be wrapped in the intestines, which had previously been carefully cleaned and dried, and cooked slowly over the fire.

AGNELLO CACIO E OVO O BRODETTATO

LAMB STEW WITH CHEESE AND EGG SAUCE

ABRUZZO

2 lbs. leg of lamb (or boneless lamb), cut in cubes

All-purpose flour for dredging

½ cup extra-virgin olive oil

1 medium onion, sliced

Pinch grated nutmeg

1 cup meat broth

1 cup dry white wine

1 large egg, beaten

1 tbsp. grated pecorino

1 tbsp. lemon juice

Salt and pepper

For the wine use Trebbiano.

Dredge the cubes of meat in the flour. Heat the olive oil in a pan (preferably earthenware) and add the lamb, onion, nutmeg, salt and pepper. ✦ When the meat has browned, pour in the meat broth, then the wine. Cook slowly about 2 hours. ✦ At the end of that time mix the egg and pecorino with the lemon juice and add to the pan. Serve hot as soon as the sauce has thickened.

MEAT & POULTRY

AGNELLO CACIO E UOVA ALLA MOLISANA

BAKED LAMB WITH EGG AND CHEESE

FOR 8 PERSONS

MOLISE

1 tbsp. lard

7 oz. prosciutto crudo, diced

1 medium onion, thinly sliced

CONTINUED

For the wine use Biferno or Trebbiano.

Preheat the oven to 350°F. Put the lard, prosciutto, and onion in a large pan and cook until they have taken on color. Add salt, pepper, and nutmeg. ✦ Dredge the pieces of lamb in the flour and add to the pan, browning them on all sides; pour in the broth and as soon as the

Pinch grated nutmeg

4½ lbs. suckling lamb, cut in rough pieces

All-purpose flour for dredging

1 cup broth

1 cup dry white wine

3 large egg yolks, beaten

Juice of ½ lemon

Salt and pepper

broth cooks down by half, add the white wine. ✦ Salt and pepper again and cook at low heat. ✦ When the lamb is well cooked, transfer it to a baking pan. Put its cooking juices in a small pan with the egg yolks and lemon juice, stir to blend at low heat, then pour this sauce over the meat. ✦ Bake until it forms a golden crust. Serve immediately.

AGNELLO CON OLIVE

LAMB WITH OLIVES

MOLISE

2 lbs. milk-fed lamb

All-purpose flour for dredging

½ cup extra-virgin olive oil

⅔ cup pitted black olives, chopped

Pinch oregano

1 *diavolillo* (hot chili pepper, see note, page 22), minced

Juice of 1 lemon

Chop the lamb in large chunks and dredge the pieces in flour. ✦ Heat the olive oil in a pan over high heat and add the lamb, cooking until it's brown. ✦ Lower the heat and add the olives, oregano, and chili pepper. ✦ Pour over the lemon juice and let it cook a minute longer. Serve warm.

AGNELLO CON PATATE

LAMB AND POTATOES

FOR 6 PERSONS

PUGLIA

2 lbs. milk-fed lamb (shoulder or hock)

Juice of 4 lemons

¼ cup extra-virgin olive oil

1¾ lbs. yellow potatoes, peeled and cut in chunks

Pinch chili pepper flakes

2 garlic cloves, minced

⅔ cup breadcrumbs

Salt

This dish is typical of Foggia.

Marinate the lamb in the lemon juice for about 2 hours, then cut it in pieces. ✦ Preheat the oven to 400°F. Grease a large earthenware pan (preferably a *tajedda*) with olive oil and add the lamb and potatoes. ✦ Add salt, chili pepper, garlic, breadcrumbs, and the remaining olive oil. ✦ Add ½ cup water and bake for about 45 minutes, then turn up the heat to 450°F for a few minutes to brown the surface. Serve hot.

EASTER LAMB

PUGLIA

⅔ cup olive oil

1 medium onion, minced

2 lbs. boneless leg of lamb,
cut in 6 equal pieces

⅔ cup dry white wine

3 cups fresh tender peas

2 large eggs, beaten

½ cup grated pecorino

Flat-leaf parsley

Preheat the oven to 350°F. Heat the olive oil in a terra-cotta pan and add the onion. ✦ As soon as the onion has browned, add the pieces of lamb, stirring often, and pour in the wine. ✦ When the lamb has browned, cover the pot and bake. ✦ After about 1 hour, add the peas and bake about 5 minutes. ✦ Remove from the oven, then mix the eggs, pecorino, and parsley, and pour the egg mixture over the lamb. Wait for the eggs to set before serving.

AGNELLO E PATATE AL FORNO

BAKED LAMB
AND POTATOES

PIEMONTE

3 lbs. boneless leg of lamb

2 sprigs rosemary, finely minced

2 garlic cloves, finely minced

¾ cup olive oil

1 cup white wine

2 tbsp. cognac

1⅓ lbs. potatoes, peeled and cubed

1 cup lamb or chicken broth
(if necessary)

For the wine use Gari or Arneis.

Preheat the oven to 350°F. Cut the lamb in chunks and roll them in the rosemary and garlic. ✦ Heat the olive oil in an ovenproof pot with a lid, add the lamb, and brown. Mix the wine and cognac and pour over the lamb. ✦ Add the potatoes. Cover the pot and bake for about 2 hours, taking it out and stirring it from time to time, adding broth if necessary to maintain the same level of liquid.

AGNELLO E PISELLI

LAMB AND PEAS

MOLISE

½ cup extra-virgin olive oil

1 medium onion, thinly sliced

4 tbsp. chopped flat-leaf parsley

2 lbs. lamb, cut in small pieces

½ cup dry white wine

1¾ lbs. fresh peas

6 large eggs, beaten

⅔ cup grated pecorino

Salt and pepper

Preheat the oven to 325°F. Heat the olive oil in an ovenproof pot over medium heat and add the onion and half the parsley. ✦ When the onion has browned, add the lamb. ✦ As the lamb browns, pour in the wine, add salt, cover, and bake. ✦ Meanwhile, shell the peas, wash in running water, and add them to the lamb when it is almost cooked. ✦ Add a pinch each of salt and pepper and continue cooking. ✦ Mix the eggs, pecorino, a pinch of salt, and the remaining parsley. Add this to the lamb and peas and bake until the eggs have set and the top has formed a nice crust.

MEAT & POULTRY

AGNELLO E TANNE VITACCHIE | LAMB WITH HOPS

MOLISE

½ cup extra-virgin olive oil

2 lbs. boneless lamb, cut in pieces

1 garlic clove, minced

½ cup wine

1 lb. *tanne vitacchie* (shoots of wild hops)

Salt

The bitter taste of the hops offsets the fat of the lamb in this dish. Hops vines grow well in a shaded garden.

Preheat the oven to 350°F. Heat the olive oil in an oven-proof pot with a lid. Add the lamb and brown it with the garlic; add the wine and let it evaporate. Cover and bake 30 minutes. ✦ Meanwhile, clean the shoots of wild hops, boil them in lightly salted water to cover until half cooked, about 5 minutes, and add them to the lamb. ✦ Bake 15 minutes more to cook the hops and blend the flavors.

AGNELLO FORMAGGIO E UOVA | LAMB WITH EGG AND CHEESE

CAMPANIA

2 lbs. lamb stew meat

2 cups red wine vinegar

3 sprigs rosemary

¼ cup olive oil

1 medium onion, minced

½ cup white wine

3 large eggs, beaten

½ cup grated Parmigiano-Reggiano

3 tbsp. chopped flat-leaf parsley

Juice of 1 large lemon

Wash the pieces of lamb under running water. Mix the vinegar and rosemary with 2 cups water. Add the lamb and marinate 2 hours. ✦ Rinse and dry with a cloth. ✦ Heat the olive oil in a large pan; add the onion. As soon as the onion has browned, add the lamb and raise the heat to brown it, turning it with a wooden spoon. ✦ When the meat is properly browned, begin slowly adding the wine a little at a time. Cover and cook over low heat for 1 hour, until tender. ✦ Mix the eggs with the Parmigiano-Reggiano, parsley, and lemon juice. Remove the lamb from the heat and add the egg mixture. ✦ Mix and serve immediately in a warmed serving bowl.

AGNELLO IN FRICASSEA | LAMB FRICASSEE

UMBRIA

¼ cup extra-virgin olive oil

1 ½ lbs. lamb stew meat

1 garlic clove

1 ¼ cups tomato purée (optional)

1 carrot, chopped

1 medium onion, chopped

1 large egg, beaten

Juice of 1 lemon

Salt and pepper

The use of tomato in this dish is controversial, so it is presented here as optional. In its absence the dish is prepared using nothing more than water (and without wine).

Heat the olive oil in a large pan and brown the meat with the garlic. When the garlic is golden, remove it and add the tomato purée (optional), carrot, onion, and salt and pepper to taste. Continue cooking until the lamb is cooked and tender, about 30 minutes. ✦ Mix the egg and lemon juice and add to the dish at the end of the cooking, mixing it in well. Let stand until the egg is set.

LAMB WITH WHITE SAUCE

SARDEGNA

¼ cup extra-virgin olive oil

2 lbs. milk-fed lamb stew meat

1 medium onion, chopped

4 large eggs, beaten

Juice of 1 lemon

Salt

Preheat the oven to 300°F. Combine the oil, lamb, and onion in a baking pan and season with salt to taste. ✦ Cover and bake for about 1 hour, stirring often and keeping the lamb from coloring, for at the end of the cooking the meat should be white and the onion creamy. Remove from the oven and let stand while making the sauce. ✦ Set up a double boiler over medium heat. Mix the eggs and lemon juice in the top of the double boiler, stirring until thickened but being careful not to let the eggs scramble. Add the egg sauce to the lamb just before serving.

AGNELLO TARTUFATO

LAMB WITH TRUFFLE

FOR
6 PERSONS

UMBRIA

½ cup extra-virgin olive oil

3 lbs. boneless lamb stew meat, cut in pieces

2 garlic cloves

2 sprigs rosemary

2 cups dry white wine

6 oz. black truffle

Salt and pepper

This dish is typical of the Valnerina. For the wine use Orvieto.

Heat the olive oil in a cast-iron pot. Add the lamb, salt, pepper, garlic, and rosemary and cook all of it together. ✦ When the lamb has browned, add the wine and continue cooking at low heat until the lamb is cooked and tender. ✦ Put the lamb on a serving plate and shave the truffle onto it, mixing it in; cover a few minutes before serving.

ANATRA DISOSSATA
CON ROSOLINE

DUCKLING FILLET
WITH POPPIES

FOR
8 PERSONS

VENETO

1 duckling

1 sprig rosemary, minced

4 sage leaves, minced

1 garlic clove, minced

9 oz. *rosoline* (wild poppies)

½ cup (¼ lb.) unsalted butter

4 oz. pancetta

½ garlic clove, chopped

½ cup breadcrumbs

CONTINUED

Traditionally, only a female duckling would be used for this recipe.

Put the duck on a cutting board, chest side down. ✦ Bone it, beginning with the back, and put it in a pan breast-side down. ✦ Salt and pepper the duck and sprinkle with most of the rosemary, sage, and garlic. ✦ Set aside a small portion of the poppies and boil the remainder in lightly salted water to cover. Heat 2 tablespoons of the butter in a pan, then cook the boiled poppies with the pancetta and garlic. Add a little water to the pan, reduce the heat to low, and stew them for 20 minutes; let cool. Preheat the oven to 300°F. ✦ When they are cool enough

2 large eggs, beaten

4 oz. soppressata, diced

⅔ cup grated Parmigiano-Reggiano

4 oz. *lardo,* diced

½ cup white wine

Salt and pepper

to handle, chop them. Combine them with the bread-crumbs, eggs, 2 tablespoons of the butter, soppressata, and Parmigiano-Reggiano. ✦ Mix in the *lardo,* then spread the mixture over the inside of the duck. ✦ Roll up the duck and tie it closed. ✦ Add the remaining garlic, rosemary, sage, and reserved poppies to the pot, cover, and bake. ✦ As soon as the duck has browned, pour the white wine over it. ✦ Uncover and bake for 1½ hours. ✦ Lift the duck out of the pot and place on a serving dish; pass the cooking juices though a fine sieve, cook down a few minutes to reduce, then pour over the duck before serving.

ANITRA FARCITA

STUFFED DUCK

FOR
6 PERSONS

PIEMONTE

½ lb. ground veal

½ lb. ground pork

4 oz. sausage meat, crumbled

2 oz. *lardo*

2 oz. pancetta, chopped

1 large onion, thinly sliced

⅔ cup cooked rice

2 tbsp. chopped flat-leaf parsley

1 garlic clove, chopped

3 large eggs, beaten

Pinch grated nutmeg

3½ lbs. young duck, cleaned

3 tbsp. olive oil

1 sprig rosemary

Broth (if necessary)

Salt and pepper

Preheat the oven to 325°F. In a bowl, combine the veal, pork, sausage meat, *lardo,* pancetta, and onion. ✦ Add the rice, parsley, garlic, eggs, salt, pepper, and nutmeg. ✦ Stuff the duck with this mixture, then sew it closed with kitchen thread. ✦ Add the olive oil to a baking pan and add the rosemary. Place the duck on top of the rosemary. Cover the pan and bake for about 2 full hours, adding water or broth if necessary.

ANATRA MUTA
A PORCHETTA

STUFFED ROAST DUCK

UMBRIA

1 duck with its giblets

CONTINUED

Preheat the oven to 300°F. Chop the duck giblets in small pieces, add the potatoes, fennel, salt, pepper, and garlic, and cook in an ovenproof pan with the olive oil. ✦ When half cooked, remove from the heat and use this

1 lb. potatoes, peeled and cubed
1 bunch wild fennel
2 garlic cloves
2 tbsp. extra-virgin olive oil
Dry white wine
Salt and pepper

mixture to stuff the duck, then carefully close the opening. ✦ Put the duck thus prepared in a pan and roast for at least 2 hours, adding wine if needed. ✦ When cooked, cut the duck in 8 pieces and put on a serving plate with its stuffing, pouring over it the thickened cooking juices. Serve hot.

ANITRA FARCITA | DUCK STUFFED WITH VEAL AND PORK

FOR
8 PERSONS

PIEMONTE

½ lb. pork shoulder, cut into chunks
½ lb. veal shoulder, cut into chunks
Meat of 1 sausage, crumbled
2 oz. pancetta, diced
2 oz. *lardo,* chopped
1 medium onion, thinly sliced
⅔ cup rice
4 oz. crustless bread, softened in milk and squeezed dry
2 tbsp. chopped flat-leaf parsley
1 garlic clove, chopped
Yolks of 3 large hard-boiled eggs, crumbled
Pinch grated nutmeg
1 duck, about 3¼ lbs.
3 tbsp. extra-virgin olive oil
1 sprig rosemary
3 sage leaves
¼ cup broth
¼ cup white wine
Salt and pepper

This dish is typical of Novara.

Pass the pork and veal through a meat grinder and combine with the sausage meat, pancetta, *lardo*, and onion and sauté in a pan until the meat is lightly browned. ✦ Separately, boil the rice in lightly salted water to cover by 1 inch until tender; drain. ✦ Put the meat mixture in a bowl and add the cooked rice, bread, parsley, garlic, egg yolks, salt, pepper, and nutmeg. ✦ Blend well and use to stuff the duck, then sew up the opening with kitchen twine. ✦ Mix the olive oil, rosemary, and sage leaves in an oval saucepan, then put in the duck. ✦ Cook the duck at low heat, uncovered, for about 2 hours. ✦ After an hour, add the broth and wine. Serve the duck cut up into about 10 pieces arranged on the serving plate.

ANITRA RIPIENA | DUCK STUFFED WITH SAUSAGE AND LIVER

VENETO

Duck was once the primary dish at every winter festivity, and the housewives and peasants throughout the valleys made certain the grounds near their homes had ranks of ducks ready to be sacrificed to the good name of the family's kitchen. This recipe calls for butter, but in the past, goose fat or pork lard was used throughout the Valli Grandi area.

1 duck with its liver (about 4 lbs.)
¾ lb. pork liver
2 oz. pancetta, diced
Meat of 1 large sausage
½ cup extra-virgin olive oil
Bread of 2 rolls, soaked in milk and squeezed dry
1 large egg, beaten
1 garlic clove, crushed
1 medium onion, chopped
1 bouquet garni (flat-leaf parsley, rosemary, sage, thyme, bay leaf)
1 sprig rosemary
½ cup white wine
3 tablespons unsalted butter
Salt and pepper

Serve with side dishes of salted cabbage and slices of polenta roasted on a grill.

Preheat the oven to 300°F. Clean the duck, removing the feet and head. Open it along its chest. ✦ Finely chop the duck liver and pork liver. Combine with the pancetta and sausage meat, olive oil, bread, egg, garlic, onion, bouquet garni, salt, and pepper. ✦ Knead this well to achieve a homogeneous filling. ✦ With this fill the duck and smear some along the outside, tie it closed, and place it in a baking pan with the rosemary. Roast for 2 hours, basting from time to time with the cooking liquid and addng the wine and butter at the end of the first hour. ✦ When the meat comes away from the bones, the duck is done. Serve the duck piping hot.

| # ROAST PORK LOIN

FOR
6 PERSONS

TOSCANA

1 pork loin with bone (about 3½ lbs.)
3 garlic cloves, minced
2 sprigs rosemary, minced
¼ cup extra-virgin olive oil
Salt and pepper

It is best to cook cubed potatoes together with the pork. There is also the alternative of using the cooking juices to flavor turnips or *cavolo nero* (black kale) boiled and roughly chopped. The recipe Artusi gives calls for the addition of a few cloves and indicates that the loin should be cooked "on a spit, as is best." He may be right, but cooking it in the oven also works quite well.

Preheat the oven to 350°F. Bone the pork loin. ✦ Combine the garlic and rosemary with salt and pepper and insert half of the mixture into the space left by the bone. ✦ Tie up to reform the loin. ✦ Massage the rest of the mixture into the meat and put it in a baking pan. ✦ Pour the olive oil over and roast for about 1½ hours. ✦ When the meat is cooked, untie it, slice it, and serve in its cooking juices.

ARROSTICINI | # SKEWERED LAMB

ABRUZZO

Meat of mutton or sheep (as much as desired)
Salt and pepper

The meat should be served with peasant-style bread spread with olive oil.

Heat the grill to medium-high. Cut the meat into 1½-inch cubes. Thread the meat onto wooden skewers about 10 to 15 inches long. ✦ Grill directly over coals until the outside is browned and crisp; the inside should still be pink. Season to taste with salt and pepper.

MILK-ROASTED VEAL

LOMBARDIA

4 tbsp. unsalted butter

1 tbsp. all-purpose flour

2 oz. prosciutto crudo, in thin slices

1¾ lbs. veal rump,
rolled into a uniform piece

4 cups milk

Salt

This cooking method can also be applied to beef.

Preheat the oven to 350°F. Heat the butter in a roasting pan over low heat and whisk in the flour and prosciutto. ✦ When this begins to take on color, add the veal and brown it, seasoning with salt. ✦ Cover and roast until cooked through, about 1 hour, adding milk from time to time to keep it from drying out. Serve the meat with its cooking juices.

✦ **LOCAL TRADITION** ✦

BECCACCE ALLA ARZIGNANESE

Prized in the Veneto Prealps, wild woodcock were hunted during their migration season in the late fall. In this rustic recipe typical of the area of Arzignano, the birds were first hung in a cool, dry place, such as a basement, to age the meat before cooking. It took the expert eye of an experienced hunter and cook to know the precise moment when the birds were ready for cooking. Once this point was determined, the woodcock would be cleaned and wrapped in a large slice of salted *lardo*. They were then roasted on a spit over an open fire, with a drip pan beneath to catch the precious cooking juices. Once the birds had taken on just the right telltale red color, they would be removed from the spit, halved, and their entrails and fresh lemon juice mixed into the drippings to make a savory sauce. The birds would finish cooking slowly in the sauce in a wide earthenware dish over low heat and would be served with bread warm from the hearth.

MEAT & POULTRY

STEAK FLORENTINE

TOSCANA

1 porterhouse steak
(preferably from a Chiana cow),
weighing at least 2 lbs.

Salt

This dish is typical of Florence. Have your butcher cut the steak at least 1½ to 2 inches thick. The porterhouse is similar to a T-bone, but includes a large section of tenderloin.

Heat a grill to hot. Add the steak and cook 5 minutes, then turn and cook 5 minutes on the other side. ✦ Then turn it again, salt, and serve. Do not add olive oil or lemon juice.

BECCACCE ALLA CHIAMPESE

In this recipe popular in the town of Chiampo, also in the Veneto, the woodcocks would be aged and roasted as in the style of Arzignano (see page 519), but when removed from the spit halfway through cooking, they were instead quartered and the entrails mixed with a little olive oil in a separate dish. The birds were then cooked slowly in a pan over embers for another two hours with black pepper and lemon juice added at the very end. The sauce would be used only according to taste during the second cooking, and the birds would be served with black bread traditional to the area of Vincenza.

BISTECCA DEL CURATO

VEAL CUTLETS IN SAUCE

UMBRIA

¼ cup extra-virgin olive oil

4 veal *nodini*

1 bunch basil leaves, chopped

1 tbsp. chopped fresh marjoram

4 mint leaves, chopped

1 sprig rosemary, chopped

5 tbsp. white wine vinegar

Juice of 5 lemons

3 anchovies, desalted, boned, and cut in pieces

5 garlic cloves, minced

½ medium onion, finely chopped

Pinch dry mustard

Salt and pepper

This dish is typical of Orvieto. *Nodini* is a special cut of veal with the bone in the middle, from the shank.

Heat the olive oil in a pan. Add the veal and sprinkle with salt and pepper. Cook over low heat, turning halfway through cooking. ✦ Grind together the herbs in a mortar. Make a sauce by combining the herbs with vinegar, lemon juice, anchovies, garlic, onion, and mustard. ✦ When the cutlets are cooked, pour the sauce over them, remove from the heat, and serve immediately.

BISTECCHE AL RAFANO

STEAKS WITH HORSERADISH SAUCE

ALTO ADIGE

---

3 tbsp. unsalted butter

CONTINUED

Heat the grill to hot. Melt the butter in a saucepan and whisk in the flour to form a paste, then dilute with the broth. ✦ Taste for salt and pepper and cook 15 minutes. ✦ Remove the sauce from the heat and add the horse-

⅓ cup all-purpose flour

2 cups meat broth, heated

2 tbsp. grated horseradish

½ cup golden raisins,
soaked in ¼ cup Marsala

1 tbsp. red wine vinegar

1 tsp. sugar

4 steaks, about 7 oz. each

Salt and pepper

radish, raisins with their liquid, vinegar, and sugar, stirring to blend. ✦ Put the steaks on the hot grill and cook until rare (2 to 3 minutes per side). ✦ Put them on a warmed serving plate, salt and pepper them, then spoon over the horseradish sauce.

MARROW SAUCE WITH PEPPER

VENETO

7 oz. marrow (equal parts beef, veal, and pork marrow, or only beef)

3 tbsp. unsalted butter

2 cups beef broth (preferably the unskimmed remains of boiling a good piece of beef), heated to boiling

2 cups breadcrumbs

Pepper, half of it very finely ground, the rest peppercorns

How much pepper? In preparing this sauce, with its wonderful flavor, the amount of pepper is left up to the cook. Even so, it is best not to overdo it with the spicy taste of this mixture. This is the ideal complement to boiled meats, also boiled capon, as on festive occasions. It is also perfect with slices of polenta toasted on a grill.

In an earthenware or enameled cast-iron pan over low heat, slowly cook the marrow. (You can also use the marrow from boiled veal shanks.) ✦ Mix in the butter. ✦ When the marrow melts from the heat, slowly pour in ½ cup of boiling broth per person, but a little at a time so as not to interrupt the cooking. ✦ Let this boil a few minutes, then add ½ cup breadcrumbs per person and let this simmer very gently for at least 1½ hours. ✦ Fifteen minutes before removing this from the heat, add the finely ground pepper and peppercorns. ✦ At this point, to give the sauce the right creamy consistency, add either more broth or more breadcrumbs. ✦ Bear in mind that the consistency of the sauce will change if cooled even a little. If it is already dense while being cooked it will certainly turn out too thick when served, and vice versa. Bring it to the table as hot as possible, if necessary making use of a catering warmer or hot plate. Also remember that the marrow will tend to stiffen as it cools.

MEAT & POULTRY

| # MIXED BRAISED MEATS

EMILIA-ROMAGNA

3 medium onions, chopped
4 carrots, chopped
4 celery stalks, chopped
1¾ lbs. beef (chuck, shoulder, or loin)
1 lb. veal breast
½ hen (or large chicken)
Veal head, foot, and tongue
2 marrow bones
1 cotechino (see note)
Salt

Carve the meat at the table and reserve the broth for use in another recipe. Serve with *Salsa verde* (see page 5), *mostarda di Cremona*, or a tomato sauce. This serves a crowd of at least 12. Cotechino is a fresh pork sausage from Modena.

Put the vegetables in a large pot. Add about 20 cups of lightly salted water and turn on the heat; when the water boils add the beef and veal and cook at low heat. ✦ After 1 hour add the hen and the remaining meat except the cotechino and cook for another hour. Cook the cotechino separately in water to cover, simmering slowly for at least an hour. ✦ When the meats are fork-tender, turn off the heat, add the cotechino, and let stand 5 minutes before serving.

| # BOILED STUFFED CAPON OR HEN

EMILIA-ROMAGNA

⅔ cup breadcrumbs
1 cup broth, boiling, plus more as needed
2 tbsp. unsalted butter
2 large eggs, beaten
⅔ cup grated Parmigiano-Reggiano
2 whole cloves
1 1-inch piece ginger, peeled and grated
Pinch grated nutmeg
1 capon or hen (about 3 lbs.)
Salt

This dish is typical of Parma.

Put the breadcrumbs in a bowl and add the broth; while stirring, add the butter, eggs, Parmigiano-Reggiano, cloves, ginger, and nutmeg. ✦ Add salt, then mix to blend. ✦ Fill the capon or hen with the filling and sew it closed with kitchen twine. Bring a large pot of water to a boil. To achieve good results, add the stuffed bird to water that is already boiling. Cook until the meat and stuffing are cooked through.

| # PORK CUTLETS IN WINE

TOSCANA

4 pork cutlets, about 7 oz. each
1 garlic clove, chopped
Pinch ground fennel seeds
½ cup red wine (preferably Chianti)

Salt and pepper the cutlets as desired and put them in a dry pan with the garlic and fennel seeds. ✦ Brown the meat at high heat on both sides, then pour in the wine. ✦ Cover the pan and continue cooking at low heat until the wine has completely evaporated. Serve hot.

BEEF IN SAUCE

CAMPANIA

1 tbsp. extra-virgin olive oil

2 oz. lard

4 oz. *lardo*

1 onion, chopped

4 oz. tomato paste

½ cup dry red wine

1 ¼ lbs. beef rump in 6 slices

½ cup chopped flat-leaf parsley

1 garlic clove

4 oz. prosciutto crudo, sliced

4 oz. provolone, cut in strips

⅔ cup mixed raisins and pine nuts

Salt and pepper

In Naples, *braciola* is a dish, whereas to the north of that city the word refers to a cut of meat (usually a cutlet). Even so, if you go into a Neapolitan restaurant and ask for *braciola*, you may be served roll-ups like the ones here or you may just as easily receive a *granatina* of ground meat, pine nuts, raisins, garlic, bread, and parsley. This is because in the nineteenth century both preparations were known as *braciolette*.

Heat the olive oil in a large pan. Add the lard and half the *lardo* and cook on low heat until the *lardo* is crisp and has given up most of its fat. Add the onion and cook until golden. Stir in the tomato paste, then stir in the wine. Stir in water to make a thin sauce. Keep warm while preparing the meat. ✦ Trim away any fat or sinew from the meat and pound each slice well until the slices are about ¼ inch thick. ✦ Finely chop the remaining *lardo*, parsley, and garlic and add salt and a pinch of pepper. ✦ Set out the six slices of meat, lay a slice of prosciutto on each, then add (always dividing the ingredients in six portions) some of the *lardo* mixture, strips of provolone, and the raisins and pine nuts. ✦ Roll up each slice around this filling and tie it closed with twine, as you would a salame, being careful to make certain the ends are closed. ✦ Add these to the sauce, reduce the heat to low, and cook for approximately 1½ hours. ✦ As soon as they are cooked, lift them out of the sauce and set them aside to drain, letting the sauce continue to slowly cook until it reaches the right thickness. ✦ At that point return the roll-ups to the sauce and heat them for about 10 minutes before serving them with side dishes of broccoli and fried potatoes.

GRILLED VEAL MESSINA-STYLE

SICILIA

1 ¼ cups breadcrumbs

2 tbsp. chopped flat-leaf parsley

1 garlic clove, finely chopped

⅔ cup grated caciocavallo

Olive oil

CONTINUED

This dish is typical of Messina.

Heat a grill to medium hot. Put the breadcrumbs in a bowl and season them with parsley, garlic, caciocavallo, and salt and pepper, mixing the ingredients well. Add just enough olive oil to moisten the mixture. ✦ Spread a little lard over each slice of meat, then top each one with 2 to 3 tablespoons of the filling. ✦ Roll up each slice, making sure to close them well. Thread them on

2 tbsp. lard
1 lb. veal roast, thinly sliced
Salt and pepper

skewers, putting 5 on each, spread more lard over them, then grill over charcoal until cooked through.

**BRASATO DI MANZO
AL BAROLO**

BEEF BRAISED
IN BAROLO

FOR
8 PERSONS

PIEMONTE

2 lbs. boneless beef sirloin
1 bottle Barolo wine
(or other full-bodied red wine)
1 medium onion, quartered
1 carrot, chopped
1 celery stalk, chopped
2 bay leaves
8 to 10 peppercorns
4 tbsp. unsalted butter
1 oz. prosciutto fat, minced
2 garlic cloves
1 sprig rosemary
1 tsp. potato starch
Salt

Serve with mashed potatoes.

Place the meat in a large pan and pour over it the bottle of Barolo. ✦ Add the onion, carrot, celery, bay leaves, and peppercorns. ✦ Leave the meat in this marinade for 24 hours, turning a few times. ✦ Using tongs, lift the meat out of the marinade, pat dry, and tie with butcher's twine to maintain its shape. ✦ In a large casserole heat the butter and prosciutto fat; add the garlic and rosemary, then the meat. Brown the meat on all sides. ✦ Meanwhile, strain the marinade, discarding the bits of solid matter. Put the liquid in a pot and boil it to reduce it by half. ✦ Season the browned meat with a little salt and slowly pour the marinade over the meat a little at a time. ✦ Cover and finish cooking over moderate heat. ✦ When the meat is medium rare, remove the twine and place it on a serving plate to let it rest. ✦ Degrease the pan juices, then thicken with the potato starch. Slice the meat carefully and pour some of the sauce over the slices.

BRODETTO PASQUALE

EASTER LAMB STEW

BASILICATA

¼ cup extra-virgin olive oil
2 lbs. boned leg of lamb,
cut into pieces
1 medium onion, finely sliced
1 lb. peeled plum tomatoes
2 lbs. wild cardoons (or asparagus
or other similar vegetable),
boiled and chopped
12 large eggs, beaten
½ cup grated pecorino
3 tbsp. chopped flat-leaf parsley
Salt

This dish is typical of Venosa. The size of the baking pan will determine the depth of the *brodetto*.

Preheat the oven to 350°F. Heat the olive oil in a large pan over medium heat. Add the lamb and onion; when the meat is half-cooked, stir in the tomatoes and cardoons (or other vegetable). ✦ Meanwhile, mix the eggs, cheese, parsley, and salt. ✦ Transfer the meat and vegetables to a baking pan and pour over the egg mixture. Bake until the egg mixture is set, about 10 minutes.

BUDELLINE DI AGNELLO DI FAICCHIO

In this recipe for lamb intestines stuffed with parsley and pepper, typical of Campania, the intestines would first be split open and cleaned with warm, salted water. The membrane attached would then be cut into many smaller pieces and each section stuffed with a parsley-pepper mixture and made into a small roll-up. The roll-ups would then be cooked either on a medium-hot grill or included in a stew.

MEAT BRAISED WITH CABBAGE

BRUSCITT

PIEMONTE

1 ¼ lbs. beef stew meat
2 tbsp. unsalted butter
2 oz. pancetta, chopped
1 garlic clove
1 ¼ cups chopped Savoy cabbage (only the inner parts)
¼ cup red wine (preferably Barbera)
Salt and pepper

This dish is eaten by local countryfolk in Bellinsago. Serve with warm, soft polenta.

Cut the meat in slices, then in smaller pieces, then dice it. ✦ Put it in a saucepan with 1 tablespoon butter, pancetta, and garlic and cook at very low heat. ✦ Add the cabbage and cook until tender, stirring from time to time. Add the remaining butter. ✦ Remove the garlic, pour in the wine, and cook at high heat until the liquid evaporates. Salt and pepper to taste.

LAMB INTESTINES VITERBO-STYLE

BUDELLINI DI AGNELLO ALLA VITERBESE

LAZIO

In the Viterbo dialect, the intestines of milk-fed lambs are called *capomazzi*, because they are *capati*, meaning "chosen," from the *mazzo*, or "bundle," of the intestines. They are prepared without interior cleaning, but the fatty parts are removed and they are woven to form braids. They can be found on sale commercially most easily during the period of the lamb slaughtering, when a great number of milk-fed lambs are killed, but in Viterbo they are available during other periods of the year since the use of lamb is very widespread there. As indicated, the intestines can be cooked in a variety of ways.

On the grill

2 lbs. braided lamb intestines

2 cups extra-virgin olive oil

Juice of 1 lemon

Salt and pepper

Heat the grill to medium. Marinate the lamb intestines in a bowl with olive oil to cover, lemon juice, salt, and pepper. ✦ When the time comes to cook them, arrange them on a grill directly over the coals. ✦ To keep them from burning without cooking, bathe them from time to time with a half lemon dipped in the oil of the marinade. ✦ When they are well cooked and browned, serve warm with lemon juice.

In a pan with potatoes

½ cup extra-virgin olive oil

2 or 3 garlic cloves

2 lbs. braided lamb intestines

¼ cup white wine

2 lbs. potatoes, peeled and cubed

2 tbsp. dried wild fennel flowers

Salt and pepper

In a good-sized pan, heat the olive oil until hot. Add the garlic and cook until golden. Add the intestines and wine. ✦ When the wine evaporates, add the potatoes, salt, pepper, and fennel flowers. Cover and cook until the potatoes are browned and flavorful and the intestines are well cooked.

In a pan with onions

½ cup extra-virgin olive oil

1 oz. prosciutto fat

2 or 3 garlic cloves

2 lbs. lamb intestines, cut in pieces of various lengths

½ cup white wine

4 medium onions, sliced

¼ cup tomato purée

Pinch chili pepper flakes

Pinch fennel seeds

Salt

If desired, cubed potatoes can be added to this dish before the onions go in. Doing so requires increasing the amount of both the tomato purée and the warm water, since the potatoes will need this increased liquid to cook. The resulting dish will have greater consistency, taking on the traits of a true one-dish meal.

In a pan, preferably earthenware, heat the olive oil and prosciutto fat. Add the whole garlic cloves, then add the intestines and wine. ✦ When the wine has evaporated, add the onions, tomato purée, salt, chili pepper, fennel, and a few tablespoons of warm water and continue cooking to obtain a somewhat dense sauce that will flavor both the onions and the intestines.

BUDINO DI CERVELLA | # BRAIN SOUFFLÉ

TRENTINO

4 tbsp. unsalted butter, plus more for the pan

½ cup breadcrumbs

1 calf's brain

1 medium onion, finely chopped

CONTINUED

Serve with a kidney and mushroom sauce.

Preheat the oven to 350°F. ✦ Use some of the butter to grease a deep round baking dish, then sprinkle with breadcrumbs. Set aside. ✦ In a separate pan, roast the calf's brain with the onion and parsley for 20 minutes. Let cool and finely dice. ✦ Beat the egg yolks with the remaining butter and bread, then stir in the brains. ✦ Beat the egg whites until soft peaks form, then fold into

2 tbsp. finely chopped
flat-leaf parsley

4 large eggs, separated

Bread of 4 rolls, soaked in milk,
then squeezed dry

the yolk mixture. Transfer the mixture to the prepared baking dish. Place it in a larger, deep baking pan and place in the oven. Fill the larger pan with hot water that reaches at least halfway up the sides of the dish. Bake until the soufflé is set.

LAMB STEW WITH TOMATOES

4½ lbs. mixed lamb
(shank, shoulder, loin)

¾ cup extra-virgin olive oil

1 large onion, chopped

½ cup dry red wine

2 garlic cloves, crushed

2 sprigs rosemary

Pinch chili pepper flakes

1 lb. peeled plum tomatoes,
without liquid or seeds

1 tbsp. tomato paste

Broth, as needed

Slices of peasant-style bread

This dish is typical of Manciano.

Cut the lamb in pieces that are not too small. Heat the olive oil in a large pan over low heat. Add the onion, then the lamb and brown. ✦ When the lamb has taken on color, add the wine, garlic, rosemary, and a pinch of chili pepper. ✦ When the wine evaporates, add the tomatoes and tomato paste. ✦ Continue cooking, adding broth as needed to maintain a couple inches of liquid in the pan. ✦ Meanwhile, toast the sliced bread, and arrange them in the bottom of a large serving bowl. ✦ When the lamb is cooked, pour some of the sauce onto the bread slices in the bowl. Over this add the pieces of meat, then pour in the remaining sauce. Serve hot.

TYROLEAN CHAMOIS

2 lbs. chamois loin or leg
(can use goat)

3 medium onions, sliced

2 bay leaves

7 juniper berries

4 whole cloves

1 lemon, sliced

Pinch thyme leaves

About 5 cups red wine

About 3 cups vinegar,
brought to a boil

4 oz. white *lardo*, finely sliced

CONTINUED

Chamois is a small hooved animal native to the Alps. Its meat is similar to venison or goat. For the wine use Lagrein.

Cut the chamois in large pieces. Mix 2 onions, the bay leaves, juniper berries, cloves, lemon, and thyme. Add the meat and equal parts red wine and boiling vinegar enough to cover the meat. ✦ Put a lid or plate directly on the meat. Place a weight on that and refrigerate for 5 days. ✦ At the end of that time remove the meat from the marinade and lard it with the *lardo*. ✦ Put the meat in a saucepan with the remaining onion, all the herbs from the marinade, 2 cups of the same wine, cream mixture, salt, and pepper. ✦ Put the pan over moderate heat and reduce the sauce, stirring often and adding more wine and cream from time to time as needed. ✦ When the meat is cooked, remove it from the sauce and keep it

½ cup heavy cream acidulated with 1 tbsp. lemon juice, plus more cream as needed

Broth

Salt and pepper

warm. ✦ Dilute the sauce with a little broth, skim off the fat, pass it through a sieve, and put it back on the heat in a different pan. When it is boiling, pour it over the meat.

CHAMOIS IN ONION SAUCE

1¾ lbs. chamois, in pieces (can use goat)

For the marinade:
1 bottle red wine
1 medium onion, sliced
1 carrot, chopped
1 celery stalk, chopped
1 garlic clove, chopped
A few sage leaves
2 sprigs thyme
1 tsp. dried marjoram
2 bay leaves
1 tsp. whole cloves
1 tbsp. juniper berries, lightly crushed
All-purpose flour for dredging
3 or 4 tbsp. extra-virgin olive oil
2 tbsp. unsalted butter
Salt and peppercorns

The dialect name for this dish, typical of Courmayeur, *Civet de tsamos*, refers to the onion in the sauce: *civet* is derived from the Latin *cepa* (onion). Serve with polenta. For the wine use Rouge de Morgex or Barolo.

Clean and dry the pieces of chamois, put them in a large bowl, and cover with red wine. ✦ Add the onion, carrot, celery, garlic, sage, thyme, marjoram, bay leaves, cloves, juniper berries, salt, and peppercorns. ✦ Cover and refrigerate for 12 hours, stirring the meat from time to time. ✦ Remove the meat from the marinade, dry it, and lightly flour each piece. ✦ Heat the olive oil and butter in a large pan and add the pieces of meat, browning them well. ✦ At this point add the marinade with its vegetables and cook, covered, for about 2 hours at low heat. ✦ When the meat is cooked, remove it from the sauce and pass the cooking juices through a sieve. ✦ Return the meat and any juices to the pan and reheat for half an hour.

ROAST CAPON

FOR
8 PERSONS

4½-lb. capon
6 oz. sliced prosciutto, both fatty pieces and lean
4 oz. *lardo*, sliced
5 tbsp. unsalted butter

CONTINUED

Serve this dish with puréed carrots.

Cut the head and feet off the capon and remove the giblets. ✦ Singe, rinse, and dry it, then wrap it in slices of prosciutto and attach these to the bird with a few stitches of kitchen twine. ✦ Cover the bottom of a large saucepan with slices of *lardo*, then add 4 tablespoons of the butter, celery, carrot, thyme, marjoram, and bay leaf. ✦ Rest the capon on this bed and add the Marsala and broth; season to taste with salt. ✦ Cover the pan with foil and then

1 celery stalk, chopped
1 carrot, chopped
1 sprig thyme
A few marjoram leaves
1 bay leaf
¼ cup Marsala
1 cup broth
1 tbsp. potato starch
1 small truffle, sliced
Salt

with the lid, making sure there is a tight seal. ✦ Put the saucepan over moderate heat and let it cook about 1 hour. ✦ At the end of this time delicately remove the capon from the pan, free it of the prosciutto slices and twine, and keep it warm. ✦ Spoon off any fat from the pan and remove the pieces of *lardo*. ✦ Transfer the cooking juices to a strainer set over a pan and press down well with a wooden spoon on all the herbs to collect as much sauce as possible, then pour this into a small saucepan. ✦ Stir together the potato starch with a couple tablespoons warm water until dissolved. Put this over heat for a few minutes to thicken, adding the sauce mixture. Stir until it reaches the desired density. ✦ Add to the sauce a small truffle in slices and the pat of butter. ✦ Put the capon back in the saucepan, pour the sauce over it, and let it cook over low heat for a few minutes. ✦ Then slice the capon in pieces, arrange them on a serving plate, and serve hot.

| ## STUFFED CABBAGE

16 Savoy cabbage leaves
1 bunch flat-leaf parsley
1 garlic clove
6 oz. leftover meat, boiled or roast
4 oz. cooked salame
2 large eggs, beaten
2 tbsp. grated Parmigiano-Reggiano
6 tbsp. unsalted butter

Parboil the Savoy cabbage leaves for a few minutes, then drain and set out on a cloth. ✦ Finely chop the parsley together with the garlic, leftover meat, and salame and put this mixture in a bowl; add eggs and Parmigiano-Reggiano and mix well. ✦ Shape this mixture into small cylinders and put them on the cabbage leaves, folding in the leaves to form roll-ups. ✦ Heat the butter in a pan and delicately add the roll-ups, browning them on both sides. ✦ Put them on a plate covered with paper towels to absorb the fat, then serve.

| ## STUFFED ZUCCHINI FLOWERS

½ lb. pork shoulder
¼ lb. veal breast
¼ lb. sausage
CONTINUED

This dish is typical of Alba.

Preheat the oven to 350°F. Cook the pork, veal, and sausage separately, then finely chop together and put in a bowl. ✦ Add the bread, nutmeg, raisins, Parmigiano-Reggiano, and salt and pepper to taste. ✦ Work in the eggs. ✦ Parboil the zucchini flowers just until wilted. ✦

8 oz. crustless bread, soaked in milk
and squeezed dry

Pinch grated nutmeg

⅔ cup raisins,
softened in warm water

1 tbsp. grated Parmigiano-Reggiano

2 large eggs, beaten

18 zucchini flowers

2 tbsp. unsalted butter

2 tbsp. extra-virgin olive oil

Salt and pepper

Place 2 tablespoons of the mixture on each flower, rolling them closed. ✦ Arrange the flowers in a baking pan with pats of the butter and olive oil and bake for about 20 minutes until the filling is hot and the flowers are lightly browned. Serve hot.

SPICED CAPON

EMILIA-ROMAGNA

1 capon

1 garlic clove

2 tsp. juniper berries

2 tbsp. lard

For the sauce:

2 tbsp. capers

2 tbsp. chopped flat-leaf parsley

5 anchovies

Pinch grated nutmeg

Juice of ½ lemon

¼ cup olive oil, or as needed

1 tbsp. unsalted butter

½ cup balsamic vinegar

Salt and pepper

This recipe, from a nineteenth-century cookbook, is somewhat complex and has a wonderfully offhand approach. It calls for quite an array of ingredients, and capons are rare; the result, however, is delicious. It is typical of Reggio Emilia. Ideally the bird should should be marinated in the sauce for 3 or 4 hours, refrigerated; then you may reheat the bird before serving.

Place the capon in a pot and add water to cover, then simmer over low heat. When it has cooked for 2 hours remove it. ✦ Preheat the oven to 350°F. ✦ Grind together garlic, juniper berries, and salt and spread this mixture the over the capon inside and out. Add the lard to a roasting pan and add the capon. Roast in the oven; when it is golden brown cut it in pieces. ✦ Reassemble the pieces on a serving plate and transfer the pan juices to a saucepan. ✦ Grind the capers, parsley, anchovies, nutmeg, and a little pepper in a mortar with enough of the olive oil to make a smooth paste. Add this mixture to the pan juices with the lemon juice, 2 tablespoons olive oil, butter, and balsamic vinegar. ✦ Simmer the mixture for half an hour, stirring constantly to prevent it from sticking, then pour over the capon on its serving plate.

CAPPELLO DA PRETE CON ZABAIONE

This sausage, which is typical of Reggio Emilia, gets its name from its special shape, which resembles the three-pointed hat of a priest. Its filling and mode of cooking are the same as those for *zampone*, another sausage that is typical of this region. However, *cappello da prete* is made with a different casing—the very soft pork rind that comes from the pig's throat. The *cappello da prete* is to be eaten with a rich zabaglione sauce, one that is reinforced with brandy. The combination of these two, both sumptuous and princely, ranks among the noblest examples of *dolcebrusco,* the "sweet and sour" taste brought from central Europe to the Po Valley. Some claim zabaglione was invented in the kitchens of the Medici family in Florence during the 1500s. Others say it was invented by French cooks brought to Parma by Marie Louise. According to Numa Ciripiglia in her *Cucina Tradizionale Reggiana,* zabaglione was invented in the area of Reggio Emilia when the condottiere Gian Paolo Baglioni (decapitated at Rome in 1520 by Pope Leo X—and only four years earlier he'd made him a count!) set up camp along with his famished soldiers. Eggs, sugar, and white wine were the only foods that could be found, so they were dutifully whisked together, heated, and distributed. The dish met an enthusiastic reception from the troops. The mixture was given the dialect version of the condottiere's name, *Zuan Bajour,* and in some dialects it is still called *zambajoun.*

**CAPPONE ALLO SPIEDO
CON ERBA LIMONCELLA**

CAPON WITH LEMON BALM

FOR
8 PERSONS

FRIULI-VENEZIA GIULIA

1 capon
10 lemon balm leaves
4 sage leaves
½ cup extra-virgin olive oil
½ medium onion, finely chopped
1 carrot, finely chopped
1 celery stalk, finely chopped
4 cups dry white wine, such as Tocai
Salt and pepper

Set up a rotisserie, placing a drip pan under the cooking area. Clean the capon and salt and pepper it. ✦ Stuff it with half the lemon balm and half the sage, then tie it shut with twine. ✦ In a large heavy pot, heat the olive oil, then add the onion, carrot, celery, and remaining sage, and cook until fragrant. ✦ Add the capon and cook on low heat for about 30 minutes; pour in the wine and cook another half hour. ✦ Impale the capon on a rotisserie skewer and roast it very slowly for 3 hours, basting it from time to time with the cooking juices left in the pan from the first hour of cooking. ✦ When cooked, serve hot, cut in pieces, pouring over it some of the cooking juices. Garnish with the remaining lemon balm.

CAPRA ALLA MOLISANA | GOAT IN SAUCE

MOLISE

2 lbs. goat

4 cups red wine (such as Montepulciano d'Abruzzo)

5 sage leaves

1 bay leaf

1 sprig rosemary

1¼ cups extra-virgin olive oil

1 medium onion, finely sliced

1 lb. plum tomatoes, peeled, seeded, and roughly chopped

Salt

This sauce can be used on cavatelli or *malefante*.

Clean the meat and cut it in small pieces, and place in a pot. Add the wine and sage, bay leaf, and rosemary. Cover and refrigerate overnight. ✦ The next morning remove the meat from the marinade, setting aside the liquid. ✦ Drain the meat and pat it dry with paper towels. ✦ Heat the olive oil in an earthenware pan and add the onion. ✦ When the onion begins to change color, add the meat and cook, drizzling from time to time with a little of the wine from the marinade. ✦ When the wine has evaporated, add salt to taste, the tomatoes, and 3 cups lightly salted warm water. ✦ Cook with the pan covered until the meat is cooked through and the sauce is thick.

CAPRA ALLA NERETESE | GOAT WITH TOMATOES AND PEPPERS
FOR 6 PERSONS

ABRUZZO

½ cup olive oil

1 medium onion, minced

1 celery stalk, chopped

1 whole clove

3¼ lbs. goat, in small pieces

2 lbs. fresh plum tomatoes, peeled and chopped

2 lbs. red peppers, cut in strips

This dish is typical of Nereto.

Heat the olive oil in a large pan. Add the onion, celery, and clove and cook until the onion begins to take on color. ✦ Add the meat and water to cover and cook over low heat for about 1½ hours. ✦ When the liquid has cooked down and the meat has browned, add the tomatoes and cook another hour; add the peppers after 45 minutes and cook until they are soft.

CAPRA ALLA VUTANA | GOAT STEW
FOR 6 PERSONS

CALABRIA

4½ lbs. stew meat from a young goat (but not a kid)

½ cup extra-virgin olive oil

4 cups red wine vinegar, or as needed

CONTINUED

Cut the goat in small pieces. Heat the olive oil in a saucepan. Add the meat and cook it, generously sprinkling it with vinegar until it no longer gives off water. ✦ Transfer the meat to a pot (traditionally copper), along with the onions, bay leaf, chili pepper to taste, and wine; cook it until the liquid has evaporated. ✦ At that point add the tomatoes and tomato purée mixture. ✦ Cook at very low

4 medium onions, chopped
1 bay leaf
Chili pepper flakes, to taste
4 cups white wine
4 ½ lbs. plum tomatoes, peeled, seeded, and chopped
1 ½ cups tomato purée, mixed with 1 ½ cups water

heat for 5 or 6 hours. Serve the meat dripping in sauce accompanied by boiled potatoes.

CAPPONE ALLA CANEVERA

Commonly made during the Christmas season in the Valle del Chiampo in the Veneto, this traditional rustic dish of capon in pig's bladder required a capon that had been purged by spending at least two months in a chicken coop. After cleaning and removing the innards, the bird would be filled with aromatic herbs and seasoned with salt and pepper and then stuffed into a fresh pig's bladder. The hole in the bladder would then be tightly sewn shut with hemp and a slender stalk of *canevera* (bamboo) would be inserted into the natural opening of the bladder to release steam and permit evaporation during cooking. After boiling for 2½ hours in salted water, the capon would be removed from the bladder and allowed to rest for about half an hour before being cut up and served with sauce collected from inside the bladder.

MEAT & POULTRY

CAPRA CON I FAGIOLI

GOAT AND BEANS

LIGURIA

8 lbs. goat meat (a *bima* is needed, meaning a female no longer milk fed but not yet adult)
3 tbsp. extra-virgin olive oil
4 oz. *lardo* (or pancetta)
2 large onions, minced
4 celery stalks, finely chopped
4 carrots, finely chopped
CONTINUED

This dish is typical of the Riviera di Ponente.

Cut the goat in pieces and rinse for at least 12 hours (24 is better) in water, changing it every 2 hours. This cleaning serves to eliminate the animal's wild flavor. ✦ Heat olive oil and *lardo* (or pancetta) in a pan and sauté the onion (there should be twice as much onion as the other vegetables), celery, and carrots. ✦ Salt and pepper the pieces of goat, put them in a large pan (earthenware, if possible, with a wide mouth), and add the cooked vegetables. ✦ Cook at high heat for a few minutes, then add

1 bottle red wine (such as Dolcetto), plus more as needed

¼ cup tomato paste

Aromatic herbs

2 cups beef broth

Dried cannellini beans (or borlotti if they are in season), soaked overnight

Salt and pepper

1 bottle of wine. Lower the heat, cover the pan, and let it cook for at least 45 minutes. ✦ At this point add the tomato paste, herbs, and broth; you can also add more red wine to keep the bottom from sticking. ✦ Separately cook the beans in water to cover for 1½ hours. Drain and add them to the pan with the goat so that the beans will pick up the flavor of the sauce. ✦ Cover again and cook at low heat for another half hour. ✦ This stew should be checked continually and stirred carefully. When done the meat should be extremely tender and beginning to dissolve. Bring the pan to the table and serve hot.

CAPRETTO A BRODETTO

STEWED KID

FOR
8 PERSONS

SICILIA

1 medium onion, sliced

3¼ lbs. kid (or lamb), in small pieces

6 artichoke hearts, boiled and quartered

2 oz. asparagus tips, boiled

¼ cup chopped flat-leaf parsley

2 plum tomatoes, peeled, seeded, and chopped

2 tbsp. tomato paste, dissolved in ¼ cup water

½ cup grated pecorino

2 large eggs

2 tbsp. breadcrumbs

Salt and pepper

Preheat the oven to 400°F. In a large pan, cook the onion in a little water over low heat until soft. Then add the pieces of kid (or lamb) and cook at low heat. ✦ As the kid cooks add half each of the artichokes and asparagus tips, and all of the parsley, tomatoes, salt, and pepper. ✦ Add the tomato paste mixture to the pan and cook, covered, 30 minutes. ✦ When the mixture has become a stew, mix in half the cheese and transfer it to a roasting pan, alternating pieces of kid with the remaining artichoke quarters and asparagus tips. ✦ Beat the eggs and pour them over the mixture, then the remaining cheese and breadcrumbs. ✦ Bake for 10 minutes; the surface should have a golden color, not burned. Serve hot.

CAPRETTO ALL'ORIGANO

LEG OF KID
WITH OREGANO

FOR
6 PERSONS

CALABRIA

1 leg of kid (4½ lbs.)

1 cup extra-virgin olive oil

½ cup white wine vinegar

Chili pepper flakes to taste

1 sprig oregano

Salt

This simple and very tasty specialty should be prepared in the open on a grill. Serve the goat with potatoes baked beneath the ashes of the grill.

Heat a grill to medium, building the fire with olive branches. When the coals are glowing without flames, set up the grill and arrange the pieces of goat on it. ✦ In a bowl mix the olive oil, vinegar, and red pepper. Use the branch of oregano to brush this mixture on the meat during the cooking, thus adding some of the oregano aroma. ✦ Do not add salt until near the end of the cooking time.

GRILLED KID

6 lbs. kid
1 garlic clove, cut in half
6 oz. fresh *lardo*
¼ cup rosemary leaves
½ cup dry white wine
Salt and pepper

Serve accompanied by new potatoes baked in the oven and a salad.

Set up a rotisserie to medium-high heat. Clean out the insides of the kid and wash and dry it. ✦ Rub the skin with the garlic, salt and pepper it, and lard it with *lardo* and rosemary leaves. ✦ Impale it on a rotisserie skewer, tie it on, and put in the rotisserie. ✦ When it begins to take on color, sprinkle with white wine. ✦ Cook at moderate heat for about 2½ hours. ✦ Remove, cut in pieces, and serve warm.

KID IN OIL AND VINEGAR

2¼ lbs. kid
4 garlic cloves
1½ cups extra-virgin olive oil
1¼ cups white wine vinegar
2 sprigs rosemary
Salt and pepper

This dish is typical of Calabritto.

Having carefully cleaned the kid, cut it in pieces. ✦ Put the garlic in a pan with the olive oil and sauté over low heat. As soon as the garlic browns add the meat and cook at low heat. ✦ Toward the end of the cooking add the vinegar and rosemary, taste for salt, and add pepper if needed. Serve at room temperature.

KID IN WINE

4 tbsp. unsalted butter
2 oz. *lardo*, finely chopped
3 lbs. kid, cut in pieces
1 medium onion, roughly chopped
4 cups red wine
Broth (if needed)
Salt and pepper

For the wine use Barbera.

Heat the butter and *lardo* until hot. Add the kid and brown. ✦ Add the onion, salt, and pepper, then pour in the red wine and, if necessary, a little broth so the liquid nearly covers the meat. ✦ Cover and cook at low heat for about 3 hours.

GOAT BRAISED WITH MUSHROOMS

SICILIA

4 ½ lbs. goat kid meat

¼ cup lard

2 medium onions, finely sliced

2 cups good dry red wine

Light meat broth

7 oz. dried mushrooms, soaked in warm water, drained, and chopped

¼ cup chopped flat-leaf parsley

Salt and pepper

Cut the goat meat in pieces and carefully clean and dry each piece. ✦ Melt the lard in a pan, add the onions, and cook until golden. ✦ Add the meat, and as soon as it has taken on a good golden color, pour in the wine and let it evaporate; then taste for salt and pepper. ✦ Pour in enough broth to just cover the kid and continue cooking for at least 45 minutes. ✦ Add the mushrooms and parsley and continue cooking. ✦ When the kid is tender and cooked through, remove the pan from the heat, let it rest a few minutes, then serve hot.

STUFFED KID

CALABRIA

½ cup extra-virgin olive oil

1 whole milk-fed kid, with its offal (heart, liver, lungs)

1 garlic clove, minced

1 bunch flat-leaf parsley, finely chopped

1 ¼ cups tomato purée

2 bay leaves

Pinch chili pepper flakes

1 lb. potatoes, peeled, cut in chunks, and parboiled

Salt

Preheat the oven to 350°F. Grease a roasting pan (preferably earthenware) with olive oil. Clean the offal and chop it into small pieces. ✦ Heat the olive oil in a pan and sauté the garlic and parsley. Add the offal, then ¼ cup tomato purée. ✦ Add the bay leaves, salt to taste, and chili pepper. ✦ Cook this for about 20 minutes over medium heat. ✦ Put the kid in the roasting pan, filling its interior with the offal mixture. ✦ Pour over this the remaining tomato purée, arrange the parboiled potatoes around the kid, add more salt, and bake 1 ½ hours until tender. Check the cooking often, basting the kid with its sauce. Serve hot.

VENISON WITH BERRIES

ALTO ADIGE

2 lbs. roe deer meat, cut in small pieces

2 sprigs rosemary

8 juniper berries

2 bay leaves

CONTINUED

In an earthenware container combine the deer meat with the rosemary, juniper berries, bay leaves, and sage leaves. ✦ Pour in enough wine to cover. ✦ Let the deer marinate in this mixture at least 2 days. ✦ Lift the meat from the marinade, filter out the herbs, and set aside the liquid. Drain and dry the meat. ✦ Heat the *lardo* over low heat to render the fat without burning it. Sauté the onions in

4 sage leaves
1 bottle red wine (such as Lagrein),
or as needed
5 ½ oz. white *lardo*
2 medium onions, thinly sliced
1 cup heavy cream
Red currant jam, for serving
Salt and pepper

the *lardo*, then add the pieces of deer and brown them slightly. ✦ Add the herbs from the marinade, then slowly pour in the marinade itself. Salt and pepper to taste. ✦ Cook at low heat, stirring from time to time, until tender. ✦ When the meat is tender, remove it from the sauce and set it aside. ✦ Pass the sauce through a sieve and whisk in the cream. ✦ Return the sauce to the pan, add the meat, and cook slowly to blend the flavors, then serve with red currant jam.

CAPRIOLO IN SALMÌ

VENISON IN SAUCE

FRIULI-VENEZIA GIULIA

3 lbs. young roe deer

For the marinade:
8 cups red wine
1 cup red wine vinegar
2 celery stalks, chopped
2 carrots, chopped
2 medium onions, chopped
4 garlic cloves
4 sprigs rosemary
8 sage leaves
4 bay leaves
½ cup chopped flat-leaf parsley
2 tbsp. juniper berries
2 cinnamon sticks
2 tsp. whole cloves
1 tsp. peppercorns
4 sprigs thyme

4 oz. prosciutto fat
2 tbsp. unsalted butter
8 oz. leftover cooked meat
2 green chili peppers, or to taste
4 gherkins, or to taste
3 anchovies, or to taste

Serve with potato gnocchi, ideally cooked in the same sauce as the venison. For the wine use Refosco, Tazzelenghe, or Merlot from Friuli.

Cut the deer into pieces. Mix together half of all the marinade ingredients, adjusting the amounts to taste. Add the deer and let marinate 12 hours, refrigerated. ✦ Remove the deer meat from the marinade and drain it, reserving the liquid from the marinade and discarding the solids from it. Pat the meat dry. Heat the prosciutto fat and butter, add the deer meat, and brown it, adding the other half of the marinade ingredients. ✦ While the meat browns, mix the reserved liquid from the marinade, the leftover meat, chili peppers, gherkins, and anchovies and heat over low heat, letting the liquid reduce slightly to make a sauce. ✦ Add the venison to this sauce and continue to cook over low heat until the venison is tender.

MEAT & POULTRY

BEEF CARBONNADE

1¾ lbs. beef rump, in 3 slices (about 9 oz. per slice)

2 garlic cloves

1 sprig rosemary

Several sage leaves

1 bay leaf

¼ lb. (½ cup) unsalted butter

1 large onion, finely sliced

¼ lb. (1 stick) unsalted butter

2 cups dry white wine

2 cups full-bodied red wine

Several cloves

Several juniper berries

1 tsp. all-purpose flour (if necessary)

Salt

In making this dish some people prefer to use only white wine or only superior red wines, choosing among Blanc de Mortex et de La Salle, Petit Rouge, Enfer, Torrette, or also Donnaz. Serve with polenta (just made or grilled leftover) or with mashed or boiled potatoes.

Have a butcher cut you three slices of beef from the rump. ✦ Arrange the slices of meat in a container with a lid and add the garlic, rosemary, sage, bay leaf, and salt. ✦ Seal the container and put it in the refrigerator for 2 to 6 days, as desired. ✦ Begin the sauce for the carbonnade by heating 3 tablespoons butter in a pan over low heat. Add the onion and cook. ✦ When the onion begins to become creamy, add the wines and salt. ✦ Simmer; add several cloves and juniper berries. ✦ Meanwhile, cut the meat into small cubes, removing any skin or sinews. ✦ Heat half of the remaining butter over high heat in a nonstick pan. ✦ Add half the meat cubes arranged to cover only the bottom of the pan, and turn them with a spatula (the meat shouldn't cook too long). ✦ Add this cooked meat to the wine sauce, then repeat the operation with the remaining meat and continue cooking the mixture for 10 more minutes. ✦ If the sauce is too thin, mix 2 tablespooons of the sauce with the flour and add back to the pan. Cook until thickened.

MUSHROOMS IN LAMB SAUCE

Heart, liver, and lungs of 1 lamb

1 garlic clove

1 lb. *cardoncelli* (oyster mushrooms)

6 large eggs, beaten

2 tbsp. pecorino (preferably *pecorino dolce* from Puglia)

Salt and pepper

This dish is usually eaten for Easter in Dauno.

Cut the heart, liver, and lungs of the lamb into small pieces. Put them in a pan with the garlic and cook, adding salt to taste. ✦ Clean the mushrooms, delicately scraping them with a knife, removing any leaves and the stalk. Cut a cross on the top (it should look like a small cotton wad). ✦ Clean them well and boil them in lightly salted water to cover, draining while still al dente and adding them to the pan with the meat sauce; add a few cups of water and bring to a boil. ✦ Meanwhile, mix the eggs with a pinch of salt, pepper, and pecorino. Pour this over the mushrooms when they return to a boil, then turn off the heat. ✦ Cover and wait for the eggs to set before serving.

NEAPOLITAN RAGÙ

FOR
12 PERSONS

CAMPANIA

7 oz. lard

⅔ cup extra-virgin olive oil

3 lbs. first cut of beef, in pieces

1 lb. *tracchiolelle* (pork ribs from which some of the meat has been removed), in pieces

1 lb. prosciutto, diced

4 oz. pancetta, diced

1 medium onion, finely chopped

Red wine as needed

4 oz. tomato paste, diluted with 2 tbsp. water

1 lb. tomato purée

Pepper

This sauce can be used to dress lasagne, rigatoni, *zitoncini*, gnocchi, etc., and it is typical of Naples.

Heat the lard and olive oil over low heat. Add the beef, pork, prosciutto, pancetta, and onion and cook, stirring often and adding a little wine when necessary, cooking it away each time. ✦ When, after 2 hours, the onion has nearly melted, raise the heat, add the tomato paste mixture and pepper. After another 15 minutes of cooking add a third of the tomato purée, cooking until it thickens. Repeat with the second third and the last, then let cook for 30 minutes. ✦ Add a cup of warm water, lower the heat, and cook 20 minutes. Let the sauce cook until it has become dark and shiny. Serve with the meat.

VEAL IN WHITE WINE

FOR
6 PERSONS

VALLE D'AOSTA

3 medium onions, sliced

¼ cup extra-virgin olive oil

3¼ lbs. veal stew meat, cubed

2 cups white wine (if possible Blanc de Morgex)

4 whole cloves

About 10 juniper berries

Salt and pepper

Cook the onions in a saucepan with the olive oil over low heat until the onions are soft. ✦ Add the meat and raise the heat to high. Pour in half the wine and add the cloves, juniper berries, and salt and pepper to taste. ✦ Add the remaining wine and cook the meat over low heat until cooked through. Serve with a vegetable timbale or boiled potatoes.

MEAT & POULTRY

BEEF IN PIZZA SAUCE

FOR
6 PERSONS

CAMPANIA

1¾ lbs. beef rib meat, sliced

1 lb. plum tomatoes, peeled, seeded, and without liquid

½ cup extra-virgin olive oil

¼ cup white wine

2 garlic cloves, chopped or whole

1 tbsp. dried oregano

Salt and pepper

This dish is typical of Naples. For the wine use Fiano di Avellino or Falanghina.

Pound the slices of meat and remove any sinews while leaving a little of the fat. ✦ Put them in a large pan and add the tomatoes, olive oil, wine, garlic, oregano, and salt and pepper. ✦ Cover the pan and simmer at medium heat for about 1 hour, or until the sauce has cooked down and is shiny.

SHEPHERD'S STYLE PORK

CALABRIA

1 lb. lean boneless pork (shoulder or loin), cut in chunks
3 garlic cloves, halved
½ cup extra-virgin olive oil
1 tbsp. lard
2 medium onions, sliced
12 oz. fresh pecorino, sliced
Salt and pepper

Rub the meat with garlic, salt and pepper it, and cover it with olive oil. Set aside to marinate for several hours. ✦ Preheat the oven to 350°F. Brown the meat in the oil of the marinade in a large ovenproof pan, then roast until cooked through, about 1 hour. Heat the lard in a pan; add the onions and cook until golden. Spoon the onions over the meat, then add the pecorino and bake for 5 minutes until the cheese melts.

PORK WITH CHERVIL SAUCE

UMBRIA

2 tbsp. extra-virgin olive oil
4 slices pork loin (about 1 lb.)
1 sage leaf, minced
1 juniper berry, crushed
2 tbsp. dry red wine

For the sauce:
10 sprigs chervil
¼ garlic clove
1 tbsp. balsamic vinegar
2 tbsp. extra-virgin olive oil
Salt and pepper

Heat the olive oil in a pan, add the pork, and brown it. ✦ Add the sage, juniper berry, and wine. ✦ Cook, covered, at low heat until the meat is no longer pink in the center. ✦ Meanwhile, chop the chervil and garlic and add salt, pepper, vinegar, and olive oil. Mix well. ✦ Arrange the meat on a warmed serving plate and pour the chervil sauce over it.

MEAT PIE

TRENTINO

3 tbsp. unsalted butter
1½ lbs. veal rump
2 oz. prosciutto, minced
8 oz. crustless bread, soaked in milk
3 large eggs, beaten
2 tbsp. grated Parmigiano-Reggiano
Shaved truffle (or porcini mushrooms)
Salt and pepper

Preheat the oven to 350°F. Butter a pie pan. Cut thin slices from the veal rump, enough to cover the bottom of the pie pan. ✦ Finely chop the remaining meat. Squeeze dry the bread. Mix the chopped meat with the prosciutto and bread. ✦ Work into this the eggs, cheese, salt, pepper, and 1 tablespoon butter. ✦ Blend these ingredients together well and spread the resulting mixture over the meat in the pie pan. ✦ Dot the remaining butter on top along with slices of truffle or porcini mushrooms. ✦ Bake 45 minutes and cut in slices to serve.

STEWED PORK

1¾ lbs. pork (mixed lean meat,
sausages, rib meat)

Several sage leaves

1 bay leaf

Several whole cloves

Pinch grated nutmeg

½ cup milk

2 tbsp. all-purpose flour

1 2-inch piece pork rind

Salt

In salted water to cover, boil all the meat except the sausages in one pot for 15 to 20 minutes. Separately boil the sausages for 10 to 15 minutes. Remove and cut the sausages into bite-size pieces and the meat into larger pieces, discarding any fat. Mix the pieces with their cooking liquid in a large pot, add the sage, bay leaf, cloves, nutmeg, and salt, and cook for about 45 minutes. ✦ Mix the milk and flour to form a paste. Stir this mixture and the pork rind into the pan and cook 15 minutes more.

MEAT AND
ARTICHOKES

FOR
10 PERSONS

½ cup extra-virgin olive oil

1 garlic clove, minced

1 medium onion, chopped

10 oz. beef stew meat, cubed

10 oz. pork shoulder, cubed

10 oz. veal roast, cubed

7 oz. veal sweetbreads,
finely chopped

2 cups white wine

2 cups tomato purée

8 tender artichokes,
cleaned and cut into sections

½ cup chopped flat-leaf parsley

Salt

For the wine use Falanghina or Fiano di Avellino.

Heat the olive oil in an earthenware pan and add the garlic and onion. Cook until soft. ✦ Add the beef and cook 10 minutes before adding the pork, veal, and sweetbreads. ✦ Once the meat has browned, add the wine. ✦ When the wine has evaporated, add the tomato purée and salt. Cook for 15 minutes, then add the artichokes and parsley and cook for about 30 minutes. Serve hot.

MEAT & POULTRY

VEAL AND POTATOES

8 slices veal (about 1¾ lbs.),
flattened

CONTINUED

Arrange the slices of meat in a pan with the olive oil and cover them in layers with the onion, potatoes, and tomatoes, seasoning each layer with salt, pepper, basil, and oregano. ✦ Cover and cook over moderate heat for about

¼ cup extra-virgin olive oil

1 medium onion, chopped

1 lb. medium potatoes, peeled and
not too thinly sliced

4 ripe plum tomatoes, peeled,
seeded, and chopped

¼ cup basil leaves (or chopped
flat-leaf parsley)

2 tbsp. chopped fresh oregano

Salt and pepper

30 minutes. Do not stir the meat during this time but keep an eye on the liquid and add a little water if necessary. Serve hot.

CARNE STECCATA
ALLA CACCIATORA

HUNTER'S STYLE
MARINATED BEEF

FOR 6 TO 8
PERSONS

FRIULI-VENEZIA GIULIA

2 lbs. beef roast

For the marinade:

4 cups red wine

1 medium onion, cut into quarters

CONTINUED

For the wine use Refosco or Friulian Merlot.

Place the beef in a large nonreactive container. Make the marinade, pour over the beef, and refrigerate for 24 hours, then remove it and set aside to drain, preserving the marinade. ✦ Heat the butter and olive oil and cook the onion until translucent. Add the meat with the garlic and *lardo*. ✦ When the meat has browned on all sides, add the flour and stir to blend. ✦ Remove the meat and continue

1 garlic clove, crushed

1 sprig rosemary

Several sage leaves

1 tsp. juniper berries

1 carrot, chopped

1 tbsp. red wine vinegar

For the preparation:

1 tbsp. unsalted butter

1 tbsp. extra-virgin olive oil

1 small onion, finely sliced

1 garlic clove, minced

2 oz. *lardo*, cut into pats

2 tbsp. all-purpose flour

2 tbsp. minced capers, if desired

Salt and pepper

cooking the onion. ✦ After 15 minutes return the meat to the pan with some of its marinade. Reduce the heat to low and cook until tender, about 2 hours. ✦ When the meat is cooked adjust for salt and pepper and add the capers (if desired).

CASSOEULA OR
CAZZOEULA

PORK AND
CABBAGE STEW

FOR
6 PERSONS

LOMBARDIA

2 oz. *lardo*, diced (or pancetta or unsalted butter)

2 tbsp. olive oil

3 carrots, diced

2 celery stalks, diced

2 medium onions, minced

1 tbsp. tomato paste

2 lbs. pork rib meat

8 oz. pork rind (or pig's foot or parts of the pig's snout), carefully cleaned, parboiled, and cut in pieces

1 small soft salame per person

2 winter cabbages, cored and shredded

Salt and pepper

You can choose to add a small glass of grappa, cognac, or wine immediately after browning the meat. In some places, people add to the ribs, rind, and cabbages other parts of the pig: feet, ears, guanciale, or throat. If the cabbages have not gone through a frost, clean them carefully and blanch them in salted water for a few minutes; finally, dry well before adding to the pork.

Heat the *lardo* and olive oil in a pan over low heat. Add the carrots, celery, and onions and sauté; as an alternative, cook pork rib meat from a local pig in the pan, then remove it and cook the vegetables in the remaining fat. ✦ Add the tomato paste, then add all the pork. Cook 30 minutes, then add the salame. ✦ Add the cabbage and continue cooking slowly until the meat is tender and nearly falling apart. The cooking time is determined by the cooking time of the pork ribs, which depends on the breed and provenance of the pig: no more than 3 hours for pigs of intensive breeding, up to 4 hours for local pigs. Adjust for salt and pepper and serve.

HUNTER-STYLE MUTTON

CASTRATO
ALLA CACCIATORA

ALTO ADIGE

2 cups robust red wine
(such as Lagrein)
1 sprig rosemary
4 sage leaves
2 bay leaves
1 tsp. juniper berries
2 lbs. boneless mutton stew meat
2 oz. speck
2 tbsp. lard
1 medium onion, chopped
1 garlic clove, chopped
⅓ cup all-purpose flour
½ cup light cream
Salt

Serve with *gnocchetti* (spätzle), see page 248.

Mix the wine, rosemary, sage, bay leaves, and juniper berries in a container made of enameled iron or stainless steel. Add the lamb and marinate for several days. ✦ Remove the meat from the marinade, setting aside the marinade, then dry the meat. Put it in a pan with the speck, lard, all the herbs from the marinade, onion, and garlic. ✦ Brown the meat, season with salt, and cook, adding some of the wine from the marinade from time to time as the meat cooks. ✦ When the meat is cooked through, remove it from the marinade and cut it in slices; pass the marinade in the pan through a sieve. ✦ Return the marinade and meat to the pan. Add the flour and cream and heat again for a few minutes to cook out the raw flavor of the flour.

ROAST YOUNG LAMB

CASTRATO ARROSTITO
IN UMIDO

MARCHE

4 oz. *lardo*, finely minced
2 garlic cloves, finely minced
8 young male lamb steaks
Salt and pepper

For the sauce:
2 tbsp. olive oil
1 small onion, minced
1 celery stalk, chopped fine
2 sprigs rosemary,
needles separated
1 sprig marjoram
1 ¼ lbs. fresh plum tomatoes
or canned peeled plum tomatoes,
chopped in small pieces

Chop together the *lardo* and garlic, spread it over both sides of the lamb steaks, and let them sit for a few hours. ✦ Heat the grill to medium-high. Heat the olive oil in a large pan. Add the onion, celery, rosemary needles, and marjoram and sauté the mixture until fragrant. ✦ Add the tomatoes and cook until the mixture is thickened. ✦ Salt and pepper the steaks, then grill them until very medium-rare, about 4 minutes per side. Arrange the lamb steaks in the pan with the sauce and let them take on its flavor for a few minutes. Serve hot.

LAMB WITH FAVA BEANS

FOR 8 PERSONS

SICILIA

4½ lbs. boneless leg of male lamb
Juice of 1 lemon
1 garlic clove
½ cup chopped flat-leaf parsley
¼ cup extra-virgin olive oil
4½ lbs. fresh fava beans
Salt and pepper

This dish is typical of Enna.

Place the lamb in a large bowl. Add water to cover and season with lemon juice and salt. Let stand several hours, then rinse under running water, pat dry, and cut into hunks. ✦ Finely chop together the garlic, parsley, and pepper to make a paste, make slits in the meat, and insert this mixture. ✦ Heat 3 tablespoons of the olive oil in a large pan. Season the lamb with salt and brown at medium heat. ✦ Meanwhile, remove the fava beans from their pods and cook them in a pan with 1 tablespoon olive oil and salt. ✦ When the lamb is well browned, add a little water and, as soon as this boils, add the fava beans and cook until the meat is tender, adding a little water from time to time as needed.

PAN-BRAISED LAMB

CASTRATO IN PADELLA

FOR 6 PERSONS

EMILIA-ROMAGNA

2 garlic cloves
1 medium onion
1 tbsp. lard
(or ½ stick unsalted butter)
2 lbs. male lamb, cut in pieces
¼ cup dry white wine
½ lb. plum tomatoes,
peeled, seeded, and diced
Salt and pepper

Begin this typically Romagno dish by finely chopping together the garlic and onion. Heat the lard or butter and cook the mixture; when the onion has taken on color, add the pieces of meat and brown them for a few minutes. ✦ Then add the wine and let it slowly evaporate. ✦ Wait until the meat is about half cooked before adding the tomatoes, along with salt and a good amount of pepper. ✦ Continue cooking at low heat, stirring from time to time, until the meat is tender.

FRIED NEAPOLITAN SAUSAGE AND FRIARIELLI

CERVELLATINE E FRIARIELLI SOFFRITTI

FOR 6 PERSONS

CAMPANIA

1 lb. *friarielli* (shoots of broccoli rabe), cleaned
2 tbsp. extra-virgin olive oil

CONTINUED

Cervellatine are a kind of thin sausage sold in butcher shops in Naples. You can substitute another thin, spicy sausage.

Steam the *friarielli* in lightly salted water until tender; drain, pressing them in a colander with a slotted spoon. ✦ Heat the olive oil and sauté the garlic until golden. Add the *friarielli*. Add the chili pepper, a pinch of salt,

MEAT & POULTRY

545

1 garlic clove, slivered
1 *diavolillo* (hot chili pepper, see note, page 22)
1 lb. *cervellatine* (see note)
Salt

and cook 10 minutes at high heat until the *friarielli* are dark green. ✦ Meanwhile, in another pan, heat a little olive oil and cook the *cervellatine*. ✦ When they are cooked, puncture them with the tines of a fork and serve with the *friarielli* as a side dish.

CHIODINI CON LOMBO E SALSICCIA

MUSHROOMS WITH PORK LOIN AND SAUSAGE

LOMBARDIA

1 ½ lbs. honey mushrooms
1 tbsp. red wine vinegar
2 tbsp. olive oil
1 medium onion, sliced
2 tbsp. unsalted butter
10 oz. pork loin, in slices
10 oz. sausage meat, in chunks
¼ cup dry white wine
2 bay leaves
½ cup chopped flat-leaf parsley
Pinch grated nutmeg
Pork or chicken broth
Salt and pepper

Polenta is the ideal companion to this dish, typical of the Lomellina area.

The mushrooms should be fresh and are best when not overly large. Clean them well and several times, eliminating all residues of dirt. ✦ Boil the mushrooms in 2 tablespoons lightly salted water and the vinegar. ✦ In a few minutes the mushrooms will be cooked down, having given up much liquid; drain them and set them aside. ✦ While the mushrooms cook, heat the olive oil in another pan and sauté the onion, removing it from the pan when browned and setting it aside. ✦ Add the butter to the same pan and lightly brown the meat with the pieces of sausage. ✦ Cover these meats with the onion and mushrooms, add the wine, bay leaves, and parsley, taste for salt and pepper, and finish this off with the nutmeg. ✦ Cover the pan and slowly cook for about 1 hour, stirring from time to time and adding a little broth when necessary.

CIBREO

GIBLET STEW

TOSCANA

¾ lb. chicken giblets
1 garlic clove
1 medium onion
½ cup chopped flat-leaf parsley
4 tbsp. unsalted butter
1 tbsp. fresh tomato purée
1 salted anchovy, boned
CONTINUED

This dish goes well with crostini.

Clean and wash the chicken livers, hearts, cocks' combs, and testicles, peeling and chopping them as needed. ✦ Finely chop the garlic, onion, and parsley. Heat the butter in a pan and sauté the mixture. ✦ When this has colored, add the cocks' combs, hearts, salt, and pepper. ✦ As soon as these are brown add the tomato purée. ✦ Add the livers and testicles, cook 5 minutes, then add the anchovy and let it dissolve. ✦ Combine the egg yolks with the flour, lemon juice, and 1 tablespoon boiling water.

2 large egg yolks, beaten

½ tsp. all-purpose flour

1 tbsp. lemon juice

½ cup chicken broth, or as needed, boiling

Salt and pepper

Mix vigorously and pour into the stew, stirring constantly. ✦ If the result seems a little too thick, add broth as needed. Serve hot.

CIF E CIAF

PORK WITH ONION SAUCE

FOR
6 PERSONS

ABRUZZO

About 2 lbs. pork (usually the rib meat and the cheek)

½ cup extra-virgin olive oil

1 medium onion, minced

½ cup dry white wine

2 tbsp. chopped flat-leaf parsley

1 tbsp. chopped marjoram

1 garlic clove, chopped

1 dried spicy chili pepper, crumbled, or ½ tsp. chili pepper flakes

Salt

This dish is usually prepared and consumed on the day when the slaughter of a pig is celebrated. For the wine use Trebbiano or Orvieto.

Clean the meat and cut it in small pieces. Heat the olive oil in a cast-iron skillet and sauté the onion until translucent. Add the meat and cook until browned. ✦ When the meat has browned, add the wine and continue cooking at low heat, stirring continuously with a wooden spoon and adding the parsley, marjoram, garlic, chili pepper, and salt. ✦ Serve hot in the skillet it was cooked in so the diners can dip the meat in the sauce.

CINGHIALE AI FRUTTI DI BOSCO

BOAR WITH FOREST BERRIES

FOR
6 PERSONS

PIEMONTE

2 lbs. boneless boar meat, cut in pieces

1 medium onion, chopped

2 carrots, chopped

2 celery stalks, chopped

2 garlic cloves, minced

1 sprig rosemary

A few sage leaves

2 sprigs thyme

Several juniper berries

1 cinnamon stick

Several whole cloves

CONTINUED

This dish is typical of the Valle Antrona. Serve it warm with polenta. For the wine use Barbera or Dolcetto. For the forest berries you can substitute what is available, such as huckleberries, blackberries, or blueberries.

Put the boar meat in a large nonreactive container with the onion, carrots, celery, garlic, herbs, and spices. Pour in the wine; refrigerate at least 2 days. ✦ At the end of that time remove the meat, drain on paper towels, and set aside. ✦ Strain the vegetables from the marinade, reserving the liquid. Heat the *lardo* and butter in a saucepan over low heat and add the vegetables from the marinade. Sauté them briefly. Flour the meat and season it with salt and pepper, then add it to the saucepan. Cook, slowly adding the wine of the marinade; cover and let this cook at low heat, for about 2 hours. ✦

4 cups good red wine

2 oz. *lardo*

2 tbsp. unsalted butter

All-purpose flour

¾ lb. dried mushrooms, soaked in warm water, drained, and chopped

1¼ cups forest berries (see note)

Salt and black pepper

Separately heat a pat of butter in another pan. Add the mushrooms and sauté, then add to the meat. ✦ Mix in berries.

CINGHIALE ALLA CONTADINA

BOAR COUNTRY-STYLE

CAMPANIA

2 garlic cloves, chopped

4 sprigs rosemary

1¾ lbs. loin of boar, divided in 4 pieces

½ cup extra-virgin olive oil

1 small onion, thinly sliced

2 apples, peeled, cored, and cut in sections

1 cup dry red wine

Salt

This dish is typical of Calitri.

Put some of the garlic and rosemary in the middle of each piece of boar and roll up; tie closed with kitchen twine. ✦ Heat the olive oil in a pan, add the roll-ups, and brown, adding the onion and apples when you turn the roll-ups the first time. ✦ When the meat has browned, pour in the wine, cover the pan with a lid, and cook at moderate heat. ✦ Before turning off the heat taste for salt and heat without the lid to reduce the sauce.

CINGHIALE ALLA VITERBESE

BOAR VITERBO-STYLE

LAZIO

1¾ lbs. boar meat (loin or saddle)

1 bottle red wine

2 garlic cloves

2 sprigs rosemary

1 tbsp. marjoram leaves

½ medium onion

¼ cup olive oil

¾ lb. plum tomatoes, peeled and drained, chopped

Chili pepper

Salt

Wash the boar meat in cold water and place in a large nonreactive container. Mix the wine, half the garlic, 1 sprig rosemary, marjoram leaves, and onion in a pot and heat until warm. Pour over the meat and let marinate overnight. ✦ The next day lift the meat out of the marinade (setting aside the liquid) and cut the meat in small pieces. ✦ Finely chop the remaining garlic and rosemary. Heat the olive oil in a pan and brown the garlic mixture. Add the boar meat, season with salt, and let it brown for several minutes. ✦ Add a little of the wine from the marinade. ✦ When the liquid has nearly evaporated, add the tomatoes and chili pepper and continue cooking with the pan covered, adding warm water as needed to maintain a quantity of sauce to accompany the boar when it is served.

CIMA

This recipe for stuffed calf's breast is typical of Alessandria in Piedmont. The preferred portion to use is the *cappucina*, but the part along the ribs could be used instead. The *cappucina* would be softened with a mallet and sewn up with thread, leaving just enough of an opening for inserting the stuffing. Pine nuts are sautéed with the calf's sweetbreads and spinal marrow as the base of the filling; ground veal could also be added and browned along with the marrow. Off the heat, grated Parmigiano-Reggiano, peas, parsley, fresh marjoram, and as many beaten eggs as necessary to bind the rest were added to complete the filling. A few pieces of prosciutto crudo or cotto and salt and pepper would be used to season the filling before it was sewn into the *cappucina*. A piece of cheesecloth moistened in milk was then wrapped around the *cima* to prevent the filling from escaping in the event the *cappucina* tore. The *cappucina* would then be placed in a pot of cold water and gently boiled over low heat; to keep the eggs from expanding and bursting the *cima*, from time to time the cheesecloth would be punctured with a pin. The finished *cima* would be sliced and served hot in the winter or cool in the summer.

CINGHIALE IN AGRODOLCE

SWEET-AND-SOUR BOAR

LAZIO

3½ lbs. skinned boar (loin or saddle)

For the marinade:
4 cups red wine
¼ cup red wine vinegar
1 celery stalk, chopped
1 carrot, chopped
1 medium onion, chopped
½ bunch flat-leaf parsley, chopped
A few marjoram leaves, chopped
A few sprigs thyme, chopped
4 bay leaves
2 tablespoons juniper berries
3 cloves
2 garlic cloves, chopped

CONTINUED

This dish is typical of the Maremma Laziale. There are some who also add sour cherries or dried prunes with the raisins. For the wine use Sagrantino or Chianti Classico.

Place the boar in a large pot. Combine the marinade ingredients in a saucepan and bring to a boil; reduce the heat and simmer 15 minutes. ✦ Turn off the heat and let the marinade cool, then bring it back to its original volume by adding more wine and vinegar. Pour over the boar and refrigerate overnight. ✦ The next day remove the meat from the marinade and tie it up with string to keep it together; strain the solids from the marinade and reserve the liquid. ✦ In a large pan, heat the olive oil and butter over medium heat. Fry the prosciutto until just starting to change color; then add the boar meat. ✦ Take the solids from the marinade and add them to the pan along with enough of the marinade liquid to partially cover the meat. ✦ Add 2 teaspoons sugar and continue

2 tbsp. peppercorns

To cook the boar:
4 tbsp. olive oil
2 tbsp. unsalted butter
1 slice prosciutto, diced
4 tsp. sugar
Red wine vinegar
1 oz. unsweetened chocolate
1 tbsp. golden raisins, soaked in warm water and drained
1 tbsp. dried sour cherries or prunes (optional)
1 tbsp. pine nuts, or as desired

cooking with the pan covered, checking from time to time to keep it from sticking to the bottom. ✦ Separately, in a small pan heat the remaining sugar with 1 tablespoon water, then pour in vinegar to a depth of about 1 inch and, constantly stirring, add the chocolate and raisins (and cherries or prunes, if using). When the mixture is smooth (apart from the raisins), remove the pan from the heat. ✦ When the meat is tender, remove it from the pan and slice it. ✦ Put the cooking juices through a colander to strain off the solids and add the liquid to the sweet-and-sour sauce, which should be reheated if necessary. ✦ Sprinkle with pine nuts as desired and serve the sauce over the slices of boar.

CINGHIALE IN DOLCE E FORTE

"SWEET-AND-STRONG" BOAR

TOSCANA

3¼ lbs. lean boar (saddle or loin)
6 cups red wine (ideally Morellino di Scansano)
1 cup white wine vinegar
2 juniper berries
4 peppercorns
2 bay leaves
All-purpose flour
½ cup extra-virgin olive oil
2 carrots, minced
1 medium onion, minced
1 celery stalk, minced
6 cups beef broth
3 *cavallucci* (cookies from Siena), soaked overnight in meat broth
4 oz. black panforte (Sienese fruitcake), chopped and soaked overnight in beef broth
4 oz. bittersweet chocolate
2 oz. unsalted butter
½ cup chopped walnuts plus whole walnuts, for garnish
½ cup pine nuts
½ cup raisins
Salt and pepper

This dish is typical of the Maremma.

Place the boar in a large nonreactive container. Mix the wine, ⅔ cup vinegar, juniper berries, peppercorns, and bay leaves and pour over the boar. Let stand several hours. ✦ Remove the boar from the marinade, reserving the liquid. ✦ Cut the boar in 1-inch cubes and season with salt and pepper, then roll in flour. Heat the olive oil in a pan and brown the boar. ✦ Add the carrots, onion, and celery. ✦ Continue browning the meat, then deglaze the pan with the broth. ✦ Continue cooking at low heat, adding some of the marinade liquid. ✦ When the meat is cooked remove it from the pan and set it aside, keeping it warm. Strain the liquid in the pan and set aside. ✦ Meanwhile, prepare the "sweet-and-strong" sauce. Put the *cavallucci* and panforte in a pan over low heat. Melt the chocolate and the butter in a pan over low heat and add this to the cookie mixture. Add the remaining vinegar, chopped walnuts, pine nuts, raisins, and strained cooking liquid. ✦ Mix well to obtain a homogeneous sauce. ✦ Put some of this sauce at the center of each plate. Add the boar around the pool of sauce, and garnish with whole walnuts.

CINGHIALE D'ASPROMONTE

From the mountains of Calabria, especially the Aspromonte area from which it takes its name, this very rustic recipe for saddle of boar used the entire animal. Typically, the boar would be aged for a full week before the hide was removed and the carcass well salted and peppered. It would then be roasted whole on a rotisserie skewer set over a medium-hot fire, the drippings collecting in a pan set beneath. A paste of finely chopped parsley, bay leaves, garlic, and olive oil would be rubbed all over the boar and used to baste the meat while cooking. This strongly flavored specialty was often served with roasted peppers and spicy sausages.

CINGHIALE STUFATO

STEWED BOAR

FOR
6 PERSONS

CALABRIA

2 lbs. boar meat (from thigh or ribs)

8 cups red wine

4 cups red wine vinegar

2 oz. lard

½ cup extra-virgin olive oil

1 medium onion, finely chopped

½ tbsp. finely chopped
flat-leaf parsley

2 bay leaves, finely chopped

4 sage leaves, chopped

2 tbsp. tomato paste,
mixed with ¼ cup water

½ tsp. dried chili pepper,
ground in a mortar

Salt

For the wine use Cirò or Aglianico.

The meat should be aged for a few days. Place it in a nonreactive container and cover it with a mixture of 4 cups wine and 4 cups vinegar and marinate for about 12 hours; drain it well. ✦ Heat the lard and olive oil in a saucepan and sauté the onion; then add the parsley, bay leaves, and sage. ✦ Add the boar meat to the pan and brown on all sides, then add the remaining wine and season with salt. Cover the pan and cook at low heat. ✦ After about 1 hour, add the tomato paste mixture and chili pepper and cook until the meat is tender.

BRAISED VEAL

TOSCANA

Snout, cheeks, and tail from 1 calf

¼ cup extra-virgin olive oil

1 medium onion, finely chopped

1 celery stalk, finely chopped

1 carrot, finely chopped

½ bunch flat-leaf parsley, finely chopped

Several basil leaves, finely chopped

½ cup white wine

1 tbsp. tomato purée

1 *diavolillo* (hot chili pepper, see note, page 22), chopped

Salt

This dish is typical of Pescia and the Valdinievole. For the wine use Vernaccia, San Gimignano, or Orvieto.

Clean the pieces of meat, cut them in pieces, then blanch them in lightly salted boiling water for about 30 minutes. ✦ Heat the olive oil in a large pan over low heat and cook the onion, celery, carrot, parsley, and basil, then add the pieces of meat, browning them well and stirring for about 30 minutes. ✦ Add the wine and tomato purée. Cover and cook at low heat for about 3 hours. ✦ Taste for salt and add the chili pepper. Serve hot.

GIBLET STEW WITH EGGS

CIPRÉ

UMBRIA

1 medium onion, thinly sliced

1 sprig rosemary

10 oz. chicken or rabbit giblets, cleaned

4 tbsp. extra-virgin olive oil

½ cup dry white wine (Orvieto), plus more as needed

3 large eggs, beaten

Salt and pepper

This dish is typical of Orvieto.

Put the onion and rosemary in a saucepan and add several inches of water; when the water boils add the giblets. ✦ Simmer until cooked through, then drain and chop in small pieces. Heat the olive oil in a pan (earthenware if possible) and add the giblets; cook until colored. ✦ Season with salt and pepper and pour in the wine. ✦ Complete the cooking, adding more wine from time to time, then add the eggs and season again with salt and pepper. Mix well and serve immediately.

OXTAIL STEW

CODA ALLA VACCINARA

FOR 6 PERSONS

LAZIO

½ cup extra-virgin olive oil

1 garlic clove, chopped

1 medium onion, chopped

CONTINUED

This dish is typical of Rome. For the wine use Frascati.

Heat the olive oil in a pan and sauté the garlic, onion, carrot, *lardo*, and chili pepper. ✦ Flour the pieces of oxtail and add them to the pan, browning each piece thoroughly. ✦ Add the wine and allow it to evaporate, then add the peeled tomatoes; season with a little salt and

1 carrot, chopped

2 oz. *lardo*

1 *diavolillo* (hot chili pepper, see note, page 22)

All-purpose flour for dredging

3 ½ lbs. oxtail, cut in small pieces

½ cup white wine

3 ½ lbs. peeled plum tomatoes

Pinch grated nutmeg

2 cups veal broth

8 celery stalks, parboiled and cut into 2 ½-inch lengths

Salt

nutmeg. ✦ Cook slowly 4 hours, adding broth from time to time so that the sauce does not reduce too much. ✦ When the meat begins to pull away from the bone, add the celery. ✦ Cook another 15 minutes. The sauce should be dense and dark.

PORK WITH POTATOES AND FENNEL

1 lb. pork tail and ears

2 tbsp. extra-virgin olive oil

2 or 3 garlic cloves, minced

2 lbs. potatoes, peeled and cut in pieces

1 tbsp. fennel seeds

Salt and pepper

This dish is typical of Viterbo.

Clean the tail and ears, singeing them and scraping the skin. ✦ Immerse them in lightly salted boiling water for a few minutes, then cut them in small pieces. ✦ Heat the olive oil in a pan and sauté the garlic, then add the tail and ears and potatoes. ✦ Season with salt, pepper, and fennel, cooking until the potatoes have browned and the tail and ears are well cooked. Serve hot.

MEAT & POULTRY

BEEF ROLL-UPS

8 slices beef tenderloin

2 oz. *lardo*, finely chopped

2 garlic cloves, finely chopped

½ cup chopped flat-leaf parsley

¼ cup extra-virgin olive oil

1 cup beef broth

3 tbsp. white wine

Salt and pepper

Pound out the meat slices and salt and pepper them to taste. ✦ Combine the *lardo*, garlic, and parsley to form a paste; spread this paste on the slices of meat. ✦ Roll the slices up and seal them with a toothpick or kitchen string. ✦ Heat the olive oil, add the beef rolls, and brown them. When they are well colored, pour in the broth and continue cooking with the pan covered at very low heat. ✦ A few minutes before the end of the cooking, add the wine, remove the lid, and cook a few minutes longer. Remove the toothpicks or string and serve.

COLLO DE CASTRATO, RISI, E PISELLI

For this recipe from the Veneto, the neck of male lambs from the Astico, Arzignano, Chiampo, and Valdagno valleys is preferred. The sheep were raised in an enclosure but out in the open, with abundant nutrition and access to clear spring water, as this and a minimum of movement favored the fattening of the animal and would in turn enhance the flavor of this dish. To prepare this recipe, the neck would be boiled with celery and onion until cooked. The resulting broth would often be used to prepare a "rice and peas soup," and the neck would traditionally be served alongside tender peas in a sauce made from grated horseradish, olive oil, vinegar, and sugar.

CONIGLIO A BUJONE | # RABBIT IN BROTH | FOR 6 PERSONS

LAZIO

1 skinned rabbit, about 3¼ lbs.
2 tbsp. extra-virgin olive oil
2 garlic cloves
4 sprigs rosemary
½ cup red wine
1¼ cups tomato purée
Chicken broth (as needed)
A few sage leaves
¼ cup white wine vinegar
Salt and pepper

This preparation, used in various areas of central Italy and in particular in Tuscia, differs from the *alla cacciatore* recipe (see page 557) because it is cooked in a pan and because of the addition of tomatoes. The term *a bujone*, used in the dish's dialect name, is presumably derived from the French *bouillon* and would refer to the fact that the rabbit is cooked in a generous amount of broth (or a thin sauce). For the wine use Chianti Classico.

Remove the intestines, head, and feet from the rabbit and soak it overnight in water. ✦ The next day cut the rabbit in pieces and dry them. ✦ Heat the olive oil in a pan and add the garlic, discarding the garlic when browned; add the pieces of rabbit with salt, pepper, and 3 sprigs of rosemary and let the rabbit brown. ✦ Add the red wine and let the meat cook a few minutes; then add the tomato purée and simmer over medium-low heat with the pan covered, adding broth or warm water if the liquid cooks down too much. ✦ Cook for about 1 hour. After 45 minutes, mix the sage, remaining rosemary, and vinegar, and pour over the rabbit. Cook 15 minutes more to let this flavor the dish, then serve hot.

RABBIT WITH WILD FENNEL

LAZIO

¼ cup extra-virgin olive oil

1 skinned rabbit, about 4 ½ lbs., with giblets

5 garlic cloves, 3 sliced and 2 whole

1 piece chili pepper

3 potatoes, peeled and cut in pieces

1 tsp. dried wild fennel flowers

1 bunch fresh fennel flowers

Lard (if desired)

Salt and pepper

In the Viterbo area, the term *a porchetta* is applied to any preparation that includes the flavor of wild fennel, whether fresh or as dried flowers, as in the pig in *porchetta*; the flowers of wild fennel, dried in the sun, are a specialty frequently used in the area. They should not be confused with fennel seeds.

Preheat the oven to 300°F. Grease a roasting pan with olive oil. Clean the rabbit, remove the innards, and chop them. Wash and dry the rabbit; chop the giblets. ✦ Heat 2 tablespoons olive oil in a pan and cook the sliced garlic and chili pepper until the garlic is golden, then add the giblets. ✦ Add the potatoes and dried fennel flowers and let the mixture cook. ✦ Stuff the belly of the rabbit with this mixture, add the fresh fennel, whole garlic, salt, and pepper, and sew up the sides of the abdominal cavity with kitchen twine. ✦ Brush the body of the rabbit with the remaining olive oil (or lard) and season with salt and pepper. Roast for a couple of hours, turning it several times, until cooked through and tender.

RABBIT WITH FENNEL

UMBRIA

1 rabbit, weighing about 4 lbs., with its giblets

Extra-virgin olive oil

A few sage leaves

2 garlic cloves

1 cup dry white wine (Orvieto)

2 potatoes, peeled and cubed

2 large slices prosciutto crudo

1 sprig rosemary

1 large head fresh fennel

10 or 12 black olives

Salt and pepper

This dish is typical of Orvieto.

Preheat the oven to 300°F. Remove the giblets from the rabbit, clean them, and chop them in small pieces. ✦ Put the chopped giblets in a pan with 2 tablespoons olive oil, salt, pepper, sage, and 1 garlic clove. As soon as this begins to brown add ½ cup wine and let it evaporate. ✦ Add the potatoes and mix into the giblets, then take the pan off the heat. ✦ Remove the mixture from the pan, wrap it in the prosciutto, and insert it in the rabbit with the rosemary and fennel. ✦ Sew up the rabbit with kitchen twine. ✦ Put the rabbit in a pan with 2 tablespoons olive oil, a garlic clove, salt, and pepper and put it in the oven to roast for a couple of hours. ✦ When the rabbit is half cooked, add the olives and the remaining wine. If the rabbit is very small, wrap the front and rear legs in aluminum foil to keep them from drying out.

CONIGLIO AL VINO ROSSO | RABBIT IN RED WINE

PIEMONTE

1 tbsp. unsalted butter

4 or 5 tbsp. extra-virgin olive oil

2 medium onions, sliced

2 slices pancetta, diced

1 rabbit, 4½ lbs., cut in pieces

Tied herbs: 1 sprig rosemary,
1 sprig sage, 2 bay leaves,
and 1 sprig thyme

1 cup red wine

½ cup chicken broth, or as needed

1 chicken liver

2 garlic cloves

½ cup flat-leaf parsley leaves

3 sage leaves

2 salted anchovies, mashed

1 tbsp. all-purpose flour

Salt

This dish is typical of Asti. Serve the rabbit accompanied by soft polenta. Grignolino or Freisa are ideal for the wine in this dish.

Heat the butter and olive oil in a saucepan and sauté the onions and pancetta over high heat until browned. ✦ Sprinkle the rabbit pieces with salt, add them to the pan, and brown them. ✦ Add the bundle of herbs; pour in the wine and let it evaporate. ✦ Reduce the heat to low, cover the pan, and cook the rabbit for 1 hour, adding broth as needed. ✦ Meanwhile, chop together the rabbit's liver, chicken liver, garlic, parsley, sage, and anchovies. ✦ Add this mixture to the rabbit 10 minutes before turning off the heat, also adding the flour and wine as needed to thicken the sauce, and turn the heat to high so the pieces of rabbit will "soak up" the flavor of the liver and herbs.

CONIGLIO ALL'ASTIGIANA | RABBIT ASTI-STYLE

PIEMONTE

2 tbsp. extra-virgin olive oil

1 tbsp. unsalted butter

1 rabbit, 4½ lbs., cut in pieces

3 medium onions, finely minced

7 oz. *lardo*, finely diced

1 sprig rosemary, minced

1 bottle red wine

2 bay leaves

2 rabbit livers (or 1 rabbit liver
and 1 chicken liver), finely chopped

2 garlic cloves, minced

2 anchovies, minced

½ cup chopped flat-leaf parsley

A few sage leaves, finely chopped

1 tbsp. all-purpose flour

½ cup broth

Nebbiolo wine is best in this dish, as is the pink variety of *lardo*.

Heat the olive oil and butter over high heat in a large earthenware pan and brown the pieces of rabbit. ✦ Lower the heat and add the onions, *lardo*, and rosemary. ✦ Cook 10 minutes to let the onions brown and the pieces of rabbit soak up the flavors, then add the wine and bay leaves. Cover the pan and simmer for 1 hour. ✦ Combine the livers, garlic, anchovies, parsley, and sage and add to the pan. ✦ Add the flour and ½ cup broth. ✦ Let the rabbit cook for 5 minutes in this mixture, after which it is ready to be brought to the table.

RABBIT BRAISED IN THE STYLE OF ISCHIA

CONIGLIO ALL'ISCHITANA

FOR 6 PERSONS

CAMPANIA

1 rabbit, 4 to 4 ½ lbs., cleaned
1 cup white wine vinegar
¼ cup extra-virgin olive oil
2 garlic cloves
¼ cup white wine
1 lb. plum tomatoes, peeled and chopped
Basil leaves, chopped (to taste)
Thyme, chopped (to taste)
Marjoram (to taste)
Rosemary (to taste)
Pinch chili pepper flakes
Salt and pepper

Cut the rabbit into small pieces; rinse in equal parts water and vinegar and dry. ✦ Heat the olive oil in a pan and sauté the garlic until browned; remove and discard the garlic, then turn up the heat and sauté the pieces of rabbit, turning them in the pan so they brown evenly on all sides. ✦ Add the wine and let it evaporate. ✦ Add the tomatoes, then salt and pepper to taste; add the herbs and chili pepper. ✦ Simmer for about 30 minutes over medium-low heat until tender. Serve warm.

HUNTER-STYLE RABBIT

CONIGLIO ALLA CACCIATORA

FOR 6 PERSONS

SICILIA

1 rabbit, about 2 ¼ lbs., cut in pieces
1 bottle red wine
¼ cup extra-virgin olive oil
1 garlic clove, slivered
1 small sprig fresh oregano
Salt and pepper

This dish is typical of Enna. For the wine use Nero d'Avola.

Soak the pieces of rabbit in the wine for 30 minutes, then drain and pat dry. Heat the olive oil in a heavy pot and brown the rabbit pieces. ✦ When the meat has taken on color, add the garlic, salt, pepper, and oregano with 1 cup water. ✦ Reduce the heat to low and continue cooking for about 40 minutes, adding more warm water as needed (in the end the sauce should be cooked down).

MEAT & POULTRY

STEWED RABBIT WITH POTATO

CONIGLIO ALLA CANAVESANA

FOR 6 PERSONS

PIEMONTE

1 rabbit, weighing about 3 ¼ lbs.
2 cups white wine vinegar
⅔ cup all-purpose flour
¼ cup extra-virgin olive oil
4 tbsp. unsalted butter
CONTINUED

Cut the rabbit into serving-size pieces. Mix the vinegar with 2 cups water. Soak the pieces of rabbit in this solution, leaving them to marinate at least half a day in the refrigerator. ✦ Remove the rabbit pieces from the liquid, dry them well, and dredge them in the flour. Heat the olive oil in a large pan and brown them. ✦ Remove the pieces of meat from the oil, dust them with salt and pepper to taste, then set them aside in a warm place. ✦ Add

1 large onion, sliced

2 celery stalks, chopped

1 carrot, chopped

1 potato, cut into matchsticks

4 cups beef or veal broth, warmed

Salt and pepper

the butter to the pan and cook the onion, celery, and carrot. Stir in the potato. ✦ When this is browned, add 4 cups of the broth and season with salt and pepper; return the pieces of rabbit to the pan, cover, and cook at low heat until tender, about 1 hour, adding a little more of the broth from time to time if needed.

CONIGLIO ALLA
MURIALDINA

STEWED RABBIT

LIGURIA

1 rabbit, weighing about 6 lbs.,
liver removed and set aside

1 sprig rosemary

1 bay leaf

½ cup extra-virgin olive oil

1 medium onion, sliced

½ cup flat-leaf parsley leaves

2 garlic cloves

2 tbsp. tomato purée

1 cup red wine (preferably
fine aged Dolcetto)

1 tbsp. ground cinnamon

3 cups veal or beef broth,
or as needed

Salt and pepper

Cut the rabbit in small pieces (27, if you cut it up well), trim away any fat, then clean and dry the pieces and heat them (except the liver) in a pan with the rosemary and bay leaf to make them "give up their water." ✦ In another pan heat the olive oil and sauté the onion; when the rabbit has given up its liquid, add it to the onion and sauté until dark golden. ✦ Chop together the parsley, garlic, and liver and add them to the pan. ✦ Mix the tomato purée, wine, salt, pepper, and cinnamon. Add this to the rabbit and slowly cook until the liquid evaporates. ✦ Then cook over low heat, adding broth a little at a time until the rabbit is cooked, about 1 hour.

CONIGLIO ALLA
PAESANA

TRENTINO-STYLE RABBIT

TRENTINO

Mixture of aromatic herbs:
1 tbsp. sweet paprika, pinch
grated nutmeg, pinch ground
cumin, ½ bay leaf, rosemary leaves,
5 juniper berries

1½ cups dry white wine, plus more
as needed

1 rabbit, skinned, about 3 lbs.

2 oz. *lardo*, finely chopped

1 tbsp. unsalted butter

CONTINUED

Serve the rabbit with polenta or mashed potatoes. Fresh seasonal vegetables and a good bottle of Trentino merlot complete a dish that is flavorful, tasty, and always new. For the wine in the dish use Pinot Grigio or Riesling Italico.

Mix the herbs and stir them into 1 cup of the wine. Remove the rabbit's head and giblets, then cut the rabbit in 8 pieces. ✦ Heat the *lardo*, butter, and olive oil over very low heat. Add the onion and sauté; then add the pieces of rabbit. This initial browning, like the rest of the cooking, must be done at very low heat and thus will take a long time. ✦ Add the remaining wine, and before it has completely evaporated, add the herbs mixture and salt

1 tbsp. olive oil
1 medium onion, minced
Meat broth
Salt and white pepper

For the sauce:
2 tbsp. extra-virgin olive oil
1 medium onion, finely minced
1 carrot, finely minced
2 tbsp. finely minced
flat-leaf parsley
Rabbit giblets, finely chopped
1 tbsp. tomato purée
1 tbsp. all-purpose flour
1 heaping tbsp. grated
Parmigiano-Reggiano

and white pepper. ✦ As the rabbit cooking liquid reduces, add broth, making sure that the meat is always partially covered by a quantity of liquid. ✦ Meanwhile, prepare the sauce. Heat olive oil in another pan, add the onion, carrot, and parsley, then brown the giblets; add the tomato purée, then whisk in the flour and cook 5 minutes. Dilute, if needed, with some of the meat broth. ✦ Add this sauce to the rabbit after it has cooked about 1 hour, then let the sauce and rabbit cook another 30 to 45 minutes, at the end of that time add the Parmigiano-Reggiano. ✦ Check that the sauce is at the desired density, and dilute, if needed, with broth and simmer briefly.

CONIGLIO ALLA
SANREMASCA

SAN REMO RABBIT

LIGURIA

1 rabbit, weighing 2 ¼ lbs.
¼ cup extra-virgin olive oil
1 medium onion, sliced
½ cup dry white wine
Broth
⅓ cup pine nuts
1 garlic clove
3 sprigs rosemary
1 cup olives (about 24; preferably
small dark ones from Taggia)
Salt

This dish is typical of San Remo.

Cut the rabbit in pieces; salt to taste. Heat the olive oil in a saucepan over low heat and brown the onion and rabbit pieces. ✦ Add the wine, cover the pan, and continue cooking, adding broth if needed. ✦ Meanwhile, chop the pine nuts, garlic, and rosemary together; set aside 15 whole olives and pit and chop the remainder. ✦ After about 40 minutes of cooking, add the pine nut mixture and chopped olives to the pan and continue cooking for another 15 minutes. ✦ Add the whole olives and let stand until it reaches room temperature.

CONIGLIO ALLA
VALLE D'ITRIA

RABBIT AND ONIONS

FOR
6 PERSONS

PUGLIA

1 rabbit, weighing 2 lbs.
Juice of 1 lemon
All-purpose flour for dredging
CONTINUED

Preheat the oven to 350°F. Clean the rabbit in water acidulated with lemon juice, drain, dry well, and cut in pieces no larger than about 2½ ounces each. ✦ Lightly flour the meat. Heat the olive oil in an earthenware pan and add the meat to brown it, turning to cook lightly on both sides. ✦ Add the wine, let it evaporate, then add the celery, onion, and tomatoes. ✦ Add the *muscari*, salt, pepper, and broth. Cover the pan and place in the oven to finish cooking, about 1 hour. Serve warm.

1 cup olive oil

¾ cup white wine (preferably Locorotondo)

½ cup minced celery

⅔ cup minced onion

A few plum tomatoes, cut in pieces

1 lb. *muscari* (bulb of the wild hyacinth), slightly blanched

1 ½ cups broth (or lightly salted water)

Salt and pepper

CONIGLIO CON I PEPERONI

RABBIT WITH PEPPERS

PIEMONTE

½ cup extra-virgin olive oil

4 tbsp. unsalted butter

1 sprig rosemary, minced

1 garlic clove, minced

2 ½ lbs. rabbit meat, cut in regular pieces

Broth

3 large yellow peppers, cored, seeded, and cut in long strips

3 tbsp. white wine vinegar

Heat half the olive oil and all of the butter over low heat, then add the rosemary and garlic and cook until fragrant. Add the pieces of rabbit. ✦ As the meat cooks, add broth as needed to keep it from drying out. ✦ In a separate pan heat the remaining olive oil, then add the peppers. ✦ When these are cooked, add the vinegar, and when this has evaporated add the peppers to the pan and simmer until the rabbit is cooked and the peppers are soft. Serve warm.

CONIGLIO CON PEPERONI E OLIVE

RABBIT WITH PEPPERS AND OLIVES

FOR 6 PERSONS

PUGLIA

⅔ cup extra-virgin olive oil

1 medium onion, finely sliced

1 2-lb. rabbit, cut in pieces

½ cup dry white wine

2 green peppers, seeded and quartered

⅔ cup pitted black olives, chopped

Salt and pepper

Heat ⅓ cup oil in a large pan and sauté the onion; add the rabbit pieces and brown. ✦ Add the wine and let it evaporate, then continue cooking, adding a little water and covering the pan; let cook 15 minutes. ✦ Meanwhile, heat the remaining oil in another pan and sauté the peppers. Once cooked, add them to the rabbit. ✦ Then add the pitted olives. ✦ After 30 minutes the rabbit should be cooked; adjust for salt and pepper and serve warm.

RABBIT WITH PEPPER SAUCE

CONIGLIO CON SALSA DI PEPERONI

FOR 6 PERSONS

PIEMONTE

2 tbsp. unsalted butter
1 medium onion, finely sliced
1 young rabbit, cut in pieces
¼ cup white wine
½ cup broth
4 red peppers, cored, seeded, and sliced
1 ripe plum tomato
½ cup olive oil
1 handful pine nuts, crushed
Salt and pepper

This dish is typical of Cremolino (Ovada).

Heat the butter in a pan and sauté half of the onion. Add the pieces of rabbit and brown them lightly. ✦ Add salt, pepper, and wine. ✦ When the wine has evaporated, add the broth and cook at low heat for 30 minutes. ✦ Meanwhile, prepare the sauce: cook the peppers, tomato, and remaining onion with the olive oil over low heat for 20 minutes, then put it through a sieve. ✦ Add the sauce to the rabbit along with the pine nuts and continue cooking for a few minutes more.

PAN-COOKED RABBIT

CONIGLIO DI DOCCIA

FOR 6 PERSONS

TOSCANA

Legs and loins of 2 young rabbits
¼ cup olive oil
2 bay leaves
1 sprig rosemary
1 garlic clove
1 cup white wine (preferably from the Colline Pisane)
½ cup meat broth
Salt and pepper

This dish is typical of Volterra.

Drizzle the rabbit pieces with half the olive oil, add the bay leaves, rosemary, and garlic, then sprinkle the meat with salt and pepper. ✦ Heat the remaining olive oil in a large pan and brown the meat until it has a fine golden color. ✦ Add the wine and broth; cover the pan and simmer 30 minutes. ✦ Remove the lid and cook down the pan liquids at low heat to obtain a sauce. ✦ Add salt and pepper and serve hot, spooning the sauce over the meat.

STUFFED RABBIT

CONIGLIO FARCITO

EMILIA-ROMAGNA

1 rabbit, weighing 3¼ lbs., with its giblets
½ lb. ground pork
4 oz. mortadella
1 large egg, beaten
2 tbsp. grated Parmigiano-Reggiano

CONTINUED

This dish is typical of Castrocaro.

Bone the rabbit and set it under running water for 1 hour. ✦ Dry the rabbit, then salt and pepper its cavity. ✦ Chop together the giblets, pork, and mortadella. ✦ Work into this the egg, Parmigiano-Reggiano, pancetta, hard-boiled eggs, and olives. ✦ Stuff this mixture into the rabbit and sew it closed. ✦ Heat the olive oil in a pan over low heat and brown the stuffed rabbit. Cover and cook over low

4 oz. pancetta, minced

3 large hard-boiled eggs, chopped

¼ cup pitted green olives, chopped

¼ cup olive oil

Dry white wine, such as Trebbiano

Shallots, minced, for garnish

Sprigs wild fennel, for garnish

Salt and pepper

heat for about 2 hours, adding wine from time to time. ✦ Put the cooked rabbit under a weight for 4 hours to make the stuffing compact. ✦ Serve the rabbit sliced, cold or warm, garnished with shallots and sprigs of wild fennel.

CONIGLIO IN PORCHETTA

ROAST STUFFED RABBIT WITH FENNEL

MARCHE

2 tbsp. olive oil

1 rabbit, with its giblets

2 oz. *lardo*

2 wild fennel stalks, chopped

2 garlic cloves, chopped

1 2-inch piece pork rind, parboiled

¼ cup black olives, pitted

Salt and pepper

Preheat the oven to 400°F. Grease a baking pan with a little of the olive oil. Carefully clean, wash, and dry the rabbit, then season inside and out with *lardo*, salt, pepper, and half the fennel and garlic. ✦ Begin making the stuffing by heating the remaining oil in a sauté pan. Brown the giblets; add the remaining fennel, garlic, salt, and pepper and mix well. ✦ Add the pork rind and olives, then cook at low heat until all the liquid has evaporated. ✦ Stuff the rabbit with this filling and roast for 1 hour, or until cooked through and tender.

CORATELLA CON CARCIOFI

LAMB OFFAL WITH ARTICHOKES

UMBRIA

1½ lbs. lamb offal

½ cup extra-virgin olive oil

2 garlic cloves, finely sliced

1 sprig rosemary

½ cup dry white wine

1 lb. artichokes, cleaned and cut in ½-inch sections

Salt and pepper

Clean the offal, cut it in small pieces, and set it out to dry on a cloth. ✦ Heat the olive oil in a pan and sauté the garlic and rosemary. ✦ When the garlic takes on color, add the offal, season with salt, and cook, covered, at low heat, sprinkling with wine from time to time. ✦ When about half cooked (after 30 minutes), add the artichokes along with a pinch of salt and a pinch of pepper. ✦ Complete the cooking with the pan uncovered, adding more wine from time to time. Serve hot.

HUNTER'S STYLE
KID OFFAL

FOR
6 PERSONS

TOSCANA

½ cup extra-virgin olive oil

1 large onion, sliced

The offal of a kid or small lamb,
cut in pieces

½ cup white wine

2 bay leaves

1-inch piece ginger,
peeled and chopped

2 or 3 plum tomatoes,
peeled and finely sliced

2 tbsp. minced flat-leaf parsley

1 garlic clove, minced

Salt

This dish is typical of Elba. For the wine use Vernaccia di San Gimignano.

Heat the olive oil in a skillet and add the onion. ✦ When the onion changes color, add the offal and brown well, stirring to keep the pieces from offal to the pan. ✦ Add the wine. ✦ When the wine has evaporated, add the bay leaves, salt to taste, ginger, tomatoes, parsley, and garlic. ✦ Cook at high heat, adding warm water if necessary to keep the mixture from sticking, until a sauce has formed, about 10 minutes.

OVEN-ROASTED VENISON

LOMBARDIA

¼ cup extra-virgin olive oil

1 deer haunch, about 5 lbs.

2 carrots, cut into 2-inch lengths

1 celery stalk, cut into 2-inch lengths

1 medium onion, cut into wedges

1 garlic clove

¼ cup whiskey

½ cup cognac

2 cups red wine
(Barolo would be good)

1 cup light cream

Salt

This dish is typical of the Valtellina.

Preheat the oven to 300°F. Heat the olive oil in a large roasting pan over medium-high heat. Brown the haunch, then add the carrots, celery, onion, and garlic. ✦ Pour in the whiskey and cognac. ✦ When these have evaporated, add the wine and salt and roast, frequently basting the haunch in its juice. ✦ When cooked (about 4 hours), remove the meat from the pan, pass the sauce through a sieve, whisk in the cream, and serve.

MEAT & POULTRY

LEG OF LAMB
WITH CHESTNUTS

FOR
8 PERSONS

PIEMONTE

Leg of lamb, weighing about 5½ lbs.

CONTINUED

Preheat the oven to 350°F. Wash and dry the leg of lamb and place it in a large roasting pan. ✦ Season with olive oil, salt, *lardo*, rosemary, and garlic. ✦ Arrange the carrots, onion, and celery around the meat. ✦ Roast for 1 hour,

½ cup extra-virgin olive oil

4 tbsp. *lardo*, finely minced

1 sprig rosemary

1 garlic clove, sliced

3 carrots, chopped

1 large onion, sliced

1 celery heart, cut in rounds

1 lb. shelled chestnuts

Pinch sugar

½ cup rum

2 tbsp. Marsala

Salt

turning the leg often and piercing it with the tines of a fork. ✦ Boil the chestnuts in water with a little salt and sugar until tender, then peel them and add them to the lamb. ✦ Return the lamb to the oven for another 10 minutes, then add the rum and Marsala. Serve hot.

LARDED LEG OF LAMB

COSCIOTTO D'AGNELLO LARDELLATO

FOR 6 PERSONS

CALABRIA

1½ cups lard

2 garlic cloves

1 bunch flat-leaf parsley

1 leg of lamb, weighing about 5½ lbs.

Oregano sprigs

3 tbsp. extra-virgin olive oil

The ideal side dish for this is fried potatoes served with the pan drippings from the cooked meat.

Chop together the lard, garlic, and parsley and use this mixture to lard the meat by cutting slits in the meat and stuffing them with the mixture. ✦ Close the openings with oregano sprigs. Add the lamb to a large pot, then add the olive oil and water to cover. Heat over medium, bring to a boil, then immediately reduce to a gentle simmer and cook until very tender when prodded with the tines of a fork, about 2 hours. ✦ Remove the meat from the cooking water, increase the heat to high, and boil the liquid to reduce it to the consistency of a sauce.

BEEF STEAKS WITH ONION

COSTATA DI MANZO CON CIPOLLA

ALTO ADIGE

2 tbsp. unsalted butter

⅓ cup olive oil

1 large onion, thinly sliced

All-purpose flour for dredging

4 well-aged beef steaks

½ cup white wine, such as Pinot Grigio

Salt and pepper

Heat the butter and olive oil in a pan at low heat. ✦ Add the onion. When the onion is golden brown, lightly flour the steaks and add them to the pan. ✦ Raise the heat to medium and sprinkle with the wine, adding salt and pepper. ✦ When the steaks have taken on color on one side, turn them to cook on the other. ✦ Put the steaks on a serving plate, cover with the onion, and serve.

COSTICINE CON VERZE SOFEGADE

PORK CUTLETS WITH SAVOY CABBAGE

VENETO

2 tbsp. unsalted butter

2 oz. *lardo*, diced

1 medium onion, sliced

1 lb. pork cutlets

1 Savoy cabbage (best if dark green with curly leaves), outer leaves removed and inner leaves washed and torn by hand

¼ cup white wine vinegar

Salt and pepper

Serve this dish with good, soft polenta.

In a high-sided pan, heat the butter over low heat and sauté the *lardo* and onion until golden. Add the cutlets and cook them at low heat. ✦ After a few minutes, add the cabbage leaves. ✦ Cover the pan and let the mixture cook at low heat for about 30 minutes, stirring every so often, until the pork is cooked through and the cabbage is soft. ✦ Taste for salt and pepper and sprinkle with vinegar near the end of the cooking time.

COSTICINE DI MAIALE ALLA MONTANARA

PAN-COOKED PORK CUTLETS

FRIULI-VENEZIA GIULIA

1 tbsp. unsalted butter

Pork cutlets (lightly smoked), cut into 2-inch pieces

½ cup white wine, such as Tocai

1 tbsp. cornmeal, mixed into 2 cups water

Salt and pepper

These cutlets go well with polenta.

Heat the butter in a terra-cotta pan over low heat. Add the pork and brown, seasoning with salt and pepper. ✦ Add the wine and continue cooking at low heat; after about 30 minutes add the cornmeal mixture. Cook until the sauce thickens slightly, about 10 minutes.

MEAT & POULTRY

COSTOLETTA ALLA MILANESE

BREADED VEAL CHOPS

LOMBARDIA

4 veal rib chops (cut to the thickness of the bone)

2 large eggs, beaten

2 cups fresh breadcrumbs

¼ lb. (1 stick) unsalted butter

1 lemon, sliced

Salt

Meat of the very best quality is absolutely essential for this dish. Each chop must have a bone, with the meat forming a "flag" on it.

Score the chops to prevent them from curling during cooking and pound them a little with a meat pounder. ✦ Add no salt at this point, since doing so would affect the tenderness of the meat; the time to salt is later, when the meat is on the serving plate. ✦ Immerse the chops (but not the bone "handle") one at a time in the eggs, then dip them in the breadcrumbs (which should be prepared only a few minutes before beginning the recipe using dry bread free of all stale odors). ✦ Press your hand against each one to make the breadcrumbs adhere well and thus keep them from coming off during cooking. ✦ Using a large pan, melt (do not fry!) the butter over low heat and arrange a single layer of chops in the pan, raising the heat a little and maintaining the pale color of the butter. ✦ Cook 7 to 8 minutes on each side (the meat should be tender and the coating slightly golden), put them on a serving plate, salt, and garnish with lemon slices. These are also excellent eaten cold.

CHEESE-FILLED VEAL CHOPS

COSTOLETTE ALLA FONTINA

VALLE D'AOSTA

4 veal chops
8 oz. fontina (from the Valle d'Aosta), in thin slices
1 cup all-purpose flour
2 large eggs, beaten
2 cups breadcrumbs
¼ lb. (½ cup) unsalted butter
Salt and pepper

Cut the chops lengthwise to the bone to create two flaps still attached to the bone. ✦ Insert the slices of fontina in this opening, close the flaps, then delicately pound the chops with a meat pounder. ✦ Salt and pepper the chops and dip them first in the flour, then the beaten eggs, then in the breadcrumbs. ✦ Heat half the butter over low heat, then raise the heat to medium and fry the chops until they have a golden crust. ✦ Melt the remaining butter and pour over the chops.

COTECHINO "IN PRISON"

COTECHINO IN GALERA

FOR
6 PERSONS

EMILIA-ROMAGNA

1 precooked cotechino, weighing about 1 lb.
1 lb. beef in a single slice, pounded thin
4 oz. pancetta, sliced
3 cups red wine
⅔ cup chopped carrots
½ cup chopped onions
⅔ cup chopped celery
2 bay leaves

CONTINUED

Cotechino is a fresh pork sausage that contains pork rind or cooked pork skin (*cotica*), which imparts an unctuous texture. It is often boiled and served with lentils. Here the cotechino is "in prison" because it is inside the rolled-up beef. This dish is typical of Modena. For the wine use Sangiovese di Romagna.

Remove the meat from the casing of the cotechino. ✦ Spread this meat over the slice of beef and roll up the beef; cover it with the slices of pancetta, then tie closed with kitchen twine. ✦ Mix the red wine with the carrots, onions, celery, and bay leaves; add the meat and marinate for 5 to 6 hours in the refrigerator. ✦ Heat the butter in a pan and add the meat, browning it. ✦ Pour in the broth, then the marinade. ✦ Bring to a boil, then reduce the heat and simmer. After about 1 hour, add the toma-

¼ lb. (½ cup) unsalted butter

4 cups beef broth

½ lb. peeled plum tomatoes

Pinch salt

toes and salt. ✦ Simmer for about 3 hours. ✦ Remove the meat from the sauce and pass the sauce through a sieve. Serve the meat sliced with the sauce.

COTOLETTE ALLA
BOLOGNESE

VEAL BOLOGNESE

EMILIA-ROMAGNA

4 boneless veal cutlets

2 large eggs, beaten

1 cup breadcrumbs

6 tbsp. unsalted butter

4 slices prosciutto crudo

⅔ cup Parmigiano-Reggiano,
in shards

2 tbsp. broth

Shaved truffle

Pound the veal slices until they are uniformly thin, dip them in the eggs, then in the breadcrumbs. ✦ Heat about half of the butter in a pan and brown the veal; cover each slice with a slice of prosciutto, then top with a little Parmigiano-Reggiano. ✦ Pour in the broth, add more butter, and cover until the cheese melts. ✦ Top with truffle before serving.

CROCCHETTE DI POLLO
E RICOTTA

CHICKEN AND RICOTTA
CROQUETTES

FOR
6 PERSONS

PIEMONTE

¾ lb. cooked boneless chicken
(roast or boiled), finely chopped

1⅔ cups ricotta

2 tbsp. chopped flat-leaf parsley

A few sage leaves, chopped

1 small onion, finely minced

1 tsp. each lemon juice
and grated lemon zest

All-purpose flour, if necessary

1 large egg, beaten

Breadcrumbs

Extra-virgin olive oil, for frying

Salt and pepper

This dish is typical of Turin.

Combine the chicken, ricotta, parsley, sage leaves, onion, lemon juice and zest, salt and pepper to taste, and work to blend well. ✦ If the mixture seems soft, add a little flour. ✦ Shape the mixture into croquettes, dip them in the egg, then in the breadcrumbs. ✦ Heat 1 inch of olive oil until hot and fry the croquettes until they are golden. Serve warm, or at room temperature in the summer.

LAMB STEW

PUGLIA

2 ¼ lbs. boneless leg of lamb,
cut in small pieces

1 bunch celery, chopped

2 oz. pecorino dolce, cubed

½ lb. plum tomatoes, lightly crushed

1 medium onion, chopped

7 or 8 bay leaves

1 bunch flat-leaf parsley, chopped

1 *diavolicchio* (spicy chili pepper,
see note, page 22)

Salt

This dish is typical of Turi.

Put all the ingredients in a copper pot with a wide bottom and narrow neck and cover with 12 to 14 cups of water. ✦ Cover and cook at low heat for about 2 hours, or until the lamb is tender.

FAGIANO IN SALMÌ | **PHEASANT IN
SPANISH SAUCE**

LOMBARDIA

1 pheasant

Several juniper berries, crushed

1 garlic clove, crushed

A few sprigs thyme

A few sprigs marjoram

1 bay leaf

1 medium onion, sliced

½ cup Marsala

4 tbsp. unsalted butter

4 oz. prosciutto crudo, diced

4 quail

1 cup white wine,
such as Arneis or Lugane

1 cup Spanish sauce (see note)

4 slices peasant-style bread

Salt and white pepper

Spanish sauce is also called *sauce Espagnole*. Heat ¼ cup (½ stick) butter in a saucepan. Add 2 tablespoons finely chopped lean raw ham, 2 tablespoons chopped celery, 2 tablespoons chopped carrot, and 1 tablespoon chopped onion and sauté. Sprinkle with ¼ cup flour, then add 1⅓ cups beef broth and ⅔ cup stewed and strained tomatoes. Cook until the sauce has thickened and the flavors have blended, about 10 minutes. Strain and season with salt and pepper.

Clean the pheasant. Heat the juniper berries, garlic, herbs, and onion in a pan until fragrant. Pour the mixture over the pheasant, cover, and refrigerate at least 24 hours. ✦ On the morning of the day it will be cooked, add half the Marsala to the mixture. After a few hours, put it in a pan over medium heat with the butter, prosciutto, quail, and marinade. ✦ When the cooking mixture and pheasant have taken on color, add the wine and simmer for about 30 minutes. ✦ Shortly before the end of the cooking remove the pheasant and pass the cooking liquid through a sieve. Save quail for another use and discard all other solids. ✦ Return the pheasant to the pan, add the strained cooking liquid, Spanish sauce, the remaining Marsala, salt, and a pinch of white pepper. ✦ Cook a few minutes more. Serve with bread that is not overly toasted.

FAGIANO OR
FARAONA CERANI

PHEASANT OR GUINEA HEN IN SAUCE

LOMBARDIA

1 whole pheasant, with its giblets
4 oz. prosciutto crudo, minced
Several sage leaves, chopped
¼ cup (4 tbsp.) unsalted butter
2 oz. veal (or chicken) liver
Pinch grated nutmeg
½ cinnamon stick
1 whole clove
3 bay leaves
2 cups chicken broth
¼ cup Marsala
Salt and pepper

This dish is typical of Magenta. If you have extra sauce, it can be used to dress fresh tagliatelle. Guinea hen may be used in place of the pheasant.

Chop the giblets and set aside. Stuff the pheasant with half the prosciutto and half the sage. ◆ Heat the butter in a pan and brown the pheasant, then add the remaining prosciutto and sage to the pan. Stir in the veal liver, giblets, nutmeg, cinnamon, clove, and bay leaves. ◆ Then add the broth, Marsala, salt, and pepper. ◆ Cover the pan and cook at low heat for 1 hour if the pheasant was young and for up to 2 hours otherwise. ◆ Remove the pheasant from the pan and slice. Pass the sauce through a sieve and pour it over the sliced pheasant to serve.

FAGIANO TARTUFATO

PHEASANT WITH TRUFFLE

PIEMONTE

1 pheasant, cleaned
1 oz. truffle

CONTINUED

Spinach purée is the ideal accompaniment to this dish, typical of Alba.

Lard the pheasant (under the skin) with a few slices of truffle. Mix the ground pork and a little diced truffle and stuff the pheasant with the mixture. ◆ Close the opening

MEAT & POULTRY

¾ lb. ground pork

1 recipe béchamel sauce (see page 339)

1 tbsp. Marsala

with kitchen twine and refrigerate for 24 hours. ✦ Preheat the oven to 350°F. Roast the pheasant for about 50 minutes and serve it warm. ✦ Prepare the béchamel sauce as in the recipe on page 339, adding the Marsala with the milk. ✦ Cut the bird in small pieces and then recompose them on the serving plate. Serve with the béchamel sauce and a shaving of truffle.

FARAONA AL MASCARPONE

GUINEA HEN WITH MASCARPONE

LOMBARDIA

1 guinea hen, cleaned

⅔ cup mascarpone cheese

2 tbsp. Ligurian extra-virgin olive oil

¼ lb. (1 stick) unsalted butter

1 celery stalk, chopped

1 carrot, chopped

1 medium onion, chopped

½ cup white wine

Chicken broth (or milk), hot (if needed)

Salt and pepper

Season the cavity of the hen with salt and pepper and fill it with mascarpone. ✦ Put the olive oil, butter, celery, carrot, and onion in a large pan, preferably earthenware. ✦ Add the hen and pour in the wine. ✦ Turn on the heat to low and simmer, turning the hen from time to time to keep it from burning. Add broth or milk if needed. ✦ After about 1½ hours take the pan off the heat and pass the sauce and vegetables through a sieve. ✦ Return the strained sauce and hen to the pan and cook for no more than 10 minutes. Serve hot on warmed plates with boiled potatoes.

FARAONA ALLA GHIOTTA

GUINEA HEN PÂTÉ

UMBRIA

1 guinea hen, with its giblets

1 tbsp. unsalted butter

4 oz. prosciutto crudo, half of it diced and half of it sliced

1 tbsp. capers

6 anchovy fillets, chopped

Juice of 1 lemon, plus more for the sauce

1 celery stalk, finely chopped

1 carrot, finely chopped

1 medium onion, minced

2 garlic cloves, minced

5 sage leaves

CONTINUED

Preheat the oven to 400°F. Prepare the hen, emptying its interior, cleaning it thoroughly, and removing its head and feet. Chop the giblets. ✦ Mix the butter, diced prosciutto, and giblets with salt and half of each of the following: the capers, anchovies, lemon juice, celery, carrot, onion, garlic, sage, and bay leaves. Stuff the hen with this mixture and place in a roasting pan. ✦ Cover the hen with the sliced prosciutto and salt lightly. ✦ Surround the bird with the remaining other half of the ingredients, pour in the wine, and roast for about 1 hour. ✦ While the hen is roasting, baste it from time to time with the liquid in the pan. ✦ When the bird is cooked through, cut it in small pieces. ✦ Bone the back and neck and pull off the meat. Pass the meat obtained through a meat grinder together with all the other ingredients from the pan; add

2 bay leaves
½ cup dry white wine
Toasted bread
Salt

additional lemon juice. ✦ This mixture should be served spread on toasted bread bathed in the cooking juices. Serve it hot on a serving plate.

FARAONA ARROSTO

ROAST GUINEA HEN

EMILIA-ROMAGNA

1 2-lb. guinea hen
1 sprig rosemary
1 sage leaf
1 oz. prosciutto crudo
3 tbsp. unsalted butter
1 pork caul
Salt and pepper

This dish is typical of Modena.

Carefully singe the guinea hen and clean it. ✦ Stuff it with rosemary, sage, salt, pepper, prosciutto crudo, and 1 tablespoon of the butter. Wrap the hen with the caul and tightly bind the ends to keep in place. ✦ Melt the remaining butter in a pan and brown the guinea hen. Season with salt, cover the pan, and cook at low heat, turning the hen every so often, for about 2 hours. ✦ When cooked, remove the caul and cut the guinea hen into pieces. Reduce the remaining liquid, pass it through a sieve, and pour it over the hen cut in pieces. Serve hot.

FARAONA GRIGLIATA
ALL'AROMA DI ALLORO

GRILLED GUINEA HEN
WITH BAY LEAVES

VENETO

1 guinea hen
14 bay leaves, plus more for garnish
1 cup extra-virgin olive oil
Salt

Cut the hen in 4 pieces, bone them, and arrange in a bowl with salt, 6 crumbled bay leaves, and 1 tablespoon olive oil. ✦ Separately chop the remaining bay leaves and put them in a container with the remaining olive oil. Let all of this stand while preparing the grill. ✦ Prepare a hot grill and let it burn down just until it is mostly embers. Grill the hen, first on one side, then on the other, until cooked through, about 20 minutes total. ✦ When cooked, arrange the pieces on separate plates and brush them well with the olive oil in which the bay leaves soaked. Decorate the plates with more bay leaves.

FARAONA IN
SALSA PEVERADA

GUINEA HEN WITH
PEPPER SAUCE

VENETO

1 guinea hen, roasted as in the recipe on page 569, with its giblets

CONTINUED

Prepare the roast hen as in the recipe on page 569, omitting the truffles and pork. When it has cooled slightly, cut it in pieces. Meanwhile, prepare the sauce: heat the olive oil in a pan and cook the liver and gizzard

For the sauce:

¼ cup extra-virgin olive oil

The hen's liver, chopped

The hen's gizzard, chopped

4 oz. soppressata (optional), minced

1 or 2 tbsp. white wine vinegar
or lemon juice

Salt and freshly ground pepper

(add some soppressata to this if desired, but if so diminish the amount of salt). ✦ Add salt and a generous sprinkling of pepper. Flavor at the end with vinegar or lemon juice. Serve with the hen.

FARRO AND
PIGS' TROTTERS

TOSCANA

1¼ cups dried cranberry beans,
soaked overnight and drained

1 garlic clove

A few sage leaves

1⅔ cups farro

4 pigs' trotters

Extra-virgin olive oil

1 medium onion, minced

½ cup chopped aromatic herbs

Pepper

This dish is typical of Lucca.

Cook the beans with the garlic and sage in water to cover by several inches until tender. Drain the beans and cook the farro in the bean liquid, adding water as necessary to cover the farro by 1 inch. Bring to a boil, then reduce the heat and simmer until tender, about 1 hour. ✦ Meanwhile, simmer the pigs' trotters in water to cover. Add them to the farro near the end of its cooking time, after about 45 minutes. Heat the olive oil in a pan, add the onion and herbs, and cook until fragrant. Stir into the farro when it has about 5 minutes left to cook. ✦ Remove the trotters and keep them warm to serve as a second course along with the farro and the beans seasoned with olive oil and a pinch of freshly ground pepper. Serve hot.

HEN WITH
PHEASANT STUFFING

VENETO

1 medium-size hen, about 3 lbs.

Juice of 3 lemons

⅔ cup olive oil

⅔ cup grated Parmigiano-Reggiano

5 oz. prosciutto crudo (if possible
from the Veneto), cubed

2 carrots, in thin strips

10 fresh shelled pistachios

3 slices sweet pepper

Salt

The *fasanà* of this dish's name is from *fagiano* ("pheasant"); this is, in fact, a filling made to be used for pheasant.

Remove the bones from the hen without cutting it up, thus leaving its shape intact (or have your butcher do this). ✦ Combine the lemon juice, olive oil, and salt (as much as needed) and marinate the hen in this liquid for several hours. ✦ Preheat the oven to 350°F. Remove the hen from the marinade, stuff the cavity of the hen with the Parmigiano-Reggiano, prosciutto, carrots, pistachios, and sweet pepper, and place in a roasting pan. ✦ Roast for 2 hours without adding any other seasoning, or until cooked through.

SAUSAGE AND FAVA BEAN STEW

SARDEGNA

½ lb. pork rib meat
½ lb. Sardinian (or fennel) sausage, sliced
½ lb. fresh pork rind, cut in pieces
1½ cups dried fava beans, soaked in water 12 hours, drained, and rinsed
¼ cup extra-virgin olive oil
½ cup finely chopped *lardo*
1 medium onion, finely chopped
¼ cup finely chopped flat-leaf parsley
Salt and pepper

Put 6 cups of water in a pot, add the pork meat, sausage, and pork rind, and salt to taste. Bring to a simmer and cook for about 1 hour. ✦ Add the fava beans and cook another hour. ✦ Heat the olive oil in a pan and add the *lardo*, onion, and parsley, cooking until the onion begins to color. Add to the meat mixture, then let the stew simmer another 5 minutes. Stir carefully, taste for pepper, and serve.

BREADED PORK LIVER

FOR 6 PERSONS

TOSCANA

1½ cups breadcrumbs
¼ cup fennel seeds
1¾ lbs. pork liver, cut in 2-inch pieces
½ cup extra-virgin olive oil
1 lb. caul fat (1 for each piece of liver)
Bay leaves (1 for each piece of liver)
Salt and pepper

Combine the breadcrumbs and fennel seeds in a bowl with as much salt and pepper as desired. ✦ Add the pieces of liver and mix them to flavor well. ✦ Heat the olive oil in a pan over medium heat. Wrap each piece of liver in caul fat, tucking a bay leaf into each one. Cook the pieces a couple at a time until golden and serve hot.

MEAT & POULTRY

PORK-LIVER SKEWERS

EMILIA-ROMAGNA

Olive oil
1 cup lemon juice
1 tbsp. ground rosemary
1 tsp. ground sage plus sage leaves
1½ lbs. pig livers, cut in 1-oz. pieces
CONTINUED

This dish is named for St. Petronius, patron saint of Bologna.

Preheat the oven to 350°F. Grease a baking pan with olive oil. Mix the lemon juice with the rosemary and sage, then season with salt and pepper. Add the liver pieces and mix well, then wrap each piece of liver in a section of the softened caul fat. ✦ Using 10-inch wooden skewers, first thread a slice of bread, then a sage leaf, a wrapped piece of liver, another sage leaf, and so on to

12 to 16 oz. pig's caul fat, softened in tepid water and cut in rectangles 6 inches long and 4 inches wide

Slices stale bread, about ½ inch thick

A few tbsp. dry white wine

Salt and pepper

the end of the skewer, ending with a piece of bread. ✦ Arrange the skewers across the pan and sprinkle with olive oil. ✦ Roast about 20 minutes, turning the skewers every now and then. ✦ Arrange the skewers on a warmed serving plate. ✦ Pour wine into the cooking juices left in the pan and reduce it by two thirds, then pour this over the livers and serve immediately.

FEGATINO E SCAROLA

LIVER AND ESCAROLE

MOLISE

½ cup extra-virgin olive oil

1 medium onion, thinly sliced

1 whole lamb's liver, cut in very small pieces

½ cup wine

1 *diavolillo* (spicy chili pepper; see note, page 22)

2¼ lbs. escarole

4 large eggs, beaten

1 cup grated aged pecorino

Salt

This dish is typical of Oratino.

Heat the olive oil in a pan and sauté the onion over moderate heat until translucent, then add the pieces of liver. ✦ Wait until these begin to "crackle" in the pan before adding the wine. ✦ Add salt and chili pepper and cook at low heat. ✦ Clean the escarole, removing the harder outer leaves, then boil in lightly salted water to cover until tender, about 5 minutes. ✦ As soon as it is cooked, drain it, reserving the liquid, and chop it. ✦ When the pieces of liver are starting to give off blood, add the escarole with a few cups of its cooking water. ✦ Add salt, if necessary, and let the liquid boil for 15 minutes. ✦ Mix the eggs, pecorino, and a pinch of salt, then pour over the liver and escarole mixture. Let the flavors blend a few minutes before serving.

FEGATO ALLA PAESANA

COUNTRY-STYLE LIVER

PIEMONTE

2 oz. *lardo*, chopped

4 tbsp. unsalted butter

2 medium onions, thinly sliced

½ cup chopped flat-leaf parsley

2 garlic cloves, minced

All-purpose flour for dredging

1½ lbs. calf's liver, sliced

½ cup dry red wine (preferably Barbera)

Salt and pepper

Heat the *lardo* and butter over low heat, add the onions, parsley, and garlic, and sauté until well cooked. ✦ Lightly flour the slices of liver, then add them to the pan. Brown on one side, then add the wine, salt, and pepper. ✦ Cook at low heat for about 10 minutes, stirring from time to time. Serve hot.

LIVER AND ONIONS VENETIAN-STYLE

FEGATO ALLA VENEZIANA

VENETO

½ cup olive oil
2 tbsp. unsalted butter
½ cup beef or veal broth
1 lb. medium onions, thinly sliced
1 lb. calf's liver, in narrow slices
2 tbsp. dry white wine
Salt and pepper

Serve with very soft yellow polenta. One variation is to add minced parsley and lemon juice with the wine.

Heat the olive oil, butter, broth, and onions in a pan over low heat until the onions are translucent. ✦ Add the liver. ✦ After 1 minute, sprinkle in the wine, add salt and pepper, and cook at high heat for about 5 minutes.

SKEWERED PORK LIVER

FEGATO DI MAIALE ALLO SPIEDO

CALABRIA

½ cup breadcrumbs
½ cup grated aged pecorino
2 tbsp. finely chopped flat-leaf parsley
1 lb. pig's liver, in 1-inch cubes
1 pork caul
Bay leaves, as needed
Salt

Prepare a grill to medium-hot. In a large bowl, combine the breadcrumbs, pecorino, a pinch of salt, and parsley. ✦ Dredge the cubes of liver in this mixture, then wrap them in pieces of the caul fat. ✦ Thread the pieces on skewers, alternating them with pieces of bay leaves. ✦ Grill until cooked through (about 5 minutes total, depending on the heat of the grill) and serve hot.

VEAL RUMP IN ASPIC

FESA DI VITELLO IN GELATINA

LOMBARDIA

2 lbs. veal rump
1 carrot, chopped
1 celery stalk, chopped
4 oz. prosciutto crudo in a single slice
2 tbsp. unsalted butter
1 oz. pancetta, minced
1 bay leaf
Beef or veal broth
2 veal trotters, in small pieces
Salt and pepper

Traditionally this dish is garnished with slices of black truffle and pickled or boiled calf's tongue.

Rub the meat with half of the carrot and half the celery, then wrap it with the prosciutto. Heat the butter in a pot, add the pancetta, remaining carrot and celery, bay leaf, salt, and pepper and sauté until the pancetta is lightly browned. ✦ Add the veal and brown evenly. Once brown, cover with broth, add the veal trotters, and let simmer gently for 2 hours. ✦ Turn off the heat and let the meat cool in its liquid. ✦ Cut the soft, well-cooked meat in thick slices (about ½ inch) and cover with the gelatin that will have formed on the chilled broth mixture.

FILETTO ALLA CARBONADE | OX IN WINE SAUCE

VALLE D'AOSTA

2 cups robust red wine
1 carrot, minced
1 medium onion, minced
1 celery stalk, minced
2 garlic cloves, minced
3 sprigs rosemary, minced
2 tbsp. unsalted butter
4 ox fillets
4 disks firm polenta, for serving
Salt and pepper

For the wine use Rouge de Morgex, Barolo, or Barbaresco.

Boil the wine with the vegetables and half the garlic and half the rosemary until reduced by half. Pass this through a sieve. ✦ Heat half the butter in a pan and brown the fillets. Add the remaining rosemary and garlic, salt and pepper, and reduced wine. ✦ Turn off the heat and let the meat sit in the sauce for a few minutes. ✦ Melt the remaining butter. Remove the meat from the sauce and season the meat with melted butter. Strain the sauce. ✦ Arrange disks of polenta (naturally made ahead of time) slightly larger than the fillets on a serving platter; place the fillets on the polenta and spoon the sauce over.

FILETTO ALLA TIROLESE | **TYROLEAN STEAK**

ALTO ADIGE

2 ¼ lbs. aged beef tenderloin
1 ½ oz. white *lardo*, cut in strips (or as needed)
¼ cup extra-virgin olive oil
1 medium onion, sliced
1 carrot, coarsely chopped
1 celery stalk, coarsely chopped
6 pitted prunes
4 slices black bread
4 juniper berries, crushed
4 peppercorns
2 whole cloves
1 garlic clove, chopped
2 tbsp. red currant sauce (see note)
3 tbsp. unsalted butter
1 cup red wine
1 cup beef broth
½ cup light cream
Salt and pepper

For the wine use Lagrein or Marzemino. You can substitute for the currant sauce currant preserves thinned slightly with water.

Preheat the oven to 400°F. Trim any fat off the meat; cut the fat in thin slices and set aside. ✦ Salt and pepper the tenderloin, lard it with the strips of *lardo,* and brush with olive oil. ✦ Arrange the slices of fat from the tenderloin in the bottom of a baking pan (or line it with a few slices of *lardo*); over this place the onion, carrot, celery, prunes, bread, juniper berries, peppercorns, cloves, garlic clove, and currant sauce. ✦ Place the tenderloin on top of this, add the butter, and bake for about 30 minutes. ✦ Add the wine and broth and return to the oven until the meat is well cooked. ✦ Remove the meat from the sauce that will have formed and set it aside. ✦ Add the cream to the sauce, bring just to a boil, stirring often, then pass through a sieve. ✦ Cut the meat in ¼-inch slices, arrange on a serving plate, and pour the sauce over it.

BEEF WITH BALSAMIC VINEGAR

FILETTO DI MANZO
ALL'ACETO BALSAMICO

EMILIA-ROMAGNA

1 lb. beef tenderloin,
cut in four slices

⅓ cup all-purpose flour

1 tbsp. olive oil

4 tbsp. balsamic vinegar,
aged at least 12 years

1 ½ cups beef broth

Salt

This dish is typical of Reggio Emilia.

Flatten the tenderloin slices with a meat pounder and dredge them in the flour, shaking them to remove any excess. ✦ Heat a griddle to high and grease it lightly with olive oil. Salt the slices, then cook them at high heat on both sides, sprinkling with 1 tablespoon balsamic vinegar. ✦ Prepare a thin sauce by combining the remaining vinegar, broth, and the remaining flour. ✦ When the meat is cooked, cover with the sauce and serve piping hot.

✦ **LOCAL TRADITION** ✦

FINANZIERA ALLA PIEMONTESE

This dish is a tour de force from the Turinese kitchen. First, chicken kidneys, wattles, and cocks' combs are boiled together. Then veal rump, beef tenderloin, sweetbreads, and spinal marrow (*filoni*) are sliced and dredged in flour. The rump and tenderloin are browned in a copious amount of butter. After that the cocks' combs, wattles, spinal marrow, sweetbreads, and chicken livers are added. Once all of this has browned, one adds a little vinegar, a handful of green peas, some pickled porcini mushrooms, and about 6 gherkin pickles. This is left to stew together for half an hour, after which one adds a half of a glass of Marsala wine and a teaspoon of sugar. The stew is served hot.

MEAT & POULTRY

BOILED BEEF STEW

FRANCESINA

FOR
6 PERSONS

TOSCANA

½ cup extra-virgin olive oil

1 sage leaf

1 lb. white onions, cut in thin slices

2 ¼ lbs. boiled beef, prepared
the day before and sliced

7 oz. peeled plum tomatoes

Salt and pepper

This recipe came into being as a means to make use of two or three leftover meats.

Heat the olive oil and sage in a pan. Add the onions and sauté. ✦ Add the beef and brown, then add the tomatoes and salt and pepper to taste. ✦ Cook for a few minutes to thicken the sauce slightly, then serve warm.

FRATTAGLIE DI CAPRIOLO IN UMIDO | STEWED ROEBUCK OFFAL

FRIULI-VENEZIA GIULIA

The offal of a roebuck
2 cups white wine vinegar
2 tbsp. extra-virgin olive oil
2 tbsp. unsalted butter
1 medium onion, sliced
2 carrots, chopped
1 celery stalk, chopped
A few whole cloves
1 cinnamon stick
½ cup white wine
1 lb. peeled plum tomatoes
3 cups venison or chicken broth
Salt and pepper

Serve on a bed of soft polenta.

Rinse the offal in running water and vinegar, then dice. ✦ Heat the olive oil and butter in a pan and cook the onion, carrots, and celery until the onion is golden, then brown the pieces of offal. ✦ Add salt, pepper, cloves, and cinnamon. ✦ Add the wine and when it has evaporated, add the tomatoes and broth. Bring to a boil and remove from the pan. ✦ Serve hot.

FRICANDÓ DAMA BIANCA | VEAL STEW "WHITE LADY"

VALLE D'AOSTA

1 leek, washed and cut in thin disks
(white and pale green parts only)
4 tbsp. unsalted butter
1 lb. veal loin, cut in chunks
¾ cup white wine
2 tbsp. all-purpose flour, if needed

This dish is typical of Issime and is a classic part of the feast of the Virgin of the Snow (August 5), known in the local dialect as Weiss-Weijbie or Dama bianca. The term *fricandó (fricandeau)* is of uncertain etymology but appears as early as Rabelais in 1522 and is registered in 1651 in Lavarenne's *Cuisinier françois*. Serve it accompanied by polenta, perhaps sliced and fried.

Sweat (soften without browning) the leek in a pan with the butter. Add the meat and brown, then add the white wine, stirring to scrape up any browned bits from the pan. ✦ If the sauce seems too thin, thicken it with a little flour, letting it cook a few more minutes. Serve hot.

FRICASSEA D'AGNELLO CON I CARCIOFI | LAMB AND ARTICHOKE FRICASSEE

LIGURIA

1 garlic clove
1 sprig rosemary
CONTINUED

Mince together the garlic and rosemary needles. Heat the olive oil in a pan and add the lamb. Brown, then add the wine and simmer gently for about 30 minutes, adding broth if needed. ✦ Salt to taste and add the artichokes, garlic, and rosemary, then continue cooking until the

½ cup extra-virgin olive oil

2 ¼ lbs. leg of lamb, cut in pieces

½ cup white wine

1 cup broth, warmed (if needed)

4 artichokes,
cleaned and cut in sections

Salt

artichokes are tender, about 30 minutes more. ✦ Add more broth if needed to complete the cooking. Serve hot.

FRIGGIONE ALLA ROMAGNOLA

PAN-FRIED BEEF AND VEGETABLES

FOR
6 PERSONS

EMILIA-ROMAGNA

½ cup olive oil

1 lb. potatoes,
peeled and cut in chunks

2 or 3 medium zucchini, cut in disks

1 large eggplant,
trimmed and chopped

1 large or 2 small peppers, chopped

1 large onion, sliced

1 lb. plum tomatoes, blanched,
peeled, seeded, and chopped

1 ½ lbs. leftover boiled beef,
cut in large cubes

1 tbsp. unsalted butter

Salt

A good broth results in a more or less highly appreciated—but always "lower class"—*lesso* ("boiled meats"), not to be confused with the elegant *bollito*. It is this *lesso* that is used for the *friggione*. In his celebrated *Arte di utilizzare gli avanzi della mensa* (1918), Olindo Guerrini (Lorenzo Stecchetti) gives this recipe for *Friggione alla Romagnola*: "Fry sliced onion in lard; when it colors add tomato cut in pieces, left-over potatoes (best if previously roasted or fried), rosemary, salt, and pepper, a glass of white wine, flour to bind it all, and meat extract. Last of all add the *lesso*, cut in pieces the size of a half egg." There are still families in Bologna that follow this recipe.

Heat the olive oil in a pan, then cook separately the potatoes, zucchini, eggplant, and peppers until golden, seasoning each with salt to taste. ✦ In another (large) pan, cook the onion in a little lightly salted water until it is soft. ✦ When the onion is cooked, add the other vegetables, tomatoes, and beef. ✦ Cook this for 15 minutes (or longer), stirring from time to time. ✦ When the tomatoes are cooked and the mixture has lost its liquid, add the butter, give it one last stir, and serve.

MEAT & POULTRY

FRITÀ DI GROP

SAUSAGE FRITTATA

PIEMONTE

1 *salame d'la duja* (pork sausage
covered in lard)

2 tbsp. unsalted butter

6 large eggs, beaten

Serve this warm in the winter and at room temperature in the summer. You may substitute for the salame another spicy somewhat soft sausage.

Carefully peel the sausage then cut it in ¼-inch slices. ✦ Melt the butter in a pan, add the slices, and cook, stirring. ✦ Add the beaten eggs and make a frittata as in the recipe on page 31.

MIXED FRY
ALBA-STYLE

PIEMONTE

Olive oil

1 ½ lbs. mixed vegetables (zucchini, sliced apples, squash blossoms, mushrooms, carrots cut in strips)

2 tbsp. unsalted butter

2 lbs. mixed meats (sliced liver, brains parboiled and cleaned, small slices of loin, lamb ribs)

2 large eggs

All-purpose flour

½ tsp. baking powder

Milk

3 apples, peeled and sliced into ½-inch wedges

Breadcrumbs

Lemon slices

Salt

Heat ¼ cup olive oil in a pan, cook the vegetables separately until golden, and set them aside in a warm place. ✦ Heat the butter in a pan and cook the liver until lightly browned. ✦ Heat several inches of oil in a high-sided pan until it shimmers. Combine 1 egg, ½ cup flour, baking powder, ¼ cup milk, and salt to make a batter. Dip the apple slices in this batter, fry them until golden, and set them aside in a warm place. ✦ Beat the remaining egg. Dip the meats in the flour, remaining egg, and breadcrumbs and fry in olive oil until golden. ✦ Serve meats, vegetables, and apples very hot on a serving plate with lemon slices.

FRIED LAMB OFFAL

MARCHE

Offal from 1 lamb: heart, sweetbreads, liver, kidneys, and/or intestines

¼ cup extra-virgin olive oil

1 medium onion, minced

1 garlic clove, chopped

2 tbsp. chopped flat-leaf parsley

Several sprigs marjoram, chopped

A few sprigs rosemary, chopped

A few sage leaves, chopped

A few sprigs thyme, chopped

¼ cup chopped basil

1 bay leaf

1 chili pepper

2 tbsp. good-quality white wine vinegar (or lemon juice)

Coratella is a generic term for all of the offal (heart, lungs, spleen, sweetbreads, liver, kidneys, and the delicate intestines, which are tied in small braids). Of course this dish can be made with just one or two types of the offal, depending on what is available at the market.

Cut all of the offal in small pieces. Heat the oil and brown the offal, with the exception of the liver, which should be added only at the very end and cooked for just a few minutes. ✦ Mix the onion, garlic, parsley, marjoram, rosemary, sage, thyme, basil, bay leaf, and chili pepper. ✦ When the offal meats are cooked through, cover them with this mixture and let them rest a few minutes off the heat. Then slowly stir and heat up with the addition of the vinegar or lemon juice. Serve very hot.

FRICEU 'D SANGH

To make these blood fritters, typical of Biella in Piedmont, a layer of breadcrumbs (*pan pist*) and grated cheese (*gru ra*) would be placed into a saucepan and then mixed with an equal amount of fresh pigs' blood. These two layers would be mixed and then left to rest so the mixture would solidify. Any resulting watery liquid would be discarded. The solid mixture would then be sliced thinly and typically fried in one of three fats: the lard used to preserve salame (*ant la grassa di salam*), the caul fat of the slaughtered pig (*reisela*), or a mixture of butter and olive oil. The hot fritters would then be served with a sprinkling of pepper.

FRITTURA DI MAIALE | # PAN-FRIED PORK

LOMBARDIA

About 2 lbs. onions, thinly sliced

4 tbsp. unsalted butter or the same quantity chopped lard or *lardo*

3 tbsp. broth

1 lb. pork loin, sliced

1 lb. pork sausages, cut in 3-inch lengths

1 lb. pork liver, in thick slices

1 tbsp. tomato paste, or as desired

Salt

The heart, spleen, and sweetbreads can be added to this recipe, proportionally reducing the other ingredients. With greater or lesser variations this dish can be encountered throughout the area above Milan, especially Cernusco Lombardone, and is known variously as *rustida* or *rostisciada*. Serve with polenta.

Slowly cook the onions in half the butter (or in lard or *lardo*) and the broth over low heat; when softened, set them aside. ✦ Add the remaining butter to the pan and briefly brown the loin, sausages, and liver (save for last). ✦ Return the cooked onions to the pan, add a little salt along with only a tablespoon tomato paste, more broth if necessary, and continue cooking for half an hour or so.

MEAT & POULTRY

PAN-FRIED CHICKEN GIBLETS

FRITTURA DI POLLO

FRIULI-VENEZIA GIULIA

1 chicken liver, heart, and stomach
½ cup chicken blood
1 cup breadcrumbs
2 tbsp. olive oil
2 tbsp. unsalted butter
1 medium onion, sliced
A few sage leaves
1 tsp. all-purpose flour,
or as needed
Salt and pepper

Serve with polenta.

Clean the liver, heart, and stomach and boil them. Mix the blood with breadcrumbs and briefly boil it to form a paste. ✦ All this should then be cubed. ✦ Heat the olive oil and butter and cook the onion. When it darkens, pour in the chicken parts and cubed blood, adding the sage, salt, pepper, and flour as needed to thicken the mixture. Sauté, stirring, until cooked through.

✦ LOCAL TRADITION ✦

FRITTO MISTO ALLA BOLOGNESE

A fritto misto is mainly a collection of various ingredients that change according to availability, custom, and season, which are fried until crunchy in strained olive oil and served very hot as a one-dish meal. A Bolognese fritto misto would typically contain meats, such as lamb ribs, chicken croquettes, pieces of mortadella, and sweetbreads; numerous vegetables, including artichokes, cauliflower florets, slices or chunks of eggplant, plum tomatoes, zucchini, and zucchini blossoms; and even sweet ingredients, such as apples and croquettes made with ricotta and semolina flour.

MIXED FRY ASCOLI-PICENO-STYLE

FRITTURA MISTA
ALL'ASCOLANA

MARCHE

For the pastry cream:
2 cups milk
½ cup all-purpose flour
½ cup sugar
CONTINUED

To make the pastry cream, bring the milk to a boil in a saucepan. ✦ Meanwhile, mix the flour, sugar, and eggs in a second saucepan until blended. Slowly pour in the milk, whisking; let this cool slowly, then stir in the lemon zest. Cook at low heat for at least half an hour, slowly stirring; do not let it boil. ✦ Whisk in the butter, and spread the mixture out in a baking pan to form a single

3 large eggs, beaten
1 tsp. grated lemon zest
1 tbsp. unsalted butter

Meat and vegetables:
2 large eggs, beaten
1 tbsp. grated Parmigiano-Reggiano
1 lb. lamb ribs
2 cups breadcrumbs
1 lb. seasonal vegetables
(artichoke sections, zucchini slices,
squash blossoms, etc.)
1 cup all-purpose flour
Extra-virgin olive oil

sheet about 1 inch high. ✦ As soon as it cools, cut it in cubes. ✦ Meanwhile, mix the eggs and cheese. ✦ Dip the ribs in the egg mixture, then in the breadcrumbs. ✦ Repeat this operation for the cream; dip the vegetables in flour only. ✦ Heat several inches of olive oil and fry the meat, vegetables, and cubed cream. ✦ Drain on paper towels and keep warm. Serve together on a serving plate.

GALLETTO ALLA
CALASCIBETTANA

SICILIA

1 rooster, cut in pieces
½ cup chicken broth, or as needed
¼ cup white wine vinegar
Juice of 1 lemon
2 bay leaves, crumbled
Salt and pepper

BRAISED ROOSTER

This is a very common way of cooking chicken in Calascibetta in the province of Enna.

Arrange the rooster pieces in a large pan in a single layer; do not let them touch. Mix the broth, vinegar, lemon juice, salt, pepper, and bay leaves and pour over the rooster. ✦ Cover the pan and cook at low heat for 1 hour, or until cooked through, watching to keep the pieces from burning. ✦ Add more broth from time to time if needed, but the final dish should have very little liquid.

GALLINA RIPIENA ALLA
CREMONESE

LOMBARDIA

Bread of 2 soft rolls
1 oz. sausage meat, crumbled
1½ oz. mortadella, chopped
3 large eggs, beaten
2 oz. leftover meat, chopped
⅔ cup grated Parmigiano-Reggiano
1 tbsp. minced flat-leaf parsley
Grated nutmeg
1 hen
Salt and pepper

STUFFED HEN CREMONA-STYLE

Serve with *mostarda di Cremona* and pickled mushrooms.

Soak the bread in water, squeeze it dry, and put it in a bowl. ✦ Add all the other ingredients except the hen and mix well. ✦ Stuff the mixture into the hen, sew the opening closed with kitchen twine, and place in a large pot. Add water to cover and bring to a boil. Then reduce the heat to low and simmer until cooked through, about 1 hour.

DRUNKEN HEN

VENETO

1 hen
All-purpose flour for dredging
4 tbsp. unsalted butter
½ cup brandy
1 tbsp. chopped flat-leaf parsley
1 bottle red wine
(Cabernet from Veneto if possible)
4 oz. smoked pancetta
1 cup white mushrooms
1 medium onion, thinly sliced
1 small sprig rosemary
Salt

Serve the hen with yellow or white polenta.

Cut the hen in 4 or 8 pieces and flour them. Heat half of the butter in a heavy-bottomed pan and brown the hen pieces over high heat, turning the pieces from time to time. ✦ Add the brandy, parsley, salt, and wine. ✦ Bring to a boil, then lower the heat to a gentle simmer and cook slowly for about 2 hours. ✦ Chop together the pancetta, mushrooms, and onion and put in a separate pan. Add the remaining butter and rosemary and cook about 15 minutes at low heat. ✦ Pour it over the hen and cook for about 10 minutes more. Serve the hen with the sauce.

CAPON WITH ANCHOVIES

FOR
6 PERSONS

GALLO ALLA CALABRESE

CALABRIA

1 capon, weighing about 4½ lbs.
8 anchovy fillets, cleaned
¼ lb. (1 stick) plus 1 tbsp. unsalted butter
Juice of ½ lemon
Pinch grated nutmeg
½ cup dry Marsala
Salt and pepper

Set up a rotisserie with a drip pan. Clean the capon and remove the breastbone. ✦ Mix the anchovies, 3 tablespoons butter, lemon juice, and nutmeg. ✦ Stuff this mixture into the capon, sew closed all openings, season with salt and pepper, and coat the bird with the remaining butter. ✦ Impale the capon on the rotisserie skewer over a drip pan to collect the fat. Add the Marsala to the drip pan. ✦ Cook at low heat for about 3 hours, basting the capon with the juices collected in the pan.

BEEF STEW WITH CLOVES

GAROFOLATO DI MANZO

LAZIO

1 garlic clove, finely chopped
1 sprig marjoram, chopped
2 oz. *lardo*, cut in thin slices
2¼ lbs. beef chuck roast
½ cup extra-virgin olive oil
CONTINUED

The Roman beef stew known as *garofolato* owes its name to the cloves with which it is seasoned, providing not just an excellent second course of meat but also a flavorful sauce to dress fettuccine. A poem by the Roman poet Augusto Jandolo begins, "Oh, egg fettuccine made with garofolato sauce—how delicious!"

Blend the garlic, marjoram, salt, and pepper with the *lardo* and insert this mixture into slits cut into the meat

1 small onion, sliced

1 carrot, sliced

2 celery stalks, sliced

1 level tbsp. chopped flat-leaf parsley

Pinch grated nutmeg

3 whole cloves

½ cup red wine

2 lbs. plum tomatoes, peeled and puréed

Salt and pepper

one at a time at regular distances. Tie the roast so it keeps its shape while cooking. ✦ Heat half the olive oil, sauté the onion, carrot, celery, and parsley, and add to this the meat. Turn the meat so it browns on all sides. Season with salt and pepper, nutmeg, and cloves. ✦ Add the wine and let it evaporate. ✦ Add the tomato purée, cover the pot, and lower the heat. Cook at low heat for 3 hours. ✦ Remove the meat from the pot and let the sauce reduce. To serve, slice the meat, arrange on a warmed serving plate, and cover with sauce.

MEAT & POULTRY

GARRETTO DI VITELLO | # VEAL HOCK

PIEMONTE

1 veal hock, weighing about 3 lbs.

Garlic cloves, sliced (as many as needed)

Rosemary leaves (as much as needed)

4 tbsp. unsalted butter

½ cup white wine

Salt and pepper

The special detail of this dish, typical of the Valle Ossolana, is the cut of meat. For the wine use Arneis or Gavi.

Preheat the oven to 350°F. Lard the entire hock with garlic and rosemary. ✦ Heat the butter in a roasting pan and brown the meat, then add the wine, salt, and pepper, and put in the oven. Roast until the meat is tender, about 2½ hours. Remove the hock from the pan and place it on a serving plate. Heat the sauce to reduce it and serve with the veal.

BAKED MALLARD

FRIULI-VENEZIA GIULIA

1 mallard, weighing about 2 lbs.,
with its giblets

1 bunch aromatic herbs

1 tbsp. unsalted butter

1 garlic clove

1 orange, sliced

4 oz. *lardo*

Sage leaves

1 sprig rosemary

½ cup white wine

Salt and pepper

Mallard ducks are larger and have a more robust flavor than the standard domesticated ducks usually used for cooking. Serve with baked new potatoes and, if desired, a little polenta. For the wine use Tocai or Ribolla Gialla.

Preheat the oven to 325°F. Remove the giblets from the duck and any remaining plumage, then salt and pepper the inner cavity and insert the herbs, butter, garlic, and a slice of orange. ✦ Rub the breast with *lardo* to keep it soft, insert some sage and rosemary between the skin and breast, then tie up the bird and put it in a pan. ✦ Roast until browned, about 20 minutes. ✦ Add the wine and let it evaporate, then turn up the heat to 375°F and roast for 2 more hours. ✦ Baste the duck from time to time with a little *lardo*. ✦ Serve the baked mallard accompanied with the remaining orange slices.

GERMANO REALE IN SUGO

MALLARD IN SAUCE

VENETO

4 oz. pancetta (or *lardo*), chopped

2 tbsp. unsalted butter

1 medium onion, sliced

2 garlic cloves

1 mallard, weighing about 3 lbs.,
in pieces

5 sage leaves

1 sprig rosemary

⅓ cup diced celery

1 carrot, diced

⅔ cup tomato purée

⅔ cup Prosecco

Duck or chicken broth, as needed

Salt and pepper

The dish can be made more flavorful by cooking minced soppressata or salame in the broth, or by adding a few boned anchovies to the duck as it cooks. The celery, carrots, and tomato can be replaced by slices of apple or quince.

Sauté the pancetta (or *lardo*) with the butter in a large pan over low heat. Add the onion and garlic and sauté. ✦ Add the duck, then add the sage, rosemary, celery, carrot, tomato, Prosecco, and salt and pepper. ✦ Cook slowly, adding broth as needed, until juices from the meat run clear when it is pricked with a fork.

BEEF POT ROAST

SARDEGNA

4 oz. *lardo*

2 cups dry red wine,
such as Cannonau

¼ cup fresh seasonings
(thyme, marjoram, myrtle)

2 tbsp. chopped flat-leaf parsley

2 ¼ lbs. lean beef chuck roast

Extra-virgin olive oil

1 tbsp. all-purpose flour

2 cups beef broth

½ cup tomato purée

1 lb. potatoes, peeled and chopped

Salt and pepper

Cut the *lardo* in thin strips. Mix the wine with the seasonings, a pinch of salt, and a little pepper. Add the *lardo* and marinate overnight. ✦ The next day drain the *lardo*, reserving the marinade liquid, and combine it with the parsley. ✦ Use this to lard the beef. ✦ Preheat the oven to 300°F. Heat 2 tablespoons olive oil in a roasting pan, and as soon as it sizzles add the larded meat. ✦ When the meat has browned, remove it from the pan and set aside for a few minutes. Pour the juice from the meat that has collected into the pan, add ¼ cup of olive oil, and heat it over low heat. ✦ Stir in the flour and brown it. ✦ Add the reserved liquid from marinating the *lardo* and reduce it by about one third, then add the meat. ✦ Pour in the broth and tomato purée. ✦ When this comes to a boil, lower the heat, cover the pan, and roast for 2½ hours. ✦ Remove the meat from the pan, pass the sauce through a sieve, then return both to the pan and add the potatoes. ✦ Return to the oven until the meat is fully cooked, about 1 hour more. Serve hot.

GRAN BOLLITO ALLA PADOVANA

BOILED MEATS PADUA-STYLE

VENETO

3 ½ lbs. beef chuck or brisket

1 medium onion, cut into wedges

5 or 6 cloves

1 carrot, cut into 2-inch pieces

3 celery stalks, cut into 2-inch pieces

3 garlic cloves

Flat-leaf parsley, roughly chopped

2 or 3 bay leaves

1 capon or hen

1 pickled calf's tongue

1 ⅓ lb. calf's head

This is a historic dish, having been based on a butcher's bill of the Italian astronomer Galileo during the period in 1604 and 1605 when he gave food and lodging to Paduan students. Word got out that one ate well at Galileo's table, and it was visited by such illustrious guests as Carlo Gonzaga, the leading nobles of Venice, Tommaso Morosini, Gregorio Moro, and other leading lights of the time. Accompany this with Green Sauce (see page 5), horseradish sauce, and coarse salt.

Place the beef in a very large pot. Stud the onion with cloves and add it and the vegetables, garlic, parsley, and bay leaves to the pot. ✦ All these ingredients must then be fully covered by cold water (about 20 cups). ✦ Bring this to a boil, then reduce the heat to a simmer and cook for about 3 hours. ✦ Add the capon or hen and simmer for another 2 hours. ✦ Separately simmer the tongue in 20 cups of water for 2 hours. ✦ Use the water in which the tongue was boiled to cook the calf's head until it is tender, about 1½ hours. ✦ On a big plate serve the beef and tongue cut in slices, the head in pieces, and the capon in 8 pieces.

BRAISED SNOUT

2 lbs. *grifi* (see note), cleaned and chopped

1 medium onion, quartered and studded with 3 or 4 cloves

Pinch thyme leaves

Pinch marjoram leaves

½ cup red wine

1 tbsp. tomato paste, mixed with 2 tbsp. water

Salt and pepper

This dish is typical of Arezzo and Siena. *Grifi* are discarded parts of the snout of veal and pork.

Heat the *grifi* in an earthenware pan with ½ cup water. ✦ When the water begins to evaporate, add the clove-studded onion, thyme, marjoram, and salt and pepper to taste. ✦ When the liquid has completely evaporated, add the wine, and when it evaporates add the tomato paste mixture. ✦ Cook until tender, adding water as needed and keeping the pan covered. Discard the onion and serve the *grifi* with the pan sauce.

BEEF CHEEK WITH CUMIN

½ cup *ont* (see note)

2 large onions, thinly sliced

1 garlic clove

Pinch cumin

2 ¼ lbs. beef cheek, cut in small pieces

1 tbsp. all-purpose flour

1 tbsp. red wine vinegar

Pinch chili pepper flakes

Broth, as needed

Salt

Ont is clarified butter. To make ½ cup, heat ¾ cup unsalted butter over very low heat until it is melted, spooning off the white foam that forms while it melts. Turn off the heat and let it rest, then pour the golden liquid only into a heatproof container, leaving behind the white liquid and any solids on the bottom of the pan. It can be stored in the refrigerator for a few months.

Melt the *ont* in a pan and add the onions, garlic, and cumin. ✦ Dredge the meat in the flour and add it to the pan. ✦ When the meat begins to brown, sprinkle in the vinegar, let it evaporate, then add the chili pepper flakes and a little broth or water. ✦ After about 15 minutes, add salt to taste and more broth as necessary. Cook until the meat is tender, about 30 minutes total.

GOULASH

3 tbsp. olive oil

5 medium onions, chopped

1 ½ lbs. lean beef stew meat,
cut in bite-size cubes

1 tsp. all-purpose flour

1 tsp. red (sweet) paprika

½ cup red wine

1 sprig rosemary

1 bay leaf

1 sprig marjoram

1 garlic clove, crushed

1 tbsp. grated lemon zest

1 tbsp. tomato paste

Salt and pepper

This dish goes particularly well with polenta, boiled potatoes, or flour gnocchi. For the wine use Lagrein or Teroldego.

Heat the olive oil in a large pan and sauté the onions. Add the meat, browning for several minutes. ✦ Dissolve the flour and paprika in a little water and pour over the meat; pour in the wine. ✦ When the wine has evaporated, add the rosemary, bay leaf, marjoram, and garlic. ✦ When these have been blended in, add the lemon zest and tomato paste. ✦ At this point add 1 cup of water and cook, uncovered, for at least 2 hours. Add more water if the mixture looks dry.

VEAL TENDON SALAD

FOR
6 PERSONS

4 veal knees or leg tendons
and gristle (cartilage)

1 bouquet garni

⅔ cup extra-virgin olive oil

1 tbsp. red wine vinegar

1 medium onion, finely sliced

2 tbsp. finely chopped
flat-leaf parsley

Salt and pepper

This dish is typical of Caserta.

Put the knees (or leg cartilage) in water perfumed with a bouquet garni and simmer for several hours, until the cartilage comes away from the bone. ✦ Drain, remove the bones, put the meat in a strainer, and drain. ✦ Before the meat cools completely put it on a plate, top with a second plate, and put a weight over them. After a few hours the meat will have formed a solid block. ✦ Put the block on a cutting board and cut it in thin strips. ✦ Combine salt, pepper, olive oil, and vinegar in a small bottle or jar; cover and shake until the ingredients are fully blended. ✦ Arrange the meat strips on a sufficiently large serving plate and pour this liquid over them; add the onion and parsley. ✦ Mix until blended and let rest a few hours before serving so the flavors can blend.

BEEF ROLLS ROMAN-STYLE

LAZIO

8 slices lean beef top or bottom round, about 3 oz. each

8 slices prosciutto crudo

2 celery stalks, cut into 2-inch matchsticks

2 carrots, cut into 2-inch matchsticks

¼ cup extra-virgin olive oil

1 medium onion, chopped

½ cup dry white wine

1½ lbs. plum tomatoes, peeled, seeded, and chopped

Salt and pepper

This dish is typical of Rome and Lazio.

Pound flat the slices of beef and salt and pepper them. ✦ Remove the fat from the prosciutto, setting it aside. ✦ Place one slice of prosciutto on each slice of beef. ✦ Top each with 3 strips of celery and 3 strips of carrot. ✦ Roll up the beef slices, being careful not to lose the contents, and tie closed with kitchen twine, which must later be removed before serving. (There are those who use toothpicks in place of the twine; toothpicks must also be removed before serving.) ✦ In a sauté pan combine the olive oil and the reserved prosciutto fat and onion. Place over medium-high heat and cook until onion is golden. ✦ Add the beef rolls and cook at high heat for 1 or 2 minutes. ✦ Pour in the wine, and when the wine has evaporated add the tomatoes. ✦ Cook over low heat to keep the sauce from thickening; if it cooks down too much add 2 tablespoons lukewarm water, repeating this if necessary. ✦ When the rolls and filling have cooked, about 20 minutes, adjust for salt and serve hot.

✦ **LOCAL TRADITION** ✦

INVOLTINI DI INTERIORA DI AGNELLO

This recipe for roasted lamb offal comes from Basilicata. The offal, excluding the intestines, would be chopped and mixed with grated cheese, orange zest, parsley, garlic, olive oil, and salt and pepper; chili pepper was also sometimes added. The mixture was then stuffed into the omentum (part of the peritoneum, which is the membrane that lines the abdomen of the animal) and the intestines were used to tie it off into sections. After pricking the omentum to prevent its bursting during cooking, it would be placed into a greased roasting pan on top of a layer of sliced potatoes and cooked either in the oven or over a hot grill for about an hour.

VEAL ROLL-UPS

4 veal scaloppine

2 oz. *mocetta* (cured goat or beef), sliced

2 oz. fontina, sliced

All-purpose flour for dredging

1 large egg, beaten

¼ lb. (½ cup) unsalted butter

½ cup brandy

1 cup meat broth

½ cup light cream

Salt

This dish is typical of the Valpelline. *Mocetta* is meat cured with herbs, often made with pork but also with beef, goat, or lamb. There is no adequate substitute, but if you used slices of prosciutto crudo instead, the result would still be tasty.

On each scaloppine place a slice of *mocetta* and a slice of fontina, then roll up, closing with a wooden toothpick. ✦ Dredge the roll-ups in flour, then dip in the egg. ✦ In a pan melt the butter over medium heat, add the veal rolls, and cook until browned on all sides. Add the brandy and broth. ✦ Pour in the cream and let the sauce cook down over low heat. Adjust the seasoning and serve hot.

PORK ROLL-UPS

Outer leaves of Savoy cabbage

10 oz. pork liver

4 oz. pork lungs or kidneys

3 medium onions, chopped

1 tsp. ground cinnamon

½ cup dark raisins, softened in liquid

4 tbsp. unsalted butter

1 cup red wine

All-purpose flour (optional)

Salt

These roll-ups, typical of Pont St. Martin, Donnaz, Bard, and in the Walser communities, were traditionally prepared and eaten on the day on which a pig was slaughtered. In fact, the meats were wrapped in a section of the pig's peritoneum (omentum), which was in turn covered by a cabbage leaf. The Roman gourmet Apicius describes a similar preparation. Serve with polenta or boiled potatoes. For the wine use Rouge de Morgex, Donnaz, or Dolcetto.

Cook the cabbage leaves in boiling water to cover for a few minutes, until slightly wilted. ✦ Remove them with a strainer and let dry on a cloth. ✦ Finely chop the meats and mix with 2 onions. ✦ Add salt, cinnamon, and raisins. ✦ Place a small amount of this mixture over each cabbage leaf and roll it up; close with a wooden toothpick. ✦ Heat the butter in a high-sided pan and sauté the remaining onion. ✦ Add the roll-ups and brown them. ✦ Pour in the wine and let it evaporate. ✦ If desired, the sauce can be thickened with the addition of 2 teaspoons flour, stirring well to avoid lumps.

INVOLTINI DI SALSICCIA | SAUSAGE ROLL-UPS

CALABRIA

8 to 12 cabbage leaves
¾ to 1 lb. spicy sausage meat, crumbled
2 tbsp. extra-virgin olive oil
3 cups tomato purée
Salt

This dish is typical of Celico.

Parboil the cabbage leaves in boiling water until wilted, then set them out on a cloth to dry. ✦ Cook the sausage meat in a pan without any seasonings, let it cool, then divide among the cabbage leaves, rolling them up and closing with toothpicks. ✦ Heat a little olive oil in the same pan, then add the rolls and brown them. Add the tomato purée and cook about 15 minutes. Add salt to taste and serve hot.

INVOLTINI SARDI | MEAT ROLL-UPS

SARDEGNA

1 garlic clove
A few sage leaves
½ cup flat-leaf parsley leaves
1 ¼ lbs. ground lean beef or pork
8 to 12 large cabbage leaves
Extra-virgin olive oil
1 cup white wine, such as Vermentino

Finely chop the garlic, sage, and parsley and combine with the meat. ✦ Shape this mixture into 3-inch loaf shapes. ✦ Parboil the cabbage leaves in salted boiling water for a few minutes. Drain well and wrap a leaf around each loaf. ✦ Heat the olive oil in a large pan and brown the roll-ups. ✦ Add wine, then cover the pan and stew them over low heat until the meat is cooked through, about 20 minutes. Serve at room temperature.

LA GALLOT | HEN GALANTINE
FOR 6 PERSONS

ABRUZZO

1 free-range hen
10 oz. very lean ground beef
2 large eggs, beaten, plus 2 large hard-boiled eggs, peeled and sliced
¼ cup grated fresh pecorino
Pinch grated nutmeg
7 oz. mortadella (or prosciutto cotto), sliced thin
⅔ cup pitted green olives, chopped
¼ cup extra-virgin olive oil
¼ cup white wine
Salt and pepper

Remove the backbone from the hen, and cut away the wings and feet to obtain a large hunk of meat. ✦ In a bowl combine and work together the ground meat, beaten eggs, cheese, nutmeg, salt, and pepper. ✦ Butterfly out the hen and line it with the mortadella (or prosciutto), then spoon in the meat mixture, olives, and hard-boiled eggs. ✦ Roll up the hen and sew closed with kitchen twine. ✦ Tightly wrap the hen in a cloth and place it in a pot. Add water to cover, season with salt, and stir in the olive oil and wine. Heat over medium heat and bring to a boil, then reduce the heat to low and simmer for 3 hours. Serve sliced.

INVOLTINI DI MUSSO ALLA PANCETTA

Typical of the Veneto, this recipe for donkey steak roll-ups involves first pounding the steaks flat and cooking them in a fragrant sauce. After being pounded thin, the steaks would be rolled closed, enclosing a slice of pancetta and two cloves. The sauce was made by grinding rosemary, garlic, and bay leaves in a mortar and pestle, and sautéing this mixture in olive oil and butter, to which a chopped onion and a cinnamon stick were added. The roll-ups would then be added to the pan, seasoned with salt and pepper, and browned. Red wine was added and the dish left to simmer gently, covered, for about two hours. Once the meat was cooked, the roll-ups were removed and the sauce finished with a little tomato paste added to the pan juices.

LEPRE ALLA CACCIATORA

HUNTER'S STYLE HARE

FRIULI-VENEZIA GIULIA

1 hare, about 4 lbs., with its giblets

3 tbsp. white wine vinegar

1 celery stalk, julienned

½ cup chopped flat-leaf parsley

2 carrots, julienned

2 potatoes, cut into chunks

1 medium onion, chopped

2 garlic cloves

3 juniper berries, lightly crushed with a knife

A few sage leaves

1 sprig rosemary

4 tbsp. olive oil

2 tbsp. unsalted butter, or as needed

4 oz. prosciutto, cubed

2 cups white wine, such as Tocai

1 sprig marjoram

1 tsp. ground cinnamon

Salt and pepper

Clean the hare, cut it in pieces, and rinse them in cold running water. ✦ In a large pot, mix 2 tablespoons vinegar with 3 cups water and add the celery, parsley, carrots, potatoes, onion, 1 garlic clove, the juniper berries, half the sage, and rosemary. ✦ Heat to a simmer. When the potatoes are just starting to soften, remove the mixture from the heat. Let the mixture cool slightly; when it is just warm, add the pieces of hare. Cool and refrigerate for about half a day. ✦ Bring to a simmer again, cool, and let stand, refrigerated, for another 4 or 5 hours so the hare will become tender. ✦ Remove the hare from the liquid with a slotted spoon; discard the marinade and vegetables. Then put the following in a pan: the olive oil, half the butter, half the prosciutto, the remaining garlic, and the remaining sage. Heat over medium heat. ✦ When the garlic has turned slightly golden, add the hare and season with salt and pepper. ✦ When the meat begins to brown, add the remaining vinegar and 1 cup of the wine. Reduce the heat to low and let simmer while preparing the sauce. ✦ Chop the giblets. Heat the remaining butter in a pan over low heat and when it melts add the giblets, remaining prosciutto, the marjoram, and cinnamon. ✦

Cook slowly, adding the remaining wine and stirring to form a rich sauce, adding a little more butter if necessary. ✦ When cooked, arrange the hare in a serving bowl and pour the giblet sauce over it and then the pan juices from the hare.

LEPRE ALLA TERAMANA

HARE IN SAUCE

ABRUZZO

¼ cup extra-virgin olive oil
2 garlic cloves, chopped
1 sprig rosemary
1¾ lbs. hare (back and thighs), cut in pieces
¾ cup chicken broth
4 salt-cured anchovy fillets, rinsed and chopped
1 tbsp. capers, chopped
⅔ cup mixed pickles, roughly chopped
Salt and pepper

This dish is typical of Teramo.

Heat the olive oil in a large pan and sauté the garlic, rosemary, and pieces of hare until the hare is golden. ✦ Add the broth, salt, and pepper. Bring to a boil, then reduce the heat to low, cover, and simmer for 1½ hours. ✦ Add the anchovy fillets, capers, and pickles and continue cooking for another 30 minutes until the meat is tender.

✦ LOCAL TRADITION ✦

LABBRITTI CON I FAGIOLI

This recipe, typical of the area of Terni in Umbria, has all but disappeared today since it calls for a piece of meat called the *labritti*, which is the serrated inner part of a cow's mouth, distinguished from the outer *labbri* (lips). Possible substitutions for the *labritti* could include pigs' trotters or the boiled cartilage from cows' hooves. To prepare the dish per its traditional methods, the *labritti* would first be cleaned and cut into small pieces, no larger than the beans that were its typical accompaniment, and then boiled in salted water. The pieces would then be added to beans cooked in the traditional manner, in an earthenware dish beside the fire, and the mixture dressed like a salad with olive oil, salt, pepper, and either a little vinegar, or, more traditionally, the juice of *melangola* oranges—sour oranges similar to Seville oranges that were once commonly grown in kitchen gardens and yards around Terni and used exclusively to season bean dishes.

LEPRE ALLA TRENTINA | TRENTINO-STYLE HARE

TRENTINO

1 bottle red wine (750 ml)

¼ cup pine nuts

¼ cup raisins

1 tsp. ground cinnamon

Grated zest of ½ lemon

3 tbsp. sugar

1 hare, skinned, and cut in pieces, with its giblets (about 3 ½ lbs.)

2 tbsp. unsalted butter

2 tbsp. lard

1 medium onion, chopped

1 tbsp. all-purpose flour

4 cups broth, plus more as needed

Salt and pepper

For the wine use Lagrein.

Mix the wine, nuts, raisins, cinnamon, lemon zest, and sugar in a nonreactive container. Add the giblets and marinate for 4 hours. ✦ Heat the butter and lard in a large pan until hot, then add the pieces of hare and onion; add salt and pepper. ✦ When the onion has darkened, stir in the flour until blended. Add the giblets with their marinade and reduce the heat to low. ✦ Add broth to cover (add more as needed) and slowly cook the hare (which will be exquisite), about 2 hours.

LEPRE IN SALMÌ 1 | JUGGED HARE 1

PIEMONTE

1 hare (about 3 lbs.)

2 cups ordinary red wine, plus 2 bottles high-quality red wine (preferably aged Barbera)

2 carrots, roughly chopped

2 celery stalks, roughly chopped

2 medium onions, roughly chopped

2 or 3 bay leaves

Pinch ground cinnamon

6 tbsp. unsalted butter

Broth

Salt and peppercorns

Cut the hare in pieces that are not too large and rinse them in the ordinary red wine (which should then be discarded). ✦ Arrange the meat in a large container, earthenware if possible, and add the carrots, celery, onions, bay leaves, cinnamon, and a few peppercorns. ✦ Pour in the 2 bottles of red wine (Barbera) and set aside to marinate in the refrigerator for about 48 hours. ✦ Remove the pieces of meat from the marinade and filter the liquid, setting it aside. ✦ Heat the butter in a pan and add the vegetables from the marinade and then the pieces of hare, browning well. ✦ Add salt and pour in the wine used in the marinade. ✦ Cover and simmer at low heat, and has soon as the wine has evaporated, add some broth and continue cooking until the meat is tender. ✦ Remove the pieces of hare and set aside; pass the sauce with the vegetables through a sieve, then return the hare and its sauce to the pan, cover, and let it rest a few hours. Reheat before serving.

MEAT & POULTRY

JUGGED HARE 2

LOMBARDIA

2 celery stalks, chopped

2 carrots, chopped

2 medium onions, chopped

1 garlic clove

4 sprigs thyme

1 bunch sage

2 sprigs marjoram

6 bay leaves

6 juniper berries

1 bottle red wine
(Barbera of the best quality
or Barolo)

1 hare (4½ lbs.), cut in pieces,
with giblets and blood

All-purpose flour for dredging

6 tbsp. unsalted butter

1 scallion, sliced

4 oz. pancetta, diced

6 oz. veal or pork liver, minced

Fat from a roast (if needed)

2 tbsp. Marsala, mixed with
1 teaspooon cornstarch

Salt and pepper

Serve with polenta, and cover with truffle slices.

Combine half the celery, carrot, onion, garlic, thyme, sage, marjoram, bay leaves, and juniper berries in a suitable container with salt and pepper to taste. Add the wine and pieces of hare and marinate for 24 hours. ✦ Remove the pieces of hare from the marinade, setting aside the liquid. ✦ Drain the pieces of hare, pat dry, then dredge in flour. ✦ Heat the butter until melted and sauté the scallion; remove the scallion and set aside. Add the hare, a few pieces at a time, along with the pancetta. ✦ Add the wine of the marinade and the remaining vegetables and herbs. ✦ Add the hare's blood and giblets, then the veal liver and cook at low heat (a gentle simmer) for a few hours. The cooking time will depend on the size of the hare and most of all on whether it was old or young; it may require as many as 4 hours. (For this reason it is best to prepare it ahead of time and then reheat it to serve.) ✦ When the meat is cooked, remove it from the pan and pass the sauce through a sieve. The sauce should be thick; if the result does not seem perfect, add 1 tablespoon of fat from a roast and the Marsala mixture. Cook 5 minutes to thicken and serve.

JUGGED HARE 3

FRIULI-VENEZIA GIULIA

8 cups red wine

½ cup red wine vinegar

A few sage leaves

1 carrot

1 celery stalk

2 bunches flat-leaf parsley

2 bay leaves

1 sprig rosemary

1 sprig oregano

CONTINUED

Serve very hot with polenta. For the wine use Refosco or Merlot from Friuli.

Prepare the marinade by pouring the red wine into a pan and adding the vinegar, 4 peppercorns, a few sage leaves, carrot, celery, parsley, bay leaves, rosemary, and oregano. ✦ Let this boil for 15 minutes, then let it cool. ✦ Clean the hare, cut it in pieces, and place them in a container. Pour in the cooled marinade and refrigerate for 12 hours. ✦ At the end of that time remove the hare from the marinade, filtering the liquid and setting it aside. ✦ Flour the pieces of hare. ✦ Heat the olive oil and butter in a large pan and add the hare. ✦ Sauté at high

1 hare, about 4½ lbs.
(or 4½ lbs. roebuck)
All-purpose flour for dredging
2 tbsp. extra-virgin olive oil
¼ lb. (1 stick) unsalted butter
4 oz. prosciutto fat, chopped
2 medium onions, sliced
1 garlic clove
½ cup dry white wine
½ cup sour cream
Salt and peppercorns

heat to brown evenly, then lower the heat and add the prosciutto fat, onions, garlic, filtered marinade, and white wine. Let simmer until tender, about 1½ hours. Remove the hare from the pan, season the sauce with salt and pepper, then bind the sauce with the sour cream. Cover the pan and heat gently (do not let the sauce boil or the sour cream will separate).

HARE IN PEPPER SAUCE

VENETO

1½ cups white wine vinegar
1 sprig rosemary
1 sprig sage
1 hare, with its giblets,
about 4½ lbs.
4 oz. lard
4 tbsp. olive oil
1 celery stalk, chopped
¼ cup chopped flat-leaf parsley
¼ cup white wine
4 oz. salame in one piece
Pinch grated nutmeg
½ tsp. ground cinnamon
¼ cup grated Parmigiano-Reggiano
Juice of ½ lemon
(and grated zest,
if desired)
½ cup golden raisins
Salt and freshly ground pepper

The hare is the most famous of game, as depicted on the mosaics of Roman villas (the museum of Opitergim in Oderzo near Treviso) and memorialized in proverbs, such as *"'Na bota ore el can, 'na bota el lievaràl!"* meaning, roughly, "Sooner or later the hunter becomes the hunted."

Mix the vinegar, rosemary, and sage with 1½ cups water in a nonreactive container. Add the hare and refrigerate overnight. ✦ The next day, remove the hare from the marinade, dry it, and cut it in pieces. Heat half the lard and 3 tablespoons olive oil over low heat and brown the hare pieces. Add the celery and parsley, then wine. Cover and simmer on low heat until the hare is tender, about 1 hour. ✦ Separately dice the giblets. Heat the remaining lard and olive oil in another pan and cook the salame, salt, a very generous amount of pepper, nutmeg, and cinnamon. Add the giblets and brown. ✦ When this sauce—the famous *peverada*—is cooked (in only a very short time), remove from the heat and stir in the cheese and lemon juice (you can add the zest if you wish). ✦ According to tradition, which calls for sweet and sour, add the raisins. ✦ When the hare is served, it should be accompanied by the *peverada*, each diner spooning some to cover his or her portion.

MEAT & POULTRY

597

| # STEWED HARE

1 hare, including giblets,
about 4 ½ lbs.

1 bottle red wine, such as Teroldego

2 medium onions, finely chopped

2 carrots, chopped

1 garlic clove

2 tbsp. juniper berries, crushed

1 bay leaf

1 tbsp. red wine vinegar

¼ cup extra-virgin olive oil

2 tbsp. lard

3 tbsp. breadcrumbs

Salt

Cut the hare in pieces and put them and the giblets in a nonreactive container; pour in enough red wine to cover and add 1 onion, the carrots, garlic, juniper berries, bay leaf, vinegar, and salt. ✦ Leave the hare in this marinade 4 days during the winter and 2 in the summer, stirring from time to time. ✦ Remove the hare, drain, and set aside, reserving the wine of the marinade. ✦ Heat half the olive oil in a casserole and add the lard and the other chopped onion; add the pieces of hare and sear them until they take on a good golden color. ✦ Pour in most of the wine of the marinade and simmer for about 2 hours. ✦ Finely chop the giblets. ✦ Separately heat the remaining olive oil in a pan and sauté the breadcrumbs until golden. ✦ Pass the remaining marinade through a sieve and add it to the breadcrumbs along with the chopped giblets. ✦ Sauté, stirring, for about 15 minutes, and when the sauce is ready, add it to the pan with the hare and let it cook 10 minutes.

| # BEAN STEW WITH BEEF AND HAM

FOR
6 PERSONS

4 oz. *lardo* (or prosciutto fat),
finely chopped

1 medium onion, minced

6 oz. lean beef bottom round
or chuck, cut in large chunks

6 oz. lean pork shoulder or loin,
cut in large chunks

4 oz. prosciutto (preferably
from near the bone), cubed

⅔ cup fresh shelled
cranberry beans

1 cup dried chickpeas,
soaked overnight

⅔ cup fresh shelled peas

Grated pecorino piccante

Salt

If desired, when adding the peas you can also add chard, chicory, lettuce, or any other suitable vegetable.

Heat the *lardo* (or, if preferred, prosciutto fat) in a stockpot and sauté the onion. Add the meats and brown them. ✦ Add the beans and chickpeas and fill the pot with water. Season with salt and cook until the beans are tender, about 1 hour. Add the peas and let cook just until bright green, about 5 minutes. Serve piping hot with pecorino piccante.

LESSO MISTO

This traditional Lombardian dish of boiled meats is distinguished from other similar recipes in its use of fine cuts of meat and was often served at Christmas in Milan. Another distinction is that the boiled meat was to be served alone and was not the by-product of making broth. The heart of the dish was always beef (most commonly *codone*, or rump roast), to which a calf's head and *biancostato* (a special cut from the breast, or flank steak) were most often added, occasionally accompanied by capon for larger parties, as well as *zampone* from Modena (though this was cooked separately). The meats were boiled according to their cooking time, in the barest minimum amount of water needed to cover, seasoned with some slices of pancetta and/or garlic. At the table, the meat would be sliced across the grain in somewhat thick slices and dusted with salt. The dense broth, which would have become the color of strong tea, would be poured over the meat and served alongside as a condiment—though for any other uses it would need to be diluted, as it was typically quite salty. As with many rustic, simple dishes, the ultimate success of the *lesso misto* depended on the cook precisely following the recipe's instructions.

TRIPE SAUSAGES
LI NNUIE

ABRUZZO

3½ lbs. pork tripe, from the last part of the intestine
½ lb. lean beef
Grated zest of 1 orange
1 sprig rosemary
2 garlic cloves
1 bay leaf
Pinch chili pepper flakes
4 feet of 1-inch hog sausage casings, cleaned

The name of this dish, which is typical in Montorio al Vomano and of the Isola del Gran Sasso, is of French origin.

Using separate pots, simmer the tripe and beef in water to cover, let them cool, then cut them in strips. ✦ Chop the orange zest, rosemary, garlic, bay leaf, and chili pepper, blending them with the meat to make a thick paste. ✦ Cut the casings into pieces about 5 inches long. ✦ Using kitchen thread, tie off one end of each casing. Scoop the paste into a sausage stuffer or pastry bag with a large (½-inch) tip. Fill each casing with the paste, pulling the casing away from the tip as you fill it. Leave 1 inch at the open end. Tie the open end, thus obtaining the highly tasty *nnuie*, which are then refrigerated for 3 or 4 days. ✦ Cook over coals, in the oven, or in a pan until very firm to the touch. Cooking time will depend on the method used.

VENISON LOIN WITH RED CABBAGE TIMBALE AND CURRANTS

ALTO ADIGE

For the red cabbage timbale:

2 tbsp. unsalted butter

½ cup breadcrumbs

2 tbsp. olive oil

1 medium onion, finely chopped

1 lb. fresh red cabbage, finely chopped

1¼ cups good red wine

1 bay leaf

½ apple, peeled and chopped

Salt and pepper

For the venison and currant sauce:

1¼ lbs. venison loin

Pinch dry mustard

¼ cup olive oil

¼ cup (4 tbsp.) unsalted butter, plus more as needed

1 cup venison broth

7 oz. fresh red currants, removed from their stems, plus more on the stems for garnish

⅔ cup currant-flavored grappa

Salt and pepper

For the red wine use Lagrein or Teroldego.

Butter 6 to 8 ramekins and dust with breadcrumbs. To make the timbale, heat the olive oil and butter and sauté the onion until soft. Add the cabbage and cook for a few minutes; add the red wine, bay leaf, and apple. ✦ Season with salt and pepper and cook at low heat for about 1 hour, letting the liquid evaporate. ✦ Fill the ramekins with the cabbage mixture, packing it tightly, and keep warm. ✦ Season the venison loin with salt, pepper, and mustard. ✦ Heat the olive oil and butter over medium-low heat, add the meat, and sauté just until medium-rare, maintaining the meat's rosy color (remove it from the pan before it's true medium-rare; the meat will contiue to cook while the sauce is made). Set aside. ✦ For the sauce, add the broth and all but 1 tablespoon of the fresh currants to the venison cooking juices and cook for a few minutes. ✦ Add the grappa, bring to a boil, then whisk in enough butter to make a velvety sauce. ✦ Strain the sauce, then stir in the reserved currants. ✦ Pour some of the sauce in the center of a serving plate, slice the loin, and add the timbale of red cabbage. Decorate with more currants on stems.

CHRISTMAS SNAILS

VENETO

2 lbs. snails

A sack of bran or sawdust to purge the snails

2 tbsp. olive oil

2 tbsp. unsalted butter

½ cup flat-leaf parsley leaves

CONTINUED

This dish is traditional on Christmas Eve. It is to be made with snails from the valleys of Posina, Pasubio, and Chiampo. Also, the larger snails, called *bovoloni* are preferred for this recipe, instead of the smaller *bovoletti*. For the wine use Soave.

Collect the snails and set them to purge for 5 or 6 days in a sack of bran or sawdust. ✦ Immerse them in a pan of boiling water and fish them out as soon as they rise to the surface. ✦ Shell them and put in an earthenware pan

3 garlic cloves

1 cup white wine

along with the olive oil, butter, parsley, and garlic. ✦ Cook this at low heat for about 6 hours, adding the wine about halfway through that period.

LUMACHE DI SAN GIOVANNI | ST. JOHN'S SNAILS

LAZIO

3 ½ lbs. snails (preferably vineyard snails)

Lettuce leaves, damp bread, and bran for purging the snails

Vinegar, as needed

3 sprigs mint (or *nepitella*; see note, page 92)

½ cup extra-virgin olive oil

3 garlic cloves, crushed

1 chili pepper

2 anchovies

1 tbsp. finely chopped flat-leaf parsley

½ cup white wine

1 lb. plum tomatoes, peeled, seeded, and chopped

Salt and coarse salt

This dish is typical of Rome, where it is served to celebrate the feast of Saint John on June 24.

Place the snails in a covered basket for two days with lettuce leaves, damp bread, and bran. ✦ After that purge them in water, vinegar, and salt, rinsing them repeatedly until they no longer emit foam. ✦ Prick them one by one to see if they are alive, discarding those that are dead. ✦ Arrange them in a large saucepan with 1 inch of water, 1 tablespoon coarse salt, and mint, and over medium heat bring the water to a boil. ✦ As soon as the snails extend from the shells, raise the heat and cook for 15 minutes. ✦ Take the snails out of the water, cool them under running water, and heat them in another pan with olive oil, garlic, chili pepper, anchovies, and parsley. Add the wine; when it evaporates, add the tomatoes and salt and cook for 1 hour, adding a tablespoon of water from time to time if necessary.

LUMACHE DI SAN QUIRINO | SAN QUIRINO SNAILS

FRIULI-VENEZIA GIULIA

2 lbs. snails, purged as above

¼ cup extra-virgin olive oil

2 garlic cloves

½ cup white wine

2 tbsp. chopped flat-leaf parsley

2 bay leaves

Salt and pepper

Serve with toasted polenta. For the wine use Tocai.

Put the purged snails in boiling water and remove them after 5 to 10 minutes when the water returns to a boil. ✦ Cool them in cold water, extract them from their shells, cut away any black portions, and rinse a single time. ✦ Heat the olive oil and cook the garlic until lightly golden; discard the garlic. Add the snails, salt, and pepper, and when the sauce becomes dense, add the wine. ✦ When the sauce becomes dense again, pour in enough water to cover the snails and simmer at low heat for about 2 hours, adding parsley and bay leaves after 1 hour.

PAN-COOKED SNAILS

LUMACHE IN PADELLA

FRIULI-VENEZIA GIULIA

2 tbsp. extra-virgin olive oil

2 tbsp. unsalted butter

1 garlic clove

2 lbs. snails, cleaned as in recipe on page 601, removed from their shells, and chopped

Dry white wine

1 tbsp. minced flat-leaf parsley

1 tbsp. all-purpose flour

1½ cups milk

Salt and pepper

For the wine use Malvasia Istriana or Tocai.

Heat the olive oil and butter in a pan, then sauté the garlic until golden and discard. ✦ Add the snails, stir, and add the wine to a depth of 1 inch. ✦ Add salt, pepper, and parsley. ✦ Dissolve the flour in the milk and pour the mixture over the snails. ✦ Continue cooking at very low heat for 2 hours.

SNAILS WITH FENNEL

LUMACHE IN PORCHETTA

MARCHE

3½ lbs. snails

Semolina flour, lettuce, and vinegar for the purging

½ cup olive oil

1 bunch wild fennel

A few mint leaves

1 sprig rosemary

A few sage leaves

½ cup chopped flat-leaf parsley

1 celery stalk, chopped

1 carrot, chopped

2 garlic cloves

1 small onion, chopped

½ cup white wine, plus more as needed

1 tbsp. tomato paste, diluted with ¼ cup water

Salt

For the wine use Verdicchio.

Purge the snails for a few days with a diet of semolina flour and lettuce, then put them in a pail with vinegar and salt. They will give off a white, viscous foam; eliminate this with repeated rinsing with clear water. ✦ Thus cleaned, let the snails sit in a pan covered with water for 20 minutes, then begin cooking at low heat. ✦ At this point the snails will leave their shells; immediately raise the heat and boil the water for 15 minutes. ✦ Drain the snails and rinse them several times. ✦ At this point put another pan over medium heat with the olive oil and add the fennel, mint, rosemary, sage, parsley, celery, carrot, garlic, and onion. ✦ Cook a few minutes and then add the snails and 1 cup water. ✦ After the snails have cooked a while, add the wine. ✦ When the wine evaporates, add the tomato paste mixture. ✦ Cover the pan and continue cooking at low heat for a few more hours, adding more wine if the mixture seems dry.

STEWED SNAILS

EMILIA-ROMAGNA

40 snails

Bran for purging the snails

Lemon juice (to acidulate the water)

½ cup red wine vinegar

½ cup dry white wine

1 carrot, chopped

1 medium onion, chopped

3 garlic cloves, chopped

1 shallot, chopped

1 bunch flat-leaf parsley, half of it chopped

2 tbsp. olive oil

Pat of unsalted butter

½ cup white wine vinegar

½ lb. fresh mushrooms, thinly sliced

1 lb. peeled plum tomatoes, chopped

2 tbsp. tomato paste

Coarse salt

This dish is typical of Ferrara. For the wine use Trebbiano.

The best way to go about the purging is to put the snails in a container full of bran for at least 1 day. ✦ When they are fully purged, put them in a pot full of acidulated water, add the red wine vinegar, and let them soak in that for at least 2 hours, stirring often. ✦ Add ½ cup coarse salt to the water and change the water 5 or 6 times over the course of 2 hours. ✦ Boil the snails in water to cover by several inches for 15 to 20 minutes, drain, and rinse them under cold water. ✦ Arrange in a pan, add the white wine, half of the carrot, half of the onion, 1 garlic clove, the shallot, and the parsley leaves. ✦ Cook at low heat for about 2½ hours, then drain the snails and remove them from their shells. ✦ In another pan, heat the olive oil and butter and sauté the remaining onion, carrot, and garlic. ✦ When they have cooked about 5 minutes, add the snails, then the white wine vinegar. ✦ Let this evaporate, then add the mushrooms, tomatoes, and tomato paste. ✦ Add about ½ cup of warm water to the pan and continue cooking for another 30 minutes. Before serving, taste for salt and add the remaining chopped parsley.

STEWED SNAILS WITH HERBS

LUMACHE IN UMIDO ALLE ERBE

LOMBARDIA

1 lb. snails

Bran for purging the snails

1½ cups white wine vinegar

2 tbsp. extra-virgin olive oil

1 garlic clove, crushed

1 large bunch flat-leaf parsley, finely chopped

Basil, finely chopped

Chives, finely chopped

Fresh tarragon, finely chopped

3 tbsp. unsalted butter

CONTINUED

This recipe can be made *"alla milanese"* by using (in place of the herbs) several salt-cured anchovies, boned and chopped, with a few fennel seeds, browned in the oil with garlic and parsley.

Purge the snails in bran for 8 days, then put them in water with 1 cup vinegar and 1 tablespoon salt for 3 hours. ✦ Clean them again in cold running water. ✦ Boil them in water to cover with the remaining vinegar and salt for a few minutes. ✦ Remove them from their shells (there is a special utensil for doing so). ✦ Heat the olive oil, then add the garlic and cook briefly until golden; discard. Add the herbs, snails, and butter; test for salt and pepper. ✦ After about 1 hour, add the wine, then cover the pan and cook for a few more hours. ✦ Serve the

¼ cup dry white wine
Toasted bread
Salt and pepper

snails warm with their sauce accompanied by slices of toasted bread.

CREMONA-STYLE SNAILS

LOMBARDIA

2 lbs. snails
2 tbsp. unsalted butter
2 tbsp. olive oil
1 medium onion, sliced
1 garlic clove, sliced
1 cup white wine, such as Lugana
1 cup chicken broth
1 cup tomato purée
½ cup chopped flat-leaf parsley
1 cup red wine, such as Bonarda
Salt and pepper

Clean and boil the snails in water to cover, shell them, then clean them again. ✦ Heat the butter and oil and sauté the onion and garlic; add the snails. ✦ Add the wine, broth, and tomato purée and simmer over low heat. ✦ After 1 hour, add the parsley and red wine. Season with salt and pepper. ✦ Cook until the sauce is thick and flavorful, 1 hour more.

DUCK BREAST
WITH CHERRY SAUCE

VENETO

2 tbsp. rosemary leaves
Juice of 1 lemon
½ cup extra-virgin olive oil
1 duck breast (about 1 lb.), fat scored
⅓ cup Sangue Morlacco
(cherry liqueur from Padua)
2 tbsp. unsalted butter
Salt and peppercorns

For the sauce:
2 tbsp. unsalted butter
3 oz. grated golden delicious apple
⅓ cup minced onion
½ cup chicken broth
1½ cups chopped pitted cherries
(fresh or thawed frozen)
Toasted bread slices

Grind a few peppercorns with the rosemary leaves in a mortar, then combine with lemon juice and olive oil; spread this mixture on the duck breast and let stand 3 hours. ✦ Make the sauce: heat the butter and cook the apple and onion. Add the broth and cherries. ✦ Boil slowly until it reaches the desired density and set aside. ✦ Put the duck in a cold pan fat-side down and heat over high heat (without butter or oil) for 8 minutes, or until the fat just starts to color. ✦ Take the pan off the heat, add salt and cherry liqueur, and after a few minutes return the pan to the heat and continue cooking the same area of the duck until the skin begins to form pearls of liquid. ✦ Add the butter, turn the duck, and cook another minute. ✦ Reheat the sauce and serve with the duck. ✦ Make a layer of bread on a serving plate. Cut the breast in slices, place them on the bread, and serve with the cherry sauce.

PORK SCRAPS
AND PEPPERS

CAMPANIA

¼ cup extra-virgin olive oil

1¾ lbs. pork scraps and chitterlings

10 oz. *papaccelle* (pickled peppers)

1 *diavolillo* (hot chili pepper, see note, page 22)

Salt

This typical local dish is made after the slaughter of a pig and is composed of the less highly valued parts, which in no sense detracts from its flavor.

In a *sartana* (a pan, from the Spanish *sarten*, a holdover of an ancient name), heat the oil and cook the pork scraps and chitterlings. ✦ When they are almost fully cooked add the *papaccelle*, *diavolillo*, salt, and cook for another 5 minutes. Serve hot.

MAIALE ALL'AGRODOLCE

SWEET-AND-SOUR PORK

UMBRIA

2 tbsp. olive oil

1 garlic clove

1 lb. pork loin, cut in small pieces

1 tsp. sugar

½ cup white wine

7 oz. scallions, chopped

7 oz. carrots, chopped

4 oz. celery, chopped

3 tbsp. white wine vinegar

Heat the oil in a pan and cook the garlic; as soon as it turns blond, remove it and add the meat. ✦ When the meat begins to brown, add the sugar and wine. ✦ Add the scallions, carrots, and celery, stirring often. ✦ When the meat and vegetables are nearly cooked, add the vinegar. Bring to a boil, then remove from the heat and serve.

MAIALE CON I CECI
DEL 2 NOVEMBRE

PORK AND CHICKPEAS
FOR ALL SOUL'S DAY

LOMBARDIA

1⅔ cup dried chickpeas

Pinch baking soda

2 lbs. pig's head (even better is lean fresh ham)

6 scallions

2 carrots

2 celery stalks

1 sage leaf

1 sprig rosemary

Grated cheese, for serving

Gherkins and pickled green peppers, for serving

Salt

Soak the chickpeas in water with baking soda for 48 hours. ✦ Rinse them thoroughly, then put them in cold unsalted water, bring to a boil, and simmer them for 4 hours. ✦ Separately combine the pork, scallions, carrots, celery, sage, rosemary, and salt in a pot with water to cover; simmer until the pork is cooked. Add the pork to the beans and cook for another 30 minutes to blend the flavors. ✦ Serve the chickpeas without the meat in their cooking broth sprinkled with cheese as a first course; serve the meat as a second course, accompanied by gherkins and pickled green peppers.

PORK AND PICKLED PEPPERS

MAIALE CON I PEPERONI
SOTT'ACETO

CAMPANIA

1 ½ lbs. pork loin, with its fat

1 tbsp. olive oil

6 pickled peppers,
seeded and chopped

1 *diavolillo* (hot chili pepper,
see note, page 22), optional

Salt

Cut the meat in pieces that weigh about 2 ounces each. Heat the olive oil and brown the meat at high heat. Reduce the heat and add the peppers and salt and cook until the meat has cooked through. ✦ Add some spicy chili pepper during the cooking according to the tastes of the diners.

MANZO ALL'OLIO OR
MANZO DI ROVATO

BRAISED BEEF

FOR
6 PERSONS

LOMBARDIA

1 ½ cups olive oil

4 lbs. beef chuck roast

1 celery stalk, chopped

2 carrots, chopped

2 medium onions, chopped

2 zucchini, chopped

4 cups good beef broth

7 oz. anchovies

½ cup chopped flat-leaf parsley

1 garlic clove

Heat 1 cup olive oil in a soup pot over low heat and add the meat, celery, carrots, onions, and zucchini. ✦ When the meat is browned, add the broth, cover the pot, and simmer at low heat for 3 hours. ✦ Remove the meat from the pot and set aside; put the vegetables and 1 cup broth in a blender and purée. ✦ Prepare a sauce by heating the remaining olive oil in a pan. Add the anchovies, parsley, and garlic (remove the garlic at the end of the cooking). ✦ Return the meat to the pan along with the vegetable purée and cook for another hour. ✦ Slice the meat and serve it with its sauce and fresh polenta.

MANZO ALLA CALIFORNIA

BEEF IN SAUCE

FOR
6 PERSONS

LOMBARDIA

2 lbs. beef chuck roast

1 oz. pancetta, cut in strips

4 tbsp. unsalted butter

1 medium onion, sliced

½ cup red wine vinegar

1 cup meat broth

1 cup heavy cream

California is a small town that is part of the district of Lesmo, near Monza.

Lard the beef with strips of pancetta. Heat the butter in a soup pot, add the onion and beef, and brown it. ✦ Pour in the vinegar and cook it off, then add the broth and half the cream. ✦ Cover the pot and simmer gently for a few hours, then uncover the pot, add the remaining cream, and stir well with a wooden spoon to blend in the pan juices. Slice the meat and arrange on a serving plate. Spoon the sauce over.

STEWED BEEF
MILAN-STYLE

LOMBARDIA

2 lbs. beef bottom round roast

2 oz. pancetta

1 carrot, chopped

1 small onion, finely sliced

2 celery stalks, chopped

2 bay leaves

2 cloves

Pinch grated nutmeg

4 cups wine, such as a red
from Valtellina

All-purpose flour for dredging

4 tbsp. unsalted butter

1 tbsp. potato starch (if necessary)

According to tradition, to maintain the aroma of the stew, there is the custom of putting a little cold water on the outside of the lid. The idea is that as this evaporates it will keep the temperature at the top of the pot lower and it will keep the liquid inside from evaporating.

Rub the beef with half the pancetta and put it in a container with the chopped vegetables and spices (using only 1 of the bay leaves); pour in the wine and marinate for 24 hours, refrigerated. ✦ At the end of that time drain the meat (setting aside the marinade, removing and discarding the bay leaf and cloves). ✦ Dust the meat with the flour. Heat the butter in a soup pot and brown the meat in it with the remaining pancetta. ✦ When the meat has taken on color, pour in the reserved wine and vegetables from the marinade, adding the other bay leaf. Cover and cook at low heat for 4 hours. ✦ Remove the meat from the pot. If the sauce seems too thin when the meat is completely cooked, dissolve the potato starch in 2 tablespoons broth and stir into the pot. Simmer until thickened.

✦ LOCAL TRADITION ✦

MARRO

From Puglia comes this traditional recipe for rostisserie-roasted stuffed caul. The caul would first be softened in vinegar and water, dried, and spread flat on a table or cooking surface. The intestines, liver, and lights (lungs) of the same animal—typically a kid or lamb—would be thoroughly cleaned in lukewarm water, cut into pieces, seasoned with salt, pepper, and parsley, and wrapped in the caul. After being tied shut with a leftover length of intestine, the stuffed caul would be roasted on a skewer over a wood fire. A variation of this dish used a pounded-thin slice of meat in place of the caul and added hard-boiled eggs and vegetables to the stuffing. This variation was usually stewed in an earthenware dish instead and sliced once cool.

MEDAGLIONI DI CERVO | VENISON MEDALLIONS

ALTO ADIGE

1 ½ lbs. aged deer steak

4 oz. *lardo*, for larding

All-purpose flour for dredging

4 tbsp. extra-virgin olive oil

¼ cup brandy

1 cup beef broth

2 pats unsalted butter

Salt and pepper

Serve with porcini mushrooms and pear halves in syrup stuffed with berry preserves. If you don't have a larding needle, use a skewer to insert strips of the fat into slits cut into the meat.

Cut the meat into medallions weighing 2 to 4 ounces, pound out lightly, and lard using a larding needle. ✦ Add salt and pepper and lightly flour the pieces. ✦ Heat the olive oil in a pan. Add the medallions and brown them on all sides (the outside of the meat should be well browned while the inside is still very pink). ✦ Remove all the meat and set aside. ✦ Pour the brandy into the pan and stir to loosen any browned bits from the bottom of the pan. ✦ Add the broth and bring to a boil. ✦ Incorporate the butter, stirring well. ✦ Arrange the meat on a warmed serving platter and pour over the sauce.

MEDAGLIONI ALLA ROSSINI | BEEF MEDALLIONS

MARCHE

2 tbsp. extra-virgin olive oil

2 tbsp. unsalted butter

4 medallions beef tenderloin, about 1 inch thick

1 tbsp. all-purpose flour

¼ cup Marsala

4 slices prosciutto crudo

4 slices Gruyère

½ cup béchamel sauce (on the thick side, see page 339)

4 slices bread, toasted in unsalted butter

White truffle (optional)

Salt and pepper

Preheat the oven to 400°F. Heat the olive oil and butter over medium heat and brown the beef. ✦ When the meat begins to take color, add the flour, then pour in the Marsala and let it evaporate. ✦ Salt and pepper the meat generously on both sides. ✦ Let the meat cook until it has absorbed the liquid, then transfer it to a baking pan. ✦ Place a slice of prosciutto crudo over each medallion, then a slice of Gruyère; pour in the béchamel sauce and bake for a few minutes, just until the cheese melts. ✦ Serve the medallions atop a slice of bread browned in butter and, if the season permits, dust with truffle.

MILZA IMBOTTITA | STUFFED VEAL SPLEEN

CAMPANIA

1 veal spleen

CONTINUED

This dish is typical of Salerno.

Clean the spleen and skin it; make a hole in the center to form a pocket. ✦ Mix together the parsley, garlic, chili pepper, mint, and salt and stuff it in the pocket. ✦ Sew

½ cup chopped flat-leaf parsley

1 garlic clove, minced

1 *diavolillo* (hot chili pepper, see note, page 22), chopped

1 bunch mint, chopped

¼ cup extra-virgin olive oil

¼ cup vinegar

Salt

the spleen closed with kitchen twine. ✦ Heat the olive oil in a pan and brown the spleen; add the vinegar, then add 2 tablespoons water and braise until it is cooked. ✦ Remove the spleen from the pan, cut it in slices, then return it to the sauce in the pan and cook it again to take on flavor for a few minutes. ✦ Serve cold, covered with its sauce.

MILZA RIPIENA | **STUFFED PORK SPLEEN**

PIEMONTE

1 pork spleen

½ cup chopped flat-leaf parsley

1 garlic clove, minced

1 cup chopped leftover meat

Parmigiano-Reggiano

1 or 2 large eggs, beaten

1 medium onion, cut in pieces

1 carrot, cut in pieces

1 celery stalk, cut in pieces

Salt and pepper

Have your butcher cut the spleen in a way to form a pocket, then turn it inside out and scrape with a knife. ✦ Put the part that comes away in a bowl and add the parsley, garlic, leftover meat, and Parmigiano-Reggiano. ✦ Add the eggs and mix well, adding salt and pepper. ✦ Stuff the pocket with this mixture, then sew the spleen closed and add to a pot with the onion, carrot, and celery. Add water to cover and season with salt. Bring to a boil, reduce the heat, and simmer for about 2 hours. ✦ When the spleen is cooked, let it cool in its broth, then cut in thin slices and serve with whichever vegetables are desired.

MISCISCHIA | **BAKED MUTTON**

MOLISE

2 lbs. mutton, in pieces

½ cup red wine vinegar

2 cups red wine

2 or 3 garlic cloves

Chili pepper to taste

Pepone (spicy pepper relish from Pugliese), to taste

1 sprig rosemary

Salt

This dish is typical of Guardialfiera. For the wine use Biferno or Montepulciano d'Abruzzo.

Marinate the pieces of meat for 1 day and 1 night in vinegar and wine flavored with garlic, chili pepper, *pepone*, salt, and rosemary. ✦ The next day preheat the oven to 300°F. Roast the meat until it is completely cooked, about 1 hour, basting with its marinade from time to time.

SWEET-AND-SOUR VEAL SNOUT

MUSETTO IN AGRODOLCE

TRENTINO

1 veal snout
2 tbsp. unsalted butter
1 heaping tbsp. all-purpose flour
2 tbsp. sugar
¼ cup red wine vinegar
Salt

Serve with yellow polenta.

Simmer the veal snout in water to cover for a few hours. ✦ Heat the butter in one pan and brown the flour in it. In another pan heat the sugar and vinegar. ✦ When the sugar is completely dissolved, pour it over the browned flour and bring this to a boil, whisking it. ✦ Cut the snout in slices and add to the sauce; let them simmer for 15 minutes. Add salt to taste. Serve hot.

PORK STEW

'NDOCCA 'NDOCCA

ABRUZZO

Pork cheeks, snout, ears, and trotters
1 heaping tbsp. white wine vinegar
Bay leaves
Rosemary
Garlic
Spicy chili pepper
Salt and pepper

This dish is typical of Montorio.

Marinate the various pig pieces in an earthenware pan in water acidulated with vinegar, leaving them there for 1 night. ✦ The next morning roughly chop the pieces of pig and put in a soup pot. Add the other ingredients and water to cover. Simmer for about 4 hours. ✦ During the cooking time skim off any fat that forms on the surface.

STUFFED TRIPE

NOD' RA D'TRIPPA

FOR 6 PERSONS

MOLISE

5 pieces lamb tripe
4 oz. *lardo*, finely chopped
1 garlic clove, minced
½ cup chopped flat-leaf parsley
2 tbsp. tomato paste
Salt and pepper

Heat lightly salted water to a boil. Plunge the pieces of tripe one by one into the water, then scrape them clean with a knife. ✦ Place them in a container and add cold water to cover. Let stand for 1 night. ✦ The next day cut each piece into 5 or 6 small pieces. Mix the *lardo*, salt, pepper, garlic, and parsley. Use this mixture to stuff the pieces of tripe. ✦ Roll up each piece and tie closed with kitchen twine. ✦ Simmer in water to cover for about an hour, adding the tomato paste and salt after 30 minutes. Serve at room temperature.

SMOKED GOOSE CONFIT

1 goose
Salt and pepper

Remove the skin and fat (reserve the fat) from the goose, cut it in pieces, and put these in a container with salt and pepper. Refrigerate for a few days, taking care to mix them around every so often. ✦ At the end of that time set up a smoker and smoke the meat until it is cooked through. Heat the fat and 3 tablespoons water in a pan over very low heat to melt the fat. Put the meat in terracotta jars and pour the melted fat over. Cover and refrigerate up to 2 months.

GOOSE CONFIT CONTADINA-STYLE

3 or 4 garlic cloves
2 sprigs rosemary
1 young goose, cleaned, gutted, and cut in somewhat regular pieces
Coarse salt

The meat will last a long time and is excellent reheated and accompanied by polenta.

Heat 1 cup of water in a pot over low heat with the garlic, rosemary, and 1 tablespoon coarse salt. ✦ Add the goose pieces, cover the pot, and simmer over very low heat for about 3 hours. ✦ When the goose is cooked, skim off and preserve all the fat. ✦ Put the pieces of goose in a bowl and cover with the fat while it is still hot, then refrigerate.

GOOSE WITH CABBAGE

¼ cup (4 tbsp.) unsalted butter
1 carrot, sliced
1 medium onion, sliced
1 celery stalk, sliced
1 goose, cut in pieces
1 can peeled plum tomatoes
Inner leaves of 1 cabbage
Salt and pepper

This dish is typical of the area around Crema.

Heat the butter in a pan and cook the carrot, onion, and celery until softened. Add the pieces of goose and brown them. ✦ Add the tomatoes, salt, and pepper, and add water to almost cover. ✦ Cook for about 1 hour, then add the cabbage. ✦ Continue cooking until the cabbage is tender, but preventing the cabbage from becoming mushy. ✦ Skim off the fat if there seems to be too much during cooking.

PRESERVED SMOKED GOOSE

VENETO

1 goose
Several sprigs rosemary
Olive oil as needed
Coarse salt

Remove all the fat from a good-size goose and melt it. ✦ Select the meatier parts of the goose and remove the skin and bones. ✦ Put the pieces of goose meat in a crock under salt for 2 days, turning them over and stirring every day. ✦ Dry the pieces of meat and smoke them in front of a fireplace for 12 hours. ✦ Put them in an earthenware pot with sprigs of rosemary. Melt the fat again and pour over the goose; if this is not enough to cover the meat, add olive oil. ✦ Let a month pass before eating this, keeping it in a container in the refrigerator, tightly sealed with a sheet of parchment.

GOOSE WITH FENNEL

OCA IN PORCHETTA

MARCHE

1 goose
1 bunch wild fennel
3 garlic cloves
1 cup minced *lardo*, plus more for basting
Olive oil as needed
Salt and pepper

This dish is typical of the period of the wheat harvest and was made in country houses using wood-burning ovens. The collected goose fat was used to make roast potatoes.

Preheat the oven to 400°F. Carefully clean the goose, cut open its belly, and gut it. ✦ Break its bones, being careful not to break the skin surrounding them. ✦ Make deep incisions in the cavity of the goose and fill them with salt and pepper, wild fennel, and garlic. ✦ Spread the inside of the goose with *lardo*. ✦ Let the goose rest 1 hour, then sew it up and roast it, every so often sprinkling on salt and basting the bird with olive oil and *lardo*. Put a container of water in the oven near the goose and keep it there, adding water to replace the water that evaporates. The steam from the water will cook the skin of the goose without drying it out. ✦ When the goose is almost cooked, about 1½ hours, and the water has completely evaporated, raise the heat to 450°F and brown the bird. Remove it from the oven. Remove the stuffing and serve hot.

PORK SHANKS

PIEMONTE

4 tbsp. unsalted butter
3 tbsp. olive oil
1 medium onion, finely minced
1 garlic clove, finely minced
1 carrot, finely minced
1 celery stalk, finely minced
2 oz. pancetta, finely diced
All-purpose flour for dredging
8 pork shanks (ossobuco)
½ cup white wine, such as Gari
3 tbsp. tomato purée
1 cup chicken broth, heated
Salt and pepper

This dish is excellent with a good risotto.

Heat the butter and olive oil in a pan and sauté the onion, garlic, carrot, celery, and pancetta. ✦ Lightly flour the pork shanks, then add them to the pan. ✦ Brown the shanks on both sides, add salt and pepper, and pour in the wine. ✦ Dissolve the tomato purée in the broth and when the wine has evaporated, add this to the pan. ✦ Cook at low heat for about 1 hour with the pan covered, turning the shanks every so often.

VEAL SHANKS MILAN-STYLE

OSSOBUCO ALLA
MILANESE

LOMBARDIA

For the veal shanks:
4 tbsp. unsalted butter
1 small onion, sliced
4 veal shanks, weighing ¾ lb. each
All-purpose flour for dredging
½ cup veal or chicken broth
1 small plum tomato, peeled and chopped
Salt

For the gremolata:
Grated zest of 1 lemon
2 tbsp. chopped flat-leaf parsley
1 small piece of garlic clove, minced
1 salt-cured anchovy, boned and finely chopped

Serve with Risotto alla parmigiana or alla milanese (page 354 or 355).

Heat the oven to 300°F. In a large casserole, heat the butter and sauté the onion. ✦ Dredge the shanks lightly in the flour, then add them to the casserole; brown them on both sides without piercing them. ✦ Add the broth, tomato, and salt and cover the pan. ✦ Roast for about 1½ hours. ✦ Remove from the oven and let stand while preparing the gremolata. Mix the lemon zest, parsley, garlic, and anchovy until blended. ✦ Serve the shanks with the sauce.

PORK AND SWEETBREADS WITH BEANS

PADELLACCIA

UMBRIA

¼ cup olive oil

1 garlic clove, chopped

2 medium onions, finely sliced

1 lb. pork scraps

2 sweetbreads

2 cups red wine

3 cups cooked beans

Salt and pepper

This is the traditional dish for the day of the pig's "funeral" in Terni. For the wine use Torgiano or Sangiovese.

Heat the oil in a pan and add the garlic and onions. Add the *pacche* (pork scraps) and sweetbreads. ✦ Add salt and pepper and red wine, then cook slowly. ✦ When it is almost done, add the beans. Stir and serve very hot.

SPIT-ROASTED SQUAB

PALOMBA ALLA TODINA

UMBRIA

1 squab

3 oz. prosciutto

A few sage leaves

¼ cup extra-virgin olive oil

1 ½ cups dry red wine, such as Montepulciano

1 small onion, chopped

½ cup black olives, such as Gaeta

1 tbsp. capers

Salt and pepper

This can be made into a spread for crostini: Bone the squab and chop it together with some prosciutto; add to this mixture the sauce passed through a sieve and spread the result over slices of toasted peasant-style bread.

Set up a rotisserie to medium heat. Preheat the oven to 350°F. Pluck the squab and scorch it to burn off any down. ✦ With a sharp knife cut the skin of the neck to empty it, at the same time removing the tongue and crop. ✦ Rinse the squab well, dry it with a cloth, and without gutting it impale it on the rotisserie skewer with a slice of prosciutto and sage leaves on both sides of it. ✦ Put the skewer over the heat and begin cooking the squab, turning it over the flame, basting with olive oil, and seasoning with salt. ✦ After 30 minutes, by which time the bird should be half cooked, take if off the skewer, chop it in 4 pieces, and put these in a roasting pan (if possible earthenware). ✦ Pour in the remaining olive oil and the wine, add the remaining prosciutto and sage, onion, olives, capers, a pinch of salt, and pepper. ✦ Cover the pan and roast for about 1 hour. ✦ Make certain that some sauce remains in the pan with the bird, adding more red wine if it seems dry. ✦ Remove the squab from the sauce and strain the sauce. Put the squab on a serving plate and cover with the sauce.

PAMPANELLA | ROAST PORK

MOLISE

2 lbs. pork shoulder

2 garlic cloves, chopped

Chili peppers (sweet and hot), to taste

2 tbsp. white wine vinegar

Salt

This dish is typical of San Martino in Pénsilis.

Preheat the oven to 350°F. Cut the meat into similar-size pieces and season with salt, garlic, and chili pepper to taste. ✦ Arrange in a roasting pan, cover with a sheet of aluminum foil, and roast for about 2 hours. ✦ Ten minutes before the end of that time, remove the pan from the oven, discard the foil, skim off the fat, and drain the liquid. ✦ Sprinkle the meat with vinegar and return to the oven to finish cooking, 10 minutes more.

PAPERA CON L'OLIVA | DUCK WITH OLIVES

MARCHE

2 tbsp. extra-virgin olive oil

1 small onion, minced

1 celery stalk, chopped

¼ cup chopped flat-leaf parsley

1 carrot, chopped

1 female duck, weighing about 2 lbs., cut in pieces

2 cups duck or chicken broth, warmed

16 large olives (4 chopped, 4 ground in a mortar, 8 whole)

3 ripe plum tomatoes, peeled and chopped

Salt

Heat the olive oil and cook the onion, celery, parsley, and carrot. ✦ Add the duck pieces and salt. Brown the pieces on all sides, turning them often, then add the warm broth, stirring to deglaze the pan. ✦ Add the olives and tomatoes and bring to a simmer. ✦ Let the sauce reduce, and when the duck is cooked through, arrange it on a serving plate and top with the sauce. Serve hot.

MEAT & POULTRY

PAPERO ALLA FRUTTA | DUCK WITH FRUIT

VENETO

1 young male duck

2 lemons, peeled

1 tbsp. extra-virgin olive oil

3 pears, peeled, cored, and sliced

CONTINUED

This preparation is from the seventeenth-century Bavarian-born Paduan cook Mattia Giegher. It is given in the *Tre Trattati*, printed in Padua around 1639.

Preheat the oven to 300°F. Clean and singe the duck and put 1 lemon in the chest cavity. ✦ Put the duck breast-side down in a roasting pan; add the olive oil and juice of the other lemon. ✦ Roast for 3 hours. After 1½ hours

| 1 cup seedless red grapes or pitted cherries |
| 1 tbsp. unsalted butter |
| 1 tbsp. sugar |
| 1 tbsp. capers |
| Salt |

turn the duck breast-side up. ✦ Add 2 pears and half the grapes or cherries and cook for 1½ hours more. ✦ Put the third pear in a pan with the remaining grapes or cherries. Add the butter and stir gently to coat the fruit, then sprinkle with sugar. ✦ Pass the cooking juices from the duck through a sieve. ✦ For each serving put a little sauce on a warmed plate, add a quarter of the duck, and garnish with the glazed fruit and capers.

✦ **LOCAL TRADITION** ✦

PALIATA

This very simple dish for grilled calf's intestines comes from the area of Abruzzo. Typically only the outer part would be cleaned before stuffing the intestine with the meat of a young lamb or milk-fed veal. The stuffed intestines would be cut into approximately six-inch lengths and grilled, brushed occasionally with olive oil and white wine and seasoned with salt.

PARMIGIANA DI CARNE
CON MELANZANE

VEAL PARMIGIANA WITH EGGPLANT

ABRUZZO

¼ cup extra-virgin olive oil

2 lbs. plum tomatoes, chopped

Basil leaves

1 lb. roasted veal, sliced (see page 519)

4 cups roasted eggplant (see page 699, omitting the topping)

1 lb. mozzarella, sliced

Grated Parmigiano-Reggiano

Preheat the oven to 400°F. Heat the oil, add the tomatoes and basil, and cook over medium heat until slightly thickened, about 15 minutes. Spoon some of the sauce into the bottom of a baking pan. ✦ Cover this with slices of veal. ✦ Cover with the eggplant, then mozzarella, and more tomato sauce. ✦ Repeat this process to form another series of layers, cover with more tomato sauce, olive oil, basil, and top with Parmigiano-Reggiano. ✦ Add a few more basil leaves and bake for a few minutes, or until the top forms a golden crust.

VEAL CASSEROLE WITH TOMATO AND CHEESE

MARCHE

1 top round of veal (about 2 lbs.)

3 garlic cloves

½ cup extra-virgin olive oil

1 cup diced pancetta

2 oz. *lardo*

1 carrot, finely chopped

1 celery stalk, finely chopped

½ medium onion, finely chopped

1 ripe plum tomato, chopped

½ cup dry white wine

2 tbsp. tomato paste, stirred into 2 tbsp. broth

Pinch marjoram

Salt and pepper

Use good meat, such as a top round of veal. Make a long incision down the full length of the meat and open it like a book. Cut the garlic cloves in half, then roll them in olive oil and then salt and pepper. Fill the veal with the pancetta and garlic. ✦ Tie up the round with kitchen twine. ✦ Heat the remaining olive oil and *lardo* in a saucepan and sauté the carrot, celery, and onion, then tomato. ✦ When this has browned a little, add the meat, taste for salt and pepper, and cook at low heat for about 2 hours, turning the meat from time to time. ✦ When the meat is well cooked on all sides, pour in the wine, and when this has evaporated, add the tomato paste mixture and marjoram. ✦ Continue cooking the meat at low heat until done. ✦ Remove it from the sauce, and when it has cooled cut it in thin slices. ✦ Arrange the meat slices on a serving plate and pour over the warmed sauce. Serve immediately.

BAKED MEAT AND VEGETABLES

VALLE D'AOSTA

3 sage leaves, chopped

1 sprig rosemary, chopped

2 garlic cloves, chopped

2 bay leaves, chopped

1 lb. meat (good veal roast would be best)

½ lb. Savoy cabbage, cut in thin strips

1 lb. white potatoes, peeled and roughly chopped

6 oz. fontina

¼ cup (4 tbsp.) unsalted butter

Coarse salt

Those who find the classic taste of the Valdostan marinated meat a little excessive can instead simmer the meat fresh, cut in large chunks, in salted water to which some garlic, sage, and bay leaves have been added.

Mix 3 tablespoons coarse salt, sage, rosemary, garlic, and bay leaves; add the meat and turn to coat. Marinate for a period of 2 to 6 days, as desired. ✦ Remove the meat from the marinade, cut it in pieces, and simmer them in lightly salted water to cover. ✦ After 30 minutes add the cabbage; after 1 hour add the potatoes. ✦ Preheat the oven to 350°F. When the potatoes are soft proceed in one of two ways, as you prefer:

1) Put half the stew in a single baking pan, alternating it with layers of sliced fontina. ✦ Top it off with more fontina and pats of butter.

2) Divide the stew among individual baking pans, covering each with slices of fontina and a few pats of butter. In either case bake for a few minutes, long enough to melt the cheese but not to further cook the stew.

HORSEMEAT STEW

VENETO

2 lbs. horsemeat
(use beef brisket if you prefer)
4 cups red wine, such as Valpolicella
½ cup olive oil
1 tbsp. unsalted butter, if desired
1½ lbs. onions, thinly sliced
4 carrots, finely chopped
3 celery stalks, finely chopped
Several whole cloves
3 oz. *lardo*
All-purpose flour
2 bay leaves
1 sprig tarragon
Broth, as needed
Salt and pepper

This example of Veronese cuisine has been around for more than a thousand years, ever since, according to tradition, a battle between Lombards and Veronese left hundreds of dead horses on the battlefield. In those thrifty times it seemed a waste to let all that meat rot, and to preserve it the Veronese salted it and marinated it in wine and spices, perhaps also to cover possible bad odors not suitable for meat that would eventually be eaten. Accompany the dish with fresh polenta.

Marinate the meat in the red wine for at least 2 days. ✦ Heat the olive oil and, if desired, a pat of butter in a soup pot and sauté the onions, carrots, and celery. ✦ Remove the meat from the marinade (reserve the marinade), make small cuts in it, and insert the cloves and *lardo*, larding it well. ✦ Flour the meat and add it to the pan. ✦ After 1 hour of cooking add the wine from the marinade, bay leaves, tarragon, and salt and pepper and continue cooking at moderate heat for at least 3 hours, turning the meat from time to time, adding broth if necessary. ✦ In the end the meat should be soft and fall apart when you press it with a fork. ✦ Remove the meat and slice it; pass some of the vegetables through a sieve. Thicken the sauce with 1 tablespoon flour and some butter. ✦ Add the puréed vegetables until reaching the desired thickness; the amount of pepper can also be adjusted to give the sauce more body. Serve the slices hot with their sauce.

CHICKEN-STUFFED TURKEY

SARDEGNA

1 chicken
Lardo
½ cup chopped aromatic herbs
(juniper berries, myrtle leaves, sage leaves, rosemary)
1 medium turkey

A small rabbit or duck can be used in place of the chicken in this recipe.

Build a fire in a pit with myrtle and juniper branches and let it burn down to embers. Clean the chicken, lard it inside and outside with *lardo*, and season it with aromatic herbs. Stuff the turkey with the chicken. ✦ Sew closed the turkey and lower it onto the embers. ✦ Cover with more embers and when it is cooked extract the chicken from the turkey and serve both warm.

PECORA IN UMIDO | MUTTON SAUCE

TOSCANA

3 lbs. mutton
½ cup extra-virgin olive oil
2 medium onions, chopped
1 sprig rosemary
2 garlic cloves
Pinch grated nutmeg
2 oz. prosciutto crudo, minced
1 tbsp. tomato paste
2 or 3 peeled plum tomatoes, chopped
Grated zest of ½ lemon
Salt and pepper

This dish is typical of Prato.

The fat must be removed from the meat, as well as any sinew. Cut it in pieces. Heat half the oil in a pan and cook the mutton at high heat for 10 minutes to make it lose its dampness and wooly smell. ✦ In another pan heat the remaining olive oil and cook the onions, rosemary, garlic, nutmeg, and salt and pepper. ✦ When this has browned, add half the mutton and prosciutto crudo, cook for a few minutes, then add the remaining pieces of mutton and stir in the tomato paste, tomatoes, 1 cup water, and lemon zest. ✦ Cook at least an hour, until the sauce is reduced and the meat is falling apart. Use the sauce to dress short pasta, such as penne.

PERNICI ALLA CACCIATORA | HUNTER-STYLE PARTRIDGES

PIEMONTE

4 partridges (can use 4 squabs or 2 Cornish game hens)
½ cup olive oil
1 carrot, sliced
½ cup breadcrumbs
Juice and grated zest of 1 lemon
½ cup good red wine
½ cup chicken broth
2 anchovies, boned and cut in pieces
Salt

This dish is typical of the Valle Anzasca. Serve with toasted bread and a side dish of stewed potatoes.

Prepare the partridges: pluck, gut, and singe them. Wash and dry them. ✦ Heat the olive oil over medium heat and add the partridges and carrot, cover the pan, and brown them. ✦ Add salt, and as soon as the meat is tender (about 20 minutes), remove the birds, cut them in four parts, and set them aside. ✦ Boil the cooking juices for 10 minutes, add the breadcrumbs, lemon juice and zest, red wine, broth, and anchovies. ✦ Stir well, skim off any fat, and pass the sauce through a sieve. ✦ Return the sauce to the heat in a pan together with the partridges and cook for another 10 minutes. ✦ Serve warm.

PERNICI CON POLENTA | PARTRIDGES AND POLENTA

LOMBARDIA

4 partridges, with giblets (can use 4 squabs or 2 Cornish game hens)

CONTINUED

Preheat the oven to 350°F. Pluck and gut the partridges. Chop the giblets. ✦ Wrap the birds in the pancetta, then put them in an ovenproof pan; add enough water to make ½ inch of liquid. ✦ Add the sage, rosemary, garlic,

4 oz. pancetta, in very thin slices

A few sage leaves

1 sprig rosemary

1 garlic clove

½ medium onion, sliced

2 bay leaves

2 tbsp. unsalted butter

1 bottle white wine (preferably Cortese di Gavi), or as needed

onion, and bay leaves and roast for about 15 minutes. ✦ Meanwhile, in another pan, heat the butter and brown the giblets. ✦ As soon as the water in the pan is almost evaporated, remove the partridges and add the cooked giblets. ✦ Pass the cooking juices through a sieve (discarding the giblets) and return them to the oven at very low heat. ✦ Brown the partridges in the giblet pan at high heat, adding a little butter if necessary. ✦ As soon as they are browned return them to the pan in the oven with the juices. ✦ Cover and bake in the oven for about 2 hours at moderate heat, adding some of the white wine as needed to keep them from browning more. Serve over hot polenta.

CHICKEN CUTLETS WITH MONTASIO CHEESE

PETTO DI POLLO DORATO AL MONTASIO

FRIULI-VENEZIA GIULIA

2 skinless, boneless chicken breast halves

Juice of 1 lemon

3 large eggs, beaten

2 tbsp. grated Parmigiano-Reggiano, plus more as needed

2 tbsp. chopped flat-leaf parsley

All-purpose flour for dredging

½ lb. (2 sticks) unsalted butter

2 oz. young Montasio cheese, grated

2 oz. aged Montasio cheese, grated

½ cup milk

1½ lbs. field herbs, cleaned and parboiled

8 white asparagus stalks

Salt and pepper

Cut the chicken breast halves into 4 thin cutlets. ✦ Salt and pepper the cutlets, sprinkle with lemon juice, and let them marinate for 5 minutes. ✦ In a blender, mix 2 eggs with 2 heaping tablespoons Parmigiano-Reggiano and parsley, obtaining a batter. ✦ Flour the cutlets, then press them into the batter to make it adhere to both sides; then dip them in the remaining egg. ✦ Heat 2 tablespoons butter in a pan and add the cutlets, frying them until they are golden. ✦ Prepare a sauce by stirring the fresh Montasio with the aged Montasio in a pan with the milk and 2 tablespoons butter over very low heat. ✦ Take the chicken off the heat, pat off any excess liquid with paper towels, then pour the cheese sauce over the cutlets and return them to a warm oven for 5 minutes. ✦ Heat the field herbs in a pan with 1 tablespoon butter and a little salt over low heat just until starting to brown. ✦ Melt the remaining butter and keep hot. Boil the asparagus in water to cover until tender; drain and arrange on a plate, sprinkling the stalks with Parmigiano-Reggiano. Pour over melted butter. ✦ Prepare warmed serving plates, putting some field herbs to one side, 2 asparagus stalks per person to the other, and a chicken cutlet in the middle. Serve very hot.

TURKEY BREAST WITH PROSCIUTTO AND FONTINA

PETTO DI TACCHINO AL PROSCIUTTO E FONTINA

EMILIA-ROMAGNA

1 lb. turkey breast, sliced into 4 slices

1 large egg, beaten

4 tbsp. breadcrumbs

2 tbsp. extra-virgin olive oil

3 tbsp. unsalted butter

3 oz. prosciutto crudo, in 4 slices

4 oz. fontina, in 4 slices

This dish is typical of Bologna.

Preheat the oven to 400°F. Pound the slices of turkey breast to flatten them. ✦ Dip each slice of turkey in the egg, then in breadcrumbs. Heat the olive oil and butter in an ovenproof pan at high heat and fry the turkey pieces until golden. ✦ Drain the slices of turkey, let them rest a few minutes in the pan, then put a slice of prosciutto and a slice of cheese over each one. ✦ Bake just until the cheese melts, then serve.

SMOKED MEAT WITH POLENTA "SAUCE"

PETUCCIA DI BARCIS COL SUF DI POLENTA

FRIULI-VENEZIA GIULIA

⅔ cup cornmeal

1⅔ cups milk

1 *petuccia* (see note)

4 tbsp. unsalted butter

Petuccia is a kind of processed minced meat made of mixed mutton and beef. It is spiced with *kummel* (liqueur spiced with cumin, caraway, and fennel) and lightly smoked. As a preservation measure it is covered with hand-cracked black pepper. This dish can resemble a *polenta concia*, that is, a very rich and soft polenta made with fontina and toma cheeses.

Use the cornmeal and 3 cups water to prepare a polenta as in the recipe on page 289. ✦ When the polenta is cooked, whisk in the milk. Cut the *petuccia* in slices about 1½ inches thick. ✦ Heat the butter in a pan, cook the slices for a few seconds on each side, and cover with the polenta, which should be very liquid.

SQUAB BAKED IN POTATO

PICCIONE IN SCRIGNO

FRIULI-VENEZIA GIULIA

2 tbsp. unsalted butter

1 very large baking potato, large enough to hold the squab

1 young squab, with its liver and gizzard

3 oz. lean prosciutto crudo

A few sage leaves

1 sprig rosemary

CONTINUED

Serve with black grapes.

Preheat the oven to 300°F. Grease a baking pan with butter. Wrap the potato in aluminum foil and bake it in the oven until soft, about 1 hour. Remove from the oven and let cool. ✦ Meanwhile, clean and dry the squab, salt and pepper it, then wrap it in the prosciutto and put it in a saucepan with half the sage, half the rosemary, and half the olive oil. ✦ Cook at low heat 20 minutes, then add the wine and brandy and transfer it to the oven. ✦ Meanwhile, finely chop together the liver, gizzard, *lardo*,

¼ cup olive oil
¼ cup dry white wine
1 tbsp. brandy
2 oz. *lardo*
2 oz. porcini mushrooms
5 or 6 flat-leaf parsley stalks
5 or 6 capers
2 or 3 gherkins
Salt and pepper

mushrooms, parsley, capers, and gherkins with the remaining sage and rosemary and cook slowly over low heat with the butter, adding salt and pepper to taste. ✦ Cut the potato in half lengthwise, hollow out the halves, put the squab with the sauce in one half and close it with the other. ✦ Return the filled potato to the oven for 10 minutes in the greased pan. Serve very hot.

✦ **LOCAL TRADITION** ✦

PEZZATA

Traditionally served on the first Sunday in August, the celebration of hospitality, this dish, typical of the Prato Gentile in Molise, was also common following the transhumance, when the shepherds would move their herds down from the mountains to the lowlands pastures. A simple preparation, it called for chopped mutton, celery, chili pepper, onion, chopped plum tomatoes, seasoned with salt, to be simmered in just enough water to cover over low heat in either a copper cauldron or, more traditionally, a clay pot. During the long cooking time, any foam would be immediately skimmed from the surface.

PICCIONI DI TORREGLIA | STUFFED SQUAB

VENETO

1 sprig rosemary
A few sage leaves
½ cup chopped flat-leaf parsley
8 juniper berries
4 oz. pancetta, thinly sliced
4 plump squabs
¼ cup dry white wine, or as needed
2 tbsp. unsalted butter
Salt and pepper

Serve with fine warm polenta. For the wine use Soave.

Set up a rotisserie with a drip pan or preheat the oven to 300°F. Chop together the rosemary, sage, parsley, juniper berries, and 3 slices of pancetta with a little salt and a pinch of pepper. ✦ Stuff the squabs with this mixture, then wrap them in the remaining pancetta slices. ✦ Cook the birds on a rotisserie or in the oven, basting them from time to time with a little wine. ✦ Add the butter to the cooking juices to make a sauce.

ROAST SQUAB WITH BLACK OLIVES

PICCIONI IN TEGAME

MARCHE

2 squabs
2 slices pancetta
¼ cup (4 tbsp.) unsalted butter
1 medium onion, sliced
2 tbsp. all-purpose flour
½ cup white wine
1 cup chicken broth
⅔ cup pitted black olives
Salt

Preheat the oven to 350°F. Clean the birds, removing any feathers or down, and gut them. ✦ Salt them inside and outside and stuff each with a slice of pancetta. ✦ Put them in a roasting pan with half of the butter and roast them for 30 minutes. ✦ Meanwhile, in another pan, heat the remaining butter and sauté the onion; add the flour to make a paste, then whisk in the white wine. ✦ When the wine has evaporated, add the broth and olives and cook, stirring to blend, over low heat. ✦ Pour this sauce over the squab for the last 10 minutes of their cooking time.

SQUAB STUFFED WITH MEAT

PICCIONI RIPIENI

MARCHE

Extra-virgin olive oil
2 tbsp. unsalted butter
2 squabs with giblets
6 oz. ground beef
6 oz. ground pork
2 oz. prosciutto crudo
Pinch grated nutmeg
2 tsp. brandy
1 small onion, minced
1 small carrot, minced
1 garlic clove, minced
1 tbsp. grated Parmigiano-Reggiano
1 large egg, beaten
1 sprig rosemary
½ cup dry white wine
Salt and pepper

The squabs should be young, so young they have never flown. They should be plucked, delicately gutted, and singed to remove any remaining feathers. For the wine use Verdicchio.

Preheat the oven to 400°F. Grease a baking dish with olive oil. ✦ To make the stuffing, melt the butter over low heat and cook the giblets briefly, then chop them together with the beef, pork, and prosciutto crudo. Mix in the nutmeg, salt and pepper, brandy, onion, carrot, garlic, cheese, and egg. ✦ Fill the cavities of the birds with this mixture, carefully sew closed the openings in the birds to keep the stuffing from coming out during cooking, salt them, brush them with olive oil, and put them in the baking dish with a sprig of rosemary. ✦ Roast 30 minutes; halfway through the cooking, add the wine. ✦ Serve the squabs hot, cut in half lengthwise and placed cut side down to hide the filling.

SQUAB ON SKEWERS

PICCIONI SPIEDATI

UMBRIA

4 squabs
CONTINUED

This dish is typical of Amelia.

Set up a rotisserie with a drip pan. The squabs, about 30 days old, should be prepared for cooking. After being plucked and cleaned, put them on the rotisserie skewers

1 bunch sage
1 cup extra-virgin olive oil
Salt

whole with sprigs of sage tucked into them. ✦ During the slow cooking, add salt to the birds when they swell up, then complete the cooking, basting with olive oil. ✦ When the birds are cooked cut them in half, remove the intestines, and chop this together with the sage, working in olive oil to create a sauce. ✦ Put the sauce into the squab halves, put the halves back together, and keep them warm. ✦ Pour a little warmed olive oil over them to serve.

PICÙLA AD CAVAL | **HORSEMEAT STEW** | FOR 6 PERSONS

EMILIA-ROMAGNA

1 tbsp. chopped *lardo* (some recipes use lard instead to flavor the meat)

2 medium onions, chopped

1½ lbs. horsemeat, coarsely ground (can use skirt steak)

4 cups broth (or white wine)

1 lb. plum tomatoes (also peeled tomatoes)

2 cups chopped sweet peppers

1 tbsp. aromatic herbs (rosemary, sage, flat-leaf parsley, basil, etc.)

½ garlic clove

This dish is typical of Piacenza. Unlike other stews, *picùla* does not improve when reheated and instead should be served immediately.

Heat the *lardo* over low heat to render the fat. Add the onions and cook slowly, then add the meat and brown it. ✦ Add broth (some recipes call for white wine instead, and perhaps it is better, your choice) and cook for about 1 hour. ✦ Add the tomatoes and sweet peppers and cook another 40 minutes, then add the aromatic herbs and garlic and cook 10 minutes more.

PIGNATA DI PECORA | **MUTTON POT**

BASILICATA

2 lbs. mutton, cut in pieces

¾ lb. potatoes, peeled and chopped

¾ lb. onions, sliced

1 celery stalk, sliced

½ lb. plum tomatoes, peeled, seeded, and chopped

4 oz. soppressata, diced

Grated pecorino

Salt and pepper

Put all the ingredients (except the cheese) in a pot with an airtight seal. ✦ Pour in 1 cup of water and seal the pot closed. ✦ Cook at moderate heat for about 1½ hours. Serve with pecorino.

| **BRAISED PORK RIBS**

SARDEGNA

4½ lbs. pork ribs

2 lbs. potatoes, cut into chunks

8 medium onions, chopped

1 cabbage, cored and chopped

A few bunches wild fennel, chopped

A few sheets *carasau* bread
(music-paper bread)

Coarse salt

Put the pork under coarse salt and refrigerate for at least 2 days. ✦ Remove from the salt and rinse in running water the night before use. ✦ Simmer the pork for about 1 hour in water to cover, then add the potatoes, onions, cabbage, and as much wild fennel as desired. ✦ Cook for another 15 to 20 minutes. ✦ Before serving, spoon some of the broth over the *carasau* bread; serve these on another plate.

POLLO ALLA 'NCIP 'NCIAP | **PAN-ROASTED CHICKEN**

MARCHE

1 chicken, weighing 2 lbs.

¼ cup lard or extra-virgin olive oil

½ cup white wine,
such as Verdicchio

1 sprig rosemary

Several sage leaves

10 or more garlic cloves, unpeeled

Salt and pepper
or chili pepper flakes

Fresh plum tomato (if necessary)

The name for this dish, *'Ncip 'nciap*, is probably onomatopoetic, derived from the sound of a knife chopping the chicken into pieces. In other places the same dish is called *Pollo all'arrabiata* or *Pollo in padella*.

Cut the chicken into somewhat small pieces. Heat the lard (or olive oil) in a pan and brown them. ✦ Pour in the wine and raise the heat to let it evaporate. ✦ When the wine has evaporated, add the rosemary, sage leaves, garlic, salt and pepper or chili pepper. ✦ Reduce the heat to low, cover, and simmer 20 minutes more. If the chicken seems overly dry, add a few pieces of fresh tomato. Serve immediately.

MEAT & POULTRY

**POLLO ALLA BELLUNESE
IN BIANCO** | **CHICKEN IN WHITE WINE**

VENETO

1 chicken, about 2 lbs., with giblets

¼ lb. (1 stick) unsalted butter

½ medium onion, sliced

¼ cup chopped flat-leaf parsley

1 garlic clove

1 cup white wine

1 cup mushrooms

2 oz. salame (optional)

Salt and pepper

For the wine use Pinot Bianco or Soave. Serve with polenta. This dish is typical of Belluno, in the Dolomites.

Wash the chicken, pat dry, and cut in 8 pieces, setting aside the giblets. ✦ In a saucepan, heat the butter. Add the onion, parsley, and garlic. ✦ Add the chicken and salt and pepper to taste, then pour in the wine and let it evaporate. ✦ Finely chop the giblets together with the mushrooms and, if desired, salame and add to the pan. ✦ Cover and cook at low heat for about 1½ hours.

POLLO ALLA CACCIATORA 1

HUNTER-STYLE CHICKEN 1

PIEMONTE

¼ cup extra-virgin olive oil

⅔ cup sliced onions

1 lb. carrots, sliced

1 celery stalk, sliced

3½ lbs. chicken, cut in pieces

½ cup dry white wine, such as Gari

½ lb. ripe plum tomatoes, peeled and chopped

Chicken broth, if necessary

Salt and pepper

This is excellent served with hot polenta.

Heat half the olive oil in a large pan and add the onions, carrots, and celery. ✦ When they have taken on color, remove them and set aside. ✦ Put the pieces of chicken in the pan with the remaining olive oil and when the pieces have colored, add the white wine. ✦ When the wine has evaporated, add the tomatoes and reserved vegetables. Continue cooking at low heat for about 40 minutes, adding a little broth, if necessary. ✦ Adjust for salt and pepper.

POLLO ALLA CACCIATORA 2

HUNTER-STYLE CHICKEN 2

EMILIA-ROMAGNA

2 tbsp. unsalted butter

2 tbsp. extra-virgin olive oil

1 medium onion, finely chopped

1 young chicken, cut in pieces

½ cup dry white wine

½ lb. plum tomatoes, peeled and chopped

1 green or yellow sweet pepper, cleaned of seeds and chopped

Salt and pepper

This dish is typical of Colorno. For the wine use Trebbiano.

Heat the butter and olive oil in a pan and add the onion. ✦ When it is golden, add the chicken pieces and let them brown. ✦ Pour in the wine, add the tomatoes and sweet pepper, and adjust for salt and pepper. ✦ Cover and cook at low heat until the chicken is cooked through, about 20 minutes.

POLLO ALLA CACCIATORA 3

HUNTER-STYLE CHICKEN 3

TOSCANA

2 tbsp. extra-virgin olive oil

1 garlic clove, chopped

2 medium onions, chopped

1 young chicken, cut in pieces

½ cup white wine

2 plum tomatoes, peeled and without seeds (or 1 tbsp. tomato paste, diluted in 1 tbsp. white wine)

Salt and chili pepper flakes

This is good served with green beans or potatoes. For the wine use Vernaccia di San Gimignano.

Heat the olive oil in a pan and cook the garlic and onions. ✦ Add the chicken (cleaned and, if necessary, singed) and brown, adding salt and chili pepper flakes to taste. ✦ When the chicken begins taking on color, pour in the white wine together with the tomatoes (if the season isn't right for fresh tomatoes use the tomato paste mixture). ✦ Cook at low heat to reduce the sauce and cook the chicken through. Serve hot.

CHICKEN IN TOMATO SAUCE

POLLO ALLA POTENTINA

BASILICATA

1 chicken, weighing about 2 lbs.

1 oz. lard

2 tbsp. extra-virgin olive oil

1 medium onion, sliced

½ cup dry white wine

Pinch chili pepper flakes

1⅔ cups tomato purée

⅓ cup chopped flat-leaf parsley

Several basil leaves, chopped

Salt

This dish is typical of Potenza. Serve with a side dish of roast potatoes. For the wine use Cirò or Fiano.

Clean the chicken, singe it, wash it well, and cut in pieces. ✦ Heat the lard in a pan with a little olive oil, add the chicken and onion, and brown. Then add the wine and chili pepper. ✦ When the wine has evaporated, add the tomato purée, parsley, and basil. ✦ Season with salt, cover, and cook over low heat for 1 hour, adding a little water if necessary.

CHICKEN WITH ONION AND TOMATO SAUCE

POLLO IN POTACCHIO

MARCHE

1 free-range chicken, weighing about 2 lbs.

2 garlic cloves, cut in half

¼ cup olive oil

1 medium onion, minced

1 *diavolillo* (hot chili pepper, see note, page 22)

2 tbsp. tomato paste, dissolved in ½ cup dry white wine

½ cup flat-leaf parsley leaves

1 sprig rosemary

Salt and pepper

Rinse the chicken, dry, and cut in pieces. ✦ Rub each piece with 1 garlic clove. ✦ Heat the olive oil and sauté the onion together with the remaining garlic clove and chili pepper. Sauté well, then add the pieces of chicken, removing and discarding the garlic and chili pepper. ✦ Add salt and pepper, then add the tomato paste mixture. ✦ Cook for 30 minutes at low heat, adding warm water if necessary. ✦ Chop the parsley and rosemary together and sprinkle over the chicken before removing it from the heat. Serve hot.

SWEET-AND-SOUR MEATBALLS 1

POLPETTE IN AGRODOLCE 1

PIEMONTE

¼ cup raisins, softened in warm water, drained, and chopped

6 oz. sausage meat, crumbled

4 amaretti cookies, soaked in milk, then crumbled

CONTINUED

Mix the raisins, sausage meat, amaretti, and veal. ✦ Add the soaked bread and blend to create a homogeneous mixture. ✦ Season with salt and pepper and add the Parmigiano-Reggiano and egg. ✦ Knead this together well, then use to create meatballs, giving them the shape of small flattened mandarin oranges. ✦ Heat the butter in a pan. Dip the meatballs in the flour and then in the breadcrumbs, then cook them in the butter until golden

10 oz. ground veal

The bread of a roll, softened
in milk, then squeezed dry
(and left somewhat damp)

1 tbsp. grated Parmigiano-Reggiano

1 large egg, beaten

¼ lb. (1 stick) unsalted butter

½ cup all-purpose flour

4 oz. breadcrumbs

2 tbsp. sugar

2 tsp. white wine vinegar

Salt and pepper

and cooked through. ✦ Meanwhile, prepare a sauce, dissolving the sugar in 2 tablespoons warm water, then stir in the vinegar. ✦ Pour this over the meatballs when they are golden brown. Serve warm.

POLPETTE IN
AGRODOLCE 2

SWEET-AND-SOUR
MEATBALLS 2

FOR
6 PERSONS

CALABRIA

7 oz. ground pork

7 oz. ground beef

2 large eggs, beaten

4 oz. stale, crustless bread,
softened in milk and squeezed dry

1 tbsp. chopped flat-leaf parsley

1 garlic clove, minced

½ cup grated pecorino

Extra-virgin olive oil

⅔ cup slivered almonds

1 small onion, minced

4 cups tomato purée

2 tbsp. cooked grape must *saba*

Salt and pepper
(preferably ground in a mortar)

Work together the meats, eggs, bread, parsley, garlic, pecorino, salt, and pepper. ✦ Heat ½ inch olive oil until hot. Shape the meat mixture into meatballs, then insert almond slivers in each meatball to give them the appearance of chestnut husks. Fry them in the olive oil until browned. ✦ Meanwhile, prepare a sauce by heating a little more olive oil in a second pan. Add the onion and cook, then add the tomato purée. ✦ When the meatballs are cooked, pour the grape must over them, then the tomato sauce. ✦ Let them sit a few minutes before serving.

POLPETTINE OR
MONDEGHILI

LEFTOVER MEATBALLS

LOMBARDIA

10 oz. leftover cooked meat

1 large egg, beaten

CONTINUED

This typical Milanese dish is an example of the use of leftovers, a traditional custom of the Lombard population.

Knead together the meat, egg, bread, parsley, and lemon zest in a bowl to form a homogeneous mixture, then shape into balls about the size of walnuts and flatten them slightly. ✦ Place the butter in a pan over medium

The bread of a roll, soaked in milk, squeezed dry, and pressed through a sieve

2 tbsp. chopped flat-leaf parsley

Grated zest of 1 lemon (or to taste)

1 cup (½ lb.) unsalted butter

½ cup breadcrumbs

heat. Roll the meatballs in the breadcrumbs, then fry them until golden and cooked through.

POLPETTONE DI CONIGLIO

RABBIT ROULADE

LOMBARDIA

1 rabbit (about 3¼ lbs.), with giblets

1 cup Marsala

1 tbsp. chopped basil

1 tbsp. chopped marjoram

1 garlic clove, minced

½ cup breadcrumbs

1 tbsp. unsalted butter

2 tbsp. milk

1 large egg

1 tbsp. grated Parmigiano-Reggiano

Extra-virgin olive oil

Unsalted butter

Salt and pepper

Bone the rabbit and soak its giblets in the Marsala with the basil, marjoram, and garlic. ✦ Make a filling by combining the breadcrumbs, butter, and milk and cook over low heat to thicken to a paste. ✦ Drain the giblets and other solids from the marinade (reserving the liquid), chop them, and add them to the breadcrumb mixture. ✦ Blend well and add salt and pepper to taste. ✦ Add the egg and Parmigiano-Reggiano. ✦ Insert this stuffing in the rabbit, wrapping the meat around the filling and rolling it up like a big salame. ✦ Heat olive oil and butter in a large pan and add the rabbit, seasoning with salt and pepper. ✦ As the meat browns, sprinkle the Marsala from the marinade over it. Cover and cook until tender, about 1½ hours.

POLPETTONE DI TACCHINO ALLA REGGIANA

TURKEY-VEAL ROULADE

EMILIA-ROMAGNA

1½ lbs. turkey breast, butterflied and pounded to ½ inch thick

10 oz. veal head, boiled and finely chopped

Pinch grated nutmeg

1 medium onion, chopped

1 carrot, chopped

1 bunch flat-leaf parsley

1 celery stalk, chopped

Salt and pepper

This is a typical example of Jewish cooking.

Remove the skin from the turkey and reserve. Place the turkey breast on a board and cover with a ½-inch layer of veal head. ✦ Season with salt and a little pepper and dust with nutmeg, then roll up tightly. ✦ Wrap the roll in the skin of the turkey, tie (or sew) it closed with kitchen twine, place it in a pot, and add water to cover. Season the water with salt and add the onion, carrot, parsley, and celery. Bring the water to a boil, then reduce the heat and simmer until cooked through. ✦ Cool and cut in slices. Serve cold.

PORCHETTA

To prepare this traditional Umbrian recipe for a whole spit-roasted pig, the animal, optimally weighing between 70 and 100 pounds, would first be carefully cleaned and all bristles scraped from the hide. The entrails would be removed and cleaned: the intestines and tripe defatted and placed under salt with a little vinegar, later rinsed and chopped; the heart, lungs, spleen, and liver cleaned and chopped. The combined entrails would then be seasoned with salt and pepper and mixed with a generous amount of parboiled fennel and garlic to make a savory filling. Numerous deep cuts would be made into the skin of the pig and the filling both stuffed into the cavity and rubbed into the cuts. After sewing the pig closed and securing it with wire, it would be roasted in a very hot wood-burning oven on two metal sawhorses, usually for about 2½ hours. While the exact cooking time was extremely difficult to predict, expert butchers would test the meat for doneness by inserting a skewer into one leg—if it came out dry, the meat was done.

PORCHETTA | # ROAST SUCKLING PIG

MARCHE

7 oz. wild fennel

Garlic to taste

1 sprig rosemary

A few sage leaves

Pinch grated nutmeg

½ cup *vino cotto*

1 milk-fed pig, disemboweled and cleaned

½ cup extra-virgin olive oil

1 cup dry white wine, such as Verdicchio, or as needed

Salt and pepper

This is a family recipe that does not follow the usual pork-butcher's method of adding all the offal, including the heart, kidneys, and liver, and marinating the pig for at least 12 hours if it is no longer milk fed. Even more, it leaves out the use of a wood-burning oven with the heat supplied by fragrant branches of pine, oak, and fir. But even with a family recipe there is sure to be plenty of flavor.

Preheat the oven to 350°F. Finely chop together the fennel, garlic, rosemary, and sage; add salt, pepper, and nutmeg; work this together with the *vino cotto*. ✦ Spread this mixture over all of the inside cavity of the pig, then insert a long stick in the pig from end to end and tie it closed with kitchen twine. ✦ Set the ends of the stick on the edges of a large, deep roasting pan. ✦ Brush the pig with olive oil, then place the pan and suspended pig in the oven and roast for 2 to 3 hours, basting its hide with white wine from time to time. ✦ Turn off the heat when the pig is golden, but leave the pig in the oven to cool.

VEAL BRAIN "SANDWICHES"

TRENTINO

1 bunch flat-leaf parsley
1 medium onion
¼ cup (4 tbsp.) unsalted butter
¾ lb. veal brains, membrane
removed and chopped
1 rectangular loaf of bread
1 cup milk
1 large egg, beaten
⅔ cup all-purpose flour
Olive oil, for frying
Salt

Serve with a salad.

Finely chop together the parsley and onion. ✦ Melt the butter in a pan over low heat and cook the brains, adding the parsley mixture and a little salt and mixing it to create a paste. ✦ Cut the bread in thick (¾-inch) slices and dampen one side of each slice with milk. ✦ Cover the damp side of a slice with the brains mixture and top with another slice, damp-side down. ✦ Prepare a batter with the egg, flour, remaining milk, and salt. ✦ Heat ¼ inch of olive oil until hot. Dip the "sandwich" in the batter and then fry until golden. Drain on paper towels and serve.

PROSCIUTTO IN BREAD DOUGH

FRIULI-VENEZIA GIULIA

1 small prosciutto
Bread dough (see page 13)

Cooking meat inside bread was a widespread custom during the Middle Ages and in fact even earlier. Apicius's recipe says, "Chop flour worked in olive oil and give the prosciutto back its skin, then when the flour is cooked it can be removed from the oven as it is." Formerly made with a variety of flours, today the prosciutto is wrapped exclusively in wheat flour, and many buffets in Trieste prepare it hot every morning.

Soak a small prosciutto in water for 12 hours. Preheat the oven to 400°F. Dry the prosciutto, prick it with a fork, and wrap it in bread dough. Bake it for about 1 hour, or until the dough is golden. Slice and serve hot.

MEAT & POULTRY

MYRTLE-SCENTED HEN

SARDEGNA

1 medium-size hen
1 medium onion, chopped
1 carrot, chopped
1 celery stalk, chopped
1 bunch chopped flat-leaf parsley
1 bunch myrtle leaves
Salt

This dish is typical of Campidano.

Clean, sear, and rinse the hen. Place it in a soup pot and cover it with water, then add the onion, carrot, celery, parsley, and salt to taste. ✦ As soon as it is cooked remove it from the pot, drain it, put it, while still warm, in a large bowl, and cover it on all sides with myrtle leaves. ✦ Cover the hen so that the perfume of the myrtle will penetrate its skin and refrigerate overnight. Serve cold.

MEATBALLS

PUGLIA

1 lb. ground horsemeat

9 oz. crustless bread, soaked in milk and squeezed dry

½ cup grated pecorino (preferably from Puglia)

1 garlic clove, minced

1 large egg, beaten

½ cup extra-virgin olive oil

1 medium onion, sliced

1 lb. tomato purée

Salt and pepper

These meatballs can be made just as well from mixed meats or pork.

Combine the meat, bread, pecorino, garlic, and egg. Work together well, then shape into balls the size of walnuts. Heat half the olive oil until hot and cook the meatballs until browned, then set aside on paper towels to drain. ✦ Meanwhile, prepare the sauce. Heat the remaining olive oil in a pan; add the onion and cook until golden. When the onion darkens, remove it and pour in the tomato purée. Add a cup of water and continue cooking. When it comes to a boil, add the fried meatballs. Reduce the heat to low and continue cooking 5 minutes, remove from the heat, and serve immediately.

STUFFED VEAL BREAST

PUNTA DI PETTO

EMILIA-ROMAGNA

6 tbsp. unsalted butter

1 bunch flat-leaf parsley, finely chopped

½ cup breadcrumbs

3 oz. Parmigiano-Reggiano, grated

2 large eggs, beaten

2 or 3 tbsp. milk

Pinch grated nutmeg

1½ lbs. boned veal breast

½ medium onion

1 celery stalk

Salt and pepper

This dish is typical of Parma. Use the remaining broth to make soup.

In a saucepan, heat the butter and lightly sauté the parsley, then add the breadcrumbs and cook for a few minutes. ✦ Remove from the heat and add the Parmigiano-Reggiano, eggs, milk, salt, pepper, and nutmeg. ✦ Work these together thoroughly. ✦ Make a slit along one side of the breast and create a pocket. Stuff this pocket with the mixture. ✦ Sew shut the pocket with kitchen twine and tie up the piece of meat. ✦ Pierce it in several places with a fork. ✦ Bring a large pot of lightly salted water to a boil and add the stuffed meat with the onion and celery. Reduce the heat and let it simmer for about 1½ hours. ✦ Let the stuffed breast cool before being sliced and served.

STUFFED SHEEP TRIPE

QUAGGHIARIIDE

PUGLIA

This is a truly ancient preparation from the shepherds of the Murgia mountains. Possible side dishes include boiled vegetables (arugula or wild chicory) seasoned with the cooking juices.

Extra-virgin olive oil
7 oz. sheep liver and heart
4 oz. sausage (preferably Puglian)
⅔ cup grated pecorino
2 large eggs, beaten
1 sheep's tripe
Salt and pepper

Preheat the oven to 400°F. Grease a baking pan with olive oil. Clean the liver and heart and finely chop them together with the sausage; season with salt, pepper, and pecorino, then work in the eggs. ✦ Lay out the cleaned tripe and put the mixture on it, fold the tripe over, and sew it shut with kitchen twine. ✦ Arrange the tripe in the pan, season with salt, pepper, and olive oil, and bake for about 30 minutes. ✦ Serve sliced.

QUAGLIE ALLA SCALIGERA

QUAIL VENETO-STYLE

VENETO

8 quail, cleaned and washed
⅓ cup extra-virgin olive oil
⅓ cup (5 tbsp.) unsalted butter
4 oz. *lardo*, in slices
8 bay leaves
¼ cup dry white wine
Salt and pepper

Serve with roasted polenta.

Heat a grill to high heat. Cut open the quail along the backbones and spread them open as far as possible. ✦ Heat the olive oil and butter in a pan over low heat and brown the quail for 10 minutes, giving them a uniform coloring. ✦ Remove them from the heat, lard them, insert a bay leaf in each of them, and salt and pepper. ✦ Put them on the hot grill for a couple of minutes. As they cook, sprinkle them with wine. Serve hot.

QUAGLIE CON PISELLI

QUAIL WITH PEAS

MARCHE

8 quail
6 oz. prosciutto fat, minced
1 cup dry white wine, or as needed, such as Verdicchio
9 oz. tomato purée
2 lbs. fresh shelled peas
2 tablespoons unsalted butter
Salt and pepper

Clean the quail, eliminating the heads, wing tips, and giblets. ✦ Melt about half of the prosciutto fat in a large pan and add the quail, browning them and adding wine from time to time. ✦ Cook off the last of the wine and add the tomato purée; add salt and pepper and continue cooking at low heat. ✦ Meanwhile, cook the peas in the remaining prosciutto fat and butter and add them to the quail in the pan, stirring them to blend for a few minutes.

QUAGLIE IN CROSTA
ALLA CANNELLA

QUAIL IN PASTRY WITH MUSHROOMS

FOR
6 PERSONS

VENETO

Preheat the oven to 450°F. Combine the quail in a roasting pan with salt, pepper, garlic, rosemary, sage, half the wine, and olive oil. Roast the quail for 10 minutes. Reduce the oven temperature to 375°F. ✦ Pass the resulting

6 quail, with giblets
1 garlic clove
1 sprig rosemary
1 sprig sage
1 cup white wine, such as Soave
¼ cup extra-virgin olive oil
1 medium onion, sliced
1 celery stalk, chopped
2 carrots, chopped
¼ cup chopped flat-leaf parsley
2 large egg yolks
2 tbsp. grated Parmigiano-Reggiano
⅓ cup heavy cream
1¼ cups all-purpose flour, plus more for rolling
¼ lb. (1 stick) plus 6 tbsp. unsalted butter, chilled and cut into small cubes
1 tsp. ground cinnamon
7 oz. porcini mushrooms, finely chopped
Salt and pepper

cooking juices through a sieve. ✦ Bone the quail, leaving the breasts whole and slicing up the rest of the meat after removing the skin. ✦ Put the skin and bones in the strained cooking juices, add the onion, celery, carrots, and parsley, and bring to a boil. ✦ Pass this through a sieve again, then add the remaining wine and cook it down. Reserve half of this liquid for the finishing sauce. ✦ Combine the other half of this liquid with the chopped-up quail meat, add the livers and hearts, chopped, and work in 1 egg yolk, the Parmigiano-Reggiano, and cream. Add salt and pepper to taste. This will be the filling for the pastry. ✦ Using your fingers, rub together the flour and 1 stick of the butter until the mixture resembles wet sand. Add 1 tablespoon ice water (or more as needed) and knead to form a smooth dough. ✦ On a floured surface, with a floured rolling pin, roll out a sheet of dough ¼ inch thick. Cut out of it twelve 3-inch heart-shaped sections (you may have to reroll the scraps to get all 12). Divide the filling among half the dough hearts, top each with a quail breast, then dust with cinnamon and dot each with about ½ tablespoon butter. Cover with another piece of dough, moisten the edges with the remaining egg yolk, and seal the edges. ✦ Bake for 20 minutes, until browned. ✦ Heat the remaining butter and cook the mushrooms, then add them to the reserved cooking liquid. ✦ Pour some of this mushroom sauce onto serving plates and arrange the quail in their crusts over it.

RAGÙ ALLA ROMAGNOLA | ROMAGNA-STYLE RAGÙ

EMILIA-ROMAGNA

2 tbsp. olive oil
1 carrot, chopped
1 celery stalk, chopped
½ medium onion, chopped
4 oz. fresh pancetta, diced
¾ lb. sausage meat, crumbled
¾ lb. stew beef, chopped
½ cup dry white wine
1 lb. ripe plum tomatoes, crushed

Heat the olive oil and cook the carrot, celery, and onion. ✦ Add the pancetta, sausage, and the meat. ✦ Add the wine and let it evaporate. ✦ Add the tomatoes and cook at low heat for about 1 hour until the meat has broken down and the sauce is uniform.

GOOSE RAGÙ

RAGÙ D'OCA

LOMBARDIA

¼ cup olive oil
1 fat goose, cut in pieces
2 medium onions, sliced
2 carrots, chopped
1 cup red wine
1 tbsp. all-purpose flour
Broth
1 garlic clove
⅔ cup tomato purée
Bouquet garni
4 oz. lard
1 bunch Swiss chard, rinsed, chopped, and parboiled
4 oz. sausage, cut in small pieces

This dish is typical of the area of the Lomellina. For the wine use Gutturnio or a Valtellina red.

Heat the olive oil in a saucepan until hot. Sauté the pieces of goose with the onions and carrots until browned. ✦ Add the wine and stir in the flour. ✦ Add broth to cover, the garlic, tomato purée, and bouquet garni. ✦ Cover the pan and cook over low heat for 1 hour. ✦ In a separate pan heat the lard and cook the chard until wilted. ✦ Remove the pieces of goose from the saucepan and set in a bowl; pour the cooked chard over them. ✦ Pass the cooking juices from the chard through a sieve and add them. ✦ Continue cooking the sauce for another hour, adding the sausage about 15 minutes before serving.

MUTTON RAGÙ

RAGÙ DI CASTRATO

CAMPANIA

3 tbsp. extra-virgin olive oil
1½ oz. pancetta, diced
1 medium onion, sliced
1½ lbs. mutton, cut in pieces
½ cup red wine
1 lb. tomato purée

This excellent sauce, typical of Roccadaspide, is good on rigatoni. Traditionally it is made from the meat of a male sheep.

Heat the olive oil in a pan and fry the pancetta and onion. ✦ Add the mutton pieces, then pour over the wine, stirring until it evaporates. ✦ Add the tomato purée and cook about 2 hours. The sauce is ready when it has become thick and the oil rises to the surface.

MOLISE-STYLE RAGÙ

RAGÙ MISTO ALLA MOLISANA

MOLISE

2 oz. *lardo*
1 medium onion, chopped
3 garlic cloves, slivered
½ cup chopped flat-leaf parsley
2 tbsp. olive oil
½ pound pork loin, sliced
CONTINUED

Use the sauce to dress pasta cooked al dente, adding grated cheese. For the wine use Montepulciano.

Chop half the *lardo* together with half of the onion, garlic, and parsley. Heat the olive oil over low heat and cook the mixture. Remove from the heat. ✦ Meanwhile, pound out the three sliced meats and divide among the slices the remaining onion, garlic, parsley, a few grindings of pepper, some salt, and the remaining *lardo*. ✦ Roll up each slice and tie closed with kitchen string. ✦

MEAT & POULTRY

½ pound veal loin, sliced

1 pound lamb loin, sliced

2 oz. pork rind, scraped and cleaned

½ pound fresh sausage,
casing removed

½ cup red wine

8 cups tomato purée

Pinch *diavolillo* (spicy chili pepper;
see note, page 22)

Salt and pepper

Add the roll-ups along with the pork rind and sausage to the pan with the onion mixture, and brown. ✦ Pour in the red wine and as soon as it evaporates add the tomato purée. ✦ Salt to taste and simmer gently at very low heat for about 2 hours, so that the meat cooks slowly and gives its flavor to the sauce. ✦ The sauce is ready when it has become dark and has a velvety consistency. At that point give it another touch of flavor by adding a little *diavolillo*.

RANE IN GUAZZETTO

SAUTÉED FROGS

LOMBARDIA

3½ lbs. frogs, cleaned

1 medium onion, chopped

1 celery stalk, chopped

1 carrot, chopped

¼ lb. (1 stick) unsalted butter

½ cup dry white wine,
such as Lugana

1 tbsp. all-purpose flour,
dissolved in 2 tbsp. water

1 bunch chopped flat-leaf parsley

Juice of ½ lemon

Salt and pepper

Certain refined souls eliminate the flour and use instead an egg yolk, which they add at the end so that its cooking will bind together the various elements, resulting in a more compact dish. There are then those who use beef broth to flavor the liquid, doing so most of all when fresh, local frogs are not available.

Remove the legs from the frogs and set aside. Put the remaining frog parts in a pot and add the onion, celery, and carrot. Add water to cover and bring to a boil. Reduce the heat and simmer for 30 minutes. ✦ Heat about three-quarters of the butter in a pan and brown the legs. Add salt, wine, and the flour mixture. Add the parsley. Strain the frog broth and stir it into the pan. ✦ Cook this for about 10 minutes, then add the remaining butter, a little pepper, and lemon juice.

RISTRETTO DI PECORA

MUTTON STEW

ABRUZZO

1 lb. mutton

1 sprig rosemary

1 sprig marjoram

5 basil leaves

1 sprig thyme

⅔ cup tomato purée

¼ cup white wine

Cut the meat in somewhat small pieces, put them in a pan with a little water, and simmer for 15 minutes. ✦ Take the pan off the heat, drain the meat, then rinse it in cold water. ✦ Put the meat and herbs in a pan (preferably earthenware), add the tomato purée, cover, and simmer at moderate heat for about 2 hours. ✦ Stir every so often with a wooden spoon, and after the first hour add the white wine. ✦ Continue cooking until the sauce has thickened and the meat has become tender and flavorful. Serve hot.

RANOCCHI FRITTI

This recipe for fried frogs, typical of Lucca in Tuscany, calls for an unusual ingredient: nettles. The powerfully stinging hairs of the herb are used in the first step of the recipe, when the skinned and cleaned frogs are soaked in cold water, to "puff up" the small legs. This step not only makes them appear more voluminous, but will also help the meat come off the bone more easily. After soaking, the frogs would simply be dredged in all-purpose flour and fried in hot olive oil a few at a time, until golden. The fried frogs would be drained and salted and served hot.

ROGNONATA

SAUTÉED KIDNEYS ON TOAST

FOR
6 PERSONS

ABRUZZO

2 lbs. sheep's kidneys
1 medium onion, chopped
1 *diavolillo* (hot chili pepper, see note, page 22)
¼ cup olive oil
Cubed toasted bread
Salt

Cut the kidneys in small pieces and put in a pan with the onion, chili pepper, olive oil, and salt. ✦ Cook at low heat, adding a little water so the sauce does not cook down too much. ✦ As soon as they lose their raw color, spoon the mixture over cubes of toasted bread.

ROSA DI PARMA

PARMA-STYLE BEEF ROAST

FOR
6 PERSONS

EMILIA-ROMAGNA

1 ½ to 2 lbs. beef flank steak
6 thin slices prosciutto
½ cup shards of Parmigiano-Reggiano
¼ cup olive oil
2 tbsp. unsalted butter
3 garlic cloves

CONTINUED

This dish is typical of Parma.

Beat the meat with a pounder or cut it spirally and open it out, forming a large slice. Salt and pepper. ✦ Cover the meat with the prosciutto and Parmigiano-Reggiano, then roll it up and tie it with kitchen twine. ✦ Heat the olive oil, butter, garlic (the garlic can be removed at the end), and rosemary. Add the meat and brown it. ✦ Add the wine and Marsala and simmer for about 30 minutes. ✦ Remove the meat from the pan and stir in the cream.

MEAT & POULTRY

1 sprig rosemary

3 cups red wine
(preferably dry Lambrusco)

1 cup Marsala

⅔ cup light cream

Salt and pepper

✦ Raise the heat and reduce the liquid for a few minutes. The meat should be served sliced and covered with the sauce.

✦ **LOCAL TRADITION** ✦

ROBA COTTA

Known colloquially as "cooked stuff," this dish from Gubbio in Umbria was once quite common, most often offered by butchers—on a fig leaf—following the slaughter of a pig. The "cooked stuff" was the less-favored portions that would be left over: the head, intestines, trotters, tripe, tail, and so forth. These would be boiled together with flavorings, such as fennel, generous amounts of onion, garlic, marjoram, salt, pepper, and, according to taste, occasionally lard.

RUSTIDA | # STEWED PORK

PIEMONTE

4 tbsp. unsalted butter

1 large onion, sliced

6 oz. pork loin, sliced

6 oz. pork heart, sliced

6 oz. sausage meat, crumbled

½ cup tomato purée

1 cup broth

Salt and pepper

Heat the butter in a large pan and sauté the onion. When it takes color, add the loin, heart, and sausage meat. ✦ Let this cook a few minutes, then add the tomato purée, broth, and salt and pepper to taste. Continue cooking over low heat until it has formed a thick sauce.

SALAME WITH VINEGAR

SALAME ALL'ACETO

FRIULI-VENEZIA GIULIA

2 tbsp. unsalted butter
½ medium onion, finely sliced
¾ lb. salame, in medium-thick slices
⅓ cup red wine vinegar
1 cup broth

This dish is typical of the Carnic Alps. The salame should be a semisoft pork sausage. Serve accompanied by baked polenta.

Heat the butter in a pan and sauté the onion. Add the salame. ✦ Cook, turning the pieces of salame frequently to cook on both sides, then pour in the vinegar. ✦ After a few minutes, dilute with the broth and serve hot.

✦ **LOCAL TRADITION** ✦

SALAMA DA SUGO

An artisan product of ancient origins, *salama da sugo*—also known as *salama* or *salamina*—is a typical sausage of Ferrara, composed of various cuts of pork meat, often including the liver and tongue, mixed with aged red wine, flavored with salt, black pepper, nutmeg, cinnamon, and cloves—the precise proportions depended on the sausage-maker—stuffed into a pig's bladder and hung to dry.

Before cooking, the *salama* would be soaked overnight in cold water and delicately cleaned with a soft brush to remove any encrustations. It would then be wrapped in a clean cotton cloth and tied at one end to a wooden stick or spoon—so that when placed into the cooking pot it would not touch the bottom or sides. The *salama*, thus suspended, would be gently simmered for approximately two hours for every pound of weight. After cooking, the top would be sliced away and the filling scooped out with a spoon. In winter, the *salama* would be eaten with mashed potatoes; in summer, with cream fritters or melon slices. The Ferrarese, however, preferred nothing so much as this specialty sausage alongside a slice of traditional Ferrara bread.

BAKED GAME

SALMÌ DEL PRETE

MARCHE

6 lbs. game (hare, rabbit, squab)
7 oz. sliced prosciutto
CONTINUED

This elegant dish, which requires a lengthy preparation, was served with a certain frequency in the homes of well-to-do families in the inland areas.

Cook the game on a rotisserie. Build a charcoal fire in a fire pit and let it burn down to embers. ✦ As soon as the

½ cup capers

6 anchovies, boned and chopped

2 tbsp. juniper berries

2 medium onions, sliced

8 whole unpeeled garlic cloves

1 bunch sage leaves

1 tbsp. peppercorns

1 cup extra-virgin olive oil, or as needed

1 cup red wine vinegar, or as needed

meat is cooked, cut it in pieces and arrange enough of these in a reasonably large earthenware pan to cover the bottom, keeping the pieces close to one another. ✦ Cover this layer of meat with strips of prosciutto and top with capers, anchovies, juniper berries, onions, garlic, sage, and peppercorns. ✦ Form a second and third layer of meat, vegetables, and herbs until using up all the meat. ✦ Press down on this firmly and pour over the olive oil and vinegar. ✦ Cover the pan with a sheet of parchment paper and over this place a plate with vinegar. Place the container in the embers. The heat must come from the sides of the pan, not from beneath. ✦ When the vinegar in the plate evaporates, the dish is done. Remove from the heat and serve the next day at room temperature.

✦ **LOCAL TRADITION** ✦

SALAME DI AGNELLO

Salame di agnello is a traditional shepherd's dish from Lucera in Puglia, most often eaten during the transhumance, the seasonal movement of the herds from Abruzzo toward Puglia. To make this rustic lamb sausage, the animal's intestines would first be opened and cleaned in several rinses of salted water and dried. The chopped lamb sweetbreads, garlic, parsley, salt, pepper, and pecorino cheese would then be mixed together and wrapped in the lamb's liver, which had been split open with a single slice. The stuffed liver would then be rolled up and wrapped in the intestines. After securing it with kitchen twine, the salame would be baked in a hot oven in a pan over sliced potatoes and several bunches of muscari. Smaller versions of this salame, about the length and width of a finger and known as *turcinielli* or *gnummarelli*, were typically grilled over hot coals.

SALSICCE IN PADELLA CON BROCCOLI

LAZIO

1 reasonably large broccoli

CONTINUED

SAUSAGES AND BROCCOLI

This dish is typical of Rome.

Carefully clean the broccoli, removing the outer leaves and cutting the florets in small pieces. Parboil in a pan and set aside. ✦ Heat the olive oil and cook the garlic

2 tbsp. extra-virgin olive oil

2 garlic cloves

8 fresh sausages, in pieces and
pierced with a fork

½ cup white wine

Salt and pepper

until lightly golden, then add the sausages. ✦ Brown the sausages for a few minutes, add the wine and bring to a boil, and add the broccoli. ✦ Season with salt and pepper, cover, and continue cooking at low heat until the sausages are cooked through. Serve hot.

SALSICCE MAGRE E
BROCCOLI DI RAPE

SAUSAGES WITH
BROCCOLI RABE

FOR
6 PERSONS

CAMPANIA

This dish is typical of Naples.

1 lb. *friarielli* (shoots of
broccoli rabe), cleaned

¼ cup olive oil

1 garlic clove

Pinch chili pepper flakes

1 lb. *cervellatine* (thin sausages
available from Neapolitan butchers)

Salt

Blanch the *friarielli*; drain them well, pressing against a colander with a slotted spoon. ✦ Heat half the olive oil and sauté the garlic until golden, then add the *friarielli*. ✦ Add the chili pepper, a pinch of salt, and cook for 10 minutes at high heat. ✦ In another pan heat the remaining olive oil and cook the *cervellatine* until browned. ✦ Pierce them with the tines of a fork and serve them with the *friarielli* as a side dish.

SALSICCIA CON BROCCOLI
DI RAPA RIPASSATI IN
PADELLA

PAN-FRIED SAUSAGES
AND BROCCOLI

FOR
6 PERSONS

CALABRIA

1 head broccoli (about 1 lb.)

½ cup extra-virgin olive oil

2 garlic cloves, crushed

Pinch chili pepper flakes

1 lb. fresh sausages

Broth

Salt

Carefully clean the broccoli, chopping the stalks and removing the tender florets. Rinse under cold running water and drain well in a colander. ✦ Heat half the olive oil in a pan and sauté the garlic and chili pepper. When the garlic colors, remove it and add the broccoli. ✦ Salt and cook at low heat, stirring the bottom of the pan often. ✦ In another pan, heat the remaining olive oil and brown the sausages, then add them to the broccoli. ✦ Deglaze the sausage pan with broth and add the liquid to the broccoli. Cover and cook at low heat until the sausages are cooked through.

SALSICCIA E PATATE

SAUSAGES
AND POTATOES

FOR
6 PERSONS

CALABRIA

1 lb. sausages

CONTINUED

Form the sausages into the spokes of a wheel, holding them in this shape with skewers inserted crosswise through them. ✦ Heat half the olive oil in a pan and add half of the potatoes. ✦ Place the skewered sausages on

¼ cup extra-virgin olive oil

1 lb. potatoes, peeled and cut into ½-inch cubes

Pepper

top of the potatoes and cover the pan. Reduce the heat to low and cook, stirring from time to time with a wooden spoon. ✦ When the potatoes are done, take them out and carefully drain them of the olive oil. ✦ Repeat with the remaining oil and potatoes. ✦ Combine the batches of potatoes and arrange them on a serving plate with the sausages at the center. Serve hot with pepper.

VEAL CUTLETS WITH PROSCIUTTO AND SAGE

SALTIMBOCCA
ALLA ROMANA

LAZIO

8 slices veal (approximately 1 lb.)

4 oz. prosciutto crudo, sliced and cut in half crosswise

8 sage leaves

All-purpose flour for dusting

3 ½ tbsp. unsalted butter

⅔ cup dry white wine

Salt and pepper

This dish is typical of Rome. *Saltimbocca* means "leap into the mouth." For the wine use Frascatio or Castelli Romani.

Pound the veal slices into thin scallops. ✦ Lay a half slice of prosciutto and a sage leaf atop each slice and hold with a toothpick; dust with flour. ✦ Melt the butter in a pan over high heat and cook the veal, seasoning with a little salt and pepper. ✦ Brown on both sides, cooking for slightly less time on the side with the prosciutto. ✦ Remove from the pan and arrange on a serving plate. ✦ Deglaze the pan with the wine and stir to make a sauce. Pour over the saltimbocca. Serve hot.

LAMB STEW WITH EGGS

SBRODETTATO
DI AGNELLO

MARCHE

1 lb. lamb stew (pieces of meat in sauce, see page 647)

2 tbsp. extra-virgin olive oil

1 plum tomato, peeled and chopped

3 large eggs, beaten

This is a very interesting way to use leftover lamb stew, the result being a worthy dish. A variation consists of using lemon juice instead of the tomato and beating the eggs before adding them.

Heat the lamb stew with the olive oil and tomato; when the liquid has cooked down, add the eggs and stir, letting the mixture thicken, then serve.

VEAL CUTLETS WITH FONTINA

SCALOPPA ALLA
DE TILLIER

VALLE D'AOSTA

2 tbsp. unsalted butter

4 veal scaloppini

CONTINUED

This recipe is from the Aosta bourgeoisie.

Heat the butter in a pan over medium-high heat. Add the scaloppini and cook on both sides until lightly browned. ✦ Add salt and the wine, letting it evaporate. ✦ Place a slice of cheese over each piece of veal, dust with

¼ cup white wine
4 slices fontina
Grated nutmeg
Salt and pepper

pepper and as much nutmeg as desired. ✦ Cover the pan and turn off the burner, but do not move the pan. Let stand for about 10 minutes, so the cheese will melt without cooking. Serve hot in the same pan.

SCALOPPA DI FEGATO GRASSO D'OCA | FOIE GRAS

LOMBARDIA

4 scaloppine of foie gras
Salt

This dish is typical of the territory of Crema, where, sad to say, the local raising of geese for making foie gras has been reduced to the minimum. Serve with polenta or on mashed potatoes.

Heat a dry pan over medium-high heat. Add the slices of foie gras and cook each one for only a few seconds, then add some salt.

✦ **LOCAL TRADITION** ✦

SANGUINACCIO DI CAPRA

Typical of San Nicola da Crissa in Calabria, this recipe for stuffed goat's intestine first involved dicing and parboiling coagulated goat's blood. The parboiled blood would then be mixed with various seasonal vegetables that had also been diced and boiled, commonly chard, cabbage leaves, and chicory. Cleaned, cooked, and chopped tripe would then be added to the blood and vegetable mixture and seasoned with olive oil and powdered chili pepper. This mixture would be stuffed into the goat's intestine, cooled, and then served in slices.

SCALOPPINE ALLA ABETONESE | VEAL CUTLETS WITH MUSHROOM CAPS

TOSCANA

1 garlic clove, chopped, plus more for serving
½ medium onion, minced

CONTINUED

For the wine use Vernaccia di San Gimignano.

Mix the garlic, onion, and *nepetella* (or mint) with the olive oil and butter. Heat half of this mixture in a pan over low heat, then lay the veal on top and cook. ✦ Salt and pepper to taste. ✦ Add ½ cup of the wine and the broth, cover, and simmer. ✦ Meanwhile, add the thyme to the remaining garlic mixture and cook the mushroom

1 tsp. *nepetella* (see note, page 92)
or a few mint leaves, chopped,
plus more for serving
1 tbsp. extra-virgin olive oil
1 tbsp. unsalted butter
8 veal scaloppini (about 1 lb.)
1 cup white wine
½ cup broth
1 sprig thyme, chopped
1 ¼ lbs. mushroom caps, cleaned
1 tbsp. grappa
Salt and pepper

caps the same way as the veal but in a separate pan. ✦ By the time the meat is nearly cooked the mushroom caps should be done. ✦ Transfer the mushroom caps and their sauce to the pan with the meat and pour in the remaining white wine and the grappa. ✦ Stir so that the meat will be fully "embraced" by the mushrooms. Serve hot with additional mint and garlic.

SCALOPPINE ALL'ACETO BALSAMICO

PORK CUTLETS WITH BALSAMIC VINEGAR

EMILIA-ROMAGNA

1 lb. pork loin, sliced
All-purpose flour for dredging
¼ cup extra-virgin olive oil
1 tbsp. balsamic vinegar
Salt

This dish is typical of Castelvetro.

Pound the slices of pork to make them very thin, then flour them lightly. ✦ Heat the olive oil in a pan, add the pork, and brown on both sides. ✦ Salt and sprinkle with balsamic vinegar. ✦ Serve immediately while the heat is still making the vinegar give off all its fragrance.

SCIUSCEDDU

MEAT AND CHEESE SOUFFLÉ

FOR 8 PERSONS

SICILIA

Tiny meatballs made of meat, grated caciocavallo cheese, flat-leaf parsley, eggs, bread, milk, chopped onion, and salt (see page 105)
Beef broth, skimmed of fat

For the soufflé:
1 ¼ lbs. sheep's-milk ricotta
4 large eggs, separated, plus 3 large egg whites
4 tbsp. grated caciocavallo
2 tbsp. grated Emmental cheese
Salt and pepper

Preheat the oven to 450°F. Simmer the meatballs in broth just to cover until cooked through and set aside. ✦ Pass the ricotta through a sieve and combine it with the egg yolks, caciocavallo, Emmental, and salt and pepper. ✦ Beat the egg whites until stiff peaks form and delicately fold them into the ricotta mixture. ✦ Put the cooked meatballs and their broth in a straight-sided ovenproof pan (a soufflé dish), making certain the meatballs are completely covered by the liquid. ✦ Add the ricotta mixture. ✦ Since this is a soufflé, opening the oven while it is cooking is out of the question; it should bake for 40 to 45 minutes. The result should be a delicate wonder, puffy and delicious, a mixture of ricotta and cheese sprinkled with the tiny meatballs.

SCANNATURE D'ABBACCHIO IN PADELLA

Scannature refers to the blood collected from the slaughter of an animal—in this case a goat—and allowed to coagulate in several small bowls. In this recipe, from Lazio, for cooked goat's blood, garlic cloves were first sautéed whole in olive oil and then discarded. Four or five whole pieces of *scannature* would then be added to the garlic-infused oil to brown slightly, before dry white wine was added to the pan. After the wine had evaporated, sliced onions, tomato purée, salt, and pepper would be added to the pan, with more wine or water added as needed.

SCOTTIGLIA

MIXED BRAISED MEATS

TOSCANA

1 lb. chicken, cut into pieces

1 lb. duck, cut into pieces

1 lb. rabbit, cut into pieces

1 lb. squab, cut into pieces

1 lb. lamb, cut into cubes

¾ cup extra-virgin olive oil

1 medium onion, minced

2 tbsp. chopped fresh basil

1 celery stalk, chopped

1 garlic clove, minced

1 carrot, chopped

½ chili pepper

1 lb. fresh tomato purée

1 cup red wine, such as Chianti Classico

Salt

This dish is typical of the Maremma. You will need a certain variety of meats: chicken, duck, rabbit, even squab and lamb—but a fine *scottiglia* can be made with a more limited variety. Serve the *scottiglia* alone, with potatoes, or even better, follow the ancient Maremma tradition and serve it on slices of toasted peasant-style bread rubbed with plenty of garlic.

Clean and cut up the meats, singeing the birds if necessary to eliminate any remaining feathers. ✦ Heat the olive oil in a very large pan and sauté the onion, basil, celery, garlic, carrot, and chili pepper for a few minutes, then add the meats and cook until they begin to take on color. ✦ Pour in the tomato purée. ✦ Simmer over low heat for at least 1 hour, pouring in red wine and letting the sauce reduce only when the meats are so well cooked they are beginning to come away from the bone. Taste for salt.

MEAT & POULTRY

ROAST SADDLE OF VENISON

LOMBARDIA

¾ cup extra-virgin olive oil
1 medium onion, chopped
1 celery stalk, chopped
½ lb. venison stew meat, cut in tiny pieces
2 bottles red wine (preferably Inferno)
1 saddle roe deer, weighing 2 lbs.
2 sprigs rosemary
½ lb. (1 cup) unsalted butter
1 tbsp. all-purpose flour
Salt and pepper

This dish is typical of the Valtellina.

Preheat the oven to 350°F. Heat half of the olive oil in a pan and sauté the onion and celery until golden. Add the stew meat and brown. ✦ After a few minutes add the wine and bring to a steady simmer. ✦ In an ovenproof pan, heat the remaining oil and brown the saddle, adding salt and pepper and rosemary. ✦ Roast the saddle in the oven, basting it from time to time with some of the wine mixture. ✦ After 20 minutes remove the saddle from the oven, since it should be served rare, and set it aside, keeping it warm. ✦ Cook down the sauce, whisk in the butter and flour to thicken it, then pass it through a food mill. ✦ Remove the loin from the saddle and slice it, then reassemble it on the bone. ✦ Serve with some of the sauce over the meat, the rest on the side.

MEAT AND SALAME PIE

FOR
10 PERSONS

SICILIA

6½ cups all-purpose flour
1 tsp. active dry yeast
8 oz. lard, plus more for the pan
9 large eggs, lightly beaten
4 tbsp. extra-virgin olive oil
2 lbs. ground pork or veal
⅔ cup grated fresh pecorino
2 oz. aged pecorino, sliced
4 oz. salame, in small cubes
Salt and pepper

This dish is typical of Mussomeli.

Stir 3 cups of the flour with 1 tablespoon salt and yeast and as much lukewarm water as necessary to form a smooth dough. Let it rest overnight at room temperature. ✦ The next morning (4 hours before baking) work the remaining flour into the dough, along with the lard and eggs, but without adding water. ✦ Knead the dough as long as necessary to make it elastic and soft. ✦ Grease a baking pan with lard. Divide the dough into two equal parts and from one half, roll out a sheet 1 inch thick and place it in the baking pan. ✦ Heat 3 tablespoons of the olive oil in a pan at low heat and cook the meat with salt and pepper until it browns. ✦ Spread half the cooked meat across the sheet of dough in the baking pan, sprinkle with pecorino, and add slices of the aged cheese, then the salame, and cover with the other half of the ground meat. ✦ Roll out the second sheet of dough and use it to seal and completely enclose the filling. ✦ Grease the top of the dough with the remaining olive oil, cover with waxed paper, and let it rise 4 hours, refrigerated. ✦ Preheat the oven to 325°F. Bake for about 1 hour; it should swell up with a golden crust.

| **FRIED PORK** |

CALABRIA

¼ cup extra-virgin olive oil

2 bay leaves

1⅓ cups tomato purée

1 garlic clove

1½ lbs. fresh guanciale and other cuts of pork with a high percentage of fat

¼ cup red wine vinegar

Salt

This dish is typical of San Giovanni in Fiore. There is a variation on this dish: The meat is cooked in a little olive oil with a few garlic cloves; when half cooked, instead of vinegar, pickled peppers cut in pieces are added to the meat.

In an earthenware pan heat the olive oil and add the bay leaves, tomato purée, garlic clove, and salt. Cut the guanciale and other pork into medium-size pieces and add to the pan. Cook until browned, about 10 minutes. ✦ After 5 minutes, stir in the vinegar.

SOPPRESSA IN TECIA | **COOKED SOPPRESSATA**

VENETO

1 lb. soppressata (preferably the Venetian type: *soppressa*)

2 tbsp. extra-virgin olive oil

2 tbsp. unsalted butter

1 medium onion, sliced

3 tbsp. red wine vinegar

5 bay leaves

1 sprig rosemary

Salt

Cut the soppressata into somewhat thick slices and trim them. ✦ Heat half of the olive oil and butter in a pan and sauté the onion until it colors. ✦ Turn off the heat, pour in the vinegar, and add a little salt. ✦ In another pan, heat the remaining oil and butter, bay leaves, and rosemary. ✦ Add the soppressata in an orderly way to make it easier to turn them. Cook quickly, then turn and cook on the other side. ✦ Pour the vinegar mixture into this pan and cook rapidly to keep the slices from getting too crisp. Serve with somewhat soft fresh polenta or with toasted slices of polenta.

SPEZZATINO D'AGNELLO | **LAMB STEW**

MOLISE

1 slice *lardo*, chopped

2 garlic cloves, chopped

1 tbsp. extra-virgin olive oil

A few sage leaves

1 sprig rosemary

2¼ lbs. lamb stew meat, cut in pieces

Pinch chili pepper flakes

½ cup white wine, or as needed

Salt

This dish is typical of Termoli. For the wine use Biferno or Trebbiano.

Using a wide terra-cotta pan, heat the *lardo*, garlic, and olive oil at very low heat. ✦ Add the sage leaves and rosemary, and as soon as the *lardo* melts add the meat, salt, and chili pepper. ✦ Cover and cook at low heat, adding wine from time to time, until the meat is cooked. ✦ As soon as it is ready bring it to the table in the cooking pot.

MEAT & POULTRY

SPEZZATINO DI CAPRA | GOAT STEW

CALABRIA

1½ lbs. tender goat meat
(preferably from the shoulder),
in pieces
1½ cups white wine vinegar
2 garlic cloves, chopped
Pinch oregano
1 *diavolillo* (hot chili pepper,
see note, page 22)
1¼ cups extra-virgin olive oil
2 lbs. tomato purée
Salt

This stew can also be made with lamb.

Soak the pieces of meat in a mixture of equal parts water and vinegar to cover for a few hours, then dry them with a cloth and put them in a terra-cotta pan. ✦Add the garlic, oregano, salt, and chili pepper. ✦Add the olive oil and tomato purée and cook at very low heat, with the pan covered, for at least 2 hours, adding a little water if necessary to maintain the level of liquid.

SPEZZATINO DI CODA DI MANZO | OXTAIL STEW

ALTO ADIGE

1 oxtail (beef), cut in pieces
1 medium onion, coarsely chopped
1 garlic clove, coarsely chopped
1 tsp. peppercorns
1 tbsp. juniper berries
2 bay leaves
Pinch thyme leaves
3 cups strong dry red wine,
such as Lagrein
½ cup extra-virgin olive oil
1 cup broth
1 tbsp. tomato paste
1 tbsp. potato starch (if necessary)
Salt and pepper

This is excellent with *canederli* (see page 222, hot sauce).

Put the pieces of oxtail in a large bowl. ✦ Add the onion, garlic, peppercorns, juniper berries, bay leaves, and thyme. ✦ Cover with the red wine and let marinate for 2 days. ✦ For the preparation, remove the pieces of oxtail from the marinade, setting aside the liquid, and dry them. ✦ Brown the pieces of oxtail in a pan with olive oil, adding salt and pepper. ✦ Add the onion and garlic from the marinade along with some of the wine of the marinade and the broth. ✦ Add the tomato paste and cook slowly for at least 3 hours. ✦ Test the meat, which should be soft, then cut it in pieces. ✦ Skim any fat from the sauce, thickening it with potato starch if needed. ✦ Pass the sauce with all its contents through a sieve, then pour it over the meat in a pan and cook again at low heat just until hot and serve.

SPEZZATINO DI INTERIORA | TRIPE AND SWEETBREAD STEW

CALABRIA

This dish, typical of Catanzaro, is based on sweetbreads and veal scraps cooked in a tomato sauce made piquant by spicy red chili pepper. Its dialect name, *morseddu*, from *morso* ("bite"), reflects the fact that it was originally held in the

About ½ lb. of each of the following: tripe, veal liver, lungs, heart, sweetbreads (veal or pork), spleen

1 bunch flat-leaf parsley

¼ cup extra-virgin olive oil

2 tbsp. tomato paste

1 sprig oregano

1 bay leaf

1 medium onion, chopped

1 *diavolillo* (hot chili pepper, see note, page 22)

Salt

hand and bitten into, along with *pitte* (soft focaccias made of bread dough). Serve this stew with focaccia (page 28).

Bring a pot of water to a boil and add the tripe. ✦ After a few minutes remove the tripe (setting aside the water) and cut it in pieces, beginning the process of cleaning it, which should be done with great care. ✦ Put the tripe in another pot of water and simmer it with the parsley and a pinch of salt. Add all the other meat parts (except the spleen, which should be boiled separately). ✦ When all of this is cooked, drain it and chop it into strips. Heat the olive oil and cook all the meats with the tomato paste, oregano, bay leaf, onion, and chili pepper. ✦ From time to time add a ladleful of the liquid from boiling the tripe.

SPEZZATINO DI VITELLO | VEAL STEW

PIEMONTE

A few sage leaves

1 sprig rosemary

2 tbsp. unsalted butter

2 tbsp. extra-virgin olive oil

1 ½ lbs. veal loin, in small pieces

1 tbsp. tomato purée

1 cup warm veal broth

1 lb. potatoes, peeled and cut in pieces

Salt and pepper

Combine the sage, rosemary, butter, and oil in a pan. Heat over medium heat and cook until fragrant. ✦ Add the meat and salt. ✦ When the meat has browned well on all sides, add the tomato purée and warm broth. ✦ Cover the pot and cook at low heat. ✦ After the meat has cooked about 10 minutes, add the potatoes and continue cooking at low heat. ✦ Continue cooking slowly, tasting for salt and pepper, and serve when the meat and potatoes are cooked, about 25 minutes.

SPEZZATO DI MONTONE | MUTTON STEW

ABRUZZO

2 tbsp. lard

1 oz. *lardo*, minced

1 celery stalk, chopped

1 carrot, chopped

1 medium onion, sliced

1 lb. mutton, cut in pieces

½ cup white wine

¾ lb. plum tomatoes, peeled, seeded, and chopped

Salt and pepper

Use this sauce on spaghetti or homemade pasta. For the wine use Trebbiano.

Heat the lard in a pan and sauté the *lardo*, celery, carrot, and onion. Add the meat. ✦ When the meat has browned, add salt and pepper and pour in the white wine; then add the tomatoes. Simmer until the meat is cooked through, about 30 minutes.

SKEWERED CHICKEN GIZZARDS

1 lb. chicken gizzards
Juice of 1 lemon
Chicken broth, as needed
Coarse salt
Sliced peasant-style bread, toasted

This dish is typical of Reggio Calabria.

Clean the gizzards; rub them with coarse salt, then carefully rinse in water acidulated with lemon juice. ✦ Put the gizzards on reed or wooden skewers and simmer in broth to cover. ✦ Serve hot with slices of toasted peasant-style bread.

✦ **LOCAL TRADITION** ✦

SPIEDO BRESCIANO OR POLENTA E UCCELLI

Two schools of thought divide the preparation of this dish, from the province of Brescia in Lombardy, known as polenta and birds. Closer to the province of Bergamo, the birds and pork loin are cooked in a large pan. Conversely, in the area between Brescia and Lake Garda, the birds and loin are cooked exclusively on a rotisserie. Other ingredients, including ribs, rabbit, potatoes, and even eel, are sometimes added in the area between the Valsabbia and the Valtenesi. In the more traditional preparation that involved only the birds and pork loin, the birds would first be thoroughly cleaned and the pork loin sliced, then the slices pounded thin and rolled up. A few sage leaves would be lightly fried in butter and olive oil in a hot pan; these fried sage leaves would be threaded onto the skewer between the different meats. Slices of potato were also commonly used to separate the portions of meat. The birds, if small, would be put on either end of the skewer. The skewers would then be cooked on a rotisserie over a drip pan atop a fire of olive or vine wood, basted regularly with the drippings, for at least four hours. Finally, the cooked meats would be served with fresh polenta, and commonly a salad.

ROAST INTESTINES

FOR
6 PERSONS

2 oz. lard
2 lbs. lamb or kid intestines
CONTINUED

This dish will be even tastier if, in addition to the parsley and garlic, the intestines are filled with hard-boiled eggs, salame, and fresh provola or provolone.

Preheat the oven to 350°F or heat a grill to medium-high. Grease a baking pan with lard. Clean the intestines

1 bunch flat-leaf parsley
2 garlic cloves, cut in large pieces
Salt and pepper

in tepid salted water, then rinse well under cold running water. ✦ Wrap them around several stalks of parsley and garlic and tie them shut like roll-ups. ✦ Put them in the baking pan, add salt and pepper, and bake in the oven or roast on a grill until cooked through, about 30 minutes.

STINCO DI MAIALE
AL FORNO

BAKED PORK SHANKS

ALTO ADIGE

4 young pork shanks (hocks)
4 oz. lard
½ cup olive oil
1 medium onion, cut in half
2 garlic cloves
1 sprig rosemary
½ cup dry white wine,
such as Pinot Bianco
Broth (optional)

Serve accompanied by roast potatoes or a fresh green salad.
Preheat the oven to 400°F. Set the shanks in a baking pan and sprinkle over the lard, olive oil, onion, whole garlic cloves, and rosemary. ✦ Turn the shanks to coat them well and put the pan in the oven. ✦ When they have browned, add the white wine; when the wine evaporates add 2 inches of broth or water: the shanks should never be without liquid. ✦ Reduce the heat to 325°F and braise for about 1½ hours, turning the shanks and basting from time to time. Serve the shanks when cooked and tender.

STINCO DI MONTONE
AL FORNO

BAKED MUTTON SHANK

ABRUZZO

2 tbsp. extra-virgin olive oil
2 tbsp. unsalted butter
Several sprigs herbs
(rosemary, sage, bay leaves, etc).
1 mutton shank
2 cups white wine, such as Trebbiano

Preheat the oven to 475°F. Heat the olive oil, butter, and whatever herbs you prefer in an ovenproof pan; add the shank and cook until browned, then add the wine. ✦ Transfer the pan to the oven and bake for about 3 hours, turning and basting the shank often and lowering the heat to 325°F halfway through the cooking time. ✦ Slice just before serving.

STINCO DI VITELLO
AL BAROLO

VEAL SHANK
WITH BAROLO WINE

PIEMONTE

1 veal shank
4 carrots, chopped
1 sprig rosemary
CONTINUED

Preheat the oven to 350°F. Lard the shank with half the carrots and rosemary. Heat the olive oil and the *lardo* in an ovenproof pan and brown the shank. ✦ Add the remaining vegetables and herbs, and salt and pepper. ✦ When everything has browned, add the wine and bring to a boil. ✦ After a few minutes transfer the pan to the

½ cup olive oil
4 oz. *lardo*, diced
2 celery stalks, chopped
3 medium onions, sliced
1 leek, chopped
3 garlic cloves, chopped
A few sage leaves
1 bay leaf
1 bottle Barolo wine
Broth (if needed)
1 tbsp. potato starch (if needed)
Salt and pepper

oven and bake for 3 hours, turning the meat from time to time so that it remains moist and soft; if necessary, add a little broth. ✦ When the meat is cooked remove it from the pan and pass the cooking juices through a sieve, thickening them with a little potato starch if needed. ✦ Slice the shank and serve warm, covered with its sauce.

STRACOTTO ALLA
PARMIGIANA

PARMA-STYLE BEEF STEW

FOR
6 PERSONS

EMILIA-ROMAGNA

3 ¼ lbs. beef (from the leg)
1 medium onion, finely chopped
1 carrot, chopped
1 celery stalk, chopped
1 garlic clove, minced
4 cloves
Pinch ground cinnamon
3 bay leaves
Red wine (enough to cover the meat)
3 tbsp. olive oil
3 tbsp. unsalted butter
2 oz. *lardo*, finely chopped
All-purpose flour for dredging
8 cups broth, warmed
Salt and pepper

This is the principal player in the preparation of stuffing for *anolini* (see pages 97 and 98), but it is also an excellent meat dish on its own. For the wine use Valpolicella or Sangiovese.

Put the meat in a saucepan with the onion, carrot, celery, and garlic. ✦ Add the cloves, cinnamon, and bay leaves and cover with the wine. ✦ Cover the pan and refrigerate for 24 hours. ✦ At the end of that time remove the meat from the marinade and drain it; strain the vegetables from the marinade and set aside; also set aside the liquid. ✦ Heat the olive oil, butter, and *lardo* in a saucepan; flour the meat, add it to the pan, and brown for about 15 minutes. ✦ Add the vegetables from the marinade and sauté them. ✦ Salt and pepper to taste, then pour in the liquid from the marinade and broth. ✦ Cover and cook at low heat for 5 hours. ✦ Then remove the meat from the pan and slice it; pass the cooking juices through a sieve and pour over the meat before serving.

STRACOTTO ALLA
PIACENTINA

PIACENZA-STYLE BEEF STEW

EMILIA-ROMAGNA

1 small piece *lardo*
1 garlic clove

CONTINUED

For the wine use Gutturnio or Sangiovese.

Prepare a good Piacenza-style *pestata di lardo* ("finely chopped *lardo*"), finely chopping together the *lardo*, garlic, and parsley. ✦ Heat the butter in a pan and add the onion and *lardo* mixture. ✦ Salt the meat and add it to

1 small bunch flat-leaf parsley
¼ cup (4 tbsp.) unsalted butter
1 small onion, minced
1 lb. beef leg
1 celery stalk, finely chopped
1 carrot, finely chopped
Tomato purée
Aged red wine (enough to cover the meat)
Broth, as needed
Salt

the pan along with the celery and carrot. ✦ Add to this as much tomato purée as desired. ✦ Add the wine. ✦ Let this simmer gently for 4 to 5 hours, adding broth as needed to keep the meat moist and cooking with the pan covered.

STRACOTTO DI ASINO ALLA PAESANA

DONKEY STEW

LOMBARDIA

2 tbsp. extra-virgin olive oil
2 tbsp. unsalted butter
2 medium onions, finely sliced
1 celery stalk, chopped
1 lb. carrots, chopped
4½ lbs. donkey meat
3 whole cloves
3 garlic cloves
Pinch grated nutmeg
1 bottle red wine (preferably aged Barbera)
Broth, as needed

Typical and ancient rural tradition, both on the plains and in the hills, this is a method of using the meat of quadrupeds (donkey or horse) after their lifetime of service. The dish has spread to rural restaurants in the area of Mantua and along the banks of the Po River, where it is frequently encountered. Beef can be used.

In a large pan, heat the olive oil and butter and sauté the onions, celery, and carrots. ✦ Stud the meat with the cloves and garlic cloves. ✦ Add the meat to the pan, sprinkle with nutmeg, and brown for about 10 minutes. ✦ Pour in the entire bottle of wine. ✦ Simmer over low heat for 2 hours, with the pan covered. If it dries out too much, add broth as needed. ✦ When cooked, remove the meat, cut it in slices, and cover with its sauce before serving.

STRACOTTO DI MANZO AL FORNO NEL PIGNATTO

THE "FIFTH QUARTER" BEEF STEW

LAZIO

This dish's dialect name, *Pignattaccia*, refers to the earthenware pot in which it is traditionally cooked. It is made using lesser cuts of beef (belly, diaphragm), which are muscular and thus less costly, along with those referred to as the *quinto quarto* ("fifth quarter") on the theory that the weight of these parts, which no one usually wants—including the head, tail, hooves, and tripe—was equal to one quarter of the slaughtered animal's weight. Because of their collagen, these pieces together with the various vegetables (most of all the celery) give this dish its special, pleasing flavor. Today, it is made with more expensive muscular parts, but

½ cup white wine

2 whole cloves

2 lbs. mixed beef (belly, shank, head, tail, tongue, tripe), cut in pieces

4 potatoes, peeled and cut in 1-inch-thick slices

Extra-virgin olive oil

1 celery stalk, chopped

2 carrots, chopped

1 large onion, chopped

4 plum tomatoes, peeled and chopped

1 *diavolillo* (hot chili pepper, see note, page 22), chopped

Salt and pepper

always with the addition of those from the *quinto quarto*. It is typical of Viterbo.

Mix the white wine and cloves. Add the beef and enough lightly salted water to cover. Refrigerate a few hours. ✦ At the end of that time drain the meat, reserving the liquid. ✦ Preheat the oven to 300°F. In the bottom of a large earthenware baking dish (*pignatta*), make a layer of potatoes. Cover this with a layer of meat, season with olive oil, salt, and pepper, then make a layer of vegetables (celery, carrots, onion, tomatoes, chili pepper). ✦ Continue making layers in this way, using up the various components and ending with a layer of potatoes. ✦ Pour over this the liquid from the marinade, enough to cover it all, then cover the pot with a sheet of aluminum foil and cover with the lid. ✦ Bake until the beef is tender, about 3 hours.

STRACOTTO DI SOMARO

DONKEY STEW

EMILIA-ROMAGNA

2 cups dry red wine

5 sage leaves

5 cloves

1 bay leaf

3 garlic cloves

Pinch grated nutmeg

1 celery stalk, chopped

1 carrot, chopped

1 lb. loin of donkey

¼ cup extra-virgin olive oil

1 lb. peeled plum tomatoes

Salt and pepper

This dish is typical of Modena. Serve with a side dish of slices of toasted polenta. Beef can be used in place of the donkey. For the wine use Sangiovese or Valpolicella.

Mix half the wine with the sage, cloves, bay leaf, garlic, salt, pepper, nutmeg, celery, and carrot. Add the meat and refrigerate for several hours. ✦ At the end of that time drain the meat. Heat the olive oil in a large saucepan and brown the meat. Add the remaining wine. ✦ After about 10 minutes, add the tomatoes and simmer for about 2 hours, tasting for salt and pepper. ✦ When the meat is cooked set it aside and strain the cooking juices through a sieve; serve the meat hot, covered with its sauce.

STRACOTTO ROMAGNOLO

BEEF STEW

EMILIA-ROMAGNA

¼ cup (4 tbsp.) unsalted butter

¼ cup extra-virgin olive oil

CONTINUED

In the past it was the custom to add red wine to this dish (typical of Imola) together with the water.

Heat half the butter and olive oil in a large pan and sauté the carrots and onions. ✦ Make a small incision in the meat and insert the garlic clove into it. ✦ When the

2 carrots, finely chopped
2 medium onions, finely chopped
1 lb. beef leg
1 garlic clove
1 ½ cups tomato purée
¼ cup dry white wine

vegetables have taken a little color, add the meat, turning it constantly. ✦ After a few minutes add water (1 or 2 cups as needed), tomato purée, and the remaining butter and olive oil. ✦ Simmer gently until tender, about 3 hours. When the meat is almost cooked, add the wine.

STRACOTTO DI PECORA

This very basic rustic recipe for lamb stew traces its origins back centuries to the Hungarian and Saracen shepherds who occupied the Alpine pass within the valley of Corteno Golgi, in the upper Val Camonica, in Lombardy, reaching its height during the late nineteenth century at the instigation of Albanian immigrants. Then, as now, tradition saw this dish most often eaten during festive occasions and celebrations at home, accompanied by smoked ricotta (in modern times, grated Parmigiano-Reggiano) and polenta. Preference is given to the local breed of small "Cortenese" sheep, although this unique and indigenous breed is slowly disappearing through crossbreeding with larger and more common Bergamo sheep.

As with the lamb or mutton dishes common during the transhumance, this stew's recipe would begin with cutting a lamb or sheep weighing between 50 and 65 pounds into portions and placing it into a pot or cauldron with some fat and sage or rosemary. The stew would be cooked at low heat over a wood fire that had been allowed to burn down to embers for five to six hours, until the meat was tender. Any leftovers would traditionally be salted and preserved under fat to be eaten as a room temperature snack later with boiled potatoes.

STUFATINO COL SELLERO

BEEF STEW WITH CELERY

FOR
6 PERSONS

LAZIO

4 oz. prosciutto fat
3 tbsp. extra-virgin olive oil
1 medium onion, finely sliced
2 garlic cloves, finely chopped
CONTINUED

This dish is typical of Rome. It was originally made from lean meat taken from the front quarter of an ox, known in the jargon of Roman butchers as *pulcio*.

Heat the prosciutto fat in the olive oil over low heat and sauté the onion and garlic. ✦ When this begins to turn golden, add the meat, salt, and a pinch of pepper. ✦ When the meat has browned, turn up the heat to medium-high

2 lbs. lean beef chuck, cut crosswise in ½-inch-thick slices

½ cup dry red wine, such as Chianti Classico

⅔ cup tomato purée

1½ cups plum tomatoes, peeled, seeded, drained, and chopped

4 basil leaves, chopped

1 lb. celery, cut in 4-inch lengths

Salt and pepper

and pour in the red wine. ✦ When the wine evaporates, add the tomato purée, tomatoes, and basil. Reduce the heat to low and simmer gently for 3 hours. ✦ If during that time the sauce cooks down too much, add 2 table-spoons of water, doing this as often as necessary but being careful not to overly dilute the sauce. ✦ After the first hour add the celery. ✦ Remove the pan from the heat and, with the lid removed, let it rest for another 30 minutes. Serve on warmed plates.

STUFATO DI CASTRATO CON PATATE

MUTTON STEW WITH POTATOES

FOR 6 PERSONS

PUGLIA

¼ cup extra-virgin olive oil

2¼ lbs. mutton or kid, cut in pieces

1 medium onion, finely chopped

½ cup red wine

1 bunch celery, cut in small pieces

½ lb. plum tomatoes, peeled

1 lb. potatoes

Salt and pepper

Heat the olive oil in a large pan and sauté the meat and onion. ✦ When the meat has browned and the onion is translucent, add the wine. ✦ Salt and pepper to taste and add ½ cup warm water and the celery. ✦ Cook for 30 minutes, add the tomatoes, and continue cooking over medium-low heat. ✦ Meanwhile, boil the potatoes in lightly salted water to cover until about half done; re-move them from the water and when cool enough to handle, peel them and chop them into large chunks. Add them to the meat for the last 15 minutes of its cooking time. Stir well and serve hot.

STUFATO DI MAIALE

PORK STEW

LOMBARDIA

2 lbs. pork or boar loin

3 carrots, cut in short lengths

1 oz. pancetta, diced

3 bay leaves

2 cups dry red wine (preferably a strong Barbera)

All-purpose flour for dredging

3 tbsp. unsalted butter

¼ cup grappa

Bread dough (see page 13)

This dish is typical of Lecco and the Valsassina. Serve with polenta and Barbera.

Cut slits in the meat and insert the carrots and pancetta. Put it in an earthenware or stainless-steel baking pan with the bay leaves and wine. ✦ Refrigerate 24 hours. ✦ Preheat the oven to 300°F. Drain the marinade, reserving the liquid. Dry the meat, tie it up, and flour it. Heat the butter in a large pan and brown the meat. ✦ When it has colored, add the grappa and let it evaporate. ✦ Transfer the meat to the pan in which it marinated; use a little wine to loosen the cooking juices in the pan in which the meat browned and add them to the meat. ✦ Cover, sealing the edge of the lid with some rolled bread dough, and bake 4 hours.

ROAST TURKEY WITH POMEGRANATE

VENETO

1 young turkey,
weighing about 6 lbs., with giblets

½ cup (¼ lb.) unsalted butter

Pancetta

2 pomegranates

2 tbsp. extra-virgin olive oil

Salt and pepper

Traditionally, a female turkey is used for this dish. Serve the roast bird with potatoes, a green salad, and accompany it with an aromatic red wine.

Prepare a rotisserie with a drip pan. Remove the giblets, chop them, and set aside. ✦ Wash the turkey inside and out and pat dry; butter the cavity and then lard the bird well using strips of pancetta. ✦ Put the turkey on the spit and roast it on the rotisserie for about 1½ hours. ✦ Meanwhile, prepare the pomegranate sauce: peel the pomegranates, extracting the seeds, and use a potato masher (or food processor) to crush them, collecting the juice (which should then be strained). ✦ About halfway through the cooking time pour about half of this juice over the turkey. Heat the olive oil and sauté the giblets, seasoning with pepper, salt, and some of the pomegranate sauce. ✦ When the turkey is cooked, cut it in pieces and cover with the sauce.

✦ **LOCAL TRADITION** ✦

TACCHINO ALLA CANZANESE

This delicious and seductive recipe, typical of Canzano in Abruzzo, has long been admired for its flavor, lightness, and nutrition. A turkey weighing approximately eleven to thirteen pounds would be well cleaned and halved lengthwise. The breastbones would be removed and the other bones, especially the longer ones, crushed. The turkey would then be placed into a terra-cotta pot with some garlic, a sprig of rosemary, white wine, and salt and black peppercorns and just covered with boiling water. The pot would then be placed into a wood-burning oven to cook for four hours, after which time more wood would be added to the fire and the turkey turned and left to cook another four hours. After removing the turkey from the oven, it was traditionally allowed to rest up to twelve hours before serving, which helped preserve the dish, another of its many virtues.

| # CHRISTMAS TURKEY

LOMBARDIA

1 turkey, weighing about 13 lbs.

4 oz. pancetta, chopped

4 tbsp. unsalted butter

2 sprigs rosemary

The fat from inside a veal kidney, from which the film has been removed, finely chopped

3 tbsp. extra-virgin olive oil

Salt

This is eaten hot on Christmas in Monza; the leftovers are eaten cold on the day of the Epiphany, with fruit *mostarda* and a salad made of greens grown under the snow.

Preheat the oven to 300°F. Fill the empty place of the turkey's gullet with chopped pancetta and put the rest of the pancetta inside the turkey with a lot of salt (turkey is more bland than other birds), half the butter, and rosemary. ✦ Cover the bottom of a pan (preferably copper) with the kidney fat, remaining butter, and olive oil. ✦ Tie up the turkey, cover, and roast at low heat for at least 6 hours, until it has taken on a good golden color on all sides. ✦ When the bird is cooked, take the lid off the pan and raise the heat to 450°F to dry up the remaining liquid and make the skin crisp.

TAPULONE | # DONKEY AND CABBAGE STEW

PIEMONTE

3 tbsp. unsalted butter

1 tbsp. olive oil

1½ oz. *lardo*, chopped

2 garlic cloves

2 bay leaves

1 head Savoy cabbage, outer leaves removed and the head cored and cut in strips

1 lb. lean donkey meat

Pinch ground cloves

½ cup dry red wine (preferably Barbera)

1 cup beef froth

Salt and pepper

Tapulone is derived from *tapulé*, meaning the knife that was used to cut up the hard meat of an old donkey, which could be rendered edible only in this way. Beef or pork can be used in place of the donkey.

In a large pan, heat the butter, olive oil, and *lardo* and sauté the garlic cloves and bay leaves. ✦ When the garlic cloves have browned, remove and discard them; add the cabbage. ✦ Let this cook, adding the meat and breaking it up with a fork. ✦ Add the cloves and salt and pepper. ✦ Brown until the meat is well broken up and dry, then add the wine. ✦ When the wine has evaporated, add the broth, cover the pan, and cook at low heat for 30 to 40 minutes. In the end the meat should be very soft.

TEGAMACCIO CON L'ANATRA | # FISH STEW WITH DUCK

TOSCANA

This stew can also be used to sauce homemade pappardelle and is typical of Chiusi. For the wine use Chianti Classico.

Heat a grill with a charcoal fire and cook the duck over it as though roasting it. ✦ Baste with half the garlic,

1 duck

2 tsp. minced garlic

1 sprig rosemary

2 lbs. mixed lake fish: carp, tench, pike, eel, etc., cleaned and boned

½ cup extra-virgin olive oil

½ cup tomato purée

½ cup red wine

1 medium onion, finely sliced

2 tbsp. chopped flat-leaf parsley

Chili pepper flakes

Juice of 1 lemon

Salt and pepper

rosemary, and salt and pepper to taste. ✦ When it is almost done, cut it into small pieces (the cooking having helped remove the fat) and set aside. ✦ Then prepare the classic *tegamaccio*, mixing the lake fish with the olive oil, tomato purée, half the wine, ½ teaspoon garlic, onion, 1 tablespoon parsley, and chili pepper in a pot and heating over low heat. Simmer, and when the liquid cooks down lift out the pieces of fish with a strainer and set aside; add the remaining wine to the cooking juices, then add the pieces of duck along with the lemon juice. ✦ Then return the fish to the pan. ✦ Add the remaining garlic, chili pepper (to taste), and the remaining parsley.

TEGAMINI DI ROGNONI
AL VINO D'ORVIETO

KIDNEYS IN WINE

UMBRIA

¼ cup extra-virgin olive oil

¼ cup chopped flat-leaf parsley

Several sage leaves

Pinch chili pepper flakes

1 anchovy, finely chopped

2 beef kidneys, cut in 4 or 6 pieces

½ cup white wine

For the wine use Orvieto.

Heat the olive oil and add the parsley, sage, chili pepper, and anchovy. Add the kidneys and brown lightly. ✦ Add the wine. ✦ When the wine has evaporated, cover the pan with aluminum foil and continue cooking at low heat until the kidneys are tender, about 10 minutes.

TIELLA ALLA SILANA

PORK WITH POTATOES AND MUSHROOMS

FOR
6 PERSONS

CALABRIA

3 oz. lard

3 garlic cloves

1¼ lbs. pork shoulder, cut in pieces

1 lb. potatoes, peeled and sliced

1 lb. porcini mushrooms, cleaned and chopped

1 tbsp. chopped flat-leaf parsley

1 sprig rosemary

Pinch chili pepper flakes

Salt

Using an earthenware pan (a *tiella*), heat the lard and cook the garlic. When the cloves turn blond, remove and discard them. ✦ Add the meat and cook for about 15 minutes. ✦ Add the potatoes, mushrooms, parsley, rosemary, chili pepper, and salt. ✦ Cover the pan and simmer over low heat until tender, about 2 hours, adding a little warm water from time to time as needed.

TESTARELLE D'ABBACCHIO IN TEGLIA

This ancient Roman specialty for lambs' heads is typical of Lazio. Two lambs' heads would be cut in half and very carefully cleaned, leaving only the prized brains and tongue. The rest of the necessary cleaning involved making specific cuts and or scrapes in the internal cartilage of the ears, the tongue, and eyes. Chopped garlic, parsley, breadcrumbs, and salt and pepper would be used to season the inside of each half, and they would then be drizzled with a bit of olive oil. The heads would then be baked in a pan with more olive oil for approximately half an hour and served immediately with lemon halves.

TOMAXELLE | # VEAL ROLL-UPS

LIGURIA

1 oz. dried mushrooms, soaked in tepid water, drained, and squeezed dry

½ cup chopped flat-leaf parsley

Several sage leaves

1 sprig marjoram

The bread of a roll, without the crust, soaked in broth

¼ cup unsalted butter

⅓ lb. lean veal, parboiled and chopped

⅓ lb. veal breast, chopped

2 tbsp. grated Parmigiano-Reggiano

1 large egg, beaten

A few tbsp. milk

8 veal cutlets, pounded thin

2 tbsp. extra-virgin olive oil

1 cup chicken broth

Salt and pepper

Chop together the dried mushrooms, parsley, sage, and marjoram. + Put this mixture in a bowl and add the soaked bread (squeezed dry). + Heat half the butter in a pan, brown the chopped veal, and add to the mixture; add the veal breast, Parmigiano-Reggiano, and egg and stir the ingredients to combine them, adding a little milk as needed to bind the mixture. + Divide this stuffing among the slices of veal, then roll up each slice, and seal with a toothpick. + Heat the remaining butter and olive oil and brown the roll-ups. + When they are brown, add salt and pepper to taste, then pour in the broth, cover, and simmer over low heat 30 to 40 minutes. Serve at room temperature.

TORTINO DI PATATE E CARNE | POTATO AND MEAT PIE

ALTO ADIGE

3 tbsp. unsalted butter

⅓ cup olive oil

1 small onion, finely chopped

¾ lb. mixed boiled or roasted
meat (veal, beef, chicken),
cut in pieces

1 lb. potatoes, peeled,
sliced, and boiled

2 bay leaves

Pinch marjoram

1 tbsp. chopped flat-leaf parsley

Salt and pepper

Heat the butter and oil in a pan and sauté the onion until it turns golden. ✦ Add the meat, then the potatoes, bay leaves, and marjoram. ✦ Stir well, browning all the ingredients. ✦ Add the parsley and salt and pepper to taste, then using a wooden spoon work the mixture into the shape of a pie. Serve warm.

TRIPPA ALLA CAGLIARITANA | SARDEGNAN STEWED TRIPE

SARDEGNA

2 lbs. pork tripe

¼ cup extra-virgin olive oil

1 medium onion, finely sliced

2 lbs. plum tomatoes, peeled,
drained, and chopped

Pinch Sardinian saffron,
toasted and crumbled

6 mint leaves

Grated aged pecorino

Salt

Many believe that the best saffron comes from Sardinia, where it has long grown wild.

Clean the tripe and cut it in thin strips. ✦ Put the strips in a pan with lightly salted cold water to cover. Bring to a boil, then simmer at medium heat for about 2 hours. ✦ At the end of that time remove the pieces of tripe and set them aside to drain. ✦ Heat the olive oil and sauté the onion. Add the tripe and let it cook for a few minutes, stirring carefully, then add the tomatoes. Taste for salt and continue cooking for half an hour. ✦ Add the saffron and continue cooking with the pan uncovered until the tripe is perfumed, about 15 minutes. Just before serving add the mint leaves and season with pecorino.

MEAT & POULTRY

TRIPPA ALLA CAMPOBASSANA | TRIPE WITH POTATOES

MOLISE

2 ¼ lbs. veal tripe

2 medium onions

CONTINUED

This dish is typical of Campobasso.

After carefully cleaning the tripe, put it in a pan full of lightly salted boiling water. ✦ Add salt, an onion (halved), and the celery. ✦ When the tripe is tender, about 30 minutes, drain it well and cut into small cubes. ✦ Heat the

1 celery stalk

½ cup extra-virgin olive oil

1 slice prosciutto fat, minced

1 garlic clove, minced

¼ cup minced flat-leaf parsley

1 lb. ripe plum tomatoes, peeled and chopped

Grated pecorino

1 chili pepper (*diavolillo*, see note, page 22), chopped

Salt

olive oil in a pan, add the prosciutto fat, remaining onion (minced), garlic, and parsley and sauté for a minute. Add the tripe and toss to coat with oil. ✦ Add the tomatoes and cook 30 minutes, then serve the tripe immediately in the pan it was cooked in, dusting it with pecorino and *diavolillo*.

TRIPPA ALLA CANEPINA

TRIPE IN SAUCE

MARCHE

2 ¼ lbs. veal tripe

4 oz. *lardo*, minced

1 medium onion, minced

1 garlic clove, minced

1 celery stalk, chopped

¼ cup chopped flat-leaf parsley

1 carrot, chopped

Grated zest of 1 lemon

Pinch ground marjoram

4 oz. pork rind, parboiled

1 prosciutto bone

1 tbsp. tomato paste, diluted in 2 tbsp. warm water

Grated Parmigiano-Reggiano

Salt

Clean and rinse the tripe, then boil it in lightly salted water to cover; drain when half cooked and cut into pieces. ✦ In a saucepan (preferably terra-cotta), heat the *lardo* and sauté the onion, garlic, celery, parsley, carrot, and lemon zest. ✦ Add a pinch of marjoram, then add the tripe, pork rind, and prosciutto bone. ✦ Add the tomato paste mixture and salt and cook slowly for 2 hours, stirring frequently. When cooked, remove the prosciutto bone and serve with cheese.

TRIPPA ALLA CROTONESE

LAMB TRIPE
IN TOMATO SAUCE

CALABRIA

Several sprigs rosemary

1 ½ lbs. lamb tripe

¼ cup extra-virgin olive oil

1 medium onion, chopped

CONTINUED

This dish is typical of Crotone. For the wine use Cirò or Fiano.

Add the rosemary to a large pot of salted water and bring to a boil. Add the tripe and cook until it is tender. ✦ Drain the tripe and cut it in thin strips. ✦ Using a terra-cotta pan, heat the olive oil and sauté the onion, sage, and chili pepper; add the tripe. ✦ When all the

A few sage leaves
1 spicy chili pepper
¼ cup dry white wine
2 cups tomato purée
Salt

liquid has been cooked out of the tripe, add the wine. ✦ When the wine has evaporated, add the tomato purée. ✦ Taste for salt and cook at low heat until the sauce is thick, about 30 minutes.

| TRIPPA ALLA FIORENTINA | **TRIPE FLORENTINE-STYLE** |

TOSCANA

½ cup extra-virgin olive oil
1 medium onion, minced
2 lbs. tripe, cut in short sections about ½ inch wide
1 lb. ripe plum tomatoes or canned peeled plum tomatoes
2 or 3 tbsp. grated Parmigiano-Reggiano
Salt and pepper

True *Trippa alla Fiorentina* wants neither wine nor broth nor long and exhausting cooking. The only variation permitted is the addition of a carrot and a little chopped celery. If you use garlic and parsley instead of the celery and carrot, the dish you're making will become *Trippa alla Livornese*.

Heat the oil in a saucepan and sauté the onion; as soon as the onion pales, add the tripe. ✦ Brown, stirring often, for about 15 minutes, then add the tomatoes. ✦ Salt and pepper to taste and cook, covered, for about 40 minutes, or until the liquid has cooked down, leaving the tripe with a creamy consistency. ✦ Turn off the heat, sprinkle with Parmigiano-Reggiano, and let rest for 5 minutes. Serve the tripe with more Parmigiano-Reggiano. The tripe is even better a few hours later, reheated.

| TRIPPA ALLA MARCHIGIANA | **VEAL TRIPE IN TOMATO SAUCE** |

MARCHE

2 ¼ lbs. pre cooked veal tripe
1 oz. *lardo*
1 medium onion, finely chopped
1 celery heart, finely chopped
1 carrot, finely chopped
¼ cup chopped flat-leaf parsley
2 or 3 garlic cloves, finely chopped
Pinch ground marjoram
1 ½ lbs. plum tomatoes, peeled, seeded, and chopped
1 cup broth
Grated Parmigiano-Reggiano
Salt and pepper

Cut the tripe in long, narrow strips, then rinse in warm water many times and dry. ✦ Heat the *lardo* in a pan and sauté the onion, celery heart, carrot, parsley, and garlic. Add the marjoram. ✦ When the mixture has browned, add the tripe, season with salt and pepper, and cook at low heat for about 15 minutes; add the tomatoes and broth. ✦ Cover the pan and cook at low heat for about 1 hour. Serve hot, dusted with Parmigiano-Reggiano.

MEAT & POULTRY

TRIPE WITH TOMATOES AND PEPPERS

CALABRIA

2 ½ lbs. tripe
2 tbsp. extra-virgin olive oil
1 medium onion, finely chopped
1 celery stalk, chopped
1 lb. ripe plum tomatoes, seeded and sliced
2 lbs. red and yellow peppers, cored, seeded, and cut in thin strips
Salt

This dish is typical of Mormanno.

Cook the tripe in lightly salted water to cover until done; drain and allow to cool. ✦ Heat the olive oil in a saucepan and sauté the onion and celery. ✦ When these have browned add the tomatoes. ✦ Cook at low heat for about 15 minutes, then add the peppers. ✦ Taste for salt then cover the pan and simmer, stirring often. ✦ Cut the tripe in strips, add to the sauce, and continue cooking until the sauce has thickened. Serve piping hot.

TRIPE ALLA PARMIGIANA

EMILIA-ROMAGNA

2 lbs. beef tripe
1 sprig rosemary
A few sage leaves
1 bay leaf
2 celery stalks, chopped
¼ cup chopped flat-leaf parsley
2 garlic cloves
2 medium onions, chopped
⅔ cup lard, chopped
2 tbsp. unsalted butter
2 tbsp. olive oil
2 carrots, chopped
¼ cup tomato purée
Grated Parmigiano-Reggiano
Salt

Carefully clean and rinse the tripe. Add it to a large pot and add the rosemary, sage, bay leaf, half the celery, parsley, garlic, and half the onions. Add water to cover, season with salt, and then boil it for about 30 minutes. ✦ When cooked drain well, discarding the vegetables and cutting the tripe in strips. ✦ Heat the lard with the butter and olive oil in a saucepan. Add the carrots and the remaining onion and celery. ✦ When the vegetables have taken on a little color, add the tripe. ✦ Cook for about 15 minutes, then add a little water and salt to taste; after an hour add as much tomato purée as desired. ✦ The cooking should take a total of about 2½ hours. Serve with Parmigiano-Reggiano.

TRIPE IN TOMATO SAUCE

ABRUZZO

2 lbs. tripe, already boiled
2 tbsp. extra-virgin olive oil
CONTINUED

This dish is typical of Penne.

Cut the tripe in strips. Heat the olive oil and sauté the onion and celery. Add the tripe and cook. ✦ When browned, add the other ingredients (except the cheese);

1 medium onion, chopped

1 celery stalk, chopped

¼ cup chopped flat-leaf parsley

1 bay leaf

Several mint leaves, chopped

1 pepper, cored,
seeded, and chopped

1 sprig marjoram

¼ cup tomato purée

Grated Pecorino

cook for 2 hours. ✦ When cooked, season with pecorino and serve hot.

TRIPPA ALLA PISANA | # TRIPE PISA-STYLE

FOR
6 PERSONS

TOSCANA

½ cup extra-virgin olive oil

2 medium onions, finely chopped

1 celery stalk, finely chopped

2 carrots, finely chopped

2 garlic cloves, finely chopped

4 oz. pancetta, diced

2 ¼ lbs. veal tripe,
cooked in boiling water and
cut in small pieces

½ cup white wine

⅔ cup tomato purée

1 bouquet garni (flat-leaf parsley,
sage, bay leaves, basil, mint, thyme)

Beef broth (as needed)

½ cup grated Parmigiano-Reggiano

Salt and pepper

For the wine use Vernaccia di San Gimignano.

Heat the olive oil in a large pan and sauté the onions, celery, carrots, and garlic. Stir in the pancetta, and after a few minutes add the tripe. ✦ Add the wine and let it evaporate. ✦ Add the tomato purée and salt and pepper to taste. ✦ Add the bouquet garni and continue cooking, adding warm broth or warm water if needed; the sauce should cook down and the tripe should be very soft when cooked. Add the cheese and serve.

TRIPPA ALLA RAGUSANA | # TRIPE WITH EGGPLANT
AND WALNUTS

FOR
6 PERSONS

SICILIA

2 ¼ lbs. pre cooked tripe

1 tbsp. lard

5 tbsp. extra-virgin olive oil

2 or 3 cups broth

2 eggplants, cut in strips

CONTINUED

Clean and rinse the tripe well, dry it, and cut it in strips. ✦ Put the lard in a saucepan with 3 tablespoons olive oil. As soon as the oil begins to smoke add the tripe with a little salt and cook for a few minutes. ✦ Pour in the broth, lower the heat, and cook 1 hour. ✦ Meanwhile, in a separate pan, heat the remaining olive oil and brown the eggplant, and set aside. ✦ When the tripe is almost done

3 or 4 tbsp. grated caciocavallo

1 heaping tbsp. toasted and chopped almonds

1 tbsp. chopped walnut meats

Pinch ground cinnamon

Pinch sugar

Salt

(there should be only a little remaining sauce), add the caciocavallo and stir it in well; then add the eggplant, almonds, walnuts, cinnamon, and sugar. Stir, taste for salt, and serve piping hot.

TRIPE ROMAN-STYLE

TRIPPA ALLA ROMANA

LAZIO

2 lbs. cooked tripe

½ cup extra-virgin olive oil

4 oz. prosciutto (or ham) fat

½ medium onion, chopped

2 garlic cloves, chopped

½ carrot, chopped

½ celery stalk, chopped

½ cup dry white wine

2 lbs. plum tomatoes, peeled and seeded

2 tbsp. tomato purée

5 mint leaves (Roman mint if possible), chopped

⅔ cup grated pecorino

Salt and pepper

This dish is typical of Rome. For the wine use Frascati or Castelli Romani.

Rinse and dry the tripe and cut it into square chunks about 2 inches on a side. ✦ In an earthenware pot heat the olive oil and prosciutto fat, then sauté the onion, garlic, carrot, and celery. ✦ Add the tripe and wine and season for salt and pepper. ✦ Cook over moderate heat, stirring often with a wooden spoon. ✦ Add the tomatoes, tomato purée, and mint leaves. ✦ Cook until the tripe is still slightly chewy, rather than melt in the mouth. It is supposed (in the word of the experts) to "slither." Serve hot with pecorino.

TRIPE IN SPICED TOMATO SAUCE

TRIPPA COMODA

PIEMONTE

2 tbsp. extra-virgin olive oil

1 medium onion, minced

1 celery stalk, minced

1 sprig rosemary

2⅓ cups tomato purée

1 lb. tripe, finely chopped

1 tbsp. unsalted butter

Pinch ground cinnamon

1 tbsp. potato starch (if needed)

Salt and pepper

This dish is typical of Novara.

Heat the olive oil in a pan and sauté the onion, celery, rosemary, and tomato purée. ✦ Separately parboil the tripe in lightly salted water to cover for 15 minutes, then add it to the pan. Add the butter (not much since tripe is already fatty), a dusting of pepper, salt to taste, and cinnamon. ✦ Cook at moderate heat until tender, about 1 hour. If necessary, add a tablespoon of potato starch to thicken the sauce. Serve hot.

TRIPE WITH
CHILI PEPPERS

FOR
6 PERSONS

CALABRIA

1 ¼ lbs. cooked veal tripe,
cut in strips

½ celery stalk, chopped

1 carrot, chopped

½ medium onion, chopped

1 lb. potatoes (not mealy)

⅔ cup extra-virgin olive oil

2 red chili peppers
(best are the famous *diavuliddi*,
see note, page 22), chopped

Salt

Although you should use cooked tripe, parboil it again in lightly salted water to cover with the celery, carrot, and onion. ✦ Drain well and let it cool, discarding the vegetables. ✦ Boil the potatoes until tender, peel while still hot, and let them cool. ✦ Before serving, slice the potatoes and put them on a serving plate, delicately mixing in the pieces of tripe. ✦ Heat the olive oil in a pan and add the chili peppers. Pour over the tripe and potatoes while still sizzling. Serve the dish very hot.

TRIPPA DI MAIALE

TRIPE AND BEANS

FOR
6 PERSONS

PIEMONTE

1 ¼ cups dried white beans,
soaked in water for 12 hours

¼ cup (4 tbsp.) unsalted butter

2 oz. pancetta, diced

Sage leaves, chopped

1 medium onion, finely sliced

1 carrot, chopped

1 celery stalk, chopped

2 lbs. pork tripe,
cleaned and cut in pieces

1 lb. plum tomatoes,
peeled, seeded, and chopped

2 cups broth, or as needed

Grated Parmigiano-Reggiano

Salt and pepper

Drain the beans, put them in a pan with cold water to cover by several inches, and boil. ✦ Meanwhile, heat the butter in a saucepan and fry the pancetta and sage. Add the onion, carrot, and celery and cook for about 10 minutes. ✦ Add the tripe, stir, and cook off some of the liquid that will have formed. ✦ Add the tomatoes, salt, and pepper. ✦ Cook with the pan covered, at low heat, for about 2 hours, adding broth if necessary and stirring often to keep it from sticking to the bottom. ✦ After 1 hour drain the beans, add them to the pot, and finish cooking. ✦ Transfer to a serving bowl, sprinkle with Parmigiano-Reggiano, and serve hot.

MEAT & POULTRY

TRIPPA DI MAIALE AL
CIALDELETTO

BAKED TRIPE IN CRUST

UMBRIA

Preheat the oven to 400°F. Grease a baking dish with olive oil. ✦ Clean the tripe and trim away all fat. Boil the tripe in lightly salted water to cover for 30 minutes, then cut it in thin strips. ✦ Combine it with the olive oil, lemon

¾ cup extra-virgin olive oil
3 ¼ lbs. pork tripe
Juice of 1 lemon
1 tbsp. fresh breadcrumbs
2 tbsp. grated pecorino
2 tbsp. chopped marjoram

For the dough:
3 cups all-purpose flour
2 cups lard
Salt and pepper (or chili pepper)

juice, breadcrumbs, pecorino, and marjoram, then mix well. ✦ Meanwhile, mix the flour with the lard and season with salt and pepper or chili pepper. Knead until a smooth dough forms. Let rest 30 minutes, then roll out to a sheet large enough to line the baking pan, making certain it extends up the sides. ✦ Spread the tripe mixture into the pan and cover. Bake until the dough is golden, about 30 minutes.

UCCELLETTI SCAPPATI

VEAL "BIRDS"

TRENTINO

2 lbs. veal rump, cut into thin slices
Pancetta (or prosciutto)
10 sage leaves, or as needed
Juniper berries
¼ cup (4 tbsp.) unsalted butter
Salt

The name *Uccelli scappati* literally means "the birds that got away." They are on toothpicks "so they won't escape," someone says, interpreting *scappati* to mean "escaped," whereas perhaps it should be written *scapati*, meaning "headless." Serve with polenta made with cornmeal (page 318) or with buckwheat flour (page 324).

Cut the veal rump in thin slices (about ¼ inch), calculating 4 to 5 per person. ✦ Pound the slices flat with the side of a knife, salt them, and cover each with a slice of pancetta (or prosciutto), a sage leaf, and several juniper berries. ✦ Roll them up and close with a toothpick. ✦ Melt the butter in a pan and add the "fake birds," along with another 5 to 6 sage leaves. Brown the "birds" at high heat, then turn down the heat to complete the cooking.

UMIDO ALLA
MARCHIGIANA

VEAL STEW

MARCHE

1 ½ lbs. veal
2 oz. prosciutto crudo, diced
2 garlic cloves, minced
Grated zest of 1 lemon
6 oz. *lardo*
1 carrot, chopped
CONTINUED

For the wine use Rosso Conero or Sangiovese.

Using the tip of a knife, make incisions in the meat. ✦ In a bowl, mix the prosciutto, half the garlic, the lemon zest, and salt and pepper. ✦ Combine these ingredients and insert the mixture in the incisions in the meat. ✦ Tie up the meat with twine. Heat the *lardo* in a large pan over low heat and add the carrot, onion, celery, and remaining garlic, salt and pepper, and marjoram. ✦ Add the meat and brown on all sides. ✦ When the meat has

1 medium onion, chopped

1 small celery stalk, chopped

Pinch marjoram

½ cup red wine

2 ⅓ cups plum tomatoes, peeled and chopped

4 cups veal broth

¼ cup (4 tbsp.) unsalted butter

Salt and pepper

colored, pour in the wine, let it evaporate, then add the tomatoes. ✦ Add the broth, cover the pan, and cook at low heat for about 2 hours. Stir in the butter and serve immediately.

BEEF ROLL-UPS

EMILIA-ROMAGNA

1 lb. beef rump roast or chuck roast

1 slice prosciutto crudo

4 oz. ground veal

4 oz. ground chicken

⅔ cup grated Parmigiano-Reggiano

½ cup breadcrumbs

2 large eggs

½ cup all-purpose flour

¼ cup chopped flat-leaf parsley

Pinch nutmeg

½ cup (¼ lb.) unsalted butter

1 cup beef or veal broth

Pepper

This dish is typical of Reggio Emilia and Parma. A simple but very tasty dish can be made by using cabbage leaves in place of the beef. Another variation is the *Uccellini scappati* (see page 668), which should be made with slices of pork and pancetta. These roll-ups are usually held together with a toothpick. Another variation of this dish is made using pork liver.

Cut the beef in thin slices. Finely chop together all the remaining ingredients except the butter and the broth to form a paste. Spread the paste on one side of each slice. ✦ Tightly roll up each slice and tie closed with kitchen twine. ✦ Heat the butter in a pan and brown the roll-ups. Add the broth and simmer for about 30 minutes.

VITELLO ALL'UCCELLETTO

VEAL STEWED IN WINE

LIGURIA

1 lb. lean veal, in slices

2 tbsp. extra-virgin olive oil

1 tbsp. unsalted butter

1 garlic clove, crushed

2 bay leaves

¼ cup dry white wine

Fried potatoes (or artichoke slices)

Salt and pepper

For the wine use Pigato or Vermentino.

Tear the slices of veal into irregular pieces, put them in a pan with the olive oil, butter, garlic, and bay leaves, and cook over low heat. ✦ When the meat is almost cooked add salt and pepper and sprinkle with the wine, letting it partially evaporate. ✦ At the moment of serving mix in fried potatoes or, in season, thin slices of artichoke.

MEAT & POULTRY

CHAPTER
SIX

VEGETABLES

SCRAMBLED EGGS WITH PEPPERS

MOLISE

½ cup extra-virgin olive oil

1 medium onion, finely sliced

1 lb. bell peppers, washed, dried, core and seeds removed, and chopped

8 ripe plum tomatoes, peeled, seeded, and chopped

1 tbsp. chopped flat-leaf parsley

1 *diavolillo* (hot chili pepper see note, page 22), minced

Several basil leaves

8 large eggs, beaten

Salt

Heat the olive oil in a pan, add the onion, and sauté it at low heat; add the peppers. ✦ After a few minutes, add the tomatoes, parsley, *diavolillo*, and basil. Salt to taste and cook for about 10 minutes. ✦ When the sauce has become somewhat dense, add the eggs. ✦ As soon as the eggs set, bring the dish to the table in its cooking pot.

ASPARAGUS WITH FRIED EGGS

ASPARAGI CON LE UOVA IN CEREGHIN

LOMBARDIA

2 lbs. asparagus, woody ends trimmed

Grated Parmigiano-Reggiano

2 tbsp. unsalted butter

4 large eggs

This is best using asparagus from the Bassa Brianza, large stalks that are white up to a few inches from the end, which is first green and then reddish, tending to white.

Cook the asparagus upright in the basket of an asparagus pot or in a large saucepan with water to cover until bright green. Drain well and lay out on 4 plates. Sprinkle each generously with Parmigiano-Reggiano. Heat the butter in a pan, fry the eggs sunny-side up, and top each serving of asparagus with one so that the cheese melts.

ASPARAGUS WITH EGG SAUCE

ASPARAGI DI BASSANO CON SALSA DI UOVA SODE

VENETO

2 lbs. asparagus, woody ends trimmed

3 large hard-boiled eggs, shells removed, cut in half

2 tbsp. lemon juice, or as needed

1 cup extra-virgin olive oil

CONTINUED

The asparagus can be served very hot, in which case they can be dipped one at a time in the sauce in a bowl; or they can be cooled and then tossed with the sauce, decorating the plate with additional chopped egg whites.

Tie the asparagus stalks in small bunches and stand them up in a high, narrow pan. ✦ Add water to about two-thirds up the length of the stalks and simmer them until bright green (about 8 minutes). ✦ Meanwhile, make the sauce. Press the hard-boiled yolks through a

2 salt-cured anchovy fillets, chopped

1 tbsp. capers, rinsed and chopped

Salt and pepper

sieve. ✦ Stir in the lemon juice and then, stirring constantly, slowly drizzle in as much olive oil as necessary to obtain a somewhat fluid sauce. ✦ Chop the egg whites and add them to the sauce. Add the anchovies, capers, and pepper. ✦ Taste the mixture to make sure the salt and lemon are right.

BRAISED WILD ASPARAGUS

SICILIA

¼ cup extra-virgin olive oil

1 garlic clove, coarsely chopped

½ lb. asparagus tips
(the top 2 inches of the stalks)

½ cup white wine

1 tsp. tomato paste

Salt

Riddle: *"Mastru Tanu, chi faciti 'nta 'ssu chiànu? Non manciati e nun viviti e chiù longu vi faciti!"* ("Master Gaetano, what are you doing in that piazza? You don't eat, don't drink, and all the time just grow longer!") Answer: "I'm wild asparagus." Wild asparagus is the rarest and most precious gift surrendered by the stingy soil of Sicilia's coastline. It has a special, very pleasant bitter flavor.

In an earthenware pan, heat 3 tablespoons of the olive oil. Add the garlic, then add the asparagus tips. ✦ Lower the heat and stir the asparagus with a wooden spoon just to coat with oil. ✦ Add the wine and a few tablespoons of water, the tomato paste, and salt. ✦ Cover the pan so none of the bitter aroma will be lost and cook, checking to keep the asparagus from drying out (add more wine and a tiny amount of water if necessary). ✦ When the asparagus are cooked, about 5 minutes, dress them with the remaining olive oil and serve warm.

BROCCOLI NERI STUFATI

BRAISED BROCCOLI

MOLISE

1 head *broccolo nero* (or broccoli),
weighing about 2 lbs.

4 tbsp. extra-virgin olive oil

2 or 3 garlic cloves, slivered

Pinch chili pepper flakes

½ cup dry white wine

Salt

For the wine use Biferno or Trebbiano d'Abruzzo.

Cut away the hard leaves of the broccoli and core it. Cut off the florets; cut the big ones in half lengthwise and leave the smaller ones as they are. ✦ Heat the olive oil in a sauté pan and add the garlic; when it changes color, add the broccoli, salt, and chili pepper, adding a little water as needed. ✦ When the broccoli is cooked, add the wine and turn up the heat; when the wine has evaporated, serve the broccoli.

VEGETABLES

BRAISED BROCCOLI WITH VINEGAR

CALABRIA

2 lbs. broccoli
½ cup extra-virgin olive oil
2 or 3 garlic cloves
1 tbsp. white wine vinegar
Salt

This can be used to dress pasta (vermicelli), but in that case omit the vinegar and add, if desired, black pepper.

Clean and rinse the broccoli and select only the most tender florets. Rinse well.✦ Heat the olive oil in a pan and add the garlic. When they become transparent, add the broccoli dripping with water. Add a pinch of salt and put the lid on the pan. ✦ Cook at moderate heat, adding a ½ cup of water from time to time and stirring frequently. ✦ After about 30 minutes, pour in the vinegar and let it evaporate rapidly. Serve hot as a side dish.

STEAMED ARTICHOKES

SARDEGNA

7 artichokes
Juice of 1 lemon
¼ cup extra-virgin olive oil
1 medium onion, sliced
½ cup chopped flat-leaf parsley
Salt

Clean the artichokes, trimming off the pointed outer leaves and slicing off the stems; immerse them in water acidulated with lemon juice. ✦ Heat the olive oil in a sauté pan and add the onion; while it cooks, quarter the artichokes, then add them to the pan and sauté them at high heat. ✦ Pour in enough water to cover the artichokes, add the parsley, salt to taste, and cover. Let them cook at low heat until the water has evaporated, by which time the artichokes will be cooked without being overdone. Serve at room temperature. Eat only the tender leaves, leaving behind the fuzzy choke.

WINTER CAPONATA

SICILIA

12 artichokes
Juice of 1 lemon
Extra-virgin olive oil
2 carrots, cut into coins
2 celery stalks, chopped
6 scallions
6 medium onions, sliced
CONTINUED

Preheat the oven to 350°F. Cut the artichokes in thin slices and soak them in water with lemon juice. Heat a pot of water to boiling; this will be used several times and may need to be replenished. Heat ½ inch of olive oil in a pan. Parboil the artichokes and then fry them in the olive oil; set aside. ✦ Repeat with the carrots, celery, and scallions. Cook the onions in the olive oil until golden. ✦ Put the tomato purée in an ovenproof baking dish; add the vinegar, sugar, and salt, then add the cooked vegetables,

4 tbsp. tomato purée

1 tbsp. white wine vinegar

1 tsp. sugar

16 green olives, pitted

¼ cup capers

6 large eggs, hard-boiled and chopped

Salt

olives, and capers. Stir this to blend, stir in the eggs, and bake until heated through, about 8 minutes.

CAPONATA DI CARCIOFI | **ARTICHOKE CAPONATA**

SICILIA

8 artichokes, trimmed of the larger leaves, chokes removed

1 celery stalk, chopped

1 tbsp. extra-virgin olive oil

1 garlic clove, minced

½ cup raisins, soaked in warm water and drained

A few mint leaves

1 tbsp. sugar

½ cup white wine vinegar

½ cup pine nuts

Salt and pepper

Cook the artichokes in lightly salted boiling water until al dente, then remove, drain, and set aside. ✦ Boil the celery in lightly salted water until bright green and tender, drain. Heat the olive oil in a pan, and sauté the celery until lightly browned. ✦ Add the artichokes to the pan along with the garlic, raisins, pepper, and mint. Stir this for a few minutes, then add the sugar and let it caramelize, stirring constantly. ✦ Add the vinegar and cook it off, then add the pine nuts and serve warm or cold.

CAPONATA DI NATALE | **CHRISTMAS CAPONATA**

FOR 8 PERSONS

SICILIA

10 large heads celery, chopped

½ cup olive oil

1 lb. green olives, pitted and chopped

1¼ cups salted capers, rinsed

1⅔ cups raisins

½ cup white wine vinegar

¼ cup sugar

1⅔ cups chopped almonds, toasted

2 tbsp. breadcrumbs or crumbled toasted bread

Seeds of 1 pomegranate

Boil the celery in salted water, draining it when al dente. ✦ Heat the olive oil in a large pan and sauté the celery, olives, and capers. Add the raisins and let this cook a little while. ✦ Make the sweet-and-sour sauce by stirring the vinegar and sugar into the pan; bring this to a boil and evaporate the liquid at high heat. ✦ When this has cooked, add 1 cup of the almonds and the breadcrumbs. Arrange the mixture on a serving plate, and sprinkle with the remaining almonds and pomegranate seeds.

VEGETABLES

| # SICILIAN CAPONATA

4 firm medium-size eggplants, peeled, sliced, sprinkled with salt, and allowed to rest to lose the bitter taste, then cut into 1-inch cubes

4 green peppers, seeded and cut in cubes

1 head celery, chopped

4 plum tomatoes, peeled and cut in small dice

1½ tbsp. capers, rinsed

1 large onion, chopped

20 green olives, pitted and chopped

1½ tbsp. sugar

½ cup olive oil

¼ cup white wine vinegar

Salt

This makes a wonderful side dish and can also be preserved in sterilized glass jars (absolutely clean and dried in a hot oven); to do so you must, however, add 1 drop of salicylic acid for every 2 pounds of caponata.

Combine all of the ingredients except the vinegar in a large pan. Cover and cook at very low heat. ✦ When the vegetables have cooked for about 15 minutes, turn up the heat to medium; add the vinegar and cook until it evaporates. Serve immediately.

| # SWEET-AND-SOUR BRAISED CABBAGE

2 tbsp. unsalted butter

2 tbsp. olive oil

1 medium onion, chopped

1 or 2 garlic cloves

6 oz. speck, minced

1 good-size Savoy cabbage, cored and cut in strips

1 apple, cored and thinly sliced

2 tbsp. white wine vinegar

Broth (if needed)

¼ cup raisins (best if muscatel), plumped in boiling water and drained (optional)

Salt and pepper

This makes a good side dish to pork.

Heat the butter and olive oil in a sauté pan and sauté the onion, garlic, and speck, then add the cabbage and apple. ✦ When the cabbage has cooked down, lower the heat and add the vinegar, salt, and pepper and cook for 30 minutes. Add a little broth if necessary. ✦ For those who like sweet-and-sour flavors, add raisins. Remove the garlic before serving.

CARCIOFI AL FORNO | BAKED ARTICHOKES

BASILICATA

8 artichokes, cut in thin sections
2 tbsp. breadcrumbs
1 tbsp. minced fresh oregano
2 tbsp. chopped flat-leaf parsley
1 garlic clove
¼ cup olive oil
Salt

If desired, potatoes can be added to this recipe, cut in slices and sprinkled with grated cheese.

Preheat the oven to 400°F. Arrange the artichokes in an ovenproof sauté pan, sprinkle over them salt, bread-crumbs, oregano, parsley, garlic (which can be removed after cooking), olive oil, and ¼ cup of water. ✦ Put the pan over medium heat and cook a while to dry up some of the liquid and thus soften the artichokes, then transfer the pan to the oven and cook until the artichokes are easily pierced with the tip of a knife.

CARCIOFI ALLA CAVOUR | BAKED ARTICHOKES WITH EGG SAUCE

PIEMONTE

8 artichokes
½ cup (¼ lb.) unsalted butter, melted
Grated Parmigiano-Reggiano

For the sauce:
2 large hard-boiled eggs, shelled and chopped
¼ cup chopped flat-leaf parsley
2 anchovies, rinsed, boned, and chopped

Choose somewhat small, tender artichokes for this dish. Preheat the oven to 375°F. Clean the artichokes, remov-ing the outer leaves and scooping out the choke. Boil them in lightly salted water until al dente. ✦ Drain them well, drizzle them with half the butter, then roll them in Parmigiano-Reggiano. Arrange them in an ovenproof pan and bake for 10 minutes, until the butter is sizzling. ✦ Meanwhile, make the sauce. Chop the eggs, parsley, and anchovies together. Heat the remaining butter in a saucepan and when it is bubbly add the egg mixture. Stir well and immediately pour over the artichokes. Serve hot.

CARCIOFI ALLA GIUDIA | JEWISH-STYLE ARTICHOKES

LAZIO

4 large globe artichokes
1 lemon and its juice
4 cups extra-virgin olive oil
Salt and pepper

This dish is typical of Rome.

Remove the hard outer leaves from the artichokes, cut back the stems, leaving only 1 inch, and with a very sharp knife begin to shape the artichokes from the bot-tom upward, turning to remove only the hard part of the leaves; at the end each artichoke should be similar to a flower. Rub the artichokes all over with half a lemon and put them in a bowl of water acidulated with the juice. ✦ Drain the artichokes, dry them, and press them top-down against a hard surface to expand the leaves. Salt and pepper the insides. ✦ Heat the olive oil in a saucepan and when it is hot immerse the artichokes, stem up, and fry for about 10 minutes; turn them over and cook the other side for the same period. ✦ When they are cooked sprinkle them with a little cold water to draw out the olive oil and make them even more crisp. Drain on paper towels and serve hot.

VINE-ROASTED ARTICHOKES

CARCIOFI ALLA
MATTICELLA

LAZIO

½ bundle *matticella*
(vine shoots; see note)

4 garlic cloves, minced

5 sprigs mint, minced

½ cup extra-virgin olive oil

8 globe artichokes

Salt

Matticella is the small bundle of dried vine shoots considered indispensable for making the right kind of bed of embers, due to the fragrance it imparts. This dish is typical of Velletri and Rome.

Prepare a fire of dried vine shoots (or a charcoal grill). ✦ While this cooks down to embers, make the filling. Mix the garlic, mint, salt, and olive oil. Remove the tough outer leaves from the artichokes, cutting away the stalks to leave only about 1 inch. ✦ Pound the artichokes on a table so that the leaves separate, then stuff them with the filling ✦ Thus prepared, place them on the fire. ✦ They are cooked when the outer leaves turn a good brown color and are crisp. Serve hot.

ROMAN-STYLE ARTICHOKES

CARCIOFI ALLA ROMANA

LAZIO

2 tbsp. finely chopped
flat-leaf parsley

3 garlic cloves, finely chopped

3 bunches fresh mint,
finely chopped

1 cup extra-virgin olive oil

8 large globe artichokes

Juice of 1 lemon

Salt and pepper

This dish is typical of Rome and Lazio.

Combine the parsley, garlic, and mint in a bowl. Add 1 tablespoon olive oil and season with salt and pepper. ✦ Peel the external leaves off the artichokes, then use a knife to trim them from the bottom upward, removing the leaves and giving them a rounded shape; clean the stems. ✦ To prevent blackening soak them in water acidulated with lemon juice. ✦ Gently open the artichokes and with a teaspoon remove any of the central downy heart (the "choke"). ✦ Fill the interior with the prepared mixture. ✦ Close and arrange in tight rows in a wide pan with relatively high sides. ✦ Pour over them the remaining extra-virgin olive oil, then add water until they are nearly completely submerged. ✦ Cover the pan and cook over moderate heat until they are tender and the sauce has reduced. They can be served hot or cold.

CARDOONS WITH TRUFFLES

CARDI AL TARTUFO

PIEMONTE

For the cardoons:
¾ lb. cardoons
Juice of 1 lemon
3 tbsp. unsalted butter
Grated Parmigiano-Reggiano
4 large eggs, beaten
2 or 3 tbsp. heavy cream
1 white truffle, finely shaved
Salt and pepper

For the béchamel sauce:
3 tbsp. unsalted butter
2 tbsp. all-purpose flour
1 cup milk
Salt

This dish is typical of Alba.

Preheat the oven to 350°F. Clean the cardoons, eliminating all the outer fibers, hard outer leaves, and green parts. ✦ Cut the stalks in lengths of about 8 inches and boil them in salted water acidulated with lemon juice so they do not turn black. ✦ When they are tender, drain them and arrange them on a cloth to let them dry well. ✦ Meanwhile, use the butter, flour, and milk to prepare a béchamel sauce as in the recipe on page 339, cooking the butter and flour together to make a paste, then whisking in the milk and a pinch of salt, and set it aside. ✦ Heat the remaining butter in an ovenproof pan. Dice the cardoon stalks and sauté them. ✦ Dust them with Parmigiano-Reggiano and add salt and pepper to taste. ✦ Add the eggs to the pan and, immediately afterward, the béchamel sauce along with the cream to obtain a soft mixture; sprinkle with the truffle. ✦ Bake until the top is golden brown, about 20 minutes.

CARDOONS WITH EGG 1

CARDI ALL'UOVO

BASILICATA

2 lbs. cardoons
2 tbsp. extra-virgin olive oil
2 tsp. chili pepper flakes
3 large eggs, beaten
4 or 5 tbsp. grated pecorino
2 tbsp. chopped flat-leaf parsley

Clean the cardoons, cut them in ½-inch chunks, and boil them until tender. ✦ Remove them from the liquid, drain them, heat the olive oil in a pan, and sauté them. Sprinkle with the chili. ✦ Just before serving add the eggs to the pan along with the pecorino and parsley; stir this together quickly, then remove it from the heat to prevent the eggs from cooking too much. Serve piping hot.

VEGETABLES

CARDOONS WITH EGG 2

BASILICATA

3 lbs. cardoons, best if gathered
during the period of Easter
Beef broth
4 large eggs, beaten
Grated aged pecorino
Salt

This dish is typical of Atella.

Preheat the oven to 350°F. Clean the cardoons, saving only the ribs of the leaves. ✦ Boil these in salted water until tender, about 30 minutes. ✦ Arrange the cardoons in an ovenproof pan and pour in enough broth to half cover them, then bake until almost all of the broth has evaporated, about 45 minutes. Remove the pan from the oven and cover the cardoons with the eggs, salt to taste, and pecorino. ✦ Return the pan to the oven and bake until the eggs are set.

ABRUZZO-STYLE CARDOONS IN SAUCE

CARDI ALL'ABRUZZESE

ABRUZZO

3 lbs. large white cardoons
2 tbsp. olive oil or unsalted butter
½ cup white wine vinegar
2 tsp. sugar, or as needed
1 tbsp. all-purpose flour
½ cup heavy cream, or as needed
½ cup golden raisins
½ cup pine nuts
Salt

Boil the cardoons in salted water to cover until tender, then drain them and cut them in pieces. ✦ Heat the olive oil or butter in a pan, add the cardoons, and sauté. ✦ Sweeten the vinegar to taste with the sugar. When the cardoons have browned, sprinkle and toss with the flour. Add cream to cover, then the vinegar mixture. Add raisins and pine nuts, taste for salt, stir, and continue cooking to reduce the liquid to a creamy sauce. Serve hot.

CARDOONS GRATINÉE

CARDI GRATINATI

PUGLIA

3 lbs. cardoons
2 garlic cloves, chopped
1 bunch flat-leaf parsley, chopped
2 tbsp. extra-virgin olive oil
1 cup breadcrumbs
Salt and pepper

If desired, add some grated pecorino to the breadcrumbs before sprinkling them over the cardoons.

Preheat the oven to 400°F. Use the ribs and stalks of the cardoons, eliminating the leaves. Cut away any hard parts from the stalks and strip off the filaments and stringy parts. ✦ Cut the remaining sections into lengths of about 8 inches. ✦ Boil these in salted water until tender and, without draining them completely, arrange them in layers in a baking pan; season with garlic, parsley, pepper, olive oil, and breadcrumbs. ✦ Bake for 20 minutes, or until the breadcrumbs are golden.

CARDI IN UMIDO OR FRITTI

BRAISED OR FRIED CARDOONS

SICILIA

This dish is typical of Enna.

To braise:
12 cardoons
12 anchovy fillets
4 oz. pecorino, cut in short strips
2 tbsp. extra-virgin olive oil
1 medium onion, minced
Juice of 1 lemon
Salt and pepper

Clean the cardoons and boil them in lightly salted water. ✦ Drain well and let them cool. ✦ Stuff the cardoons with anchovies and cheese. ✦ Heat the oil in a pan, add the onion, and cook until it has taken on color. Add the cardoons, pepper, and lemon juice. Cook at low heat for several minutes until tender.

To fry:
Cardoons, as above
Olive oil, for frying
All-purpose flour for dredging
3 large eggs, beaten
1 cup breadcrumbs

Clean, boil, and stuff the cardoons as above. Heat several inches of olive oil in a deep pan. Dredge the cardoons in flour, dip them in the eggs and breadcrumbs, then fry until golden. Serve hot.

CAVOLFIORE ALLA FANESE

CAULIFLOWER AND OLIVES

MARCHE

1 cauliflower
4 anchovy fillets
2 tbsp. capers
2 tbsp. pitted black olives
¼ cup extra-virgin olive oil
Salt and pepper

Clean and core the cauliflower and boil it in lightly salted water to cover until al dente. ✦ Drain it and when it is cool enough to handle, cut it into pieces. ✦ Arrange these in a salad bowl, and add the anchovies, capers, and olives. ✦ Season with salt, pepper, and olive oil.

CIAMBOTTA

VEGETABLE STEW

BASILICATA

¼ cup extra-virgin olive oil

CONTINUED

Heat half of the olive oil in a large pan and when it is hot cook the eggplant until golden. ✦ Heat the remaining olive oil in a second pan and cook the potato and pepper

½ lb. eggplant, sliced and salted to drain the bitter taste, then rinsed

½ lb. potato, peeled and cubed

½ lb. sweet peppers, seeded, rinsed and dried, and cut in strips

1 ¼ cups tomato purée

1 garlic clove, chopped

Salt

until the potato takes on a little color, then add them to the eggplant. ✦ Add the tomato purée, garlic, and salt and stir. ✦ Cook at low heat for 1 hour, until the vegetables have formed a stew.

VEGETABLE STEW WITH CELERY

CIAMBOTTA

CALABRIA

1 tbsp. extra-virgin olive oil

1 medium onion, sliced

2 sweet peppers, sliced and seeded

3 potatoes, peeled and cubed

2 eggplants, peeled and sliced

2 plum tomatoes, peeled, seeded, and chopped

2 celery stalks, chopped

8 pitted green olives, chopped

Pinch chili pepper flakes

Basil leaves

Salt and pepper

Heat the olive oil in a pan and add the onion. ✦ As it colors, add the remaining vegetables. ✦ Add salt and pepper and chili pepper and cook at low heat, adding a little water if necessary. Serve hot, garnished with basil leaves.

ARTICHOKE AND FAVA BEAN STEW

CIAUREDDA

BASILICATA

¼ cup extra-virgin olive oil

2 medium onions, minced

6 oz. pancetta, diced

3 lbs. fresh fava beans, shelled

7 artichokes, trimmed and cut in 4 sections

3 medium potatoes, peeled and sliced

Salt

Heat the olive oil in a pan and add the onions and pancetta. When the onions change color, add the fava beans, artichokes, and potatoes. ✦ Salt and stir, then cover the pan and cook at low heat until the vegetables are tender, adding a little warm salted water if necessary. Serve hot.

CAROTE DI VITERBO IN BAGNO AROMATICO

Jams and preserves made with various vegetables cooked in sugar and flavored with exotic spices are an ancient tradition. In Viterbo, the local, and increasingly rare, purple carrots were especially prized not only for their intense violet color but also for their flavor as early as the fifteenth century—according to records from a local convent as well as recipes unearthed from libraries and archives. Important guests and dignitaries would often be served various *confeture* made from the famous local carrots, and history shows that they were included in meals served in Viterbo in honor of Giuseppi Garibaldi in 1876.

This preserve, made in the traditional manner, takes several days to prepare and requires a great deal of the rare purple carrots. Several pounds of the carrots—and it has been shown that even using ordinary orange or yellow carrots will produce an excellent result—would be cleaned, peeled, and briefly blanched in boiling water before being set out to dry in the sun for several days. After the carrots had reduced slightly in size and curled, they would then be covered with a generous amount of high-quality vinegar in an earthenware pan and left to soak for several days. The carrots would then be drained and the vinegar put into a cooking pot with cinnamon sticks, cloves, and nutmeg, along with a lot of sugar, and boiled down slightly. The carrots would be added back to the reduced vinegar and cooked briefly. This step would be repeated a few times until the liquid reached a syrupy density but the carrots still retained a bit of crunch. According to family tastes, occasionally other sweet ingredients, such as chocolate, pine nuts, raisins, or candied fruit, would be added. The finished confection would be poured into glass jars, making sure to fully submerge the carrots; historically it was kept in special earthenware jars and aged for years. Viterbo carrots were a favorite accompaniment to boiled meats.

DRUNKEN CAULIFLOWER

CIOFFA 'MBRIICA

ABRUZZO

3 lbs. cauliflower, cut in florets and rinsed

¼ cup extra-virgin olive oil

¼ cup white wine

2 bay leaves

2 garlic cloves

Chili pepper flakes, to taste

Salt

This dish is typical of Giulianova. For the wine use Trebbiano or Orvieto.

Put the ingredients in a pan and add enough water to cover them fully. + Cover the pan and slowly cook at low heat, stirring, until the cauliflower is tender, about 20 minutes.

SWEET-AND-SOUR ONIONS

2 tbsp. unsalted butter
1 tbsp. sugar
⅓ cup finely chopped pancetta
1 tbsp. white wine vinegar
1 lb. small white onions, peeled
Salt

This dish is typical of the area of Brianza.

Heat the butter and sugar in a pan, stirring until the sugar begins to darken. ✦ Add the pancetta, then immediately add the vinegar. Stir, then add the onions and a pinch of salt. ✦ Cover the pan, lower the heat, and let cook about 1 hour, by which time the onions should be completely cooked and caramelized, looking shiny and somewhat dark.

✦ **LOCAL TRADITION** ✦

CIPOLLINE D'IVREA

Ivrea onions have been renowned for their small size and fine, delicate flavor for centuries—so famous were they that the great Artusi himself would use them in his recipes. Connoisseurs prefer the nut-brown onions to the red-violet varieties, and most are no larger than hazelnuts. Once exported to cities all across Piemonte and farther-flung locales in Switzerland, France, Spain, and the Americas, they are famously used in this rustic glazed-onion side dish, a favorite accompaniment to braised or roasted meats. The peeled onions would be added to a hot pan to sauté in melted butter and olive oil; once they had achieved a nice color, salt and white wine would be added. After the wine evaporated, the onions would be glazed with the addition of sugar until caramelized. A few drops of broth or meat drippings could be used to soften the cooked onions.

POTATO PANCAKES WITH BLOOD SAUSAGE

For the pancakes:
3 large eggs
3 potatoes, peeled, cubed, and boiled
2 tbsp. olive oil
CONTINUED

Preheat the oven to 350°F. Separate one of the eggs and whisk the white until soft peaks form. Pass the potatoes through a sieve, then mix into them the remaining 2 whole eggs, 1 remaining egg yolk, and olive oil. Fold in the egg white. ✦ Cook this mixture in a pancake pan or other small pan, using ¼ cup batter per pancake and flipping to cook the pancakes on both sides. Keep them

For the filling:

4 potatoes, peeled and cubed

1 leek, chopped and rinsed well

2 tbsp. extra-virgin olive oil

2 links blood sausage (available in specialized food shops), chopped

Salt

warm. ✦ Make the filling by simmering the potatoes, leek, and olive oil in lightly salted water to cover until the potatoes are tender. Purée the mixture in a blender, then pass it through a sieve. ✦ Work this mixture together with the blood sausage and cook in a pan until the mixture is bubbling, about 20 minutes. Spoon the mixture over the pancakes and serve.

CUCULLI

POTATO BALLS

PIEMONTE

1½ lbs. potatoes

½ cup pine nuts

¼ cup unsalted butter

1 sprig marjoram, minced

2 tbsp. grated Parmigiano-Reggiano

3 large eggs (1 fewer than the number of diners)

Extra-virgin olive oil, for frying

1 cup breadcrumbs

Salt

Cuculli are often confused with *frisciêu* (see page 689) but differ because they include potatoes.

Boil the potatoes in water to cover until soft, then drain. ✦ When they are cool enough to handle, grind them in a mortar with pine nuts, butter, marjoram, and Parmigiano-Reggiano. ✦ Separately whip the egg whites until frothy. ✦ Add the egg yolks to the potato mixture and stir energetically with a wooden spoon to obtain a soft and creamy texture that is not too solid. ✦ Heat several inches of olive oil in a high-sided pan. Shape the potato mixture into balls, dip them in egg whites, then in breadcrumbs, and fry until golden. ✦ Drain on paper towels, sprinkle with salt, and serve.

ERBE DI CAMPO AL BURRO

FIELD GREENS IN BUTTER

FRIULI-VENEZIA GIULIA

2 tbsp. unsalted butter (or minced *lardo*)

1 or 2 garlic cloves

About 4 lbs. mixed field herbs: dandelion (*Taraxacum officinale*), corn poppy (*Papaver rhoeas*), hawkbit (*Leontodon hostilis*), maiden's tears or bladder campion (*Silene vulgaris*), thistle (*Cirsium arvense*), white campion (*Lychnis alba*), Venus' looking glass (*Specularia speculum*)

Salt and pepper

This should be served as a side dish traditionally on June 24, the feast day of St. John. No exact quantities can be given for the use of field herbs and greens. Mix those you have, taking into account their sweet or bitter flavors and aiming for a suitable final quantity.

Heat the butter or *lardo* and sauté 1 or 2 garlic cloves until golden. ✦ Cook the herbs in lightly salted water for a few minutes just until wilted. ✦ Drain them, let them cool, then roughly chop them. ✦ Add them to the pan. ✦ Add a little pepper and cook for about 30 minutes, or until tender.

| # BEANS AND GRAINS

LAZIO

1 lb. mixed dried legumes: beans, chickpeas, lentils, fava beans, farro

1 tbsp. finely chopped prosciutto fat

¼ cup finely chopped pancetta

small piece salame, chopped

2 tbsp. tomato paste

Slices of whole-wheat bread

For the salame try to use Genoa or Finoccchiona.

Soak the legumes in water for 1 day to soften them, then boil each type separately until tender. ✦ Heat the prosciutto fat, pancetta, and salame until lightly colored, then stir in the tomato paste. ✦ Add the legumes with a little of their cooking liquid and cook to blend the flavors. This should be served with slices of whole-wheat bread.

FAGIOLI CON PEPERONI SECCHI ARROSTITI | BEANS AND ROASTED DRIED PEPPERS

CALABRIA

½ lb. dried beans

4 dried red peppers, seeded and stemmed

Extra-virgin olive oil

2 garlic cloves, coarsely chopped

¼ cup coarsely chopped flat-leaf parsley

Salt

Soften the beans in water for 1 night, then cook them in lightly salted water until tender; drain off most of the liquid and pour into a salad bowl. ✦ Heat a grill or broiler until hot. Cook the peppers on a grill or under a broiler until puffy, turning them to cook all sides, then chop them and add to the beans. ✦ Season with salt and olive oil and flavor with garlic and parsley.

FAGIOLINI DELL'OCCHIO CON COTENNE | BEANS AND PORK

LOMBARDIA

1 lb. dried beans

2 tbsp. extra-virgin olive oil

1 tbsp. unsalted butter

½ oz. *lardo*

2 celery stalks, chopped

2 carrots, chopped

2 medium onions, finely sliced

2 garlic cloves, minced

½ cup tomato purée

1 lb. pork rind, parboiled and cut in ½-inch-strips

Grated Parmigiano-Reggiano

Salt and pepper

Soak the beans overnight, drain them, and then boil them in fresh lightly salted water to cover, taking them off the heat when almost tender. ✦ Heat the oil, butter, and *lardo* until hot; add the vegetables, 1 cup water, salt, and tomato purée. ✦ Add the pork rind and beans, along with a little of their cooking water. ✦ Cook for another 20 minutes and serve hot with a little pepper and Parmigiano-Reggiano.

FAGIOLI INFIASCATI

This recipe from Toscana for beans cooked in a glass flask should ideally be made with an authentic Chianti *fiasco* (with or without the straw), but any flask-shaped bottle with nothing attached to the inside will do. The dried cannellini beans would be soaked overnight and then poured into the bottle with sage, olive oil, a garlic clove, and salt and pepper, and the bottle filled only three-quarters full of water. Since it was to be put over heat and the water boiled, the bottle should be stoppered with a wad of cotton to allow any steam to escape. The bottle would then be set into smoldering embers in the hearth at a 45-degree angle. After an hour, the water would start to boil, and after two more hours the beans should be cooked—at which time a length of wire hooked on one end would be sent down the bottle to spear a single bean to test doneness. The beans would be carefully poured or shaken out of the bottle and into a bowl just before serving.

FAVA BEANS AND GUANCIALE 1

FAVE AL GUANCIALE

LAZIO

4 ½ lbs. fresh small fava beans
½ cup extra-virgin olive oil
1 medium onion, thinly sliced
1 cup diced guanciale
Salt and pepper

This dish is typical of Rome. Guanciale is cured pork cheek.

Shell and clean the fava beans and soak them in water until the moment of cooking. ✦ In a pan (best if earthenware), heat the olive oil and sauté the onion and guanciale. ✦ After a few minutes, add the fava beans, still damp, along with salt and pepper to taste. ✦ Cook 20 minutes at high heat, adding 1 tablespoon of warm water from time to time if necessary.

FAVA BEANS AND GUANCIALE 2

FAVE AL GUANCIALE

LAZIO

4 ½ lbs. fresh fava beans, best if not too large
½ cup extra-virgin olive oil

CONTINUED

If you use dried fava beans previously boiled, cook them for a shorter time and add a little dry white wine during the cooking. This dish is typical of Rome.

Shell the fresh fava beans and rinse them in running water. ✦ Heat the olive oil in a pan (best if earthenware) and add the guanciale. ✦ When this begins to color, add

VEGETABLES

6 oz. guanciale, diced

Salt and pepper

the fava beans with salt and pepper and continue cooking until the beans are tender, adding a little warm water from time to time if necessary. Serve hot.

FAVA BEANS AND ANCHOVIES

MARCHE

2 lbs. fresh fava beans, shelled

2 anchovy fillets, boned and chopped

2 garlic cloves, minced

Pinch marjoram

2 tbsp. white wine vinegar

¼ cup plus 2 tbsp. extra-virgin olive oil

Salt and pepper

Variations: parboil the fava beans in boiling salted water, then season them with garlic, olive oil, marjoram, and pepper; or season the beans with a sauce of chopped fresh chives, olive oil, salt, and pepper.

Cook the fava beans in a little lightly salted boiling water, draining them when al dente. ✦ Combine the anchovies, garlic, and marjoram, chopping to blend. Add the vinegar, olive oil, salt, and pepper to make a sauce and pour it over the drained favas.

FAVA BEANS IN VINEGAR SAUCE

CALABRIA

1¾ lbs. fava beans, shelled

2 tbsp. olive oil

2 garlic cloves

1 cup stale bread, crust removed

½ cup white wine vinegar

½ cup grated pecorino

1 cup fresh mint leaves

Using a sharp knife, cut away the fibrous edge of the beans without opening them, then rinse them and boil them whole in lightly salted water; drain and set aside. ✦ Heat the olive oil in a pan and add the garlic; when it changes color, add the beans and cook over low heat. ✦ Meanwhile, combine the bread, vinegar, cheese, and mint and work together well until blended ✦ When the beans are just tender, turn off the heat and add the bread sauce, blending and letting the dish rest before serving it hot or cold.

FAVA BEANS AND CHICORY 1

PUGLIA

This dish is typical of the area of Daunia. There are local variations of this recipe in several areas of Puglia. There are those who change the texture of the fava purée by adding a boiled potato. In other places the favas and chicory are worked together before being served. There are also those who drizzle the dish with *olio santo* (olive oil infused with spicy chili pepper).

1 ¼ cups dried fava beans

1 lb. chicory (if possible wild, can substitute escarole)

Extra-virgin olive oil

Salt

Soak the favas for at least 12 hours. ✦ Drain them and cook them for about 3 hours in lightly salted water at low heat. ✦ Separately cook the chicory in lightly salted boiling water until tender. ✦ Once cooked, the beans should be crushed, drizzled with olive oil, and mashed with a wooden spoon. ✦ Serve the mashed beans on a bed of chicory, drizzled with more olive oil.

FAVETTE E CICORIA | # FAVA BEANS AND CHICORY 2

BASILICATA

2 lbs. chicory

1 lb. dried fava beans

1 celery stalk, chopped

1 medium onion, chopped

2 tsp. chili pepper flakes

A few tbsp. extra-virgin olive oil

Slices of toasted bread

Salt and pepper

Cook the chicory in lightly salted boiling water. ✦ Cook the fava beans, celery, and onion in lightly salted boiling water to cover, then purée them in a blender and combine them with salt, pepper, chili, and enough olive oil to make a smooth purée. ✦ Drain the chicory when tender and season it with olive oil. ✦ Mix the chicory and favas and serve on toasted bread.

FRISCIÊU | # VEGETABLE FRITTERS

LIGURIA

3 ⅓ cups all-purpose flour

2 ¼ tbsp. active dry yeast

4 large eggs, beaten

Extra-virgin olive oil, for frying

2 lbs. mixed vegetables: lettuce, radicchio, *preboggion* (see page 292), cut in strips

4 large egg whites, beaten until frothy

2 cups breadcrumbs

Salt

This dish is typical of Genoa. Another classic variation of *friscêu* consists of using chickpea flour. This must be worked in warm water with 1 tablespoon active dry yeast. This batter, traditionally prepared the evening before use, must rest, rising, for the entire night. Before frying it, use a spoon to shape it into balls a little larger than a walnut, and add salt (not too much since it is better to sprinkle it on the hot *friscêu* in the plate) and minced (or dried) marjoram. Fry and serve.

Combine the flour, yeast, and eggs in a bowl, adding as much salt as desired. ✦ Combine with just enough water to make a batter, then let it rest 30 minutes until it has increased in volume. ✦ Heat several inches of olive oil in a deep pan until hot. Add the desired vegetables to the batter only at the last moment, then shape the batter into small balls (using a spoon), dip these in the egg whites, then in the breadcrumbs. ✦ Fry to a nice golden color. Drain on paper towels and serve hot.

BAKED OMELET WITH PORK AND POTATOES

FRITTATA
ALL'AMATRICIANA

ABRUZZO

2 tbsp. extra-virgin olive oil (or lard)

½ medium onion, finely sliced

4 oz. guanciale, cubed

2 potatoes, peeled, boiled, and finely sliced

10 large eggs, beaten

1 *diavolillo* (spicy chili pepper, see note, page 22)

Salt

Heat the olive oil (or lard) in a pan and add the onion. ✦ As soon as the onion changes color, add the guanciale and potatoes and stir well with a wooden spoon to keep the mixture from sticking to the bottom of the pan. ✦ After a few minutes, stir in the eggs, then add the *diavolillo* and a pinch of salt. Stir quickly, always using the wooden spoon. ✦ As soon as the eggs begin to set, shake the pan slightly to detach the frittata from the bottom, turn it over, and cook it on the other side. ✦ The heat should be kept high during all of these operations so that the frittata will be golden on the outside and soft on the inside and will not absorb too much fat. Serve the frittata immediately, while it is still hot.

SPRING VEGETABLES WITH VINEGAR

FRITTEDDA

SICILIA

2 tbsp. extra-virgin olive oil

3 small onions, finely sliced

2 lbs. mixed vegetables, divided equally among fresh peas, fava beans, and artichoke hearts, sliced

2 or 3 tbsp. white wine vinegar

2 tbsp. chopped flat-leaf parsley (optional)

Salt and pepper

In general, *frittedda* is more flavorful if eaten cold, even more so if allowed to rest for 24 hours before being eaten. Usually eaten as a one-dish evening meal, it can just as well serve as an antipasto or side dish.

Heat several cups of water to boiling. Heat the olive oil in a sauté pan; add the onions, mixed vegetables, salt, and pepper, and cook for a few minutes. ✦ Add the vinegar and stir constantly until it evaporates, then continue cooking, adding small amounts of boiling water as needed. ✦ The dish is finished when the mixture becomes creamy. If desired, finish with parsley.

WILD ONION FRITTERS

FRITTELLE DI CIPOLLINE
SELVATICHE

CALABRIA

¾ lb. muscari (wild onions; can use ramps or scallions if necessary)

1⅓ cups all-purpose flour

2 large egg yolks

CONTINUED

Remove the outer layer from the onions and cut them in short lengths. ✦ Parboil them a few minutes in lightly salted water, then drain and dry them. ✦ Prepare a batter, combining the flour, egg yolks, wine, a pinch of salt, parsley, and pepper. ✦ Stir with a wooden spoon to mix evenly. Add the tablespoon of olive oil and a little cold water, working with the spoon to obtain a somewhat dense

½ cup dry white wine

2 tbsp. finely chopped
flat-leaf parsley

1 tbsp. extra-virgin olive oil,
plus more for frying

Salt and freshly ground pepper

liquid. ✦ Let this rest about 10 minutes, then mix in the onions. ✦ Heat about ½ inch of olive oil in a high-sided pan. Drop in the batter by spoonfuls and fry until golden on both sides. Drain on paper towels and serve hot.

FUNGHI FRITTI | # FRIED MUSHROOMS

CALABRIA

1 lb. *lattaruli* (mushrooms)

½ cup extra-virgin olive oil

2 garlic cloves, minced

1 red or green pepper, seeded,
stemmed, and chopped

Salt

Clean the mushrooms, then chop them. Blanch them for 5 minutes in lightly salted boiling water. ✦ Drain and set aside. ✦ Heat the olive oil in a pan, add the garlic, and sauté; when it begins to color, add the mushrooms. ✦ Add the pepper and salt and finish cooking. The mushrooms should be lightly browned and wilted. Drain on paper towels and serve at room temperature.

GATTÒ DI PATATE | # POTATO AND CHEESE GALETTE

FOR
8 PERSONS

CAMPANIA

¼ lb. (1 stick) unsalted butter,
softened

5 tbsp. breadcrumbs

3 lbs. all-purpose potatoes

6 large eggs, beaten

½ cup grated Parmigiano-Reggiano

½ cup milk

6 oz. prosciutto, cubed

8 oz. mozzarella, in small cubes

4 oz. smoked provola, in small cubes

Salt and pepper

This dish is typical of Naples.

Preheat the oven to 350°F. Grease a 10- or 12-inch round cake pan with some of the butter and dust with some of the breadcrumbs. Boil the potatoes in salted water to cover until they are easily pierced with a knife. While they are still warm, peel them and put them through a food mill or sieve to purée them. ✦ Put the purée in a bowl and mix in the eggs, a pinch of salt, pepper, 6 tablespoons of the butter, Parmigiano-Reggiano, milk, and prosciutto. ✦ Spread half of the potato mixture into the prepared pan and cover it with mozzarella and provola. Cover with the remaining potato mixture, using a fork to spread it evenly and form a flat surface. ✦ Sprinkle with the remaining breadcrumbs, dot with the remaining butter, and bake for about 30 minutes, or until it has developed a nice brown color. ✦ Let the casserole rest for 15 minutes before serving.

CHICORY GALETTE

GLIË ZEPPOLONE

LAZIO

2 lbs. chicory or other wild greens

2 tbsp. olive oil

2 garlic cloves

1 bunch flat-leaf parsley, chopped

¼ cup chopped mint leaves

1 fresh chili pepper, minced

2 tbsp. white wine vinegar

¼ cup cornmeal

Salt and pepper

This dish is typical of Spigno Saturnia.

Clean the chicory or other greens well, roughly chop, and boil them in water to cover until tender. ✦ Wring them dry. Heat the olive oil in a pan and add the greens, garlic, parsley, mint, and chili pepper and season with salt and pepper. ✦ Sprinkle with vinegar. ✦ Stir in the cornmeal with a wooden spoon and cook for 2 minutes. ✦ Using a small pan lid, press down on the mixture to shape it into a large cake and brown it on both sides.

BRAISED CARDOON

GOBBO IN UMIDO

MARCHE

4 oz. *lardo*

1 medium onion, sliced

1 sprig fresh marjoram

1 cardoon, cut in strips and parboiled

¼ cup white wine

1 tbsp. tomato paste, dissolved in 2 tbsp. warm water

¼ tsp. ground cinnamon

Grated Parmigiano-Reggiano

Grated zest of 1 lemon

Salt and pepper

For the wine use Verdicchio or Trebbiano.

Heat the *lardo* in a pan over low heat until the fat is rendered, then add the onion and marjoram and cook until fragrant. Add the cardoon. ✦ Sprinkle with the wine. When the wine has evaporated, add the tomato paste mixture, salt, pepper, and cinnamon. ✦ Cook slowly and serve sprinkled with cheese and lemon zest to taste.

SCRAMBLED EGGS WITH ARTICHOKES

IMBROGLIATA DI CARCIOFI

LIGURIA

¼ cup extra-virgin olive oil

6 artichokes, cleaned and finely chopped

3 large eggs, beaten

½ cup grated Parmigiano-Reggiano

1 tbsp. unsalted butter

Salt and pepper

This dish is typical of Oneglia.

Heat the olive oil in a pan and add the artichokes. Cook for 5 minutes, then add the eggs, Parmigiano-Reggiano, and butter, stirring to scramble. Season with salt and pepper to taste. ✦ Cook for only a few minutes, until the eggs are just set.

| # CAPRI SALAD

1 lb. plum tomatoes,
sliced lengthwise

10 oz. *fior di latte* cheese
(preferably from Agerola or *treccia*
from Sorrento; fresh mozzarella
could also be used)

½ cup basil leaves,
whole or cut into strips

Extra-virgin olive oil

Salt

Use large, round plum tomatoes so that when sliced length-wise the slices of tomato will be almost as large as the slices of *fior di latte*. An even simpler method is to dice both the cheese and tomatoes and mix them with the olive oil in a salad bowl. In that case, serve with chopped basil.

On a serving plate alternate slices of tomato with those of *fior di latte*, overlapping them; top with basil leaves. ✦ At the table each diner should season the salad with olive oil and salt to taste.

INSALATA CON SPECK | # BITTER GREENS SALAD WITH WARM BACON DRESSING

4 heads red radicchio or 2 of
curly endive, outer leaves removed

1 tbsp. extra-virgin olive oil

6 oz. speck (or pancetta), diced

2 tbsp. white wine vinegar

Salt and pepper

Rinse the radicchio and dry it well; place in a serving bowl. ✦ Heat the olive oil in a sauté pan and add the speck; heat over low heat to render the fat. ✦ When the speck turns golden yellow, stir in the vinegar. ✦ Use this sauce to season the salad, adding salt and pepper to taste. Serve immediately.

INSALATA DI CICORIA DEI
PRATI ALLA PANCETTA | # DANDELION AND PANCETTA SALAD

2 oz. pancetta, in small dice

8 small bread rounds

About 8 cups (1 lb.) dandelion
greens, cleaned and dried

2 tbsp. red wine vinegar
(or as much as desired)

2 large hard-boiled eggs, sliced

Salt

This local recipe is very old and is shared with Switzerland and Savoy.

Cook the pancetta in a skillet at low heat without burning it. ✦ When all the fat has melted, remove the pancetta from the pan, add the bread rounds, and brown them. ✦ Toss the bread and the fat from the pan with the dandelion. Sprinkle with vinegar, salt, and hard-boiled eggs. Serve warm.

VEGETABLES

| # CHRISTMAS SALAD

SICILIA

About 8 cups chicory

2 lbs. celery, chopped (about 8 cups)

⅓ cup olive oil

2 tbsp. capers, well rinsed

1 tbsp. green olives, pitted and chopped

Orange slices, for garnish

Lemon slices, for garnish

Seeds from 1 pomegranate

The quantities of the ingredients can be changed, but use chicory and celery in equal quantities.

Separately boil the chicory and the celery until tender, drain them, and let them cool. ✦ Mix them and season them with olive oil, capers, and olives. ✦ Arrange this on a serving plate and decorate with orange and lemon slices. Sprinkle with pomegranate seeds.

INSALATA DI OLIVE VERDI SCHIACCIATE | # SALAD OF CRUSHED OLIVES

SICILIA

1 lb. green olives

⅔ cup chopped celery leaves

⅔ cup chopped mint leaves

3 tbsp. extra-virgin olive oil

1 tbsp. white wine vinegar

Salt

A variation calls for the addition of some spicy chili pepper cut in tiny pieces.

Crush the olives, removing their pits, and set them aside to soften in water for 3 days, changing the water every day. ✦ At the end of this time put the olives in a salad bowl and add the celery leaves and mint. Season with olive oil, vinegar, and salt and serve.

✦ **LOCAL TRADITION** ✦

INSALATA DI LAMPASCIONI

This rustic salad recipe from Basilicata uses the *lampascioni*, the bulb of the wild hyacinth. To prepare the salad, first the outer leaves must be cut away. The bulb would then be thoroughly cleaned and soaked for a day in several changes of cold water. On the next day, the *lampascioni* would be boiled and then left to cool in the water. Once cool, it would be drained and seasoned with salt, pepper, vinegar, olive oil, and parsley, tossed, and served as a refreshing salad.

EGGPLANT ROLL-UPS

4 medium-size eggplants
1 cup fresh tomato purée
¾ cup grated Parmigiano-Reggiano
1 cup extra-virgin olive oil
4 oz. crustless bread
1 tbsp. or more grated pecorino (optional)
1 garlic clove, finely chopped
½ cup chopped flat-leaf parsley
1 large egg, beaten
Salt and pepper

Peel the eggplants, cut them in slices that are not too thin, salt them, and set them aside for an hour to lose their bitter taste. ✦ Preheat the oven to 400°F. Cover the bottom of a baking dish with some of the tomato purée, sprinkle the purée with 2 tablespoons of the Parmigiano-Reggiano, and set aside. ✦ Rinse and dry the eggplant slices. Heat ½ cup olive oil in a pan and add the egg-plant. Cook until lightly browned, then set them out on paper towels to drain away the grease. ✦ Prepare the fill-ing: combine the bread with ½ cup of the Parmigiano-Reggiano (and the pecorino if desired), garlic, parsley, egg, salt, and pepper. ✦ Work this together well with the remaining olive oil to make a dense and moist mixture. ✦ Distribute this filling on the slices of eggplant, roll them up around it, and arrange them in the prepared baking dish. ✦ Cover with more of the tomato purée and dust with the remaining Parmigiano-Reggiano. ✦ Bake for 10 minutes, until golden.

PEPPER ROLL-UPS

¼ cup olive oil
2½ lbs. peppers
6 oz. stale bread, soaked in milk and squeezed dry
3 large eggs, beaten
1⅔ cups mozzarella, cut in small bits
1¼ cups Emmental, cut in small bits
1 cup prosciutto cotto, minced
½ cup grated Parmigiano-Reggiano
¼ cup basil, torn in small pieces
½ cup breadcrumbs
Salt and pepper

This dish is typical of Naples.

Preheat the oven to 350°F. Lightly grease a baking pan with olive oil. Roast the peppers over a flame, skin them, and cut each one in half, removing the seeds. ✦ Com-bine the bread with the eggs and all the other ingredients (except the breadcrumbs). ✦ Divide this mixture in equal parts among the pepper halves and wrap them up around it. ✦ Arrange these roll-ups in the baking pan, dust with breadcrumbs, and bake for about 20 minutes, or until the filling is hot. Let rest 10 minutes and serve warm.

VEGETABLES

LAMPASCIONI FRITTI

For this recipe from Basilicata, the *lampascioni* (wild hyacinth bulbs) would be cleaned, scored lightly, and rinsed under cold running water to remove some of the bulbs' characteristic bitterness. After rinsing, the bulbs would be parboiled to mellow the flavor further, and then drained. A second cooking in fresh water would soften them until tender. Once they were tender, the *lampascioni* would be dredged lightly in flour, then in a beaten egg, and again in breadcrumbs and fried till golden in a little olive oil. The fried *lampascioni* then needed only a little salt before being served hot.

LARDARI AL POMODORO

LARDARI WITH TOMATOES

CAMPANIA

1 lb. *lardari* (see note)
2 tbsp. olive oil
1 garlic clove, chopped
¼ cup chopped basil leaves
2 or 3 plum tomatoes, peeled, seeded, and chopped
Salt

This dish is typical of Salerno. *Lardari* are large green beans that get their name from lard: it was once common custom to boil them and then fry them along with basil and salt in lard. Giant fava beans can be used instead.

Cook the *lardari* in a pan with boiling water to cover until tender. Drain very well. ✦ Heat the olive oil in a pan and add the garlic. Cook until it turns light brown, then add the basil, tomatoes, salt, and *lardari*. ✦ When a uniform sauce has formed, remove the pan from the heat and serve.

LUNETTE DI PATATE

POTATO CRESCENTS

FRIULI-VENEZIA GIULIA

1¾ lbs. potatoes, peeled
2 tbsp. unsalted butter
1 large egg yolk
⅓ cup all-purpose flour
Olive oil, for frying
Coarse salt

Boil the potatoes, drain them, then crush with a potato ricer or sieve. Add salt. ✦ When the purée has cooled, add the butter and egg yolk. ✦ Next, blend the flour into the mixture and work this into a soft dough. ✦ Roll out the dough into cylinders about the length and width of a pinky and curl them to form *lunettes* (crescents). ✦ Heat 1 inch of olive oil until moderately hot, add the *lunettes*, and fry for about 20 minutes, until they swell up and have taken on a golden color. Drain on paper towels and serve them warm sprinkled with coarse salt.

MARINATED LETTUCE

1 head lettuce
1 garlic clove, minced
1 small, fresh, mildly hot chili pepper, chopped
2 tbsp. extra-virgin olive oil
½ tsp. sea salt

Serve this dish, which is typical of Cosenza, as you would any normal salad. The lettuce wilts as it becomes infused with the marinade but retains some refreshing crispness. Choose a sturdy type of lettuce such as frisée (curly endive), romaine, or green leaf.

Separate the leaves of the lettuce. Rinse well, drain, and dry it as best as possible. ✦ Tear the lettuce into bite-size pieces. Place the lettuce in a large bowl and toss with the garlic, chili pepper, and salt. Drizzle with the oil. ✦ Set a plate, just smaller in size than the bowl, on top of the salad. Then place a weight, such as a large heavy jar or can, on top of the plate to apply pressure. Place this in the refrigerator for a few hours. Toss the lettuce again before serving.

✦ **LOCAL TRADITION** ✦

LAMPASCIONI IN AGRODOLCE

Sweet-and-sour muscari is another rustic dish from Basilicata that makes use of the *lampascioni*, or the bulb of the wild hyacinth. In this dish, it would be cleaned and parboiled as is common to remove most of its bitterness and to tenderize it. Two peeled, seeded, and chopped plum tomatoes would then be lightly cooked in a hot pan with olive oil; after a few minutes, the muscari would be added and crushed with a fork. Sugar, vinegar, and salt would follow and be cooked together for a few minutes to make a true *agrodolce*.

VEGETABLES

EGGPLANT BOATS

3 eggplants (about 1 ½ lbs.)
2 tbsp. breadcrumbs
CONTINUED

Cut the eggplants in half lengthwise, scoop out the pulp, and set it aside. ✦ Salt the hollowed halves and set them out to dry in the sun for several hours. ✦ Preheat the oven to 350°F. Meanwhile, chop up the eggplant pulp and mix with salt, breadcrumbs, parsley, salame, provola,

⅓ cup chopped flat-leaf parsley
½ lb. salame, diced
½ lb. provola, diced
⅔ cup grated pecorino
1 or 2 large eggs, beaten
½ cup olive oil
5 tbsp. tomato purée
Salt

pecorino, and eggs. Heat half the olive oil in a pan and cook the eggplant halves until golden; place in a baking pan. Heat the remaining olive oil in the same pan and cook the pulp mixture until the eggs are just set. ✦ Fill the halves with the pulp mixture; pour the tomato purée over them. ✦ Bake for 30 minutes, or until the sauce is bubbling and the stuffing is browned.

FRIED EGGPLANT SANDWICHES

MELANZANE A BECCAFICO

SICILIA

4 eggplants (about 2 lbs.)
1¼ cups pecorino, cubed
6 oz. salt-cured anchovies, rinsed and chopped
Basil leaves
Olive oil, for frying
2 large eggs, beaten
Salt

This dish is typical of Enna.

Trim and peel the eggplants, and cut them lengthwise to form ¼-inch-thick slices, trying for an even number of slices. ✦ Sprinkle with salt and set them aside to dry for about 1 hour. ✦ At the end of that time, wipe the slices dry, and set them on a work surface. On half of the slices arrange a filling composed of a few cubes of the pecorino, a small amount of the anchovies, and a leaf of basil. ✦ Cover each of these with another slice of eggplant and secure each sandwich with a toothpick. ✦ Heat 1 inch of olive oil in a sauté pan over medium heat until hot. Dip the sandwiches in the eggs, then fry them. ✦ Turn to cook on the other side until golden. Remove the toothpicks and serve hot.

TWICE-FRIED EGGPLANT SANDWICHES

MELANZANE A BECCAFICO

SICILIA

3 eggplants (about 1½ lbs.)
Olive oil, for frying
7 oz. (about 1¼ cups) tuma (soft, tangy cheese), cubed
6 oz. salt-cured anchovies, rinsed and chopped
1 bunch basil
4 large eggs, beaten
Salt

Trim and peel the eggplants and cut them lengthwise into ¼-inch-thick slices, trying for an even number of slices. ✦ Salt them and set them out to dry for about 2 hours. ✦ Wipe the slices dry. Heat ⅛ inch olive oil in a pan. Fry the eggplant on one side only. ✦ Lay out half the slices with the cooked side down and arrange across them equal quantities of the cheese, anchovies, and basil leaves; cover each with another slice, cooked side up. Secure these "sandwiches" with toothpicks. ✦ Heat ½ inch of olive oil in a sauté pan over medium heat until hot. Coat the sandwiches with egg, then fry them in the olive oil until they are golden brown, turning them very carefully. Remove the toothpicks and serve piping hot.

MELANZANE
A FUNGHETTO

FRIED EGGPLANT WITH TOMATO SAUCE

CAMPANIA

3 lbs. eggplant (about 6 medium)
Extra-virgin olive oil, for frying
2 garlic cloves, chopped
1 cup fresh chopped tomato
¾ cup chopped basil leaves
Salt

This dish is typical of Naples. There are no mushrooms in this dish; instead, eggplant is cooked as though it were mushrooms. A variation calls for the addition (along with the tomato sauce) of rinsed capers and pitted olives.

Trim and rinse the eggplants, dry them with a cloth, and without peeling them cut them into ½-inch cubes. ✦ Put these in a colander and sprinkle with salt. After about half an hour, the eggplants will have given up most of their liquid; squeeze them slightly to dry them. ✦ Heat ½ inch of olive oil in a high-sided pan until hot, then deep-fry the eggplant pieces, a few at a time. ✦ When they begin to brown, lift them out of the pan with a skimmer or slotted spoon and set them on a plate lined with paper towels so the excess oil will drain off. ✦ Pour out the olive oil from the pan, leaving enough to cook the garlic. ✦ When the garlic begins to darken, add the tomatoes to the pan and, after 2 to 3 minutes, the eggplant. ✦ Salt to taste, turn off the heat, and add the basil. Serve warm.

MELANZANE AL FORNO

BAKED EGGPLANT

BASILICATA

2 lbs. eggplant (about 4 medium)
1 stale roll, crust removed
1 cup pitted black olives
1 bunch flat-leaf parsley, chopped
4 oz. salt-cured anchovies, rinsed and chopped
½ cup capers, rinsed and chopped
Pinch oregano
2 ripe plum tomatoes, peeled, seeded, and chopped
Extra-virgin olive oil
Salt

Peel the eggplants, cut them in half lengthwise, and make several lengthwise incisions in the pulp. ✦ Salt them and set them out to dry for 1 hour. ✦ Preheat the oven to 400°F. Crumble the bread into a bowl and mix in the olives, parsley, anchovies, capers, and oregano. ✦ Rinse the eggplant halves, dry them well, and arrange them in an ovenproof pan with the cut side up. ✦ Cover each half with some of the filling, topping it with some tomatoes. ✦ Drizzle with olive oil, then bake for about 1 hour, or until tender.

VEGETABLES

EGGPLANT AND SAUSAGE

MELANZANE
ALLA FINETESE

CALABRIA

2 lbs. eggplant (about 4 medium)
6 oz. provolone, thinly sliced
6 oz. spicy cured sausage,
thinly sliced
Olive oil, for frying
3 or 4 large eggs, beaten
All-purpose flour for dredging
Salt

Cut the eggplants into ¼-inch slices and parboil them in lightly salted water until tender, about 8 minutes. ✦ Dry the slices and set them out on a work surface in pairs. ✦ Cover half of each pair with slices of provolone and sausage, then cover with the remaining eggplant slices. ✦ Heat 1 inch of olive oil in a high-sided pan. Dip the paired slices in egg, then in flour, then fry them in olive oil until golden.

EGGPLANT AND MINT

MELANZANE ALLA MENTA

CALABRIA

3 eggplants (about 1½ lbs.)
¼ cup extra-virgin olive oil
6 fresh mint leaves, chopped
1 tbsp. white wine vinegar
3 tbsp. breadcrumbs
Salt

Trim off the ends of the eggplants, then cut them in four parts lengthwise. ✦ Scoop out a little of the pulp, then slice the quarters to create short sticks about ¼ inch thick. ✦ Heat 1 inch of olive oil in a pan and fry until golden. Lift them out of the oil and set aside on paper towels to drain, sprinkling with salt. ✦ Pour out most of the oil, leaving only a few tablespoons, then add the mint to the pan and cook it for a few minutes. Return the eggplant sticks to the pan and add the vinegar. ✦ Stir well to blend, then add the breadcrumbs to soak up some of the cooking liquid. Serve cold.

EGGPLANT BRAISED WITH TOMATOES

MELANZANE
ALLA PARMIGIANA

EMILIA-ROMAGNA

4 firm eggplants, peeled
(about 2 lbs.)
2 tbsp. unsalted butter
2 tbsp. extra-virgin olive oil
1 medium onion, finely sliced
3 oz. prosciutto crudo,
cut in cubes
⅔ cup tomato purée

Cut the eggplants in long, lengthwise slices and simmer in water to cover until slightly wilted. ✦ When cooked, drain them well and set them aside to dry, if possible on a cutting board in the sun. ✦ Heat the butter and olive oil in a pan; add the onion and cook until it changes color. Add the prosciutto crudo and brown it. ✦ Add the tomato purée and eggplant slices. ✦ Cook this at low heat for about 1 hour until the eggplant is soft, then serve.

MELANZANE SOTT'ACETO

This recipe for pickled eggplant comes from Calabria. The eggplants are cleaned, trimmed, peeled, cut into long strips, and salted in a large bowl for a few hours to remove excess liquid and bitterness. Once squeezed dry, the strips are covered with white wine vinegar and set aside again. After a couple of hours in the vinegar, the strips are once again squeezed to remove any excess vinegar and layered into terra-cotta vases between fresh mint leaves and the shoots of wild fennel. They are then pressed down gently and covered with olive oil and aged for at least two months.

**MELANZANE
DAI CENTO SAPORI**

100-FLAVOR EGGPLANT

CALABRIA

2 lbs. eggplant (about 4 medium)

3 tbsp. sugar

4 tbsp. white wine vinegar

1 oz. unsweetened chocolate, chopped

¼ cup walnuts, chopped

¼ cup pine nuts

Pinch ground cinnamon

½ cup raisins, soaked in warm water, then drained

1 tbsp. grated citron zest (can use lemon)

¾ cup extra-virgin olive oil

Salt

Trim and peel the eggplants, then cut them into small cubes. ✦ Put these in a saucepan with the sugar, vinegar, chocolate, walnuts, pine nuts, cinnamon, raisins, and citron zest. ✦ Add the olive oil, salt to taste, and stir to blend. ✦ Cook at medium-low heat until the eggplant is soft.

MELANZANE E POMODORI

EGGPLANTS
AND TOMATOES

CALABRIA

4 eggplants (about 2 lbs.)

4 large eggs, beaten

CONTINUED

Clean the eggplants and cut them in small cubes. ✦ Put the cubes in salted water for about 1 hour. ✦ Meanwhile, mix the eggs and pecorino and set aside. ✦ Rinse and drain the eggplant cubes. Heat ¼ inch of olive oil in a high-sided pan and fry the eggplant cubes until golden.

VEGETABLES

2 tbsp. grated pecorino

Olive oil

4 plum tomatoes,
peeled, seeded, and chopped

Salt

✦ Add the tomatoes and egg mixture and stir to cook the eggs until they are set. Serve immediately.

MELANZANE RIPIENE | # STUFFED EGGPLANTS

PUGLIA

Extra-virgin olive oil

4 medium-size eggplants
(about 2 lbs.)

8 plum tomatoes,
peeled, seeded, and chopped

2 garlic cloves, chopped

12 black olives, pitted and chopped

1 dried chili pepper

½ cup capers, rinsed

Pinch oregano

½ cup breadcrumbs

½ cup tomato purée

Salt

This dish is typical of Brindisi.

Preheat the oven to 400°F. Grease a baking pan with olive oil. ✦ Cut the eggplants in half lengthwise and scoop out the pulp. ✦ Chop the pulp into small pieces. Heat about ¼ inch of olive oil in a pan and cook the tomatoes and garlic. ✦ When cooked, add the black olives, chili pepper, capers, and oregano. ✦ Meanwhile, cook the scooped-out eggplant halves in one of two ways: boil them in lightly salted water or fry them lightly until pale golden in olive oil. ✦ Arrange the cooked halves in the prepared pan, then fill them with the pulp mixture; sprinkle with breadcrumbs, brush with olive oil, and cover each with a tablespoon of tomato purée. ✦ Bake for 20 minutes, basting with the cooking liquid halfway through that time if necessary. ✦ Heat the broiler and broil for 5 minutes, or until the breadcrumbs are browned. Let cool slightly before serving.

✦ **LOCAL TRADITION** ✦

MELANZANE SOTT'OLIO

Another recipe for eggplant comes from Le Marche, where the eggplants would be sliced into rounds, or if smaller, segments. Instead of salting the eggplants first, the vinegar would be brought to a boil in a cooking pot, perhaps diluted with water just enough to cover the sliced eggplant. The eggplant rounds would then be added to the boiling vinegar along with salt and nearly cooked through. While still firm, the eggplant rounds would be removed from the vinegar and dried on a cloth for about thirty minutes. Once dry, the eggplant would be placed into glass jars along with chopped parsley and topped with olive oil, a bay leaf, a garlic clove, and a single anchovy fillet. After steeping for about two weeks, the pickled eggplant would be ready to eat.

MISTICANZA

Misticanza is a dialect term from Lazio simply meaning mixed greens dressed in olive oil, vinegar, salt, and pepper. The basic ingredient is wild greens gathered from springtime fields in the Lazio: field chicory, *crespigno* (or *crespino* or *lattuga pungente*), *caccia-lepre, cresta di gallo, dente di leone* (or *pisciacane* or *tarassico*), *pimpinella, raponzoli* (or *rapenzoli*), *erba noce* (or *erba San Pietro*: costmary), *cipiccia* (*lattughetta* or *radicchiello*), *valeriannella* (*dolcetta*), *papala* (poppy plant), *cordone del frate, orecchio d'asino*, and so on. It is still possible, with a little experience, to assemble the ingredients from any field outside Rome or in the Colli Cimini; one can also often find *misticanza* at fruit and vegetable stands. It appears on menus all over, particularly in Rome. When sold in stores, fresh garden greens are used, with cultivated *righetta* (arugula) as the base of the salad along with *riccioletta, scarola, punarelle di catalogna, indivia, radicchi, chicory da taglio* (or *cicorne*), the *barba di frate*, fava buds, and so on.

MORZI | # PEAS WITH SAUTÉED BREAD

PUGLIA

1 lb. dried peas
1 medium onion, sliced
2 plum tomatoes, peeled, seeded, and chopped
1 bunch flat-leaf parsley, chopped
Extra-virgin olive oil
6 oz. stale bread, cut in cubes
Salt

To the peasants of the Salento area *morzi* (Italian: *morsi*, "bites") were pieces of stale bread fried in olive oil and combined with leftover vegetables (boiled or stewed). All this was stirred together over heat with a good dose of chili pepper. Sometimes a bay leaf was added to render the blend more digestible. This preparation is typical of Martano.

Soak the peas in cold water for 12 hours. ✦ Drain them and put them in an earthenware pan, cover with water, and cook over medium heat. ✦ After 15 minutes, drain the peas, discarding the water, then return them to the pan and add enough warm water to cover them. ✦ Add the onion, tomatoes, parsley, and salt. ✦ Cook at low heat, adding water from time to time as needed, until the beans are tender. ✦ Heat ¼ inch of olive oil in a pan and sauté the bread cubes until golden. Add them to the peas, stirring to blend. Let this cook together a few moments, then serve hot.

VEGETABLES

| **FRIED BROCCOLI RABE**

1 ¾ lbs. broccoli rabe

¼ cup extra-virgin olive oil

3 oz. pork belly (or bacon), diced

½ garlic clove

Pinch chili pepper flakes

1 lb. stale peasant-style bread, in small cubes

Salt

This dish is typical of Marcianise.

Cook the broccoli rabe in lightly salted boiling water until very bright green; drain and dry well. ✦ Heat the olive oil in a pan and cook the pork belly, garlic, and chili pepper. ✦ Remove and discard the garlic when it darkens and add the broccoli rabe. ✦ Cook this for 5 minutes, then add the bread cubes and cook at high heat until the liquid is absorbed.

✦ **LOCAL TRADITION** ✦

MOSTARDA MANTOVANA

Difficult to find commercially, *mostarda mantovana,* or Mantuan *mostarda,* is the only correct cooked-fruit sauce for filling *tortelli di zucca* (see page 417) and differs from most other varieties by being composed entirely of apples and by its cooking method. To prepare true *mostarda mantovana,* first peel, core, and slice the apples and let stand covered with sugar in a container for 48 hours. The resulting mixture is then briefly boiled and then fried in olive oil in a cast-iron skillet while still warm. A small amount of mustard syrup is added to the fried apples and the mixture transferred into sterilized glass jars, sealed, and processed through a pressure canner. Besides being used to fill *tortelli di zucca, mostarda mantovana* is also a common accompaniment to boiled or roasted meats.

| **EGGPLANT PARMIGIANA 1** | FOR 8 PERSONS

This is the version of this dish most famous outside of Italy. To remove the excess oil from the eggplant slices after frying set them out in a colander for 1 hour. Alternatively, you could use the mixed procedure: half fried in oil, half roasted. Doing so diminishes the amount of fat in the dish while maintaining the traditional Neapolitan flavor.

2 lbs. eggplant (about 4 medium)
½ cup extra-virgin olive oil
1 medium onion, sliced
2 lbs. tomato purée
1 bunch basil
5 oz. *fior di latte* cheese
or mozzarella, cubed
⅔ cup grated Parmigiano-Reggiano
Salt

Trim the ends of the eggplants, peel them, and slice them. ✦ Salt them and set them aside for half an hour to lose their bitter taste; rinse and pat dry. ✦ Preheat the oven to 400°F. In a saucepan, heat 2 tablespoons olive oil. Add the onion and cook until translucent. Add the tomato purée, salt, and a few basil leaves, then cook down at very low heat until thickened. ✦ Meanwhile, heat the remaining olive oil in another pan, cook the eggplant slices a few at a time, and drain well. ✦ Pour some of the tomato sauce into a baking dish and cover it with a layer of the fried eggplant slices along with cubes of *fior di latte*, basil leaves, and Parmigiano-Reggiano. ✦ Cover with more sauce and make another layer of eggplant, *fior di latte*, basil, and Parmigiano-Reggiano, ending with a layer of tomato sauce and Parmigiano-Reggiano. ✦ Bake until the surface is crisp. Serve at room temperature.

✦ **LOCAL TRADITION** ✦

'NDUGGHIA DI CASTROVILLARI

This recipe from Calabria is a rustic single-dish meal in which the *'ndugghia di* Castro-villari (*'ndugghia* is from the French *andouille* and here refers to a similar spicy pork sausage) is boiled in a pot of lightly salted water. After boiling, the sausage is removed, cut into pieces, and set aside; any fat is skimmed off of the surface and mixed with greens (commonly chicory, wild fennel, and cardoons) and fresh beans are cooked in the same water. The sausages are then nestled into the hot, cooked vegetables and served together.

VEGETABLES

PARMIGIANA
DI MELANZANE 2

EGGPLANT
PARMIGIANA 2

PUGLIA

Zucchini can be used in place of the eggplant. The procedure to follow remains the same, but the zucchini should be sliced lengthwise. Mortadella can be used in place of the sausage, arranged in slices to make a single layer.

1 lb. eggplant (about 2 medium)

Extra-virgin olive oil

All-purpose flour for dredging

2 large eggs, beaten

1½ cups tomato purée

¾ cup cubed mozzarella

⅓ cup crumbled cooked sausage meat

¾ cup grated Parmigiano-Reggiano

Salt

Preheat the oven to 350°F. Peel the eggplants, cut them lengthwise in thin slices, then salt and drain for 20 minutes. Rinse and pat them dry. ✦ Heat ½ inch of olive oil in a high-sided pan. Dip the eggplant slices in flour and egg and fry until golden on both sides. ✦ Cover the bottom of an ovenproof pan with a thin layer of tomato purée and cover this with a layer of fried eggplant. ✦ Add mozzarella, a little sausage meat, and more tomato purée. ✦ Sprinkle with Parmigiano-Reggiano, then make another layer of eggplant, continuing the layers until the ingredients are used up, ending with a layer of tomato purée and Parmigiano-Reggiano. Bake until the top is golden brown, about 20 minutes.

✦ **LOCAL TRADITION** ✦

OVOLI IN FRICASSEA

From Calabria comes this mushroom fricassee cooked with garlic, parsley, and eggs. First the mushrooms—traditionally "Caesar's mushrooms" (*Amanita caesarea*)—would be cleaned and cut into pieces. Cloves of garlic would be lightly sautéed until they just begin to brown in olive oil, then the mushrooms would be added, followed by salt, pepper, and parsley. Once the mushrooms were cooked, three beaten eggs would be added to the dish and lightly cooked just until set. The warm mushrooms and eggs would be spritzed with fresh lemon juice and could be served hot or cold.

PARMIGIANA
DI MELANZANE 3

EGGPLANT PARMIGIANA 3

SICILIA

4 eggplants (about 2 lbs.)

Extra-virgin olive oil

1 garlic clove

8 ripe plum tomatoes, peeled, seeded, and chopped

CONTINUED

Clean the eggplants without peeling them, cut them in thin slices, and sprinkle them with salt for at least 30 minutes to make them lose their bitter liquid. ✦ Preheat the oven to 350°F. Grease a baking dish with olive oil. Heat 2 tablespoons olive oil in a pan and add the garlic. When golden, add the tomatoes and cook until reduced to a thick sauce. Stir in the sugar. ✦ Rinse the salt off the eggplants and dry them. Heat 1 inch of olive oil in a

1 tsp. sugar

4 large hard-boiled eggs, sectioned

6 oz. tuma (a soft, tangy cheese), cut in cubes

1 bunch basil

1 cup grated caciocavallo

Salt and pepper

high-sided pan and fry the eggplant slices until they are golden and crisp. ✦ Set them out on paper towels to drain. ✦ Spoon a few tablespoons of tomato sauce across the bottom of the baking dish; over this arrange a layer of eggplant, eggs, tuma, basil leaves, caciocavallo, and more sauce. ✦ Continue with these layers to end with a layer of eggplant, using the last of the caciocavallo to cover the top. ✦ Bake for about 10 minutes. Serve at room temperature or even cold.

PASTICCIO DI VERDURE

VEGETABLE PIE

VALLE D'AOSTA

4 tbsp. unsalted butter

⅔ cup minced onion

1¾ lbs. green beans or fresh peas

1 slice pancetta (about 5 oz.)

1¾ lbs. potatoes, peeled and thinly sliced

1 tbsp. chopped basil

1 tbsp. thyme leaves

1 tbsp. savory

1 celery stalk, chopped

Salt

This is a classic single-dish meal for summer Sundays, put on the stove in the morning and slowly cooked in its cast-iron pan to be ready at noon when the head of the household returns from High Mass. One variation includes the use of a little tomato sauce, only enough to color the dish (blended into the cooking water). In Vartney the dish is made without potatoes. Serve with slices of cotechino or Valdostan sausage, cooked separately.

Heat the butter in a saucepan or cast-iron skillet and sauté the onion until translucent. ✦ Add the green beans (or peas), pancetta, and potatoes. ✦ Add a little salt, the herbs, and celery. ✦ Add just enough water to cover and cook slowly for 1 or 2 hours, by which time the water should have cooked away.

PATATE AL TARTUFO

TRUFFLED POTATOES

PIEMONTE

1 lb. potatoes

2 tbsp. unsalted butter

1 white truffle

1 heaping tbsp. grated Parmigiano-Reggiano

Juice from 1 lemon

Salt and pepper

This dish is typical of Alba.

Boil the potatoes in lightly salted water until al dente; drain. ✦ When cool enough to handle, peel and slice them. ✦ Heat the butter in a pan until hot. Add the potatoes and sauté them, stirring them delicately so as not to break them. ✦ When they are well browned, shave the truffle over them, then add salt and pepper and Parmigiano-Reggiano. ✦ Finish them with a squeeze of lemon juice and serve at room temperature.

VEGETABLES

POTATO AND TRUFFLE GRATIN

PATATE CON I TARTUFI

MARCHE

Unsalted butter

2 lbs. potatoes

1 recipe béchamel sauce (see page 339)

½ cup grated Parmigiano-Reggiano

Shaved truffle

Preheat the oven to 350°F. Grease a baking dish with butter. Peel the potatoes and slice them in thin rounds. ✦ Arrange some of these across the bottom of the baking dish. ✦ Pour a layer of béchamel sauce over the potatoes, dust with Parmigiano-Reggiano, and follow with truffle shavings. ✦ Repeat this operation layer by layer, ending with a layer of truffles. ✦ Bake until the potatoes are cooked, about 40 minutes.

POTATO AND BEAN STEW

PATATE E FAGIOLI

BASILICATA

1 lb. dried beans, soaked overnight and drained

1 celery stalk, chopped

1 garlic clove

1 tbsp. lard

1½ lbs. potatoes, peeled and coarsely chopped

Salt

Put the beans, celery, garlic, salt, and lard in an earthenware pot. Add water to cover and simmer at low heat. ✦ When the beans are almost tender, about an hour and a half, add the potatoes and simmer until the potatoes are cooked through, another 20 minutes.

POTATOES AND PEARS

PATATE E PERE LESSE ALLA VALDOSTANA

VALLE D'AOSTA

¾ lb. potatoes, peeled and chopped in pieces

2 oz. pancetta

1 bay leaf

3 medium-firm pears (preferably St. Martin), halved and seeded

4 tbsp. unsalted butter

1 medium onion, finely sliced

Salt

This dish is typical of the valley of Gran San Bernardo. You may use another type of pear, but preferably one that is fragrant and has a red skin.

Boil the potatoes in water with the pancetta and bay leaf until cooked through; drain well and set aside. ✦ Cook the pears in lightly salted boiling water just until tender, about 10 minutes, and drain well. ✦ Heat the butter in a large pan; add the onion and cook until golden. Pour the onions over the cooked potatoes, then add the pears and toss gently to mix.

PAN-FRIED POTATOES

FRIULI-VENEZIA GIULIA

2 lbs. potatoes
4 tbsp. lard
1 medium onion, thinly sliced
4 oz. pancetta, diced

This dish is typical of Trieste, where it is called *patate in tecia*. Boil the potatoes until tender, peel them, and set them aside. ✦ Heat the lard in a cast-iron skillet and when it liquefies, add the onion and pancetta. Cook until the pancetta has taken a little color. ✦ Add the potatoes, crushing them with a fork and working them to blend with the other ingredients. ✦ When the potatoes have browned on one side, turn them over to brown on the other. Serve hot.

CRUSHED POTATOES

PATATE SCHIACCIATE

CALABRIA

1 lb. potatoes
2 tbsp. extra-virgin olive oil
1 garlic clove
1 dried chili pepper
Salt

Boil the potatoes in lightly salted water until tender. ✦ Drain them and when cool enough to handle, peel them and crush them. ✦ Heat the olive oil in a pan and cook the potatoes in a pan with the garlic for 10 minutes. ✦ Add the chili pepper and cook 5 minutes longer over medium heat. Remove the garlic and chili pepper and serve hot.

CALABRIAN PEPPERS

PEPERONI
ALLA CALABRESE

CALABRIA

8 peppers
2 tbsp. extra-virgin olive oil
1½ cups chopped plum tomatoes
Salt and pepper

Roast the peppers over a gas burner until completely black. Place in a plastic bag, seal, and let steam for 15 minutes. Skin them, remove their seeds, and cut them in strips. ✦ Heat the olive oil in a pan and add the tomatoes. ✦ Cook at moderate heat for about 15 minutes, then add the peppers and salt and pepper. Stir, then serve immediately.

VEGETABLES

SPICY STUFFED PEPPERS

MOLISE

4 meaty peppers

2 tbsp. extra-virgin olive oil

1½ cups breadcrumbs

7 fillets salt-cured anchovies, rinsed, boned, and chopped

2 tbsp. chopped flat-leaf parsley

2 tbsp. chopped basil leaves

1 fresh chili pepper, seeded and diced

⅔ cup tomato purée

Salt

Preheat the oven to 350°F. ✦ Roast and peel the peppers as in the recipe on page 712. ✦ Trim off an inch from the stem end, scrape out the seeds and any internal membranes, and dry them. ✦ Make the filling. Heat the olive oil in a pan and toast the breadcrumbs until just browned, stirring with a wooden spoon. ✦ In a bowl, mix the breadcrumbs, anchovies, parsley, basil, chili pepper, and a little salt. ✦ Stuff this mixture into the peppers, drizzle with olive oil, and arrange them in a terra-cotta pan. ✦ Pour the tomato purée over them, adjusting for salt and adding a little water. ✦ Bake for 1 hour, basting the peppers from time to time with the cooking liquid. Serve hot.

✦ **LOCAL TRADITION** ✦

PATATE LESSE SFRITTE

This simple recipe for fried boiled potatoes comes from Basilicata. The potatoes would first be boiled, drained, and roughly crushed with a fork, then added to hot oil in a skillet that had been flavored with a dried spicy chili pepper. While the potatoes fried, they would be crushed further, almost to a coarse purée, to absorb the seasonings. Additional chili pepper, salt, and parsley would be added toward the end of cooking for a brighter flavor.

PEPPERS STUFFED WITH EGGPLANT

CAMPANIA

4 yellow or red peppers

¼ cup extra-virgin olive oil

2 medium eggplants, diced

1 garlic clove

CONTINUED

Preheat the oven to 400°F. Roast the peppers and skin them as in the recipe on page 712. Cut the peppers in half and scrape away the seeds. ✦ Heat half of the olive oil in a sauté pan and add the eggplant. Cook until golden, then remove from the pan and set aside. ✦ Add the remaining olive oil to the pan and cook the garlic (later discarded), tomato purée, and salt. ✦ Add the oregano

2 cups tomato purée
1 tbsp. chopped oregano
1 tbsp. chopped basil
⅓ cup capers, rinsed
½ cup pitted Gaeta olives, chopped
2 or 3 tbsp. breadcrumbs
Salt

and basil. ✦ Add the eggplant, stirring for a few minutes. ✦ Add the capers and olives. ✦ Remove from the heat and stir in just enough breadcrumbs to bind the ingredients. ✦ Stuff the roasted peppers with this mixture, then arrange them in a baking pan. ✦ Brush the filling with olive oil and season with salt. ✦ Bake for about 30 minutes, or until the filling is lightly browned. Serve at room temperature.

STUFFED PEPPERS CAPRI-STYLE

PEPERONI IMBOTTITI
ALLA CAPRESE

CAMPANIA

4 large peppers
¾ lb. bucatini pasta
2 tbsp. extra-virgin olive oil, plus more as needed
1 garlic clove
1½ cups tomato purée
⅓ cup pitted black olives, chopped
⅓ cup capers, rinsed
4 salt-cured anchovies, rinsed and chopped
¼ cup chopped flat-leaf parsley
½ cup breadcrumbs (optional)
Salt and pepper

Preheat the oven to 450°F. Roast the peppers until the skin has bubbled. Then place them in a plastic bag and let the peppers steam 15 minutes. Peel them, slice off the tops, and scrape out the seeds. Reduce the oven temperature to 350°F. ✦ Cook the bucatini in lightly salted boiling water until very al dente. ✦ Meanwhile, heat the olive oil in a pan, add the garlic, and cook until it turns light brown. Remove the garlic and add the tomato purée to the pan. ✦ Cook this at low heat for 10 minutes, then add the olives, capers, anchovies, and a little salt and pepper. ✦ After a few minutes, add the parsley. ✦ Drain the bucatini and dress with the tomato sauce. ✦ Stuff the peppers with the bucatini mixture and arrange them in a baking pan. Drizzle with olive oil, season with a little salt, and top with breadcrumbs (if desired). ✦ Bake for 30 minutes.

SWEET-AND-SOUR STUFFED PEPPERS

PEPERONI IN AGRODOLCE

SICILIA

8 round pickled peppers
10 oz. crustless stale bread, crumbled
1 cup extra-virgin olive oil
2 garlic cloves, chopped
¼ cup chopped flat-leaf parsley
½ cup golden raisins

CONTINUED

Choose firm, fleshy peppers for this recipe. Cherry peppers can be used, but you may have to use more peppers to accommodate all of the stuffing.

Trim off the tops of the peppers and remove the seeds. ✦ Mix the bread, ⅓ cup olive oil, garlic, parsley, raisins, capers, and olives. Use this mixture to stuff the peppers. Heat the remaining olive oil in a large pan, add the peppers, and cook at medium heat, closely watching them. ✦ When the undersides of the peppers have browned thoroughly (about 10 minutes), very carefully turn them

⅓ cup capers, rinsed

¾ cup pitted Gaeta olives

2 tbsp. *vino cotto* or *saba* (wine "cooked" down to a sweet syrup)

upside down to cook the top until the stuffing is golden. ✦ Turn them back over, add the *vino cotto*, and let cook another 10 minutes.

STUFFED PEPPERS WITH TUNA

PEPERONI RIPIENI 1

PIEMONTE

2 peppers, roasted and peeled (see recipe)

4 oz. mozzarella, cubed

3 oz. ricotta, cut in small pieces

½ tbsp. grated Parmigiano-Reggiano

2 oz. canned tuna, drained and crumbled

1½ salt-cured anchovies, rinsed, boned, and chopped

2 tbsp. chopped flat-leaf parsley

2 sage leaves, chopped

3 tbsp. tomato purée, sweetened with ½ tsp. sugar

½ tsp. red wine vinegar

2 basil leaves, chopped

Pinch oregano or thyme

1 large egg plus 1 yolk

A few tbsp. breadcrumbs (to bind the filling)

2 tbsp. extra-virgin olive oil

Salt

This dish is typical of Asti.

To roast peppers: You may cook them either directly over the flame of a gas stovetop burner, or, less efficiently, in an oven preheated to 450°F. Use tongs to turn the peppers occasionally and cook until the skin is completely blistered and blackened. Place in a plastic bag or small container and seal. Let the peppers steam this way for 15 minutes. Gently rub off the skin, leaving some of the charred membrane underneath if you like, for flavor. Cut the peppers in half and remove the seeds. Set aside. ✦ Lower the oven to 400°F. Make the stuffing by combining all the ingredients (except the olive oil) and blend well. ✦ Stuff the pepper halves and arrange them in a baking pan. Add the olive oil and ¼ inch of water to the pan. Cover with foil and bake 20 minutes. Remove the foil and bake until the stuffing is cooked through and golden, about 10 minutes more. Serve hot or at room temperature.

STUFFED PEPPERS

PEPERONI RIPIENI 2

PUGLIA

Extra-virgin olive oil

4 large peppers (preferably yellow)

1¼ cups breadcrumbs

2 tbsp. grated pecorino (preferably from Puglia)

1 tbsp. chopped flat-leaf parsley

CONTINUED

Preheat the oven to 375°F. Grease a baking pan with olive oil. Cut the tops off the peppers (setting aside the tops with their stems to serve as lids) and remove the seeds; rinse and dry them and set upside down to drain. ✦ Heat 2 tablespoons olive oil in a pan, add the breadcrumbs, and toast until golden. Mix the breadcrumbs, pecorino, anchovies, parsley, olives, and capers; mix in just enough olive oil to bind. ✦ Stuff this mixture into the peppers and close them with their stem-lids. ✦ Arrange

4 anchovies, rinsed,
boned, and chopped
½ cup pitted black olives, chopped
¼ cup capers, rinsed,
dried, and chopped

them in the baking pan. Drizzle them with more olive oil and bake them for about 25 minutes. These can be eaten hot or cold.

PEPERONI RIPIENI 3

STUFFED PEPPERS WITH CACIOCAVALLO

SICILIA

Extra-virgin olive oil
4 large peppers
1 ½ cups breadcrumbs
¼ cup chopped basil
½ cup grated caciocavallo
2 tbsp. capers, rinsed
4 ripe plum tomatoes,
peeled, seeded, and chopped
4 salt-cured anchovies,
rinsed, boned, and chopped
Salt and pepper

Preheat the oven to 400°F. Grease a baking pan with olive oil. Cut off the tops of the peppers. With the tip of a small, sharp knife scrape away the seeds and inner membranes of the peppers, being careful not to break them, then set them aside. ✦ Briefly toast the breadcrumbs in a dry pan until golden brown. In a bowl, mix them with salt, pepper, basil, caciocavallo, capers, tomatoes, and anchovies. ✦ Add a few tablespoons olive oil to bind, then stuff the mixture into the peppers. ✦ Put them in the baking pan and drizzle with oil. Cover the pan with a sheet of aluminum foil. Bake for 15 minutes, then remove the aluminum foil and continue cooking for 10 minutes, adding more olive oil if necessary. Serve at room temperature or cold.

PEPERONI SOTT'ACETO

PICKLED PEPPERS

CAMPANIA

Cherry peppers
White wine vinegar

Cherry peppers are a variety of small, sweet peppers with a meaty flesh that are grown in the area of Avellino. They are almost always red and are roundish in shape with a circumference of 4 to 4½ inches. When preserved in vinegar they are called in the Avellino dialect *papaccelle* or *pepaine*. They are easy to make at home. Cut in strips, they make a side dish to roast pork, cooked sausages, and cod and are also an ingredient in many traditional dishes.

You will need a large-mouthed container made of enameled terra-cotta. Buy enough peppers to fill the container, choosing those that are firm and free of scratches. ✦ Rinse them in cold water and carefully dry with a cloth. ✦ Before putting the peppers in the container, fill it with boiling water and let it rest several minutes before pouring the water out. ✦ Then add the peppers (with their stems still on). ✦ Meanwhile, bring equal parts of water and vinegar

VEGETABLES

to a boil and pour this, still boiling, over the peppers, making certain it covers all of them. (If more liquid is needed during the process of pickling the peppers, add more pure vinegar.) ✦ Cover the container with its lid and refrigerate at least 20 days before eating the peppers.

SPICED CABBAGE WITH EGG

PIPETTO

LOMBARDIA

1 head Savoy cabbage, outer leaves removed
¼ cup (4 tbsp.) unsalted butter
1 garlic clove, crushed
Pinch ground cloves
Pinch ground cinnamon
1 large egg, beaten
Grated Parmigiano-Reggiano
Salt

This side dish is typical of the area around Crema, most often served with dishes using goose.

Rinse the cabbage and cook it in lightly salted water, about 5 minutes. ✦ Drain and chop. ✦ Melt the butter in a pan over low heat and add the garlic, cabbage, cloves, and cinnamon. Season with salt. ✦ Cook for 30 minutes, until the cabbage is tender. ✦ A few minutes before the end of that time, add the egg and 1 tablespoon Parmigiano-Reggiano. Cook until the egg is set but still soft. Serve hot, sprinkling with more Parmigiano-Reggiano.

ARTICHOKE PIZZA

PIZZA DI CARCIOFI

CAMPANIA

For the dough:
About 3⅓ cups all-purpose flour, plus more as needed
½ cup extra-virgin olive oil
1 large egg yolk, beaten with ½ tsp. water

For the filling:
12 medium-size artichokes
Juice of 1 lemon
2 tbsp. extra-virgin olive oil
1 garlic clove
1 or 2 tbsp. chopped flat-leaf parsley
2 large eggs, beaten
2 tbsp. grated Parmigiano-Reggiano
CONTINUED

A modern variation of this blends the cooked artichokes with a béchamel sauce (see page 339) made using 1½ cups milk to which the other ingredients (except the bread) are added. The mixture will be more flavorful if you use prosciutto crudo and cook it yourself in a little lightly salted water.

Stir together the flour and oil until a smooth dough forms, adding a little water if necessary. Let the dough rest, covered with a cloth, 30 minutes. ✦ Clean the artichokes, cut them in eighths, and soak them for 20 minutes in water acidulated with lemon juice to maintain their color. ✦ Preheat the oven to 350°F. Grease a round baking pan with olive oil. Heat the remaining olive oil in a pan, cook the garlic clove until golden, then add the artichoke sections directly from the water (do not drain them too much). Cover the pan and cook the artichokes at low heat, adding salt and 1 tablespoon of warm water as needed to maintain the level of liquid. ✦ When the artichokes are almost cooked (about 20 minutes), take

Bread of 1 stale roll,
without the crust, finely crumbled
(about ¼ cup)
¼ cup milk
Pinch grated nutmeg
4 oz. prosciutto cotto, diced
Salt and pepper

the lid off the pan, remove the garlic, and add the parsley and a good pinch of pepper. ✦ Turn up the heat and stir the mixture to evaporate the moisture. Push the artichokes to one side of the pan, then turn off the heat and tilt the pan, resting it on a support, to make the oil drain from the artichokes. Carefully discard the oil and lay the pan flat again. ✦ Stir in the eggs, Parmigiano-Reggiano, bread, milk, and nutmeg. (The bread serves to keep the eggs from draining to the bottom of the pan.) ✦ Last, add the prosciutto cotto. ✦ Divide the dough in two parts, one larger than the other, and roll out on a floured board to form two ¼-inch-thick sheets: the large one to line the baking pan, the smaller one to cover it. ✦ The eventual pizza should be about 2 inches thick. ✦ Line the baking pan with the larger dough sheet. ✦ Spoon in the filling, spreading it out evenly, then cover with the smaller sheet. Seal the edges of the two sheets, pressing down with the tines of a fork for a decorative edge. ✦ Brush the surface with the yolk mixture and make a hole about 1 inch across at the center of the pizza to allow steam to escape during the baking. ✦ Bake for about 40 minutes.

POLPETTE DI
MELANZANE 1

EGGPLANT BALLS

LOMBARDIA

4 eggplants (about 4 lbs.)
4 tbsp. grated Parmigiano-Reggiano
1 cup breadcrumbs
1 large egg, beaten
Pinch grated nutmeg
Extra-virgin olive oil, for frying
Salt

Select fine, firm medium-size eggplants for this recipe. These are excellent served at room temperature, and can also be served cold.

Peel the eggplants and cut them lengthwise into four wedges. ✦ Cook them in lightly salted boiling water for no more than 5 minutes, being careful not to overcook them. ✦ Drain thoroughly, patting dry to eliminate every bit of water. ✦ In a bowl, mash the eggplant with cheese, 1 tablespoon breadcrumbs, egg, and nutmeg. ✦ Form this mixture into balls, not too large (about the size of a walnut), and dredge them in the remaining breadcrumbs. ✦ Heat ½ inch of olive oil in a large pan. Fry just until light golden (do not overcook) and drain on paper towels.

EGGPLANT BITES

¾ lb. eggplant (about 1 medium)

1 cup breadcrumbs

1 garlic clove, minced

1 tbsp. chopped flat-leaf parsley

1 tbsp. chopped basil leaves

⅓ cup grated pecorino

1 large egg, beaten

Extra-virgin olive oil, for frying

Salt

These can be served either hot or cold or covered with a tomato sauce as a side dish.

Peel the eggplant, slice in half, put in a pot, and cover with water. ✦ Bring the water to a boil and cook for about 45 minutes, until very soft, then drain and let cool. ✦ In a large bowl, combine the breadcrumbs, garlic, parsley, basil, cheese, and salt. ✦ Dry off the eggplant sections and work them into the mixture with the egg, kneading well to make a homogeneous mixture. ✦ Shape this mixture into 2-inch flat logs. Heat about ½ inch of olive in a pan and fry until golden. Drain on paper towels.

CAULIFLOWER BALLS

1 small head cauliflower

½ cup grated caciocavallo

Bread of 1 roll, soaked in milk, then squeezed dry

2 large eggs

Pinch grated nutmeg

1 cup breadcrumbs

Olive oil, for frying

Salt and pepper

In Sicilia *broccolo* means "cauliflower."

Trim the outer leaves off the cauliflower, then put it in a pot of cold, lightly salted water to cover and bring the water to a boil. ✦ Cook until tender, about 20 minutes. As soon as it is cooked, drain it and chop it in small pieces. ✦ Put the pieces of cauliflower in a bowl and add the caciocavallo, bread, 1 egg, nutmeg, and a little pepper. ✦ Work the ingredients well to blend them, then shape into 1-inch balls. ✦ Heat 2 inches of olive oil until hot. Season the remaining egg with a little salt, then dip the balls in the egg, roll them in breadcrumbs, and fry until golden. Drain on paper towels and serve hot.

OREGANO TOMATOES

1¾ lbs. large, round plum tomatoes

3 tbsp. extra-virgin olive oil, or as needed

1 cup breadcrumbs

1 garlic clove, minced

1 tbsp. chopped oregano (or flat-leaf parsley)

This dish is typical of Naples.

Preheat the oven to 350°F. Wash the tomatoes, dry them, cut them in half, remove the seeds, and let them drain for 30 minutes. ✦ Salt the tomato halves and set aside. ✦ Mix 1 tablespoon of the olive oil (or more if needed) with the breadcrumbs, garlic, oregano (or parsley), and capers, if desired (if not using the capers add salt). ✦ Spread a little of this mixture on each tomato half and

²⁄₃ cup capers (optional), rinsed

Salt

arrange them in a baking pan. Drizzle them with the remaining olive oil and bake until the breadcrumbs are brown, about 20 minutes.

POMODORI RIPIENI

STUFFED TOMATOES

CALABRIA

8 large tomatoes

1 cup breadcrumbs

1 cup grated pecorino

1 tsp. chopped oregano

4 or 5 basil leaves, minced

4 tbsp. extra-virgin olive oil

Salt and pepper

Preheat the oven to 400°F. Slice the tomatoes in half, remove the seeds, and set them out upside down to drain. ✦ In a bowl, combine the breadcrumbs, cheese, oregano, basil, salt, and pepper; work these ingredients together with 1 tablespoon water and 3 tablespoons olive oil until blended ✦ Fill the tomato halves with this mixture, then arrange them in a baking pan. ✦ Drizzle them with the remaining olive oil and bake until golden, about 15 minutes.

PROSCIUTTO CRUDO
E FAGIOLINI DELLA NONNA

GRANDMA'S PROSCIUTTO AND BEANS

VALLE D'AOSTA

1 prosciutto crudo
(if possible from Bosses)

½ cup white wine

¼ lb. (½ cup) unsalted butter

1 large onion, finely sliced

2 lbs. green beans (best if just gathered in the garden)

2 cups meat broth

Salt

This recipe was a family tradition in the area known as the "Grand Saint Bernard" where Napoleon Bonaparte spent three days during his crossing of the Alps.

Using a flame, burn away any bristles on the prosciutto crudo. ✦ Clean it and cook it for 2 hours in water to cover, to which the wine has been added. ✦ Heat the butter in a cast-iron pot and add the onion. Cook until golden, then add the green beans. ✦ Add a little salt and the broth and cook at low heat for 1 hour. ✦ Drain the prosciutto and add it to the beans. ✦ Continue cooking another 10 minutes so the remaining fat will help to season the beans.

VEGETABLES

PUNTARELLE
IN SALSA D'ALICI

PUNTARELLE SALAD WITH ANCHOVY DRESSING

LAZIO

½ lb. *puntarelle* (see note)

1 garlic clove

7 anchovy fillets,
boned and chopped

CONTINUED

Meaning "little tips"(and also called *catalogna*), this is a kind of green akin in taste to celery and chicory, with a pleasingly bitter flavor; the tender shoots up to the head are used, harvested in the period before flowering, to make a very tasty salad. This is typical of Rome and Lazio.

Clean the *puntarelle*, cutting away the stringy parts and working from the bottom up, then cut lengthwise to

4 tbsp. white wine vinegar,
or as needed

4 tbsp. extra-virgin olive oil,
or as needed

create, depending on the thickness of the shoots, two, three, or four parts. Long shoots should be shortened, but no shorter than 4½ to 6 inches. ✦ Rinse these and put them in a bowl of cool water to make them curl, about 2 hours. ✦ Meanwhile, prepare the dressing in a mortar, preferably of wood: grind together the garlic, anchovies, vinegar, and olive oil to form a paste. ✦ Add more oil and vinegar to form a somewhat liquid dressing. ✦ Pour this over the *puntarelle* and let them steep in a covered container for at least 1 hour. Serve in a bowl with the addition of more of the dressing and mix well.

✦ **LOCAL TRADITION** ✦

POMODORI SOTT'OLIO

These pickled tomatoes are a Pugliese favorite. The largest and firmest tomatoes available are halved, heavily salted, and then set in the sun to dry. Once dry, they are soaked in lukewarm vinegar for about twenty minutes, and then arranged in glass or earthenware jars with fresh mint leaves and a garlic clove. The mixture is lightly pressed to eliminate any air pockets and then covered with olive oil, enabling the pickled tomatoes to keep for a long time as a favorite condiment to boiled meats, fish, or simply with bread.

PUREA DI FAVE | # FAVA PURÉE

PUGLIA

1⅔ cups dried fava beans

2 large potatoes, peeled and cubed

1½ cups extra-virgin olive oil,
or as needed

Salt

The secret to making this purée is to refrain from stirring the fava beans. This purée can be served with boiled field greens.

Rinse the fava beans and put them in an earthenware pot with the potatoes; cover with water and bring to a boil over low heat. Cover and simmer for about 20 minutes. ✦ Drain away the water and cover the favas with more cold water, adding salt. ✦ Bring to a second boil, then simmer for another 30 minutes. ✦ Pass the beans and potatoes through a food mill, then return them to the earthenware pan and mash them vigorously with a wooden spoon, adding olive oil a little at a time as needed to form a smooth purée. Season with salt.

PUREA DI ZUCCA

SQUASH PURÉE

SARDEGNA

1 lb. dried beans

2 oz. *lardo*, minced

1 lb. winter squash, peeled and diced

Salt

This dish, typical of Gavoi, is even better if the squash is cooked and passed through a food mill before being added.

Soak the beans overnight in water to cover. Drain them, rinse them, and add water to cover by a few inches. Add the *lardo* and boil them for about 1½ hours, or until nearly tender. ✦ Add the squash and continue cooking, adding water and salt as desired, until the squash is completely cooked, about 30 minutes. Mash the beans and squash to form a thick purée. Season with salt and serve.

PURGATORIO ALLA CALABRESE

CALABRIAN "PURGATORY" VEGETABLE SANDWICHES

CALABRIA

3 medium plum tomatoes

2 tbsp. shredded basil leaves

½ cup olive oil

2 eggplants, cut in sections and soaked in salted water for about 30 minutes

4 young potatoes, peeled and cut in quarters

4 peppers, coarsely chopped

1 loaf country bread

Salt

Parboil the tomatoes, peel them, and cut them in pieces. ✦ Put the tomatoes in a saucepan with the basil and 2 tablespoons of olive oil and cook for 15 minutes over medium heat, adding salt to taste. ✦ In another pan, heat the remaining olive oil. Add the remaining vegetables and cook until the potatoes are soft. Transfer them to the tomato sauce, and stir together for a few minutes to evaporate some of the liquid. ✦ Cut the loaf lengthwise, scoop out some of the bread, then stuff it with the *purgatorio*; close it, slice it, and serve immediately.

VEGETABLES

RADICCHIO DI CAMPO CON LARDO

WILD GREENS WITH LARDO

FRIULI-VENEZIA GIULIA

2 heads *radicchio di campo* (see note), outer leaves removed and remaining leaves rinsed and dried

CONTINUED

This delicious spring dish goes very well with hard-boiled eggs. *Radicchio di campo* is not red radicchio but a wild green with small leaves. You could substitute wild arugula.

Tear the greens and place in a salad bowl. Heat the *lardo* over low heat until the fat is rendered and the *lardo* is

4 oz. *lardo*, diced
2 tbsp. white wine vinegar
Salt

lightly browned. Add the vinegar, then pour the mixture over the greens. Toss until the leaves are wilted.

RAPE CON LO ZUCCHERO | # CARAMELIZED TURNIPS

FRIULI-VENEZIA GIULIA

2 oz. lard
1½ tbsp. sugar
1½ lbs. violet turnips, peeled and cubed
Salt and pepper

White turnips can be used in this recipe in place of the violet ones, if necessary.

Heat the lard in a pan over low heat and add the sugar. ✦ When the sugar melts, whisk in 2 tablespoons of water. Immediately add the turnips, stirring to keep the sugar from caramelizing too quickly. ✦ The turnips should soon turn a brownish color. ✦ Season with salt and pepper and cook at low heat until the turnips are tender.

RADICCHIO AI FERRI TREVIGIANO | # GRILLED RADICCHIO, TREVISO-STYLE

VENETO

Radicchio di Treviso (½ head for each person)
Extra-virgin olive oil
Salt and pepper

Radicchio from Treviso has the characteristic red and white color of the ball-shaped radicchio from Chiogga, but it is shaped like a head of green Romaine lettuce.

Heat a grill until hot. Divide the individual heads of radicchio into four parts, leaving about 2 inches of the root to hold the leaves together. ✦ Season with olive oil, salt and pepper and arrange on the grill. ✦ Cook rapidly, letting the heat eliminate all the water in the radicchio. When the radicchio is marked and wilted, it is ready.

RAPE STRASCINATE | # BRAISED TURNIPS

ABRUZZO

½ cup olive oil
1 garlic clove
1 dried chili pepper
1½ lbs. turnips, washed but not dried and cut into quarters
Salt

These are excellent in the winter after the frosts.

In a cast-iron skillet, heat the olive oil. Add the garlic, salt, and chili pepper; stir, then add the turnips and stir to coat with the oil. ✦ Cook at slow heat with the skillet uncovered, stirring often to cook them evenly.

BROVADA

One of the most common Friulian dishes since time immemorial, this dish calls for marinating white turnips in unfermented wine pressings for a few months, during which time the pressings will ferment and bestow a dark pink color onto the turnips. First the roots and leaves of the turnips would be cleaned, then the turnips would be packed into a container in alternating layers with the pressings. The turnips and pressings would be left for a few months until they took on the desired color, then they would be grated and cooked along with onion and garlic in *lardo*, with meat broth added as desired. The flavors of the dish improved the longer the turnips cooked, and this was a favorite side dish for any kind of meat, especially pork.

RATATUIA

RATATOUILLE PIEMONTE-STYLE

PIEMONTE

1½ lbs. broccoli, chopped

¾ lb. cardoons, cut in small pieces

¾ lb. yellow summer squash, peeled and cut in slices

2 tbsp. extra-virgin olive oil

2 tbsp. unsalted butter

½ garlic clove

6 oz. salt-cured anchovies, rinsed and boned

1 tbsp. cornstarch

Cauliflower can be used in place of the broccoli in this dish, which is typical of Domodossola.

Preheat the oven to 350°F. Boil the broccoli and cardoons in water to cover until they are half cooked. ✦ In an ovenproof pan, cook the squash in water to cover until fork-tender but still firm, then transfer the pan to the oven. ✦ Heat half the olive oil and the butter in a pan and add the garlic. When the garlic is golden, add the broccoli and cardoons and cook at high heat, stirring constantly. ✦ Heat the remaining olive oil in a second pan over low heat, add the anchovies, and cook until they have basically disintegrated. Stir in the cornstarch and cook for a few minutes. At the moment of serving toss together the squash with its liquid, the broccoli mixture, and the anchovy mixture.

VEGETABLES

ESCAROLE WITH MEATBALLS

CALABRIA

2 lbs. curly escarole
¾ lb. ground pork
2 large eggs
1 tbsp. chopped flat-leaf parsley
⅔ cup grated pecorino
Extra-virgin olive oil
1 cup breadcrumbs
6 oz. cooked *ciccioli* (see note, page 12)
Salt and pepper

Use only the green part of the escarole. Parboil it in lightly salted water until tender (about 5 minutes), dry, and roughly chop. ✦ Combine the pork, 1 whole egg, 1 egg yolk, salt, pepper, parsley, and half of the pecorino until blended. Form into 1-inch meatballs. ✦ Heat ½ inch of olive oil in a large pan. Dredge the meatballs in the breadcrumbs, fry until golden, and drain on paper towels. ✦ Remove and discard most of the olive oil. Cook the escarole in the same pan until the liquid has evaporated. ✦ Beat the remaining egg white with the remaining pecorino until frothy and add this to the escarole, stirring to blend and cook. Serve immediately, topped with the *ciccioli* and the meatballs.

STUFFED AND BRAISED ESCAROLE

SCAROLA RIPIENA

LAZIO

6 heads curly escarole
½ cup pine nuts
1 or 2 salt-cured anchovies, rinsed, boned, and chopped
½ cup golden raisins
20 pitted olives
4 or 5 garlic cloves, minced
Extra-virgin olive oil
Broth

This dish is typical of Itri.

Clean and rinse the escarole without separating the leaves from the heart. Set it out upside down to drain. ✦ Mix the pine nuts, anchovies, raisins, olives, and garlic until blended. Delicately spread open each head and fill with the mixture. Drizzle the filling with olive oil. Do not add salt. ✦ Tie each head closed with kitchen twine and stand them up in a saucepan. Add 1 inch of broth. ✦ Cover and cook at medium-low heat until the escarole is tender, about 20 minutes.

STUFFED AND BAKED ESCAROLE

SCAROLE IMBOTTITE

CAMPANIA

Extra-virgin olive oil
7 heads curly escarole
3 garlic cloves, slivered
5 or 6 tbsp. breadcrumbs
⅔ cup capers, rinsed

CONTINUED

This dish is typical of Salerno.

Preheat the oven to 350°F. Grease a baking pan with olive oil. Remove the outer leaves from the escarole, rinse the hearts several times, then parboil them until tender, about 10 minutes; put them upside down in a colander to drain. ✦ Heat 5 tablespoons of olive oil in a pan and add the escarole, 1 garlic clove, and a pinch of salt. ✦ When they are tender, carefully lift them out of the pan without

2/3 cup pitted Gaeta olives

1 bunch flat-leaf parsley, chopped

3 oz. salt-cured anchovies, rinsed, boned, and chopped

Salt and freshly ground white pepper

breaking them; set them out to drain. ✦ Add more oil to the pan along with the remaining garlic and breadcrumbs. Sauté, stirring continuously with a wooden spoon, for 2 or 3 minutes; add the capers, olives, parsley, and white pepper. ✦ Stir for a few minutes, then add the anchovies. ✦ Fill the escarole with this mixture without breaking them and arrange them in the pan, one beside the next. ✦ Dust them with more breadcrumbs, drizzle with more olive oil, and bake for about 20 minutes, or until golden.

VEGETABLES

SCAROLE STUFATE

BAKED ESCAROLE

CAMPANIA

This dish is typical of Salerno.

1 ½ lbs. escarole, outer leaves removed

2/3 cup extra-virgin olive oil

3 garlic cloves

5 tbsp. breadcrumbs

1/3 cup capers, rinsed

¾ cup pitted Gaeta olives

1 bunch flat-leaf parsley, chopped

1 oz. salt-cured anchovies, rinsed, boned, and chopped

Salt and pepper

Preheat the oven to 350°F. Parboil the escarole for about 10 minutes and drain in a colander. ✦ When dry, heat 2 tablespoons of the olive oil in a large pan and add the escarole, 1 garlic clove, and a little salt. ✦ When the escarole is wilted, remove from the heat and let drain. ✦ In an ovenproof pan, heat the remaining olive oil, remaining garlic, and the breadcrumbs, stirring with a wooden spoon. Cook for 2 or 3 minutes, then add the capers, olives, parsley, pepper, and anchovies. ✦ Add the escarole, stir to blend well, then transfer to the oven and bake for 20 minutes, until browned.

STUFFED CELERY

TOSCANA

8 celery stalks

4 tbsp. unsalted butter

1 small onion, finely sliced

6 oz. chicken livers

¾ lb. lean ground veal

3 large eggs, beaten

½ cup grated Parmigiano-Reggiano

Olive oil, for frying

All-purpose flour for dredging

1 lb. meat sauce (see page 331)

Salt and pepper

Carefully clean the celery, rinsing away any dirt and trimming off the leaves. ✦ Parboil the ribs for a few minutes in lightly salted boiling water until slightly softened. Let them cool, then clean them again, cutting away any fibrous parts and chopping them in equal lengths of 3 or 4 inches. ✦ Heat the butter in a saucepan, add the onion, and sauté until translucent, then add the chicken livers and veal. ✦ Cook this for a few minutes, then take the pan off the heat and add 1 egg, Parmigiano-Reggiano, and salt and pepper. Stir to blend well. ✦ Distribute this filling over each stalk, then put the stalks together in pairs, filling side in. ✦ Press them together well and tie each pair together with kitchen twine but without making any difficult knots: this way they will stay together during cooking. ✦ Heat 1 inch of olive oil until hot. Dredge the celery pairs in flour, then in the remaining eggs, then fry until golden. ✦ Heat the meat sauce in a pan, add the celery, and cook until the sauce has reduced slightly and the celery has taken on a fine red color. Remember to untie the bundles before serving.

ARTICHOKE AND CHEESE CASSEROLE

LIGURIA

1 garlic clove, minced

½ cup chopped flat-leaf parsley

½ cup extra-virgin olive oil

5 artichokes, cleaned and cut in thin slices

2¼ cups *quagliata* (see note)

5 large eggs, beaten

⅔ cup grated Parmigiano-Reggiano

.   Salt and pepper

*Quagliata (*prescinsoeua* in dialect) is a soured-milk product very popular in Liguria. Ricotta thinned with a little yogurt (or quark cheese) can be substituted.*

Preheat the oven to 400°F. Mix the garlic and parsley. ✦ Heat the olive oil in a sauté pan and add the garlic mixture. ✦ After a few minutes, add the artichokes, salt, and pepper, and cook at moderate heat for 10 minutes. ✦ Off the heat, add the *quagliata*, eggs, cheese, and salt and pepper to taste. ✦ Pour this mixture into a nonstick baking pan and bake for about 20 minutes, or until the eggs are set and lightly golden.

SAVOY CABBAGE FLANS WITH FONDUTA

VALLE D'AOSTA

For the flans:
Unsalted butter
1 medium onion, finely chopped
½ Savoy cabbage, outer leaves removed and finely chopped
2 bay leaves
1 bunch basil
4 large eggs
1¼ cups heavy cream
Salt

For the fonduta:
1½ lbs. fontina, diced
Milk (enough to cover the fontina)
3 large egg yolks
Pepper

Preheat the oven to 350°F. Butter four 8-ounce ramekins and arrange them in a baking pan that is at least 2 inches deep and allows for 1 inch of space around each of them. Combine the onion and cabbage in a saucepan, add water to cover, and season with salt and bay leaves. Cook the onion and cabbage together until very soft. ✦ Remove the bay leaves and put the mixture in a blender, adding the basil. ✦ Pass the result through a very fine sieve (preferably a chinois), then whisk in the eggs and cream. ✦ Pour the mixture into the ramekins and place the pan in the oven. Fill the baking pan halfway up the sides of the ramekins with cool water. Bake until set, about 1 hour. ✦ To prepare the fonduta: Combine the fontina with milk to cover and a pinch of pepper in the top of a double boiler, stirring with a wooden spoon until it is perfectly blended. ✦ Blend in the egg yolks, but do not let them scramble. Once the fonduta has thickened slightly, serve it with the flans.

SAVOY CABBAGE FLAN

VALLE D'AOSTA

Unsalted butter
2 tbsp. extra-virgin olive oil
½ Savoy cabbage, outer leaves removed and finely chopped
1 large onion, finely chopped
2 bay leaves
Several basil leaves, shredded
4 large eggs, beaten
⅔ cup heavy cream
Salt and pepper

This recipe shows its Piemontese origins; in fact, Vialardi, cook for the Turin royal household, cites similar preparations, referring to them as vegetable flans. In the Valle d'Aosta such flans were often accompanied, as in Piemonte, by fondues, sometimes using white Piemontese truffles.

Preheat the oven to 400°F. Butter a baking dish and place it in a larger baking pan, making sure there is at least 1 inch of room on all sides. Heat the olive oil in a large pan on low heat; add the cabbage, onion, bay leaves, and basil. ✦ When the cabbage has cooked, remove the bay leaves and pass the mixture through a food mill. ✦ Stir in the eggs, cream, and salt and pepper. ✦ Stir this mixure well to blend. ✦ Pour the mixture into the smaller pan, place the whole thing in the oven, then fill the larger pan halfway with cool water. Bake for about 30 minutes, or until set.

VEGETABLES

POTATO AND
TOMATO CASSEROLE

CALABRIA

Extra-virgin olive oil

2 tbsp. breadcrumbs

½ cup grated pecorino

1 tbsp. oregano

½ tsp. chili pepper flakes

2 lbs. fresh plum tomatoes, peeled, seeded, and chopped in small pieces

4 or 5 large potatoes (preferably from Calabria), peeled and cut into thick rounds

1 medium onion, sliced

Several basil leaves, shredded

Salt

The name *tieddra* (also called *teglia*) is from the Latin *tigella*, meaning "the pan in which the dish is prepared." There are many versions of *tieddra* in Calabria, for example, with mushrooms from the Sila Massif or with wild artichokes. Another variation consists of adding to the potatoes and tomatoes a little pasta, usually broken-up bucatini. The addition of this ingredient alone makes the *tieddra* even more flavorful.

Preheat the oven to 450°F. Grease an earthenware baking dish with olive oil. Combine the breadcrumbs, cheese, oregano, and chili pepper in a bowl and set aside. ✦ Spread a layer of tomatoes across the bottom of the dish, season with salt, and top with a layer of potatoes. ✦ Place slices of onion here and there along with some of the breadcrumb mixture; add the basil leaves, then drizzle with olive oil. ✦ Repeat, beginning with another layer of tomatoes and ending with a layer of the breadcrumb mixture. Top this with more olive oil. ✦ Add a little water, pouring it in slowly from the side, then bake for about 1 hour, or until a golden crust has formed on the top. Serve this exquisite dish at room temperature or cold.

✦ **LOCAL TRADITION** ✦

SFORMATO DI LAMPASCIONI
CON SALSA DI SEDANO

In this recipe from Puglia for timbales of muscari and potato flan, the muscari and potatoes would first be boiled separately, dried in a warm oven, and then puréed into a smooth mixture along with grated Pugliese pecorino, salt, pepper, and parsley. A beaten egg white would then be folded into the mixture. The muscari and potato purée would then be spooned into ramekins that had been greased and dusted with breadcrumbs. The filled ramekins would be baked in a cool water bath in a large roasting dish in a hot oven just until set. After coming out of the oven, the timbales would be turned out onto a serving plate on top of a smooth purée of celery, olive oil, salt, and pepper, and served immediately.

SIÔLE PIENE | STUFFED ONIONS

PIEMONTE

3 ½ lbs. onions (preferably *cipollini*)

½ cup (¼ lb.) unsalted butter

½ lb. mixed herbs and greens
(flat-leaf parsley, sage, rosemary,
bay leaves, thyme, basil, mint,
arugula, celery leaves, and so on),
finely chopped

⅔ cup breadcrumbs,
softened in ½ cup milk

½ cup raisins,
softened in lukewarm water

7 large eggs

1 cup grated Parmigiano-Reggiano

½ cup milk

Salt

This dish is typical of Ivrea. Ground meat can be used in place of the herbs.

Preheat the oven to 350°F. Boil the onions in lightly salted water to cover until tender, cut them in half horizontally, and scoop out their insides to form small bowls, setting aside the pulp. ✦ Heat half the butter in a pan and add the herbs/greens and onion pulp. Sauté, adding salt to taste. ✦ Take the mixture off the heat and mix in the breadcrumbs and raisins, along with 4 eggs and half of the Parmigiano-Reggiano. ✦ Stuff the onion bowls with this mixture and arrange them in a baking pan. ✦ Beat the remaining 3 eggs with the remaining Parmigiano-Reggiano and the milk. ✦ Drizzle this over the onions: it should almost cover them. ✦ Top each onion with a pat of the remaining butter and bake until the surface is browned.

SPINACI ALLA GENOVESE | SPINACH GENOA-STYLE

LIGURIA

1 ¼ lbs. spinach

2 tbsp. extra-virgin olive oil

1 garlic clove, chopped

1 tbsp. pine nuts

1 tbsp. raisins, soaked in
lukewarm water

4 slices peasant-style bread,
toasted

Salt

Clean and rinse the spinach, squeeze dry, and steam it, using only the moisture that remains in it. ✦ Drain and squeeze it again. ✦ Heat the olive oil in a pan and add the spinach and garlic. Season with salt, then add the pine nuts and raisins. ✦ Cook for about 10 minutes at moderate heat. Serve the spinach over slices of toasted bread.

SPOLLICHINI IN BISACCIA | BEANS IN SAUCE

CAMPANIA

1 lb. fresh shelled beans

½ lb. green beans, tips cut off

CONTINUED

This dish is typical of Salerno.

Boil the beans in a large pot with water to cover by a couple of inches until tender, about 15 minutes. Add the green beans after 10 minutes. ✦ Meanwhile, in a terracotta pan heat the olive oil and add the garlic, tomato

5 tbsp. olive oil

2 garlic cloves, crushed

1½ cups tomato purée

5 basil leaves

1 small bunch flat-leaf parsley, chopped

Several celery stalks, chopped

1 dried chili pepper

Slices of peasant-style bread, toasted

purée, basil, parsley, celery, and chili pepper. Cook just until blended. ✦ Transfer the beans to a bowl, pour the sauce over, and toss to mix. Let stand 30 minutes so the flavors can blend. Serve on toasted slices of peasant-style bread.

STUFATO DI VERDURE PRIMAVERA | SPRING VEGETABLE STEW

SICILIA

1 small onion, finely chopped

2 oz. pancetta (or prosciutto), diced

1⅔ cups fresh shelled peas

1⅔ cups fresh shelled fava beans

6 artichokes, cleaned, trimmed of outer leaves, and cut in thin sections

¼ cup white wine

½ cup extra-virgin olive oil, or as needed

1 tbsp. finely chopped flat-leaf parsley

1 tbsp. finely chopped basil

Salt and pepper

Serve this dish as a one-dish entrée or as a side dish, or use as a sauce for pasta (*pennette*, for example). For the wine use a Sicilian white that has been aged in barrels.

In a somewhat large saucepan, cook the onion with 2 tablespoons water. ✦ Add the pancetta (or prosciutto) and after a few minutes the peas, fava beans, and artichokes. ✦ Add the wine and turn the heat up to high for a few minutes to evaporate it. ✦ Add half of the olive oil; stir in the parsley, cover, and cook at low heat, stirring from time to time, for about 20 minutes. ✦ When the vegetables are tender, add salt and pepper, more olive oil if needed, and basil. Serve hot.

TARTRÀ | ARTICHOKE FLAN | FOR 6 PERSONS

PIEMONTE

2 tbsp. unsalted butter

All-purpose flour

1 medium onion, chopped

4 large eggs plus 2 yolks, beaten

2 cups lukewarm milk

1 cup heavy cream

3 tbsp. grated Parmigiano-Reggiano

CONTINUED

This dish is typical of Asti.

Preheat the oven to 350°F. Butter and flour an earthenware baking dish and place it in a larger baking pan, making sure there is at least 1 inch of room on all sides. Heat the remaining butter in a pan over medium-low heat and add the onion, cooking until golden. ✦ In a large bowl, beat the eggs and egg yolks, milk, cream, cheese, herbs, salt, pepper, and nutmeg. ✦ Add the onion and artichokes and stir well to blend. ✦ Pour the mixture into the prepared dish. Place the whole thing in the oven,

2 tbsp. mixed chopped herbs
(sage, fresh bay, rosemary)

Pinch grated nutmeg

1 cup finely chopped cooked
artichoke hearts

Salt and freshly ground black pepper

then fill the larger pan halfway with cool water. Bake 30 minutes, or until set.

TIMBALLO DI PATATE

POTATO TIMBALE

BASILICATA

¼ cup unsalted butter

2 lbs. potatoes

¾ cup grated pecorino

2 tbsp. chopped flat-leaf parsley

Milk (if necessary)

2 large hard-boiled eggs,
shelled and cut in rounds

1½ cups cubed provolone

6 oz. sausage, sliced

Preheat the oven to 350°F. Grease a baking dish with butter. ✦ Boil the potatoes until soft, peel them, and put them through a potato ricer. ✦ Mix the resulting purée with the pecorino and parsley. If the mixture is too thick, add a little milk. It should be creamy and not too stiff. ✦ Put the mixture in the baking dish and top it with the eggs, provolone, and sausage. ✦ Top with pats of the remaining butter. ✦ Bake for about 30 minutes, or until golden, then serve.

SWISS CHARD AND RICOTTA

TORTA DI BIETOLE E RICOTTA

SICILIA

2 tbsp. extra-virgin olive oil
1 ¼ lbs. Swiss chard
10 oz. ricotta
3 large eggs, beaten
Salt and pepper

Preheat the oven to 350°F. Grease a baking dish with olive oil. Parboil the Swiss chard until tender, about 5 minutes, and drain well. Heat the remaining olive oil in a large pan and add the chard. Cook until totally wilted. ✦ In a bowl, crush the ricotta with the tines of a fork, add the eggs and chard, and salt and pepper lightly. ✦ Put this mixture in the baking dish and bake for 10 minutes.

EGGPLANT PIE

TORTA DI MELANZANE

LOMBARDIA

2 tbsp. unsalted butter, melted and cooled slightly
2 tbsp. breadcrumbs
5 or 6 firm eggplants
2 large eggs, beaten
1 heaping tbsp. grated Parmigiano-Reggiano
⅛ tsp. grated nutmeg
Salt

Preheat the oven to 400°F. Grease a baking dish with butter and sprinkle it with some of the breadcrumbs. Peel the eggplants, cut them in quarters, and immediately cook them in a little salted water for no more than 10 minutes. ✦ Drain and press down on them to remove the water; also remove the larger seeds. ✦ Mix the eggplant, eggs, cheese, and the remaining breadcrumbs. ✦ Mix in the remaining butter and nutmeg and pour into the baking dish. ✦ Bake for about 20 minutes, until the breadcrumbs are golden, and serve piping hot.

EASTER SPRING GREENS PIE

TORTA DI PASQUA

VALLE D'AOSTA

4 oz. *lardo*, minced
¼ lb. (1 stick) unsalted butter
1 small onion, thinly sliced
3 lbs. mixed spring greens, from a garden or wild: sage, rosemary, wild spinach, nettles, hop buds, dandelion, plantain, chives, wild arugula, meadow salsify, lovage, leaves of costmary, lamb's quarter, parboiled and chopped
4 large eggs, beaten in 3 cups milk
2 cups cornmeal (or whole-wheat flour)
1 ¼ cups all-purpose flour
3 small Valdostan sausages (mixed beef and lard)
Salt

This dish is typical of Arnaud and is much like the Tourte d'Espinoche known from the Middle Ages.

Begin the preparation the night before (traditionally the eve of Easter). Heat the *lardo* and butter in a pan, add the onion, and sauté until translucent. Put it into a large baking pan or cast-iron skillet. ✦ Add the greens and egg mixture. ✦ Sift together the cornmeal and flour with salt. Blend into the egg mixture and add the sausages at the center. Cover and refrigerate overnight. ✦ The next day (Easter) preheat the oven to 350°F. Bake for about 2 hours, checking its progress often. The final result should be firm but not dry.

RUSTIC TORTE
WITH ARTICHOKES

ABRUZZO

For the dough:

1 ¼ cups all-purpose flour,
plus more if needed

7 oz. ricotta (about ¾ cup)

⅔ cup extra-virgin olive oil

For the filling:

4 tbsp. unsalted butter

12 artichokes, trimmed and
quartered

6 oz. prosciutto crudo, diced

2 small balls mozzarella, diced
(about ½ lb.)

3 large eggs, beaten

½ cup grated aged pecorino

4 oz. fontina, cut in very thin slices

Salt

Preheat the oven to 400°F. Knead together the flour, ricotta, and olive oil to make a very soft dough. Divide it into two small loaves and let rest. ✦ Heat the butter in a large pan and cook the artichokes until they start to take on a little color. Remove from the heat. Add the prosciutto and mozzarella. ✦ Mix the eggs and pecorino; season with salt. ✦ Roll out the small loaves on a floured board to form sheets of dough and use the first to line a baking pan. ✦ Cover the bottom with the slices of fontina, then top with the vegetable mixture; pour over the egg mixture. Cover with the remaining sheet of dough and seal the edges. ✦ Bake for about 45 minutes, or until the crust is golden brown.

LAYERED PIE
WITH ARTICHOKES

CALABRIA

Extra-virgin olive oil

½ cup breadcrumbs

8 artichokes

Lemon juice (or vinegar)

2 oz. spicy salame, cubed

1 ball mozzarella, cubed

½ cup grated pecorino

1 tbsp. oregano

Salt

This dish is typical of Vibo Valentia.

Preheat the oven to 400°F. ✦ Grease a round baking pan with olive oil and dust with breadcrumbs. Boil the artichokes in lightly salted water acidulated with lemon juice, drain when three-quarters done (about 15 minutes), cool, and cut in small sections. ✦ Lay some of the artichokes across the bottom of the baking pan. ✦ Mix the salame, cheeses, remaining breadcrumbs, and oregano, then make a layer of this mixture over the artichokes. ✦ Repeat the layers, alternating the artichokes and salame mixture. ✦ Drizzle olive oil over the top and bake until it forms a light golden crust.

VEGETABLES

VEGETABLES AND PANCETTA

VERDURA 'SSETTATA CON VENTRESCA DI MAIALE

PUGLIA

¼ cup extra-virgin olive oil

2 tbsp. breadcrumbs

2 lbs. *catalogna* chicory (a cultivated relative of wild chicory) or wild chicory

1 small onion, thinly sliced

7 oz. fresh pancetta, thinly sliced

1 ¼ cups tomato purée

1 tbsp. grated pecorino

Slices of peasant-style bread, toasted

Preheat the oven to 350°F. ✦ Grease the bottom of a baking pan with olive oil and sprinkle with half the breadcrumbs. ✦ Clean the chicory and parboil, until half cooked, about 10 minutes. Drain. ✦ Heat the remaining olive oil in a pan over low heat, add the onion, then pancetta. ✦ After a few minutes, add the tomato purée and cook until slightly thickened. ✦ Add the half-cooked chicory to the pan. ✦ Pour the chicory-tomato mixture into the prepared baking pan. Mix the remaining breadcrumbs and pecorino and sprinkle this on top of the chicory. ✦ Bake for 20 minutes. Serve warm on slices of toasted bread.

"STRANGE" GREENS

VERDURA STRANGHIATA

CALABRIA

1 ¼ lbs. mixed wild or cultivated greens: chicory, spinach, beets, broccoli florets

¼ cup extra-virgin olive oil

1 garlic clove

2 slices peasant-style bread, toasted and finely crumbled

Salt

Boil the greens for about 1 minute, drain, and lightly squeeze them dry. ✦ Heat the olive oil in a pan, add the garlic, and cook until fragrant. Add the greens and bread and cook for 5 minutes, stirring. Serve hot.

PAN-FRIED GREENS

VERDURE MISTE IN PADELLA

FRIULI-VENEZIA GIULIA

3 lbs. mixed greens: spinach, chard, leeks, chicory, celery leaves, radicchio

2 oz. *lardo*, finely minced

2 garlic cloves

1 tbsp. all-purpose flour

Salt and pepper

Cook the greens in lightly salted boiling water for about 2 minutes; drain and, without drying, roughly chop. ✦ Heat the *lardo* in a pan with the garlic cloves, add the flour, and brown. ✦ Add the chopped greens, salt, and pepper and cook for about 5 minutes.

VERDURE RIPIENE | VEGETABLE STUFFING

LIGURIA

¼ cup extra-virgin olive oil

1 oz. dried mushrooms, softened in warm water and drained

1 garlic clove, chopped

1 tbsp. chopped fresh marjoram

Crustless bread of a roll, softened in milk and squeezed dry

2 large eggs

¼ cup grated Parmigiano-Reggiano

¼ cup grated pecorino

2 oz. ricotta

Salt and pepper

This dish is typical of Savona and can be used to stuff zucchini, eggplant, boiled onions, or raw peppers or tomatoes.

Preheat the oven to 350°F. Grease a baking pan with olive oil. ✦ Combine the mushrooms, garlic, and marjoram and finely chop them together. Heat the remaining olive oil and cook the mushroom mixture. ✦ When these have cooked well, add all the other ingredients and salt and pepper to taste. ✦ Stuff the chosen vegetables, arrange them in the baking pan, and bake for about 40 minutes, or until the stuffing is golden. Serve warm on a serving plate.

ZUCCA ALLA SCAPECE | MARINATED SQUASH

CAMPANIA

1 ¼ lbs. yellow winter squash, peeled and seeds removed

½ cup extra-virgin olive oil

1 bunch mint leaves

1 tbsp. chili pepper flakes

¼ cup white wine vinegar

2 garlic cloves

Salt and pepper

Cut the squash into rectangles ½ inch by 2 inches and about ¼ inch thick. ✦ Sprinkle with salt and set aside in a warm place (out in the sun is ideal) for about an hour. ✦ Heat the olive oil and cook the squash pieces a few at a time until they take on color. ✦ Drain them, reserving their cooking oil, then form them into several layers in a container, alternating each layer with a layer of mint leaves, pepper, chili pepper, and a pinch of salt. ✦ Pour the vinegar into a saucepan, add the garlic cloves and ½ cup water, and bring to a boil. ✦ Let this boil about 10 minutes then pour it over the squash, adding about 3 tablespoons of the oil the squash was cooked in. ✦ Cover the container and let this marinate for about 12 hours in the refrigerator. Serve cold.

ZUCCHINE ALLA SCAPECE | MARINATED ZUCCHINI WITH MINT

CAMPANIA

3 ½ lbs. medium zucchini, cut in thick rounds

CONTINUED

This dish is typical of Salerno. *Scapece* is even better served the next day.

Arrange the zucchini rounds on a plate and set them out to dry in a warm place (out in the sun if possible). ✦ Heat the olive oil and cook the rounds a few at a time

½ cup olive oil

2 garlic cloves, sliced

1 bunch mint leaves

½ cup white wine vinegar

until they take on color. ✦ Using a skimmer or slotted spoon, lift them out of the oil and transfer them to a bowl, alternating layers of zucchini with layers of garlic and mint leaves. ✦ Pour the vinegar over the whole thing and let it rest about 2 hours. Do not stir until the moment of serving.

SWEET-AND-SOUR ZUCCHINI

ZUCCHINE IN AGRODOLCE

SARDEGNA

Olive oil, for frying

1 ½ lbs. small zucchini, sliced in rounds

4 tbsp. sugar

4 tbsp. white wine vinegar

This dish is typical of Nuoro and is delicious warm in the autumn or cold in the summertime.

Heat ¼ inch of olive oil in a large pan. Add the zucchini in batches and fry, transferring them when done to another pan large enough to hold them in a single layer. ✦ When all the zucchini has been fried, melt the sugar and vinegar together in a saucepan over low heat and pour it over the zucchini. ✦ Put them back over heat for a minute and serve hot.

MARINATED ZUCCHINI STRIPS

ZUCCHINI IN CAÔDA

PIEMONTE

Extra-virgin olive oil

1 ½ lbs. zucchini

2 garlic cloves, chopped

2 anchovies, rinsed, boned, and chopped

1 dried chili pepper, crumbled

½ cup white wine vinegar

Salt and pepper

This dish is typical of Monferrato.

Heat ¼ inch of olive oil in a pan. Cut the zucchini lengthwise to form long strips and briefly cook them in the oil until lightly golden. Transfer them to a container. ✦ Make the marinade by combining 2 tablespoons olive oil, the garlic, anchovies, chili pepper, salt, pepper, and vinegar. Pour the marinade over the zucchini, making sure the zucchini is completely covered. ✦ Marinate for at least 24 hours, covered, in the refrigerator. Serve hot or cold according to the season.

SAUTÉED ZUCCHINI

ZUCCHINE IN CARPIONE

PIEMONTE

3 tbsp. extra-virgin olive oil

CONTINUED

Heat the olive oil over low heat, add the onions, and cook, adding salt to taste. ✦ When the onions have colored, add the zucchini and cook until golden. ✦ Add the bread and cook 10 to 15 minutes, adding a little warm

2 medium onions, finely sliced

1 ½ lbs. zucchini, cut in small pieces and seeded

Bread of a roll, soaked in vinegar and squeezed dry

Salt

water if needed to keep the mixture sufficiently soft. Serve hot.

MARINATED ZUCCHINI

ZUCCHINE MARINATE

LAZIO

1 lb. zucchini

Extra-virgin olive oil

2 garlic cloves, sliced

¼ cup white wine vinegar

1 tbsp. finely chopped flat-leaf parsley

Salt

This dish is typical of Rome.

Clean the zucchini, trim off the ends, and cut them into disks. ✦ Heat ½ inch of olive oil in a sauté pan over high heat. Fry the zucchini, removing them as soon as they begin to brown and putting them in a container. ✦ Heat 5 tablespoons olive oil in a second pan and sauté the garlic until golden; add the vinegar, parsley, and a pinch of salt. ✦ Turn off the heat, stir the marinade, and pour it over the zucchini. ✦ Let them marinate in this liquid at least one full day before serving. Serve cold.

STUFFED ZUCCHINI

ZUCCHINE RIPIENE

LIGURIA

12 small zucchini

¼ cup extra-virgin olive oil

1 ½ garlic cloves, minced

¼ oz. dried mushrooms, soaked in lukewarm water, drained, and chopped

2 large eggs, beaten

⅔ cup grated Parmigiano-Reggiano

2 oz. crustless bread, soaked in milk and squeezed dry

1 tbsp. fresh oregano

1 ½ cups breadcrumbs

Salt and pepper

Eggplant can be prepared in the same manner.

Preheat the oven to 350°F. Clean the zucchini, parboil them in lightly salted water to cover until they just start to soften, about 6 minutes, and drain. ✦ When they are cool enough to handle, cut them in half lengthwise. Scoop out the pulp with a spoon, setting aside the emptied halves. Finely chop the pulp and set it aside. ✦ Heat the olive oil until hot, then cook the garlic and mushrooms until the mushrooms have wilted and the moisture has evaporated. Remove from the heat and let cool. ✦ When this mixture has cooled, add the zucchini pulp, eggs, cheese, bread, oregano, salt, and pepper. ✦ Fill the zucchini halves with this mixture and arrange them in a baking pan. Drizzle with olive oil and sprinkle with breadcrumbs, then place in the oven. Pour about ¼ inch of water into the pan. ✦ Bake for about 25 minutes, or until the filling is golden.

VEGETABLES

CHAPTER
SEVEN

CHEESE DISHES

FONDUE WITH WHITE TRUFFLES

PIEMONTE

1⅔ cups cubed high-quality fontina (preferably from the Valle d'Aosta)

2 cups milk, plus more as needed

1¼ cups cubed lower-fat fontina

¾ lb. (3 sticks) unsalted butter

4 egg yolks, lightly beaten

3 oz. white truffles from Alba, shaved

Put the high-quality fontina in a bowl, add 1 cup of milk (or enough to cover the cheese completely), and let sit for 3 hours. ✦ Pour off and discard the milk, replacing it with an equal quantity of fresh milk. ✦ Meanwhile, melt the lower-fat fontina with the butter in the top of a double boiler. Add the egg yolks, then pour in the milk and fontina mixture. ✦ Cook, whisking constantly, until it is a thick, creamy liquid. ✦ Serve the fondue hot, with a dusting of the truffles.

VALDOSTAN FONDUE

VALLE D'AOSTA

2⅓ cups cubed fontina (preferably from the Valle d'Aosta)

2 cups milk

2 tbsp. unsalted butter

4 large egg yolks, beaten

This recipe dates back to the 1800s and was probably invented by the cook of Count Cavour, who had spent time at Forte di Bard (in Aosta) in his youth. However, the term *fondue* had already appeared in the *Cuisinier Moderne* by Vincent La Chapelle in 1735, used for a preparation of French cheeses and truffles with eggs. This fondue is also excellent as a sauce for boiled rice. The fondue can be served in earthenware bowls with slices of white bread toasted or sautéed in butter, simply dusting it with black pepper ground at the table, or it can be served with white Piemonte truffles sliced using a truffle slicer.

Put the fontina in a bowl, cover with milk, and refrigerate overnight. ✦ When you are ready to make the fondue, drain off most of the milk. ✦ In the top of a double boiler, melt the butter. Add the fontina with its remaining milk and cook at low heat until melted, stirring constantly with a wooden spoon. ✦ Add the egg yolks all at once and cook, stirring and never letting the mixture boil, until it has become a smooth, dense cream. ✦

CHEESE SAUCE WITH POTATOES AND ONIONS

FRIULI-VENEZIA GIULIA

3 tbsp. extra-virgin olive oil

1 lb. potatoes, peeled and cubed

⅔ cup chopped onions

This sauce, typical of the area of Carnia, goes quite well with polenta.

Heat the olive oil in a pan and cook the potatoes and onions over low heat until the potatoes begin to fall apart, adding water as needed to keep them from taking on any

9 oz. fresh Montasio, cut in pieces
9 oz. aged Montasio, cut in pieces
Salt

color. ✦ When the potatoes have nearly disintegrated, add both cheeses, stirring to form a homogeneous mixture and adding salt to taste.

FRICO | **CHEESE CRISP**

FRIULI-VENEZIA GIULIA

4 oz. fresh Montasio, finely cubed
4 oz. aged Montasio, finely cubed

If you place the disk of cheese while still hot atop an upside-down bowl, it will take on a nice basket shape as it cools.

Mix the cheeses together. Heat a large nonstick pan over medium heat. Sprinkle the two cheeses in the pan so that they cover the entire surface. Cook until the cheese melts but does not take on color. Gently turn over to cook on the other side briefly, until crisp.

✦ **LOCAL TRADITION** ✦

FRICO

In this simple recipe from Friuli-Venezia Giulia for fried cheese disks, thin slices of fresh mountain cheese are sautéed in a little olive oil or butter until they form a single disk with a crust. Popular variations include the additions of sliced onions, tomatoes, potatoes, or even apples, first fried and then added to the cheese as it melts to become part of the final crispy disk.

FRICO CON PATATE | **CHEESE CRISP WITH POTATOES**

FRIULI-VENEZIA GIULIA

6 oz. smoked pancetta, diced
1 medium onion, cut in thin slices
4 large potatoes, peeled and cubed
10 oz. Montasio (if possible, aged 3 months), cut in small cubes
Salt and pepper

Heat the pancetta in a large pan over low heat until it begins to give off fat. Add the onion and cook until translucent. ✦ Add the potatoes, salt, pepper, and 1 cup water; cook 30 minutes. Add the cheese and blend. ✦ Transfer this to an 8- or 9-inch pan, leaving behind as much fat as possible. Sauté the *frico* on both sides until it has a golden crust. ✦ Cut in quarters and serve.

MARINATED TOMINO CHEESE

VALLE D'AOSTA

1 bunch flat-leaf parsley, finely chopped

2 garlic cloves, finely chopped

1 dried chili pepper, finely chopped

A few sage leaves, finely chopped

2 sprigs thyme, finely chopped

1 celery stalk, finely chopped

Pinch grated nutmeg

5 tbsp. extra-virgin olive oil

3 tbsp. white wine vinegar

8 fresh tomino cheeses from the Valle d'Aosta, cubed

16 slices bread, toasted

Pepper

The amounts of ingredients in this recipe, typical of Courmayeur, can be adjusted to your personal tastes. Tomino cheese comes in small disks.

Put the chopped ingredients in a bowl and add the nutmeg and pepper. ✦ Add olive oil and vinegar to make a sauce; put the tomino cheese in this sauce and let it stand for a few hours. ✦ Serve with slices of toasted bread.

FOCACCIA WITH CHEESE

FUGASSA CÖ FORMAGGIO

LIGURIA

1 tbsp. extra-virgin olive oil

1⅔ cups hard durum flour

1 lb. cheese (see note), cubed

Coarse salt

For the cheese you can use Crescentina, Invernizzina, or Stracchino from Liguria.

Preheat the oven to 400°F. Grease a baking sheet with olive oil and sprinkle with salt. Use the flour to prepare a pasta dough as in the recipe on page 10, using 5 tablespoons water in place of the eggs; roll out two sheets about ⅛ inch thick (see note, page 212). ✦ Arrange the cubes of cheese across one of the sheets and cover with the other. Place on the prepared pan and bake until the dough has formed a golden crust and the cheese has melted, about 15 minutes.

LARGE TOMATO AND MOZZARELLA RAVIOLI

PANZEROTTI, MOZZARELLA E POMODORO

PUGLIA

5 cups all-purpose flour

¼ oz. active dry yeast

CONTINUED

Use the flour and yeast to prepare a dough as on page 10, using 1¾ cups water (and add the potato if desired) in place of eggs. Cover and let the dough rise for about 2 hours. ✦ Meanwhile, crush the tomatoes and drain them in a colander. When the tomatoes are well drained,

1 large potato, boiled and put through a sieve (optional)

1 lb. plum tomatoes, peeled

10 oz. mozzarella (best if aged), diced

Extra-virgin olive oil, for frying

Salt and pepper

add them to the mozzarella and season with salt and pepper. ✦ Divide the dough into balls, then roll out each ball into a disk about 8 inches in diameter and ⅛ inch thick. ✦ Put a few tablespoons of the mozzarella and tomato mixture at the center of each, fold the dough over to form a half moon, and close with a pasta wheel, pinching the edges to seal. ✦ Heat 1 inch of olive oil in a large pan, add the *panzerotti*, and fry until golden, moving them around to prevent them from taking on too much color.

✦ **LOCAL TRADITION** ✦

PALLOTTE

From Trivento in Molise comes this old recipe for cheese and sausage dumplings in tomato sauce. The dumplings would be made with stale bread without the crust, grated pecorino, finely chopped dried sausage, and parsley worked together with egg to yield a soft dough. This dough would then be shaped into meatball-size dumplings and the balls lightly rolled in flour. A simple tomato sauce of onion and *lardo* slowly sautéed together, tomato purée, water, and salt would be prepared alongside and used to cook the dumplings, undisturbed, for about twenty minutes. The trick was not to stir the sauce at all or remove the lid from the pan until just before serving, otherwise the delicate dumplings would go flat.

PEYLA D'ORZO

POTATO PURÉE WITH CHEESE

VALLE D'AOSTA

1½ lbs. potatoes, peeled

1⅔ cups soft wheat flour

1⅔ cups barley flour

2 oz. fontina

4 oz. toma (soft, fresh cheese, can substitute ricotta)

¼ cup (4 tbsp.) unsalted butter, melted

Salt

This dish is typical of Cogne.

Boil the potatoes in a pot of lightly salted water to cover, drain them (reserving the water), peel them, and put them through a potato ricer. ✦ Mix the flours and whisk them into the potato water; when they are well mixed add the mashed potatoes. Cook over low heat, stirring occasionally with a wooden spoon, for about 30 minutes. ✦ Transfer to another pot and add the cheese, stirring until all the cheese has melted. Pour the melted butter over the top and serve.

RICOTTA MANTECATA CON CIALDE

Once a traditional dish for the feast of Our Lady Help of Christians held in late May, this recipe for marinated ricotta (or *seirass*—the local name meaning "curd" for Piemontese ricotta) comes from the area of Quincinetto and was typical throughout the upper Canavese. The fresh, soft *seirass* would be mixed with salt, pepper, cumin seeds, a crumbled hot chili pepper, and, according to taste, wild fennel seeds. The resulting grainy mixture, now a straw color, was called *salignon* in the local dialect, and could either be left to sit for a few days and eaten fresh or be dried by hanging it near the hearth in a canvas bag to absorb the smoke. If smoked, it became known as *mortret* and could be bought in round bundles about the size of a small apple.

PIZZA COL FORMAGGIO | # CHEESE ROLLS

FOR 6
CHEESE ROLLS

MARCHE

¼ lb. (½ cup) unsalted butter

7 large eggs

3 tsp. sugar

5 cups all-purpose flour

⅔ cup grated pecorino

4 oz. ricotta

2 ¼ tsp. active dry yeast, dissolved in 3 tbsp. warm milk

Grated zest of 1 lemon

10 oz. fresh pecorino, cut in 6 sticks

Salt and pepper

Butter 6 ramekins, if possible made of terra-cotta. Beat the eggs with salt, pepper, and sugar. ✦ Gradually add the flour, pecorino, ricotta, yeast mixture, and lemon zest. ✦ Fill each ramekin halfway with the mixture and push a stick of pecorino into the middle of each one, then set aside in a warm place and wait for the dough to rise until doubled in volume. ✦ Preheat the oven to 400°F. Bake for about 30 minutes, then lower the heat to 325° and bake another 30 minutes until golden.

RICOTTA FRITTA | # FRIED RICOTTA

MOLISE

Olive oil, for frying

CONTINUED

Prepared this way, ricotta is golden and crunchy on the outside while on the inside it maintains all its soft creaminess.

In a pan, heat 3 inches of olive oil until hot. Dip the ricotta slices in flour, then in eggs, then in breadcrumbs. Fry

1 lb. ricotta (preferably sheep's milk), in somewhat thick slices

2 tbsp. all-purpose flour

2 large eggs, beaten

1 cup breadcrumbs

Salt

them until golden, then remove them with a slotted spoon and set them out to drain on paper towels. Sprinkle with salt.

SCAMORZA AFFUMICATA CON FUNGHI CARDONCELLI ALL'OLIO

SMOKED SCAMORZA SALAD WITH MUSHROOMS

PUGLIA

1 lb. smoked scamorza cheese

½ lb. salad greens (radicchio, lettuce, arugula)

7 oz. oil-packed *cardoncelli* mushrooms, drained

Heat a grill or grill pan until hot. Cut the scamorza into thick slices and arrange these over the grill for a few minutes; meanwhile, wash and tear up the salad greens and arrange in a serving bowl. ✦ Top with the scamorza and mushrooms and serve immediately.

SCHIZ CON POLENTA

HOMEMADE CHEESE

VENETO

2½ gallons fresh whole milk

¼ oz. rennet (available as rennin in most supermarkets)

Unsalted butter

Salt

Schiz is the typical daily cheese of the mountain communities around Feltre and Belluno. Although in substance it is hardly more than rennet, along with polenta it represented the almost daily meal of the mountain dweller. Today *schiz* is available at some stores, but since freshness is the essential requisite for its quality, the best will always be made at home and eaten within a day. Refinements include the addition of cream or milk during the cooking phase and dipping the slices of *schiz* in beaten eggs and breadcrumbs before cooking it. Serve on a warmed plate with polenta.

Heat some fresh whole milk in a pan to a temperature of about 95°F; add the rennet and let it rest for a little more than 30 minutes. ✦ Use a whisk to separate the mass, reducing it to grains the size of a pea. ✦ After another 10 minutes of rest, heat it to 104°F, constantly stirring. ✦ After another period of rest in which the rennet will separate from the whey, drain it through a cloth, slice, and sauté in a pan with some butter and a little salt, first on one side and then on the other, until it forms a golden crust.

CHEESE DISHES

| SCHIZ IMPANATO | **BREADED CHEESE** |

| VENETO |

4 tbsp. (¼ cup) unsalted butter
Schiz (see note, page 743)
3 large eggs, beaten
1 cup breadcrumbs
Cooked wild mushrooms
Salt

Heat the butter over medium-high heat until hot. Cut the cheese in ½-inch-thick slices, dip them in egg, then in breadcrumbs, and fry them until golden, first on one side, then on the other, adding salt only at the end when the slices will have formed a nice crust. ✦ Serve immediately with cooked mushrooms.

| TARÒZ | **CRUSHED POTATOES AND BEANS WITH CHEESE** |

| LOMBARDIA |

¾ lb. potatoes, peeled
1½ lbs. green beans
1⅔ cups fresh shelled beans
1 lb. (2 cups) unsalted butter
1 or more medium onions, sliced
4 oz. young *casera*, cubed
4 oz. *grasso casera*, cubed
⅓ cup grated Parmigiano-Reggiano
Salt and pepper

Taròz is a dish unknown outside the Valtellina, where it was first created on the banks of the Davaglione. There are variations from zone to zone. *Casera* is a generic term meaning cheese. You can substitute *bitto*, Taleggio, or fontina.

Cook the potatoes and green beans together in a pot of boiling water; cook the shelled beans separately. ✦ When the vegetables are tender, drain them and set them aside together in the same bowl. ✦ Heat ½ cup of the butter in a pan and add the onions; cook over medium-low heat until the onions are golden brown. ✦ Using a wooden spoon, roughly crush the vegetables and when the butter has browned, add them to the pan and mix well at low heat for 5 minutes. ✦ Add the rest of the butter, cheeses, salt, and pepper. Cook over low heat until the cheese is melted and smooth. Serve hot.

| TOMINI IN COMPOSTA | **MARINATED TOMINI** |

| PIEMONTE |

This dish is typical of Chiaverano. Fully 64 of the 403 original cheeses officially recognized in Italy are produced in Piemonte. A popular song credits the local toma cheese with having convinced many of Hannibal's Carthaginian troops to remain in Piemonte, creating new families with the local women. There is then the treatise published in Turin in 1477 by Pantaleone da Confienza, the *Summa Lacticinorum Completa Omnibus Idonei*, which includes a monograph *De caseis* that lists the typical cheeses produced in the Valle d'Aosta, the Vale di

12 dried *tomini* (see note)

2 tbsp. white wine vinegar

1 dried chili pepper, finely chopped

1 tsp. tomato paste

1 cup extra-virgin olive oil

Pepper

Lanzo, the Val di Susa, etc. Among the specialties of Piemonte, the tomini cheeses, made from cow's milk (but also from goat or sheep's milk), enjoy particular fame. Those from the Canavese area differ from the others because the rennet, before being put in molds, goes through a further process in which it is salted, removing any excess whey. This "aging" was once performed in special perforated molds. Today, instead, the mass is pressed in a cylindrical form from which it emerges as a form about 10 inches long with a diameter of about 1½ inches. The cheese is then "sliced" to divide it into the individual tomini. Thanks to this salting, these cheeses can be preserved for longer periods than other types of similar cheeses, provided, of course, they are kept in a cool place. They can be consumed fresh or dried, on their own or seasoned in various ways. If desired, add a few garlic cloves, a bay leaf, a few cloves, or a few peppercorns to the marinade.

Arrange the tomini in an earthenware pan and sprinkle with a little pepper and vinegar. ✦ Put the chili pepper in a pan, add the tomato paste, then very slowly, and while constantly stirring, pour in the olive oil. ✦ Pour this over the tomini, making certain they are fully covered, then let them soak up these flavors for at least 1 day. Store this in a cool place, making sure the tomini remain completely covered by the marinade.

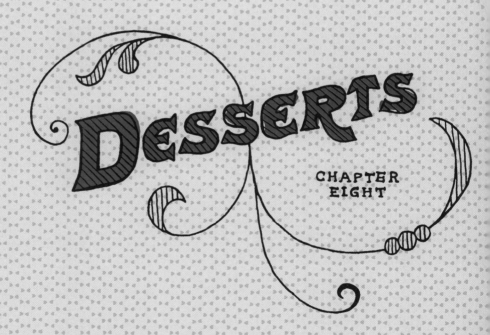

DESSERTS

CHAPTER EIGHT

GLAZED SWEET ROLLS

PUGLIA

½ cup milk
¾ lb. (1½ cups) unsalted butter
1¼ cups sugar
6⅔ cups all-purpose flour
5 large eggs
3 tsp. baking powder
1 tsp. vanilla extract
¾ cup confectioners' sugar
Juice of 1 lemon
⅔ cup dark rum

Although this is the most exquisite of Lecce's traditional desserts, it cannot be found in pastry shops. Pastry shops offer traditional desserts only for certain occasions and do not seek to repeat old ones. Literally the name means "cat-drowners."

Preheat the oven to 400°F. Heat 2 tablespoons of the milk over low heat in a large pot. Add the butter and stir until it is melted. Remove the pot from the heat and mix in the sugar, the flour, eggs, baking powder, ¾ teaspoon of the vanilla, and the remaining milk. Turn out onto a floured surface and knead until a smooth dough forms. Shape the resulting dough into 2-inch rounds. Place them 1 inch apart on a baking sheet and bake them until golden. ✦ Meanwhile, prepare the glaze: mix the confectioners' sugar with 1¼ cups water in a saucepan and bring to a boil. Reduce the heat and simmer until the mixture forms threads when the spoon is lifted from the pan (223°F to 234°F on a candy thermometer). At that point add the lemon juice, rum, and the remaining vanilla, then simmer for 3 minutes more. Brush this glaze on the warm rolls, then put them back in the oven (with the heat off but still warm) to dry, about 10 minutes.

ANICINI | ## ANISE COOKIES

LIGURIA

12 large eggs, separated
2½ cups granulated sugar
½ cup orange-flower water
1 tsp. anise seeds
4¼ cups all-purpose flour
Confectioners' sugar, for dusting

Preheat the oven to 350°F. In a large bowl, beat the egg yolks together with the granulated sugar, orange-flower water, and anise seeds until pale yellow. Whip the egg whites until frothy and fold into the yolk mixture. Finally, add the flour and continue mixing until blended. ✦ Grease 2 biscotti pans, then line them with parchment. Butter the parchment. Pour the dough into the pans and smooth the top. Bake for 20 minutes, then take them out and cut them in small slices. ✦ Increase the oven temperature to 400°F. Arrange the slices on a baking sheet and return to the oven for another 20 minutes. Dust with confectioners' sugar.

SARDINIAN ORANGE SLICES

ARANCIATA SARDA

SARDEGNA

1 lb. orange peels, preferably from organic fruit

1 ⅓ cups honey, preferably from Sardegna

⅔ cup sugar

1 cup almonds, shelled and ground into paste

This recipe is typical of Nuoro.

After carefully scraping away the pith from the orange peels, cut them in strips about 2 inches long and ⅛ inch wide. ✦ Put the peels in a large pot and add water to cover. Soak the peels for 5 days, changing the water daily, until the peels lose their bitter aroma. ✦ After the fifth day, drain away the water and put the strips of orange peel in a pot over low heat and slowly add the honey, stirring often and carefully until the strips have absorbed the honey. ✦ At this point add the sugar and the almond paste and stir until blended. ✦ Spread out this mixture on a sheet of aluminum foil and level it off with a rolling pin to the thickness desired (usually about ½ inch). Let this rest a few hours. Then cut with a knife into the shapes and sizes desired.

BABAS WITH RUM

BABÀ

FOR 6 PERSONS

CAMPANIA

½ lb. (1 cup) unsalted butter, plus more for greasing the dish

¾ cup milk

2 ¼ tsp. active dry yeast

2 cups all-purpose flour, plus more as needed

6 large eggs

1 ½ cups sugar

½ cup rum

This recipe is typical of Naples. *Babà* is usually served accompanied by cherries in pastry cream. Another excellent accompaniment is whipped cream and strawberries or just cream and zabaglione with Marsala.

Heat the oven until warm (about 200°F). Use some of the butter to grease a baba mold or round high-sided baking dish. Heat 2 tablespoons of the milk until just warm. Dissolve the yeast in the lukewarm milk. Work it into the flour, then turn the mixture out onto a floured surface and knead, adding flour as needed, to create a smooth ball of dough. Place in a bowl, cover with a kitchen towel, and set this to rise in the barely heated oven. ✦ When the dough has doubled in size, about half an hour, work in the remaining butter and the eggs. Put the dough in the baba mold and let the baba rise a second time. Increase the oven temperature to 375°F, then place the baba in the oven to bake. ✦ While the baba bakes prepare the syrup. Dissolve the sugar in ¾ cup water in a saucepan over low heat; simmer it until it begins to form threads when the spoon is lifted from the pan (223°F to 234°F on a candy thermometer). Remove

DESSERTS

749

from the heat and let cool slightly, then whisk in the rum. ✦ Remove the baba from the oven when it is golden brown all over. Using a small ladle or spoon pour the syrup over the warm baba, doing so several times by collecting the syrup that falls to the bottom of the baba.

BAICOLI | VENETIAN BISCOTTI

VENETO

1 tsp. active dry yeast
¼ cup milk, warmed, or as needed
1¼ cups all-purpose flour
⅔ cup sugar
½ lb. (2 sticks) plus 4 tbsp. unsalted butter
3 egg whites, beaten until frothy
Salt

Dissolve the yeast in 2 tablespoons milk and work it into the flour; form this into a ball and inscribe a cross on the top of it. Set aside to let rise 30 minutes. ✦ At the end of that time knead in the remaining ingredients adding enough lukewarm milk to obtain a smooth dough the consistency of bread dough. ✦ Knead until smooth, then shape into long cylinders. Place them on a baking sheet and let them rise 1½ hours. ✦ Preheat the oven to 400°F. Then bake for 10 minutes. Remove from the oven and set aside to rest for 48 hours. ✦ At the end of that time cut the cylinders into thin slices and bake them until lightly browned and crisp, 10 minutes more.

BARBAJADA | BARBAJADA

LOMBARDIA

4 oz. (4 squares) bittersweet chocolate, chopped
½ cup brewed espresso coffee
½ cup milk or cream

This dish seems to bear the name of its inventor, a certain Neapolitan theatrical impresario named Barbaja (1778–1841), who concocted it at the Caffè dei Virtuosi in Milan's Via Manzoni. Rather than a dessert, this is really a sweet drink consumed warm that was once adored by the Milanese. A place called Samarani seems to have been the last Milanese café famous for its way of preparing it. During the summer this is excellent cold.

Combine the chocolate, coffee, and milk or cream in a saucepan; whisk this over medium-low heat until the chocolate melts and the mixture begins to foam. Pour into 4 espresso cups and serve.

ALMOND TART WITH CHOCOLATE GLAZE

PUGLIA

For the short pastry:

1 ¼ cups all-purpose flour, plus more as needed

¼ lb. (1 stick) unsalted butter

⅔ cup sugar

3 egg yolks

Salt

For the filling:

6 oz. blanched almonds

3 large eggs, separated

¾ cup sugar

1 pinch ground cinnamon

Grated zest of 1 lemon

¼ cup pear jelly, warmed to liquid

For the glaze:

1 ¼ cups sugar

1 oz. (1 square) unsweetened chocolate

Prepare the short pastry, forming a well with the flour and putting the butter in pieces in the middle. Work together the flour and butter until they become a mass of small lumps. ✦ Make the well again, adding the sugar to the center, a pinch of salt, and the egg yolks. Work these ingredients together to form a smooth dough, adding flour as needed. ✦ Spread out the dough with the palms of your hands, fold it over on itself, then repeat. Shape it into a ball, wrap it in waxed paper, and refrigerate for at least 1 hour. ✦ Preheat the oven to 350°F. Butter a round cake pan. For the filling: finely chop the almonds. Beat the egg yolks with the sugar and add the almonds, a little salt, cinnamon, and lemon zest. Beat the egg whites until soft peaks form and gently fold them into the mixture. ✦ Roll out the dough to about ¹⁄₁₆ of an inch and use it to line the bottom of the pan; spread the pastry with the pear jelly across the bottom then pour in the filling. Bake for about 30 minutes. It is ready when a toothpick inserted in the center comes out clean. Let it cool. ✦ For the chocolate glaze: Dissolve the sugar in ¾ cup water in a saucepan over low heat and simmer it until it begins to form threads when a spoon is lifted from the pan (223°F to 234°F on a candy thermometer). Remove from the heat and let cool slightly. Melt the chocolate in a double boiler and add the sugar syrup. Stir until smooth and pour the warm glaze over the tart. Let stand until set, about 1 hour.

FRUITCAKE 1

TOSCANA

¾ lb. (1 ½ cups) unsalted butter, melted and cooled slightly

4 large eggs, beaten

1 ⅔ cups sugar

⅔ cup golden raisins, soaked in warm water, dried, and lightly floured

CONTINUED

This recipe is typical of the Garfagnana, north of Lucca.

Preheat the oven to 400°F. Butter a high-sided baking dish. Beat the eggs with the sugar with a mixer on medium speed until pale yellow. Add the butter; blend well with a wooden spoon and add the raisins (flouring the raisins keeps them from sinking to the bottom). Add the lemon and orange zest. ✦ At this point add the candied fruit. Then gradually add the potato starch and flour (a little at a time), and, if necessary, add a little milk to soften the

Grated zest of 1 lemon
Grated zest of 1 orange
½ cup candied fruit, chopped
⅔ cup potato starch
1⅔ cups all-purpose flour
½ cup milk (if necessary)

dough. ✦ Place the dough in the baking dish and bake for about 30 minutes (it is always best to test with a toothpick, which should come out clean from the middle of the pastry).

TUSCAN SWEET BREAD

TOSCANA

¼ lb. (½ cup) unsalted butter, melted and cooled slightly
3⅓ cups all-purpose flour, plus more as needed
2 large eggs
1¼ cups sugar
2 tsp. baking powder
Grated zest of 1 lemon
3 tbsp. milk, or as needed
Salt

This recipe is typical of Lamporecchio.

Preheat the oven to 350°F. Butter and flour a baking pan. In a bowl, mix the flour, eggs, sugar, butter, baking powder, lemon zest, and a pinch of salt. Add the milk 1 tablespoon at a time until you obtain a soft dough. ✦ Place the dough in the prepared pan and bake for about 40 minutes until lightly browned.

BLANCMANGE

FOR
6 PERSONS

CAMPANIA

½ cup cornstarch
2 cups milk
2 scant cups sugar
Peel from 1 lemon

This dessert is best accompanied by cookies. The blancmange can be flavored with almond milk.

Dissolve the cornstarch in a pan with the milk, pour the sugar in slowly, and add the lemon peel (which will later be removed). ✦ Cook over low heat, stirring constantly with a wooden spoon, until the mixture thickens and coats the back of the spoon when it is removed from the pan. Remove the lemon peel. ✦ When the blancmange has thickened, pour it into a large glass dish or, in keeping with tradition, into small individual molds. As soon as it has cooled put it in the refrigerator to chill for several hours. ✦ When ready to serve, turn the mold or molds upside down. The blancmange should slide out easily. If it does not, slip a knife around the edges of the mold to loosen.

BIASCIA

CORNMEAL FRUITCAKE

LOMBARDIA

10 oz. stale bread, diced

6 cups milk

3 tbsp. unsalted butter

3 large eggs

Grated zest of 1 lemon

3 pears, peeled, cored, and chopped

3 apples, peeled, cored, and chopped

1 or 2 tbsp. raisins

2 tbsp. all-purpose flour

1 tbsp. cornmeal

1 cup plus 1 tbsp. sugar

1 tbsp. extra-virgin olive oil

1 sprig rosemary, chopped

This recipe is typical of the Brianza area north of Milan and seems to be a combination of two ancient recipes, the *meascia*, originally from Tremezzo at Lake Como, and the *Torta del Michelasc*, of which there are several variations. In the Brianza these are made using mixed flour and cornmeal; the *Torta paesana* or *Torta del Michelasc* from farther north is instead made from a base of stale bread soaked in milk. It is made of *mich* (bread) and *lacce* (milk), hence *michelasc*.

Soak the bread in the milk for 1 hour. Preheat the oven to 350°F and butter a cake pan. Add the eggs to the bread mixture, working them in gently, then add the lemon zest, pears, apples, raisins, flour, cornmeal, and 1 cup sugar. ✦ Mix well then transfer to the cake pan, smoothing the top; the dough should be about about 1½ inches thick. ✦ Dot with butter and drizzle with olive oil, then sprinkle with 1 tablespoon sugar and rosemary. ✦ Bake for 1 hour until golden.

BIGNÈ DI SAN GIUSEPPE

ST. JOSEPH'S DAY FRITTERS

LAZIO

3 tbsp. unsalted butter

⅔ cup all-purpose flour

2 large eggs plus 1 yolk

1½ tsp. sugar

Grated zest of ½ lemon

4 cups extra-virgin olive oil, for frying

½ cup vanilla sugar

Salt

This recipe is typical of Rome.

In a saucepan combine 1 cup cold water, butter, and a pinch of salt; bring this to a boil over medium heat. Remove from the heat and add all the flour in all at once, stirring vigorously with a wooden spoon. ✦ Place the pan back over the heat and stir to obtain a ball that easily comes away from the wooden spoon and from the sides of the pan. When the mixture begins making a slight "sizzling" sound, as though it were frying, remove it from the heat and let it cool. ✦ When it has cooled, mix in the eggs and yolk one at a time and knead the dough. The dough must be worked a long time in order for this recipe to succeed. When the dough begins to produce scattered air bubbles, add the sugar and the lemon zest. Continue working the dough to incorporate these last two ingredients, then wrap it in a clean cloth and set it aside in a cool spot for 45 minutes. ✦ Heat the olive oil in a deep frying pan over medium heat. Drop in the dough in walnut-size pieces. Fry a few at a time on both sides. As they swell, turn up the heat to medium-high; as soon as they are a good blonde color remove them and let them drain on paper towels. Return the heat to medium between each batch. ✦ Arrange them in a pyramid on a serving plate, sprinkle with vanilla sugar, and cover them with a napkin. Serve immediately.

BISCOTTI ALLA GENOVESE

GENOA BISCOTTI

LIGURIA

2 ¼ tsp. active dry yeast
3 ⅓ cups all-purpose flour
¾ cup (1 ½ sticks) unsalted butter
1 ¼ cups sugar
⅓ cup fennel seeds
3 tbsp. milk, or as needed
Salt

This recipe is typical of Genoa.

Dissolve the yeast in 2 tablespoons lukewarm water and combine it with as much flour as necessary to obtain a soft dough. Shape this into a ball and set it aside to rise for a few hours, covered with a clean dishcloth. ✦ Knead the remaining flour with the butter, sugar, fennel seeds, salt to taste, and a little milk to form a smooth dough. Combine the two doughs, knead together, and set them aside to rise for 1 hour. ✦ Butter a baking sheet. Form the dough into large loaves, put them on the baking sheet, and let them rise for 1 hour. ✦ Preheat the oven to 350°F. Make long shallow crosswise cuts in the dough about 1 inch apart. Bake the loaves for about 30 minutes and let them cool to just warm (do not turn off the oven). Separate the loaves into biscotti by completing the cuts already made in the surface. ✦ Place them on the baking sheet and return them to the oven for a second baking of about 15 minutes, or until lightly browned and crisp.

BISCOTTI CASERECCI

HOME-STYLE BISCOTTI

PUGLIA

6 ⅔ cups all-purpose flour
2 cups sugar
4 large eggs, 1 yolk reserved
½ cup extra-virgin olive oil
1 ½ tbsp. baking powder
Grated zest of 1 lemon
1 ¼ lbs. almonds, boiled, shelled, and lightly roasted
A few tbsp. milk (if necessary)

Preheat the oven to 400°F. Combine the ingredients except the reserved egg yolk to obtain a soft dough, adding milk by the tablespoon if necessary. ✦ Shape this into a loaf and place it on a baking sheet. Beat the reserved yolk and brush it over the loaf. Bake until light golden, about 15 minutes. ✦ Remove from the oven and cut the loaf into large slices. Return these to the oven for 15 minutes more until crisp.

ALMOND BISCOTTI 1

4 cups all-purpose flour
2⅓ cups sugar
1 tsp. baking powder
6 large eggs
2⅓ cups blanched almonds
Salt

Preheat the oven to 350°F. Mix the flour, sugar, baking powder, and a pinch of salt in a mixing bowl. Blend in the eggs to form a smooth dough. Knead in the almonds, then shape the dough into a cylinder, like a baguette. ✦ Place on a baking sheet and bake until the surface is light brown, about 20 minutes. ✦ Remove from the oven and cut crosswise into slices. Place these, without overlapping, on the baking sheet. Put back in the oven for their second baking. Bake until crisp, about 20 minutes.

MOIANO BISCOTTI

FOR
6 PERSONS

¼ cup (4 tbsp.) unsalted butter
2 cups all-purpose flour
⅔ cup sugar
¾ tsp. baking powder
2 large eggs
Grated zest of 1 lemon
Salt

Preheat the oven to 400°F. Butter a baking sheet. Mix the flour, sugar, baking powder, and a pinch of salt in a mixing bowl. Blend in the butter, eggs, and lemon zest to make a soft, compact dough, adding a little warm water if necessary. Form into a log. ✦ Slice this into biscotti and arrange them on the baking sheet and bake for half an hour until golden.

BISCOTTI FROM PROSTO

6⅔ cups all-purpose flour
2 cups sugar
1 lb. (4 sticks) unsalted butter

This recipe is typical of Sondrio. The complete recipe for the *biscotín* is still the secret of the owners of the mill at Prosto, alongside the parish church.

Preheat the oven to 350°F. Combine the ingredients to make a smooth dough, then shape into cylinders about 1½ inches in diameter. ✦ Cut these into slices about ¼ inch thick. Place on a baking sheet and bake about 10 minutes until golden.

DESSERTS

FERRARA BISCOTTI

Unsalted butter
3⅓ cups all-purpose flour
15 egg yolks
2 cups sugar
Grated zest of 1 lemon

Preheat the oven to 350°F. Butter and flour a baking sheet. Beat the yolks and sugar with a mixer on medium speed until pale yellow, then stir in the lemon zest and flour and blend to obtain a very soft dough. ✦ Put the dough on a lightly floured surface and roll it into a long cylinder. Cut this in small pieces, roll them into small ropes, then shape them into "S" shapes. ✦ Arrange the cookies on the baking sheet, leaving 2 inches between them, and bake for about 40 minutes until golden brown.

BLANCMANGE WITH AMARETTI

The bread of 1 roll, without crust
(about ½ cup)
2 cups milk
4 large eggs
¼ cup grated Parmigiano-Reggiano
6 amaretti, finely ground
1 cup sugar
¼ lb. (1 stick) unsalted butter,
melted and slightly cooled
Salt

This recipe is typical of Ivrea and differs from the blancmange recipe on page 752 in that bread is the thickener here, not cornstarch.

Preheat the oven to 350°F. Soften the bread in ½ cup milk, squeeze dry, then pulse a few times in a blender. ✦ Beat the eggs and add them to the blender along with the remaining milk, cheese, amaretti, a pinch of salt, ½ cup sugar, and butter. ✦ Blend these ingredients well, then put them into a saucepan and heat to a boil. ✦ Remove the pan from the heat and pour the mixture into a baking dish. Bake for about 20 minutes, until the mixture thickens. ✦ Caramelize a ring mold as in the recipe on page 791 (wear oven mitts if your mold is metal), using the remaining sugar. ✦ Pour the baked custard into the caramelized ring mold and put it in the refrigerator for a few hours. Turn out the pudding and serve cold.

RING CAKE

This cake is called *Bosilàn* in almost all of the area of Parma, but also *Bissolàn* in the area near Piacenza. In Reggio-Emilia it is made without the central hole and is called *Bucellato*, in Modena *Bensone*. The result should be a soft and delicate dough, tasty, and in a shape somewhat reminiscent of the more refined and recent *Pandoro* of Verona. About ¼ cup of a dry liquor such as dry sherry can be added to the dough if

3 ⅓ cups all-purpose flour

½ cup milk, lukewarm

1 ¼ cups sugar

4 oz. lard, melted (or 1 stick unsalted butter)

Grated zest of 1 lemon

2 large eggs (or 1 egg plus 3 yolks)

2 ¼ tsp. active dry yeast

Sugar or vanilla sugar (if desired)

Salt

desired. A similar recipe is made in Veneto and goes by the name *Ciambella*.

Shape the flour into a well and pour into it the milk, sugar, melted lard (if using butter instead, it should be warmed), a pinch of salt, and the lemon zest. Beat the eggs until blended, then add those to the flour. ✦ Blend all of this to obtain a dough that is not overly soft. Blend in the yeast and set it aside to rest until it has doubled in size. ✦ Preheat the oven to 400°F. Butter a round cake pan and the outside of a small ovenproof bowl. Add the dough to the pan, to form a ring, and place the bowl in the center to maintain the hole. Bake for 45 minutes. Dust the surface with sugar or vanilla sugar before serving, if desired.

BOSSOLÀ

VANILLA RING CAKE

LOMBARDIA

½ cup milk

½ vanilla bean

2 tsp. active dry yeast

¼ lb. (1 stick) plus 6 tbsp. unsalted butter, softened

1 ⅔ cups all-purpose flour

1 ¼ cups potato starch

4 large eggs, separated

1 ¼ cups sugar

Grated zest of 1 lemon

This is a homemade-style ring cake from the area of Brescia, similar to the *Bussolano* of Cremona and Mantua. The recipe can be enriched with the addition of raisins and candied fruit.

Heat the milk just to a boil and add the vanilla bean; remove the pan from the heat. Cover and let stand for 30 minutes, then remove the vanilla bean. Add the yeast. ✦ Butter a tube pan. Sift together the flour and potato starch, then whisk the egg whites until frothy. Whip the softened butter with the sugar until fluffy, then add the yolks and flour-starch mixture. ✦ Mix this together carefully, add the grated lemon zest, then add this mixture to the milk mixture. Fold in the whipped egg whites and pour into the buttered tube pan. ✦ Set it aside to rise for 1 hour. Preheat the oven to 325°F. Bake for about 40 minutes, until golden.

BOSTRENGO

BAKED RICE PUDDING WITH CHOCOLATE

MARCHE

2 ½ cups white rice

CONTINUED

Preheat the oven to 350°F. Cook the rice in salted water (or milk) to cover just until al dente. ✦ Meanwhile combine the sugar (or honey), eggs, orange and lemon zests, raisins and pine nuts, chocolate (or cocoa), coffee, and

1⅔ cups sugar (or honey)

3 large eggs

Grated zest of 1 orange

Grated zest of 1 lemon

1¼ cups mixed raisins and pine nuts

1¼ cups grated chocolate or cocoa powder

1 cup strong black coffee

6 oz. dried figs, finely chopped

2 tbsp. rum (or *alchermes*, see note, page 786)

Confectioners' sugar

Salt

figs in a saucepan. ✦ Pour in the rum (or *alchermes*). Mix well, heating if necessary to blend it well; add the drained rice. ✦ Combine this thoroughly then put in a baking pan and bake for about 1 hour, or until it forms a golden crust. ✦ Remove from the oven, let it cool, and serve sliced, sprinkled with confectioners' sugar.

BRICCIOLANI

SPICED SHORTBREAD

PIEMONTE

3⅓ cups all-purpose flour

1 cup sugar

Pinch ground cinnamon

Pinch ground cloves

Pinch grated nutmeg

¼ lb. (½ cup) plus 2 tbsp. unsalted butter

This recipe is typical of Vercelli.

Mix the flour with the sugar and the spices. Add the butter and knead, working it until a smooth dough forms. Refrigerate for at least 6 hours. ✦ Preheat the oven to 400°F. Butter a baking sheet and dust it with flour. ✦ Roll the dough to a thickness of about ⅛ inch. Cut grooves across the surface using a pastry wheel or a serrated bread knife. Cut the dough into rectangles about 1 by 3 inches and arrange on the pan. ✦ Bake for about 10 minutes, until golden.

BROTIE

RUM FRITTERS

FOR 6 TO 7 PERSONS

PIEMONTE

5 large eggs

¼ cup rum

¼ lb. (1 stick) plus 6 tbsp. unsalted butter, melted

5 cups all-purpose flour

2 tsp. baking powder

Extra-virgin olive oil, for frying

Sugar, for dusting

This recipe is typical of the Val Formazza.

Beat the eggs in a medium bowl with a mixer on medium speed until pale, then add the rum, butter, flour, and baking powder; work this together for at least 15 minutes to obtain a compact dough. ✦ Heat several inches of oil in a deep saucepan. Shape the dough into balls and fry them until golden. Drain on paper towels and dust with sugar.

UGLY AND GOOD COOKIES

BRUTTI E BUONI

VENETO

2 tbsp. unsalted butter

⅓ cup ground dry biscuits (zwieback)

⅓ cup all-purpose flour, plus more as needed

½ cup sugar

1 tbsp. ground cinnamon

1 egg plus 1 yolk

½ cup coarsely chopped almonds

½ cup chopped candied orange peel

Preheat the oven to 375°F. Butter a baking sheet. Combine all the ingredients and knead them together well to form a smooth dough. Shape this into long, thin cylinders about 1 inch in diameter and 14 inches long. ✦ Sprinkle the cylinders with flour and arrange them on the baking sheet. Bake until they are golden brown. ✦ While they are still warm cut them diagonally into 2-inch lengths.

UGLY BUT GOOD MACAROONS

BRUTTI MA BUONI

PIEMONTE

Unsalted butter

3¾ cups almonds

12 egg whites

2 cups sugar

1 tbsp. ground cinnamon

½ tsp. vanilla extract

This recipe is typical of Borgomanero. These can be preserved for a while if stored in airtight containers.

Preheat the oven to 350°F. Butter a baking sheet. Toast the almonds on an ungreased baking sheet until lightly browned, then finely chop them. Reduce the oven temperature to 300°F. ✦ Whip the egg whites until opaque and frothy, then stir in the almonds, sugar, cinnamon, and vanilla extract. Transfer the mixture to a saucepan and put it over very low heat, stirring constantly, for about 30 minutes, or until the liquid has evaporated. ✦ Use a tablespoon to scoop up lumps of the mixture, then place them on the buttered baking sheet and give them a roundish shape. ✦ Bake about 40 minutes, until slightly cracked and dry. ✦ Remove from the oven and let cool before serving.

LUCCA RING CAKE

BUCCELLATO

TOSCANA

3⅓ cups all-purpose flour, plus more as needed

¾ cup sugar

CONTINUED

This cake has been popular in Lucca for quite a while: food writer Waverley Root reports a reference to it in that city dating back to 1485. It tastes wonderful when dipped in white wine.

Mix the flour, sugar, 1 egg, butter, milk, and yeast with a pinch of salt. Knead to obtain a soft dough, then knead

DESSERTS

759

2 large eggs

4 tbsp. unsalted butter, melted and slightly cooled

½ cup milk

2 ¼ tsp. active dry yeast, dissolved in 1 tbsp. warm water

¼ cup raisins, softened in warm water and drained

2 tsp. anise seeds

Salt

in the raisins and anise seeds. Shape the dough into a ball, cover it with a cloth, and let it rise for a few hours in a warm spot. ✦ After the dough has risen, shape it into a round cake on a baking sheet, making a shallow incision along its full length with a knife. Let it rest for another hour. ✦ Preheat the oven to 375°F. Beat the remaining egg and brush on the dough. Bake for 1 hour. Serve lukewarm.

BUDINO DI LIMONE | # LEMON PUDDING

SICILIA

4 oz. sugar cubes

Peel of 3 ripe lemons, in strips

1 ¼ cups sugar

6 tbsp. cornstarch

Lemon leaves, for garnish

Rub the sugar cubes on the lemon peels so they will soak up the juice the peels secrete. ✦ Meanwhile, heat 4 cups water in a pot, add the sugar and cornstarch, and bring to a boil at low heat, stirring constantly. Add the sugar cubes, then continue cooking (it should become a dense cream). ✦ Still stirring, pour into a mold that has been dipped in water then drained, and refrigerated for at least 1 night. ✦ Cover the serving plate with lemon leaves, then turn the pudding out of the mold onto the plate.

BUDINO DI NOCI | # WALNUT PUDDING

ALTO ADIGE

¼ lb. (½ cup) unsalted butter, softened

½ cup breadcrumbs

⅔ cup sugar

½ cup walnuts, chopped

4 large eggs, separated

3 rolls without crust, crumbled and soaked in milk

Preheat the oven to 325°F. Butter pudding molds or ramekins and sprinkle them with breadcrumbs. Cream the butter and sugar together, then mix in the walnuts and egg yolks. Whisk the egg whites until stiff, then add the rolls, then the egg whites, to the mixture and combine. ✦ Pour the mixture into the molds, then place them in a baking pan large enough to hold them with 1 inch of space around each one. Place the pan on the oven rack, then fill the pan halfway with water. Bake until set, about 1 hour. When set, run a knife around the edges of the puddings, then turn the puddings out on a plate.

| # RICE PUDDING 1

¾ cup rice

2 cups milk

4 tbsp. (¼ cup) unsalted butter, in pieces

½ cup rum

Grated zest of 1 orange

½ cup golden raisins

⅓ cup chopped citron

⅔ cup sugar

3 large eggs, 2 separated

Semolina flour (or breadcrumbs)

Salt

Put the rice and a little salt in water to cover and heat over medium heat. When it comes to a boil drain the rice, discard the water, and combine the rice with the milk. Cook, stirring, on low heat. ✦ After about 40 minutes, by which time the rice should be becoming tender and thick, remove it from the heat and let it cool. Put the rice in a bowl and mix in the butter, then add the rum, orange zest, raisins, citron, and sugar. Add 1 egg and 2 yolks, setting aside the remaining whites. ✦ Preheat the oven to 350°F. Grease a baking dish with butter and dust with semolina flour or breadcrumbs. Whip the remaining egg whites until soft peaks form, add them to the rice mixture, and pour the mixture into the mold, smoothing the top. ✦ Place the mold in a baking pan large enough to hold it with 1 inch of space on all sides. Place the pan on the oven rack, then fill the pan halfway with water. Bake for 45 minutes or until set.

| # SEMOLINA PUDDING

FOR 6 TO 9 PERSONS

4 tbsp. (¼ cup) unsalted butter, in pieces

⅔ cup coarse semolina, plus more for the pan

2 cups milk

½ vanilla bean

⅔ cup sugar

Grated zest of 1 small orange

3 large eggs, 2 separated

½ cup chopped citron

2 tbsp. cognac

Salt

Serve this with raspberry sauce.

Preheat the oven to 350°F. Grease a Bundt pan with butter and dust it with semolina. Pour the milk into a saucepan with the vanilla bean. Add a little salt and heat. When the milk boils pour in the semolina in a steady stream, stirring, until the mixture becomes smooth. ✦ After a few minutes, add the sugar and cook for another 2 to 3 minutes. Remove from the heat and add the orange zest and butter. Remove the vanilla bean. Then stir in 1 whole egg and 2 yolks, one at a time. Add the chopped citron and the cognac. Beat the egg whites until stiff, then fold into the mixture and pour the batter into the Bundt pan. ✦ Place the Bundt pan in a baking pan large enough to hold it with 1 inch of space on all sides. Place the pan on the oven rack, then fill the pan halfway with water. Bake for 1 hour or until set. Serve lukewarm.

DESSERTS

ROSE PUDDING

FRIULI-VENEZIA GIULIA

6 large eggs
6 tbsp. sugar
⅔ cup ground almonds
1 tbsp. rose water
½ tsp. vanilla extract
Grated zest of 1 lemon
2¾ cups milk

The highly popular *rosada* is enjoyed most of all by the elderly, the ill, and children.

Preheat the oven to 350°F. Beat the eggs, add the sugar, almonds, rose water, vanilla extract, and lemon zest, and add the milk. ✦ Pour the mixture into a large ovenproof mold, smoothing the top. ✦ Place the mold in a baking pan large enough to hold it with 1 inch of space on all sides. Place the pan on the oven rack, then fill the pan halfway with water. Bake until set, about 1 hour.

BUNÊT

AMARETTI PUDDING

PIEMONTE

4 cups milk
⅔ cup crumbled ladyfingers
⅔ cup crumbled amaretti
1 cup black coffee
4 tbsp. Marsala
4 tbsp. rum
1¼ cups plus 2 tbsp. sugar
3½ tbsp. cocoa powder
5 large eggs

This recipe is typical of Asti.

Preheat the oven to 400°F. Bring the milk to a boil in a pot, then take it off the heat and let it cool. ✦ Add the ladyfingers and amaretti to the milk; then add the coffee, Marsala, and rum. ✦ In another bowl beat 1¼ cups sugar, cocoa, and eggs with a mixer on medium speed until the mixture is creamy. Then incorporate the milk mixture a little at a time, stirring well. ✦ Caramelize a pudding mold with the remaining sugar (see page 791), then pour the mixture into the mold. Place the mold in a baking pan large enough to hold it with 1 inch of space on all sides. Place the pan on the oven rack, then fill the pan halfway with water. Bake until set, for 30 to 40 minutes. ✦ Cool and refrigerate for a few hours. Turn it out on a plate and serve at room temperature.

BUSECCHINA

CHESTNUTS WITH CREAM

LOMBARDIA

1 lb. dried chestnuts
½ cup dry white wine (optional)
½ cup sweet wine (optional)
2 cups heavy cream

A variation can be added to this easy dessert: when the chestnuts are cooked, drain them in a bowl and cover them with sweet white wine, such as a Moscato. Let them absorb as much of the wine as possible, then arrange them in cups, as indicated.

Soak the chestnuts in lukewarm water overnight. ✦ The next day drain them, rinse them in running water, clean them with a cloth or brush to remove any remaining film, and rinse again. ✦ Put the chestnuts in a pan, add enough water to just cover them, and cook at low heat until they have absorbed all the liquid, never letting the liquid boil, to avoid breaking them. (If you want to add dry white wine or sweet wine do not do so until the chestnuts are half cooked.) ✦ Meanwhile, whip the cream to soft peaks. When cooked put the chestnuts in cups, spoon any of their own sweet sauce over them, then add whipped cream.

CAFFÈ ALLE MANDORLE

ALMOND COFFEE

VALLE D'AOSTA

2 tbsp. unsalted butter
4 tbsp. ground almonds
4 cups brewed coffee

Serve in large cups accompanied by breadsticks or biscotti.

Melt the butter in a small copper pan over medium-low heat and sauté the almonds until golden. ✦ Pour the hot almonds into the coffee and reheat the coffee, taking if off the heat before it boils. Pour into coffee cups and serve.

CAGGIUNITTI

SWEET RAVIOLI

MOLISE

For the dough:
3 cups all-purpose flour, plus more as needed
2 large eggs
3 oz. (6 tbsp.) unsalted butter
⅔ cup sugar
½ cup milk, or as needed
1 tbsp. baking powder
Salt

For the filling:
½ lb. chestnuts, shelled, parboiled, and peeled
4 oz. (4 squares) chocolate, finely chopped
½ cup chopped candied fruit
½ cup chopped almonds
1 tsp. grated lemon zest

For frying:
Extra-virgin olive oil
Lard

Some people use chickpeas instead of chestnuts.

Use the flour and eggs to prepare a pasta dough as in the recipe on page 10, adding the butter and sugar with the eggs and using milk as needed in place of the water. ✦ Set the dough aside to rest for about 1 hour, then knead in the baking powder. ✦ Crush the chestnuts; put them through a sieve and mix the resulting purée in a bowl with the chocolate pieces, candied fruit, almonds, and lemon zest. ✦ At this point roll out the dough to form a sheet (see page 212), and cut it in long strips about 2 inches wide. Spoon filling down the centers of the strips then roll up the strips of dough like small salami and join the ends to form doughnut shapes. Heat equal parts olive oil and lard in a saucepan to a depth of several inches. Fry the ravioli until golden brown, drain on paper towels, and serve hot.

DESSERTS

CALZONCELLI

Olive oil
3⅓ cups all-purpose flour
1½ cups sugar
3 large eggs
6 oz. lard
1⅔ cups chestnuts
1½ cups bittersweet chocolate

Preheat the oven to 375°F. Grease a baking sheet with olive oil. Combine the flour, sugar, eggs, and lard and knead it thoroughly, making the dough smooth and homogeneous. ✦ Let it rest for about 20 minutes, then roll out a sheet about ⅛ inch thick. ✦ Using a glass or cookie cutter, cut it into disks. ✦ Chop together the chestnuts and chocolate to make a filling and place lumps of it at the center of each disk. ✦ Fold over to form half-moons, place on the baking sheet, and bake until golden, about 10 minutes.

CHESTNUT CALZONI

FOR
10 PERSONS

For the filling:
1¼ cups dried chickpeas
2 lbs. chestnuts
Pinch ground cinnamon
⅔ cup semisweet chocolate chips
⅔ cup sugar
1 tbsp. herb-infused liqueur, such as anisette or *alchermes* (see note, page 786)

For the dough:
6⅔ cups all-purpose flour
1¼ cups sugar
10 oz. lard
9 large eggs
Sweet white wine (or Marsala), as needed
Salt

For frying:
Lard

This recipe is typical of Melfi. In Abruzzo, a similar recipe is made using almonds in place of the chickpeas and honey in place of the sugar to sweeten the filling.

Boil the chickpeas and chestnuts, peel them, and remove any inner film. ✦ Combine them and pass them through a sieve, reducing them to a purée, then mix in the cinnamon, chocolate, sugar, and liqueur. ✦ Use the flour to make a dough as in the recipe on page 10, adding the sugar and lard with the eggs, and using wine in place of the water as needed to obtain an elastic and compact dough. ✦ Roll out the dough to ¹⁄₁₆ of an inch thick (see note, page 212) and cut the resulting sheet into squares. ✦ Arrange the filling on the squares, fold them over to close, and seal the edges. ✦ Heat 1 inch of lard in a saucepan and fry until golden. Drain on paper towels.

CANASTRELLI OF PIEMONTE

This recipe is typical of Borgofranco d'Ivrea. Flour, butter, eggs, chocolate, hazelnuts, cognac, lemon zest, and Marsala are mixed together into a dough, which is then rested overnight. Then the dough is shaped into balls the size of hazelnuts and placed 4 or 5 at a time in the special iron used for *cialde* (a type of wafer). We are told the *canastrelli* are cooked for the length of time "for an Ave Maria," then flipped to cook on the other side. In Molise, larger versions about the size of walnuts, called *cancelle*, are made using olive oil in place of butter and flavored with lemon zest and anise or white wine.

CANESTRELLI

SUGAR COOKIES

LIGURIA

½ lb. (1 cup) plus 2 tbsp. unsalted butter, chopped and softened
⅔ cup sugar
1 egg, separated
1 ⅔ cups all-purpose flour
Confectioners' sugar

This recipe is typical of Torriglia di Genova. *Canestrelli* are meant to be pale, so do not let them get too dark when baking.

Preheat the oven to 325°F. Cream the butter with the sugar until pale, then stir in the egg yolk. Gradually stir in the flour to make a smooth dough (you may not use all of the flour). Beat the egg white until frothy. ✦ On a floured surface, with a floured rolling pin, roll out the dough to form a sheet about ½ inch thick. Cut this into cookies with a cookie cutter with a scalloped edge. Place the cookies on a baking sheet and brush them with egg white. Bake until pale golden, about 20 minutes. ✦ Dust with confectioners' sugar while still warm, then dust them again when cool.

CANNOLI RIPIENI

FILLED CANNOLI

SICILIA

Cassata (see page 768) and cannoli are the two traditional products of Sicilian pastry making. Once associated with the period of Carnival, cannoli can be found today at any time of the year in any respectable bakery. The average cannoli are also similar in terms of size; in the area of Palermo, how-

DESSERTS

765

1 ½ cups fresh ricotta
½ cup sugar
A few tbsp. milk
1 tbsp. vanilla extract
⅛ tsp. ground cinnamon
⅓ cup diced candied fruit
¼ cup bittersweet chocolate chips
1 recipe cannoli shells (see below)

For the garnish:
Ground pistachios
Confectioners' sugar

ever, one can find tiny *cannulicchi* hardly bigger than a finger. At the other end are those from Piana degli Albanesi, which can reach large sizes that are quite unusual. The shells should not be filled until shortly before serving. After a few hours they soften and lose the crunchiness that is part of their appeal, being one aspect of the exquisite harmony that is a cannoli.

Using a fork blend the ricotta and sugar. Stir in the milk a tablespoon at a time, just to make a smooth mixture. Add the vanilla extract and cinnamon, then pass the result through a sieve. Mix in the candied fruit and chocolate chips. ✦ Transfer the mixture to a pastry bag with a large (½-inch) tip attached or without a tip. Pipe the filling into 1 end of the shell until it is halfway filled, then pipe filling into the other end to fill completely. Dust the ends with pistachios and sprinkle with confectioners' sugar.

CANNOLI SHELLS

CALABRIA

1 ⅔ cups all-purpose flour
1 tbsp. sugar
½ cup white wine
Olive oil, for frying
½ cup honey
Salt

Cannoli molds are metal tubes usually made of aluminum or stainless steel that are used to shape the cannoli during frying. The standard size mold (about 1 inch thick by 5½ inches long) is widely available. Be sure to regulate the temperature of the oil carefully between batches so it does not get too hot and burn the dough; it should hover around 350°F.

Mix the flour, sugar, a pinch of salt, and the wine to obtain a smooth, firm dough. Form the dough into a ball, wrap in a clean kitchen towel, and let it rest for 2 hours. ✦ Roll out the dough on a floured surface to form a sheet ⅛ inch thick. ✦ Divide this sheet into large (6-inch) squares. Heat several inches of olive oil in a wide saucepan. Grease cannoli molds (see note, or use lightly floured lengths of 1-inch dowel). Working in batches, wrap squares of dough around the molds, pressing the overlap together to seal (so it does not come apart while frying). Fry until golden brown and crispy, turning as necessary. ✦ Drain on paper towels, and when they are cool enough to handle remove the mold (or dowel). Repeat with the remaining dough. ✦ Meanwhile, heat the honey and 2 tablespoons water over low heat until a thin syrup forms; brush the fried shells with the mixture and let stand until dry.

ALMOND BISCOTTI 2

TOSCANA

1 ¼ cups almonds

Unsalted butter

3 ⅓ cups all-purpose flour,
plus more as needed

½ tsp. baking powder

2 cups sugar

1 tsp. grated orange zest

½ tsp. vanilla extract

4 large eggs, beaten

Salt

This recipe is typical of Prato.

Preheat the oven to 375°F. Toast the almonds until fragrant and lightly golden, then chop them. Leave the oven on, grease a baking sheet with butter, and sprinkle it with flour. ◆ Combine the flour, baking powder, salt, sugar, and orange zest. Stir in the vanilla and eggs. Knead in the almonds. ◆ Pat out the dough to form long, flat loaves about 3 inches wide. Place them on the baking sheet and bake about 15 minutes. ◆ Remove from the oven and cut the "fingers" in diagonal slices ½ inch thick. ◆ Return them to the sheet and bake unti crisp, about 25 minutes.

CARTELLATE

WINE PINWHEELS

PUGLIA

3 ⅓ cups all-purpose flour

⅓ cup dry white wine

⅔ cup extra-virgin olive oil,
plus more for frying

4 cups *vin cotto* (see note, page 818)

Anicini (candy-coated fennel seeds)

Salt

One variation is to use 3 cups honey instead of *vin cotto*. Heat the honey with 1 cup water to make a thin syrup and drizzle it over the *cartellate*. They can also be dusted with the *anicini*. These are a specialty of the Christmas season. They stay good for several weeks.

Use the flour to make a dough as in the recipe on page 10, using the wine and ⅔ cup olive oil in place of the eggs. Let the dough rest 1 hour. ◆ Roll out the dough to form a thin sheet and cut this into strips 6 inches long and 1 inch wide. Make a cut halfway through the strips every inch or so, alternating sides. Roll the strips into loose spirals. Cover them loosely and set them out to dry overnight. ◆ The next day heat several inches of olive oil in a saucepan and fry the pinwheels until golden. Drain on paper towels. ◆ Heat the *vin cotto* in a pan to thin slightly, then dip in the pinwheels; remove them with a slotted spoon and let the excess drip back into the pan. Arrange on a serving plate and dust with *anicini*. Let stand, covered, 2 days before eating them.

DESSERTS

CASCIATELLA | RICOTTA TART

LAZIO

Extra-virgin olive oil
1 ¼ cups all-purpose flour
1 lb. ricotta
4 large eggs
2 tbsp. sugar
1 tsp. ground cinnamon
¼ cup cognac or other aromatic liquor
Grated zest of 1 lemon
Salt

This recipe is typical of Maenza.

Preheat the oven to 350°F. Grease a round baking pan with olive oil and flour it lightly. Combine the ricotta with 2 of the eggs, sugar, cinnamon, a little salt, cognac (or other liquor), and lemon zest. ✦ While this mixture rests, make pastry dough (see page 773) with the flour, 1 egg, and a little water. Roll out two thirds of the dough to form a disk and use the disk to line the baking pan. Pour in the ricotta mixture. ✦ Roll out the remaining dough and use a pastry wheel to cut it into ½-inch strips. Use these strips to create a latticework covering for the filling. Beat the remaining egg and brush it over the pastry strips. ✦ Bake for 20 minutes, or until the surface turns golden.

CASSATA NAPOLETANA | CASSATA FROM NAPLES

CAMPANIA

2 lbs. ricotta
2 cups sugar
2 tbsp. Maraschino (or other liqueur)
¼ cup chocolate chips
1 ¾ cups chopped candied fruit, plus more as needed
1 10-inch sponge cake (see page 843)

Using the tines of a fork work the ricotta together with the sugar, adding the Maraschino or other liqueur. Pass this mixture through a sieve. ✦ Set aside half of this mixture. Blend the other half with the chocolate chips and the candied fruit. ✦ Slice the sponge cake into two layers. Hollow out some of the cake from the cut sides of the two halves. Fill these hollows with the ricotta-chocolate mixture and re-form the cake. ✦ Top with the remaining portion of the ricotta mixture (that is, without the chocolate chips). Sprinkle the cake with with more candied fruit. ✦ Let the cake chill in the refrigerator a few hours before serving.

CASSATA SICILIANA | CASSATA FROM SICILIA

SICILIA

Cassata is the traditional Sicilian dessert for Easter. The name seems to be derived from the Arabian *quas'at*, although there are two different meanings: a round bowl (in reference to the shape) or a cheesecake. In the past, Palermo's monastery of Valverde was famous for its *cassata*. The an-

2 lbs. ricotta

2 cups sugar

½ cup Maraschino liqueur
(or other sweet liqueur)

⅔ cup chocolate chips

1 10-inch-round sponge cake
(see page 843)

2 tbsp. apricot preserves,
heated until melted

Sugar glaze (made with
confectioners' sugar mixed with just
enough water to make spreadable,
colored green with pistachio,
if desired)

⅔ cup chopped candied fruit

cient tradition of the *cassata* in Sicilia is supported by a document from the Synod of Mazara (1575), which refers to the *cassata* as being among the sweets "unfailingly present at all festivities."

Put the ricotta in a bowl and work in the sugar, Maraschino or other liqueur, and chocolate chips. ✦ Slice the sponge cake crosswise to form three disks, each about ½ inch thick. ✦ Line a cake pan with wax paper; coat the paper lightly with some of the apricot preserves (it will act as an adhesive). Put one of the disks of sponge cake in the bottom of the pan; slice another disk into strips, then cut those into 1-inch pieces and use them to line the sides of the pan. ✦ Pour in the ricotta mixture, smooth the top to make it level, and cover with the remaining disk of sponge cake. ✦ Refrigerate for at least 2 hours. ✦ Turn the cake out on a plate; remove and discard the wax paper. Reheat the remaining apricot preserves and use them to coat the sides of the cake. ✦ Cover the top and sides with sugar glaze, decorate with candied fruit, and return to the refrigerator for at least another hour before serving.

CASSATINE RIPIENE

MARZIPAN-FILLED COOKIES

SICILIA

For the dough:
Unsalted butter
10 oz. lard
7 ¼ cups pastry flour
1 ¼ cups sugar

For the filling:
3 ¾ cups blanched almonds
2 ⅓ cups sugar
1 tbsp. unsweetened cocoa powder
1 tbsp. ground cinnamon
Grated zest of 1 lemon

For the glaze:
1 egg white
1 ¼ cups confectioners' sugar
1 tsp. lemon juice

Preheat the oven to 350°F. Grease two sheet pans with butter. In a large bowl combine the lard with the flour and sugar and make a soft dough, adding water by the tablespoon as needed. Set aside while making the filling. ✦ Grind the almonds in a mortar, adding ¼ teaspoon water to keep them from giving off their oil. Work them into the sugar, adding a little water to obtain a somewhat solid paste. ✦ Add the cocoa, cinnamon, and lemon zest. ✦ Divide the dough in half and roll each piece out to form a thin, rectangular sheet. Arrange teaspoons of the almond filling in regularly spaced rows along one sheet of dough; cover with the other sheet. ✦ Cut out filled cookies in the shape of hearts, mushrooms, flowers, or other shapes as you like. ✦ Arrange the cookies on the baking sheets and bake until the cookies are just colored, 10 to 12 minutes, rotating the pans from top to bottom halfway during baking. ✦ Whisk the egg white until frothy, then whisk in the confectioners' sugar and lemon juice. ✦ Remove the baking sheet with the cookies and turn off

DESSERTS

the oven. Brush the hot cookies with the glaze and return them to the oven, which will still be warm enough to dry the glaze in about 5 minutes.

CASTAGNACCIO

CHESTNUT CAKE

TOSCANA

1⅔ cups chestnut flour

3 tbsp. extra-virgin olive oil

½ cup raisins, soaked in warm water, drained, and squeezed dry

⅓ cup walnuts, broken up

⅓ cup pine nuts

1 tbsp. rosemary

Salt

This recipe is typical of Lucca.

Sift the chestnut flour and put it in a bowl; gradually whisk in about 2 cups warm water to make a thick batter free of lumps. ✦ Whisk in 2 tablespoons olive oil, a little salt, and raisins; blend well. ✦ Pour into a greased cake pan. Sprinkle with the walnuts, pine nuts, rosemary leaves, and the remaining olive oil. ✦ Bake for about 30 minutes.

CASTAGNE AL CUCCHIAIO

CHESTNUT FUDGE

ABRUZZO

½ cup (¼ lb.) plus 1 tbsp. unsalted butter, plus some for the mold

1 ¼ lbs. chestnuts

6 oz. chocolate, chopped in pieces

⅔ cup sugar

Whipped cream, for serving

Salt

Butter a baking pan and line it with wax paper. Cook the chestnuts in lightly salted boiling water to cover until soft. Drain, peel, and put through a sieve. ✦ Melt the chocolate in the top of a double boiler and add it to the chestnuts; stir in the sugar and butter and mix until thoroughly blended. ✦ Pour the mixture into the prepared pan, smooth to make even, and cover with more wax paper. ✦ Refrigerate for at least 4 hours, then serve with whipped cream on the side.

CASTAGNE SECCHE LESSATE

BOILED CHESTNUTS

LOMBARDIA

1 lb. dried chestnuts

½ cup sugar, or as much as desired

2 tbsp. honey

Soak the chestnuts in water for 1 night. ✦ Remove any remaining film. Boil in 4 cups water until tender; add the sugar and honey and cook for another 15 minutes. ✦ Serve the chestnuts with their dark reddish cooking liquid.

LAZIO

4 large eggs

¼ cup sugar

¼ cup extra-virgin olive oil (or unsalted butter)

1½ tsp. baking powder

Grated zest of 1 lemon

2 cups all-purpose flour, or as needed

Olive oil, for frying

Liqueur (such as rum or *alchermes*, see note, page 786)

Confectioners' sugar

The term *castagnole* ("little chestnuts") and this recipe, the origin of which is attributed to various regions of Italy (Veneto, Emilia-Romagna, Lazio), until now was known only from nineteenth-century cookbooks. A manuscript volume from the end of the 1700s, found in the Viterbo state archives by that city's delegate Italo Arieti, contains four recipes for *castagnole*, one of which has them baked. In the face of this evidence one must also add that, even today, in many towns of Tuscia *castagnole* are called *struffoli*, a term today considered to be of Neapolitan origin that refers to small fried balls held together by honey. Examining old texts we find that Nascia, famous cook at the Farnese court, in his manuscript, dated 1684, presents a recipe entitled *Struffoli alla Romana*, which describes fried balls with ingredients similar to those of *castagnole*, prepared with a paste of flour, butter, sugar, and aromatic water with which one makes small gnocchi that are then fried in lard and served with a dusting of sugar; there is then—and from not much later (1692)—a recipe from Latini, who was cook to the dukes of Altemps at Soriano nel Cimino (not far from Viterbo) before serving the Anjou court in Naples, also entitled *Struffoli alla Romana* and also similar to today's Neapolitan *struffoli*.

In a bowl beat the eggs with the sugar until pale yellow, then slowly add the olive oil (or butter), baking powder, lemon zest, ¼ cup water, and enough flour to make a very soft dough (more like a very thick batter). ✦ Heat ½ inch of olive oil in a large pan and, using a teaspoon, drop balls of the batter into the oil (do not crowd them, but fill the pan). While cooking lift and carefully swirl the pan. Doing so will give the lumps of batter their characteristic spherical shape, while taking the pan off the heat will keep the dough soft and not too greasy. This will also keep the balls from cooking too quickly. With a little patience, prolonging the cooking to 5 or 6 minutes, you will obtain big, soft balls. ✦ After cooking drain on paper towels, then sprinkle with liqueur and dust them with confectioners' sugar.

DESSERTS

| # CUSTARD

LOMBARDIA

1⅔ cups milk
6 egg yolks
3 tbsp. sugar

In the well-to-do areas above Milan this is made using cream. The "whipped" version of *caulatt*, a kind of *zuppa inglese*, is made with half cream and half milk.

Mix the milk, egg yolks, and sugar in a heavy saucepan until blended. Heat over medium-low heat, stirring, but do not let the mixture boil. ✦ As soon as the liquid coats the back of the spoon, turn off the heat, cover the pan, and let it thicken 10 minutes.

CENCI | # FRIED PASTA RIBBONS

TOSCANA

1½ cups all-purpose flour
1 egg
⅓ cup sugar
1 tsp. vanilla extract
2 tbsp. unsalted butter, melted
3 tbsp. *vin santo*
(or other sweet white dessert wine)
Olive oil, for frying
Confectioners' sugar
Salt

This recipe is typical of Florence. *Cenci* means "rags," from the shape of the cut ribbons of dough.

Use the flour and egg to make a dough as in the recipe on page 10, adding the sugar, vanilla extract, butter, and a little salt with the egg. When the dough is smooth, knead in the *vin santo*. ✦ Cover with a clean kitchen towel and let it rest for about 1 hour. ✦ Roll out the dough on a floured surface to a sheet about ⅛ inch thick. Use a knife or pastry wheel to cut it in long ribbons about 1 inch wide and 8 inches long; twist each one into a loose knot, crossing the ends like a scarf. ✦ Heat 2 inches of olive oil in a saucepan and fry the ribbons a few at a time until they puff up and turn golden brown. ✦ Drain on paper towels and dust with confectioners' sugar.

CEPPELLIATE | # CHERRY MARMALADE COOKIES

MOLISE

For the dough:
6⅔ cups all-purpose flour
18 egg yolks
2 cups sugar
CONTINUED

Very sweet marmalade is not recommended for these because it can cause them to open and lose the filling.

Preheat the oven to 350°F. Use the flour and egg yolks to make a dough as in the recipe on page 751, adding the sugar, lard, and lemon zest with the egg yolks. Add the baking powder and quickly knead together all the ingredients to form a smooth dough. ✦ Form a sheet with a rolling pin and cut out 2-inch disks, filling each with

14 oz. lard

Grated zest of 2 lemons

1½ tsp. baking powder

Confectioners' sugar

For the filling:

Cherry marmalade, as needed

cherry marmalade (about 1 tablespoon each). ✦ Fold the dough over the filling and seal the edges, then bend them to give them the shape of small crescents. ✦ Bake until golden, then let them cool and dust them with confectioners' sugar.

CHARLOTTE | **PEAR PIE** | FOR 8 PERSONS

PIEMONTE

For the short pastry:

3⅓ cups all-purpose flour

1¼ cups sugar

¼ lb. (½ cup) plus 6 tbsp. unsalted butter, chilled and cut into pieces

4 egg yolks

¼ cup Marsala

1 tsp. grated lemon zest

For the filling:

2 lbs. pears (if possible "Martin sech"), cored but not peeled and cut in half lengthwise

½ lb. prunes, pitted

2 cups Barolo (or other hearty red wine)

1 tsp. grated lemon zest

5 tbsp. sugar

1 tsp. ground cinnamon

1 pinch ground cloves

Salt

Prepare the short pastry: sift together the flour and sugar, then cut in the butter. Stir in the egg yolks, Marsala, and lemon zest until the mixture comes together in a ball. Knead gently a few times. ✦ Refrigerate the pastry for one hour. ✦ Prepare the filling: Combine the pears, prunes, Barolo, lemon zest, sugar, spices, and salt. Cook until the the liquid has reduced to a thick syrup and the pears are tender. ✦ Preheat the oven to 350°F. Butter a deep pie plate. Roll out half of the pastry to ⅛ inch thick. Use it to line the pie plate, then fill it with the cooked fruit and liquid. ✦ Roll out the other half of the pastry and cover the fruit. Use a fork to seal the edges well. ✦ Bake until golden, about 40 minutes. Cool for a few minutes, then transfer to a serving plate. Serve warm.

CHARLOTTE ALLA MILANESE | **APPLE CHARLOTTE** | FOR 6 PERSONS

LOMBARDIA

¼ cup (4 tbsp.) unsalted butter

¾ cup sugar

CONTINUED

Preheat the oven to 350°F. Mix 2 tablespoons butter and ¼ cup sugar and use this mixture to coat the inside of a round cake pan. Cut the apples into ¼-inch slices. Arrange them in a single layer in a sauté pan; dust with the remaining sugar, then add the lemon zest, wine, and

2 lbs. apples, peeled and cored

Grated zest of 1 lemon

¼ cup white wine, such as Moscato from the Oltrepò Pavese

½ cup golden raisins

Stale French bread, cut into thin slices (enough to line the baking pan)

½ cup rum

enough water to cover them. ✦ Cook the apples for several minutes, just until they are tender but not soft. Drain the apple slices (set aside to let them drain completely). ✦ Meanwhile soak the raisins in a little warm water for 15 minutes, then drain and set aside. ✦ With the remaining butter, butter both sides of the slices of bread, then use them to line the bottom and sides of the pan; arrange a layer of apple slices in the middle of the mold; sprinkle with raisins. ✦ Sprinkle with 2 tablespoons rum, then make another layer of apple slices and sprinkle with raisins and 2 tablespoons rum. Cover with the remaining slices of bread. Dust this with sugar so that it will caramelize when baking. ✦ Bake for 1 hour until dark golden. When it is done, turn out the mold onto a heatproof plate and, in the style of great chefs everywhere, sprinkle the charlotte with rum, strike a match, and serve it flambé!

CHIACCHIERE
DI CARNEVALE

CARNIVAL COOKIES

FOR
6 PERSONS

CAMPANIA

6⅔ cups all-purpose flour

6 tbsp. sugar

6 large eggs

¼ lb. (½ cup) plus 1 tbsp. unsalted butter, melted

2 tbsp. rum

2 tbsp. almond oil

Sunflower oil, for frying

Confectioners' sugar

Salt

This recipe is typical of Benevento. Similar fried pastries are made all over Italy with different names and different ingredients: *chiacchiere, bugie, galani, frappe* (see page 795), *crostoli*, and *guanti*.

Mix the flour and the sugar, then use them and the eggs to make a dough as in the recipe on page 751, adding the butter, rum, and almond oil with the eggs. ✦ Knead the mixture energetically, adding a little lukewarm water if necessary. ✦ When the dough is smooth and elastic roll it into a sheet with a rolling pin and cut it into strips 4 inches long and 1 inch wide. ✦ Heat 2 inches of sunflower oil in a saucepan and fry the dough until golden. Drain on paper towels and let cool. Dust with confectioners' sugar and serve.

| # WINE DOUGHNUTS

FRIULI-VENEZIA GIULIA

6⅔ cups all-purpose flour

10 oz. (1¼ cups) unsalted butter, softened

¼ cup white wine

1⅔ cups sugar

Preheat the oven to 350°F. Thoroughly blend the flour with the butter and pass it through a sieve. ✦ Heat the wine and sugar, stirring just until the sugar dissolves, then stir the mixture into the dough. Shape the dough into thin ropes, cut into lengths, and form rings about 3 inches in diameter. Place the rings on a baking pan. ✦ Bake for 20 minutes until lightly browned.

CIAMBELLE DOLCI | # RING BREADS WITH EGGS

CALABRIA

3¾ cups all-purpose flour

2¼ tsp. active dry yeast

4 large eggs plus about 10 more hard-boiled (depending on the number of loaves)

¼ cup anisette

1¼ cups sugar

4 oz. lard, softened

Salt

Mix about 2 cups of the flour and the yeast dissolved in 2 tablespoons warm water to form a sticky dough. Cover and let this rest in a warm spot. ✦ When the dough has doubled form a well with the remaining flour and work it into the dough along with the raw eggs, anisette, sugar, and a pinch of salt. Then blend in the lard. ✦ Knead this energetically for a long time to obtain a firm and elastic dough. ✦ Flour a baking sheet. Shape the dough into small loaves about 4 inches long and press a hard-boiled egg into each. ✦ Arrange them on the baking sheet and let them rise a few hours. ✦ Preheat the oven to 400°F and bake until golden, about 30 minutes.

CIAMBELLINE ALL'ACQUA MELATA | # HONEY DOUGHNUTS

LAZIO

This recipe is typical of the Viterbo area. Honey water is nothing more than the water used to rinse out honeycombs after extracting the honey. In times gone by, the producers of honey sold this water for a few cents or even gave it away to the less well-to-do, who used it as a sweetener in place of the more costly honey. Those who had the means to do so made these doughnuts with honey instead of honey water. Today, like many of the sweets made with honey, these are almost completely forgotten, also because their hard texture made them less appealing to both children and adults. The various dialect names by which they are known—*stracca-ganasse, ferri d'asino, cazzo melato, birolli*—all make reference to this particular characteristic. There are also certain

DESSERTS

3¾ cups all-purpose flour, or as needed

2 cups honey water (see note)

1 or 2 tbsp. olive oil

Pepper (if desired)

places in Italy where these same names are also used to identify those who are "hard of understanding."

Preheat the oven to 300°F. Grease a baking sheet. Knead the flour with the honey water, adding olive oil to form a dough the consistency of bread dough. (A little ground pepper can be added to dough made for adults.) Shape this dough into cylinders 3 inches long and ½ inch thick and join the ends to form doughnuts. ✦ Bake until golden and crunchy, about 40 minutes.

CIAMBELLINE
ALL'ANICE

ANISE RING COOKIES

LAZIO

3½ cup all-purpose flour

½ cup sugar

½ cup white wine, such as Frascati, Castelli Romani, or Orvieto

½ cup olive oil

2 tbsp. anise seeds

This recipe is typical of Rome.

Preheat the oven to 300°F. Use the flour to make a dough as in the recipe on page 751, using the sugar, wine, and olive oil. Fold in the anise seeds. ✦ Roll out a sheet of dough to ¹⁄₁₆ inch thickness, cut it into 3-inch lengths, and wrap these around your finger to form little doughnuts. ✦ Place on a baking sheet and bake until they are golden and crunchy, about 15 minutes.

CIARAMILLE

BOILED AND BAKED COOKIES

LAZIO

3 cups all-purpose flour, plus more as needed

1 egg, beaten

1 tbsp. sugar

1 tbsp. olive oil

1 tsp. grated lemon zest

Salt

This recipe is typical of Villa San Giovanni in Tuscia. Boiling the dough before baking makes the cookies look shiny, as though they had been brushed with egg white.

Preheat the oven to 400°F. Use the flour and egg to prepare a dough as in the recipe on page 751, adding the sugar, a pinch of salt, olive oil, and lemon zest with the egg. ✦ Shape the dough into cylinders the thickness of your thumb, about ½ inch. Form these cylinders into various shapes, joining the ends, tying them in knots, splitting the ends, etc. Heat a pot of lightly salted water to boiling and immerse the shaped dough into it. ✦ When they float extract them with a skimmer, make a small shallow incision in the surface of each one, and bake until they are golden brown.

APPLE TART

CAMPANIA

For the short pastry:

1⅔ cups all-purpose flour

6 oz. (1½ sticks) unsalted butter, chilled

⅔ cup sugar

3 egg yolks

Grated zest of 1 lemon

For the filling:

1 lb. apples, peeled, cored, and cut into wedges

1⅔ cups sugar

½ cup Cointreau

1 tsp. vanilla extract

Crystallized violets

Mint leaves

The short pastry in this recipe is perfect for every kind of filling.

Combine the pastry ingredients just until mixed; shape into a ball and let it rest, covered, in a cool place for about 30 minutes. ✦ Preheat the oven to 400°F. Butter a 9-inch baking pan, then roll out the pastry on a floured surface and use it to line the baking pan. Cover the dough with aluminum foil and bake for 20 minutes. ✦ At the end of that time remove the aluminum and bake for another 5 minutes, or until the dough is golden brown. ✦ Toss the apples with the sugar and arrange in a single layer in a large sauté pan. Cook over medium-high heat without stirring so the sugar caramelizes and the apples keep their shape (they will look "candied"). Remove the pan from the heat and add the Cointreau and vanilla extract. Spoon the apple mixture into the short-pastry mold. Decorate with crystallized violets and mint leaves.

ANISE FRITTERS WITH HONEY

CALABRIA

7 large eggs plus 3 yolks

⅔ cup sugar

5 oz. lard

½ cup anise seeds

6⅔ cups all-purpose flour

4½ tsp. active dry yeast

Olive oil, for frying

1⅔ cups honey

Salt

In a large bowl beat together the eggs and yolks, sugar, lard, anise, and a pinch of salt, beating until the mixture is pale yellow. ✦ Gradually add the flour, working the dough to obtain a fine but firm consistency. Knead in the yeast, cover with a cloth, and let rise for 1 hour. ✦ Roll out the dough to a thickness of ¾ inch and cut it into shapes (stars, circles, sticks, etc.). Heat several inches of oil in a saucepan and fry the dough, a few pieces at a time until golden. Drain on paper towels. ✦ Heat the honey and ¼ cup water in a small saucepan over medium heat and let it simmer for 10 minutes. Transfer the *ciccitielli* to a wire rack and pour the honey syrup over, carefully turning them to coat both sides. Let stand until dry, about 30 minutes.

DESSERTS

HONEY FRITTERS

CICERCHIATA

LAZIO

6⅔ cups all-purpose flour
5 large eggs
Olive oil, for frying
1⅓ cups honey
Candied fruit, chopped
Blanched sliced almonds
Candy-coated almonds

This recipe is typical of Rieti. A similar recipe from Larino in Molise is a specialty of the feast day of St. Anthony Abbot.

Use the flour and eggs to prepare a soft dough as in the recipe on page 751. ✦ Shape the dough into long sticks as though about to prepare gnocchi, but instead cut them into small lumps the size of chickpeas. ✦ Heat 2 inches of olive oil in a saucepan and fry the dough until golden, then drain on paper towels. ✦ Put them on a serving plate in any arrangement desired, such as a pyramid or ring or oval. ✦ Heat the honey in a saucepan over low heat just until bubbles form on the edges of the pan. Pour the honey over the fritters, then sprinkle them with candied fruit, sliced almonds, and candy-coated almonds. Let stand until set, about 1 hour.

CARNIVAL RING CAKE

CICERCHIATA
DI CARNEVALE

ABRUZZO

1½ cups all-purpose flour, plus more as needed
2 large eggs
¼ cup dry white wine, such as Trebbiano d'Abruzzo or Orvieto
¼ cup extra-virgin olive oil, plus oil for frying
3 tbsp. sugar
⅔ cup honey
⅔ cup slivered almonds

Use the flour and eggs as in the recipe on page 751 to make a soft dough, adding the wine, ¼ cup olive oil, and 2 tablespoons sugar with the eggs to obtain a dense but soft dough. Let this rest 15 minutes, covered by a cloth. ✦ Divide the dough and work them into pieces about the size and shape of a pinky. Cut these into short chunks and roll them in your palms to form balls. ✦ Dust these balls with flour, then fry them in olive oil until golden. Drain and set them aside to dry on paper towels. ✦ Put the honey and the remaining sugar in a saucepan and heat over medium heat just to thin it. Add in the dough balls, toss to coat, then stir in the almonds. ✦ Let this cool a few hours (on a windowsill or in the refrigerator) before serving.

ALMOND SHORTBREAD

CIPRÉN

EMILIA-ROMAGNA

When she arrived in Parma, Marie Louise (empress of the French as consort of Napoleon) was accompanied by a court composed almost entirely of Austrians. Among them was a baker named Cipperech, responsible for preparing the

1⅔ cups pastry flour
1¼ cups almond flour
⅔ cup confectioners' sugar
½ lb. (1 cup) plus 2 tbsp.
unsalted butter
Grated lemon zest

famous Viennese bread. This man later went into business, selling his goods to the public, and his most popular products included certain small loaves made of semolina flour in a distinctive half-moon shape. The French called these *croissants*; the people of Parma named them for the baker and called them *gipperic*. The same name was also applied for the shape of bread the Austrians called *gipfel* or *kipferln*, which evolved into *giprén* and, finally, *ciprén*.

Preheat the oven to 325°F. Whisk together the flours and sugar. Work in the butter until the mixture forms a dough; knead in the lemon zest. Shape the dough into a thin (½-inch) cylinder and cut into pieces about 2 inches long. ✦ Bake until lightly colored, about 12 minutes.

COLAC | # NUT CRESCENTS

MOLISE

For the filling:
½ cup stale bread without crust
(or ½ cup coarse breadcrumbs)
¾ cup finely chopped almonds
½ cup finely chopped walnuts
4 dried figs
1 apple, peeled, cored, and minced
Grated zest of 1 orange
Pinch ground cloves
Pinch ground cinnamon
½ cup honey, plus more as needed

For the short pastry:
3⅓ cups all-purpose flour
4 large eggs
⅔ cup sugar
5½ oz. lard, softened
½ cup wine

This recipe is typical of Montemitro.

Crumble the bread into a saucepan and add the almonds, walnuts, figs, apple, orange zest, cloves, and cinnamon. Mix until blended. Add the honey and cook at low heat, stirring until a paste forms, adding more honey as needed. ✦ Meanwhile prepare the short pastry: use the flour and eggs as in the recipe on page 773 to make a dough, adding the sugar, lard, and wine with the eggs. Wrap the dough in a clean kitchen towel and set this aside to rest for about 30 minutes. ✦ Preheat the oven to 350°F. On a floured surface, with a floured rolling pin, roll out the dough to ⅟₁₆ inch thick. ✦ Using a glass cut the dough into disks and place a heaping tablespoon of the filling at the center of each. Fold the disks over on themselves, sealing the edges with the tines of a fork and bending them to give them the shape of horseshoes. ✦ Arrange these on the baking sheet and bake for 30 minutes, until golden.

DESSERTS

COPATE BIANCHE

These sweet sandwich wafer cookies come from Toscana. To make the *copate*, or filling, first the sugar and honey would be cooked down in a saucepan over low heat to form a thick paste. Stiffly whipped egg whites would then be stirred into the mixture, followed by toasted and finely chopped almonds and vanilla-flavored confectioners' sugar. While keeping the saucepan over low heat, scoops of the *copate* would be rolled into cylinders (with cornstarch used to keep them from sticking) and then cut into short lengths. These lengths then would be sandwiched between two *cialde*, or wafers, to form the finished *copate bianche*. After resting a few hours, these cookies were served at room temperature.

COPETE | **ALMOND WAFERS** | TO MAKE 30

BASILICATA

¾ cup blanched almonds
2 egg whites
1⅓ cups confectioners' sugar, plus more for sprinkling
Pinch ground cinnamon
30 (3-inch-diameter) wafers

Preheat the oven to 400°F. Toast the almonds just until starting to take on a little color. ✦ Let cool and chop well. ✦ Whip the egg whites until stiff, then fold in the confectioners' sugar, almonds, and cinnamon. Distribute this mixture by the teaspoonful on the wafers and spread the mixture to the edges of the wafers. Place on baking sheets (at least two sheets will be needed). ✦ Dust with confectioners' sugar and bake for 15 minutes. ✦ Let cool and trim away any area of wafer that extends beyond the filling. These can be stored in an airtight container for a long time.

COTOGNATA | **QUINCE PASTE**

SICILIA

1 lb. whole quinces
1½ lemons
Sugar, as needed

Select firm quinces that are not quite ripe. Use utensils of earthenware, Pyrex, or stainless steel for this recipe; do not use aluminum.

Cook the quinces in a saucepan with half a lemon in water to cover. ✦ After about 30 minutes they should be soft. Drain and let stand just until cool enough to handle, then peel them (the skin is thin) and seed them. Slice and pass through a small-holed nonreactive sieve. ✦ Measure the resulting purée, then transfer to a saucepan and add an equal amount of sugar. Stir this well and add the juice of 1 lemon. ✦ Heat over medium heat and stir constantly until the mixture begins to boil. ✦ Remove from the heat and pour into molds (the best are the earthenware ones called *formi*, but any flat mold will do). ✦ Let the paste dry in the refrigerator for 8 days; when it is almost dry to the touch, it is ready. Loosen it from the mold and turn it out. Tightly wrapped, this paste can be stored a long time.

✦ **LOCAL TRADITION** ✦

COPATE NERE

Similar to the *copate bianche*, these Tuscan sandwich cookies were made by pressing a sweet filling between two wafers. In this recipe, the sugar and honey were instead cooked over high heat until almost burned, achieving the dark reddish brown color from which the dessert takes its name. Toasted and chopped almonds and walnuts were then added to the thickened mixture, and the filling was spread between two of the wafers.

ICE CREAM WITH CHOCOLATE SAUCE

COPPA DELL'APE

VALLE D'AOSTA

¼ cup milk
4 oz. chocolate, chopped
1 lb. ice cream
12 walnuts, shelled
⅔ cup honey
Whipped cream
12 wild cherries in syrup

This recipe is typical of Cervinia.

Make chocolate syrup by heating the milk and chocolate over low heat, stirring until smooth. Remove the pan from the heat. Scoop ice cream into four bowls. ✦ Crumble the walnuts over and drizzle with honey, then with chocolate syrup. ✦ Decorate each with whipped cream, wild cherries, and a little of the cherry syrup.

| # CHOCOLATE PARFAITS

CAMPANIA

4 large eggs, separated
½ cup sugar
¼ cup rum
2 tbsp. unsweetened cocoa powder
1¾ cups pastry cream (see page 843)

This recipe is typical of Naples.

Whip the whites of the eggs until soft peaks form and gradually fold in ¼ cup sugar. ✦ Beat the yolks and the remaining ¼ cup sugar with a mixer on medium speed until thickened and pale yellow, then add the rum. Fold the egg whites into the egg yolks until blended, then divide the mixture in two parts. ✦ To one of these parts add the cocoa powder and half of the pastry cream; to the other add only the pastry cream. ✦ Put a few tablespoons of both mixtures in dessert glasses or, even better, in chocolate molds (sold in gourmet stores). Refrigerate and serve the next day.

CREMA DI ARANCE | # ORANGE CUSTARD

CAMPANIA

4 egg yolks
⅔ cup sugar
⅓ cup cornstarch
2 cups milk
Juice and grated zest of 4 oranges, preferably organic

This recipe is typical of Naples. Serve this highly fragrant cream decorated with a dollop of whipped cream and a twist of candied orange, dusted with cinnamon.

Make a cream by heating the egg yolks, sugar, cornstarch, and milk over medium-low heat, stirring constantly. ✦ When this reaches the consistency of thick pudding remove it from the heat and add the orange juice and zest. Spoon into dessert cups and put in the refrigerator. Serve cold.

CREMA DI COGNE | # CHOCOLATE CUSTARD

VALLE D'AOSTA

6 egg yolks
2 cups sugar
1 tsp. unsweetened cocoa
4 cups milk
2 cups plus 2 tbsp. heavy cream
2 oz. (2 squares) chocolate, grated
¾ tsp. corn syrup

This should be served with slices of *pan dolce* from Cogne (Lo Macoulen), *tegole* from the Valle d'Aosta, or even with simple ladyfingers.

Set up a double boiler. In a heatproof bowl, beat the egg yolks and half the sugar with a mixer on medium speed until thickened and pale yellow, then add the cocoa and stir in the milk and 2 cups cream. ✦ Cook over simmering water, whisking until thick, then whisk in the chocolate. ✦ Meanwhile, combine the remaining sugar with the corn syrup and 1 tablespoon water in a saucepan.

Heat over high heat without stirring until the mixture is a dark golden color. Remove the pan from the heat and whisk in the remaining cream (the mixture will steam and bubble vigorously). Whisk until the mixture is smooth, then whisk it into the chocolate mixture. Remove the custard from the heat and chill. Serve cold.

RUM CUSTARD

CREMA DI COURMAYEUR

VALLE D'AOSTA

1 ¼ cups whole milk
4 egg yolks
½ cup sugar
¼ cup rum
Grated zest of 1 lemon
Black Valdostan rye bread, crumbled

This recipe is typical of Courmayeur.

Combine all the ingredients except the bread in a copper bowl or in the top of a double boiler. Set the bowl over simmering water and stir until the mixture thickens and it is very creamy. ✦ Pour the mixture into individual cups, then top with the bread.

BERRY-CHEESE CREAM

CREMA DI FORMAGGIO BIANCO AI MIRTILLI

VALLE D'AOSTA

10 oz. *reblec* (fresh white cheese; can use *fromage blanc* if necessary)
½ cup milk
3 tbsp. heavy cream
3 tbsp. berry jam
Toasted almonds or hazelnuts, crushed (optional)

This is a simple and healthy dessert that is made with fresh products, except for the jam and the nuts. It cannot be made with products with preservatives. Serve with cookies.

Mix the *reblec*, milk, cream, and berry jam in a bowl until blended. Spoon into individual cups. Refrigerate for 1 hour. ✦ If desired, decorate with crushed almonds or hazelnuts before serving.

MASCARPONE CREAM

CREMA DI MASCARPONE

LOMBARDIA

2 large eggs, separated, plus 1 egg yolk
½ cup sugar
10 oz. mascarpone
4 tbsp. rum

You can reduce the amount of sugar in this recipe to suit your taste. Serve this with a sweet bread; panettone is a good choice, whether fresh or toasted on the grill.

In a bowl, beat the 3 egg yolks and the sugar with a mixer on medium speed until thickened and pale yellow. ✦ In another bowl whip the 2 egg whites until stiff then fold into the yolk mixture. ✦ Gently stir in the

DESSERTS

mascarpone and rum. ✦ Spoon into teacups and refrigerate until serving.

CRESCIA FOGLIATA

BAKED APPLE PASTRY

MARCHE

For the dough:

1 ¼ cups all-purpose flour
¼ lb. (½ cup) unsalted butter, chilled
1 egg
Salt

For the filling:

1 lb. apples, peeled, cored, and sliced
⅔ cup raisins
1 ¼ cups sugar
¾ cup chopped walnuts
¾ cup chopped dried figs
Pinch ground cinnamon
½ cup Marsala
¼ cup anisette
½ cup apricot jam
⅔ cup heavy cream

This recipe is typical of Laverino. It was invented by peasants long ago. The name is composed of *crescia*, meaning "cake," and *fogliata*, meaning "short pastry."

Preheat the oven to 400°F. Blend ½ cup flour with the butter until a dough forms. Shape into a ball and set aside. ✦ Combine the remaining flour, salt, ½ cup water, and egg to form a soft mixture, then knead with the dough to create a unifom mixture. ✦ Meanwhile cook all the ingredients for the filling in a saucepan over low heat. When the apples are slightly tender, remove the pan from the heat and let the mixture cool. ✦ Roll out the dough to form a large rectangle that is about ⅛ inch thick. Arrange the filling down the length of one side. Starting with the same side, roll up the dough to form a long cylinder. ✦ Place on a baking sheet and bake for 20 to 25 minutes until golden. Let stand and serve at room temperature.

CRESPELLE
CON MARMELLATA

PALATSCHINKEN WITH PRESERVES

FRIULI-VENEZIA GIULIA

These pancakes, ennobled in the rest of Italy by the pompous name *crêpes*, are in truth one of the most authentic yet humble sweets from the Trieste area. Considering the poverty in the area and the scarcity of ingredients, the poor families of Trieste saved eggs by adding more flour, resulting in crespelle that are larger and heavier than their French cousins. Filled with apricot preserves, folded in four or rolled up—in certain trattorias in the Carso area they are filled with walnut cream or pastry cream—and dusted with confectioners' sugar, then pressed with the tines of a hot fork, they are a special sweet and in truth highly satisfying. The recipe has remained unchanged in time and the people of Trieste insist that their crespelle must never be confused with crepes.

In a bowl mix the flour, 2 cups water, and eggs to form a smooth batter. Melt 1 tbsp. butter in a pan and pour in enough batter to cover the bottom of the pan with a thin layer. Cook until lightly golden on the bottom, then turn over to complete the cooking. Repeat with the remaining batter, adding more butter to the pan as needed, until all the batter has been used up. Fill these with preserves, roll up, and sprinkle with confectioners' sugar.

For the filling:

Apricot preserves

Confectioners' sugar

CROSTATA
CON LA RICOTTA

RICOTTA CROSTATA

LAZIO

This recipe is typical of Upper Lazio. Once upon a time lard was used in place of butter.

For the pastry:

1⅔ cups all-purpose flour

1 large egg plus 2 yolks

¼ lb. (1 stick) plus 3 tbsp. unsalted butter, cut into pieces

¾ cup sugar

Grated zest of ½ lemon

Salt

For the filling:

1 lb. fresh ricotta

1½ cups sugar

3 large eggs, 2 separated

Grated zest of 1 orange and 1 lemon

2 oz. (2 squares) bittersweet chocolate, grated

Pinch ground cinnamon

½ cup rum

Diced candied fruit

Confectioners' sugar

Use the flour and whole egg to prepare a dough as in the recipe on page 751, adding the egg yolks, butter, sugar, pinch of salt, and lemon zest with the whole egg. Let the dough rest for about 1 hour in the refrigerator. ✦ Preheat the oven to 425°F. Butter a pie pan. In a bowl combine the ricotta, sugar, 2 egg yolks (reserve the whites), 1 whole egg, orange and lemon zest, chocolate, cinnamon, rum, and candied fruit until mixed. ✦ Divide the pastry dough in two parts, one slightly larger than the other. Roll out the larger portion to form a circle about 11 inches in diameter and use it to line the pie pan. Cover this with the ricotta mixture. ✦ Roll out the remaining portion of pastry dough and cut it into 1-inch-thick strips. Arrange some of the strips over the ricotta to form a lattice, using other strips to create a border. ✦ Beat the egg whites until frothy and brush the pastry strips with them. Bake for about 30 minutes, or until the pastry strips are golden brown. Let cool to room temperature, then refrigerate until cold. Dust with confectioners' sugar before serving.

CROSTATA DI SEIRÀSS
(RICOTTA)

RICOTTA CHEESECAKE

FOR
6 PERSONS

PIEMONTE

This recipe is typical of Cuneo.

Butter the bottom and sides of a round baking pan and sprinkle it with breadcrumbs. Whisk together the flour, sugar, baking powder, and a pinch of salt. Work in the

DESSERTS

For the dough:

¼ lb. (½ cup) unsalted butter

½ cup breadcrumbs

2 cups all-purpose flour, plus more as needed

1 tbsp. sugar

1 tsp. baking powder

4 egg yolks

1 cup heavy cream

¼ cup Marsala

¼ cup cognac

Grated zest of 2 or 3 lemons

Salt

For the filling:

1¾ lbs. ricotta (*seiràss*, if available)

⅔ cup raisins, softened in lukewarm water and drained

½ cup chopped candied fruit

2 oz. torrone (nougat), crumbled

1 tbsp. vanilla sugar

1 tbsp. lemon zest

2 tbsp. heavy cream

butter until the mixture looks like coarse crumbs, then mix in the egg yolks, cream, Marsala, and cognac until a smooth dough forms. Let the dough rest 30 minutes. ✦ Roll out a sheet about ½ inch thick and use it to line the bottom and halfway up the sides of the pan. Let this rise 1 hour. ✦ Preheat the oven to 350°F. Mix together the filling ingredients except the cream. Spoon the mixture into the pastry; it should be between 1 and 1½ inches thick. ✦ Drizzle with the cream and bake for 35 to 40 minutes. Let cool to lukewarm and serve.

CROSTINI UBRIACHI

DRUNKEN TOASTS

UMBRIA

3 tsp. chopped semisweet chocolate

½ cup chopped bittersweet chocolate

2 cups brewed black coffee

¾ cup *alchermes* (see note)

¾ cup rum

Slices of stale bread, crust removed

⅔ cup toasted and chopped almonds

Alchermes is a liqueur infused with floral and spicy flavors. To achieve its characteristic red color, it is dyed with cochineal. You can substitute another sweet liqueur of your choice. This sweet is typical of the Carnival celebrations in Città di Castello.

Melt the two kinds of chocolate in a saucepan at low heat. Remove the pan from the heat, then stir in the coffee, then ½ cup of the *alchermes* and ½ cup of the rum. ✦ Dip the slices of bread in the liquid then arrange on a serving plate. Add the almonds to the remaining liquid in the saucepan along with the remaining rum and *alchermes*, stir to blend, then spoon the mixture over the slices of bread. ✦ Let stand 15 minutes before serving.

| # CRESCENT COOKIES

PIEMONTE

½ lb. (2 sticks) plus 2 tbsp. unsalted butter

1 ¼ cups all-purpose flour

1 ⅔ cups cornmeal

1 cup sugar

4 large eggs

The name, also spelled *krumiri*, comes from the name of a liqueur popular in the late nineteenth century.

Preheat the oven to 400°F. Butter and flour a baking sheet. Mix the flour, cornmeal, and sugar, then blend in the butter. Add the eggs one at a time and blend thoroughly to make a smooth, soft dough. ✦ Let it rest, covered, for 30 minutes, then divide it into four portions. Put one portion at a time into a pastry bag with a large star tip. Pipe out half-moons about 4 inches long onto the prepared baking sheet. ✦ Bake for 20 minutes until lightly browned.

CUCCÌA | # WHEAT-BERRY PUDDING 1

SICILIA

1 ⅔ cups wheat berries

1 lb. ricotta

¼ cup anise liqueur

1 ⅔ cups sugar

1 tbsp. sweet ground chocolate

Ground cinnamon, as desired

1 ½ oz. bittersweet chocolate, chopped

2 tbsp. chopped citron

⅔ cup chopped candied pumpkin (see note)

Salt

This is a traditional sweet for the feast of St. Lucy, December 13. Candied pumpkin is sold in jars packed in syrup, or you can make your own. To make candied pumpkin, cut enough squash or pumpkin into 1-inch cubes to make ¾ cup. Combine 1 cup sugar, ¾ cup water, and ½ teaspoon orange-flower water in a medium-size saucepan over medium heat. Bring the mixture to a boil, stirring so that the sugar dissolves. When it is clear and boiling nicely, add the cubed squash and return to a boil. Let boil for 6 minutes, or until the squash is tender but still firm when pierced with a knife. Remove the squash with a slotted spoon to a bowl and set aside to cool. Another version of this dessert flavors the wheat berries with milk, dried orange peel, cinnamon, cloves, raisins, walnuts, and grated chocolate.

Soak the wheat berries in a saucepan with cold water to cover for an entire night. ✦ The next day, change the water and begin cooking the wheat berries in the same pan with a pinch of salt. ✦ When this has cooked (at low heat this will take about half a day), drain it and cool it. ✦ Pass the ricotta through a sieve into a bowl. Mix in the liqueur, then the sugar, ground chocolate, and cinnamon. Stir in the chopped chocolate and the citron, then fold in the candied pumpkin. ✦ Add the wheat berries and mix well. ✦ Pour into cups or molds and refrigerate until cold. Dust with cinnamon before serving.

DESSERTS

ALMOND- AND FIG-FILLED CHRISTMAS COOKIES

CUCCIDDATI

SICILIA

For the dough:

3 ⅓ cups all-purpose flour

9 oz. lard

1 ¼ cups sugar

For the filling:

½ lb. almonds, shelled, peeled, toasted, and finely chopped

1 lb. dried figs, finely chopped

1 ½ cups golden raisins

¼ cup honey, or as needed

Pinch ground cinnamon

1 or 2 tbsp. unsweetened cocoa powder

2 egg yolks, beaten

This is a traditional Christmas sweet.

Use the flour to prepare a firm dough as in the recipe on page 751, using the lard, sugar, and a few tablespoons water (or as needed) in place of the eggs. Set it aside to rest. ✦ In a saucepan combine the almonds, dried figs, raisins, the honey, and cinnamon until blended. ✦ Stir in the cocoa and cook at very low heat, stirring continuously, until it forms a homogeneous paste. ✦ Refrigerate the filling. Preheat the oven to 350°F and grease a baking sheet. Shape the filling into cylinders about 1½ inches in diameter. ✦ On a floured surface, roll out the dough to ⅛ inch thick and cut it into rectangular strips about 2 inches wide. Place the cylinders of filling on these rectangles, folding over the dough to enclose them to make lengths of filled dough. Cut these into 8-inch lengths and press the ends together to form doughnut shapes. ✦ Make incisions on the surface with the tip of a knife to let steam escape during cooking. Place the cookies on the baking sheet and brush them with the egg yolks. Bake for 20 minutes, or until they are golden brown. Serve either hot or cold.

APOSTLES' FINGERS (RICOTTA-STUFFED CREPES)

DITA DEGLI APOSTOLI

PUGLIA

For the filling:

1 lb. sheep's-milk ricotta

⅔ cup superfine sugar

Juice of 1 lemon

Grated zest of 2 lemons

½ cup chopped candied orange

For the crepes:

3 ⅓ cups all-purpose flour

⅓ cup confectioners' sugar

6 large eggs

4 cups milk

CONTINUED

In Brindisi this was once made with ricotta and sugar, coffee powder, cherries in liquor, pitted and chopped, along with the alcohol from the cherries.

Wrap the ricotta in cheesecloth, place it in a strainer, and put it in the refrigerator for 4 hours to drain. ✦ At the end of that time combine the drained ricotta with the other filling ingredients, working well to obtain a homogeneous mixture. ✦ Whisk together the flour and sugar in a bowl, then whisk in the eggs until smooth, then whisk in the milk and orange zest to make a smooth batter. Heat a 10-inch nonstick pan over medium-high heat and add 1 tablespoon of butter, swirling to coat the bottom of the pan. Pour ¼ cup batter into the pan and immediately swirl and tilt the pan so the batter coats the surface evenly to make a crepe 8 inches in diameter.

Grated zest of 1 orange

Unsalted butter, as needed for cooking the crepes

⅔ cup chopped semisweet chocolate

Cook for about 2 minutes until the bottom is light brown (the top will start to look set). Turn and cook the other side. Cook the rest of the batter, adding more butter to the pan as needed. ✦ Spoon the filling onto the crepes and roll them up, then cut each one in three parts. Arrange them on a serving plate. Top with the chopped semisweet chocolate.

DOLCE AMOR

HAZELNUT TRIFLE

EMILIA-ROMAGNA

½ lb. ladyfingers (about 30)
½ cup Marsala
6 yolks of large hard-boiled eggs
1 tbsp. sugar
¼ lb. (1 stick) unsalted butter
1¼ cups toasted and chopped hazelnuts
1 tsp. unsweetened cocoa powder
30 almonds, chopped

Soak all but 1 ladyfinger in the Marsala. Mix the hard-boiled yolks with the sugar, butter, hazelnuts, cocoa, and 1 ladyfinger; pass through a sieve and blend again. ✦ On a serving plate alternate layers of this mixture with layers of ladyfingers. ✦ End with a layer of the egg mixture, spreading it over the sides. ✦ Top with almonds and refrigerate for a few hours before serving.

DOLCE CON MIELE E NOCI

HONEY-NUT STICKS

TOSCANA

1 cup honey
3 cups all-purpose flour
1½ cups sugar
⅔ cup white wine
¼ cup (or less) extra-virgin olive oil
¾ lb. walnuts, finely chopped
Grated zest of 1 orange
Pinch ground cinnamon
Pinch ground cloves
Salt and pepper

These resemble sticks, but their dialect name, *sfratti* ("evicted"), reflects a far-from-sweet reason, since it refers to the sticks or clubs used to evict peasants who fell behind on their rent payments. For the wine, use Vernaccia di San Gimignano or Orvieto.

Combine the honey with the flour, sugar, a pinch of salt, wine, olive oil, and a pinch of pepper in a deep saucepan. Slowly cook the mixture until a thick batter has formed. ✦ Combine the walnuts, orange zest, cinnamon, and cloves and add to the honey mixture. Let this cool, then shape it into short sticks. Serve at room temperature.

DESSERTS

| # LAYERED SPONGE CAKE

½ cup *alchermes*
(see note, page 786)

½ cup cognac

½ cup plus 2 tbsp. rum

½-lb. sponge cake, cut in half
horizontally (see page 843), or
ladyfingers

1½ tbsp. sugar

1 large egg yolk

6 oz. fresh mascarpone

This recipe is typical of Milan and the Milanese lowland and is the forerunner of *tiramisù* but is by no means as elegant. Bear in mind that the mascarpone mixture does not give off moisture so the slices of cake should be well soaked before assembling.

Mix the *alchermes*, cognac, and ½ cup rum in a shallow bowl and soak the sponge cake in it. ✦ Use 1 slice of the cake to line the bottom of a cake pan. ✦ Beat the sugar and egg yolk with a mixer on medium speed until thickened and pale yellow, then whisk in the mascarpone and the remaining rum. ✦ Fill the pan with this mixture then cover with the other half of the soaked sponge cake. ✦ Wrap the whole thing in plastic wrap and refrigerate for at least 24 hours. Serve cold.

| # TUSCAN CHESTNUT LOAF

Unsalted butter

Breadcrumbs

3 large eggs

1⅔ cups sugar

Juice of 1 lemon

½ cup milk

3 cups chestnut flour,
plus more as needed

1½ tsp. active dry yeast,
mixed with ¼ cup warm water

Salt

Butter a baking pan and dust it with breadcrumbs. In a large bowl beat the eggs together with the sugar. Add the lemon juice and mix again, then add the milk. ✦ Sift the chestnut flour and very slowly work it into the egg mixture. Add the yeast dissolved in ¼ cup warm water and a pinch of salt. ✦ Press the dough into the prepared pan, spreading it to a uniform thickness. Let it rise, covered, for 2 hours in a warm place. ✦ Preheat the oven to 350°F. Bake for 40 minutes, until lightly browned.

| # ALMOND CANDY

FOR
6 PERSONS

3 cups almonds

2 cups sugar

CONTINUED

Put the almonds and sugar in a large saucepan and bring this mixture to a boil over low heat, stirring constantly until the sugar completely melts and coats the almonds. ✦ Grease a work surface (preferably marble) with olive oil and pour the mixture onto it. Level the surface first

Olive oil
1 large lemon, cut in half
Candy-coated almonds, crushed

using a wooden spoon and then smooth by rubbing it lightly with the cut sides of the lemon. ✦ When it has cooled completely cut it in pieces and dust with candy-coated almonds.

VALDOSTAN APPLE CAKE

¼ lb. (1 stick) unsalted butter
½ cup sugar
4 ripe rennet apples, peeled, cored, and cut in thin slices
10 slices stale white bread
2 large eggs, beaten
2 cups milk, mixed with ⅔ cup sugar
½ cup chopped walnuts

The dialect name for this, *gatò*, comes from the twelfth-century word *gastel*, a modification of the word *wastil*, which in France meant "food."

Preheat the oven to 350°F. Butter a pie pan. Sprinkle half the sugar over the apple slices. ✦ Use some of the butter to butter the bread slices and use half of them to line the bottom of the pie pan. Cover with a layer of apple slices. Dot the apples with the remaining butter. Repeat this operation. ✦ Mix the eggs and milk mixture and pour this into the pie pan. ✦ Bake for about 30 minutes. ✦ Let cool, invert onto a plate, and decorate with the remaining sugar and the walnuts.

PUMPKIN CAKE

FOR
6 PERSONS

1¾ lbs. pumpkin or yellow winter squash, peeled, seeded, and cut into pieces
½ cup milk
4 tbsp. (½ stick) plus 1 tbsp. unsalted butter
⅔ cup honey
¾ cup all-purpose flour
2 large eggs, separated
½ cup sugar
Salt

Boil the pumpkin or squash pieces in the milk, ½ cup water, and a pinch of salt in a pot. ✦ When the squash is tender, transfer it to a blender and purée it, adding a little of the cooking liquid if necessary to form a smooth purée. Return the purée to the pot. ✦ In a separate pot, heat the butter, honey, a pinch of salt, and ¼ cup warm water until a homogeneous liquid forms. Add this to the squash purée. ✦ Stirring constantly, gradually add the flour and cook until the mixture is thick. Let it cool. ✦ Preheat the oven to 350°F. Caramelize the baking pan: Spread out the sugar in the bottom of the cake pan and place in the oven. Check it every couple of minutes and remove the pan from the oven as soon as the sugar has taken on a light amber color. ✦ Add the egg yolks to the pumpkin mixture, then whip the whites until stiff and gently fold them into the mixture. Put the mixture in the prepared pan and bake for 20 to 25 minutes. Let it cool and turn out on a serving plate.

DESSERTS

DOLCETTI
CON L'UVA PASSA | # RAISIN COOKIES

CALABRIA

Unsalted butter
2½ cups raisins
1½ cups blanched almonds
1½ cups walnut halves
Grated zest of 1 lemon
½ tsp. ground cloves
½ tsp. ground cinnamon
½ cup honey (or as needed), warmed
⅔ cup all-purpose flour
(or as needed)
Lemon leaves
Salt

Preheat the oven to 400°F. Grease a baking sheet with butter. Soften the raisins in lukewarm water to cover for 15 minutes, then drain. ✦ Toast the almonds until golden and chop together with the walnuts and raisins, then mix with the lemon zest, cloves, cinnamon, and a pinch of salt. Mix into this enough honey and flour to make a firm dough. ✦ Roll out this dough into a somewhat thick sheet and cut it into squares. Place each square on a lemon leaf, arrange on the baking sheet, and bake until golden.

DOLCETTI DI MANDORLE | # ALMOND COOKIES

CALABRIA

Lard (or unsalted butter)
2 lbs. blanched almonds
6⅔ cups all-purpose flour
3¾ cups sugar
1½ tbsp. baking powder

Preheat the oven to 350°F. Cover a baking sheet with aluminum foil, then grease the foil with lard or butter. Toast the almonds on an ungreased baking sheet until golden and let stand until cool enough to handle. ✦ Combine them with the flour, sugar, baking powder, and water as needed to form a dough. ✦ Roll out this dough to a sheet the thickness of a finger. Cut the sheet of dough in squares and arrange them on the baking sheet. ✦ Bake until golden, about 12 minutes.

DOLCI NATALIZI | # CHRISTMAS SWEETS

CALABRIA

¼ lb. (1 stick) plus 6 tbsp.
unsalted butter
6⅔ cups all-purpose flour
Sugar
8 large eggs, 4 separated
10 tbsp. milk
CONTINUED

The dialect name *cuzzupa* is from the Greek. This type of sweet, also part of the Greek and Jewish traditions, is used by Calabrians as devotional offerings on Christmas Day, in particular as gifts to loved ones.

Preheat the oven to 400°F. Grease a baking sheet with butter. Mix the flour and sugar and use it and 4 whole eggs to make a dough as in the recipe on page 751, adding 4 egg yolks, butter, milk, lemon and orange zest, and baking powder with the whole eggs. ✦ Divide the dough

Grated zest of 1 lemon plus 1 tbsp. lemon juice
Grated zest of 1 orange
1½ tsp. baking powder
¾ lb. confectioners' sugar

and give the pieces the desired shape (doughnuts, knots, bowties, fish, etc.). Beat 2 of the eggs whites until frothy and brush the cookies with them. ✦ Bake until golden, about 10 minutes. ✦ Meanwhile, make the glaze by energetically beating together the remaining egg whites, confectioners' sugar, and lemon juice until smooth. When the cookies are golden, brush them with the glaze and let rest until dry.

GRAPPA FRITTER

FARTAIES

VENETO

3 large eggs
2 tbsp. sugar
3⅓ cups all-purpose flour
½ cup milk (or as needed)
¼ cup grappa
Grated zest of 1 lemon
1½ tsp. baking powder (optional)
¼ cup sunflower oil (or lard)
Confectioners' sugar
Salt

The success of the *fartaies* consists in the density of the batter, which should be neither too liquid nor too thick.

Put the eggs, sugar, flour, a pinch of salt, and as much milk as needed in a bowl and whisk this mixture to make a smooth batter; add the grappa and lemon zest (also the baking powder if desired). ✦ Heat the sunflower oil (or lard) in a frying pan and pour in the batter in concentric circles, beginning at the center. Cook until golden on the bottom, then turn it over to cook the other side and make it puff up. ✦ Remove from the pan, drain on paper towels, and dust with confectioners' sugar. Serve warm.

FIGS WITH CHOCOLATE

FICHI AL CIOCCOLATO

CALABRIA

3 cups almonds, lightly toasted in the oven and chopped
1 tbsp. cloves, crushed
1½ cups diced candied citron
1 lb. semisweet chocolate, grated
1½ cups sugar
1 tsp. ground cinnamon
4½ lbs. sun-dried figs

Another method is to put the figs, just removed from the oven, in a saucepan in which the chocolate has been melted in a little water with a pinch of cinnamon.

Preheat the oven to 350°F. Mix the almonds, cloves, and candied citron and set aside. ✦ Mix the chocolate, sugar, and cinnamon and set aside. ✦ Cut open the figs and fill them with the almond mixture. Close them tightly, put them on a baking sheet, and bake. As soon as they change color remove them from the oven and, while they are still warm, roll them in the chocolate mixture. ✦ These figs can be kept in an airtight container lined with waxed paper.

FERRATELLE ALLO ZAFFERANO

These cookies, typical of L'Aquila in Abruzzo, are called *ferratelle* after the iron used to cook them. In the past, and to a certain degree also today, families "personalized" their iron with the family coat of arms, the monogram of the head of the household, or some special design that served as a distinctive element. A dough is made of flour and eggs, then flavored with saffron, sugar, and orange liqueur. It is divided into cylinders that are cut into 1-inch lengths. These lengths are then cooked, one by one, in the hot oiled iron in the fireplace. How do you know how long it takes to cook them? Say the "Ave Maria" prayer. When you are halfway through, it is time to flip the cookie. When you are finished with the prayer, the cookie is done.

FICHI RIPIENI | **STUFFED FIGS**

CALABRIA

1½ cups chopped almonds
1¼ cups chopped walnuts
1¼ cups grated bitter chocolate
1 cup chopped candied citron
⅔ cup sugar
Pinch cinnamon
(or ground cloves)
4½ lbs. sun-dried figs
1 cup sweet white wine
Fresh bay leaves

For the wine, use Moscato di Pantelleria or Malvasia della Lipari.

Preheat the oven to 350°F. Mix the almonds, walnuts, chocolate, and citron until blended. ✦ Mix the sugar and cinnamon (or cloves) and set aside. ✦ Cut the figs open and stuff them with the almond mixture, then close them, dust with the sugar mixture, sprinkle with sweet wine, and dry them in the oven for 10 minutes. ✦ These can be preserved by wrapping groups of them in bay leaves. They can also be preserved in containers lined with wax paper.

FOCACCIA DI SEIRÀSS
(RICOTTA) | **FOCACCIA WITH RICOTTA**

PIEMONTE

Unsalted butter, for buttering
the baking pan
1¼ cups all-purpose flour
CONTINUED

Preheat the oven to 425°F. Butter and flour a baking pan. Combine the flour, ricotta, sugar, lemon zest, yeast, drained raisins, and chocolate in a bowl until blended; let this mixture rest for 30 minutes in a cool place. ✦ Spread the mixture across the baking pan. ✦ Bake for

7 oz. firm ricotta (*seiràss*)

1 ¼ cups sugar

Grated zest of 1 lemon

1 ½ tsp. active dry yeast

½ cup raisins, soaked in rum, diluted with an equal amount of water, and drained

½ cup grated chocolate

Confectioners' sugar

about 1 hour until golden. Let cool in the pan. When it has cooled, turn it out on a serving plate and dust with confectioners' sugar.

FOCACCIA PASQUALE

EASTER FOCACCIA

FRIULI-VENEZIA GIULIA

4 ½ tsp. active dry yeast

3 tbsp. milk

⅔ cup sugar

6 ⅔ cups all-purpose flour

4 large eggs plus 8 yolks

¼ lb. (½ cup) plus 3 tbsp. unsalted butter, softened

2 tbsp. rum

2 tbsp. Marsala

1 tsp. vanilla extract

Grated zest of 1 lemon

Grated zest of 1 orange

Salt

Dissolve the yeast in the milk with 1 teaspoon of the sugar and enough flour to form a small loaf; when this loaf has risen combine it with 1 egg and 3 yolks, ⅓ cup of the sugar, ¼ cup of the butter, a pinch of salt, and enough flour to make a soft dough. Let this rise again. ✦ After about 2 hours add all the remaining ingredients and knead on the work surface to obtain an elastic dough. ✦ Divide the dough in two balls. Shape these balls into the classic flat focaccia shape and let them rise again. ✦ Preheat the oven to 350°F. Before putting the focaccias in the oven make deep incisions in them to divide them in thirds. ✦ Put in the oven and bake 45 minutes, lowering the temperature to 300°F and covering the focaccias with aluminum foil halfway through that time.

FRAPPE OR CHIACCHIERE DELLE MONACHE

NUNS' FRITTERS FOR CARNIVAL

LOMBARDIA

3 ⅓ cups all-purpose flour

1 large egg plus 2 yolks

Olive oil, for frying

Confectioners' sugar

Salt

This is a classic Carnival sweet. Some recipes use lard as the fat for the frying, but it is not a traditional component in Milanese cooking.

Use the flour, egg, and yolks to prepare a dough as in the recipe on page 751. Roll out a thin sheet of dough and cut it in squares with a pastry wheel, also making diagonal cuts inside the squares. ✦ Heat 2 inches of olive oil in a saucepan and fry until golden. Drain on paper towels and dust with confectioners' sugar. Serve hot.

BUTTER CRUMBLE

FREGOLOTTA

VENETO

¼ lb. (1 stick) unsalted butter, melted

1 ¼ cups all-purpose flour

⅔ cup sugar

Grated zest of 1 lemon

This recipe is typical of Salvarosa di Castelfranco. There are versions of it that call for the addition of chopped almonds or lard in place of the butter. Another version: add the yolks of 2 hard-boiled eggs to the mixture.

Preheat the oven to 350°F. Butter and flour a 12-inch-square baking pan. Mix the butter, sugar, lemon zest, and flour until blended. ✦ Stir briskly, pass the mixture through a food mill, then pour it into the pan. ✦ Bake until set and cut in slices while still hot. The slices should be no more than ¾ inch thick.

EMPEROR'S FRITTATA

FRITTATA DELL'IMPERATORE

FOR 2 PERSONS

ALTO ADIGE

8 large eggs, separated

6 tbsp. all-purpose flour, sifted

2 tbsp. sugar

½ cup raisins
(or as many as desired)

1 tbsp. unsalted butter

Confectioners' sugar, for dusting

Red currant jam

Salt

This is a one-dish dessert that is economical and easy to prepare.

Lightly beat the egg yolks in a large bowl and slowly add the sifted flour, a pinch of salt, sugar, and raisins, beating the mixture energetically with a whisk. ✦ Whip the egg whites until stiff and fold them gently into the batter. ✦ In a large skillet heat the butter until bubbling. Pour in the batter and cook it on one side then turn and cook the other. ✦ Using two forks tear up this omelet and serve it hot, dusted with confectioners' sugar and topped with jam.

SEMOLINA FRITTERS

FRITTELLE

BASILICATA

Extra-virgin olive oil

1 bay leaf

2 ¼ cups all-purpose flour

⅓ cup coarse semolina

Confectioners' sugar

Salt

Grease a baking pan with olive oil. Combine 3 cups of water in a saucepan with 3 tablespoons olive oil, a pinch of salt, and the bay leaf and bring to a boil. ✦ When the mixture boils remove the pan from the heat and add all at once the flour and the semolina, stirring briskly with a wooden spoon. ✦ Return the pan to the heat and cook, constantly stirring. When the mixture is smooth and compact, remove the bay leaf and pour the mixture into the greased pan. Let it cool, then cut it into squares. Heat 2 inches of olive oil in a pan and fry until golden.

Drain them on paper towels, then arrange on a serving plate and dust with confectioners' sugar. Serve hot.

RAISIN FRITTERS

LAZIO

1½ tsp. active dry yeast
1 cup milk, warmed
3 large eggs, beaten
3 tbsp. sugar
½ cup golden raisins (or as many as desired)
Grated zest of 1 lemon
Grated zest of 1 orange
½ to ¾ cup all-purpose flour
Olive oil, for frying
¼ cup rum
Confectioners' sugar

This recipe is typical of Rome. *Zibibbo*, by way of an Arabic word, means "raisin." Pine nuts can be added in addition to the raisins.

Dissolve the yeast in the milk and add the beaten eggs, sugar, raisins, and lemon and orange zests. Stir this to blend, adding the flour a little at a time to obtain a firm and homogeneous batter. Let this rise until nearly doubled. ✦ Heat 1 inch of olive oil in a saucepan and fry tablespoonfuls of the batter, swirling the pan to give them a spherical shape. ✦ Drain on paper towels, then brush with rum and dust with confectioners' sugar. These are most flavorful when eaten warm.

FRITTELLE
DI CASTAGNACCIO
CHESTNUT FRITTERS

EMILIA-ROMAGNA

3 cups chestnut flour
⅔ cup raisins, softened in water and dried
1 tsp. vanilla extract
½ cup extra-virgin olive oil (or lard)
Confectioners' sugar

Pour the chestnut flour into a bowl and add the raisins, vanilla extract, and enough water to make a somewhat soft batter; set this aside and let it rest for a few hours. ✦ Heat olive oil (or lard) in a skillet and fry the batter 1 tablespoon at a time until puffed and golden. ✦ As the fritters are ready set them out on paper towels to drain and serve hot with a dusting of confectioners' sugar.

FRITTELLE DI MELE
APPLE FRITTERS

FRIULI-VENEZIA GIULIA

Various kinds of fruit can be fried in this kind of batter, such as plums, prunes, peaches, pears, bananas, apricots, and so on. The batter can be made with yeast—flour, milk, yeast, eggs, olive oil, and rum—or it can be made with only flour and wine.

⅔ cup all-purpose flour

1⅓ cup sugar

1 tbsp. rum

1 tbsp. olive oil, plus more for frying

1 large egg, separated, plus 1 yolk

Lemon juice, as needed

4 large apples, peeled, cored, and cut crosswise in ½-inch-thick slices

Confectioners' sugar

Make a batter with the flour, ⅓ cup sugar, rum, olive oil, and egg yolks. Whisk the egg white until stiff. Add the egg white to the batter, working it in spoonful by spoonful. ✦ Mix the remaining sugar and enough lemon juice to make a mixture the consistency of wet sand. Roll the apple slices in the sugar mixture, then dip them one at a time in the batter and fry in oil until golden. Serve dusted with confectioners' sugar.

APPLE FRITTERS WITH MOSCATO WINE

LOMBARDIA

1 large egg

½ cup Moscato wine (preferably from the Oltrepò Pavese area)

1 tsp. baking powder

1 tbsp. honey, preferably acacia

Extra-virgin olive oil, for frying

4 large apples (best would be from the Valtellina), peeled, cored, and sliced

1¾ cups all-purpose flour

Confectioners' sugar

Salt

Prepare a batter with the egg, a pinch of salt, and Moscato. Add the baking powder and the honey, then let this rest for about 30 minutes. ✦ Heat the olive oil until hot. ✦ Dip the apple slices one at a time in the flour, then in the batter and fry until golden. ✦ Serve hot, dusted with confectioners' sugar.

PANE CARASAU FRITTERS

SARDEGNA

1⅔ cups all-purpose flour

3 large eggs

Milk

Pane carasau (music-paper bread, see note), crumbled, as needed

Extra-virgin olive oil, for frying

Honey

Salt

This recipe is typical of Nuoro. Music-paper bread is a cracker-thin flatbread typical of Sardinia.

Knead the flour with the eggs, a little milk, and a little warm salted water. ✦ When the batter is soft but thick let it rest a few minutes. ✦ Add the *pane carasau* to the batter to make it very dense. ✦ Heat 1 inch of olive oil in a pan. Using a spoon scoop out walnut-size balls and fry them. ✦ When golden, remove with a slotted spoon and drain on paper towels. Serve hot, drizzled with a little honey.

RICE FRITTERS FOR SAINT JOSEPH'S DAY

LAZIO

1 ½ cups superfine rice

1 ½ cups milk

⅔ cup all-purpose flour

⅔ cup sugar, or as needed

3 large eggs, separated

1 cup golden raisins,
soaked in wine to soften

1 tsp. ground cinnamon

Grated zest of 1 lemon

Grated zest of 1 orange

3 tbsp. rum

2 tsp. vanilla extract

1 tbsp. baking powder

Olive or peanut oil, for frying

Confectioners' sugar

Salt

Throughout the Viterbo area these rice fritters are prepared on St. Joseph's Day, which is celebrated with so many similar fried sweets in so many of Italy's regions that the saint has been nicknamed St. Joseph *frittellaro*.

Cook the rice in the milk diluted with a little water and salt until tender; drain, reserving the milk, and let the rice cool. ✦ Dissolve the flour and sugar in ½ cup milk. In a bowl work the 3 egg yolks together with the milk mixture, then add the raisins, cinnamon, lemon and orange zests, rum, vanilla, and baking powder. Whip the egg whites until stiff and fold into the mixture. ✦ Incorporate the rice and add additional sugar and salt if desired. Its consistency should be that of a somewhat dense batter. Let it rest about an hour. ✦ In a deep skillet or fryer heat 2 inches olive or peanut oil until hot, then carefully drop in egg-size scoops of this batter to make fritters. ✦ When they have cooked on all sides and are golden brown, remove with a slotted spoon and let dry on paper towels. Before serving dust with confectioners' sugar and serve hot.

POTATO FRITTERS

CALABRIA

1 lb. potatoes

3 tsp. active dry yeast,
dissolved in lukewarm water

3 ⅓ cups all-purpose flour

Olive oil, for frying

Confectioners' sugar

Salt

These sweet fritters are a traditional dish on Christmas Eve.

Peel the potatoes and boil them until tender. Drain them completely, then put them through a potato ricer. Add the yeast. ✦ Knead this mixture to obtain a soft dough, then add the flour with a little lukewarm water and a pinch of salt. ✦ Knead the dough and shape into cylinders a little more than ½ inch in diameter and about 1 foot long. Join the ends of each of these long cylinders to form thin doughnuts. Let them rise, covered by a cloth, for several hours. ✦ Heat 2 inches of olive oil and fry until they are so puffed up they double their volume. ✦ Drain on paper towels and dust them with confectioners' sugar before serving.

DESSERTS

ABRUZZO

1½ cups sugar

1¾ cups all-purpose flour,
plus more for dipping the fritters

Pinch ground cinnamon

Grated zest of 1 lemon

1 tsp. vanilla extract

4 cups milk

Olive oil

3 large egg whites

Fine breadcrumbs

Rum (optional)

Salt

This recipe is typical of Torricella and Montorio.

Whisk together the sugar, flour, cinnamon, a pinch of salt, and lemon zest in a saucepan. Stir the vanilla into the milk, then add to the sugar mixture, stirring to avoid the formation of lumps. ✦ Put this mixture in a saucepan and cook over low heat for a few minutes, stirring until it forms a paste. ✦ Grease a work surface (preferably marble) with olive oil and spread out this paste to a thickness of ¾ inch. Let it cool for about 5 hours. ✦ Beat the egg whites until frothy. Cut the paste into small squares, dip them in flour, then in egg whites, and finally in the breadcrumbs. Heat 2 inches of olive oil in a pan. Fry the fritters until golden and drain on paper towels. Serve at room temperature (they are exceptional drizzled with rum).

FROSCIA O MALASSATA | **RICOTTA CHEESECAKE**

SICILIA

1 lb. ricotta

2 cups sugar

10 large eggs, beaten

1¼ cups grated fresh
caciocavallo cheese

20 mint leaves

Pinch ground pepper

Breadcrumbs (if needed)

This recipe is typical of Gela. This Easter sweet has very ancient origins. The name *froscia*, or *floscia*, meaning "limp" or "soft," refers to a particular version made in western Sicilia, most of all in the interior of the island.

Preheat the oven to 400°F. Grease a round baking pan. Mix together all the ingredients (except the breadcrumbs) in such a manner to make a wet dough. Add breadcrumbs if needed to stiffen the dough slightly (it should be wet but not runny). ✦ Pour this into the baking pan and top with more breadcrumbs. ✦ Bake and remove when the surface is golden.

FRUSTINGO | **FRUITCAKE WITH NUTS**

MARCHE

1¼ cups extra-virgin olive oil

1 lb. dried figs,
soaked in water overnight

⅔ cup golden raisins, soaked in
lukewarm water, drained, and dried

CONTINUED

Preheat the oven to 325°F. Grease a pie pan with olive oil. Boil the figs in water until they soften completely. Remove from the water, chop, and add the raisins, honey, sugar, lemon (or orange) zest, candied fruit (if desired), nutmeg, and cinnamon. ✦ Toast the almonds, finely chop together with the walnuts, and add to the fig mixture. ✦ Knead the mixture together with the olive oil until

⅔ cup honey
⅔ cup sugar
Grated lemon (or orange) zest
Candied fruit (optional)
Pinch grated nutmeg
Pinch ground cinnamon
⅔ cup almonds
⅔ cup walnut halves

blended. Pour the mixture into the pie pan. ✦ Bake until it has a good golden color. Serve at room temperature.

FRUTTARA DI CAMPAGNA

POLENTA FRUITCAKE

VENETO

1⅔ cups cornmeal
⅔ cup all-purpose flour
½ cup raisins
½ cup pine nuts
½ cup chopped dried figs
1¼ cups sugar
Grated zest of 1 orange
2 apples, peeled, cored, and minced
1½ cups plus 2 tbsp. unsalted butter
Breadcrumbs
Coarse sugar
Salt

Preheat the oven to 300°F or light a grill and let it burn down to embers. Use the cornmeal, a pinch of salt, and 5 cups water to make a polenta as in the recipe on page 289, but cook it just until it is beginning to soften, about 15 minutes. Remove from the heat and stir in the remaining ingredients except the coarse sugar; transfer the mixture to a baking pan. ✦ Cook over coals or in the oven for about 1½ hours, until set. ✦ After baking sprinkle with coarse sugar.

GASSE

FRIED KNOTS

LIGURIA

3⅓ cups all-purpose flour
1 large egg
2 tbsp. unsalted butter
½ cup sugar
½ cup milk
Olive oil, for frying
Confectioners' sugar

This recipe is typical of the Valle Bormida. To make them puffy and crumbly, so that they almost melt in the mouth, use only a little butter, a single egg, and a little sugar.

Use the flour and egg to prepare a dough as in the recipe on page 751, adding the butter, sugar, and milk with the egg. The dough should be firm and soft, with a smooth appearance. ✦ Roll out to form a very thin sheet. ✦ Using a pastry wheel cut strips of dough 1 inch wide and 6 to 8 inches long then cross the ends to form knots (*gasse*). Heat 2 inches of olive oil in a saucepan and fry until golden. ✦ Drain them on paper towels and dust with confectioners' sugar.

DESSERTS

CHOCOLATE ROLLED CAKE

TOSCANA

6 large eggs, separated

1⅔ cups sugar

⅔ cup all-purpose flour

1½ tsp. baking powder

2 oz. bittersweet chocolate, chopped

1 tbsp. milk

1 tbsp. heavy cream

¼ cup *alchermes*
(see note, page 786)

Confectioners' sugar

This recipe is typical of Arezzo. As an alternative: After baking, cover half the cake with chocolate sauce and put plain pastry cream on the other half and cover with a light layer of cream. This results in a filling more varied to both taste and sight. Roll up the cake. Dust the roll with confectioners' sugar or pour over whipped cream.

Line a jelly roll pan with a sheet of wax paper, letting the ends extend above the pan. Butter the wax paper. Preheat the oven to 450°F. Whip the egg yolks and sugar with a mixer on medium speed until pale and very thick; separately, whip the egg whites until stiff. Fold the whites into the yolks, then fold in the flour very slowly to avoid lumps. Add the baking powder. ✦ Pour the mixture into the pan and level it off. The batter should cover the bottom without being more than ½ inch in depth. Bake for 5 minutes. ✦ Melt the chocolate in the top of a double boiler until smooth. Gradually stir in the milk and cream to make a smooth sauce. Take the pan out of the oven and immediately lift the cake out of the pan by grasping the ends of the wax paper. Put the cake on a damp dishcloth paper-side up and let stand until cool enough to handle. Carefully peel off the waxed paper. ✦ Sprinkle the cake with *alchermes* then spread it with the chocolate mixture. Starting at a short end and using the cloth as a guide, roll up the cake. Dust with confectioners' sugar before serving.

GELATINA DI ARANCE SANG-SANG

BLOOD-ORANGE GELATIN

SICILIA

1 oz. gelatin, soaked in cold water and drained

2 cups sugar

3½ cups juice of blood oranges, mixed with the juice of 4 lemons

½ cup rum

Sliced oranges and strawberries for garnish

The gelatin of Sicilian mandarins is a variation of the gelatin of blood oranges: proceed as below, substituting the juice of sweet mandarins for the juice of the blood oranges. Add the lemon juice and the rum. The two gelatins can be served together in matching containers; the difference in color makes them spectacular. This is an excellent dessert in place of the usual fruit, which can also be served along with this gelatin. Indeed, you can use a round mold with a hole at the center to make the gelatin and then fill the center with fruit salad.

Wipe the inside of a mold with a damp paper towel. Heat the drained gelatin and sugar to melt them, but do not let the mixture boil (which would give it a bitter taste). ✦ Remove from the heat and mix in the juice and rum. Pour this into the mold and refrigerate until set. ✦ Using a warm cloth unmold the gelatin onto a plate of a color that complements the color of the oranges. Garnish with slices of orange and strawberry.

WATERMELON ICE

GELO DI COCOMERO

SICILIA

1 quart watermelon juice
1 cup sugar
½ cup cornstarch
1 tsp. essence of jasmine (see note)
1 cinnamon stick
4 oz. chocolate chips
⅓ cup chopped pistachios
⅓ cup diced candied pumpkin (see note, page 787)

Make the essence of jasmine by soaking a bunch of jasmine flowers in a little water for 2 hours.

Thoroughly blend the watermelon juice with the sugar and cornstarch to obtain a smooth and homogeneous mixture, adding the essence of jasmine. ✦ Pour this into a saucepan, add the cinnamon stick, and cook to make it thicken, stirring continuously. ✦ When thickened, remove from the heat and pour into small molds garnished with chocolate chips, pistachios, and candied pumpkin. ✦ Refrigerate and serve cold.

✦ **LOCAL TRADITION** ✦

GELATINE DI FICHI D'INDIA

Typical of Ponza in Lazio, this sugarless dessert is made by slow-cooking the pulp of the sun-ripened prickly pears that grow wild on the island. The cooked pulp is passed through a fine sieve to remove the many small seeds. Back on the heat, semolina flour is added to thicken the pulp. This second, longer cooking results in a dense cream that is then spread on a table to dry in the sun, after which the pulp can be cut into lozenges and further dried in an oven if still too soft. These "gummy" sweets were most often stored in tightly sealed glass jars.

| # MANDARIN GELATIN

SICILIA

15 mandarin oranges
¼ cup plus 3 tbsp. cornstarch
⅔ cup sugar
Mandarin leaves
Seasonal fruit for decoration
(strawberries, apricots, pears,
cherries, or others)

Remove the peel from 1 mandarin, making sure not to remove the bitter white pith, and slice. Squeeze the mandarins through a strainer. ✦ Add enough water to make a total of 4 cups liquid and using a whisk (to avoid the formation of lumps) stir the cornstarch and sugar into the liquid, then pass the mixture through a sieve. ✦ Pour the resulting mixture in a saucepan and add the slices of mandarin peel. Stirring constantly with a wooden spoon, cook until it begins to boil, at which point remove the mandarin peel. ✦ Pour into a damp mold and cool in the refrigerator for a few hours. At the moment of serving turn out on a serving plate and decorate with mandarin leaves and seasonal fruit as desired.

GIALLETTI

CORNMEAL RAISIN COOKIES

LAZIO

3 oz. lard
1⅔ cups cornmeal
⅔ cup all-purpose flour
2 large eggs, beaten
¼ lb. (1 stick) plus 3 tbsp. unsalted butter, softened
1¼ cups sugar
Grated zest of 1 lemon
⅔ cup raisins

Preheat the oven to 400°F. Grease a baking sheet with lard. Mix together the cornmeal and flour and use them and the eggs to make a dough as in the recipe on page 751, adding the butter, sugar, lemon zest, and lard with the eggs ✦ Fold in the raisins so that they are uniformly distributed in the mixture. ✦ Roll it out with a rolling pin to the thickness of about ¾ inch. With a knife cut lengthwise into strips, then cut crosswise into squares. ✦ Arrange these on the baking sheet and bake until cooked through and golden, about 10 minutes.

GNOCCHETTI RICOPERTI DI MIELE

HONEYED GNOCCHI

CALABRIA

3⅓ cups all-purpose flour
1 tbsp. extra-virgin oil plus olive oil for frying

CONTINUED

This is traditional on December 13, feast day of St. Lucy.

Use the flour to make a dough as in the recipe on page 751, using the olive oil, wine, cinnamon, and orange zest in place of the eggs. The resulting dough should be soft. ✦ Form the dough into a cylinder about 1 inch in diameter and cut it in pieces, making them into large gnocchi. ✦ Heat 2 inches of olive oil in a pan and fry the gnocchi until golden. ✦ Meanwhile put the honey and orange juice in a separate pan and simmer, stirring, until the honey melts. ✦ Add the fried gnocchi to the honey mixture, stir to coat, then arrange them on a serving plate. Serve hot.

1 cup white dessert wine (preferably Moscato)

Pinch ground cinnamon

Grated zest and juice from 1 orange

1¼ cups honey

PLUM GNOCCHI

GNOCCHI DI SUSINE

FRIULI-VENEZIA GIULIA

1½ tsp. active dry yeast

¼ cup sugar, or as needed

4½ cups all-purpose flour

2 large eggs

1 cup milk

3 tbsp. unsalted butter, softened

10 plums (preferably Italian or Santa Rosa), pitted and cut in half lengthwise

1 tbsp. breadcrumbs

In a large bowl dissolve the yeast in ¼ cup warm water with 1 tablespoon sugar and 1 tablespoon flour. ✦ In a separate bowl beat the eggs with another tablespoon sugar then add the milk, 1 tablespoon of the butter, and remaining flour. Add this to the yeast and knead well to form dough; set aside and let rise. ✦ Roll the plum halves in the remaining sugar. ✦ Bring a pot of water to a boil. Take 1 tablespoon of the dough and wrap it around a plum half, pinching the seam to seal completely. Immerse the whole thing in boiling water. When the gnocchi float they are done. ✦ Drain them well. ✦ Heat the remaining butter in a pan and toast the breadcrumbs; add the gnocchi and toss to coat. Dust with sugar and serve hot.

WHEAT-BERRY PUDDING 2

GRANO DEI MORTI

PUGLIA

1 lb. wheat berries

Seeds of 1 pomegranate

¾ cup shelled and chopped walnuts

¾ cup chopped chocolate

⅔ cup chopped candied citron

1 cinnamon stick, broken into pieces

2 or 3 tbsp. sugar

Vin cotto (see note, page 818)

This recipe is typical of Foggia. This dessert is made for the celebration of the Day of the Dead.

Soak the wheat berries in lukewarm water for 2 days in the refrigerator, then boil them for about 1 hour. ✦ Drain and cool. ✦ When they have cooled add all the other ingredients except the *vin cotto*, then, at the moment of serving, add *vin cotto* as desired (if added earlier it will stiffen the mixture).

DESSERTS

FRIULIAN FILLED CAKE

FRIULI-VENEZIA GIULIA

For the dough:

1⅔ cups all-purpose flour, plus more as needed

1 tbsp. unsalted butter, plus more for the pan

For the filling:

1½ cups raisins, soaked in grappa, slivovitz, or Marsala and drained

2 cups chopped walnuts

1 cup pine nuts

½ cup chopped dried figs

¼ cup chopped prunes

1 tbsp. chopped candied citron

⅔ cup grated chocolate

½ cup breadcrumbs, fried in unsalted butter

Grated zest of 1 lemon

Grated zest of 1 orange

1 large egg separated, egg white whipped stiff

Salt

Use the flour to make a dough as in the recipe on page 751, using ½ cup water and the butter in place of the eggs. The dough will be soft. Let it rest 30 minutes. ✦ Preheat the oven to 350°F. Butter and flour a baking sheet. Roll out the dough to form a very thin sheet to make it nearly transparent. ✦ Combine all of the filling ingredients except the egg yolk. Spread the filling down one edge of the dough, then roll up the dough to form a large salame shape, curving in its ends to form a spiral. ✦ Place on the baking sheet and brush with the reserved egg yolk. Bake for 45 minutes, or until golden.

APPLE-RAISIN PANCAKES

VENETO

5 large eggs

3 tbsp. sugar

3⅓ cups all-purpose flour

Milk

4 apples, peeled, cored, and cut into thin slices

½ cup raisins, soaked in warm water until soft and drained

¼ cup lard (or olive oil or unsalted butter)

Salt

Serve with red currant or lingonberry jam or, when in season, cherries cooked in their juice.

Beat the eggs with the sugar and a pinch of salt until well blended, then whisk in the flour and milk to make a somewhat liquid, smooth, and homogeneous batter. ✦ Add the apple slices and raisins to the batter and mix well. ✦ Heat 1 tablespoon lard, olive oil, or butter in a cast-iron skillet and pour in some of the batter, enough to cover the bottom to a thickness of ⅛ inch. ✦ Cook until golden brown on one side then flip it over to cook the other side. Break it up into small pieces. ✦ Transfer these pieces to a bowl and repeat with the remaining batter, oiling the pan again from time to time.

APRICOT DUMPLINGS

ALTO ADIGE

2 lbs. potatoes (best if starchy)

1⅔ cups all-purpose flour, sifted

3 large eggs

¼ lb. (1 stick) plus 6 tbsp. unsalted butter

16 apricots, pitted

⅔ cup breadcrumbs

Sugar

Ground cinnamon

Salt

Some people today insert a sugar cube inside each apricot in place of its pit, especially if the apricots are not totally ripe.

Boil the potatoes until tender then peel them, pass them through a potato ricer, and put the purée on a work surface to cool. ✦ When the potato purée has cooled, add the flour, eggs, 1 tablespoon butter, and a pinch of salt and knead to form a smooth dough that is not sticky. ✦ Shape the dough into a long cylinder and cut this into sixteen 6-inch lengths. ✦ Push down on each length to form a large rectangle then place an apricot in the middle of each. ✦ Using floured hands close over the dough to form each rectangle into a ball. ✦ Bring salted water to a boil and drop in the apricot balls, cooking them until they float, then setting them out to drain. ✦ Meanwhile melt the remaining butter in a saucepan. When the butter begins to brown add the breadcrumbs, stir, and after a minute or two add the cooked apricot dumplings, rolling them around with a wooden spoon to uniformly coat them. ✦ Serve hot with a dusting of sugar and cinnamon.

KNÖDEL CON LE MELE

APPLE DUMPLINGS

ALTO ADIGE

2 lbs. apples, peeled, cored, and chopped

2 large eggs

1¼ cups all-purpose flour

½ cup unsalted butter

2 tbsp. breadcrumbs

2 tbsp. sugar

Salt

Put the apples in a bowl and add the eggs, flour, and a little salt. Mix to form a soft dough. ✦ Shape this mixture into balls and boil them in lightly salted water for 8 to 10 minutes, until they float. ✦ Heat the butter in a pan, add the breadcrumbs and sugar, and stir to mix. Add the apple dumplings, rolling them around to coat thoroughly. Serve hot.

CHOCOLATE IN PIEMONTE

Chocolate is the primary ingredient in many of the traditional sweets of the Canavese area. This should surprise no one since not far away is Turin, renowned as the "capital of chocolate." Sandro Doglio relates that the first chocolate beans to reach Italy from the New World, not long after its discovery, arrived in Turin from the Madrid court in 1559. Records indicate that by the opening years of the 1600s companies had been founded in Turin for the production and sale of chocolate, then used exclusively as a beverage. During the second half of that century chocolate *en pastille* appeared, as well as *en liqueur*. By the end of the century Turin was producing 750 pounds of chocolate a day, with exports to Austria, Switzerland, Germany, and France. Turin was the birthplace of chocolate bars, such that in the early nineteenth century even the famous Swiss chocolatiers did their apprenticeships in Turin, the city which invented *Gianduja* during that same period, a creation in which hazelnut powder took the place of some of the chocolate, which had become harder to come by because of an English naval blockade. Not even the arrival of coffee managed to affect the deeply rooted taste for chocolate, leading to the creation of *bicerin*, a beverage combining milk, chocolate, and coffee. Alexandre Dumas *père*, who arrived in Piemonte in 1859, wrote of this treat that it was something he "would never forget." Even today there are large and small chocolate companies in Piemonte, evidence of the continuation of a taste and a tradition.

LASAGNE DA FORNEL | SWEET LASAGNE

VENETO

1 ¼ cups all-purpose flour

1 ¼ cups semolina flour

3 large eggs

¼ lb. (1 stick) plus 6 tbsp. unsalted butter, melted

½ lb. apples, peeled, cored, and thinly sliced

½ cup chopped figs

⅔ cup chopped walnuts

1 tbsp. ground cinnamon

½ cup raisins

1 tbsp. poppy seeds

Salt

Preheat the oven to 350°F. Mix together the flours and use them and the eggs to prepare a dough as in the recipe on page 10. Cut it into lasagne strips a little narrower than the length of a finger. ✦ Boil these strips in salted water then add half the butter. ✦ Combine the apples, figs, walnuts, cinnamon, raisins, and poppy seeds. ✦ In a baking pan alternate layers of the cooked lasagne with the apple mixture, ending with a layer of apples. Cover this with the remaining butter and bake for about 20 minutes.

LATTAIOLO | CUSTARD TART

MARCHE

Unsalted butter

1 recipe pastry dough made with
only flour, butter, and water
in place of the eggs (see page 773)

2 large eggs (or 6 yolks)

⅔ cup sugar

Grated zest of 1 lemon

1 pinch ground cinnamon

1 pinch grated nutmeg

4 cups milk

Confectioners' sugar (optional)

This recipe is based on antique versions with names like *lat-taccioﬂu* or *lattaruolo*. This custard is typical of the Marche, such that its preparation follows a kind of ritual.

Preheat the oven to 350°F. Butter a baking dish and line the bottom and sides with the dough. Refrigerate until needed. Beat the eggs together with the sugar, adding the lemon zest, cinnamon, and nutmeg. ✦ Cook this mixture in the top of a double boiler, slowly adding the milk while constantly stirring in one direction. ✦ When the mixture has thickened, pour it into the pastry-lined baking dish. Cover with aluminum foil and bake for about 30 minutes. ✦ Remove the tart from the pan, place the result on a plate, and let cool, dusting (if desired) with confectioners' sugar. Cut into squares to serve.

LATTE DI MANDORLE | ALMOND SPAGHETTI

PUGLIA

1 cup all-purpose flour

3 cups blanched almonds

¼ cup cornstarch

2 cups sugar

Ground cinnamon

This recipe is typical of the Salento area and is usually made for Christmas lunch.

Use the flour to prepare a dough as in the recipe on page 10, using 6 tablespoons water in place of the eggs. ✦ Take small bits of this and work them between the hands to make short lengths of spaghetti, about ½ inch long. ✦ Grind the almonds in a food processor to obtain a smooth paste. ✦ Mix the almond paste with 6 cups of water. Pour this liquid into a fine cheesecloth and squeeze out as much liquid as possible, collecting it in a bowl. ✦ Repeat this procedure using another 6 cups of water and collecting the liquid in the same bowl. ✦ In a small bowl combine the cornstarch with some of the almond liquid to make a paste, then add this back into the bowl with the almond water. Pour the almond water into a saucepan, add the sugar, and heat over moderate heat until it boils. ✦ Add the spaghetti and stir constantly until they are cooked. Transfer to a serving bowl and dust with cinnamon. Let this rest a few hours and serve at room temperature.

DESSERTS

| # FRIED CUSTARD SQUARES

LIGURIA

4 cups milk
1 cup all-purpose flour
1 cup sugar
Grated zest of 1 lemon
4 large eggs, beaten
Unsalted butter
Olive oil, for frying
Lard, for frying
Breadcrumbs

In a saucepan gradually mix the milk into the flour, then add the sugar, lemon zest, and 3 eggs. ✦ Cook over low heat, stirring constantly, until it reaches a thick and creamy consistency. ✦ Butter a work surface, then pour the mixture out on it. Spread evenly and let cool. ✦ Heat ½ inch olive oil and ½ inch lard in a wide pan. Cut the cooled cream in squares, dip them in the remaining egg, then breadcrumbs, then fry them until golden. Serve hot.

LAURINO | # LAUREL LIQUEUR

EMILIA-ROMAGNA

1⅔ cups sugar
2⅓ cups high-proof alcohol
7 oz. bay berries

Dissolve the sugar in 2 cups boiling water. ✦ When the syrup has cooled, pour it in a glass jar along with the alcohol and bay berries and seal. ✦ Let this macerate for about a month, shaking the jar every so often. ✦ After this period, pass the contents through a sieve and strain through paper. Put it in a bottle with a cork or other stopper. Let this age at least four months before using.

LIMONCELLO | # LIMONCELLO

CAMPANIA

5 medium lemons or limes, preferably organic
4 cups high-proof alcohol
⅔ cup sugar

This recipe is typical of Salerno.

Remove the peel from the lemons and try not to get any of the white pith. Put the peels along with the alcohol in a container with a hermetic seal. Let this sit for 7 days. ✦ At the end of the seventh day heat the sugar with 6 cups water until dissolved. Strain the peels from the alcohol. Add the lemon peels to the sugar mixture and cook until they break down. Remove from the heat, then pour in the alcohol, which in the meantime will have assumed a yellow or greenish color. ✦ Let this rest two or three days and then strain before use.

LEMON VERBENA LIQUEUR

2 cups sugar

120 leaves of lemon verbena

Peel from 3 lemons, in strips, white pith removed

4 cups high-proof alcohol

Bring 4 cups of water to a boil in a pot, remove the pot from the heat, and add the sugar, stirring with a wooden spoon. ✦ Wait until the sugar has dissolved and the liquid has completely cooled before adding all the other ingredients. ✦ Pour this into a ceramic or glass jar and let sit 30 days in a cool, dark place. Strain the resulting liquid, bottle it, and let it age at least 6 months before using.

CHRISTMAS MACARONI WITH WALNUTS

For the honey bread:

6⅔ cups all-purpose flour

½ cup extra-virgin olive oil

1½ cups honey

For the macaroni sauce:

8¾ lbs. shelled walnuts, toasted and chopped

1⅔ cups sweet ground chocolate

⅔ cup sugar

1 tsp. ground cinnamon

1 lb. macaroni (see note)

Salt

This recipe is typical of Viterbo. Macaroni with walnuts is the most typical Christmas dish of the Tuscia area and it appears in several variants between one town and another. Years ago it was eaten as the first serving for "Christmas Dinner" (and in some towns this is still the case), but later the dish came to represent the favorite dessert at the end of the meal on Christmas Eve. The generic term *macaroni*, once used to identify any type of pasta, is here meant to indicate the variety of shapes that were used in the past. The oldest was the sheet of dough made at home using flour and water, in later times enriched with egg and cut into fettuccine; with the arrival of industrial pasta the most common shape used for this dish is linguine.

Make the honey bread. Preheat the oven to 350°F. Use the flour to make a dough as in the recipe on page 751, using the oil and honey in place of the eggs. Form this into a loaf, then bake it until browned. ✦ Remove the bread from the oven and let it stand until it is cool enough to handle then grate it. ✦ Make the macaroni sauce. Measure the walnuts after chopping them then measure the grated bread and use enough of both to make a mixture of 2 parts bread to 1 part nuts. ✦ In another bowl mix the chocolate, sugar, and cinnamon. (These two mixtures can be prepared a day in advance but should be stored in separate bowls.) ✦ Cook the macaroni in lightly salted boiling water, letting them cook a little longer than normal so they are slightly overcooked. Using a large fork, tongs, or slotted spoon lift out some of the macaroni and, without letting it drain too much, put it in a serving bowl. ✦ Add some of the chopped nuts and

DESSERTS

honey bread mixture and toss well to blend. ✦ Cover with a thin layer of the chocolate mixture and with another layer of the nuts and honey bread mixture. Repeat this operation until all the macaroni is used up, pressing down on the various layers.

MANDORLATO
DI COLOGNA VENETA

ALMOND NOUGAT 1

VENETO

2 oz. white wafers
2 cups wildflower honey
2 large egg whites
2 lbs. peeled almonds
⅔ cup diced candied citron
Pinch ground cinnamon

This is meant to be stored and eaten a little at a time. In truth, the *mandorlato* of Cologna Veneta is one of Italy's national specialties. Although the recipe is simple, the preparation is actually quite complex. It owes its fame primarily to the quality of the ingredients (the honey and almonds), which must be the very best. If you cannot find the wafers, you can line the pan with parchment.

Line a baking pan with the wafers, breaking them as necessary to cover the whole surface. Heat the honey in a heatproof bowl set over a pot of simmering water (do not let it touch) for about 30 minutes, stirring constantly. ✦ Meanwhile, whip the egg whites until stiff and fold into the honey. ✦ Put the honey back over the heat in the water bath and cook, stirring, another 30 minutes. Let this cool until it is lukewarm. ✦ Add the almonds, citron, and cinnamon. Stir to blend well and pour this mixture into the pan lined with wafers. ✦ Wait for the mixture to cool then break it in pieces and store them in a closed jar.

MARITOZZI

SWEET BUNS

FOR
8 PERSONS

LAZIO

1½ tsp. active dry yeast
1¼ cups all-purpose flour
1 large egg
¼ cup extra-virgin olive oil
3 tbsp. sugar
2 tbsp. pine nuts
⅓ cup raisins
Grated zest of 1 orange
Salt

Maritozzi are typical of the Lenten period in Rome. In the past they were made in an elongated shape and also in the shape of a heart decorated with doves made with cotton candy because many buyers were young men who got them for their sweethearts. There were then the famous *maritozzi* from Giobbe, a well-known pastry shop in Piazza Navona, where they made them larger than usual and where they cost three *soldi* instead of two.

Dissolve the yeast in ¼ cup lukewarm water and combine with ½ cup of the flour to make a soft dough. Set this aside to rise, covered, in a warm spot for 30 minutes. ✦ When the dough has risen add the remaining flour, the egg, olive oil, and a pinch of salt. Knead energetically, then add the sugar. ✦ Knead the dough for another 30 minutes, then form it into a ball and keep it covered and floured in a warm spot for 1 hour. ✦ As soon as the dough begins to swell, add the pine nuts, raisins, and orange zest and work all this together on a work surface dusted with flour. ✦ Shape the dough into 12 oval buns, arrange them evenly on a baking sheet greased with olive oil, and let them rise again for 6 hours in a lukewarm spot. ✦ Preheat the oven to 400°F. Bake until golden and serve at room temperature.

MARMELLATA DI ARANCE | # ORANGE MARMALADE

PUGLIA

1 lb. organic oranges
(preferably those with thin rinds)
2 cups sugar
Juice of 1 lb. organic lemons

This recipe is typical of the Salento area.

Peel half of the oranges and slice thinly. Slice the remaining half without removing the peel. Put them in a bowl, alternating layers of orange slices with sugar. Let this sit 8 to 10 hours. ✦ At the end of that time add the lemon juice and transfer the mixture to a pan and cook at moderate heat, skimming the surface from time to time and stirring often until it reaches the right density: the marmalade should not drip from a wooden spoon when lifted out of the mixture. ✦ While the mixture is still hot pour it into sterilized jars with bands and lids, leaving about ½ inch at the top of the jar. Do not tighten the lids completely. Process in boiling water to cover for 6 minutes. Let cool completely before using.

MARMELLATA D'UVA | # GRAPE JAM

PUGLIA

1 lb. red grapes

This jam is suitable for the preparation of pies and cakes. Any kind of ripe red or black grape suitable for making *mostarda* or grapes for making wine will do.

Remove the seeds without skinning them and heat them in a large pot until the juice cooks away completely. Do not add any sugar since the grapes are already well supplied. ✦ While the mixture is still hot pour it into sterilized jars with bands and lids, leaving about ½ inch at the top of the jar. Do not tighten the lids completely. Process

DESSERTS

in boiling water to cover for 6 minutes. Let cool completely before using.

MASCARPONE CAKE WITH MARSALA

MASCARPONE
ALLO ZABAGLIONE

LOMBARDIA

3 large eggs
4 tbsp. sugar
2 tbsp. plus ½ cup Marsala
1 cup mascarpone
1 10-inch sponge cake (see page 843)

Make a zabaglione, whisking together the eggs, sugar, and 2 tablespoons Marsala in the top of a double boiler. Cook 10 minutes, whisking until thick and a little foamy. Fold the warm zabaglione into the mascarpone, which will melt on contact with the heat. Mix well. ✦ Cut the sponge cake in slices and soak them in the remaining Marsala; use the slices to line a mold. ✦ Pour in the mascarpone mixture, smooth the surface with a spatula, and cover with more slices of sponge cake. ✦ Put in the refrigerator until the next day and serve by turning the cake over onto a plate.

✦ **LOCAL TRADITION** ✦

MARMELLATA DI CASTAGNE

Marmellata di castagne, typical of the Agno valley, Montecchio, Schi, and Tretti in the Veneto, is a sweet spread made from wild chestnuts and apples. The apples are diced and cooked down until their liquid is released and thickened, then the shelled chestnuts are added. After two hours of steady cooking, sugar, or more traditionally, honey, is added and the mixture stirred until homogeneous.

EGGPLANT WITH CHOCOLATE

MELANZANE
AL CIOCCOLATO

CAMPANIA

2 lbs. medium eggplants, peeled
Extra-virgin olive oil
2 cups sugar
CONTINUED

This recipe is typical of Maiori on the Amalfi Coast.

Cut the eggplants into ½-inch slices. Heat ¼ cup of olive oil in a pan and fry the eggplant until soft, not letting them brown. Set them aside to cool. ✦ Prepare a syrup by heating sugar in an equal amount of water just until the sugar is dissolved (making certain the sugar does not

Crustless bread from a roll

⅔ cup cocoa, dissolved in
½ cup warm water

1¼ cups grated chocolate

⅔ cup pine nuts

⅔ cup chopped almonds

⅔ cup chopped candied citron

caramelize). Shred the bread into this syrup, stirring, and when it thickens mix in the cocoa and 1 cup of the chocolate and stir a long time to blend. ✦ Pour a good portion of this syrup into a baking pan. ✦ Dip the eggplant slices in the syrup one at a time and use some of them to form a first layer over the syrup in the pan. Sprinkle over this some pine nuts, almonds, and citron. Continue with these layers until using up the ingredients. ✦ Dust the last layer with the remaining chocolate, pine nuts, almonds, and citron. ✦ Bake at 200°F for 10 minutes. Serve lukewarm or cold from the refrigerator.

MERINGHE | # MERINGUES

LIGURIA

Unsalted butter

2 large egg whites

1¼ cups sugar

Preheat the oven to 300°F. Line a baking sheet with parchment, then butter the parchment. Whip the egg whites stiff while adding the sugar a little at a time until it has dissolved completely. The mixture should have a smooth consistency. ✦ Drop tablespoons of the mixture on the baking sheet, leaving 1 inch of space around them. ✦ Bake for 20 minutes or until crisp on the outside.

MIASCIA | # FRUITCAKE 3

LOMBARDIA

2 tbsp. unsalted butter

10 oz. stale bread, without crust

6 cups milk

3 large eggs

Grated zest of 1 lemon

3 pears, cored and chopped

3 apples, peeled, cored, and finely sliced

1 or 2 tbsp. golden raisins

2 tbsp. all-purpose flour

1 tbsp. cornmeal

4 sugar cubes

Extra-virgin olive oil

¼ cup sugar

1 sprig rosemary, chopped

Preheat the oven to 350°F. Butter a baking pan. Dice the bread and soak it in the milk for 1 hour; add the eggs, working them in delicately, then add the lemon zest, pears, apples, raisins, flour, cornmeal, and sugar cubes. ✦ Blend well, then pour into the pan, smoothing it out to a thickness of 1½ inches. ✦ Dot with butter and drizzle with olive oil; add a dusting of sugar and rosemary. ✦ Bake for 1 hour or until golden and set.

DESSERTS

SEMOLINA CAKE

CAMPANIA

¼ cup (4 tbsp.) unsalted butter

5 tbsp. sugar

4 cups whole milk

Grated zest of 1 lemon and peel of 1 lemon, cut in strips

1 cinnamon stick

¾ cup coarse semolina

5 large eggs, 4 separated

¼ cup citrus liqueur or limoncello

1⅔ cups ricotta

Confectioners' sugar

Preheat the oven to 350°F. Grease a baking pan with butter and sprinkle with sugar. Pour the milk into a saucepan and add the strips of lemon peel, sugar, and cinnamon stick; bring to a boil. ✦ When the milk boils take the pan off the heat and add the semolina, pouring it in a steady stream and stirring. ✦ Return the pan to the heat and boil again for 5 minutes. Stir in the butter and let it cool. ✦ Add 1 whole egg and 4 egg yolks, setting aside the whites. ✦ Remove the lemon peel and cinnamon stick; add the citrus liqueur, ricotta, and the grated zest. Whip the egg whites until stiff and fold them in. ✦ Pour the mxture into the pan. ✦ Bake for 45 minutes, or until a toothpick comes out clean when inserted in the center of the cake. Turn out on a serving plate and dust with confectioners' sugar.

MISTOCCHINE

CHESTNUT DUMPLINGS

EMILIA-ROMAGNA

1⅔ cups chestnut flour

½ cup milk

Lard or extra-virgin olive oil, for frying

Salt

Until about thirty years ago these were sold in Bologna during the winter by street vendors.

Mix the flour with the milk and 2 tablespoons water. Season with salt and knead to form a soft dough; shape this into balls and press them to form rounds about 4 inches in diameter. ✦ Heat the lard (or olive oil) and fry the dough. Drain on paper towels and serve hot.

MONTBLANC

CHESTNUT "MOUNTAIN"

PIEMONTE

1 lb. chestnuts

4 cups whole milk, or as needed

½ vanilla bean

1¼ cups sugar

½ cup rum

CONTINUED

This recipe is typical of Cuneo.

Boil the chestnuts in lightly salted water, drain, and peel while they are still hot. ✦ Put them in a pan with the milk and vanilla and cook very slowly until they are tender. ✦ Drain them and pass them through a potato ricer. ✦ Using a wooden spoon incorporate the sugar and rum into the resulting purée. Adjust for sugar and, if necessary, add a few tablespoons of milk. ✦ Pass the mixture through the

3 cups sweetened whipped cream

Salt

For decoration:

Meringues

Marrons glacés

Candied violets

potato ricer again, this time through the strainer plate with the largest holes, thus forming long strands. ✦ Arrange these strands on a serving plate shaping them into a peak—the mountain the dish is named for—and covering with "snow" made of whipped cream, smoothing it to cover the entire structure. ✦ Decorate with meringues and pieces of *marrons glacés* and candied violets.

WALNUT COOKIES

LAZIO

Unsalted butter

½ cup all-purpose flour

1 ¾ cups chopped walnuts

⅔ cup honey

2 large egg whites

1 tsp. ground cinnamon

Freshly ground pepper

Mostaccioli, a sweet typical of Christmas, is derived from the ancient *mustacea* of the Romans, made of cooked wine must, flour, walnuts, almonds, and other flavors. The name *mostaccioli* is a later addition. In keeping with tradition they are sold at open stalls in Piazza Navona on the Epiphany.

Preheat the oven to 350°F. Butter a baking sheet. Mix the flour with the walnuts, honey, egg whites, a pinch of pepper, and cinnamon. ✦ Mix well to form a smooth dough and roll it out on a work surface to form a sheet about ½ inch thick. ✦ Cut this into rectangular strips and cut these crosswise to form diamond shapes about 3 inches long. ✦ Arrange these on the baking sheet and bake for 20 minutes. Let them cool before removing from the sheet.

✦ **LOCAL TRADITION** ✦

MIGLIACCI DOLCI DI MAIALE

Typical of Prato in Toscana, this unique dessert is made by combining pig's-head broth with white bread, and after cooling, adding in fresh, strained pig's blood. Before cooking, orange zest, cinnamon, and salt are added, as well as a little flour, if needed, to obtain a thick, somewhat liquid consistency. The mixture, traditionally about ⅓ broth and bread to ⅔ blood, would then cook on both sides in a little melted *lardo* in a hot pan. The finished *migliaccio* would then be slid out onto a plate to cool, while another was prepared in the same pan. While stacking the *migliacci* one atop the next, sugar, grated bitter chocolate, or even grated cheese could be added between the layers to make a popular variation on the original recipe.

DESSERTS

MOSTACDIOLI DE VIN COTTO

Making these wine-must cookies from Calabria is a two-step process. Vin cotto—also called saba or sapa—is the dense, intensely-flavored result of cooking down wine must into a concentrated state. To make the mostaccioli, first the wine must would be combined with a smaller amount of water, flavored with orange zest and cinnamon, and heated on the stovetop. Enough flour would be slowly stirred into the warm mixture to form a soft dough, and this would be turned out onto a work surface to knead into short cylinder shapes. The resulting cookies would be briefly baked, then cooled. A second pot of vin cotto and water, this time with a higher proportion of vin cotto so as to be almost a syrup, would be brought to a boil and the mostaccioli cooked in this mixture for about five minutes. While these dried, more orange zest and chopped and toasted almonds and walnuts would be sprinkled over the cookies.

MOSTO COTTO | # COOKED WINE (SABA)

CAMPANIA

4½ lbs. grapes
(preferably somewhat sweet)

In southern Italy, cooked wine must is called *vin cotto* ("cooked wine") while in other areas of Italy it is called *sapa, saba,* or *calamich*. An ancient preparation, it is obtained by cooking down wine must over low heat until it has reduced in volume by one third to one eighth. The resulting liquid will be more or less dense and of a brownish color. Today the use of *vin cotto* is restricted to the preparation of certain traditional dishes. Various wine companies make their own industrially because it is part of the preparation for Marsala-like wines. In the past it was the most common and economic of sweeteners, used for making a great number of desserts. It was also used to make sorbets for children.

Crush the grapes in a food mill or potato ricer. ✦ Strain the resulting juice of all pits and skins then bring it to a boil over low heat in a tin-plated copper pot or, if that is not available, in a stainless-steel pot. The liquid must be continuously stirred with a wooden spoon to keep any of it from sticking to the walls or bottom of the pot (any that sticks will burn and give the remainder an off odor; if some does stick pour the liquid into another pot and begin again). ✦ At the same time, skim off the foam that forms on the surface. ✦ After about 1 hour the liquid will be ready. Let it cool before pouring it into a sterilized bottle with a somewhat wide mouth; seal the bottle. In this way it can be preserved for a long time.

| MOUSSE DI ARANCE | **ORANGE MOUSSE** | FOR 12 PERSONS |

CAMPANIA

10 large eggs, separated

Grated zest and strained juice of 5 oranges, preferably organic

½ cup orange liqueur

2 cups heavy cream, whipped until stiff

1½ cups sugar

Candied orange peels

This recipe is typical of Naples.

Beat the egg yolks with a mixer on medium speed until pale and thick. Whisk in the juice and half the liqueur. ✦ Fold in the whipped cream. Whip the 10 egg whites until stiff and add them to the mixture. ✦ Pour this mixture into a plum-cake mold and refrigerate overnight. ✦ Shortly before serving prepare the syrup. Boil the sugar with ¾ cup water until the liquid thickens slightly. Turn off the heat and add the zest and remaining liqueur. ✦ Turn the mousse out and decorate with candied orange peels and syrup.

| NATALINO | **STAR CAKE** |

VENETO

4½ tsp. active dry yeast

1⅔ cups sugar

3⅓ cups all-purpose flour

4 large eggs

6 oz. (1½ sticks) unsalted butter, softened

¼ cup vanilla sugar

Salt

This typically Veronese dessert is a forerunner of the more famous *pandoro*.

Dissolve the yeast and 1 teaspoon sugar in 1 cup warm water. Let rest 15 minutes. ✦ Use the flour and yeast mixture to make a dough as in the recipe on page 13, adding the eggs, butter, sugar, and a pinch of salt with the yeast mixture. Knead to obtain a smooth and homogeneous dough. ✦ Place this in a star-shaped mold. Cover with a clean kitchen towel and let it rise for about 50 minutes in a cool place. ✦ Preheat the oven to 350°F. Bake for 40 minutes, until golden. ✦ When it is done turn it out on a plate and sprinkle it with vanilla sugar while still warm. Let it cool slowly.

DESSERTS

NECCI

These traditional chestnut-flour crepes, typical of Pisoia in Toscana, were made from a simple batter of chestnut flour, water, sugar, and salt. Following the traditional method of preparing the crepes, first the special 2-sided iron pan is heated; a single chestnut leaf would be placed onto the hot plate and a ladleful of the crepe batter poured over; the batter would be topped by a second leaf and then the heated iron plate would be closed. Each crepe would be removed when just brown and another made in the same manner. The finished crepes were often served with pecorino, ricotta, or pork sausage.

NEPITELLE

BAKED FIG AND NUT CALZONE

CALABRIA

3 ⅓ cups all-purpose flour
5 large eggs
1 cup sugar
5 ½ oz. lard, softened
1 cup toasted and chopped almonds
1 cup chopped walnuts
1 ⅔ cups chopped, parboiled dried figs
1 tbsp. cinnamon
Pinch ground cloves
⅔ cup golden raisins
Zest of 2 oranges
1 ¼ cups orange marmalade (see page 813)
Salt

Use the flour and 4 of the eggs to make a dough as in the recipe on page 10, adding the lard, sugar, and a pinch of salt with the eggs. Knead to obtain a homogeneous dough and let rest 30 minutes in a cool spot. ✦ Preheat the oven to 350°F. Grease a baking sheet with lard. Beat the remaining egg. Combine the almonds, walnuts, figs, cinnamon, cloves, raisins, zest, a pinch of salt, and marmalade to form the filling. Mix until thoroughly blended. ✦ Roll out the dough to form a sheet about ¼ inch thick and cut out disks about 4 inches in diameter. ✦ Arrange a dollop of the filling on each disk, dampen the edges with a little water (or egg white), and close, forming half-moons. Seal the edges with the tines of a fork and make two or three short cuts across the upper part of each half-moon. ✦ Put these on the baking sheet, brush the surface of each with a little beaten egg, and bake for about 30 minutes or until golden.

VANILLA FRITTERS

CALABRIA

6⅔ cups all-purpose flour
10 large eggs
4 oz. lard, mixed with 1 tbsp. warm water
⅔ cup sugar
1 tsp. vanilla extract
Grated zest of 1 lemon
Olive oil, for frying
Confectioners' sugar
Ground cinnamon

Use the flour and eggs to form a dough as in the recipe on page 751, adding the lard mixture, sugar, vanilla, and lemon zest with the eggs. ✦ Using a floured rolling pin roll out a sheet of dough about ⅛ inch thick. Cut this in rectangles 2½ to 3 inches long and 1 to ½ inches wide. ✦ Heat 2 inches of olive oil in a saucepan and fry until golden. ✦ Drain on paper towels. Mix the confectioners' sugar and cinnamon to taste and sprinkle over the fritters. Serve immediately.

WALNUT NOUGAT

NOCIATA

UMBRIA

2⅔ cups honey
5⅔ cups shelled walnuts
Grated zest of ½ orange
Grated zest of ¼ lemon
6 large egg whites
Fresh bay leaves

In a copper pot combine the honey, walnuts, zests, and egg whites and cook at low heat, stirring constantly, until the mixture thickens and becomes opaque. ✦ Pour it out onto a work surface (preferably marble) and shape into lozenge-shaped pieces about 2 inches wide and 3 inches long. ✦ Wrap these in bay leaves while they are still hot. Let cool completely before serving.

FRIED WINE KNOTS

ORECCHIE DI AMMAN

TOSCANA

2 large eggs, beaten
2 tbsp. sugar
¼ cup white wine
3 tbsp. extra-virgin olive oil plus olive oil for frying
1 tsp. vanilla extract (or 1 tsp. grated lemon or orange zest)
1½ cups all-purpose flour, plus more as needed
Vanilla sugar
Salt

This recipe is typical of Livorno. The name literally means "Amman's ears." For the wine, use Vernaccia di San Gimignano, Vermentino, or Orvieto.

Beat the eggs and sugar with a mixer on medium speed until pale, then mix in the wine, olive oil, vanilla (or lemon or orange zest), a pinch of salt, and as much flour as necessary to form a smooth dough. ✦ Roll out the dough to form a sheet and cut it into strips about 6 inches long. Twist them between your hands to form twists or shape them into knots. ✦ Heat 2 inches of oil in a saucepan and fry until golden. Drain completely on paper towels, then dust with vanilla sugar.

"BONES OF THE DEAD" COOKIES

2⅔ lbs. all-purpose flour
10 large eggs
⅔ cup anise liqueur
⅔ cup sugar
⅓ cup olive oil
⅓ cup lard
Grated zest of ½ lemon

These are traditionally made for the Day of the Dead, November 2.

Preheat the oven to 400°F. Use the flour and eggs to make a dough as in the recipe on page 751, adding the anise, sugar, olive oil, lard, and lemon zest with the eggs. ✦ Pinch off lumps of dough, shape into 3-inch sticks, and twist them in the middle to form shapes similar to figure eights. ✦ Boil them in a pot of water a few at a time and drain as soon as they float. ✦ Arrange on a baking sheet and bake for about 20 minutes.

PALLINE DI BUCCE D'ARANCIA

ORANGE-PEEL BALLS

SICILIA

Orange peels from organic oranges, preferably
Sugar

These are served after dinner as an aid to digestion.

Soak the orange peels in water to cover for 4 days, changing the water often each day. ✦ At the end of that time drain them, dry them, coarsely chop, then weigh them; add to them an equal weight of sugar. ✦ Put the orange peels and sugar over low heat and stir to blend, keeping the mixture from boiling or caramelizing. Cook until the sugar is dissolved and the mixture has thickened. ✦ Remove from the heat, form into balls, and roll in sugar. Serve at room temperature.

PALLINE DI CASTAGNE

CHESTNUT BALLS

CAMPANIA

2 lbs. chestnuts
1 cup whole milk
5 tbsp. sugar
2 tbsp. bitter cocoa powder
¼ cup rum or Marsala
Confectioners' sugar

This recipe is typical of Cassano Irpino.

Boil the chestnuts, then peel them and pass them through a sieve. Work the resulting purée together with the other ingredients (except the confectioners' sugar). Shape into balls and roll in the confectioners' sugar.

NOCINO

This walnut liqueur from Modena comes from a very old recipe. The first step in making the *nocino* is to combine a gallon of a neutral high-proof alcohol with fresh walnuts, ground with their shells in a mortar and pestle, in a wide-mouthed glass jar. Tradition dictates using summertime walnuts, ideally those gathered on St. John's Day, June 24. To the alcohol and walnut mixture was added the grated zest of one lemon, cinnamon, and cloves. The jar would then be sealed, shaken occasionally, and left in the sun for about two months to steep. After the steeping period, the alcohol would be strained and the nuts and shells squeezed or pressed to extract as much liquid as possible. To this was added a thick syrup made by boiling down hearty red wine with a quantity of sugar, also flavored with cinnamon and cloves and filtered through a piece of clean wool. The walnut-steeped alcohol and the cooled wine syrup are then combined in an earthenware container, shaking again from time to time to keep the syrup from separating.

PALPITÒN | # PEAR CAKE | FOR
8 PERSONS

PIEMONTE

¼ lb. (1 stick) unsalted butter

10 tbsp. sugar

Grated zest of 1 lemon and peel of 1 lemon, cut in strips

4 ½ lbs. pears, peeled and cut lengthwise in strips

Bread of 2 stale rolls, soaked in water

1 ⅔ cups finely ground amaretti

⅔ cup unsweetened cocoa powder

1 tbsp. *amaro* (preferably Fernet Branca)

6 large eggs

⅔ cup raisins, soaked in water, drained, and dried

Salt

This recipe is typical of Biella.

Preheat the oven to 350°F. Grease a large baking pan with butter. Melt the butter in a large pan and add the sugar; add the lemon peel and a pinch of salt. ✦ Add the pears and cook them at low heat until they are thoroughly cooked and all of the liquid has evaporated. ✦ Remove the pan from the heat and let cool. ✦ Remove the lemon peel and blend in the bread. Add the amaretti, cocoa powder, grated lemon zest, and *amaro*. ✦ Mix this, adding the eggs and raisins, and working to obtain a dense and homogeneous mixture. ✦ Pour the mixture into the pan (ideally so that it extends up to about 1 inch below the lip of the pan). Dot with butter evenly across the surface and bake until the surface is golden brown. Turn out on a serving plate and let cool. Serve at room temperature.

DESSERTS

| # SPICE CAKE

2 cups sugar

4 ½ cups all-purpose flour

1 lb. candied melon

1 ¼ cups candied orange

3 cups almonds, blanched, toasted, and chopped

½ cup ground spices (5 parts coriander, 3 parts mace, 1 part ground cloves, 1 part grated nutmeg)

¼ cup ground pepper

⅓ cup plus 1 tbsp. ground cinnamon

3 tbsp. coriander seeds

Preheat the oven to 350°F. Dissolve the sugar in 1 cup water in a copper pan and heat it until it forms threads when the spoon is lifted from the pan (223°F to 234°F on a candy thermometer). ✦ When it reaches that density stir it into the flour, then add the candied fruits, almonds, mixed spices, pepper, and ⅓ cup cinnamon. ✦ Pat out the dough to ¾ inch thick, then use 2- to 2½-inch cookie cutters to cut circles of dough. ✦ Place on baking sheets, spacing them 2 inches apart. Mix the coriander seeds and 1 tablespoon cinnamon and sprinkle over the cookies. ✦ Bake between 20 and 30 minutes according to their size.

| # SPICED NUT CAKE FROM TERNI

Olive oil

5 lbs. shelled walnuts

1 ¼ cups shelled almonds

1 ¼ cups shelled hazelnuts, lightly toasted

¾ lb. dark chocolate, chopped

¾ lb. milk chocolate, chopped

1 ⅔ cups sugar

2 nutmegs, grated

1 tsp. ground cinnamon

1 cup honey

1 ½ cups chopped candied citron

1 ¼ cups raisins

1 cup cooked grape must (see note, page 818)

3 tbsp. *alchermes* (see note, page 786)

2 tbsp. rum

2 tbsp. *rosolio* (can substitute 1 tbsp. rose water)

1 ¼ cups sifted all-purpose flour

2 cups strong coffee

Pinch pepper

Preheat the oven to 400°F. Grease a baking sheet with olive oil. Combine the walnuts, almonds, and hazelnuts, then add the remaining ingredients, working them together until blended. ✦ Divide the mixture into loaves weighing about ½ pound each and about 6 inches in diameter. ✦ Arrange the loaves on the baking sheet. Cover with aluminum foil and bake 10 minutes. Remove the foil and bake 5 minutes more, until golden.

PAN DE MEI

LOMBARDIA

⅔ cup all-purpose flour

1¼ cups fine-grain cornmeal

1¼ cups coarse-grain cornmeal

3 large eggs

½ oz. elderberry flowers

⅔ cup sugar

¼ lb. (1 stick) plus 3 tbsp. unsalted butter

2¼ tsp. active dry yeast, dissolved in 4 tbsp. warm milk

2 tbsp. vanilla sugar

Salt

SWEET CORNMEAL BREAD

The Italian name means "millet bread," but this is also called *paniga* (from the elderberry). Since the eighteenth century the millet flour has been replaced by cornmeal. There are many variations varying the yeast and the formula for the short pastry. In fact the yeast is a somewhat recent addition. This sweet is found throughout Lombardia known by different local names, such as *sbrisolona mantovana* near Mantua, *torta di polenta* around Varese, *melegòt* in Cremona, and so on.

Preheat the oven to 375°F. Sift and combine the flour and cornmeals, then use them and the eggs to make a dough as in the recipe on page 751, adding the elderberry flowers, a pinch of salt, sugar, and butter with the eggs, then add the yeast mixture. ✦ Work into a ball and put in a bowl. Cover with a kitchen towel and let rise for 1 hour in a warm place. ✦ Shape the dough into small loaves about 4 inches in diameter, slightly flattening them, and place them on a baking sheet. ✦ Dust with vanilla sugar and bake for 30 minutes.

PAN DI ATRI

ABRUZZO

6 large eggs, separated

1 cup sugar

1 cup semolina flour

1½ tsp. baking powder

Juice of 1 lemon

1 cup chopped almonds

SEMOLINA BREAD

Preheat the oven to 350°F. Using a mixer on medium speed, whip the egg yolks and sugar until pale and thickened, then sift in the semolina flour and baking powder. ✦ Whip the whites until stiff and fold them in, then add the lemon juice and almonds. ✦ Shape into a loaf and bake for 40 minutes, until golden.

PAN DOLCE

LIGURIA

2¼ tsp. active dry yeast, dissolved in 2 tbsp. lukewarm milk

3⅓ cups all-purpose flour

CONTINUED

SWEET BREAD WITH FRUITS AND NUTS

This is a classic Christmas sweet typical of Genoa.

Combine the yeast mixture with as much of the flour as it will absorb without becoming too stiff to work with, shape into a small loaf, and set aside to rise for a few hours. ✦ Combine the remaining flour with the Marsala, orange-flower water, and butter. ✦ Knead in the small

DESSERTS

¼ cup Marsala

1 tbsp. orange-flower water

3 oz. (6 tbsp.) unsalted butter, softened

1 cup sugar

1 tbsp. fennel seeds

1 tbsp. crushed pistachios

⅓ cup pine nuts

½ cup raisins

½ cup chopped candied citron

½ cup chopped candied orange

Salt

loaf and all the remaining ingredients. Form the result into a loaf and let it rise again, tightly covered by a cloth. ✦ Preheat the oven to 400°F. Make three triangular incisions in the center of the loaf and bake for about 1 hour. Serve lukewarm.

SWEET BREAD FROM COGNE

PAN DOLCE DI COGNE

FOR 3 LOAVES

VALLE D'AOSTA

1 ¼ cups raisins

⅔ cup rum

2 ¼ tsp. active dry yeast

3 ⅓ cups all-purpose flour

2 cups whole milk

⅔ cup heavy cream

4 large eggs

1 ½ cups sugar

4 tbsp. unsalted butter

½ cup extra-virgin olive oil

Grated zest of 3 lemons

Salt

This recipe is typical of Cogne. These should be eaten with whipped cream seasoned with Valdostan grappa or Crema di Cogne (see page 782). If possible bake them in a wood-burning oven.

Soak the raisins in the rum for at least 2 hours. ✦ Combine the yeast and flour in a large bowl. ✦ Separately heat the milk with all the other ingredients (including the raisins and rum and a pinch of salt), stir well, gradually whisk in the flour, and knead this well to obtain a firm dough. ✦ Remove from the bowl, place on a pan, cover with a kitchen towel, and let rise for about 6 hours (it should double in size). ✦ Knead the mixture on a floured surface for a few minutes then divide it into three equal parts. Shape each of these into a round loaf. ✦ Preheat the oven to 400°F. Bake for at least 1 hour, or until the loaves are golden.

CHARTERHOUSE-STYLE SWEET BREAD

PAN SPEZIALE ALLA CERTOSINA

EMILIA-ROMAGNA

1 tsp. ground coriander

1 tsp. anise seeds

½ tsp. ground cloves

2 ¼ tsp. active dry yeast

CONTINUED

This is named for the charterhouse of Bologna, where it was prepared by the friars as a sweet during the Christmas period.

Combine the spices, yeast, honey, and sugar with ½ cup boiling water; add the flour and blend. Turn out onto a floured surface and knead in the raisins, almonds, citron and orange, pine nuts, and chocolate. Let rise, covered

⅔ cup honey

⅔ cup sugar

1 ¼ cups all-purpose flour

½ cup raisins, soaked in
lukewarm water and drained

½ cup almonds

½ cup candied citron and orange

½ cup pine nuts

½ cup chopped bittersweet chocolate

with a kitchen towel, until nearly doubled in volume. Preheat the oven to 350°F. ✦ Shape the dough into a loaf and place on a baking sheet. Bake for 30 to 40 minutes.

PANE DI NATALE | # CHRISTMAS BREAD

EMILIA-ROMAGNA

¼ lb. (½ cup) unsalted butter,
softened

3 ⅓ cups all-purpose flour

1 ¼ cups sugar

2 large eggs

⅔ cup ground sweet chocolate

⅓ cup unsweetened cocoa powder

½ cup anisette

1 ⅛ tsp. active dry yeast

2 tbsp. wine must
(see note, page 818)

1 ⅔ cups chopped walnuts

⅓ cup chopped almonds

⅔ cup pine nuts

⅔ cup raisins, softened in
warm water and drained

1 tsp. fennel seeds

⅔ cup chopped candied citron

½ cup chopped candied
red and green cherries

This recipe is typical of Modena. If the cake is prepared a few days before Christmas, keep it moist by periodically brushing it with more wine must.

Butter a baking sheet. Mix the butter, flour, and sugar, then use the mixture and eggs to prepare a dough as in the recipe on page 751, adding the chocolate, cocoa, anisette, yeast, and half the wine must with the eggs. ✦ Knead this for a long time then add the walnuts, almonds, pine nuts, raisins, fennel seeds, candied citron, and candied cherries. ✦ Shape into a round loaf and let rise. ✦ Preheat the oven to 350°F. Put the loaf on the baking sheet and bake for 1 hour. When it is baked and still hot glaze it with the remaining wine must.

PANE DI ZUCCA | # PUMPKIN BREAD

EMILIA-ROMAGNA

1 lb. cooked pumpkin
(or winter squash)

CONTINUED

Make sure the oven is no hotter than called for because the loaves should bake without letting the surface burn.

Combine the ingredients except the flour until blended. Work in the flour and a pinch of salt to make a smooth dough. ✦ Let the dough rest for about 30 minutes. ✦

DESSERTS

1 ¼ cups sugar

¼ lb. (1 stick) unsalted butter

4 ½ tsp. active dry yeast

3 cups all-purpose flour,
plus more as needed

Salt

Shape the dough into loaves and let them rise another 30 minutes. ✦ Preheat the oven to 350°F. Bake until just golden, but do not let the outside get too brown. Let cool and serve.

FRIED BREAD

FOR
6 PERSONS

FRIULI-VENEZIA GIULIA

Milk, as needed

¼ cup sugar,
plus more for sprinkling

1 10-oz. loaf peasant-style bread,
sliced

1 large egg, beaten

1 tbsp. white wine

Juice of ½ lemon

¼ cup (4 tbsp.) unsalted butter

Pour the milk into a mixing bowl and stir in half the sugar. Add the bread and soak 30 minutes, rotating the slices from top to bottom halfway through. ✦ Mix the egg with the wine, lemon, and remaining sugar. Drain the bread and dip the slices in the egg mixture. Heat 2 table-spoons butter in a nonstick pan and sauté half the bread. Repeat with the remaining butter and bread. Sprinkle with sugar and serve warm.

PANE INDORATO

FRIED BREAD
WITH BULIDE

FRIULI-VENEZIA GIULIA

2 tbsp. all-purpose flour

1 cup milk

2 tbsp. sugar

3 large eggs

8 oz. bread, in thick slices

¼ cup unsalted butter or lard

Bulide (see note)

Bulide is a sort of cooked wine product. You can substitute *vin cotto* (see note, page 818).

In a mixing bowl, whisk together the flour and milk, then add the sugar and eggs. ✦ Add the bread and turn to coat thoroughly. Let stand 15 minutes. ✦ When the bread has soaked up the egg mixture, heat half the butter in a non-stick pan and cook half the bread, turning, until golden brown. Repeat with the remaining butter and soaked bread. Drizzle each slice with *bulide* and serve hot.

PÀNERA

COFFEE ICE CREAM

LIGURIA

⅔ cup coarsely ground coffee beans

CONTINUED

Mix the coffee and cream in a saucepan. Put this over heat and when it boils add the sugar, stirring with a wooden spoon. Remove the pan from the heat and let stand until the coffee settles to the bottom. ✦ At that

8 cups heavy cream
2⅓ cups sugar

point drain it through a very fine sieve, making sure no coffee grounds get into the liquid. Refrigerate until cold. Put this liquid in an ice-cream machine and freeze according to the manufacturer's instructions.

RAISIN BUNS

CAMPANIA

Grated zest of 1 lemon
1¼ cups milk
3⅓ cups all-purpose flour
1½ cups sugar
2¼ tsp. active dry yeast, dissolved in 2 tbsp. warm milk
7 large eggs
½ cup raisins
½ cup candied fruit
½ lb. (2 sticks) unsalted butter

Soak the lemon zest in the milk for 6 hours, then pass the mixture through a sieve. ✦ Combine the flour with the sugar and yeast mixture, then blend in the eggs. Fold in the raisins and candied fruit. ✦ Knead on a floured surface to form a smooth dough. Place in a bowl, cover with a kitchen towel, and let rise. ✦ Grease a baking sheet with butter. Shape the dough into balls and arrange them on the baking sheet. Let rise again 2 to 3 hours. ✦ Preheat the oven to 350°F. Bake until golden, then let cool completely before serving.

PANETTONE

LOMBARDIA

10 cups all-purpose flour
¾ oz. (3 packets) active dry yeast, dissolved in ½ cup warm water
¼ cup milk, warmed
1 lb. (2 cups) unsalted butter
2 cups sugar
3 large eggs plus 10 or 12 large egg yolks
1 cup golden raisins, soaked in water and drained
½ cup diced citron
½ cup diced candied orange
Salt

So many legends surround the origin of this Christmas sweet that we hardly dare go near the subject! Suffice to say it is typical of Milan. This recipe, among the most traditional, has been adapted for home use.

Place about 1 cup of flour and a pinch of salt on the work surface and add the yeast mixture. Work these together to form a homogeneous mixture, then shape into a little loaf. ✦ Cover this little loaf with a cloth, put it in a floured bowl, and let it rise 3 hours. ✦ At the end of that period put about 1½ cups of flour on the work surface and at the center of this place the little risen loaf. Soften the loaf with a few tablespoons of the milk and combine it with the flour. Knead this well and shape into a ball. ✦ Let this rise, as before, in a covered bowl for 2 hours. ✦ Heat a pot of water to a boil. Melt about half of the butter in a pan without burning it. In another pan heat the sugar with 1 cup warm water to obtain a syrup. Transfer the syrup to a heatproof bowl and whisk in the eggs and egg yolks. Place the bowl on top of the

DESSERTS

829

pot of water (making sure it does not touch the water) and whisk until thickened. ✦ Pour about 6 cups of the remaining flour on a work surface or in a large bowl, sprinkle with a little salt, and form a well in the center. ✦ Put the risen ball of dough at the center of the well, then add the melted butter and blend well. ✦ Add the egg mixture and incorporate the remaining flour a little at a time. ✦ Knead energetically for a good 20 minutes, blending all the ingredients to obtain a firm, smooth, and elastic dough. Knead in the raisins and candied fruit. ✦ Unless you have a very large oven, you'll need to divide the mixture into two or more loaves. ✦ Butter and flour a baking sheet, then grease your hands with butter and round off the loaves, place them on the baking sheet, and place them in a warm dry place free of drafts to rise for about 6 hours (they have risen when they have more than doubled in volume). ✦ Preheat the oven to 400°F. Put the loaves in a cool place for a few minutes then bake. Melt the remaining butter and after 5 minutes baking drizzle with the melted butter. Bake until golden, about 1 hour, lowering the temperature by 25 degrees every 15 minutes.

✦ **LOCAL TRADITION** ✦

PANFORTE MARGHERITA

This traditional fruitcake recipe from Toscano closely follows the preparation for *Pampetato* (see page 824), with some differences in the ingredients and procedure. To make the *Margherita*, a large amount of sugar was first combined with a similarly large amount of cubed classic candied citron and toasted almonds, smaller portions of candied orange peel, and marzipan paste, as well as all-purpose flour, vanilla sugar and chopped vanilla beans, cinnamon, and nutmeg, giving it its characteristic flavor. Both before and after baking the cake should be covered with confectioners' sugar, with the final coating traditionally flavored with vanilla. The *Margherita*, again like the *Pampetato*, should be wrapped in aluminum foil once finished to avoid spoiling, and can be kept for several months.

PANGIALLO

YELLOW CAKE WITH FRUIT

LAZIO

For the cake:

1 ¼ cups all-purpose flour

4 oz. risen bread dough; see page 13 (or 1 ⅛ tsp. active dry yeast, dissolved in 2 tbsp. warm water)

1 cup sugar

1 tsp. ground cinnamon

¼ cup extra-virgin olive oil

½ cup chopped candied orange peel

½ cup chopped candied citron

½ cup pine nuts

⅔ cup almonds

⅔ cup hazelnuts

½ cup shelled, peeled, lightly toasted, and chopped walnuts

2 large egg whites

1 ¼ cups raisins, soaked in water and drained

For the glaze:

1 tbsp. all-purpose flour

2 tbsp. olive oil

¼ tsp. saffron

This cake is usually served on Christmas.

Form the flour into a well on the work surface or in a bowl and add the bread dough (or yeast mixture), sugar, cinnamon, and olive oil. Knead to form a dough softer than that for bread. ✦ In a separate bowl combine the candied orange peel, candied citron, pine nuts, almonds, hazelnuts, and walnuts. Stir in the egg whites and the raisins. Thoroughly combine these ingredients then add them to the dough. ✦ Knead this dough, then shape into two medium-size loaves and set them aside to rise, covered with a cloth, in a warm place for 12 hours. ✦ Preheat the oven to 350°F. Prepare the glaze, blending ½ cup water with the flour, olive oil, and saffron. Brush this glaze on the loaves then bake for 45 minutes.

PANIERINI DI CREMA

CREAM BASKETS

FOR 8 PERSONS

SICILIA

2 ½ cups sugar

Juice and grated zest of ½ lemon

1 ¼ lbs. almonds, peeled and coarsely chopped

1 recipe pastry cream (see page 843)

Pistachios

Lightly grease a work surface (marble would be best). Heat the sugar, 2 tablespoons water, and the lemon juice in a saucepan until the sugar is dissolved. ✦ Add the almonds and lemon zest and heat, stirring slowly, until the sugar has caramelized. ✦ Pour this on the work surface and spread smooth with a spatula. ✦ When it has cooled but not hardened cut into 4-inch circles, then form on a cup to make baskets about the size of an orange with flat bottoms. ✦ Fill each basket with pastry cream (or ricotta cream) and garnish with green pistachios.

VANILLA PANNA COTTA

4 gelatin sheets

Sugar for caramelizing the mold plus 3 tbsp.

4 cups heavy cream

½ cup whole milk

1 tsp. vanilla extract (or better, two vanilla beans, slit lengthwise)

This is typical of Alba.

Soak the gelatin in cold water to cover for about 30 minutes; drain and set aside. ✦ Caramelize sugar to coat the bottom of a large mold or several small molds (such as dariole molds) as in the recipe on page 791. ✦ Mix the cream, milk, and 3 tablespoons sugar in a saucepan and bring almost to a boil; add the vanilla and gelatin, stirring well to combine (if using vanilla beans remove them before pouring into the mold). ✦ Pour into the mold or molds; let cool, then put in the refrigerator for several hours before serving. ✦ To unmold, pass the mold over a flame for a second (or dip in hot water), then invert on a serving plate, letting the caramelized sugar drip over the panna cotta.

CHESTNUT PANZAROTTINI

For the filling:

1 lb. chestnuts

1 sprig rosemary

Pinch ground cinnamon

¼ cup strong brewed coffee

2 tbsp. Strega liqueur

½ cup unsweetened cocoa powder

¾ cup sugar

Grated zest of 1 lemon

Salt

For the dough:

1¼ cups all-purpose flour

1 large egg plus 1 large egg white

Olive oil, for frying

⅔ cup honey

Confectioners' sugar

Boil the chestnuts in water to cover with a sprig of rosemary and a little salt. ✦ Drain the chestnuts, shell them, and pass them through a food mill. ✦ Combine the resulting purée with the remaining ingredients for the filling. ✦ Use the flour and whole egg to prepare a dough as in the recipe on page 10, adding ¼ cup water with the egg. ✦ Roll this out to make a thin sheet (see note, page 212). Using a pastry wheel cut this into small squares about 1½ inches on a side. ✦ Place a teaspoon of filling on each square, brush the edges with egg white, and fold over to create triangles. Seal well with the tines of a fork. ✦ Heat 2 inches of olive oil in a saucepan and fry until golden. Heat the honey until it is thinned and drizzle over the *panzarottini* while they are still warm. Sprinkle with confectioners' sugar and serve.

NUT AND RAISIN CANDY

3 cups almonds

⅔ cup walnut halves

2 cups raisins

2 cups cooked wine must
(see note, page 818)

Confectioners' sugar

Candy-coated almonds, crushed

This recipe is typical of Nuoro.

Chop together the almonds and walnuts and transfer to a saucepan. Add the raisins and blend in the wine must. ✦ Cook over low heat until thickened. When this has become homogeneous, pour it onto a damp work surface and cut into squares. ✦ Set these out on a board, cover with a cloth, and let them dry for 2 days. Just before serving, sprinkle with confectioners' sugar and crushed candy-coated almonds.

APPLE PANCAKES

4 cups cold milk

3⅓ cups all-purpose flour

4 large eggs

⅔ cup sugar, plus more for dusting

4 apples, peeled, cored, and sliced

⅔ cup raisins, softened in water
and drained

½ cup pine nuts, toasted

Extra-virgin olive oil, for frying

Salt

This recipe is typical of the middle zone of Lake Como.

Whisk the milk, flour, and eggs to make a batter; add the sugar, a pinch of salt, apples, raisins, and pine nuts. ✦ Heat 2 tablespoons olive oil in a skillet and pour in about 1 cup of this batter: each fritter should not be more than ½ inch thick. Repeat with the remaining batter, adding olive oil to the pan as needed. Dust with sugar before serving.

RICOTTA-STUFFED COOKIES

1⅔ cups all-purpose flour

2 large eggs, separated

1 tbsp. lard

1 lb. ricotta

⅔ cup sugar

Pinch saffron

Grated zest of 1 orange

Confectioners' sugar (or honey)

Salt

Preheat the oven to 350°F. Use the flour and egg whites to make a dough as in the recipe on page 751, adding the lard with the egg whites. ✦ Combine the ricotta in a bowl with the sugar, egg yolks, saffron, a pinch of salt, and orange zest and mix well with a wooden spoon. ✦ Roll out the dough to form a ⅛-inch-thick sheet and cut it into disks about 3 inches in diameter. ✦ Put a dollop of the filling in the center of each disk then lift the disk and place it in your palm. Squeeze your palm to make a small cup without a lid, like a small open-faced pie. ✦

DESSERTS

833

Place these on a baking sheet and bake until the filling browns. Dust with confectioners' sugar or honey before serving.

ALMOND CAKE GLAZED WITH CHOCOLATE

PARROZZO DI PESCARA

ABRUZZO

3 oz. (6 tbsp.) unsalted butter
⅔ cup blanched almonds
¾ cup sugar
5 large eggs, separated
¾ cup all-purpose flour
½ cup cornstarch
8 oz. bittersweet chocolate

This recipe is typical of Pescara. The poet Gabriele D'Annunzio (a native of Pescara) had much to say in praise of this sweet.

Preheat the oven to 400°F. Butter a cake pan. Sprinkle the almonds with 2 tablespoons sugar and grind them in a mortar. ✦ Melt the butter in the top of a double boiler, then add the egg yolks and the remaining sugar. Cook, stirring, until thickened, then stir in the ground almonds. ✦ Add the flour and the cornstarch. Whip the egg whites until stiff and fold them into the mixture. ✦ Pour the mixture into the cake pan and bake for 45 minutes. ✦ When the cake is cool, melt the chocolate in the top of a double boiler, then pour over the cake.

ALMOND PASTE

PASTA DI MANDORLE

SICILIA

2 cups sugar
3 cups almonds, ground into a fine meal
⅔ cup all-purpose flour

The primary use of almond paste is in the creation of fruit-shaped sweets. Tradition ascribes the invention of these realistic-looking sweets, or fruits, to the Benedictine sisters of the monastery of Martorana in Palermo, which was so famous for these colorful creations in the Middle Ages that they were known as *"frutti alla Martorana."* Used in the past for commemoration of All Saints' Day and Christmas, they can today be found more or less year-round. Other sweets made using almond paste include the *picureddi* ("little sheep") found everywhere at Easter time, the horses and donkeys at Acireal for St. Anthony (January 17), and the little pigs made around Palermo for St. Sebastian (January 20).

Melt the sugar at very low heat in ½ cup of water. ✦ As soon as it starts to form threads when the spoon is lifted from the pan (223°F to 234°F on a candy thermometer), pour in the almond meal and all-purpose flour. Stir this, still at low heat, and cook until the mixture pulls away from the sides of the pan, becoming dense and very firm. ✦ Remove from the heat and let cool slightly. Knead until smooth, put in molds, and color as desired.

1) The first variation uses different ingredients but follows the same method of preparation: 2 cups sugar, 3 cups ground almonds, 1¼ cups flour, and 1 tablespoon cream of tartar (added with the flour).

2) The second variation also has different ingredients, but uses the same preparation: 2 cups sugar, 2 tablespoons water, 1½ cups ground almonds, and 1⅔ cups flour.

3) This third variation consists of simply adding ½ teaspoon vanilla extract with the almond flour and proceeding as above.

WHEAT-BERRY RICOTTA TART

FOR 10 PERSONS

CAMPANIA

For the filling:
1½ cups soft white wheat berries
2⅓ cups milk
1½ cups sugar
2 tbsp. lard
1½ tsp. vanilla extract
Grated zest of ½ orange
2 cups ricotta
4 large eggs, separated
1 to 2 tsp. orange-flower water
½ tsp. cinnamon
⅔ cup chopped candied fruits

For the pastry dough:
3⅓ cups all-purpose flour
1¼ cups sugar
4 oz. lard
¼ lb. (1 stick) unsalted butter
4 large egg yolks
Grated zest of 1 lemon
Confectioners' sugar

This recipe is typical of Naples. The tart improves if allowed to rest for 2 or 3 days in a box at room temperature.

The day before, simmer the wheat berries with the milk, ¼ cup of the sugar, lard, vanilla, and orange zest at low heat for several hours until the mixture becomes creamy and the wheat has softened. Refrigerate overnight. ✦ Make the pastry: Blend the flour, sugar, lard, and butter until the mixture looks like coarse sand. Blend in the egg yolks and lemon zest and let it rest for at least 1 hour. ✦ Preheat the oven to 325°F. Grease a pie pan with butter. Mix the ricotta in a bowl with the remaining 1¼ cups of sugar then add the egg yolks one at a time, half the orange-flower water, and cinnamon. Add to this the wheat mixture and the candied fruit. Stir well to blend. ✦ Beat 3 of the egg whites until stiff and fold them into the mixture; when the mixture is blended check to see if there is enough orange-water flavor and if not add the remaining teaspoon. ✦ Roll out two-thirds of the pastry dough to form a ¼-inch-thick sheet and use it to line the baking pan. ✦ Pour the mixture in the pan, leveling it off. ✦ Roll out the remaining third of the pastry dough on a sheet of waxed paper, forming it into a rectangle as long as the diameter of the pan. Using the tip of a knife make incisions in the dough that divide it into ¾-inch-wide strips. Following these incisions cut through the waxed paper, creating strips of dough attached to waxed paper. ✦ Take one of the strips, turn it over, and position it along the

DESSERTS

center of the cake where the diameter is greatest, then delicately pull off the waxed paper. Continue with a second and third strip, putting each of these parallel to the central one and about 1 inch to the side of it. Put on the next strips but apply these crosswise, forming a lattice over diamond-shaped openings. ✦ Bake until a toothpick inserted comes out dry and the dough is browned. Let it cool and dust with confectioners' sugar.

SWEET CHESTNUT POLENTA

PATTONA

FOR 6 PERSONS

TOSCANA

1 lb. chestnut flour
Salt

Bring 4 cups of lightly salted water to a boil in a pot. As soon as the water begins to boil pour in all the flour all at once: do not stir, do not touch. ✦ Let this simmer for about 30 minutes, then drain off the water, setting it aside nearby. ✦ With the pan off the heat, stir the mixture with a wooden spoon while slowly adding back the cooking water. When the mixture is smooth, transfer it to another pan, even off the surface with a wooden spoon dampened in fresh water, and put back on the heat. ✦ Cover a work surface with a cloth. As soon as this mixture begins to "puff up" from boiling (bubbles will rise to the surface and break) turn it out on the work surface. Let it cool before cutting and serving.

LAYER CAKE

PAZIENTINA

FOR 6–8 PERSONS

VENETO

¼ lb. (1 stick) plus 2 tbsp. unsalted butter
1 cup sugar
⅔ cup all-purpose flour
⅔ cup finely ground blanched almonds
½ cup finely ground toasted bitter almonds (see note)
3 large egg whites, beaten stiff

CONTINUED

If you cannot find bitter almonds, use 1 cup almonds and ½ teaspoon almond extract. Decorate the finished cake with chocolate leaves, if desired.

Preheat the oven to 350°F. Cream the butter and the sugar until fluffy, then add the flour in a steady stream, then add a pinch of salt. Add the blanched and bitter almonds, then fold in the egg whites. ✦ Spread this dough in a round pan to a thickness of about ½ inch. ✦ Bake for 30 minutes, remove from the oven, and let cool. ✦ Make the zabaglione. Bring a pot of water to a simmer. In a heatproof bowl, whisk together the egg yolks and sugar until the sugar is dissolved. Place over the simmering water and whisk in the Marsala and flour. Continue

1 baked Polentina di Cittadella (see page 846), sprinkled with 1 tbsp. *alchermes* (see note, page 786)

2 oz. semisweet chocolate, melted

Salt

For the zabaglione:

5 large egg yolks

1⅔ cups sugar

2 cups Marsala

⅔ cup all-purpose flour

whisking until the mixture is frothy and thick and falls in mounds when the whisk is lifted out of the mixture. Let cool. ✦ Spread half of the zabaglione over the almond cake. Top with the *Polentina di Cittadella*. Top with the remaining zabaglione and set aside in a cool place. ✦ Level off the surface and drizzle with melted chocolate.

PEPATELLI

HONEY BISCUITS

ABRUZZO

6⅔ cups all-purpose flour

1 tbsp. unsweetened cocoa powder

Grated zest of 1 orange

1⅓ cups honey

1⅔ cups chopped almonds

Pepper

Preheat the oven to 300°F. Whisk together the flour, cocoa, zest, and a pinch of pepper. Stir in the honey, then knead in the almonds (the dough will be relatively firm). ✦ Form the dough into long cylinders then press them to slightly flatten. ✦ Bake until lightly browned, about 25 minutes. While still very warm, cut the cylinders into cookies ½ to ¾ inch thick. Let cool completely.

✦ **LOCAL TRADITION** ✦

PEVARINI DI TREGNANO

Typical of the Veneto, the elegant cookies known as *pevarini di Tregnano* get sweetness from molasses and a subtle bite from white pepper. Flour, sugar, baking powder, and pepper are mixed with lard and a generous amount of molasses to form a smooth dough, then cut into long strips. The long strips are baked just until cooked through, and the cooling cookies would be brushed with a glaze of simple syrup.

PEARS IN WINE

VALLE D'AOSTA

8 pears (preferably Martin Sec;
Bosc can also be used)

1 cup red wine (preferably from the
Valle d'Aosta: Petit Rouge, Torrette,
Enfer d'Arvier, Donnaz)

⅔ cup sugar

½ cinnamon stick

1 whole clove

Peel of ½ lemon, in strips

Serve the pears with their cooking liquid only or with whipped cream.

Place the pears in a saucepan and pour over the red wine. Add the sugar, cinnamon, clove, and lemon peel. ✦ Cover the pan and cook at low heat for about 30 minutes or until it forms a thick syrup not unlike cherries jubilee. Let cool completely before serving.

BAKED AMARETTO PEACHES

PESCHE RIPIENE 1

LIGURIA

Unsalted butter

4 large, ripe peaches

1⅔ cups crushed amaretti

20 hazelnuts

½ cup pastry cream (see page 843)

1 tbsp. amaretto liqueur

2 tbsp. sugar, or as needed

½ cup dry white wine,
such as Pigato or Vermentino

Confectioners' sugar

Preheat the oven to 350°F. Butter a round cake pan. Rinse the peaches and cut them in half, removing the pit. Scoop out most of the pulp and reserve it. (Leave a little pulp to help the peaches keep their shape.) ✦ Finely chop the amaretti and 12 of the hazelnuts, then add them to the peach pulp and blend. ✦ Add the pastry cream and liqueur. Use this mixture to stuff the peach halves; arrange them in the cake pan. ✦ At the center of each peach half press one of the remaining hazelnuts; sprinkle with sugar. ✦ Pour the white wine into the pan and bake for about 10 minutes. Let cool and sprinkle with confectioners' sugar just before serving.

STUFFED PEACHES

PESCHE RIPIENE 2

EMILIA-ROMAGNA

Unsalted butter

8 large, ripe peaches

3 large eggs, separated

1 cup sugar

1 cup blanched almonds,
ground to a flour

CONTINUED

This recipe is typical of Modena. You can use finely crushed amaretti in place of the almonds.

Preheat the oven to 300°F. Butter a baking sheet. Cut the peaches in half and remove the pits and most of the pulp so as to enlarge the space for the filling, reserving the pulp in a mixing bowl. ✦ Whisk the egg yolks and sugar until pale and thick, then add to the peach pulp. Mix in the almonds and bread. Whip the whites of 2 eggs and fold into the mixture. ✦ Fill the peach halves with the

Bread of 1 roll, soaked in milk and squeezed dry

Confectioners' sugar

mixture and place them on the baking sheet. Bake for 30 minutes. Let cool slightly and dust with confectioners' sugar. Serve warm.

STUFFED PEACHES WITH ALMONDS

PESCHE SCALIGERE

VENETO

8 firm, yellow peaches

3 tbsp. unsalted butter

¾ cup blanched almonds, toasted and finely chopped

10 amaretti, crumbled and ground

1 tbsp. grappa

½ cup sugar

⅓ cup honey

This recipe is typical of Verona.

Preheat the oven to 350°F. Peel the peaches, cut them in half, and remove the pits. ✦ Butter a baking sheet and arrange the peach halves across it. ✦ Meanwhile prepare the filling by combining the almonds with the amaretti, grappa, sugar, and honey. ✦ Fill the peach halves with this mixture and put them in the oven. Bake for at least 2 minutes according to the size of the peaches. ✦ Serve the peaches at room temperature, perhaps with whipped cream on the side.

✦ **LOCAL TRADITION** ✦

PESCHE DI CASTELBOTTACCIO

"Stuffed peaches," typical of Molise, were baked sweet rolls filled with a sweet yellow cream that resembled the luscious peaches of the Italian countryside. The dough was made from flour, eggs, olive oil, sugar, and yeast dissolved in milk and shaped into balls the size of walnuts. The dough was set aside to rest and rise until the balls doubled in volume and were then baked at low heat without browning. After the "peaches" were removed from the oven and had cooled, a small hole would be made in each and the cream piped into the center. Each "peach" was then bathed in sugar syrup, and finally brushed with a little red liqueur to give them the perfect red-gold color. The final step was to roll each "peach" in confectioners' sugar; they would traditionally be arranged in straw baskets and decorated with bay leaves to look almost like real peaches gathered from the orchard.

| # CHRISTMAS RING CAKES

For the dough:
3⅓ cups all-purpose flour
2¼ tsp. active dry yeast

For the filling:
⅔ cup raisins
⅔ cup shelled walnuts
3 cups chopped dried figs
⅔ cup shelled and finely chopped almonds
Pinch ground cinnamon
1 cup honey, plus more as needed
Olive oil
2 large egg yolks

This recipe is typical of Corleone.

Knead together the flour, yeast, and 1 cup water to prepare a somewhat soft and homogeneous dough. Cover with a clean kitchen towel and let rise for a few hours. ✦ In a saucepan combine the raisins, walnuts, figs, almonds, and cinnamon. Add the honey and cook at low heat, stirring constantly. Cook until the mixture forms a soft paste, adding more honey if needed. Set aside to cool. ✦ Preheat the oven to 325°F. Grease a baking sheet with olive oil. Roll out the dough to form a sheet ⅛ inch thick and cut it in long strips 2 to 2½ inches wide. ✦ When the filling has cooled, form it into small cylinders about 1½ inches thick and place these on the strips of dough, rolling them up like a salame to enclose the filling. Cut these into sections about 8 inches long and join the two ends to form rings. Make incisions along the lengths of the rings to allow heat to escape during cooking. Brush with egg yolks. ✦ Place on the baking sheet and bake for 30 minutes, or until they are golden. Serve hot or cold.

| # RING CAKE

3⅓ cups all-purpose flour
½ cup sugar
1⅛ tsp. active dry yeast
¼ lb. (1 stick) unsalted butter
3 large eggs
½ cup milk
Vanilla sugar
1 large hard-boiled egg, for serving
Salt

For Easter every family in Formia prepares its own *pigna*. In the past these ring cakes were made using native yeast, the same used for baking bread, but today the dish is made using active dry yeast.

Whisk together the flour, sugar, a pinch of salt, and yeast. Then blend in the butter, eggs, and milk. Knead for a long time to form a soft, smooth dough. Form into a ball, cover with a cloth, and set aside in a cool spot to rise. ✦ Preheat the oven to 350°F. Butter a baking sheet. Form the dough into a ring and place the sheet in the oven. Bake until the surface browns. ✦ Let cool completely. A few minutes before serving dust with the vanilla sugar and place the traditional shelled, hard-boiled egg in the center.

HONEY COOKIES

3 ⅓ cups all-purpose flour

⅔ cup plus 1 tbsp. sugar

3 tsp. active dry yeast

½ tsp. ground cinnamon

½ cup orange liqueur

Grated zest of 1 orange and peel of 1 orange, cut in strips

3 large eggs

1 oz. lard, melted

2 tbsp. unsalted butter, softened

Olive oil, for frying

2 tbsp. honey

Salt

Whisk together the flour, ⅔ cup sugar, yeast, cinnamon, a pinch of salt, liqueur, and grated zest. Use the mixture and eggs to make a dough as in the recipe on page 751, adding the lard and butter with the eggs. Cover with a cloth and set aside to rise for 1 hour. ✦ Roll the dough out to a ½-inch-thick sheet. Heat 2 inches of olive oil in a saucepan. Cut the dough into squares and fry them until golden; drain on paper towels. ✦ Heat the honey, remaining sugar, and orange peels in a large skillet at low heat. Add the fried squares and stir them around to soak up the honey, then arrange on a serving plate. Serve cool.

EASTER CAKE

3 ⅓ cups all-purpose flour

1 ½ cups sugar

2 ¼ tsp. active dry yeast

1 ½ cups whole milk

⅔ cup unsalted butter, melted and cooled slightly

2 large eggs plus 9 yolks

1 tbsp. rum

1 tbsp. citron essence (see note)

Salt

This Easter cake is prepared in three stages. If you cannot find the citron essence, use 1 tablespoon grated lemon zest instead. This recipe is typical of Gorizia.

First leavening: combine ⅔ cup flour, 2 tablespoons sugar, a pinch of salt, and the yeast with just enough milk to form a small loaf. Set aside to rise for about 30 minutes. ✦ Second leavening: combine half the remaining flour, the remaining sugar, butter, 1 egg plus 6 yolks, salt, the loaf from the first stage, and enough milk to again make a loaf. This time let it rise 1 hour. ✦ Third leavening: on the work surface knead the remaining flour with the remaining egg yolks, the rum and citron essence, the risen loaf, and remaining milk. Knead this dough until smooth and not sticky. Shape it into a round, and set it aside to rise for 1 hour. ✦ Preheat the oven to 325°F. Beat the remaining egg and brush on the dough. Bake for 40 minutes, until light golden.

OLIVE OIL NUT CAKE

CALABRIA

For the dough:

6 cups all-purpose flour

3 tbsp. sugar

3 large eggs

12 tbsp. lard

Grated zest of 1 lemon

Salt

For the filling:

¼ cup extra-virgin olive oil

¼ cup *vin cotto*
(see note, page 818)

1½ cups raisins

1⅔ cups chopped walnuts

¼ tsp. ground cinnamon

Grated zest of 1 orange

1¼ cups sugar

This recipe is typical of Crotone. This is made for the feast of the Madonna, May 8.

Preheat the oven to 400°F. Grease a round cake pan with olive oil. Mix the flour, sugar, and a pinch of salt and use them and the eggs to prepare a dough as in the recipe on page 751, adding the lard and lemon zest with the eggs. Divide the dough into two loaves, the larger one using ¾ of the dough. ✦ Roll out the larger loaf to form two sheets about 30 inches in diameter and about ¹⁄₁₆ inch thick. Lightly grease one of these sheets with a little olive oil and sprinkle with *vin cotto*. Mix together the raisins, walnuts, cinnamon, and orange zest. Sprinkle this mixture over the sheet of dough and dust with sugar. ✦ Cover with the remaining sheet and cut into strips, being careful to keep the filling from coming out; shape the strips into rosettes. ✦ Roll out the smaller loaf to form a sheet 1 inch larger than the diameter of the pan and use it to line the bottom and sides of the pan; brush it with olive oil. ✦ Arrange the stuffed rosettes in the pan, pressing them in so they touch. Press the sheet lining the pan in to adhere to the rosettes. Dust with sugar and bake until dark golden, about 20 minutes.

WALNUT-FILLED PIZZA

ABRUZZO

1⅔ cups all-purpose flour

4 tbsp. extra-virgin olive oil

4½ cups ground walnuts

2 tbsp. bitter cocoa

1¼ cups chopped bitter chocolate

4 tbsp. sugar

Pinch ground cinnamon

¼ cup chopped candied citron

1¼ cups honey

1¼ cups raisins

1 tbsp. rum

1 large egg yolk

Salt

Preheat the oven to 400°F. Line a baking sheet with parchment. Use the flour and olive oil to make a dough as in the recipe on page 751 using the olive oil in place of the eggs. Roll out into a thin sheet. ✦ Mix the walnuts, cocoa, chocolate, sugar, cinnamon, and candied citron. ✦ Spread this mixture down the side of the sheet of dough, then sprinkle with the honey, raisins, and rum. Roll up the mixture like a salame, then fold in on itself to form a spiral. Place on the baking sheet and press to flatten slightly. Brush with the egg yolk and bake for about 45 minutes, or until golden. ✦ Let it cool and serve sliced.

PIZZA DI RICOTTA

RICOTTA PIE

1 lb. ricotta

1 ½ cups sugar

3 large egg yolks

Grated zest of 1 orange

2 tsp. vanilla extract

⅔ cup diced candied fruit

½ cup anise liqueur (or Strega)

Pastry dough (packaged or prepared as in the recipe on page 773)

Confectioners' sugar

Vanilla sugar

Salt

Preheat the oven to 350°F. Mix the ricotta and sugar in a mixing bowl, working well to obtain a smooth mixture without lumps. ✦ Incorporate the egg yolks one at a time, then stir in the orange zest, vanilla, candied fruit, a pinch of salt, and liqueur. ✦ Roll out half of the pastry dough and use it to line a 9-inch pie pan. Spoon in the filling, smoothing to an even layer. Roll out the remaining pastry and cover the filling, using a fork to seal the edges. ✦ Pierce the surface with the tip of a knife and bake for about 1 hour, until golden. ✦ Let cool completely, dust with confectioners' sugar and vanilla sugar, and serve.

PIZZA DOLCE

ALMOND AND CHOCOLATE LAYER CAKE

FOR 6 PERSONS

ABRUZZO

Olive oil and all-purpose flour, for the baking pan

For the sponge cake:

10 large eggs, separated

½ cup sugar

10 tbsp. all-purpose flour

1 tsp. baking powder (optional)

Grated zest of 1 lemon

1 tsp. vanilla extract

For the pastry cream and chocolate cream:

8 large egg yolks

¾ cup sugar

4 tbsp. all-purpose flour

4 cups whole milk

Grated zest of 1 lemon

2 tsp. ground cinnamon

½ cup cocoa powder

CONTINUED

This recipe is typical of Pescara. In place of *alchermes* you can use strong coffee. Serve with whipped cream and cherry syrup if desired.

Preheat the oven to 325°F. Grease a round 10-inch cake pan with olive oil and dust with flour. Make the sponge cake: beat the yolks of the eggs with the sugar, add the flour and baking powder, if using, in a steady stream, constantly stirring, then add the lemon zest and vanilla; whip the egg whites stiff and fold them in. ✦ Pour the mixture into the pan and bake until set, about 40 minutes. Let cool completely in the pan. ✦ For the pastry cream: beat the egg yolks and ¼ cup sugar with a mixer on medium speed until pale and thick, then whisk in the flour in a steady stream. Whisk in the milk. Pour this into a saucepan and cook over low heat. When the mixture begins to thicken (after about 5 minutes), add the lemon zest and half the cinnamon. ✦ Stir and continue cooking at low heat to thicken to the consistency of pudding. Remove from the heat and let stand until cool, then make the chocolate cream. Whisk together the remaining ½ cup sugar, cocoa, and remaining cinnamon and mix in half of the pastry cream, whisking until blended. Set

For the almond paste:

1 ⅔ cups sugar

1 cup finely ground
blanched almonds

Grated zest of 1 lemon

For assembly:

2 tbsp. rum

2 tbsp. milk

Alchermes (see note, page 786)

1 large egg white, beaten

Confectioners' sugar

1 tsp. lemon juice

aside. ✦ For the almond paste: heat the sugar in 1¼ cups water until the mixture forms threads (223°F to 234°F on a candy thermometer), then gradually add the almond meal and lemon zest, stirring to form a dense paste. Remove from the heat and set aside to cool slightly. ✦ Cut the cooled sponge cake crosswise to create 4 disks of the same thickness. Place the first of these on a serving plate. Mix together the rum and milk and brush the first disk generously (you should use all of the liquid). Spread evenly with pastry cream, then top with the second disk of cake. Brush the second disk with *alchermes* and cover with a layer of the almond paste. Top with the third layer and brush as before with either additional rum-milk mixture or additional *alchermes*. Spread evenly with the chocolate cream; top with the last disk of cake. Whisk together the egg white with enough confectioners' sugar to make a thin glaze, then whisk in the lemon juice. Pour this glaze over the top of the cake, spreading to make a little of the glaze drip down the sides of the cake.

CORNMEAL AND RAISIN CAKE

LAZIO

Lard or olive oil

1 ¼ cups all-purpose flour

1 ¼ cups cornmeal

½ cup sugar

½ cup raisins, soaked in water
and drained

½ tsp. cinnamon

½ cup pine nuts (optional)

1 tbsp. extra-virgin olive oil

Salt

In the past this cake was baked in wood-burning ovens when the fire (dried branches) was at its hottest: when it "flamed up," to translate the dialect word. In some towns in the province of Viterbo (Tuscania, Tarquinia, and so on), it is made using only cornmeal or leftover polenta, which is softened with water to become creamy. This is then seasoned on the surface with sugar, cinnamon, and olive oil. The dialect name of this cake, *Diomeneguardi* ("may God watch over it"), may have been intended to reflect the special appreciation given this cake during a period of simple tastes suited to the absence of resources.

Preheat the oven to 400°F. Grease a sheet pan with lard or olive oil. Mix the flour and cornmeal in a bowl with 1 cup water, a pinch of salt, and ¼ cup sugar. You should have a thick batter that is almost a wet dough. ✦ Add the raisins and mix to blend. Work this together with a wooden spoon to make it homogeneous and pour into the pan. Mix the remaining sugar and cinnamon and dust the dough with the mixture. Sprinkle with pine nuts, as desired. ✦ Before putting this in the oven drizzle with olive oil. ✦ Bake until dark golden, about 20 minutes.

PIZZA DOLCE DI PASQUA | EASTER BUNS

UMBRIA

4½ tsp. (2 packets) active dry yeast

½ cup milk, warmed slightly

6 cups all-purpose flour, or as much as needed

12 large eggs

3½ cups sugar

¼ lb. (1 stick) plus 6 tbsp. unsalted butter

Grated zest of 2 lemons and 2 oranges

½ cup *vin santo* (see note)

½ cup Marsala

1 tsp. *rosolio* liqueur with cinnamon (see note)

½ tsp. vanilla extract

Vin santo is a golden, sweet dessert wine. If you can't find *rosolio*, you can use ½ teaspoon rose water and ½ teaspoon ground cinnamon.

Mix half the yeast with the milk. Form a well with half the flour and add the yeast mixture. Knead to form a soft dough and let rise at least 2 hours (overnight is best). ✦ The next morning preheat the oven to 350°F. Beat the eggs and sugar with an electric mixer on medium speed until pale and thick. Whisk in the butter, lemon and orange zests, *vin santo*, Marsala, *rosolio*, and vanilla. Mix this with the remaining flour, remaining yeast, and yeasted dough and knead to form a soft dough. Let rest for 2 hours. Divide into 6 equal balls and place each one in a 6-inch-high mold, filling them up to three-quarters. ✦ Bake for about 45 minutes or until golden.

POLENTA DI MARENGO | CORNMEAL SPONGE CAKE

PIEMONTE

¼ lb. (½ cup) unsalted butter, softened

All-purpose flour

3 large eggs, separated

1 cup sugar

⅔ cup cornmeal

⅓ cup cornstarch

½ cup potato starch

2 tbsp. almond flour

Grated zest of 1 lemon

½ cup golden raisins

For the covering:

½ cup almond paste (see page 834)

½ cup sponge cake crumbs (see page 843)

Preheat the oven to 350°F. Butter and flour a cake pan. Beat the egg yolks and sugar with a mixer on medium speed until pale and thick. Beat the egg whites until stiff but not dry, then fold into the yolk mixture. ✦ Fold in the cornmeal, starches, almond flour, and lemon zest until smooth. Fold in the raisins and softened butter. ✦ Pour the mixture into the pan and bake for about 1 hour. ✦ Let cool completely, then cover the cake with a thin layer of almond paste and sprinkle with finely crumbled sponge cake.

DESSERTS

PIZZE DI PASQUA

Easter pizzas are a long-standing tradition in Lazio; the gleaming copper pans used to bake them were hung on the kitchen wall throughout the year and became prized heirlooms for daughters when they married. Each family would have particular favorite variations or "secret recipes" (such as adding or using fewer eggs, adding butter, or the choice of liqueurs) depending on taste, but the most basic recipe, typical of Viterbo, involved using natural yeast—aged yeast left over from bread making—and flour to yield a very soft, pliant dough. After the dough rested for at least twelve hours, up to two dozen eggs, sugar, cinnamon, vanilla, grated orange and lemon zest, and various sweet liqueurs would be carefully incorporated during several hours of laborious kneading. The special copper pans would be greased and then filled at most halfway with portions of the dough, which would then be set aside in special chests to rest and rise again. An egg wash was brushed atop the risen dough before the pizzas were baked to create a shiny brown burnish. During baking, the pizzas would expand farther than the rims of the copper pans, giving them their characteristic mushroom shape.

POLENTINA DI
CITTADELLA

SPONGE CAKE

FOR 6–8
PERSONS

VENETO

1 ¼ cups all-purpose flour
⅔ cup potato starch
6 or more tbsp. milk
4 large eggs, separated
1 tsp. baking powder
1 ⅛ tsp. active dry yeast
4 tbsp. unsalted butter, for the pan
Breadcrumbs
Salt

Dissolve the flour and starch in the milk. Add the yolks of the eggs, baking powder, and the yeast. ✦ Whip the egg whites stiff and add them to the mixture with a pinch of salt. ✦ Wrap the resulting dough in a warm cloth and let rest about 1 hour. ✦ Preheat the oven to 300°F. Butter a round pan with 3-inch sides and sprinkle with breadcrumbs. Pour the mixture into the pan and bake, gradually increasing the temperature 25 degrees every 15 minutes until the cake rises above the sides of the pan, about 1 hour.

TRIESTINE YEAST CAKE

FRIULI-VENEZIA GIULIA

1⅛ tsp. active dry yeast

¾ cup milk, warmed slightly

3⅓ cups all-purpose flour

1½ cups sugar

¾ cup (1½ sticks) unsalted butter, melted, plus 1 tbsp., softened slightly

1 large egg plus 2 yolks

4 oz. (4 squares) semisweet chocolate

1⅔ cups chopped walnuts

1 tbsp. rum

½ cup raisins

½ cup pine nuts

In a large bowl, dissolve the yeast in ¼ cup milk. Stir in ½ cup flour and 1 teaspoon sugar; set this aside to rise. ✦ When the mixture has doubled, stir in the melted butter, 1 cup sugar, egg yolks, and 1 egg. Knead in the remaining flour and work to make a firm dough. ✦ Melt the chocolate and whisk in the remaining milk. Stir in the walnuts, remaining sugar, softened butter, rum, raisins, and pine nuts until blended. Roll the dough out to form a sheet ¹⁄₁₆ inch thick. Sprinkle this mixture along one side of the sheet of dough. Roll this up to form a cylinder and set aside to rise 1 hour. ✦ Preheat the oven to 400°F. Bend in the ends of the cylinder to form a spiral and place it on a baking sheet. Bake for 20 minutes, then reduce the oven temperature to 350°F and bake until golden, about 20 minutes more.

SPICED WINE

LAZIO

1 lb. black cherries (wild, if possible), pitted (pits reserved)

2 cups red wine

A few cinnamon sticks

A few whole cloves

Pinch whole coriander seeds

2 cups sugar, or as needed

1½ cups high-proof alcohol, or as needed

This recipe is typical of Maenza, Prossedi, Pisterzo, and Cisterna.

Crush the cherry pits to obtain about ½ cup of crushed seeds. Combine all the ingredients except the sugar and liqueur in a large stoppered bottle or sterilized wine bottle (without its straw covering). ✦ Close the bottle with its stopper or a cork. Let stand 40 days, opening the bottle twice a day and shaking the bottle from time to time. ✦ After this period of fermentation strain the liquid through cheesecloth, then measure it and return it to the bottle. ✦ Add 2 cups sugar and 1½ cups alcohol for every 4 cups of liquid. Let stand 3 more days, shaking the liquid every so often, then strain into a sterilized bottle and let it rest another 40 days in a dark, cool, dry place before tasting.

JAM RAVIOLI

EMILIA-ROMAGNA

1¼ cups all-purpose flour

1 large egg

⅔ cup sugar

¼ lb. (1 stick) unsalted butter

1 cup apricot jam, or as needed

1 cup Bolognese *mostarda*
(see note, page 877), or as needed

Confectioners' sugar

Salt

These are also called *Raviole di San Giuseppe* because of their use on the feast day of St. Joseph, March 19. The *mostarda* in this recipe is a sweet kind; you could substitute any type of fruit preserves of your choice.

Preheat the oven to 350°F. Use the flour and egg to make a dough as in the recipe on page 10, adding the sugar, butter, and salt with the egg. Roll out to a ½ inch thickness (see note, page 212). Cut the dough into 4-inch disks. ✦ At the center of each disk put 1 teaspoon of jam and 1 teaspoon of *mostarda*. Fold the disks over and seal with the tines of a fork. Place on a baking sheet and bake until well browned. Sprinkle with confectioners' sugar and serve warm.

BAKED SWEET RAVIOLI

LAZIO

Unsalted butter

For the dough:

3 cups all-purpose flour

1 cup sugar

Pinch baking powder

¼ cup extra-virgin olive oil

1 cup white wine

For the filling:

1¾ lbs. ricotta

1½ cups sugar

½ tsp. cinnamon

⅔ cup finely diced candied fruit

1 large egg plus 1 egg, separated

Grated zest of 1 lemon

⅔ cup chocolate chips

¼ cup white rum

Confectioners' sugar

For the wine, use Frascati or Castelli Romani.

Preheat the oven to 350°F. Butter a baking sheet. Use the flour, sugar, and baking powder to make a dough as in the recipe on page 10, using the olive oil and wine in place of the eggs. ✦ Roll out a sheet and cut it in strips about 6 inches wide. ✦ Mix the ricotta, sugar, cinnamon, candied fruit, egg, egg yolk, lemon zest, chocolate, and rum. When this mixture is well blended distribute large spoonfuls of it along the strips of dough, placing them about 4 inches apart. ✦ Fold over the strips to cover the filling, making the edges match, then pressing them to seal. ✦ Using a pastry wheel cut out half-moon-shaped ravioli and place on the baking sheet. Beat the remaining egg white and brush on the ravioli. ✦ Bake for about 20 minutes or until golden, then dust with confectioners' sugar. Serve cold.

QUARESIMALI

The spice trade has a long and storied history in the city of Genoa. As early as 1369, the courts of Ferrara and Mantua held the cakes and pastry from Genoa's community of spice vendors in high regard and these Lenten cookies are one of the oldest recipes from that group. A combination of both sweet and bitter almonds would first be ground in a mortar with sugar, vanilla, and lemon zest. This ground mixture would then be kneaded with egg whites to form a dough, which would be rolled out onto a greased work surface, traditionally marble. After an hour of resting, the dough would be cut into circle shapes, often using a drinking glass, and the remaining scraps would be cut into smaller squares. After baking, some of the round cookies would be topped with small *finocchetti* and some with a glaze flavored with chocolate, mint, and lemon. The squares were then made into sandwich cookies with a little marmalade.

RAVIOLI DOLCI CON LA RICOTTA (TACCONI)

SWEET RAVIOLI WITH RICOTTA

LAZIO

For the dough:

3 cups all-purpose flour, plus more as needed

2 large eggs, 1 separated

1 tbsp. unsalted butter

1 or 2 tbsp. sugar

½ cup milk (more or less)

Salt

For the filling:

1 ¼ lbs. ricotta

1 ½ cups sugar, or to taste

½ tsp. ground cinnamon

2 large eggs, beaten

Grated zest of 1 lemon

¼ cup rum

Olive oil, for frying

Confectioners' sugar

This recipe is typical of the Viterbo area. These are called *tacconi* ("heels") because they are shaped like shoe heels; they are traditionally prepared during the Carnival period. Not everyone loves fried food and, in fact, there is a variation of this recipe in which the ravioli are simply boiled. In that case, put a large pot with slightly salted water on the stove and when it boils immerse the ravioli with a skimmer or slotted spoon, not letting them overlap. Cook them for 5 minutes then strain them and arrange on a clean, dry kitchen cloth to dry. When they are dried use the usual pastry wheel to cut away as much of the border of each raviolo as possible, since the dough there will be thick and not overly pleasing; of course, as you do so avoid opening the ravioli. Arrange them on a serving plate and dust with sugar and cinnamon then sprinkle with a mixture of liquors, traditionally rum and *alcherme* (see note, page 786).

Use the flour and 1 egg to make a dough as in the recipe on page 10, adding just the yolk of the second egg, the butter, sugar, salt, and as much milk (about ½ cup) as needed with the whole egg. ✦ Let it rest for 30 minutes, then roll out a thin sheet (see page 212) and cut it in strips 6 inches wide. ✦ Make the filling: Combine the ricotta, sugar, cinnamon, eggs, lemon zest, and rum and mix until thoroughly blended. ✦ Arrange small lumps of this filling along the sheets of dough, spacing them 4 to 4½ inches apart, then fold over the sheets to cover the filling and align the edges. ✦ Cut the ravioli in the shape of half-moons with a pastry wheel, sealing the edges and piercing each ravioli with the tip of a fork. ✦ Heat 1 inch of olive oil in a pan and fry until golden. Drain on paper towels and dust with confectioners' sugar.

CHICKPEA RAVIOLI

RAVIOLONI DI PUREA DI CECI

CALABRIA

For the filling:

1 cup dried chickpeas, soaked in water overnight and drained

½ cup *vin cotto* (see note, page 818)

Pinch ground cinnamon

Pinch ground cloves

For the dough:

1½ cups all-purpose flour

1 large egg plus 1 large egg yolk

¼ cup extra-virgin olive oil, plus olive oil for frying

2 tbsp. sugar

¼ cup vermouth

Confectioners' sugar (optional)

These ravioli, traditionally eaten at Christmas, vary from place to place in terms of their shape and their filling (which could include ricotta, jam, or chocolate). What remains the same is their characteristic of being a fried, stuffed pasta, considered good luck in Calabria.

Cook the chickpeas in lightly salted water until tender, drain, and pass them through a sieve. Mix in the wine must, cinnamon, and cloves. ✦ Use the flour and whole egg to make a dough as in the recipe on page 10, adding the egg yolk, olive oil, sugar, and vermouth with the egg. ✦ Roll out this dough to form a thin sheet (see note, page 212), and using a pastry wheel cut it into rounds about 2 inches in diameter. ✦ Spoon the filling onto the disks of dough, then fold them over to form half-moons. Dampen the edges and press down to seal. ✦ Heat 1 inch of olive oil and fry until golden. Drain on paper towels, and if desired, dust with confectioners' sugar.

ALMOND PASTE COOKIES

RICCIARELLI

TOSCANA

2 cups blanched almonds

⅔ cup all-purpose flour

4 cups sugar

2 large egg whites

CONTINUED

This recipe is typical of Siena.

Industrial manufacturers have their refineries; at home we must make do with an old marble mortar and a wooden pestle. Use this to turn the almonds into a paste, adding the flour and about 2⅔ cups of the sugar. ✦ Make a simple syrup by mixing the remaining sugar with about ⅔ cup water and adding it to the almond mixture. ✦

½ cup vanilla sugar

½ tsp. baking powder

½ cup confectioners' sugar, or as needed

½ cup cornstarch, or as needed

Refrigerate for at least 8 hours. ✦ Preheat the oven to 300°F. Whip the egg whites and vanilla sugar until stiff peaks form. Fold into the almond mixture, then stir in the baking powder. Mix together the confectioners' sugar and cornstarch. Add to the almond mixture and knead to create a dough. ✦ Roll out the dough and divide it into small portions, and from these shape the *ricciarelli*, small cylinders as large as a thumb with the ends squeezed to form diamonds; you can also use the special lozenge-shaped mold. ✦ Place on a baking sheet, dust with confectioners' sugar, and bake about 20 minutes.

RISO MANTECATO | **RICE PUDDING 2** | FOR 8 PERSONS

SICILIA

4 cups milk

Heaping ½ cup sugar

1 heaping cup rice

1 ¼ cups toasted almonds, coarsely chopped

1 ¼ cups chopped candied squash (see note, page 787), plus more as needed

½ cup chocolate chips, plus more as needed

Put the milk in a saucepan with the sugar and rice. ✦ Bring to a boil at low heat, stirring constantly, until the rice is cooked (the liquid should be completely absorbed). ✦ Remove the pan from the heat and stir in the almonds, candied squash, and chocolate. ✦ Mix well and put on a serving plate. Cover with more candied squash and chocolate and serve cold.

RÜSSÜMADA OR ROSSÜMADA | **EGG COCKTAIL**

LOMBARDIA

4 large egg yolks

¼ cup sugar (optional)

White wine or lemon, as needed

This is an ancient beverage-snack widespread in northern Lombardia. Its name refers to its basic ingredient, egg, *russ d'oof* or *rüssümm*. It depends on the absolute freshness of the eggs, a rarity these days. There are even special glasses with pierced covers and small whisks so that the drinker can whip up the drink as it is consumed. Note that if you are concerned about salmonella and egg safety, then you should avoid this recipe, since the eggs are used raw.

To make the popular version, whip 1 egg yolk with 1) 1 tablespoon sugar and ¼ cup white wine or 2) with ¼ cup water and ¼ cup white wine or 3) with ¼ cup water and ¼ cup lemon in a blender until frothy and pale.

DESSERTS

ROSE FRITTE

This recipe for "fried roses" involves deep-frying pastry in the shape of flowers and is typical of Oderzo in the Veneto. A soft pastry dough made with many egg yolks would first be rolled out to a large sheet. The "roses" would be cut out of the dough using cutters or molds in the shape of clovers and stacked concentrically. Pressing down in the center with a stick, each rose would then be fried separately before being drained and dusted with sugar. Marmalade or cream could be piped or spread between the "petals" of each finished rose.

SALAME DEL RE

ROLLED CHOCOLATE CAKE

FOR
11 PERSONS

UMBRIA

Unsalted butter

For the dough:
6 large egg yolks
1⅔ cups sugar
1⅔ cups all-purpose flour
Juice and grated zest of ½ lemon
1 tsp. baking powder

For the filling:
¼ cup *alchermes*
(see note, page 786)
1½ cups chopped bitter chocolate
¼ cup milk
1 recipe pastry cream
(see page 843)

This recipe is typical of Città di Castello and is commonly prepared for baptismal celebrations.

Preheat the oven to 350°F. Butter a baking sheet and line it with parchment. Cover a work surface with a clean kitchen towel. Beat the egg yolks and sugar with a mixer on medium speed until pale and thickened. Whisk in the flour and lemon juice and zest until blended. Add the baking powder. ✦ Pour the dough on the baking sheet and spread to ¼ inch thick. ✦ Bake until set, about 15 minutes, then remove from the oven and invert on the cloth. Peel off the parchment and brush with *alchermes*. ✦ Place the chocolate in a heatproof bowl. Heat the milk just to boiling and pour the milk over the chocolate, then stir until smooth. Spread the cake with the chocolate mixture, then spread with pastry cream. ✦ Roll up the sheet to form a sort of flat salame shape and let stand a few minutes before slicing and serving.

| # CHOCOLATE SALAME

LOMBARDIA

¾ cup sugar

1 large egg plus 1 large egg yolk

¼ lb. (1 stick) plus 1 tbsp. unsalted butter

¾ cup chopped unsweetened chocolate

½ cup peeled and chopped hazelnuts (or almonds)

⅔ cup crumbled dried biscuits (zwieback)

Sweet almond oil

Note that if you are concerned about egg safety, then you should avoid this recipe.

In a bowl combine the sugar, egg, and yolk, stirring for 15 minutes. ✦ Melt the butter and add it, then add the chocolate, hazelnuts (or almonds), and biscuits and stir gently just to mix. ✦ Grease a sheet of waxed paper with almond oil, spread the mixture across it, then roll it up to give it the shape of a salame. ✦ Let it cool in the refrigerator overnight. Cut in slices to serve.

ALMOND-CHOCOLATE TARTLETS

SALIERINE

SICILIA

Unsalted butter, for the pan

For the dough:

3 cups all-purpose flour, plus more as needed

6 oz. lard

2 large egg yolks

1 cup sugar

Grated zest of 1 lemon

For the filling:

3 cups blanched almonds

4 cups plus 1 tbsp. sugar

⅔ cup chocolate chips

½ cup unsweetened cocoa powder

Pinch ground cinnamon

3 large egg yolks, beaten

For the meringue:

6 large egg whites

1½ cups granulated sugar

Preheat the oven to 375°F. Butter the cups of a muffin pan. Use the flour and lard to make a dough as in the recipe on page 751, adding the egg yolks, sugar, and lemon zest with the lard. ✦ Roll out a sheet of the dough, cut it into circles, and use these to line the muffin cups and bake until golden. ✦ When baked, let cool slightly, then remove from the cups and set aside. ✦ Meanwhile toast the almonds and finely chop them. Reduce the oven temperature to 275°F. Put the almonds in a saucepan with 3 cups water and bring to a boil. ✦ As soon as the water boils add 4 cups sugar, chocolate chips, cocoa powder, and cinnamon. Cook for about 45 minutes at moderate heat, stirring continuously. ✦ Remove the pan from the heat and incorporate the beaten egg yolks a little at a time. ✦ Return the pan to the heat and add the remaining 1 tablespoon sugar. ✦ Let cool slightly (it should still be warm), then fill the dough cups. Refrigerate them until cold. ✦ Whip the egg whites and sugar until stiff peaks form, then top each tartlet with this meringue, making sure the meringue reaches the dough shells. ✦ Bake until the meringue is dry to the touch, about 30 minutes.

DESSERTS

HONEY ALMOND COOKIES

LAZIO

Olive oil
1 ½ cups sugar
1 ½ cups honey
4 cups all-purpose flour,
or as needed
Grated zest of 1 orange
½ cup candied citron
1 ⅔ cups chopped almonds

This recipe is typical of Gaeta.

Preheat the oven to 350°F. Grease a baking sheet with olive oil. In a saucepan big enough to hold about 8 cups combine the sugar and honey; put this over very low heat, adding 1 tablespoon water. ✦ When this mixture is well blended take the pan off the heat and add 1 tablespoon flour. ✦ Pour out the remaining flour on a work surface (marble is best) or in a bowl and mix in the sugar syrup, creating a firm and homogeneous paste. If it is too soft add a few more tablespoons of flour. ✦ Add the orange zest, candied citron, and almonds. ✦ Divide this into 30 pieces and place on the baking sheet. ✦ Bake for about 10 minutes.

"STAIRWAY TO HEAVEN" COOKIES

SCALETTE

CALABRIA

4 large eggs, beaten
¼ lb. (½ cup) unsalted butter
1 tbsp. sugar
2 ¼ tsp. baking powder
1 tsp. vanilla extract
¼ cup anise seeds
2 cups all-purpose flour,
or as much as needed, sifted
Olive oil, for greasing and frying
½ cup honey
Salt

These Christmas sweets are named *scalette*, or "stairs," because they are shaped to be symbolic of the "stairway to heaven."

In a bowl mix the eggs, butter, sugar, baking powder, vanilla, salt, and anise, then add the sifted flour a little at a time until blended and smooth, to obtain a soft but firm dough. ✦ Knead the dough on the work surface until smooth, then divide in small portions to roll out to form cylinders about the size of breadsticks but thicker. ✦ Wrap these around a pencil or wooden spoon handle (greasing it with olive oil from time to time) to form long spirals. Carefully remove them from the pencil and set them out on a floured cloth. ✦ Heat 2 inches of olive oil and fry until golden. Drain on paper towels. Heat the honey over low heat just until melted and brush on the golden cookies. Let stand until dry, about 20 minutes.

SAVÔR

Savôr is a traditional cooked-fruit compote made from unfermented grape must, typical of Forli in Emilia-Romagna, with roots that reach back to ancient times. Traditionally, *savôr* is made just after the grape harvest in the early fall. The concentrated grape must from sweet, ripe red- or white-wine grapes would be very carefully cooked down in a copper pot for about four hours, at which point the additional ingredients were added for continued slow cooking.

The more careful the choice of ingredients, the richer and more flavorful the resulting compote would be. These ingredients symbolized a synthesis of the summer and autumn seasons and traditionally included nuts gathered in late summer, such as walnuts, hazelnuts, pine nuts, and almonds (all peeled and chopped fine); late-summer fruit, such as apples and quinces; sun-dried fruit, such as apple slices, apricots, raisins, and figs; fresh fruit, such as summer peaches; candied fruit, including citrus peel or watermelon rind; and even some traditional peasant fare, now rarely seen, such as diced carrots or squash. Sugar was added only occasionally, and not in the more authentic, original recipes. All of these ingredients, added halfway through cooking, were kept under the surface of the grape must to obtain a dense, concentrated liquid after six more hours of cooking. Constant stirring with a long wooden spoon ensured that the *savôr* wouldn't burn or stick to the bottom of the cauldron.

The finished *savôr* was cooled overnight and hermetically sealed in glass or earthenware jars, to be used in dessert recipes or as a sweet accompaniment on the table through the cold months.

SCALITÙ | # BUTTER CAKE | FOR 10 PERSONS

LOMBARDIA

3 ⅓ cups all-purpose flour

2 cups sugar

2 ¼ tsp. baking powder

10 oz. (2 ½ sticks) unsalted butter, softened

1 tsp. milk

Salt

Mix the flour, sugar, baking powder, and a pinch of salt in a bowl. Mix in the butter and milk and knead until a smooth dough forms. Cover with a clean kitchen towel and let rest for about 30 minutes. ✦ Preheat the oven to 400°F. Grease a 9-inch cake pan and place the dough in it. Bake for about 45 minutes or until golden. Let cool completely.

DESSERTS

SWEET EASTER BREAD

PUGLIA

⅔ cup extra-virgin olive oil

3 cups all-purpose flour,
or as needed

1½ tsp. active dry yeast

1 cup sugar

Grated zest of 1 lemon

3 large eggs

⅔ cup whole milk, warmed

For the glaze:

1 large egg white

½ tsp. lemon juice

1¼ cups confectioners' sugar

Candy-coated almonds, crushed

Preheat the oven to 350°F. Grease a baking sheet with olive oil. Mix the flour, yeast, sugar, and lemon zest and use them and 1 egg to make a dough as in the recipe on page 751, adding the olive oil and milk with the egg. Let the dough rest in a bowl, covered with a kitchen towel, for about 1 hour, until almost doubled in volume. ✦ Divide the dough in three parts and roll into cylinders. Braid the three cylinders, then form the cake into a ring or a figure eight. ✦ Place on the baking sheet; gently press the remaining 2 eggs (in their shells) into the dough. ✦ Bake for 1 hour or until cooked through and golden. Remove from the sheet and let it cool. ✦ Whisk together the egg white and lemon juice, then whisk in the confectioners' sugar a little at a time to make a thick but spreadable glaze. ✦ Spread it over the cake evenly but without covering the two eggs, and before the glaze sets dust it with candy-coated almonds. Let stand until set.

ZUCCHINI CAKE

TOSCANA

Unsalted butter

1⅔ cups all-purpose flour

2 cups whole milk

1¼ cups sugar

1 lb. zucchini, trimmed and
shredded

Grated zest of 1 lemon

1 tsp. vanilla extract

½ tsp. Marsala

1½ tsp. baking powder

1 tbsp. extra-virgin olive oil

Preheat the oven to 400°F. Butter a baking pan. Mix all the ingredients except the olive oil until blended. Pour the batter into the pan, drizzle with olive oil, and bake for 1 hour, or until the bread springs back when lightly pressed.

CHRISTMAS SPICE COOKIES

ABRUZZO

6⅔ cups all-purpose flour

8 oz. (8 squares) unsweetened chocolate

1½ cups sugar

1¼ cups chocolate chips

3 cups wine must (see note, page 818)

1 tbsp. baking powder

1 tsp. cinnamon

3 large eggs

1 tbsp. rum

1 tsp. Sambuca

¼ cup extra-virgin olive oil

1¼ cups raisins

⅔ cup chopped candied citron

Grated zest of 2 oranges

Grated zest of 2 lemons

4½ lbs. coarsely chopped toasted walnut halves

This recipe is typical of Sulmona.

Preheat the oven to 400°F. Sprinkle a baking sheet with flour. Melt the unsweetened chocolate in a saucepan with the sugar and chocolate chips, stirring until smooth. In another pot heat the wine must, stirring constantly to avoid lumps. ✦ Whisk together the flour, baking powder, and cinnamon in a bowl or on a work surface and form into a well. Beat the eggs in the center, then slowly add the wine must, then the melted chocolate mixture, rum, Sambuca, and olive oil. Stir in the raisins, citron, orange and lemon zests, and walnuts. ✦ Blend this together to form a thick dough. ✦ Arrange tablespoon-size lumps of the dough in even rows across the baking sheet, spacing them so that they will not touch when they puff up. ✦ Bake for 20 to 25 minutes, until the surface is dry and the cookies are set.

SEMOLINA BREAD WITH WINE MUST AND ALMONDS

SCAVUNISCU

CALABRIA

3 cups semolina flour, plus more as needed

1 cup wine must (see note, page 818)

⅔ cup coarsely chopped almonds

Peel of 1 orange, cut in thin strips

Lard

Salt

This dish, flour mixed with wine must, is an ancient peasant sweet. Its Italian name comes from *schiavonesco*, meaning "dark in color."

Combine the semolina flour with the wine must and a little warm water. ✦ Add to this the salt, almonds, and orange peel. Work the resulting mixture to blend well and form into the shape of a loaf. Let the loaf rest for 1 hour. ✦ Preheat the oven to 400°F. Grease a baking sheet with lard and place the loaf on it. Bake until dry to the touch and cooked through, about 35 minutes.

DESSERTS

FLATBREAD WITH DRIED FIGS

TOSCANA

2 ¼ tsp. active dry yeast
3 ⅓ cups all-purpose flour
1 tsp. sugar
1 tsp. extra-virgin olive oil
16 dried figs
Salt

This recipe is typical of the Chianti area.

Dissolve half the yeast in 2 tablespoons warm water. On the work surface combine half the flour with the yeast mixture, sugar, and olive oil, adding ½ cup water. Knead to form a smooth dough. ✦ Shape this into a loaf and set aside in a warm place to rise for about 2 hours, covered by a cloth. ✦ Chop the figs in small pieces and soak them in warm water to soften. ✦ Pour the remaining flour out on the work surface and add the remaining yeast and ½ cup warm water. Knead together with the dried figs and a pinch of salt to form a soft smooth dough. ✦ Add the loaf prepared earlier, and knead them together. Set aside to rest for 1 hour. ✦ Grease a baking sheet with olive oil, then press the dough evenly into the pan. ✦ Using the tip of a knife score squares into the surface then cover with a cloth and let rest again for 1 hour. ✦ Preheat the oven to 400°F. Bake for about 40 minutes or until golden and cooked through.

SWEET FLATBREAD

VENETO

3 ⅓ cups all-purpose flour
4 oz. lard (or 1 stick butter)
3 large eggs
⅔ cup sugar
Salt

Preheat the oven to 350°F. Knead together the flour and lard (or butter), then blend in the eggs, sugar, and a pinch of salt. Knead until smooth. ✦ Press the dough into a baking sheet to form a flat focaccia. Using the tip of a knife, make incisions in the surface to form double crosses. ✦ Brush with cold water and bake until the surface is a pretty golden color, about 40 minutes.

FLATBREAD WITH ROSEMARY AND RAISINS

TOSCANA

3 ⅓ cups all-purpose flour
1 ½ tsp. active dry yeast, dissolved in 1 cup warm water

CONTINUED

This recipe is typical of Florence.

Put the flour in a bowl and knead with the yeast mixture; shape into a loaf and let it rise, covered by a cloth, in a warm place for about 2 hours. ✦ Coarsely chop the rosemary needles. Preheat the oven to 350°F. Grease a baking sheet with 1 tablespoon olive oil. Heat the remaining

Needles from 1 sprig rosemary

¼ cup extra-virgin olive oil

2 oz. lard

1 large egg, beaten

¾ cup sugar

1⅔ cups raisins, soaked in water and drained

olive oil in a saucepan and cook the rosemary needles just until fragrant, then remove from the heat and let cool. When this has cooled add half of it (both rosemary and oil) to the leavened dough, setting aside the other half. Also blend in the lard, egg, ½ cup of the sugar, and raisins. ✦ Knead until smooth then press into the baking sheet (it should be about ½ to ¾ inch thick) then brush with the remaining olive oil mixture and sprinkle with the remaining sugar. ✦ Bake for about 30 minutes or until golden. Serve at room temperature.

SCARSELLA

In various parts of Italy, though especially in Lazio, it was the tradition to make small shaped sweet pastries from the leftover scraps of dough from Easter pizzas—these would be given to children during Easter Monday picnics, while the adults enjoyed the pizzas or various salame themselves, or just relaxed. General traditions abounded, such as decorating the pastries with sugar or peppercorns, and usually a shelled hard-boiled egg formed the center of each, surrounded by the shaped strips of dough. Each area usually had a characteristic shape or form. In Viterbo, for instance, the *scarsella* were most often baked in the shape of money bags or purses with handles; in Maremma, they took the form of a pot-bellied man. Animal shapes were common, too, and included mice and doves.

SCHIACCIUNTA

SWEET FLATBREAD

TOSCANA

10 oz. lard

1⅔ cups flour, plus more as needed

3 large eggs, beaten

1⅔ cups sugar, plus more for dusting

1½ tsp. baking powder

Grated zest of 1 lemon

This recipe is typical of Elba.

Preheat the oven to 350°F. Grease a baking sheet with lard and dust with flour. Stir together the eggs and sugar until blended, then stir in the lard, baking powder, and lemon zest. ✦ Slowly add the flour, constantly stirring until the mixture has a soft consistency. ✦ Press the dough into the pan to a height of about ½ inch. ✦ Bake for about 30 minutes or until golden. Remove from the oven and dust with sugar.

DESSERTS

FLOATING ISLANDS

6 large eggs, separated

4 tbsp. unsalted butter, melted and cooled

1 teaspooon vanilla extract

8 cups whole milk

½ tbsp. all-purpose flour

⅔ cup sugar

½ cup pistachios

Ground cinnamon

You can decorate the serving plate with cookies of your choosing.

Whip the 6 egg whites until stiff, add the butter, then add the vanilla. ✦ Heat 7¾ cups milk in a wide pan and when it bubbles around the edges, spoon in the egg white mixture slowly and carefully so they form small lumps that quickly harden. ✦ Turn off the heat and lift the egg white "islands" out of the pan with a skimmer and set them out to drain. ✦ Whisk the flour and sugar into the milk. ✦ Beat the 6 remaining yolks until thick and pale and whisk them into the milk (which by now should be almost cold). ✦ Grind the pistachios and boil them in the remaining milk; pass the result through a sieve and add it to the milk mixture. ✦ Put the pan back over heat and heat without letting it boil, stirring with a wooden spoon, until it has thickened slightly and coats the back of the spoon. ✦ Arrange the egg white "islands" in soup plates or a large serving bowl and pour the heated milk mixture around them—without submerging them (the egg whites should seem to float)—and dust with cinnamon. Serve immediately.

ANISETTE FRITTERS

For the batter:

5 ½ cups all-purpose flour

5 large eggs

⅔ cup sugar

1 or more tbsp. extra-virgin olive oil

1 tbsp. anisette

Grated zest of 1 lemon

For frying:

Extra-virgin olive oil

For serving:

Vanilla sugar

Alchermes (see note, page 786)

Combine all the batter ingredients and work them together thoroughly to create a light dough. ✦ Form this dough into balls the size of walnuts and set them aside to rest for 30 minutes. ✦ There are two methods of cooking them, in the oven or fried, but in both cases they must first be immersed in boiling water and removed as soon as they float (set them out on a cloth to dry). ✦ To bake them, preheat the oven to 325°F and grease a baking sheet. Arrange on the baking sheet and bake for about 30 minutes, until golden and crisp. ✦ As for frying, heat 2 inches of fat (lard was once used, but today preference goes to olive oil) over moderate heat until golden. While still hot they can be sprinkled with vanilla sugar and *alchermes.*

SWEET CHEESE PASTRIES

1 ¼ cups grated *fiore sardo* cheese

Grated zest of 1 orange

Grated zest of 1 lemon

3 tbsp. *fil'e ferru* (Sardinian grappa)

1 ½ cups all-purpose flour

1 tbsp. lard

Extra-virgin olive oil, for frying

1 ¼ cups *ranzigo* (chestnut honey)

Confectioners' sugar

Put the grated cheese in a bowl, add the orange and lemon zests and the grappa, and knead to obtain a soft dough. ✦ Use the flour and lard to make a dough as in the recipe on page 10, using ¼ cup warm water in place of the eggs and gradually blending in the lard. ✦ When the dough is very elastic roll out a thin sheet (see note, page 212) and cut into disks about 4½ inches in diameter. On half of these put a tablespoon of the cheese mixture; cover with another disk, pressing well to eliminate any air. Finish the edges with a pastry wheel. ✦ Heat 1 inch of olive oil in a wide pan and fry until golden. Drain on paper towels. Meanwhile, heat the honey in a pan until melted. Spoon honey over the pastries and sprinkle with confectioners' sugar.

SEMIFREDDO DI PESCHE ED AMARETTI

PEACH AND AMARETTI SEMIFREDDO

2 lbs. ripe yellow peaches

⅔ cup chopped amaretti

⅔ cup sugar

1 cup heavy cream, whipped

1 large egg white, beaten until stiff

Line a loaf pan with plastic wrap. Peel and pit the peaches, chop them, and put them in a blender with the amaretti and sugar. Purée until smooth, about 2 minutes. ✦ Pour the result into a bowl and fold in the whipped cream and the egg white. ✦ Pour into the loaf pan and freeze for 4 hours. Turn out onto a serving plate, remove the plastic wrap, and serve immediately.

SFOGLIATELLE FROLLE

FILLED COOKIES

FOR 12 SFOGLIATELLE

For the dough:

1 ¼ cups all-purpose flour

½ cup sugar

3 oz. lard

1 large egg yolk, for brushing

CONTINUED

This recipe is typical of Naples.

Form a well with half the flour in a bowl or on a work surface; at the center mix in the sugar, 3 tablespoons water, lard, and the remaining flour, stirring in a little at a time and working small portions of the dough by hand. ✦ When all the flour has been absorbed, knead, working the dough but doing so without pulling on it, so that it will become homogeneous and smooth. Let it rest for 30 minutes. ✦ Preheat the oven to 275°F. Prepare the filling by mixing the ingredients given. ✦ Divide the dough

DESSERTS

For the filling:

1 cup semolina flour

1 cup ricotta

1¼ cups sugar

1 large egg, beaten

½ cup chopped candied citron and orange peel

½ tsp. vanilla extract

2 drops cinnamon oil

Salt

Confectioners' sugar

into 12 equal portions and shape these into ovals about ¼ inch thick. ◆ Divide the filling in 12 portions and put each portion on one of the ovals; fold the dough over the filling, press well to seal the edges, then using a glass (4 to 4½ inches in diameter) or, better, a pastry wheel, cut out the *sfogliatelle* to make them round. ◆ Transfer them to a baking sheet, brush them with egg yolk, and bake in the top of the oven, checking from time to time to make certain they do not burn on the bottom. After about 15 minutes they will be golden; remove from the oven, let cool, and dust with confectioners' sugar.

SFOGLIATINE DI VILLAFRANCA

PUFF PASTRIES

VENETO

½ lb. (1 cup) plus 2 tbsp. unsalted butter, softened

1½ cups all-purpose flour

2 large egg yolks, beaten

1 cup sugar

This recipe is typical of Villafranca Veronese.

Preheat the oven to 400°F. Melt 6 tablespoons of the butter, mix in the flour, and add as much water as needed to make a soft dough (about 3 tablespoons). Knead the dough to make it smooth and homogeneous. Shape it into a ball and let it rest in a cool place under a cloth for 10 minutes. ◆ Roll out the dough to the thickness of about ¼ inch. ◆ Divide the remaining butter in 6 equal portions (3 tablespoons each). Spread a portion of the butter on the sheet of dough, let it rest 5 minutes, then fold over the dough and roll it out with the rolling pin to form a sheet about ¼ inch thick. ◆ Spread another portion of butter across the sheet of dough, fold it over, and again roll it out. ◆ Repeat this operation four more times, using the remaining portions of butter. ◆ Then roll out the dough in a very thin sheet (about ⅛ inch) and cut it in doughnut shapes, using a round mold to make the outer ring and a small one to make the hole in the middle. ◆ Arrange these rings on a baking sheet and brush with the 2 egg yolks. ◆ Sprinkle with sugar and bake until puffed up and golden.

FRIED DOUGH KNOTS

EMILIA-ROMAGNA

1⅔ cups all-purpose flour

2 large eggs

½ cup sugar

Grated zest of 1½ lemons

4 tbsp. (¼ cup) unsalted butter

2 tbsp. rum (or to taste)

Olive oil, for frying

Salt

Confectioners' sugar

This sweet is eaten during the Carnival season in Bologna. In other places they are called *galani, cenci, fiocchi, nastrini di monache, donzellini,* and so on. Food writer Waverley Root reports that *sfrappole* were considered so "inexcusably luxurious" that they were banned by a sumptuary law in 1294.

Use the flour and eggs to make a dough as in the recipe on page 751, adding the sugar, lemon zest, butter, rum, and a pinch of salt with the eggs. Let the dough rest 30 minutes. ✦ Roll out the dough to form a sheet about ¹⁄₁₆ of an inch thick; using a toothed pastry wheel cut this into strips 6 inches long and 1½ inches wide. ✦ Tie the strips into knots. Heat 2 inches of olive in a saucepan and fry them until golden. ✦ Drain on paper towels and serve warm, dusted with confectioners' sugar.

SGONFIOTTI ALLA FRUTTA | FRUIT RAVIOLI

ALTO ADIGE

For the dough:

3 cups rye flour, plus more as needed

1 large egg yolk

¼ lb. (½ cup) unsalted butter, softened

2 tbsp. heavy cream

2 tbsp. milk (as much as needed)

Salt

For the filling:

1 cup red currants

1 cup grated apples

2 tbsp. breadcrumbs

Lard (or olive oil), for frying

Confectioners' sugar

Use the flour and egg yolk to make a dough as in the recipe on page 10, adding the butter, cream, milk, and a pinch of salt with the egg yolk. Let it rest for about 1 hour. ✦ Roll out the dough to form a very thin sheet (see note, page 212). ✦ Prepare the filling by combining the currants, apples, and breadcrumbs until blended. ✦ Cut out a small portion of the dough to make a disk about 2 to 3 inches in diameter, put a little of the filling in the middle of this, and fold it over to form a large ravioli. Proceed in this way until all the dough and filling have been used up. ✦ Heat 1 inch of lard (or olive oil); when it is hot fry the ravioli until golden. Drain on paper towels. Dust with confectioners' sugar and serve hot.

DESSERTS

GRIDDLE CAKES

FRIULI-VENEZIA GIULIA

1 ¼ cups all-purpose flour
4 large eggs
1 tbsp. sugar
Grated zest of 1 lemon
¼ cup milk (or as needed)
Extra-virgin olive oil
Salt

Serve these with black currant jam or warm raspberry sauce.

Combine the flour, eggs, sugar, lemon zest, and a pinch of salt in a bowl and add enough milk to obtain a batter that is not too thick. Stir it well to blend. ✦ Heat 1 tablespoon olive oil in a skillet and pour in about ¼ cup of the batter and cook until set. Repeat with the remaining batter and olive oil. Serve warm.

LEMON SORBET

CAMPANIA

1 lb. lemons
1 ½ cups sugar
3 large egg whites, beaten until stiff (optional)

Serve the sorbet in champagne flutes for an elegant presentation.

Remove the zest from 3 of the lemons and set aside. Squeeze the lemons and strain their juice. ✦ Make a syrup by mixing the sugar and lemon zest with 3 cups water in a saucepan. Bring to a boil, then simmer for 5 to 6 minutes. Remove from the heat and let cool completely. ✦ When this cools strain it, then stir in the lemon juice. Pour into a loaf pan. ✦ Put this in the freezer, removing it to stir it from time to time to avoid the formation of ice crystals. ✦ When it begins to solidify you can fold in the beaten egg whites to make it more frothy. Freeze until nearly solid, about 4 hours.

FRUITCAKE 2

EMILIA-ROMAGNA

For the filling:
1 ⅓ cups honey
1 ½ cups chopped walnuts
⅔ cup toasted and chopped almonds
¾ cup pine nuts
⅔ cup chopped citron
1 ½ cups chopped biscuits (zwieback)

CONTINUED

This is an ancient sweet, dating back to Roman times and even mentioned in Petronius's famous "Trimalchio's Feast." In the area of Reggio its birthplace is Brescello, the oldest Gallo-Roman city in Emilia. References to *spongata* can be found in local records from the fifteenth and sixteenth centuries when it was variously prepared for illustrious guests or banned, during periods of famine, because it was considered too luxurious. Elsewhere it is usually made at Christmastime, but at Brescello it can be found throughout the year, looked upon as a local specialty.

Heat the honey with ½ cup water in a large saucepan; bring to a boil and let it boil for 2 minutes. Add the other

1 tsp. ground cinnamon

½ tsp. ground cloves

½ tsp. grated nutmeg

1⅔ cups apricot jam

For the dough:

4½ cups pastry flour

½ tsp. baking powder

½ lb. (2 sticks) plus 2 tbsp. unsalted butter

1½ cups honey (or sugar)

1 large egg yolk

½ cup white wine, or as needed, such as Trebbiano or Albana

Confectioners' sugar

filling ingredients and refrigerate for 15 days, stirring every day. ✦ Preheat the oven to 350°F. Mix the flour and baking powder to make a dough as in the recipe on page 751, using the butter, honey, egg yolk, and wine in place of the eggs. ✦ Roll out the dough to form two sheets about ¼ inch thick, piercing them with a fork. Use one to line a baking pan and spread the filling across it. Cover with the other sheet. ✦ Bake for about 30 minutes. Sprinkle with confectioners' sugar before serving.

SPUMINI

BAKED MERINGUES

EMILIA-ROMAGNA

Butter, for the baking sheet

4 large egg whites

1⅔ cups sugar

Preheat the oven to 325°F. Butter a baking sheet. Heat the egg whites and sugar in a saucepan until the sugar is dissolved, then beat them together with a whisk. ✦ As soon as the mixture becomes firm, after about 10 minutes, transfer it to a pastry bag and pipe out walnut-size lumps of the mixture well spaced on the baking sheet. ✦ Bake until the *spumini* are thoroughly dried, as long as 1 hour if necessary.

STACCADENTI

ALMOND BISCOTTI 3

BASILICATA

Olive oil, for the pan

1½ cups all-purpose flour

1¼ cups sugar

1½ cups whole blanched almonds

4 large eggs, beaten

It's true, the Italian name means "tooth-pullers."

Preheat the oven to 350°F. Grease a square cake pan. Mix the flour, sugar, whole almonds, and eggs until blended. ✦ Pour into the pan, leveling it off with the back of a knife. ✦ Bake until golden. Remove the pan from the oven and break up the mixture to the size of cookies, then return to the oven to complete the baking, until crisp.

DESSERTS

HONEY SQUARES

Olive oil

1 ¼ cups honey

4 cups all-purpose flour, or as needed

This recipe is typical of the Viterbo area.

Preheat the oven to 400°F. Grease a baking sheet with olive oil. In a pan, melt the honey with ¼ cup warm water and stir in 2 tablespoons olive oil. Stir in as much flour as needed to obtain a dough that is softer than normal bread dough. ✦ Roll out this dough to form a sheet about ¼ inch thick. Using a floured knife or a pastry wheel cut this into strips about 2 inches wide then cut these cross-wise to form squares. ✦ Arrange these on the baking sheet and bake until they are slightly blond and firm.

FRIED SMALL DUMPLINGS

For the dough:

3 large eggs, beaten

1 ¼ cups sugar

3 cups all-purpose flour, plus more as needed

¼ lb. (1 stick) unsalted butter

1 ½ tsp. active dry yeast

Grated zest of 1 lemon

2 tbsp. grappa

Salt

For the filling:

⅓ cup sugar

4 tbsp. (¼ cup) unsalted butter

1 tbsp. grappa

Pinch grated nutmeg

1 ⅔ cups ground walnuts

½ cup raisins

½ cup chopped pine nuts

½ cup breadcrumbs

For frying and serving:

Lard (or peanut oil) for frying

Superfine sugar

This recipe is typical of the Natisone-Stregna valleys. A similar recipe from the same area is made with potatoes in the dough and is boiled not fried.

Beat the eggs and sugar until pale and thick, then gradually add the flour, butter, yeast, lemon zest, grappa, and a pinch of salt. Knead to obtain a smooth and homogeneous dough. ✦ Roll out the dough to the thickness of 1 inch. Cut it into disks (3 to 4 inches in diameter). ✦ Combine the indicated ingredients to make the filling and put a small lump of it to the side of each disk. Fold the disks in half to cover. Using the tines of a fork push down the edges to seal. ✦ Heat 1 inch of lard (you may prefer to use peanut oil) and fry until they are golden brown. Drain on paper towels. Arrange, hot or at room temperature, on a serving plate and sprinkle with superfine sugar.

CHERRY STRUDEL

FRIULI-VENEZIA GIULIA

For the filling:

1 lb. ripe cherries, pitted

1 cup sugar

Juice and grated zest of 1 lemon

5 tbsp. (¼ cup plus 1 tbsp.)
unsalted butter

⅔ cup breadcrumbs
or crumbled biscuits

Pinch ground cinnamon

For the dough:

1½ cups all-purpose flour

1¼ cups sugar

2 tbsp. sunflower-seed oil
(or 3 tbsp. butter)

Salt

Do not make this dish if cherries are not in season since the result would not have the right flavor and the liquid in unripe cherries would ruin the dough.

Preheat the oven to 350°F. Combine the cherries with the sugar, lemon juice, and zest. ✦ Heat the butter in a pan and toast the bread until golden, then add both to the mixture along with the cinnamon. ✦ Mix the flour and sugar and use them to make a dough as in the recipe on page 10, using the oil and 6 tablespoons water in place of the eggs. ✦ Roll out the dough to a thin sheet (about ¹⁄₁₆ inch) and spread the filling along one long side. Starting with that side, roll up to form a log. Place on a baking sheet and bake for 40 minutes.

APPLE STRUDEL

ALTO ADIGE

For the dough:

1⅔ cups all-purpose flour

2 or 3 tbsp. extra-virgin olive oil

Salt

For the filling:

3 tbsp. unsalted butter, plus more
for brushing the outside
of the strudels

½ cup breadcrumbs

4½ lbs. apples, peeled,
cored, and cut in thin slices

1¼ cups raisins

⅔ cup pine nuts

⅔ cup sugar

3 tbsp. rum

1 level tsp. cinnamon

Pinch ground cloves

Confectioners' sugar

Use the flour to prepare a pasta dough as in the recipe on page 10, using the oil and ½ cup water in place of the eggs. ✦ Divide the dough in three parts, shape them into balls, grease with olive oil, and set aside to rest, covered with a cloth, for about 30 minutes. ✦ At the end of that time preheat the oven to 425°F. Butter a baking sheet or line it with parchment. Roll out one of the balls to form a sheet as thin as possible, almost transparent. Lay this out on a cloth and roll it out farther, giving it a square shape. ✦ At this point heat the butter in a pan and sauté the breadcrumbs. Spread one third of the mixture across two-thirds of the square of dough, leaving a strip free, which should be greased with olive oil. ✦ Proceed in this way with the other two balls of dough and remaining breadcrumbs. ✦ Mix the apple slices, raisins, pine nuts, sugar, rum, cinnamon, and cloves. (Measure out the cinnamon with care since it should not overwhelm the other flavors.) ✦ Sprinkle out this filling across the part of the dough covered with breadcrumbs.

DESSERTS

Then, lifting an edge of the cloth from the side of the filling, roll up the strudel on itself. The area greased with olive oil will serve as the final, closing layer. Cut away any extra dough on the ends that is not spread with filling. ✦ Put the three strudels on the baking sheet, leaving space between them. Melt the remaining butter and brush on the strudels. Bake for 30 to 40 minutes or until they are golden. Before serving sprinkle with confectioners' sugar.

STRUFFOLI

FRIED PASTRIES

FOR
6 PERSONS

CAMPANIA

For the dough:
3 ⅓ cups all-purpose flour
3 large eggs plus 3 large egg yolks
⅔ cup sugar
3 oz. (6 tbsp.) unsalted butter
Salt
Olive oil, for frying

For the finishing:
1 ½ cups honey
⅔ cup sugar
⅔ cup candy sprinkles
Candied citron peel
Candied orange slices

This recipe is typical of Naples.

Use the flour and whole eggs to prepare a pasta dough as in the recipe on page 751, adding the yolks, sugar, and butter with the eggs. Knead the dough, form it into a ball, and let it rest, covered, for 2 hours. ✦ On a floured work surface pull off small bits of the dough and roll them to form cylinders about the size of a piece of chalk. Cut these in lengths somewhat larger than chickpeas. ✦ Heat 1 inch of olive oil over moderate heat and fry the dough until golden. Drain on paper towels. ✦ Put the honey and sugar in a saucepan with ¼ cup water and heat until it becomes a brownish-gold syrup. ✦ Turn off the heat (but leave the pan on the burner) and pour in the *struffoli*, stirring well to coat them. Transfer them to a serving plate and by hand or with a wooden spoon work them into the shape of a dome. ✦ Top with sprinkles and decorate with thin slices of citron peel and candied orange slices.

SUSAMIELLI

SPICED HONEY TWISTS

CAMPANIA

Unsalted butter
1 ⅓ cups honey
1 ¼ cups sugar
CONTINUED

This recipe is typical of Naples.

Preheat the oven to 350°F. Grease a baking sheet with butter. Heat the honey and the sugar until melted. Form the flour into a well in a bowl or on the work surface and add the honey mixture. ✦ Add the cinnamon, nutmeg, and cloves and knead well. ✦ Shape this into sticks about

3⅓ cups all-purpose flour
Pinch ground cinnamon
Pinch grated nutmeg
Pinch ground cloves

4 inches long, twist these into S shapes, and lay out on the baking sheet. ✦ Bake for 30 minutes or until golden.

JAM-FILLED HORSESHOE COOKIES

SUSUMELLI

ABRUZZO

½ cup extra-virgin olive oil
¼ cup white wine, such as Trebbiano
1 tbsp. sugar
2 cups all-purpose flour, plus more as needed
1½ cups grape jam, or as needed
Confectioners' sugar

Preheat the oven to 350°F. Grease a baking sheet with olive oil. Mix the olive oil, wine, and sugar. Use the flour to make a dough as in the recipe on page 10, using the wine mixture in place of the eggs. ✦ Roll this out into a thin sheet (see note, page 212) and cut into rectangles (6 inches by 2½ inches). ✦ Spoon a line of jam down the center of each square and then fold it over like a long ravioli. Twist these into horseshoe shapes and arrange on the baking sheet. ✦ Bake for 30 minutes or until golden. Sprinkle with confectioners' sugar as soon as they are taken from the oven.

GLAZED S COOKIES

TARALLI

SICILIA

For the dough:
4 oz. lard
4½ cups pastry flour
¾ cup sugar
2 tbsp. baking powder
4 tbsp. anise seeds
10 large egg yolks
2 tbsp. milk, or as needed

For the glaze:
3 large egg whites, beaten stiff but not dry
1 cup confectioners' sugar, or as needed
1 tsp. lemon juice

Preheat the oven to 325°F. Grease a baking sheet with lard. Combine the flour, sugar, lard, baking powder, anise, egg yolks, and a little milk to make a somewhat soft and smooth dough. ✦ Shape this into cylinders about 1 to 1½ inches thick and cut them into lengths of 2 to 2½ inches. ✦ Immerse these cookies, a few at a time, in lightly salted boiling water, removing them as soon as they float. Drain and shape into S shapes, then arrange them on the baking sheet. ✦ Bake for about a half hour, paying attention not to let them take on too much color. ✦ Meanwhile prepare the glaze. Mix the egg whites, confectioners' sugar, and lemon juice to make a thick but spreadable glaze. Brush this on the cookies as soon as they are baked, then return them to the oven to dry with the heat turned off but still warm.

DESSERTS

BRAIDED COOKIES

TARALLI DI SORIANO

CALABRIA

Extra-virgin olive oil
1 lb. bread dough (see page 13)
2 large eggs
2 tbsp. lard
⅔ cup honey

Preheat the oven to 350°F. Grease a baking sheet with olive oil. Combine the dough with the eggs, lard, and honey until blended and shape into small logs. ✦ Shape these into doughnuts or figure eights and immerse them for a few seconds, a few at a time, in a pot of boiling water until they float. ✦ Arrange them on the baking sheet and bake until golden.

CHIETI COOKIES

TARALLUCCI
ALLA CHIETINA

ABRUZZO

1⅔ cups all-purpose flour
1 cup sugar
1 cup extra-virgin olive oil
Dry red wine
Salt

Shape the flour into a well in a bowl or on the work surface and put in the middle the sugar, olive oil, and a pinch of salt. Add some wine a little at a time to obtain an elastic dough. ✦ Form the dough into a ball, wrap it in a cloth, and let it rest 30 minutes. ✦ Preheat the oven to 350°F. Grease a baking sheet with olive oil. Flour a work surface. Divide the dough in pieces and put them on the floured work surface. Roll out each piece by hand into the shape of a cylinder about 1 inch thick and 8 inches long; join the ends to make rings. Arrange the *tarallucci* on the baking sheet and bake for about 20 minutes.

ALMOND NOUGAT 2

TORRONE

MOLISE

1⅓ cups honey
5 large egg whites
2½ cups sugar
2 tsp. vanilla extract
Grated zest of ½ mandarin orange
3 cups almonds, toasted
As many wafers as desired
or 2 sheets of pastry dough, baked

This recipe is typical of Santo Stefano.

Liquefy the honey in the top of a double boiler. Remove from the heat and let it cool to lukewarm. Beat the egg whites until stiff, then fold into the honey. ✦ Return the mixture to the double boiler and cook for 2 hours, stirring with a wooden spoon until it becomes dense and shiny. (Be sure to check the water level in the bottom pot from time to time so it does not dry out.) ✦ Meanwhile, prepare a syrup by heating the sugar with ½ cup water for about 20 minutes, or until it begins to turn golden and is at the brittle thread stage, 300°F to 310°F on a candy thermometer. (To see if it is done put a drop of the liquid sugar on a spoon and dip the spoon in a glass of water or put it under running water from a faucet. If the thread of sugar does not drop off the spoon but is so solidified that it breaks, the syrup is ready.) ✦ Stir the syrup into the honey mixture. Cook the two together for a few minutes, then add the vanilla, mandarin zest, and almonds. ✦ Spread the sheet of wafers or pastry dough on a baking sheet and pour the mixture over. Wet your hands (so as not to burn or to stick) and press the mixture into an even layer. ✦ Let cool completely, then cover it with another sheet of wafers or pastry and press well.

CHRISTMAS NOUGAT

TORRONE DI NATALE

SICILIA

Olive oil
3 cups blanched almonds
2 cups sugar
Candy sprinkles

Grease a work surface with olive oil. Coarsely chop the almonds, then combine them with the sugar in a pan over low heat and, stirring continuously with a wooden spoon, cook until the mixture has taken on a reddish-brown color. ✦ Immediately pour the mixture out onto the work surface. ✦ Level the surface with the dampened blade of a large knife. Let this cool, then cut in pieces of the desired size. Decorate as desired with sprinkles.

SESAME NOUGAT

TORRONE DI SEMI
DI SESAMO

CALABRIA

Olive oil
1 ¼ cups honey
½ cup sesame seeds
(or as many as desired)
½ cup almonds, shelled,
toasted, and chopped

Grease a cutting board or work surface with olive oil or line it with parchment. Put the honey in a saucepan and heat it over low heat until thinned. ✦ Immediately add the seeds and almonds, stirring continuously with a wooden spoon until the honey is a dark caramel color. ✦ Pour out on the cutting board or a marble surface and let it cool, then cut in pieces of the desired shape.

ORANGE CAKE

TORTA ALL'ARANCIA

SICILIA

5 large eggs, separated
1¼ cups sugar
1⅔ cups all-purpose flour
3 oz. (6 tbsp.) unsalted butter
Grated zest of 1 orange
2¼ tsp. baking powder
Juice of 4 oranges, strained
2 tbsp. orange liqueur
½ cup confectioners' sugar

Garnish with slightly caramelized orange slices, if desired.

Preheat the oven to 350°F. Make a dough with the egg yolks, sugar, flour, butter, and orange zest. Blend in the baking powder. Beat the egg whites until stiff and fold them into the mixture. ✦ Spread this into a cake pan, place on a baking sheet, and bake until set. Remove and let it cool. ✦ Blend the orange juice, orange liqueur, and confectioners' sugar to make a thin glaze. Drizzle over the cake and serve.

ALMOND TART

TORTA BIANCA

EMILIA-ROMAGNA

Butter, to grease the pan
Flour, to flour the pan
Pastry for a single-crust pie
1⅔ cups blanched almonds
1⅔ cups sugar
½ cup anisette
Grated zest of 1 lemon
3 large egg whites
1 oz. (1 square) semisweet chocolate

This recipe is typical of Reggio Emilia.

Preheat the oven to 400°F. Butter and flour a 9-inch springform cake pan, then line the bottom and sides with pastry. ✦ Finely chop the almonds, then combine them in a bowl with the sugar, anisette, and lemon zest. ✦ Separately whip the egg whites until stiff then fold them into the mixture. ✦ Grate the chocolate square over the pastry then pour in the almond mixture and level off the top. ✦ Bake until the filling is set, about 45 minutes.

CAPRI CHOCOLATE-ALMOND CAKE

FOR 8 PERSONS

TORTA CAPRESE

CAMPANIA

¼ lb. (1 stick) plus 6 tbsp. unsalted butter
1¼ cups sugar
6 large eggs, beaten
1⅔ cups chopped almonds
2 oz. (2 squares) semisweet chocolate, finely chopped
3 tbsp. Strega liqueur
1 tsp. baking powder
Confectioners' sugar

Preheat the oven to 350°F. Butter a 10-inch round pan. Cream the sugar with the butter until fluffy, then add the eggs and blend well. Stir in the almonds, chocolate, and liqueur; thoroughly blend all the ingredients, then add the baking powder. ✦ Pour the mixture into the pan. Bake for 50 to 55 minutes, or until set. When done invert on a serving plate and remove the pan. Let it cool, then dust with the confectioners' sugar before serving.

| # PISA-STYLE RICE TART

TOSCANA

For the dough:

4 cups all-purpose flour

¾ cup sugar

2 ½ sticks (1 ¼ cups) unsalted butter

2 large eggs plus 2 large egg yolks

Salt

For the filling:

6 cups milk

¾ cup sugar

1 ¼ cups rice

⅔ cup unsweetened cocoa powder

¾ cup raisins

½ cup pine nuts

¾ cup diced candied fruit

Grated zest of 1 lemon

Confectioners' sugar

This recipe is typical of Pisa.

Mix the flour, sugar, and a pinch of salt, then blend in the butter and whole eggs plus 1 egg yolk. Let the dough rest for 20 minutes. ✦ Meanwhile prepare the filling, bringing the milk and sugar to a boil in a saucepan. Add the rice and cook until the liquid has been absorbed and the rice is soft. Stir in the cocoa powder, raisins, pine nuts, candied fruit, and lemon zest. Let it cool. ✦ Preheat the oven to 400°F. Roll out the dough to make a sheet about ⅛ inch thick and use it to line a pie pan, letting the extra dough hang over the sides. Put in a little over an inch of the filling. Cut the remaining dough into strips and place these all around the pan. ✦ The filling can remain exposed in the middle or it can be covered with strips of dough. Brush the dough strips with the remaining egg yolk and bake for 20 minutes. Let it cool, then sprinkle it with confectioners' sugar.

TORTA COLONNE | # CHERRY-ALMOND TART

PUGLIA

1 ¼ cups all-purpose flour

1 ¼ cups sugar

1 tbsp. unsweetened cocoa powder

1 tbsp. ground cinnamon

1 ½ cups chopped almonds

¼ lb. (1 stick) plus 6 tbsp. unsalted butter

2 large eggs, 1 separated

1 tsp. vanilla extract

1 tbsp. cherry liqueur or kirschwasser

1 cup sour cherry jam, or as needed

Whisk together the dry ingredients, then work in the almonds, butter, 1 egg, vanilla, and cherry liqueur to form a smooth dough. Let it rest for 1 hour in the refrigerator. ✦ Preheat the oven to 350°F. Roll out two-thirds of the dough on a baking sheet, cover with a layer of cherry jam, then cover with the remaining dough cut in strips. ✦ Brush with the remaining egg yolk and bake for 1 hour. Serve cold.

DESSERTS

PEAR TART

1⅔ cups all-purpose flour

1 cup sugar

2 large egg yolks

¼ lb. (1 stick) plus 3 tbsp. butter, melted

1 ½ cups red wine, such as Bonarda or Gutturnio

6 pears, peeled, cored, and cut in thin slices

A few whole cloves

2 or 3 pieces cinnamon stick

Salt

The tart comes into its true fragrance 24 hours after being baked.

Combine the flour with ⅔ cup sugar, the egg yolks, butter, and a pinch of salt. Knead the dough well and set aside to rest for about 30 minutes in a cool spot (even the refrigerator). ✦ Preheat the oven to 350°F. Butter and flour a pie pan. Combine the red wine, pears, 3 tablespoons sugar, cloves, and cinnamon in a pan. Simmer at low heat so the wine will not caramelize and the pears will soften without coming apart. Remove the cloves. ✦ Roll out the dough to form 2 sheets about ⅛ inch thick. Use one sheet to line the pie pan. Over this dough arrange the pears, distributing them evenly. ✦ Cover with the other sheet of dough or cut the sheet into strips and arrange them across it in a lattice pattern. ✦ Bake for about 30 minutes, until golden, then let it remain in the oven with the heat off for another 10 minutes.

ALMOND CAKE 1

8 large eggs, separated

1 ¼ cups sugar

½ cup almond liqueur

½ cup finely chopped almonds

4 oz. crumbled dry bread (or ½ cup breadcrumbs)

This recipe is typical of Cremona.

Preheat the oven to 300°F. Beat the egg yolks with the sugar until thick and pale, then add the liqueur and almonds. Stir in the bread. Whip 5 egg whites until stiff, then fold into the mixture. ✦ Pour into a cake pan and bake until set, about 25 minutes.

WALNUT CARAMEL PIE

For the dough:

¾ cup finely chopped walnuts

1 cup all-purpose flour

¼ lb. (1 stick) unsalted butter

CONTINUED

Begin the dough by combining the walnuts with the flour. ✦ Separately work the butter and the sugar together with the egg yolk; add this to the flour and nuts without kneading it too much. Set this aside in a cool place for 2 hours to rest. ✦ Preheat the oven to 350°F. Heat the sugar and lemon juice over medium heat until golden.

⅓ cup sugar
1 large egg yolk

For the filling:
2 cups sugar
Juice of 2 lemons
1⅔ cups heavy cream
⅓ cup honey
2 tbsp. black coffee
2¼ cups finely chopped walnuts

Bring the cream to a boil, then mix in the honey and coffee; whisk this mixture into the sugar mixture. Stir in the walnuts and let the mixture cool. ✦ Roll out the dough to form two sheets. Use one to cover the bottom and sides of a pie pan. Spread the walnut mixture over this, leveling it off, then cover with the second sheet of dough, pinching the edges to seal. ✦ Bake for about 30 minutes, or until the dough is dark golden.

TORTA DI AMANDOLE

ALMOND CAKE 2

EMILIA-ROMAGNA

1½ lbs. (2 sticks) plus 4 tbsp.
unsalted butter
⅔ cup finely chopped almonds
1⅔ cups sugar
3 large egg yolks
3⅓ cups all-purpose flour
Grated zest of 1 lemon

This recipe is typical of Castell'Arquato.

Preheat the oven to 350°F. Butter a pie pan. Toss the almonds with half the sugar and spread on a baking sheet. Toast until lightly caramelized, then let cool. ✦ In a bowl cream the butter and the remaining sugar until fluffy, then add the egg yolks, flour, and lemon zest. Stir in the toasted almonds, working all these ingredients to blend them well. ✦ Pour the mixture into the pie pan and bake for about 45 minutes, or until set. ✦ Remove from the oven and let rest, still in the pan, 10 to 15 minutes before turning it out and serving.

TORTA DI FARINA
DI GRANO SARACENO

BUCKWHEAT CAKE

ALTO ADIGE

1¼ cups (½ lb. plus 4 tbsp.)
unsalted butter, softened
3 tbsp. all-purpose flour
1⅔ cups sugar
6 large eggs, separated
1⅔ cups buckwheat flour
2¼ tsp. baking powder
1 cup red currant jam
1½ cups heavy cream

The most recent version of this most excellent cake includes a quantity of ground almonds equal to the amount of flour. To make a cake with a 12-inch diameter use 1½ cups buckwheat flour, the same quantity almonds, ½ pound (2 sticks) plus 2 tablespoons butter, and 1½ cups sugar.

Preheat the oven to 350°F. Butter and flour a 9-inch cake pan. Cream the butter until it's fluffy, then slowly add the sugar and, one at a time, the egg yolks, mixing well after each addition to make the sugar dissolve completely. ✦ Sift the buckwheat flour together with the all-purpose flour and the baking powder then add to the butter mixture 1 tablespoon at a time. ✦ Whip the egg whites stiff and fold them in. ✦ Pour the dough into the cake pan and bake for about 40 minutes. If a toothpick inserted comes out clean the cake is done. ✦ Let the cake cool completely, then cut it in half and spread the bottom half with the jam. Whip the cream until stiff, then spread over the reassembled cake.

ALMOND CAKE 3

LOMBARDIA

1 cup blanched almonds
1½ sticks (12 tbsp.) unsalted butter
1⅔ cups all-purpose flour
1 cup sugar
1 large egg yolk
Grated zest of ½ lemon
¼ tsp. baking powder

Tradition calls for making crosswise lines across the surface of the cake with a fork before putting it in the oven.

Preheat the oven to 400°F. Finely chop the almonds. ✦ Heat 2 tablespoons of the butter in a pan and as soon as it changes color add the almonds and give them a quick toasting. Remove from the heat and set aside. ✦ Mix together the flour, remaining butter, sugar, egg yolk, lemon zest, and baking powder. Fold in the almonds. ✦ Put the mixture in a baking pan and bake for about 30 minutes, until golden.

✦ **LOCAL TRADITION** ✦

TORTA DI FARINA GIALLA

This cornmeal cake from Lombardia was once a traditional sweet treat for children around the holidays and is distinguished by its use of a larger-than-usual amount of natural yeast, which is the leftover yeast from making homemade bread. This extra yeast made these cakes lighter and crustier than similar recipes. To make the cake, cornmeal, rye flour, and all-purpose flour were mixed with sugar, water, and the natural yeast. Raisins, ripe figs, and salt were added and the cakes would be baked in several small loaves at a high temperature, as though baking whole-wheat bread.

APPLE TART
WITH MOSTARDA

Unsalted butter and flour,
for the pan

For the short pastry:

1⅔ cups all-purpose flour

3 large egg yolks

1 cup sugar

¼ lb. (1 stick) plus 3 tbsp.
unsalted butter, softened
and cut into pieces

Grated zest of 1 lemon

Salt

For the filling:

8 apples, peeled,
cored, and chopped

2 tbsp. sugar

2 tbsp. *mostarda di carpi*
(see note)

When serving, top each slice with a scoop of apple or vanilla ice cream and a few fresh apple slices. *Mostarda di Carpi* is a sweet-style *mostarda*, fruit preserves in grape must.

Butter and flour a 9-inch pie pan. Use the flour and egg yolks to make a dough as in the recipe on page 751, adding the sugar, butter, salt, and lemon zest with the egg yolks. ✦ Refrigerate for about 30 minutes. ✦ Meanwhile prepare the filling. Put the apples and sugar in a saucepan with 2 tablespoons water. Cook for 10 minutes then add the *mostarda*. ✦ Roll out the short pastry on the work surface to about ¼ inch thick. Setting aside one section to use as the top crust, use the pastry to line the pie pan. ✦ Fill the pastry with the apple mixture and cover with the remaining sheet of dough, closing the edges tightly. ✦ Bake until golden, about 40 minutes.

TORTA DI MELE E PERE

APPLE AND PEAR CAKE

¼ lb. (1 stick) unsalted butter

1 cup all-purpose flour

1 large egg

1¼ cups sugar

1½ tsp. baking powder

Grated zest of 1 lemon

1¼ cups milk, or as needed

2 lbs. apples, peeled,
cored, and thinly sliced

1¼ lbs. pears, peeled,
cored, and thinly sliced

Preheat the oven to 400°F. Butter and flour a cake pan. Melt 5 tablespoons of the butter. Mix the flour, egg, melted butter, ½ cup plus 2 tablespoons sugar, baking powder, lemon zest, and as much milk as needed to make a soft dough. ✦ Roll out this dough about ½ inch thick and use it to cover the bottom of the cake pan. ✦ Spread the fruit slices over the dough, dust with the remaining sugar, and dot with the remaining butter. ✦ Bake and after 15 minutes lower the heat to 350°F. The cake should require a good hour in the oven to permit the dough to cook, the fruit to blend, and the sugar and butter to form a light crust on the top. Serve warm.

DESSERTS

HAZELNUT CAKE

PIEMONTE

¼ lb. (1 stick) butter, softened

1⅔ cups shelled hazelnuts

1 cup sugar

1¼ cups all-purpose flour

3 large eggs, beaten

½ cup coffee

½ cup milk

1 tbsp. extra-virgin olive oil

2 tbsp. rum

½ tsp. vanilla extract

1½ tsp. baking powder

This recipe is typical of the Langhe area.

Preheat the oven to 350°F. Butter a cake pan. Spread the hazelnuts in an even layer on a baking sheet, then toast until fragrant and lightly golden, about 7 minutes. Rub the hazelnuts in a dish towel to loosen the skins, then remove the skins. Let cool slightly and chop them. ✦ Increase the oven temperature to 400°F. Mix the sugar and flour and add the nuts. Stir in the eggs, coffee, milk, olive oil, rum, vanilla, and baking powder until blended. Blend in the butter. ✦ Spread the mixture in the cake pan; it should have a thickness of ¾ inch. ✦ Bake for 30 minutes. Serve at room temperature.

SWEET POTATO CAKE

VENETO

Olive oil and breadcrumbs, for the pan

4 large sweet potatoes

½ cup all-purpose flour

3 large apples, peeled, cored, and sliced

⅔ cup chopped dried figs

½ cup milk

⅔ cup raisins

4 tbsp. sugar

1 tbsp. honey

2 large eggs

3 tbsp. anisette (or rum or plum brandy)

Salt

If you wish you can decorate the baked cake with orange and lemon peels and citrus flowers. Anisette is a liqueur flavored with anise seeds. If you do not have it, you could substitute 1 tablespoon of crushed aniseed.

Preheat the oven to 350°F. Grease a cake pan with olive oil and dust with breadcrumbs. Boil the sweet potatoes until soft, then peel them. Crush them by hand, then mix them in a bowl with the other ingredients in order. Pour into the pan and bake until set, about 1 hour.

OLD-FASHIONED RICE PUDDING CAKE

VALLE D'AOSTA

¼ cup (4 tbsp.) unsalted butter
½ cup breadcrumbs
1½ cups rice
4 cups milk
1 cup sugar
Grated zest of 1 lemon
½ cup raisins, softened in warm water, dried, and lightly floured
2 large eggs, beaten
Salt

The cake can be eaten warm or cold. This recipe is typical of Aosta.

Preheat the oven to 375°F. Butter a cake pan and sprinkle with breadcrumbs. Cook the rice in milk and a pinch of salt, stirring to keep it from sticking to the bottom of the pan. ✦ When the rice is done add 3 tablespoons of the butter, the sugar, lemon zest, raisins, a pinch of salt, and the eggs. Mix with care. ✦ Pour the rice mixture into the pan. Dust with the remaining breadcrumbs and dot with butter. ✦ Bake for 20 minutes or until golden.

BAKED RICE CUSTARD FROM CARRARE

TOSCANA

Butter and flour, for the pan
1 cup rice
15 large eggs
2 cups sugar
4 cups milk
Grated zest of 1 lemon
Salt

Preheat the oven to 350°F. Butter and flour a cake pan. Boil the rice in lightly salted water to cover for 5 minutes then set aside. ✦ Beat the eggs and sugar until pale and thick, then add a pinch of salt. Gradually whisk in the milk and lemon zest. ✦ Spread the cooked rice across the bottom of the pan and pour over the milk mixture. ✦ Bake for about 50 minutes.

RICE PUDDING CAKE

EMILIA-ROMAGNA

4 tbsp. unsalted butter
2 cups milk
⅔ cup sugar
Grated zest of 1 lemon
1¼ cups rice
3 large eggs
½ cup chopped candied citron
½ cup chopped almonds
Maraschino liqueur

The *addobbi* (sacred church vessels and statuary) were celebrated with a procession in the parishes of Bologna every 10 years in June and the windows along the streets down which the procession moved were decorated.

Preheat the oven to 400°F. Butter a round cake pan. Heat the milk with 2 cups water, the sugar, lemon zest, and a little salt; when it boils add the rice and cook until it has absorbed the liquid. ✦ Add the eggs, butter, candied citron, and almonds. ✦ Pour into the pan and bake for 30 minutes. Let cool slightly, then cut the cake into diamond shapes, brush them with the liqueur, and serve warm.

DESSERTS

TORTA DI SUSINE RAMASSIN

PLUM CAKE

PIEMONTE

Unsalted butter and
all-purpose flour, for the pan

1¾ lbs. dried yellow or green plums

1 lb. amaretti

2 cups milk

⅔ cup unsweetened cocoa powder

1 cup sugar

12 large eggs

½ tsp. grated lemon zest

3 tbsp. rum

Confectioners' sugar

Preheat the oven to 350°F. Butter and flour a pie pan. Soak the plums in lukewarm water and soak the amaretti in the milk. ✦ Squeeze the plums until dry, then coarsely chop them. ✦ Pour the milk and amaretti into a saucepan and add the cocoa, sugar, eggs, plums, lemon zest, and rum. Stir until blended, then pour into the pie pan. ✦ Bake for about 40 minutes, until set. Serve with a dusting of confectioners' sugar.

TORTA DI TAGLIOLINI

TAGLIOLINI PIE

EMILIA-ROMAGNA

For the dough:

1¼ cups all-purpose flour

⅔ cup sugar

1½ tsp. baking powder

1 large egg

¼ cup (4 tbsp.) unsalted butter

1 tbsp. bitter almond liqueur,
plus more for sprinkling

For the tagliolini:

1¼ cups all-purpose flour

1 large egg

For the filling:

⅔ cup blanched almonds

½ cup candied citron

Grated zest of 1 lemon

1 cup sugar

3 tbsp. unsalted butter,
cut into pieces

Preheat the oven to 425°F. Mix the flour, sugar, and baking powder. Use it and the egg to make a dough as in the recipe on page 751, adding the butter and liqueur with the egg. Roll out a sheet of dough and use it to line a deep pie pan. ✦ Use the flour and egg to make a pasta dough as in the recipe on page 10, then cut into fine tagliolini; set aside. ✦ For the filling, finely chop the almonds together with the candied citron and lemon zest. Add the sugar. This will have a powdery consistency. ✦ Spread a thin layer of the almond filling over the dough in the pie pan. Arrange over this a layer of the tagliolini and continue alternating layers of filling and tagliolini. Dot the final layer with butter. ✦ Bake for 30 minutes, or until the dough is well cooked and the tagliolini is golden. When this has cooled sprinkle with bitter almond liqueur.

TORTA DI VIGILIA
FRIULI-VENEZIA GIULIA

¼ lb. (½ cup) plus 6 tbsp.
unsalted butter, softened

Juice and grated zest of 1 lemon

1¼ cups sugar

1 tsp. vanilla extract

1¼ cups finely chopped almonds

1¼ cups all-purpose flour

1 cup raspberry, black currant,
or strawberry jam

CHRISTMAS EVE CAKE

Preheat the oven to 400°F. Whip the butter until fluffy and add the lemon juice and zest with 1 tablespoon ice water. Add the sugar, vanilla, almonds, and flour. ✦ Working quickly, divide the dough in two parts, one larger than the other. Pat the large one in an even layer across the bottom of a pie pan, about ½ inch thick. ✦ Cover this with a layer of jam. ✦ Roll or pat out the remaining dough to about ½ inch thickness. Slice out strips about ½ inch wide. Cover the jam with these strips, interlacing them to form a latticework. ✦ Bake for 30 minutes, or until the dough is golden brown.

TORTA NERA
EMILIA-ROMAGNA

¼ lb. (½ cup) plus 2 tbsp.
unsalted butter, softened

1¼ cups blanched almonds

5 large eggs, separated

1¼ cups sugar

⅔ cup unsweetened cocoa powder

¼ cup powdered instant
espresso coffee

Grated zest of 1 lemon

2 tbsp. anisette

1⅔ cups all-purpose flour

Salt

COFFEE AND CHOCOLATE PIE

This recipe is typical of Reggio Emilia. This is also called *Torta Barozzi* in Modena after a recipe by the architect Giacomo Barozzi, known as "Il Vignola."

Preheat the oven to 350°F. Grease a pie pan with butter. Toast the almonds in the oven until lightly browned, then grind them in a mortar to a paste. ✦ Beat 4 of the egg yolks and ½ cup of the sugar with a mixer on medium speed until thick and pale, then add the other ingredients one at a time: cocoa, coffee, lemon zest, 5 tablespoons of the butter, and the anisette. Beat 4 of the egg whites until stiff, then fold them into the mixture. ✦ Let this rest while preparing the pastry. Blend together the flour and remaining butter, then blend in the remaining sugar, remaining whole egg, and a pinch of salt until a smooth dough forms. Cover with a clean kitchen towel, then set it aside to rest for about 15 minutes. ✦ Roll it out to form a sheet and use it to line the pie pan, cutting away all the dough that extends beyond the edges. ✦ Pour the almond mixture into this, filling it to the top. Reroll the dough scraps to a sheet and cover the filling, sealing the edges, but making a few vents in the top crust. Bake for about 40 minutes or until golden. Let cool before serving.

PARADISE CAKE

½ lb. (2 sticks) plus 4 tbsp. unsalted
butter, at room temperature
6 large egg yolks
plus 2 large egg whites
1⅔ cups sugar
Grated zest of 1 lemon
⅔ cup all-purpose flour, sifted
1¼ cups potato starch, sifted
Vanilla sugar

This recipe is typical of Pavia. If kept wrapped in aluminum foil the cake will last a long time and improve in flavor. Add the vanilla sugar just before serving each time.

Preheat the oven to 400°F. Butter a 10-inch pie pan. Whip the butter in a bowl with a wooden spoon or, even better, with an electric beater until very soft and almost white. ✦ Add the egg yolks, one at a time, waiting for each to be completely blended before adding the next. ✦ While constantly beating the mixture add the sugar, then the lemon zest, then the flour and potato starch. ✦ When all the ingredients are blended, clean the beaters and whip the egg whites in a separate bowl until stiff. Add 2 tablespoons egg whites to the butter mixture, then fold in the rest, gently mixing from the bottom up. ✦ Pour the mixture into the pan and bake for about 1 hour. Use a toothpick to determine when it is cooked (it will come out clean when inserted into the center of the cake). Invert onto a wire rack and remove the pan. Let cool completely. ✦ Serve with a dusting of vanilla sugar.

SANDY CAKE

½ lb. (1 cup) plus 2 tbsp.
unsalted butter, softened
All-purpose flour, for the pan
1⅔ cups sugar
3 large eggs, separated
1⅔ cups potato starch
1½ tsp. baking powder
Grated zest of 1 lemon
Confectioners' sugar
Salt

Variation: use equal parts of potato starch and yellow polenta flour (*fioretto* cornmeal). The result will be very similar to the *Polentina di Cittadella* (see page 846), a cake that is well known even outside regional borders.

Preheat the oven to 350°F. Butter and flour a 9-inch cake pan. Cream the butter and sugar until fluffy, then add the egg yolks with the mixer running. ✦ Add the potato starch, baking powder, a pinch of salt, and lemon zest. ✦ Whip the egg whites until stiff, then fold into the mixture. ✦ Pour the mixture into the pan and bake for about 30 minutes without ever opening the oven. When it is baked, invert onto a serving plate. Let it cool and dust with confectioners' sugar.

TORTA NOVECENTO

At the beginning of the twentieth century, famed Canavese pastry chef Ottavio Berti-notti created this highly original sponge cake to celebrate the year 1900. The "1900 cake" quickly became famous throughout Italy; so much so, in fact, that by 1964, Ber-tinotti, tired of seeing impostors trading on the now-famous name, finally patented the recipe. Though the method of combining the ingredients remains a mystery, it is distinguished by the use of chocolate in both the sponge itself and in the cream filling. In 1971, however, he taught the secrets of the "torta novecento" to his Umberto Balla, whose eponymous pastry company has been making it ever since. What is known about this exquisite confection is that the sponge cake consists of eggs, butter, sugar, and a mixture of flour, potato starch, cocoa, and yeast. The delectable cream filling contains milk, vanilla, eggs, butter, sugar, shards of real chocolate, and flour. The renowned cake has become a culinary landmark of Ivrea.

TORTA SBRISOLONA

CRUMBLY ALMOND CAKE

FOR
6 PERSONS

LOMBARDIA

Olive oil, for the pan

3⅓ cups all-purpose flour

½ pound (2 sticks) plus 4 tbsp. butter, at room temperature

1⅔ cups peeled, toasted, and chopped almonds

⅓ cup sugar

To peel almonds, you must first blanch them in boiling water for about 30 seconds. Remove and drain them. They should pop out of their peels easily when pressed.

Preheat the oven to 350°F. Grease a large baking pan (at least 10 inches in diameter) with olive oil and dust it with flour. Combine all the ingredients, mixing just until blended. Do not work the dough too much. ✦ Spread the mixture in the pan. It should be about 1½ inches thick. ✦ Bake until golden, 30 to 40 minutes. Let it cool slightly, then unmold onto a wire rack to cool completely.

| # CARNIVAL FRITTERS

FOR
6 PERSONS

PIEMONTE

1 cup milk

¼ lb. (1 stick) unsalted butter, melted

2 large eggs

Juice of 1 lemon

1½ tsp. baking powder

1 tsp. vanilla extract

2 tbsp. grappa

All-purpose flour
(as much as needed)

Olive oil, for frying

Sugar, for dusting

Salt

This recipe is typical of the Antigorio Valley and Formazza.

Heat the milk over medium heat until bubbles form on the edges of the pan. Stirring constantly, add the salt, butter, eggs, lemon juice, baking powder, vanilla, and grappa. Gradually stir in enough flour to make a soft dough. ✦ Transfer it to a work surface and knead for 10 minutes. ✦ Roll out the dough to form a thin sheet and use a pastry wheel to cut strips as long and wide as desired. ✦ Heat several inches of olive oil in a saucepan and fry the *tortelli* until golden. Drain on paper towels, dust with sugar, and serve warm.

✦ **LOCAL TRADITION** ✦

TORTOLI

The recipe for this anise cake from Terracina in Lazio is very simple. Sugar and eggs are beaten together, then yeast is added to the mixture. After the addition of the yeast, all of the other ingredients are added to make the dough: olive oil, rum, vanilla, grated bread, anise seeds, and flour. The dough is then left to rest and rise for twenty-four hours, after which time it is divided into different baking dishes and left to rise again—ultimately tripling in volume. The different anise cakes are then baked in a hot oven until golden. In Fondi, a very similar cake was called *Tortone*.

| # ALMOND-FRUIT BISCOTTI

UMBRIA

Unsalted butter

1 large egg plus 3 large egg yolks

CONTINUED

Preheat the oven to 350°F. Grease a baking sheet with butter. Beat the egg and egg yolks with the sugar until thickened and pale. Blend in the flour and other ingredients to make a firm dough, adding more flour if needed. ✦ Shape this into a cylinder, place on the baking sheet,

1¼ cups sugar

3 cups all-purpose flour, plus more as needed

¾ cup olive oil

⅔ cup chopped blanched almonds

⅔ cup chopped candied fruit

¼ cup anisette

Pinch baking powder

and bake for 15 minutes. ✦ Let it cool, then cut cross-wise to make the *tozzetti*.

TOZZETTI
CON LE NOCCIOLE

HAZELNUT COOKIES

LAZIO

½ cup extra-virgin olive oil

6⅔ cups all-purpose flour

7 large eggs

2½ cups sugar

1½ tsp. baking powder

Grated zest of 1 lemon

½ cup milk (optional)

1¼ lbs. hazelnuts, baked in the oven and skinned; half whole, half coarsely chopped

This recipe is typical of the Viterbo area and that of the Monti Cimini. The area of the Cimini Mountains is a center of hazel-nut production, and the nuts are used to make many regional dishes. Among the most common of these are *tozzetti*, for which there are numerous recipes that vary in terms of in-gredients and proportions. The one given here is one of the most widespread.

Preheat the oven to 350°F. Grease a baking sheet with olive oil and dust with flour. Beat 6 of the eggs together in a bowl with the sugar until thickened and pale. Blend in the olive oil, baking powder, lemon zest, and, if de-sired, milk. ✦ Mix well, then add the hazelnuts. Add the flour a little at a time to obtain a soft dough. Form the dough into cylinders ¾ inch in diameter and 4 inches long. ✦ Arrange these on the baking sheet. Beat the re-maining egg and brush on the dough. Bake until golden, about 15 minutes. ✦ Remove the pan from the oven, and before the cylinders have had time to cool completely cut them crosswise to form ¾-inch-long cookies. ✦ Re-turn them to the sheet and put them back in the oven for a few minutes to brown, about 15 minutes more.

UOVA RIPIENE
AL CIOCCOLATO

CHOCOLATE-STUFFED EGGS

BASILICATA

10 large hard-boiled eggs plus 1 large egg white

1 tsp. cinnamon

CONTINUED

Peel the hard-boiled eggs, cut them in half lengthwise, and remove the yolks, setting aside the whites. ✦ Work the yolks together with the cinnamon, vanilla, cocoa, sugar, and liqueur to obtain a mixture that is not overly soft. ✦ Use this to fill the egg-white halves. ✦ Heat 2 inches of olive oil in a saucepan. Whip the remaining egg

DESSERTS

2 tsp. vanilla extract
¾ cup unsweetened cocoa powder
Sugar (to taste)
Aromatic liqueur (as desired)
Olive oil, for frying
All-purpose flour, for dredging
Confectioners' sugar

white until stiff, lightly flour the halves, dip them in the whipped egg white, then fry until golden. Arrange on a serving plate and dust with confectioners' sugar.

ZABAGLIONE

ZABAIONE 1

PIEMONTE

8 large egg yolks
8 tbsp. sugar
16 half eggshells of dry Marsala

Serve accompanied by ladyfingers or similar cookies.

Bring a pot of water to a simmer. In a heatproof bowl whisk together the egg yolks and the sugar until thick and pale. Gradually whisk in the Marsala; place over the simmering water and beat the mixture to make it soft and foamy. ✦ Continue beating until it begins to bubble slightly, then pour into cups and serve hot.

ZABAGLIONE WITH RUM

ZABAIONE 2

EMILIA-ROMAGNA

5 large egg yolks
2¼ cups sugar
¼ cup dry Marsala
3 tbsp. rum

This recipe is typical of Parma. A variation uses only white wine in place of both the Marsala and the rum.

Combine the egg yolks, sugar, Marsala, and rum in a pan, put it over low heat, and begin stirring without whipping it up too much. ✦ Let it cook a few minutes, stirring, so the zabaglione will be firm and not overly foamy. Serve hot or lukewarm (even as a side dish to *zampone*).

CORNMEAL COOKIES

ZALETI

VENETO

1¼ sticks butter (or 5 oz. lard), softened
2 large eggs, beaten
⅔ cup sugar
2 cups cornmeal
CONTINUED

Preheat the oven to 375°F. Butter a baking sheet. Beat the eggs and sugar until thick and pale, then blend in the butter (or lard). ✦ Mix the cornmeal and flour with the baking powder and stir into the egg mixture. Stir in the raisins, pine nuts, milk, lemon zest, and vanilla to obtain a smooth dough. ✦ Shape the dough by hand into small ovals about 3 inches long. ✦ Arrange the ovals in rows on the baking

1 ½ cups all-purpose flour

2 tsp. baking powder

⅔ cup raisins, soaked in warm water, drained, and squeezed dry

½ cup pine nuts

½ cup whole milk

2 tbsp. grated lemon zest

½ tsp. vanilla extract

sheet and bake until golden, 20 to 25 minutes (cooking time will vary according to the size of the *zaleti*).

✦ **LOCAL TRADITION** ✦

TREDICI ERBE

This digestif, known poetically as "thirteen herb liqueur," is typical of Graglia in the Biella area of Piemonte. A quantity of sugar would be dissolved in tepid water and then mixed with a quart of pure alcohol. The mixture would be poured into a glass jar or bottle and the thirteen herbs—traditionally also thirteen leaves of each—would be added: rue, *archibus*, sage, *limonina*, mint, lemon balm, (1 sprig of) rosemary, basil, lemon peel (without any pith), chives, juniper berries, a pinch of cinnamon, and gentian root. After thirteen days of steeping, the liqueur would be strained, the herbs discarded, and the *tredici erbe* bottled and left to rest in a cool, dark place for at least three months. This was a popular digestive.

ZEPPOLE CALABRESI

CALABRIAN FRITTERS

CALABRIA

2 tbsp. extra-virgin olive oil, plus more for the work surface

¾ cup sugar

1 bay leaf

1 ½ cups all-purpose flour, mixed with ¼ cup semolina flour

4 large egg yolks

⅔ cup dry white wine

Lard, for frying

CONTINUED

These are a Christmas tradition.

Grease a work surface (marble is best) with olive oil. Pour 2 cups of cold water into a saucepan, add the sugar, olive oil, bay leaf, and a pinch of salt, and bring to a boil. ✦ When it boils remove the pan from the heat and all at once add the mixture of flours, stirring rapidly and energetically with a wooden spoon. ✦ Put the pan back on the heat and continue to work the mixture without pause for about 10 minutes. When the mixture is smooth and compact, remove the bay leaf and incorporate the egg yolks and wine. ✦ Turn the mixture out onto the

DESSERTS

Vanilla sugar or sugar flavored
with cinnamon

Salt

work surface and let it cool. ✦ Shape it into doughnuts. Heat 2 inches of lard in a saucepan and fry the doughnuts until golden. As they cook pierce them from time to time with the tines of a fork to release the particles of dough that characterize these zeppole. ✦ When they are golden and crunchy drain them well on paper towels. Dust with vanilla sugar or sugar flavored with cinnamon.

YEASTED FRITTERS

ZEPPOLE DI SAN GIUSEPPE

CAMPANIA

¾ lb. potatoes

2½ cups all-purpose flour

2¼ tsp. active dry yeast

3 tbsp. lukewarm milk,
plus more as needed

Grated zest of ½ lemon

½ cup olive oil (or 4 tbsp. butter)

1 large egg

Olive oil, for frying

Sugar

Salt

This recipe is typical of Naples.

Boil the potatoes until tender, peel them, and pass them, still hot, through a sieve or food mill. ✦ Arrange the flour in a well and dissolve the yeast at the center in 3 tablespoons milk. Add the potatoes and all the other ingredients (except the sugar in which the zeppole will be rolled), working them into the flour and, if the dough seems too hard, add a little more milk as needed. ✦ Knead for 10 minutes and divide the dough in 6 equal parts. Roll out each piece on the work surface to form thick cords, as thick as a finger and about 8 inches long. ✦ Sprinkle a clean kitchen towel with flour. Form these into doughnuts, making the ends meet and sealing by pressing one end down atop the other. One by one place these zeppole on the floured cloth, then over this rest a dish towel but in such a way that it does not rest its weight on the dough. ✦ Let it rise 1 to 1½ hours. Heat 2 inches of olive oil in a saucepan and fry the zeppole, one or two at a time, over low heat so they do not brown. Drain them on a wire rack, then roll them in sugar. Let cool completely.

HONEY-FILLED FRITTERS

ZIPPULAS

SARDEGNA

¼ lb. (1 stick) plus 6 tbsp.
unsalted butter

1⅔ cups all-purpose flour

CONTINUED

There are those who prefer to soak the balls in grappa in which honey has been dissolved.

Bring 2 cups of water to a boil in a pan with the butter and a pinch of salt. When the water boils remove the pan from the heat and pour in all the flour, stirring with a wooden spoon to create a ball of dough that easily comes

9 large eggs
Olive oil, for frying
Lard, for frying
1 cup honey
2 tbsp. grappa
Sugar
Salt

away from the sides of the pan. ✦ Add the eggs to this, working them in one at a time. As soon as the dough forms bubbles on its surface wrap it in a cloth and let it rest for about 45 minutes. ✦ Heat equal parts olive oil and lard in a skillet and drop balls of the dough into this, letting them swell as they fry. As soon as they brown remove them from the skillet, let them drain on paper towels, and let cool slightly. Mix the honey and grappa until blended and transfer to a squeeze bottle. As soon as they can be handled make an incision in each and pipe in a little of the honey mixture. ✦ Sprinkle the balls with sugar and serve.

ZUCCOTTO

CREAM-FILLED SPONGE CAKE

FOR
6 PERSONS

TOSCANA

1½ cups light whipping cream
⅔ cup confectioners' sugar
1⅔ cups ricotta cheese
⅔ cup chopped candied fruit
3 oz. bittersweet chocolate, chopped
1 oz. (1 square) unsweetened chocolate, melted and cooled slightly
1½-lb. sponge cake (see page 843)
½ cup mixed liqueurs (Maraschino, rum, kirsch, *alchermes* [see note, page 786], etc.), diluted with 2 tbsp. water

Line a bombe mold or small mixing bowl with plastic wrap, leaving several extra inches on the edges. Whip the cream and confectioners' sugar until stiff peaks form. Press the ricotta through a sieve and fold into the cream mixture. ✦ Divide this mixture in two portions, one slightly larger than the other. Add the chopped candied fruit and the bittersweet chocolate to the larger portion; fold the unsweetened chocolate into the smaller portion. ✦ Cut the sponge cake in thin slices and brush them with the liqueur mixture. ✦ Line the mold or bowl with these slices and cover them with the smaller portion of the whipped cream mixture. Fill the cavity with the other mixture, spreading it out to fill the space and covering with more slices of soaked sponge cake. ✦ Wrap the plastic around the cake and refrigerate this for several hours before serving.

ZUPPA ALLE MANDORLE

ALMOND BREAD PUDDING

VALLE D'AOSTA

6 oz. blanched almonds
⅔ cup confectioners' sugar
Ground cinnamon, to taste

CONTINUED

This recipe is typical of Valgrisenche.

Preheat the oven to 350°F. Grind the almonds in a mortar, gradually adding the confectioners' sugar and up to 2 cups lukewarm water from time to time. ✦ Add cinnamon to this according to taste. ✦ Strain this mixture through cheesecloth. ✦ Heat the butter in a pan and toast

1½ sticks (12 tbsp.) unsalted butter
8 slices bread

the bread until golden. Arrange in a single layer in a baking pan. Pour the almond mixture over them, then dust with more cinnamon. ✦ Bake for about 15 minutes.

| ZUPPA DI AREY | # WALNUT SOUP |

VALLE D'AOSTA

1 large egg
4 cups milk
4 tbsp. red wine
½ cup sugar
25 walnut halves, finely ground
½ cinnamon stick
Pinch grated nutmeg
3 oz. breadsticks
Salt

This recipe is typical of Courmayeur. A variation consists of adding a shot of liqueur at the last moment (grappa, kirsch, rum).

In a large copper pan beat together the egg, milk, wine, and sugar until blended. ✦ Add the walnuts, cinnamon, nutmeg, and salt. ✦ Break the breadsticks in pieces and incorporate them. ✦ Put the pan over high heat and cook, stirring constantly with a wooden spoon. ✦ When the mixture begins to thicken and foam like zabaglione (it must never boil), remove the pan from the heat and serve immediately while hot.

✦ **LOCAL TRADITION** ✦

ZUPPETTA DI VINO

The name of this rustic recipe from the Valle d'Aosta, *seupa frieda de l'âno*, translates literally as "donkey's soup," a reference to the pastoral tradition of rewarding a farm animal's particularly hard labors with black bread soaked in red wine. "Wine soup," as it's called for people, was made using a traditional implement of the Italian kitchen, the *copa-pan*, a breadboard fitted with a blade, used to break up stale bread. To make the "wine soup," half a loaf of stale black rye bread would be broken up on the *copa-pan* and marinated in a large bowl with about a cup of sugar and two cups of local red wine for at least two hours.

CHOCOLATE CUSTARD TRIFLE

ZUPPA INGLESE 1

EMILIA-ROMAGNA

4 cups milk

Peel of 1 lemon, in strips

8 large egg yolks

1 ¼ cups sugar

⅔ cup all-purpose flour

4 oz. bitter chocolate, chopped

1 1-lb. sponge cake, sliced in 3 horizontal rounds (see page 843)

1 cup *alchermes* (see note, page 786)

¾ cup rum, mixed with 2 tbsp. water

A variation of this recipe is made with ladyfingers, arranged in layers, in place of the sponge cake.

Heat the milk and lemon peel in a saucepan over medium heat until bubbles form around the edge of the pan. Remove the pan from the heat and set aside to steep for 10 minutes, then divide in half. Thoroughly combine half the egg yolks with half the sugar and half the flour; slowly add to this half of the milk infusion. ✦ Heat this mixture over low heat, stirring constantly to avoid lumps, until thickened. ✦ Repeat with the remaining egg yolks, sugar, flour, and milk to make another batch of pastry cream; mix in the chocolate and stir until smooth. ✦ Put a round of sponge cake on a large plate and brush generously with *alchermes*, then top with a layer of plain pastry cream; follow with a round of sponge cake. Brush with the rum mixture and top with chocolate cream. Top with the remaining cake layer and remaining plain cream. ✦ Cool the *zuppa* in the refrigerator for at least half a day before serving.

ORANGE CUSTARD TRIFLE

ZUPPA INGLESE 2

FOR 8 PERSONS

LAZIO

1 ½-lb. sponge cake, cut in half horizontally (see page 843)

¼ cup *alchermes* (see page 786)

2 tbsp. rum, diluted with 2 tbsp. water

For the custard:

3 large egg yolks

⅔ cup sugar

½ cup all-purpose flour

2 cups milk

1 tbsp. chopped candied fruit

3 large egg whites, whipped to soft peaks

⅓ cup confectioners' sugar

This recipe is typical of Rome.

Preheat the oven to 300°F. Put each half of the sponge cake on a plate. ✦ Brush the *alchermes* liqueur over one half, and the rum mixture over the other. ✦ Meanwhile prepare the pastry cream as in the recipe on page 843; it should not be too thick but lightly runny. Mix in the finely chopped candied fruit. ✦ Preheat the oven to 300°F. Spread 2 tablespoons of pastry cream across the bottom of a round ovenproof 12-inch serving plate; place on top of this the slice of sponge cake soaked in the *alchermes*, then spread with pastry cream, forming a slight dome in the center, and on top of this place the cake round soaked in rum. ✦ Cover the surface with the whipped egg whites, smoothing them across with a spatula and sprinkling with confectioners' sugar. ✦ Transfer to the oven and bake it long enough to dry and lightly brown the meringue. Serve cold.

DESSERTS

CONVERSION CHARTS

ALL CONVERSIONS ARE APPROXIMATE.

LIQUID CONVERSIONS

U.S.	Metric
1 tsp	5 ml
1 tbsp	15 ml
2 tbsp	30 ml
3 tbsp	45 ml
¼ cup	60 ml
⅓ cup	75 ml
⅓ cup + 1 tbsp	90 ml
⅓ cup + 2 tbsp	100 ml
½ cup	120 ml
⅔ cup	150 ml
¾ cup	180 ml
¾ cup + 2 tbsp	200 ml
1 cup	240 ml
1 cup + 2 tbsp	275 ml
1¼ cups	300 ml
1⅓ cups	325 ml
1½ cups	350 ml
1⅔ cups	375 ml
1¾ cups	400 ml
1¾ cups + 2 tbsp	450 ml
2 cups (1 pint)	475 ml
2½ cups	600 ml
3 cups	720 ml
4 cups (1 quart)	945 ml
	(1,000 ml = 1 liter)

WEIGHT CONVERSIONS

U.S./U.K.	Metric
½ oz	14 g
1 oz	28 g
1½ oz	43 g
2 oz	57 g
2½ oz	71 g
3 oz	85 g
3½ oz	100 g
4 oz	113 g
5 oz	142 g
6 oz	170 g
7 oz	200 g
8 oz	227 g
9 oz	255 g
10 oz	284 g
11 oz	312 g
12 oz	340 g
13 oz	368 g
14 oz	400 g
15 oz	425 g
1 lb	454 g

OVEN TEMPERATURES

°F	Gas Mark	°C
250	½	120
275	1	140
300	2	150
325	3	165
350	4	180
375	5	190
400	6	200
425	7	220
450	8	230
475	9	240
500	10	260
550	Broil	290

INDEX *of* RECIPES

BY REGION

ABRUZZO

Appetizers
Cheese and egg fritters, 50
Marinated squid, 26
Mussels au gratin, 21
Pickled fish 1, 77
Polenta pie with sausage and raisins, 54
Squash-blossom sauce, 72–73

Desserts
Almond and chocolate layer cake, 843–844
Almond cake glazed with chocolate, 834
Carnival ring cake, 778
Chestnut fudge, 770
Chieti cookies, 870
Christmas spice cookies, 857
Ferratelle allo zafferano, 794
Honey biscuits, 837
Jam-filled horseshoe cookies, 869
Milk fritters, 800
Semolina bread, 825
Sweet ravioli, 763
Walnut filled pizza, 842

Fish
Anchovy frittata, 461
Fish soup Pescara-style, 447
Grilled trout, 503
Mullet baked in parchment 1, 499

Meat
Baked leg of lamb, 510
Baked mutton shank, 651
Goat with tomatoes and peppers, 532
Hare in sauce, 594
Hen galantine, 592
Lamb stew with cheese and egg sauce, 511
Mutton stew 1, 636
Mutton stew 2, 649
Paliata (grilled calf's intestines), 616
Pork stew, 610
Pork with onion sauce, 547
Sautéed kidneys on toast, 637
Skewered lamb, 518
Tacchino all canzanese (turkey), 657
Tripe in tomato sauce, 664–665
Tripe sausages, 599
Veal parmigiana with eggplant, 616

Pasta, polenta, rice
Baked cheese pie, 241
Baked layered crepes with artichoke, 409
Beef and vegetable pie, 410
Bucatini in mackerel sauce, 221
Cannarozzetti with ricotta and saffron, 223–224
Cornmeal pasta with tomatoes, 271
Gnocchi with rabbit sauce, 252
Homemade pasta in pork sauce, 281
Homemade pasta with meat and tomato, 278
Linguine with seafood, 273–274
Maccheroni alla mulinara, 280
Pappardelle in duck sauce, 295–296
Pasta and fava beans, 305
Pasta stuffed with beef and sausage, 244
Pasta with beans, 373
Polenta and beans, 322
Risotto with trout and saffron, 356–357
Spaghetti baked in foil, 380
Spaghetti with garlic and chili pepper, 280
Spaghetti with guanciale, 380
Sweet ricotta ravioli, 336–337
Truffle ravioli, 402

Soups
Bean and pasta soup, 197
Bean and pork soup, 197
Cardoons in broth 2, 110
Crepes in broth, 178
Farro soup 1, 134–135
Le virtù (Virtues Soup), 185
Lentil and crostini soup, 200
Pasta and prawns in broth, 184
Potato and pasta soup, 143
Sausage soup, 193
Tiny square pasta and peas, 172

Vegetables
Abruzzo-style cardoons in sauce, 680
Baked omelet with pork and potatoes, 690
Braised turnips, 720
Drunken cauliflower, 683
Rustic torte with artichokes, 731

ALTO ADIGE. *See*
TRENTINO-ALTO ADIGE

BASILICATA

Appetizers
Cheese tart, 84

Desserts
Almond biscotti, 865
Almond wafers, 780
"Bones of the dead" cookies, 822
Calzoncelli, 764
Chestnut calzoni, 764
Chocolate-stuffed eggs, 885–886
Semolina fritters, 796–797

Meat
Chicken in tomato sauce, 627
Easter lamb stew, 524
Involtini di interiora di agnello (roasted lamb offal), 590
Mutton pot, 624

Pasta, polenta, rice
Bucatini in tomato sauce, 275
Cavatelli and beans, 230
Cavatelli con cime di cocozze, 229
Ferretti in meat sauce, 239
Ferretti with anchovies and bread, 239
Manatelle, 286
Pasta and chickpeas, 266
Pasta and white beans, 307
Pasta in mint, 388–389
Pasta with dried peppers, 282
Pasta with guanciale, 376
Pasta with turnip tops, 304–305
Ricotta calzoni, 223
Ricotta ravioli, 333
Spinach-ricotta ravioli, 337

Soups
Bean soup with chicory and fennel, 127
Bean soup with mushrooms, 134
Beans and grain mush, 109
Bread soup 5, 159
Chicory soup, 191
Potato and celery soup, 168
Ricotta and egg soup, 97
"Salted water" soup 2, 96
Shepherd's bread soup, 161
White celery soup, 126
Wild herbs and meat soup, 153

Vegetables
Artichoke and fava bean stew, 682
Baked artichokes, 677
Baked eggplant, 699
Cardoons with egg 1, 679
Cardoons with egg 2, 680
Eggplant boats, 697–698

Fava beans and chicory 2, 689
Insalata di lampascioni (rustic muscari salad), 694
Lampascioni fritti (fried muscari), 696
Lampascioni in agrodolce (sweet-and-sour muscari), 697
Patate lesse sfritte (fried boiled potatoes), 710
Potato and bean stew, 708
Potato timbale, 729
Vegetable stew, 681–682

CALABRIA

Appetizers

Anchovy fritters, 34
Bianchetti fritters, 35
Bread rings and baked eggs, 9
Carne 'ncartarata ("aged meat"), 15
Filled focaccia, 28
Focaccia with oil, tuna, and tomato, 29
Focaccia with ricotta, 29
Fried squash, 89
Frittelle di anemoni di mare (sea anemone fritters), 35
Gelatina, 37
Mushroom meatballs, 66
Mushrooms with tomatoes, 37
Olive oil, lemon, and garlic sauce 1, 74
Pan-cooked mushrooms, 48
Pizza con fiori di sambuco (pizza with elderberry flowers), 64
Pizza with anchovies and capers, 60
Pizza with artichokes and ricotta, 60–61
Pizza with cracklings and raisins, 61

Desserts

Almond cookies, 792
Anise fritters with honey, 777
Baked fig and nut calzone, 820
Braided cookies, 870
Calabrian fritters, 887–888
Cannoli shells, 766
Chickpea ravioli, 850
Christmas sweets, 792–793
Figs with chocolate, 793
Honey cookies, 841
Honeyed gnocchi, 804–805
Olive oil nut cake, 842
Potato fritters, 799
Raisin cookies, 792
Ring breads with eggs, 775
Semolina bread with wine must and almonds, 857
Sesame nougat, 871
"Stairway to heaven" cookies, 854
Stuffed figs, 794
Vanilla fritters, 821
Wine-must cookies, 818

Fish

Anchovy balls, 478
Anchovy roll-ups, 445
Baked anchovies, 428–429
Baked swordfish 1, 473
Baked swordfish 2, 476
Boiled tuna, 498
Cod and potato stew 2, 492
Cod with green olives, 466
Diamante-style grouper, 456–457
Fried fish, 477
Fried tope, 470
Mustica di crucoli (sardine spread), 468
Octopus in wine 2, 478
Pan-fried whitebait, 444
Pike croquettes, 460
Sole with peppers, 489
Steamed swordfish 1, 473
Stockfish with capers, 495
Stuffed gar fish or pike, 458
Swordfish in salmoriglio sauce, 476
Swordfish roll-ups, 472
Swordfish with capers 1, 473–474
Swordfish with capers 2, 475
Swordfish with capers and lemon, 475
Swordfish with mint, 474
Swordfish with olives and capers, 475
Tuna Calabria-style, 497
Tuna Cosenza-style, 497–498
Tuna Reggio-style, 498
Ventricieddi di stocco al pomodoro, 502

Meat

Capon with anchovies, 584
Cinghiale d'aspromonte (saddle of boar), 551
Fried pork, 647
Goat stew, 532–533, 648
Lamb tripe in tomato sauce, 662–663
Larded leg of lamb, 564
Leg of kid with oregano, 534–535
Pan-fried sausages and broccoli, 641
Pork with potatoes and mushrooms, 659
Sanguinaccio di capra (stuffed goat intestines), 643
Sausage roll-ups, 592
Sausages and potatoes, 641–641
Shepherd's-style pork, 540
Skewered chicken gizzards, 650
Skewered pork liver, 575
Stewed boar, 551
Stuffed kid, 536
Sweet-and-sour meatballs 2, 628
Tripe and sweetbread stew, 648–649
Tripe with chili peppers, 667

Tripe with tomatoes and peppers, 664

Pasta, polenta, rice

Baked pasta and potatoes, 307–308
Baked pasta with eggplant 1, 297
Baked pasta with eggplant 2, 339
Baked ravioli, 332
Calabrian-style pasta with lardo and onion, 280
Fusilli with mushrooms and olives, 244
Homemade pasta with pork sauce, 308
Linguine with swordfish, 299–300
Pan-cooked pasta with pork, tomato, and red wine, 283
Pasta in anchovy sauce, 242
Pasta with beans and mushrooms, 283
Pasta with bottarga 1, 303
Pasta with potatoes and eggs, 308
Pasta with sardines, anchovies and breadcrumbs, 304
Pasta with snails, 315–316
Polenta with salted green tomatoes, 320
Polenta with salted pork, 319
"Priest caps," 225
Rice with fennel and ricotta, 348
Rigatoni with sausage and mushrooms, 338–339
Spaghetti with baby anchovies, 385
Spaghetti with cuttlefish ink, 380–381
Spaghetti with peppers, tomatoes, and guanciale, 299
Stuffed lasagna, 269–270
Tagliatelle and chickpeas with dried peppers, 396
Tagliatelle with broccoli, 396
Tagliatelle with wild fennel, 394
Tagliatelle with zucchini, roasted peppers, and tomatoes, 393
Vegetable timbale, 377
Ziti with tuna sauce, 423

Soups

Asparagus soup, 192
Bean, cabbage, and potato soup, 156–157
Borage soup, 193
Chard in broth, 99
Fava bean purée 1, 121
Onion soup with bread, 196
Ricotta dumplings in broth, 171
Stuffed-bread soup, 202–203
Tagliatelle with chickpeas, 181–182
Vegetable soup, 201
Wedding soup 1, 151
Wheat berry soup, 137
Wild onion soup, 189
Zuppa di pesce (fish soup), 202

Vegetables
Beans and roasted dried peppers, 686
Braised broccoli with vinegar, 674
Calabrian peppers, 709
Calabrian "Purgatory" vegetable sandwiches, 719
Crushed potatoes, 709
Eggplant and mint, 700
Eggplant and sausage, 700
Eggplant bites, 716
Eggplants and tomatoes, 701–702
Escarole with meatballs, 722
Fava beans in vinegar sauce, 688
Fried mushrooms, 691
Layered pie with artichokes, 731
Marinated lettuce, 697
Melanzane sott'aceto (pickled eggplant), 701
'Ndugghia di Castrovillari (pork sausage), 705
100-flavor eggplant, 701
Ovoli in fricassea (mushroom fricassee), 706
Potato and tomato casserole, 726
"Strange" vegetables, 732
Stuffed tomatoes, 717
Vegetable stew with celery, 682
Wild onion fritters, 690–691

CAMPANIA
Appetizers
Baked calzone, 12–13
Baked polenta with turnips and sausages, 65–66
Baked truffles, 81
Bread with pork bits, 86
Caponata 1, 14
Cornmeal fritters, 75
Crostini with anchovies and provatura, 24
Fasting day (meatless) calzone, 13
Fried bread puffs, 89
Layered pizza, 58
Meat pizza, 64
Neapolitan pâté, 55–56
Neapolitan pizza, 58
Pizza with escarole, 61–62
Rice balls, 48–49
Seafood salad 1, 39–40
Stuffed brioche, 7–8
Stuffed eggs, 87–88
Stuffed peppers, 53
Stuffed pizza, 63
Desserts
Almond candy, 790–791
Apple tart, 777
Babas with rhum, 749–750
Blancmange, 752
Capri chocolate-almond cake, 872
Carnival cookies, 774
Cassata from Naples, 768
Chestnut balls, 822
Chestnut panzarottini, 832
Chocolate parfaits, 782

Cooked wine (saba), 818–819
Eggplant with chocolate, 814–815
Filled cookies, 861–862
Fried pastries, 868
Lemon sorbet, 864
Limoncello, 810
Moiano biscotti, 755
Orange custard, 782
Orange mousse, 819
Raisin buns, 829
Semolina cake, 816
Spiced honey twists, 868–869
Wheat berry ricotta tart, 835–836
Yeasted fritters, 888
Fish
Baked mullet, 500
Braised cod and potatoes, 440–441
Eel with wild chicory, 435
Mullet baked in parchment 2, 500
Mussels au gratin with lemon, 459
Poached cod, 442–443
Salt cod fritters, 504
Sautéed clams, 483
Sea bass stuffed with seafood, 490
Stewed octopus, 479
Stockfish and potatoes 1, 494
Stuffed squid, 499
Sweet-and-sour cod stew, 504
Meat
Beef in pizza sauce, 539
Beef in sauce, 523
Boar country-style, 548
Budelline di agnello di faicchio (rolled lamb intestines), 525
Fried Neapolitan sausage and friarielli, 545–546
Kid in oil and vinegar, 535
Lamb with egg and cheese, 514
Meat and artichokes, 541
Mutton ragù, 635
Neapolitan ragù, 539
Pork and pickled peppers, 606
Pork scraps and peppers, 605
Rabbit braised in the style of Ischia, 557
Roast intestines, 650–651
Sausages with broccoli rabe, 641
Stuffed veal spleen, 608–609
Veal tendon salad, 589
Pasta, polenta, rice
Baked fusilli and orecchiette, 246
Baked gnocchi with fior di latte cheese and tomato sauce, 253–254
Baked polenta with sausage and ciccioli, 289
Baked seafood risotto, 243–244
Benevento-style lasagna with veal meatballs and eggs, 267–268
Bucatini with caciocavallo cheese, 288
Cannelloni with meat sauce, 224
Cauliflower ravioli, 337–338

Cavatelli with walnuts, 230
Conglufi, 234
Ditali with zucchini and ricotta, 236–237
Fioroni filled with salame and cheese, 242
Leftover pasta omelet, 244
Linguine with anchovies, olives, and capers, 273
Linguine with lobster, 273
Linguine with mushrooms, 271
Linguine with walnuts, 271
Little stuffed dumplings, 294
Macaronara di Montemarano, 276
Macaroni au gratin, 278
Neapolitan lasagna, 268–269
Pasta and cheese pie, 412
Pasta and meat pie, 411
Pasta timbale, 378–379
Pasta with anchovies and tuna, 423
Pasta with cauliflower, 307
Pasta with chickpeas, 231
Pasta with meat and onions, 279
Penne with tomatoes and basil, 315
Peppers stuffed with pasta, 315
"Priest-chokers" with meat sauce, 390
Rice timbale 1, 374
Rice timbale 2, 375
Spaghetti alla colatura (spaghetti with colatura sauce), 384
Spaghetti with clams, 386
Spaghetti with fried eggs, 383
Spaghetti with garlic and oil, 277
Stuffed dumplings, 293
Tagliolini croquets, 289–290
Trilli pasta in walnut sauce, 419
Vermicelli and seafood baked in foil, 420
Vermicelli in garlic and oil, 420
Ziti with lardo, 283
Soups
Bean, escarole, and pork soup, 198
Cabbage and rice soup, 149
Cardoon soup, 193
Cardoons in broth 1, 110
Chestnut and leek soup, 130
Fresh fava bean soup, 198
Minestra maritata 2 (wedding soup), 151
Onion and fava bean soup, 195
Pasta and bean soup 1, 166
Soupy Pasta with cauliflower and black olives, 164
St. Lucy's soup, 206
Vegetable ragù, 172–173
Vegetable Stew, 112
Zuppa di soffritto, 206
Vegetables
Artichoke pizza, 714–715
Baked escarole, 723

Beans in sauce, 727–728
Capri salad, 693
Eggplant Parmigiana 1, 704–705
Fried broccoli rabe, 704
Fried eggplant with tomato sauce, 699
Lardari with tomatoes, 696
Marinated squash, 733
Marinated zucchini with mint, 733–734
Oregano tomatoes, 716–717
Pepper roll-ups, 695
Peppers stuffed with eggplant, 710–711
Pickled peppers, 713–714
Potato and cheese galette, 691
Stuffed and baked escarole, 722–723
Stuffed peppers Capri-style, 711

EMILIA-ROMAGNA
Appetizers
Bèlecòt ("already cooked" salame), 8
Flatbread with greens and sausage, 23
Fried bread, 38
Fried Flatbread, 9
Grape syrup, 69
Green-pepper sauce, 73–74
Horseradish sauce, 71
Mostarda di Carpi, 48
Mushrooms in broth, 36–37
Prosciutto mousse, 45
Spalla cotta di San Secondo (boiled pork salame), 79
Spinach pie, 26
Sweet-and-sour sauce Parma style, 70
Unleavened flatbread, 57
White truffles with Parmigiano-Reggiano, 81
Desserts
Almond cake 2, 875
Almond shortbread, 778–779
Almond tart, 872
Baked meringues, 865
Charterhouse-style sweet bread, 826–827
Chestnut dumplings, 816
Chestnut fritters, 797
Chocolate custard trifle, 891
Christmas bread, 827
Coffee and chocolate pie, 881
Ferrara biscotti, 756
Fried dough knots, 863
Fruitcake 2, 864–865
Hazelnut trifle, 789
Jam ravioli, 848
Ladyfinger trifle, 890
Laurel liqueur, 810
Lemon verbena liqueur, 811
Nocino (walnut liqueur), 823
Pumpkin bread, 827–828
Rice pudding cake, 879

Ring cake, 756–757
Savôr, 855
Spice cake, 824
Stuffed peaches, 838
Tagliolini pie, 880
Zabaglione with rum, 886
Fish
Braised catfish 1, 471
Eel with Savoy cabbage, 432
Fish soup Ravenna-style, 447
Fried catfish, 470–471
Grilled eel in grape leaves, 452
Grilled sole 1, 488
Grilled sole 2, 489
Marinated eel, 434–435
Pike in tomato sauce, 464
Sautéed baby sardines, 482–483
Sole in wine, 489
Stewed eel with peas, 434
Stuffed small cuttlefish 1, 486
Meat
Beef roll-ups, 669
Beef stew, 654–655
Beef with balsamic vinegar, 577
Boiled stuffed capon or hen, 522
Cappello da prete con zabaione, 531
Cotechino "in prison," 566–567
Donkey stew, 654
Fritto misto alla bolognese (mixed fry Bologna-style), 582
Horsemeat stew, 624
Hunter-style chicken 2, 626
Mixed braised meats, 522
Pan-braised lamb, 545
Pan-fried beef and vegetables, 579
Parma-style beef roast, 637–638
Parma-style beef stew, 652
Piacenza-style beef stew, 652–653
Pork cutlets with balsamic vinegar, 644
Pork-liver skewers, 573–574
Roast guinea hen, 571
Romagna-style ragù, 634
Salama da sugo, 639
Spiced capon, 530
Stewed snails, 603
Stuffed rabbit, 561–562
Stuffed veal breast, 632
Tripe alla Parmigiana, 664
Turkey breast with prosciutto and fontina, 621
Turkey-veal roulade, 629
Veal bolognese, 567
Pasta, polenta, rice
Baked polenta with meat sauce 2, 325
Baked tagliolini, 217
Baked tortellini, 313
Capon with anolini and prosciutto sauce, 226
Garganelli with peas and prosciutto, 247
Green lasagna with meat sauce, 270

Macaroni pie 1, 310–311
Pasta stuffed with squash, 224–225
Piacenza tortelli, 414
Potato gnocchi 1, 256
Potato gnocchi 2, 256
Potato gnocchi Romagna-style, 257
"Priest-chokers" with salsify sauce, 390
Pumpkin ravioli 1, 416
Rice bombe with squab, 220
Rice with squash, 343
Ricotta tortelli with sage sauce, 416
Risotto with clams, 363–364
Risotto with Parmigiano-Reggiano, 355
Risotto with sausage 1, 361
Romagna-style meat sauce, 330
Romagna-style polenta, 318
Sfoglia (homemade pasta), 377
Tagliatelle, 397
Tagliatelle pie, 396–397
Tagliatelle with herb sauce, 392
Tagliatelle with meat sauce, 392
Tagliatelle with Romagna-style meat sauce, 394
Tortelli filled with Swiss chard, 415
Wild duck risotto, 352
Soups
Anolini with beef filling, 97
Bean soup, 106
Bread soup 1, 158
Cappelletti in broth, 108–109
Chicken broth with grated pasta, 167
Manfrigùl pasta balls, 123
Mushroom soup, 199
Passatelli in broth, 163
Pasta and bean soup 3, 169
Pasta with beans, 179
Piacenza-style anolini, 98
Rice with egg and cheese, 173
Risotto with eels, 176
Soup with bread dumplings 1, 124
Spinach soup, 207
Tiny pasta in bean broth, 169–170
Tortellini bolognese in broth, 183–184
Vegetables
Eggplant braised with tomatoes, 700

FRIULI-VENEZIA GIULIA
Appetizers
Eggs and mushrooms, 88
Fried sage leaves, 30
Frittata con le erbe (herb frittata), 31
Frittata with whitebait, 31
Prosciutto di Sauris, 68

Salame d'oca (goose salame), 70
Spicy cheese spread, 80
Spider crab canapes, 38
Cheese
Cheese crisp, 739
Cheese crisp with potatoes, 739
Cheese sauce with potatoes and
    onions, 738–739
Frico (fried cheese disks), 739
Desserts
Almond biscotti, 755
Apple fritters, 797–798
Cherry strudel, 867
Christmas Eve cake, 881
Easter cake, 841
Easter focaccia, 795
Fried bread, 828
Fried bread with bulide, 828
Fried small dumplings, 868
Friulian yeast cake, 806
Griddle cakes, 864
Palatschinken with preserves,
    784–785
Plum gnocchi, 805
Rice pudding 1, 761
Rose pudding, 762
Semolina pudding, 761
Triestine yeast cake, 847
Wine doughnuts, 775
Fish
Anguilla infilzata (skewered eel),
    436
Cod in sauce, 438
Sea bass and shellfish in dough,
    446
Sea bass in salt, 446
Squillfish with garlic, 451
Stockfish with tomato sauce,
    494
Trout baked in tomato sauce with
    polenta, 503
Meat
Baked mallard, 586
Beef cheek with cumin, 588
Capon with lemon balm, 531
Chicken cutlets with Montasio
    cheese, 620
Grilled kid, 535
Hunter's-style hare, 593–594
Hunter's-style marinated beef,
    542–543
Jugged hare 3, 596–597
Pan-cooked pork cutlets, 565
Pan-cooked snails, 602
Pan-fried chicken giblets, 582
Prosciutto in bread dough, 631
Salame with vinegar, 639
San Quirino snails, 601
Smoked goose confit, 611
Smoked meat with polenta
    "sauce," 621
Squab baked in potato, 621–622
Stewed pork, 541
Stewed roebuck offal, 578
Venison in sauce, 537

Pasta, polenta, rice
Buckwheat pasta with toasted
    cornmeal, 219–220
Butternut-squash gnocchi 2, 259
Half-moon pasta with potato
    filling, 214
Half-moon pasta with ricotta and
    prune filling, 213
Handcut pasta with cheese and
    sage sauce, 372
Medieval gnocchi, 261
Pasta and prosciutto pie, 312
Pasta roll with spinach, 372–373
Rice with crabs and razor clams,
    342
Risotto with campion, 360–361
Seas and mountains risotto,
    369–370
Stuffed gnocchi in cheese sauce,
    258
Stuffed potato gnocchi, 250–251
Soups
Barley and potato soup, 155
Barley and vegetable soup, 142
Bean soup 1, 131
Bean soup with fermented
    turnips, 134
Bean soup with musetto, 133
Beans with dumplings, 114
"Burned broth," 104
Corn, bean, and potato soup, 137
Fish soup Marano-style, 101
Grated pasta with broth, 167
Minestrone with basil, 126
Montasio cheese soup, 138–139
Pasta and bean soup 2, 166
Pea soup, 143–144
Rice and potato soup 2, 146
Spinach-cornmeal soup, 161
Squash soup, 150
Toasted broth, 104
Tripe soup 2, 207–208
Turbot Grado-style, 103
Winter vegetable soup, 100
Zuppa di pane (bread soup), 200
Vegetables
Brovada (turnips marinated in
    wine pressings), 721
Caramelized turnips, 720
Field greens in butter, 685
Pan-fried greens, 732
Pan-fried potatoes, 709
Potato lunettes (crescents), 696
Sweet-and-sour braised cabbage,
    676
Wild greens with lardo, 719–720

LAZIO
Appetizers
Baked dumplings with sausage
    and cheese, 10
Bruschetta, 8
Ciarla (pizza dough), 18
Fried mozzarella sandwich, 46
Meat jerky, 21

Pizza with turnip greens, 60
Rice croquettes, 80–81
Ring-shaped fritters, 23
Desserts
Anise ring cookies, 776
Baked sweet ravioli, 848
Boiled and baked cookies, 776
Christmas macaroni with walnuts,
    811–812
Cornmeal and raisin cake, 844
Cornmeal raisin cookies, 804
Fritters, 771
Gelatine di fichi d'India (prickly
    pear gelatin), 803
Hazelnut cookies, 885
Honey almond cookies, 854
Honey doughnuts, 775–776
Honey fritters, 778
Honey squares, 868
Orange custard trifle, 891
Pizze di Pasqua (Easter pizzas),
    846
Raisin fritters, 797
Rice fritters for St. Joseph's Day,
    799
Ricotta crostata, 785
Ricotta tart, 768
Ring cake, 840
St. Joseph's Day fritters, 753–754
Scarsella, 859
Spiced wine, 847
Sweet buns, 812–813
Sweet ravioli with ricotta,
    849–850
Tortoli (anise cake), 884
Walnut cookies, 817
Yellow cake with fruit, 831
Fish
Anchovies with endive, 429
Batter-dipped whitebait, 444
Bolsena eels in the style of
    Bisentina, 430
Cod with tomatoes, raisins, and
    pine nuts, 442
Crayfish soup, 504–505
Eels Labrese-style, 431
Fried cod fillets, 460–461
Hunter-style eels, 430
Marinated eel, 452
Octopus in wine 1, 478
Meat
Abbuoto, 511
Beef rolls Roman-style, 590
Beef stew with celery, 655
Beef stew with cloves, 584–585
Boar Viterbo-style, 548
The "fifth quarter" beef stew,
    653–654
Hunter-style suckling lamb, 508
Lamb intestines Viterbo-style,
    525–526
Oxtail stew, 552–553
Pork with potatoes and fennel,
    553
Rabbit in broth, 554

Rabbit with wild fennel, 555
Roast suckling lamb with
    potatoes, 508
St. John's snails, 601
Sausages and broccoli, 640–641
Scannature d'abbacchio in
    padella (cooked lamb's blood),
    645
Stewed suckling lamb Roman-
    style, 508–509
Sweet-and-sour boar, 549–550
Testatelle d'abbacchio in teglia
    (lambs' heads), 660
Tripe Roman-style, 666
Veal cutlets with prosciutto and
    sage, 642

Pasta, polenta, rice
Baked meat ravioli, 333
Bucatini with guanciale, hot
    pepper, and tomato, 221
Fettuccine "Alfredo," 240
Fettuccine with meat sauce, 331
Fettuccine with ricotta, 240
Homemade pasta with tomatoes
    and garlic, 313
Pasta "snakes" with sausage, 423
Penne with hot chiles, prosciutto,
    and tomato, 314
Pizziconi (dumplings in tomato
    sauce), 317
Polenta with pork and turnips,
    322
Polenta with pork loin, 320
Polenta with pork sauce, 320–321
Rice-stuffed tomatoes 1, 327–328
Rice-stuffed tomatoes 2, 328–329
Rigatoni con la pagliata (rigatoni
    with calf intestines), 338
Roman-style gnocchi, 253
Rome-style potato gnocchi,
    257–258
Spaghetti with anchovies, olives,
    and capers, 384
Spaghetti with Carbonara Sauce,
    382–383
Spaghetti with garlic, olive oil,
    and hot pepper, 379
Spaghetti with guanciale and chile
    pepper, 383
Spaghetti with guanciale sauce,
    382
Spaghetti with pecorino and
    pepper, 384
Thick pasta with tomato ragù,
    274
Tiella de Gaeta, 406
Timbale all Bonifacio VIII, 410

Soups
Acquacotta laziale, 94
Bathed bread, 98–99
Bean and wild fennel soup,
    196–197
Cardoon soup, 128–129
Chestnut and chickpea soup 1,
    194

"Cooked water" soup with wild
    herbs, 93
Escarole soup, 147
Farro Porridge, 114–115
Fava bean soup, 190
Italian egg-drop soup, 180–181
Lamb soup, 189–190
Maremma-style "Cooked water"
    soup 1, 95
Pasta and chickpea soup 1,
    164–165
Pasta with beans, 119
Polenta and beans, 170
Skate soup with pasta, 127–128
Spring vegetable stew, 185
Tagliolini with pork gullets,
    182–183
Tench and tagliolini soup 1, 148
Tiny dumplings in broth, 116
Tiny square pasta and fava beans,
    171
Turnip and bean soup, 190–191
Zuppa di pesce di lago (lake fish
    soup), 204

Vegetables
Beans and grains, 686
Carote di Viterbo in bagno
    aromatico (Viterbo carrots),
    683
Chicory galette, 692
Fava beans and guanciale 1, 687
Fava beans and guanciale 2,
    687–688
Jewish-style artichokes, 677–678
Marinated zucchini, 735
Misticanza (wild salad), 703
Puntarelle salad with anchovy
    dressing, 717–718
Roman-style artichokes, 678–679
Strigoli (bladder campion), 729
Stuffed and braised escarole, 722
Vine-roasted artichokes, 678

LIGURIA

Appetizers
Bormida sauce, 72
Caponata 3, 15
Chickpea crepe, 26–27
Chickpea Flatbread, 27
Chickpea-flour fritters, 35
Chickpea polenta, 53
Cialde (fried wafers), 17
Easter tart, 85
Focaccia, 28
Focaccia with olives, 28–29
Fried milk, 42–43
Fried potato dumplings, 43
Fried squash ravioli, 6–7
Pissaladière, 57–58
Potato salad with anchovies,
    olives, and tomato, 20
Small focaccias with tomato
    sauce, 78
Walnut sauce, 73
Zeaia (meat gelatin), 86

Cheese
Focaccia with cheese, 740

Desserts
Anise cookies, 748
Baked amaretto peaches, 838
Coffee ice cream, 828–829
Floating islands, 860
Fried custard squares, 810
Fried knots, 801
Genoa biscotti, 754
Meringues, 815
Quaresimali (Lenten cookies), 849
Sugar cookies, 765
Sweet bread with fruits and nuts,
    825–826

Fish
Boiled stockfish with potatoes,
    493
Fish stew, 448
Fried stuffed anchovies, 427
Marinated anchovies, 427
Mariner's stockfish, 493
Seafood and vegetable platter,
    453
Soused bream, 445
Stewed cuttlefish 1, 484
Stockfish and potato stew, 491
Stockfish with potatoes and
    onions, 495
Stuffed cuttlefish 1, 485
Whitebait frittata, 461

Meat
Goat and beans, 533–534
Lamb and artichoke fricassee,
    578–579
San Remo rabbit, 559
Stewed rabbit, 558
Veal roll-ups, 660
Veal stewed in wine, 669

Pasta, polenta, rice
Baked rice and meat, 341
Fish ravioli, 335–336
Genoese meat sauce, 413
Genoese rice, 341–342
Griddled pasta, 403–404
Herb-stuffed pasta, 292–293
Le trofie Recchesi, 420
Maltagliati with artichoke sauce,
    329
Meatless ravioli 1, 334–335
Mixed meat ravioli, 331–332
Mushroom sauce, 412
Pasta "crosses," 233–234
Potato dumplings with mushroom
    sauce, 216
Rice with meat sauce, 347
Riso co-i fidê (rice with sea
    anemones), 342
Trenette with pesto sauce,
    418–419

Soups
Anchovy soup, 99
Black kale and rice soup, 200
Chickpea and bean soup,
    124–125

Chickpea stew, 186
Christmas macaroni, 121
Fish soup with herbs, 113
Lettuce rolls, 120
Minestrone with pesto, 155
Mussel soup, 201
Rice and wild herbs, 174
Tripe soup, 177
Whitebait soup, 136–137

Vegetables
Artichoke and cheese casserole, 724
Scrambled eggs with artichokes, 692
Spinach Genoa-style, 727
Stuffed zucchini, 735
Vegetable fritters, 689
Vegetable stuffing, 733

LOMBARDIA
Appetizers
Alborelle or sardine salate, 3
Aspic, 5
Buckwheat fritters, 78–79
Hops frittata, 32
Insalata di nervetti (tendon salad), 41
Mortadella di fegato, 49
Pork roll-ups, 41–42
Sausage frittata, 30–31
Squash cake, 85

Cheese
Crushed potatoes and beans with cheese, 744

Desserts
Almond cake 1, 874
Almond cake 3, 876
Apple and pear cake, 877
Apple charlotte, 773–774
Apple fritters with Moscato wine, 798
Apple pancakes, 833
Barbajada, 750
Biscotti from Prosto, 755
Boiled chestnuts, 770
Butter cake, 855
Chestnuts with cream, 762–763
Chocolate salame, 853
Cornmeal fruitcake, 753
Crumbly almond cake, 883
Custard, 772
Egg cocktail, 851
Fruitcake 3, 815
Layered sponge cake, 790
Mascarpone cake with Marsala, 814
Mascarpone cream, 783–784
Nuns' fritters for Carnival, 795
Panettone, 829–830
Paradise cake, 882
Pear cake, 874
Sweet cornmeal bread, 825
Torta di farina gialla (cornmeal cake), 876

Vanilla ring cake, 757
Fish
Agoni alla navett (shad "boat-style"), 429
Pike in anchovy sauce, 465
Pike-perch in shrimp and mushroom sauce, 477
Shad in green sauce, 428
Soused fish, 476–477
Soused shad, 428
Stewed eel, 433
Whitefish in white wine, 463

Meat
Beef in sauce, 606
Braised beef, 606
Breaded veal chops, 565–566
Christmas turkey, 658
Cremona-style snails, 604
Donkey stew, 653
Foie gras, 643
Goose ragù, 635
Goose with cabbage, 611
Guinea hen with mascarpone, 570
Jugged hare 2, 596
Leftover meatballs, 628–629
Lesso misto (boiled meats), 599
Milk-roasted veal, 519
Mushrooms with loin and sausage, 546
Oven-roasted venison, 563
Pan-fried pork, 581
Partridges and polenta, 619–620
Pheasant in Spanish sauce, 568
Pheasant or guinea hen in sauce, 569
Pork and cabbage stew, 543
Pork and chickpeas for All Soul's Day, 605
Pork stew, 656
Rabbit Roulade, 629
Roast saddle of venison, 646
Sautéed frogs, 636
Spiedo bresciano or polenta e uccelli (polenta and birds), 650
Stewed beef Milan-style, 607
Stewed snails with herbs, 603–604
Stracotto di pecora (lamb stew), 655
Stuffed hen Cremona-style, 583
Veal rump in aspic, 575
Veal shanks Milan-style, 613

Pasta, polenta, rice
Baked crepes with bread and cheese filling, 287
Baked polenta with meat sauce 1, 324–325
Bergamo-style stuffed pasta, 227–228
Black polenta, 324
Brescia-style stuffed pasta, 228
Buckwheat and cornmeal polenta taragna with cheese, 325–326
Buckwheat pasta with cabbage, 318

Country-style risotto, 355
"Drowned" polenta, 326
Frog leg risotto, 352–353
La frigolada, 245
Pasta with mascarpone, 298
"Priest stranglers" green gnocchi in butter and sage sauce, 387–388
Pumpkin ravioli 2, 417
Rice and asparagus, 343–344
Rice and turnips, 346
Risotto with beans, 360
Risotto with bladder campion and onion, 359
Risotto with salame, 355–356
Risotto with salame and onion, 366
Risotto with sausage 2, 366–367
Risotto with squash and beans, 363
Rough-cut pasta with beans, 285
Saffron risotto with mushrooms, 354
Sausage-filled pasta with butter sauce, 227
Tortelli Cremasco-style, 417

Soups
Barley soup 4, 140–141
Bread soup, 142
Bread soup 2, 158
Cheese and onion bread in broth, 160
Chestnut mash 1, 122
Chicken and pasta soup, 154
Minestra di sondalo (elderberry soup), 146
Rice and egg soup, 127
Soup of the dead, 128
Soup with bread dumplings 2, 124
Soup with shaved pasta 1, 142
Soup with shaved pasta 2, 143
Tripe and Bean Stew, 115

Vegetables
Asparagus with fried eggs, 672
Beans and pork, 686
Eggplant balls, 715
Eggplant pie, 730
Mostarda mantovana, 704
Spiced cabbage with egg, 714
Sweet-and-sour onions, 684

MARCHE
Appetizers
Fried baccalà balls, 66
Stuffed olives, 46–47

Cheese
Cheese rolls, 742

Desserts
Anisette fritters, 860
Baked apple pastry, 784
Baked rice pudding with chocolate, 757–758
Custard tart, 809
Fruitcake with nuts, 800–801

Fish
Clams in parsley and wine, 503
Meat
Baked game, 639–640
Beef medallions, 608
Chicken with onion and tomato
sauce, 627
Duck with olives, 615
Fried lamb offal, 580
Goose with fennel, 612
Hunter-style lamb, 510
Lamb stew with eggs, 642
Mixed fry Ascolo-Piceno-style,
582–583
Pan-roasted chicken, 625
Quail with peas, 633
Roast pigeon with black olives,
623
Roast stuffed rabbit with fennel,
562
Roast suckling pig, 630
Roast young lamb, 544
Snails with fennel, 602
Squab stuffed with meat, 623
Tripe in sauce, 662
Veal casserole with tomato and
cheese, 617
Veal stew, 668–669
Veal tripe in tomato sauce, 663
Pasta, polenta, rice
Baked polenta and sausage, 327
Bucatini with mullet sauce, 221
Duck with rice, 215
Gnocchi with duck sauce, 254
Green rice, 348
Marche-style lasagna, 422
Mariner's spaghetti, 386
Pappardelle with quail and fennel,
296
Pasta with black olives and
mushrooms, 376
Pasta with Campofilone-style
meat sauce, 277
Pasta with white mullet, 281–282
Shrimp risotto with zucchini
flowers, 369
Spaghetti with black truffle, 381
Tagliatelle with baby squid, 395
Tagliatelle with beans, 395
Tagliolini with black truffle, 399
Tagliolini with squid and shrimp,
399–400
Thin tagliatelle with squid and
shrimp, 398
Soups
Anchovy and cauliflower stew, 103
Chickpea soup, 130
Farro soup 2, 135
Farro with zucchini flowers, 115
Fish soup Ancona-style, 100–101
Fish soup Fano-style, 102
Fish soup from Porto Recanati,
102–103
Marche-style "cooked water"
soup, 93

Passatelli in fish broth, 163–164
Vegetables
Braised cardoon, 692
Cauliflower and olives, 681
Fava beans and anchovies, 688
Melanzane sott'olio (pickled
eggplant), 702
Potato and truffle gratin, 708

MOLISE
Appetizers
Calcioni (fried dumplings with
prosciutto and cheese), 11
Caponata 2, 14
Crostini with mussels, 24–25
Oranges with anchovies, 3
Pickled fish 2, 77
Pizza di verdure (pizza with
vegetables), 62
Pork salad, 39
Stuffed mussels, 22
Cheese
Fried ricotta, 742–743
Pallotte (cheese and sausage
dumplings), 741
Desserts
Almond nougat 2, 870–871
Cherry marmalade cookies,
772–773
Nut crescents, 779
Pesche di Castelbottaccio
("stuffed peaches"), 839
Fish
Cod in wine, 437
Marinated skate, 480
Sea bass with tomato, 490
Stewed octopus "in Purgatory,"
479
Stuffed mullet, 501
Stuffed squid 1, 450
Meat
Baked lamb with egg and cheese,
511–512
Baked mutton, 609
Goat in sauce, 532
Lamb and peas, 513
Lamb stew, 647
Lamb with hops, 514
Lamb with olives, 512
Liver and escarole, 574
Molise-style ragù, 635–636
Pezzata, 622
Roast pork, 615
Stuffed tripe, 610
Tripe with potatoes, 661–662
Pasta, polenta, rice
Cavatelli with eggs and pancetta,
230–231
Corn Pone with turnips, 317
Fusilli alla molisana, 245
Pasta squares with John Dory, 391
Pasta squares with meat sauce,
391
Pasta with beans, 284
St. Joseph's lunch, 328

Torcinelli (stuffed lamb's
intestines), 415
Vermicelli with eel sauce, 421
Whole wheat spaghetti with
anchovies and breadcrumbs,
387
Soups
Baked pasta with hen and broth,
176–177
Bread soup with bay leaf, 160
Cardoon and meatball soup, 105
Cheese balls in broth, 157–158
Farro soup 3, 135
Fish and vegetable soup, 106
Fish soup Termoli-style, 104
Pappone di tornola ("Fisherman's
Dinner"), 162
Pasta water pick-me-up, 177
Pesce fuiute ("fake fish" soup),
170
Vegetables
Braised broccoli, 673
Scrambled eggs with peppers, 672
Spicy stuffed peppers, 710

PIEMONTE
Appetizers
Anchovies in tomato sauce, 2
Asparagus with Gorgonzola, 5
Bagna caôda, 6
Beef roll-ups with tuna sauce, 42
Breadsticks, 38
Buckwheat flatbread, 69
Caesar's mushrooms with truffles,
47
Duck terrine, 82
Fried eggs in sauce, 87
Gorgonzola-stuffed celery, 79
Green sauce for boiled meat, 5
Insalata di gallina cotta nel fieno
(hen cooked in hay), 40
Marinated trout, 87
Meatless stuffed onions, 18–19
Mushroom and truffle salad, 39
Onions in the Piedmontese
tradition, 19
Onions stuffed with meat, 18
Pan-cooked peppers, 56
Rabbit and pork pâté, 55
Rice salad with anchovies, 41
Salame frittata 1, 33
Stewed frittata strips, 86
Stuffed zucchini blossoms, 27
Vegetable pie, 54
Winemaker-style snails, 44
Cheese
Fondue with white truffles, 738
Marinated tomini, 744–745
Ricotta mantecata con cialde
(marinated ricotta), 742
Desserts
Amaretti pudding, 762
Blancmange with amaretti, 756
Canestrelli of Piemonte, 765
Carnival fritters, 994

Chestnut "mountain," 816–817
Chocolate, 808
Cornmeal sponge cake, 845
Crescent cookies, 787
Focaccia with ricotta, 794–795
Hazelnut cake, 878
Peach and amaretti semifreddo, 861
Pear cake, 823
Pear pie, 773
Plum cake, 880
Pumpkin cake, 791
Ricotta cheesecake, 785–786
Rum fritters, 758
Spiced shortbread, 758
Torta novecento (1900 cake), 883
Tredici erbe ("thirteen herb liqueur"), 887
Ugly but good macaroons, 759
Vanilla panna cotta, 832
Zabaglione, 886

Fish
Anchovies in green sauce, 426–427
Anchovies in red sauce, 426
Cod and potato stew 1, 492
Pike-perch in cream, 471–472
Tuna roll, 480

Meat
Baked lamb and potatoes, 513
Beef braised in Barolo, 524
Boar with forest berries, 547–548
Chicken and ricotta croquettes, 567
Cima (stuffed calf's breast), 549
Country-style liver, 574
Donkey and cabbage stew, 658
Finanziera all piedmontese (braised beef), 577
Friceu 'd sangh (pig's blood fritters), 581
Goose confit contadina-style, 611
Hunter-style chicken 1, 626
Hunter-style partridges, 619
Jugged hare 1, 595
Kid in wine, 535
Leg of lamb with chestnuts, 563–564
Meat braised with cabbage, 525
Mixed fry Alba-style, 580
Pheasant with truffles, 569–570
Pork shanks, 613
Rabbit Asti-style, 556
Rabbit in red wine, 556
Rabbit with pepper sauce, 561
Rabbit with peppers, 560
Roast capon, 528–529
Sausage frittata, 579
Stewed pork, 638
Stewed rabbit with potato, 557–558
Stuffed cabbage, 529
Stuffed duck, 516

Stuffed duck with veal and pork, 517
Stuffed pork spleen, 609
Stuffed zucchini flowers, 529–530
Sweet-and-sour meatballs 1, 627–628
Tripe and beans, 667
Tripe in spiced tomato sauce, 666
Veal hock, 585
Veal shank with Barolo wine, 651–652
Veal stew, 649

Pasta, polenta, rice
Agnolotti gobbi astigiani-Albesi ai tre arrosti (agnolotti with three roasts), 213
Bigoli with duck 1, 218
Brusarol, 222
Buckwheat porridge, 376
Fondue-stuffed pasta with veal broth, 267
Fontina gnocchi with sage cream, 419
Fried small gnocchi, 249–250
Frog risotto, 365
Gnocchi in meat sauce, 252–253
Half-Moon Pasta with meat-and-spinach filling, 212
Half-Moon Pasta with Spinach and Ricotta Filling, 214–215
Homemade rough-cut pasta with leeks, 285
Pasta stuffed with sweetbreads and borage, 285–286
Pasta with potatoes and pancetta, 309
Polenta with leeks, 319–320
Polenta with spring greens, 326–327
Polenta with white beans and cabbage, 319
Pumpkin-potato gnocchi, 254
Rice and mushrooms, 348
Rice with beans, 292
Rice with beans, cabbage, and pork, 292
Rice with beans, cabbage, and salame, 291
Rice with cheese sauce, 347
Rice with smoked cheese, 378
Risotto with baked sole, shrimp, and hollandaise, 370
Risotto with Barbera, 349–350
Risotto with Barolo, 350
Risotto with cream of leek, 353
Risotto with fennel, 349
Risotto with freshwater prawns, 358–359
Risotto with giblets, 365
Risotto with Gorgonzola, 350
Risotto with mushrooms, 349
Risotto with perch and zucchini flowers, 358
Risotto with red wine, 352

Risotto with saffron and zucchini flowers, 358
Risotto with sausage and rum, 356
Risotto with snails, 363
Risotto with Spumante, fontina, and mushrooms, 357
Risotto with tench, 362
Saffron risotto soufflé, 351
Small gnocchi with ricotta and porcini, 248–249
Tagliatelle in egg sauce, 397–398
Tagliatelle with truffle, 401
Taglierini in meat sauce, 400

Soups
Barley soup, 202
Bean and chestnut soup, 106
Bean and rice soup, 107
Bean soup 2, 132
Bread soup 3, 159
Cabbage and cheese soup, 180
Cabbage and pork-rind soup, 149
Cardoon and Jerusalem artichoke soup, 129
Chestnut mash 2, 122–123
Chickpea and pork soup, 156
Chickpea soup, 112
Cream of zucchini soup, 113
Leek and chestnut soup, 144
Lentil soup, 138
Minestra di riso (rice soup), 144
Onion soup, 195
Pasta and bean soup, 180
Pork and beans, 114
Potato and leek soup, 203
Rice, beans, milk, and salame, 175
Rice and chestnut soup, 206
Rice and pansies, 174
Rice soup with squash, 145
Rice with milk and chestnuts, 174
Tagliatelle and chestnut soup, 147
Tagliatelle with chicken livers, 125
Tripe soup, 107
Trippa del "Vecchio Salera," 182
Vegetable soup, 157
Walnut soup, 139
Wedding soup 3, 152

Vegetables
Artichoke flan, 728–729
Baked artichokes with egg sauce, 677
Cardoons with truffles, 679
Cipolline d'Ivrea (Ivrea onions), 684
Marinated zucchini strips, 734
Potato balls, 685
Ratatouille Piedmont-style, 721
Salam ad patati (potato salami), 723
Sautéed zucchini, 734–735
Stuffed onions, 727
Stuffed peppers with tuna, 712
Truffled potatoes, 707

PUGLIA

Appetizers
Bread with olives, 51
Carnival calzone, 12
Olio santo (peppered olive oil), 50
Olive and ricotta calzones, 11–12
Olive bread, 67
Pizza with potatoes and olives, 64–65
Spicy tomato sauce, 80
Stuffed pizza, 76

Cheese
Large tomato and mozzarella ravioli, 740–471
Smoked scamorza salad with mushrooms, 743

Desserts
Almond spaghetti, 809
Almond tart with chocolate glaze, 751
Apostles' fingers (ricotta-stuffed crêpes), 788–789
Cherry-almond tart, 873
Glazed sweet rolls, 748
Grape jam, 813–814
Home-style biscotti, 754
Orange marmalade, 813
Ricotta pie, 843
Sweet Easter bread, 856
Wheat-berry pudding 2, 805
Wine pinwheels, 767

Fish
Angler in tomato sauce, 479
Baked whitebait, 444
Cuttlefish baked in foil, 455
Fish cooked in salt, 469
Grilled cod, 438
Halibut and seafood stew, 457
Herb-stuffed gilthead bream, 469
Mackerel in vinegar, 488
Mussels au gratin, 459
Puglia-style mussels, 458
Stuffed cuttlefish 2, 485–486
Stuffed mussels, 459
Stuffed sardines 2, 482
Stuffed squid 2, 450
Sweet-and-sour mussels, 457

Meat
Easter lamb, 513
Lamb and potatoes, 512
Lamb stew, 568
Marro, 607
Meatballs, 632
Mushrooms in lamb sauce, 538
Mutton stew with potatoes, 656
Rabbit and onions, 559–560
Rabbit with peppers and olives, 560
Salame di agnello (lamb sausage), 640
Stuffed sheep tripe, 632–633

Pasta, polenta, rice
Baked rice Foggia-style, 404–405

Baked rice with mussels and potatoes, 404
Baked rice with seafood, 406
Baked seafood linguine, 272
Bread balls in tomato sauce, 327
Buckwheat Pasta with Zucchini, 389
Capunti with lamb sauce, 226–227
Chicory timbale, 407
Fettuccine with white fava beans, 238
Fillings for tiellas, 340–341
"Gendarme hat" pasta pie, 225–226
Lasagne in meat sauce, 373
Linguine with cuttlefish ragù, 272
Linguine with razor clams, 272
Long-cooked pasta with stew and broth, 279–280
Macaroni with arugula, 276
Mignuic or cavatielli, 288
Orecchiette with artichokes, 290
Orecchiette with ricotta, 291
Orecchiette with turnip tops, 290
Panzerotti, 295
Pasta asciutta alla pugliese, 301
Pasta with breaded tomatoes, 306
Pasta with broccoli 3, 302
Pasta with chickpeas and onion, 231–232
Potato and vegetable gratin, 405–406
Potato-mushroom gratin, 405
Puglian meat sauce, 329–330
St. Joseph's pasta, 266
Sardine and artichoke casserole, 418
Troccoli al ragù di polpo (thick-cut pasta with octopus sauce), 418
Ziti and meatballs, 309

Soups
Baked lasagna with broth, 120
Bean soup 5, 196
Bread soup with arugula and potatoes, 160
Callariedde, 107
Cannelicchje e fafe, 109
Cavatelli with arugula and potatoes, 111
Chickpea purée with shrimp and clams, 162
Fava, broccoli, and chicory soup, 191
Fava bean soup, 118
Fish soup Brindisi-style, 205
Pasta and chickpea soup 2, 165
Pasta and lentil soup, 167
Pastina in fish sauce, 168
Peasant soup, 111
"Salted water" soup 1, 96
Tomato soup, 156

Vegetable soup with squash and barley, 199
Wedding soup 4, 152
Zuppa di pesce gallipolina (fish soup Gallipoli-style), 205

Vegetables
Cardoons gratinée, 680
Eggplant Parmigiana 2, 705–706
Fava beans and chicory 1, 688–689
Fava purée, 718–719
Peas with sautéed bread, 703
Pomodori sott'olio (pickled tomatoes), 718
Sformato di lampascioni con salsa di sedano (timbales of muscari and potato flan), 726
Stuffed eggplants, 702
Stuffed peppers, 712–713
Vegetables and pancetta, 732

SARDEGNA

Appetizers
Music-paper-bread salad, 52
Onion pizzas, 2

Desserts
Nut and raisin candy, 833
Pane carasau fritters, 798
Ricotta-stuffed cookies, 833–834
Sardinian orange slices, 749
Sweet cheese pastries, 861

Fish
Boiled lobster, 436–437
Eels and trout in a spicy sauce, 435
Fish in walnut sauce, 448
Fish soup, 455
Mullet with Vernaccia, 501
Roast striped mullet, 455–456
Sea bass in wine sauce, 490

Meat
Bean stew with beef and ham, 598
Beef pot roast, 587
Beef roll-ups, 553
Braised pork ribs, 625
Chicken-stuffed turkey, 618
Lamb with white sauce, 515
Meat roll-ups, 592
Myrtle-scented hen, 631
Sardegnan stewed tripe, 661
Sausage and fava bean stew, 573

Pasta, polenta, rice
Baked bread and cheese with broth, 391
Meat (or vegetable or fish) pastries 1, 262
Meat pastries 2, 263
Music-paper bread with poached eggs, 291
Sardinian-style pasta stuffed with potato and mint, 235–236
Sardinian-style stuffed pasta with spinach, 235

Small Sardinian gnocchi with
meat sauce, 284
Stuffed pasta, 215–216
Soups
Beef broth with barley flour, mint,
and pecorino, 181
Clam soup, 125
Fregula soup, 117
Soup with salt cheese, 150
Vegetables
Squash purée, 719
Steamed artichokes, 674
Sweet-and-sour zucchini, 734

SICILIA
Appetizers
Almond-and-anchovy sauce, 75
Bread and tomato salad, 51
Fava-bean fritters, 52
Fried cheese, 9
Green sauce, 74
Meat pie with elderberry, 83
Mixed fried vegetables, 36
Olive oil, lemon, and garlic sauce
2, 74–75
Pasta and fava-bean cubes, 44
Prosciutto and cheese fritters, 68
Rice balls with meat and peas, 4
Ricotta and sausage dumplings,
82
Rolled pizza, 59
Sausage timbale, 82–83
Seafood rice balls, 3–4
Seafood salad 2, 40
Sicilian pizza 1, 59
Sicilian pizza 2, 65
Snails with picchi pacchi sauce,
16
Desserts
Almond and fig-filled Christmas
cookies, 788
Almond-chocolate tartlets, 853
Almond paste, 834–835
Blood-orange gelatin, 802–803
Cassata from Sicilia, 768–769
Christmas nougat, 871
Christmas ring cookies, 840
Cream baskets, 831
Filled cannoli, 765–766
Glazed S cookies, 869
Lemon pudding, 760
Mandarin gelatin, 804
Marzipan-filled cookies, 769–770
Orange cake, 872
Orange-peel balls, 822
Quince paste, 780–781
Rice pudding 2, 851
Ricotta cheesecake, 800
Watermelon ice, 803
Wheat-berry pudding 1, 787
Fish
Baked anchovies, 466
Baked fresh tuna, 460
Cod in sauce, 437

Crespelle di "mucco rosso," 463
Fish in vegetable sauce, 472
Fried tuna with lemon and
parsley, 458
Grouper in sauce, 456
Marinated tope (shark), 469
Monkfish with olives, 491
Sarde salate (salted sardines), 482
Sardine and lettuce soup, 505
Steamed swordfish 2, 473
Stuffed small cuttlefish 2, 486
Stuffed sardines 1, 480–481
Swordfish pie, 468
Swordfish steaks, 445–446
Swordfish with peppers, 474
Tuna and onions, 499
Meat
Braised rooster, 583
Goat braised with mushrooms,
536
Grilled veal Messina-style,
523–524
Hunter-style rabbit, 557
Lamb with fava beans, 545
Meat and cheese soufflé, 644
Meat and salame pie, 646
Onion-glazed beef, 509
Stewed kid, 534
Tripe with eggplant and walnuts,
665–666
Veal and potatoes, 541–542
Pasta, polenta, rice
Baked macaroni and rice with
pork, 408
Baked macaroni with eggplant,
407
Baked rice mold, 401–402
Baked rigatoni with braised pork
and eggs, 402–403
Baked winter pasta, 297–298
Busiati with pesto, 222
Crown of rice with squid, 233
Curly lasagne with ricotta and
cauliflower, 270
Cuscus, 236
Cuscus con zuppa di pesce, 237
Cuscus siciliano, 238
Ditalini with anchovies and sun-
dried tomatoes, 237
Gnoccoli with tuna sauce, 261
Homemade pasta with baby
anchovies, 282
Lasagne with ricotta e melanzane,
269
Pasta for hard times (with
broccoli and anchovies),
265–266
Pasta with bottarga 2, 303
Pasta with breadcrumbs and
anchovies 1, 303–304
Pasta with breadcrumbs and
anchovies 2, 304
Pasta with broccoli 1, 301
Pasta with broccoli 2, 302

Pasta with broccoli and
anchovies, 300–301
Pasta with eggplant and ricotta
salata, 299
Pasta with fried broccoli,
302–303
Pasta with fried eggplants, 300
Pasta with sardines 1, 305–306
Pasta with sardines 2, 306
Polenta with broccoli and
pancetta, 321
Rice and pasta baked with
meatballs, 408–409
Sicilian-style Vermicelli, 421
Seafood risotto, 353–354
Spaghetti and lobster, 387
Spaghetti with cuttlefish ink, 298
Spaghetti with tuna, 381
Tagliatelle with squash blossoms,
395–396
Uncle Vincenzo's rigatoni
(rigatoni with anchovies,
broccoli, and breadcrumbs),
309
Soups
Beef soup with meatballs and
eggs, 184
Fava bean purée 2, 122
Rice balls in soup 1, 117
Rice balls in soup 2, 117–118
Veal meatballs with ricotta in
broth, 178
Vegetables
Artichoke caponata, 675
Braised or fried cardoons, 681
Braised wild asparagus, 673
Cauliflower balls, 716
Christmas caponata, 675
Christmas salad, 694
Eggplant Parmigiana 3, 706–707
Eggplant roll-ups, 695
Fried eggplant sandwiches, 698
Salad of crushed olives, 694
Sicilian caponata, 676
Spring vegetable stew, 728
Spring vegetables with vinegar,
690
Stuffed peppers with caciocavallo,
713
Sweet-and-sour stuffed peppers,
711–712
Swiss chard and ricotta, 730
Twice-fried eggplant sandwiches,
698–699
Winter caponata, 674–675

TOSCANA
Appetizers
Barberina sauce, 72
Chicken-liver paté canapes, 25
Crostini with liver and spleen, 25
Eggs in garlic sauce, 88
Frittata di Vitalba, 32
Marinated bread salad, 53

Migliaccio (baked blood
pudding), 45
Myrtle cream crostini, 24
Pastry leaves, 52
Sage-and-anchovy fritters, 2
Sausage sauce, 73
Smoked spiced veal, 21
Sweet-and-sour sauce, 70
Tarragon sauce, 71
Vegetable tart, 78
Desserts
Almond biscotti 1, 767
Almond paste cookies, 850–851
Baked rice custard from Carrare,
879
Chestnut cake, 770
Chocolate rolled cake, 802
Copate bianche (almond wafers),
780
Copate nere (wafer cookies), 781
Cream-filled sponge cake, 889
Flatbread with dried figs, 858
Flatbread with rosemary and
raisins, 858–859
Fried pasta ribbons, 772
Fried wine knots, 821
Fruitcake 1, 751–752
Honey-nut sticks, 789
Lucca ring cake, 759–760
Migliacci dolci di maiale, 817
Necci (chestnut-flour crepes),
820
Panforte Margherita (fruitcake),
830
Pisa-style rice tart, 873
Sweet chestnut polenta, 836
Sweet yeasted flatbread, 859
Tuscan chestnut loaf, 790
Tuscan sweet bread, 752
Zucchini cake, 856
Fish
Boiled cod, 483
Cod Arezzo-style, 441
Codfish Florence-style, 438–439
Eel in sauce, 436
Eels Giovi-style, 430–431
Fish stew Livorno-style, 449
Fish stew Viareggio-style,
449–450
Fried eel marinated in vinegar
sauce, 483–484
Mullet with plum tomato, 500
Stewed cuttlefish 2, 484
Stockfish with tomatoes and
potatoes, 495
Tope and mushrooms, 470
Tuna-and-anchovy crepes, 467
Tuscan seafood stew, 451
Meat
Boiled beef stew, 577
Braised snout, 588
Braised veal, 552
Breaded pig livers, 573
Farro and pig's trotters, 572

Fish stew with duck, 658–659
Giblet stew, 546–547
Hunter-style chicken 3, 626
Hunter's-style kid offal, 563
Lamb stew with tomatoes, 527
Leg of lamb baked in embers,
510
Mixed Braised Meats, 645
Mutton sauce, 619
Pan-cooked rabbit, 561
Pork cutlets in wine, 522
Ranocchi fritti (fried frogs), 637
Roast pork loin, 518
Steak Florentine, 519
"Sweet-and-strong" boar, 550
Tripe Florentine-style, 663
Tripe Pisa-style, 665
Veal cutlets with mushroom caps,
643–644
Pasta, polenta, rice
Black risotto with cuttlefish ink
and chard, 370–371
Chestnut-flour gnocchi, 255
Griddled pasta, 403–404
Homemade twisted pasta, 316
Layered polenta with sausage and
mushrooms, 287–288
Macaroni with chard sauce, 413
Meatless ravioli 2, 335
Pappardelle in hare sauce,
294–295
Pappardelle with boar, 296–297
Polenta with beans and cabbage,
263
Polenta with beans and *cavolo
nero*, 324
Tuscan ragù, 331
Tuscan tortelli, 414
Twisted pasta in bread sauce, 316
Soups
Bean soup 3, 132
Bread soup 4, 159
"Cooked water" Casentino-style
soup, 92
"Crazy water" soup, 92
Farro soup 4, 136
Lucca spring veal and vegetable
stew, 118
Maremma-style "Cooked water"
soup 2, 95–96
Marjoram broth with poached
eggs, 168–169
Minestrone, 154
Polenta soup with *cavolo nero*, 116
Polenta with black kale, 99–100
Sweet onion soup, 109–110
Tagliolini in broth with chicken
giblets, 183
Tomato soup, 161
Vegetable and bean stew, 173
Vegetables
Fagioli infiascati (beans in a
bottle), 687
Stuffed celery, 724

TRENTINO-ALTO ADIGE
Appetizers
Potato pie or "tartlets," 84
Desserts
Apple dumplings, 807
Apple strudel, 867–868
Apricot dumplings, 807
Buckwheat cake, 875–876
Emperor's frittata, 796
Fruit ravioli, 863
Walnut pudding, 760
Fish
Cod Trentino-style, 439
Stockfish and potatoes 2, 494
Meat
Baked pork shanks, 651
Beef steaks with onion, 564
Brain soufflé, 526–527
Carne salata (salted meat), 542
Goulash, 589
Hunter-style mutton, 544
Meat pie, 540
Oxtail stew, 648
Potato and meat pie, 661
Steaks with horseradish sauce,
520–521
Stewed hare, 598
Sweet-and-sour veal snout, 610
Trentino-style hare, 595
Trentino-style rabbit, 558–559
Tyrolean chamois, 527–528
Tyrolean steak, 576
Veal "birds," 668
Veal brains "sandwiches," 631
Venison loin with red cabbage
timbale and currants, 600
Venison medallions, 608
Venison with berries, 536–537
Pasta, polenta, rice
"Appetite-buster" sausage
casserole, 379
Baked mushroom crespelle, 310
Black-bread gnocchi with hops,
264
Cheese gnocchi, 250
Cheese-stuffed dumplings, 264
Fried sauerkraut ravioli, 334
Gnocchi with sardines, 255
Polenta and snails, 322–323
"Priest stranglers" green gnocchi
in butter sauce, 388
Small butter gnocchi in broth, 248
Small spinach gnocchi in
prosciutto sauce, 249
Spätzle, 248
Spinach dumplings 1, 265
Spinach ravioli, 336
Soups
Barley soup 2, 140
Barley soup 3, 140
Crostini all milza per minestra
(spleen crostini), 111
Dumplings with speck in broth,
119

Goulash soup, 138
Mushroom soup, 105
Piquant tripe soup, 187
Potato and mushroom soup, 203
Rice and frankfurter soup, 147
Tripe soup, 149
Wine soup, 208
Vegetables
Bitter greens salad with warm
bacon dressing, 693

UMBRIA
Appetizers
Barbazza scottata (fried pork
cheek), 7
Bread with walnuts, 51
Coppa (pork sausage), 20
Cornmeal pizza, 62
Easter cheese bread, 22
Easter frittata, 33
Easter pizza with cheese, 63
Pizza with cracklings, 61
Ring cakes with cheese, 17
Truffle frittata, 32
Truffle sauce, 71
Desserts
Almond-fruit biscotti, 884–885
Drunken toast, 786
Easter buns, 845
Rolled chocolate cake, 852
Spice nut cake from Terni, 824
Walnut nougat, 821
Fish
Carbonaretti del Lago di
Piediluco (fire-scorched
perch), 454
Carp roasted in wild fennel,
453–454
Cod fritters, 462
Cod with raisins and prunes, 441
Fried shad, 427
Shrimp in green sauce, 462
Spit-roasted eel, 432
Stewed eels and perch, 496–497
Tench soup, 447
Trout with parsley sauce, 502
Trout with truffle sauce, 502
Meat
Baked tripe in crust, 667–668
Giblet stew with eggs, 552
Guinea hen pâté, 570–571
Kidneys in wine, 659
Labbritti con i fagioli (labbritti
and beans), 594
Lamb fricassee, 514
Lamb offal with artichokes, 562
Lamb with truffle, 515
Porchetta (spit-roasted pig), 630
Pork and sweetbreads with beans,
614
Pork with chervil sauce, 540
Rabbit with fennel, 555
Roba cotta ("cooked stuff"), 638
Spit-roasted squab, 614
Squab on skewers, 623–624

Stuffed roast duck, 516–517
Sweet-and-sour pork, 605
Veal cutlets in sauce, 520
Pasta, polenta, rice
Baked pasta pie, 375
Gnocchi with goose sauce, 251
Homemade pasta with chicken
giblets, 281
Homemade pasta with guanciale
and sausage, 314
Lamb ragù, 330
Pasta Scheggino-style, 275
Pasta "snails" with sausage, 275
Pasta with mushrooms and garlic,
232–233
Risotto with wild greens, 359
Small gnocchi made with
breadcrumbs in bean sauce,
247
Spaghetti with guanciale and
tomato sauce, 385
Spaghetti with truffles, 385
Strengozzi with garlic, chili, and
tomatoes, 389
Tagliolini with black truffle from
Norcia, 399
Terni-style pasta with garlic and
oil, 232
Soups
Bean soup 4, 132–133
Chestnut and chickpea soup 2,
195
Cicerchia soup, 131
Farro soup 5, 136
Pasta and chickpea soup 3, 165
Tench and tagliolini soup 2, 148

VALLE D'AOSTA
Appetizers
Boiled chestnuts with butter,
15–16
Carnesecca valdostana (Valdostan
cured meat), 16
Cured chamois on crostini, 45
Lardo di Arnad (marinated lard),
42
Mammella di mucca (brined
udders), 43
Marinated toma cheese, 30
Polenta balls, 50
Prosciutto di Bosses (jambon de
Bosses), 67
Sanguinaccio valdostano (blood
pudding), 76
Cheese
Marinated tomino cheese, 740
Potato purée with cheese, 741
Valdostan fondue, 738
Desserts
Almond bread pudding, 889–890
Almond coffee, 763
Berry-cheese cream, 783
Chocolate cream, 782–783
Ice cream with chocolate sauce,
781

Old-fashioned rice pudding cake,
879
Pears in wine, 837
Rum custard, 783
Sweet bread from Cogne, 826
Valdostan apple cake, 791
Walnut soup, 890
Zuppetta di vino ("donkey's
soup"), 889
Fish
Trout in red wine, 501
Meat
Baked meat and vegetables, 617
Beef carbonnade, 538
Chamois in onion sauce, 528
Cheese-filled veal chops, 566
Ox in wine sauce, 576
Pork roll-ups, 591
Veal cutlets with fontina, 642–643
Veal in white wine, 539
Veal roll-ups, 591
Veal stew "White Lady," 578
Pasta, polenta, rice
Barley polenta, 326
Buckwheat gnocchi with speck,
255–256
Butternut-squash gnocchi 1, 259
Chestnut fettuccine with cabbage
and pork, 241
Polenta with fontina, 321
Valdostan baked polenta, 323
Soups
Baked rice and beans with cheese,
175
Baked vegetable soup with black
bread and barley, 188
Barley soup 1, 139
Cheese soup, 187
Chestnut and rice soup, 129–130
Minestra di riso alla valdostana
(Valdostan rice soup), 146
Minestra primaverile di erbe di
Prato (spring herb soup), 153
Mountain soup from Valpelline,
188–189
Peasant soup, 209
Rice soup, 145
Rye-flour porridge, 171
Soup from Cogne, 178–179
Wild herb soup, 131
Zuppa al raperonzolo (rampion
soup), 186
Vegetables
Dandelion and pancetta salad,
693
Easter spring greens pie, 730
Grandma's prosciutto and beans,
717
Potato pancakes with blood
sausage, 684–685
Potatoes and pears, 708
Savoy cabbage flan, 725
Savoy cabbage flans with fonduta,
725
Vegetable pie, 707

VENETO

Appetizers

Frittata with ground meat, 34
Frittelle di maresina (herb
 fritters), 36
Liver pâté, 55
Marrow sauce, 56
Salame frittata 2, 34
Vol-au-vent with radicchio and
 cheese, 88–89

Cheese

Breaded cheese, 744
Homemade cheese, 743

Desserts

Almond nougat 1, 812
Apple-raisin pancakes, 806
Apple tart with mostarda, 877
Butter cake, 796
Cornmeal cookies, 886–887
Grappa fritters, 793
Layer cake, 836–837
Marmellata di castagne, 814
Polenta fruitcake, 801
Prune or apricot knödel, 11910
Puff pastries, 862
Rose fritte ("fried roses"), 852
Sandy cake, 882
Sponge cake, 846
Star cake, 819
Stuffed peaches with almonds,
 838–839
Sweet flatbread, 858
Sweet lasagna, 808
Sweet potato cake, 878
Ugly and good cookies, 759
Venetian biscotti, 750
Walnut caramel pie, 874–875
White pepper cookies, 839

Fish

Baked pasta with anchovies,
 487
Baked sturgeon, 496
Boiled pike, 466
Braised catfish 2, 471
Cod in parsley, 442
Cod Vicenza-style, 439–440
Creamed cod Veneto-style, 443
Creamed cod Vicenza-style,
 443–444
Eel with plums, 432
Fried eel, 433
Fried pike croquettes, 464–465
Fried soft-shell crabs, 467
Glassmaker's eel, 431–432
Pike—fried, grilled, and baked,
 464
Pike in sauce, 465
Roast cod, 440
Sardines in vinegar, 481
Schille or cragnoni con aglio e
 olio (shrimps in garlic and
 oil), 485
Shrimp and porcini gratin,
 487–488
Soused fish, 454

Stewed eel with peas, 433–434
Sturgeon with capers and olives,
 496
Treviso shrimp, 462

Meat

Beccacce all chiampese
 (woodcock Chiampo-style),
 520
Beccacce alla arzignanese
 (woodcock Arzignano-style),
 519
Boiled meats Padua-style,
 587–588
Cappone alla canevera (capon in
 pig's bladder), 533
Chicken in white wine, 625
Christmas snails, 600–601
Collo de castrato, risi, e piselli
 (lamb's neck), 554
Cooked soppressata, 647
Drunken hen, 584
Duck breast with cherry sauce,
 604
Duck stuffed with sausage and
 liver, 517–518
Duck with fruit, 615–616
Duckling fillet with poppies,
 515–516
Gallina cotta nel capretto (hens
 cooked in a kid), 585
Grilled guinea hen with bay
 leaves, 571
Guinea hen with black pepper
 sauce, 571–572
Hare in pepper sauce, 597
Hen with pheasant stuffing, 572
Horsemeat stew, 618
Involtini di musso alla pancetta
 (donkey roll-ups), 593
Liver and onions Venetian-style,
 575
Mallard in sauce, 586
Marrow sauce with pepper, 521
Pork cutlets with Savoy cabbage,
 565
Preserved smoked goose, 612
Quail in pastry with mushrooms,
 633–634
Quail Veneto-style, 633
Roast turkey with pomegranates,
 657
Stuffed squab, 622

Pasta, polenta, rice

Baked prosciutto and herb pie,
 312
Beet stuffed pasta with poppy
 seeds, 229
Bigoli with anchovies, 219
Bigoli with duck 2, 218
Bigoli with salted freshwater
 sardines, 217
Black risotto with cuttlefish ink,
 351
Black tagliatelle with cuttlefish,
 398

Butternut-squash gnocchi
 Belluno-style, 260
Cheese dumplings, 223
Feltre-style rice and beans, 344
"Free-range" risotto with
 gizzards, 368
Gnocchi stuffed with mushrooms,
 260
Macaroni pie 2, 311
Potato gnocchi Verona-style, 258
Radicchio crepes, 234–235
Rice and beans, 344
Rice and celery, 346
Rice and peas 1, 345
Rice and peas 2, 345
Rich risotto Padua-style, 371–372
Riso con i fegatini (rice and
 livers), 343
Risotto with honey mushrooms,
 360
Risotto with hop shoots, 368
Risotto with Lake Garda tench,
 363
Risotto with pork and veal, 357
Risotto with sausage and cabbage,
 362
Risotto with sausage and
 cauliflower, 367
Risotto with sea bass, 367
Risotto with *sècole*, 366
Risotto with shrimp and
 asparagus, 368–369
Spiced risotto with salame, 361
Spinach dumplings 2, 265
Spring risotto, 371
Tagliatelle in squab sauce, 393
Thick bigoli with goose and
 mushroom sauce, 219
Veronese rice and tripe, 346–347

Soups

Barley soup 5, 141
"Brooding" Pigeons (squab)
 Stew, 179
Fish soup, 204
Lake Garda fish soup, 192
Lamon bean soup, 133
Razor clams in broth, 108
Rice and potato soup 1, 145
Rice with celery and tomato, 176
Rice with chicken livers, 175
"Roots" and bean soup, 172
Scaliger soup, 187–188
Tripe soup 1, 207
Tripe soup 3, 208
Turnip greens soup, 113–114
Wedding soup 5, 152–153
White bean purée, 123

Vegetables

Asparagus with egg sauce,
 672–673
Grilled radicchio Treviso-style,
 720

INDEX *of* RECIPES

BY PRINCIPAL INGREDIENT

Almonds

Almond and chocolate layer cake, 843–844
Almond and fig-filled Christmas cookies, 788
Almond biscotti (Abruzzo), 755
Almond biscotti (Basilicata), 865
Almond biscotti 1, 767
Almond bread pudding, 889–890
Almond cake 1, 874
Almond cake 2, 875
Almond cake 3, 876
Almond cake glazed with chocolate, 834
Almond candy, 790–791
Almond coffee, 763
Almond cookies, 792
Almond nougat 1, 812
Almond nougat 2, 870–871
Almond paste, 834–835
Almond paste cookies, 850–851
Almond shortbread, 778–779
Almond spaghetti, 809
Almond tart, 872
Almond tart with chocolate glaze, 751
Almond wafers, 780
Almond-and-anchovy sauce, 75
Almond-chocolate tartlets, 853
Almond-fruit biscotti, 884–885
Baked fig and nut calzone, 820
Buckwheat cake, 875–876
Capri chocolate-almond cake, 872
Charterhouse-style sweet bread, 826–827
Cherry-almond tart, 873
Christmas Eve cake, 881
Christmas nougat, 871
Christmas ring cakes, 840
Coffee and chocolate pie, 881
Copate bianche (wafer cakes), 780
Cornmeal sponge cake, 845
Cream baskets, 831
Crumbly almond cake, 883
Drunken toasts, 786
Fruitcake 2 (Emilia-Romagna), 864–865
Fruitcake with nuts, 800–801
Home-style biscotti, 754
Honey almond cookies, 854
Honey biscuits, 837
Honey fritters, 778
Layer cake, 836–837
Marzipan-filled cookies, 769–770
Nut and raisin candy, 833
Nut crescents, 779

Panforte Margherita (fruitcake), 830
Quaresimali, 849
Raisin cookies, 792
Rose pudding, 762
"St. Joseph's Lunch," 329
Sardinian orange slices, 749
Semolina bread, 825
Semolina bread with wine must and almonds, 857
Sesame nougat, 871
Spice cake, 824
Spiced nut cake from Terni, 824
Squash cake, 85
Stuffed figs, 794
Stuffed peaches, 838
Stuffed peaches with almonds, 838–839
Sweet-and-sour meatballs 2 (Calabria), 628
Sweet-and-sour mussels, 457
Tagliolini pie, 880
Ugly and good cookies, 759
Ugly but good macaroons, 759
Yellow cake with fruit, 831

Amaretti cookies

Amaretti pudding, 762
Baked amaretto peaches, 838
Blancmange with amaretti, 756
Peach and amaretti semifreddo, 861
Pear cake, 823
Plum cake, 880
Stuffed peaches with almonds, 838–839
Sweet-and-sour meatballs 1 (Piemonte), 627–628
Tortelli Cremasco-style, 417

Anchovies

Almond-and-anchovy sauce, 75
Anchovies in green sauce, 426–427
Anchovies in red sauce, 426
Anchovies in tomato sauce, 2
Anchovies with endive, 429
Anchovy and cauliflower stew, 103
Anchovy balls, 478
Anchovy frittata, 461
Anchovy fritters, 34
Anchovy roll-ups, 445
Anchovy soup, 99
Bagna caôda, 6
Baked anchovies (Calabria), 428–429
Baked anchovies (Sicilia), 466
Baked pasta with anchovies, 487

Bigoli with anchovies, 219
Ditalini with anchovies and tomatoes, 237
Fava beans and anchovies, 688
Ferretti with anchovies and bread, 239
Fillings for *tiellas*, 340–341
Fried stuffed anchovies, 427
Green sauce for boiled meat, 5
Homemade pasta with baby anchovies, 282
Hunter's-style suckling lamb, 508
Linguine with anchovies, olives, and capers, 273
Little stuffed dumplings, 294
Marinated anchovies, 427
Mariner's spaghetti, 386
Oranges with anchovies, 3
Pasta for hard times (with broccoli and anchovies), 265–266
Pasta in anchovy sauce, 242
Pasta with anchovies and tuna, 423
Pasta with breadcrumbs and anchovies 1 (Sicilia), 303–304
Pasta with breadcrumbs and anchovies 2 (Calabria), 304
Pasta with broccoli and anchovies, 300–301
Pasta with sardines, anchovies, and breadcrumbs, 304
Pickled fish 2 (Molise), 77
Pike in anchovy sauce, 465
Pizza with anchovies and capers, 60
Puntarelle salad with anchovy dressing, 717–718
Ratatouille Piedmont-style, 721
Rice salad with anchovies, 41
Sage-and-anchovy fritters, 2
St. Joseph's pasta, 266
Soused bream, 445
Spaghetti alla colatura, 384
Spaghetti with anchovies, olives, and capers, 384
Spaghetti with baby anchovies, 385
Tielle de Gaeta, 406
Tuna-and-anchovy crepes, 467
Uncle Vincenzo's rigatoni (rigatoni with anchovies, broccoli, and breadcrumbs), 309
Whole wheat spaghetti with anchovies and breadcrumbs, 387

Anise liqueur and anisette

Almond-fruit biscotti, 884–885
Anisette fritters, 860
"Bones of the dead" cookies, 822

Coffee and chocolate pie, 881
Ricotta pie, 843

Anise seeds
Anise cookies, 748
Anise fritters with honey, 777
Anise ring cookies, 776
Charterhouse-style sweet bread,
    826–827
Glazed S cookies, 869
Lucca ring cake, 759–760
"Stairway to heaven" cookies, 854
Tortoli, 884

Apples
Apple and pear cake, 877
Apple Charlotte, 773–774
Apple dumplings, 807
Apple fritters, 797–798
Apple fritters with Moscato wine,
    798
Apple pancakes, 833
Apple strudel, 867–868
Apple tart, 777
Apple tart with mostarda, 877
Apple-raisin pancakes, 806
Baked apple pastry, 784
Valdostan apple cake, 791

Artichokes
Artichoke and cheese casserole, 724
Artichoke and fava bean stew, 682
Artichoke caponata, 675
Artichoke flan, 728–729
Artichoke pizza, 714–715
Baked artichokes, 677
Baked artichokes with egg sauce,
    677
Baked layered crepes with artichoke,
    409
Beef and vegetable pie, 410
Jewish-style artichokes, 677–678
Lamb and artichoke fricassee,
    578–579
Lamb offal with artichokes, 562
Layered pie with artichokes, 731
Maltagliati with artichoke sauce, 329
Meat and artichokes, 541
Orecchiette with artichokes, 290
Pizza with artichokes and ricotta,
    60–61
Rice timbale 1 (Campania), 374
Roman-style artichokes, 678–679
Rustic torte with artichokes, 731
Sardine and artichoke casserole, 418
Scrambled eggs with artichokes,
    692
Spring vegetable stew (Sicilia), 728
Steamed artichokes, 674
Vine-roasted artichokes, 678
Winter caponata, 674–675

Arugula
Bread soup with arugula and
    potatoes, 160

Cavatelli with arugula and potatoes,
    111
Macaroni with arugula, 276

Asparagus
Asparagus soup, 192
Asparagus with egg sauce, 672–673
Asparagus with fried eggs, 672
Asparagus with Gorgonzola, 5
Braised wild asparagus, 673
Frittata di Vitalba, 32
Rice and asparagus, 343–344
Risotto with shrimp and asparagus,
    368–369

Aspic
preparation of, 5
Veal rump in aspic, 575

Barley
Baked vegetable soup with black
    bread and barley, 188
Barley and potato soup, 155
Barley and vegetable soup, 142
Barley polenta, 326
Barley soup 1 (Valle d'Aosta), 139
Barley soup 2 (Alto Adige), 140
Barley soup 3 (Trentino), 140
Barley soup 4 (Lombardia),
    140–141
Barley soup 5 (Veneto), 141
Barley soup 6 (Piemonte), 202
Beef broth with barley flour, mint,
    and pecorino, 181
Vegetable soup with squash and
    barley, 199

Basil
Minestrone with basil, 126
Penne with tomatoes and basil, 315

Beans
Bean, cabbage, and potato soup,
    156–157
Bean, escarole, and pork soup, 198
Bean and chestnut soup, 106
Bean and pasta soup, 197
Bean and rice soup, 107
Bean and wild fennel soup, 196–197
Bean soup, 106
Bean soup 1 (Friuli-Venezia Giulia),
    131
Bean soup 2 (Piemonte), 132
Bean soup 3 (Toscana), 132
Bean soup 4 (Umbria), 132–133
Bean soup 5 (Puglia), 196
Bean soup with chicory and fennel,
    127
Bean soup with fermented turnips,
    134
Bean soup with musetto, 133
Bean soup with mushrooms, 134
Beans and pork, 686
Beans and roasted dried peppers,
    686

Beans in sauce, 727–728
Beans with dumplings, 114
Cannelichhje e fafe, 109
Cavatelli and beans, 230
Chickpea and bean soup, 124–125
Cicerchia soup, 131
Corn, bean, and potato soup, 137
Crushed potatoes and beans with
    cheese, 744
Fagioli infiascati (beans in a bottle),
    687
Feltre-style rice and beans, 344
Goat and beans, 533–534
Labbritti con i fagioli, 594
Lamon bean soup, 133
Lardari with tomatoes, 696
Le virtù (Virtues Soup), 185
Pasta and bean soup 1 (Campania),
    166
Pasta and bean soup 2 (Friuli-
    Venezia Giulia), 166
Pasta and bean soup 3 (Emilia-
    Romagna), 169
Pasta and bean soup 4 (Piemonte),
    180
Pasta and white beans, 307
Pasta with beans (Abruzzo), 373
Pasta with beans (Emilia-Romagna),
    179
Pasta with beans (Lazio), 119
Pasta with beans (Molise), 284
Pasta with beans and mushrooms,
    283
Polenta and beans (Abruzzo), 322
Polenta and beans (Lazio), 170
Polenta with beans and cabbage, 263
Polenta with beans and *cavolo nero*,
    324
Polenta with black kale, 99–100
Polenta with white beans and
    cabbage, 319
Pork and bean soup, 197
Pork and beans, 114
Pork and sweetbreads with beans,
    614
Pork roll-ups, 41–42
Potato and bean stew, 708
Rice, beans, milk, and salame, 175
Rice and beans (Valle d'Aosta), 175
Rice and beans (Veneto), 344
Rice with beans, 292
Rice with beans, cabbage, and pork,
    292
Rice with beans, cabbage, and
    salame, 291
Risotto with beans, 360
Risotto with squash and beans, 363
"Roots" and bean soup, 172
Rough-cut pasta with beans, 285
"St. Joseph's Lunch," 329
Small gnocchi made with
    breadcrumbs in bean sauce, 247
Tagliatelle with beans, 395
Tiny pasta (*pistadein*) in bean broth,
    169–170

Tripe and beans, 667
Turnip and bean soup, 190–191
Vegetable and bean stew, 173

Beef
Agnolotti gobbi astigiani-albesi ai tre arrosti, 213
Half-moon pasta with meat-and-spinach filling, 212
Anolini with beef filling, 97
Baked fusilli and orecchiette, 246
Baked lasagna with broth, 120
Baked layered crepes with artichoke, 409
Bean stew with beef and ham, 598
Beef and vegetable pie, 410
Beef braised in Barolo, 524
Beef carbonnade, 538
Beef cheek with cumin, 588
Beef in pizza sauce, 539
Beef in sauce (Campania), 523
Beef in sauce (Lombardia), 606
Beef medallions, 608
Beef pot roast, 587
Beef rolls Roman-style, 590
Beef roll-ups (Emilia-Romagna), 669
Beef roll-ups (Sardegna), 553
Beef roll-ups with tuna sauce, 42
Beef soup with meatballs and eggs, 184
Beef steaks with onion, 564
Beef stew, 654–655
Beef stew with celery, 655–656
Beef stew with cloves, 584–585
Beef with balsamic vinegar, 577
Bergamo-style stuffed pasta, 227–228
Boiled beef stew, 577
Boiled meats Padua-style, 587–588
Brain soufflé, 526–527
Braised beef (Lombardia), 606
Brescia-style stuffed pasta, 228
Cannelloni with meat sauce, 224
Cotechino "in prison," 566–567
Fettuccine with meat sauce, 331
The "fifth quarter" beef stew, 653–654
Finanziera alla piemontese, 577
Gelatina (gelatin), 37
Goulash, 589
Goulash soup, 138
Green lasagna with meat sauce, 270
Horsemeat stew (Emilia-Romagna), 624
Horsemeat stew (Veneto), 618
Hunter's-style marinated beef, 542–543
Kidneys in wine, 659
Leftover meatballs, 628–629
Lesso misto (boiled meats), 599
Macaroni pie 1 (Emilia-Romagna), 310–311
Macaroni pie 2 (Veneto), 311
Marrow sauce, 56

Meat and artichokes, 541
Meat and cheese soufflé, 644
Meat braised with cabbage, 525
Meat pastries 1 (Sardegna), 262
Meat pastries 2 (Sardegna), 263
Meat roll-ups, 592
Meatballs, 632
Mignuic or cavatielli, 288
Mixed braised meats, 522
Mushroom meatballs, 66
Neapolitan lasagna, 268–269
Neapolitan ragù, 539
Onion-glazed beef (or chicken), 509
Ox in wine sauce, 576
Oxtail stew (Alto Adige), 648
Oxtail stew (Lazio), 552–553
Pan-fried beef and vegetables, 579
Pappardelle in duck sauce, 295–296
Parma-style beef roast, 637–638
Parma-style beef stew, 652
Pasta and meat pie, 411
Pasta asciutta alla pugliese (pasta Puglia-style), 301
Pasta stuffed with beef and sausage, 244
Pasta with meat sauce and onions, 279
Piacenza-style anolini, 98
Piacenza-style beef stew, 652–653
Potato and meat pie, 661
Potato gnocchi Romagna-style, 257
Puglian meat sauce, 329–330
Rice croquettes, 80–81
Risotto with sècole, 366
Romagna-style meat sauce, 330
Romagna-style ragù, 634
Saffron risotto with mushrooms, 354
Smoked meat with polenta "sauce," 621
Squab stuffed with meat, 623
Steak florentine, 519
Steaks with horseradish sauce, 520–521
Stewed beef Milan-style, 607
Stuffed lasagna, 269–270
Stuffed olives, 46–47
Sweet-and-sour meatballs 2 (Calabria), 628
Tagliatelle with Romagna-style meat sauce, 394
Tripe sausages, 599
Tripe soup 1 (Veneto), 207
Tripe soup 2 (Friuli-Venezia Giulia), 207–208
Tripe soup 3 (Veneto), 208
Tuscan ragù, 331
Tyrolean steak, 576
Wild herbs and meat soup, 153
Zeaia, 87

Black kale (*cavolo nero*)
Black kale and rice soup, 200
Polenta soup with *cavolo nero*, 116

Polenta with beans and *cavolo nero*, 324
Polenta with black kale, 99–100

Boar
Boar country-style, 548
Boar Viterbo-style, 548
Boar with forest berries, 547–548
Cinghiale d'Aspromonte (saddle of boar), 551
Pappardelle with boar, 296–297
Pork stew, 656
Stewed boar, 551
Sweet-and-sour boar, 549–550
"Sweet-and-strong" boar, 550

Bread
Acquacotta laziale, 94
Almond bread pudding, 889–890
Apple pancakes, 833
Apple-raisin pancakes, 806
Apricot dumplings, 807
Baked bread and cheese with broth, 391
Baked calzone, 12–13
Baked crepes with bread and cheese filling, 287
Baked dumplings with sausage and cheese, 10
Baked polenta with turnips and sausages, 65–66
Bathed bread, 98–99
Black-bread gnocchi with hops, 264
Braided cookies, 870
Bread and tomato salad, 51
Bread balls, 327
Bread rings with baked eggs, 9
Bread soup (Lombardia), 142
Bread soup 1 (Emilia-Romagna), 158
Bread soup 2 (Lombardia), 158
Bread soup 3 (Piemonte), 159
Bread soup 4 (Toscana), 159
Bread soup 5 (Basilicata), 169
Bread soup with arugula and potatoes, 160
Bread soup with bay leaf, 160
Bread with olives, 51
Bread with pork bits, 86
Bread with walnuts, 51
Breadsticks, 38
Brusarol (grilled polenta balls), 222
Bruschetta, 8
Buckwheat flatbread, 69
Buckwheat fritters, 78–79
Buckwheat porridge, 376
Calcioni (fried dumplings with prosciutto and cheese), 11
Caponata 2 (Molise), 14
Carnival calzone, 12
Cheese and egg fritters, 50
Cheese and onion bread in broth, 160
Cheese dumplings, 223
Cheese gnocchi, 250

Chicken-liver paté canapes, 25
Chickpea crepe, 26–27
Chickpea flatbread, 27
Chickpea polenta, 52
Chickpea-flour fritters, 35
Christmas bread, 827
Ciarla (pizza dough), 18
Conglufi, 234
Cornmeal fritters, 75
Cornmeal pizza, 62
Crepes in broth, 178
Crostini with anchovies and
    provatura, 24
Crostini with liver and spleen, 25
Crostini with mussels, 24–25
Cured chamois on crostini, 45
Dumplings with speck in broth, 119
Easter cheese bread, 22
Easter focaccia, 795
Easter pizza with cheese, 63
Fasting day (meatlesss) calzone, 13
Filled focaccia, 28
Flatbread with dried figs, 858
Flatbread with greens and sausage,
    23
Flatbread with rosemary and raisins,
    858–859
Focaccia, 28
Focaccia with cheese, 740
Focaccia with oil, tuna, and tomato,
    29
Focaccia with olives, 28–29
Focaccia with ricotta (Calabria), 29
Focaccia with ricotta (Piemonte),
    794–795
Fried bread (Emilia-Romagna), 38
Fried bread (Friuli-Venezia Giulia),
    828
Fried bread puffs, 89
Fried bread with Bulide, 828
Fried flatbread, 9
Griddle cakes, 864
Homemade twisted pasta in bread
    sauce, 316
La frigolada, 245
Layered pizza, 58
Marinated bread salad, 53
Meat pizza, 64
Medieval gnocchi, 261
Mountain soup from Valpelline,
    188–189
Music-paper bread with poached
    eggs, 179
Music-paper-bread salad, 52
Myrtle cream crostini, 24
Neapolitan pizza, 58
Olive and ricotta calzones, 11–12
Olive bread, 67
Onion soup with bread, 196
Palatschinken with preserves,
    784–785
Pane carasau fritters, 798
Panettone, 829–830
Pastry leaves, 52
Peasant soup (Puglia), 111

Peasant soup (Valle d'Aosta), 209
Pissaladière, 57–58
Pizza con fiori di sambuco (pizza
    with elderberry flowers), 64
Pizza di verdure, 62
Pizza with anchovies and capers, 60
Pizza with artichokes and ricotta,
    60–61
Pizza with cracklings, 61
Pizza with cracklings and raisins, 61
Pizza with escarole, 61–62
Pizza with potatoes and olives,
    64–65
Pizza with turnip greens, 60
Pizze di Pasqua (Easter pizza), 846
Pizziconi, 317
Polenta balls, 50
Polenta pie with sausage and raisins,
    54
"Priest stranglers" green gnocchi in
    butter and sage sauce, 387–388
"Priest stranglers" green gnocchi in
    butter sauce, 388
Prosciutto in bread dough, 631
Pumpkin bread, 827–828
Radicchio crepes, 234–235
Ricotta and sausage dumplings, 82
Ricotta dumplings in broth, 171
Ring breads with eggs, 775
Ring cakes with cheese, 17
Ring-shaped fritters, 23
Rolled pizza, 59
Romagna-style polenta, 318
Rye-flour porridge, 171
"Salted water" soup 1 (Puglia), 96
"Salted water" soup 2 (Basilicata),
    96
Sausage soup, 193
Semolina bread, 825
Semolina bread with wine must and
    almonds, 857
Shepherd's bread soup, 61
Sicilian pizza 1 (pizza alla Siciliana),
    59
Sicilian pizza 2 (pizza Siciliana), 65
Small focaccias with tomato sauce,
    78
Soup from Cogne, 178–179
Soup with bread dumplings 1
    (Emilia-Romagna), 124
Soup with bread dumplings 2
    (Lombardia), 124
Spleen crostini (Crostini all milza
    per minestra), 111
Stuffed brioche, 7–8
Stuffed peaches, 838
Stuffed pizza (Campania), 63
Stuffed pizza (Puglia), 76
Stuffed-bread soup, 202–203
Sweet bread from Cogne, 826
Sweet bread with fruits and nuts,
    825–826
Sweet cornmeal bread, 825
Sweet Easter bread, 856
Sweet flatbread, 858

Sweet yeasted flatbread, 859
Tiny dumplings in herb broth, 116
Toasted broth, 104
Tuscan sweet bread, 752
Unleavened flatbread, 57
Whole wheat spaghetti with
    anchovies and breadcrumbs, 387
Yellow cake with fruit, 831
Zuppa di pane (Friuli-Venezia
    Giulia), 200
Zuppetta di vino ("donkey's soup"),
    889

Broccoli
Braised broccoli, 673
Braised broccoli with vinegar, 674
Fava, broccoli, and chicory soup,
    191
Fried broccoli rabe, 704
Fried neapolitan sausage and
    friarielli, 545–546
Pan-fried sausages and broccoli, 641
Pasta for hard times (with broccoli
    and anchovies), 265–266
Pasta with broccoli 1 (Sicilia), 301
Pasta with broccoli 2 (Sicilia), 302
Pasta with broccoli 3 (Puglia), 302
Pasta with broccoli and anchovies,
    300–301
Pasta with fried broccoli, 302–303
Polenta with broccoli and pancetta,
    321
Ratatouille Piedmont-style, 721
"St. Joseph's Lunch," 329
Sausages and broccoli, 640–641
Sausages with broccoli rabe, 641
Tagliatelle with broccoli, 396
Uncle Vincenzo's rigatoni (rigatoni
    with anchovies, broccoli, and
    breadcrumbs), 309

Cabbage
Baked meat and vegetables, 617
Buckwheat pasta with cabbage, 318
Cabbage and cheese soup, 180
Cabbage and pork-rind soup, 149
Cabbage and rice soup, 149–150
Chestnut fettuccine with cabbage
    and pork, 241
Donkey and cabbage stew, 658
Eel with Savoy cabbage, 432
Fried sauerkraut ravioli, 334
Goose with cabbage, 611
Meat braised with cabbage, 525
Mountain soup from Valpelline,
    188–189
Polenta with white beans and
    cabbage, 319
Pork and cabbage stew, 543
Pork cutlets with Savoy cabbage,
    565
Rice with beans, cabbage, and pork,
    292
Rice with beans, cabbage, and
    salame, 291

Risotto with sausage and cabbage, 362

Savoy cabbage flan, 725

Savoy cabbage flans with fonduta, 725

Spiced cabbage with egg, 714

Stuffed cabbage, 529

Sweet-and-sour baised cabbage, 676

Venison loin with red cabbage timbale and currants, 600

Capers

Linguine with anchovies, olives, and capers, 273

Pizza with anchovies and capers, 60

Spaghetti with anchovies, olives, and capers, 384

Stockfish with capers, 495

Sturgeon with capers and olives, 496

Swordfish with capers 1 (Calabria), 473–474

Swordfish with capers 2 (Calabria), 475

Swordfish with capers and lemon, 475

Swordfish with olives and capers, 475

Capon

Boiled meats Padua-style, 587–588

Boiled stuffed capon or hen, 522

Capon with anchovies, 584

Capon with anolini and prosciutto sauce, 226

Capon with lemon balm, 531

Capppone alla canevera (capon in pig's bladder), 533

Lesso misto (boiled meats), 599

Roast capon, 528–529

Spiced capon, 530

Cardoons

Abruzzo-style cardoons in sauce, 680

Braised cardoon, 692

Braised or fried cardoons, 681

Cardoon and Jerusalem artichoke soup, 129

Cardoon and meatball soup, 105

Cardoon soup (Campania), 193

Cardoon soup (Lazio), 128–129

Cardoons gratinée, 680–681

Cardoons in broth 1 (Campania), 110

Cardoons in broth 2 (Abruzzo), 110

Cardoons with egg 1 (Basilicata), 679

Cardoons with egg 2 (Basilicata), 680

Cardoons with truffles, 679

Ratatouille Piedmont-style, 721

Cauliflower

Anchovy and cauliflower stew, 103

Cauliflower and olives, 681

Cauliflower balls, 716

Cauliflower rigatoni, 337–338

Curly lasagne with ricotta and cauliflower, 270

Drunken cauliflower, 683

Pasta and cauliflower (Campania), 307

Pasta with broccoli 3 (Puglia), 302

Risotto with sausage and cauliflower, 367

Soupy pasta with cauliflower and black olives, 164

"St. Joseph's Lunch," 329

Celery

Beef stew with celery, 655–656

Christmas caponata, 675

Christmas salad, 694

Gorgonzola-stuffed celery, 79

Potato and celery soup, 168

Rice and celery, 346

Rice with celery and tomato, 176

Stuffed celery, 724

Vegetable stew with celery, 682

White celery soup, 126

Chamois

Chamois in onion sauce, 528

Tyrolean chamois, 527–528

Chard. *See* **Swiss chard**

Cheese

Apostles' fingers (Ricotta-stuffed crêpes), 788–789

Artichoke and cheese casserole, 724

Baked cheese pie, 241

Baked crepes with bread and cheese filling, 287

Baked dumplings with sausage and cheese, 10

Berry-cheese cream, 783

Black polenta, 324

Breaded cheese, 744

Bucatini with caciocavallo cheese, 288

Buckwheat and cornmeal polenta with cheese, 325–326

Cabbage and cheese soup, 180

Calcioni (fried dumplings with prosciutto and cheese), 11

Cannarozzetti with ricotta and saffron, 223–224

Capri salad, 693

Cassata from Naples, 768

Cassata from Sicilia, 768–769

Cheese and egg fritters, 50

Cheese and onion bread in broth, 160

Cheese balls in broth, 157–158

Cheese crisp, 739

Cheese crisp with potatoes, 739

Cheese rolls, 742

Cheese sauce with potatoes and onions, 738–739

Cheese soup, 187

Cheese tart, 84

Cheese-stuffed dumplings, 264

Chicken cutlets with Montasio cheese, 620

Cream-filled sponge cake, 889

Crushed potatoes and beans with cheese, 744

"Drowned" polenta, 326

Filled cannoli, 765–766

Filled cookies, 861–862

Fillings for *tiellas*, 340–341

Fiorini filled with salame and cheese, 242

Focaccia with cheese, 740

Focaccia with ricotta (Calabria), 29

Focaccia with ricotta (Piemonte), 794–795

Fondue-stuffed pasta with veal broth, 167

Frico (fried cheese), 739

Fried cheese, 9

Fried mozzarella sandwich, 46

Fried ricotta, 742–743

Gorgonzola-stuffed celery, 79

Half-moon pasta with ricotta and prune filling, 213

Handcut pasta with cheese and sage sauce, 372

Homemade cheese, 743

Lamb with egg and cheese, 514

Large tomato and mozzarella ravioli, 740–741

Lasagne with ricotta e melanzane, 269

Marinated *toma* cheese, 30

Marinated tomini, 744–745

Marinated tomino cheese, 740

Mascarpone cake with Marsala, 814

Mascarpone cream, 783–784

Meat and cheese soufflé, 644

Montasio cheese soup, 138–139

Olive and ricotta calzones, 11–12

Orecchiette with ricotta, 291

Pallotte (cheese and sausage dumplings), 741

Pasta and cheese pie, 412

Pasta au gratin, 278

Pasta with mascarpone, 298

Peasant soup (Valle d'Aosta), 209

Pizza with artichokes and ricotta, 60–61

Polenta with fontina, 321

Potato and cheese galette, 691

Potatoe purée with cheese, 741

Rice with eggs and cheese, 173

Rice with smoked cheese, 378

Ricotta and egg soup, 97

Ricotta and sausage dumplings, 82

Ricotta calzoni, 223

Ricotta cheesecake (Piemonte), 785–786

Ricotta cheesecake (Sicilia), 800
Ricotta crostata, 785
Ricotta dumplings in broth, 171
Ricotta mantecata con cialde
  (marinated ricotta), 742
Ricotta pie, 843
Ricotta ravioli, 333
Ricotta tart, 768
Ricotta tortelli with sage sauce, 416
Ricotta-stuffed cookies, 833–834
Risotto with Gorgonzola, 350
Risotto with Parmigiano-Reggiano,
  355
Risotto with spumante, fontina, and
  mushrooms, 357
Soup with salt cheese, 150
Spaghetti with pecorino and pepper,
  384
Spicy cheese spread, 80
Spinach-ricotta ravioli, 337
Stuffed dumplings, 293
Sweet cheese pastries, 861
Sweet ravioli with ricotta, 849–850
Sweet ricotta ravioli, 336–337
Swiss chard and ricotta, 730
Tripe alla Parmigiana, 664
Turkey breast with prosciutto and
  fontina, 621
Valdostan baked polenta, 323
Valdostan fondue, 738
Veal cutlets with fontina, 642–643
Wheat berry ricotta tart, 835–836
White truffles with Parmigiano-
  Reggiano, 81

Cherries
Cherry marmalade cookies, 772–773
Cherry strudel, 867
Cherry-almond tart, 873
Duck breast with cherry sauce, 604

Chestnuts
Bean and chestnut soup, 106
Boiled chestnuts, 770–771
Boiled chestnuts with butter, 15–16
Calzoncelli, 764
Chestnut and chickpea soup 1
  (Lazio), 194
Chestnut and chickpea soup 2
  (Umbria), 195
Chestnut and leek soup (Campania),
  130
Chestnut and rice soup, 129–130
Chestnut balls, 822
Chestnut cake (Toscana), 770
Chestnut calzoni, 764
Chestnut dumplings, 816
Chestnut fettuccine with cabbage
  and pork, 241
Chestnut fritters, 797
Chestnut fudge, 770
Chestnut mash 1 (Lombardia), 122
Chestnut mash 2 (Piemonte),
  122–123

Chestnut "mountain," 816–817
Chestnut panzarottini, 832
Chestnut-flour gnocchi, 255
Chestnuts with cream, 762–763
Leek and chestnut soup (Piemonte),
  144
Leg of lamb with chestnuts,
  563–564
Marmellata di castagne, 814
Necci (chestnut-flour crêpes), 820
Pumpkin-potato gnocchi, 254
Rice and chestnut soup, 206
Rice with milk and chestnuts, 174
St. Joseph's pasta, 266
Sweet chestnut polenta, 836
Sweet ravioli, 763
Sweet-and-sour mussels, 457
Tagliatelle and chestnut soup, 147
Tuscan chestnut loaf, 790

Chicken
Boiled stuffed capon or hen, 522
Braised rooster, 583
Chicken, veal, pork and guinea hen
  cooked with tomatoes and herbs,
  645
Chicken and pasta soup, 154
Chicken and ricotta croquettes, 567
Chicken cutlets with Montasio
  cheese, 620
Chicken in tomato sauce, 627
Chicken in white wine, 625
Chicken with onion and tomato
  sauce, 627
Chicken-liver pâté canapes, 25
Chicken-stuffed turkey, 618
Crostini with liver and spleen, 25
"Free-range" risotto with gizzards,
  368
Fritto misto alla bolognese, 582
Giblet stew, 546–547
Giblet stew with eggs, 552
Homemade pasta with chicken
  giblets, 281
Hunter-style chicken 1 (Piemonte),
  626
Hunter-style chicken 2 (Emilia-
  Romagna), 626
Hunter-style chicken 3 (Toscana),
  626
Liver pâté, 55
Mixed braised meats, 522
Neapolitan pâté, 55–56
Onion-glazed beef (or chicken), 509
Pan-fried chicken giblets, 582
Pan-roasted chicken, 625
Potato and meat pie, 661
Rice with chicken livers, 175
Risotto with giblets, 365
Skewered chicken giblets, 650
Taglierini in meat sauce, 400
Tagliolini in broth with giblets, 183
Timballo alla Bonifacio VIII, 410
Wedding soup 5 (Veneto), 152–153

Chickpeas
Bean stew with beef and ham, 598
Chestnut and chickpea soup 1
  (Lazio), 194
Chestnut and chickpea soup 2
  (Umbria), 195
Chickpea and bean soup, 124–125
Chickpea and pork soup
  (Piemonte), 156
Chickpea crepe, 26–27
Chickpea flatbread, 27
Chickpea-flour fritters, 35
Chickpea polenta, 52
Chickpea purée with shrimp and
  clams, 162
Chickpea ravioli, 850
Chickpea soup (Marche), 130
Chickpea soup (Piemonte), 112
Chickpea stew, 186
Pasta and chickpea soup 1 (Lazio),
  164–165
Pasta and chickpea soup 2 (Puglia),
  165
Pasta and chickpea soup 3
  (Umbria), 165
Pasta and chickpeas, 266
Pasta with chickpeas and onion,
  231–232
Pasta with chickpeas, 231
Pork and chickpeas for All Soul's
  Day, 605
St. Lucy's soup, 206
Soup of the dead, 128
Tagliatelle and chickpeas with dried
  peppers, 396
Tagliatelle with chickpeas, 181–182

Chicory
Bean soup with chicory and fennel,
  127
Callariedde, 107
Chicory galette, 692
Chicory soup, 191
Chicory timbale, 407
Christmas salad, 694
Eel with wild chicory, 435
Fava, broccoli, and chicory soup, 191
Vegetables and pancetta, 732
Wedding soup 4 (Puglia), 152

Chocolate
Almond and chocolate layer cake,
  843–844
Almond cake glazed with chocolate,
  834
Almond tart with chocolate glaze,
  751
Almond-chocolate tartlets, 853
Baked rice pudding with chocolate,
  757–758
Barbajada, 750
Capri chocolate-almond cake, 872
Chocolate custard, 782–783
Chocolate in the Piedmont, 808

Chocolate parfaits, 782
Chocolate rolled cake, 802
Chocolate salame, 853
Chocolate-stuffed eggs, 885–886
Christmas spice cookies, 857
Coffee and chocolate pie, 881
Cream-filled sponge cake, 889
Drunken toasts, 786
Eggplant with chocolate, 814–815
Figs with chocolate, 793
Friulian yeast cake, 806
Honey biscuits, 837
Ice cream with chocolate sauce, 781
Ladyfinger trifle, 890
Rolled chocolate cake, 852
Spiced nut cake from Terni, 824
Stuffed figs, 794
Sweet ravioli, 763
Torta Novecento (sponge cake), 883
Triestine yeast cake, 847
Walnut filled pizza, 842
Watermelon ice, 803
Wheat-berry pudding 1, 787
Wheat-berry pudding 2, 805

Clams
Cannelichhje e fafe, 109
Chickpea purée with shrimp and
    clams, 162
Clam soup, 125
Clams in parsley and wine, 503
Linguine with razor clams, 272
Razor clams in broth, 108
Rice with crabs and razor clams,
    342
Risotto with clams, 364–365
Sautéed clams, 483
Sea bass and shellfish in dough, 446
Seafood risotto, 353–354
Seafood salad 1 (Campania), 39–40
Seafood salad 2 (Sicilia), 40
Spaghetti with clams, 386
Vermicelli and seafood baked in foil,
    420–421

Codfish
Acquacotta laziale, 94
Bathed bread, 98–99
Boiled cod (Toscana), 483
Boiled stockfish with potatoes, 493
Braised cod and potatoes, 440–441
Cod and potato stew 1 (Piemonte),
    492
Cod and potato stew 2 (Calabria),
    492
Cod fritters (Umbria), 462
Cod in parsley, 442
Cod in sauce (Friuli-Venezia
    Giulia), 438
Cod in sauce (Sicilia), 437
Cod in wine, 437
Cod with green olives, 466
Cod with raisins and prunes, 441
Cod with tomatoes, raisins, and pine
    nuts, 442

Codfish Arezzo-style, 441
Codfish Florence-style, 438–439
Codfish Trentino-style, 439
Codfish Vicenza-style, 439–440
Creamed cod Veneto-style, 443
Creamed cod Vicenza-style, 443
Fillings for *tiellas*, 340–341
Fried baccalà balls, 66
Fried cod fillets, 460–461
Grilled cod, 438
Maremma-style "cooked water"
    soup 1 (Lazio), 95
Mariner's stockfish, 493
Poached cod, 442–443
Roast cod, 440
"St. Joseph's Lunch," 329
Salt cod fritters (Campania), 504
Stockfish and potato stew, 491
Stockfish and potatoes 1
    (Campania), 494
Stockfish and potatoes 2 (Alto
    Adige), 494
Stockfish with capers, 495
Stockfish with potatoes and onions,
    495
Stockfish with tomato sauce, 494
Stockfish with tomatoes and
    potatoes, 495
Sweet-and-sour cod stew, 504
Ventricieddi di stocco al pomodoro,
    502

Coffee
Almond coffee, 763
Coffee and chocolate pie, 881
Coffee ice cream, 828–829

Cornmeal
Buckwheat and cornmeal polenta
    with cheese, 325–326
Buckwheat pasta with toasted
    cornmeal, 219–220
Cornmeal and raisin cake, 844
Cornmeal cookies, 886–887
Cornmeal fritters, 75
Cornmeal fruitcake, 753
Cornmeal pasta with tomatoes, 271
Cornmeal pizza, 62
Cornmeal raisin cookies, 804
Cornmeal sponge cake, 845
Corn pone with turnips, 317
Spinach-cornmeal soup (Friuli-
    Venezia Giulia), 161
Sweet cornmeal bread, 825

Couscous
Cuscus, 236
Cuscus con zuppa di pesce, 237
Cuscus siciliano, 238

Crabs
Fried soft-shell crabs, 467
Rice with crabs and razor clams,
    342
Spider crab canapes, 38

Curly endive
Wedding soup 4 (Puglia), 152

Donkey
Donkey and cabbage stew, 658
Donkey stew (Emilia Romagna), 654
Donkey stew (Lombardia), 653

Duck
Baked mallard, 586
Bigoli with duck 1 (Piemonte), 218
Bigoli with duck 2 (Veneto), 218
Duck breast with cherry sauce, 604
Duck stuffed with sausage and liver,
    517
Duck stuffed with veal and pork,
    517
Duck terrine, 82
Duck with fruit, 615–616
Duck with olives, 615
Duck with rice, 215
Duckling fillet with poppies,
    515–516
Fish stew with duck, 658–659
Gnocchi with duck sauce, 254
Mallard in sauce, 586
Pappardelle in duck sauce, 295–296
Stuffed duck, 516
Stuffed roast duck, 516–517
Wild duck risotto, 352

Eel
Anguilla infilzata (skewered eels),
    436
Bolsena eels in the style of Bisentina,
    430
Eel in sauce, 436
Eel with plums, 432
Eel with Savoy cabbage, 432
Eel with wild chicory, 435
Eels and trout in a spicy sauce, 435
Eels Giovi-style, 430–431
Eels Labrese-style, 431
Fried eel, 433
Fried eel marinated in vinegar sauce,
    483–484
Glassmaker's eel, 431
Grilled eel in grape leaves, 452
Hunter-style eels, 430
Marinated eel (Emilia-Romagna),
    434–435
Marinated eel (Lazio), 452
Risotto and eels, 176
Spit-roasted eel, 432
Stewed eel, 433
Stewed eel with peas (Emilia-
    Romagna), 434
Stewed eel with peas (Veneto),
    433–434
Stewed eels and perch, 496–497
Vermicelli with eel sauce, 421

Eggplant
Baked eggplant, 699
Baked macaroni with eggplant, 407

914

Baked pasta with eggplant 1 (Calabria), 297
Baked pasta with eggplant 2 (Calabria), 339
Calabrian "Purgatory" vegetable sandwiches, 719
Eggplant and mint, 700
Eggplant and sausage, 700
Eggplant balls, 715
Eggplant bites, 716
Eggplant boats, 697–698
Eggplant braised with tomatoes, 700
Eggplant Parmigiana 1 (Campania), 704–705
Eggplant Parmigiana 2 (Puglia), 705–706
Eggplant Parmigiana 3 (Sicilia), 706–707
Eggplant pie, 730
Eggplant roll-ups, 695
Eggplant with chocolate, 814–815
Eggplants and tomatoes, 701–702
Fried eggplant sandwiches, 698
Fried eggplant with tomato sauce, 699
"Gendarme hat" pasta pie, 225–226
Lasagne with ricotta e melanzane, 269
Melanzane sott'aceto (pickled eggplant), 701
Melanzane sott'olio (pickled eggplant), 702
Minestrone with pesto, 155
100-flavor eggplant, 701
Pan-fried beef and vegetables, 579
Pasta with fried eggplants, 300
Peppers stuffed with eggplant, 710–711
Potato and vegetable gratin, 405–406
Sicilian caponata, 676
Sicilian-style vermicelli, 421
Spaghetti with eggplant and ricotta salata, 299
Spring risotto, 371
Stuffed eggplants, 702
Tomato soup, 156
Tripe with eggplant and walnuts, 665–666
Twice-fried eggplant sandwiches, 698–699
Veal parmigiana with eggplant, 616
Vegetable ragù, 172–173
Vegetable soup (Piemonte), 157
Vegetable stew, 112
Vegetable stew (Basilicata), 681–682
Vegetable stew with celery, 682

Eggs
Anise cookies, 748
Asparagus with egg sauce, 672–673
Asparagus with fried eggs, 672
Baked artichokes with egg sauce, 677
Baked meringues, 865

Baked omelet with pork and potatoes, 690
Baked rigatoni with braised pork and eggs, 402–403
Benevento-style lasagne with veal meatballs and eggs, 267–268
Cavatelli with eggs and pancetta, 230–231
Cheese and egg fritters, 50
Easter frittata, 33
Egg cocktail, 851
Eggs and mushrooms, 88
Eggs in garlic sauce, 88
Emperor's frittata, 796
Floating islands, 860
Fried eggs in sauce, 87
Frittata di Vitalba, 32
Frittata with ground meat, 34
Frittata with whitebait, 31
Frittati con le erbe (herb frittata), 31
Hops frittata, 32
Italian egg-drop soup, 180–181
Lamb stew with eggs, 642
Lamb with egg and cheese, 514
Leftover pasta omelet, 244
Marjoram broth with poached eggs, 168–169
Meringues, 815
Music-paper bread with poached eggs, 291
Orange mousse, 819
Pizze di Pasqua (Easter pizza), 846
Rice and egg soup, 127
Rice with eggs and cheese, 173
Ricotta and egg soup, 97
Ring breads with eggs, 775
Salame frittata 1 (Piemonte), 33
Salame frittata 2 (Veneto), 34
Sausage frittata (Lombardia), 30–31
Sausage frittata (Piemonte), 579
Sausage soup, 193
Scrambled eggs with artichokes, 692
Scrambled eggs with peppers, 672
Shepherd's bread soup, 61
Spaghetti with carbonara sauce, 382–383
Spaghetti with fried eggs, 383
Spiced cabbage with egg, 714
Stewed frittata strips, 86
Stuffed dumplings, 293
Stuffed eggs, 87–88
Tagliatelle in egg sauce, 397–398
Toasted broth, 104
Vegetable fritters, 689
Vol-au-vent with radicchio and cheese, 88–89
Zabaglione, 886
Zabaglione with rum, 886

Elderberries and elderberry flowers
Meat pie with elderberry, 83
Minestra di sondalo, 146

Pizza con fiori di sambuco (pizza with elderberry flowers), 64
Sweet cornmeal bread, 825

Endive
Anchovies with endive, 429

Escarole
Baked escaraole, 723
Bean, escarole, and pork soup, 198
Escarole soup, 147
Escarole with meatballs, 722
Fillings for tiellas, 340–341
Liver and escarole, 574
Meatless ravioli 1 (Liguria), 334–335
Mixed meat ravioli, 331–332
Pizza with escarole, 61–62
Stuffed and baked escarole, 722–723
Stuffed and braised escarole, 722
Wild herbs and meat soup, 153

Farro
Beans and grains, 686
Farro and pig's trotters, 572
Farro porridge, 114–115
Farro soup 1 (Abruzzo), 134–135
Farro soup 2 (Marche), 135
Farro soup 3 (Molise), 135
Farro soup 4 (Toscana), 136
Farro soup 5 (Umbria), 136
Farro with zucchini flowers, 115

Fava beans
Artichoke and fava bean stew, 682
Fava, broccoli, and chicory soup, 191
Fava bean purée 1 (Calabria), 121
Fava bean purée 2 (Sicilia), 122
Fava bean soup (Lazio), 190
Fava bean soup (Puglia), 118
Fava beans and anchovies, 688
Fava beans and chicory 1 (Puglia), 688–689
Fava beans and chicory 2 (Basilicata), 689
Fava beans and guanciale 1 (Lazio), 687
Fava beans and guanciale 2 (Lazio), 687–688
Fava beans in vinegar sauce, 688
Fava purée, 718–719
Fava-bean fritters, 52
Fettuccine with white fava beans, 238
Fresh fava bean soup, 198
Lamb with fava beans, 545
Onion and fava bean soup, 195
Pasta and fava beans, 305
Pasta and fava-bean cubes, 44
Sausage and fava bean stew, 573
Spring vegetable stew (Lazio), 185
Spring vegetable stew (Sicilia), 728

Tiny square pasta and fava beans,
171
Wedding soup 1 (Calabria), 151

Fennel
Bean and wild fennel soup, 196–197
Bean soup with chicory and fennel,
127
Callariedde, 107
Carp roasted with wild fennel,
453–454
Goose with fennel, 612
Pappardelle with quail and fennel,
296
Pork with potatoes and fennel, 553
Rabbit with fennel, 555
Rabbit with wild fennel, 555
Rice with fennel and ricotta, 348
Risotto with fennel, 349
Roast stuffed rabbit with fennel, 562
Snails with fennel, 602
Tagliatelle with wild fennel, 394
Wedding soup 4 (Puglia), 152

Fennel seeds
Genoa biscotti, 754
Sweet bread with fruits and nuts,
825–826

Figs
Almond and fig-filled Christmas
cookies, 788
Baked fig and nut calzone, 820
Figs with chocolate, 793
Flatbread with dried figs, 858
Stuffed figs, 794

Fish. *See also* **Mixed seafood**
Agoni alla navett (shad), 429
Angler in tomato sauce, 479
Baked sturgeon, 496
Baked whitebait, 444
Batter-dipped whitebait, 444
Bianchetti fritters, 35
Boiled pike, 466
Braised catfish 1 (Emilia-Romagna),
471
Braised catfish 2 (Veneto), 471
Bucatini in mackerel sauce, 221
Caponata 1 (Campania), 14
Carbonaretti del Lago di Piediluco
(perch), 454
Carp roasted with wild fennel,
453–454
Diamante-style grouper, 456–457
Fish ravioli, 335–336
Fried catfish, 470–471
Fried fish, 477
Fried pike croquettes, 464–465
Fried shad, 427
Fried tope (shark), 470
Frittata with whitebait, 31
Grouper in sauce, 456
Halibut and seafood stew, 457
Herb-stuffed gilthead bream, 469

Mackerel in vinegar, 488
Marinated skate, 480
Marinated tope (shark), 469
Missoltini alla gratella (shad), 46
Monkfish with olives, 491
Pan-fried whitebait, 444
Pasta squares with John Dory, 391
Pickled fish 1 (Abruzzo), 77
Pike croquettes, 460
Pike in anchovy sauce, 465
Pike in sauce, 465
Pike in tomato sauce, 464
Pike—fried, grilled, and baked, 464
Pike-perch in cream, 471–472
Pike-perch in shrimp and
mushroom sauce, 477
Risotto with Lake Garda tench, 363
Risotto with perch and zucchini
flowers, 358
Risotto with tench, 362
Shad in green sauce, 428
Skate soup with pasta, 127–128
Soused bream, 445
Soused shad, 428
Squillfish with garlic, 451
Stewed eels and perch, 496–497
Stuffed gar fish or pike, 458
Sturgeon with capers and olives, 496
Tench and tagliolini soup 1 (Lazio),
148
Tench and tagliolini soup 2
(Umbria), 148
Tench soup, 447
Tope (shark) and mushrooms, 470
Turbot Grado-style, 103
Whitebait frittata, 461
Whitebait soup, 136–137
Whitefish in white wine, 463
Zuppa di Pesce di lago (lake fish
soup), 204

Fowl
Baked mallard, 586
Baked pasta pie, 375
Baked pasta with hen and broth,
176–177
Beccacce all chiampese (woodcock),
520
Beccacce alla arzignanese
(woodcock), 519
Boiled meats Padua-style, 587–588
Braised rooster, 583
Capon with anolini and prosciutto
sauce, 226
Drunken hen, 584
Gallina cotta nel capretto (hens
cooked in a kid), 585
Grilled guinea hen with bay leaves,
571
Guinea hen pâté, 570–571
Guinea hen with black pepper sauce,
571–572
Guinea hen with mascarpone, 570
Hen galantine, 592
Hen with pheasant stuffing, 572

Insalata di gallina cotta nel fieno
(hen cooked in hay), 40
Mallard in sauce, 586
Myrtle-scented hen, 631
Pheasant in Spanish sauce, 568
Pheasant or guinea hen in sauce, 569
Pheasant with truffle, 569–570
Rich risotto Padua-style, 371–372
Roast guinea hen, 571
Scaliger soup, 187–188
Spiedo bresciano or polenta e uccelli
(polenta and birds), 650
Stuffed hen Cremona-style, 583

Frogs
Frog leg risotto, 352–353
Frog risotto, 365
Ranocchi fritti (fried frogs), 637
Sautéed frogs, 636

Gelatin
Blood-orange gelatin, 802–803
Gelatina (beef gelatin), 37
Gelatine di fichi d'India (prickly
pear gelatin), 803
Mandarin gelatin, 804

Goat
Abbuoto, 511
Chamois in onion sauce, 528
Goat and beans, 533–534
Goat braised with mushrooms, 536
Goat in sauce, 532
Goat stew, 532–533
Goat with tomatoes and pepper, 532
Grilled kid, 535
Hens cooked in a kid, 585
Hunter's-style kid offal, 563
Kid in oil and vinegar, 535
Kid in wine, 535
Leg of kid with oregano, 534–535
Marro (Puglia), 607
Mutton stew with potatoes, 656
Roast intestines, 650–651
Sanguinaccio di capra (stuffed goat's
intestine), 643
Scannature d'abbacchio in padella
(cooked goat's blood), 645
Stewed kid, 534
Stuffed kid, 536
Tyrolean chamois, 527–528

Goose
Foie gras, 643
Gnocchi with goose sauce, 251
Goose confit contadina-style, 611
Goose ragù, 635
Goose with cabbage, 611
Goose with fennel, 612
Maccheroni alla mulinara, 280
Preserved smoked goose, 612
Salame d'oca (goose salame), 70
Smoked goose confit, 611
Thick bigoli with goose and
mushroom sauce, 219

Grape leaves
Grilled eel in grape leaves, 452
Vine-roasted artichokes, 678

Grape must
Mostarda di carpi (fruit sauce), 48
Savôr, 855

Grapes
Grape jam, 813–814
Grape syrup, 69

Grappa
Grappa fritters, 793

Greens
Butter greens salad with warm
    bacon dressing, 693
Dandelion and pancetta salad, 693
Easter spring greens pie, 730
Field greens in butter, 685
Misticanza (mixed greens), 703
'Ndugghia di Castrovillari, 705
Orecchiette with turnip tops, 290
Pan-fried greens, 732
Pasta with turnip tops, 304–305
Pizza with turnip greens, 60
Polenta with spring greens, 326–327
Risotto with bladder campion and
    onion, 359
Risotto with campion, 360–361
Risotto with wild greens, 359
"Strange" greens, 732
Strigoli (sautéed campion), 729
Turnip greens soup, 113–114
Vegetable pie (Piemonte), 54
Wild greens with lardo, 719–720
Zuppa al raperonzolo, 186

Hare
Baked game, 639–640
Hare in pepper sauce, 597
Hare in sauce (Abruzzo), 594
Hunter's-style hare, 593–594
Jugged hare 1 (Piemonte), 595
Jugged hare 2 (Lombardia), 596
Jugged hare 3 (Friuli-Venezia
    Giulia), 596–597
Mignuic or cavatielli, 288
Pappardelle in hare sauce, 294–295
Stewed hare, 598
Trentino-style hare, 595

Hazelnuts
Baked amaretto peaches, 838
Canastrelli of Piemonte, 765
Hazelnut cake, 878
Hazelnut cookies, 885
Hazelnut trifle, 789
Spiced nut cake from Terni, 824
Yellow cake with fruit, 831

Herbs
Acquacotta laziale, 94
Baked prosciutto and herb pie, 312

Beef broth with barley flour, mint,
    and pecorino, 181
Borage soup, 193
Chicken, veal, pork and guinea hen
    cooked with tomatoes and herbs,
    645
"Cooked water" Casentino-style
    soup, 92
"Cooked water" soup with wild
    herbs, 93
"Crazy water" soup, 92
Eggplant and mint, 700
Fish soup with herbs, 113
Frittati con le erbe (herb frittata), 31
Frittelle di maresina, 36
Herb-stuffed gilthead bream, 469
Herb-stuffed pasta, 292–293
Marche-style "cooked water" soup,
    93
Maremma-style "cooked water"
    soup 1 (Lazio), 95
Maremma-style "cooked water"
    soup 2 (Toscana), 95–96
Marinated zucchini with mint,
    733–734
Minestra di riso (rustic soup with
    wild plants), 144
Minestra maritata 2 (wedding soup
    2, Campania), 141
Minestra primaverile di erbe di
    Prato (spring herb soup), 153
Pasta stuffed with sweetbreads and
    borage, 285–286
Pasta with mint, 388–389
Rice and wild herbs, 174
Ricotta and egg soup, 97
Stewed snails with herbs, 603–604
Swordfish with mint, 474
Tagliatelle with herb sauce, 392
Tiny dumplings in herb broth, 116
Tredici erbe ("thirteen herb
    liqueur"), 887
Wild herb soup, 131
Wild herbs and meat soup, 153

Hops (luvértis)
Black-bread gnocchi with hops, 264
Hops frittata, 32
Lamb with hops, 514
Risotto with hop shoots, 368

Horsemeat
Horsemeat stew (Emilia-Romagna),
    624
Horsemeat stew (Veneto), 618
Meatballs, 632

Lamb
Abbuoto, 511
Baked lamb and potatoes, 513
Baked lamb with egg and cheese,
    511–512
Baked leg of lamb (Abruzzo), 510
Baked mutton, 609
Baked mutton shank, 651

Budelline di agnello di faicchio
    (lamb intestines), 525
Capunti with lamb sauce, 226–227
Collo de castrato, risi, e piselli
    (lamb's neck), 554
Easter lamb (Basilicata), 524
Easter lamb (Puglia), 513
Fried lamb offal, 580
Fritto misto alla bolognese, 582
Homemade pasta with meat and
    tomato, 278
Hunter's-style suckling lamb, 508
Hunter-style lamb (Marche), 510
Hunter-style mutton, 544
Involtini di interiora di agnelli
    (roasted lamb offal), 590
Lamb and artichoke fricassee,
    578–579
Lamb and peas, 513
Lamb and potatoes (Puglia), 512
Lamb fricassee, 514
Lamb in white sauce, 515
Lamb intestines Viterbo-style,
    525–526
Lamb offal with artichokes, 562
Lamb ragù, 330
Lamb soup, 189–190
Lamb stew (Molise), 647
Lamb stew (Puglia), 568
Lamb stew with cheese and egg
    sauce, 511
Lamb stew with eggs, 642
Lamb stew with tomatoes, 527
Lamb tripe in tomato sauce,
    662–663
Lamb with fava beans, 545
Lamb with hops, 514
Lamb with olives, 512
Lamb with truffle, 515
Larded leg of lamb, 564
Leg of lamb baked in embers, 510
Leg of lamb with chestnuts,
    563–564
Maccaronara di Montemarano, 276
Marro (Puglia), 607
Mixed fry Alba-style, 580
Mixed fry Ascolo-Piceno-style,
    582–583
Molise-style ragù, 635–636
Mushrooms in lamb sauce, 538
Mutton pot, 624
Mutton ragù, 635
Mutton sauce, 619
Mutton stew 1 (Abruzzo), 636
Mutton stew 2 (Abruzzo), 649
Mutton stew with potatoes, 656
Paliata (grilled calf's intestines), 616
Pan-braised lamb, 545
Pezzata, 622
Roast intestines, 650–651
Roast suckling lamb with potatoes,
    508
Roast young lamb, 544
Salame di agnello (lamb sausage),
    640

Sautéed kidneys on toast, 637
Skewered lamb, 518
Smoked meat with polenta "sauce," 621
Stewed suckling lamb Roman-style, 508–509
Stracotto di pecora (lamb stew), 655
Stuffed sheep tripe, 632–633
Stuffed tripe (Molise), 610
Testarelle d'abbacchio in teglia (lambs' heads), 660
Torcinelli, 415
Zuppa di soffritto, 206

Lampascioni (wild hyacinth bulbs)
Insalata di lampascioni, 694
Lampascioni fritti, 696
Lampascioni in agrodolce (sweet-and-sour muscari), 697
Sformato di lampascioni con salsa di sedano (muscari and potatoes), 726

Lard
Calabrian-style pasta with lardo and onion, 280
Country-style liver, 574
Country-style risotto, 355
Larded leg of lamb, 564
Lardo di Arnad, 42
Wild greens with lardo, 719–720
Ziti with lardo, 283

Leeks
Chestnut and leek soup (Campania), 130
Leek and chestnut soup (Piemonte), 144
Polenta with leeks, 319–320
Potato and leek soup, 203
Risotto with cream of leek, 353
Rough-cut pasta with leeks, 285
Veal stew "White Lady," 578

Lemons
Lemon pudding, 760
Lemon sorbet, 864
Lemon verbena liqueur, 811
Limoncello, 810
Semolina cake, 816

Lentils
Bean and grain mush, 109
Beans and grains, 686
Le virtù (Virtues Soup), 185
Lentil and crostini soup, 200
Lentil soup, 138
Pasta and lentil soup, 167

Liver
Abbuoto, 511
Breaded pork liver, 573
Chicken-liver pâté canapes, 25
Country-style liver, 574
Crostini with liver and spleen, 25
Duck stuffed with sausage and liver, 517
Foie gras, 643
Liver and escarole, 574
Liver and onions Venetian-style, 575
Liver pâté, 55
Pork-liver skewers, 573–574
Rice with chicken livers, 175
Riso con i fegatini (rice and livers), 343
Skewered pork liver, 575
Tagliatelle with chicken livers, 125
Taglierini in meat sauce, 400
Tagliolini in broth with giblets, 183

Lobster
Baked seafood risotto, 243–244
Boiled lobster, 436–437
Linguine with lobster, 273
Seafood and vegetable platter, 453
Spaghetti and lobster, 387

Milk and cream
Amaretti pudding, 762
Blancmange, 752
Blancmange with amaretti, 756
"Burned broth," 104
Coffee ice cream, 828–829
Cream baskets, 831
Custard, 772
Custard tart, 809
Floating islands, 860
Fried custard squares, 810
Fried milk, 42–43
Homemade cheese, 743
Ice cream with chocolate sauce, 781
Ladyfinger trifle, 890
Milk fritters, 800
Orange custard, 782
Peach and amaretti semifreddo, 861
Rice with milk and chestnuts, 174
Rose pudding, 762
Rum custard, 783
Semolina pudding, 761
Vanilla panna cotta, 832

Mixed seafood
Baked seafood linguine, 272
Baked seafood risotto, 243–244
Crespelle di "mucco rosso," 463
Fish and vegetable soup, 106
Fish in walnut sauce, 448
Fish pastries, 262
Fish soup (Sardegna), 455
Fish soup (Veneto), 204
Fish soup Ancona-style, 100–101
Fish soup Brindisi-style, 205
Fish soup Fano-style, 102
Fish soup from Porto Recanati, 102–103
Fish soup Marano-style, 101
Fish soup Pescara-style, 447
Fish soup Ravenna-style, 447
Fish soup with herbs, 113
Fish stew, 448
Fish stew Livorno-style, 449
Fish stew Termoli-style, 104
Fish stew Viareggio-style, 449–450
Fish stew with duck, 658–659
Fritelle di anemoni di mare (sea anemone fritters), 35
Lake Garda fish soup, 192
Linguine with seafood, 273–274
Pappone di tornola (Fisherman's Dinner), 162
Seafood risotto, 353–354
Tuscan seafood stew, 451
Vermicelli and seafood baked in foil, 420–421
Zuppa di Pesce (fish soup), 202
Zuppa di Pesce di lago (lake fish soup), 204
Zuppa di pesce gallipolina (Gallipoli-style fish soup), 205

Mixed vegetables
Baked vegetable soup with black bread and barley, 188
Easter tart, 85
Fritto misto alla bolognese, 582
Grandma's prosciutto and beans, 717
Half-moon pasta with spinach and ricotta filling, 214–215
Minestrone, 154
Minestrone with basil, 126
Minestrone with pesto, 155
Mixed fried vegetables, 36
Mixed fry Alba-style, 580
Spring vegetable stew (Lazio), 185
Spring vegetable stew (Sicilia), 728
Spring vegetables with vinegar, 690
Vegetable and bean stew, 173
Vegetable fritters, 689
Vegetable pastries, 262
Vegetable pie (Valle d'Aosta), 707
Vegetable ragù, 172–173
Vegetable soup (Calabria), 201
Vegetable soup (Piemonte), 157
Vegetable soup with squash and barley, 199
Vegetable stew, 112
Vegetable timbale, 377
Vegetables and pancetta, 732
Winter vegetable soup, 100

Mullet
Baked mullet, 500
Bucatini with mullet sauce, 221
Mullet baked in parchment 1 (Abruzzo), 499
Mullet baked in parchment 2 (Campania), 500
Mullet with plum tomato, 500
Mullet with Vernaccia, 501
Pasta with bottarga 2 (Sicilia), 303

Pasta with whitemullet, 281–282
Roast striped mullet, 455–456
Stuffed mullet, 501

Mushrooms
Baked mushroom crespelle, 310
Baked polenta with meat sauce 1
    (Lombardia), 324–325
Baked polenta with meat sauce 2
    (Emilia-Romagna), 325
Caesar's mushrooms with truffles,
    47
Eggs and mushrooms, 88
Fried mushrooms, 691
Fusilli with mushrooms and olives,
    245
Gnocchi stuffed with mushrooms,
    260
Layered polenta with sausage and
    mushrooms, 287–288
Linguine with mushrooms, 271
Little stuffed dumplings, 294
Mushroom and truffle salad, 39
Mushroom meatballs, 66
Mushroom sauce, 412
Mushroom soup (Emilia-Romagna),
    199
Mushroom soup (Trentino), 105
Mushrooms in broth, 36–37
Mushrooms in lamb sauce, 538
Mushrooms with loin and sausage,
    546
Mushrooms with tomatoes, 37
Ovoli in fricassea, 706
Pan-cooked mushrooms, 48
Pasta with beans and mushrooms,
    283
Pasta with black olives and
    mushrooms, 376
Pasta with mushrooms and garlic,
    232–233
Pork with potatoes and mushrooms,
    659
Potato and mushroom soup, 203
Potato-mushroom gratin, 405
Quail in pastry with mushrooms,
    633–634
Rice and mushrooms, 348
Rigatoni with sausage and
    mushrooms, 338–339
Risotto with honey mushrooms, 360
Risotto with mushrooms, 349
Risotto with spumante, fontina, and
    mushrooms, 357
Saffron risotto with mushrooms, 354
Shrimp and porcini gratin, 487–488
Small gnocchi with ricotta and
    porcini, 248–249
Smoked scamorza salad with
    mushrooms, 743
Thick bigoli with goose and
    mushroom sauce, 219
Timballo alla Bonifacio VIII, 410
Tope and mushrooms, 470

Veal cutlets with mushroom caps,
    643–644
Vegetable stuffing, 733

Mussels
Baked rice with mussels and
    potatoes, 404
Baked rice with seafood, 406
Crostini with mussels, 24–25
Halibut and seafood stew, 457
Mariner's spaghetti, 386
Mussel soup, 201
Mussels au gratin (Abruzzo), 21
Mussels au gratin (Puglia), 459
Mussels au gratin with lemon, 459
Puglia-style mussels, 458
Sea bass and shellfish in dough, 446
Stuffed mussels, 22
Stuffed mussels (Puglia), 459
Sweet-and-sour mussels, 457
Vermicelli and seafood baked in foil,
    420–421

Octopus
Fillings for *tiellas*, 340–341
Octopus in wine 1 (Lazio), 478
Octopus in wine 2 (Calabria), 478
Stewed octopus "in purgatory,"
    479
Stewed octopus, 479
Troccoli al ragù di polpo, 418
Vermicelli and seafood baked in foil,
    420–421

Olive oil
Acquacotta laziale, 94
Olio santo, 50
Olive oil, lemon, and garlic sauce 1
    (Calabria), 74
Olive oil, lemon, and garlic sauce 2
    (Sicilia), 74–75
Olive oil nut cake, 842

Olives
Bread with olives, 51
Cauliflower and olives, 681
Cod with green olives, 466
Duck with olives, 615
Focaccia with olives, 28–29
Fusilli with mushrooms and olives,
    245
Lamb with olives, 512
Linguine with anchovies, olives, and
    capers, 273
Monkfish with olives, 491
Olive and ricotta calzones, 11–12
Olive bread, 67
Pasta with black olives and
    mushrooms, 376
Rabbit with peppers and olives, 560
Salad of crushed olives, 694
San Remo rabbit, 559
Soupy pasta with cauliflower and
    black olives, 164

Spaghetti with anchovies, olives, and
    capers, 384
Stuffed olives, 46–47
Sturgeon with capers and olives, 496
Swordfish with olives and capers,
    475
Tielle de Gaeta, 406

Onions
Beef steaks with onion, 564
Calabrian-style pasta with lardo and
    onion, 280
Cheese sauce with potatoes and
    onions, 738–739
Cipolline d'Ivrea, 684
Fillings for *tiellas*, 340–341
Liver and onions Venetian-style, 575
Meatless stuffed onions, 18–19
Onion and fava bean soup, 195
Onion pizzas, 2
Onion soup (Piemonte), 195
Onion soup with bread, 196
Onion-glazed beef (or chicken), 509
Onions in the Piedmontese tradition,
    19
Onions stuffed with meat, 18
Pasta with meat sauce and onions,
    279
Rabbit and onions, 559–560
Risotto with salame and onion, 366
Stockfish with potatoes and onions,
    495
Stuffed onions, 727
Sweet onion soup, 109–110
Sweet-and-sour onions, 684
Tuna and onions, 499
Wild onion fritters, 690–691
Wild onion soup, 189

Oranges
Blood-orange gelatin, 802–803
Chocolate custard, 782–783
Mandarin gelatin, 804
Orange cake, 872
Orange custard, 782
Orange marmalade, 813
Orange mousse, 819
Orange-peel balls, 822
Oranges with anchovies, 3
Sardinian orange slices, 749

Parsley
Clams in parsley and wine, 503
Cod in parsley, 442
Fried tuna with lemon and parsley,
    458
Green sauce for boiled meat, 5
Trout with parsley sauce, 502

Pasta
Baked fusilli and orecchiette, 246
Baked gnocchi with fior di latte
    cheese and tomato sauce, 253
Baked pasta with eggplant, 297

Baked pasta with hen and broth, 176–177
Baked sweet ravioli, 848
Baked tagliolini, 217
Baked tortellini, 313
Baked winter pasta, 297–298
Bean and pasta soup, 197
Benevento-style lasagne with veal meatballs and eggs, 267–268
Bucatini in mackerel sauce, 221
Bucatini in tomato sauce, 275
Bucatini with caciocavallo cheese, 288
Bucatini with guanciale, hot pepper, and tomato, 221
Buckwheat pasta with toasted cornmeal, 219–220
Busiati with pesto, 222
Calabrian-style pasta with lardo and onion, 280
Cannarozzetti with ricotta and saffron, 223–224
Cappelletti in broth, 108–109
Cavatelli with arugula and potatoes, 111
Chicken and pasta soup, 154
Chicken broth with grated pasta, 167
Chickpea ravioli, 850
Christmas macaroni, 121
Cornmeal pasta with tomatoes, 271
Ferretti in meat sauce, 239
Ferretti with anchovies and bread, 239
Fettuccine "Alfredo," 240
Fettuccine with ricotta, 240
Fregula soup, 117
Fried pasta ribbons, 772
Fried small gnocchi, 249–250
Fruit ravioli, 863
Fusilli alla molisana, 246
Fusilli with mushrooms and olives, 245
Garganelli with peas and prosciutto, 247
"Gendarme hat" pasta pie, 225–226
Gnocchi in meat sauce, 252–253
Gnoccoli with tuna sauce, 261
Grated pasta in broth, 167
Griddled pasta, 403–404
Homemade pasta with meat and tomato, 278
Homemade pasta with tomatoes and garlic, 313
Homemade twisted pasta, 316
Honeyed gnocchi, 804–805
Jam ravioli, 848
Large tomato and mozzarella ravioli, 740–741
Le trofie recchesi, 420
Long-cooked pasta with stew and broth, 279
Macaroni with arugula, 276
Maccaronara di Montemarano, 276

Manatelle, 286
Pan-cooked pasta with pork, tomato, and red wine, 283
Panzerotti, 295
Passatelli in broth, 163
Passatelli in fish broth, 163–164
Pasta and bean soup (Piemonte), 180
Pasta and bean soup 3 (Emilia-Romagna), 169
Pasta and prawns in broth, 184
Pasta au gratin, 278
Pasta "crosses," 233–234
Pasta for hard times (with broccoli and anchovies), 265–266
Pasta "snails" with sausage, 275
Pasta squares with John Dory, 391
Pasta squares with meat sauce, 391
Pasta stuffed with squash, 224–225
Pasta stuffed with sweetbreads and borage, 285–286
Pasta with beans (Abruzzo), 373
Pasta with Campofilone-style meat sauce, 277
Pasta with guanciale, 376
Pasta with mascarpone, 298
Pasta with mint, 388–389
Pasta-water pick-me-up, 177
Pastina in fish sauce, 168
Plum gnocchi, 805
Potato and pasta soup, 143
"Priest caps," 225
"Priest chokers" with meat sauce, 390
"Priest chokers" with salsify sauce, 390
Rice and pasta baked with meatballs, 408–409
Roman-style gnocchi, 253
"St. Joseph's Lunch," 329
St. Joseph's pasta, 266
Sardinian-style stuffed pasta with spinach, 235
Sausage-filled pasta with butter, 227
Sfoglia, 377
Small butter gnocchi in broth, 248
Small gnocchi made with breadcrumbs in bean sauce, 247
Small Sardinian gnocchi with meat sauce, 284
Soup with shaved pasta 1 (Lombardia), 142
Soup with shaved pasta 2 (Lombardia, also called gratin), 143
Spaghetti baked in foil, 380
Spaghetti with garlic, olive oil, and hot pepper, 379
Spaghetti with garlic and chili pepper, 280
Spaghetti with garlic and oil, 277
Spaghetti with guanciale, 380
Spaghetti with peppers, tomatoes, and guanciale, 299
Spätzle, 248

Strengozzi with garlic, chili, and tomatoes, 389
Stuffed gnocchi in cheese sauce, 258
Stuffed pasta, 215–216
Sweet lasagne, 808
Sweet ravioli with ricotta, 849–850
Tagliatelle, 397
Tagliatelle and chestnut soup, 147
Tagliatelle pie, 396–397
Tagliatelle with chickpeas, 181–182
Tagliatelle with meat sauce, 392
Tagliolini croquettes, 289–290
Terni-style pasta with garlic and oil, 232
Thick pasta with tomato ragú, 274
Tiny pasta in bean broth, 169–170
Tiny square pasta and fava beans, 171
Tiny square pasta and peas, 172
Tortellini Bolognese in broth, 183–184
Trenette with pesto sauce, 418–419
Vermicelli in garlic and oil, 420
Ziti with lardo, 283
Ziti with meatballs, 309

Pastry
Almond and fig-filled Christmas cookies, 788
Almond tart with chocolate glaze, 751
Anise fritters with honey, 777
Anise ring cookies, 776
Anisette fritters, 860
Apostles' fingers (Ricotta-stuffed crêpes), 788–789
Apple and pear cake, 877
Apple Charlotte, 773–774
Apple dumplings, 807
Apple fritters, 797–798
Apple fritters with Moscato wine, 798
Apple strudel, 867–868
Apple tart, 777
Apple tart with mostarda, 877
Babas with rhum, 749–750
Baked apple pastry, 784
Baked sweet ravioli, 848
Biscotti from Prosto, 755
Boiled and baked cookies, 776
"Bones of the dead" cookies, 822
Braided cookies, 870
Buckwheat cake, 875–876
Butter cake (Lombardia), 855
Butter cake (Veneto), 796
Calabrian fritters, 887–888
Canastrelli of Piemonte, 765
Cannoli shells, 766
Carnival cookies, 774
Carnival fritters, 884
Carnival ring cake, 778
Cescent cookies, 787
Cherry marmalade cookies, 772–773
Cherry strudel, 867

Chieti cookies, 870
Chocolate rolled cake, 802
Christmas sweets, 792–793
Cornmeal and raisin cake, 844
Cornmeal cookies, 886–887
Cornmeal fruitcake, 753
Cornmeal raisin cookies, 804
Cornmeal sponge cake, 845
Cream-filled sponge cake, 889
Custard tart, 809
Easter buns, 845
Easter cake, 841
Ferrara biscotti, 756
Ferratelle allo zafferano, 794
Filled cookies, 861–862
Fried dough knots, 863
Fried knots, 801
Fried pasta ribbons, 772
Fried pastries, 868
Fried small dumplings, 866
Fritters, 771
Friulian yeast cake, 806
Fruit cake (Emilia-Romagna),
    864–865
Fruit ravioli, 863
Fruitcake 1, 751–752
Fruitcake 2, 815
Fruitcake with nuts, 800–801
Glazed S cookies, 869
Glazed sweet rolls, 748
Grappa fritters, 793
Honey cookies, 841
Honey doughnuts, 775–776
Honey fritters, 778
Honey squares, 866
Jam ravioli, 848
Jam-filled horseshoe cookies, 869
Layer sponge cake, 790
Lucca ring cake, 759–760
Marzipan-filled cookies, 769–770
Migliacci dolci di maiale (sweet
    migliacci with pork), 817
Milk fritters, 800
Moiano biscotti, 755
Nuns' fritters for Carnival, 795
Orange cake, 872
Palatschinken with preserves,
    784–785
Paradise cake, 882
Pear cake, 823
Pear pie, 773
Pear tart, 874
Pesche di Castelbottaccio (baked
    sweet rolls), 839
Pisa-style rice tart, 873
Pizze di Pasqua (Easter pizza), 846
Plum cake, 880
Polenta fruitcake, 801
Puff pastries, 862
Raisin buns, 829
Raisin fritters, 797
Ricotta cheesecake (Piemonte),
    785–786
Ricotta cheesecake (Sicilia), 800

Ricotta crostata, 785
Ring cake (Emilia-Romagna),
    756–757
Ring cake (Lazio), 840
Rose fritte ("fried roses"), 852
Rum fritters, 758
St. Joseph's Day fritters, 753–754
Sandy cake, 882
Scarsella, 859
Semolina fritters, 796–797
Spiced honey twists, 868–869
Spiced shortbread, 758
Sponge cake, 846
Star cake, 819
Sugar cookies, 765
Sweet buns, 812–813
Sweet cheese pastries, 861
Sweet lasagne, 808
Sweet ravioli with ricotta, 849–850
Tagliolini pie, 880
Torta di farina gialla, 876
Torta Novecento (sponge cake),
    883
Tortoli, 884
Tuscan sweet bread, 752
Valdostan apple cake, 791
Vanilla fritters, 821
Vanilla ring cake, 757
Venetian biscotti, 750
Wheat berry ricotta tart, 835–836
White pepper cookies, 839
Wine doughnuts, 775
Wine pinwheels, 767
Yellow cake with fruit, 831

Peaches
Baked amaretto peaches, 838
Peach and amaretti semifreddo,
    861
Stuffed peaches, 838
Stuffed peaches with almonds,
    838–839

Pears
Apple and pear cake, 877
Pear cake, 823
Pear pie, 773
Pear tart, 874
Pears in wine, 837
Potatoes and pears, 708

Peas
Collo de castrato, risi, e piselli
    (lamb's neck), 554
Garganelli with peas and prosciutto,
    247
Lamb and peas, 513
Pea soup, 143–144
Peas with sautéed bread, 703
Quail with peas, 633
Rice and peas 1 (Veneto), 345
Rice and peas 2 (Veneto), 345
Stewed eel with peas (Emilia-
    Romagna), 434

Stewed eel with peas (Veneto),
    433–434
Tiny square pasta and peas, 172

Pine nuts
Charterhouse-style sweet bread,
    826–827
Fried small dumplings, 866
Friulian yeast cake, 806
Fruit cake (Emilia-Romagna),
    864–865
Sweet bread with fruits and nuts,
    825–826
Sweet-and-sour cod stew, 504
Yellow cake with fruit, 831

Pistachios
Cream baskets, 831
Sweet bread with fruits and nuts,
    825–826
Watermelon ice, 803

Pork
Agnolotti gobbi astigiani-albesi ai tre
    arrosti, 213
"Appetite-buster" sausage casserole,
    379
Baked dumplings with sausage and
    cheese, 10
Baked macaroni and rice with pork,
    408
Baked meat ravioli, 333
Baked omelet with pork and
    potatoes, 690
Baked polenta and sausage, 327
Baked polenta with meat sauce 1
    (Lombardia), 324–325
Baked polenta with meat sauce 2
    (Emilia-Romagna), 325
Baked polenta with sausage and
    ciccioli, 289
Baked pork shanks, 651
Baked prosciutto and herb pie, 312
Baked ravioli, 332
Baked rigatoni with braised pork and
    eggs, 402–403
Baked tripe in crust, 667–668
Barbazza scottata, 7
Bean, escarole, and pork soup, 198
Bean stew with beef and ham, 598
Beans and pork, 686
Braised pork ribs, 625
Bread with pork bits, 86
Breaded pork liver, 573
Bucatini with guanciale, hot pepper,
    and tomato, 221
Cabbage and pork-rind soup, 149
Calcioni (fried dumplings with
    prosciutto and cheese), 11
Cappello da prete con zabaione,
    531
Carne 'ncartarata ("aged meat"), 15
Chestnut fettuccine with cabbage
    and pork, 241

Chicken, veal, pork and guinea hen cooked with tomatoes and herbs, 645

Chickpea and pork soup (Piemonte), 156

Coppa (Umbrian pork sausage), 20

Duck stuffed with sausage and liver, 517

Duck stuffed with veal and pork, 517

Eggplant and sausage, 700

Escarole with meatballs, 722

Farro and pig's trotters, 572

Fava beans and guanciale 1 (Lazio), 687

Fava beans and guanciale 2 (Lazio), 687–688

Friceu 'd sangh (blood fritters), 581

Fried neapolitan sausage and friarielli, 545–546

Fried pork, 647

Garganelli with peas and prosciutto, 247

Grandma's prosciutto and beans, 717

Homemade pasta in pork sauce, 281

Homemade pasta with guanciale and sausage, 314

Homemade pasta with meat and tomato, 278

Homemade pasta with pork sauce, 308

Lasagne with meat sauce, 373

Layered polenta with sausage and mushrooms, 287–288

Marche-style lasagne, 422

Meat and artichokes, 541

Meat and salame pie, 646

Meat pie, 540

Meat pie with elderberry, 83

Meat roll-ups, 592

Meatballs, 632

Migliaccio (baked blood pudding), 45

Minestra maritata 2 (wedding soup 2, Campania), 141

Mixed braised meats, 522

Mixed meat ravioli, 331–332

Molise-style ragù, 635–636

Mortadella di fegato, 49

Mushrooms with loin and sausage, 546

Neapolitan pâté, 55–56

Pallotte (cheese and sausage dumplings), 741

Pan-cooked pasta with pork, tomato, and red wine, 283

Pan-cooked pork cutlets, 565

Pan-fried pork, 581

Pan-fried sausages and broccoli, 641

Pasta and prosciutto pie, 312

Pasta "snails" with sausage, 275

Pasta "snakes" with sausage, 423

Pasta timbale, 378–379

Pasta with Campofilone-style meat sauce, 277

Pasta with guanciale, 376

Pasta with potatoes and pancetta, 309

Penne with hot chiles, prosciutto, and tomato, 314

Piquant tripe soup, 187

Pizza with cracklings, 61

Pizza with cracklings and raisins, 61

Polenta with broccoli and pancetta, 321

Polenta with pork loin, 320

Polenta with pork sauce, 320–321

Polenta with salted pork, 319

Porchetta (whole spit-roasted pig), 630

Pork and bean soup, 197

Pork and beans (Piemonte), 114

Pork and cabbage stew, 543

Pork and chickpeas for All Soul's Day, 605

Pork and pickled peppers, 606

Pork and sweetbreads with beans, 614

Pork cutlets in wine, 522

Pork cutlets with balsamic vinegar, 644

Pork cutlets with Savoy cabbage, 565

Pork roll-ups (Lombardia), 41–42

Pork roll-ups (Valle d'Aosta), 591

Pork salad, 39

Pork scraps and peppers, 605

Pork shanks, 613

Pork stew (Abruzzo), 610

Pork stew (Lombardia), 656

Pork with chervil sauce, 540

Pork with onion sauce, 547

Pork with potatoes and fennel, 553

Pork with potatoes and mushrooms, 659

Pork-liver skewers, 573–574

"Priest chokers" with salsify sauce, 390

Prosciutto and cheese fritters, 68

Prosciutto di bosses (jambon di bosses), 67

Prosciutto di sauris, 68

Prosciutto in bread dough, 631

Prosciutto mousse, 45

Rabbit and pork pâté, 55

Rice with beans, cabbage, and pork, 292

Ricotta and sausage dumplings, 82

Rigatoni with sausage and mushrooms, 338–339

Risotto with pork and veal, 357

Risotto with sausage 1 (Emilia-Romagna), 361

Risotto with sausage 2 (Lombardia), 366–367

Risotto with sausage and rum, 356

Roast pork, 615

Roast pork loin, 518

Roast suckling pig, 630

Roba cotta ("cooked stuff"), 638

Salama da sugo, 639

Salame d'oca, 70

Sanguinaccio valdostano (blood pudding, blood sausage), 76

Sardegnan stewed tripe, 661

Sausage and fava bean stew, 573

Sausage frittata, 579

Sausage roll-ups, 592

Sausage timbale, 82–83

Sausages and broccoli, 640–641

Sausages and potatoes, 641–642

Sausages with broccoli rabe, 641

Shepherd's-style pork, 540

Skewered pork liver, 575

Small Sardinian gnocchi with meat sauce, 284

Spaghetti with carbonara sauce, 382–383

Spaghetti with guanciale, 380

Spaghetti with guanciale and chile pepper, 383

Spaghetti with guanciale and tomato sauce, 385

Spaghetti with guanciale sauce, 382

Spaghetti with peppers, tomatoes, and guanciale, 299

Spiedo bresciano or polenta e uccelli (polenta and birds), 650

Squab stuffed with meat, 623

Stewed pork (Friuli-Venezia Giulia), 541

Stewed pork (Piemonte), 638

Stuffed pork spleen, 609

Stuffed squab, 622

Stuffed zucchini flowers, 529–530

Sweet-and-sour meatballs 2 (Calabria), 628

Sweet-and-sour pork, 605

Tagliatelle with Romagna-style meat sauce, 394

Taglierini in meat sauce, 400

Tagliolini with pork gullets, 182–183

Timballo alla Bonifacio VIII, 410

Tortellini Bolognese in broth, 183–184

Tripe and beans, 667

Tripe and sweetbread stew, 648–649

Tripe sausages, 599

Tripe soup 2 (Friuli-Venezia Giulia), 207–208

Turkey breast with prosciutto and fontina, 621

Veal stew, 668–669

Vegetables and pancetta, 732

Wedding soup 1 (Calabria), 151

White bean purée, 123

Wild herbs and meat soup, 153

Zeaia, 87

Potatoes

Apricot dumplings, 807

Baked lamb and potatoes, 513

Baked meat and vegetables, 617
Baked omelet with pork and potatoes, 690
Baked pasta and potatoes, 307–308
Baked rice Foggia-style, 404–405
Baked rice with mussels and potatoes, 404
Barley and potato soup, 155
Bean, cabbage, and potato soup, 156–157
Boiled stockfish with potatoes, 493
Bread soup 5 (Basilicata), 169
Bread soup with arugula and potatoes, 160
Buckwheat gnocchi with speck, 255–256
Cavatelli with arugula and potatoes, 111
Cheese crisp with potatoes, 739
Cheese sauce with potatoes and onions, 738–739
Cod and potato stew 1 (Piemonte), 492
Cod and potato stew 2 (Calabria), 492
Cod and potatoes 1 (Campania), 494
Corn, bean, and potato soup, 137
Crushed potatoes, 709
Crushed potatoes and beans with cheese, 744
Fontina gnocchi with sage cream, 419
Fried potato dumplings, 43
Gnocchi stuffed with mushrooms, 260
Gnocchi with duck sauce, 254
Gnocchi with goose sauce, 251
Gnocchi with rabbit sauce, 252
Gnocchi with sardines, 255
Half-moon pasta with potato filling, 214
Lamb and potatoes (Puglia), 512
Leg of lamb baked in embers, 510
Mutton stew with potatoes, 656
Pan-fried beef and vegetables, 579
Pan-fried potatoes, 709
Pasta with potatoes and eggs, 308
Pasta with potatoes and pancetta, 309
Patate lesse sfritte (fried boiled potatoes), 710
Pork with potatoes and fennel, 553
Pork with potatoes and mushrooms, 659
Potato and bean stew, 708
Potato and celery soup, 168
Potato and cheese galette, 691
Potato and leek soup, 203
Potato and meat pie, 661
Potato and mushroom soup, 203
Potato and pasta soup, 143
Potato and tomato casserole, 726
Potato and truffle gratin, 708

Potato and vegetable gratin, 405–406
Potato balls, 685
Potato crescents, 696
Potato dumplings with mushroom sauce, 216
Potato fritters, 799
Potato gnocchi 1 (Emilia-Romagna), 256
Potato gnocchi 2 (Emilia-Romagna), 256
Potato gnocchi Romagna-style, 257
Potato gnocchi Verona-style, 258
Potato pancakes with blood sausage, 684–685
Potato pie or "tartlets," 84
Potato salad with anchovies, olives and tomato, 20
Potato timbale, 729
Potato purée with cheese, 741
Potatoes and pears, 708
Potato-mushroom gratin, 405
Pumpkin-potato gnocchi, 254
Rice and potato soup 1 (Veneto), 145
Rice and potato soup 2 (Friuli-Venezia Giulia), 145
Roast suckling lamb with potatoes, 508
Roasted cod and potatoes, 440–441
Roman-style potato gnocchi, 257–258
Salam ad patati (potato salame), 723
Sardinian-style pasta stuffed with potato and mint, 235–236
Sausages and potatoes, 641–642
Squab baked in potato, 621–622
Stewed rabbit with potato, 557–558
Stockfish and potatoes 2 (Alto Adige), 494
Stockfish with potatoes and onions, 495
Stockfish with tomatoes and potatoes, 495
Stuffed potato gnocchi, 250–251
Sweet potato cake, 878
Truffled potatoes, 707
Veal stew, 649
Vegetable soup (Piemonte), 157
Vegetable stew (Basilicata), 681–682
Vegetable stew with celery, 682
Vegetable timbale, 377
Yeasted fritters, 888

Prunes
Cod with raisins and prunes, 441
Friulian yeast cake, 806
Half-moon pasta with ricotta and prune filling, 213
Pear pie, 773
Sweet-and-sour cod stew, 504

Quail and partridge
Hunter-style partridges, 619

Pappardelle with quail and fennel, 296
Partridges and polenta, 619–620
Quail in pastry with mushrooms, 633–634
Quail Veneto-style, 633
Quail with peas, 633

Quinces
Quince paste, 780–781

Rabbit
Agnolotti gobbi astigiani-albesi ai tre arrosti, 213
Baked game, 639–640
Giblet stew with eggs, 552
Gnocchi with rabbit sauce, 252
Hunter-style rabbit, 557
Meatball-stuffed rabbit, 629
Pan-cooked rabbit, 561
Rabbit and onions, 559–560
Rabbit and pork pâté, 55
Rabbit Asti-style, 556
Rabbit braised in the style of Ischia, 557
Rabbit in broth, 554
Rabbit in red wine, 556
Rabbit with fennel, 555
Rabbit with pepper sauce, 561
Rabbit with peppers, 560
Rabbit with peppers and olives, 560
Rabbit with wild fennel, 555
Roast stuffed rabbit with fennel, 562
San Remo rabbit, 559
Stewed rabbit, 558
Stewed rabbit with potato, 557–558
Stuffed rabbit, 561–562
Trentino-style rabbit, 558–559

Radicchio
Grilled radicchio Treviso-style, 720
Radicchio crepes, 234–235

Raisins
Apple-raisin pancakes, 806
Cod with raisins and prunes, 441
Cod with tomatoes, raisins, and pine nuts, 442
Cornmeal and raisin cake, 844
Cornmeal raisin cookies, 804
Flatbread with rosemary and raisins, 858–859
Nut and raisin candy, 833
Pizza with cracklings and raisins, 61
Polenta pie with sausage and raisins, 54
Raisin buns, 829
Raisin cookies, 792
Raisin fritters, 797

Rice, risotto
Baked rice and meat, 341
Baked rice custard from Carrare, 879

Baked rice mold, 401–402
Baked rice pudding with chocolate, 757–758
Baked rice with mussels and potatoes, 404
Bean and rice soup, 107
Black risotto with cuttlefish ink (Veneto), 351
Black risotto with cuttlefish ink and chard, 370–371
Cabbage and rice soup, 149–150
Country-style risotto, 355
Crown of rice with squid, 233
Duck with rice, 215
Fava bean soup, 118
Feltre-style rice and beans, 344
"Free-range" risotto with gizzards, 368
Frittelle di maresina, 36
Frog leg risotto, 352–353
Frog risotto, 365
Genoese rice, 341–342
Green rice, 348
Minestra di riso (Piemonte), 144
Minestra di riso alla Valdostana (Valdostan rice soup), 146
Old-fashioned rice pudding cake, 879
Pisa-style rice tart, 873
Rice, beans, milk, and salame, 175
Rice and asparagus, 343–344
Rice and beans (Valle d'Aosta), 175
Rice and beans (Veneto), 344
Rice and celery, 346
Rice and chestnut soup, 206
Rice and egg soup, 127
Rice and frankfurter soup, 147
Rice and mushrooms, 348
Rice and pansies, 174
Rice and pasta baked with meatballs, 408–409
Rice and peas 1 (Veneto), 345
Rice and peas 2 (Veneto), 345
Rice and potato soup 1 (Veneto), 145
Rice and potato soup 2 (Friuli-Venezia Giulia), 146
Rice and turnips, 346
Rice and wild herbs, 174
Rice balls, 48–49
Rice balls in soup 1 (Sicilia, typical of Enna), 117
Rice balls in soup 2 (Sicilia), 117–118
Rice balls with meat and peas, 4
Rice bombe with squab, 220
Rice croquettes, 80–81
Rice fritters for St. Joseph's Day, 799
Rice pudding 1, 761
Rice pudding 2, 851
Rice pudding cake, 879
Rice salad with anchovies, 41
Rice soup (Valle d'Aosta), 145
Rice soup with squash, 145
Rice timbale 1 (Campania), 374
Rice timbale 2 (Campania), 375

Rice with beans, 292
Rice with beans, cabbage, and pork, 292
Rice with beans, cabbage, and salame, 291
Rice with celery and tomato, 176
Rice with cheese sauce, 347
Rice with chicken livers, 175
Rice with crabs and razor clams, 342
Rice with eggs and cheese, 173
Rice with fennel and ricotta, 348
Rice with meat sauce, 347
Rice with milk and chestnuts, 174
Rice with smoked cheese, 378
Rice with squash, 343
Rice-stuffed tomatoes 1 (Lazio), 327–328
Rice-stuffed tomatoes 2 (Lazio), 328–329
Rich risotto Padua-style, 371–372
Riso co-i fidê (rice with sea anemones), 342
Riso con i fegatini (rice and livers), 343
Risotto and eels, 176
Risotto with baked sole, shrimp, and hollandaise, 370
Risotto with Barbera, 349–350
Risotto with Barolo, 350
Risotto with beans, 360
Risotto with bladder campion and onion, 359
Risotto with campion, 360–361
Risotto with clams, 364–365
Risotto with cream of leek, 353
Risotto with fennel, 349
Risotto with freshwater prawns, 358–359
Risotto with giblets, 365
Risotto with Gorgonzola, 350
Risotto with honey mushrooms, 360
Risotto with hop shoots, 368
Risotto with Lake Garda tench, 363
Risotto with mushrooms, 349
Risotto with Parmigiano-Reggiano, 355
Risotto with perch and zucchini flowers, 358
Risotto with pork and veal, 357
Risotto with red wine, 352
Risotto with saffron and zucchini flowers, 358
Risotto with salame, 355–356
Risotto with salame and onion, 366
Risotto with sausage 1 (Emilia-Romagna), 361
Risotto with sausage 2 (Lombardia), 366–367
Risotto with sausage and cabbage, 362
Risotto with sausage and cauliflower, 367
Risotto with sausage and rum, 356
Risotto with sea bass, 367
Risotto with sècole, 366

Risotto with shrimp and asparagus, 368–369
Risotto with snails, 364
Risotto with spumante, fontina, and mushrooms, 357
Risotto with squash and beans, 363
Risotto with tench, 362
Risotto with trout and saffron, 356–357
Risotto with wild greens, 359
Saffron risotto soufflé, 351
Saffron risotto with mushrooms, 354
"St. Joseph's Lunch," 329
Seafood rice balls, 3–4
Seafood risotto, 353–354
Seas and mountains risotto, 369–370
Shrimp risotto with zucchini flowers, 369
Soup from Cogne, 178–179
Spiced risotto with salame, 361
Spring risotto, 371
Veronese rice and tripe, 346–347
Wedding soup 3 (Piemonte), 152
Wedding soup 5 (Veneto), 152–153
Wild duck risotto, 352

Rocks
Pesce fuiute ("fake fish" soup), 170

Rum
Babas with rhum, 749–750
Carnival cookies, 774
Drunken toasts, 786
Fritters, 771
Layer sponge cake, 790
Risotto with sausage and rum, 356
Rum custard, 783
Rum fritters, 758
Sweet bread from Cogne, 826
Zabaglione with rum, 886

Sage leaves
Fried sage leaves, 30
Sage-and-anchovy fritters, 2

Salame
Bèlecòt (fresh salame), 8
Chocolate salame, 853
Cooked soppressata, 647
Fiorini filled with salame and cheese, 242
'Ndugghia di Castrovillari, 705
Rice, beans, milk, and salame, 175
Rice with beans, cabbage, and salame, 291
Risotto with salame, 355–356
Risotto with salame and onion, 366
Salam ad patati (potato salame), 723
Salama da sugo, 639
Salame di agnello (lamb sausage), 640
Salame d'oca, 70
Salame frittata 1 (Piemonte), 33
Salame frittata 2 (Veneto), 34

Sausage frittata (with raw salame), 30–31
Spalla cotta di San Secondo (boiled pork salame), 79
Spiced risotto with salame, 361
Stuffed dumplings, 293

Sardines
Alborelle or sardine salate, 3
Bigoli with salted freshwater sardines, 217
Fillings for *tiellas*, 340–341
Gnocchi with sardines, 255
Homemade pasta with baby anchovies, 282
Mustica di Crucoli (sardine spread), 468
Pasta with sardines, anchovies, and breadcrumbs, 304
Pasta with sardines 1 (Sicilia), 305–306
Pasta with sardines 2 (Sicilia), 306
Sarde salate (salted sardines), 482
Sardine and artichoke casserole, 418
Sardine and lettuce stew, 505
Sardines in vinegar, 481
Sautéed baby sardines, 482–483
Soused bream, 445
Soused fish (Lombardia), 476–477
Soused fish (Veneto), 454
Stuffed sardines 1 (Sicilia), 480–481
Stuffed sardines 2 (Puglia), 482

Sauces and syrups
Almond-and-anchovy sauce, 75
Barberina sauce, 72
Bormida sauce, 72
Genoese meat sauce, 413
Grape syrup, 69
Green sauce, 74
Green-pepper sauce, 73–74
Horseradish sauce, 71
Marrow sauce with pepper, 521
Mostarda di carpi (fruit sauce), 48
Mostarda mantovana, 704
Mushroom sauce, 412
Mutton sauce, 619
Olive oil, lemon, and garlic sauce 1 (Calabria), 74
Olive oil, lemon, and garlic sauce 2 (Sicilia), 74–75
Sausage sauce, 73
Spicy tomato sauce, 80
Squash-blossom sauce, 72–73
Sweet-and-sour sauce (Toscana), 70
Sweet-and-sour sauce Parma style, 70
Tarragon sauce, 71
Truffle sauce, 71
Walnut sauce, 73

Sea bass
Fish cooked in salt, 469
Fish in vegetable sauce, 472
Risotto with sea bass, 367

Sea bass and shellfish in dough, 446
Sea bass in salt, 446
Sea bass in wine sauce, 490
Sea bass stuffed with seafood, 490
Sea bass with tomato, 490
Seafood and vegetable platter, 453

Sesame seeds
Sesame nougat, 871

Shrimp, crustaceans
Chickpea purée with shrimp and clams, 162
Crayfish soup, 504–505
Halibut and seafood stew, 457
Pasta and prawns in broth, 184
Risotto with baked sole, shrimp, and hollandaise, 370
Risotto with freshwater prawns, 358–359
Risotto with shrimp and asparagus, 368–369
Schille or cragnoni con aglio e olio, 485
Seafood and vegetable platter, 453
Seas and mountains risotto, 369–370
Shrimp and porcini gratin, 487–488
Shrimp in green sauce, 462
Shrimp risotto with zucchini flowers, 369
Taglionlini with squid and shrimp, 399–400
Thin tagliatelle with squid and shrimp, 398
Treviso shrimp, 462
Vermicelli and seafood baked in foil, 420–421

Snails
Christmas snails, 600–601
Cremona-style snails, 604
Pan-cooked snails, 602
Pasta with snails, 315–316
Polenta and snails (Trentino), 322–323
Risotto with snails, 364
St. John's snails, 601
San Quirino snails, 601
Snails with fennel, 602
Snails with picchi pacchi sauce, 16
Stewed snails, 603
Stewed snails with herbs, 603–604
Winemaker-style snails, 44

Sole
Grilled sole 1 (Emilia-Romagna), 488
Grilled sole 2 (Emilia-Romagna), 489
Risotto with baked sole, shrimp, and hollandaise, 370
Sole in wine, 489

Spinach
Fillings for *tiellas*, 340–341

Green lasagna with meat sauce, 270
Green rice, 348
Manfrigùl pasta balls, 123
Pasta roll with spinach, 372–373
Piacenza tortelli, 414
"Priest stranglers" green gnocchi in butter and sage sauce, 387–388
"Priest stranglers" green gnocchi in butter sauce, 388
Sardinian-style stuffed pasta with spinach, 235
Spinach Genoa-style, 727
Spinach gnocchi in prosciutto sauce, 249
Spinach dumplings 1, 265
Spinach dumplings 2, 265
Spinach pie, 26
Spinach ravioli, 336
Spinach soup (Emilia-Romagna), 207
Spinach-cornmeal soup (Friuli-Venezia Giulia), 161
Spinach-ricotta ravioli, 337
Wedding soup 3 (Piemonte), 152

Spreads
Foie gras, 643
Mustica di Crucoli (sardine spread), 468
Spicy cheese spread, 80

Squab
Baked game, 639–640
"Brooding" pigeons (squab) stew, 179
Rice bombe with squab, 220
Roast squab with black olives, 623
Spiedo bresciano or polenta e uccelli (polenta and birds), 650
Spit-roasted squab, 614
Squab baked in potato, 621–622
Squab on skewers, 623–624
Squab stuffed with meat, 623
Stuffed squab, 622
Tagliatelle in squab sauce, 393

Squash, winter. *See also* **Zucchini (summer squash)**
Buckwheat pasta with zucchini, 389
Butternut-squash gnocchi 1 (Valle d'Aosta), 259
Butternut-squash gnocchi 2 (Friuli-Venezia Giulia), 259
Butternut-squash gnocchi Belluno-style, 260
Cavatelli con cime di cocozze, 229
Fried squash, 89
Fried squash ravioli, 6–7
Marinated squash, 733
Minestrone with pesto, 155
Mixed fry Ascolo-Piceno-style, 582–583
Pan-fried beef and vegetables, 579
Pasta stuffed with squash, 224–225
Pumpkin bread, 827–828

Pumpkin cake, 791
Pumpkin ravioli 1 (Emilia-
Romagna), 416
Pumpkin ravioli 2 (Lombardia), 417
Pumpkin-potato gnocchi, 254
Ratatouille Piedmont-style, 721
Rice soup with squash, 145
Rice timable 2 (Campania), 375
Rice with squash, 343
Risotto with squash and beans, 363
Squash cake, 85
Squash purée, 719
Squash soup, 150
Vegetable soup with squash and
barley, 199
Vegetable tart, 78
Watermelon ice, 803
Wheat-berry pudding 1, 787
Winter vegetable soup, 100

Squid and cuttlefish
Black risotto with cuttlefish ink
(Veneto), 351
Black risotto with cuttlefish ink and
chard, 370–371
Black tagliatelle with cuttlefish, 398
Crown of rice with squid, 233
Cuttlefish baked in foil, 455
Fillings for *tiellas*, 340–341
Linguine with cuttlefish ragù, 272
Marinated squid, 26
Spaghetti with cuttlefish ink
(Calabria), 380–381
Spaghetti with cuttlefish ink (Sicilia),
298
Stewed cuttlefish 1 (Liguria), 484
Stewed cuttlefish 2 (Toscana), 484
Stuffed cuttlefish 1, 485
Stuffed cuttlefish 2, 485–486
Stuffed small cuttlefish 1, 486
Stuffed small cuttlefish 2, 486
Stuffed squid (Campania), 499
Stuffed squid (Molise), 450
Stuffed squid (Puglia), 450
Tagliatelle with baby squid, 395
Taglionlini with squid and shrimp,
399–400
Thin tagliatelle with squid and
shrimp, 398

Sweet peppers
Beans and roasted dried peppers,
686
Calabrian peppers, 709
Goat with tomatoes and pepper, 532
Green-pepper sauce, 73–74
Pan-cooked peppers, 56
Pasta with dried peppers, 282
Pepper roll-ups, 695
Peppers stuffed with pasta, 315
Pickled peppers, 713–714
Pork and pickled peppers, 606
Pork scraps and peppers, 605
Rabbit with peppers, 560

Rabbit with peppers and olives, 560
Scrambled eggs with peppers, 672
Sole with peppers, 489
Spaghetti with peppers, tomatoes,
and guanciale, 299
Spicy stuffed peppers, 710
Stuffed peppers, 53
Stuffed peppers (Puglia), 712–713
Stuffed peppers Capri-style, 711
Stuffed peppers with caciocavallo,
713
Stuffed peppers with tuna, 712
Sweet-and-sour stuffed peppers,
711–712
Swordfish with peppers, 474
Tagliatelle with zucchini, roasted
peppers, and tomatoes, 393
Tripe with tomatoes and peppers,
664
Vegetable stew (Basilicata), 681–682
Vegetable stew with celery, 682

Sweet potatoes
Sweet potato cake, 878

Swiss chard
Black risotto with cuttlefish ink and
chard, 370–371
Chard in broth, 99
Macaroni with chard sauce, 413
Meatless ravioli 2 (Toscana), 335
"Priest chokers" with salsify sauce,
390
Swiss chard and ricotta, 730
Tortelli filled with Swiss chard, 415
Tuscan tortelli, 414

Swordfish
Baked swordfish 1 (Calabria), 473
Baked swordfish 2 (Calabria), 476
Linguine with swordfish, 299–300
Seafood rice balls, 3–4
Steamed swordfish 1 (Calabria), 473
Steamed swordfish 2 (Sicilia), 473
Swordfish in salmoriglio sauce, 476
Swordfish pie, 468
Swordfish roll-ups, 472
Swordfish steaks, 445–446
Swordfish with capers 1 (Calabria),
473–474
Swordfish with capers 2 (Calabria),
475
Swordfish with capers and lemon,
475
Swordfish with mint, 474
Swordfish with olives and capers, 475
Swordfish with peppers, 474

Tomatoes
Bucatini in tomato sauce, 275
Buckwheat pasta with zucchini, 389
Capri salad, 693
Cornmeal pasta with tomatoes, 271
Goat with tomatoes and pepper, 532

Homemade pasta with tomatoes and
garlic, 313
Lamb stew with tomatoes, 527
Large tomato and mozzarella ravioli,
740–741
Oregano tomatoes, 716–717
Pan-cooked pasta with pork, tomato,
and red wine, 283
Pasta with breaded tomatoes, 306
Penne with tomatoes and basil, 315
Polenta with salted green tomatoes,
320
Pomodori sott'olio (pickled
tomatoes), 718
Potato and tomato casserole, 726
Rice with celery and tomato, 176
Spaghetti with peppers, tomatoes,
and guanciale, 299
Spicy tomato sauce, 80
Stuffed tomatoes, 717
Tagliatelle with zucchini, roasted
peppers, and tomatoes, 393
Thick pasta with tomato ragù, 274
Tomato soup, 156
Tomato soup (Toscana), 161
Vegetable timbale, 377

Tripe
Baked tripe in crust, 667–668
Lamb tripe in tomato sauce,
662–663
Piquant tripe soup, 187
Sardegnan stewed tripe, 661
Stuffed tripe (Molise), 610
Tripe alla Parmigiana, 664
Tripe and beans, 667
Tripe and bean stew, 115
Tripe Florentine-style, 663
Tripe in sauce, 662
Tripe in spiced tomato sauce, 666
Tripe in tomato sauce, 664–664
Tripe Pisa-style, 665
Tripe Roman-style, 666
Tripe soup (Liguria), 177
Tripe soup (Piemonte), 107
Tripe soup (Trentino), 149
Tripe soup 1 (Veneto), 207
Tripe soup 2 (Friuli-Venezia Giulia),
207–208
Tripe soup 3 (Veneto), 208
Tripe with chili peppers, 667
Tripe with eggplant and walnuts,
665–666
Tripe with potatoes, 661–662
Tripe with tomatoes and peppers,
664
Trippa del "Vecchio Salera," 182
Veal tripe in tomato sauce, 663
Veronese rice and tripe, 346–347

Trout
Eels and trout in a spicy sauce, 435
Grilled trout, 503
Marinated trout, 87

Pasta Scheggino-style, 275
Risotto with trout and saffron, 356–357
Trout baked in tomato sauce with polenta, 503
Trout in red wine, 501
Trout with parsley sauce, 502
Trout with truffle sauce, 502

Truffles
Baked truffles, 81
Caesar's mushrooms with truffles, 47
Cardoons with truffles, 679
Fondue with white truffles, 738
Lamb with truffle, 515
Mushroom and truffle salad, 39
Pheasant with truffle, 569–570
Potato and truffle gratin, 708
Spaghetti with black truffle, 381
Spaghetti with truffles, 385
Tagliatelle with truffle, 401
Tagliolini with black truffle (Marche), 399
Tagliolini with black truffle from Norcia (Umbria), 399
Trout with truffle sauce, 502
Truffle frittata, 32
Truffle ravioli, 402
Truffle sauce, 71
Truffled potatoes, 707
White truffles with Parmigiano-Reggiano, 81

Tuna
Baked fresh tuna, 460
Beef roll-ups with tuna sauce, 42
Boiled tuna, 498
Caponata 3, 15
Focaccia with oil, tuna, and tomato, 29
Fried tuna with lemon and parsley, 458
Gnoccoli with tuna sauce, 261
Pasta with anchovies and tuna, 423
Pasta with bottarga 1 (Calabria), 303
Pasta with bottarga 2 (Sicilia), 303
Spaghetti with tuna, 381
Stuffed peppers with tuna, 712
Tuna and onions, 499
Tuna Calabria-style, 497
Tuna Cosenza-style, 497–498
Tuna Reggio-style, 498
Tuna roll, 480
Tuna-and-anchovy crepes, 467
Ziti with tuna sauce, 423

Turkey
Cardoon and meatball soup, 105
Chicken-stuffed turkey, 618
Christmas turkey, 658
Roast turkey with pomegranates, 657
Scaliger soup, 187–188

Tacchino alla canzanese, 657
Turkey breast with prosciutto and fontina, 621
Turkey-veal roulade, 629

Turnips
Bean soup with fermented turnips, 134
Beet stuffed pasta with poppy seeds, 229
Braised turnips, 720
Bread soup 3 (Basilicata), 159
Bread soup 5 (Basilicata), 159
Brovada (turnips marinated in wine pressings), 721
Carmelized turnips, 720
Corn pone with turnips, 317
Minestra di riso alla Valdostana (Valdostan rice soup), 146
Polenta with pork and turnips, 322
Rice and turnips, 346
Rice soup (Valle d'Aosta), 145
Turnip and bean soup, 190–191

Variety meats
Carnesecca Valdostana, 16
Fried lamb offal, 580
Hunter's-style kid offal, 563
Insalata di nervetti, 41
Involtini di interiora di agnelli (roasted lamb offal), 590
Lamb offal with artichokes, 562
Mammella di mucca (brined udders), 43
Meat jerky (coppiette), 21
Pasta stuffed with sweetbreads and borage, 285–286
Roast stuffed rabbit with fennel, 562
Stewed roebuck offal, 578

Veal
Agnolotti gobbi astigiani-albesi ai tre arrosti, 213
Baked meat and vegetables, 617
Baked ravioli, 332
Baked rice and meat, 341
Baked rice mold, 401–402
Benevento-style lasagne with veal meatballs and eggs, 267–268
Braised snout, 588
Braised veal, 552
Breaded veal chops, 565–566
Carne salata (salted meat), 542
Cheese-filled veal chops, 566
Chicken, veal, pork and guinea hen cooked with tomatoes and herbs, 645
Cialde (fried wafers stuffed with veal), 17
Cima (stuffed calf's breast), 549
Duck stuffed with veal and pork, 517
Fondue-stuffed pasta with veal broth, 167

Genoese meat sauce, 413
Grilled veal Messina-style, 523–524
Homemade pasta with meat and tomato, 278
Lettuce rolls, 120
Lucca spring veal and vegetable stew, 118
Meat and artichokes, 541
Meat and salame pie, 646
Meat pie, 540
Milk-roasted veal, 519
Mixed braised meats, 522
Mixed meat ravioli, 331–332
Molise-style ragù, 635–636
Neapolitan pâté, 55–56
Paliata (grilled calf's intestines), 616
Pasta timbale, 378–379
Pasta with Campofilone-style meat sauce, 277
Piquant tripe soup, 187
Potato and meat pie, 661
Rigatoni con la pagliata, 338
Risotto with pork and veal, 357
Small Sardinian gnocchi with meat sauce, 284
Smoked spiced veal (coppietta), 21
Spleen crostini (Crostini all milza per minestra), 111
Stuffed veal breast, 632
Stuffed veal spleen, 608–609
Stuffed zucchini flowers, 529–530
Sweet-and-sour meatballs (Piemonte), 627–628
Sweet-and-sour veal snout, 610
Timballo alla Bonifacio VIII, 410
Tripe and sweetbread stew, 648–649
Tripe in sauce, 662
Tripe Pisa-style, 665
Tripe soup 1 (Veneto), 207
Tripe soup 3 (Veneto), 208
Tripe with chili peppers, 667
Tripe with potatoes, 661–662
Turkey-veal roulade, 629
Veal and potatoes, 541–542
Veal "birds," 668
Veal bolognese, 567
Veal brains "sandwiches," 631
Veal casserole with tomato and cheese, 617
Veal cutlets in sauce, 520
Veal cutlets with fontina, 642–643
Veal cutlets with mushroom caps, 643–644
Veal cutlets with prosciutto and sage, 642
Veal hock, 585
Veal in white wine, 539
Veal meatballs with ricotta in broth, 178
Veal parmigiana with eggplant, 616
Veal roll-ups (Liguria), 660
Veal roll-ups (Valle d'Aosta), 591
Veal rump in aspic, 575

Veal shank with Barolo wine,
651–652
Veal shanks Milan-style, 613
Veal stew (Marche), 668–669
Veal stew (Piemonte), 649
Veal stew "White Lady," 578
Veal stewed in wine, 669
Veal tendon salad, 589
Veal tripe in tomato sauce, 663
Zuppa di soffritto, 206

Vegetables. *See also* **Mixed vegetables**
Beet stuffed pasta with poppy seeds,
229
Carote di Viterbo in bagno
aromatico, 683
Marinated lettuce, 697
Sardine and lettuce stew, 505

Venison
Oven-roasted venison, 563
Roast saddle of venison, 646
Stewed roebuck offal, 578
Venison in sauce, 537
Venison loin with red cabbage
timbale and currants, 600
Venison medallions, 608
Venison with berries, 536–537

Walnuts
Baked fig and nut calzone, 820
Bread with walnuts, 51
Cavatelli with walnuts, 230
Christmas macaroni with walnuts,
811–812
Christmas ring cakes, 840
Christmas spice cookies, 857
Fish in walnut sauce, 448
Fried small dumplings, 866
Friulian yeast cake, 806
Fruit cake (Emilia-Romagna),
864–865
Fruitcake with nuts, 800–801
Herb-stuffed pasta, 292–293
Honey-nut sticks, 789
Linguine with walnuts, 271
Nocino (walnut liqueur), 823
Nut and raisin candy, 833
Nut crescents, 779
Olive oil nut cake, 842
Raisin cookies, 792
Spiced nut cake from Terni, 824
Stuffed figs, 794
Sweet lasagne, 808
"Sweet-and-strong" boar, 550
Triestine yeast cake, 847
Trilli pasta in walnut sauce, 419
Tripe with eggplant and walnuts,
665–666
Walnut caramel pie, 874–875
Walnut cookies, 817
Walnut filled pizza, 842
Walnut nougat, 821

Walnut pudding, 760
Walnut sauce, 73
Walnut soup (Piemonte), 139
Walnut soup (Valle d'Aosta), 890
Wheat berry pudding 2, 805
Yellow cake with fruit, 831

Wheat berries
Wheat berry pudding 1, 787
Wheat berry pudding 2, 805
Wheat berry ricotta tart, 835–836
Wheat berry soup, 137

Wine
Apple fritters with Moscato wine,
798
Baked amaretto peaches, 838
Beef braised in Barolo, 524
Calabrian fritters, 887–888
Carnival ring cake, 778
Chicken in white wine, 625
Chieti cookies, 870
Clams in parsley and wine, 503
Cod in wine, 437
Cooked wine (saba), 818–819
Drunken hen, 584
Fried bread with Bulide, 828
Fried wine knots, 821
Honeyed gnocchi, 804–805
Jam-filled horseshoe cookies, 869
Jugged hare 1 (Piemonte), 595
Jugged hare 2 (Lombardia), 596
Jugged hare 3 (Friuli-Venezia
Giulia), 596–597
Kid in wine, 535
Kidneys in wine, 659
Mascarpone cake with Marsala, 814
Mullet with Vernaccia, 501
Nut and raisin candy, 833
Octopus in wine 1 (Lazio), 478
Octopus in wine 2 (Calabria), 478
Olive oil nut cake, 842
Ox in wine sauce, 576
Pan-cooked pasta with pork, tomato,
and red wine, 283
Pasta-water pick-me-up, 177
Pear pie, 773
Pear tart, 874
Pears in wine, 837
Pork and sweetbreads with beans,
614
Pork cutlets in wine, 522
Rabbit Asti-style, 556
Rabbit in red wine, 556
Risotto with Barbera, 349–350
Risotto with Barolo, 350
Risotto with spumante, fontina, and
mushrooms, 357
St. John's snails, 601
San Quirino snails, 601
Sea bass in wine sauce, 490
Semolina bread with wine must and
almonds, 857
Sole in wine, 489

Spiced wine, 847
Spit-roasted squab, 614
Trout in red wine, 501
Veal in white wine, 539
Veal shank with Barolo wine,
651–652
Veal stew "White Lady," 578
Veal stewed in wine, 669
Whitefish in white wine, 463
Wine doughnuts, 775
Wine pinwheels, 767
Wine soup, 208
Wine-must cookies, 818
Zabaglione, 886
Zabaglione with rum, 886
Zuppetta di vino ("donkey's soup"),
889

Zucchini (summer squash).
See also **Squash, winter**
Beef and vegetable pie, 410
Buckwheat pasta with zucchini, 389
Cream of zucchini soup, 113
Ditali with zucchini and ricotta,
236–237
Marinated zucchini (Campania),
733
Marinated zucchini (Lazio), 735
Marinated zucchini strips, 734
Marinated zucchini with mint,
733–734
Pan-fried beef and vegetables, 579
Rice timable 2 (Campania), 375
Risotto with perch and zucchini
flowers, 358
Sautéed zucchini, 734–735
Stuffed zucchini (Liguria), 735
Sweet-and-sour zucchini, 734
Tagliatelle with zucchini, roasted
peppers, and tomatoes, 393
Vegetable tart, 78
Zucchini cake, 856

Zucchini flowers
Farro with zucchini flowers, 115
Risotto with saffron and zucchini
flowers, 358
Shrimp risotto with zucchini flowers,
369
Squash-blossom sauce, 72–73
Stuffed zucchini blossoms, 27
Stuffed zucchini flowers, 529–530
Tagliatelle with squash blossoms,
395–396